GATEWAY TO LAND LAW
How To Think And Reason Like A Land Lawyer

GATEWAY TO
LAND LAW
How To Think And Reason Like A Land Lawyer

1ST EDITION

NICOLA JACKSON

Lecturer in Property Law, Leicester De Montfort Law School

SWEET & MAXWELL

London 2012

Published in 2012 by Sweet & Maxwell, 100 Avenue Road, London NW3 3PF, part of Thomson Reuters (Professional) UK Limited (Registered in England and Wales, Company No.1679046. Registered Office and address for service: Aldgate House, 33 Aldgate High Street, London EC3N 1DL)

Typeset by LBJ Typesetting Limited,
Printed in Great Britain by Ashford Colour Press, Gosport, Hants

No natural forests were destroyed to make this product; only farmed timber was used and re-planted.

A CIP catalogue record for this book is available from the British Library.

ISBN 9780414044876

CONTENTS

PREFACE

My aim in this book is to teach land law in a way that helps the reader understand how to think and reason like a land lawyer. This requires an imaginative connection with the subject. Ramsden draws a distinction between deep learning and surface learning. Deep learning forges an understanding of how the different parts of a subject relate to each other.[1] Law is a demanding subject to study at university and it is all too easy to resort to surface learning strategies, where the elements of law, facts of cases—conclusion—reasons—policy—argument, are split off from one another, put on the same level and learned as facts to be memorised.[2] This will not achieve the best marks as it programmes the meaning right out of law. As Sawyer observes

> "One can learn imitation history – kings and dates, but not the slightest idea of the motives behind it all; imitation literature – stacks of notes of Shakespeare's phrases, and a complete destruction of the power to enjoy Shakespeare".[3]

If we learn an imitation version of law we are completely lost when it comes to knowing how to solve a legal problem or create a discussion about the law in an essay. This is because the very act of splitting off the various elements of law and memorising them as facts destroys our power to understand the process of legal reasoning. Law learned in this way forges no internalised picture of how one should use a precedent case to predict the legal consequences of a novel fact scenario. To think and reason like a land lawyer we must form an image of what a reason for a judge's decision *looks like*, how it differs from a conclusion, and how to perceive when facts of a case are treated as *materially* important. These elements are more to be tasted than memorised. It is my aim here to help the reader understand the role of all these separate elements of a case and the links and connections between them. This book thereby aims to help readers understand how to solve land law problems.

Likewise, when we are asked to create an argument about land law ("discuss" or "critically evaluate"), a series of atomised and memorised facts will not help us. We need to experience the reality of the connection between "evidence" and "conclusion" before we understand how to construct an argument. In this book I present a method by which to create a compelling argument about land law: Building Blocks. The aims and policies of land law are set out in

---

1   *Learning to Teach in Higher Education* (Routledge, 2003), p.47.
2   Ramsden's "surface-atomistic" approach to learning: above pp.46–59.
3   Quoted in Ramsden, above.

Building Blocks. In the first chapter we examine these policies, such as the need to protect *residential security* and the need for *certainty and predictability* in a legal system. Throughout the book, the reader is then invited to hold the rules of land law against the relevant Building Blocks and say whether the rule supports or undermines the policies of land law. We say that the rule is good or bad accordingly. Here we are learning about the internal connections of land law argument—how to understand what makes compelling evidence for a conclusion.

Apart from Ramsden's *Learning to Teach in Higher Education*,[4] another work that has been of major influence in formulating Building Blocks has been Alec Fisher's *The Logic of Real Arguments*.[5] In this work Fisher puts forward a non-formal method of constructing and evaluating argument. It draws upon the "insights of traditional logic". I do not in any way claim that Building Blocks adapts or applies that method, but I have taken from it Fisher's "assertability question" which is clearly aimed at provoking an imaginative response to the idea of what constitutes compelling evidence for an argument. It asks *what evidence will justify me in accepting this conclusion*. He observes:

"It is possible to rely too heavily on experts and this approach to learning and knowledge tends to encourage passivity and receptiveness rather than inventiveness and imagination."[6]

For many years I have looked for a way to teach the art of creating argument about land law, at the same time disengaging surface learning strategies. During this long time, Fisher's book was a constant companion. Its influence on me has been immeasurable.

Another important work in the development of Building Blocks has been the work of Jean Piaget, who advocated that we learn as children and adolescents by a process of re-inventing and structuring our environment:

"The essential functions of intelligence consist in understanding and in inventing, in other words in building up structures by structuring reality."[7]

In short, "telling ... about the properties of materials is less effective than creating an experiment".[8] The aim of Building Blocks is to offer a very physical way of constructing an argument about land law. The student is invited to form a picture of the policies of land law as "blocks" of evidence. The idea is then to hold the rules against the Building Blocks and consider whether the rule supports or undermines the policy. This is evidence for a conclusion that the rule is good or bad. In this way the student learns about land law by structuring it for themselves: by *thinking like a land lawyer would*.

---

4   Above.
5   Cambridge University Press, 1988.
6   Above, p.1.
7   J. Piaget, *Science of Education and the Psychology of the Child* (Viking Press, 1970), pp.27–8; also Smith, Cowie and Blades, *Understanding Children's Development*, 3rd edn (John Wiley, 1998), p.359.
8   Smith, Cowie and Blades, above p.359.

Others before me have used the expression "building blocks", notably Elizabeth Cooke, *Land Law*,[9] referring to types of property right. But I use the expression in a very different sense here.

This has been a long journey and I would like to thank people who have helped me along the way. I would like to thank David Milman (Lancaster) and Joseph Jaconelli (Manchester), for continued support and encouragement. I had a particularly rewarding time whilst teaching in the law school at the University of East Anglia. I spent a year on the MA-Higher Education Practice course and undertook a project that was the start of my Building Blocks method. I would like to thank those in the Education department for their support and encouragement. My colleagues in the law school, particularly Gareth Thomas and Duncan Sheehan, were very supportive. I became Land Law module leader at Leicester De Montfort Law School in 2010 and we have now done 2 full years of "Building Blocks". We have had some astonishing results and I would like to thank my colleagues who teach with me on the team, Jenny King and Sheree Peaple, who have taught with such dedication, enthusiasm and at times great courage, also Richard Ward, now retired Head of School, who championed Building Blocks right from the beginning. Without Jenny, Sheree and Richard, and the Land Law classes of 2010–11 and 2011–12—who brought Building Blocks into reality, this book probably would never have been written. I would also like to thank my colleagues at Sweet & Maxwell, in particular my editor Amanda Strange and house editor Sarah Spooner, for the professional and creative way in which they brought the manuscript to life, and to Constance Sutherland, who supported the project from the beginning.

I have attempted to state the law as it was on March 31, 2012. On a point of terminology, in 2009 the House of Lords (the highest appeal court) became the Supreme Court. I use the description "House of Lords" to refer to cases prior to that change, but to the "Supreme Court" for cases after.

I dedicate the book to my mum and dad, in grateful acknowledgement of all that they have done for me.

Nicola Jackson
Leicester De Montfort Law School
May 2012

---

9   Oxford University Press, 2006.

ACKNOWLEDGMENTS

The author and publishers would like to thank those organisations who have allowed their copyright material to be reproduced in this work. Grateful acknowledgement is made to the following:

Incorporated Council of Law Reporting (www.iclr.co.uk)
Oxford University Press (www.oup.com)

While every care has been taken to establish and acknowledge copyright, and contact the copyright owners, the publishers tender their apologies for any accidental infringement. They would be pleased to come to a suitable arrangement with the rightful owners in each case.

All extracted materials are represented in the format and with the correct content at the time of writing the book and are subject to change.

USING THIS BOOK

The overall aim of this book is to teach the skill of critical thinking and the art of reasoning like a land lawyer. The following features are used throughout the book to support this aim:

BUILDING BLOCKS

The BUILDING BLOCKS are 6 basic principles with which to construct argument about Land Law rules.

> **BUILDING BLOCK NO 1: Residential Security**
> We can legitimately say that where the rules operate in the context of owner occupation of property, they are good and fair if they give effective protection to people's residential security. Land Law now operates in the context of owner occupation. Land Law rules should give effect to the purposes for which people buy and use land/houses. People place a good deal of importance on land ownership and the law should protect this. When people are using land ownership to build a home this is a significant part of their lives. As Atiyah says (*Rise and Fall of Freedom of Contract* (1979)) the strength of people's expectations reinforces the rigour with which the law protects them.

CRITICAL THINKING POINTS

Critical Thinking Points provide hints and examples of critical thinking and legal reasoning to help you develop your own critical perspective.

delay repossession of a family home, or use every device to make repossession a last resort, might be considered "good" in accordance with the evidence in this Building Block.[60]

> In the European Convention on Human Rights the right to peaceful enjoyment of possessions is enshrined as a basic human right alongside rights such as the right to life, liberty, fair trial, and privacy. BUILDING BLOCKS NOS 1–3 provide some justification for why this is the case.

D. BUILDING BLOCK NO 4: IDEAS OF OWNERSHIP

What does it mean when we say that we "own" land or a house? What powers do we have? What privileges do we have? Why do we need to answer this question at all? Firstly, it helps us to understand why land is so important to people and how land can give freedom of choice and

LECTURER-STUDENT DIALOGUES

Imaginary dialogues exemplify the process of legal reasoning, argument construction, problem-solving, and working effectively with judgments. Follow the dialogues to consolidate your knowledge and learn to think like a lawyer.

LECTURER: And what about small businesses?
STUDENT: Most of their start-up funding will come from banks, who may insist on a mortgage over the new directors' family home as security. If they can't repossess it and sell it if things go wrong then they will be reluctant to lend to businesses in the future.

This all sounds a bit hollow. Surely asking purchasers to make a few more enquiries when they buy the house or before a lender takes a mortgage on it, would not be too burdensome? It's not like going back to the sort of enquiries that purchasers of old used to have to make (at least according to BUILDING BLOCK NO 5: Property Rights and the Protection of Purchasers and Mortgage Lenders, where *every* right would bind a purchaser). For residential purchasers and banks, their conveyancers could always ask anyone who lived there with the vendor to fill out a form or something. That way they would find out about property rights that would bind them.
LECTURER: When you get into Land Law you will see that there are a number of cases and articles that will support you on this point. And there are ones that will help you develop it

your Building Blocks, perhaps in separate files, and hold them against the rules so that you are constantly thinking about the relationship between rules and their underlying concepts and policies.

> Read carefully and critically, think about how the authors and judges are considering the relationship between the rules and the Building Blocks. Throughout the book we will be considering extracts from judgments and articles. This is designed to help you think carefully about the reasoning in cases and about which of the Building Blocks have been used to construct the reasoning and argument. Throughout the book there are LECTURER and STUDENT dialogues to help you construct your arguments using Building Blocks.

F. SUMMARY OF THE BUILDING BLOCKS

And finally here is a summary of our Building Blocks. We will be using them throughout in order to construct arguments about, and understand, the rules of Land Law that we find in cases and statutes.

INFORMATION POINTS
Definitions, examples and other useful information is provided to further enhance your understanding.

TABLE OF CASES

TABLE OF STATUTES

Chapter 1

The Building Blocks of Land Law

CHAPTER OVERVIEW

In this Chapter you will find:

- The aims of this book and how it will help you to think like a Land Lawyer
- A brief history of Land Law and how it has developed
- Six guiding principles with which to construct a case in Land Law: the Building Blocks
- A method for constructing argument using the Building Blocks.

The aim of this book

1

The broad difference between school and university is the difference between merely learning information and the need for critical thinking.

We are going to be learning the rules of Land Law: for example, what are the requirements that we have to establish before the law says we gain the right to walk across another's land? If a bank wants to repossess someone's house, what are the legal tests they have to satisfy before the law will let them do it? If I buy a house, what paperwork do I have to complete ("formalities") before the house is put in my name?

Part of learning how to think critically and independently is to begin to understand how to form and write down a valid opinion about whether particular rules, such as the ones above, are good or bad, fair or unfair. We have to learn how to create argument about rules. Argument is important when it comes to examinations and coursework. Law examinations and coursework involve two types of question: discursive essay questions and problem questions.

A. PROBLEM SOLVING SKILLS TAUGHT IN THIS BOOK

In law examinations we often have to apply rules to a factual situation in order to predict a legal solution to the problem. It means that we have to argue about *how* a rule should apply. This involves various skills by which we have to extract rules from cases and look at how they may help us predict a solution to our problem. This book contains extracts from judgments in important Land Law cases and shows you how to interpret and apply legal rules.

Furthermore, an examiner will often create a legal problem where it is unclear whether a particular rule applies or not. It is down to the candidate to create a convincing argument for why the rule *should* or *should not* apply. Cases reach the Court of Appeal and the Supreme Court precisely because it is uncertain whether and how a particular rule applies to a set of facts.

For example, a bank may be trying to repossess your client's house. The client has failed to make his mortgage payments for six months.

> **For information: A mortgage**
> A bank will lend you money to buy a house in which you live. You will then pay the loan back on monthly instalments. If you fail to meet the repayments, the bank has the power to repossess your house and sell it in order to get its money back.

Your client is currently out of work but has a job about to start soon. A rule of Land Law provides that the court has discretion to prevent the bank from repossessing the house, but only in circumstances where the borrower has reasonable prospects of making his mortgage payments in the future, including paying off any arrears. The rule was laid down in s.36 of the Administration of Justice Act 1970 and interpreted in *Cheltenham & Gloucester Building Society v Norgan*.[1] It is currently unclear whether having a job about to start will constitute reasonable prospects. It is open to a considerable amount of argument about whether the client or the bank will win the case. If it were clear the case would not usually get to court as the solicitor would advise his or her client accordingly.[2] So, lawyers in court often have to persuade a judge that a rule should or should not apply in a particular case. They give a reasoned argument as to why the rule should apply in a particular way.

B. ARGUMENT SKILLS TAUGHT IN THIS BOOK

Law examinations will often include "essay-style questions" in which we have to "discuss" or "critically evaluate" rules, i.e. create argument about them.

---

1   [1996] 1 W.L.R. 343.
2   F. Schauer, *Thinking Like a Lawyer* (Harvard University Press, 2009), p.23.

> **Example of essay-style question:** Discuss whether you think the rules laid down in *Cheltenham & Gloucester Building Society v Norgan* [1996] 1 W.L.R. 343, and interpreted in subsequent cases, create a fair balance between borrower and lender in the law of mortgages.

For this question you will have to argue about whether the rules laid down in *Cheltenham & Gloucester v Norgan* are fair; do they create a balance between these two competing interests that is justifiable in the interests of what is fair?

C. THE BUILDING BLOCKS

When we write essays which require us to discuss or critically evaluate a particular rule, it means that we are to give a reasoned or informed opinion about whether the rule is fair or not. The aim of this book is to give you a method of creating an authentic argument about the rules of Land Law: Building Blocks. Authentic argument is about identifying evidence that supports a particular point of view, e.g. that the rules laid down in *Cheltenham & Gloucester v Norgan* are fair. It is also about how to use that evidence in a persuasive way. It is important to remember that there is no right answer. The strength of your argument, its authenticity, is assessed by the way in which you have used *evidence* to support your claims.

Alec Fisher in *The Logic of Real Arguments* (1988) considers that we can evaluate the strength of an argument by identifying those elements that the author uses to support his conclusion and then asking the question: *What evidence will justify me in accepting that evidence as true or false?* In this book Fisher constructs a method of testing the validity and strength of an argument, using examples of commonly accepted theories from many different areas of knowledge. I am not claiming in any way to apply that method to Land Law rules and to represent its intricacies here, but I take from it these two elements: firstly, his assertability question. Although I do not apply it here in quite the same senses and with the same subtleties and complexities as Fisher does, that question will give us a valuable starting point in creating authentic argument about Land Law rules.

> As a starting point for creating authentic argument about Land Law rules we may ask the question *what evidence will justify me in concluding that this rule is good or bad fair or unfair?*

Secondly, in the Preface to his book Fisher observes that we are accustomed to relying on experts, to accepting their views and pronouncements. Life is so complicated and specialist that we are used to relying on the experts, the writers and the lecturers, in our various fields. We take their pronouncements as self-evidently correct, particularly when they project the authority and finality that they so often do. We are in some sense *cowed*—blinded by science so to speak. Never has this been truer than in Land Law! I admit that when I came across Fisher's book in a little old-fashioned second-hand bookshop and I read this, I could have shouted for sheer joy. I immediately wanted to convey this idea to my students. The aim of my book is to put the Building Blocks of Land Law argument firmly in your hands. In our second-year Land Law module my students and I have a maxim that "it's all for you to play for"! I hope that this becomes as true for you as it has become for them.

D. WHAT QUALIFIES AS EVIDENCE FOR AN ARGUMENT?

We need to understand the type of evidence that can be used to construct a solid and persuasive argument about Land Law rules. In court, one usual way that a barrister aims to persuade a judge to accept his interpretation of the way a rule should apply, is to argue that their opponent's interpretation would undermine the fundamental purpose of the rule and theirs would support that purpose. This is the evidence needed for a reasoned and persuasive argument. Many judges proceed on the basis that law does not exist in a vacuum; that rules need underlying justifications[3]; that a rule should further basic policy aims. We argue that a development of a rule in a case is good or bad, fair or unfair, depending on:

- the extent to which it promotes the policy aims of Land Law;
- the extent to which the rule promotes legitimate purposes of a good legal system;
- the extent to which a rule is consistent with what "justice" means;
- the extent to which a rule is based on identified concepts that underpin land law.

All of these may be used legitimately as evidence to justify saying whether a particular rule is good or bad, fair or unfair. Some are specific to Land Law; others are not. The purpose of this chapter is to set out in detail each one of these blocks of evidence that we use to build arguments; the purposes behind Land Law rules.[4]

> These Building Blocks are your stock-in-trade for creating arguments. Keep them separate. Read them frequently, and add to them as you read about Land Law.

When we consider the various rules of Land Law, we hold the rule against the Building Blocks and consider which of them relate to the rule and which do not. We then ask whether the rule supports or undermines the policies and principles contained in these Building Blocks. We say the rule is good or bad according to this.

> Throughout this book there are imaginary LECTURER and STUDENT dialogues to help you develop your skills in constructing authentic argument with Building Blocks.

---

3   See for example, F. Schauer, *Thinking Like a Lawyer* (2009), Ch. 2 "Rules – In Law and Elsewhere", pp.13–35.
4   At least we will consider some of the main ones here. There are some purposes that will only make sense alongside the specific rule to which they relate. In such cases I defer consideration of these Building Blocks until the point in the book that I consider the relevant rules.

E. THE MAKER'S INSTRUCTIONS!

Therefore, for both essays and problems we need to know why the rules of Land Law are the way they are. We need to know the intimate concerns and purposes of Land Law rules before we can solve its problems and write essays about it. For this we need to open the book that lies behind Land Law and look at what it is trying to do. From this we get an idea of how it is supposed to work: Land Law's *Genetic Fingerprint*.

F. AN EXAMPLE

Our Building Blocks are some of the basic aims of Land Law and of a good legal system in general. They are policies and first principles. For example, one of our Building Blocks is that "There is a Need for Certainty and Predictability in Land Law Rules". When we hold a rule against this Building Block and we see that the rule is not certain and clear, then we can *legitimately* say that it is a bad rule.

Example: How to use the Building Blocks to interrogate the rules of Land Law

Rule:
Under *C&G v Norgan* the court can prevent a bank or building society from repossessing a house where a borrower can show that they have a "reasonable prospect" of being able to catch up with their mortgage payments.

BUILDING BLOCK NO 6: The Need for Certainty in Law
It is important that any rule provides certainty as to how it is going to apply in the future. No one should have to go to court to find out what the law is.

Hold the rule against the policy or Building Block and think about the connection between the two. The Building Block is your evidence for stating "yes this rule is good" or "no it is bad". Is the rule certain as to how it will apply to cases? Is it so unclear that banks would have to go to court to find out what "reasonable prospect" means?
Does the rule support or undermine the Building Block? Why?

My ARGUMENT: I submit that the rule in *Cheltenham & Gloucester BS v Norgan* is not good law.

A rule must be certain as to how it will apply in the future in order to be called "good law". In any legal system we must have certainty. When we look carefully at the rule in *C&G v Norgan* we might say that it is uncertain as to what is a "reasonable prospect", i.e. is it sufficient for a defaulting borrower to show that they have a well-paid job about to start, is it o.k. for them to show that they bought a lottery ticket for Saturday night's draw? Without going to court, which is the last thing any borrower needs at this time, it might be difficult for a lawyer to advise a client when the bank would be legally able to repossess their house. Thus, we can say legitimately that the rule in *C&G v Norgan* is not good law. This is just an example, and counter-arguments will be possible.

← My CONCLUSION

← My EVIDENCE for this conclusion: provided by one of our Building Blocks

2 A history of Land Law

Land Law is about *ownership* of land, how it is regulated, and what an owner is entitled to do. Both land and ownership has been highly prized in our culture for centuries. Land is the commodity on which we do all our working, eating, sleeping, living and dying. Land has shaped our lives, society and economy. Let us take some examples.

At the time of King Edward in the eleventh century, the land in a village was divided into strips and distributed amongst peasant farmers. Although these farmers owned their individual strip, decisions about "the crops to be grown, the dates of ploughing, sowing and reaping, and the periods during which animals might graze in the different fields, were subject to the decision of the village".[5] People had to co-operate with each other in order to get the best out of the land. One crop would be grown in one field, another in a different field, and land could not be cultivated all the time. Animals needed to graze on the land. In order to maximise their stock and food, the villagers had to co-operate with each other as a society.[6] The way in which people lived and the values by which they lived their lives were dictated by the need to live off the land.[7]

During the eighteenth and nineteenth centuries, the ownership of land was connected with social and political ambition. Land was the most "socially acceptable form of property".[8] It shaped the social and political fortunes of the landed gentry. The landed aristocracy enjoyed a great deal of political control. At the end of the eighteenth century, "[t]he peerage was certainly the most conspicuous and powerful institution of the landed aristocracy", and "a sizeable fraction of the nobility exercised a considerable degree of direct control over the composition of the House of Commons".[9] Thus, the ownership of land was important to a noble family. It gave them social and political status. The estate of a landowner would be a "mini community". Great landowners had tenants who farmed parts of the estate. This was a far cry from the landlord and tenant relationship with which we are familiar today.[10] A landowner would often take an interest in the welfare of his tenants. He was head of a large estate and his tenants participated in the important life events of the great family:

> "The birth of an heir was matter for much rejoicing in the neighbourhood of a great house. . . . A great dinner would be given for the tenantry, and the senior tenant, the steward and the owner would all make speeches".[11]

---

5   G.W.S. Barrow, *Feudal Britain* (London: Hodder & Stoughton, 1956), pp.17–20, the so-called "open field" system.
6   Barrow, above, p.21.
7   K. Gray and P.D. Symes, *Real Property and Real People* (London: Butterworths, 1981) p.15.
8   F.M.L. Thompson, *English Landed Society in the Nineteenth Century* (London: Routledge and Kegan Paul, 1963), p.50.
9   Thompson, above, p.45.
10   T. Murphy, S. Roberts and T. Flessas, *Understanding Property Law,* 4th edn (London: Sweet & Maxwell, 2004).
11   Thompson, *English Landed Society in the Nineteenth Century* (1963), pp.76–7.

This in turn reinforced the standing of the landed family.[12]

The way in which land shaped status, reputation and even our institutions of church and government, gave rise to legal forms of ownership that ensured their protection. From the seventeenth century, devices were perfected to enable the landed family to keep that land in their family for generations. These legal devices, known as strict settlements, were used by the lawyers of "the landed classes [and] shackled much of the land in England to the same families until Victorian times and beyond".[13] The idea was to make sure that land passed from the father of the family to his eldest son, on each new generation.[14] Thus, "the landed family was preserved as a powerful institution in running the whole machinery of the country's administration".[15] At the time of the Industrial Revolution, much of the land in England was owned by the aristocracy:

"The New Domesday Book, compiled in the 1870s, provided information from which it was estimated that 'a landed aristocracy consisting of about 2,250 persons own together nearly half the enclosed land in England and Wales' ".[16]

The landed gentry were instrumental in the enterprises involved in the industrial revolution because it involved the exploitation of their land:

"Being large owners of the surface, English landowners became large owners of the sub-surface minerals in an island richly endowed with mineral resources."[17]

But it was in the latter half of the nineteenth century that society's view of the importance of land changed again. Land lost its attractiveness to the gentry and aristocracy. Land no longer provided the social status that it did in former times. Once the industrial revolution got underway, land was no longer seen as the only form of socially recognised wealth. There was money and shares in new companies, such as railway companies. The great landed estates were eventually broken up. The government began to impose huge death duties, which meant that the new heir succeeding to the estate could not afford to maintain it. Also, land no longer provided the wealth that it once did. From about 1750 until 1850 there was a depression in the agricultural industry and insufficient profit could be made from the land: "in the end falling prices rather than mismanagement accounted for the break-up of the great estates".[18] The farming world was no longer a means of providing wealth:

---

12   Thompson, above, pp.76–7.
13   J.H. Baker, *An Introduction to English Legal History,* 2nd edn (London: Butterworths, 1979) p.247. In the *Parliamentary Papers,* 1847/8, S.C. on Agricultural Customs, Q.1004–5, (Chandos Wren-Hoskyns), it was said that in 1847 "'speaking generally . . . half or two-thirds of the land of England' was in encumbered estates" (settlements) (quoted and cited in Thompson, above, p.67, there was another observation made that this figure was as high as 70%).
14   J.H. Baker, *An Introduction to English Legal History* above, p.245.
15   F.M.L. Thompson, *English Landed Society in the Nineteenth Century* (1963), p.65; also "[o]ne main purpose of the settlement was indeed to protect the family estate from the worst depredations of spendthrift heads of family". A settlement would ensure that he only had limited powers to deal with the land: Thompson, above, p.66.
16   G. Broderick, *English Land and English Landlords* (1881), quoted by D. Spring, "English Landowners and Nineteenth-Century Industrialism", in J.T. Ward and R.G. Wilson (eds) *Land and Industry* (University of California, 1971), pp.16–17.
17   D. Spring, "English Landowners and Nineteenth-Century Industrialism", in *Land and Industry* (1971) p.17.
18   B. Kerr, *Bound to the Soil* (Dorset Books, 1993), p.221.

"The predicament of landowners, farmers, and of rural shopkeepers and craftsmen was one of struggling to survive in a country which no longer looked to the soil for its wealth."[19]

Thus, the strict settlement, the legal device for keeping land in the same family for generations, fell into disuse:

"The final stage in the history of the settlement realised the economic fact that, local sentiment apart, a settlement of land was a settlement of wealth which need not be tied to specific pieces of land."[20]

Whilst this decline of fortune was in operation, in the latter half of the nineteenth century the Liberal government argued that large estates of land should be broken up, divided into plots and sold to commoners. The argument was that these "small proprietorships" would do much to foster the good of society in general by instilling in an individual a sense of identity, security and worth.[21]

So we see that land has unique importance in the affairs of human beings. The legal recognition of ownership of land has been instrumental in creating communities, power, social hierarchy, government, identity and wealth.[22]

And then something happened in the twentieth century that Land Law did not expect. People started to buy houses, instead of renting them, in order to create a *home*. A considerable amount of the population of this country now *owns* their home. We call this "owner occupation".

Successive governments in the 70s and 80s placed considerable value on a home-owning democracy, particularly Margaret Thatcher's governments. Just for comparison: in the early 1900s, most ordinary people used to rent the house in which they lived.

> **"The mass diffusion of home ownership has been one of the most striking social changes of our own time."**
>
> *Midland Bank Plc v Cooke* **[1995] 4 All E.R. 562, p.575A per Waite L.J.**

So how, in financial terms, is this home-owning democracy achieved?

Most residential purchasers cannot afford to buy a house outright. They use what is called a mortgage. What is a mortgage? A bank will lend you money to buy a house in which you live,

---

19   B. Kerr, above, p.93; J.H. Baker, *An Introduction to English Legal History*, p.248.
20   J.H. Baker, *An Introduction to English Legal History*, pp.247–8, footnote omitted.
21   George Osborne Morgan, *Land Law Reform in England* (Pamphlet, London: Chapman and Hall, 1880) pp.8, 21–23.
22   There is much that has been said on this before, notably: Gray and Symes, *Real Property and Real People*; Murphy, Roberts and Flessas, *Understanding Property Law*.

usually three times your income. You will then pay the loan back on monthly instalments. You grant the bank a mortgage over the house so that if you fail to meet the repayments, the bank has the power to repossess your house and sell it in order to get its money back.

The Building Blocks of Land Law

3

A. BUILDING BLOCK NO 1: RESIDENTIAL SECURITY

The purpose for which people buy houses is to create a stable home for themselves and their families, so Land Law rules should protect this. Rules should support the rationale for owning land. It is a policy of Land Law to protect people's *residential security*. [23] So we can legitimately say that Land Law rules *ought to* protect a person's residential security, and should not be interpreted by the courts to undermine it. People become attached to the land, and through ownership of their space, come to feel a sense of security and inviolability.[24] This feeling of safety, security, protectedness, and inviolability is thought to be fundamental in the raising of children. It is therefore the bedrock of civilisation.[25] Indeed the philosopher Hume considered that the expectation of continued stability is strong within a person: "it would be greater cruelty to dispossess a man of any thing, than not to give it to him".[26] Atiyah considers that "[e]xpectations based on, and allied with, physical possession, seemed, in a stable society, to be the most natural type of expectation to be protected".[27]

> **BUILDING BLOCK NO 1: Residential Security**
> We can legitimately say that Land Law rules are good if they protect a person/family's residential security. *So how does this work?*

---

23   Expression and idea of "residential security": K. Gray and P. Symes, *Real Property and Real People*.
24   Also, Gray and Symes, above.
25   L. Payne, conference Oxford; K. Stern, *The Flight From Woman* (Farrar, Strauss & Giroux, 1965).
26   *Treatise*, Book III, Part II, Section I, quoted by P.S. Atiyah, *The Rise and Fall of Freedom of Contract* (Oxford University Press, 1979), p.107. The ideas in this paragraph are taken from an article previously published by the author of this book: [2003] 119 L.Q.R. 660.
27   P.S. Atiyah, *The Rise and Fall of Freedom of Contract*, p.109.

Example 1:   Creating an argument using BUILDING BLOCK NO 1: Residential Security

Rule:
There is a very alarming "loophole" in Land Law that allows banks to repossess a family home without first going to court to obtain a possession order: *Horsham v Clarke* [2009]

BUILDING   BLOCK   NO   1: Residential Security
Land Law rules should protect peoples' residential security and not be interpreted to undermine it. They are good and fair if they offer this protection.

Hold the rule against the policy or Building Block and think about the connection between the two.

Let's say that I CONCLUDE that *Horsham Properties Group Ltd v Clarke* [28] is bad law. But what is the EVIDENCE that I need to make my conclusion into an argument? The rule undermines the policy of protecting residential security (BUILDING BLOCK NO 1) because it denies a residential occupier any defence to repossession proceedings. They should have the chance to prove that they can catch up on their mortgage payments. Because we live in a social climate of owner occupation and the reason why many people buy land is to buy a family home, Land Law should as far as possible protect the stability of that home. Rules should always reflect their functions. If Land Law allows repossessions of those homes to take place so readily and families to be evicted accordingly, Land Law rules are not giving adequate protection to the need for residential security. This will provide persuasive evidence for my CONCLUSION that *Horsham v Clarke* is bad law.

BUILDING BLOCK NO 1: Residential Security
If a rule of Land Law undermines people's residential security too much, and allows banks to repossess houses too readily then this is a legitimate reason for arguing that the rule is bad law.

---

28   [2008] EWHC 2327.

Example 2:   Another one involving banks and building societies

James owns a house with his partner Janet, and unbeknown to Janet he mortgages the house, runs off with the money and defaults on the payments due under the mortgage. Rules of Land Law have to answer the question of whether Janet can stop the bank from repossessing the house because she did not know about the mortgage. If the rules allow the bank to take possession *too easily* then they might be criticised on the basis of this Building Block.

Rules: If the rules allow Janet to stay in the house and refuse to allow the bank to repossess the house: Good or bad law?

BUILDING BLOCK NO 1: Residential Security
A law is good if it protects a person's residential security

Hold the rule against the BUILDING BLOCK and think about the connection between them.

I might CONCLUDE that a rule that prevents the bank from repossessing the house and evicting Janet in this situation is good law. But what is the EVIDENCE that I put forward to make my conclusion into an ARGUMENT? The rule protects Janet's residential security. She was powerless. She did not know that a mortgage had been created over the house and no doubt the repossession proceedings were a shock to her. She was living in the house as her home. Whether Land Law likes it or not, it's rules determine the outcome of this kind of dispute all the time, between people who have purchased land as a home, and not for investment, and who need residential stability. Because we live in a social climate of owner occupation and the reason why many people buy land is to buy a family home, Land Law should reflect this. Rules should always promote their purposes. If Land Law allows repossessions of those homes to take place so readily and families to be evicted accordingly, Land Law rules are not giving adequate protection to the need for residential security.

But we must also consider counter-arguments: Is there anything Janet, and many like her, could have done to protect herself further? Why should the law intervene to protect her? After all, the courts have to consider the bank (and many like them) as well.

Example 3:   Here's an example involving co-ownership

Five vets together purchase "Herriot House" in order to run a practice and provide living accommodation. They will own the property jointly. The law of co-ownership is very important as it provides rules that answer questions like: What happens when one of the co-owners dies—who gets his share? Let's say that his share is inherited by his brother. Can his brother, the new owner of that share, force the other co-owners to sell the house? Rules have to provide a resolution to the dispute when co-owners fall out and one wants to sell the land and the others don't.

Rule: Let's say that the court allows Herriot House to be sold very quickly at the request of the new co-owner who has only just inherited his share I would CONCLUDE that this is bad law.

BUILDING BLOCK NO 1: Residential Security
The EVIDENCE for my conclusion (which turns it into an ARGUMENT) is that the court has not considered, before ordering sale of Herriot House, that the other co-owners, who owned it for much longer, want to stay living there. Rules now operate in the context of owner occupation and should reflect this purpose. In this case they didn't so this is bad law.

(1) Imaginative argument: Does the rule undermine the Building Block?

So far we have seen that for a good argument we need evidence to support our conclusion. We get our evidence from our Building Blocks.[29] Much land is owned for the purpose of residential security, the rules of Land Law should reflect this. Land Law does not and should not exist as an abstract entity. It should reflect the uses in society to which land is put. We can argue that a development of a rule in a case or statute is good or bad, fair or unfair, depending on the extent to which it supports or undermines people's expectation that their residence in the house will continue. So we have blocks of evidence. Now we need cement to build our argument. When constructing our arguments we should practice ASKING QUESTIONS. Return to Example 2 above:

EVIDENCE

Rules: If the rules allow Janet to stay in the house and refuse to allow the bank to repossess the house: this is good law.

BUILDING BLOCK NO 1: Residential Security
A law is good if it protects a person's residential security.

---

29   Alec Fisher's "assertability question" in *The Logic of Real Arguments* (Cambridge University Press, 1988) (adapted here): *What evidence will justify me in accepting the proposition that this rule is good or bad fair or unfair?* I am not in any way attempting to set down his method of argument evaluation and construction. However, at various stages throughout the process he uses this question. I found it a useful starting point to introduce what it is that makes a strong and persuasive argument.

But residential security is not an absolute, immutable, article of faith. It would be supremely unconvincing to say that all repossession law is bad just because it impacts on a person's residential security. You have to determine the point at which the rules *really do* undermine residential security. And we do this by asking questions.

Let's check out the evidence:

> The bank should only be allowed to succeed if they themselves have taken adequate precautions that the house is good security. Does the law require banks in this situation to conduct enough "checks" etc?

> Is there something that all occupiers in this situation could have done to protect themselves (we can't just go on a case-by-case basis and ask about Janet)? For example could they have registered their interest in the house so that the bank would have known about it? They should not be able to rely on the law simply to bail them out. We can often find information/arguments of this kind in articles.

There are other equally important policies and principles that Land Law must bear in mind. Do the rules perhaps offer too much protection so that a bank will have difficulty repossessing a house and getting its money back even though borrowers have not acted reasonably responsibly? We must consider the boundaries of protection of continued stability.

> What do the academic authors say about this? Look at a couple of articles for each topic. We will be considering extracts from judgments and articles. So you have some raw material to interrogate.

> Would protection of residential security involve a massive departure from an existing system of rules and their other functions—in which case your argument will have to be extremely strong?

B. BUILDING BLOCK NO 2: IDEAS OF JUSTICE

Justice is a virtue. It is an absolute good. It is something that we can hold against any form of conduct as a standard by which we say that conduct is good or bad. So in this sense it is the easiest of our Building Blocks. If we can form some articulated idea of what justice might mean in the context of the possession of land then we can hold up the rules of Land Law against this and say whether or not they are good or bad. A logical starting point is to try and work out where the idea of justice comes from.

> *"Justice is the settled and permanent intention of rendering to each man his rights."*
> (Roman, Justinian, *Institutions*, I.i.)

According to the twentieth century moral philosopher Josef Pieper, justice "is the notion that each man is to be given what is his due".[30] But why should he be? Pieper affirms the view that God created us as separate beings with a creative will of our own: " '[i]t is through creation that the created being first comes to have his rights' ".[31] And it is for this reason that each person should be respected as "master of his own actions" and choices. This is a person's "due" respect.

A person's freedom of will should be respected because he or she

> "is a *person* – a spiritual being, a whole unto himself, a being that exists for itself and of itself, that wills its own proper perfection. Therefore, and for *that very reason* something *is* due to man in the fullest sense, *for that reason* he does inalienably have a *suum*, a 'right' which he can plead against everyone else, a right which imposes upon everyone of his partners the obligation at least not to violate it. [...] [T]he concept of the personality is set forth in all its elements: its freedom, imperishability, and responsibility for the whole of the world. If on the contrary, man's personality is not acknowledged to be something wholly and entirely real, then right and justice cannot possibly be established."[32]

"Their due" or "justice" inalienably belongs to a human being. So much so that:

> "[T]he man who does not give a person what belongs to him, withholds it or deprives him of it, is really doing harm to himself; *he* is the one who actually loses something – indeed, in the most extreme case, he even destroys himself. At all events, something incomparably worse befalls him than happens to the one who suffers an injustice: that is how inviolable the right is! [...] [j]ustice belongs to man's true *being*".[33]

Examples of not rendering to another their due:
- Mockery, because it causes shame—or anything that lowers a person in their own eyes
- Coercion/undue influence—because it violates a person's will and denies that he or she is "master of their own actions"

---

30   Josef Pieper, *The Four Cardinal Virtues* (first paperback edition University of Notre Dame Press, 1966, reprinted 2006), p.44.
31   Above, p.46, affirming Aquinas.
32   Josef Pieper, *The Four Cardinal Virtues*, p.50. Thus human beings are capable of having something "belong to" them, in contrast with other created beings such as plants and animals, which are not "wholes in this sense": Pieper, p.47.
33   Above pp.47–8.

"Pious declamation on solemn occasions is not enough. Fundamental truths must constantly be pondered anew lest they lose their fruitfulness." [34] I think it amounts to this—that I might look at this information "dead on the page"—but unless I practice it, justice will remain an *abstraction*. To be a good lawyer justice must enter my *heart*. Therefore, it is something that has to be *practised*.

(1) The moral duty not to violate the will

The will in a person is everything they call "myself". When the will is properly active, the personality can move forward, direct, press through difficulty, initiate change. Thus, a person must be accorded freedom of the will.[35] Justice is to accord someone their due of being recognised as a separate entity, in possession of a creative will. We might say that a principle of justice is to accord a person his due and not violate his will. If such harm is done, restitution must be made.[36]

Example 1:   *Blackhill Farm*

David owns Blackhill Farm. He forms a friendship with Peter. Over a long period of time, David tells Peter that he does not have to worry about his future. That he will leave Blackhill Farm to him when he dies. David encourages Peter to rely on this promise. Peter moves into the Farmhouse and spends his own money renovating it and making it habitable. After 10 years of David's promises and Peter's reliance, David and Peter fall out. David changes his will and tells Peter to move out of the farmhouse.

In short David has systematically overcome Peter's will and by his continuous promises influenced Peter's life-choices. David has also influenced Peter into spending money on improving his (David's) farm. This influence, and David's eventual gain from it, violates moral justice which says that a person should have freedom of his will.

Broadly under the rules of Land Law Peter would obtain a remedy against David. He may get a part share of Blackhill Farm. We might conclude then that this is good law

CONCLUSION

BUILDING BLOCK NO 2: Ideas of Justice

Hold a rule or set of cases up against these ideas of justice. If the rule/cases reflect these ideas of justice they are good. If they undermine them they are bad. If the law gives Peter a remedy it is supporting these ideas of moral justice

EVIDENCE

---

34   Pieper, p. 51
35   D. Rose, *Hegel's "Philosophy of Right": A Reader's Guide* (Continuum, 2007). Of course, Hegel identifies proper constraints on the exercise of the will, such as criminal activity; also J.W. Harris, *Property and Justice* (Oxford: Clarendon Press, 1996).
36   Pieper, above, p.80.

So giving others freedom of choice is inherently morally justifiable.[37] Let's try another example.

(2) A non-Land Law example

I would like you to think about whether justice has been violated in this example: Jane makes a promise to Alison, an 18-year-old who lives next door, that she will give her Jane's bicycle, provided that she will repair it. Alison then gives up her weekend to work on repairing the bicycle and sells her old car. When Alison comes round to Jane's house to claim the bicycle, can we say that Jane's refusal to hand it over is an act of moral injustice? From the above, the quality of the act as unjust lies in the fact that Jane has interfered with Alison's freedom of will. Jane's statements about what she would do with her bicycle influenced Alison's choices about her conduct. Therefore, if Jane profited from her influence at Alison's expense, the person whose will she had power over, then moral justice demands that Jane makes restitution, i.e. she either gives Alison the bicycle or does whatever is in her power to compensate her. Jane has not given Alison her due as an independent being with free choices.

As the quality of the act as just or unjust depends on Jane's influence over Alison's will, there will be factors that enter the equation and impact on whether or not justice has been violated. The quality of Jane's refusal as unjust will diminish in direct proportion to her influence over Alison's conduct in repairing the bicycle. So if Alison is a shrewd businesswoman and well aware that she is taking a risk that Jane may not hand over the bicycle, Jane's refusal to do so will be less unjust.[38] Similarly, if Jane said "repair the bicycle and I *might* give it to you".

Thus, it is said that a good person is one who "must learn to be faithful to his superiors and to keep promises".[39] One of Atiyah's arguments in *Promises, Morals and Law*,[40] is that a promise becomes morally binding on the maker when it is relied upon by the recipient. It is in reliance on a promise that this element of influence is shown. "The foundation of justice is good faith".[41] It is surprising just how many rules of Land Law seek to give effect to this principle of moral justice. We will be examining some of those rules and will be able to hold them against this Building Block to determine whether they do reflect moral justice or not.

(3) Respecting "autonomous choice"[42]

From this we can say that freedom of choice is inherently morally justifiable. Harris observes that "autonomous choice" is "an aspect of personhood" and that "respecting personhood is intrinsic to just treatment".[43] From this, he argues that the ownership of property gives a person

---

37   J.W. Harris, *Property and Justice*. There are obviously public policy limits to this.

38   This is the moral principle that appeared to underpin the House of Lords decision in *Cobbe v Yeoman's Row Management Ltd* [2008] UKHL 55. We will consider this below in Chapter 3.

39   Ancient Chinese, *Analects*, I .8, quoted C.S. Lewis, *The Abolition of Man—Reflections on Education*, University of Durham (1946), p.62.

40   P.S. Atiyah, *Promises, Morals and Law* (Oxford University Press, 1983).

41   Roman. Cicero, *De Off*, I vii, quoted C.S. Lewis, *The Abolition of Man—Reflections on Education* (1946), p.62.

42   Expression J.W. Harris, *Property and Justice*, p.230, see Chapter 13 "Property and Freedom".

43   J.W. Harris, *Property and Justice*, p.173; Harris' conception of justice is that "autonomous choice is of value to all human beings": p.230.

freedom to make choices. Therefore, where a rule operates to protect a person's ownership of property it is just.[44]

Gray and Symes argue that ownership of property and money gives a person independence. The effect of not owning a resource that is valued by society is "dependence" on others who possess that resource.[45] Pipes observes that[46]:

"It is the sense of economic independence and that of personal worth which it generates that give rise to the idea of freedom. That the ancient Greeks realized this is suggested by a passage in the *History* of Herodotus which attributes the valor of the Athenians in the war against the Persians to the fact that they no longer 'worked for a master'. Herodotus meant specifically that they had liberated themselves from the whims of tyrants. But the concept had broader implications than the political one, defining also the person who worked for himself, who was economically independent. . . . . And such self-sufficiency is possible only in societies that recognise private ownership."

Thus a person who is master of his own money is free in the sense that he is able to choose his own course of action and follow it through. For example, a woman who has given up work to look after the children has not the financial independence to choose what commodities to use and what services to employ.[47] The adult son of the owner sometimes feels his lack of power and dependence on the choices of his parents because he, as yet, does not have a home of his own; just at a time when his need to assert his independence is felt most keenly. The owner of property has power over things; non-owners are dependent.[48] Owners can use those things as they wish, sell them, keep them, buy other things etc. All of this entails choice. If the ownership of the family home is at stake, there are a variety of choices that the owner can make. It is the owner's choice that determines whether the family stays there or moves elsewhere. Stability is in the owner's choice.[49] Of course, ownership of property does not guarantee that a person will make the *right* choices. But it gives them a wider sphere in which to make decisions: to take action, to do what they believe to be the right thing, and to pursue right courses of action. It thus enables them to develop as a human being.[50] Ownership gives them the ability to exercise their free will. It accords them existence and respect as a human being: "a consciousness with a conscience".[51] Consequently, the recognition of private property is part of what constitutes "justice".[52]

---

44 He argues that this is Hegel's fundamental argument in favour of the recognition of private property in societies: Harris, above, p.220.
45 Gray and Symes, *Real Property and Real People*, p.5.
46 Pipes, *Property and Freedom* (Vintage Books USA, 1999), p.119 (footnotes omitted).
47 Harris, *Property and Justice*, p.231.
48 Gray and Symes, *Real Property and Real People*, p.5.
49 Harris, above.
50 Harris, above, p.234.
51 L. Payne, *Pastoral Care Ministries* Conference August 2001, Oxford University.
52 Harris, above, Ch.13, a valuable discussion on the role of property in relation to freedom and choice.

(4) How do the rules of Land Law interact with the ideas of justice?

Freedom of will that comes with property takes on peculiar significance in the context of the family home and owner-occupation. In a culture where many people now own the houses in which they live, the rules that regulate home ownership and mortgages should not be interpreted to restrict unduly the owner's freedom of choice. But how might someone's freedom of will and free choice be threatened by Land Law rules so that they need to offer some level of protection? Here are some examples.

It is still often the case that a couple's family home is put into the name of one of the spouses or partners. This means that the other person in the couple lacks any part of the ownership of the house. There are rules of Land Law by which a non-owning partner can acquire part of the ownership of the house by conduct alone. When we look at these rules we can ask whether they are sufficiently generous. Do they allocate ownership of the house in a way that reflects the input and work of those non-owning partners towards the welfare of the family? Do the rules that give non-owning cohabitees and family members a part share of the ownership of the house reflect the social and financial input of these family members so that they are then given real choices over what happens to the home and their residential security?[53]

For another example, Jake is the owner of a house. When his wife moves in after they are married, he promises that "the house and everything in it is as much yours as mine". In reliance on this, she spends a large sum of money on a new kitchen. Thus, Jake's promise influenced his wife's freedom of choice. If he goes back on his promise and refuses to acknowledge that the house is hers, this has been a violation of her free will. According to the moral principles that we have considered in this section, he should make restitution accordingly and give her the share of the ownership of the house that he promised her. If the rules of Land Law do not give Jake's wife some form of remedy against him, or part-ownership of the house, they are unfair when measured against this Building Block. It is a case of moral injustice.

Further, we have essentially said that "property is power", or at least that power resides in the ownership of property. This is open to abuse. Thus, as Jake is the sole owner of the house, he can sell or mortgage the house without the consent of his wife. She may be evicted as a result of Jake's actions. Harris argues that the law must offer some protection against the "domination potential" that comes with ownership of property.[54]

(5) Imaginative argument: Does the rule undermine the Building Block?

> **BUILDING BLOCK NO 2: Ideas of Justice**
> Rules are good and fair if they take account of moral justice, freedom of the will, autonomous choice. They are bad and unfair if they do not.

---

53   This issue was raised in Harris, *Property and Justice*, p.211.
54   Harris, above, pp.270–275.

Remember that we are using our Building Blocks to critically evaluate Land Law, i.e. to create valid and persuasive arguments about the rules. We need evidence to support our conclusion that the rule is good or bad fair or unfair. We get our evidence from the Building Blocks. So we can say that a rule is good or bad fair or unfair, depending on the extent to which it supports or undermines these basic ideas of justice.

> So we have blocks of evidence. Now we need cement to build our argument. When constructing our arguments we should practice asking questions and cross-examining BUILDING BLOCK NO 2: Ideas of Justice. Let's check out the evidence—see how strong it is.

We may argue that legal rules should follow these principles of moral justice. But using the Building Block to create a persuasive argument is quite another thing. Would you be convinced by an argument that just said "any rule that does not give a family member an ownership right in every circumstance will necessarily be bad"? There must be a cut off point somewhere. Ask questions like: In what sense do you think the law is or is not protecting a person's freedom of choice, i.e. the ability to make uninfluenced choices? Are there any policies or principles (see your other Building Blocks) that might dictate that the law's intervention in this situation ought to be limited? Although justice is very definitely an article of faith for any legal system, the rules inevitably have to take into consideration competing concerns, as we shall see below. You then decide whether the rules strike the right balance. For the person who is claiming that their freedom of choice is being threatened by a rule of Land Law, are they relying passively on the rules when they could have done something to protect themselves? If someone could have exercised their will to protect their interests, is there much justice in allowing them to remain passively reliant on the legal system to invent a rule to protect their interests?

C. BUILDING BLOCK NO 3: PROPERTY AND IDENTITY

Rules of Land Law are good and fair if they give effect to the idea that people express their personalities and derive identity from property.

This Building Block is a shorter one and is more limited in scope. Sometimes a link is drawn between the ownership of property and a person's sense of their own identity. William James states that "it is clear that between what a man calls *me* and what he calls *mine* the line is difficult to draw".[55] Winnicott shows that a child develops a sense of identity through possessing property. A child, at the age of two "possesses as many things as possible. [This shows a] strong feeling of ownership, especially in toys. 'It's mine' is a constant refrain".[56] "The 'this is mine' of a

---

55   James, *The Principles of Psychology*, 1 (New York, 1890), Chapter x, 291 at p.293, quoted by Pipes, *Property and Freedom*, p.72.
56   Winnicott, *The International Journal of Psycho-Analysis* 34, Part 2 (1953) at pp.89–97, quoted and cited in Pipes, above, p.73.

two-year-old implies 'this is not yours', and so conveys that 'I am I' and 'you are you' ".[57] It has been said also that property shapes a person's sense of personhood and identity as they get older. James states:

"We feel and act about certain things that are ours very much as we feel and act about ourselves. Our fame, our children, the work of our hands, may be as dear to us as our bodies are, and arouse the same feelings and the same acts of reprisal if attacked . . . *In its widest possible sense . . . a man's Self is the sum total of all that he CAN call his*, not only his body and his psychic powers, but his clothes and his house, his wife and children, his ancestors and friends, his reputation and works, his lands and horses, and yacht and bank-account. All these things give him the same emotions. If they wax and prosper, he feels triumphant; if they dwindle and die away, he feels cast down . . . [I]n every case [of loss of possessions] there remains . . . a sense of the shrinkage of our personality, a partial conversion of ourselves to nothingness."[58]

Thus, ownership of property may become part of a sense of value and worth. Harris is sceptical, contending that the idea is idiosyncratic. But "we can register the presence of the phenomenon in modern societies, intuitively, at least if we regard it as a matter of degree".[59]

(1) How do the rules of Land Law interact with ideas of property and identity?

> **BUILDING BLOCK NO 3: Property and Identity**
> Rules are good if they take proper account of the fact that people gain a sense of value and worth from ownership of land, particularly in the context of owner occupation.

Remember that for a good argument we need justification. We need evidence to support our conclusion that a rule is good or bad fair or unfair. We get our evidence from our Building Blocks. The evidence of BUILDING BLOCK NO 3 tells us that people derive a sense of identity from the ownership of their land. Thus, rules should not deprive them of that possession without adequate safeguards. So we can say that a rule is good or bad fair or unfair, depending on the extent to which it protects a person's ownership from interference.

However, for the argument to be at all convincing we must limit this one. Otherwise it could be used to justify any form of ownership over anything. Perhaps the best way of using this Building Block is to ask—*in what situation might it be convincing to argue that people should be allowed to continue in possession of land or a house?* For example, an elderly couple are living in a house,

---

57   Harris, above, pp.270–275.

58   James, *The Principles of Psychology*, 1 (New York, 1890), Chapter x, pp.291 and 293, quoted by Pipes, above, p.72 (editing supplied). This, although true, may signify that the individual's sense of security, value and worth was not strong from the start and these factors taken as "filling the gap". See the principles of developmental psychology and the various personality theories cited and discussed by Frank Lake, *Clinical Theology* (1986), abridged edition M.H. Yeomans ed.)

59   Harris, *Property and Justice*, p.223, citing Margaret Radin.

and have done so for a long time, when the person in whose name the house is legally registered mortgages the house behind the couple's back. The couple have invested much of their lives and personalities in the house. When the legal owner is no longer able to meet the repayments due under the mortgage, the bank tries to repossess the house and sell it. The first that the couple hear about the mortgage is when the bank commences legal action against them to evict them from the house. They had nothing to do with the mortgage. Rules which in some way delay repossession of a family home, or use every device to make repossession a last resort, might be considered "good" in accordance with the evidence in this Building Block.[60]

> In the European Convention on Human Rights the right to peaceful enjoyment of possessions is enshrined as a basic human right alongside rights such as the right to life, liberty, fair trial, and privacy. BUILDING BLOCKS NOS 1–3 provide some justification for why this is the case.

D. BUILDING BLOCK NO 4: IDEAS OF OWNERSHIP

What does it mean when we say that we "own" land or a house? What powers do we have? What privileges do we have? Why do we need to answer this question at all? Firstly, it helps us to understand why land is so important to people and how land can give freedom of choice and residential security. So knowing what ownership means gives us an understanding of our other BUILDING BLOCKS. It also justifies why English Law recognises ownership rights. Thus it will help us argue about Land Law. Secondly, the courts must sometimes determine whether someone has a *right* to claim property. So in this case we say that in order for the claimant to establish that he has a right at all, the conduct or agreement on which he relies to establish the right must exhibit all the characteristics of ownership. Rights in land must have the qualities of ownership. Otherwise they are not rights at all. So when we are confronted with cases that decide whether someone has a right in the land, this is often a meaningful way of arguing whether the court made the right decision or not.

So what is ownership? Bright observes:

> "Ownership itself is a set of open-ended use privileges and open-ended powers to control the use made by others of the property. . . . It is simply not possible to list all the potential uses which the owner may make of the property — she can live on it, use it for growing crops, climb trees on it, and so on."[61]

---

60   Harris, *Property and Justice*, p.223 refers to the exemption of very personal items from the bankruptcy rules.
61   S. Bright, "Of Estates and Interests: A Tale of Ownership and Property Rights" in *Land Law Themes and Perspectives* (Willan Publishing (now Routledge), 1998), p.529.

An owner can sell the land, can leave it by will, give it away, and destroy it. They can include or exclude anyone they please.[62] As Gray and Gray observe, the key factor of possession is *control*.[63]

> "Far from denoting a mere factual presence upon land, possession comprises a range of inner assumptions as to the power relationships generated by such presence . . . [These] encapsulate the possessor's own perception of the force and defensibility of his rights in relation to the land. Thus, for instance, no 'possession' can properly be attributed to a mere 'overnight trespasser' or to a friend who has expressly agreed to look after a house during its owner's absence on holiday."[64]

Ownership gives the owner control over what happens on their land without interference from others. The owner can exercise their freedom to include or exclude anyone they wish, feel that their privacy and residential security is protected, and have the ability to express their identity through their home.

For example, *Hunter v Canary Wharf Ltd*[65] concerned the construction of the Canary Wharf Tower, London's Docklands. It is one of the tallest office blocks in Europe (it is 800 feet tall) and has its own station. The owners of the land on which it was built were taken to court because the Tower interrupted the local inhabitants' television reception. The House of Lords stated that it was a basic rule that an owner of land is entitled "to build what he likes on his land".[66] Unless the claimants could establish that the building of the tower infringed an established right then they could not object to its presence. The House of Lords held that there was no right known in English law to receive television signals.

Building on this idea, a landowner can destroy his house without incurring any obligation to his neighbour to rebuild the house. He does not have to offer any form of protection from damage caused by exposure to the weather.[67] The owner of land is entitled to sell it; to transfer all ownership he has in that property to another person. An owner of land is entitled to take the profit from that land; to exploit its value economically. This might be done by renting out the property. It might be done by taking out a loan and in return giving the bank or building society a mortgage over the house, for example, to finance a business. In this way the ownership of land can be very useful. It thus provides much needed start up capital for small businesses.[68] The use privileges of ownership are numerous. The owner of a house can refurbish the house in any way

---

62   Naturally enough, ownership in English law is not absolute. Just as there are policy reasons why someone should not have absolute freedom of contract, and for that contract to be then enforceable through the courts (e.g. contracts for the undertaking of criminal endeavours are unenforceable), there are public policy reasons why ownership might be limited.

63   K. Gray and S.F. Gray, *Land Law Core Text* (Oxford University Press, 2006), p.90.

64   ibid.

65   [1997] 2 W.L.R. 684.

66   [1997] 2 W.L.R. 684, p.712, per Lord Hoffman: quoted Gray and Gray, "The Idea of Property in Land", in S. Bright and J. Dewar (eds) *Land Law Themes and Perspectives* (Oxford University Press, 1998), p.34. This right is subject to the grant of planning permission from the local council, where necessary.

67   *Phipps v Pears* [1965] 1 Q.B. 76.

68   K. Gray and S.F. Gray, *Elements of Land Law*, 4th edn (Oxford University Press, 2004), pp.1625–6.

he/she wishes, subject to local authority controls on what may be done, such as building extensions and altering listed buildings.

(1) How does Land Law enforce the rights of a landowner/householder?

If someone comes onto my land and I do not wish them to be there, the law will allow me to enforce my ownership and to evict them on the basis that they are committing a trespass.[69] It does not matter that they trespass for only a short time.[70] And it is not necessary to prove that they caused any annoyance or damage.[71] Even if they have an important reason to be there, such as undertaking repairs on neighbouring land, if I deny them entry they are committing trespass.[72] I can enforce my right and the court will usually grant an injunction to prevent the trespass.[73] This is why it was necessary for parliament to intervene and pass the Access to Neighbouring Land Act 1992, to ensure that it was possible for the owners of property to gain access to adjacent land, by applying to the court, in order to conduct necessary repairs to their own property.[74]

(2) It is arguable that a person who controls property should be the recognised owner

There are arguments that suggest that when a person controls things and land they almost become part of that person. If this is the case it would be wrong to evict them from the land or take the thing away from them. Harris argues that

> "The . . . driving force of the argument is the analogy with assault. If I am there already, it is a manifest wrong for some stranger to come along and push me out just as would be any other attack on my person; so I have a just claim to remain in possession of that which I have first occupied."[75]

So there is a form of "analogy with physical assault".[76] The Australian Aborigines had the same idea: "If the native made a 'find' of any kind (e.g. a honey tree) and marked it, it was thereafter safe for him, as far as his own tribesmen were concerned, no matter how long he left it".[77] He has taken trouble over it and controlled it.

---

69   *Kelsen v Imperial Tobacco Co (of Great Britain and Ireland) Ltd* [1957] 2 Q.B. 334; *Bernstein of Leigh (Baron) v Skyviews & General Ltd* [1978] Q.B. 479.

70   *Pickering v Rudd*, 4 Camp. 219; *Bernstein of Leigh (Baron) v Skyviews & General Ltd* [1978] Q.B. 479, p.482.

71   *Wandsworth Board of Works v United Telephone Co Ltd* (1883–4) L.R.13 Q.B.D. 904; *Gifford v Dent* [1926] W.N. 336; *Woollerton and Wilson Ltd v Richard Costain Ltd* [1970] 1 W.L.R. 411; *Bernstein of Leigh (Baron) v Skyviews & General Ltd* above, p.482; *Kelsen v Imperial Tobacco Co (of Great Britain and Ireland) Ltd* [1957] 2 Q.B. 334.

72   *John Trenberth Ltd v National Westminster Bank Ltd* (1980) 39 P. & C.R. 104, cited for this point in Stevens and Pearce, *Land Law*, 3rd edn (London: Sweet & Maxwell, 2005), p.13.

73   *Kelsen v Imperial Tobacco Co (of Great Britain and Ireland) Ltd* [1957] 2 Q.B. 334.

74   Stevens and Pearce, *Land Law*, p.14.

75   J.W.Harris, *Property and Justice*, p.214.

76   Harris, above p.168.

77   Australian Aborigines *ERE* v 441, quoted C.S.Lewis, *The Abolition of Man — Reflections on Education*, University of Durham (1946), p.61.

This may provide some justification for saying that a person should be recognised as owner of property over which he has assumed control, either where the competing claimant has no better claim to the property or where the person's control has manifested for a considerable period of time.

(3) Deciding whether a right in land exists

The courts use ownership qualities to decide whether a right in land exists. For example, the case of *Street v Mountford*[78] used ownership qualities to identify rules by which to distinguish a tenancy from a licence. A tenancy is a right in the land. It is ownership "for a time". A licence is not in any sense ownership of the land. It is mere permission from the owner to be there. It is not a right at all. If you occupy a house, you *might* be a tenant, but it is not necessarily the case that you *are* a tenant. It may be that you just have permission to be there. Determining the difference between a tenancy and a licence has been the cause of many legal disputes, not the least because a tenant cannot be evicted as easily as someone with only bare permission to be there. This is an important issue of Housing Law.

In *Street v Mountford*, the House of Lords said that it did not matter what was written on the document. [There were too many unscrupulous landlords around for that!] Whether you had a tenancy or not depended on the substance of *what* was agreed. Exactly *what* were you given the right to do with the land? Essentially if the occupier was given the right to *control* the land, i.e. exclude all including the landlord, then this meant he was a tenant.

> "The traditional view that the grant of exclusive possession for a term at a rent creates a tenancy is consistent with the elevation of a tenancy into an estate in land. The tenant possessing exclusive possession is able to exercise the rights of an owner of land, which is in the real sense his land albeit temporarily and subject to certain restrictions. A tenant armed with exclusive possession can keep out strangers and keep out the landlord unless the landlord is exercising limited rights reserved to him by the tenancy agreement to enter and view and repair. A licensee lacking exclusive possession can in no sense call the land his own and cannot be said to own any estate in the land. The licence does not create an estate in the land to which it relates but only makes an act lawful which would otherwise be unlawful."[79]

So we see here that the House of Lords recognised the fact that a tenancy was an ownership right in the land. The occupier, before she could be recognised as having a tenancy, must therefore have been granted the rights of exclusivity and control associated with ownership. She had been. Thus, she had a tenancy and not a mere licence.

---

78   [1985] A.C. 809.
79   [1985] A.C. 809, p.816 per Lord Templeman.

> **BUILDING BLOCK NO 4: Ideas of Ownership**
> Land Law rules should reflect its underlying concepts, such as ownership. The courts must sometimes determine whether someone has a right in land. Rights such as leases are rights of ownership over the land, albeit temporary. So the conduct or agreement on which the claimant relies to establish the right must exhibit all the characteristics of ownership, e.g. *Street v Mountford*. If it does not then the court should not have recognised a right in the land. When cases decide whether someone has a right in the land, this is often a meaningful way of arguing whether the court made the right decision or not.

(4) Different types of right in land

Numerous rights can exist in land. So far we have been looking at ownership of a house or land.[80] It is possible to have a right in someone else's land. Land is very different from other types of property. It is fixed; immovable, as well as physically unavoidable. We have to live and work on it and we have to co-operate with others in so doing.

(a) Co-ownership rights and mortgages

Land is often owned by more than one person. For example, if John and Mary decide to get married and live together in a house that Mary already owns, she may grant John a share of the ownership.[81] They will then become co-owners of the house. A landowner can take out a loan and grant the lending bank a mortgage over his land. A mortgage is an important interest in land because it confers rights to possess and sell the land should the owner not be able to make the repayments due under the loan. This will enable the bank to get its investment back.

(b) Smaller rights in land

The law has created different types of smaller right in land, many more than would arise in other types of property such as shares in a company or jewellery. Neighbours need to live in close proximity to each other. One may need to have access round the back of the other's house, a right of storage on his land, a right to park his car, a right to a certain amount of light through his window that his neighbour is not allowed to block etc. He will need an "easement", which is a limited right to do something on land belonging to another.

If a builder has developed a piece of land into five new executive houses, he may want to ensure that the value of the houses is not diminished by further building on the estate. He may wish to impose restrictions on the new owners of the executive houses providing that they cannot build another house on their land. This is a limited right that one landowner (x) has over the land of another (y) — y promises to refrain from doing something on his land. And x can enforce that promise. This right is known as a "restrictive covenant".

---

80   They are both classed as "land" for the purposes of Land Law rules.
81   Jackson, Pearce and Stevens, *Land Law,* 4th edn (London: Sweet & Maxwell, 2008).

Easements and covenants are enforced in much the same way as larger ownership rights. If the owner of the land refuses to give effect to the right, damages or an injunction can be granted to make him do so. In *Wrotham Park Estate Ltd v Parkside Homes*, the court awarded damages to the owner of the benefit of a restrictive covenant when the landowner built houses on his land in breach of the covenant.[82] In *Daniells v Mendonca*[83] the claimant's neighbour was ordered to knock down an extension that intruded on his right to light. When we looked at *Hunter v Canary Wharf Ltd*[84] earlier in this section we saw that the only factor that could have stopped the defendants from building the Canary Wharf Tower, which had interfered with the claimants' television signals, was where the claimants could establish that they had an easement to receive those signals: a limited right to curtail the freedom of ownership belonging to the defendants. This they could not do.

(c) The difference between ownership and smaller rights

There are significant differences between larger ownership rights, such as outright ownership, co-ownership, and, to a similar extent, mortgages, and smaller rights in the land. With smaller rights, such as easements and covenants, ownership of the right is not exclusive. The owner of an easement can enforce it against the landowner, but cannot prevent others from lawfully exercising the same right:

> "An easement holder can prevent her right from being interfered with but apart from that she has no say over who is allowed onto the land. This right to exclude, and the territorial control inherent to it, distinguishes . . .. . . ownership from [these smaller rights]".[85]

There is another point of distinction: Smaller ownership rights concern one purpose only, e.g. the right to gain access over another's land, the right to prevent another from building on his land. These are limited privileges. In distinction from ownership of the land:

> "[i]t is the open-endedness of the use privileges that ownership brings that sets estates [large ownership rights] apart from other [smaller] interests in land".[86]

(d) Determining whether a small right exists

The courts may refer to ownership qualities and underpinning ideas of smaller rights in land to determine whether a small right exists. The case of *Copeland v Greenhalf*[87] provides a good example. The question was whether X had an easement over the land of Y. This is a smaller right in land. It is not a claim to the whole ownership of the land. By nature an easement is a limited right to do some activity on your neighbour's land, e.g. to walk across it to gain access to your

---

82   [1974] 1 W.L.R. 798, pp. 810–811.
83   (1999) 78 P. & C.R. 401.
84   [1997] 2 W.L.R. 684.
85   S. Bright, "Of Estates and Interests: A Tale of Ownership and Property Rights" in *Land Law Themes and Perspectives*, p.538.
86   S. Bright, above, p.534.
87   [1952] Ch. 488.

land, or do some other limited activity, such as park a car or store items. Easements can be expressly granted by your neighbour, e.g. as a condition attached to sale of part of their land to you. Easements can also come into being by implication of law, on the circumstances of the case, without any express grant.

Often people will go to court seeking to establish that they have an easement, usually in response to the landowner neighbour who is seeking to stop them using his land to walk across, store things on, park a car on etc. So there is a dispute. In order to prove to the satisfaction of the court that the litigant has an easement, they must prove that their use of their neighbour's land *is only limited*, i.e. that it does not push the neighbour off his own land. The rule that the courts apply is that the claimant's use of the land must not amount to *excessive use* of the neighbour's land. Otherwise it would look like full ownership of the land and not a smaller right.

The facts of *Copeland v Greenhalf* were as follows: the claimant, Mrs Copeland, was the owner of an orchard and an adjoining strip of land 150ft by 15–35ft. The defendant was a wheelwright with a business across the road from the orchard and he used the strip of land to store his customers' vehicles awaiting repair and collection. Mrs Copeland brought an action against the defendant preventing him from using the land. The wheelwright claimed that he had an easement in the land, i.e. he had a right to use the land irrespective of whether he had permission. The extent to which the wheelwright used the land was undefined: he left the vehicles all over the land in different places and leaving Mrs Copeland an "ill defined" access.[88] Effectively his use amounted to possession of the strip, excluding Mrs Copeland.[89] Because of this Upjohn J. held that the right claimed by the wheelwright could not be an easement, which, by nature, is a smaller right to undertake a limited activity on someone else's land. What the wheelwright was claiming resembled ownership of the land, and not a smaller right in it.

We can see here that Upjohn J. relied on essential ideas about the nature of ownership and smaller rights in the land, and used these ideas to interpret the rules that determine whether the wheelwright could properly claim an easement.

> An easement is a more limited right than full ownership so it cannot look like this

> **BUILDING BLOCK NO 4: Ideas of Ownership**
> Land Law rules should reflect its underlying concepts, such as ownership. The basic idea of ownership is that it confers *control* over the land. The owner can use it in a variety of ways and can stop anyone else using it. The owner has *exclusive possession* of the land.

---

88   [1952] Ch. 488, p.497, per Upjohn J., discussing the arguments of counsel.
89   Above p.498, per Upjohn J.

LECTURER: So can we form an argument about whether the court made the right decision or not.

STUDENT: It is good law if the judge's reasoning conformed to our BUILDING BLOCK NO 4: Ideas of Ownership, and to our ideas about the nature of smaller rights.

LECTURER: That's right. So why did the judge hold that the claimant had no easement in *Copeland*?

STUDENT: Because he was exercising full control over that plot of land and effectively excluding the owner from it.

LECTURER: And why was this not in the nature of an easement?

STUDENT: Because an easement is only a very limited right to use the land in one sense only.

LECTURER: That's right. It should not look like ownership as it is a limited right. Therefore . . . what is our conclusion? Did *Copeland v Greenhalf* make good or bad law?

STUDENT: It was good law because it reflected underlying ideas of what ownership looks like and what smaller rights should look like. The nature of the right claimed in *Copeland* did not look like a limited right so the judge was correct to hold that no easement had been created.

E. BUILDING BLOCK NO 5: PROPERTY RIGHTS AND THE PROTECTION OF PURCHASERS AND MORTGAGE LENDERS

(1) What is a property right?

Rights in land, both large and small, such as those we have just discussed, are "property rights" or "proprietary rights". This might seem fairly obvious, but the expression "property right" does not mean "you legitimately own property", although of course this is true in another context. The expression relates to the juristic nature of the right, i.e. how it is enforced by the court. Property rights are different from personal rights, e.g. a right arising under a contract. A personal right is a right to sue a *person* who owes you an obligation, e.g. if you have entered into a contract with a trader to supply you with goods and they have defaulted on this, you have a right under the contract to sue them. But that right is only enforceable between you and the trader, i.e. the parties who entered into the contract. It will not affect anyone else. This is not so with rights in land. These are so-called property rights or proprietary rights. They are enforced not against the owner of the land themselves or any person in particular, but against the *land itself*. You are not saying "you have breached your obligation and I'm going to sue *you*" (a right *in personam* (against the person)), but "that is Mine! I am entitled to have it back"[90] Technically you are saying "I have a right in that land—you must let me exercise it".

> ✓   "That's mine—I am entitled to have it back"
> ✗   "You have breached your obligation and I'm going to sue you"

---

90   P.Birks, "Five Keys to Land Law" in Bright and Dewar (eds) *Land Law Themes and Perspectives* (Oxford University Press, 1998), p.471.

This is not a legal technicality. It transforms the nature of the right. The right is asserted against the land itself and not against the owner for the time being of that land. This means that any future owner of the land will have to give effect to the right. It does not matter who owns the land. It might have been sold several times over. You have a right in the *land itself* and thus any future owner must allow you to exercise it. We call this a right *in rem* (a right to a thing). A contractual right, such as the one in the above example, is called a right *in personam* (a right against the person). So a purchaser of land is bound by the rights that already exist in that land, or as we sometimes say "takes his title to the land subject to"[91] them, *even if the purchaser is unaware of them*.[92]

> **Legal nature of a property right**
> If I have a right of way (an easement) over your land next door, my right is a "proprietary right" that I assert against your land: "that is my right to walk across the land. Don't interfere with it!" Therefore, if you sell your land, I can still assert my easement against the land and the new owner will have to give effect to it. My right is not purely personal against you. It is *in the land itself* and as such will bind every subsequent owner.

(2) The drastic effects of property rights[93]

The idea that rights in land are property rights and bind the land itself and affect every subsequent purchaser is an important concept that judges often have to bear in mind when deciding cases. Whenever judges have to consider the rules by which rights in land, such as easements, restrictive covenants, and co-ownership rights, come into being, this is always at the back of their minds and informs their development of the rules. They will often impose strict rules that limit the number of interests in land that can come into being, and the way in which they come into being. The restrictive nature of those rules might mean that it seems unfair to deny a person a right of way or co-ownership right. A Land Law judge will always be thinking:

"Here I may be formulating a rule that too easily allows the creation of rights that may affect the title of an innocent third party purchaser of that land."

Let's take some examples of rights in land and see how they can potentially affect purchasers. Firstly, there is a very common smaller right that can exist: a restrictive covenant. Like easements, this is a topic of Land Law that we will study on its own later in the book. A restrictive covenant is a promise not to do something on your land.

> **Restrictive covenants**
> A very usual form of restrictive covenant is a promise not to build on your land. Property developers who are building an executive housing estate may use covenants to ensure that none of the future owners can build any more houses.

---

91 "Title" is the lawyer's word for ownership: Murphy, Roberts and Flessas, *Understanding Property Law*, p.54.
92 This is subject to the rules of Land Transfer Law which we look at in later chapters.
93 Often you will find this concept of property right called proprietary right. It is the same idea that is being described.

If a property developer is planning on purchasing a large plot of land on which to build a housing estate, she will have to make very sure that there are no restrictive covenants attached to the land because they are property rights and will bind her as a purchaser of the land.[94] How would a property developer feel if they had bought land and found that the land is subject to covenants restricting building on that land?

Another very common smaller right in land is an "option to purchase". This is a type of right known as an "estate contract".[95] Broadly, this is a contract, a legally enforceable agreement between two parties, for one to grant some form of right in the land to the other. An option to purchase is where one party grants to the other the right to purchase land, usually within a specified time period and at a particular price.

In *Midland Bank Trust Co Ltd v Green*[96] a father with five grown up children owns several farms and has throughout his life farmed the land. He lets one of his sons, Geoffrey, occupy a farm and work it over a long period of time. During that time, his son and his family became attached to the land and their lives and well-being probably become deeply entwined with the farm. The father, in order to help his son towards independence, went to a solicitor and granted him a right in the land known as an "option to purchase". This meant that the son could purchase the farm at any time during the next ten years, and the terms of this option were particularly favourable. Geoffrey had an enforceable (and extremely valuable) right in the farm.

An option to purchase land is a property right and can be enforced *against the property itself no matter who comes to own it*. Without more therefore, Farmer Geoffrey could have purchased the land at a reduced price not only from his father, *but from anyone who purchased the land from his father*. We will return to *Midland Bank v Green* when we look at the land transfer system later in the book. Then we will see the (perhaps surprising!) outcome of the case.

It is also possible to people to acquire a right to co-own a house: a right to part ownership. In certain circumstances they can acquire this right without any formal document, for example, by contributing financially to the purchase of the house which is then registered in the name of another (such as a spouse). How people can acquire a share of the ownership in a way that is entirely informal, by their conduct alone and not by having the owner write anything down, is (like easements and covenants) a topic in its own right.[97]

For an example of an informal co-ownership right, lets look at *In Re Sharpe*.[98] A man owned a house. As we know from BUILDING BLOCK NO 4: Ideas of ownership, this gave him control over the land. He exercised this control by selling it. However, prior to this his mother had given him

---

94   As with all rights this is subject to the rules that we will consider in the chapters on Land Transfer Law.
95   Estate contracts must be properly executed in writing in accordance with s.2 of the Law of Property (Miscellaneous Provisions) Act 1989, which we consider in Chapter 3.
96   [1981] A.C. 513.
97   See Chapter 3.
98   *In Re Sharpe* [1980] 1 W.L.R. 219, the facts of the case are simplified here.

a large sum of money towards its purchase, and had thereby acquired part ownership of it. This is a property right that will affect all subsequent purchasers. The son's name was still the only name on the documents so the law allows him to sell the house without asking the informal co-owner's permission.

So what happened in this case? The purchaser from the son was bound by the mother's property right. The purchaser was thus unable to live in the house because the mother was living there and had the prior right. The purchaser ended by living in a caravan whilst the legal issues were sorted out. Fortunately this does not happen very often.

(3) Protection for purchasers

As you probably appreciated from looking at *In Re Sharpe*, these cases involve considerable pain for some parties. As we have seen, there are many different rights that can exist in the land, e.g. rights such as that belonging to Farmer Geoffrey (the option to purchase) and Mrs Sharpe (informally acquired co-ownership right), easements, i.e. limited rights to do something on land belonging to another (such as store coal), restrictive covenants, leases, mortgages, and so on. They are all property rights that can be enforced against the land. Thus, whenever someone buys that land, if any of those rights exist, the new owner will be bound by them.[99] He will have to give effect to those rights. It is obviously in the new owner's interests to be bound by as few rights as possible. If he acquires a title that is bound by several rights that he did not know about, this may have the effect of devaluing the land.

Why is this situation so difficult for purchasers? Investment in our house/land is possibly the most important and expensive investment we shall ever make in our lives, apart from our pensions. Thus, a purchaser of land will have a big stake in wanting to make sure that he has a clean or clear title to the house, with no Mrs Sharpes, Farmer Geoffreys: no prior rights that can be asserted against him—or at least no interests that are likely to affect the value of the house or that he did not know about. After all, this purchaser will probably be buying the house to provide residential security for himself and his family.

But it is also difficult for people with the small rights: Yet on the other hand, the people with the prior rights, the Mrs Sharpes and Farmer Geoffreys of Land Law, co-owners who want to live in the house, neighbouring owners of a restrictive covenant who want to preserve their peace or the character of the neighbourhood, will not want their rights to be destroyed when the ownership of the house is transferred to the new purchaser.[100] What value would their interests be if they could not attach to the land—land is bought and sold all the time?

How does Land Law resolve this clash of interest?: A great deal of Land Law concerns this question of land transfer from one owner to another. One important issue of conveyancing is to establish a certain, coherent, and fair set of rules that determines whose right, the

---

99   Subject to the rules of land transfer which we will consider in a later chapter.
100   K.Gray, *Elements of Land Law*, 2nd edn (Oxford University Press, 1993).

purchaser's or another's, will take priority upon a sale of that land: will it be the farmer's son, Farmer Geoffrey, or the new purchaser of the farm; will it be the purchaser in *Re Sharpe* or Mrs Sharpe? Which side of the line would Land Law fall?

(4) The 1925 property legislation

Perhaps the most important policy of Land Law is to protect the purchaser of land.

> The great policy of 1925 is to ensure the simplification of conveyancing: House of Lords, *Abbey National Building Society v Cann* [1991] 1 A.C. 56.
>
> The policy of 1925 is that a purchaser or mortgage lender should gain a good title free from encumbrances: House of Lords, *City of London Building Society v Flegg* [1988] A.C. 54.

Prior to 1925, in order for a purchaser to make sure he had a good title, i.e. that he did not have all these people asserting rights against his newly purchased land, he would have to conduct exhaustive and expensive enquiries. Parliament's concern around the time of the 1925 land law reforms, and that of the Lincoln's Inn conveyancing barristers instrumental in constructing the legislation, was to ensure that a purchaser's land was worth what he paid for it.[101] As we have seen, even in twenty-first century terms, land is the largest investment most of us are likely to make. We do not want to lose part of its value as soon as the purchase is made. The 1925 legislation laid down two systems of rules that were aimed at simplifying the conveyancing process: transfer of land where the title (ownership) to land is registered at the Land Registry, and transfer of land where it is not. We will look at the land transfer system later in the book. The rules make sure that a purchaser of land can acquire the ownership (title) of the land free from prior rights that may be claimed against the land, very easily and without having to make a great number of enquiries through a lawyer about the possibility of other rights being asserted against his land.

> **The 1925 Property Legislation**
>
> The main structure of these land law rules is laid down by the 1925 Property Legislation: a scheme of legislation with which we will become deeply acquainted. For now, the 1925 Property Legislation is a number of Acts of Parliament that were designed to reform Land Law: the Law of Property Act 1925; the Land Charges Act 1925 (amended and updated by the Land Charges Act 1972); the Land Registration Act 1925 (now replaced in its entirety by the Land Registration Act 2002); the Settled Land Act 1925 (now made largely redundant by the Trusts of Land and Appointment of Trustees Act 1996); Administration of Estates Act 1925.

---

101   J.S.Anderson, *Lawyers and the Making of English Land Law* 1832–1940 (Oxford University Press, 1992) gives a full account of this.

Hence the purchaser's concerns are given precedence over those of anyone else who might need (even for justifiable reasons) to establish a prior right in the land. Sir Arthur Underhill, senior conveyancing counsel, wrote of the then new legislation:

"The reader will no doubt have grasped the great and salient fact that . . . a *bona-fide* purchaser . . . may, in the words of Shakespeare, 'Close up his eyes and draw the curtain close' – in other words, deal with the owner . . . without troubling himself with the [interests] of third parties, even if he [knew about] them".[102]

> **BUILDING BLOCK NO 5: Property Rights and the Protection of Purchasers**
> We can legitimately say that rules of Land Law are good if they make it easy for a purchaser of land to acquire that land free from as many prior property rights as possible.

(5) Banks and building societies

Where the owner of a house has granted a mortgage to a bank or building society, in return for a loan (e.g. to buy or improve that house), the bank will want to force a sale of the house if the owner does not keep up the repayments due under the loan agreement. This is in order that the bank can recoup its investment. Thus, the bank will want to make sure that they can sell the land and there is no person asserting a prior right in that land who can stop it from doing so, such as Mrs Sharpe and Farmer Geoffrey in our example.

> **The 1925 Legislation: Mortgage lender = "purchaser"**

Under the 1925 legislation banks and building societies, when they are granted their mortgages, have the same protection against prior rights in the land that a *purchaser* has. In fact, a mortgage lender is defined as a purchaser under the legislation. From the above, we now know broadly that the rules laid down by the 1925 legislation ensure that a purchaser of land can acquire the ownership (or title) to his land free from many prior rights that may be claimed against the land. The rules aim to ensure that he can do this very easily and without having to make a great number of enquiries through a lawyer about the possibility of other rights being asserted against his land.

But why should banks and building societies be able to gain houses as security for the loan they make to the owner, in such a straightforward and inexpensive way? A large institutional lender can afford to make expensive enquiries that ordinary residential purchasers cannot. A lender can bear the loss if in one or two cases they are not able to gain ready access to their investment.

---

102   Sir Arthur Underhill, *A Concise Explanation of Lord Birkenhead's Act* (1922), p.91.

There is a justification for giving protection to banks and building societies. Finance from banks and building societies helps us to buy the houses in which we live. It also funds a great many small businesses. In return for this finance banks have a mortgage on the house. The purpose of this is to make sure the bank can readily get its money back by repossessing and selling the house should the borrower(s) default on the loan repayments. Gray and Gray observe that "finance released by second mortgages of family homes has become a significant source of start-up capital for the small business sector, which in this country accounts for some 95 per cent of all businesses and nearly one-third of all employment". If the law does not give the bank the ability to sell the house easily free from prior property rights, such as Mrs Sharpe's, then they will be reluctant in future to lend money to the owners and purchasers of family homes: "institutions will be unwilling to accept such security, thereby reducing the flow of loan capital to business enterprises."[103]

Therefore, Land Law rules must make it a straightforward matter for the lender to sell the mortgaged house should the borrower default on the loan repayments. The lender must be able to gain rights over the house and not be prevented from selling it by people with prior rights in the house, such as Farmer Geoffrey or Mrs Sharpe.

> **BUILDING BLOCK NO 5: Property Rights and the Protection of Purchasers and Mortgage Lenders**
> Unless the rules of Land Law make sure that lenders can readily get their money back by selling houses, banks and building societies may become reluctant to give loans to small businesses or ordinary house purchasers in the future. This would have significant impact on the country's economy, as we have seen in the recent credit crunch.

(6) Constructing an argument using BUILDING BLOCK NO 5

Remember that we are using our Building Blocks to critically evaluate Land Law, i.e. to create valid and persuasive arguments about the rules. For this we need justification and evidence to support our conclusion that the rule is good or bad fair or unfair. We get our evidence from the Building Blocks. We can argue that a development of a rule in a case or statute is good or bad, fair or unfair, depending on the extent to which it supports or undermines the idea that rules of Land Law should protect a purchaser or mortgage lender from being bound by prior interests in the land. A rule of Land Law is good if when applied in future cases it would not make life difficult for purchasers buying land, i.e. the rule would not mean that the land, when it is transferred to them, will be bound by rights (such as Mrs Sharpe's informal co-ownership right or Farmer Geoffrey's estate contract) that a purchaser or mortgage lender could not have found out about in advance.

---

103   Gray and Gray, *Elements of Land Law,* 4th edn, (2004), pp.1625–6, quoting *Barclays Bank Plc v O'Brien* [1994] 1 A.C. 180, per Lord Browne-Wilkinson; *Royal Bank of Scotland Plc v Etridge (No. 2)* [2002] A.C. 773 paras 34–35.

BUILDING BLOCK NO 5: Property Rights and the Protection of Purchasers and Mortgage Lenders
A rule is good or bad fair or unfair, depending on the extent to which it supports or undermines the policy that Land Law should protect purchasers and mortgage lenders from being bound by prior interests in the land.

Example 1:   Returning to *Re Sharpe:* good or bad law?

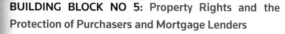

Re Sharpe [1980] 1 W.L.R. 219 – revisit the facts and decision at pp.30–31 above

BUILDING BLOCK NO 5: Property Rights and the Protection of Purchasers and Mortgage Lenders
Land Law rules are good if they make it a straightforward matter for the purchaser to acquire a house free from prior property rights in the land. The underlying justification for this policy is to protect one of the most important investments we will ever make.

Hold the case up against BUILDING BLOCK NO 5 and think about the connection between them.

I CONCLUDE that the case is bad law. My EVIDENCE for this conclusion is that Land Law rules should not have this effect. It should protect purchasers from being bound by prior rights because of the importance of the purchase of land. In *Re Sharpe* this did not happen so therefore it is bad law.

---

(7)   Imaginative argument—asking questions

So we have blocks of evidence. Now we need cement to build them into an argument. Look again at my conclusion about *Re Sharpe*. It is not very imaginative is it? Therefore it is not very convincing. Before we use the Building Blocks as evidence we need to interrogate them—cross-examine the evidence. We might ask questions like:

Was the purchaser negligent? Is there anything the law does or should expect purchasers and mortgage lenders to do in order to protect their own interests, rather than remain passively reliant on a rule that says that they can take free from a prior property right? Would these actions be reasonable? If the case had been decided the other way and the rules said that the purchaser could take free from the prior property right, would this be too much protection? Thus, BUILDING BLOCK NO 5 may not be strong evidence for saying that the law is bad.

If there was a rule that allowed the purchaser to take free from the right more easily, as there is in some situations, does the law make it too easy for purchasers at the expense of BUILDING BLOCK NO 1: Residential Security. Mrs Sharpe's residential security was at stake – the purchaser would have evicted her even though she knew nothing about the sale.

Is there anything all *Mrs Sharpes could do in such cases* to protect their own interest? Would their failure to take such action be negligent? In which event, the purchaser *ought to have won the case.*

When the time comes and you work out what Building Blocks you are going to use for what arguments, look at a couple of articles and see whether they help you to take your points any further. There are LECTURER and STUDENT dialogues throughout this book designed to help you with this process of creating and evaluating an argument.

F. BUILDING BLOCK NO 6: THE NEED FOR CERTAINTY AND PREDICTABILITY IN LAND LAW RULES

Land Law rules must provide certainty. It must be clear how a rule that is applied and articulated in one case will apply to several others. Judges cannot simply do what they think is fair. So a rule is good if it is certain how the rule will apply to similar cases in the future. You should not have to go to court to find out what the rule is and how it works. For example, let's say that a rule stated that a bank or building society can only repossess a residential property *as a last resort*. As a general principle it is a good idea—banks should not be allowed to repossess family homes too readily as this will affect the borrowers' residential security: essentially in a repossession action the borrowers are evicted from their house. In this sense repossession *should* be a last resort. However, if this was the rule to be applied by the courts it is hopelessly inadequate. A bank who wants to repossess a house would not really know whether it could do so or not without going to court. My opinion as to what is a "last resort" differs from theirs and judges' opinions. There is nothing about this as a rule that will guide the bank and their legal advisors as to whether they can legally take action for repossession. So we have to have rules that state exactly what action the bank must take before starting proceedings for possession and what the borrower must prove in order to prevent repossession.

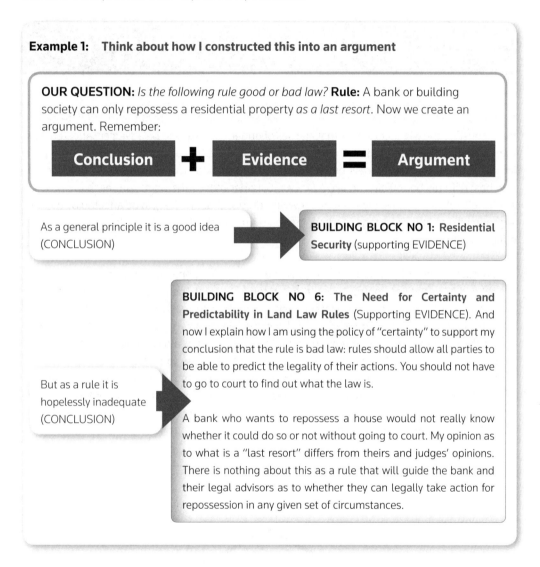

Example 1:   Think about how I constructed this into an argument

OUR QUESTION: *Is the following rule good or bad law?* **Rule:** A bank or building society can only repossess a residential property *as a last resort*. Now we create an argument. Remember:

Conclusion ✚ **Evidence** ═ **Argument**

As a general principle it is a good idea (CONCLUSION) ➤ **BUILDING BLOCK NO 1: Residential Security** (supporting EVIDENCE)

BUILDING BLOCK NO 6: The Need for Certainty and Predictability in Land Law Rules (Supporting EVIDENCE). And now I explain how I am using the policy of "certainty" to support my conclusion that the rule is bad law: rules should allow all parties to be able to predict the legality of their actions. You should not have to go to court to find out what the law is.

But as a rule it is hopelessly inadequate (CONCLUSION) ➤ A bank who wants to repossess a house would not really know whether it could do so or not without going to court. My opinion as to what is a "last resort" differs from theirs and judges' opinions. There is nothing about this as a rule that will guide the bank and their legal advisors as to whether they can legally take action for repossession in any given set of circumstances.

Because human beings attach so much importance to land ownership, Land Law rules *must* create a certain and predictable system. Atiyah says that strong expectations in society reinforce "the rigour with which they [are] protected by law".[104] Thus, the stronger the human expectation

---

104   Atiyah, *The Rise and Fall of Freedom of Contract*, pp.109–110. Atiyah dismisses the suggestion that could be made that expectation is derived solely from the extent of legal protection, at least in a contractual context.

of things or situations, the more certain and predictable the system of rules relating to the allocation of those things needs to be. Rules must tell people as clearly as possible where they stand.

> So we must ask how will this judge's interpretation and application of the rule affect whole classes of litigant? F.Schauer, *Thinking like a Lawyer* (2009), p.8

Each court deciding a property case must consider not only the facts of the immediate case. It must consider the wider context. What classes of litigant are likely to be adversely affected if the rule is changed or extended in order to do justice to a particular occupier? What is the likely impact on future litigants' residential security if a particular rule is extended in favour or a purchaser? In his book *Thinking like a Lawyer*, Schauer makes the point that each court, when applying a rule, must have regard to the relevant groups that are likely to be affected by the rule, e.g. purchasers and mortgage lenders. It should not bend rules to do justice in a particularly difficult case:

> "Although disputes, in court and out, involve particular people with particular problems engaged in particular controversies, the law tends to treat the particulars it confronts as members of larger categories. Rather than attempting to reach the best result for each controversy in a wholly particularistic and contextual way, law's goal is often to make sure that the outcome for *all* or at least most of the particulars in a given category is the right one. . . . Lord Coke is illuminating: 'It is better saith the Law to suffer a mischief (that is particular to one) than an inconvenience that may prejudice many.' In other words, for Coke it was better to reach the wrong result in the particular controversy than to adopt a rule that would produce what would seem to be the correct result for this case but at the cost of producing the wrong result in many others."[105]

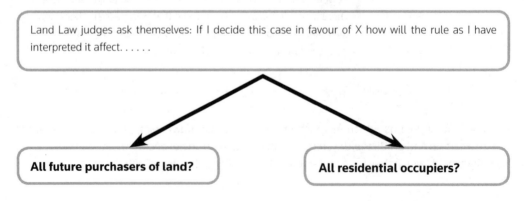

Land Law judges ask themselves: If I decide this case in favour of X how will the rule as I have interpreted it affect. . . . . .

All future purchasers of land?   **All residential occupiers?**

---

105   (2009), p.8, footnote omitted from quoted text.

So we have to ask ourselves, who is going to be affected by a decision in the future and how? The law must consider the effect of a rule on a class of individuals who might be affected, such as banks and building societies lending money on mortgages: just the way that we did in our first example. Banks need to be able to predict the legal outcome of their actions.[106]

> **BUILDING BLOCK NO 6: The Need for Certainty and Predictability in Land Law Rules**
>
> A rule of Land Law can be said to be good and fair if it provides certainty as to how it will apply to relevant classes of litigant in the future. It must allow them to be able to predict the legal consequences of their actions or inactions. Hold this as a gold standard against the cases that you read in this book.

(1) The Practice Statement 1966

Whilst studying a "Legal Method" course, you will have come across the Practice Statement 1966, in which the House of Lords (now the Supreme Court) sought to regulate its practice. The 1966 Statement provided that the House of Lords should have freedom to depart from its own decisions. This was necessary because under normal rules of precedent, if the House of Lords had laid down a rule it must follow that rule in all its subsequent cases. The reason behind this change in practice was to make sure that the law did not stagnate. It should be adaptable to changes in society. As part of the Practice Statement, the House of Lords laid down the warning that a rule should not lightly be departed from. If the law were constantly being changed in this way, it would not be possible to predict the outcome of a case or for a lawyer to order his client's affairs in accordance with established law. The House of Lords identified a few categories of case where certainty and predictability of law was particularly important. One of these was where *property rights* were concerned.

(2) Constructing an argument using BUILDING BLOCK NO 6

> **BUILDING BLOCK NO 6: The Need for Certainty and Predictability in Land Law Rules**
>
> If the rules are clear as to how they will apply in future cases, i.e. if they allow people (e.g. purchasers or occupiers) to predict the outcome of their actions, then they are good law.

We can argue that a development of a rule in a case or statute is good or bad fair or unfair, depending on the extent to which it provides certainty and predictability.

---

106   Harris, *Property and Justice*, p.329.

EXAMPLE 2:   What a nice view!

In *William Aldred's Case* (1610) 9 Co. Rep. 57b it was held that the right to a "nice view" is not a proper right in land. Therefore someone can build on their land and block your view. Is this good law?

BUILDING BLOCK NO 6: The Need for Certainty and Predictability in Land Law Rules

If the rules are clear as to how they will apply in future cases, i.e. if they allow people (e.g. purchasers or occupiers) to predict the outcome of their actions, then they are good law.

Hold the rule up against the BUILDING BLOCK and think about the connection between them. To understand whether a rule is certain or not you have to imagine who is likely to be affected by it.

OUR ARGUMENT: So we think—who is likely to be affected by this rule? Our answer: Anyone using land or purchasing it. Does the rule provide clear guidance to them as to what they can do with their land? Let's say that this case had been decided the other way. If you bought land and someone at the back of it could stop you from building anything that took away from their "nice view" you would never be able to do anything on your land. The word "nice" is hopelessly uncertain, as is the word "view". You would never know when you were breaking the law!

The case is good law—such a rule allowing such a right in land would violate the policy of certainty.

(3) Imaginative argument: does the rule undermine the Building Block?

So if you can establish that a rule is uncertain as to how it might apply in the future than this is evidence that justifies you in saying that the rule is not good. In one sense this looks like the easiest of our Building Blocks to use. It does however require a lot of thought about how Land Law rules work. Only then will you be properly equipped to make convincing predictions about the classes of litigant likely to be affected by a court decision. A sustained amount of regular reading and thought will suffice, e.g. one or two articles for each topic and some judgments from the cases. This book will provide you with many extracts that will be useful tools.

So how do we go about asking questions to determine whether a case really does violate legal certainty? Here are some possibilities:

* What is the "rule" that you think has been distorted? What concepts and principles is it based on?

- What classes of Land Law litigant might be affected in the future by the distorted rule? How might they be affected?
- Was the law prior to this case tolerably certain? Which way would you have decided the case?
- Might a small amount of legal uncertainty be tolerable? Does there need to be a trade off with other Building Blocks, e.g. BUILDING BLOCK NO 2: Ideas of Justice?

Constructing an argument with the Building Blocks

4

Consider the following extract from *Williams & Glyn's Bank Ltd v Boland*,[107] and the LECTURER and STUDENT dialogue. We are going to construct an argument using the BUILDING BLOCKS. The question for you to argue about is:

> **Discuss whether you think *Williams & Glyn's Bank v Boland* is a good decision.**

A. READING THE EXTRACT

I have included below an extract from the case. *Boland* is one of the most significant Land Law cases of the twentieth century, so we will be returning to it again. It is not necessary at this early stage for you to understand the precise context of the rule that Lord Wilberforce was applying and developing. We will study this when we consider the land transfer system in a later chapter. There will be parts of the extract from Lord Wilberforce's judgment that you will not understand. I want you *not to worry about this*. Try to see beyond the technicalities for the moment to the bare bones of the rules and argument. There are two factors on which I want you to concentrate. Firstly, the change in the law that the House of Lords was making and, broadly speaking, how this was done; and secondly, making sure that you read the extract thoroughly, relating all the different parts together, in order to *get the information you need from it*. So throughout your work you should be aiming to formulate a clear idea of what you want to know.

> The important thing is for you to "get the feel" of the decision.

---

107   [1981] A.C. 487 (HL).

B. USING YOUR BUILDING BLOCKS

When you are reading the extract, have your Building Blocks beside you. Make sure that you have a reasonable grasp of their content, particularly BUILDING BLOCK NO 5: Property Rights and the Protection of Purchasers. During his judgment Lord Wilberforce bases his reasoning directly on some of the Building Blocks. So you can use them to help you understand what he is saying.

C. IDENTIFYING THE REASONS FOR THE DECISION

First you have to have some understanding of what the case is about. Then you need to be able to identify the conclusion. Often a person making a conclusion will use words like "therefore", "in consequence", "the result" etc,[108] but often you just get a feel for when a conclusion is made from a chain of reasoning.

Make sure that you separate the conclusion from Lord Wilberforce's *reasons* for his conclusion. It is never a precise art to try and identify reasons for a decision.[109] There may be more than one reason and judges often do not order them into a nice neat chain. Many reasons are based on the Building Blocks, and this is true of Lord Wilberforce's judgment. A useful way of identifying a judge's reasons for his decision is to ask the question: *what were the factors that were so important to the judge that they led him to decide what he did AND WHY? Or: what were the factors about the case without which the case would have been decided the other way?*[110] Remember that this is not a precise art. There is much colour to notice in a legal case and we may come to slightly different conclusions about what those reasons are.

> **Identify the reasons for Lord Wilberforce's conclusion:**
> *What were the factors that were so important to Lord Wilberforce that they led him to decide what he did AND WHY? What were the factors about the case without which the case would have been decided the other way?*
> Hold the case against the Building Blocks: Were any of Lord Wilberforce's reasons based on the Building Blocks? Can you use the Building Blocks to explain the reasoning more fully? Can you use *Boland* to add to and explain the Building Blocks? You will now have a legal citation in support of some of the Building Blocks. Write it on and already you are adding to them.

---

108   A.Fisher, *The Logic of Real Arguments*, Ch.1.
109   See for example McBride, *Letters to a Law Student* (Longman, 2006).
110   L.Elder's article "I Think Critically Therefore I Am" *Times Higher Education Supplement* (August 2009) and A.Fisher's book *The Logic of Real Arguments* (1988) was of great help in formulating these questions.

D. WILLIAMS & GLYN'S BANK LTD V BOLAND[111]

(1) The social context

Women started going out to work and now possessed spending power. Thus, they would often contribute financially to the purchase and running of the house. To some extent, as we shall see when we study this area, the law responded to this development. Although when the family home is purchased it is often put in the name of one of the partners (usually in earlier days, the husband), the wife or other non-owning partner still contributes financially. Because of this Land Law gives her rights to part ownership of the house. This is a property right (the precise type of right we will also consider later). It is not necessary to write anything down. Co-ownership can come into existence simply by contributing financially to the purchase of a house that is then put legally into the name of another.

However, because the husband's name is the sole name on all the documents, he is able to mortgage the house to a bank or building society in order to obtain finance, e.g. for a business or for home improvements.[112] The informal co-owner does not have to give permission or even be aware of the mortgage. Thus, if the owner does not keep up the payments due under the mortgage, the bank can sell the house in order to get its money back. The letter from the bank advising the husband of their intent to start proceedings for repossession may often be the first time that an informal co-owner learns of the existence of the mortgage. So a bank may use the house as security for a loan in this way irrespective of the fact that it may be a home that provides residential security for the couple and their children. The house is treated solely as tradable property, like any other form of property. No special consideration is made for the fact that it is a matrimonial or family home. It is treated as the commercial asset of the owner. And if he wants to raise money on the security of it—English Land Law lets him do it.[113]

Before you go any further make sure that you understand:

- what a property right is, the parties that may be affected by it, and the problems that this may cause for purchasers of the house from the husband, or mortgage lenders when (unbeknown to the wife) the husband takes out a loan and mortgages the house. You need to consult BUILDING BLOCK NO 5: Property Rights and the Protection of Purchasers; and
- think about the position if the wife's rights *did not* bind the purchaser or bank: She would be evicted, even though she did not know about the mortgage, and even though she has rights of her own in the house. What other Building Blocks could you use as evidence to establish a conclusion as to whether or not this would be a good or a bad thing?

---

111 [1981] A.C. 487.
112 We will look at what a mortgage of land is and how it comes into being in a later chapter.
113 I express my thanks for the point in this paragraph to one of the anonymous reviewers of this chapter.

(2) The facts and summary

Mr and Mrs Boland were a married couple and Mr Boland was the sole legal owner of their matrimonial home. If you remember Land Law recognises that a person can become a joint owner of a house in a way that is totally informal, e.g. simply by contributing financially to the purchase of a house that is then put into another's name. This was the case with Mrs Boland. She had made a sizeable financial contribution to the purchase of the matrimonial home. However, because Mr Boland's name was still the sole name on all the documents, he was able to (and did) mortgage the house to the bank in order to finance his business.[114] Mr Boland did not keep up the payments due under the mortgage. So the bank wanted to sell the house in order to get its money back.

> Who was the dispute between?

Mrs Boland knew nothing about the bank's interest in the house and had not consented to the mortgage. This was a contest between the bank and Mrs Boland, who did not want to lose her home.

The only way in which Mrs Boland could legally stop the bank from selling the house is if she could establish that her property right, acquired informally through her contribution to the purchase price, bound the bank. BUILDING BLOCK NO 5: Property Rights and the Protection of Purchasers and Mortgage Lenders tells us that the 1925 legislation made it easy for banks to repossess and sell property without being bound by pre-existing property rights that might stop them from doing so. And this legislation had been interpreted in the following way. The precise rules need not concern you at this early stage, and you are not to worry if you do not understand all the technicalities. Just try to get the gist of the dispute.

Prior to this point, the law tended to remove any impediment to banks and building societies repossessing family homes, and this law would have held that Mrs Boland's right to part ownership of the house made no difference. The husband, as the sole owner on the documents, had the full power to

> **The previous law**
>
> Is this law supported by any of the Building Blocks?

mortgage the house,[115] and people living with that sole owner had no right to prevent the bank from selling the matrimonial home if the husband defaulted on the loan.[116]

The House of Lords in *Williams & Glyn's Bank v Boland* stated that the time had come to reset the balance. People bought houses in order to live in them. Women went out to work and contributed to the purchase of the home and its upkeep. This was now a stable feature of our society that the law could not afford to ignore. So the law should no longer give automatic priority to banks

---

114   We will look at what a mortgage of land is and how it comes into being in a later chapter.

115   Don't worry about the technicalities of how and why this is the case. There is more information we will need to put in place before you can understand this fully.

116   See *Caunce v Caunce* [1969] 1 W.L.R. 286; *Bird v Syme-Thompson* [1979] 1 W.L.R. 440.

at the expense of occupiers with property rights in the house, such as Mrs Boland, who needed residential security.[117] The House of Lords held that Mrs Boland had a right to remain in the house and that therefore, the bank could not sell it. The bank should have taken greater pains to protect its own interest by making sure that there were no other people living in the house who could claim any prior property rights that would stop it from selling the house.

The relevant rule was that if Mrs Boland could establish that she 1) had a property right in the house before the time the bank was granted the mortgage, and 2) was in actual occupation of it, then her right would bind the bank. They would not be able to repossess and sell the house because Mrs Boland had the prior right.

> **This was the rule that the House of Lords were rethinking and redeveloping**

(3) The judgment[118]

LORD WILBERFORCE: "My Lords, these appeals . . . raise for decision the same question: whether a husband or a wife (in each actual case a wife) who has a [property right] in the matrimonial home, by virtue of having contributed to its purchase price but whose spouse is the legal and registered owner, has an . . . interest binding on a mortgagee who claims possession of the matrimonial home under a mortgage granted by that spouse alone. Although this statement of the issue uses the words 'spouse,' 'husband and wife', 'matrimonial home,' the appeals do not, in my understanding, involve any question of matrimonial law, or of the rights of married women or of women as such. Exactly the same issue could arise if the roles of husband and wife were reversed, or if the persons interested in the house were not married to each other. [. . . . .]

> **The entries in square brackets [ ] are my editing and explanations designed to help you understand the text of Lord Wilberforce's judgment.**

The system of land registration [this is part of the land transfer system that we will be studying later] as it exists in England . . . is designed to simplify and to cheapen conveyancing. It is intended to replace the often complicated and voluminous title deeds of property by a single land certificate, of the strength of which land can be dealt with. In place of the lengthy and often technical investigation of title to which a purchaser was committed, all he has to do is to consult the register; from any burden [property right] not entered on the register, with one exception, he takes free. [The previous systems] involved him in enquiries, often quite elaborate, failing which he might be bound by [property rights]. [The land registration system] enables a purchaser to take free from all interests unless they are first registered against the title when he buys the property, **with just the one exception**.]

117 Expression Gray and Symes, *Real Property and Real People* (1981).
118 [1981] A.C. 487, pp.503–508, substantial editing supplied. It is worth repeating the warning not to get bogged down in the technicalities of the rules. We will be looking at these when we study the land transfer system.

BUILDING BLOCK NO 5: Property Rights and the Protection of Purchasers
Re-read this Building Block. Lord Wilberforce is describing the changes made by the 1925 property legislation, of which the system of land registration is one. Can you form an argument on the basis of this Building Block for why these changes are a good thing?

[Lord Wilberforce went on to explain that the legislation provided that Mrs Boland's property right could be brought within this exception, meaning that it would bind the bank and they would not be able to repossess the house, **only** if she was 'in actual occupation'. Such was the wording of the legislation. It was now up to the court to interpret it. What did 'in actual occupation' mean? Could the words be taken literally or did they bear some other technical meaning more favourable to banks? Lord Wilberforce continued . . .]

Now I deal with the. . . question, [was Mrs Boland] in 'actual occupation'? [. . .] I ask: why not? There was physical presence. . . . . . . The house was a matrimonial home, intended to be occupied, and in fact occupied by both spouses, both of whom have an interest [or property right] in it: It would require some special doctrine of law to avoid the result that each is in occupation. . . . It was said that if the vendor (I use this word to include a mortgagor) is in occupation [Mr Boland in this case], that is enough to prevent [a person living with the vendor proving 'actual occupation']. . . . [N]o doubt, if correct, this would be very convenient for purchasers and intending mortgagees. But the presence of the vendor, with occupation, does not exclude the possibility of others. There are observations which suggest the contrary in. . . *Caunce v Caunce* [1969] 1 W.L.R. 286, but I agree with the disapproval of these. . . . Then it was suggested that the wife's occupation was nothing but the shadow of the husband's – a version I suppose of the doctrine of unity of husband and wife. This expression and the argument flowing from it was used by Templeman J. in *Bird v Syme-Thomson* [1979] 1 W.L.R. 440, 444. . . The argument appears to me to be heavily obsolete. . . . A wife may, and everyone knows this, have rights of her own; particularly, many wives have a share in a matrimonial home. . . And if she has rights, why, just because she is a wife (or in the converse case, just because an occupier is the husband), should these rights be denied protection? . . . If one looks beyond the case of husband and wife the difficulty of all these arguments stands out if one considers the case of a man living with a mistress, or of a man and a woman—or for that matter two persons of the same sex—living in a house in separate or partially shared rooms. [Can the rights of all these persons] be disregarded? The only solution which is consistent with the Act. . . and with common sense is to read the [Act] for what it says. Occupation, existing as a fact, may protect rights if the person in occupation has rights. On this part of the case I have no difficulty in concluding that a spouse, living in a house, has an actual occupation capable of conferring protection. . . upon rights of that spouse.[119] [Lord Wilberforce then considered at length another issue which is not relevant here.]

---

119   By "protection" is meant that the right will bind a purchaser so they will have to give effect to it (like *In Re Sharpe* [1980] 1 W.L.R. 219, above) and banks will be unable to repossess houses where there is an occupier with a right.

BUILDING BLOCK NO 1: Residential Security

We can legitimately say that where the rules operate in the context of owner-occupation of property, they are good and fair if they give effective protection to people's residential security. In this paragraph Lord Wilberforce seems to be saying that other factors than purchaser protection should be borne in mind. Can you justify his conclusion on the basis of this Building Block?

I would only add, in conclusion. . . a brief observation on the conveyancing consequences of dismissing the appeal. These were alarming to Templeman J.,[120] and I can agree with him to the extent that whereas the object of a land registration system is to reduce the risks to purchasers from anything not on the register [e.g. Mrs Boland had acquired her co-ownership right entirely informally with nothing written down], to extend (if it be an extension) the area of risk so as to include possible [property rights] of spouses, and indeed, in theory, of other members of the family or even outside it, may add to the burdens of purchasers [and mortgage lenders], and involve them in enquiries which in some cases may be troublesome.

But conceded, as it must be, that the Act, following established practice, gives protection to occupation, the extension of the risk area follows necessarily from the extension, beyond the paterfamilias, of rights of ownership, itself following from the diffusion of property and earning capacity. What is involved is a departure from an easy-going practice [on the part of banks and building societies] of dispensing with enquiries as to occupation [and whether any occupiers have Property Rights that could potentially bind them] beyond that of the vendor and accepting the risks of doing so. To substitute for this a practice of more careful enquiry. . . as to the rights of occupiers can not, in my view of the matter, be considered as unacceptable except at the price of overlooking the widespread development of shared interests of ownership."

As part of his concurring judgment in *Boland*, Lord Scarman added: "The courts may not. . . put aside as irrelevant, the undoubted fact that if [Mrs Boland] succeeds, the protection of the beneficial interest which English law now recognises that a married woman has in the matrimonial home will be strengthened whereas, if [she loses], this interest can be weakened, and even destroyed, by an unscrupulous husband [who mortgages the matrimonial home behind her back]."[121]

(4) Constructing an argument

LECTURER: The question we are arguing about is "*discuss whether you think Williams & Glyn's Bank v Boland is a good decision*". Often in exams essay questions are not quite as direct as this. An essay-style question might take the following form:

---

120   Templeman J. was the judge in the court of first instance in *Boland* this was the appeal to the House of Lords.

121   [1981] A.C. 487.

"To substitute for this a practice of more careful enquiry as to the fact of occupation, and if necessary, as to the rights of occupiers can not . . . be considered as unacceptable except at the price of overlooking the widespread development of shared interests of ownership . . ." (*Williams & Glyn's Bank v Boland* [1981] A.C. 487, p.508H)

Discuss or "critically evaluate this statement"

Actually both questions amount to more or less the same thing. The second gives a statement of opinion, that Purchaser Protection is no longer a sufficient justification by itself on which to base the rules. The first asks the question in a more open way: on what Building Blocks can the decision be justified? When you are constructing an argument about a rule or series of rules, i.e. you are asked to *critically evaluate* the rules, this entails building up evidence that shows whether a particular rule or interpretation is good or bad, fair or unfair. We ask the question, *what evidence will justify me in accepting that the rule is fair?*[122] Now you have identified and mapped Lord Wilberforce's reasoning, hold this against the Building Blocks. We use these as our fields of evidence by which we can say whether the case is good or not. Keep your Building Blocks to hand so that you can pick them up, measure them against the rule and almost physically construct an argument.

> **BUILDING BLOCK NO 1: Residential Security**
> We can legitimately say that where the rules operate in the context of owner-occupation of property, they are good and fair if they give effective protection to people's residential security.

STUDENT: The purchase of a house is significant in society today. The reason is that people buy houses in order to live with their families. Their ownership gives them privacy and identity as citizens. This is not something that should be taken away lightly. This is what Hume was saying—it is a greater cruelty to a person to take away something from them, than it is not to give it to them in the first place. The law should reflect this.

LECTURER: How was *Boland* based on this idea?

STUDENT: The law made it harder for banks to repossess houses. It used to be the case that for someone to show that they had a prior right to be in the house, which would stop the bank from repossessing it, they had to show actual occupation—which they could not do if the owner (Mr Boland here) was there as well. Families live together and the person in whose name the house is registered (and the one who mortgages it without his wife knowing) will invariably be living there. But *Boland* said that this did not matter anymore. If someone had a property right in the house, like Mrs Boland (which she had gained by contributing a large

---

122   A.Fisher, *The Logic of Real Arguments*: Fisher's "Assertability Question".

amount of money to its purchase), then if she could prove occupation in the ordinary sense of the word, then she had a right to stop the bank from repossessing the house.

LECTURER: Does this give better protection to the residential security of families?

STUDENT: Well for one thing it stops a forced sale of the family home.

LECTURER: And do you think it would affect a lot of people?

STUDENT: I should think that many spouses and partners whose spouses are the formal owner of the house would acquire property rights in this way. It may be fairly common to contribute financially to the purchase of your home, even though your name is not on the deeds. If the owner then mortgaged the house without telling them their residential security is protected. *Boland* is good law.

LECTURER: It would still be a nasty surprise when the letter from the bank plops onto the doormat saying that they are going to repossess the house! It happens frequently enough.

STUDENT: But actually, looking at the "**Imaginative Argument**" section of the Building Block I think we should ask whether there is anything occupiers could do to protect their property rights. Shouldn't we expect all future Mrs Bolands to have to do something to protect themselves against repossession or do they just sit tight and the law will protect them? I don't really know at the moment, but it's the sort of thing I would ask if I knew the rules and the other cases in this area. If there is something that all future Mrs Bolands could be expected to do to protect their own interests, the case may have gone too far at the expense of banks.

LECTURER: Are occupiers who have contributed to the purchase price of a house (where that house is put in someone else's name) even aware that they have rights in the land? Imagine Land Law as a big pendulum that must not swing too far in the direction of one Building Block at the expense of another. The scales of justice must be balanced. Can you identify any of the Building Blocks that seem to pull in opposite directions?

BUILDING BLOCK NO 5: Property Rights and the Protection of Purchasers and Mortgage Lenders

A rule is good or bad fair or unfair, depending on the extent to which it supports or undermines the idea that Land Law should protect purchasers and mortgage lenders from being bound by prior interests in the land.

STUDENT: If an ordinary residential purchaser, like a family, a couple, or a first-time buyer, is bound by property rights that existed in the land prior to the purchase, then this will devalue their house—someone else may have a claim on it first! Like Mrs Sharpe in BUILDING BLOCK NO 5: Property Rights and the Protection of Purchasers and Mortgage Lenders, and now Mrs Boland. And as I said before, this might be quite a common situation. And banks and building societies who lend money, have to be able to recoup their investment if things go wrong and the borrower defaults on the loan repayments. So at least under the old law people knew where they stood.

LECTURER: You have not said *why* it is important that banks should be able to repossess houses in order to get their money back.

STUDENT: They might be reluctant to lend to homebuyers in the future. This will lead to a slump in the housing market because many people need mortgages in order to buy houses.

LECTURER: And what about small businesses?

STUDENT: Most of their start-up funding will come from banks, who may insist on a mortgage over the new directors' family home as security. If they can't repossess it and sell it if things go wrong then they will be reluctant to lend to businesses in the future.

　　This all sounds a bit hollow. Surely asking purchasers to make a few more enquiries when they buy the house or before a lender takes a mortgage on it, would not be too burdensome? It's not like going back to the sort of enquiries that purchasers of old used to have to make (at least according to BUILDING BLOCK NO 5: Property Rights and the Protection of Purchasers and Mortgage Lenders, where *every* right would bind a purchaser). For residential purchasers and banks, their conveyancers could always ask anyone who lived there with the vendor to fill out a form or something. That way they would find out about property rights that would bind them.

LECTURER: When you get into Land Law you will see that there are a number of cases and articles that will support you on this point. And there are ones that will help you develop it further.

STUDENT: But just for now, Lord Wilberforce supports it. He says that at the moment the practices of banks and purchasers is "easy-going", which means that they could with little trouble be made to make more inquiries along the lines I suggested above. Banks should not longer be able to rely on a general proposition that people in occupation can be disregarded and that any property rights those people may have will not in any case bind them.

LECTURER: Very good—you have done well here.

BUILDING BLOCK NO 6: The Need for Certainty and Predictability in Land Law Rules:

If the rules are clear as to how they will apply in future cases, i.e. if they allow people (e.g. purchasers or occupiers) to predict the outcome of their actions, then they are good law.

LECTURER: Just as a little exercise here: You also have to make sure that your evidence *really does* support your conclusion. To take the famous example from the film *Witness for the Prosecution*, the accused had bloodstains on his jacket. When the blood was analysed it was proven to be of the same group as the victim's. This looked like it was strong support for the Prosecution's conclusion that the accused had killed the victim, that is, until the defence barrister pointed out that the accused's own blood was of the same group and he had cut himself accidentally that morning with a bread knife. Evidence supports conclusion (and thereby creates an argument) *if the conclusion follows from the evidence*. This means that it must be the only likely conclusion from that evidence. If another is possible the argument is invalid.[123] You need to practice examining *possibilities*.

STUDENT: Ah, this is what it means when we say that the argument must be *watertight*.

---

123   S.Guttenplan, *The Languages of Logic*, 2nd edn (Wiley-Blackwell, 1997), Ch. 14.

LECTURER: I will put an argument to you, based on BUILDING BLOCK NO 6: The Need for Certainty and Predictability in Land Law Rules, and see if you can say whether the evidence *in fact* really does support my conclusion.

> **PREMISE:** *Boland* means that banks have to look at the house and enquire of occupiers before they can repossess a house and get their money back.
>
> **PREMISE:** *Boland* undermines certainty
>
> **PREMISE:** Land Law rules must create a certain and predictable system. Property rights are so important to people and to the operation of the banking system that it must be predictable how the rule will apply in future.
>
> **CONCLUSION:** *Boland* is bad law.

STUDENT: It should be clear how a rule is going to apply to *all banks* in the future. The rule must create a stable system in which all (or most) banks will be able to order their affairs and know when they will be able to repossess a house and get their money back . . . . . .Oh! It's Premise 2 that's wrong. *Boland* is not unpredictable just because it says that banks must make *more* enquiries. It is only unpredictable if it is unclear how banks are supposed to act, i.e. what sort of enquiries should be made how many etc.

LECTURER: So let's see if we can do any better. The outcome of a case must not merely do justice between the parties of that case, the bank and Mrs Boland, but it must be clear what kind of a precedent the case will create for all lenders and all Mrs Bolands.

STUDENT: If the sort of inquiry that the lender would need to make in order to make sure that they could evict the occupier and sell the house, was certain, then this might add a little to the cost of domestic conveyancing, but the law itself would still be certain. They could be required to ask all occupiers to fill out a form, as I argued above, and this would be perfectly certain in what they are required to do in the future. Lenders would know what they had to do in order to repossess a house. There must be cases decided *after Boland* that have expanded further of this issue. I also think I need to know more about these cases and the rule itself.

E. BUILDING BLOCKS IS A PROCESS—NOT AN ANSWER

There is much more that you can argue about in *Boland*, particularly when you look at *imaginative argument* and cross-examining the evidence in each of the Building Blocks. It is important to remember that the Building Blocks do not give you a magic formula for writing a 2(i) or first class essay. They are *forms* of evidence that can be used to establish a good argument. If you want to gain these high marks, you need to keep thinking about and refining your ideas about the rules and the Building Blocks. What you have got at the moment is "flat pack" argument: deconstructed first class Land Law argument (like on *MasterChef* you might see a deconstructed cheesecake). You have the ingredients for an argument. What you need to do now is to keep your Building Blocks, perhaps in separate files, and hold them against the rules so that you are constantly thinking about the relationship between rules and their underlying concepts and policies.

> Read carefully and critically, think about how the authors and judges are considering the relationship between the rules and the Building Blocks. Throughout the book we will be considering extracts from judgments and articles. This is designed to help you think carefully about the reasoning in cases and about which of the Building Blocks have been used to construct the reasoning and argument. Throughout the book there are LECTURER and STUDENT dialogues to help you construct your arguments using Building Blocks.

Summary of the Building Blocks

And finally here is a summary of our Building Blocks. We will be using them throughout in order to construct arguments about, and understand, the rules of Land Law that we find in cases and statutes.

> **BUILDING BLOCK NO 1: Residential Security**
> We can legitimately say that where the rules operate in the context of owner occupation of property, they are good and fair if they give effective protection to people's residential security. Land Law now operates in the context of owner occupation. Land Law rules should give effect to the purposes for which people buy and use land/houses. People place a good deal of importance on land ownership and the law should protect this. When people are using land ownership to build a home this is a significant part of their lives. As Atiyah says (*Rise and Fall of Freedom of Contract* (1979)) the strength of people's expectations reinforces the rigour with which the law protects them.

BUILDING BLOCK NO 2: Ideas of Justice

Rules are good and fair if they take account of moral justice: Every person should be accorded the freedom of their will and autonomous choice. Thus, if people deal with each other and with their property in a way that violates the will of another then the law should offer that other some remedy. We may legitimately say that Land Law is bad if it does not do so. As property gives a person choice over their life, Land Law rules should distribute ownership adequately, e.g. a family member should be able to acquire an informal co-ownership right in the home where they have joint responsibility for the family. Land Law should decide its rules to guard against the potential for the legal owner, e.g. the husband, to deal with the land in a way that dramatically affects the life of the other spouse, e.g. by mortgaging the house behind her back and then defaulting on the repayments: "domination-potential": Harris, *Property and Justice*, p.273. We have already seen how *Boland* was a step in this direction, as Harris also observes: above.

BUILDING BLOCK NO 3: Property and Identity

Rules are good if they take proper account of the fact that people gain a sense of value and worth from ownership of land, particularly in the context of owner occupation. Thus, Land Law rules should not deprive people of that possession without adequate safeguards. So we can say that a rule is good or bad fair or unfair, depending on the extent to which it protects a person's ownership from interference. This principle is not absolute. It may justify an argument against allowing banks to repossess family homes without making sure that they have exhausted every other avenue first, or, as in *Boland* without taking reasonable care to make sure, when it accepted the house as security for the mortgage, that there was no spouse or other person who could potentially assert a prior property right and stop it repossessing the house.

BUILDING BLOCK NO 4: Ideas of Ownership

This Building Block shows us how Land Law rules should be made. They ought to be based on, and rooted in, underlying concepts of Land Law, such as ownership. So this Building Block will give us an understanding of how some of the rules come into being. We have seen in *Street v Mountford* and *Copeland v Greenhalf* that this Building Block is useful in helping us to understand what a lease or tenancy *is* and what an easement *is*. Thus when deciding when someone has acquired particular rights in land, e.g. by their conduct or by an agreement, they should not be held by a judge to have done so unless their conduct displays, or the agreement confers, characteristics that resemble *ownership*. Sometimes when we are looking at smaller rights in land the court will have regard to the ideas of ownership. If the right confers the large and all embracing qualities of control of the land (ownership), then it cannot be a smaller right, which, by definition, entails a more limited use of the land. Thus, in deciding whether the various rights in land have come into being—the courts should look at fundamental ideas of ownership. If not then we can say that the case is bad.

BUILDING BLOCK NO 5: Property Rights and the Protection of Purchasers and Mortgage Lenders

We can argue that a development of a rule in a case or statute is good or bad fair or unfair, depending on the extent to which it supports or undermines the idea that rules of Land Law should protect a purchaser or mortgage lender from being bound by prior interests in the land. This is the policy behind the 1925 property legislation. A rule of Land Law is good if when applied in future cases it would not make life difficult for purchasers buying land, i.e. the rule would not mean that the land, when it is transferred to them, will be bound by rights (such as Mrs Sharpe's informal co-ownership right or Farmer Geoffrey's estate contract (see BUILDING BLOCK NO 5 for details of these examples)) that a purchaser or mortgage lender could not have found out about in advance. Banks and building societies often lend to small businesses on the security of family homes. If they cannot be sure of their security, i.e. that the courts will not recognise rights that will bind them and stop them from selling the house if the borrower defaults—as in *Boland*, then they may become reluctant to lend money. This will affect our economy.

BUILDING BLOCK NO 6: The Need for Certainty and Predictability in Land Law Rules

If the rules are clear as to how they will apply in future cases, i.e. if they allow people (e.g. purchasers or occupiers) to predict the outcome of their actions then they are good law. Atiyah says that this is particularly important where people have strong expectations that their rights will be protected. This is the case with property because people attach so much importance to it.

Chapter 2

Land Ownership in English Law

CHAPTER OVERVIEW

In this Chapter you will find:

- The answer to two abiding mysteries of Land Law
- Definitions of land ownership
- The three legal structures of land ownership
- A constructed argument about equity using the Building Blocks.

Introduction:
Two mysteries of Land Law

1

We have opened the book that lies behind Land Law and looked inside at what it is trying to do. We have got some idea of how it is supposed to work and what it is supposed to do: Land Law's Genetic Fingerprint. In this Chapter we build on these foundations and look at *what* is owned when we say we own land and *how* we own land (the legal forms of ownership). But first, a short introduction to help us understand a couple of the mysteries surrounding Land Law.

A. WHY DISTINGUISH LAND FROM OTHER TYPES OF PROPERTY?

Why do not we study the law of ownership of all forms of property? Why study Land Law separately? Some of the forms of ownership are the same for all types of property. You can have a mortgage on land and a similar arrangement in relation to other property. Similarly it is possible to have a trust fund for a child, where a fund of money is looked after by adults for the child, and for land to be held on trust for that same child. But land itself is different from other types of property, and this requires some different forms of ownership. Land is immoveable. There is only one lot of it, i.e. it is not in constant manufacture like many other forms of property, such as cars, shares, jewellery, furniture, money etc. And we have to live out our lives upon it. Thus, land has to go further and do more. We have to live co-operatively with our neighbours. Thus, my neighbour might have a right of way across my back yard in order to be able to get to their house, and vice versa. It is difficult to imagine this being true of other types of property, such as a car.[1]

In Chapter 1 we saw that the possession of land went hand-in-hand with power and status. This was not the case with other types of property, such as money and shares, at least not until the Industrial Revolution and the agricultural depression of the nineteenth century. The seventeenth and eighteenth centuries saw complex family settlements whereby land was kept in the family for generations. As well as ensuring that land passed to the eldest son each generation, provisions were made for widows and younger children. Thus "[s]chemes of provision for the interests of members of landed families led in due course to an elaborate doctrine of estates and rules of inheritance.[2] Personal property, on the other hand, was not subject to [such rules]".[3] And thus "[t]he common law relating to movable property was totally separate and distinct from the law of [land]".[4]

B.　REAL PROPERTY AND PERSONAL PROPERTY

Another way of referring to land is real property. All other forms of property are called personal property.

In English legal procedure in the 1700s, litigants first selected a "form of action", which was "a choice between methods of procedure adapted to cases of different kinds",[5] one for a broken promise, another for a trespass etc. Actions for recovery of property were classified as real, personal or mixed.[6] If the plaintiff was claiming that the defendant had dispossessed him of his land he would have to bring a real action or action *in rem*. The remedy available was that the defendant would have to give up the land to the plaintiff, who would thereby be put back in possession of it.[7] But real actions could only be brought in relation to land. In relation to other types of property, the plaintiff had to proceed on the basis of a personal action. The remedy available to the plaintiff under a personal action was less satisfactory: the defendant who was in wrongful possession of a thing had a choice of whether to give the thing up or pay to the claimant its equivalent price.[8] Because real actions were only available for land, land gradually

---

1　　R.Smith, *Property Law*, 6th edn (Longman, 2009), Ch.1
2　　This book is not concerned with the detail of many of these rules as they are largely defunct today.
3　　J.H Baker, *An Introduction to English Legal History*, 2nd edn (London: Butterworths, 1979), p.193.
4　　Baker, above, p.315.
5　　F. Maitland, *The Forms of Action at Common Law* (1936), Lecture I, p.2.
6　　F. Maitland, above, Lecture I, p.7.
7　　Maitland, above, Lecture VII, p.74.
8　　Maitland, above, Lecture VII, p. 74.

became known as real property. All other types of property became known as personal property. This classification of land as real property was thus nothing to do with the nature of land *as land* in itself.[9]

What is owned when we say we own "land"?   2

A. THE AIRSPACE ABOVE THE LAND AND THE SOIL BELOW?

In *Bernstein of Leigh (Baron) v Skyviews & General Ltd*[10] the court had to consider the rule that governed trespass cases in ancient common law: *cujus est solum ejus est usque ad coelum et ad inferos*,[11] which means whoever owns the land owns up to the highest heaven and down to the depths of the earth. Technically therefore this maxim meant that whoever enters into any of this space without the landowner's permission is guilty of trespass. Thus, parliament passed the Civil Aviation Act 1982, s.76(1), which allows aircraft to fly over land without threat of a trespass action, provided they are flying over as a result of "innocent passage".[12] No court prior to this case had been called upon to consider directly the extent to which a landowner could sue a person for trespass for incursion into the airspace above their land. Up to what height could a landowner claim exclusive rights? The facts of the case were as follows:

> **THE FACTS:** Skyviews & General Ltd were aerial photographers who took photographs of houses from a sky viewpoint and then offered them for sale to the owners. This happened with Coppings Farm, Leigh, owned by Baron Bernstein, who alleged that Skyviews had committed a trespass by flying into his airspace.

> **THE CONCLUSION:** Griffiths J. held that Skyviews & General had not committed a trespass. The landowner's rights did not extend to this height.

STUDENT: Have I got all the information I need now?

LECTURER: You need to know *why* Griffiths J. decided what he did. This gives you the way in which the rule was developed and shows you how to apply it to future cases. But more than this—examining a judge's *reasoning* shows you the law as it ought to be seen: as a process of developing rules to govern the needs of society. Law is under construction all the time—it is not cast in stone.

---

9   The forms of action have now been abolished. Early writers on English common law imported the terms "real action" and "personal action" from Roman Law, which had an entirely different system of classification: F. Maitland, above, Lecture VII, pp.73–4.

10   [1978] Q.B. 479.

11   A maxim "first coined by Accursius in Bologna in the 13th century": per Griffiths J. *Bernstein v Skyviews & General Ltd*, above p.485.

12   K. Gray and S.F. Gray, *Land Law Core Text Series* (Oxford University Press, 2011), Ch.1.

STUDENT: So it's the process of reasoning that I need to learn.

LECTURER: It's like remembering all the reasons why you wanted to do law in the first place. Law is a process of development; it meets the needs of society; you loved the way in which lawyers formed their argument, the way in which nothing was cast in stone, and the way it was a question of representing the interests of *people*. So you will want to see law in action, and not merely learn a series of facts *about law*.

So we will read an extract from the judgment of Griffith J. in *Bernstein v Skyviews*.

STUDENT: Can you give me a starting point—what am I looking for?

How to identify and analyse a judge's chain of reasoning

When we are attempting to extract a rule and reasons from a judgment we need to identify a chain of reasoning and its conclusion. The first thing we do is extract what the judge is reasoning *about*. One way of doing this is to work backwards and identify what conclusion they came to. The conclusion has an air of "the result" or "completion of the process" about it, a certain "air of finality". It may follow expressions such as "therefore", "thus", "in conclusion", "in consequence" etc. (A.Fisher, *The Logic of Real Arguments* (1988)).

Then we need to identify what *reasons* the judge gives in support of his or her conclusion. Identifying factors that a judge puts forward as reasons for his or her conclusion is far from being a precise art. We might ask the question: *what were the factors that the judge seemed to regard as supporting their conclusion? What did they feel was so important that it led them to that particular conclusion?* (A.Fisher, *The Logic of Real Arguments* (1988)). In formulating questions to help identify a judge's chain of reasoning, I am indebted to L. Elder's article "I Think Critically Therefore I Am" in the *Times Higher Education Supplement*, August 2009.

LECTURER: Let's see how we get on. Here is a short extract from Griffiths J.'s judgment in *Bernstein v Skyviews*[13]:

THE REASONING: "The plaintiff claims that as owner of the land he is also owner of the air space above the land, or at least has the right to exclude any entry into the air space above his land. He relies upon the old Latin maxim, cujus est solum ejus est usque ad coelum et ad inferos. . . There are a number of cases in which the maxim has been used by English judges, but an examination of those cases shows that they have all been concerned with structures attached to the adjoining land, such as overhanging buildings, signs or telegraph wires, and for their solution it has not been necessary for the judge to cast his eyes towards the heavens; he has been concerned with the rights of the owner in the air space immediately adjacent to the surface of the land . . . [. . .]

---

13   [1978] Q.B. 479, pp.485–488.

I can find no support in authority for the view that a landowner's rights in the air space above his property extend to an unlimited height. In *Wandsworth Board of Works v United Telephone Co. Ltd.*, 13 Q.B.D. 904 Bowen L.J. described the maxim, usque ad coelum, as a fanciful phrase, to which I would add that if applied literally it is a fanciful notion leading to the absurdity of a trespass at common law being committed by a satellite every time it passes over a suburban garden. . . The problem is to balance the rights of an owner to enjoy the use of his land against the rights of the general public to take advantage of all that science now offers in the use of air space. This balance is in my judgment best struck in our present society by restricting the rights of an owner in the air space above his land to such height as is necessary for the ordinary use and enjoyment of his land and the structures upon it, and declaring that above that height he has no greater rights in the air space than any other member of the public.

Applying this test to the facts of this case, I find that the defendants' aircraft did not infringe any rights in the plaintiff's air space, and thus no trespass was committed. It was on any view of the evidence flying many hundreds of feet above the ground and it is not suggested that by its mere presence in the air space it caused any interference with any use to which the plaintiff put or might wish to put his land . . . [There is no] principle of law or authority that would entitle Lord Bernstein to prevent someone taking a photograph of his property for an innocent purpose, provided they did not commit some other tort such as trespass or nuisance in doing do."

LECTURER: What maxim is Griffiths J. speaking of?

STUDENT: *Cujus est solum ejus est usque ad coelum et ad inferos*, which means whoever owns the land owns up to the highest heaven and down to the depths of the earth.

LECTURER: And what was the question that the judge had to answer in relation to it?

STUDENT: The question for Griffiths J. was whether the landowner (Baron Bernstein in this case) should be able to sue Skyviews & General for damages in trespass because they flew their aircraft into the upper airspace over his land, or whether the rights of the landowner should be restricted in some way—if so in what way?

LECTURER: What was his conclusion?

STUDENT: Apart from the fact that it is at the end, the conclusion, given away by the language "this balance is in my judgment best struck", was that the landowner should not be able to sue for trespass regarding the entire airspace above the land—only that necessary to protect his ordinary use and enjoyment of his land.

LECTURER: What were the judge's reasons for this decision?

STUDENT: There was never any authority for the extension of claims to trespass to the entire airspace over the land. Secondly, unless the owner's rights to bring a claim against potential trespassers were limited to a certain height, the law would be unbalanced. It would unduly restrict "the rights of the general public to take advantage of all that science now offers in the use of air space".

LECTURER: A good Building Block if ever I saw one! Let's create an argument.

STUDENT: I definitely agree that had the decision in *Bernstein* gone the other way, we might have said that it created bad law because aircraft would be subject to claims of many landowners in trespass. This would mean that flights would not be economically viable. Thus, it would restrict science.

LECTURER: On the other hand, as seen above, the Civil Aviation Act 1982, s.76(1), allows aircraft to fly over land without threat of a trespass action, provided they are flying over as a result of "innocent passage". Thus, we might argue that it is unnecessary to have restricted the claimant's ownership rights any further.

STUDENT: There is no *positive* reason to protect ownership rights that high up. But at least every outcome in the future would be predictable. The rule that Griffith J. laid down was that the rights of an owner in the air space above his land should extend no further than is necessary for the ordinary use and enjoyment of his land. This to me sounds quite vague. It may be difficult for people to understand how this rule would apply in the future. So they would not know what rights they have.

LECTURER: So you are saying that on the basis of BUILDING BLOCK NO 6: The Need for Certainty and Predictability in Land Law Rules, Griffith J.'s judgment created bad law.

> **BUILDING BLOCK NO 6: The Need for Certainty and Predictability in Land Law Rules**
> If the rules are clear as to how they will apply in future cases, i.e. if they allow people to predict the outcome of conduct, then they are good law.

LECTURER: But on this certainty point, many rules are successfully formulated on the basis of what is "reasonable use". Think of it this way: How do you think the rule that a claimant can only assert rights to airspace above his land to the extent that it is necessary for the *reasonable enjoyment of his land*, would apply to cases in the future? Remember that we have to argue *imaginatively* and ask questions—cross examine the evidence in the Building Block.

STUDENT: It would depend on what the landowner wanted to use his land for. It would depend on the type of property. If he was running a park which involved putting things in the air, or needed extra quiet, such as a nature reserve, it might be arguable that his right to exclude, say a low-flying aircraft, might extend into higher regions than an ordinary landowner.

Actually I see now that the law does need some flexibility here. Even if you cannot say *exactly* how a rule may apply, it would be easy for a barrister to formulate an argument on the basis of the rule. They would show how an alleged trespass did in fact affect what the claimant wanted to use the land for. For example, in a nature reserve the presence of a low-flying aircraft may interfere with the quiet that is needed for observation.

LECTURER: I agree. I think that this is what Griffiths J. is saying. Now let's look at the case from a problem-solving angle:

What does it mean when we are asked to "solve a legal problem"? Examiners expect you to be able to apply the law to a factual scenario. What this means is that you have to predict the legal consequences of the events in the scenario. And the legal consequences follow from a proper *identification* and *application* of the legal rules in the cases and statutes.

Reasoning by analogy

If we are presented with a set of facts that are materially the same as a case in which a current rule of law has been applied (here *Bernstein*) then this provides a reason to support the conclusion that our case would be decided in the same way as the "analogue" case. This is what lawyers call "reasoning by analogy": F.Schauer, *Thinking Like a Lawyer* (2009), Ch.5 "The Use and Abuse of Analogies".

LECTURER: Let's say we are presented with a problem scenario in which Mario flew an aeroplane over Jane's land for photographic purposes. Do you think Mario is liable or not? What evidence would you put forward for your conclusion?

Identifying legal analogies

To give rise to the same conclusion as *Bernstein v Skyviews & General Ltd* our facts must have *materially similar properties* to that case (expression and idea: Schauer (2009), above). These material factors are identified by asking questions like: *what would have to have been different about the case for the judge to decide it the other way*—in favour of Baron Bernstein? (L.Elder, *I Think Critically Therefore I Am*, THES, 2009.)

STUDENT: In *Bernstein v Skyviews* the factors without which the case would have been decided the other way were that the aircraft was flying at such a height that it did not interfere with the reasonable use of the claimant's land (p.488).

LECTURER: That's good. Now we hold the facts of our problem (Mario and Jane's case) against these material facts of *Bernstein* and see whether the same factors are present.

Applying and distinguishing a case

We use the material properties of the precedent case (or "analogue") to give us a conclusion to our problem case. If the same material properties are present in the *Jane v Mario* case then the rule in *Bernstein* applies in the same way and Mario will not be liable. But if the *material* properties are not the same in our *Jane v Mario* problem, then we distinguish *Bernstein v Skyviews* and we conclude that Mario *is* liable in trespass. Here we are saying, in effect, that whilst this is the rule that should apply, the *result* would be different in our case because the case itself is different from *Bernstein*. This is how the legal system strives to treat "like cases alike".

STUDENT: So if Mario's aircraft were flying much lower we may be justified in saying our case was different and that Jane would have the right to exclude Mario from the land. Also, Mario might have been making a pest of himself by taking lots of photographs. In which case, he would be interfering with Jane's use and enjoyment of her land. This means that unlike

Bernstein, where the defendants were not so interfering, Jane would be able to claim against Mario for coming into her airspace.

LECTURER: Very good. I see you are getting the idea of legal reasoning.

(1) The airspace immediately above the land

Ownership rights are enforced with full vigour when there is an invasion into the airspace *immediately above* the land, for example, where a neighbour has erected a sign over his neighbour's land,[14] allowed a crane to swing over neighbouring land,[15] grown a tree that overhangs adjacent land, or passed a telephone line over another's land.[16] "Of such stuff is the endless saga of neighbour disputes."[17] In *Kelsen v Imperial Tobacco Co Ltd*,[18] the defendant tobacco company displayed three advertising signs which intruded into the claimant's airspace by four inches. The claimant, a retail tobacconist, claimed an injunction to force the defendants to remove the signs. The defendants argued that it was necessary for the claimant to prove that the presence of the sign caused him harm, which it had not. McNair J. held that an intrusion into the airspace immediately above land amounted to a trespass. It was thus not necessary for the claimant to establish harm.[19] The claimant was awarded an injunction: the defendants had to remove the signs.[20]

(2) The soil below

In *Bocardo SA v Star Energy UK Onshore Ltd*[21] the Supreme Court affirmed that the owner of land owns the strata beneath the soil, which includes minerals found there.[22] In *Edwards v Lee's Administrator*[23] there was a cave that was discovered underneath the claimant's and the defendant's adjoining lands. The defendant had permitted tourists to visit the cave and the claimant was arguing that this constituted a trespass on his land. Stites J. held that he was entitled to a proportion of the profit made by the defendant from the tourists.[24] However, the landowner does not have absolute control. In *Bocardo* Lord Hope made the point that there would come a depth at which it would be meaningless to talk about ownership of the strata below the soil. Furthermore, gas and coal belong to the Crown, as do items defined as "treasure".[25]

(3) Damages in lieu of an injunction

Whilst a claimant will be able to sue for violation of their rights over land, it is by no means always the case that they will be awarded an injunction. The court has discretion to award

---

14   *Gifford v Dent* [1926] W.N. 336.
15   *Anchor Brewhouse Developments Ltd v Berkley House (Docklands Developments) Ltd* [1987] 38 B.L.R. 82.
16   *Wandsworth District Board of Works v United Telephone Co Ltd* (1883–84) L.R. 13 Q.B.D. 904.
17   Gray and Gray, *Land Law Core Text Series*, 4th edn (2006), p.8.
18   [1957] 2 Q.B. 334.
19   [1957] 2 Q.B. 334, p.345.
20   "In such cases the well-known rule is . . . . . . to grant the injunction sought, for the plaintiff's legal right has been invaded, and he is prima facie entitled to an injunction", per McNair J., quoting A.L.Smith L.J. in *Shelfer v City of London Electric Lighting Co* [1895] 1 Ch. 287.
21   [2010] UKSC 35.
22   Lord Hope, approving *Mitchell v Mosley* [1914] 1 Ch. 438.
23   96 S.W. 2d 1028 (1936, Court of Appeals of Kentucky); B.McFarlane, N.Hopkins, S.Nield, *Land Law, Text, Cases and Materials* (Oxford University Press, 2009), pp.34–35.
24   McFarlane, Hopkins, Nield, above p.35.
25   Petroleum (Production) Act 1934; Coal Industry Act 1994; Treasure Act 1996: M.Thompson, *Modern Land Law*, 4th edn (Oxford University Press, 2009), p.7.

damages instead of an injunction.[26] In *Kelsen v Imperial Tobacco*, McNair J. awarded an injunction even though both parties accepted that no significant harm had been suffered.[27] In this case there was no "accidental invasion of the plaintiff's rights". The defendants had insisted throughout that they had a right to display the sign.[28] McNair J. wished to prevent the defendant trespassers from effectively buying the right to trespass. But there are cases where the award of an injunction would be harmful and in such cases damages may be awarded instead. For example, where houses have been built in breach of a restrictive covenant. In *Wrotham Park Estate Co Ltd v Parkside Homes Ltd*, Brightman J. reasoned that

"The erection of the houses, whether one likes it or not, is a fait accompli and the houses are now the homes of people. . . . I cannot close my eyes to the fact that the houses now exist. It would, in my opinion, be an unpardonable waste of much needed houses to direct that they now be pulled down."[29]

(4) Nuisance and public rights

We have seen from this that the protection of ownership rights can never be absolute. The law prevents me from enjoying my land in ways that unreasonably interfere with my neighbour's use of his land. I cannot play loud music all night in my house because this would cause a nuisance to my neighbours. The law protects their quiet enjoyment of their land.[30] The law has circumscribed the freedom of certain types of landowner because it is necessary to ensure that the public can make use of the land. For example, the owner of a shopping centre complex does not have the same rights of exclusion as other landowners.[31]

B. THE DEFINITION OF LAND AND WHAT IT INCLUDES UNDER THE LAW OF PROPERTY ACT 1925

The Law of Property Act 1925 tells us the meaning of "Land":[32]

" 'Land' includes land of any tenure, and mines and minerals, whether or not held apart from the surface, buildings or parts of buildings (whether the division is horizontal, vertical or made in any other way) and other corporeal hereditaments, also a manor, an advowson, and a rent and other incorporeal hereditaments, and an easement, right, privilege, or benefit in, over or derived from land".

---

26   *Shelfer v City of London Electric Lighting Co* [1895] 1 Ch. 287. The assessment of damages is flexible, and the standard approach is to award damages on the basis of a reasonable fee for the use of the claimant's land. Only in rare cases would an account of profits made be appropriate: *Stadium Capital Holdings v St Marylebone Properties Co Plc* [2010] EWCA Civ 952.

27   [1957] 2 Q.B. 334, p.347, per McNair J. relying on *Goodson v Richardson* (1874) L.R. 9 Ch. 221.

28   [1957] 2 Q.B. 334, p.347.

29   [1974] 1 W.L.R. 798, pp. 810–811.

30   P.Giliker and S.Beckwith, *Tort,* 4th edn (London: Sweet & Maxwell, 2011), p.294.

31   K.Gray and S.F.Gray, "The Idea of Property in Land" in S.Bright and J. Dewar (eds) *Land Law: Themes and Perspectives* (Willan Publishing, 1998), p.15.

32   Law of Property Act 1925 s.205(1)(ix).

"Buildings or parts of buildings": So when I purchase a house, I have bought the land, but I also own the house built upon it. When the land is transferred to me, so is the house. The buildings upon it are defined as part of the land.

"And other corporeal hereditaments": Any other physical entities as well as buildings.

"Also a manor, an advowson": An advowson was the ancient right to appoint a clergyman to a living (an appointment at the parish church).

"Whether the division is horizontal, vertical or made in any other way": Land is not just defined as the surface of the earth. It includes the space above the earth. When I own a flat, I still own land. What I own is the space in the air that the flat occupies, and, of course, the flat itself. This is a horizontal division of the land, sometimes called a "flying freehold".

"Other incorporeal hereditaments; and an easement, right, privilege, or benefit in, over or derived from land": Just as "corporeal" means property of a physical nature; something material,[33] like a building on land, "incorporeal" means a type of property that does not have a physical existence. A right of access over your neighbour's land to get to your house (an easement), is an example of an incorporeal right. It has no physical existence. You cannot touch, slap, or bang your head against a right of way. It is defined as land.

(1) Fixtures and structures on the land[34]

When ownership of land changes hands people may dispute over what is intended to form part of the transfer of ownership from one to another. For example:

> **Sarah v Alfred**
> Sarah transfers her house "Heath Green" to Alfred. On this transfer, Alfred owns everything that forms part of that land. On the day Alfred is due to move in and Sarah to move out, he finds Sarah removing a small summerhouse from the garden, some paving slabs from the patio, and a sprinkler system in the garden that she uses to water her prize tomatoes. Alfred is annoyed because he had thought that he was entitled to these items: the sprinkler system would be particularly good for his chrysanthemums. **Who is entitled to what?**

Alfred is only entitled to items that are deemed to be part of the "land". Section 62(1) of the Law of Property Act 1925 provides that:

> "A conveyance of land shall be deemed to include and shall by virtue of this Act operate to convey, with the land, all buildings, erections, fixtures, commons, hedges, ditches, fences, ways, waters, water-courses, liberties, privileges, easements, rights, and advantages whatsoever, appertaining or reputed to appertain to the land, or any part thereof, or, at the

---

33   *Collins English Dictionary.*

34   See e.g. *Elitestone Ltd v Morris* [1997] 1 W.L.R. 687, per Lord Lloyd; B.McFarlane, N.Hopkins, S.Nield, *Land Law, Text, Cases and Materials* (2009).

time of conveyance, demised, occupied, or enjoyed with, or reputed or known as part or parcel of or appurtenant to the land or any part thereof."

Thus Alfred will be able to claim the summerhouse, the paving slabs, and the sprinkler system, if they can be defined as fixtures appertaining to the land (appertaining meaning to be part of or connected to). Otherwise they will be chattels that the outgoing occupier is entitled to take with them.[35]

(a) From landed gentry to owner occupation

Disputes as to whether items are fixtures and thus pass with the land have arisen in many different contexts. Historically, they arose in the context of large houses and estates that passed from father to son. The question then, was whether the son inherited items affixed to the house, such as statues in the grounds, tapestries hanging on the wall, valuable carvings, etc.[36] Were these fixtures and therefore part of the land which was to be kept in the family and passed from generation to generation?

In Chapter 1, we saw that society now has different reasons for wanting to own land. In the twentieth century there was a transition. From a society in which most people rented the house in which they lived, we became a home owning democracy. People often borrow money from a bank or building society in order to fund the purchase of a house. The bank takes a mortgage on the house and, if the borrower defaults, it has the power to sell the house in order to recoup its money. The house is the bank's security for the loan. It is not surprising therefore to find cases in this modern context that involve disputes between a defaulting borrower, who wants to take items such as bathroom fittings, carpets, and kitchen goods with him when he leaves, and a bank that argues that these items are fixtures and therefore form part of the house that the borrower offered as security in the first place.[37] This is less likely to be an issue when the value of the house will in any event exceed the debt owed by the borrower to the bank.[38]

So how does the law determine whether an item is a fixture or part and parcel of the land? There is a two-part test: the degree of annexation test and the purpose of annexation test. The first raises a presumption as to the classification of the item; the second is decisive.

(b) The degree of annexation test

In *Holland v Hodgson*[39] Blackburn J. explained the way in which the law determines whether an item is a "fixture", and thus part of the land, or a mere "chattel": a personal possession that the outgoing occupier can take with them:

---

35 It is standard practice for conveyancers to issue fixtures and contents lists to vendors in order to make clear what items are or are not included in the contract of sale. This would be definitive.

36 *D'eyncourt v Gregory* (1866–67) L.R.3 Eq. 382; *Leigh v Taylor* [1902] A.C. 157; *Re Lord Chesterfield's Settled Estates* [1911] 1 Ch. 237 respectively: E.H.Burn, *Maudsley & Burn's Land Law Cases and Materials*, 8th edn (Oxford University Press, 2004), p.97, fn.11.

37 *Botham v TSB Bank Plc* (1997) 73 P. & C.R. D1.

38 In *Botham* there was a £170,000 shortfall. It was a case that involved an owner-occupier. However, *Maudsley and Burn* cites many earlier cases that involved mortgage lenders making similar claims: e.g. *Holland v Hodgson* (1871–72) L.R. 7 C.P. 328; *Lyon & Co v London City and Midland Bank* [1903] 2 K.B. 135: E.H.Burn, *Maudsley & Burn's Land Law Cases and Materials*, 8th edn, p.97, fn.10.

39 (1871–72) L.R. 7 C.P. 328.

"Perhaps the true rule is, that articles not otherwise attached to the land than by their own weight are not to be considered as part of the land, unless the circumstances are such as to shew that they were intended to be part of the land, the onus of shewing that they were so intended lying on those who assert that they have ceased to be chattels, and that, on the contrary an article which is affixed to the land even slightly is to be considered as part of the land, unless the circumstances are such as to shew that it was intended all along to continue a chattel, the onus lying on those who contend that it is a chattel."

So where an item rests on its own weight it is prima facie a chattel. And if it is affixed, albeit to a slight degree only, it is prima facie a fixture. *Prima facie* means that it is a presumptive classification only. Thus, if an item is resting on its own weight, i.e. not affixed to the land at all, then it is classified as a personal possession that the outgoing occupier can take with them *unless the new owner can prove that it was intended to form part of the land*. And the same is true the other way around.

LECTURER: So in our problem case involving Sarah and Alfred, if the sprinkler system was not attached to the garden in any way, but was heavy enough to stand by its own weight, what would be its prima facie classification?

STUDENT: It is classed as a personal possession and not part of the land.

LECTURER: Unless? The degree of annexation test is not decisive of the issue.

STUDENT: Unless it is proven that the sprinkler system was intended to form part of the land.

LECTURER: Good, but our problem solving and legal reasoning technique require us to be more precise than this. Look again at the extract from Blackburn J.'s judgment in *Holland v Hodgson*. If, under the degree of annexation test the sprinkler system is classified as a chattel because it is resting on its own weight, we know this is not decisive. *Who* must prove that it was intended to be part of the land in order for it to be classified as a fixture?

STUDENT: Sarah can take it with her as a chattel unless Alfred proves it is intended to form part of the land. He would be the one contending that the circumstances are such that the sprinkler system was no longer intended to be a chattel but intended to be part of the land.

LECTURER: Good. And if the sprinkler is attached, even to a small degree, then Sarah has to prove that it is *not* intended to form part of the land.

STUDENT: So how would Alfred go about proving that the sprinkler system, or any other item that was not attached, was intended to form part of the land?

LECTURER: We shall now see.

(c) The purpose of annexation test

The degree to which something is attached to the land is not the end of the story. How is it to be proven whether something was intended to form part of the land or not? This depends on what it is that has been brought onto the land, and on the type of property or land it is.

(d) Structures which have become "part and parcel" of the land

In *Billing v Pill*[40] Lord Goddard C.J. said "[t]he commonest fixture is a house which is built into the land, so that in law it is regarded as part of the land. The house and the land are one thing". But we need to understand why and from what material we can infer that structures such as houses are intended to form part of the land.

(i) Elitestone Ltd v Morris

In order to do this we will look in detail at a decision of the House of Lords: *Elitestone Ltd v Morris*.[41] First we must look at the facts and conclusion.

> **THE FACTS**: In *Elitestone Ltd v Morris* Mr Morris was the occupier of a chalet bungalow that was resting on its own weight on Elitestone Ltd's land. Mr Morris was claiming that he was a protected tenant under the Rent Act 1966, which would mean that Elitestone Ltd would be unable to get him off their land. Elitestone Ltd could only evict Morris if the chalet bungalow was held *not* to form part of the land.[42]

> **THE CONCLUSION**: Lord Lloyd held that the bungalow formed part of the land. But this does not tell us what we need to know in order to solve our *Sarah v Alfred* problem. We need to know *why* the bungalow was held to be part of the land: the judge's REASONING.

> **The reasoning:** To understand the law applied in a case and how to use it to solve our problem, we need to identify how the judge got from A (the facts of the case) to C (the conclusion or outcome of the case). We need to identify the judge's reasons for his conclusion. We can do this by asking questions like: *what were the factors that were so important to the judge that they led him to this particular conclusion? What would have to have been different for the judge to come to a different conclusion?* L.Elder, "I Think Critically Therefore I Am", *THES* (August 2009).

> **THE REASONING**: LORD LLOYD: "[T]he photographs show very clearly what the bungalow is, and especially what it is not. It is *not* like a Portakabin, or mobile home. The nature of the structure is such that it could not be taken down and re-erected elsewhere. It could only be removed by a process of demolition. This . . . is a factor of great importance in the present case. If a structure can only be enjoyed in situ, and is such that it cannot be removed in whole or in sections to another site, there is at least a strong inference that the purpose of placing the structure on the original site was that it should form part of the realty at that site, and therefore cease to be a chattel . . . [. . .]

---

40 [1954] 1 Q.B. 70, p.75, relied on in *Elitestone Ltd v Morris* [1997] 1 W.L.R. 687, per Lord Lloyd.
41 [1997] 1 W.L.R. 687, from p.690.
42 It is not important that you understand *why* this is the case. The information here is provided for context only.

[T]he question in the present appeal is whether, when the bungalow was built, it became part and parcel of the land itself. The materials out of which the bungalow was constructed, that is to say, the timber frame walls, the feather boarding, the suspended timber floors, the chipboard ceilings, and so on, were all, of course, chattels when they were brought onto the site. Did they cease to be chattels when they were built into the composite structure? [. . .]

[Lord Lloyd proceeded to consider the purpose of annexation test] A house which is constructed in such a way so as to be removable, whether as a unit, or in sections, may well remain a chattel, even though it is connected temporarily to mains services such as water and electricity. But a house which is constructed in such a way that it cannot be removed at all, save by destruction, cannot have been intended to remain as a chattel. It must have been intended to form part of the realty. I know of no better analogy than the example given by Blackburn J in *Holland v Hodgson*, L.R. 7 C.P. 328, 335:

'Thus blocks of stone placed one on the top of another without any mortar or cement for the purpose of forming a dry stone wall would become part of the land, though the same stones, if deposited in a builder's yard and for convenience sake stacked on the top of each other in the form of a wall, would remain chattels.'

Applying that analogy to the present case, I do not doubt that when Mr Morris's bungalow was built, and as each of the timber frame walls were placed in position, they all became part of the structure, which was itself part and parcel of the land. The object of bringing the individual bits of wood onto the site seems to be so clear that the absence of any attachment to the soil (save by gravity) becomes an irrelevance."

Finally, Lord Lloyd distinguished two cases that concerned whether greenhouses could be held to be part of the land. In *Deen v Andrews*[43] a greenhouse was held not to be part of the land. Hirst J. relied on the decision in *H.E.Dibble Ltd v Moore*[44] in which Megaw L.J. had observed that 'it was customary to move such greenhouses every few years to a fresh site'."

LECTURER: What was Lord Lloyd's conclusion about the bungalow?

STUDENT: That it was part of the land itself. It was a fixture and, for the purposes of problem-solving, would pass with the ownership of the land.

LECTURER: And what was his reason for this conclusion? This gives us the *law* that we then apply to future problems.

STUDENT: Lord Lloyd came to his conclusion that the bungalow was part and parcel of the land, because the bungalow had been constructed on the land and now could not be separated from it without the complete destruction of the bungalow. This showed that they were one entity.

LECTURER: And as this is a piece of *legal* reasoning you will find that Lord Lloyd relied on past cases that articulated this reason, or rule.

---

43   [1986] 1 E.G.L.R. 262.
44   [1970] 2 Q.B. 181.

> **Legal Reasoning**
>
> SELECT AN ANALOGY: Lawyers will first select an "analogy". The analogue cases used by Lord Lloyd are the greenhouse cases, a dry stone wall example, and an analogy based on a Portakabin. It is from these analogies that he will arrive at his conclusion in *Elitestone* itself.
>
> IDENTIFY THE MATERIAL FACTORS OF THE ANALOGUE CASE: To give rise to the same conclusion as the analogies, the facts of the present case must have the same significant features or *materially similar properties* to those cases: Schauer, *Thinking Like a Lawyer* (2009), Ch.5
>
> DISTINGUISHING THE ANALOGIES: If the significant features of the present case are not the same as those in the analogue case, the same conclusion cannot be reached.

STUDENT: Lord Lloyd considered this rule as it applied in some cases that involved greenhouses.

LECTURER: What were the "material properties" or what we might say "significant features" of the greenhouse cases?

STUDENT: The greenhouses could be more easily moved. They would not cease to be greenhouses if they were moved. Their greenhouseness did not depend on the land. Therefore they were chattels and not fixtures.

LECTURER: Lord Lloyd "distinguished" the greenhouse cases from the bungalow that he was considering. He was saying that he did not have to come to the same conclusion as the greenhouse cases because there was a significant difference. What was it?

STUDENT: Because the bungalow *could not be* removed and re-erected elsewhere—its removal would cause it to be destroyed.

LECTURER: And he said the bungalow was like a dry stone wall, using the authority of *Holland v Hodgson*, why?

STUDENT: Its entity as a wall would be destroyed if the pieces were taken away. Its wallness depended utterly on the land. Just like the bungalow.

(e) Objects brought onto the land

These cases do not always involve large structures, such as buildings, bungalows, or greenhouses. They can involve smaller items, such as paintings, tapestries, kitchen and bathroom fitments etc. When such items are brought onto the land how do we determine whether they are fixtures that pass with the ownership of the land? Such items are not likely to become unrecognisable in their identity when removed. The law has found more suitable ways of determining the purpose for bringing the item onto the land. One way is to ask "whether the object which has been fixed to the property has been so fixed for the better enjoyment of the object as a chattel, or whether it has been fixed with a view to effecting a permanent improvement of the freehold".[45]

---

45   *Elitestone Ltd v Morris* [1997] 1 W.L.R. 687, p.692 per Lord Lloyd, citing *Leigh v Taylor* [1902] A.C. 157.

In *Leigh v Taylor*[46] tapestries were tacked to a wall on canvas. It was held that they were not fixtures, i.e. they had not become part of the land. They remained chattels and did not pass with the ownership of the house. The reason why they had been fixed to the wall of the house was so that they could be enjoyed by the present owners. There was no intrinsic connection with the house itself.[47] In *Re Whaley*[48] the current owner of a house had created a "complete specimen of an Elizabethan dwelling-house". As part of this design, the owner had attached tapestries to the dining room wall. The owner had left all his land (realty) to one person and chattels to another.[49] The reason for attaching the tapestries was that they should form part of the Elizabethan design of the house. Thus, the tapestries were deemed to be part of the land. In *Berkley v Poulett*[50] the same test was applied to a large statue, a sundial, and paintings screwed onto a wall. All were held to be chattels because the paintings were put on the wall, and the statues put in the garden in order to better enjoy them as chattels.

STUDENT: Taking the tapestries away would make the house much less a "complete specimen of an Elizabethan dwelling-house". Wouldn't this be a matter of opinion though? I mean, it's easy to tell whether a structure can be removed without destruction, you either end up with a pile of rubble or you don't, but how do you determine whether an *idea* is destroyed?

LECTURER: I should imagine that there would be common ground in the middle.

STUDENT: But what if the owner in *Re Whaley* had said that he never intended the tapestries to form part of the Elizabethan design. Then, every person moving out of a house would be able to take whatever they liked with them.

LECTURER: A person would not be allowed to ride roughshod over Land Law in this way. The test is objective. In *Elitestone Ltd v Morris*, Lord Lloyd stated that "the intention of the parties is only relevant to the extent that it can be derived from the degree and object of the annexation. The subjective intention of the parties cannot affect the question whether the chattel has, in law, become part of the freehold".

(i) Botham v TSB Bank Plc

The more recent case of *Botham v TSB Bank Plc*[51] applied these tests in a more modern context. What we begin to see when we examine subsequent cases that apply the basic principles of law is that the judges will interpret and re-interpret the rule. This gives depth to our understanding of the legal tests concerned and enhances our ability to apply them. Don't therefore look for exact, word-for-word reiterations of the tests above. Look to see how the judge's reasoning in *Botham v TSB Bank Plc* can be mapped onto your existing understanding.

---

46   [1902] A.C. 157.
47   E.H.Burn, *Maudsley & Burn's Land Law Cases and Materials*, p.97, fn.11.
48   [1908] 1 Ch. 615.
49   Burn, above, p.97, fn.11.
50   (1977) 241 E.G. 911.
51   (1997) 73 P. & C.R. DI, McFarlane, Hopkins, Nield, *Land Law, Text, Cases and Materials*.

THE FACTS: Mr Botham owned a flat in Chelsea, which he had bought with the aid of a mortgage from the TSB Bank. He defaulted on the repayments to the bank and it sought possession of the flat. The value of the flat fell short of the debt owed by Mr Botham by £170,000. The dispute surrounded certain items in the flat and whether they formed part of the bank's security, i.e. whether they formed part of the land. The disputed items were: bathroom fittings (namely, the taps, plugs, and showerhead, together with the towel rails, soap dishes and lavatory roll holders); kitchen units, including the sink; carpets, curtains and blinds; oven, the dishwasher, the hob, the fridge, and the freezer.

THE CONCLUSION: Some of the items were held to be fixtures; others, chattels. We now need to understand *why*. This will tell us the law.

THE REASONING: ROCH L.J. "The tests . . . seem to be the purpose of the item and the purpose of the link between the item and the building. If the item viewed objectively is intended to be permanent and to afford a lasting improvement to the building, the thing will have become a fixture. If the attachment is temporary and is no more than necessary for the item to be used and enjoyed, then it will remain a chattel.

Some indicators can be identified. For example, if the item is ornamental and the attachment is simply to enable the item to be displayed and enjoyed as an adornment that will often indicate that this item is a chattel. Obvious examples are pictures. But this will not be the result in every case; for example ornamental tiles on the walls of kitchens and bathrooms. The ability to remove an item or its attachment from the building without damaging the fabric of the building is another indicator. The same item may in some areas be a chattel and in others a fixture. For example a cooker will, if freestanding and connected to the building only by an electric flex, be a chattel. But it may be otherwise if the cooker is a split level cooker with the hob set into a work surface and the oven forming part of one of the cabinets in the kitchen. It must be remembered that in many cases the item being considered may be one that has been bought by the mortgagor [borrower] on hire purchase, where the ownership of the item remains in the supplier until the instalments have been paid. Holding such items to be fixtures simply because they are housed in a fitted cupboard and linked to the building by an electric cable, and, in the cases of washing machines, by the necessary plumbing would cause difficulties and such findings should only be made where the intent to effect a permanent improvement in the building is incontrovertible. . . . ."

LECTURER: How does this add to your knowledge of the tests?

STUDENT: Whether an item is a fixture or a chattel depends on the purpose of the link between the item and the building. The court was considering utilitarian items, such as bathroom fittings, and items such as bathroom tiles. The question was whether the item was attached to or brought onto the land simply to enjoy it as an ornament or to improve the room as a kitchen or a bathroom. However, this did not cover all situations for example where ornamental tiles had been attached to bathroom or kitchen walls.

LECTURER: And so Roch L.J. "borrowed" part of the test from *Elitestone v Morris*.

STUDENT: And held that such items *could* be fixtures where their removal would cause damage to the fabric of the wall.

LECTURER: The same could be said of electrical items. Where they are freestanding and attached only by an electric cable they would ordinarily be chattels. But where they are an integrated unit in the kitchen and their removal would damage the kitchen then they would be fixtures. However, Roch L.J. saw that there is another "novel" point that arises in relation to these items. What was it?

STUDENT: Electrical items are often purchased from the supplier in instalments. Finding that they became part of the land would mean that ownership in the items transferred to the new purchaser of the house. This was thought to be impractical and (possibly) unjust so that Roch L.J. considered that it was unlikely in this situation that they would be held to be fixtures.

LECTURER: So this is the law. Roch L.J. now applied the law to the facts of *Botham*.

> **ROCH L.J.'s JUDGMENT CONTINUES**: "I have no hesitation in agreeing that . . . . . . the bathroom fittings namely the taps, plugs and showerhead together with the towel rails, soap dishes and lavatory roll holders . . . . are fixtures. . . . Those items are attached to the building in such a way as to demonstrate a significant connection with the building, and are of a type consistent with the bathroom fittings such as the basins, baths, bidets and lavatories, as to demonstrate an intention to effect a permanent improvement to the flat. They are items necessary for a room which is used as a bathroom. They are not there, on the evidence which was before the judge and which is before us, to be enjoyed for themselves, but they are there as accessories which enable the room to be used and enjoyed as a bathroom. Viewed objectively, they were intended to be permanent and to afford a lasting improvement to the property."

LECTURER: Consider how the purpose of annexation text was applied here. Roch L.J. applies the ordinary test, seen in *Leigh v Taylor* that the items were not brought into the flat to be enjoyed in themselves. They were intended to affect a lasting improvement to the building. How was this shown?

STUDENT: The permanent improvement was demonstrated in a practical way. The items were necessary to enable the bathroom to function *as a bathroom*.

> **ROCH L.J.'S JUDGMENT CONTINUES**: "[Concerning] the kitchen units, including the sink . . . Again in my judgment the degree of annexation, the fact that between the working surfaces and the underside of the wall cupboards of the wall units there is tiling, demonstrates both a degree of annexation and an intention to effect a permanent improvement to the kitchen of the flat so as to make those units fixtures. Further, as a matter of common sense, those units could not be removed without damaging the fabric of the flat, even if the damage is no more than the leaving of a pattern of tiling which is unlikely to be of use if different units had to be installed."

LECTURER: How does the judge apply the purpose test?

STUDENT: He found that because the kitchen units were part of an integrated whole, demonstrated by the tiling in between the units, this showed that the units were intended to be part of the flat as a whole. This was shown by the fact that their removal would cause damage to the building, even if only the cosmetic damage, i.e. new units would not go with the old tiling.

LECTURER: So here, Roch L.J. is applying a more sophisticated version of the test in order to cover the novel facts in this case. This is how we see the law develop.

> **ROCH L.J.'S JUDGMENT CONTINUES**: "I would allow the appeal with regard to the fitted carpets and the curtains and blinds. These items, although made or cut to fit the particular floor or window concerned, are attached to the building in an insubstantial manner. Carpets can easily be lifted off gripper rods and removed and can be used again elsewhere. In my judgment neither the degree of annexation nor the surrounding circumstances indicate an intention to effect a permanent improvement in the building. Although many people take with them their curtains and carpets when they move, it is true that others leave curtains and carpets for the incoming occupier, but normally only where the incoming occupier has bought those items separately from the purchase of the property itself. Curtains are attached merely by being hung from curtain rails. The removal of carpets and curtains has no effect damaging or otherwise on the fabric of the building. In my opinion, the method of keeping fitted carpets in place and keeping curtains hung are no more than is required for enjoyment of those items as curtains and carpets." [. . . . .]

LECTURER: Here we see that the carpets were chattels because they can be removed easily and used again. Roch L.J. also inferred that such items are usually intended to be chattels on the basis that it is standard conveyancing practice to treat these items as separate from the land. Can you think of a scenario in which this decision could be easily distinguished?

STUDENT: If someone were to fit carpets as part of a contemporary theme of a trendy flat in Portobello Road, then by analogy with *Re Whaley* (above) they may be held to be fixtures. Here we would distinguish (see p.69 above on "Legal Reasoning") Roch L.J.'s decision in *Botham*.

> **ROCH L.J.'S JUDGMENT CONTINUES**: "[Concerning the oven, the dishwasher, the hob, the fridge, and the freezer], . . . no one, I venture to suggest would look on these as fixtures. Here the judge should have reminded himself that the degree of annexation was slight: no more than that which was needed for these items to be used for their normal purposes. In fact these items remain in position by their own weight and not by virtue of the links between them and the building. All these items can be bought separately, and are often acquired on an instalment payment basis, when ownership does not pass to the householder immediately. Many of these items are designed to last for a limited period of time and will require replacing after a relatively short number of years. The degree of annexation is therefore slight.

Disconnection can be done without damage to the fabric of the building and normally without difficulty. The purpose of such links as there were to the building was to enable these machines to be used to wash clothes or dishes or preserve or cook food. . . these items were [not] installed with the intention that they were to be a permanent or lasting improvement to the building."

LECTURER: How did Roch L.J. apply the purpose of annexation test in relation to the oven, dishwasher, hob, fridge etc?

STUDENT: Their removal would not cause damage. They were only brought into the flat in order to be used for their own purposes, and attached to no greater degree than that necessary for this purpose. The items by nature are short lived and often purchased by instalments. These factors added up to the conclusion that there was no objective intention that they should become part of a permanent improvement to the flat.

(f) Problem solving: applying and distinguishing cases

We now return to our example problem scenario where Alfred bought Heath Green from Sarah. Sarah transfers ownership of her house "Heath Green" to Alfred. On the day Alfred is due to move in and Sarah to move out, he finds Sarah removing some paving slabs from the patio and a sprinkler system for watering her prize tomatoes. Since then, three other things are in dispute:

- A summerhouse, resting on its own weight. It is a basic timber frame with glass in the windows. The timber frame locks into place and in not glued.
- A tapestry of Heath Green, placed in the breakfast room in order to be viewed against the local landscape.
- A breakfast bar attached by a screw to the wall in the breakfast room.

Sarah says that she did not intend the tapestry to be in anyway part of the house. Use the advice given in this chapter on applying and distinguishing cases, and on selecting analogies in order to discover who is entitled to what.

LECTURER: Before we begin, how did you get on with that last section?

STUDENT: It is a little bit strange. I'm used to reading a passage in a textbook or lecture handout and then that tells me what the law is.

LECTURER: Well, it tells you facts *about* what the law is. This way you get to see the picture of law exactly as it is—as a process of development. Let's have a go at the *Alfred v Sarah* problem. There is no right answer. It's all down to how well you argue

Always remember that what you are doing is *solving a legal problem*. As with problem solving outside the context of law you should do two things: identify what the problem actually *is*, and secondly, identify the factors that will help you solve the problem: the analogue cases.

STUDENT: The problem has arisen because s.62 of the Law of Property Act 1925 tells us that items classified as fixtures pass with a transfer of the land. Sarah, the transferor, wants to take certain items with her, which she cannot do if they are classified as fixtures. Otherwise they are classed as her personal possessions and she can take them with her.

LECTURER: Good, you explain how a problem has arisen. Because legal problems are often used as coursework, many forget the reality of what they are doing and will begin by simply talking about the law—as if it were a fact and not a process of solving a problem: "The law of fixtures and chattels was laid down in *Holland v Hodgson* (1871–72) L.R. 7 C.P. 328 and it says. . . . etc".

Now we need the analogies that will help us solve this problem.

STUDENT: The general test that we apply to decide whether an item is a fixture or a chattel was established in *Holland v Hodgson* that if an item is resting on its own weight (degree of annexation) then the item is presumptively a chattel unless the person claiming that ownership has passed on conveyance, here Alfred, can establish that it was intended to become part and parcel of the land.

LECTURER: Good. You must now select the most appropriate cases to help us resolve the dispute. Let's start with the summerhouse. What are the cases with the most materially similar properties to a summerhouse resting on its own weight?

STUDENT: Alfred must show that the summerhouse was intended to become "part and parcel of the land": *Elitestone v Morris*. This he must do by showing that its structural identity depends on the land. In *Elitestone* the bungalow was a fixture because its removal would cause it to be destroyed. In the *Holland v Hodgson* analogy the stones that were used to make the dry stone wall would not be individual chattels because they now formed an entity, a wall, which would be demolished by its removal. In the two "greenhouse" cases, *Deen v Andrews* and *H.E.Dibble Ltd v Moore*, the greenhouses were held to be chattels and not fixtures because they could easily be removed and used elsewhere.

LECTURER: Well done. You have given all the relevant "analogies", i.e. the reason for the decisions in the cases that are closest to our summerhouse.

> **Use of the facts of past cases**
> Have you noticed that the only time we refer to "case facts" is when we use them to better help us articulate the *reason* for the decision in that case? Students will often simply recite case facts without quite knowing why they are doing it. They will often ask *how much should we include the facts of cases?* Once you properly grasp the process of legal reasoning you will use only those facts that you need to help you articulate the rules and, for the next stage, apply and distinguish the selected analogue cases.

LECTURER: So having identified our analogies we now need to use them to predict a legal outcome for Sarah and Alfred. Hold the analogue cases up against our problem (the summerhouse). It must have the same *material facts* as these cases in order to justify our arriving at the same conclusion. Otherwise we must distinguish them and come to a different conclusion.

STUDENT: We could apply the greenhouse cases and distinguish *Elitestone v Morris* if we can fully establish that the summerhouse would not be destroyed by removing it. The timber frame is only locked into place, so it could be deconstructed and reassembled elsewhere. On the rule in all these cases the Summerhouse would be a chattel.

LECTURER: Good, but a counter argument may be possible on the basis of the glass in the window. We don't know what effect this might have. Sometimes the facts of a problem do not give you enough information for you to be 100 per cent sure about applying or distinguishing. In this situation the best you can do is to state this. Now—what about the paving slabs in the garden.

STUDENT: Applying first the "degree of annexation" test (*Holland v Hodgson*), because the paving slabs are attached to the land, prima facie they are fixtures and pass with the land unless Sarah can prove that they were not objectively intended to affect a permanent improvement.

LECTURER: So turning to the "purpose of annexation" test, which cases would be the closest analogies to use to solve the problem?

STUDENT: I would use *Leigh v Taylor*; *Re Whaley*; *Botham v TSB Bank Plc*. In *Leigh v Taylor* tapestries were held to be chattels on the basis that they had been fixed to the wall only to be better enjoyed as pictures and not to improve the building. The opposite conclusion was reached on the same reason in *Re Whaley*, in which tapestries formed part of the integral design of the house. Perhaps the closest analogy is *Botham v TSB* in which tiling and attachments were held to be fixtures where they enabled a room to be used in accordance with its proper function. One reason for this is that the removal of the tiles may leave some damage to the fabric of the building.

LECTURER: So having identified our analogies we now need to use them to predict a legal outcome for Sarah and Alfred. Hold the analogue cases up against our problem (the paving slabs) and apply these cases or distinguish them, if they are sufficiently materially different.

STUDENT: It seems that the majority of the reasons in the cases point to the conclusion that the paving slabs are fixtures, and therefore pass on transfer of the land to Alfred. If the slabs were an integrated part of the design so that their removal would diminish that design then on *Re Whaley* they would be held to be fixtures. Sarah would not be able to take them with her. I would apply rather than distinguish *Botham*. Even if the paving slabs were not part of any special design, they arguably help the garden function better as a garden (by analogy with the bathroom fitments in *Botham*). It is also quite likely that the paving slabs are attached in some way and that their removal would cause some form of damage to the land. In *Botham* Roch L.J. thought that damage did not have to be very significant.

LECTURER: Good—you are getting very adept at selecting and applying analogue cases. For now, I will leave you to the rest of the problem.

(g) Tenants fixtures

Where a tenant has attached an item that has become a fixture then the general rule is that these "must be left for the landlord at the end of the lease".[52] However a tenant has a power to remove fixtures in certain circumstances during the tenancy. A tenant may remove items that

---

52   C.Harpum, S.Bridge, M.Dixon, *Megarry & Wade, Law of Real Property*, 7th edn (London: Sweet & Maxwell, 2008), para.23–010.

they have attached for the purposes of the tenant's trade or business.[53] In *Mancetter Developments Ltd v Garmanson*[54] a tenant was permitted to remove an extractor fan that he used in his business. A tenant may also remove an item that has been attached for ornamental purposes, provided significant damage would not be caused by its removal.[55] The tenant must repair any damage caused by the removal of the item.[56]

C. FINDINGS AND TREASURE

> **In this section, we are going to learn how to create a "map" of the law, i.e. a picture of how cases relate together.**

This type of dispute is all about who is entitled to keep items of property found on the land or under its surface. Here are some examples:

- In 1722, a boy chimney sweep found a jewel. He took it to a goldsmith's shop, whereupon the master offered the boy money but refused to return the jewel to him. The boy argued that he had the right to keep the jewel. Does he have a right to keep it?[57]
- A man was using a metal detector in a local park. He found a medieval brooch below the surface of the earth. He dug it out and claimed it as his. The council owned the land and say that the brooch is theirs.[58]
- A commercial traveller was doing business in a shop. On the premises he found a parcel of Bank of England notes, which no one came forward to claim. The firm, whose shop it was, said that the notes were theirs. The commercial traveller wanted to keep them himself.[59] Does the person on whose land the find is made get to keep the bank notes?

In *Armory v Delamirie* (the first of our examples above) the judge's conclusion was that the boy could keep the jewel. But this gives us nothing that we can use to solve a problem, should a case with similar facts arise in the future. For this, we need to know how the judge got from A (the facts) to C (the conclusion): the judge's *reasoning*:

> "the finder of a jewel, though he does not by finding acquire an absolute property or ownership, yet he has such a property as will enable him to keep it against all but the rightful owner".[60]

Thus, a person who finds an object and takes control of it has a better right to it than anyone except the true owner of it. This is our "rule"—*why* the judge decided what he did.

---

53   Above, para.23–012.
54   [1986] Q.B. 1212.
55   *Megarry & Wade*, above, para.23–012, citing *Martin v Roe* (1857) 7 E. & B. 237.
56   *Mancetter Developments*, above.
57   *Armory v Delamirie* (1722) 5 Stra. 505, cited in *Hannah v Peel* [1945] K.B. 509.
58   *Waverley Borough Council v Fletcher* [1996] Q.B. 334.
59   *Bridges v Hawkesworth* (1851) 21 L.J. QB 75.
60   [1722] 5 Stra. 55.

LECTURER: What is your opinion about this case? Do you think it was the right decision? Does the judge's reasoning support or undermine any of the Building Blocks?

BUILDING BLOCK NO 4: Ideas of Ownership

The basic characteristic of ownership is exclusive control. If someone has taken control of something and taken it into his care, there is an argument for saying that he should be recognised as the owner. By his efforts of control the thing may be said to be an extension of himself.

STUDENT: The boy had taken control of the item before anyone else. So I think it is a good decision.

LECTURER: But of course the boy would have had no claim against the real owner of the jewel.

STUDENT: But BUILDING BLOCK NO 4 would provide a good justification for allowing the boy to keep the jewel against a stranger who was claiming it.

(1) Disputes between landowners and finders: Hannah v Peel[61]

This next case has a potential "distinguishing" feature.

THE FACTS: During the Second World War, Mr Hannah, who was a lance corporal, was stationed in the house of Mr Peel. During this time, he found a brooch lodged near a window frame and gave it in to the police. As no one came forward to claim the brooch the police gave it back to Mr Peel (the landowner), who kept it but offered Mr Hannah a reward. Mr Hannah claimed that he was now the rightful owner of the brooch.[62]

THE CONCLUSION: The potential distinguishing feature is that Mr Peel owned the house in which the brooch was found. This might mean that he had a stronger claim to the brooch. Notwithstanding this the judge concluded that Mr Hannah could keep the brooch. Why? We need to know the judge's reasoning.

THE REASONING: The judge reasoned that the landowner does not automatically acquire ownership of a thing found on his land. Birkett J. relied on the reasoning in *Bridges v Hawkesworth*,[63] in which banknotes had been found by a travelling salesman in the defendant's shop (so *Hannah v Peel* had the same material factors as this case), in which the judge had stated:

"The notes never were in the custody of the defendant (landowner), nor within the protection of his house, before they were found, as they would have been had they been intentionally deposited there; and the defendant has come under no

---

61   [1945] K.B. 509.
62   B.McFarlane, N.Hopkins, S.Nield, *Land Law Text, Cases, and Materials*, pp.46–55.
63   (1851) 21 L.J. QB 75 quoted in *Hannah v Peel*, p.517.

responsibility, except from the communication made to him by the plaintiff, the finder, and the steps taken by way of advertisement. . . . . We find, therefore, no circumstances in this case to take it out of the general rule of law, that the finder of a lost article is entitled to it as against all persons except the real owner."

Birkett J. in *Hannah v Peel*[64] followed this reasoning that the place in which the brooch had been found made no difference. There were no special circumstances to take the case out of the general rule: "The defendant was never physically in possession of these premises [he had yet to move in after having bought the house] . . . It is clear that the brooch was never his, in the ordinary acceptation of the term, in that he had the prior possession. He had no knowledge of it". [65] Neither landowner in these cases had exerted any degree of control or care over the item found.

So the courts are using basic ideas of ownership to decide who should be entitled to the item found. The finders in both these cases took control of the item. The landowners did not. Thus, there were no circumstances to take the case out of the general rule in *Armory v Delamirie* that the finder has the better claim against all but the true owner. The courts so far have decided that the person who exerts the most control over an item found has the better claim, i.e. unless the true owner comes forward.

LECTURER: If we were presented with a legal problem involving similar facts, how could we potentially distinguish it? *What features of these cases would have to be different for the cases to be decided the other way?*

STUDENT: If the brooch were deposited in Peel's (the landowner's) custody; if he knew about its existence; if he somehow would come under a responsibility to look after it. In those situations he would, according to the judge, have asserted a claim to *possession* of the brooch prior to the person finding it.

LECTURER: Can you see what is so especially decision-changing about these situations?

STUDENT: They are all situations in which the landowner would have somehow "controlled" the item.

(2) Parker v British Airways Board[66]

Now we will consider another development in the law.

THE FACTS: The claimant was a passenger waiting in the executive lounge at Heathrow airport. He found a gold bracelet and handed it in to an official from British Airways, who were the occupiers of the premises where it was found. He asked for it to be returned to him if no one claimed it. No one claimed the bracelet and the airline sold it for £850, keeping the proceeds. Mr Parker claimed the £850 plus interest on the basis that he had a better right to the bracelet than the airline.[67]

---

64   [1945] K.B. 509.
65   p.521.
66   [1982] Q.B. 1004.
67   B.McFarlane, N.Hopkins, S.Nield, above p.49.

THE CONCLUSION: Donaldson L.J. held that Mr Parker had the better claim to the bracelet.

THE REASONING: Donaldson L.J. held that on the ordinary principles, Parker, as the finder of the bracelet, acquired the right to it "against all but the true owner". British Airways, the occupier of the premises, could only have established that their claim was superior if it had manifested

"an intention to exercise control over a building and the things which may be upon or in it . . . The manifestation of intention may be express or implied from the circumstances including, in particular, the circumstance that the occupier manifestly accepts or is obliged by law to accept liability for chattels lost upon his 'premises' ".

As far as this case was concerned, British Airways could establish no such intention simply by their "right to decide who should and who should not be permitted to enter and use the lounge". It was insufficient also that they could have excluded individuals such as drunks, and confiscated objects such as guns: "this control has no real relevance to a manifest intention to assert custody and control over lost articles".[68] Was this the correct decision? Consider Building Block 4:

> **BUILDING BLOCK NO 4: Ideas of Ownership**
> Ownership is all about having control over something. Therefore, it is appropriate that a landowner who has manifested an intention to control items found on his land, should be able to have the better legal claim to those items, in the absence of the true owner. Otherwise it is the finder who has de facto control over the item.

(3) The rights of trespassers as finders

But what about the situation where the finder is a trespasser who manifests control over an item when the landowner does not? The general rule does not apply with the same force. According to Donaldson L.J. in *Parker v British Airways Board* a trespasser acquires only "very limited rights over" an article that they find in the course of trespassing on another's land, as does one who takes the item "into his care and control with dishonest intent", e.g. where he makes no attempt to find the true owner. As Donaldson L.J. observes "Wrongdoers should not benefit from their wrongdoing". Although Thompson considers that this is a "highly questionable" basis on which to give the *landowner* a stronger claim[69] it is done simply to avoid a "free-for-all situation" whereby anyone can claim the item.[70]

In *Waverley Borough Council v Fletcher*[71] Mr Fletcher had been using a metal detector in a public park owned by Waverley Borough Council. He found a medieval brooch a few inches below the surface and dug it out. The Council claimed the brooch. Auld L.J. held that the council had the better right to the brooch. There were "sound and practical" reasons why a distinction must be drawn between items found *on* the land and items found *in* the land. Where an object is found

---

68   [1982] Q.B. 1004, p.1018.
69   M.Thompson, *Modern Land Law*, p.11.
70   *Parker v British Airways Board* [1982] Q.B. 1004.
71   [1982] Q.B. 1004, p.1017.

in the land the object is treated as forming part of the land itself. It therefore belongs to the landowner: the council. Secondly, "the finder in detaching the object [from the land] would, in the absence of licence to do so, become a trespasser". As we have already seen, a trespasser will have a weaker claim to the item than the landowner.

(4) Where the finder is acting in the course of his employment

Finally, where an item is found by an employee acting in the course of his employment, he is deemed to take it into his care "on behalf of his employer or principal who acquires a finder's rights to the exclusion of those of the actual finder".[72]

Let's see how the principles fit together:

PRINCIPLE OF OWNERSHIP: WHO WAS THE FIRST TO CONTROL THE ITEM?

> *Armory v Delamirie* (1722): a person who finds an object and takes control of it, has a better right to it than anyone except the true owner of it: reaffirmed in *Hannah v Peel* [1945].

A BETTER CLAIM THAN THE LANDOWNER ON WHICH IT WAS FOUND:

> *Hannah v Peel* [1945]: because of this the owner/occupier of the land on which the object was found will not be able to assert a better claim.

UNLESS THE LANDOWNER MANIFESTS AN INTENTION TO CONTROL AREA AND ITEMS ON THE LAND

> *Parker v British Airways Board*: the landowner can only assert the better claim if he manifested an intention to control the area in which the object was found and to control any objects found thereon.

FINDER'S CLAIM NEGATED BY

> As a matter of public policy, if he is dishonest (does not hand item in or search for true owner), or if he is a trespasser, then landowner will have a better claim: *Parker v BAB; Waverley BC v Fletcher*.

Item goes to landowner

A DISTINCTION MUST BE DRAWN WITH ITEMS FOUND *IN* THE LAND

> *Waverley*: in detaching the item, the finder may become a trespasser. In any case, the item is treated as an integral part of the land against all but the true owner of the item.

---

72   *Parker v British Airways Board* [1982] Q.B. 1004, per Donaldson L.J., p.1017.

3

The legal structures of land ownership: tenures, estates, equity and the trust

I said at the beginning of the previous section that this chapter is all about answering two questions.

Firstly, *what* do we own when we say we own land—how is "land" defined and what is included within this definition. Section 2 was concerned with this issue, and we looked at what constituted a fixture so as to pass with the ownership of the land. We also considered the extent of land ownership, i.e. into the airspace above and the soil below. Our second question is with *how* we own land: the legal forms of ownership. There are two important doctrines that have shaped the form of land ownership for centuries: the doctrine of tenures and the doctrine of estates.[73]

A. THE DOCTRINE OF TENURE

From 1066[74] the system of tenure was how land in England was used and enjoyed by her subjects. No subject owns the land itself, the land is owned by the king. The king gives possession of parcels of land to "tenants",[75] so they hold the land *of* the king, who was "lord paramount". Very soon these tenants started to grant a parcel of land to tenants of their own and themselves become a "mesne (middle) lord".[76] This tenant holds the land *of* the mesne lord. Thus, a "feudal pyramid" is formed with the king at the top. The grant of land would be in return for services. These could take many forms, including knight service, "whereby the tenant was obliged in time of war to provide one soldier in combat order"; Castlegard (or "garrison duty"); Cornage (or "border patrol"); "Divine service, or the general duty of saying prayers for the soul of the lord". There were also agricultural services ("socage"), which may involve "helping the lord with sowing or reaping".[77]

So the land, or the use of it, became deeply entwined with an obligation of loyalty and service to the feudal lord. The relationship between lord and tenant was ideally "a bond lasting for life; it was personal to the tenant, inalienable and uninheritable".[78] "It was a life-long status, comparable in some respects with marriage, which also began by contract".[79] The tenant would undertake to provide services and to be faithful, and in return the lord would offer his

---

73 J.H.Baker, *An Introduction to English Legal History,* 2nd edn (London: Butterworths, 1979) Chapter 13; Jackson, Stevens and Pearce, *Land Law,* 4th edn (London: Sweet & Maxwell, 2008) Chapter 3.

74 Baker observes that although "feudal institutions of a kind existed in Anglo-Saxon England", the lawful conquest of the realm by William I in 1066 "led to the regularisation and centralisation of those institutions": *An Introduction to English Legal History*, p.194.

75 The description "tenant" has nothing to do with the modern "lease" or "tenancy"; the landlord and tenant relationship. The word derives from "tenure", meaning "to hold" or "holding". Here I am using it to convey the idea that the tenant has possession of the land: Baker, above, p.194.

76 Baker, above, p.195.

77 J.H.Baker, above, pp.195–7.

78 Baker, above, p.197.

79 Baker, above, p.195.

protection, rule over him, and hold "court for him".[80] The obligations were moral, as well as contractual, in nature.[81] Not only this, the structure of land holding became an important part of meeting the fundamental needs of the realm: national security, agricultural, and spiritual.[82]

> **A special, life-long relationship**
> "The special relationship was sealed by the ceremony of homage, when the tenant knelt and placed his hands between those of his lord and swore to become his man in life and limb and earthly honour against all men except the king": (Baker, *An Introduction to English Legal History* (2nd edn 1979), p.195.)

The process of "subinfeudation", whereby a tenant could become a lord himself by granting part of his land to a tenant, was abolished in 1290. Following this, the only way in which a tenant could dispose of an interest in the land was to transfer his tenure to another tenant, i.e. put another tenant in *his* place.[83]

(1) The modern significance of tenure

However, about a century after the Norman Conquest, the operation of tenants' services had changed. Because the system allowed tenants to sell their holding to another, and now allowed it to be inherited, the new tenant would often not be in a position to provide personal service in battle. The new tenant may not be as able a servant as their predecessor, and a "practical solution was to commute the services to a money rent which the lord could spend on servants of his own choosing". These payments decreased in value due to inflation and thus feudal services completely lost significance by the fifteenth century.[84] Tenures were free or unfree.[85] We still hold land of the Crown, as tenants in socage, the last remaining "free"-hold tenure. But this does not affect our use of the land.[86]

(2) Possession in the feudal system

The feudal system, in its pure form, was based on possession, i.e. possession *as a fact*.[87] The lord would decide who to admit, and the fact of possession by the tenant, when he had taken possession of the land and sworn allegiance, was conclusive. The possession enjoyed by a tenant exhibited

> "few of the privileges of an owner. He could not do what he liked with the land. He could not sell it. He could not pass it on to others by will, and there was no guaranteed succession in his family after his death."[88]

---

80 Baker, above, p.195.
81 Baker, above, p.196.
82 Stevens and Pearce, *Land Law,* 3rd edn (London: Sweet & Maxwell, 2004) pp.23–4.
83 Above, p.24.
84 Baker, above, p.198.
85 Not all tenants had possession themselves but "only occupied their land on behalf of their lords": Stevens and Pearce, *Land Law* (3rd edn), p.24. These were "unfree tenants".
86 Further see Stevens and Pearce, *Land Law* (3rd edn), pp.24–5.
87 J.H.Baker, *An Introduction to English Legal History*, p.198–9.
88 Baker, above, p.198.

The tenant in the pure feudal system had very little of the control over property that we associate with ownership in today's society.[89] During the fourteenth century the common law gradually recognised such rights.[90]

B. THE DOCTRINE OF ESTATES

It is still true today that we hold land of the Crown. We do not own the land itself. However, the doctrine of tenure has little practical significance in modern land law. We own what is called an "estate" in the land. An estate in land is a period of time over which we are entitled to exercise the rights of an owner of that land.[91] It confers ownership of the land for a time. In *Walsingham's Case*[92] it was said that

"an estate in the land is a time in the land, or land for a time, and there are diversities of estates, which are no more than diversities of time ..."

The units of currency in the estates system are the life estate and the inheritable estate.[93]

(1) Freehold Estates

The life and the inheritable estates are forms of freehold estate. The expression "freehold" derives from the feudal system where there were free and unfree tenures. Now all land is held of the Crown on freehold tenure. The most common of these estates is the fee simple, which is practically indistinguishable from actual ownership of the land. For any given piece of land, somebody will own the fee simple.

Freehold estates are classified as follows:

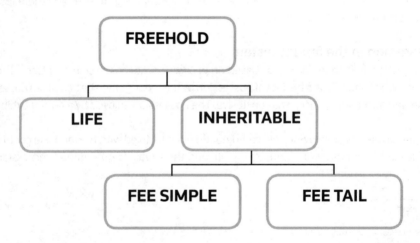

---

89   See for example J.W.Harris, *Property and Justice* (Oxford: Clarendon Press, 1996) Part 1; S.Bright, "Of Estates and Interests: A Tale of Ownership and Property Rights" in *Land Law Themes and Perspectives*, p.529.
90   For further detail see Baker, *An Introduction to English Legal History*, p.199–203.
91   It is from the word "status" we get the word "estate": Baker, *An Introduction to English Legal History*.
92   (1573) 2 Plow. 547.
93   Baker, above, p.222.

(a) The life estate

A life estate is where a person owns the rights over the land for the length of his own lifetime. A life tenant has the immediate right to possess the land. If someone trespasses on the land, the life tenant has the right to bring a legal action to be put back in possession. For all intents and purposes he is the owner, for the length of his life. The life estate is a limited interest in the land: ownership for the life of the person who was granted the interest. It can be sold, but because the right is so limited, all the grantee obtains is the land for the length of the life of the person to whom the life estate has been originally granted.[94] The estate of the purchaser is an estate *pur auter vie*. It "lasted until some other person died."[95] There was no inherent logic behind this, except that at the time of the feudal system "[a] series of such [sales] might have kept the land from ever returning to the lord, who had only parted with it for one life".[96]

(b) The inheritable estate

The right to sell land was important from a very early date. Equally important was the ability to have land inherited by an heir. Thus, the law made it so that an inheritable estate could be transferred to a purchaser as a single entity. When the land is sold, the purchaser will get the same estate, i.e. the right to the land and the right to have it inherited by *their* heirs.[97] Thus, a grant of land "to X and his heirs forever" is a single estate.

(c) The fee simple estate—the totality of ownership

The *fee simple estate* is where we can possess the land and exercise ownership rights over it for an indefinite period and have it inherited by our heirs *forever*.[98] In *Walsingham's Case* the fee simple estate was described as "a time in the land without end".[99] The fee simple estate is practically indistinguishable from ownership of the land. It can be inherited by your heirs, any heirs—however remote. This is what the word "simple" means. "Fee" just means inheritable. Only if you had no living relatives left to inherit after your death would the Crown ever be able to claim the land. Baker observes of the fee simple estate:

> "Unlike lesser estates it was as perpetual and indestructible as the land itself, neither the subject of creation nor of determination by parties. The fee simple was a right to land for ever. It had always to be vested in someone, and if it was in no subject it would be in the Crown. All that men could do with it was to pass it from one to another or carve it up."[100]

(d) The fee tail or curtailed fee

Originally the fee tail (or "entailed") estate was a grant of land for the purpose of providing for the family or family branch of a *younger* son. That son and his family were not going to inherit (that privilege belonged to the *eldest* son). It was also the means of assisting "a daughter who was not an heiress to make a good match":

---

94   Baker, above, p.225.
95   ibid.
96   ibid.
97   Baker, above, p.222-3.
98   Stevens and Pearce, *Land Law*, p.25.
99   (1573) 2 Plow. 547, quoted Stevens and Pearce, *Land Law*, p.26.
100   Baker, above, pp.224-5.

> "Since the purpose of such gifts was to provide for the couple and their progeny, the couple were not usually given an absolute or pure fee, but an inheritance limited to their issue. This was a curtailed fee or fee tail."[101]

Under this estate, the right to possess the land could only be inherited by the direct descendants of the couple, and not by *any* relative. The estate was thus limited in time and ended when there were no more "heirs of the body".[102] Thus it was an estate shorter in time than the fee simple, which was practically indefinite.

In society, the dynastic instinct was strong. So was the "desire to control the devolution [passing] of land after death and to restrain descendants from disposing of the [land] for their own personal benefit". [103] Thus, the law made sure that no descendant in the family line could transfer the estate so as to benefit someone else's direct line of heirs. Thus, in 1285 [104] a statute made it so that if any life tenant (the heir for the time being in possession) attempted to sell the land, the future heirs could bring an action to enforce their claims. Entailed land was "a rigid, unalterable, inalienable perpetuity: a 'juridical monster'".[105] All the life tenant could ever sell was the land for his own lifetime. Few purchasers would want this. They would want the totality of ownership of the land: the fee simple. None of the heirs owned the fee simple so as to be able to convey it.

(i) The relationship between the fee simple and the fee tail

As the fee tail was inevitably a shorter estate than the fee simple, the fee simple must still exist somewhere. The two estates existed at the same time.[106] Let's say that X is the owner of land and he grants it in fee tail "to A and B and the heirs of their bodies". The fee tail was typically shorter which meant that X had not granted away all of his ownership in the land: the totality of it.

> "This fee simple would not fall into possession unless [A and B's] issue failed, which might never happen, but it was logically necessary that it should be vested in someone, to fill the residue of eternity which would be left if and when the fee tail ended." [107]

The fee tail estate was the device used by the lawyers of the landed gentry to create the so-called "strict settlements". When a son and heir came of age and married, the patriarch usually settled the land as follows: "To my son for life, remainder in fee tail to his son, remainder in fee simple to his grandson". So the son had a life estate, his son an entail [so he couldn't sell it] and the fee simple went to the grandson. However, these families never intended the fee simple ever to fall into the possession of a descendant. They would re-settle the land every

---

101 Baker, above, p.231.
102 ibid.
103 Baker, above, p.234.
104 Statute of Westminster, *De donis conditionalibus* (of conditional gifts): Baker, above, p.231.
105 Baker, above, p.235, quoting Milsom, *Historical Foundations of the Common Law*, p.146.
106 Baker, above, p.232: "an unfeudal notion, comprehensible only in the sense that the fee had become an estate or time in the land which could vest either in possession or in the future".
107 Baker, above, p.232.

generation, to make sure the land went to the eldest son on fee tail and that the land could never be sold. And to make it inalienable you had to ensure that none of the descendants ever came into possession of the fee simple, as they were then able to sell it.

(e) Possession interests, reversion interests, and remainder interests

Land Law allows the fee simple to be carved up into life estates, fees tail (entails), and into present and future interests. Thus, we have to become acquainted with a further classification.

(i) Estates in possession

Let's say that Alison is the owner of the fee simple estate in Perelandra, a small country cottage and paddock. As we know this gives her indefinite ownership. People who own the fee simple estate usually own it *in possession*. This means that they are at the present time entitled to use and enjoy the land. In fact you may well say at this point *what other way of owning land is there?*

(ii) Estates in reversion

Let's say that Alison wishes to grant to Elwin a life estate in her land. He is her father and she wants to provide him with security until he dies. But she does not want to transfer the whole of her interest in the land to him so that he can leave it by will to someone else. She wants to keep ownership of the house. So she grants him a limited estate: a life estate.[108] This, as we have seen, would give Elwin the right to possession and enjoyment of the land for his life. Thus Alison is no longer entitled to *currently* possess and enjoy the land. Alison still keeps her fee simple estate. But the right to possess it will only "revert" to her when Elwin dies. So while Elwin is still alive we say that Alison is the owner of the fee simple absolute in *reversion*.

> **There can be more than one estate in the same piece of land. All will count as current rights in the land that can be bought and sold.**

(iii) Estates in remainder

But what if Alison wanted to do something entirely different with Perelandra? Let's say she wants to create the following interests: "My house, Perelandra, to Elwin, for life, and then to Jack in fee simple".

We can see that Elwin still has a life interest. But this time she chooses not to retain the fee simple herself but grant it to Jack. Land Law only uses the description "reversion" when possession is reverting back to the original grantor (Alison). Where the possession passes to another we call this an estate *in remainder*. The word comes from the fact that once Elwin's life estate ceases, possession still *stays away* from Alison: *remanere* ("stays away"). Jack has a fee simple estate *in remainder*.

---

108   This would now take effect as a "trust of land": Trusts of Land and Appointment of Trustees Act 1996 s.2. See Chapter 5.

(2) Leasehold Estates

Freehold estates are not the only tenure recognised by Land Law. The lease is an arrangement between the freeholder of land and a tenant for exclusive use of the land for a set number of years (or less). A lease is carved out of the fee simple estate. Historically, the lease of land was an interest that fell outside the scope of the feudal system, which was concerned with interests for life or hereditary interests. As Baker observes "the letting for years .... was a temporary commercial or financial interest, commonly granted to secure a loan of money... [T]he profits [from the land] would slowly pay off the debt".[109] Thus, leases were contractual and did not involve the personal loyalty protected by the feudal system.[110] Leases were historically classified by the courts as personal property and not real property, which meant that the dispossessed tenant could not automatically be put back in possession of the land itself. [111]

(3) Commonhold

Commonhold is "a form of freehold estate". [112] Two or more freehold owners, e.g. of flats or adjacent houses, form a "commonhold". It was introduced as a method of land holding in part to overcome a particular problem, namely to ensure the continued enforceability of obligations to repair. Title to the land must be registered before a commonhold can be created, and the commonhold is then registered as a separate estate consisting of the separate units.[113]

(a) The need for reform

Enforcing repairing obligations is a particular problem in relation to freehold land. The only type of covenant that can be enforced against a purchaser of freehold land is a *restrictive* covenant, i.e. an obligation *not* to do something on the land (such as build) and which does not involve the owner in expenditure. [114] This creates a problem, e.g. in relation to a freehold block of flats. If the owner of the top floor flat sells it to a purchaser, that new owner will be under no obligation to repair the flat, e.g. the roof. This may end in causing damage to the flats underneath. This makes it difficult to obtain mortgage funding, which, in turn, will have an impact on the saleability of the flat. [115]

(b) The Commonhold and Leasehold Reform Act 2002

Commonhold is regulated by the Commonhold and Leasehold Reform Act 2002. It is a tenure that is ideal for blocks of flats and other property developments, e.g. where common facilities are provided.[116] The owners of the individual properties (or units) will form a "commonhold community" that imposes obligations on all the owners, such as repair of the common parts,

---

109   Baker, above, p.252.
110   Baker, p.252.
111   Baker, above, pp.251-2. The trespasser could take the option of paying compensation.
112   Clarke, *Commonhold–The New Law* (Jordans, 2002), p.16.
113   s.1(1)(a); D.N.Clarke, *Commonhold – The New Law*, p.17.
114   *Haywood v Brunswick Permanent Benefit Building Society* (1881-82) L.R. 8 QBD 403, CA; *Tulk v Moxhay* (1848) 18 L.J. Ch.83; *Rhone v Stephens* [1994] 2 A.C. 310; *Thamesmead Town Ltd v Allotey* (1998) 30 H.L.R. 1052.
115   D.N.Clarke, *Commonhold – The New Law*, pp.4-5.
116   Clarke, above, p.2.

e.g. roof, lifts and stairs.[117] In order to create a commonhold there must be a "commonhold community statement", which identifies and imposes these obligations.[118] This way a "local law" is created.[119] In order to create a commonhold there must be a "commonhold association", which is a private company limited by guarantee the object of which is to exercise functions in relation to the commonhold land. [120]

C. EQUITY AND THE TRUST

(1) The need for equity

Equity and the concept of the Trust are an integral part of Land Law. The rules of equity often determine who owns the land, or a property right in the land, and *how* they own it. The trust is a creation of equity and is a device by which people own property. Both equity and its creation, the trust, have roots that run very deep in Land Law. Both have considerable impact on the allocation of ownership.

Maitland, a famous professor of law in the early 1900s, began his lectures on equity by saying "I intend to speak of Equity as of an existing body of rules administered by our courts of justice".[121] By the end of the 1200s, England had three courts of law: the King's Bench, the Court of Common Pleas, and the Exchequer.[122] They administered a system of law that was common to the whole realm. This common law had been but lately established after the Norman Conquest. It had defects. A litigant must commence an action with a writ, and the common law only recognised a limited range of writs. If the subject matter of the litigant's case was not covered by one of the available writs, he could not bring the case to court. He would thus be without a remedy. Furthermore, the common law had rigid formal procedure, which often was not flexible to do justice in individual cases. For example, if you were a debtor, you needed a deed of release in order to be released from that debt. If a debtor had paid but had no deed, common law would make him pay twice! Thus a person may have "by some trick or some accident acquired an advantage of which the ordinary courts with their formal procedure will not deprive him".[123]

The procedures of the courts of common law were often abused. If a litigant's opponent was rich or powerful, he may bribe or intimidate the jury.[124]

Because of these defects in the common law a person would often complain "that for some reason or another he can not get a remedy in the ordinary course of justice".[125] But the king could

---

117 Clarke, above, p.1.
118 Commonhold and Leasehold Reform Act 2002 s.31(1).
119 Clarke, above, p.18.
120 Commonhold and Leasehold Reform Act 2002 s.34(1).
121 F.W. Maitland, *Lectures in Equity* (1936), p.1; a definition also used in Strahan and Kenrick, *A Digest of Equity*, 2nd edn (1909), p.3.
122 Maitland, p.2.
123 Maitland, p.4, and p.30.
124 ibid. F.W. Maitland, "Trust and Corporation" in D.Runciman and M.Ryan (eds) *State, Trust and Corporation* (Cambridge University Press, 2003), p.84.
125 Maitland, *Lectures in Equity*.

still do justice amongst his subjects and people would petition the king for a remedy. The king referred these petitions (matters of grace) to the Chancellor.[126] The Chancellor established a procedure for dealing with these cases. He would summon the defendant personally and examine him. Unlike ordinary common law procedure, the Chancellor would not rely on juries: Juries could be bribed by wealthy and influential defendants. He adopted the personal approach and scrutinised the defendant's conscience. The defendant would be examined by the Chancellor on oath.[127] At common law the defendant in an action could not be examined.[128]

(2) Development of a system of precedent

At this time of the early origins of equity, the Chancellor would probably not have thought that he was administering any body of rules separate "from the ordinary law of the land".[129] He would not have seen himself as applying rules that denied the common law. He would, for example, simply forbid a litigant to enforce a common law judgment because it was against good conscience for him to do so.[130] In this sense, equity operated *in personam*—against the person of the defendant. The rules and doctrines of equity are now established and governed by precedent, and have been since the end of the seventeenth century.[131] Nonetheless, the doctrines of equity that we now apply grew from early ideas that the defendant should act in good faith and with justice in relation to other people.

Aristotle defined equity as "the correction of the law, wherein it is defective"; Blackstone as "the soul and spirit of all law" (Blackstone, *Commentaries*); St Germain said of equity: "Equity is a rightwiseness, that considereth all the particular circumstances of the deed, which is also tempered with the sweetness of mercy"..."Equity is that which is commonly called equal, just and good" (St Germain *Doctor and Student*).[132] Equity is "based on the notion that there is a justice which is higher than the justice of the law, which must be observed in spite of the law".[133]

In the early days of equity persons holding the office of Chancellor tended to be churchmen, such as Cardinal Wolsey. At this time, justice was more discretionary, i.e. the Chancellor would examine the conscience of the defendant and merely do what they thought right in the individual circumstances of the case. But after this, when lawyers started to hold the office, equity was solidified into a system of rules and precedent; in much the same way as the common law.[134] It was administered through the Court of Chancery. However, its roots in moral justice are clear for anyone to see.

---

126   See A.H. Marsh, *History of the Court of Chancery and the Rise and Development of the Doctrines of Equity* (1890), p.30; Maitland described the Chancellor as the king's "prime minister": Maitland, *Lectures in Equity* (1936), pp.3, 4, 30.

127   Marsh, above pp.49–53. Maitland, *Lectures in Equity* (1936), p.5.

128   Marsh, above p.50.

129   Maitland, *Lectures in Equity* (1936), p.5.

130   Maitland *Lectures in Equity* (1936), pp.4–5.

131   Clarke and Greer, *Land Law Directions*, 2nd edn (Oxford University Press, 2010), p.34. At this time, Lord Nottingham was Chancellor and he has been called "the father of equity": Maitland, *Lectures in Equity* (1936), p.10.

132   All quoted in Story, *Commentaries on Equity Jurisprudence*, first English edition, W.E.Grigsby edn, 1884, pp.1–7.

133   Strahan and Kenrick, *A Digest of Equity*, 2nd edn (1909), p.6.

134   A.H. Marsh, *History of the Court of Chancery and of the Rise and Development of the Doctrines of Equity* (1890), p.79; Stevens and Pearce, *Land Law*, 3rd edn (2005), p.28.

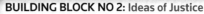

We will hold many of the rules of equity against BUILDING BLOCK NO 2 in order to examine the extent to which they reflect ideas of moral justice. We can say they are good rules if they do.

BUILDING BLOCK NO 2: Ideas of Justice
Rules are good and fair if they take account of moral justice: Every person should be accorded the freedom of their will and autonomous choice. Thus, if people deal with each other and with their property in a way that violates the will of another then the law should offer that other some remedy. We shall see that this moral idea of freedom of the will runs like a vein through many of the doctrines of equity.

(3) The administration of equity

Until the end of the nineteenth century the rules and remedies of equity and those of the common law were administered by separate courts with separate procedures. This meant that a litigant had to select the correct court in which to bring his case. And if he made a mistake he would have to start over again. There were also abuses in the Court of Chancery, which administered equity, particularly with regard to the length of time it took to obtain judgment. The Judicature Acts 1873 and 1875 restructured the legal system. The Acts formed the Supreme Court, made up from the Court of Appeal and the High Court of Justice with three divisions, the Queen's Bench, Chancery, and the Family Division. The doctrines and remedies of common law and equity can now be administered by all judges in any court.

(4) Conflict between equity and the common law judges

Can you imagine how popular this reserve of justice in the king was with the common law judges, who prided themselves on the fact that no-one was above the law, and the common law of the land applied consistently to all, even the king?

In the fourteenth century common law judges were complaining bitterly that the Chancellor had no right to set aside plain judgments of the common law courts.

"Complaints against this extraordinary justice grew loud . . . But then just at this time it is becoming plain that the Chancellor is doing some convenient and useful works that could not be done, or could not easily be done, by the courts of common law. He has taken to enforcing uses or trusts".[135]

---

135   Maitland, p.6.

> "I think it might be said that if the Court of Chancery saved the Trust, the Trust saved the Court of Chancery."
>
> F.W.Maitland, "Trust and Corporation" in *State, Trust and Corporation* (2003, ed. D.Runciman and M.Ryan), p.84.

The conflict between the Chancellor and common law judges finally came to a head in 1616 and James I settled that equity would prevail in the event of a conflict.[136]

(5) Rules and doctrines of equity

Let us consider some examples of doctrines of equity. Equity creates and administers rights and remedies not recognised by law, for example, the remedy of specific performance of a contract. The only remedy recognised by the common law is damages. However, equity would go one step further. It would make the defendant go through with what he had, by virtue of the contract, promised to do. This enforcement was on the equitable basis that the defendant *in all good conscience* should do what he had promised to do. But specific performance is not available as a remedy in all cases. The claimant must first establish that damages would be an inadequate remedy: *equity will not act in vain*.[137] For example, the parties may have contracted to sell and purchase a valuable and unique violin. Damages would not be an adequate compensation if the seller refused to honour the contract. The court could order specific performance instead.

The injunction is also an equitable remedy, awarded on the basis that damages would be inadequate as compensation for breach of a right. An injunction either prohibits a defendant from carrying out some activity, such as a noise nuisance, or forces him to undo something where the action of doing that thing has breached the claimant's right. For example, where a defendant has built an extension that significantly interferes with his neighbour's easement of light, an injunction may be awarded ordering the defendant to demolish the extension.[138]

Equity goes further than the common law, for example, prohibiting types of fraud that are not recognised by law. In this sense, equity supplements the common law.[139]

But equity's crowning achievement was the creation of the property-holding device of the trust. As Maitland observes "[p]roperty law was yet more richly glossed" by equity. "One vast appendix was added to it under the title of trusts."[140]

---

136   See also, *Earl of Oxford's Case* (1615) 1 Ch. Rep. 1; A.H.Marsh, *History of the Court of Chancery and of the Rise and Development of the Doctrines of Equity* (1890), p.90; Stevens and Pearce, *Land Law*, p.28. This is now enshrined in statute, the latest version being s.49(1) of the Supreme Court Act 1981, where there is a conflict between common law and equity, equity will prevail.

137   Hanbury and Martin, *Modern Equity*, 18th edn (London: Sweet & Maxwell, 2009); Story, *Commentaries on Equity Jurisprudence*, first English edition, (W.E.Grigsby ed., 1884), p.17.

138   The courts have discretion to award damages instead of an injunction even where the case for an injunction has been made out: *Shelfer v City of London Electric Lighting Co* [1895] 1 Ch. 287, CA.

139   Maitland, *Lectures in Equity* (1936), p.18.

140   Maitland, above, p.20.

(6) The trust

A trust is an arrangement whereby the legal owner of property (the "trustee") is obliged to hold that property for the benefit of another: the "beneficiary". The trustee holds the property legally but is not entitled to benefit from it himself. As his name suggests the trustee holds the property solely to manage it for the beneficiary, who has all the rights to enjoy and take profit from it. So the trustee has all the burdensome tasks of ownership; the beneficiary all its benefits. Indeed, Baker describes the nature of the trust as being "a separation of legal title from true ownership".[141]

| Property put in the name of X | **X** | TRUSTEE |
| But X is holding on trust for Y | **Y** | BENEFICIARY |

Where might we see a Trust ?—Answer = Everywhere!

PENSIONS: We pay into a fund that is held and managed by specialists on trust for us	CHARITIES: When we give money to charity it is held on trust for that charity's purposes	FAMILY TRUSTS: Property may be put in trust for a child until he or she comes of age
Pension fund trustees	**Charity trustees**	**Trustees**
Employees for their retirement	The purposes of the charity, e.g. relief of poverty	Child

TRUST OF A HOUSE: Zak moves in with Melissa and she decides to give him a share of the ownership of her house. She sets up a trust whereby she holds the house on trust for Zak and herself	THE LAW MAY DEEM A TRUST TO EXIST EVEN WHERE THE PARTIES DID NOT EXPRESSLY CREATE ONE: For example, if Mrs B contributes to the purchase of her family home which is then put in the name of her husband, he holds it on trust for his wife and himself.
Melissa	CASE_____ _____
Holds the house on trust for Zak and herself	**Mr B** _____ Mr B and Mrs B

---

141   Baker, *An Introduction to English Legal History*, p.210.

(a) A beneficial interest under a trust is a property right in the land

We call the beneficiary's right a "beneficial interest under a trust". It is one of a number of rights in land recognised by equity so it is sometimes referred to as an "equitable interest under a trust". The beneficiary has rights against the land. He can enforce his rights to the land, i.e. the use and enjoyment of it, the profits from it, against the trustee, who is, by equity, compelled to recognise the beneficiary's right to use and enjoy the land. Crucially however, he can also enforce his beneficial rights against the *land itself* should the trustee sell that land to a third party. A trust creates a property right. You may remember from our LECTURER and STUDENT dialogue in Chapter 1, concerning *Williams & Glyn's Bank Ltd v Boland*,[142] Mrs Boland acquired a share of the ownership of the house by contributing to its purchase. We can now know that this took effect because the law imposed a trust on Mr Boland. Although the house was registered in his sole name he held it on trust for himself and his wife. This created a property right and not just a personal obligation. Thus, when Mr Boland mortgaged the house Mrs Boland's interest under the trust was capable of binding the bank.[143]

(b) The history and origins of the trust

As to its origins, the word "trust" probably meant exactly what a non-lawyer would expect it to mean: to put faith in someone, to rely on them, to put confidence in them. In the days of the feudal system the law did not permit a landowner to leave his lands to a chosen heir by will.[144] So it became common practice for a landowner, when nearing his death, to convey his lands to trusted friends on the understanding that they will convey it after his death to a person whom he nominated as his heir.[145] Also at this time, certain religious orders were not permitted to own land, "and so a person wishing to benefit the order would grant land to a group" of people he trusted on the basis that they would permit the order to have full use and enjoyment of the land.[146] Later on, in the sixteenth and seventeenth centuries, the trust device was employed for different reasons. Land was conveyed to trustees to look after for an "unthrifty son", or a child, for example.[147] The common law did not recognise married women as having the capacity to own property in their own right.[148] So property might be conveyed to trustees to hold for the benefit of the married woman. Thus the trust was used to give married women property in their own right. Trusts had become an important part of society.[149]

---

142   [1981] A.C. 487.

143   For the concept of a property right see Chapter 1 BUILDING BLOCK NO 5: Property Rights and the Protection of Purchasers and Mortgage Lenders.

144   Maitland observes that "as regards freehold land every germ of testamentary power is stamped out in the twelfth century": *Lectures in Equity*, p.26.

145   Baker, *An Introduction to English Legal History*, p.211; Maitland, *Lectures in Equity*, pp.24–6.

146   Maitland, *Lectures in Equity*, pp.24–6; Also Maitland, "Trust and Corporation" in *State, Trust and Corporation*, p.85; The trust was originally called the use. Their existence was threatened by the Statute of Uses 1535, passed by Henry VIII because uses were depriving him of revenue due under the feudal system. Whenever land was held for the benefit of another the Act transferred the legal ownership of the land to that other. Thus it was not possible to hold land for another. Lawyers soon found ways to circumvent this and the modern version of the use, "the trust", was recognised by Lord Nottingham in the latter half of the seventeenth century: Yale, "The Revival of Equitable Estates in the Seventeenth Century: An Explanation by Lord Nottingham" [1957] C.L.J. 72, see *Mildmay & Duckett's Case* (case 822): Yale, above p.76.

147   Baker, *An Introduction to English Legal History* (1979), p.243.

148   Baker, above, pp.243–4.

149   Maitland, *State, Trust and Corporation* (from the 1911 *Collected Papers* (Cambridge), repr. 2003), p.87.

The Court of Chancery, administering the rules of equity, enforced these trusts, whereby a promise was made by the defendant that when the landowner transferred ownership of the land to him, he would hold it for the benefit of another and not keep it for himself. An early documented case involving a trust was *Mildmay & Duckett's Case*.[150] There had been an arrangement whereby the defendant had agreed to hold the estate in land for the benefit of another. The issue was whether this defendant could keep the lands for himself. Emphatically, Lord Nottingham declared that "all the deeds obtained by the defendant were in trust for the plaintiff. For else I should be obliged to set them all aside as being gained by a manifest fraud and circumvention".[151]

Thus, where land was conveyed to a trusted person, on trust for another that trusted person could not deny this position of responsibility and keep the land for himself. He was compelled to carry out the trust to which he had agreed.

But precisely *how* were trusts enforced? As we have seen above, a beneficial interest under a trust is a property right. But this did not have to be the case. Trusts could easily have been enforced by recognising a contract between the original landowner and his trustee. But "[o]ur landowner did not mean to exchange ownership of land for the . . . benefit of a promise".[152] Equity gave *the beneficiary* (the married woman, or the unthrifty son, or the dying landowner's chosen heir) the remedy and not the aggrieved landowner.[153] If the trustee misappropriates the property, not only can the beneficiary can sue him personally, but if the trustee sells the land the beneficiary can also force him to look after the proceeds of sale for him, on the same terms as the original trust. And if the trustee has absconded with the sale proceeds, the beneficiary can force the purchaser of the land to hold it for him.[154]

(c) A working definition

And so we arrive at something like a definition of a trust: It is an arrangement whereby the legal owner of property, the trustee, is to hold the property for the benefit of another: the beneficiary. The beneficiary can enforce his beneficial rights to the land, i.e. the use and enjoyment of it, the profits from it, against the trustee, who is compelled to recognise the beneficiary's right in the land. The beneficiary's right is a property right that can be enforced against a third party who comes into possession of the property from the trustee. That third party is then compelled to recognise the beneficiary's prior claim to the use and enjoyment of the land. A third party is not always bound by the beneficiary's interest in the land. He will only be so if his conscience is deemed to be affected by the transfer he has taken from the trustee.[155] The beneficiary has an

---

150   (case 822), quotation and citation: Yale, "The Revival of Equitable Estates in the Seventeenth Century: An Explanation by Lord Nottingham" [1957] C.L.J. 72, p.76 note 13.

151   Maitland referred to Lord Nottingham as "the father of Equity": *Lectures in Equity* (1936), p.10; Lord Nottingham formed and created the trust that we recognize today: Yale, "The Revival of Equitable Estates in the Seventeenth Century: An Explanation by Lord Nottingham" [1957] C.L.J. 72.

152   Maitland, *Lectures in Equity* (1936), pp.30–1.

153   Maitland, above, p.31.

154   Maitland, above, p.32, subject to the rules of Land Transfer Law.

155   The rule that has been evolved by the courts to determine whether a third party's conscience is affected by the transfer of the land to him from the trustees is known as the *bona fide purchaser* rule or the "doctrine of notice". It has largely been superseded by the 1925 legislation, which lays down rules of land transfer that determine when a purchaser is bound by pre-existing property rights, including trusts. We will look at these rules in our chapters on Land Transfer Law.

"Equitable Interest" in the land. He has "virtual ownership"[156]: he cannot say "I am the outright legal owner of the land", because the trustee is. But he can say: "you hold all the benefits of your ownership for me and I may be able to enforce them against a purchaser or donee from you". This is not quite saying "that's mine—give it back", but it is as near to it as equity could make it look.[157]

> "Thus we get a conversion of the [trust] into an incorporeal thing – in which estates and interests exist – a sort of immaterialized piece of land."[158]

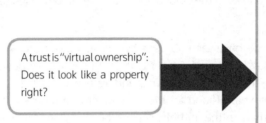

A trust is "virtual ownership": Does it look like a property right?

BUILDING BLOCK NO 5: Property Rights and the Protection of Purchasers and Mortgage Lenders
If a right is a property right, it means that it can be enforced against the land itself. Therefore, it will bind every subsequent purchaser of the land. Contrast this with a contractual right, which can only be enforced against the person you contracted with.

(d) The trust in the context of the English law of estates
Equity's creation of the trust was made so that it dovetailed into the existing common law on estates: "as the common law enabled land to be settled upon A for life, to B in fee tail, remainder to C in fee simple, equity also allowed these interests to be held on trust".[159]

(e) The trust today
The trust is an incredibly flexible device that has evolved to meet the needs of modern society. Many pension funds use the trust device because it enables a group of expert investment specialists to have control of the ownership of the fund so that they can invest it and make a profit. The funds belonging to charities are held on trust. Provision can still be made for a child in this way, so that a trustee will be appointed to look after money and invest it, for the child until they come of age. A significant amount of Trusts Law is made up of the duties that the trustees have to comply with when making investments, and the obligations that ensure they prefer the interests of the beneficiaries when dealing with the trust property.

Trusts can be implied by law, in much the same way as terms are implied into a contract, where the law deems it right that a legal owner should not have full benefit of the property but should

---

156   Maitland, *Lectures in Equity* (1936), p.31.
157   Maitland, above, p.31.
158   Above p.31.
159   M.Thompson, *Modern Land Law*, p.45.

hold it on trust for another. The parties do not have to expressly create a trust. As you have already seen, in this way, the law gives rights to non-owners of property when they have contributed to its purchase.[160] This has nothing to do with matrimonial law. It is the ordinary law of property. In this way equity devised a whole system of rules whereby cohabitees and spouses can acquire part ownership of the land or house. These implied trusts, used in other circumstances as well, are called "resulting" and "constructive" trusts. We look at these in the next chapter.

(7) Other equitable interests

Equity created other interests in land, for example, the restrictive covenant. In *Tulk v Moxhay*,[161] the claimant owned land in Leicester Square, London. He sold off part of the plot and he and the purchaser entered into a contract, a "covenant", that the purchaser would "at all times thereafter maintain the said piece of ground in an open state, uncovered with buildings". In short, the purchaser covenanted not to build on the land he was buying. The purchaser of the plot then sold it on to someone else: Purchaser 2, who knew about the covenant and deliberately ignored it. The claimant sought an injunction against Purchaser 2 to prevent him from building on the land. The idea that a covenant would bind a purchaser, who had not entered into it himself, was an idea foreign to the common law of contract.[162] The common law had long held that it was not possible for a private agreement between individuals to create new burdens on the land that would bind future purchasers.[163] But, acting on the conscience of Purchaser 2, equity held differently. The Lord Chancellor held[164] that it would be inequitable, i.e. against good conscience, to allow Purchaser 2 to ignore the covenant, because he knew of its existence and had paid less for the land because of the covenant. He then could have sold the land on without the covenant at a profit.[165]

And thus the restrictive covenant became a right that is enforceable against the land and purchasers of it, i.e. a *property right*, rather than a purely personal right that binds only the contracting parties.

D. ESTATES AND INTERESTS IN LAND AFTER THE 1925 PROPERTY LEGISLATION

The 1925 Property Legislation is a number of Acts of Parliament that were designed to reform land law.

---

160 *Williams & Glyn's Bank Ltd v Boland* [1981] A.C. 487.
161 (1848) 2 Ph. 774.
162 Story, *Commentaries on Equity Jurisprudence*, first English edition, (W.E.Grigsby ed., 1884), p.490.
163 *Keppel v Bailey* (1834) 2 My. & K. 517; *Duke of Bedford v Trustees of the British Museum*, 2 My & K 552.
164 (1848) 2 Ph. 774, per Lord Cottenham L.C.
165 ibid.

> The 1925 Property Legislation incorporates: The Law of Property Act 1925; The Land Charges Act 1925 (amended and updated by the Land Charges Act 1972); The Land Registration Act 1925 (now replaced in its entirety by the Land Registration Act 2002); The Settled Land Act 1925 (now made largely redundant by the Trusts of Land and Appointment of Trustees Act 1996); The Administration of Estates Act 1925; The Trustee Act 1925 (amended by the Trustee Act 2000).

(1) A reclassification of estates in land

For reasons connected with simplifying the transfer of land from a seller to a buyer the 1925 property legislation reclassified estates and interests in land. As we have seen, the common law recognised the existence of a variety of estates in land: the life estate, the fee tail, the fee simple. The fee fail and the fee simple could exist "in possession" (which meant that you had the right to use the land) or "in reversion" or "remainder". They were all capable of being recognised as legal estates or equitable estates. The 1925 legislation reclassified many estates in land as equitable only. In fact, the Law of Property Act 1925 s.1 provides that the only two estates capable of existing as legal estates are: the fee simple absolute in possession and the term of years absolute.[166]

(a) The fee simple absolute in possession

This is now the only freehold estate in land capable of existing as a legal estate. "Fee" means that the estate is capable of being inherited, e.g. it is possible to leave it in a will to someone. The expression "simple" originated in the context of the feudal system. In modern terms this means that "the estate continues for as long as there is anyone to inherit it, whether by will, or upon intestacy".[167] "Absolute" means unqualified and unconditional. "In possession", as we have seen, means that the owner of the estate has the present right to enjoy the land.

(i) Conditional and determinable fees

A fee simple is not "absolute" if it is subject to a condition. Where the estate is conveyed subject to a condition, in the event of the condition happening, ownership of the estate will terminate. For example, Brian grants "the fee simple of Blueacre to Alan *unless he becomes a chef*". The estate is absolute unless the condition occurs. Once the condition has occurred, the grantor has a right of re-entry, which will terminate the estate. There are certain conditions that will be held void on grounds of public policy, for example, some conditions in restraint of marriage,[168] and a condition prohibiting alienation (sale) of the land.[169] If a condition is held void the fee simple becomes absolute.[170] These conditional fees simple are not absolute and thus ordinarily they would not be capable of existing as a legal estate because of s.1 of the Law of Property Act 1925.

---

166   A minor cannot hold a legal estate in land: Law of Property Act 1925 s.1(6).
167   Clarke and Greer, *Land Law Directions*, p.66.
168   *Long v Dennis* (1767) 4 Burr. 2052.
169   *Re Brown* [1954] Ch. 39.
170   *Re Croxon* [1904] 1 Ch. 252.

However, s.7(1) of that Act, inserted by the Law of Property (Amendment) Act 1926, provides that these estates are still regarded as "absolute" for the purpose of their recognition as legal estates.

A determinable fee simple is very difficult to distinguish from a conditional one, this distinction having been called "little short of disgraceful to our jurisprudence".[171]

The best way of distinguishing a conditional fee from a determinable fee is to recognise that a conditional fee is an absolute grant that might be cut short. The parties contemplate that the estate will last indefinitely. The nature of the condition is to defeat the absolute estate. A determinable fee is where the estate continues until a "specified state of affairs comes to an end".[172] For example, Brian grants "the fee simple of Blueacre to Alan until he qualifies as a barrister". Thus, words like "until", or "whilst" will be held to create a determinable fee, words such as "unless", create a conditional fee. *Megarry & Wade* defines the determinable fee as a grant of an estate that has a natural ending, rather than an estate that is cut short:

> "[I]f the specified state of affairs comes to an end, the fee determines and the land reverts to the original grantor or his estate. The grantor's interest is called a possibility of reverter, i.e. a possibility of having an estate at a future time."[173]

(b) The term of years absolute

This is the leasehold estate. This is a lease for a certain number of years, but terms less than a year still fall within the definition.[174] It also includes leases "from year to year".[175] This is a periodic tenancy where the grant is not for a specified number of years or months but takes effect on a recurring basis: month by month, or year by year. It ends when either landlord or tenant gives notice to terminate the lease. One principal characteristic of the term of years is that the term for which it is granted must be certain. The term of a periodic tenancy is certain once it is terminated.[176] The word "absolute" seems to add little. It does not have the same meaning ascribed to a "fee simple absolute" as it is not precluded from being absolute even though it may be ended by notice of either party, or is brought to an end by the landlord through "forfeiture" proceedings.[177] This is where the tenancy can be ended by the landlord in the event that the tenant breaches a covenant under the lease, for example failure to pay rent. To fall within this definition a lease does not have to be "in possession", entitling the tenant to immediate enjoyment of the land. It might be that the tenant is granted a lease to take effect in three years time.[178] This is still capable of being a legal estate. Surprisingly it is not a requirement that rent is paid.[179]

---

171   *Re King's Trusts* (1892) 29 L.R. Ir. 401, p.410, per Porter M.R., quoted in C.Harpum, S.Bridge, M.Dixon, *Megarry & Wade, Law of Real Property* (7th edn 2008), para.3–057.
172   *Megarry & Wade*, above para.3–056.
173   *Megarry & Wade*, above paras 3–054-3–055.
174   Law of Property Act 1925 s.205(1)(xxvii).
175   s.205(1)(xxvii).
176   *Prudential Assurance Co Ltd v London Residuary Body* [1992] 2 A.C. 386.
177   Law of Property Act 1925 s.205(1)(xxvii).
178   s.205(1)(xxvii). This would be a lease taking effect "in reversion".
179   s.205(1)(xxvii).

(2) A reclassification of interests in land

Smaller interests in land, i.e. smaller property rights, such as easements and restrictive covenants, were reclassified in a similar way.[180] Section 1(2) of the Law of Property Act 1925 provides that the only interests in land capable of existing as legal interests are:[181]

"An easement, right, or privilege in or over land": as we have seen, an easement is a right to undertake a limited activity on land belonging to another. For example, a right to park a car,[182] a right to store something on your neighbour's land,[183] a right of access to neighbouring pleasure gardens,[184] and a right of way.[185] However, before the easement is capable of existing as a legal interest in land it must be either of indefinite duration ("equivalent to an estate in fee simple") or be for a set number of years ("a term of years absolute"). An easement granted for "the life of Harry" would not fall within s.1(2). Thus, the easement could not be a legal interest. This section includes a *profit à prendre*, which is the right to enter someone's land and take something from it. For example, the right to take fish is known as a profit of piscary.

"A rentcharge": is a periodic sum that the owner of land is obliged to pay to the owner of the rentcharge.[186] It does not include a tenant's obligation to pay rent to his landlord, or "any sum payable by way of interest", e.g. on a mortgage loan.[187] Again, in order to be capable of being legal, the rentcharge must be of perpetual duration or for a set term of years. It is no longer possible to create new rentcharges,[188] and existing rentcharges will be extinguished after 60 years.[189] Thus, rentcharges are of diminishing significance.

"A charge by way of legal mortgage": is what we commonly know as a mortgage on land. This is where a lender loans money to the owner of land and that owner grants the lender security for the loan, as Mr Boland did in *Williams & Glyn's Bank Ltd v Boland*.[190] This security takes the form of an interest in the borrowers land, which gives the lender the right, for example, to possess the house and sell it should the borrower default on the loan repayments. Thus, rather than relying merely on a personal remedy against the borrower, the right to sue him on his obligation to make the repayments, the lender will have another way of recouping his money: a second bite of the cherry. He can sell the borrower's house and deduct the loan amount from the proceeds of sale. This is why mortgages are called "security" interests. They "secure" the lender's investment. Prior to 1925 it was

---

180   Whether a property right is classified as legal or equitable can be significant in respect of whether the right will bind a purchaser taking a transfer of the land. We will consider this issue further in the chapters on Land Transfer Law.

181   The exact wording provides: "The only interests or charges in or over land which are capable of subsisting or of being conveyed or created at law".

182   *Moncrieff v Jamieson* [2007] 1 W.L.R. 2620; *Batchelor v Marlow* (2001) 82 P. & C.R. 36.

183   *Wright v Macadam* [1949] 2 K.B. 744; *Copeland v Greenhalf* [1952] Ch. 488.

184   *Re Ellenborough Park* [1956] Ch. 131.

185   *Wheeler v J.J.Saunders Ltd* [1996] Ch. 19.

186   Rentcharges Act 1977 s.1, s.2(4).

187   Rentcharges Act 1977 s.1.

188   Rentcharges Act 1977 s.2. There are exceptions: s.2(3).

189   s.3.

190   [1981] A.C. 487. And thus there were two property rights that competed for priority: Mrs Boland's beneficial interest under a trust and the bank's mortgage.

possible, and common, to create a mortgage by conveying the land to the lender.[191] He was then in possession of the land and would have the power to sell the land in the event of a default by the borrower. When the borrower repaid the loan the lender would reconvey the land. Section 85(1) of the Law of Property Act 1925 provides that it is no longer possible to create a mortgage in this way. A mortgage is only capable of being created (1) by granting to the lender a 3000-year lease of the land,[192] or (2) "by a charge by deed expressed to be by way of legal mortgage". This is a bundle of rights and remedies granted to the lender, including the right to sell the mortgaged property if the borrower should default.[193] It is usually referred to as a "charge". It is a property right.

"A right of entry": is where a landlord has reserved the right to repossess leased premises where there has been a breach of a tenant's covenant in the lease, for example, the covenant for the tenant to pay rent. In order to be legal, the lease or other interest to which it relates must also be legal.[194]

(3) All other estates and interests in land are equitable

The Law of Property Act 1925 s.1(3) classifies all other estates in land, e.g. the life estate, the fee tail estate, and all other interests, e.g. restrictive covenants, options to purchase,[195] beneficial interests under a trust,[196] as *equitable*. The reason why the difference between law and equity was thought so important is that estates and interests in land are *property rights*. As we have seen, property rights will bind a purchaser of land. As part of its general policy the 1925 legislation sought to make it an easy matter for a purchaser to take land free from *equitable* interests. And so to make life as easy as possible for purchasers and mortgage lenders, the Act reclassified most estates and interests therein as equitable. In this way the 1925 legislation achieved its principal objective of making easier the transfer of land from a seller to a buyer. The distinction between legal and equitable interests is less important in the system of registration of title to land.

BUILDING BLOCK NO 5: Property Rights and the Protection of Purchasers and Mortgage Lenders

This reclassification was part of a comprehensive structure of rules designed to make it easier for a purchaser of land to take that land free from pre-existing property rights. Study this Building Block to clarify your understanding of the reasons for the reclassification.

---

191 See for example, *Pilcher v Rawlins* (1871–72) L.R. 7 Ch. App. 259.
192 As far as the system of registration of title to land is concerned it is not possible to create a mortgage in this way. The grant of a first legal mortgage of land must now be registered: Land Registration Act 2002 s.4(1)(g) and s.27(2)(f). Thus it is effectively no longer possible to create a mortgage by long lease, unless it is a second mortgage of an unregistered estate.
193 Law of Property Act 1925 ss.101, 103.
194 See also, M.Thompson, *Modern Land Law*, pp.71–2; Jackson, Stevens and Pearce, *Land Law*, pp.41–2.
195 The right that had been granted to farmer Geoffrey in our example in Chapter 1, BUILDING BLOCK NO 5: Property Rights and the Protection of Purchasers and Mortgage Lenders.
196 The type of right that Mrs Boland asserted against the bank (successfully) in *Williams & Glyn's Bank Ltd v Boland* [1981] A.C. 487. See Chapter 1 section 4 "Constructing an argument with the Building Blocks".

4 Constructing an argument about equity with Building Blocks

An example of a doctrine of equity is the doctrine of proprietary estoppel. We are not concerned with the technicalities of this doctrine in this Chapter. But in looking at a decided case it shows us an example of how the rules of equity have adapted to modern ownership disputes. It also shows how notions of "justice" are central to the distribution of property, particularly where equity is concerned.

A. GILLETT V HOLT

Consider the following extract from *Gillett v Holt*[197] and we are going to construct an argument using Building Blocks. The question we will be arguing about is:

"*Gillett v Holt* is a bad decision: claimants should be told in no uncertain terms: *DON'T COUNT YOUR CHICKENS BEFORE THEY ARE HATCHED!*"
Discuss this statement.

(1) The social context

Land and property is so important to families that it becomes deeply entwined with their lives. It is usually very clear who is the legal owner of the land. This is not the issue. Families may operate solely on the basis of trust in each other. They see no need for legal documents, or they may not be aware of the need for them. There may be "understandings" between families or family members: "It was always understood that Emily would have the cottage and I would have the farm". Then people live their lives on the basis of this understanding. There may be one head of the family who holds the purse-strings. He or she may supply the needs of the others, and make promises that "after I'm gone, it will all be yours". There is not necessarily any malice or over-reliance. It is just the way things are done. Property is merely part of the family hierarchy, and it becomes the object of our trust in each other. Sometimes there may even be an unwillingness to go to a lawyer in order to formalise these arrangements, to "put it in writing", because it shows lack of trust. In some families it may even seem like a shabby thing to do.[198] Our complexities as human beings cannot be reduced to a short-form legal document and the law recognises this. It recognises that a person can become entitled to a claim against the land in all of these informal circumstances.

(2) The facts and decision of the Court of First Instance

    THE FACTS: Holt was a wealthy farmer in Lincolnshire. Gillett had been Holt's friend for over forty years. Holt had persuaded him to leave school and to work on his farm. He

---

197   [2001] Ch. 210.
198   S.Gardner, "Rethinking Family Property" (1993) 109 L.Q.R. 263.

eventually became the farm manager and Gillett and his wife and children lived in the farmhouse. Holt made many promises to the Gilletts, often during family occasions, saying that he would leave Gillett the farm business and the house and that they and their two sons would have an assured future. He made a will accordingly. Mr Gillett relied on this promise and stepped off the property ladder in order to live on the farm. He did not pursue alternative employment and was completely dependent on Holt's informal assurances. Gillett also renovated the farmhouse. However, the friendship between Holt and Gillett turned sour. Holt befriended Wood and made a new will, excluding Gillett.

Gillett brought a claim against Holt on the basis of the doctrine of "proprietary estoppel". Again it is important to remember not to get bogged down by the technicalities of the rules. Try just to get a feel for the principles on which the judge and the Court of Appeal decided the case. The law does not always allow a person to make and break promises whenever they feel like it. But the problem is ascertaining *when* a promise becomes legally binding.

THE DECISION AT FIRST INSTANCE: At first instance the judge held that a person who makes a will in favour of one person is always free to change it in favour of another. Wills only take effect on death. On a similar case, Swadling made the following criticism:

"This decision is clearly wrong, for the judge seems to have forgotten that the whole point of estoppel claims is that they concern promises which, since they are unsupported by consideration, are initially revocable. What later makes them binding, and therefore irrevocable, is the promisee's detrimental reliance on them. Once that occurs, there is simply no question of the promisor changing his or her mind."[199]

(3) The judgment on appeal

Gillett appealed and Robert Walker L.J. gave the following judgment in the Court of Appeal[200]:

ROBERT WALKER L.J. [To bring a claim in the doctrine of proprietary estoppel Gillett had to establish that 1. There was an assurance on the part of Holt that he would have the property; 2. That Gillett relied on this to his detriment; and 3. That it would be "unconscionable" for Holt to go back on the promise.] "[I]t is important to note at the outset that the doctrine of proprietary estoppel cannot be treated as subdivided into three or four watertight compartments. Both sides are agreed on that, and in the course of the oral argument in this court it repeatedly became apparent that the quality of the relevant assurances may influence the issue of reliance, that reliance and detriment are often intertwined, and that whether there is a distinct need for a 'mutual understanding' may depend on how the other elements are formulated and understood. Moreover the fundamental principle that equity is concerned to prevent

---

199   [1998] Restitution Law Review 220, commenting on *Taylor v Dickens* [1998] 1 F.L.R. 806.
200   [2001] Ch.210.

unconscionable conduct permeates all the elements of the doctrine. In the end the court must look at the matter in the round." [. . .]

"[Of the first element of the doctrine of proprietary estoppel: the requirement for an 'assurance' or promise that the claimant will have an interest in the land]. [T]he inherent revocability of testamentary dispositions (even if well understood by the parties, as Mr Gillett candidly accepted that it was by him) is irrelevant to a promise or assurance that 'all this will be yours' (the sort of language used on the occasions [on which Mr Holt made promises]) . . . Even when the promise or assurance is in terms linked to the making of a will [as Mr Holt had promised to do] . . . the circumstances may make clear that the assurance is more than a mere statement of present (revocable) intention, and is tantamount to a promise . . . Carnwath J. observed that the advice to the claimant in *Taylor v Dickens* 'not to count his chickens before they were hatched' is [1998] 3 All ER 917, 929:

> 'an apt statement of how, in normal circumstances, and in the absence of a specific promise, any reasonable person would regard − and should be expected by the law to regard − a representation by a living person as to his intentions for his will.'

In the generality of cases that is no doubt correct, and it is notorious that some elderly persons of means derive enjoyment from the possession of testamentary power, and from dropping hints as to their intentions, without any question of an estoppel arising. But in this case Mr Holt's assurances were repeated over a long period, usually before the assembled company on special family occasions, and some of them (such as 'it was all going to be [y]ours anyway' . . .) were completely unambiguous . . . I find it wholly understandable that Mr and Mrs Gillett, then 10 years married and with two young sons, may have been worried about their home and their future depending on no more than oral assurances, however emphatic, from Mr Holt. . . . But Mr Gillett, after discussing the matter with his wife and his parents, decided to rely on Mr Holt's assurances because 'Ken was a man of his word.' Plainly the assurances given on this occasion were intended to be relied on, and were in fact relied on . . ." [. . .]

[His lordship now proceeds to consider the second element required in order for the claimant to obtain a remedy under the doctrine] "It is therefore necessary to go on to consider detriment. . . . Whether the detriment is sufficiently substantial is to be tested by whether it would be unjust or inequitable to allow the assurance to be disregarded − that is, again, the essential test of unconscionability . . . [. . .]

The matters which Mr Gillett pleaded as detriment . . . included . . . (i) his continuing in Mr Holt's employment . . . and not seeking or accepting offers of employment elsewhere, or going into business on his own account; (ii) carrying out tasks and spending time beyond the normal scope of an employee's duty; (iii) taking no substantial steps to secure his future wealth, either by larger pension contributions or otherwise; and (iv) expenditure on improving The Beeches farmhouse [where the Gilletts lived] which was, Mr Gillett said, barely habitable when it was first acquired.

. . . Mr Gillett's case on detriment . . . was an unusually compelling one . . Mr Gillett had an exceptionally strong claim on Mr Holt's conscience. Mr Gillett was then 35. He had left school before he was 16, without taking any of the examinations which might otherwise have given him academic qualifications, against the advice of his headmaster and in the face of his parents' doubts, in order to work for [Mr Holt] . . . Mr Holt's influence extended to Mr Gillett's social and private life . . . [F]or 30 years Mr and Mrs Gillett and their sons provided Mr Holt with a sort of surrogate family. [. . .]

Mr Gillett also incurred substantial expenditure on the farmhouse at The Beeches, most of it after the clear assurance which Mr Holt gave him when, in 1975, he ventured to ask for something in writing: 'that was not necessary as it was all going to be ours anyway'. This was after the Gilletts had sold their own small house . . . and so had stepped off the property-owning ladder . . .

It is entirely a matter of conjecture what the future might have held for the Gilletts if in 1975 Mr Holt had (instead of what he actually said) told the Gilletts frankly that his present intention was to make a will in their favour, but that he was not bound by that and that they should not count their chickens before they were hatched. Had they decided to move on, they might have done no better . . . The fact is that they relied on Mr Holt's assurance, because they thought he was a man of his word and so they deprived themselves of the opportunity of trying to better themselves in other ways . . . Mr Gillett and his wife devoted the best years of their lives to working for Mr Holt and his company, showing loyalty and devotion to his business interests, his social life and his personal wishes, on the strength of clear and repeated assurances of testamentary benefits . . . I would find it startling if the law did not give a remedy in such circumstances."

CONCLUSION: Mr Gillett's appeal was allowed and Mr Holt was directed to convey the house to Mr Gillett and pay him £100,000 compensation for excluding him from the business.

(4) Constructing an argument

LECTURER: So the first requirement of the equitable doctrine is that the defendant must have made the claimant a promise. Will any sort of statement suffice as a promise?

STUDENT: No. I think that the point that Robert Walker L.J. is making is that normal statements about whether a person is going to leave this or that property by will do not have the necessary quality to amount to a promise.

LECTURER: What would amount to a promise, or "assurance" then?

STUDENT: Very definite assertions, maybe (as here) repeated over a long period of time.

LECTURER: Robert Walker L.J. uses the word "unambiguous". What do you think he means by this?

STUDENT: That the intention of the person making the promise should be absolutely clear and capable of one meaning only—that this is a promise on which it is reasonable for someone to rely.

LECTURER: In certain cases like this one then, it does not matter that Gillett would have known that Holt could have changed his will at any time.

STUDENT: It did not matter in this case because the quality of the assurances that Gillett and his family would inherit the farm business and the farmhouse was so definite and clear, e.g. "one day all this will be yours". Robert Walker L.J. thought it reasonable that Gillett had relied on the promise. "But Mr Gillett, after discussing the matter with his wife and his parents, decided to rely on Mr Holt's assurances because 'Ken was a man of his word' ".

LECTURER: The second element that Mr Gillett had to establish in order to bring a claim under the doctrine of proprietary estoppel was "detriment". What does this mean?

STUDENT: He had to show that he had relied on Mr Holt's promise and that he had suffered some sort of loss in so doing. The idea seems to be that the detriment that the claimant has suffered must be looked at to see whether, taking this detriment into account, it would be unjust (or "unconscionable") to allow the defendant (here Mr Holt) to go back on his promise and not leave the claimant anything.

LECTURER: And how was "detriment" established in this case?

STUDENT: The conduct of Mr Gillett showed that over his whole lifetime he had relied on these promises, e.g. he gave up school and work, he worked on Mr Holt's farm, he did not make arrangements for his future, he stepped off the property ladder and paid to renovate the farmhouse etc.

LECTURER: And all of this amounted to the conclusion that Gillett had a claim on Holt's conscience.

So having said what the law *is* and looked at how Gillett established his claim, let's now consider whether we think that *Gillett v Holt* is good or bad law.

> Remember! This is the question we are discussing: *"Gillett v Holt* is a bad decision: Claimants should be told: *DON'T COUNT YOUR CHICKENS BEFORE THEY'RE HATCHED!"* Discuss this statement.

LECTURER: First of all you need to be able to explain what this statement means.

STUDENT: I think that the statement is saying that *Gillett v Holt* is bad law because it allows someone to claim an interest in someone else's land without having been formally granted one.

LECTURER: But we may be able to prove that the case creates good law. We hold the reasoning in *Gillett v Holt* against the Building Blocks and we can say that the reasoning is good if, on balance, it supports the ideas in the Building Blocks, but bad if it undermines those ideas.

STUDENT: I think we should use BUILDING BLOCK NO 2: Ideas of Justice to say that the case is good law and perhaps an argument could be based on BUILDING BLOCK NO 6: The Need for Certainty and Predictability in Legal Rules.

> **BUILDING BLOCK NO 2: Ideas of Justice**
> Rules are good and fair if they take account of moral justice: every person should be accorded the freedom of their will and autonomous choice. The will in a person is everything he calls "myself". When the will is properly active, it can move forward, direct, press through difficulty, initiate change: e.g. Josef Pieper, *The Four Cardinal Virtues*, p.50. See Chapter 1. Thus, if people deal with each other and with their property in a way that violates the will of another then the law should offer that other some remedy. We may legitimately say that Land Law is bad if it does not do so.

STUDENT: I think that the idea of "justice" comes from the fact that we are, and should be recognised as, independent beings. We have our own wills. Moral justice lies in the obligation to recognise this. Thus, we should take care to respect and not to undermine someone's separateness as an individual.

LECTURER: So how was this idea of moral justice violated in *Gillett v Holt*?

STUDENT: Mr Holt as a landowner, used the power that came with the ownership of property, to influence the lives of Mr Gillett and his family. Effectively Mr Holt obtained what Robert Walker L.J. describes as a surrogate family. Mr Gillett made the life choices he did because of the strength of Mr Holt's promises that one day the business and the house would be his. Mr Holt had influence over Mr Gillett—his will prevailed.

LECTURER: Robert Walker L.J. remarked on all these features. How were these ideas reflected in the elements of the doctrine of proprietary estoppel?

STUDENT: Robert Walker L.J. was looking for strong and "irrevocable" assurances made by Mr Holt to Mr Gillett, and for evidence that Mr Gillett was influenced by these assurances and made his life choices and curtailed his freedom accordingly. This is proven by showing a "detriment". Robert Walker L.J. found that it was reasonable to rely on Mr Holt's promises, thus demonstrating the necessary factor or *influence* over Gillett's will: "Mr Gillett, after discussing the matter with his wife and his parents, decided to rely on Mr Holt's assurances because 'Ken was a man of his word' ".

STUDENT: Thus we can say that *Gillett v Holt* is a good decision because it reflects principles of moral justice. Mr Holt was not allowed to dominate the will of Mr Gillett to the latter's detriment, with the power that came from his being a landowner. This is why Robert Walker L.J. stated that Mr Gillett had a claim on Mr Holt's conscience.

LECTURER: Let's turn now to our other argument, based on BUILDING BLOCK NO 6: The Need for Certainty and Predictability in Land Law rules. The ideas in this Building Block are often used to form a criticism of cases like *Gillett v Holt*. Can you think why?

STUDENT: I think that where cases are decided on the basis of good conscience this is very subjective. One judge's opinion as to that might differ from another's. Therefore, the outcome of future cases might be unpredictable. Solicitors will not be able to advise their clients as to the consequences of making or relying on a promise.

> **BUILDING BLOCK NO 6: The Need for Certainty and Predictability in Land Law Rules**
> If the rules are clear as to how they will apply in future cases, i.e. if they allow people (e.g. purchasers or occupiers) to predict the outcome of their actions then they are good law.

LECTURER: I take your point. But I'm not sure that with *Gillett v Holt* you are justified in taking your argument to quite this extent. Robert Walker L.J. made it quite clear that a clear assurance and substantial detriment must be proven. And it is worth your noting that unconscionability is largely shown by the strength of the assurance and the quality of the detriment. It is not quite the vague notion that you think.

STUDENT: It might be difficult to say in future cases *when* a promise is sufficiently certain or what kind of thing a claimant would have to do to prove that they suffered "detriment", particularly as Robert Walker L.J. said that the court must "look at the matter in the round". All of this might make it difficult in advance to predict when someone was going to be able to prove that they have a claim.

LECTURER: But one thing is clear. *Gillett v Holt* sets the bar high. The courts are looking for *influence*. This is what we have argued. And Robert Walker L.J. made it clear that in most cases of this kind claimants would be told "don't count your chickens". It was the severity of the detriment, over a whole life, and the quality of assurances and promises on the part of Mr Holt, that made this an exceptional case.

STUDENT: So people would know in advance what kind of task they were up against bringing a claim of this kind. Perhaps certainty and predictability is violated less than I thought.

LECTURER: Would you agree that most people ought to know that to gain ownership over property it must be put in writing? People ought not to be encouraged to take Land Law into their own hands?

STUDENT: No I don't agree! To an extent the law should reflect what people actually do. And it is often the case that people act on the basis of trust in each other, even when they know about the legal rules. Mr Gillett knew full well that he could not rely on the promises as a matter of strict law; that something needed to be in writing. But he acted out of trust. I think the law should protect this human aspect.

LECTURER: In terms of whether *Gillett v Holt* lays down a clear enough rule for people to know in the future when they own a stake in the land or not, what other class of litigant might be affected?

STUDENT: Landowners, like Mr Holt.

LECTURER: And potentially purchasers from him. A right that arises under the doctrine of proprietary estoppel is classed as a property right that will bind a purchaser of the land from a Mr Holt.[201]

STUDENT: It might be a little difficult for purchasers to know when the seller has made a promise and it has been relied on.

LECTURER: And difficult for a bank or building society to find out about if, for example, Mr Holt had sought to raise a loan on the security of the farmhouse. The bank would only be able to

---

201   Land Registration Act 2002 s.116.

sell the property to get its money back (should Mr Holt default on the loan repayments) if there were no property rights that bound the bank.

STUDENT: So if the scope of the decision in *Gillett v Holt* is not curtailed strictly then it is potentially bad law on the basis of BUILDING BLOCK NO 5: Property Rights and the Protection of Purchasers and Mortgage Lenders.

BUILDING BLOCK NO 5: Property Rights and the Protection of Purchasers and Mortgage Lenders

We can argue that a rule in a case or statute is good or bad fair or unfair, depending on the extent to which it supports or undermines the idea that rules of Land Law should protect a purchaser or mortgage lender from being bound by prior interests in the land.

LECTURER: So far though, I think it is fair to say that there must be a balance between certainty and justice. Morality is important and because *Gillett v Holt* was identified as something of an exceptional case, certainty and predictability is maintained.

And so we are getting on quite well. We have moved to a position whereby we can say that *Gillett v Holt* is not a bad decision. It reflects legitimate principles of moral justice. It is not justifiable in every case to say *"DON'T COUNT YOUR CHICKENS BEFORE THEY'RE HATCHED"*. We have checked out the soundness of the Building Blocks as evidence by asking questions. The only thing we have not done is to look at whether the points made by academic authors support, deny, or add to, any points that we have made. This makes sure that our argument is properly *established*.

Chapter 3

Formal and Informal Ownership

CHAPTER OVERVIEW

In this chapter you will find:

- The principles by which ownership of land is transferred
- Four doctrines by which someone can own land without a written transfer
- Constructed arguments about the law using Building Blocks.

Introduction

1

In this chapter we will consider the process that must be gone through in order for ownership of an estate in land to be transferred *formally*. And then we will look at all the ways in which the law permits a person to acquire an interest in land without any document of transfer being executed in their favour, i.e. *informal ownership*.

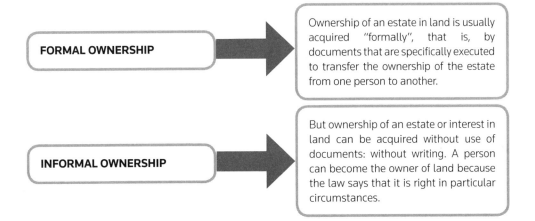

FORMAL OWNERSHIP → Ownership of an estate in land is usually acquired "formally", that is, by documents that are specifically executed to transfer the ownership of the estate from one person to another.

INFORMAL OWNERSHIP → But ownership of an estate or interest in land can be acquired without use of documents: without writing. A person can become the owner of land because the law says that it is right in particular circumstances.

Formal ownership

A. HOW OWNERSHIP OF LAND IS FORMALLY TRANSFERRED FROM ONE PERSON TO ANOTHER

Ownership of an estate in land is usually acquired formally, that is, by documents that are specifically executed to transfer the ownership of the estate from one person to another. The most common form of ownership is the freehold estate in land, i.e. the fee simple absolute in possession.[1] Ownership of the freehold estate is transferred from one person to another in a variety of different circumstances, for example land may be transferred by gift, either during the donor's lifetime or on their death by their will, or it may be transferred as a result of one person purchasing it from another.

> **An example of land transfer or conveyancing process**
> We are used to walking down the high street of a town or city and passing estate agents' windows. We may see several people looking in: a nervous first time buyer, who is wondering whether they have enough deposit saved to buy a two-bedroomed apartment, or a couple looking for a larger house in which to raise their growing family. When these people purchase their house/flat they go through a process whereby the house/flat is formally transferred from the person selling it to these buyers here.

In this section we will consider the formalities involved in a typical transaction between a buyer and a seller of the freehold estate in land. In Chapters 6, 7 and 8 we will study Land Transfer Law in depth. We are concerned here with formalities for the transfer of ownership. The principal object of Land Transfer Law is to make sure that the seller's title is proven sound and acceptable to the purchaser and that as few property rights as possible will bind the land when it is transferred to the new purchaser.

The land transfer process can be broken down into four stages. →

a) Pre-contract enquiries.
b) The contract stage.
c) "Completion"—the transfer of the legal estate.
d) Compulsory registration of the new purchaser as owner at the Land Registry.

(1) The pre-contract stage

Once a purchaser has found a property they like, they will negotiate a price with the seller. When a price is agreed the house is sold "subject to contract", although there is no legally binding

---

1   See Chapter 2, section 3D, p.97.

agreement to sell/purchase at this stage. Both seller and buyer are free to pull out of the transaction.

> The commonly used expression "sold subject to contract" means "although the parties have reached an agreement, no legally binding contract comes into existence until the exchange of formal written contracts takes place".
>
> *Christos v Secretary of State for Transport* [2003] EWCA Civ 1073, quoted Harpum, Bridge and Dixon, *Megarry & Wade Law of Real Property* 7th edn (2008), para.15–010.

And it is important that at this stage both parties *are* free to withdraw from the transaction. With sales of land, the principle of *caveat emptor* applies. This is Latin for "let the buyer beware". There is no obligation on the part of the seller to disclose defects and other matters connected with the house and land sold.[2] Thus, the purchaser should satisfy himself as to the state and condition of the house or flat, *before* he or she is contractually bound to purchase it. The purchaser will usually undertake a form of survey of the condition of the property. This can range from a simple valuation, to ensure that the property is worth the money agreed, to a full structural engineer's report.

At this stage the purchaser must also make enquiries about the state of the seller's *title* to the land, i.e. does he own what he claims to own, does he have the power to make the transfer, and are there any property rights, such as easements and restrictive covenants that affect the land? This will usually involve making inquiries at the Land Registry and inspecting the land itself for evidence of third party rights and occupation.

We will look at *how* the purchaser proves that the vendor has power to transfer the land and *how* it can be determined which third party property rights will bind the land, in Chapters 6, 7 and 8: Land Transfer Law.

The *caveat emptor* principle does not apply in the same force to matters of *title*, e.g. property rights affecting the land and which bind the purchaser. Where these defects are not visible to the purchaser on inspection or not within his actual knowledge, so are solely within the knowledge of the vendor, the latter is under a contractual duty to disclose such defects.[3]

Because at this stage neither seller nor buyer is legally bound to complete the sale, this means that *gazumping* can occur. This is where the seller accepts a higher offer from another buyer and then refuses to sell to the first purchaser.

---

2   *Lowndes v Lane* (1789) 2 Cox 363. For further detail see C.Harpum, S.Bridge and M.Dixon, *Megarry & Wade Law of Real Property*, 7th edn (London: Sweet & Maxwell, 2008) Ch.15.

3   *Peyman v Lanjani* [1985] Ch. 457; *Yandle & Sons v Sutton* [1922] 2 Ch. 199. See C.Harpum (1992) 108 L.Q.R. 280; for further detail see *Megarry & Wade Law of Real Property* 7th edn (2008), Ch.15.

(a) The role of mortgages

Many purchasers will require a loan from a bank or building society before they can afford to buy a house. In return for this loan they will grant the bank a mortgage over their new house. The lender will usually undertake a separate survey or "valuation" of the house.

> **Why does a mortgagee undertake a separation valuation?**
> This will be in order to make sure that the house is worth the money secured by the mortgage. Thus, in the event that the bank had to repossess and sell the house they need to be confident that the sale proceeds will pay off the debt.

(b) Chain sales

When a buyer has found a house which they like, it will often be the case that the seller of this house will need to purchase another house at the same time. The buyer may also have a house to sell. Thus, there are several transactions that need to happen at the same time. This is known as a "chain". All of the sellers and purchasers down the chain must enter into the contract for sale at the same moment in time. Otherwise, the situation may occur where a buyer is contractually obliged to purchase whilst he or she has yet to enter into a binding contract to sell their own house. Should their buyer then withdraw from the transaction the result is "financially catastrophic".[4]

> **Remedies for breach of contract of sale: Specific performance**
> If a purchaser breaches the contract of sale the equitable remedy of "specific performance" is available for land contracts. This is a remedy that derives from the equitable maxim *equity sees as done that which ought to be done: Walsh v Lonsdale* (1882) L.R. 21 Ch. D.9. Instead of merely awarding damages for breach of contract equity will hold the purchaser to his obligation and make him complete the purchase.
>
> *Sudbrook Trading Estate Ltd v Eggleton* [1983] 1 A.C. 444

(2) The contract stage

Once the pre-contractual searches and enquiries are completed to the purchaser's satisfaction, seller and purchaser are ready to enter into a contract for the sale of the land. This is the point at which the sale becomes legally binding.

(a) Section 2 of the Law of Property (Miscellaneous Provisions) Act 1989

The contract that the seller and buyer enter into must comply with the formalities contained in s.2 of the Law of Property (Miscellaneous Provisions) Act 1989. For contracts entered into after September 27, 1989 the contract must comply with s.2, which provides that

---

4   M.Thompson, *Modern Land Law*, 4th edn (Oxford University Press, 2009), p.165.

"(1) A contract for the sale or other disposition of an interest in land can only be made in writing and only by incorporating all the terms which the parties have agreed in one document or, where contracts are exchanged, in each.

(2) The terms may be incorporated in a document either by being set out in it or by reference to some other document.

(3) The document incorporating the terms or, where contracts are exchanged, one of the documents incorporating them (but not necessarily the same one) must be signed by or on behalf of each party to the contract."

Thus, in order to be valid, the contract must contain the terms of the transaction. Section 2 preserves the standard conveyancing practice of "exchange of contracts". This is where there are two contracts, the seller signs one that is in the possession of his conveyancer and the purchaser signs the other, which is held by her conveyancer. The contract becomes legally binding when the seller has the contract signed by the purchaser and vice versa. Exchange does not have to happen physically, in person. It can occur, for example, by telephone. The conveyancers for the buyer and seller agree with each other that contracts are "exchanged". The effect of this is that each from that point onwards considers himself as holding "his client's part of the contract . . . to the order of the other party".[5] Where contracts are exchanged in this way, as you can see from s.2(1), all the terms which the parties have agreed must be incorporated in both documents and the documents must be signed by both parties. As you see, s.2(3) provides that it is not necessary that the same document is signed by both seller and purchaser. So the seller's conveyancer will obtain the seller's signature on their copy of the contract and the purchaser's conveyancer will obtain her signature on their copy.

(b) A valid contract

Once executed in accordance with s.2, the contract is binding on the vendor and purchaser. Either can be sued on the contract. If either party defaults on the contract the remedy of specific performance is available. This means that the party in breach can be made to perform the contract. Because of this, another effect of the contract for sale is that from the moment of its execution the seller will hold the land on constructive trust for the purchaser.

---

5   *Megarry & Wade Law of Real Property*, 7th edn (2008), para.15–036.

> **The seller as constructive trustee of the land for the purchaser**
>
> Where the equitable remedy of specific performance is available equity is holding the purchaser or seller (depending which party is in breach) to the bargain. Equity makes the purchaser go through with the transaction, and is not satisfied merely by making him pay damages for breach of contract. Thus, because this important equitable remedy is available for breach of contract for the sale of land: *equity sees as done that which ought to be done: Walsh v Lonsdale* (1882) L.R. 21 Ch. D.9. Consequently, from the moment the contract is in being the seller is deemed to hold the legal estate in the land on trust for the purchaser: *Lysaght v Edwards* (1876) 2 Ch.D 499. This is a trust that the law *implies*. It is not a trust that the parties have entered into expressly. It is known as a *constructive trust*. Thus, the purchaser has a full equitable property right in the land by virtue of the contract.

> Thus, as soon as the purchaser has entered into a binding contract of sale he or she is responsible for insuring the property: *Lysaght v Edwards* (1876) 2 Ch.D. 499, p.507, per Sir George Jessel M.R.

A valid contract for the sale or other disposition of an interest in land is also regarded as a interest in the land in its own right. It is known as an "estate contract" which is a property right.

> **"The right to call for a conveyance of the land is an equitable interest or an equitable estate."**
>
> *London and South Western Rly Co v Gomm* **(1882) 20 Ch.D. 562, per Sir George Jessel M.R.**

Thus, if the seller, before completing the purchase as required by the contract, sold his legal estate to another, Purchaser 2, it is possible that Purchaser 2 will take his estate in the land subject to the original purchaser's estate contract. In short he may be forced to allow the original purchaser to buy the land at the price agreed.[6]

But what if the contract between seller and purchaser *does not* comply with s.2, e.g. if the contract is insufficiently certain as to its terms or is not signed? The effect of non-compliance with s.2 is that the contract is void, i.e. of no legal effect. The position was different under s.40 of the Law of Property Act 1925, the provision that s.2 replaced. Section 40 required contracts to be evidenced in writing and an oral contract was valid but *unenforceable*. The doctrine of "part performance" applied by which equity would enforce the oral contract where one of the parties had acted in reliance on it, e.g. where the purchaser took possession before the conveyance of the land to him.

---

6   *Midland Bank Trust Co Ltd v Green* [1981] A.C. 513. We will consider the circumstances in which estate contracts will bind a subsequent purchaser or mortgagee of the land in Chapters 7 and 8.

Because under s.2 of the Law of Property (Miscellaneous Provisions) Act 1989 a non-compliant contract is void, i.e. it is regarded as never having existed, and is not merely *unenforceable*, there is no room for the doctrine of part performance. There is nothing to "part perform".

(c) Contracts to which section 2 applies

Up until this point we have been talking about the formalities required to transfer a freehold estate in land from one person to another. And one such formality is that if the parties wish to enter into a contract prior to the transfer of the legal fee simple estate, that contract must comply with s.2 of the Law of Property (Miscellaneous Provisions) Act 1989. The transfer of the legal estate must then be made by deed, as we shall see below. But as you can see from the terms of s.2(1)[7] the formalities for contracts apply not only to contracts for the sale of the freehold estate but to contracts for the sale or other disposition of *any* interest in land, for example contracts to grant or assign leases,[8] contracts to create or transfer a mortgage over land, and contracts to grant easements.

> **Examples**
>
> 1. Alan is purchasing Blackacre. He borrows £100,000 from the Enterprise Bank in order to finance the purchase. He agrees to grant a mortgage over Blackacre to the Enterprise Bank. He enters into a contract to grant a mortgage. The Bank sends him their standard form contract, which incorporates all the terms and conditions of the mortgage. The Bank and Alan sign this contract. It complies with the s.2 requirements and is thus valid.
>
> 2. Harpreet is an artist and wishes to rent a studio. Mr Patel is the freehold owner of the studio. Harpreet and Mr Patel agree terms. Before Mr Patel actually grants the lease to Harpreet the parties may wish to enter into a contract. The contract sets out all the terms and conditions of the lease ("covenants") and it is signed by both parties. It is a valid contract to grant a lease.
>
> 3. Nicky is the freehold owner of Cherry Cottage and agrees that her neighbour, Albert, can have a right of way (an easement) over her back garden. Albert agrees to pay Nicky a fee for this. Nicky and Albert put all the terms in a single document and both sign it.

(i) Effect of a valid contract to grant a lease, mortgage or easement

The Enterprise Bank, Harpreet, and Albert all have a specifically enforceable contract for the creation of an interest in land: a mortgage, a lease and an easement. Potentially therefore they can compel Alan, Mr Patel and Nicky to grant the rights. However, they do not yet have those interests. In order to create a legal interest in land this must be done by deed (see below). But what if Alan, Mr Patel and Nicky never get around to executing a deed of grant? Because of the

---

7   "(1) A contract for the sale or other disposition of an interest in land can only be made in writing".

8   An "assignment" of a lease is where the tenant transfers his existing leasehold interest in the land to another. A "grant" of a lease is where an entirely new leasehold estate is created afresh out of a freehold estate or a larger leasehold estate. See Chapter 9.

availability of the remedy of specific performance for breach of contract, under certain circumstances equity will recognise that Harpreet has an equitable lease (see Chapter 9), the Enterprise Bank—an equitable mortgage, and Albert—an equitable easement.[9]

But in order to have a valid contract for the creation of any of these rights, it must comply with the s.2 formalities.

(ii) Section 2 and options to purchase land

An option is where the owner of land grants to another the right to purchase his land during a specified period on specified terms.[10] It is an interest in land: a property right. The option must be created in accordance with s.2, i.e. the document creating the option must incorporate all the terms, for example the period during which the option may be exercised, the price that is to be paid for the land. It must also be signed by both parties. The reason is that the grant of an option is regarded as a conditional contract of sale. "An option to buy land can properly be described as a contract for the sale of that land conditional on the exercise of the option".[11] If the grantee decides to exercise the option the document giving notice of this to the grantor does not have to comply with s.2.[12] The exercise of the option turns the conditional contract into a contract of sale as if seller and purchaser "had concluded an ordinary contract of sale".[13]

(iii) Section 2 and short leases

Short leases are exempt from the formalities in s.2. Thus, it is possible for a valid contract for the grant of a short lease to come into being without any writing at all, i.e. entirely through the oral arrangements of the parties. Where there is a contract to grant a short lease of the type mentioned in s.54(2) of the Law of Property Act 1925, then the contract does not need to comply with s.2.[14] Section 54(2) provides that a lease does not require a deed in order to come into being as a legal estate in land if it takes "effect in possession for a term not exceeding three years . . . at the best rent which can be reasonably obtained without taking a fine".

> **Example**
> Harpreet is an artist and wishes to rent a studio. Mr Patel is the freehold owner of the studio. Harpreet and Mr Patel agree terms. If the lease to which both parties agree does not exceed three years in its length, is at the market rent for that type of property, and Mr Patel does not receive a lump sum payment from Harpreet, then there is an enforceable contract even if the parties did not put their arrangements in writing.

---

9   *Walsh v Lonsdale* (1882) L.R. 21 Ch. D.9.
10   *Midland Bank Trust Co Ltd v Green* [1981] A.C. 513.
11   *Spiro v Glencrown Properties Ltd* [1991] Ch. 537, per Hoffman J. Also *Griffith v Pelton* [1958] Ch. 205. For detailed discussion of options in relation to s.2(1) see *Megarry & Wade Law of Real Property* 7th edn (2008), paras 15–012 and 15–018.
12   As Hoffman J. observed in *Spiro v Glencrown Properties Ltd* [1991] Ch. 537; *London and South Western Rly Co v Gomm* (1882) 20 Ch.D. 562, per Sir George Jessel M.R.
13   *Spiro v Glencrown Properties Ltd* [1991] Ch. 537, per Hoffman J.
14   Law of Property (Miscellaneous Provisions) Act 1989 s.2(5).

(d) Section 2 and resulting and constructive trusts

Section 2(5) of the 1989 Act provides that the formalities of s.2 do not apply to resulting or constructive trusts.[15] Resulting and constructive trusts are both species of "implied trusts". Trusts can be implied by law into the parties' dealings with land, in much the same way as terms are implied into a contract. For example, where two parties are dealing with land and one acts in reliance on a promise made by the other that they will gain an interest in the land, the law may impose a constructive trust. In such a situation it will be irrelevant that any contract between them failed to comply with the s.2 formalities, or indeed, that there was no contract at all. In *Yaxley v Gotts*[16] the Court of Appeal implied a constructive trust to give effect to an oral arrangement between two men that one would acquire an interest in the other's land in return for building work. This arrangement had not been formalised.[17]

To make sure you understand the idea of the "trust" revisit Chapter 2 section 3(c): Equity and the Trust.

(3) "Completion": The transfer of the legal estate—the deed of transfer

Although at the contract stage the purchaser becomes the owner of the house in equity, it is not until the seller conveys (transfers) the legal estate or interest to the purchaser that he becomes the full legal owner. This transfer of the legal estate must be made by deed. If there is not a deed the purchaser does not acquire the legal estate.

The requirement for a deed: Law of Property Act 1925 s.52(1)

Under s.52(1) of the Law of Property Act 1925 "all conveyances of land or of any interest therein are void for the purpose of conveying or creating a legal estate unless made by deed".

Examples

If David has contracted to buy the freehold estate in Yellowacre from Alec, Alec must execute a deed of conveyance in order for David to obtain the legal estate.

In our examples above, Harpreet will not get a legal lease until Mr Patel formally grants it by deed (if the lease is for a term exceeding three years). The Enterprise Bank will not get a legal mortgage until Alan executes a mortgage deed. And Albert will not get a legal easement until Nicky grants it by deed.

---

15   We will consider such trusts below in this Chapter.
16   [2000] Ch. 162.
17   The circumstances in which the law will imply a trust in such a way, particularly where the oral arrangement would have been enforceable *but for* the requirements of s.2, are now quite restricted: *Cobbe v Yeoman's Row Management Ltd* [2008] UKHL 55.

(a) What is required to create a deed?

It used to be required that a deed had to be written on paper or parchment and had to be executed by the affixation of a seal. This rule has now been abolished.[18] It has been replaced by the requirements that:

- The document of transfer or creation of an interest in land in order to be a deed must make it clear on the face of the document "that it is intended to be a deed by the person making it . . . whether describing itself as a deed or expressing itself to be executed or signed as a deed or otherwise"; and
- It must be validly executed as a deed. This means that the document must be signed by the transferor/creator of the estate or interest,[19] "in the presence of a witness who attests the signature", and delivered by him as a deed.[20]

> **Example**
> Alan executes a mortgage deed in order to grant a mortgage over Blackacre to the Enterprise Bank. At the bottom it states that the document is "signed as a deed by Alan". It then states that Alan signed in the presence of Daniel, who signs the document to show that he has attested Alan's signature.

A deed of transfer of the legal freehold estate is usually executed by way of the Land Registry's TR1 form. This form sets out all the information about the property to be transferred, the transferor, any interests that exist in relation to the estate, the money paid and how the purchasers, if more than one, are to hold the property. This is set out with the requirements of a deed upon which the transferor must append his signature along with that of his witness.[21]

(b) No deed required for short leases

There is an exception to this requirement for leases for a term of three years or less taking effect in possession "at the best rent which can be reasonably obtained without taking a fine".[22] Such leases can be legal without any deed. They can come into being orally.

> **Example**
> Harpreet wishes to rent a studio. Mr Patel is the freehold owner of the studio. Harpreet and Mr Patel agree terms. If the lease to which both parties agree does not exceed three years and is at the market rent for that type of property, and Mr Patel does not receive a lump sum payment from Harpreet, then a legal lease can come into being between the parties without a deed.

---

18   Law of Property (Miscellaneous Provisions) Act 1989 s.1(1).
19   Or by a person authorised to execute the deed on his behalf.
20   Law of Property (Miscellaneous Provisions) Act 1989 s.1(2) and (3).
21   For a helpful and detailed illustration see Clarke and Greer, *Land Law Directions*, 2nd edn (Oxford University Press) pp.80–83.
22   Law of Property Act 1925 s.54(2).

(c) The estate or interest must be capable of being legal

Not all estates and interests in land are capable of existing as *legal* estates and interests. You may remember from Chapter 2 that for reasons connected with simplifying the transfer of land from a buyer to a seller the 1925 property legislation reclassified estates and interests in land.

See Chapter 2, section 3(D): Estates and Interests in Land after the 1925 Property Legislation.

> **Reclassification of estates and interests in land: s.1 of the Law of Property Act 1925**
>
> Section 1 of the Law of Property Act 1925 provides that the only two estates capable of existing as legal estates are: the fee simple absolute in possession and the term of years absolute; the freehold and leasehold estates.
>
> As far as concerns smaller interests in land, such as easements and restrictive covenants, s.1(2) of the Law of Property Act 1925 provides that the only interests in land capable of existing as *legal* interests are: an easement, right or privilege, for perpetual duration or an identified period of years, a rentcharge, a mortgage, and a right of entry. The Law of Property Act 1925 s.1(3) classifies all other estates in land, e.g. the life estate and all other interests, e.g. restrictive covenants, options to purchase, beneficial interests under a trust, as *equitable*.

An estate or interest that is *capable* of being legal under s.1 must be transferred or created by deed before it *becomes legal*. But a deed cannot make an estate or interest *legal* if s.1 provides that it can only be equitable. Thus, it is usual for a restrictive covenant to be granted by deed, because this is in the nature of the interest, as we shall see in Chapter 12. But this will never make a covenant a *legal* interest in land.

(d) The effect of non-compliance with the requirement for a deed

Section 52 of the Law of Property Act 1925, which sets out the requirement that a legal estate or interest must be created by deed, provides that if there is no deed then the transferee or grantee of the estate or interest will get no legal estate. However, it is still possible that they may have an equitable interest. As we have seen, if there is a valid contract to transfer an estate, the purchaser has an estate contract. This is an equitable interest. As far as concerns leases, if there is a valid contract to grant a lease and the remedy of specific performance is available then the tenant may acquire an equitable lease, provided they give consideration (value).[23] This will be the case if a tenant pays rent. A contract to create a mortgage and an easement may give rise to an equitable mortgage or easement, if there is consideration.

---

23   *Walsh v Lonsdale* (1882) L.R. 21 Ch. D.9. We consider this further in Chapter 9.

(4) The requirement of compulsory registration

Once a deed of transfer has been executed the purchaser is the owner of the land. However, there is a requirement that certain transfers and dispositions of estates and interests in land must be registered with their own title at the Land Registry. Unless they are so registered the purchaser will not obtain the legal estate or interest.[24] Where title to the land is unregistered there are a number of dispositions of that land that trigger compulsory first registration.[25] And where title to the land is already registered, any transfer of the freehold estate, or grant of a lease for a term greater than seven years, or grant of a legal charge (mortgage), must be registered at the Land Registry.[26] Otherwise the purchaser, tenant, or mortgagee will not gain the legal estate or interest.

However, the system of registration of title to land is much more than just a final step in the process of transfer of title from seller to purchaser. It is an entirely self-contained system of land transfer law.[27]

> Registered land law provides a conclusive way for the purchaser to ascertain that the seller owns the land and has the power to transfer it to him. And it provides rules that determine which third party property rights, such as easements, restrictive covenants, and beneficial interests under trusts, will bind the purchaser once he is registered as the owner of the land.

(a) A system of proof of title

As we saw when we considered the pre-contract stage of conveyancing, the purchaser must be able to ascertain that the seller *actually owns the land*. Where title to the land is registered at the Land Registry all a purchaser needs to do is to check the land register as this records the name of the owner of that land.

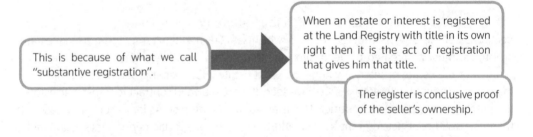

This is because of what we call "substantive registration".

When an estate or interest is registered at the Land Registry with title in its own right then it is the act of registration that gives him that title.

The register is conclusive proof of the seller's ownership.

Thus, the system of title registration does more than simply record all estates and interests that exist in relation to a particular plot of land. It *creates or confers ownership*. When a person is

---

24   Land Registration Act 2002 s.7(1) (for first registrations), s.27(1) for transactions with a registered estate.
25   Land Registration Act 2002 s.4.
26   Land Registration Act 2002 s.27, there are other estates and interests that must be registered.
27   We will consider this system in Chapter 8.

registered as proprietor of the estate, he is deemed to own that estate whether he was entitled to it under ordinary principles or not.[28]

(b) Third party property rights: the question of priority

We also saw when we were examining the pre-contract stage of conveyancing that it is important for a purchaser of land to ascertain which third party rights have priority over the land that he or she is planning to buy, i.e. which rights they will have to give effect to. In registered land law the rule that determines priority upon a transfer of the registered title, is simple and purchaser-friendly.[29] A transferee for valuable consideration will take the title subject to third party rights that have been registered as a notice against the title. He will also take subject to "overriding interests", which is a contained list of types of interest in land that will bind a purchaser.[30] The importance of overriding interests is that they will bind a purchaser automatically *even though they have not been registered* against the title. Mrs Boland's right fell into this category,[31] see Chapter 1, section 4.

The aim of the Land Registration Act 2002 is to ensure that the land register is, as far as possible, an accurate reflection of those interests that will bind a purchaser. Thus a purchaser should be able to look at the land register and ascertain those rights that will bind him. This is not the case with overriding interests. In the interests of purchaser protection, the categories of "overriding interest" were narrowed and reduced in scope by the 2002 Act.[32]

(c) Electronic conveyancing

The Land Registration Act 2002 makes provision for the future introduction of a system of electronic conveyancing.[33] The idea is that the estate in land will be transferred from seller to buyer entirely electronically. This will abolish the current two-stage system of conveyancing. There is currently a gap of time between execution of the deed of transfer to the purchaser and his registration as the new proprietor of the estate. A problem currently arises in this two-stage system because it is only at the point of *registration* that the purchaser is deemed to take his estate in the land free from most prior third party rights. Under the proposed system, the document of transfer or creation of an interest will be executed online and at the same time the transaction will be registered at the Land Registry.[34] Section 91 of the Land Registration Act 2002 allows a document that creates a disposition of a registered estate or charge, a disposition of an interest that is to be protected as a notice in the register, or a disposition which triggers compulsory registration, to take electronic form. Section 93 gives the power to require that document to be in electronic form and to be simultaneously registered before it can take effect.

---

28 s.58. Because of this, there are rules that enable the land register to be altered in order to bring it up to date or correct a mistake: Sch.4.
29 Land Registration Act 2002 ss.29 and 30. Where title is transferred and then registered for the first time the rule that determines which interests will bind that estate is contained in s.11 (freehold estates) and 12 (leasehold estates).
30 Land Registration Act 2002 Sch.3. The interests that override first registrations are contained in Sch.1.
31 *Williams & Glyn's Bank v Boland* [1981] A.C. 487.
32 Law Commission, *Land Registration for the Twenty-First Century – A Conveyancing Revolution* (2001) Law Com No.271, section 1.
33 Land Registration Act 2002 ss.92 and 93, Sch.5
34 Law Commission, above, para.2.1(2).

(5) The role of formality in trusts of land and co-ownership

Direct transfer is not the only way in which a person can come to own land. What if Betty forms a relationship with Frank and she wishes, when they decide to live together, to give him a share of the ownership of her house. She can do this in one of two ways. She can execute a deed of conveyance of the house into her and Frank's joint names. Or she can continue as the sole legal owner but give Frank a beneficial interest under a trust.

> **What is a trust?**
> A "trust" is a way of holding property. The legal owner of property, the trustee, holds the property for the benefit of another: the beneficiary. The beneficiary has an equitable (or as we sometimes say "beneficial") interest in the land. It is the equitable interest that entitles a person to the value of the land, to the proceeds of sale, to occupy the house, or to demand that the trustee(s) transfer the legal title to them.

We now need to consider what Betty would need to do in order to give Frank a beneficial interest in the house, and the problems that could arise if she chose to reconvey the property into her and Frank's joint names.

An express declaration of a trust: Betty in our above example may wish to continue as the sole owner of the house. She can still give Frank a share of the beneficial interest if she creates a trust, with herself as legal owner—holding the house on trust for herself and Frank. *So how are express trusts formally created?*

> **Formality for the creation of an express trust of land**
> Section 53(1)(b) of the Law of Property Act 1925 provides that express trusts of land must be manifested and proved by some writing before they can be enforced through the courts.

In order to create an enforceable express trust it must be proven in writing that the legal owner(s), e.g. Betty, intended to create a trust[35] and the writing must be sufficiently clear as to the terms of the trust, e.g. the size of the beneficiaries' shares. The trust is then enforceable and Frank will be entitled to a beneficial interest in the house.[36] If an intended express trust of land is not proved by writing the legal effect is that it cannot be enforced by the beneficiary.[37]

---

35   It is not necessary that the word "trust" is used, provided that the legal owner shows the intention that equates with a desire that their legal ownership should henceforth have some custodial element, i.e. looking after the legal title for the partial benefit of another: Hanbury and Martin, *Modern Equity*, 18th edn (London: Sweet & Maxwell, 2009) "The Three Certainties".

36   Law of Property Act 1925 s.53(1)(b).

37   *Rochefoucauld v Boustead* [1897] 1 Ch. 196.

As with s.2 of the Law of Property (Miscellaneous Provisions) Act 1989, this formality requirement for express trusts does not apply to "resulting and constructive trusts".[38] They can come into being without any writing at all.

> **Resulting and constructive trusts can come into being without writing**
> It would substantially defeat the purpose behind these trusts if they were required to be proved by writing before they were enforceable. Resulting and constructive trusts arise in very informal circumstances, for example where one party contributes to the purchase of the home which is then put legally in the name of her partner, for example *Williams & Glyn's Bank Ltd v Boland* [1981] A.C. 487
>
> They also arise because the law imposes them in specific circumstances and not because the parties intended to create a trust. Consequently it is highly unreal to expect there to be evidence in writing of such trusts. And the Law of Property Act 1925 recognises this.

A conveyance to joint purchasers: There are a number of problems that can exist where a house is conveyed into joint names. Whenever land is transferred into two or more people's names[39] the Law of Property Act 1925 provides that they will hold on trust for each other. This was a device imposed by the draftsman as part of an overall scheme to make land transfer easier.[40] But it does cause problems for people like Betty and Frank—who have no knowledge of the "ins and outs" of Land Law! For instance, even where the land is conveyed into the joint names of the co-owners this conveyance does not necessarily determine the size of their *beneficial* shares. The conveyance would need to stipulate the size of joint purchasers' beneficial shares in the house. An express trust is thereby created. The court will give effect to an express declaration of trust, no matter how strongly the parties argue that this is not the intended outcome, unless it can be proven that the declaration was fraudulent or procured by some fundamental mistake.[41]

The creation of an express trust of the beneficial interest is a useful device for joint purchasers if they contributed to the purchase in different size amounts. They may wish their beneficial shares to reflect their contributions. The Law imposes a trust on them if the land is conveyed legally into their joint names, but unless they stipulate expressly (i.e. create an express trust) *how* they intend to share the equitable/beneficial interest, e.g. in shares that reflect their original contributions to the purchase price, they may end up with an allocation of shares that they did not intend.[42]

---

38   Law of Property Act 1925 s.53(2).
39   The Law of Property Act 1925 provides that a maximum of four people can hold a legal estate in land: s.34.
40   We will consider the so-called statutory co-ownership trust and its purpose in detail in Chapters 4 and 5.
41   *Goodman v Gallant* [1986] Fam. 106.
42   We discuss the law of implied trusts and the distribution of beneficial shares for joint purchasers below.

> **Practice Hints**
> When conducting the ordinary process of conveyancing, a good conveyancing practitioner will make joint purchasers aware of this option, maybe as part of the initial Client Care letter.

In cases of joint purchasers the instrument by which to execute a written declaration of trust of the beneficial interest would be the deed of conveyance. There is even a box provided for an express declaration of trust by the Land Registry deed of transfer form: Form TR1. It asks joint transferees of the legal title how they hold the beneficial interest and in what shares. But lamentably this box is often left blank.

(6) Critical thinking: formality versus informality

The consequences for not complying with the formality requirements are harsh. Unless a contract for the creation or transfer of an estate or interest in land complies with s.2(1) of the 1989 Act, it is void. Likewise, unless ownership of land is transferred using a deed of transfer that complies in substance and form with s.1 of the 1989 Act, it does not operate to transfer the legal estate. An intended express trust will be unenforceable unless it is proved in writing. The presence of such a high degree of formality can lead us to think that it is a "red tape" exercise, particularly when fully intended transactions are rendered void by the courts because the person did not use the required "piece of paper".[43] Formality can seem to work an injustice.

> **Examples**
> Alison promises that she will share the ownership of her house with her mother, who then gives her £20,000 towards the deposit. The house is conveyed into Alison's sole name and there is no express declaration of trust in favour of her mother. Alison's mother takes the arrangement on face value.
>
> Richard transfers his house to a trusted friend, with whom he has built up a relationship over the years. The idea is that Richard has become infirm and the friend has promised to "look after the house" for him. Once the transfer is executed it is binding. The friend then waves the conveyance at Richard and says that he is going to keep the house and that their informal arrangement has no standing at all.

Even a cursory glance at the law reports shows us that people enter into these sorts of informal arrangements all the time. Land is the basic commodity on which we live our lives. And people will often not consider the possibility of putting these arrangements in writing or executing the

---

43   P.Birks, "Five Keys to Land Law" in Bright and Dewar (eds) *Land Law Themes and Perspectives* (Oxford University Press, 1998) pp.483–4.

correct formalities. Their ownership of their houses is an extension of their lives.[44] And people trust each other and are in the habit of relying on promises. If the law insisted upon formality 100 per cent of the time, Alison's mother and Richard in our example above would leave empty handed. If you remember from Chapter 2, in *Gillett v Holt*,[45] Mr Holt had made several strong assurances over a long period of time that Mr Gillett would inherit his farm and business. Mr Gillett relied on this promise, worked for many years on the farm and did not make other provision for his future as a result of the promise of inheritance. He did not insist that Mr Holt put the arrangement in writing. He took him to be "a man of his word". The law ought to support the ideal that people have faith and trust in each other. And it ought to send the message that fraud and deceit should not go unpunished.[46]

English law's recognition of land ownership must create a balance between formality and informality.

> "There is an inescapable tension. Formality breeds hard cases . . . there is a terrific clash between two simple principles. One is that you cannot have your cake and eat it. You cannot take the advantages of formality and at the same time let off all those who do things in their own informal way. The other is that pain should not be inflicted except in case of pressing necessity. It is not so easy to send someone away empty-handed who would have taken a fortune if only the right piece of paper had been used. Wherever there are formal requirements, there will be litigation in which these two principles meet head to head."
>
> P.Birks, "Five Keys to Land Law" in Bright and Dewar (eds) *Land Law Themes and Perspectives* (1998) pp.483–4

We will examine the nature of this balance firstly by looking at why formalities, such as written contracts and deeds, are so important. There is much to be said on this side of the argument.

(a) The functions of formality[47]

(i) *The evidentiary function of formality*[48]

Where a transaction is required to be in writing, or manifested and proved by writing, it removes the need to rely on oral testimony in court. It provides clear and enduring evidence of the intention of the transferor/parties.[49] Thus, where the terms of a transfer of land are written

---

44   P.Critchley, "Taking Formalities Seriously", in *Land Law Themes and Perspectives*, pp.524–5.

45   [2000] 2 All E.R. 289, Chapter 2, section 4, p.102.

46   P.S.Atiyah, *Promises, Morals and Law* (Oxford University Press, 1981), p.14.

47   Critchley, above, provides a checklist of "benefits" and "detriments" of formality requirements so that it is possible to see whether case law decisions have been made reasonably or have "gone seriously awry".

48   J.H.Langbein (1975) Vol.88 *Harvard Law Review* 489, p.492.

49   J.H.Langbein, above p.492; also T.G.Youdan [1984] C.L.J. 306, pp.310–311, on the functions of the formalities in the Statute of Frauds 1677.

down and agreed to in writing by both buyer and seller, this provides certainty as to the content of the agreement. There will be fewer matters to dispute about in the future.[50]

(ii) The channelling function of formality[51]

Where someone intends to dispose of their property they must do so in recognisable ways prescribed by law. In this way land is disposed of in a uniform way and using the same language. This not only ensures that like cases are treated alike, an essential requirement of any system of justice, but it makes it easier for the courts to ascertain what the transferor/parties to a contract intended.[52]

(iii) The cautionary function of formality[53]

If land or a house could be sold or given away without any need for writing of any kind, i.e. I could transfer my house by saying that "my house is now yours", I could live to regret my decision. If I have to enter into a contract and then execute a deed of transfer this gives me plenty of opportunity to reflect on what I am doing and to make sure that *this is what I really intend to do*. Land, or our house, is probably the most valuable asset most people possess.[54] Formality also ensures that anyone entering into such transactions is impressed with their "solemnity and legal significance"[55] and is likely to have much greater awareness of the consequences of what they are doing.

> **BUILDING BLOCK NO.6: The Need for Certainty and Predictability in Land Law Rules**
> All these requirements support the idea that land transfer must be a certain and predictable process. People should not have to go to court in order to know what their rights are. Formalities provide this certainty.

(iv) Formality and third party purchasers and mortgage lenders

Also, where interests in land are created in writing, and by deed, and the more important estates and interests, such as fees simple, leaseholds, and mortgages, are required to be registered at the Land Registry, a third party who is considering purchasing the land will have documentary evidence of the rights that will bind him if he goes ahead and buys the land.[56] The purchaser just needs to look at the land register. If ownership of land is allowed to come into being entirely informally, without writing and without registration of that ownership, a later purchaser of the land might be bound by rights that he could not readily have discovered—because they were not on the land register.

---

50   P.Critchley, above pp.517–8.
51   L.Fuller, "Consideration and Form", 41 *Columbia Law Review* 799.
52   J.H.Langbein (1975) Vol.88 *Harvard Law Review* 489, p.494.
53   The terminology "channelling" and "cautionary" function: L.Fuller, "Consideration and Form", 41 *Columbia Law Review* 799.
54   P.Critchley, above, pp.514–5.
55   Langbein, above, p.495.
56   P.Critchley, "Taking Formalities Seriously", in *Land Law Themes and Perspectives* (1998) pp.516–517.

As far as co-ownership is concerned, if the legal owner of land wants to create an express trust, this must be proved by writing.[57] The usual place to do this is on the Land Registry transfer form when the land is transferred to the legal owner(s).[58] This will then be sent to the Land Registry for the transfer to be registered. At the same time, if the form includes an express declaration of trust it will give the Land Registry the chance to make all the appropriate entries on the register concerning the details of the trust. These entries will be aimed at ensuring that a later purchaser or mortgage lender will know of the possibility that someone other than the legal owner ("registered proprietor") might be able to assert a beneficial interest against the land. A later purchaser or mortgage lender can then either proceed with the necessary caution or withdraw from the transaction entirely.

> If the law too readily recognises informal trusts and other types of informal ownership, this potentially threatens the position of third party purchasers and mortgage lenders. It would thus be bad law.

BUILDING BLOCK NO 5: Property Rights and the Protection of Purchasers and Mortgage Lenders
We can argue that a development of a rule in a case or statute is good or bad fair or unfair, depending on the extent to which it supports or undermines the idea that rules of Land Law should protect a purchaser or mortgage lender from being bound by prior interests in the land. This is the policy behind the 1925 property legislation. See Chapter 1 for the full text of BUILDING BLOCK NO 5.

Informal ownership

3

Now we will look at all the ways in which the law and equity permits a person to acquire an interest in land without any document of transfer, or declaration of trust, being executed in their favour, i.e. *informal ownership*.

---

57   Above, Law of Property Act 1925 s.53(1)(b).
58   Above, Chapter 3 section 2, p.125–6.

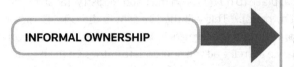

INFORMAL OWNERSHIP

Ownership of an estate or interest in land can be acquired without use of documents: without writing. A person can become the owner of land because the law says that it is right in particular circumstances.

Is the law on informal ownership good or bad law?
If rules that recognise informal ownership support or undermine any of our Building Blocks then we can say that they are good or bad law accordingly. For the full text of our Building Blocks and instructions on how to use them to build an argument, see Chapter 1.

A. THE RULE THAT EQUITY WILL NOT PERMIT FORMALITY REQUIREMENTS TO BE USED AS AN INSTRUMENT OF FRAUD

This is perhaps the courts' most direct interference with statutory formality requirements. If a person seeks to rely on the fact that an agreement was not put in writing in accordance with statutory formality requirements, and in doing so is committing a fraud, then the court will enforce the agreement even though it did not comply with formality or was not sufficiently certain.[59] Similarly, if land is transferred subject to an oral agreement that the transferee will hold the land on trust for the transferor, he or she will not be permitted to deny the trust and keep the land for themselves on the basis that s.53(1)(b) of the Law of Property Act 1925 requires trusts of land to be manifested and proved by some writing.[60]

> **Example: Rochefoucauld v Boustead [1897] 1 Ch. 196**
> The plaintiff owned land in Ceylon. She entered into an oral agreement with the defendant that he would take a transfer of the estates and hold them on trust for her. After the transfer the defendant denied the trust on the basis that it was not proved in writing. In short he tried to keep the land for himself. It was held that despite the absence of writing, the defendant held the land on trust for the plaintiff. To require otherwise would be to use as an instrument of fraud the statute that requires the trust to be evidenced in writing.
>
> Lindley L.J. observed that "it is a fraud on the part of a person to whom land is conveyed as a trustee, and who knows it was so conveyed, to deny the trust and claim the land himself": [1897] 1 Ch. 196, p.206.

---

59   *In re Duke of Marlborough* [1894] 2 Ch. 133; *Lincoln v Wright* 4 De. G. & J. 16; *Haigh v Kaye* L.R. 7 Ch. 469; *Heard v Pilley* L.R. 4 Ch. 548. *Chattock v Muller* 8 Ch.D. 177; *Pallant v Morgan* [1951] 1 Ch. 43.
60   The predecessor of this section was Statute of Frauds 1677 s.7.

For a later example of the fraud doctrine we can look at *Bannister v Bannister*.[61] In this case the elderly owner of two cottages agreed to sell them at a reduced price to her brother-in-law. However, the sale was on the condition that he would allow her to live in one of them rent free for as long as she wished. This is an agreement for a life interest in land and as such was not put in writing when the lady transferred the cottages to her brother-in-law. The arrangement between them was entirely oral. Technically therefore it was unenforceable. After she had conveyed the cottages to her brother-in-law he attempted to evict her. Scott L.J. dismissed his claim for possession:

> "[A] constructive trust is raised against a person who insists on the absolute character of a conveyance to himself for the purpose of defeating the beneficial interest, which, according to the true bargain, was to belong to another."[62]

In short the brother-in-law, now that he was the full and complete owner of the land upon the execution of the deed of conveyance, could not be permitted to retain that absolute ownership free from his sister-in-law's claims. *But why?* What was Scott L.J. really saying in this statement? He was applying the doctrine that no statutory formality provision can be used in order to help someone commit a fraud. Here, the brother-in-law was attempting to evict his sister-in-law on the ground that she did not have a properly formalised right to occupy the cottage. Although this is normally good ground for denying someone an interest in land, as we saw in section 2 above in this Chapter, this argument could not be used in this case. But why were his actions fraudulent? Scott L.J. found that his sister-in-law would not have sold the cottages at a reduced price to her brother-in-law *but for* his oral undertaking that she should be able to occupy one of them.

> "She would not have sold the two cottages to the plaintiff . . . if the plaintiff had not agreed to let her stay in No.30 as long as she liked rent free":[63]

She executed the deed of conveyance of the cottages in his favour entirely under the influence of this promise that she should be allowed to stay there. She would not otherwise have transferred ownership to him. The brother-in-law received property that he would not have received without making his promise. It would be fraudulent of him to use his technically correct form of ownership to deny his sister-in-law's formally defective rights.

Where a conveyance is made in circumstances such as this, i.e. in reliance on a promise that the transferor should thereafter have some beneficial interest, it does not matter that the transferee at the time of the conveyance intends to carry out the undertaking or does not have fraudulent intent. It is sufficient if, afterwards, he turns around and denies this beneficial interest and claims that by virtue of the conveyance he is entitled to the whole and absolute ownership.[64] Furthermore, there does not have to be an express stipulation that the transferee will hold "on

---

61   [1948] 2 All E.R. 133.
62   [1948] 2 All E.R. 133, p.136.
63   Above, p.134.
64   Per Scott L.J., above, p.136.

trust" provided that a bargain is reached "under which some sufficiently defined beneficial interest in the property was to be taken by another".[65]

A similar case applying the fraud doctrine is *Pallant v Morgan*.[66] The agents of two neighbouring landowners were both intending to bid for property in an auction. They entered into an agreement immediately before the auction that the plaintiff's agent should not bid and that the defendant would acquire the land and divide it between himself and the plaintiff. The defendant's agent obtained the property as agreed and refused to honour the agreement. The agreement would have failed for lack of certainty. However, Harman J. refused to allow the defendant to plead this rule of law and held that the defendant held the property on trust for them jointly.[67] It would be fraudulent for the defendant to retain the whole of the property in denial of the agreement. The finding of fact that appeared material to the Harman J.'s decision was that the defendant's agent's conduct influenced the plaintiff's agent's action not to bid at the auction: "I do not think he would have acted in the way he did unless he at least thought he had reached such an agreement".[68] The headnote describes this as "the true view" of the situation.

> Modern pre-occupation with "division and order" of legal doctrine means that cases applying *Pallant v Morgan* are customarily dealt with as cases of proprietary estoppel, constructive trust, or as a sui generis category: "the *Pallant v Morgan* equity". In truth, *Pallant v Morgan* was decided on the same basis as *Rochefoucauld v Boustead*, i.e. that equity will not allow a statute to be used as an instrument of fraud.

And finally, in *Hodgson v Marks*[69] Mrs Hodgson was the sole owner of her house. Her lodger, Evans, gained her trust and she transferred the house to him on the oral understanding that he would hold it for her. After the conveyance of the house to Evans, he assumed full ownership, selling it to Mr Marks, who then mortgaged it. It was held that Mrs Hodgson retained the beneficial interest of the house, even though the arrangement that he would hold the house on trust had not been put in writing.[70]

LECTURER: So we considered first in this chapter that the transfer of land or the transfer or creation of any interest therein, is hedged about with a number of formality requirements. Can you recall what these are?

---

65   Per Scott L.J., above, p.136.
66   [1951] 1 Ch. 43, applying *Chattock v Muller* 8 Ch.D. 177.
67   [1951] 1 Ch. 43, p.47.
68   [1951] 1 Ch. 43, p.47.
69   [1971] Ch. 892.
70   [1971] Ch. 892, p.908 per Ungoed-Thomas J., at first instance. In *Lyus v Prowsa Developments Ltd* [1982] 1 W.L.R. 1044 the fraud doctrine was applied to land registration. See further Chapter 8.

STUDENT: Firstly where a contract is entered into for the transfer or creation of an estate or interest in land, that contract must be in writing and comply with s.2(1) of the Law of Property (Miscellaneous Provisions) Act 1989. For the creation or transfer of the legal estate or interest, there must be a deed (s.52 of the Law of Property Act 1925) which deed itself must comply with s.1 of the Law of Property (Miscellaneous Provisions) Act 1989. Then, to obtain the legal estate, the transferee must register his title at the Land Registry. And finally we saw that an express trust of land is not enforceable unless the trust is proved by writing: Law of Property Act 1925 s.53(1)(b).

LECTURER: And we have also seen that formality requirements such as these perform important functions: The cautionary function, the evidentiary function and the channelling function.

STUDENT: They also support the aims and policies of Land Law contained in our Building Blocks, for example BUILDING BLOCK NOS 5 and 6.

LECTURER: Yet in the very next section we read about cases that effectively ignore formality requirements and allow people to claim interests in land on the basis of agreements that are entirely oral: *Rochefoucauld v Boustead, Bannister v Bannister, Pallant v Morgan* and *Hodgson v Marks*. What is your gut reaction to these decisions? Do you think they are wrong because they effectively disapplied formality requirements?

STUDENT: No, quite the opposite. I think that the court did what was fair in the circumstances.

LECTURER: Let's see if we can come up with a more precise analysis. First of all look at all the cases and see if you can find some common ground between them.

> When you get cases that are grouped together always look for a common rationale. This is the beginning of an analysis of these cases.

STUDENT: In each of the above cases the material finding appeared to be that the legal owner, e.g. the brother-in-law in *Bannister*, the defendant's agent in *Pallant v Morgan*, Evans in *Hodgson v Marks*, all made a promise that when they became the full owners of the property, they would give effect to the oral arrangement.

LECTURER: And the various judges considered it important that the transfers (or refrain from action in *Pallant v Morgan*) were made on the compulsion of the promise. For example, the sister-in-law would not have transferred ownership of the cottages at a bargain price *but for* her brother-in-law's promise that she could live in one of them.

But why do you think that it would have been *unjust* to hold that the transferees could keep the property absolutely, i.e. the brother-in-law in *Bannister* or Evans in *Hodgson*?

STUDENT: Because once the transfer of ownership had been made there was nothing more that the transferor could do—they were entirely at the mercy of the transferee. The defendant in *Rochefoucauld v Boustead*, the brother-in-law in *Bannister*, the defendant's agent in

Pallant v Morgan all had the upper hand. And they had obtained this upper hand by promising that someone else would have a claim to the property.

LECTURER: So each transfer or action was made under the influence of the transferee's promise and the execution of the deed of transfer showed that the promise was relied upon. Thus, they should not be able to profit from this ascendant position by ignoring their promise.

> Story observes: "If the means of personal control are given, they must be always restrained to purposes of good faith and personal good (Story, *Commentaries on Equity Jurisprudence* (1834, first English edn 1884, repr. 1988), para.308). This appears to spell out the basis of the fraud doctrine.

LECTURER: Can you say whether the outcome of these cases creates good or bad law?
STUDENT: I think that this is good law on the basis of BUILDING BLOCK NO 2.

BUILDING BLOCK NO 2: Ideas of Justice

Rules are good and fair if they take account of moral justice: Every person should be accorded the freedom of their will and autonomous choice. Thus, if people deal with each other and with their property in a way that violates the will of another then the law should offer that other some remedy. We may legitimately say that Land Law is bad if it does not do so.

LECTURER: So if these cases had given no remedy at all to the persons who transferred the land on the basis of the promise, why would this violate the principle in BUILDING BLOCK NO 2?
STUDENT: Because in each case the transferees had influenced the free choices of the property owners. The owners' actions in conveying their land to the transferees (pretty life-defining actions) were influenced by the oral undertaking of those transferees that they would still have interests in the land.
LECTURER: So their will, and consequently their ability to make autonomous choices, was not "free" when the transfer was made.
STUDENT: In this situation, according to this moral principle, we can at least say that this puts a person morally in a position of trust. They should act in accordance with that person's best interests.
LECTURER: Or at least carry out their promises!
STUDENT: Otherwise the transferor's will has been violated.
LECTURER: Remember that when constructing our arguments we should practice asking questions.

Asking questions and imaginative argument

In what sense do you think the law is or is not protecting a person's freedom of choice, i.e. the ability to make uninfluenced choices? Are there any policies or principles (in your other Building Blocks) that might dictate that the law's intervention in this situation ought to be limited? Although justice is very definitely an article of faith for any legal system, the rules inevitably have to take into consideration competing concerns as we shall see below. You then decide whether the rules strike the right balance. For the person who is claiming that their freedom of choice is being threatened by a rule of Land Law, are they relying passively on the rules when they could have done something to protect themselves? If someone could have exercised their will to protect their interests, is there much justice in allowing them to remain passively reliant on the legal system to invent a rule to protect their interests?

STUDENT: OK then, there is a question that we can ask: Was the transferor's reliance in these cases reasonable? Surely people like the transferors in these cases could have protected their interests by insisting that all the terms of the oral arrangements with the defendants were put in writing?

LECTURER: There are two points which we can raise in response to this. Firstly, do you think that the transferors in this case would have been aware that they should have put these arrangements in writing? Ignorance of the formality requirement may in certain situations justify the courts' not insisting upon it.[71]

> "[U]nless things be so ordered that every one shall know what formalities are required, every law or rule of law imposing, on pain of nullity, the necessity of complying with any such formality, is a breach of faith on the part of the ruling power".
>
> Bentham, *Rationale of Judicial Evidence*, quoted P.Critchley, "Taking Formalities Seriously", in *Land Law Themes and Perspectives* (1998), p.522

STUDENT: Some of the people in these cases would probably not be aware of the requirement to put the agreements in writing, particularly Mrs Bannister. But surely, someone acting as an agent, as in *Pallant v Morgan*, ought to have been able to better protect the interests of their principal without relying on the law.

LECTURER: OK so let's look for a better justification. People in family relationships and relationships of mutual trust will habitually rely on each other. Thus they may simply act on the basis of trust and not put arrangements into their legal forms.[72]

---

71   P.Critchley, "Taking Formalities Seriously", in *Land Law Themes and Perspectives* (1998), from p.522.
72   Critchley, above, pp.523–6.

STUDENT: And so what we are saying is that the law should protect this type of reliance, and recognise parties' informal arrangements when it goes wrong?

LECTURER: If there is an overbearing of the will and some irrevocable action, yes.

> **Truth and reliance**
>
> "Veracity and fidelity would be of no significance were men not disposed to have faith and to rely upon what is said to them . . . Faith and trust, on the other hand, would be very hurtful principles were mankind void of veracity and fidelity: for upon that supposition the world would be overrun with fraud and deceit".
>
> Lord Kames, *Essays on the Principles of Morality and Natural Religion* (1751), p.114, quoted by P.S.Atiyah, *Promises, Morals and the Law*, p.14.

LECTURER: Can we now look at whether any important policies or Building Blocks are being *undermined* by the rule that "equity will not permit a statute to be used as an instrument of fraud".[73] Do you remember the "cautionary function" of formality?

> **The cautionary function:** Putting arrangements in writing means that the person making the transfer is forced to think carefully about what they are doing, to make sure that it is the right course of action.

STUDENT: Well, if people are unaware of the requirement of formality in the first place then it can never have this effect. Also where people trust each other and simply think that formality is unnecessary, the formal processes cannot perform this function.[74]

LECTURER: What about BUILDING BLOCK NO 5?

> **BUILDING BLOCK NO 5: Property Rights and the Protection of Purchasers and Mortgage Lenders**
>
> We can argue that a development of a rule in a case or statute is good or bad fair or unfair, depending on the extent to which it supports or undermines the idea that rules of Land Law should protect a purchaser or mortgage lender from being bound by prior interests in the land. This is the policy behind the 1925 property legislation.

---

73   In relation to formality, Critchley says that the various functions of formality provide us with "a checklist of factors which should be taken into consideration when decisions are being taken about formality": above, p.513.

74   Critchley, above.

STUDENT: Well, the cases which we have been discussing allow an interest in land to be created under a trust—*without any writing at all*.

LECTURER: And it is certainly not the sort of interest that must be registered at the Land Registry.

STUDENT: So potentially the "rogues" in these cases, the brother-in-law in *Bannister v Bannister* for example, could sell the land or mortgage it as soon as they have obtained the transfer, which is what happened in *Hodgson v Marks*. This means that the purchaser or mortgage lender may face the possibility that they will have to give priority to the earlier interest of the transferor. So potentially it is bad law.

LECTURER: Yes, once the transfer had been made, e.g. by Mrs Bannister to her brother-in-law, equity recognises that he holds the land on trust for her. This creates a property right that is capable of binding later purchasers and mortgage lenders.[75]

LECTURER: But whether or not the equitable rule is good or bad law because of this, all depends on the protection given to purchasers and mortgage lenders under our system of land transfer. Our main system of land transfer is the system of title registration (at the Land Registry).

A question of priority

So before we could address the question of whether the rule in *Rochefoucauld v Boustead* supports or undermines BUILDING BLOCK NO 5, we need to consider in Chapter 8 what kind of protection is offered to purchasers and mortgage lenders in such situations, e.g. although it is important that the interests belonging to people such as Mrs Hodgson in *Hodgson v Marks* and the sister-in-law in *Bannister v Bannister*, are protected from disruption due to fraud, there may also be innocent third parties involved. Generally speaking the balance is struck on the basis of what the purchaser could have discovered about the presence of a person with a prior right, such as Mrs Hodgson, upon a reasonably careful inspection of the land. In *Hodgson v Marks* title to the house was registered. The rule is different in relation to unregistered land: see Chapter 7. In the Court of Appeal in *Hodgson v Marks* Russell L.J. held that Mrs Hodgson's beneficial interest had priority over that of the later mortgagee: "As to the defendant building society it is plain that it made no inquiries on the spot save as to repairs; it relied on Mr Marks, who lied to it; and I waste no tears on it": [1971] Ch. 892, p.932.

STUDENT: One more possible argument is that the courts should not be able to set aside the plain terms of a statute in the interests of fairness. This contravenes the principle of Parliamentary Supremacy.

---

75   For an explanation of the idea of a property right and its binding effects, see BUILDING BLOCK NO 5 in Chapter 1.

LECTURER: Well, at least in relation to trusts more modern cases tend to take the line of least resistance and say that the transferee, e.g. the brother in law in *Bannister v Bannister*, hold their legal title on *constructive trust*, a form of implied trust, for the transferor, e.g. the sister-in-law in that case.

> **Constructive trusts and the rule in *Rochefoucauld v Boustead***
>
> In *Bannister v Bannister* it was held that although the conveyance to the brother-in-law gave him the legal title, he held the land on constructive trust to give effect to his sister-in-law's beneficial interest. Resulting and constructive trusts are exempt from the formality that trusts of land should be manifested and proved in writing: Law of Property Act 1925 s.53(2). They can come into being entirely orally. There is an obvious appeal to this as it means that the courts can give effect to the parties' oral arrangements without appearing to contradict an Act of parliament. However, the trust enforced in *Rochefoucauld v Boustead* was an express trust: T.G.Youdan [1984] C.L.J. 306, p.330–3. It was a trust which both parties intended to create. The same may technically be said of *Bannister* as there was an express intention to give effect to Mrs Bannister's life interest.

(1) A modern take on an ancient principle

The principle that equity will not permit a statute to be used as an instrument of fraud is an ancient one.[76] However, it has been applied directly to resolve a property dispute in a recent Court of Appeal case.

De Bruyne v De Bruyne[77] concerned a trust of shares. The family agreed to dissolve an existing trust and create a new trust and H agreed to act as trustee. Under this agreement H was to act as trustee for his children. H procured a transfer of the shares on the basis of this agreement. He denied the interests of the children in the shares and transferred them to W, who knew that the transfer was not a gift to her. She sold them and together they spent the proceeds on property and other shares. The Court of Appeal imposed a constructive trust for the benefit of the children. Relying on *Rochefoucauld v Boustead*[78] and *Bannister v Bannister*[79] the Court of Appeal confirmed that because the trustees of the original trust would not have transferred the shares to H unless he had agreed to hold them on trust for the children, it would be unconscionable to allow H to keep the shares beneficially.

"In these circumstances, it is impossible, in my view, to regard [H] as having been free to deal with the shares as his own. The assurance given . . . was that the shares would belong

---

76   P.S.Atiyah, *The Rise and Fall of Freedom of Contract* (Oxford University Press, 1979); Story, *Commentaries on Equity Jurisprudence*, first English edn, W.E.Grigsby ed., 1884.

77   [2010] EWCA Civ 519.

78   [1897] 1 Ch. 196.

79   [1948] 2 All E.R. 133.

to the children and would be [transferred] for that purpose. It was not merely a statement of intention or best endeavours as to what might happen at some indeterminate point in the future."[80]

Patten L.J.[81] considered that the rule in *Rochefoucauld v Boustead* did not require detrimental reliance on the part of the would-be beneficiaries, in this case, the children.[82] The rule concentrates "on the circumstances in which the transferee came to acquire the property in order to provide the justification for the imposition of a trust". If a person acquires property and agrees that they will hold it on trust, then "equity will regard it as against conscience for the owner of the property to deny the terms upon which he received it".[83]

Patten L.J. compared the rule to the rationale for the enforcement of express trusts by equity. They are enforced because the express trustee receives the property subject to the terms in the trust instrument. Under the rule in *Rochefoucauld* the trust is imposed following the transfer in order to prevent the transferee's fraudulent conduct. However it is highly arguable that there is no appreciable difference in theory here. Lord Nottingham stated that he enforced express trusts because to do otherwise would permit "manifest fraud".[84] An early documented case involving an express trust was *Mildmay & Duckett's Case*.[85] There had been an arrangement whereby the defendant had agreed to hold the estate in land for the benefit of another. The issue was whether the defendant could keep the lands for himself. Emphatically, Lord Nottingham declared that:

"all the deeds obtained by the defendant were in trust for the plaintiff. For else I should be obliged to set them all aside as being gained by a manifest fraud and circumvention".[86]

Another point held in *De Bruyne v De Bruyne* by Patten L.J. was that it was incorrect to search for a detriment on behalf of the would-be beneficiaries, the children.[87] However, to say that there is no reliance at all in such cases is also inaccurate.[88] In effect it is the transferor who relies on the

---

80   [2010] EWCA Civ 519, para.53, per Patten L.J..
81   In the Court of Appeal, with whom Sir Paul Kennedy and Thorpe L.J. agreed.
82   Rochefoucauld, para.51.
83   Rochefoucauld, para.51.
84   The trust was originally called the "use". Their existence was threatened by the Statute of Uses 1535, passed by Henry VIII because "uses" were depriving him of revenue due under the feudal system. Whenever land was held for the benefit of another the Act transferred the legal ownership of the land to that other. Thus it was not possible to hold land for another. Lawyers soon found ways to circumvent this and the modern version of the use, "the trust", was recognised by Lord Nottingham in the latter half of the seventeenth century. The trust was enforced to prevent "manifest fraud": Yale, "The Revival of Equitable Estates in the Seventeenth Century: An Explanation by Lord Nottingham" [1957] C.L.J. 72.
85   (case 822), quotation and citation: Yale, "The Revival of Equitable Estates in the Seventeenth Century: An Explanation by Lord Nottingham" [1957] C.L.J. 72, p.76 note 13.
86   Maitland referred to Lord Nottingham as "the father of Equity": *Lectures in Equity* (1936), p.10; Lord Nottingham formed and created the trust that we recognise today: Yale, "The Revival of Equitable Estates in the Seventeenth Century: An Explanation by Lord Nottingham" [1957] C.L.J. 72.
87   [2010] EWCA Civ 519, paras 44–48.
88   As Patten L.J. says in para.51: "These cases do not depend on some form of detrimental reliance in order to re-balance the equities between competing claimants for the property".

agreement by committing the irrevocable act of transfer.[89] It is this fact that gives rise to the idea that it would be unconscionable or fraudulent for the transferee to be permitted to renege on the terms of the agreement, hence the requirement that the transfer would not have been made *but for* the promise to hold it on trust.[90] However, it is quite correct that the detrimental reliance is not required of the would-be *beneficiary*, unless that person is also the transferor. The rule is engaged because of the power imbalance that arises when the transferor is no longer in a position of control over the property and is entirely at the mercy of the transferee, which, as seen in Lord Nottingham's analysis, is also the rationale for the enforcement of express trusts. As Patten L.J. acknowledges, express trusts and trusts that arise as a result of the rule in *Rochefoucauld v Boustead*[91] impose "fiduciary obligations"[92] to hold the property for the stipulated beneficiaries.

B. THE DOCTRINE OF PROPRIETARY ESTOPPEL[93]

We had a brief look at the doctrine of proprietary estoppel at the end of Chapter 2 when we constructed arguments about Equity using the case of *Gillett v Holt*.[94]

> See Chapter 2 section 4: Constructing an argument about equity with Building Blocks.

In this case we saw that under the doctrine of proprietary estoppel Mr Gillett became the owner of a farmhouse without anything being "put in writing".

> Mr Holt, a wealthy farmer, befriended Mr Gillett whilst he was a boy at school. Mr Gillett gave up school in order to work on the farm. All through his life, **Mr Holt promised him that he would inherit the farmhouse and the farming business.** Mr Holt did not formally transfer any property to him under s.52 of the Law of Property Act 1925. He did not contract to do so in any terms that satisfied s.2(1) of the Law of Property (Miscellaneous Provisions) Act 1989. And the will that he made in Mr Gillett's favour could be revoked by Mr Holt at any time during his lifetime: wills only take effect on the death of the testator.
>
> Thus, in formal legal terms Mr Gillett was entitled to nothing. As we might say "he did not have a leg to stand on". Nevertheless, the Court of Appeal awarded Mr Gillett the farmhouse and £100,000 compensation.

---

89 In all the cases examined above it has been the transferor who has also been claiming that the land is in reality held on trust for them, e.g. Mrs Bannister in *Bannister v Bannister*.
90 Evidently considered to be a necessary finding in this case itself by Patten L.J.
91 [1897] 1 Ch. 196.
92 paras 49 and 51 respectively.
93 See E.Cooke, *The Modern Law of Estoppel* (Oxford University Press, 2000).
94 [2001] Ch. 210.

WHY? **Mr Gillett had relied heavily on the assurances and promises given to him by Mr Holt** that he would inherit the farmhouse and business. In reliance on the assurances he spent his own money renovating the farmhouse—stepping off the property ladder himself. And he worked on the farm, declining to pursue alternative employment. **Mr Gillett was granted a remedy under the doctrine of proprietary estoppel.**

(1) An outline of proprietary estoppel

One of the earlier statements of the doctrine of proprietary estoppel is that of Lord Kingsdown in *Ramsden v Dyson*[95]:

"The rule of law applicable to the case appears to me to be this: If a man, under a verbal agreement with a landlord for a certain interest in land, or, what amounts to the same thing, under an expectation, created or encouraged by the landlord, that he shall have a certain interest, takes possession of such land, with the consent of the landlord, and upon the faith of such promise or expectation, with the knowledge of the landlord, and without objection by him, lays out money upon the land, a court of equity will compel the landlord to give effect to such promise or expectation."

The doctrine of proprietary estoppel has three component parts

Firstly, a landowner makes **assurances** to another to the effect that he will gain some property right, as Mr Holt promises that Mr Gillett would inherit his farm.

Secondly, the promisee undertakes conduct that shows he acts to his **detriment** in reliance on the assurance, e.g. spending money on the land as Mr Gillett did on the farmhouse.

Thirdly, these acts must be done in **reliance** on the assurances, i.e. the promisee would not have done what he did *but for* the belief that he was going to acquire an interest in the property.

If then the landowner goes back on his promise and denies the claimant an interest in his land, the claimant will be entitled to go to court and ask for a remedy.

Once these elements of assurance, reliance and detriment are established, the court may award the claimant a remedy against the promisor. The court can award a wide variety of remedies, as we will see below.

---

95   (1866) L.R. 1 H.L. 129, p.170. This was a landlord and tenant case, hence the language.

(a) The underpinning principle of unconscionability

The basis of the doctrine of proprietary estoppel is the principle of *unconscionability*.[96] Equity expects people to deal with their property in good faith. And thus, if the assurances of the landowner that the claimant is to have an interest in his land and the claimant's detrimental reliance on these assurances, are of such a nature that it shocks the conscience of the court to allow the landowner to go back on his promises, then the court will award the claimant a remedy.[97] This must not be taken to mean that the courts will merely award the claimant a remedy when they think it is fair to do so. The doctrine of proprietary estoppel has a principled basis.[98] There must be assurances and detrimental reliance. But then the court asks whether it would be against good conscience on the part of the legal owner to go back on his promises and deny the claimant an interest in the land.[99]

(2) Two stages to the claim

As you may see from the above description the doctrine of proprietary estoppel operates in two stages:

> Firstly, the pre-court stage: Once the claimant has received assurances and relied upon them to the extent to which it becomes unconscionable for the legal owner to go back on the assurances, we say that an "equity" has arisen in favour of the claimant. He has a right to go to court and ask for a remedy.

> Secondly, the court then "satisfies the equity" by awarding the claimant a remedy.

(3) Does the estoppel "equity" bind purchasers and mortgage lenders as a property right?

How does the doctrine of proprietary estoppel fit with our current appreciation of property rights in land and how they affect purchasers? In registered land, the right (or "equity") that arises in favour of the claimant at the pre-court stage, is a property right capable of binding purchasers and mortgage lenders. At this stage the claimant's rights are "inchoate" (incomplete)[100] and these rights are capable of binding successors in title if the land is registered.[101] Thus, had Mr Holt sold the farmhouse to X in order to try to rid himself of Gillett's claims before the court action, Gillett's equity by estoppel may bind X, the purchaser. The purchaser would then have to give effect to Gillett's rights in the land, whatever they may be. In this case, he would have had a prior claim to the farmhouse, which would be potentially catastrophic for the purchaser.

---

96   See M.Dixon, "Confining and defining proprietary estoppel: the role of unconscionability" (2010) 30 L.S. 408.
97   *Thorner v Major* [2009] UKHL 18.
98   *Cobbe v Yeoman's Row Management* [2008] UKHL 55.
99   *Crabb v Arun District Council* [1976] Ch. 179, p.187, per Lord Denning M.R.
100   G.Battersby (1995) 58 M.L.R. 637, p.642.
101   Land Registration Act 2002 s.116.

> Under the registered land rules that we consider in Chapter 8, Gillett's right may bind X as an "overriding interest" irrespective of registration, if Gillett was "in actual occupation": Land Registration Act 2002 Sch.3, para.2.
>
> The case then becomes similar to *Williams & Glyn's Bank Ltd v Boland* [1981] A.C. 487.

The position is less clear where title to the land in question was unregistered, although the correct view is thought to be that the equity will bind successors in title.[102]

(4) The historical development of the doctrine of proprietary estoppel

Originally, the courts adhered to a rigid formula before a person could establish a claim under the doctrine of proprietary estoppel. This was known as the "five probanda" laid down in *Willmott v Barber*.[103] But even this case shows the centrality of the idea of *unconscionability*—or, as it used to be called "equitable fraud". In this case Fry J. observed that:

"A man is not to be deprived of his legal rights unless he has acted in such a way as would make it fraudulent for him to set up those rights. What, then, are the elements or requisites necessary to constitute fraud of that description? In the first place the plaintiff must have made a mistake as to his legal rights. Secondly, the plaintiff must have expended some money or must have done some act . . . on the faith of his mistaken belief. Thirdly, the defendant, the possessor of the legal right, must know of the existence of his own right which is inconsistent with the right claimed by the plaintiff . . . Fourthly, the defendant . . . must know of the plaintiff's mistaken belief of his rights. If he does not, there is nothing which calls upon him to assert his own rights. Lastly, the defendant . . . must have encouraged the plaintiff in his expenditure of money or in the other acts which he has done, either directly or by abstaining from asserting his legal right. Where all these

1. X thinks that he owns land adjacent to his house. In fact the land belongs to Y

2. X builds a house

3. Y knows that he owns the land not X

4. Y knows that X wrongly thinks the land belongs to X

5. Y encouraged X to build on the land Court will not allow Y to assert his rights over the land

---

102   *Inwards v Baker* [1965] 2 Q.B. 29, p.37, per Lord Denning M.R. See G.Battersby (1995) 58 M.L.R. 637, pp.641–2.
103   (1881) 15 Ch.D. 96, pp.105–6.

elements exist, there is fraud of such a nature as will entitle the court to restrain the possessor of the legal right from exercising it".

(5) The modern law of estoppel

We can see from this that the essential nature of the claim under the doctrine of proprietary estoppel is that the legal owner of property has fostered an expectation in the mind of the claimant that he will have an interest in land. And the claimant has relied upon this expectation to his detriment. It is this which makes it "fraudulent" for the legal owner of the land to deny that the claimant has any rights. As Oliver J. stated in *Taylors Fashions Ltd v Liverpool Trustees Co* "the 'fraud' in these cases is not to be found in the transaction itself but in the subsequent attempt to go back upon the basic assumptions which underlay it".[104] The *fraud* element is now referred to as *unconscionability*.[105]

BUILDING BLOCK NO 2: Ideas of Justice

Once a person influences the actions and conduct of another, that person's will is not free. It is at this point that retraction of any promise becomes immoral. Throughout our examination of the doctrine of estoppel we will consider whether the application of the rules by the courts reflects this idea of moral justice. Indeed, according to Professor Atiyah, it is detrimental reliance upon a promise which makes that promise morally binding: P.Atiyah, *Promises, Morals and Law*.

The modern law of estoppel has moved on from the rigid formula in *Willmott v Barber*.[106] It is no longer considered necessary to prove that the claimant is *mistaken* in his belief that he owns an interest in the land.[107] Indeed in most of the modern cases we shall consider neither side is mistaken as to their rights. The courts now look at the quality of the assurances and the nature of the claimant's detrimental reliance in order to ascertain whether it would be unconscionable to allow the legal owner to go back on his promises and insist on his strict legal rights.[108] In *Taylors Fashions Ltd v Liverpool Trustees Co*[109] Oliver J. stated that the doctrine of proprietary estoppel

"requires a very much broader approach which is directed rather at ascertaining whether, in particular individual circumstances, it would be unconscionable for a party to be permitted to deny that which, knowingly, or unknowingly, he has allowed or encouraged another to

---

104   [1982] 1 Q.B. 133, p.147.
105   It has been indicated that "fraud" and "unconscionability" in this context mean more or less the same thing: *Crabb v Arun D.C.* [1976] 1 Ch. 179, p.195 per Scarman L.J.
106   (1881) 15 Ch.D. 96.
107   In true cases of estoppel by acquiescence, where a landowner merely sits back and allows another to spend money on his land in the mistaken belief that he has an interest in it, it may be necessary to establish the five *Willmott v Barber probanda*, but see the doubt of this expressed by the Court of Appeal in *Shaw v Applegate* [1977] 1 W.L.R. 970.
108   *Gillett v Holt* [2001] Ch. 210, p.225, per Robert Walker L.J.
109   [1982] 1 Q.B. 133, pp.151–2.

assume to his detriment than to inquiring whether the circumstances can be fitted within the confines of some preconceived formula serving as a universal yardstick for every form of unconscionable behaviour."

(6) The elements of the doctrine of estoppel

(a) Assurance

There must be some assurance by the landowner that another will have some interest in their land.

> **Mr Holt owned a farm and kept repeating to Mr Gillett that "One day all of this will be yours". He repeated this assurance on important family occasions, which added to its solemnity and credibility.**
> *Gillett v Holt* [2001] Ch. 210

> **The legal owner of a house assured his girlfriend that "the house is yours and everything in it". This was sufficient to meet the requirement of an assurance of an interest in land.**
> *Pascoe v Turner* [1979] 1 W.L.R. 431

The assurance made by the landowner does not need to be accurate or precise as to the exact nature of the interest that the claimant can expect.[110] Indeed, the promise made might lead the claimant to expect a right of occupation for life, rather than an ownership right. In *Greasley v Cooke*,[111] the claimant was promised that she could live in the house rent free for as long as she wished.[112]

The quality of the assurance must be such that it is capable of inducing a reasonable person to rely on it. Thus, the assurance must be sufficiently strong and clear.[113] It is only where an assurance is capable of engendering a reasonable expectation, and when it is subsequently relied upon, that it could be said to be unconscionable for the legal owner to insist on his strict legal rights. Despite judicial suggestions to the contrary[114] the House of Lords in *Thorner v Major*[115] has recently held that it is not necessary for the assurances to be made with the intent that they should be relied upon.

---

110 *Thorner v Major* [2009] UKHL 18. For earlier authority for this proposition see *Inwards v Baker* [1965] 2 Q.B. 29, p.37, per Lord Denning M.R.; *Plimmer v Wellington Corporation* (1884) 9 App. Cas. 699, pp.713–4 PC.
111 [1980] 1 W.L.R. 1306.
112 See also *Matharu v Matharu* [1994] 2 F.L.R. 597.
113 *Thorner v Major* [2009] UKHL 18, para.15, per Lord Scott.
114 *Gillett v Holt*, per Robert Walker L.J.; *Crabb v Arun D.C.* [1976] 1 Ch. 179, p.188, per Lord Denning M.R.; *Brikom Investments Ltd v Carr* [1979] Q.B. 467, p.482–3 per Lord Denning M.R.
115 *Thorner v Major* [2009] UKHL 18.

"It was enough that the meaning he conveyed would reasonably have been understood as intended to be taken seriously as an assurance which could be relied upon."[116]

LECTURER: Can you relate this to BUILDING BLOCK NO 2—our ideas of moral justice?

> **BUILDING BLOCK NO 2: Ideas of Justice**
> Every person should be accorded the freedom of their will and autonomous choice. Thus, if people deal with each other and with their property in a way that violates the will of another then the law should offer that other some remedy.

STUDENT: It appears that the cases emphasise the fact that the assurance must be capable of inducing reliance, i.e. it must be reasonable for the claimant to rely on it.

LECTURER: And how does this relate to our BUILDING BLOCK NO 2?

STUDENT: If the courts are looking for the assurance to be strong enough to induce reasonable reliance, they clearly think it important to establish that the claimant's will was materially affected by the promise—i.e. he no longer had free will because his choices had been determined by the promise.

The courts consider the question of whether the assurance engenders a reasonable expectation, in the context of the facts of the case[117]: "to establish a proprietary estoppel the relevant assurance must be clear enough. What amounts to sufficient clarity . . . is hugely dependent on context".[118] For example, in *Gillett v Holt*,[119] Mr Holt treated the Gilletts as a surrogate family and promised Mr Gillett on several solemn family occasions that he would inherit his farm. Mr Gillett then acted on this promise by not making any plans for his future and by not insisting that Mr Holt put the arrangement in writing, which was quite a risk to take. However, because of the way in which Mr Holt had treated the Gilletts as his own family, this was held to be an expectation on which it was reasonable for Mr Gillett to rely.

LECTURER: Gillett's power of determining his life choices, his free will, could reasonably be said to have been affected in these circumstances.

Also in *Inwards v Baker*[120] the claimant wished to build a bungalow on land, but could not afford the price for the land. So his father said "Why not put the bungalow on my land and make the bungalow a little bigger". His father had encouraged him to give up the prospect of owning his own land. The son built on the father's land. The father contributed to the expenditure and

---

116   per Lord Hoffman, para 5; per Lord Scott, para.17.

117   In *Gillett v Holt* [2001] Ch. 210 Robert Walker L.J. said that it was important for a judge in such cases to "look at the matter in the round".

118   *Thorner v Major* [2009] UKHL 18, per Lord Walker para.56; N.Hopkins (2011) 31 L.S. 175.

119   [2001] Ch. 210.

120   [1965] 2 Q.B. 29.

visited him at the bungalow. The son remained there for over 30 years. It was held that in all these circumstances it could be found that the father had "allowed an expectation to be created in the son's mind that this bungalow was to be his home".[121]

LECTURER: It showed that the son's decision to build the bungalow and to stay living in it, was materially affected by the father's actions and statements, and in these circumstances, reasonably so. Due to the influence of his father, he was not exercising a free choice. The father may have had every intention that his promise would be carried out to the letter. This is not the point. What counts is his *influence* over the actions of his son, which then led to his son changing his life's course in this material way.

Similarly, in *Re Basham*[122] the claimant's mother and step-father lived in a cottage. The claimant helped her mother and step-father in many ways. Although she was given no payment she was given to understand that she would inherit the estate of her step-father. The judge held that the claimant was entitled to the estate under the doctrine of estoppel. The promises made to the claimant had not been exactly expressed or stated, e.g. she would not "lose by" her help. However, this was in keeping with the character of the family and the nature of their relationship with the claimant. Thus, it was held that these statements formed a reasonable expectation in the mind of the claimant.

(i) The House of Lords' decision in Thorner v Major

Given the above therefore, the finding of an assurance and the question of whether it engenders reasonable reliance depends on many factors such as how the parties' normally relate to each other on a day to day basis; their knowledge of each other; the history of the relationship, and whether it is the type of relationship in which faith and trust are habitual.

In *Thorner v Major*,[123] the claimant sought to establish a proprietary estoppel in relation to a farm. The owner of the farm was the cousin of his father and the claimant had worked unpaid on the farm for 30 years. The owner had made a will leaving his estate (after several legacies) to the claimant,[124] but revoked it because of a quarrel with one of the legatees. Thus, he died intestate and the claimant brought this action against the statutory next of kin. The circumstances of the case were unusual. There was never an express assurance that the claimant would inherit the farm. The two men were taciturn and "hardly ever spoke in direct terms". But they understood each other well and were close. The judge found that the owner made several oblique remarks[125] which, in these circumstances, led the claimant to expect reasonably that he would inherit the farm. He also found that the conduct of the two men also engendered this expectation. The owner once handed the claimant an insurance document stating "That's for my death duties".

---

121   Lord Denning M.R. above p.37.
122   [1986] 1 W.L.R. 1498.
123   [2009] UKHL 18; [2009] 1 W.L.R. 776.
124   A fact not known to the claimant.
125   For example, "[the owner] would point out to him little things about the farm which would only be of relevance to someone with [continuing long-term involvement]".

The House of Lords[126] held that given the claimant's knowledge of his cousin, and their strong relationship, it was reasonable for him to take the oblique remarks and conduct as a serious assurance that he was going to inherit the farm. Because the claimant had remained working at the farm unpaid, and did not move away as he had been considering, the estoppel claim had been made out.

LECTURER: Equity protected the faith and trust inherent in human nature, and this case shows that where one person has attracted this fidelity and consequent power over the other, the law will not allow the basis of that fidelity to be freely revoked. Although equity attaches the label that "it would be unconscionable to allow the promisee to go back on his promise", in *Thorner*, the promisor did not act against good conscience in trying to revoke the promise. He simply died without making a will and the claim was brought against his next of kin. This shows that proprietary estoppel is essentially "claimant-centred". It searches for the element of trust and confidence, which is as old as the equitable jurisdiction itself.

Lord Walker thought that a sufficiently clear promise of future inheritance was acceptable as an assurance, even though all parties would probably know that if circumstances radically altered, e.g. if it became necessary to sell the property, it would no longer be reasonable to expect that inheritance. If in the circumstances the promise can be construed as sufficiently strong that it is reasonable for the claimant to rely upon it, this can give rise to an estoppel, even if it is well understood that wills can generally be revoked.[127]

(b) Reliance

A promise that the claimant will have an interest in land becomes irrevocable once the claimant relies on that promise to their detriment. The court will infer reliance from the strength of the assurance and the quality of the acts undertaken by the claimant by way of detriment.[128] It is thus not necessary for the claimant to prove that their actions of detrimental reliance proceeded from their belief in the assurance that they would have some right in the land. This is presumed in the claimant's favour. It is for the legal owner to prove that the acts of detriment were *not* motivated by the promise.

In *Greasley v Cooke*[129] a woman had been employed as a housekeeper. Once her employer died, she stayed on to look after his family, and had a relationship with one of his sons. She took no wages and was encouraged by members of the family to believe that she would be able to live there for the rest of her life. The trial judge had stated that it was necessary for her to prove that her acts of detriment, i.e. looking after the family and taking no wages, were undertaken as a result of the belief, and not simply because she wanted to help. In the Court of Appeal Lord

---

126   Lord Walker giving the leading judgment.
127   *Gillett v Holt* [2001] Ch. 210.
128   *Gillett v Holt* [2001] Ch. 210.
129   [1980] 1 W.L.R. 1306.

Denning M.R. held this to be wrong. There is a presumption of reliance once it is proven that the representations would influence the mind of the reasonable person.[130]

(c) Detriment

Whether or not a person has suffered a detriment will be considered at the point "when the person who has given the assurance seeks to go back on it".[131] It will then be determined whether the claimant has been so prejudiced by the acts and conduct they undertook in reliance on the promise that it would be unconscionable to allow the owner to go back on their assurances. The conduct relied upon as "detriment" must be "sufficiently substantial to justify the intervention of equity".[132] Clearly the expenditure of money on land will suffice as a detriment.[133] But financial expenditure is not a pre-requisite. Robert Walker L.J. stated in *Gillett v Holt* that detriment "is not a narrow or technical concept".

> **Example**
> In *Gillett v Holt*, in reliance on repeated assurances from Mr Holt that he would inherit his farming business and farmhouse, Mr Gillett had continued to work for Mr Holt and had acted beyond the scope of an employee. He had sold his house and thereby stepped off the property ladder in order to move into the farmhouse. He had not taken steps to provide for his future, and had spent money renovating the farmhouse. This was held to be substantial detriment spanning a considerable number of years. Robert Walker L.J. held that the case was "an unusually compelling one". When considering this conduct against the repeated assurances by Mr Holt that he would inherit, often made on solemn family occasions, it became clear that "Mr Gillett had an exceptionally strong claim on Mr Holt's conscience".

LECTURER: Why do you think it is necessary for the claimant to show that they acted to their detriment?

STUDENT: Well, in these cases we see people influenced by assurances that they will gain property, and will thus be materially more secure. They demonstrate this influence by showing that they have made certain choices connected with their lives *on the basis of the assurance*. They may have decided to spend money on the land, or given up employment prospects elsewhere, as in the *Gillett v Holt* example above. They have not done this of their own free will but because they were influenced by the promises made by the landowner.

LECTURER: So "detriment" shows that the claimant *has* in fact been influenced by the legal owner and it shows that he has suffered loss as a result.

---

130   *Greasley v Cooke* [1980] 1 W.L.R. 1306, p.1311 per Lord Denning M.R. Also *Brikom Investments Ltd v Carr* [1979] Q.B. 467, p.482–3 per Lord Denning M.R.
131   *Gillett v Holt*, per Robert Walker L.J.
132   *Thorner v Major* [2009] UKHL 18, para.15, per Lord Scott.
133   *Inwards v Baker* [1965] 2 Q.B. 29; *Pascoe v Turner* [1979] 1 W.L.R. 431.

LECTURER: So the doctrine of proprietary estoppel provides the law with a means of giving effect to moral justice.

> **BUILDING BLOCK NO 2: Ideas of Justice**
> Rules can be legitimately argued to be good and fair if they take account of moral justice: Every person should be accorded the freedom of their will and autonomous choice. Thus, if people deal with each other and with their property in a way that violates the will of another, and which causes that other loss, then the law should offer that other some remedy.

(i) Examples of "detriment"

Detriment has been established when a woman worked unpaid as a housekeeper and looked after a family member who was seriously mentally ill.[134] Conversely in *Coombes v Smith*[135] a man bought a house and promised his mistress that "she would always have a roof over her head". She claimed detrimental reliance on the basis that she had left her husband in order to live with him, redecorated the house and allowed herself to become pregnant by him. It was held that this was insufficient as it was attributable not to the promise of an interest in the house but to the nature of the parties' relationship.[136] In *Wayling v Jones*[137] a homosexual couple lived together. The older partner owned a hotel and the claimant worked for him for very little money. The former had promised that he would leave the hotel to the claimant in his will. The claimant's continued work in the hotel was held to be sufficient detrimental reliance. In *Campbell v Griffin*[138] the claimant was lodger to a frail elderly couple. He came to be treated by them as a son and looked after them as their carer. He had been promised that he would have a home in the house for life and it was held that he had relied sufficiently on this to his detriment by acting as their carer in particularly demanding circumstances.

(7) The requirements of assurance, reliance and detriment—Cobbe v Yeoman's Row Management Ltd[139]

THE FACTS: The defendant owned valuable property with potential for residential development. The claimant was an experienced property developer and business man. They orally agreed that the defendant would sell the property to the claimant for £12m. He would, at his own expense, do the work required to obtain planning permission for six town houses and he would develop the land. They also agreed to divide profits from the development. This was an "agreement in principle" to enter

---

134   *Greasley v Cooke* [1980] 1 W.L.R. 1306, p.1314 per Dunn L.J.
135   [1985] 1 W.L.R. 808.
136   Compare *Maharaj v Chand* [1986] A.C. 898—sufficient detriment where a woman gave up her own secure accommodation to live with her lover: see Thompson [2003] 67 Conv. 157.
137   [1995] 2 F.L.R. 1029.
138   [2001] EWCA Civ 990.
139   [2008] UKHL 55; [2008] 1 W.L.R. 1752. See also T.Etherton [2009] Conv. 104; M.Dixon [2009] Conv. 260, p.265; N.Hopkins (2011) 31 L.S. 175; M.Dixon (2010) 30 L.S. 408.

into a binding contract for sale of the land. Both knew that it was not legally binding and that a binding contract was needed under the Law of Property (Miscellaneous Provisions) Act 1989.

After the claimant had completed the work for the planning permission, and spent considerable sums in the process, the defendant announced that she was not going to honour their oral agreement. In fact, she had made up her mind to go back on the agreement months before the defendant had completed the work for the planning permission. But she did not tell him because she wanted the preliminary work done.

LECTURER: I think most would probably agree that the defendant's behaviour was highly unethical. But the Court of Appeal held that it was *unconscionable* and that the claimant could establish a claim by proprietary estoppel.

The House of Lords overturned this decision and criticised the reasoning of the Court of Appeal. Lord Scott stated that a proprietary estoppel could not be established *solely* on the basis that a legal owner has acted *unconscionably*. This is far too subjective, as one judge's idea of what is unconscionable may differ from another's. Consequently there would be uncertainty and unpredictability in the law. The Court of Appeal had not properly considered that a claim to a proprietary estoppel is based on a sufficiently strong assurance that the claimant will have an interest in land, and the fact that the claimant has relied on this to their detriment.

The House of Lords allowed the defendant's appeal and held that the claim to a proprietary estoppel, preventing her from insisting on the fact that she was the absolute owner of the property, was not established.

LECTURER: We will look at the precise reasoning *why* the House of Lords came to this conclusion in a moment. Let us firstly consider the House of Lords' "certainty" argument. Lord Walker considered that if a proprietary estoppel could be established solely on the basis that the court considered the legal owner's behaviour to be *unconscionable* then this would give rise to uncertainty in commercial transactions. So the House of Lords was saying that the Court of Appeal's decision was bad on the basis of one of our Building Blocks.[140]
STUDENT: BUILDING BLOCK NO 6.

BUILDING BLOCK NO 6: The Need for Certainty and Predictability in Land Law Rules
It is important for legal rules to have clear and predictable outcomes so that the parties know the legal consequences of their actions. People should not have to litigate in order to find out what their rights are. We can legitimately say that rules are good or bad depending on whether they support or undermine this policy.

---

140   Remember that we can say that a rule of Land Law is good or bad fair or unfair depending on the extent to which it supports or undermines any of the policies or aims in our Building Blocks. For the full text of our Building Blocks and instructions on how to use them to create an argument about Land Law rules see Chapter 1.

LECTURER: Why do you think that the Court of Appeal's decision undermined the policy in this Building Block?

STUDENT: The case took place in the commercial context. In this context people to want to develop land. They may also want to enter into joint ventures with other business people and share the profits of developing the land, as in this case, or want to transact with land on any other commercial basis.

LECTURER: Yes, but why do you think legal certainty is important *in these situations*?

STUDENT: Parties need to know exactly when they have entered into binding agreements and what legal obligations they are under in relation to the property. If this depends on how any court at any time will interpret the vague word "unconscionable", people involved in commercial dealings with land will not know what their obligations are without going to court to find out.

> Proprietary estoppel "is not a sort of joker or wild card to be used whenever the court disapproves of the conduct of a litigant who seems to have the law on his side".
> Lord Walker, para.46.

LECTURER: And what if the defendant in *Cobbe* had sold her land to a third party in the meantime—or mortgaged it? We know that the "equity" that arises under the doctrine of proprietary estoppel is an interest in land that is capable of binding purchasers and mortgage lenders. Could you say that the Court of Appeal decision was good or bad on the basis of any other of our Building Blocks?

STUDENT: I would use BUILDING BLOCK NO 5.

> **BUILDING BLOCK NO 5: Property Rights and the Protection of Purchasers and Mortgage Lenders**
> We may legitimately say that a rule of Land Law is good or bad fair or unfair depending on the extent to which it protects a purchaser from being bound by too many property rights that could not have been discovered prior to the purchase.

STUDENT: If an estoppel claim can be established solely on the vague basis that it is *unconscionable* to allow the defendant to go back on the promise, without sufficient regard to the other elements of proprietary estoppel, then many more property rights may come into existence.

> Dixon poses the question: "Just how far can estoppel go in permitting the generation of property rights in the absence of normally required formality"? (M.Dixon, "Proprietary estoppel: a return to principle?" [2009] Conv. 260, pp.266–7).

LECTURER: And why does this situation potentially undermine BUILDING BLOCK NO 5?

STUDENT: Those rights are then capable of affecting later purchasers of the land. This will be bad for them as someone may have a prior claim to the land. The law would not be giving protection to purchasers and mortgage lenders.

LECTURER: But what questions might we need to ask before we can conclude *definitely* that the law does not protect third party purchasers of the land?

STUDENT: We need to know the circumstances in which a right acquired by proprietary estoppel will actually bind a purchaser or mortgage lender.

Asking questions and arguing imaginatively

Note that we are not just accepting that an increase in number of property rights would automatically undermine the policy of purchaser protection. We are cross-examining the evidence by asking questions!

LECTURER: This is determined by the rules of Land Transfer Law, in Chapters 7 and 8. We would need to look to see whether those rules protect purchasers from being bound by a right that they could not have discovered in advance of the purchase. If this is not the case the Court of Appeal decision in *Cobbe* would have been very threatening indeed.

Just briefly for now, under the rules of registered land law it is possible for an estoppel equity to be an "overriding interest". The claimant would have to prove that they were *in actual occupation of the land*. Effectively what this means is that their interest will bind a purchaser even though it has not been registered.[141] And at this point then, the case would look like *Williams & Glyn's Bank Ltd v Boland*, see Chapter 1, section 4.

The House of Lords overturned the decision of the Court of Appeal in *Cobbe v Yeoman's Row Management Ltd*. "Unconscionability" should not be used in a general sense as a remedy where the court disapproved of the defendant's conduct.[142] The elements of assurance and detrimental reliance must be established.

The claim failed largely on the "assurance" point. Lord Scott, with whom the other Law Lords agreed, held that the assurance made by the defendant, on which the claimant relied by working to obtain planning permission, was that she would enter into a binding contract with him in the future. Thus, there was no assurance that the claimant would get an *interest in land*, a required element of proprietary estoppel. As Lord Walker observed, the claimant was expecting to get a contract, not an interest in property.[143]

Apart from this point, both Lord Scott and Lord Walker[144] held that there was no assurance on which it was reasonable for the claimant to rely. Lord Walker considered it crucial that "the

---

141   The relevant rules are covered by Land Registration Act 2002 Sch.3 para.2. See Chapter 8. See also above in this Chapter, section 2, p.123.

142   [2008] UKHL 55, Lord Scott, para.16.

143   [2008] UKHL 55, para.87; also Lord Scott, para.20.

144   With both of whom the other Law Lords agreed.

claimant believed that the assurance on which he or she relied was binding and irrevocable".[145] Here, both parties knew that their original agreement that the land would be sold to the claimant and the profits of the development divided between them, was not legally binding.

> "The terms that had already been agreed were regarded by the parties as being 'binding in honour', but it follows that the parties knew they were not legally binding."[146]

The claimant was an experienced property developer and knew the defendant. He was aware that she would not regard the arrangement between them as legally binding. Both knew that a formal contract was necessary under s.2(1) of the Law of Property (Miscellaneous Provisions) Act 1989 before any legal rights came into being.[147] Lord Walker observed that the claimant took a calculated risk that the defendant would not honour the agreement.[148]

> The significance of these findings appears to be that it could not be said that the belief that the defendant would honour the oral agreement was a material factor in inducing the claimant's work and expenditure on the planning permission.

LECTURER: Does this reasoning reflect our ideas of moral justice in BUILDING BLOCK NO 2?

> **BUILDING BLOCK NO 2: Ideas of Justice**
> If people deal with each other and with their property in a way that violates the will of another, and which causes that other loss, then the law should offer some remedy.

STUDENT: The House of Lords, particularly Lord Walker in the point immediately above, took pains to establish that the claimant did the work on the planning permission entirely of his own free will. He was not induced to do it by the defendant.

LECTURER: Therefore we can say that the claimant's will was not overborne or controlled in any way by the promises of the defendant to enter into a binding contract for the sale of the land.

STUDENT: No. The House of Lords' reasoning is consistent with ideas of moral justice in BUILDING BLOCK NO 2.

---

145   [2008] UKHL 55, para.67.
146   para.15, per Lord Scott. The proposed property venture was, in any event, highly speculative and at a very early stage. The fact that the claimant may have made nothing from it shows that he was not trusting the defendant for any particular advantage anyway: see per Lord Walker [2008] UKHL 55, paras.88–90.
147   See also M.Dixon (2010) 30 L.S. 408.
148   [2008] UKHL 55 para.89.

> Thus, the Court of Appeal were not so much at fault for deciding for the claimant *solely* because the defendant's conduct was unconscionable, but because it ought to have made the finding that it *was not unconscionable*. So in this respect Lord Scott was also wrong. The reason the courts require the components of "assurance" and "reliance" is to ascertain whether there was a reasonable trust and confidence placed in the promisor and whether that trust and confidence had led to the claimant suffering harm. Only then would it be unconscionable for the legal owner to go back on their promise.

LECTURER: But this does show us that the finding of a relevant "assurance" will depend heavily on the context in which the statements relied upon are made, as Lord Walker observes in *Thorner v Major*.[149]

   Are there any situations you can think of in a commercial context where it might have been reasonable for the claimant to rely upon an agreement that he knew was not legally binding?

STUDENT: What if the defendant had said definitely that by doing the work on the planning permission she would regard them both as owning the land jointly and would not take any steps to evict him?[150]

LECTURER: But even then it would be difficult to show that it was reasonable to regard this informal arrangement as irrevocable. It might be different if it was a family business venture.

STUDENT: Or if the parties were less experienced.

By way of summarising the issues involved in an estoppel claim in relation to agreements for the disposition of an interest in land, in *Herbert v Doyle*[151] Arden L.J. in the Court of Appeal held that proprietary estoppel or a constructive trust cannot be imposed to give effect to an oral agreement concerning the disposition of land, where the parties intended to formalise their arrangement at a later date, or where the parties' knew, as in *Cobbe v Yeoman's Row Management Ltd*, that the oral agreement could not be enforced. Indeed, in both such cases it could be said that there would be no "assurance" of an interest in land upon which it would be reasonable to rely (for reasons given in this section). If negotiations between the parties are made expressly "subject to contract", this cannot give rise to a realistic expectation that the agreement will be honoured, even if an oral agreement is reached.[152] It will be irrelevant that the claimant relied on it to his or her detriment. The expression "subject to contract" is understood widely to mean that there is no obligation to honour the agreement.

---

149 *Thorner v Major* [2009] UKHL 18, per Lord Walker para.56. See N.Hopkins, "The relevance of context in property law: a case for judicial restraint?" (2011) 31 L.S. 175.
150 Dixon takes a similar point (2010) 30 L.S. 408.
151 [2010] EWCA Civ 1095.
152 *Haq v Island Homes Housing Association* [2011] EWCA Civ 805.

Although a proprietary estoppel claim would be difficult to establish in the commercial context, it would not be impossible. In *Yaxley v Gotts*,[153] a claim was upheld in the context of an oral commercial arrangement that a builder would acquire the ground floor flat if he renovated the entire block. Although both parties clearly knew that a formalised contract was necessary to make this agreement enforceable, the distinguishing features of this case appear to be the long-term nature of the parties' relationship and the fact that both had appeared to agree that they would not resort to legal formality.[154]

Indeed, the obiter view of Lord Scott in *Cobbe v Yeoman's Row Management*[155] that a proprietary estoppel could *never* be established in the commercial context in order to enforce a verbal agreement that was void under Law of Property (Miscellaneous Provisions) Act 1989 s.2(1) was doubted in *Thorner v Major*. It has recently been observed at first instance by Bean J. that "notwithstanding Lord Scott's dicta in *Cobbe*, proprietary estoppel in a case involving a sale of land has survived the enactment of s.2 of the 1989 Act".[156] Indeed in *Whittaker v Kinnear*,[157] Bean J. remarked on "the fact sensitivity of claims based on proprietary estoppel or constructive trust".[158] In cases where the parties' relationship is more familial and informal, and characterised by trust and fidelity, the faith in the assurance being complied with is more likely to result in a perception of irrevocability[159]—even if (when pushed on the point in court) the claimants would admit to knowing that their arrangements are not legally binding.[160]

> "The typical domestic claimant does not stop to reflect (until disappointed expectations lead to litigation) whether some further legal transaction (such as a grant by deed, or the making or a will or codicil) is necessary to complete the promised title."[161]

LECTURER: And so finally, can you create an argument about whether the House of Lords' ruling in *Cobbe v Yeoman's Row Management* is good or bad law? Hold the reasoning against our Building Blocks and see whether it supports or undermines any of them.
STUDENT: I would use BUILDING BLOCK NO 6. The House of Lords make it much clearer what is required in order to establish a claim under the doctrine of proprietary estoppel. It makes it much more predictable in advance when obligations have arisen.

---

153   [2000] Ch. 162. The Lord Justices in this case did not feel it necessary to decide whether the agreement in question would have been specifically enforceable but for the requirement for the agreement to be in writing under s.2(1) of the Law of Property (Miscellaneous Provisions) Act 1989.
154   See also M.Dixon (2010) 30 L.S. 408. Although the Court of Appeal did not appear to scrutinise the "assurance" point that carefully. Beldam L.J. considered that the Law of Property (Miscellaneous Provisions) Act 1989 was not intended to preclude reliance on the doctrine of proprietary estoppel. Indeed, in *Haq v Island Homes Housing Association* [2011] EWCA Civ 805, it was considered possible that an assurance that an oral agreement would be binding and the arrangement would no longer be "subject to contract", may give rise to a proprietary estoppel.
155   [2008] UKHL 55.
156   *Whittaker v Kinnear* [2011] 2 P. & C.R. DG20, relying on *Herbert v Doyle* [2010] EWCA Civ 1095.
157   [2011] 2 P. & C.R. DG20.
158   From the report [2011] 2 P. & C.R. DG20.
159   Dixon also takes this point: (2010) 30 L.S. 408.
160   Mr Gillett clearly knew that he had no direct legal rights and pressed Mr Holt to formalise the arrangement.
161   *Cobbe v Yeoman's Row Management* [2008] UKHL 55, para.68, per Lord Walker.

LECTURER: And what about third party purchasers of land?

STUDENT: The House of Lords' reasoning brings proprietary estoppel back into line with its principles in all the cases discussed in this chapter. So it will not give rise to a greater number of claims – as the Court of Appeal decision threatened to do. We may say that the law at least does not increase the possibility of a purchaser or mortgage lender being bound by an unregistered interest in land.

(8) Remedy[162]

Once an equity has arisen in favour of the claimant the court must determine the extent of the equity.[163] "It is for the courts of equity to decide in what way that equity should be satisfied",[164] i.e. what remedy should be awarded the claimant. It is frequently said that the courts must award the "minimum equity to do justice".[165] The court can award a wide variety of remedies, for example, it can order the conveyance of the entire fee simple estate to the claimant,[166] or the grant of a lease.[167] It can order the grant of smaller rights such as easements,[168] give the claimant a licence to occupy for life—where, usually in family relationships, they have been promised residential security,[169] order that the defendant pay financial compensation,[170] or even award no remedy at all.[171] The remedy can sometimes take the form of protection from eviction.[172] In *Inwards v Baker*[173] in which a father promised his son that if he built his bungalow on the father's land he would be able to live there for life, the court held that the son could live there as long as he wished.

The court may hold that the equity has already been satisfied. In *Sledmore v Dalby*[174] Dalby had lived rent free in the house of his mother-in-law. Although he incurred some detriment by paying rates and maintaining the house, the court said that the rent-free accommodation he and his family had enjoyed over 15 years had amply compensated for any detriment he had suffered. Thus, Dalby had not suffered an injustice. The court will weigh any advantages gained against any detriment suffered in order to determine either whether it is unconscionable to allow the legal owner to go back on an assurance, or, if it is, in order to award the fair remedy.[175]

(a) The protection of expectations or compensation for detrimental reliance?

It is clear that the court has a wide discretion to choose an appropriate remedy. But we need to consider the principles upon which the courts decide what remedy to award the estoppel

---

162 S.Gardner (1999) 115 L.Q.R. 438; (2006) 122 L.Q.R. 492; M.P.Thompson [2003] Conv. 157; E.Cooke [1997] 17 L.S. 258.

163 *Crabb v Arun District Council* [1976] 1 Ch. 179, p.193 per Scarman L.J.

164 *Greasley v Cooke* [1980] 1 W.L.R. 1306, p.1312 per Lord Denning M.R.

165 *Crabb v Arun D.C.* above p.198, per Scarman L.J.

166 *Pascoe v Turner* [1979] 1 W.L.R. 431.

167 *Yaxley v Gotts* [2000] 1 All E.R. 711.

168 *Crabb v Arun D.C.* [1976] 1 Ch. 179; *E.R. Ives Investment Ltd v High* [1967] 2 Q.B. 379.

169 *Matharu v Matharu* [1994] 2 F.L.R. 597, p.608 per Roch L.J.

170 *Gillett v Holt* [2001] Ch. 210; *Lim Teng Huan v Ang See Chuan* [1992] 1 W.L.R. 113.

171 *Appleby v Cowley* (1982) *The Times*, 14 April.

172 E.H.Burn, *Maudsley & Burn's Land Law Cases and Materials*, 8th edn (Oxford University Press, 2004) calls this "negative protection", p.654.

173 [1965] 2 Q.B. 29.

174 (1996) 72 P & C.R. 196.

175 An approach recently applied by the Privy Council (St Lucia) in *Henry v Henry* [2010] UKPC 3.

claimant. In a good number of the cases we have considered the claimant has been led to expect that they will have a definite interest in the land. And they have relied on this expectation to their detriment. A question that has emerged in the law of proprietary estoppel is whether it is appropriate for the court to award the remedy that best fulfils what the claimant had been led to expect, or to "compensate him for his detrimental reliance".[176]

Some of the older cases gave effect to the claimant's expectations.[177] For example, the claimant had expected to get the house in *Pascoe v Turner* and the court ordered to defendant to convey it to her. In *Crabb v Arun DC* the claimant had expected a right of way and this is what the court ordered.

(b) Proportionality

Recently the courts have considered the extent of the detriment and weighed it against the claimant's expectation. In *Sledmore v Dalby*[178] it was held that there must be proportionality between the remedy awarded and detriment suffered by the claimant when the assurance was retracted.

> For example, it could be seen as disproportionate to order that a valuable house be conveyed to a claimant in order to satisfy his or her expectation of inheriting it, if the claimant undertook only about £5,000 of repairs by way of reliance.

As Robert Goff J. observed in *Amalgamated Property Co v Texas Bank*,[179] "[i]t would be wholly inequitable and unjust to insist upon a disproportionate making good of the relevant assumption". This would particularly be the case if there were others expecting to inherit under a will. In *Campbell v Griffin*[180] the claimant was lodger to a frail elderly couple. He came to be treated by them as a son and looked after them as their carer. He had been promised that he would have a home in the house for live and it was held that he had relied sufficiently on this to his detriment. Given the considerable care he had provided the court awarded him £35,000 (secured on the house), which balanced his expectation of a home for life with the interests of the beneficiaries under the will of the couple, who would be due to receive the proceeds of the sale of the house.[181] As Hobhouse L.J. observed in *Sledmore v Dalby*[182]:

"the end result must be a just one having regard to the assumption made by the party asserting the estoppel and the detriment which he has experienced."

---

176   *Jennings v Rice* [2003] 1 P. & C.R. 8, per Robert Walker L.J.
177   S.Gardner (1999) 115 L.Q.R. 438.
178   (1996) 72 P & C.R. 196.
179   [1982] Q.B. 84, p.103, relied upon for this principle in *Sledmore v Dalby* (1996) 72 P. & C.R. 196.
180   [2001] EWCA Civ 990.
181   Thompson [2003] 67 Conv. 157.
182   (1996) 72 P. & C.R. 196, quoted in *Jennings v Rice* [2003] 1 P. & C.R. 8, per Robert Walker L.J. para.56.

In *Jennings v Rice*[183] the claimant was a gardener and worked for an elderly widow. Eventually he began to look after her, care for her, and to run errands. At this time he had ceased to take any payment, but she told him that "he would be alright" and "she would see to it". When she died there was no provision for him in her will. A proprietary estoppel was made out on the facts, the main question being the remedy that the court would grant to satisfy the equity. Her estate was valued at approximately £1.7m and his services represented nothing like this value. He was awarded £100,000 for his services over the period of time in question.[184]

Robert Walker L.J. considered that it is appropriate to order the remedy that best satisfies the claimant's expectations where the estoppel arose out of a clear bargain between claimant and defendant. In such a case the parties themselves "probably regarded the expected benefit and the accepted detriment as being (in a general, imprecise way) equivalent, or at any rate not obviously disproportionate".[185] However, where the claimant does not have certain expectations,[186] or has large expectations in proportion to their detriment, the court would regard the claimant's expectations as a "starting point" only.[187] "The court can and should recognise that the claimant's equity should be satisfied in another (and generally more limited) way".[188]

C. IMPLIED TRUSTS: RESULTING AND CONSTRUCTIVE TRUSTS

(1) Introduction

There is another way in which a person can acquire an interest in land belonging to another entirely *informally*, i.e. without writing. This is where the claimant establishes that they have an interest under a resulting or constructive trust. Certain circumstances surrounding dealings with property will have the effect of creating a trust even though one has not been expressly brought into being under s.53(1)(b) of the Law of Property Act 1925.[189]

Much of the law in this area is directed at determining whether a spouse, partner, or other cohabitee has acquired an interest in the family home. The law of implied trusts is relevant in two senses. Firstly, a family home may be registered legally in the name of one of the partners. The question is then whether the other has acquired an interest in the home. Secondly, where the house is registered in a couple's joint names they may not have executed an express declaration of trust. As we saw in section 2(5) of this chapter, whenever land is conveyed into two or more people's names the law will impose a trust.[190] But the joint purchasers often fail to

---

183 [2003] 1 P. & C.R. 8.
184 The Privy Council (St Lucia) in *Henry v Henry* [2010] UKPC 3 applied the principle of proportionality.
185 *Jennings*, para.45.
186 e.g. non-specific assurances of future inheritance, as was the case in *Jennings* itself: "he would be alright".
187 para.47.
188 [2003] 1 P. & C.R. 8 para.47.
189 This is the formality that requires trusts of land to be "manifested and proved" by evidence in writing. Otherwise they are unenforceable. See above in this chapter, section 2A, p.124.
190 Law of Property Act 1925 ss.34–36, see above, section 2A, p.125.

stipulate expressly in the deed of conveyance *how* they intend to share the equitable/beneficial interest.[191] And it is the beneficial ownership under a trust that entitles the beneficiary to the value and benefit of the house. Thus, the law of implied trusts is often called upon to determine how joint purchasers of land are to share the beneficial interest, i.e. do they have equal shares of the house or shares in some other proportion?

> **Law Reform**
>
> The Law Commission has said recently that the doctrines of resulting and constructive trusts are far from satisfactory as a way of resolving the issue of whether a person has acquired an interest in land belonging to another. The doctrines are ill adapted to modern purposes. They are inconsistent, difficult to apply, and can lead to injustice. It is far better that people should execute an express trust to leave beyond all doubt who has what share of the ownership of the house. However, as the Law Commission conceded in the later of these reports, it is unrealistic to expect people to act in such a formal way.
>
> Law Commission, *Sharing Homes—A Discussion Paper* (2002) Law Com No.278; Law Commission, *Cohabitation: the Financial Consequences of Relationship Breakdown* (Law Com CP No.179); Law Commission, *Cohabitation: The Financial Consequences of Relationship. Breakdown* (July 31, 2007) Law Com No.307.

(2) Resulting trusts[192]

This was the traditionally accepted way for a person to acquire a beneficial interest in land belonging to another. Where a person contributes financially to the purchase of a house which is put into the name of another, they acquire a beneficial interest under a resulting trust.[193] This is often known as a "purchase money resulting trust". There is another type of resulting trust called an "automatic resulting trust",[194] a consideration of which is beyond the scope of this book. Under a resulting trust, the beneficiary acquires an interest in the property proportionate to his or her contribution.[195]

> *Williams & Glyn's Bank v Boland* **[1981] A.C. 487**
>
> Mrs Boland contributed half of the purchase price of her matrimonial home. The house was registered in the name of her husband. She acquired a 50 per cent beneficial interest in the house.

---

191   Had they have done so this would then be an express trust which is evidenced in writing and enforceable under s.53(1)(b) of the Law of Property Act 1925.

192   See R. Chambers, *Resulting Trusts* (Oxford: Clarendon Press, 1997).

193   *Dyer v Dyer* (1788) 2 Cox Eq. Cas 92. A resulting trust is also presumed where a person transfers property voluntarily (i.e. without consideration). Equity assumes that no gift is intended: *Re Vinogradoff* [1936] WN 68.

194   *Vandervell v Inland Revenue Commissioners* [1967] 2 A.C. 291.

195   *Walker v Hall* [1984] F.L.R. 126, *Huntingford v Hobbs* [1993] 1 F.L.R. 736 and *Springette v Defoe* [1992] 2 F.L.R. 388.

(a) The resulting trust is a presumption of the contributor's intentions

The basis for imposing the resulting trust is that where someone contributes to the purchase of property which is then transferred into the name of another, equity presumes that it was not the intention of the contributor to benefit the other. In short equity imposes a resulting trust in response to what it presumes to be the intentions of the person making the contribution: "Equity, being concerned with commercial realities, presumed against gifts and other windfalls".[196] This means that the presumption of a resulting trust can be rebutted by evidence of the contributor's actual intentions.

> Thus, if it had been established that Mrs Boland intended her contribution to the purchase of the house to be a gift to her husband, this would displace the presumption of resulting trust and she would not have acquired an interest in the house.

(b) What type of contribution to the purchase suffices?

Traditional resulting trust theory holds that the beneficial interests are quantified "once and for all" at the time of acquisition of the property.[197] Thus, direct financial contributions to the purchase will suffice.[198] This has been held to include the situation where a council tenant had a substantial "right to buy" discount from the asking price.[199] It will not include superficial contributions, such as conveyancing fees and costs of removal.[200] Where the property is purchased with the aid of a mortgage it is more difficult to determine whether a person's contributions towards the monthly instalments of the mortgage will give rise to a resulting trust. In *Cowcher v Cowcher*,[201] Bagnall J. held that where the parties agree at the time the mortgage is granted that they will share the repayments a resulting trust will arise as a result of these contributions. Otherwise contributions to the mortgage will not suffice.[202] This has been questioned recently in the House of Lords.[203] In the domestic context, where spouses, partners and other cohabitants seek to establish a beneficial interest in their family home, it has recently been held by the House of Lords that the doctrine of resulting trusts no longer applies.[204] The question of the parties' beneficial shares in the house is determined by the law of *constructive trusts* (see below). So the issue of resulting trusts and mortgage contributions ceases to have much significance.

---

196   *Stack v Dowden* [2007] UKHL 17; [2007] 2 A.C. 432, per Baroness Hale, para.60; *Pettitt v Pettitt* [1970] A.C. 777, p.823.
197   *Curley v Parkes* [2005] 1 P. & C.R. DG15.
198   *Burns v Burns* [1984] Ch.317.
199   *Springette v Defoe* [1992] 2 F.L.R. 388.
200   *Curley v Parkes* [2005] 1 P. & C.R. DG15.
201   [1972] 1 W.L.R. 425.
202   *Curley v Parkes* [2005] 1 P & CR DG15 per Peter Gibson L.J.
203   *Stack v Dowden* [2007] 2 AC 432, paras 117–120, per Lord Neuberger.
204   *Stack v Dowden* [2007] UKHL 17; [2007] 2 A.C. 432 disapproved *Walker v Hall* [1984] F.L.R. 126, *Huntingford v Hobbs* [1993] 1 F.L.R. 736 and *Springette v Defoe* [1992] 2 F.L.R. 388; Lord Walker: para.31; Lady Hale: paras 56–70; also *Jones v Kernott* [2011] UKSC 53, Supreme Court, para.23 (joint judgment of Lady Hale and Lord Walker).

(c) The countervailing presumption of advancement

As you will remember from above, a resulting trust is imposed to give effect to what is presumed to be the contributor's intention. However, if a contribution is made in the context of particular relationships, i.e. husband and wife; father and child, then the presumption will be the opposite. Equity will presume, unless there is evidence of the actual intention of the party making the contribution[205] that they intend to make a gift. If a husband conveys a house to his wife, or contributes to the purchase of a house that is put legally in his wife's name, the presumption is that he intended to make a gift. He will not have a beneficial interest in it unless he proves that his intention was *not* to make a gift. The same applies in the context of father and child: "[E]ven equity was prepared to presume a gift where the recipient was the provider's wife or child".[206]

The idea behind the presumption of advancement is that because the husband has a duty to provide for his wife, and the father his child, equity assumes that any voluntary conveyance or cash contribution to a purchase in the other's name is made in furtherance of this obligation. In today's society the presumption of advancement looks increasingly outdated and unreal. "These days, the importance to be attached to who paid for what in a domestic context may be very different from its importance in other contexts or long ago."[207] Section 199(1) of the Equality Act 2010 abolishes the presumption of advancement "by which, for example, a husband is presumed to be making a gift to his wife if he transfers property to her, or purchases property in her name".[208] The abolition is prospective so that it does not affect transfers etc. that occurred prior to the commencement of s.199.[209]

(d) Resulting trust doctrine no longer appropriate in the domestic-consumer context

The House of Lords/Supreme Court has recently held that the presumptions of resulting trust and advancement are no longer appropriate as a way of determining the beneficial ownership of property in the domestic/consumer context.[210] They only take into account a limited range of contributions to the purchase of property and take a rigid approach to the quantum of the share of the contributor. The size of the interest under a resulting trust is determined by the size of the contribution. A more flexible and realistic way of allocating the beneficial ownership of the family home is through the doctrine of constructive trusts.

---

205 *Antoni v Antoni* [2007] UKPC 10—the presumption of advancement is a rule of evidence that can be rebutted with evidence of a contrary intention.

206 *Stack v Dowden* [2007] UKHL 17; [2007] 2 A.C. 432, per Baroness Hale, para.60.

207 *Stack v Dowden*, above, per Baroness Hale, para.60. Similar comments were made by three of the Law Lords in *Pettitt v Pettitt* [1970] A.C. 777.

208 At the time of writing the section had not yet come into force.

209 Equality Act 2010 s.199(2).

210 *Stack v Dowden* [2007] UKHL 17; [2007] 2 A.C. 432 disapproved *Walker v Hall* [1984] F.L.R. 126, *Huntingford v Hobbs* [1993] 1 F.L.R. 736 and *Springette v Defoe* [1992] 2 F.L.R. 388, Lord Walker: para.31; Baroness Hale: paras 56–70; also *Jones v Kernott* [2011] UKSC 53 (references in this chapter are from the official Transcript, Westlaw No. 2011 5105146, November 9, 2011, Supreme Court), para.23 (joint judgment of Lady Hale and Lord Walker).

(3) Constructive trusts

Thus, in domestic cases, where a couple, whether married or cohabiting, or others e.g. mother and son, are in dispute about whether one or more of them have acquired a beneficial interest in the house, the doctrine of constructive trusts applies.[211] It also resolves the question of the size of the parties' respective beneficial shares.

(a) Introduction: social changes and owner occupation[212]

> Throughout the twentieth century, particularly towards the end, there became an increasingly urgent need for the law to find an equitable way of giving one person part of the ownership of the house in which they lived.

As you saw in Chapter 1, during the twentieth century people started to buy houses, instead of renting them, in order to create a *home*. A considerable amount of the population of this country now *owns* their home. As Waite L.J. observed in *Midland Bank Plc v Cooke*[213] "the mass diffusion of home ownership has been one of the most striking social changes of our own time". Most residential purchasers cannot afford to buy a house outright. They put down a deposit and borrow the balance from a bank or building society, granting the latter a mortgage or "charge" on the family home. The borrower then pays back the loan on monthly instalments.

In many cases, particularly around the 1970s it was common for the house to be put in the sole name of the husband or male partner.[214] And at the same time women were becoming increasingly financially independent, going out to work and contributing to the household expenses. Once marital break-up and separation became more frequent, more disputes arose about whether the wife or other cohabitee had acquired any part of the ownership of the house.

> A house is registered in the sole name of a husband. A wife or cohabitee may have gone out to work and helped her husband pay the mortgage instalments. She may have paid the other household bills and provided clothing and holidays etc thereby freeing up his income to pay the mortgage. She may have given up work to look after the children and keep the house. She may have redecorated it and affected similar improvements. In all these situations, she will want to know whether, by these activities, she has acquired an interest in the house.

---

211   There are many situations in which a constructive trust arises, for example under the rule in *Rochefoucauld v Boustead* [1897] 1 Ch. 196 (discussed above) or where someone has received trust property knowing it to have been transferred in breach of trust: *Bank of Credit and Commerce International (Overseas) Ltd v Akindele* [2001] Ch. 437. But we are concerned here with constructive trusts that allow someone to acquire a share in the family home.

212   See for example, Pearce and Stevens, *Land Law*, 3rd edn (London: Sweet & Maxwell, 2005), p.251.

213   [1995] 4 All E.R. 562, p.575.

214   See for example, *Burns v Burns* [1984] Ch.317; The cases we are about to consider apply whether or not the house is the home of a married or unmarried couple, or whether it is occupied by relatives or friends. What we are considering here is the ordinary law of property: *Williams & Glyn's Bank Ltd v Boland* [1981] A.C. 487.

In 1973 parliament passed the Matrimonial Causes Act, which gives the court discretion to distribute property between divorcing spouses. So the law of implied trusts is no longer relevant where the dispute concerns a married couple who are getting divorced. There has been further legislation, and possible future legislation, which replaces the law of implied trusts in the situation where an unmarried couple are separating. Under the Civil Partnership Act 2004 where a homosexual couple has registered a civil partnership, the court has similar powers to redistribute the couple's property on the breakdown of that relationship.

The law of implied trusts remains relevant in two contexts: firstly where a couple are separating and they are neither divorcing spouses nor separating civil partners, the law of constructive trusts will determine what beneficial interests each has in the former home. Secondly, the law of constructive trusts applies where the legal owner(s) has executed a subsequent mortgage of the family home. The person whose name is not on the legal title is arguing that they have acquired a beneficial interest that takes priority over the mortgage. In this way the lender will be unable to repossess the house.

(b) Where a mortgage lender has become involved: the priorities context

If the legal owner has mortgaged the house and defaulted on the repayments due under the loan, the bank will seek to repossess the house in order to recoup its original investment. They will only be able to do this if the non-legal-owning spouse or partner does not have a prior beneficial interest that is held to take priority over the mortgage. In such a case it is the ordinary law of trusts that determines whether a spouse, cohabitant or other friend/family member has acquired an equitable interest in the house. This was the context of the dispute in *Williams & Glyn's Bank Ltd v Boland*.[215] The matrimonial home was registered in the sole name of Mr Boland. Mrs Boland established that she had a beneficial interest under an implied trust by virtue of her contribution to the purchase price of the house. Unbeknown to his wife, Mr Boland then executed a mortgage on the house to secure business debts. Upon default under the terms of the mortgage, the question in the case was whether Mrs Boland's equitable interest under the trust bound the bank. This would mean that she had a prior interest that would stop the lender from taking immediate possession of the house. You may remember that the House of Lords held that her interest *did* bind the bank. In order for Mrs Boland's interest to take priority over the mortgage, the relevant rule dictated that she had to prove that she was "in actual occupation".[216] She was!

The diagram below shows a typical dispute of priority in the owner occupation context.

---

215   [1981] A.C. 487.
216   See Chapter 8 for a full consideration of the rules of priority where title to the land is registered.

Legal owner (Husband) grants mortgage to   **Bank**

LAND (Family home)

Wife had contributed to the purchase but although the house is in her husband's sole name, she has, by virtue of her contribution, a beneficial interest in the land under a trust.

LAND (Family home)

Does bank take its security for the loan to husband, ie the house, free from the wife's prior interest? If not, the wife can prevent the bank from repossessing the house if the husband defaults on the loan.

(c) The modern problem—joint legal ownership

It is becoming increasingly common for the house to be registered in the joint names of a couple. The couple become joint owners of the legal title. For example, A and B purchase "Broadacres" in 1985 at a price of £30,000. The house is transferred into their joint names. For reasons that you will appreciate when you have studied the Law of Co-ownership in Chapters 4 and 5, the Law of Property Act 1925 imposes a trust whenever land is conveyed into the names of two or more people. Thus, A and B hold Broadacres on trust for each other. But merely registering the legal ownership in joint names does not determine how the equitable or beneficial interest is held. And under a trust it is the beneficial interest that is the real ownership of the land, i.e. its value. On the transfer deed there is no mention of how A and B are to own the beneficial interests in Broadacres. So this is a serious gap that must be filled. Let's say that Broadacres is currently worth £250,000 and A and B are separating. They will both urgently want to know how much of the beneficial interest they are entitled to. This determines how the proceeds of sale are divided between them. If the law decides that they are entitled to equal beneficial shares then the proceeds of sale must be distributed equally, and so forth. But what if B contributed more to the purchase than A? Is she entitled to a greater amount of the equity in the house?

It is unfortunately quite common for a house to be registered in co-owners' joint names without there being an express declaration of trust. The law of constructive trusts fills the gap and determines the size of the co-owners' beneficial shares. However, it is complex law and not without its ambiguities.

> **Practice Point**
> If you go into practice as a property lawyer remember this point. Try to get joint purchasers to agree how they want to hold the beneficial interests and record their intentions as an express declaration of trust: *Carlton v Goodman* [2002] 2 F.L.R. 259

(d) Two situations to be treated separately

So we have seen that the law of constructive trusts will determine the beneficial ownership of the family home in two situations:

Situation 1: Where the house is put legally in the name of one of the cohabitees/family members and the other is seeking to establish that they have acquired a beneficial interest; and

Situation 2: Where the house is put legally in the joint names of the couple, there is no express declaration of trust of the equitable interest and they wish to ascertain the size of their respective beneficial shares.

(4) So when will a constructive trust arise?

In Situation 1 above (where the house is put legally in the name of one of the cohabitees) the non-owning partner must prove that she has acquired a beneficial interest in accordance with the principles in *Gissing v Gissing*[217] and *Lloyds Bank Plc v Rosset*.[218] Once she has proved that she has acquired a beneficial interest, the court will have to determine the size of that interest ("quantify it") in accordance with the principles in *Midland Bank Plc v Cooke*,[219] *Oxley v Hiscock*,[220] and *Stack v Dowden*.[221]

In Situation 2 (i.e. where the house is put legally in the joint names of the couple and they wish to ascertain the size of their respective beneficial interests), the starting point is that the law presumes strongly that they intended to hold the beneficial interests in equal shares.[222] Of course the law gives way to actual intentions and this presumption can be rebutted. However, the person seeking to establish that shares are other than equal must prove to the satisfaction of the court that this is what the parties actually intended. And as the Supreme Court has very recently observed, this is not a task that should be undertaken lightly.[223] The presumption of equal beneficial shares is a strong one.[224] Therefore, we will need to consider the type of evidence that will suffice to rebut the presumption of joint beneficial ownership.

---

217   [1970] 2 All E.R. 780.
218   [1991] 1 A.C. 107.
219   [1995] 4 All E.R. 562.
220   [2004] EWCA Civ 546.
221   [2007] 2 A.C. 432.
222   *Stack v Dowden* [2007] 2 A.C. 432.
223   *Jones v Kernott* [2011] UKSC 53.
224   *Stack v Dowden* [2007] 2 A.C. 432.

> **The starting point**
> "Just as the starting point where there is sole legal ownership is sole beneficial ownership, the starting point where there is joint legal ownership is joint beneficial ownership. The onus is upon the person seeking to show that the beneficial ownership is different from the legal ownership".
>
> *Stack v Dowden* [2007] 2 A.C. 432 per Baroness Hale, paras 54–56

(5) Situation 1: sole legal ownership

In the situation where the house is put legally in the name of one of the cohabitees/ family members and the other is seeking to establish that they have acquired a beneficial interest, that other must prove that she is entitled to a beneficial interest under a constructive trust. Constructive trusts arise in specific circumstances where the law defines that it would be "unconscionable" for the legal owner to retain the entire beneficial interest themselves and deny someone an interest in their land. The law "constructs" a trust to give effect to that interest.[225] The principles were established *Gissing v Gissing*[226] and interpreted in later cases.

> Where the house is put legally in the name of one spouse/partner the other can acquire an interest in the home under a constructive trust: IF:
>
> Firstly, there was a "common intention" between the spouses that she was to acquire a share of the ownership of the home, AND
>
> Secondly, she relied on this common intention to her detriment, for example, by making significant improvements to the home.
>
> She will thereby acquire a beneficial interest in the home. The court will "construct a trust" to give effect to the common intention.

> **Constructive trusts and proprietary estoppel**
>
> There is some similarity between constructive trusts and the doctrine of proprietary estoppel, but as we shall see, the doctrine of constructive trusts has significant differences.

---

225   *Gissing v Gissing* [1970] 2 All E.R. 780; *Pettitt v Pettitt* [1970] A.C. 777.
226   [1970] 2 All E.R. 780, p.790.

(a) The principles in Lloyds Bank Plc v Rosset

The matter of whether a spouse or partner has acquired an interest in the house[227] is governed by the principles in *Lloyds Bank Plc v Rosset*.[228] These principles have been criticised as being too narrow, and there is some suggestion that the courts may follow a broader approach.[229] But *Rosset* remains good law.

In *Lloyds Bank v Rosset* the husband acquired the matrimonial home with money from a Swiss trust fund, of which he was beneficiary. The trustees insisted that the house was registered in his name only. The house was a renovation project and unbeknown to his wife he borrowed money to fund the renovations and executed a mortgage on the house. He defaulted on the repayments due under the loan and the bank claimed possession of the house so that they could sell it and recoup their investment. The wife claimed that she had acquired a beneficial interest that bound the lender. During the renovations the wife had helped with the decoration of the house and supervised the builders who were working on the house. On this basis she claimed that a constructive trust had arisen in her favour. On the facts of the case her claim failed. But the importance of the House of Lords' decision in *Rosset* lies in the fact that Lord Bridge clarified the law in this area, and articulated two ways in which a claimant whose name is not on the legal title can establish an interest in the house by way of constructive trust:

1. Where a common intention constructive trust is established as a result of express discussion and detrimental reliance;
2. Where a common intention is inferred from conduct, i.e. direct contributions to the purchase of the house.

   (i) The common intention constructive trust arising as a result of express discussion and detrimental reliance

Lord Bridge stated that[230]:

"The first and fundamental question which must always be resolved is whether . . . there has at any time prior to acquisition, or exceptionally at some later date, been any agreement, arrangement or understanding reached between [the parties] that the property is to be shared beneficially. The finding of an agreement or arrangement to share in this sense can only, I think, be based on evidence of express discussions between the partners, however imperfectly remembered and however imprecise their terms may have been. Once a finding to this effect is made it will only be necessary for the partner asserting a claim to a beneficial interest against the partner entitled to the legal estate to show that he or she has acted to his or her detriment or significantly altered his or her position in reliance on the agreement in order to give rise to a constructive trust or a proprietary estoppel."

---

227   Although it should be noted that it is possible in this way to establish a constructive trust in relation to business property: *Lloyd v Pickering* [2004] EWHC 1513.
228   [1991] 1 A.C. 107.
229   Following the decision of the House of Lords in *Stack v Dowden* [2007] 2 A.C. 432. We will examine this broader approach below.
230   *Lloyds Bank Plc v Rosset* [1991] 1 AC 107, p.132.

Summary
Therefore a constructive trust can be established where there are express discussions between the couple that reveal their common intention that the ownership of the house is to be shared between them. The claimant must then prove that she relied on this common intention to her detriment. We will deal with each of these elements in turn.

Express discussions: Firstly, the claimant must show that there were express discussions. The court will not invent or "impute" a common intention for them, however fair and reasonable it may appear from the circumstances of the case.[231] The express discussions do not have to be in technical language, or precisely formulated, or even precisely remembered by the parties.[232] However, the express discussions must establish the parties' common view that the ownership of the house was intended to be shared. Thus, the discussions relied upon must relate to the ownership of the house. In *Lloyds Bank v Rosset* itself, Mr Rosset had made only vague statements to Mrs Rosset about her *living* in the house. They had not discussed the matter of her *owning* any share of it. Given the clear intentions of the Swiss trustees that Mr Rosset should become the sole owner of the house, this was not sufficient evidence of an express common intention to the contrary.[233] Similarly, in *James v Thomas*,[234] Mr Thomas was already the owner of the property in question. When he and his partner were undertaking renovations on the property he made statements to the effect that their joint work would "benefit them both". It was held that these comments referred only to an improvement in the couple's lifestyle and did not show an intention that the ownership of the property should be shared.

Sometimes the express discussion has taken the form of an excuse for why the non-owning partner's name could not have been put on the legal title.[235] In *Eves v Eves*[236] the male partner told the female partner that the house could not be in joint names because she was under 21.[237] Otherwise, he said, he would have put the house in joint names. The implication from this was that they intended that she would have a share in the house. Brightman J. stated that:

"[The defendant] agrees that he used her age as an excuse to avoid [putting the house in joint names]. It seems to me that this . . . raises a clear inference that there was an understanding between them that she was intended to have some sort of proprietary interest in the house: otherwise no excuse would have been needed."

---

231   *Lloyds Bank v Rosset*, above p.132, per Lord Bridge.
232   *Hammond v Mitchell* [1991] 1 W.L.R. 1127.
233   Per Lord Bridge, p.128.
234   [2007] EWCA Civ 1212.
235   For criticism see Gardner, "Rethinking Family Property" (1993) 109 L.Q.R. 263.
236   [1975] 1 W.L.R. 1338.
237   Which is wrong. A minor (under 18) cannot hold a legal estate in land: Law of Property Act 1925 s.1(6).

The same conclusion was reached in *Grant v Edwards*[238] in which the male partner said to his girlfriend that he would put the house in joint names, but this might prejudice her forthcoming divorce settlement. The implication from these statements was that they intended all along that the ownership of the house would be shared.

> The relevant question is not what the legal owner subjectively intended by his or her statements. Here, the defendants were lying in order to avoid putting the house in joint names. They had no intention of sharing the ownership with their partners. The question is what inferences would the reasonable person draw from the statements made: *an objective test.*

Detrimental reliance: Once there is evidence of express discussions that the ownership of the house should be shared, the claimant must establish that "he or she has acted to his or her detriment or significantly altered his or her position in reliance on the agreement".[239]

> In is only at the point where the claimant establishes their detrimental reliance on the common intention that the law no longer insists that ownership of land must be transferred formally.

Detriment in this context can be established from a wide variety of acts. It is not necessary for the claimant to have contributed to the purchase of the house in financial terms. However, the conduct relied upon as a detriment must consist of acts that the claimant could not have been expected to have undertaken unless they were under the impression that they were to acquire an interest in the house. In *Eves v Eves*,[240] after an express discussion between the couple that led to an understanding that she was to have an interest, the claimant helped to renovate the house. She broke up concrete with a 14lb sledgehammer and filled a skip. It was held that she would not have undertaken such activities

"except in pursuance of some expressed or implied arrangement and on the understanding that she was helping to improve a house in which she was to all practical intents and purposes promised that she had an interest."

Janet Eves was awarded a one-third interest in the house. Similarly in *Grant v Edwards*[241] the claimant made a very substantial contribution from her earnings to the housekeeping. In this way she freed the legal owner's income to pay the mortgage. This was held to be sufficient

---

238   [1986] Ch. 638.
239   *Lloyds Bank Plc v Rosset* [1991] 1 AC 107, p.132, per Lord Bridge.
240   [1975] 1 W.L.R. 1338.
241   [1986] Ch. 638.

detrimental reliance on the promise that she was to have an interest in the house. It was the type of conduct that the claimant could not have been expected to undertake unless she thought she had an interest in the house.

The need for the claimant to prove a causal link is capable of working injustice, i.e. it is only conduct which goes "above and beyond" the type of activity expected within their relationship that will qualify as a "detriment". In *Grant v Edwards*, Browne-Wilkinson V.C. adopted a broader approach to the type of conduct that would prove detrimental reliance on an express agreement. It is similar to the approach under the doctrine of proprietary estoppel, where reliance is presumed in the claimant's favour. He considered that any conduct referable to the joint lives of the parties would suffice as detriment once a promise had been made that the claimant should have a beneficial interest in the house, e.g. looking after the house and raising the couple's children.

STUDENT: It seems a bit strange that for a woman to acquire an interest in the family home her conduct must go beyond that of a wife and mother!

LECTURER: So you think that a partner should be able to acquire an interest in the home in which they are living in a more straightforward manner?

STUDENT: Well, at present she must establish an express promise and detrimental reliance. If she cannot do this, which is quite a high hurdle, it may be said that the law is unfair.

LECTURER: Why?

STUDENT: Because she lives in it just as much as the legal owner does. She contributes emotionally and physically to the running of the household.

LECTURER: She may have given up work to bring up the couple's children. What other arguments can we make about the law? Perhaps you can create an argument for why the law should be left as it is. Hold the principles we have just discussed against the policies and principles in our Building Blocks and if they support or undermine the Building Blocks we may say that it would be a good or bad law accordingly.[242]

STUDENT: I think that if the law were changed to allow a broader type of detrimental reliance this would undermine BUILDING BLOCK NO 6.

BUILDING BLOCK NO 6: The Need for Certainty and Predictability in Land Law Rules
If the rules are clear as to how they will apply in future cases, i.e. if they allow people (e.g. purchasers or occupiers) to predict the outcome of their actions then they are good law.

If the law were more lenient and allowed people to establish detriment by simply doing ordinary domestic chores etc then it would be unclear when people will have acquired an interest in land. It would mean that many more property rights would come into existence.

---

242   For the full text of our Building Blocks and instructions on how to use them to create an argument see Chapter 1.

LECTURER: But a claimant will have to establish an "express discussion" that they are to have an interest in the house. This may limit the number of property rights. Do you think that the rules relating to "express discussions" are sufficiently clear?

STUDENT: From the law we have considered above it is quite difficult to say what type of conversation will amount to an "express discussion", particularly as Lord Bridge in *Lloyds Bank v Rosset* said that these conversations do not have to be "perfectly or precisely remembered". It also feels sometimes as if the courts are inventing a common intention to share on the basis that an "excuse" was made to the claimant why her name could not be put on the legal title to the house. Surely it is bending the law to say that the parties intended the claimant to have an interest in the house when the legal owner made an excuse for why her name should not be put on the legal title. The courts are clearly trying to do justice to the claimant by giving her an interest in the house. But because of this, the rules do lack clarity.

The doctrine of proprietary estoppel and the express common intention constructive trust: You may have noticed that there is a considerable similarity between the "express common intention" constructive trust in *Lloyds Bank v Rosset*[243] and the doctrine of proprietary estoppel. In *Grant v Edwards*[244] Sir Nicholas Browne-Wilkinson V.C. considered that the two doctrines should be assimilated. Indeed there are many similarities between them. Both are based on an express assertion that the claimant should have an interest in the land. However, the common intention trust requires "discussions" between the parties, although in practice there is likely to be little difference. Another potential difference is that with proprietary estoppel, provided that there is sufficient certainty that the claimant is to expect some form of right, the precise nature of the right need not be specified. With the common intention trust, the discussions must relate to the acquisition of part of the ownership of the house, although such discussions need not be precisely remembered in their terms. Both doctrines require that the claimant relies upon the express discussions/assurances to their detriment. However, with proprietary estoppel, once there are assurances made by the defendant and the claimant has acted to his or her detriment, the law presumes that the acts of detriment were done in reliance on the promise. There are also differences of a conceptual nature. With the doctrine of proprietary estoppel, once there has been an assurance and detrimental reliance, the claimant is only entitled to an "inchoate" equity, i.e. the right to go to court and ask for a remedy. The court can then award any remedy it thinks will do justice, taking into account the principle of proportionality between the claimant's expectation and their detrimental reliance. This remedy may or may not be a proprietary right. On the other hand once a constructive trust has arisen in favour of a claimant this exists as an immediate proprietary right. The court merely recognises its existence and therefore has no discretion as to remedy. Nevertheless, following the statutory recognition that in registered land law the equity arising under proprietary estoppel is capable of binding successors in title, this distinction seems less material.[245]

---

243   [1991] 1 A.C. 107.
244   [1986] Ch. 638, p.656.
245   Land Registration Act 2002 s.116.

Despite assertions to the contrary in an earlier case,[246] Lord Walker in *Stack v Dowden*,[247] indicated, obiter, that the two doctrines should be regarded as separate and distinct.

(ii) Where a common intention is inferred from conduct

Lord Bridge in *Lloyds Bank v Rosset*[248] stated that where the claimant could not show evidence of express discussion and detrimental reliance, a common intention that the ownership of the house should be shared can be inferred from the parties conduct. However, Lord Bridge took a restrictive approach and held that the only conduct that will have this effect is a financial contribution to the acquisition of the house[249] or regular and substantial contributions to the mortgage payments[250]:

"In sharp contrast with this situation [express discussions] is the very different one where there is no evidence to support a finding of an agreement or arrangement to share, however reasonable it might have been for the parties to reach such an arrangement if they had applied their minds to the question, and where the court must rely entirely on the conduct of the parties both as the basis from which to infer a common intention to share the property beneficially and as the conduct relied on to give rise to a constructive trust. In this situation direct contributions to the purchase price by the partner who is not the legal owner, whether initially or by payment of mortgage instalments, will readily justify the inference necessary to the creation of a constructive trust. But, as I read the authorities, it is at least extremely doubtful whether anything less will do."

Mrs Rosset also failed to establish a constructive trust on this ground. She had not contributed financially to the purchase of the house, and she had not made any mortgage payments. She had spent some time decorating and supervising the builders who were renovating the house. Lord Bridge held that this conduct was so trifling as to be almost *de minimis*. It certainly did not count for the purposes of establishing a common intention constructive trust.

If a claimant is relying upon paying mortgage contributions in order to raise the inference of a common intention that the house should be shared, they must show that the contributions towards the instalments are "regular and substantial".[251] The recent case of *Lightfoot v Lightfoot-Browne*[252] reminds us that in this second of Lord Bridge's categories, the courts are using the claimant's contributions to the acquisition of the house in order to evidence a *common intention* that the beneficial interest would be shared. In this case, the claimant contributed £41,000 towards paying off the mortgage, but did this without the legal owner's knowledge. Accordingly, there was no constructive trust.

---

246   *Yaxley v Gotts* [2000] Ch.162, p.177, per Walker L.J.
247   [2007] 2 A.C. 432, para.37.
248   [1991] 1 A.C. 107, pp.132–3.
249   Here Lord Bridge overlapped with the concept of the resulting trust.
250   *Lloyds Bank Plc v Rosset* [1991] 1 A.C. 107, pp.132–3.
251   *Gissing v Gissing* [1971] A.C. 886, p.908, per Lord Diplock.
252   [2005] EWCA Civ 201.

Contribution to the initial deposit of the house will be sufficient. In *Midland Bank v Cooke*[253] one half of a wedding gift of money towards the deposit on a house was treated as a direct contribution on the part of the wife. It has been less clear whether a claimant's contributions to the household budget will suffice, for example paying the gas and electric bills and council tax. If the claimant's contribution to these bills frees the legal owner's resources to meet the monthly mortgage instalments, it has been held that this will amount to a contribution sufficient to imply a common intention.[254] In *Stack v Dowden*[255] the House of Lords made certain obiter comments that this was the preferred approach.

> **The relationship between *Lloyds Bank v Rosset* and *Gissing v Gissing***
> In *Gissing* the House of Lords laid down that a person could establish a constructive trust of the family home where a) she could show a common intention that the beneficial interest in the house should be shared, and b) that she relied on this to her detriment. Lord Bridge in *Lloyds Bank v Rosset* reformulated this into the rules we have examined above. We see plainly that his first type of constructive trust, established by express discussions and detrimental reliance, fits neatly with the formula in *Gissing v Gissing*. However, it is less obvious how his second type of constructive trust fits, i.e. where common intention is inferred by conduct. It appears that the common intention and the detrimental reliance are established by the same act of contribution to the purchase of the house.

Having examined the principles in *Lloyds Bank v Rosset*[256] we can see that these principles allow a non-owner to acquire a beneficial interest in the house, but only in very narrow circumstances. A case that demonstrates the defects in the law is *Burns v Burns*.[257] This case concerned an unmarried couple who lived together for 17 years.[258] The house was legally in the name of Mr Burns. Valerie Burns stayed at home to look after the children and the house. When she began going out to work later in the relationship, she used her earnings to help pay household bills. She also provided some clothing, a dishwasher, washing machine and other such items. When she left Mr Burns she claimed that she was entitled to a beneficial interest in the house by virtue of her contributions over the 17 years. The parties had never had any express discussions that the beneficial interest in the house should be shared. The Court of Appeal held that because she had not contributed to the financial acquisition of the house, she had not acquired a beneficial interest:

---

253 [1995] 4 All E.R. 562.
254 *Gissing v Gissing* [1971] A.C. 886, per Lord Pearson p.303; *Le Foe v Le Foe* [2001] 2 F.L.R. 970.
255 [2007] 2 A.C. 432.
256 [1991] 1 A.C. 107.
257 [1984] 1 Ch. 317, CA. See Law Commission, *Sharing Homes – A Discussion Paper* (2002) Law Com No.278; Law Commission, *Cohabitation: the Financial Consequences of Relationship Breakdown* (Law Com No.179); Law Commission, *Cohabitation: The Financial Consequences of Relationship Breakdown* (2007) Law Com No.307.
258 She adopted his name.

"The mere fact that parties live together and do the ordinary domestic tasks is, in my view, no indication at all that they thereby intended to alter the existing property rights of either of them".

The case was decided prior to *Rosset*, under which her claim would also have been unsuccessful.

LECTURER: Given Valarie Burns' significant emotional and physical contribution to the running of the household, many think it unfair that the law denied her an interest in the house just because she made no financial contribution.[259] Do you think that this is good law? What Building Blocks would you use to support your conclusion?
STUDENT: I would firstly refer to BUILDING BLOCK NO 2: Ideas of Justice.

BUILDING BLOCK NO 2: Ideas of Justice
Ownership gives a person choice over what to do with the house. Effectively this will give the owner more control over what they can do with their lives: Harris, *Property and Justice*, p.273. They will have control over when to move and where, and what to do with the house, and whether to raise money by way of mortgage on it etc. Property, in this sense, confers freedom and stability. Furthermore, Land Law should decide its rules to guard against the potential for the legal owner, e.g. the husband, to deal with the land in a way that dramatically affects the life of the other spouse, e.g. by mortgaging the house behind her back and then defaulting on the repayments ("domination-potential") Harris, *Property and Justice*, p.273. See the full text of this Building Block in Chapter 1.

STUDENT: I think that where a person has joint responsibility for the family, and has contributed to the running of the family home and the household, they should have a beneficial interest in the house in which the family live. As they probably make joint decisions about their family's life, they should both have the same degree of control and choice over what is done with the house in which their family lives.
LECTURER: Can you think of any situations in which Harris' "domination potential" argument may apply? Do the rules reflect this?
STUDENT: They do. In *Williams & Glyn's Bank Ltd v Boland* if a cohabitant has an interest in the house she will be able to prevent a bank from repossessing the house, if the legal owner has mortgaged the house behind her back and defaulted on the mortgage repayments.
LECTURER: So you feel that the law relating to constructive trusts is unfair?
STUDENT: Yes, it only awards a share in the family home to a partner who has contributed financially, or where there have been express discussions and detrimental reliance. In many situations, as with Mrs Burns, a person has given up work in order to look after the home and children. Because of this they will not be *able* to contribute financially.

---

259   Gardner (1993) 109 L.Q.R. 263; Gardner (1991) 54 M.L.R. 126.

LECTURER: So you argue that the law should imply a constructive trust on the basis of a much broader range of conduct, such as running the household in the ordinary way and raising children. But can we say that the law is good on the basis of BUILDING BLOCK NO 6?

BUILDING BLOCK NO 6: The Need for Certainty and Predictability in Land Law Rules

If the rules are clear as to how they will apply in future cases, i.e. if they allow people to predict the outcome and consequences their actions and of particular situations, then they are good law. Atiyah says that certainty in law is particularly important where people have strong expectations that their rights will be protected. This is the case with property because people attach so much importance to it.

STUDENT: At least it may be said of Lord Bridge's law in *Lloyds Bank v Rosset* that it is certain and predictable.

LECTURER: Before you can use this Building Block as evidence for a conclusion that the law is good or bad you need to be able to say which classes of litigant are likely to be affected by an absence of certainty in the law.

> This is similar to what the Law Commission refers to as an "impact assessment".

STUDENT: Well, all cohabitants as a class will need to know what their property rights are without necessarily having to go to court. This will particularly be the case if their relationship breaks down, as in *Burns v Burns* itself. At least now lawyers will be able to predict when a cohabitant will have acquired a beneficial interest. Just ask them whether they have made any financial contributions to the purchase or the mortgage repayments.

LECTURER: It is perhaps less clear whether a cohabitant can establish an express discussion constructive trust, as you have argued above. But in Land Law cases what other class of litigant is affected by the rules?

STUDENT: Purchasers who buy the house from the legal owning spouse, or mortgage lenders who have taken a mortgage on the house as security for a loan to the legal owning partner, as in *Williams & Glyn's Bank Ltd v Boland*.

BUILDING BLOCK NO 5: Property Rights and the Protection of Purchasers and Mortgage Lenders

We can argue that a development of a rule in a case or statute is good or bad fair or unfair, depending on the extent to which it supports or undermines the idea that rules of Land Law should protect a purchaser or mortgage lender from being bound by prior interests in the land. This is the policy behind the 1925 property legislation. For the full text of this Building Block see Chapter 1.

The more easily the law allows a person to acquire a beneficial interest in the house, the more property rights will come into existence. And the type of property right we are talking about here is not an easement or a restrictive covenant. It is a right in equity to part ownership of the house. It will prevent a bank from repossessing a house[260] and will take part of the value of the house from a purchaser.

LECTURER: And how does this relate to your "certainty" argument?

STUDENT: The law must be very clear and predictable in the way it allows a non-owning cohabitee to acquire a beneficial interest in the house. If the law allowed such rights to come into being simply because a cohabitant had given up work to look after the children, or had done the housework, then it would become unpredictable when a cohabitee had acquired a beneficial interest.

LECTURER: Therefore?

STUDENT: A purchaser or mortgage lender would not be able to predict the rights that would bind them after any sale or mortgage of the house. Currently the law is good on the basis of BUILDING BLOCK NO 5. A purchaser or mortgage lender could simply ask any occupier of the property whether they had contributed to the purchase of the house. And then they would be able to find out whether it was likely that someone could claim a beneficial interest. But if it became easier to acquire a beneficial interest a purchaser or mortgage lender may have difficulty finding out about a right that could potentially bind them.

LECTURER: And as we shall see in Registered Land Law the beneficial owner only needs to be in "actual occupation" of the house and their right will bind a later purchaser or mortgage lender. When we look at Land Transfer Law, Chapters 7 and 8 we will see that there are various rules that protect a purchaser from being bound by earlier beneficial interests under a trust, including "overreaching". You can then see whether you think purchasers and mortgage lenders are sufficiently protected should the *Rosset* law be interpreted in a broader way.

> Notice that our STUDENT is asking questions and arguing imaginatively—not just accepting that the existence of property rights will *always* create a problem for purchasers, but asking questions about the circumstances in which property rights may not cause such a problem, i.e. where the purchaser could have found out about them.

(iii) An expanded approach[261]

In *Stack v Dowden*[262] the House of Lords made certain obiter remarks that called for an expanded approach to the type of conduct from which a common intention may be implied.

---

260 Although even where a mortgagee is bound by a beneficial interest under a trust, they can apply to the court for an order of sale under s.14 of the Trusts of Land and Appointment of Trustees Act 1996. However, if the court orders sale, the bank can only claim their interest out of what is left of the proceeds of sale: the beneficiary under the trust will have the prior claim to be satisfied out of the proceeds, if their interest is held to take priority under *Boland* principles.

261 For an advocate of this approach see M.Dixon, *Modern Land Law*, 7th edn (Routledge, 2010), pp.168–9.

262 [2007] 2 A.C. 432.

Lord Walker thought that the court should consider conduct such as manual labour and improvements to the house: "while remaining sceptical of the value of alleged improvements that are really insignificant".[263] In this respect Lord Walker stated that Lord Bridge's approach had been too narrow.

> "Whether or not Lord Bridge's observation [that he doubted whether anything less than direct contributions would do to infer a common intention] was justified in 1990, in my opinion the law has moved on, and your Lordships should move it a little more in the same direction".[264]

Baroness Hale thought that

> "The law has indeed moved on in response to changing social and economic conditions. The search is to ascertain the parties' shared intentions. . . with respect to the property in the light of their whole course of conduct in relation to it."[265]

Thus, in order to ascertain whether there is a common intention that the property should be shared the court should adopt a "holistic" approach, unrestricted by the need to find direct contributions, and ascertain the parties' common intentions from their whole course of dealings in relation to the house.[266] The court should consider any discussions the parties had about their intentions for the house, the reason why the house was purchased, the nature of the parties' relationship and whether they had any children for whom they needed to provide a home. It should consider how the house was financed and how the couple arranged their finances.[267] The court should also consider any other relevant factors. In this way the court should infer what the couple intended and whether they intended for the non legal owner to acquire an interest.[268]

Binding authority?

As to the binding nature of the authority of these statements, *Stack v Dowden* was a case involving quantification of the parties' beneficial shares where the house had been purchased in their joint names. It did not concern directly the question of whether a non legal owner could *acquire an interest in the first place*. Therefore, these remarks, as obiter dictum, are only persuasive authority. They are not binding.

---

263 [2007] 2 A.C. 432, paras 34 and 36.
264 Above, para.26. His lordship doubted whether Lord Bridge's formulation in *Lloyds's Bank Plc v Rosset* "took full account of the views (conflicting though they were) expressed in *Gissing v Gissing*", referring especially to Lord Reid [1971] A.C. 886, pp.896–7 and Lord Diplock, p.909.
265 *Stack v Dowden* [2007] UKHL 17, para.60.
266 Above, para.60.
267 Above, para.69.
268 Also Lord Walker, above para.31. This "holistic" approach is the way in which the courts quantify the claimant's beneficial share, i.e. determine the size of it, once she has proved that she has acquired one. Here the House of Lords were advocating that the same holistic approach should be adopted to ascertain whether the claimant has *acquired* a beneficial interest in the first place.

In *Abbott v Abbott*[269] Baroness Hale, in delivering the advice of the Privy Council, confirmed these statements criticising Lord Bridge's formula.[270] The case concerned directly the question of whether a wife had *acquired* a beneficial interest in the matrimonial home. The husband was the sole legal owner. The Privy Council applied the broader approach suggested in *Stack v Dowden*. It surveyed the parties' whole course of dealing with the house and held that the inference was that the couple intended to share the beneficial interest equally. The husband's mother had provided the land upon which the matrimonial home was built, and had intended it to be a gift to the couple. The couple organised their finances jointly. Although the husband was the sole legal owner of the house, they had a loan to finance the house that was paid into their joint bank account, their income was paid into this account, and they had a mortgage on the house for which they both assumed responsibility.[271]

Abbott v Abbott was a Privy Council decision, and so persuasive authority only, and the claimant could have established an interest under ordinary *Rosset* principles (para.15). Furthermore, the husband conceded that she was entitled to a beneficial interest but disputed the size of that interest. Therefore it is not a strong indicator that the courts will adopt this new approach in cases such as *Burns v Burns*.

The broader or "holistic" approach advocated in *Stack v Dowden* has been adopted in one first instance decision to award the claimant a 25 per cent beneficial share of property registered in the name of his mother and brother. In this case it was by no means definite that he could acquire an interest under the ordinary *Rosset* principles.[272] But apart from this the broader approach to establishing a common intention constructive trust, advocated in *Stack v Dowden*, has had a fairly cold judicial reception. In *De Bruyne v De Bruyne*[273] Patten L.J. in the Court of Appeal recognised that the correct approach to the acquisition of a beneficial interest in the family home, where that property belonged legally to another, was that laid down in *Lloyd's Bank v Rosset*.[274] Although he recognised that *Rosset* had been criticised as "too narrowly stated" by the House of Lords in *Stack v Dowden* and that a broader approach had been recommended, Patten L.J. considered that the "approach is not uncontroversial and has been said by some commentators and practitioners to be unworkable".[275] In *Gledhill's Trustee v Gledhill*[276] District Judge Saffman applied the *Rosset* criteria, but in a slightly broader way, inferring a common intention through payments to renovation.

---

269 [2007] UKPC 53.
270 [2007] UKPC 53, paras 5, 6 and 18.
271 para.7.
272 *Hapeshi v Allnatt* [2010] EWHC 392; M.Dixon, *Modern Land Law*, pp.166.
273 [2010] EWCA Civ 519.
274 [1991] 1 A.C. 107.
275 para.42. The point was made obiter as in *De Bruyne*, a constructive trust was imposed on the basis of the rule in *Rochefoucauld v Boustead* [1897] 1 Ch. 196.
276 [2011] B.P.I.R. 918.

LECTURER: Do you think a broader approach to the acquisition of beneficial interests in the family home will make good and fair law?

STUDENT: If the *Stack v Dowden* approach became the law, it would make it much harder to predict in advance whether a cohabitee has acquired a beneficial interest.

LECTURER: And which other class of litigant would be affected by a change in the law?

STUDENT: Purchasers and mortgage lenders.

LECTURER: A broader approach would cause difficulties for third party purchasers of the house from the sole legal owner, or mortgage lenders, where the legal owner has granted a charge over the house after the time at which the claimant has allegedly established a beneficial interest.

Can you think of why the *Stack v Dowden* broader approach to the finding of a constructive trust might make it difficult for purchasers and mortgage lenders to find out in advance whether they will be affected by someone claiming a beneficial interest under a trust?

STUDENT: How could a purchaser or mortgage lender survey the whole course of the parties' dealing in relation to the house? They could not make any meaningful inquiry that would tell them whether someone was able to claim a beneficial interest.

> **"This ... approach has generated criticism, not the least because it offers little predictability nor certainty for third parties."**
>
> *Megarry & Wade Law of Real Property* 7th edn (2008), para.11.025

(b) The Matrimonial Proceedings and Property Act 1970 section 37

Under s.37 of the Matrimonial Proceedings and Property Act 1970:

> "where a husband or wife contributes in money or money's worth to the improvement of real or personal property in which . . . either or both of them has or have a beneficial interest, the husband or wife so contributing shall, if the contribution is of a substantial nature and subject to any agreement between them to the contrary . . . be treated as having then acquired by virtue of his or her contribution a share or an enlarged share . . . in that beneficial interest of such an extent as may have been then agreed or, in default of such agreement, as may seem in all the circumstances just to any court".

By s.2 of the Law Reform (Miscellaneous Provisions) Act 1970 this applies to engaged couples and by the Civil Partnership Act 2004 s.65 to registered civil partners. It does not apply generally to other cohabitants.

(c) Quantifying the size of the claimant's share

After it has been established that the non-owning partner is entitled to a beneficial interest, it is necessary for the courts to determine the *size* of that interest. If you remember where a person is claiming an interest under a resulting trust, they obtain a beneficial interest proportionate to their contribution. With constructive trusts the courts take a more flexible approach to the question of the size of the claimant's share.

In *Midland Bank v Cooke*[277] a wife made small contribution to the purchase of the house by way of a wedding gift given to her and her husband—just over 6 per cent of the price of the house. Therefore she had established an interest in the house under principles in *Lloyds Bank v Rosset*. So what was the size of the share she was to have? The judge at first instance said that the wife should have a beneficial interest proportionate to her contribution, i.e. 6 per cent of the value of the house. This was overturned by the Court of Appeal. Waite L.J. held that when quantifying interests that have arisen under a constructive trust a court is not bound to award a proportionate interest. Applying statements from *Gissing v Gissing*,[278] he held that where there is evidence of the parties actual intentions as to the size of shares they both were to have, the court must give effect to this. For example, if the claimant had been promised a 60 per cent share then this would be sufficient evidence of their actual intentions and the claimant would be awarded 60 per cent of the beneficial interest. However, the parties may not have discussed the matter. It is possible that couples may not have intended that their shares in the property be determined immediately on acquisition of the house. They may be taken to have intended that their shares should not be assessed until a later time. In such a case, in order to throw "light on the question of what shares were intended" the court must

"undertake a survey of the whole course of dealing between the parties relevant to their ownership and occupation of the property and their sharing of its burdens and advantages".

Undertaking such a survey in the present case, Waite L.J. found that the parties had shared their lives together, committed themselves to each other through marriage, and had eventually put the property in joint names. The wife had improved the house and garden and shared her earnings. Because of all these factors, Waite L.J. held that the couple had intended to share everything equally so the wife was awarded a 50 per cent interest in the house.

However, Waite L.J. said that he arrived at the conclusion about what the couple *intended* from a survey of their whole course of dealing in relation to the ownership and occupation of the house. Yet the parties admitted that they had not given a single thought to the matter! So the search for their *intentions* as to the shares they would have is somewhat artificial. The Court of Appeal addressed this point in *Oxley v Hiscock*.[279] It was held that where there was no agreement between the couple as to their shares in the house

"the answer was that each was entitled to that share which the court considered fair having regard to the whole course of dealing between them in relation to the property, including any arrangements made to meet the various outgoings required to be met to live in the property as their home".

---

277 [1995] 4 All E.R. 562.
278 [1971] A.C. 886.
279 [2004] 3 W.L.R. 715.

Thus, the Court of Appeal suggested abandoning the potentially artificial search for what the parties intended in favour of allowing the court to impose its own solution on the parties on the basis of what was fair.[280]

In *Stack v Dowden*,[281] which we will consider more fully below, the House of Lords reviewed the law relating to quantification of beneficial interests. Baroness Hale, who gave the leading judgment for the majority,[282] stated that in the domestic-consumer context, the courts should adopt the approach in *Oxley v Hiscock*:

"[t]he search is to ascertain the parties' shared intentions, actual, inferred or imputed, with respect to the property in the light of their whole course of conduct in relation to it".[283]

However there were two qualifications: firstly, the courts must examine the conduct of the parties in so far as it related to the ownership of the house. They must not consider conduct with regard to the relationship in general. Secondly, the relevant inquiry is what shares were *intended*. If the courts used a test that awarded the interests that were in all the circumstances *fair*, then this would permit too great a use of judicial discretion.

One criticism of *Stack* is that it does not provide any guidance as to how the parties' beneficial shares should be quantified in the event that there was virtually no evidence of what the parties intended from their course of dealings.[284] In the recent case of *Jones v Kernott*,[285] the Supreme Court acknowledged that in such a case the court could impute an intention to the parties based on their whole course of dealing and award that share that was fair in all the circumstances.

> An "imputation" of an intention is to attribute to the parties an intention which they did not in fact have. To draw an "inference" of an intention from the parties' conduct is to bring in a finding of their real intentions.

The "whole course of dealing" approach to ascertaining the size of the parties' respective shares in the property, applies only in the domestic-consumer context,[286] although it is not restricted to couples sharing a house.[287]

---

280 See also *Drake v Whipp* [1996] F.L.R. 826.
281 [2007] UKHL 17; [2007] 2 A.C. 432; S.Gardner and K.Davidson (2011) 127 L.Q.R. 13; W.Swadling (2007) 123 L.Q.R. 511; M.Dixon [2007] Conv. 456; E.Cooke [2011] Fam. Law 1142; N.Piska (2008) 71 M.L.R. 120; *Stack v Dowden* was a case where the legal title was registered in the parties' joint names. We will deal with this situation below.
282 Lord Neuberger dissented on the law but agreed with the result. He considered that the resulting trust analysis should apply. Where the parties had contributed unequally then they should get an interest proportionate to their contributions.
283 [2007] 2 A.C. 432, para.60.
284 For example see *Adekunle v Ritchie* [2007] 2 P & CR DG20, where there was little evidence beyond what the parties had contributed financially, which, under the doctrine of constructive trusts, is inconclusive evidence of what the parties intended: *Stack v Dowden*.
285 [2011] UKSC 53.
286 *Stack v Dowden* [2007] 2 A.C. 432, para.60, per Baroness Hale.
287 *Adekunle v Ritchie* [2007] 2 P. & C.R. DG20; *Hapeshi v Allnatt* [2010] EWHC 392.

(i) Quantifying the size of the claimant's share: factors relevant to determining the parties' intentions

In *Stack v Dowden* Baroness Hale held that in order to determine the size of the claimant's beneficial interest the court must examine the parties' whole course of dealing in relation to the house.[288] The court would consider whether the parties had any discussions at the time of purchase of the house that could shed light on the size of the beneficial shares that were intended. Regard will be had to the nature of their relationship and whether they had children that they both had to provide a home for. This may make it more likely that they intended to own the house in equal shares. The court would also consider the way in which the couple organised their finances, e.g. how they paid for the upkeep of the house.[289] For example, if the parties contributed to the running of the house from their pooled resources, the inference would be that each intended that they would both contribute what they could and to share the benefit equally.

In *Abbott v Abbott*[290] a wife established an equitable half-share in the house. The couple arranged their finances jointly and assumed joint liability for a mortgage. Furthermore, the husband's mother had provided the land on which the matrimonial home was built and paid the construction costs, intending it to be a joint gift to the couple.

(ii) Constructing an argument with the Building Blocks

LECTURER: Do you think that the law that determines the *size* of the claimant share is good and fair law?

STUDENT: It's definitely better than the doctrine of resulting trusts, which awards a share proportionate to the financial contribution made.

LECTURER: So on what basis do you think it is good law?

STUDENT: On the basis of BUILDING BLOCK NO.2.

BUILDING BLOCK NO 2: Ideas of Justice

Property gives a person choice over what to do with the house. Effectively this will give them more control over what they can do with their lives: Harris, *Property and Justice*, p.273.

Under *Stack v Dowden* the law gives the claimant a share that better reflects her input into the running of the joint household. The house is the centre of the parties' lives, and the claimant has contributed to the parties' joint life together. Thus, both parties should have a level of ownership and control over it. The law that would award the claimant an equal share in such circumstances is good law on the basis of this Building Block.

---

288 [2007] 2 A.C. 432; We will consider this in greater detail below when we examine joint legal ownership cases.
289 [2007] 2 AC 432, per Baroness Hale, paras 69–70.
290 [2007] UKPC 53.

LECTURER: But what about certainty and the position of third party purchasers and mortgage lenders?

> **BUILDING BLOCK NO 5: Property Rights and the Protection of Purchasers and Mortgage Lenders**
> We can argue that a development of a rule in a case or statute is good or bad fair or unfair, depending on the extent to which it supports or undermines the idea that rules of Land Law should protect a purchaser or mortgage lender from being bound by prior interests in the land. This is the policy behind the 1925 property legislation.

STUDENT: Well, under *Lloyds Bank v Rosset* there must either be an express common intention, which the claimant relied upon to her detriment, or she must have contributed financially to the purchase of the house. This is what she needs to do in order to *acquire* a beneficial interest in the first place. However, when the courts are determining the size of that interest, they will survey the parties' dealings with the house and award the share that reflects their intentions. So although it would be fairly easy to predict in advance whether the claimant had acquired an interest in the house, the size of that interest would probably be rather obscure.

LECTURER: So the rules provide insufficient certainty and predictability for third party purchasers and mortgage lenders?

STUDENT: At least the rules would allow them to understand that someone *may* be claiming a beneficial interest, so that at this point they could either wait for further information or withdraw from the transaction entirely.

LECTURER: A mortgage lender would probably try to obtain the cohabitee's consent to a mortgage transaction. For the circumstances in which the claimant's beneficial interest will bind third party purchasers and mortgage lenders see Chapters 7 and 8.

(d) Reform of the property rights of cohabitees

The Law Commission has given extensive consideration to the law that determines whether a person can acquire a beneficial interest in land belonging to another. It concluded that the current law is a patchwork of legal rules which is uncertain and difficult to apply.[291] The rules also produce unfairness. The rules in *Lloyds Bank v Rosset*,[292] are overly restrictive as to when a claimant can establish that she has acquired an interest in the house. The law does not allow a cohabitant to acquire an interest in the home by ordinary relationship-based conduct, such as giving up work to look after the children, cleaning and decorating the house etc.

In its first report in this area, *Sharing Homes—A Discussion Paper*,[293] the Law Commission concluded that it was not possible to lay down a general scheme for the allocation of property

---

291   *Sharing Homes—A Discussion Paper* (2002) Law Com No.278.
292   [1991] 1 A.C. 107.
293   (2002) Law Com No.278.

rights in the family home. There were too many different types of relationship and living arrangements and it was impossible to legislate for all of them. Instead the Law Commission encouraged home owners to make express provision for their beneficial interests in the conveyance of the house.

In a later report the Law Commission reconsidered its position on reform. It published a recommended scheme for financial relief on the breakdown of a quasi-matrimonial relationship.[294] The scheme was targeted at situations such as *Burns v Burns*, where one partner has contributed a significant amount of domestic labour and possibly given up opportunities to work in order to look after the children.[295] The Law Commission no longer considered it realistic to expect couples to make express legal arrangements to formalise their interests in the home. Many couples believe in "the common law marriage myth", i.e. that people who live together outside marriage have rights in the home by virtue of this status.

The Cohabitation Bill 2009 was introduced into parliament in the 2009–2010 session. If enacted into law it would give the court extensive discretion to redistribute property belonging to a cohabiting couple on the breakdown of their relationship.

(6) Situation 2: joint names
Whenever land is conveyed to two or more people, the Law of Property Act 1925 imposes a trust. The legal owners will therefore hold on trust for themselves. However, a conveyance into joint names does not, by itself, determine what their equitable/beneficial shares are, whether 50/50 or (for example) 25/75. If the parties do not expressly state in the conveyance how the *beneficial interest* is shared, there could be disputes between them in the future as to who should have what shares in the house. After all, remember that this is the "real ownership" of the land, i.e. its value. It is crucial for parties to know *just how much* of the value of the house they are entitled to. They may be separating and wish to buy another house elsewhere.[296]

Of course it is much more straightforward if couples purchasing a house[297] can agree this at the time they buy the house and record their agreement in the conveyance. Such an express declaration will be conclusive as to the beneficial shares the parties hold.[298] But this does not always happen and there are many cases in which joint legal owners are in dispute about the size of their beneficial shares.

(a) The starting point in joint ownership cases
In such a case there is no need for the claimant to establish that she has *acquired* an interest in the property, either through the principles in *Lloyds Bank v Rosset* or otherwise. Whenever

---

294   *The Financial Consequences of Relationship Breakdown* Law Com No.307 (2007).
295   To echo recent observations in *Jones v Kernott* [2011] UKSC 53 (Official Transcript, Westlaw No. 2011 5105146, November 9, 2011), it does not appear that the recommended scheme will be enacted into law at any point in the near future.
296   See for example *Jones v Kernott* [2011] UKSC 53.
297   The law in this section is not restricted to couples who purchase a house, but applies whenever land is purchased jointly in a domestic/consumer context: *Stack v Dowden* [2007] 2 A.C. 432, per Baroness Hale.
298   *Goodman v Gallant* [1986] Fam. 106.

property is put legally in the parties' joint names there will be a strong presumption that they intended to own the property beneficially in equal shares. In *Stack v Dowden*,[299] Baroness Hale stated the law in the following way:

> "Just as the starting point where there is sole legal ownership is sole beneficial ownership, the starting point where there is joint legal ownership is joint beneficial ownership. The onus is upon the person seeking to show that the beneficial ownership is different from the legal ownership."

Thus, where the house in put in joint names there will be a "strong presumption" that the parties intended to share the beneficial ownership equally. The reason for the existence of this presumption of joint beneficial ownership was articulated in the joint judgment of Lady Hale and Lord Walker in the Supreme Court in *Jones v Kernott*[300]:

> "If a couple in an intimate relationship (whether married or unmarried) decide to buy a house or flat in which to live together, almost always with the help of a mortgage for which they are jointly and severally liable, that is on the face of things a strong indication of emotional and economic commitment to a joint enterprise."

In such cases where the house is put in joint names the parties will give little thought to how the property should be divided in the event that they separate. They will trust each other.[301] The law should protect this. And thus there is a strong presumption that they intended to share the ownership of the house equally. This is likely to represent the cohabitants' actual (though inarticulate) assumptions. Putting the house in joint names is likely to be a conscious decision involving a large financial commitment by both parties.[302] Furthermore, such a legal presumption offers a simple, inexpensive and clear solution to the property dispute that arises on separation. The *Stack v Dowden* presumption of joint beneficial ownership is intended to discourage litigation.[303]

BUILDING BLOCK NO 6: The Importance of Certainty and Predictability in Land Law Rules

The law should be clear enough for people to be able to predict the consequences of their actions. No one should have to go to court to find out what the law is. Ownership of the house in which they live is of major significance to people, both financially and emotionally. The law must give them a clear way of determining what they own. We may say that the law in *Stack v Dowden* and *Jones v Kernott* is clear and simple and predictable in its outcome. Thus it is good law so far!

---

299   [2007] 2 A.C. 432, paras 54–56.
300   [2011] UKSC 53 (Official Transcript, Westlaw No. 2011 5105146, November 9, 2011), Supreme Court, para.19.
301   Gardner and Davidson (2011) 127 L.Q.R. 13, cited in *Jones v Kernott* [2011] UKSC 53 (Official Transcript, Westlaw No. 2011 5105146, November 9, 2011), per Lady Hale and Lord Walker, para.21.
302   Lord Collins in *Jones v Kernott* [2011] UKSC 53 para.60.
303   *Jones v Kernott* [2011] UKSC 53, per Lady Hale and Lord Walker.

It is clear from Baroness Hale's judgment in *Stack v Dowden* that the presumption of equality, where the house is put in parties' joint names, applies only in the domestic-consumer context. Although this concept has itself been criticised as uncertain,[304] it has been held that the presumption of equality does not apply where the parties have acquired the property for non-domestic reasons, such as investment.[305] In this context the parties' shares are determined by the size of their financial contributions to the purchase of the house.[306] It has also been confirmed that the *Stack v Dowden* law is not restricted to cohabiting couples.[307]

The Supreme Court in *Jones v Kernott*,[308] with notable qualification which we consider below, affirmed the law in *Stack v Dowden*.

Summary
Where a house is put in joint names and there is no express declaration as to the extent or nature of the parties' beneficial shares, there is a strong presumption that they intended to own the house as joint tenants in law and in equity and to hold in equal shares. For an explanation of a joint tenancy see Chapter 4. Essentially it means that when one of the parties dies the other takes their share in the house.

(b) Rebutting the strong presumption of joint beneficial ownership

An attempted rebuttal of the strong presumption of equality is not something that should be undertaken lightly.[309] If such a task is attempted it is for the party asserting that their beneficial ownership is other than equal to prove that the beneficial interests were intended to be shared in different proportions from their legal interests. In order to ascertain this, Baroness Hale in *Stack* confirmed that the court will determine the parties' common intentions from their whole course of dealing in relation to the ownership of the house.[310] The "course of dealing" examined by the court must be only that conduct which related to the ownership of the house, and not the conduct within the relationship generally. Baroness Hale considered that it would have to be a "very unusual" case to rebut the presumption of joint beneficial ownership.[311] It could not be rebutted solely on the basis that the parties had contributed unequally to the purchase of the house. In *Jones v Kernott*,[312] the Supreme Court has recently affirmed that in order for the court

---

304   N.Hopkins, "The relevance of context in property law: a case for judicial restraint?" (2011) 31 L.S. 175.
305   In *Laskar v Laskar* [2008] 1 W.L.R. 2695, para.16, per Lord Neuberger. In this case a mother and daughter purchased a house as an investment. The *Stack v Dowden* presumption of equality did not apply because the house was not to provide a home, even though their relation was "a familial one": paras 17–19.
306   *Laskar v Laskar* [2008] 1 W.L.R. 2695, para.32, per Lord Neuberger.
307   See for example, *Adekunle v Ritchie* [2007] 2 P. & C.R. DG20, which concerned a mother and son whose house was registered in their joint names.
308   [2011] UKSC 53.
309   *Jones v Kernott* [2011] UKSC 53, per Lady Hale and Lord Walker; Lord Collins observes "it is to be expected that joint transferees would have spelled out their beneficial interests when they intended them to be different from their legal interests": para.60.
310   Confirming the law in *Midland Bank v Cooke* [1995] 4 All E.R. 562, and *Oxley v Hiscock* [2004] 3 W.L.R. 715.
311   [2007] 2 A.C. 432, para.70.
312   [2011] UKSC 53.

to arrive at the conclusion that the parties hold in other than equal shares there must be strong evidence pointing to a contrary intention. The courts' search here is initially for what the parties *actually intended*.[313]

"In the event that the evidence were to suggest that, whether by expression or by inference, the parties intended that the beneficial interests in the home should be held in certain proportions, equity would not 'impose' different proportions upon them".

(c) Inference or imputation?

Although the court's first step is to ascertain what the parties intended, either by direct evidence of their actual intentions, or by inferences of intention from the type of conduct we shall consider below, in *Jones v Kernott*[314] the Supreme Court acknowledged that it may not always be possible to divine what *exact* shares the parties intended, once the presumption of equality had been rebutted.[315]

In this respect the law in *Stack v Dowden* went radically wrong at an important point. It had said only that the court was to infer from the parties' whole course of conduct *their real intentions*. But what if there was no such evidence and it was not possible for the court to make such inferences beyond the fact that it was clear that the presumption of equality had been rebutted? How is the court to go that one final step and determine what size shares the parties in fact intended?[316] In such a situation, where there really is no further evidence of the size of shares that the parties intended the Supreme Court in *Jones v Kernott* held that the court could *impute* an intention to the parties based on their whole course of dealing in relation to the house.[317] Lord Kerr articulated the accepted view of the Supreme Court as follows:

"Where the intention as to the division of the property cannot be inferred, each is entitled to that share which the court considers fair. In considering the question of what is fair the court should have regard to the whole course of dealing between the parties."[318]

An "imputation" of intention is to attribute to the co-owners an intention which they never actually had,[319] i.e. what was reasonable or fair in the circumstances.[320] Imputation of intention was the kind of judicial discretion that Lord Bridge in *Lloyds Bank v Rosset* was keen to avoid.[321] It introduces

---

313   [2011] UKSC 53, per Lord Wilson, para.86.
314   Above.
315   Note the difficulty of the judge in *Adekunle v Ritchie* [2007] 2 P & CR DG20 and the criticism on this point in *Jones v Kernott* [2011] UKSC 53, in particular, the joint judgment of Lord Walker and Lady Hale.
316   Lord Collins in *Jones v Kernott* [2011] UKSC 53, para.63 suggested that Baroness Hale in *Stack v Dowden* had meant the search for actual intentions to be relevant to the rebuttal of the presumption only and not to the stage after, i.e. that of determining what shares the parties should then have. See also Lord Wilson, paras 84–5.
317   [2011] UKSC 53, e.g. para.68, summarising the areas in which all the judges in the Supreme Court agreed.
318   [2011] UKSC 53, para.68.
319   *Stack v Dowden* [2007] 2 A.C. 432, para.126, per Lord Neuberger.
320   The judgments of the Supreme Court in *Jones v Kernott* [2011] UKSC 53, which all discussed this issue, do not come to any coherent census on whether imputation means imposition a solution based upon what the parties would reasonably have intended in the circumstances or upon what was fair. Lord Wilson suggested there was no difference: reasonable spouses would intend what was fair.
321   [1991] 1 A.C. 107, p.132.

an element of uncertainty into the law as the judges are simply awarding the shares that they consider fair in the circumstances. In this respect, Lord Kerr in *Jones v Kernott*[322] considered that an inference of what the parties actually intended "is obviously preferable to the court's enforcing a resolution".

LECTURER: In effect the Supreme Court acknowledged that, for the sake of resolving the dispute, it may be necessary to resort to an element of judicial discretion. The court should award to the parties the shares that were fair for them to have in all the circumstances. On which of our Building Blocks might we criticise this element of discretion?

STUDENT: I would use BUILDING BLOCK NO 6.

BUILDING BLOCK NO 6: The Need for Certainty and Predictability in Land Law Rules
If the rules are clear as to how they will resolve cases in the future, i.e. if they allow people (e.g. purchases or occupiers) to predict the legal outcome of particular situations then they are good law.

Such a judicial discretion could be open to the criticism that the law is now uncertain. How will legal advisers be able to predict in advance what shares the parties may have? If judges can decide this on the basis of what if fair one would have to go to court to find out what shares the parties had.

LECTURER: That said it is a notable feature of all these cases that the results tend to be the same whether an intention is imputed on the basis of what is fair or whether it is implied to be the parties' actual intentions. Perhaps the element of uncertainty is overstated. In *Jones v Kernott* itself the Judges of the Supreme Court agreed that the parties' respective shares should be 90 per cent and 10 per cent but disagreed on whether this was a finding based on *imputation* or on inferences of real intentions derived from the parties' conduct. Thus, the distinction between inference and imputation is hardly ever likely to matter in practice.[323]

Indeed, in *Jones v Kernott*[324] Lord Wilson observed that "it was difficult to see how . . . the process could work without the court's supply of what it considered to be fair". Lord Kerr observes that "It would be unfortunate if the concept of inferring were to be strained so as to avoid the less immediately attractive option of imputation".[325] The process of inferring an intention would become unclear and somewhat artificial, given that the courts would be effectively forming a conclusion about what the parties' real intentions were (based on an inference from their whole course of dealing) when in fact it was unlikely that they had ever given the matter much thought.[326]

---

322 [2011] UKSC 53, para.72.
323 [2011] UKSC 53, para.34 (Lord Walker and Lady Hale) and para.65 (Lord Collins). Lord Kerr did not agree that the distinction would make no practical difference (para.67).
324 [2011] UKSC 53, para.87.
325 [2011] UKSC 53, para.72.
326 As in the case of *Midland Bank Plc v Cooke* [1995] 4 All E.R. 562.

(d) Factors relevant to rebutting the presumption of joint beneficial ownership: what do we mean by the parties' "whole course of dealing"?

The presumption of equality cannot be rebutted solely on the basis that the parties contributed in unequal shares to the purchase. In *Stack v Dowden* Baroness Hale identified the type of evidence that is relevant to determining the parties' intentions. For example, their discussions at the time of the purchase may reveal the reasons why the house was put in joint names.[327] The court should look at the nature of the parties' relationship, whether they had children for whom both had responsibility to provide, and how they managed their finances.

> If they arranged their finances separately, one paid most of the purchase price, they had no children to provide a home for, and thus depended on each other much less, the court may be more inclined to hold the presumption of joint interests to have been rebutted. On the other hand, if the parties discharged the outgoings on the property and their other household expenses, from their pooled resources, particularly where the couple are joint owners and jointly liable for the mortgage, the inference would be that each intended that they would both contribute what they could and to share the benefit equally.

It must also be considered whether the parties' intentions could be taken to have changed during the course of their relationship, for example, where "one party has financed (or constructed himself) an extension or substantial improvement to the property, so that what they have now is significantly different from what they had then".[328]

These then, are the factors that the court must bear in mind when considering how the parties' conduct sheds light on what beneficial shares they intended to have. However, Baroness Hale made it clear that it would take an unusual case to rebut the presumption of joint beneficial ownership.

(e) For example . . . Stack v Dowden itself and post-Stack cases

Stack v Dowden itself was just such an "unusual" case. Ms Dowden succeeded in rebutting the presumption of equality. Ms Dowden and Mr Stack were unmarried cohabitees. She had purchased the couple's first house and paid all the expenses. This house was then sold and another purchased. The couple put this second house into their joint names. Ms Dowden had contributed overall 65 per cent of the purchase price. They both contributed to lump sum payments in order to discharge a joint mortgage on the house. Otherwise they kept their finances separate. When the couple split, Mr Stack claimed a half-share of the house.

In surveying the parties' whole course of dealing in relation to the ownership of the house, it was clear that the couple kept their affairs "rigidly separate".[329] Ms Dowden had contributed

---

327   [2007] 2 A.C. 432, per Baroness Hale, para.66.
328   *Stack v Dowden* [2007] 2 A.C. 432, per Baroness Hale, paras 69–70.
329   *Stack v Dowden* [2007] 2 A.C. 432, para.92.

significantly more money to the purchase of the house. This was not a situation "in which it can be said that the parties pooled their separate resources, even notionally, for the common good . . . they undertook separate responsibility for that part of the expenditure which each had agreed to pay".[330] Mr Stack had not agreed at any time to pay for food etc. or to help towards child minding expenses. Ms Dowden was awarded a 65 per cent share and Mr Stack 35 per cent.[331]

In *Adekunle v Ritchie*,[332] a mother and son were joint registered proprietors of the house in which they lived. The mother had contributed about 75 per cent of the purchase money, partly through a "right to buy" discount from the local authority. Behrens J. held that the whole course of the parties' dealings in relation to the house showed that they did not intend equal shares. The presumption of equality had been rebutted. The purpose of the house was to give the mother a home. Mother and son kept their finances separate. The mother had a good relationship with her other children. Had there been a presumption of joint ownership this would have meant a joint tenancy, under which the son would have become the sole owner of the house upon the death of the mother.[333] This would have had the effect of disinheriting the others and is not something she would have intended. Behrens J. held that the son was entitled to a 30 per cent beneficial share of the house.

Although it is clear that the so-called *Stack v Dowden* "holistic approach" applies outside the context of cohabiting couples,[334] as here, to mother and son, Behrens J. stated that

> "it may well be, however, that where one is not dealing with the situation of a couple living together it will be easier to find that the facts are unusual in the sense that they are not to be taken to have intended a beneficial joint tenancy".[335]

(f) The Supreme Court decision in Jones v Kernott
In *Jones v Kernott*,[336] Ms Jones had originally purchased in her sole name a mobile home in 1981. She started living with Mr Kernott. In 1985 she sold her home and a house was purchased in their joint names. They financed the purchase with a joint mortgage, and jointly financed an extension. The outgoings on the house were financed from joint money. The couple had two children. Mr Kernott left in 1993 and made no further contributions either to the house or to the upkeep of his children. He purchased a property of his own in his sole name. After both properties increased significantly in value he claimed that he was entitled to a half share of the jointly owned house, over 15 years after he had left and to which he had made no contribution during that time.

---

330 Above paras 90–91.
331 For critical commentary on *Stack v Dowden* see S.Gardner and K.Davidson (2011) 127 L.Q.R. 13; W.Swadling (2007) 123 L.Q.R. 511; M.Dixon [2007] Conv. 456; E.Cooke [2011] Fam. Law 1142; N.Piska (2008) 71 M.L.R. 120.
332 [2007] 2 P. & C.R. DG20.
333 This is the "right of survivorship" inherent in the concept of the joint tenancy. See Chapter 4.
334 Confirmed by the Court of Appeal in *Laskar v Laskar* [2008] 1 W.L.R. 2695, para.16 per Lord Neuberger.
335 [2007] 2 P. & C.R. DG20.
336 Official Transcript, Westlaw No. 2011 5105146, November 9, 2011.

AT FIRST INSTANCE: the judge held that the presumption of joint beneficial ownership had been rebutted and that Mr Kernott was entitled to a 10 per cent beneficial share.

COURT OF APPEAL: A majority of the Court of Appeal, Jacob L.J. dissenting, held that they were entitled to equal shares—on the basis that until Mr Kernott left they had pooled their resources and intended to share everything equally, and there was no evidence from which to infer that the parties intended different shares after he left.

The Supreme Court overturned the Court of Appeal. When Mr Kernott left he purchased his own house, which he would have been unable to do had he carried on contributing to the jointly owned house and his family. The "logical inference" was that they intended for Mr Kernott's beneficial interest to crystallise at the time of his leaving and that he should not have the benefit of any subsequent increase in value.[337] Mr Kernott was awarded a 10 per cent beneficial share and Ms Jones 90 per cent.[338]

(7) Constructive trusts and joint venture agreements

A constructive trust may arise in other circumstances, perhaps with a more commercial origin, in which it is unconscionable to permit a legal owner to set up his legal title and deny another person a beneficial interest. If there is an express agreement that another will acquire a beneficial interest in land, and this induces reliance on that agreement, a court may impose a constructive trust. It will all depend on the quality of the statements made, the nature of the agreement, and whether reliance upon it was reasonable.[339] The usual type of case is where the parties have agreed to purchase land for a joint venture, for example, to develop land for profit. "Most of these cases concern some kind of joint venture in which there was an arrangement short of a contract under which the parties agreed to acquire property for their mutual benefit."[340]

For example, in *Pallant v Morgan*[341] the plaintiff and defendant were intending to bid for the same land at an auction. They both agreed beforehand that the plaintiff would refrain from bidding and the defendant would acquire the land on behalf of them both. The defendant then attempted to keep the land for himself. The court found that the defendant held the land on constructive trust for himself and the plaintiff. So why did the court impose a constructive trust of the land in favour of the plaintiff? The reason was connected with our BUILDING BLOCK NO 2.

---

337   para.48, per Lady Hale and Lord Walker.
338   para.49. Lady Hale and Lord Walker came to this conclusion on the basis of an inference of the parties' actual intentions. Lord Collins agreed. Lord Kerr thought that it was impossible to infer that Mr Kernott's beneficial interest should crystallise at the point at which he left, but thought that this intention should be imputed to them because it was "eminently fair" (para.77). Lord Wilson expressed a preference for imputing this intention, as inference seemed impossible (para.89).
339   *Baynes Clarke v Corless* [2010] Civ 338.
340   *Baynes Clarke v Corless*, above, para.36, per Patten L.J.
341   [1953] Ch. 43, creating the *"Pallant v Morgan* equity" from the case of that name [1953] Ch. 43. The case was originally decided on the basis that "equity will not permit a statute to be used as an instrument of fraud"; also *Chattock v Muller* (1878) 8 Ch.D 117.

> **BUILDING BLOCK NO 2: Ideas of Justice**
> Rules are good and fair if they take account of moral justice: Every person should be accorded the freedom of their will and autonomous choice. Thus, if people deal with each other and with their property in a way that violates the will of another then the law should offer that other some remedy.

The defendant's promise to acquire the land on behalf of both parties influenced the plaintiff's act of reliance (his withdrawal from the bidding process). Thus, he had been influenced in important choices in a way that permitted the defendant to acquire the land for a lower price than he might have done.

(a) The need for an agreement

There must be an agreement reached between the parties that the non-acquiring party should have an interest in the land.[342] As with proprietary estoppel, the agreement must be of such a nature that it reasonable to rely upon it.[343] In *Banner Homes Group Plc v Luff Developments Ltd*[344] Banner and Luff agreed to develop a plot of land together. Luff subsequently acquired the land in its sole name, Banner having agreed to refrain from acquiring the land in reliance of their agreement. Luff then went back on the agreement. Chadwick L.J. observed[345]:

> "It is the pre-acquisition arrangement which colours the subsequent acquisition . . . by the defendant and leads to his being treated as a trustee if he seeks to act inconsistently with it".[346]

Thus, it appears again that the courts are looking for the pre-acquisition agreement between the parties to have influenced the claimant's reliance upon it, for example, in refraining to insist that the property was purchased in joint names. It was held that Banner acted in reasonable reliance on the agreement that the land would, in reality, be owned by them both. He stood back and refrained from acquiring the land himself. The element of "equitable fraud" must be present,[347] by which, because of the influence of the pre-acquisition agreement, it would be unconscionable to permit the acquiring party to retain sole ownership of the land. It may be difficult in a strictly commercial context to establish that the agreement *influenced* the claimant's alleged reliance upon it. In this context most people contemplating joint ventures connected with the acquisition of land will know that their informal arrangements are unenforceable and that contracts for the creation or disposition of an interest in land must be in writing.[348] They will

---

342   It is not necessary for the agreement to be enforceable as a contract: *Holiday Inns Inc. v Broadhead* (1974) 232 E.G. 951. In *Pallant v Morgan* the original agreement between the plaintiff and defendant was void for uncertainty.

343   *Baynes Clarke v Corless* [2010] EWCA Civ 338, para.41, per Patten L.J. The subjective intent of the acquiring party is irrelevant: above, para.50. The relevant point is whether an agreement has been reached by *all* the joint venturers.

344   [2000] Ch. 372.

345   [2000] Ch. 372, p.397.

346   Also *Time Products Ltd v Combined English Stores Group Ltd* (December 2, 1974, unreported), referred to by Chadwick L.J. and by Lord Scott in *Cobbe v Yeoman's Row Management Ltd* [2008] UKHL 55, para.32.

347   Or as it is now called, *unconscionability: Cobbe v Yeoman's Row Management Ltd* [2008] UKHL 55, from para.30 per Lord Scott.

348   Law of Property (Miscellaneous Provisions) Act 1989 s.2(1).

not be influenced by a reasonable belief that the agreement will be honoured. In relying upon it, they will be taking a calculated risk.[349]

In *London & Regional Investments Ltd v TBI Plc*,[350] TBI owned land and agreed with the claimants that they would enter into a joint venture to develop it. The claimants relied on this agreement, which was said to be "subject to contract". Because of the "subject to contract" provision the fact of the agreement could not be said to have sufficient influence over the conduct of the claimant. Their actions could not be said to be reliance on the fact that they would acquire an interest in land, or if they could it would not be reasonable reliance.[351] The claimant would be fully aware of the possibility that the defendant's undertaking would not be enforceable and that he would be legally free to go back on it. Mummery L.J. observed that:

> "The recorded intentions as to the joint venture implicitly proceeded on the basis that no concluded agreement had been reached and contemplated that such an agreement might never be reached".[352]

Similarly, in *Cobbe v Yeoman's Row Management*,[353] the defendant owned valuable development land and orally agreed with the claimant, an experienced property developer, that the claimant should develop the land and retain any profits, subject to certain overage payments to the defendant. The defendant agreed to sell the land to the claimant. The oral agreement was an "agreement in principle", i.e. both parties knew it to be legally unenforceable. The claimant did a considerable amount of work obtaining planning permission. Once this had been obtained the defendant went back on the agreement, and said that she wanted more advantageous terms. She had even waited until the planning permission had been obtained before backing out of the agreement, to ensure that the claimant carried on with the work. The House of Lords declined to impose a constructive trust because the claimant knew the oral agreement was not legally enforceable and had therefore taken a calculated risk that it would be honoured. He cannot have said to have been influenced by an agreement that he knew to be unenforceable.[354]

(b) Demonstrating reliance—advantage/disadvantage

I think you will perceive from the above that no claim to a constructive trust can be established unless the claimant proves that they relied on the agreement that they were to have an interest in land. However, in this context there is no need to prove a disadvantage to the claimant. Indeed in *Pallant v Morgan* the plaintiff would not have had the authority to outbid the defendant.

---

349   As in the case of *Cobbe v Yeoman's Row Management Ltd* [2008] UKHL 55.

350   [2002] EWCA Civ 355.

351   "The question in every case must be whether the agreement made or the words used were reasonably relied upon by the claimants as an assurance that they would obtain an interest in the property": *Baynes Clarke v Corless* [2010] EWCA Civ 338, para.41, per Patten L.J., relying on statements made by Lord Diplock in *Gissing v Gissing* [1971] A.C. 886, p.905.

352   [2002] EWCA Civ 355, para.47, quoted and relied upon by Lord Scott in *Cobbe v Yeoman's Row Management Ltd* [2008] UKHL 55, para.35.

353   [2008] UKHL 55.

354   [2008] UKHL 55, para.37, per Lord Scott. The case was primarily decided on the basis of the doctrine of proprietary estoppel, under which the claimant's action was also dismissed.

So he suffered no disadvantage as such. He could not have acquired the land. However, it *is* necessary to show that the defendant gained an advantage. In *Pallant v Morgan* the defendant gained the land at a lower price than he otherwise would have done, because the plaintiff refrained from bidding at the auction. Either advantage or detriment will do.[355]

(c) Property owned by one of the joint venturers—an ordinary constructive trust claim?

In *Cobbe v Yeoman's Row Management*,[356] Lord Scott held obiter that a claim to a constructive trust could not succeed where one of the joint venturers already had an entitlement to the land in question.[357] Effectively this is saying that it is not possible to establish a constructive trust by way of express oral agreement and detrimental reliance in a commercial context.

However, rather than preclude *any possibility* of such a claim arising, it is probably better to consider the matter from first principles.[358] For the same reason that it is difficult to establish equitable fraud or unconscionability in most commercial cases where property is acquired in a joint venturer's sole name, it is equally difficult to establish that a person who *already owns the land* should be made liable as a constructive trustee as a result of an express agreement to transfer an interest. Such cases would usually involve experienced property developers, or commercially aware people. Thus, as most would know that the owner would have to at least execute a contract in writing under s.2(1) of the Law of Property (Miscellaneous Provisions) Act 1989, it would be difficult to establish that in relying on any oral agreement that the joint venturers will acquire ownership of the land, they would not simply be taking a calculated risk that the legal owner would not change their mind.[359] There would thus be no evidence that the non-legal owner was acting in the reasonable belief that they would acquire an interest in the land. The required element of influence would be lacking.

(d) Constructive trusts and section 2(1) of the Law of Property (Miscellaneous Provisions) Act 1989

In *Herbert v Doyle*[360] the Court of Appeal confirmed that although it was possible for a constructive trust to arise in a commercial context, one cannot be imposed to give effect to an oral agreement concerning the disposition of land, simply by virtue of the part-performance of the agreement, if that agreement was unenforceable by virtue of s.2(1) of the Law of Property (Miscellaneous Provisions) Act 1989. The agreement would be void if the parties intended to formalise their

---

355 *Banner Homes Group Plc v Luff Developments Ltd* [2000] Ch. 372, p.397, applied in *Baynes Clarke v Corless* [2010] EWCA Civ 338.

356 [2008] UKHL 55.

357 paras 33 and 37. In such circumstances the situation would be governed by the doctrine of proprietary estoppel. See also *Banner Homes v Luff Developments* [2000] Ch. 372, p.397 per Chadwick L.J.

358 The view of Lord Scott in *Cobbe v Yeoman's Row Management* [2008] UKHL 55 that a proprietary estoppel could never be established in the commercial context was doubted in *Thorner v Major* [2009] UKHL 18.

359 A possible exception is *Yaxley v Gotts* [2000] Ch. 162 in which a builder had been promised an interest in land by the defendant if, once the land had been acquired in the defendant's name, he would develop it. Both parties had intended to enter into a formal agreement but there was some suggestion that there was a promise not to insist on the formality. In such cases, there would be sufficient influence: See e.g. M.Dixon, "Confining and defining proprietary estoppel: the role of unconscionability" (2010) 30 L.S. 408.

360 [2010] EWCA Civ 1095.

arrangement at a later date, or where the parties' knew, as in *Cobbe v Yeoman's Row Management Ltd*[361] that the oral agreement could not be enforced.

However, *if* the claimant can establish an interest under a constructive trust this is exempt from the requirement that a contract for the creation of an interest in land must be in writing.[362] In *Yaxley v Gotts*[363] the owner of a block of flats agreed to give the claimant the ground floor flat if he would renovate the building and manage the lettings. The parties' arrangement was not put in writing as required by s.2(1). However, it was held that once the claimant had acted in reliance on the oral agreement, a constructive trust had arisen. This was enforceable without any writing as constructive trusts are exempt from s.2(1).

D. ADVERSE POSSESSION OF LAND[364]

(1) Introduction

If a trespasser takes possession of land belonging to another, i.e. to which he has no entitlement whatsoever, and he stays in possession for a period of 12 years continuous and uninterrupted, then after that time he acquires ownership of the land. There is no formal transfer into the trespasser's name. He acquires his ownership, or "title", entirely by possessing the land.

> You will often see this principle referred to in the newspapers as "squatters' rights".

(a) The doctrine derives from the principle of "relativity of title"

The fact that one can establish a title to land through adverse possession is because ownership of land has traditionally been a relative rather than an absolute concept.[365] It is possible to enter into possession of land, to which the squatter has no documentary title, and to acquire a form of effective "ownership" (or "title") over it. In brief, ownership, as we have seen, means that the owner of the land has the ability to exclude the whole world. A squatter in possession of land, by virtue of that possession, can exclude the whole world. He has what the law calls a "possessory title". There is, however, an important qualification. He cannot exclude anyone with a superior or better title. Thus, what you may call the "real owner" of the land, i.e. the person into whose name the land has been conveyed and registered, can come forward and evict the squatter. And he would be well advised to do so, given how the law works.

---

361   [2008] UKHL 55.
362   Law of Property (Miscellaneous Provisions) Act 1989 s.2(1). The exemption is affected by s.2(5).
363   [2000] 1 All E.R. 711.
364   E.H.Burn, *Maudsley & Burn's Land Law Cases and Materials*; Dockray, "Adverse Possession and Intention" [1982] Conv. 256.
365   *Asher v Whitlock* (1865) L.R. 1 Q.B. 1.

We see that as against the whole world the squatter has the better title, and can evict any unwanted people from the land. But as between the squatter and the owner of the documentary title, the latter has the stronger title. We call this principle "relativity of title". There is no principle of absolute ownership.[366]

> The owner of the documentary title, or the "paper owner" as we shall call him or her, has the better title. And he ought to assert that title and evict the squatter—for reasons that we will now see.

(b) The Limitation Act 1980

We have seen that a squatter acquires what is called a *possessory title*. The owner of the paper title has the right to reclaim possession of the land from that squatter. But such a right of action ceases after 12 years. So if a person enters into possession of land, dispossessing the paper owner, that owner must bring an action for recovery of the land within 12 years. The Limitation Act 1980 provides that after this time the paper owner's right to recover the land from the squatter is extinguished. His title to the land is extinguished.[367]

> Accordingly, the squatter who entered into possession of land and maintained that possession continuously and without interruption, has a possessory title to the land which now defeats any claim to ownership of the land made by the paper owner.

(c) Critical Thinking about adverse possession

LECTURER: What have you understood about the doctrine of adverse possession so far?

STUDENT: I can't believe the law would do that! Allow someone just to take land that isn't theirs to occupy and then not allow the real owner to get it back.

LECTURER: Can you see no justification for the rule whatsoever?

STUDENT: None whatsoever!

LECTURER: There are some justifications for the existence of the doctrine of adverse possession. Let's see if they convince you. The first one is that the paper owner has had 12 years to evict the squatter and to protect his own interests. And he has not acted. He has remained entirely passive.

STUDENT: Almost as if he didn't care for the land or didn't want it.

LECTURER: Yes that's right.

STUDENT: So the law should let someone take charge of it who is going to look after it.

LECTURER: Yes, the law should not allow the paper owner to "go to sleep on his rights".

---

366   *Asher v Whitlock* (1865) L.R. 1 Q.B. 1.
367   Limitation Act 1980 s.17.

> "It is a policy of the Limitation Acts that those who go to sleep upon their claims should not be assisted by the courts in recovering their property".
>
> *R.B.Policies at Lloyd's v Butler* [1950] 1 K.B. 76, p.81, per Streatfield J.

LECTURER: What if you were the squatter and had made the land your own, enclosed it with a fence, and grew things on it and so forth. Perhaps it is unclear who really owns the land. Would you want the threat of litigation hanging over your head forever?

STUDENT: It makes more sense when people are not sure who really owns the land and they want to be sure that they are not disturbed. Perhaps they need the land. But if they are blatantly aware that they are using someone else's land I still don't see why the law should give it to them.

LECTURER: A windfall so to speak!

> "[A]nother, and, I think, equal policy behind the [Limitation Act], is that there shall be an end of litigation".
>
> *R.B.Policies at Lloyd's v Butler* [1950] 1 K.B. 76, p.81, per Streatfield J.

LECTURER: But if a person has built on the land, perhaps mistakenly, and genuinely used it as if it were their own, cared for it and so forth, to have the possibility of having it taken away at any time in the future might be considered unjust on one of our Building Blocks.

STUDENT: In your example, those people could have become attached to the land. We have a deep personal connection with the land on which we live, it can become entwined with our sense of identity and well-being. If the law would allow the paper owner to take it away at any time in the future, however long into the future and despite the fact that he has not cared for the land, this is potentially bad law on the basis of BUILDING BLOCK NO 3.[368]

BUILDING BLOCK NO 3: Property and Identity

Rules are good if they take proper account of the fact that people gain a sense of value and worth from ownership of land, particularly in the context of owner occupation. Thus, Land Law rules should not deprive people of that possession without adequate safeguards. So we can say that a rule is good or bad fair or unfair, depending on the extent to which it protects a person's ownership from interference.

> "It is . . . an Act of peace. Long dormant claims have often more of cruelty than of justice in them".
>
> *A' Court v Cross* (1825) 3 Bing 329, p.332, per Best C.J.

---

368   K.Gray, *Elements of Land Law*, 2nd edn (London: Butterworths, 1993).

STUDENT: However, I don't think that this justifies the doctrine of adverse possession in all cases. It wouldn't in a case where the squatter knew full well that the land did not belong to them and was trying to take advantage of the law.

LECTURER: Another justification comes from our BUILDING BLOCK NO 5. In our economy land must be capable of being transferred easily. If the squatter sells the land to a purchaser and years later that purchaser sells the land to Purchaser 2, the original paper owner that was dispossessed by the squatter will only be able to claim the land back from the purchasers for 12 years after the squatter originally took possession. This means that the conveyances after the 12 year period can be fully relied upon by purchasers. They will have what we call a "good title".

In effect they can rely upon the person in possession of the land to convey to them a good title. The doctrine of adverse possession allows the person in control to acquire title and with it, the ability to transfer that title to a purchaser.[369]

> **BUILDING BLOCK NO 5: Property Rights and the Protection of Purchasers and Mortgage Lenders**

LECTURER: The doctrine of adverse possession is useful in another sense. It helps to resolve boundary issues between neighbours. Neighbours can often fall out over the precise location of the boundary between their properties. Have you heard of this kind of dispute?[370]

STUDENT: Definitely! One house owner may put up a fence or build a wall and the other may say that it has taken up three inches of their land.

LECTURER: And neighbours can often fall out very badly over something like this. They may go on forever arguing about where the precise boundary line should be. Can you see where the doctrine of adverse possession comes in to help this situation?

STUDENT: Well, if one neighbour had put up a fence that *did* take up some of his neighbour's land and it stayed there for 12 years, he would get the full ownership of that part of the land. There would then be no dispute.

(2) What is "adverse possession"?

As we have seen, the Limitation Act 1980 operates to extinguish the paper owner's title to the land after 12 years continuous possession by the squatter. However, this time will not start running against the paper owner until the squatter is in "adverse possession".[371]

---

369   Note that this justification for the adverse possession doctrine applies with less force in the context of registered land law, which is why the Land Registration Act 2002 restricts the ability to establish adverse possession of registered land. See below.

370   For recent examples: *Huntley v Armes* [2010] EWCA Civ 396; *Zarb v Parry* [2011] EWCA Civ 1306.

371   Limitation Act 1980 Sch.1, para.8(1).

Adverse possession
This simply means that the squatter must have a sufficient degree of factual possession of the land, coupled with the intention to possess, and without the consent of the owner of the paper title.

Slade J. in *Powell v McFarlane*,[372] stated that

"If the law is to attribute possession of land to a person who can establish no paper title to possession, he must be shown to have both factual possession and the requisite intention to possess ('animus possidendi')".[373]

The principles of the doctrine of adverse possession were reviewed and restated by Slade J. in *Powell v McFarlane*,[374] which judgment was approved by the Court of Appeal in *Buckinghamshire County Council v Moran*[375] and the House of Lords in *J.A.Pye (Oxford) Ltd v Graham*.[376]

(a) Adverse possession must be continuous

The squatter must show either that the paper owner had "discontinued" his possession of the land, i.e. he had left the land, or that the squatter has "dispossessed" the paper owner.[377] In addition the squatter's adverse possession must be continuous. It does not matter if several successive squatters possessed the land for a total of 12 years.

Example
If A adversely possesses land for three years, and B takes over possession from him for a further nine years, B will be able to establish that the paper owner's title is extinguished. However, the periods of adverse possession must be successive and continuous.

Thus, if the paper owner interrupts possession and the squatter resumes his adverse possession, then the 12 year count will start afresh. For example, if the paper owner brings a successful action for possession of the land, this will interrupt the squatter's adverse possession,[378] but this will not be the case if the possession proceedings are abandoned.[379] If the squatter starts paying rent to the paper owner or is given a licence to occupy the land by the paper owner then these are both ways in which the paper owner gives to the squatter his *consent*. Adverse possession

---

372 (1977) 38 P. & C.R. 452, p.470.
373 Otherwise the law ascribes possession to the paper owner.
374 (1977) 38 P. & C.R. 452.
375 [1990] Ch. 623.
376 [2003] 1 A.C. 419.
377 *Treloar v Nute* [1976] 1 W.L.R. 1295.
378 Clarke and Greer, *Land Law Directions*, p.183.
379 *Markfield Investments Ltd v Evans* [2001] 2 All E.R. 238.

can only be established if the squatter is in possession *without the consent of the paper owner*. Thus, the payment and acceptance of rent or the grant of a licence will stop the time from running against the paper owner. If, when the lease expires, the tenant stays in possession without the consent of the paper owner then time will start running afresh.

So what does a squatter have to show in order to bring a successful claim to adverse possession of the land?

We have seen that in order for time to start running against the paper owner the squatter must be in "adverse possession". In *Pye v Graham*[380] the House of Lords held that this simply means that the squatter must have (i) a sufficient degree of factual possession of the land, (ii) coupled with the intention to possess, and (iii) the squatter's possession of the land must be without the consent of the owner of the paper title. We will now examine each of these elements in turn.

(b) There must be factual possession[381]

The squatter must be in possession of the land *in fact*. He must show that he has taken control of the land in the way an occupying owner would: "a sufficient degree of physical custody and control".[382] In *Powell v McFarlane*[383] Slade J. looked to define the idea of "taking possession":

> "Possession of land . . . is a concept which has long been familiar and of importance to English lawyers, because (inter alia) it entitles the person in possession, whether rightfully or wrongfully, to maintain an action of trespass against any other person who enters the land without his consent, unless such other person has himself a better right to possession. In the absence of authority, therefore, I would for my own part have regarded the word 'possession' . . . as bearing the traditional sense of that degree of occupation or physical control, coupled with the requisite intention commonly referred to as animus possidendi, that would entitle a person to maintain an action of trespass in relation to the relevant land".[384]

Slade J. goes on to say that in order to show factual possession the squatter must show that he "has been dealing with the land in question as an occupying owner might have been expected to deal with it and that no-one else has done so".[385]

LECTURER: So what Slade J. is saying is that in order to understand what degree of control of the land will establish "factual possession" it must be the type of control and custody that an owner exercises over his land. So let's re-examine BUILDING BLOCK NO 4 as this one helps us to understand what an owner is entitled to do with his land.

---

380 [2003] 1 A.C. 419.
381 Dockray, "Adverse Possession and Intention" [1982] Conv. 256.
382 *J.A.Pye (Oxford) Ltd v Graham* [2003] 1 A.C. 419, para.40 per Lord Browne-Wilkinson.
383 (1977) 38 P. & C.R. 452, p.469.
384 Confirmed in *Pye v Graham* [2003] 1 A.C. 419, para.32 per Lord Browne-Wilkinson.
385 *Powell v McFarlane* (1977) 38 P. & C.R. 452, p.471.

> **BUILDING BLOCK NO 4: Ideas of Ownership**
> So what is "ownership"? Bright observes:
>> "Ownership itself is a set of open-ended use privileges and open-ended powers to control the use made by others of the property. . . . It is simply not possible to list all the potential uses which the owner may make of the property—she can live on it, use it for growing crops, climb trees on it, and so on." S.Bright, "Of Estates and Interests: A Tale of Ownership and Property Rights" in *Land Law Themes and Perspectives*, p.529.
>
> An owner can include or exclude anyone they please. As Gray and Gray observe, the key factor of possession is *control*.
>> "Far from denoting a mere factual presence upon land, possession comprises a range of inner assumptions . . . [that] encapsulate the possessor's own perception of the force and defensibility of his rights in relation to the land." Gray & Gray, *Land Law Core Text*, p.90.

LECTURER: How does Slade J.'s reasoning relate to these ideas of ownership?

STUDENT: Gray and Gray state that an owner acts exclusively. He protects his territory. And Slade J. says that a squatter, in order to establish his factual possession, must act in the same way: "that degree of occupation or physical control . . . that would entitle a person to maintain an action of trespass in relation to the relevant land".

LECTURER: So in a very real sense he must have treated the land as "his territory". So what we are looking for is that the squatter demonstrates that he is using the land and excluding all others. In what other ways can you usefully relate Slade J.'s judgment to BUILDING BLOCK NO 4?

STUDENT: As Bright observes, an owner exercises power over the land, including all the ways mentioned that make use of the land. And Slade J. says that the adverse possessor must act like an owner. So we are looking for the squatter to demonstrate these controlling acts.

LECTURER: So the squatter must act with this level of physical custody, control and exclusivity. We will come back to this important point in a moment. But before that, Slade J. makes another point: You will remember that we said at the beginning that in order to establish a successful claim to adverse possession of the land, either the paper owner must leave possession voluntarily and the squatter take over, or . . . .. can you remember the other?

STUDENT: The squatter must "dispossess" the paper owner.

LECTURER: Well done. Effectively Slade J. says that the taking of a sufficient degree of physical control with the requisite intention (the second element we examine below) without the consent of the paper owner (i.e. our definition of adverse possession), is sufficient to "dispossess" the paper owner.

> "[L]ikewise I would have regarded the word 'dispossession' in the [Limitation Act] as denoting simply the taking of possession in such sense from another without the other's licence or consent; likewise I would have regarded a person who has 'dispossessed' another in the sense just stated as being in 'adverse possession' for the purposes of the Act."
> *Powell v McFarlane* (1977) 38 P. & C.R. 452, p.469, confirmed in *Pye v Graham* [2003] 1 A.C. 419, para.32 per Lord Browne-Wilkinson.

LECTURER: Now let's return to our first point about the qualities of ownership. We have seen that the adverse possessor must display a sufficient degree of physical custody and control over the land. He must act like an occupying owner. Let's look at cases that have considered various actions on land by squatters and whether or not they amounted to a sufficient degree of "possession".

In *Pye v Graham*,[386] Pye were the owners of farmland. The Grahams owned and farmed land adjacent to this. Pye agreed to let the Grahams graze their livestock on 25 hectares of their land. After the agreement came to an end the Grahams repeatedly tried to get Pye to renew the agreement. Eventually Pye, who wished to develop the land, stopped responding to the Grahams' requests. However, the Grahams continued to use the land and claimed, after 12 years had passed, that Pye could no longer recover possession of the land. They argued that they had established title through adverse possession.[387] Lord Browne-Wilkinson held that the Grahams had satisfied the first hurdle and were able to establish factual possession, i.e. physical control. They had farmed the land and erected a gate which excluded Pye:

> "The Grahams were in occupation of the land which was within their exclusive physical control. The paper owner, Pye, was physically excluded from the land by the hedges and the lack of any key to the roadgate. The Grahams farmed it in conjunction with Manor Farm and in exactly the same way. They were plainly in factual possession".[388]

LECTURER: Do you agree that these actions were sufficient to demonstrate "factual possession" in the sense we described above?

STUDENT: Yes! Firstly, the Grahams had farmed the land in the same way that they farmed their own land. So they established the type of physical control that Bright mentions as one of the qualities of ownership in our BUILDING BLOCK NO 4.

LECTURER: Clearly Lord Browne-Wilkinson considers another quality as being important.

STUDENT: The fact that the Grahams treated the land exclusively. They put up a gate and locked it. This excluded the whole world—including the paper owner. It is that element of territorial control that Gray and Gray consider so important in our BUILDING BLOCK NO 4.

LECTURER: OK now let's consider some more examples.

Cases that have been held to establish a sufficient degree of exclusive physical control include: fencing off the land, padlocking a gate and constructing flower beds,[389] grazing cattle and storing timber on the land,[390] maintaining a compost heap, erecting a fence to keep animals in,

---

386   [2003] 1 A.C. 419.
387   E.H.Burn, *Maudsley & Burn's Land Law Cases and Materials*, p.210.
388   [2003] 1 A.C. 419, para.41.
389   *Buckinghamshire County Council v Moran* [1990] Ch. 623.
390   *Treloar v Nute* [1976] 1 W.L.R. 1295.

and cutting hedges,[391] shooting over marshland,[392] and the placing of a door on an entrance to a derelict property.[393]

From the above dialogues it will come as no surprise that there can be no legal possession unless the acts had the effect of excluding the whole world, that is, any unauthorised people.[394] Fencing indicates a strong degree of exclusive physical control of the land. It will usually establish adverse possession.[395] Even maintenance of a fence that the squatters had not erected themselves was sufficient to establish a strong case in *Barrett v Tower Hamlets LBC*[396] Similarly, establishing fixtures on the land is more readily seen as factual possession, because of their permanence.[397] The physical acts sufficient to establish factual possession depend on the nature of the land. Thus in *Roberts v Swangrove Estates Ltd*[398] there were several acts that demonstrated possession and control of riverbed, including granting fishing licences and dredging.

Trivial actions will not suffice. In *Techbild Ltd v Chamberlain*,[399] it was held that children playing on the land and the tying up of ponies were too trivial to amount to possession.

LECTURER: Can you understand why?

STUDENT: Well firstly there is not much that is exclusive about allowing children to play on the land and tying up ponies on it. This is not exclusive behaviour. Also it is not really exercising any degree of power over the land—treating it as your own. It is not the type of behaviour that Bright and Gray describe in BUILDING BLOCK NO 4.

(i) Possession must be open and unconcealed

The squatter's possession of the land must be open and unconcealed.[400] If the possession takes place so that the paper owner is not aware of it, i.e. if the adverse possessor conceals it, the paper owner cannot in any sense be said to be "sleeping on his rights". He will be unaware of any adverse claim to his land and cannot thus take proceedings to reclaim it. Thus, if the squatter deliberately conceals possession from the paper owner, there will be no adverse possession for the purposes of the Limitation Act.[401] Time will start running again from the point at which possession becomes open.

391　*London Borough of Hounslow v Mitchinton* (1997) 74 P. & C.R. 221.

392　*Red House Farms (Thorndon) Ltd v Catchpole* (1976) 244 E.G. 295.

393　*Purbrick v Hackney London Borough* [2004] 1 P. & C.R. 34: E.H.Burn, *Maudsley & Burn's Land Law Cases and Materials*, p.214.

394　*British Waterways Board v Toor* [2006] EWHC 1256.

395　*Seddon v Smith* (1877) 36 L.T. 168: "Enclosure is the strongest possible evidence of adverse possession"; also *Pye v Graham* [2003] 1 A.C. 419. But see *George Wimpey and Co Ltd v Sohn* [1967] Ch.487.

396　[2005] EWCA Civ 923, para.38, per Neuberger L.J.

397　*Roberts v Swangrove Estates Ltd* [2007] EWHC 513, para.46.

398　[2007] EWHC 513.

399　(1969) 20 P. & C.R. 633.

400　*Roberts v Swangrove Estates Ltd* [2007] EWHC 513, per Lindsay J.

401　Limitation Act 1980 s.32; *Beaulane Properties Ltd v Palmer* [2006] Ch. 79.

(ii) Must the squatter's use be inconsistent with the paper owner's intentions for the land?

It is not necessary for the squatter's use of the land to be inconsistent with, or be incompatible with, the paper owner's future plans for the land.[402] As Lord Browne-Wilkinson observed in *Pye v Graham*,[403] "[t]he suggestion that the sufficiency of the possession can depend on the intention not of the squatter but of the true owner is heretical and wrong".[404]

> "The question is simply whether the defendant squatter has dispossessed the paper owner by going into ordinary possession of the land for the requisite period without the consent of the owner."[405]

The taking of possession therefore, does not need to be confrontational. All it requires is for the squatter to "possess" the land in an ordinary sense described above.[406]

(c) The squatter must have the requisite intention to possess

The squatter must also evidence the intention to possess the land. It is not necessary for the squatter to intend to acquire title to the land. What is required is an intention to possess.[407] This means that in addition to the required element of physical custody and control the squatter must show "an intention to exercise such custody and control on one's own behalf and for one's own benefit".[408] He does not need to show "any long term intention to acquire a title".[409] In *Powell v McFarlane*,[410] Slade J. stated that the intention to possess involves:

> "the intention, in one's own name and on one's own behalf, to exclude the world at large, including the owner with the paper title . . . so far as is reasonably practicable and so far as the processes of the law will allow".

In *Pye v Graham*, Lord Browne-Wilkinson explained the nature of the intention to possess:

> "Suppose a case where A is found to be in occupation of a locked house. He may be there as a squatter, as an overnight trespasser, or as a friend looking after the house of the paper owner during his absence on holiday. The acts done by A in any given period do not tell you whether there is legal possession. If A is there as a squatter he intends to stay as long as he can for his own benefit: his intention is an intention to possess. But if he only intends to trespass for the night or has expressly agreed to look after the house for his friend he does

402   *Pye v Graham* [2003] 1 A.C. 419, paras.32–35 per Lord Browne-Wilkinson; also *Powell v McFarlane* (1977) 38 P. & C.R. 452, per Slade J. Limitation Act 1980 Sch.1, para.8(4); *Paradise Beach and Transportation Co Ltd v Price-Robinson* [1968] A.C. 1072 PC, per Lord Upjohn.
403   [2003] 1 A.C. 419, para.45.
404   Holding that *Leigh v Jack* 5 Ex. D 264 had been wrongly decided on this point.
405   *Pye v Graham*, above, para.36, per Lord Browne-Wilkinson.
406   *Pye v Graham*, above, para.38, per Lord Browne-Wilkinson.
407   *Buckinghamshire County Council v Moran* [1990] Ch. 623, p.643; *Pye v Graham* [2003] 1 A.C. 419 para.42 per Lord Browne-Wilkinson.
408   *Pye v Graham*, above, para.40, per Lord Browne-Wilkinson.
409   Above, para.42.
410   (1977) 38 P. & C.R. 452, pp.471–472.

not have possession. It is not the nature of the acts which A does but the intention with which he does them which determines whether or not he is in possession."

Thus, the overnight trespasser or the guest, do not intend to possess the land for their own benefit.

LECTURER: Can you understand why it is necessary to establish an "intention to possess" as a separate requirement? Why is it not just necessary to show factual possession without the paper owner's consent?

STUDENT: I suppose that a person can exercise control over the land for a variety of reasons, i.e. in order to look after it for a friend. And in order to do this he may manifest actions that exclude the whole world. The ideas of ownership in BUILDING BLOCK NO 4 show that you are controlling *your own territory*.

LECTURER: Thus, to establish a right to do this by virtue of a "possessory title", you must be doing the acts of possession for your own benefit.

The intention to possess may be, and often is, "deduced from the physical acts themselves".[411] Thus, actions may demonstrate an intention to exclude the whole world for the benefit of the squatter. In *Buckinghamshire County Council v Moran* the physical actions of fencing off the land, padlocking a gate, and constructing flower beds, were held to show an intention to possess to the exclusion of all including the paper owner.[412] In *Pye v Graham* the defendants had remained in possession of the land after the expiry of the grazing licence and had used and enclosed the land not just for grazing but for the same farming purposes as they used their own adjoining farm. Lord Browne-Wilkinson held that this showed a manifest intention "to assert their possession against Pye"[413] and thus, their claim to adverse possession had been established.

It did not matter that the Grahams had offered to pay to use the land. They had applied to the owners for a grazing licence. Lord Browne-Wilkinson held that because the squatter needs only to intend to possess and control the land for the time being, and not necessarily to own it, it did not matter that they had been willing to pay to use the land.[414] Consequent on this reasoning the Court of Appeal in *Ofulue v Bossert*,[415] held that if a person wrongly believes themselves to possess the land as a tenant of the paper owner this does not prevent their being in adverse possession.[416]

(d) Defeating a claim to adverse possession

It used to be said that the squatter's possession must be *adverse* to the title of the paper owner. This has recently been clarified to mean that if the squatter is occupying the land with the permission or consent of the owner of the paper title then he or she will not be able to establish

---

411   *Pye v Graham* [2003] 1 A.C. 419, para.40, per Lord Browne-Wilkinson.
412   [1990] Ch. 623, p.643.
413   [2003] 1 A.C. 419, para.64.
414   Above para.46. Also *Ocean Estates Ltd v Pinder* [1969] 2 A.C. 19.
415   [2008] EWCA Civ 7.
416   Confirmed by Lord Neuberger in the House of Lords: [2009] UKHL 16, para.67, although the appeal was not on this point.

a title under the Limitation Act 1980.[417] Thus, where a tenant is occupying under a lease, or where the paper owner gives the squatter permission to be on the land, then there will be no adverse possession. However, if the tenant or licensee remains in occupation after the expiry of the lease or licence then possession at this point may become adverse (unless consent is given to remain in possession). There can still be adverse possession if the squatter's use of the land extends beyond the scope of the permission granted by the paper owner.[418] Permission can be express or implied, but it will not be implied on the basis that the squatter's use of the land is not inconsistent with the paper owner's intentions.[419]

> In *Colin Dawson Windows Ltd v Kings Lynn and West Norfolk B.C.* [2005] 2 P. & C.R. 19 the alleged squatters were negotiating to purchase the land and the legal owner stated that they should leave the land if the sale did not complete. This was sufficient for the court to imply that the owner had given permission for the squatters to remain in the meantime.

(e) Where the squatter acknowledges the paper owner's title

An acknowledgement by the squatter of the paper owner's title will defeat the squatter's claim to adverse possession. If sometime during the 12 years the squatter acknowledges the title of the paper owner then time will start running again from the date of that acknowledgement. The time prior to the acknowledgement will not count.[420] However, in order to have this effect, "an acknowledgement must be in writing and signed by the person making it".[421]

In *Ofulue v Bossert*,[422] the defendant had occupied a house with her father under a tenancy, whilst the owners were abroad. When the lease ended they stayed in possession. The owners commenced possession proceedings, which lapsed. When the owners commenced this new action for possession they argued that the defendant's offer to purchase the property at the time of the first action was an "acknowledgement of title" for the purposes of s.29. In this case the letter had been made in response to the first proceedings and it had been made "without prejudice". It was held that in these circumstances it could not be relied upon.[423] It would

---

417 *Pye v Graham* [2003] 1 A.C. 419, paras.29 and 36, per Lord Browne-Wilkinson.
418 *Allen v Matthews* [2007] EWCA Civ 216.
419 *Pye v Graham* [2003] 1 A.C. 419, paras 32–35 per Lord Browne-Wilkinson; also *Powell v McFarlane* (1977) 38 P. & C.R. 452, per Slade J. Limitation Act 1980 Sch.1, para.8(4); *Paradise Beach and Transportation Co Ltd v Price-Robinson* [1968] A.C. 1072 PC, per Lord Upjohn. This "implied licence theory" was said by Lord Browne-Wilkinson in *Pye v Graham* [2003] 1 A.C. 419, para.45, to be "heretical and wrong". The theory had been established by Lord Denning M.R. in *Wallis Cayton Bay Holiday Camp Ltd v Shell Mex and BP Ltd* [1975] Q.B. 94.
420 Limitation Act 1980 s.29(2)(a).
421 Limitation Act 1980 s.30(1).
422 [2009] UKHL 16.
423 "The normal rule is . . . that statements made in negotiations entered into between parties to litigation with a view to settling that litigation are inadmissible and therefore cannot be given in evidence": per Lord Neuberger, para.85. It is a rule of public policy designed to encourage parties to speak freely in attempting to negotiate a compromise to court proceedings: Lord Hope para.12; Lord Walker, para.59. In the context of the first proceedings there was no question of adverse possession. Lord Scott (dissenting) considered that there were more powerful policy reasons within s.29 for allowing the acknowledgment to defeat the adverse possession claim: para.35.

otherwise have constituted a fatal admission of title. An offer to purchase property from the paper owner would amount to an express acknowledgement of title.[424]

(3) The effect of adverse possession

The effect of establishing a claim to adverse possession is different depending on whether title to the land is registered or not.

(a) Unregistered land

Once the squatter has established 12 years adverse possession the person who has been dispossessed may no longer bring an action to recover the land.[425] His title to the estate is extinguished. The squatter acquires his possessory title subject to the rights of third parties that affect the estate, e.g. restrictive covenants.[426]

(i) Where the extinguished title is leasehold

It is important to remember that it is only the person who had the right to possession at the time, the person who is dispossessed, whose title is extinguished. His action is statute barred. However, anyone whose action is not statute barred may still bring a claim. For example, if a squatter dispossesses a tenant and that tenant's action has, through passage of time, become statute barred, this does not mean that the landlord's title is also extinguished.[427] The squatter has not dispossessed the landlord and thus, time has not run against the landlord.[428]

> "The landlord's right to recover possession from the squatter on the [ending] of the lease is not barred by a squatter's adverse possession against the [tenant], however long this continues."[429]

However, time will start running against the landlord when the lease ends. This is because he now has an interest in possession of the land—so he can be dispossessed by the squatter.[430] "Only then does time start running against the landlord."[431]

The tenant who obtains a new lease is claiming a title derived from the landlord's title, which has not been statute barred. Thus, if a tenant's right to recover possession from the squatter has become time barred and he is granted a new lease, this will start time running afresh. He has acquired a new legal estate that has not been extinguished. The position is otherwise if the new lease is granted as a result of an option to renew the lease in the original lease agreement.[432]

---

424   Lord Neuberger, para.76; Lord Hope, para.3. Confirming *Edington v Clark* [1964] 1 Q.B. 367.
425   Limitation Act 1980 s.15.
426   *Re Nisbet and Potts' Contract* [1906] 1 Ch. 386, per Cozens-Hardy L.J.
427   *Fairweather v St Marylebone Property Co Ltd* [1963] A.C. 510.
428   *Asher v Whitlock* (1865) L.R. Q.B. 1.
429   *Chung Ping Kwan v Lam Island Development Co Ltd* [1997] A.C. 38, PC, per Lord Nicholls.
430   Limitation Act 1980 Sch.1 para.1.
431   *Chung Ping Kwan v Lam Island Development Co Ltd* [1997] A.C. 38, PC, per Lord Nicholls.
432   *Chung Ping Kwan v Lam Island Development Co Ltd* [1997] A.C. 38, PC, per Lord Nicholls.

A logical extension of this principle is that where the tenant "surrenders" his leasehold estate,[433] the landlord, the owner of the freehold reversion, can then take possession of the land and evict the squatter.[434]

(ii) Squatter's protection against third party purchasers

So how well are the squatter's rights protected if the owner sells and transfers the land to a third party—who then registers the land for the first time?

Under the Land Registration Act 1925, rights in the process of being acquired through adverse possession were "overriding interests" which bound any purchaser of the land from the paper owner, whether they were registered against the title or not.[435] This is no longer the case under the Land Registration Act 2002. However, until October 13, 2006 where a right to the estate was acquired through adverse possession it remained binding as an overriding interest where the land is sold and registered for the first time.[436] After October 13, 2006 the squatter's rights only bind the purchaser once he is registered as proprietor of the land if he has notice of those rights.[437]

(b) Under the Land Registration Act 1925

Where the 12 year period of adverse possession was completed prior to October 13, 2003[438] the estate of the paper owner is not extinguished but deemed to be held on trust by him for the squatter—who may then apply to be registered as proprietor. He takes his estate subject to the property rights of third parties, unless they also have been extinguished.[439]

(i) Where the title is leasehold

Clearly this does not affect the landlord's registered title, for reasons I have given above. However, if the squatter has been registered as proprietor, the tenant cannot bring his lease to an end by surrender in order that the landlord can take possession of the land. Where the squatter has registered his lease it has been held that the original tenant no longer possesses an estate to surrender.[440]

(c) Under the Land Registration Act 2002

"One of the most striking features of the Land Registration Act 2002 is that it disapplies the present law of adverse possession in relation to registered land. In its place it substitutes a new scheme that reflects the principles underlying registered conveyancing."[441]

---

433   A surrender operates to bring the lease to an end: to "determine" it. As against the landlord and tenant the leasehold estate no longer exists: *Fairweather v St Marylebone Property Co Ltd* [1963] A.C. 510.

434   *Fairweather v St Marylebone Property Co Ltd* [1963] A.C. 510, per Lord Denning.

435   Land Registration Act 1925 s.70(1)(f).

436   Land Registration Act 2002 Sch.12, para.7.

437   Land Registration Act 2002 s.11(4)(c).

438   When the Land Registration Act 2002 came into force.

439   Land Registration Act 1925 s.75.

440   *Spectrum Investment Co v Holmes* [1981] 1 W.L.R. 221.

441   C.Harpum and J.Bignell, *Registered Land—Law and Practice under the Land Registration Act 2002* (Jordan Publishing, 2004), p.353.

The Land Registration Act 2002 lays down a whole new system of rules that "confer greater protection against the acquisition of title by persons in adverse possession".[442] The Limitation Act does not apply and a squatter does not acquire a title to registered land automatically after the requisite period of adverse possession. The registered proprietor's title is not automatically extinguished.[443] Where title to the estate is registered and a squatter has been in adverse possession of the estate for a period of *ten years* ending on the date of the application, he can apply to the land registrar to be registered as the proprietor of the estate.[444]

> These new rules apply where the period of adverse possession is completed after October 13, 2003. The 2002 Act does not define the term "adverse possession" so the requirements discussed above for factual possession, intention to possess and absence of consent etc apply in exactly the same way.

(i) The notification procedure

Once such an application is made the registrar must give notice of the application to the registered owner of the estate (the person I have been referring to as the paper owner above), anyone who has a registered charge (mortgage) on the estate, and if the relevant estate is leasehold, the registrar must notify the owner of the registered freehold or any superior registered lease.[445] The registered proprietor of the land, or other person notified may then serve a counter-notice objecting to the squatter's registration as proprietor of the estate.[446]

(ii) The squatter's right to make a further application

If any of these people objects to the adverse possessor being registered as proprietor of the land after being notified of his application, the squatter cannot be registered as proprietor unless he falls within one of the limited exceptions below. If the squatter continues in adverse possession for a further two years, he can apply to the registrar again[447] and this time he is entitled to be registered as the new proprietor.[448] Thus, after being notified of the original application for registration it is important that the registered proprietor takes steps to recover possession from the squatter.

(iii) When registration can be made automatically after 10 years[449]

If the adverse possessor's application falls within one of the following limited exceptions he is entitled to be registered as proprietor of the land straight away, upon his initial application, once he has been in adverse possession for 10 years.

---

442   Law Commission Report, *Land Registration for the Twenty-First Century—A Conveyancing Revolution* (Law Com No.271), para.1.13.
443   Land Registration Act 2002 s.96.
444   Land Registration Act 2002 Sch.6, para.1(1).
445   Land Registration Act 2002 Sch.6, para.2.
446   Sch.6, para.3.
447   Land Registration Act 2002 Sch.6, para.6. He will not be so entitled if he is in the process of being sued for possession, if a possession order has been awarded against him, or if he has been evicted following a court order: Sch.6, para.6(2).
448   Sch.6, para.7.
449   C.Harpum and J.Bignell, *Registered Land—Law and Practice under the Land Registration Act 2002*.

Proprietary estoppel: If the squatter can establish a claim to the land under the doctrine of proprietary estoppel he can be registered as proprietor after 10 years. An adverse possessor will be entitled to be registered as proprietor if he can show that

> "(a) it would be unconscionable because of an equity by estoppel for the registered proprietor to seek to dispossess the applicant, and
>
> (b) the circumstances are such that the applicant ought to be registered as proprietor."[450]

As we have seen above in this chapter, a person will be able to establish an equity by estoppel if he acts to his detriment in reliance on an assurance by the paper owner that he will gain an interest in the land. The provision in the Land Registration Act reflects the fact that it must be unconscionable to deny that person a right. Only then can the squatter be registered as proprietor. Referring to part (b), if it is clear that the squatter ought to be given the estate in question, rather than some other remedy,[451] then he can be registered as proprietor.

Entitlement to registration for another reason: The squatter can be registered as proprietor if he is entitled to be so registered for another reason.[452] Someone may be present on the land as a squatter, i.e. without entitlement to be on the land, but he may have a right in the land. For example, if a purchaser has gone into adverse possession of the land after execution of a contract for sale but prior to completion, that entitles him to be registered as proprietor.[453]

The adverse possessor reasonably believes that the land is part of his boundary: An adverse possessor may be registered as proprietor of land after 10 years adverse possession where the land in question "is adjacent to land belonging to" him and "for at least ten years of the period of adverse possession ending on the date of the application, [he] . . . reasonably believed that the land" belonged to him.[454]

> For example, if A and B are neighbours and A has built a fence on his boundary that encloses a small part of B's land, and if A has believed reasonably for the last 10 years that he constructed the fence on the correct boundary line, A may be entitled to be registered as proprietor of that small part of B's land, once he has enclosed it for ten years. B will not be able to object.

---

450 Sch.6, para.5(2).

451 You may remember that under the doctrine of proprietary estoppel the court has a wide variety of remedies at its disposal in order to satisfy the equity, including financial compensation or the award of a proprietary right. So it is by no means certain that the claimant "ought" to be awarded a proprietary claim to the land. Also Harpum and Bignell, above, para.30.39. It will be the Adjudicator to the Land Registry who exercises this discretion as to which remedy to award the applicant: above, para.30.40.

452 Land Registration Act 2002 Sch.6, para. 5(3).

453 *Bridges v Mees* [1957] Ch. 475; Harpum and Bignell, above, para.30.41.

454 Land Registration Act 2002 Sch.6, para.5(4)(a) and (c).

Consequently we can see that the applicant must have a reasonable belief that the land belonged within his boundary. The applicant must have held this belief for the last 10 years immediately before the application. For example, a belief will not be reasonable if the applicant knew or ought to have known that the boundaries were incorrectly drawn.[455] Thus, if the squatter learns that the land does not belong to his plot, and the boundary line is in fact in a different place, he must make the application to be registered as proprietor. Otherwise he will lose the right to do so.[456]

There are two other qualifications to this provision. It must be the case that the exact line of the boundary between the two plots has not been drawn by the Land Registry, and the title to the land claimed has been registered for more than a year prior to the application.[457]

(iv) The effect of registration

If the squatter is registered as the new proprietor of the estate he takes the same class of title that the previous registered proprietor had.[458] However, he takes the title subject to all other estates and interests that affected the estate in the hands of the previous registered proprietor.[459]

(4) Adverse possession and human rights[460]

Recently there has been much debate in the courts as to whether the law allowing a person to acquire title to land by adverse possession, entirely without paying for it, amounts to a violation of the paper owner's human rights under the Human Rights Act 1998. In this way it is arguable that allowing adverse possession unjustly deprives the paper owner of his title to the land. Article 1 of the First Protocol provides that:

> "Every natural or legal person is entitled to the peaceful enjoyment of his possessions. No one shall be deprived of his possessions except in the public interest and subject to the conditions provided for by law and by the general principles of international law.
>
> The preceding provisions shall not, however, in any way impair the right of a State to enforce such laws as it deems necessary to control the use of property in accordance with the general interest or to secure the payment of taxes or other contributions or penalties."

In *Beaulane Properties v Palmer*,[461] Mr Nicholas Strauss Q.C. held that the law on the Limitation Act 1980 and the Land Registration Act 1925[462] constituted a violation of Article 1. It amounted

---

455 e.g. *Zarb v Parry* [2011] EWCA Civ. 1306. At the end of this case, by way of a "postscript", Arden L.J. gave advice on the difficulties associated with ongoing boundary disputes between neighbours.
456 *Zarb v Parry* [2011] EWCA Civ 1306.
457 Land Registration Act 2002 Sch.6, para.5(4)(b) and (d).
458 Sch.6(9)).
459 Sch.6(9)(2); Harpum and Bignell, para.31.5. The one exception is that the new registered proprietor will not be bound by a registered charge that affected the estate immediately before his registration, unless the squatter had brought himself within the three exceptions discussed above: paras 9(3) and (4).
460 J.Howell, "The Human Rights Act 1998: Land, Private Citizens, and the Common Law" (2007) 123 L.Q.R. 618.
461 [2005] EWHC 1071.
462 The land registration legislation then in force.

to a deprivation of possessions. Thus, he gave the law of adverse possession an interpretation that he felt was consistent with the Human Rights Act 1998 and stated that a squatter could not establish adverse possession unless his possession was inconsistent with the paper owner's intended use of the land. However, as you may remember, this "implied licence" principle was held by the House of Lords in *Pye v Graham* to be "heretical and wrong". A first instance judge could not therefore properly apply it.

However, in *J.A.Pye (Oxford) Ltd v United Kingdom*[463]—the Grand Chamber of the European Court of Human Rights held that the Limitation Act 1980 and Land Registration Act 1925 did not constitute a deprivation of possessions. The English Law was compliant with Article 1. Pye's argument had been that the Grahams had acquired the land entirely gratis and that the law which allowed them to do so therefore deprived Pye of an extremely valuable possession[464] in a way that contravened Article 1. The Grand Chamber dismissed the argument:

> "The acquisition of unassailable rights by the adverse possessor had to go hand-in-hand with a corresponding loss of property rights for the former owner."

The Land Registry, despite the decision in *Pye v United Kingdom*, applied the law in *Beaulane* and required adverse possessors of registered land to establish a use of the land inconsistent with that of the paper owner. In the recent case of *Ofulue v Bossert*,[465] the Court of Appeal stated that it would apply *Pye v United Kingdom*, and the Land Registry now appears to have reconciled itself to this.[466]

Articles for further reading

4

M.Dixon, "Proprietary estoppel: a return to principle?" [2009] Conv. 260.
M.Dixon, "Confining and Defining proprietary estoppel: the role of unconscionability" (2010) 30 L.S. 408.
N.Hopkins, "The relevance of context in property law: a case for judicial restraint?" (2011) 31 L.S. 175.
Gardner, "Family Property Today" [2008] L.Q.R. 422.
Dixon, "The Never-Ending Story—Co-ownership after *Stack v Dowden*" [2007] Conv. 456.
Gardner, "Rethinking Family Property" (1993) 109 L.Q.R. 263.
Dockray, "Adverse Possession and Intention" [1982] Conv. 256.

---

463 (2007) *The Times* October 1
464 The land had been valued at £2.5m in 2002.
465 [2008] EWCA Civ 7.
466 See also Clarke and Greer, *Land Law Directions*, pp.180–183.

Chapter 4

Principles of Co-ownership

CHAPTER OVERVIEW

In this chapter you will find:

- The two forms of co-ownership: the joint tenancy and the tenancy in common
- Instructions on problem solving and how to recognise the form of co-ownership
- The principles of severance and their application to co-ownership problems
- Constructed argument about the principles of co-ownership with Building Blocks.

Introduction

1

In Chapters 1 and 2 we considered what ownership means and how it comes into being. Ownership of land is sought after by our society. It is thought to confer freedom of choice: autonomous choice.

> **BUILDING BLOCK NO 4: Ideas of Ownership**
> What does it mean to be an owner of land? Ownership confers rights and privileges of control over land.

> **BUILDING BLOCK NO 2: Ideas of Justice**
> If you study this Building Block it will show you how ownership gives control over property. This in turn, gives a person a sense of autonomy and freedom. It gives them the power to make choices about their own lives.

In Chapter 2 we considered the basis of ownership of land in English law: the freehold and the leasehold estate.

> **The Law of Property Act 1925 s.1:**
> The only two estates in land capable of existing as legal estate in land are the fee simple absolute in possession and the leasehold estate. All the rest have been re-classified as equitable.

We have also considered the ownership of smaller rights in land belonging to third parties, such as easements, estate contracts and restrictive covenants. We have seen that Land Law recognises both legal rights and equitable rights. In Chapter 3 we looked at how legal and equitable estates and interests are brought into being, both formally and informally.

A. CONCURRENT AND SUCCESSIVE OWNERSHIP[1]

"Concurrent ownership", the main subject matter of this chapter, is where more than one person owns the same land. The law of co-ownership is a vital part of Land Law. "Successive ownership" is where land is owned by one person after another. For example, land could be left by will to "my wife for her life, with remainder in fee simple to my three children". Here, the wife will have ownership of the land for her life, and the children will own the land after she has died. Land was often passed down the family line in this way, from father to eldest son. Whilst we will briefly consider successive ownership, our main concern is co-ownership.

B. THE BUILDING BLOCKS OF CO-OWNERSHIP

(1) BUILDING BLOCK NO 1: Residential Security

Co-ownership has many different functions: married couples and cohabitees will naturally want to own houses together. There may be other family members who choose to live together. For example a son may move in with his mother in order to care for her more effectively. They may buy a house together. Three university friends may graduate and buy a house together because they want to get onto the property owning ladder and cannot afford to buy houses individually.

The law of co-ownership has assumed greater relevance due to the socio-economic phenomenon of "owner occupation". This altered the landscape of Land Law forever. People now buy land to live there and not solely for investment purposes. At the time of the 1925 legislation, the purpose of co-ownership was different. The law was required to regulate an entirely different situation. Land was left to two or more persons in a will, i.e. it provided for the financial security of the next generation, or it was conveyed to two or more persons wanting to make an

---

1   Throughout this chapter I am indebted to R. Smith's excellent book: *Plural Ownership* (Oxford University Press, 2005).

investment in land. The land was looked upon by its new co-owners as an investment. It could be used to raise money or rented out in order to provide an income. They did not usually live there.

Owner occupation is one of the social phenomena of our modern times, and the co-ownership rules now operate in this context. Houses are now routinely owned by ordinary citizens who buy them in order to make a home there.

BUILDING BLOCK NO 1: Residential Security

Residential security is now a main purpose behind the co-ownership of land in this country. If we want to create an argument about whether a rule is good or bad fair or unfair we can use our Building Blocks as evidence. If a rule undermines the purposes behind its existence, i.e. *why* we want to own land, then we can legitimately say that it is not good law. Thus, when we look at the rules of co-ownership we can say that they are good or bad depending on the extent to which they protect someone's right to continue living in the home, their *residential security*.

How do co-ownership rules impact Residential Security? FOR EXAMPLE: what happens when co-owners fall out? One may wish to remain in occupation the other may wish the land to be sold. The law has a way of determining *whose voice shall prevail*. When you study this, do you think that this is good law? Hold the rules of co-ownership against BUILDING BLOCK NO 1 (see Chapter 1 for details) and ask whether the rules give protection to people's residential security.

---

(2) Residential security, co-ownership law, and the inheritance issue

Consider this example: John and Mary co-own the fee simple of a house and live there together. John dies having made a will leaving his share of the house to his son. Does his share pass to his son under his will, rather than to Mary? Answering this question is an important issue of the law of co-ownership. If John's share does go to his son, his son may be keen to sell the house. Mary will want to continue living there. Thus the law that decides what happens to John's share on his death ought to an extent to take account of its potentially detrimental effect on another co-owner's *residential security*. A primary issue in the law of co-ownership concerns what happens to a co-owner's share of the property when they die: The rules determine whether the remaining co-owners get the deceased co-owner's share, or whether the relatives of the deceased get the share by inheritance (will or intestacy). Perhaps it is arguable on the basis of BUILDING BLOCK NO 1 that the law should not readily allow one co-owner to split off their share and leave it to someone else in their will.

(3) BUILDING BLOCK NO 5: Protection of Purchasers (secured creditors)

Another issue of the law is co-ownership arises where a co-owner is in debt and their share of the co-owned property is security for that debt. If she fails to make repayments due under the loan, then the secured creditor will want the co-owned property sold in order to repay the debt.

BUILDING BLOCK NO 5: Property Rights and the Protection of Mortgage Lenders

We are not concerned here with the fact that rights in land are property rights. The question of whether rights in land will bind a purchaser or mortgagee of that land pertains to where there has been a sale or mortgage of the *whole estate*. We are talking about a single co-owner mortgaging *their share only*. The courts and the rules of co-ownership will have to determine whether the whole house can be sold in order to pay off one co-owner's debt. This will prejudice the residential security of the other co-owners who had nothing to do with the loan. In Chapter 1, we saw that it is important for banks to be able to sell the house should the debtor default on the loan. If the law of co-ownership makes it difficult for banks and building societies to realise their security for the loan they may be reluctant to give loans to homebuyers and small businesses in the future. Thus, when we are constructing an argument about the rules of co-ownership, this Building Block provides evidence for an argument that a rule is good or bad if it allows co-owned property to be sold in order to pay off a debt. However, a balance clearly needs to be struck. Have the courts got it right?

---

(4) BUILDING BLOCK NO 7: Land Law is "facilitative" and should give effect to the co-owners' intentions

Consider the following example:

Alan, Sven, Victor, and Chloe run a business together and are looking to purchase larger premises. They are able to buy office premises and all four of them are the legal owners of the fee simple estate. They are co-owners.

The law of co-ownership determines what co-owners can do with the premises, that is what powers the co-owners have, e.g. to sell lease or mortgage the co-owned land. It also determines who will get their share if one of them dies.

But what if they fall out and Alan and Sven no longer want to be part of the business? The other two, Victor and Chloe, wish to continue running the business from the premises. The law of co-ownership determines whether Alan and Sven can get their wish and sell the land or Victor and Chloe can prevent them from doing so.

What if Victor dies what happens to his share of the business premises when he dies? Do the other business partners get his share or is it inherited by his family?

The law of co-ownership is primarily about facilitating what the co-owners want to achieve in respect of land ownership, their *intentions* regarding the land and its ownership.[2] Peter Birks argues that giving effect to what people want to achieve through ownership of land is one of the important functions of Land Law: it is "facilitative".

> "Some areas of law are primarily concerned to inhibit undesirable conduct. This is most obviously true of the law relating to wrongs, whether criminal or civil . . . By contrast, other areas are primarily facilitative. The law of contract, for example, helps people do something which by and large they want to be able to do—namely, to make reliable agreements." Land Law 'can be seen as facilitating the achievement of goals which people routinely want to achieve. It helps very much to keep in mind what landowners and would-be landowners are likely to want'".[3]

If this is one of the primary *aims and purposes* of Land Law we can legitimately say that its rules should give effect to it. Thus, rules should enable people to acquire land and to achieve what they intend to achieve by owning the land. The rules that regulate the issues of co-ownership as highlighted in our example above should give effect to what the co-owners intended with regard to their co-ownership of the property. We can say that those rules are good or bad fair or unfair accordingly.

BUILDING BLOCK NO 7: Land Law is "facilitative" and should give effect to the parties' intentions or reasonable expectations

In this context we can say that if the rules of co-ownership fail significantly to reflect the parties' intentions or reasonable expectations with regard to what should happen to the co-owned property, then those rules are bad law. Take the example of Alan, Sven, Victor and Chloe, who are business partners and together co-own their business premises. In this type of situation most people would reasonably expect his "share" of the co-owned property to go to his family and not to the other co-owners. If the rules of co-ownership say something different, this raises a question as to their adequacy.

---

2   R.Smith, *Plural Ownership*, Chs 3 and 4.
3   P.Birks, "Before we begin: Five keys to land law" in Bright and Dewar (eds), *Land Law Themes and Perspectives* (Oxford University Press, 1998), Ch. 18, p. 457.

(5) BUILDING BLOCK NO 6: The Importance of Certainty and Predictability

> **BUILDING BLOCK NO 6: The Need for Certainty and Predictability in the Law of Co-ownership**
>
> A legal system should be sufficiently certain to allow people to know where they stand with regard to their rights in co-owned property. What is the extent of their rights? Who else may claim rights? If the law of co-ownership does not allow people to know where they stand in respect of co-owned property, and order their affairs accordingly, this justifies you in saying that the rule is not good.
>
> Don't forget to ask questions and interrogate the Building Block to determine whether a case really does violate the interests of certainty and predictability:
>
> - Why does this rule mean that future classes of litigant might have trouble knowing what their rights are and ordering their affairs accordingly?
> - Might a small amount of legal uncertainty be tolerable? Does there need to be a trade off with other Building Blocks? There has to be room for flexibility. People do not generally go about their lives legalistically. There must be some room for justice to be done.

C. THE IMPORTANCE OF TRUSTS IN THE LAW OF CO-OWNERSHIP

Under English law all co-ownership of land takes effect by way of a trust. So where John and Mary bought a house together for their joint occupation, and it was conveyed into their joint names, legally they hold the fee simple estate on trust for each other. There is no magical logic behind this. The Law of Property Act 1925, as amended by the Trusts of Land and Appointment of Trustees Act 1996, provides that where land is owned by more than one person, it will be held on trust. There is a reason for it, akin to our Building Blocks, which we will examine in the next chapter.

(1) What is a trust?

> Revisit Chapter 2 for a detailed description of the nature and development of the trust device.

A trust is a way of holding property. The legal owner of property, the trustee, holds the property for the benefit of another: the beneficiary. This means that the trustee has the obligation to manage the property and the beneficiary has the right to enjoy it. The beneficiary's right is a property right that can be enforced against a third party who comes into possession of the property from the trustee, e.g. the trustee may have sold the land, given it away, left it in a will to someone else.[4] The beneficiary's interest was not enforceable in the courts of common law, which recognised only that the trustees were the absolute owners. But his interest was recognised by the court of equity. Thus, the beneficiary has an "equitable interest" in the land. We tend to call it a "beneficial interest". Trusts can be created expressly (where a person creates one deliberately). They can come into being impliedly (for example as in *Williams & Glyn's Bank Ltd v Boland*[5]). And, as we now see, they can be imposed by statute.

(2) Express trusts

A trust may be created expressly by a legal owner or purchaser of land. The size of the parties' shares will be determined by the express declaration in the conveyance. Any different combination of shares may be created. Parties can share the equitable or beneficial interest however they wish.

> **Example**
> A husband and wife, when they are buying their home, may want to ensure that the wife has a greater share of the house. She may have contributed 80 per cent of the purchase price from her inheritance. The parties can achieve this by executing a trust so that the land is conveyed "to Husband and Wife on trust in the following shares: 80/20 to the wife".
>
> Or if the Wife is already the sole owner of her own house when she meets her husband, she may wish to give him a share of the ownership of the house. One way of doing this is to execute a trust in his favour, e.g. "I hereby declare that I hold the house, as sole legal owner, on trust for myself and my husband in equal shares".

(3) The statutory trust

Where no trust is set up expressly, the Law of Property Act 1925 ss.34–36 (as amended by the Trusts of Land and Appointment of Trustees Act 1996) imposes a trust of land in all cases where more than one person owns the land, i.e. *a trust is imposed by statute in all cases of co-ownership*.

> **Example**
> Land is conveyed "to Adam, Brian and Claire". There will be a trust whereby Adam, Brian and Claire own the legal estate on trust for themselves beneficially.
> LEGAL ESTATE
>
> **Adam Brian Claire**
> _____
>
> EQUITABLE (or "beneficial") INTEREST   **Adam Brian Claire**

---

4   We will look at this in detail when we study Land Transfer Law in later chapters.
5   [1981] A.C. 487.

The statutory trust imposed in all cases of co-ownership looks slightly odd where the co-owners are both trustees and beneficiaries. However, there are sound conveyancing reasons why this trust device was adopted. We will explore these in the next chapter and in the chapters on land transfer. However, it is worth noting at this stage that the trustees and the beneficiaries will not always be the same people. The Law of Property Act 1925, s.34(2) only allows four people of full age to own the legal estate. Thus if land is conveyed to Adam, Brian, Claire, David and Erica, the statutory trust will take effect as follows:

Example

Land is conveyed "to Adam, Brian, Claire, David and Erica". There will be a trust whereby Adam, Brian, Claire and David own the legal estate on trust for themselves and Erica beneficially:

LEGAL ESTATE

$$\frac{A\ B\ C\ D}{A\ B\ C\ D\ E}$$

EQUITABLE (or "beneficial") INTEREST

There is, again, a sound conveyancing reason why this is the case, which we will examine in the next chapter.

(4) The statutory trust—trustees and beneficiaries

How do we work out who are the trustees and the beneficiaries under the statutory trust? As you will remember from Chapter 2, it is the trustees who are the legal owners of property. As far as the statutory trust is concerned, it is the legal owners of the land who become the trustees. So you need to determine in whose names the deed of conveyance and registration is made. This determines legal ownership.[6]

D. THE LAW OF CO-OWNERSHIP: AN OVERVIEW

The law of co-ownership has three significant features. Firstly, we need to understand the principles of co-ownership that regulate how the co-owners hold the land and the consequences of how they hold it. This determines "the inheritance issue", as described above. We look at the principles of co-ownership in this chapter. Secondly, we need to understand how co-ownership is regulated. For example, what powers do the co-owners have to deal with the land? They are statutory trustees. So what duties do they have in relation to the other co-owners? What happens when co-owners fall out and want to do different things with the land? Whose voice will prevail?

---

6   Law of Property Act 1925 s.52, Land Registration Act 2002 ss.4 and 27; see Chapter 3.

Co-ownership is regulated by statute: the Law of Property Act 1925 and the Trusts of Land and Appointment of Trustees Act 1996. We look at the regulation of co-ownership in the next chapter. Thirdly, where co-owned land is conveyed to a third party purchaser, or is mortgaged, there may be co-owners who are not on the legal title (as we saw in the example with Adam, Brian, Claire, David and Erica). They have a beneficial interest under the trust of land. This, as we saw in Chapter 1, is a property right. And the effect of a property right is that it can be asserted against the land itself. This means that any future purchaser, or any bank or building society who has taken a mortgage over the land, may be bound by the right. We need to know when the purchaser of the land is affected by the beneficial interests under a trust of land. This is an issue that we will explore mainly in the context of the chapters on Land Transfer Law.

E. SUCCESSIVE OWNERSHIP

Although we are principally looking at co-ownership, i.e. where land is owned by more than one person *at the same time*, a linked topic is "successive ownership", i.e. where land is owned by one person after another. We will consider successive ownership here only very briefly. Some knowledge of the strict settlement will help you to understand the 1925 legislative reforms of Land Transfer Law considered in later chapters.

As we saw in Chapter 2, many different estates are capable of existing in land. The doctrine of estates enabled the fee simple to be fragmented up into a series of life estates, or entailed interests. Because estates in land are essentially ownership "for a time",[7] it meant that people could regulate how land was held in the future and by whom. The doctrine of estates could ensure that possession of land fell to one person after another. Ownership could be *successive*. One person has the possession of the land for his lifetime; another has the interest *in remainder*, e.g. the right to possession of the land when the current incumbent dies.

> Richard dies and in his will leaves his land to his wife for life, and remainder to his daughter. Richard's wife has the current right to possession and enjoyment of the land; his daughter has the right to future enjoyment of the land. Her interest will fall into possession when her mother dies.

(1) Strict settlements and the policy of the Settled Land Act 1925

The landed gentry used successive ownership devices to ensure that land passed from father to son and was thus kept in the family. Each time the land passed from father to son (it was usually the son and usually the eldest) the son only took a limited interest. As we saw in Chapter 2, where

---

7   *Walsingham's Case* (1573) 2 Plow. 547.

land was tied up in this way, it made it very difficult to sell. For example: Harold owns a life estate, then Claude an entail which takes effect when Harold dies, and William has the fee simple, which takes effect if Claude has no more direct heirs. William might never get the fee simple. Thus, who could ensure that the purchaser got the fee simple estate? The person who had settled the land in the first place had exactly this intention: that the land could not be sold outside the family.

In the seventeenth and eighteenth centuries land represented wealth, status and power, and the patriarch of the family had designs that *his* family would stay powerful or wealthy. "Strict settlements" were usually created on marriage of the eldest son and were recreated each generation.[8] In this way the eldest son would take a limited interest and the fee simple would never fall into possession.[9]

(2) The legal structure of the Settled Land Act 1925[10]

The aim of the Settled Land Act 1925, building on its predecessor the Settled Land Act 1882, was to make land subject to a settlement easier to transfer to a purchaser. The Settled Land Act 1925 defines a "settlement" as arising where land is "limited in trust for any persons by way of succession" or on trust for persons entitled to entailed interests or other equitable estates, such as a life estate, or where land is left to an infant.[11] Following s.1 of the Law of Property Act 1925, these are mainly equitable interests and accordingly take effect under a trust. Thus, most successive ownership was subject to the Settled Land Act 1925. Under the scheme for successive and concurrent ownership laid down by the 1925 legislation, if it could be construed from the relevant documents that any of these interests were held on "trust for sale" then it would not be settled land for the purposes of the 1925 Act.[12]

The person who is currently entitled under a settlement to possess and enjoy the land for his life is defined in the Act as the "tenant for life" under the settlement.[13] The only method of creating a settlement of land was to convey the fee simple estate to the tenant for life.[14] He thus had ownership of the estate and consequently was in a position of trust, to look after the estate both for himself and for the others who were to inherit after him. But this meant that he could transfer it to a purchaser. He is not entitled to do what he likes with the land and disregard the interests of other family members under the settlement. The tenant for life is trustee of the legal fee simple estate for all parties interested. In dealing with the land in accordance with the Act, he must "have regard to the interests of all parties entitled under the settlement". He comes under the obligations of a trustee.[15] There are also rules to ensure that the tenant for life does not damage the property etc.

---

8   Flessas, Murphy and Roberts, *Introduction to Property Law*, 4th edn (London: Sweet & Maxwell, 2004), p.85.
9   J.H.Baker, *An Introduction to English Legal History* (London: Butterworths 1979), "Strict Settlements".
10   For a detailed and useful account of the Act see Thompson, *Modern Land Law* (4th edn, 2009) pp.250–263.
11   Settled Land Act 1925 s.1(1).
12   Settled Land Act 1925 s.1(7). We will look at what is a "trust for sale", how it works, and how trusts for sale and settlements have been superseded by the "trust of land" in this Chapter: Thompson, *Modern Land Law* pp.250–1 and 263.
13   s.19(1).
14   s.4(2).
15   s.107(1).

As to what the tenant for life was allowed to do with the fee simple estate, if you have been thinking ahead you may think that he had the fee simple estate and could enter into any sort of transaction with estate: sale, lease, contracts, however many mortgages he likes. And this would have been true had the Settled Land Act 1925 not "clipped his wings" a little. The Act gave limited powers to the tenant for life to deal with the estate and s.18 of the Settled Land Act 1925 renders void any transaction that is outside these powers.[16]

Whenever the tenant for life exercised his statutory powers, e.g. sale, the purchaser would take the fee simple estate free from all the interests under the settlement provided the money (called "capital money") was paid to the trustees of the settlement.[17] But the interests of those entitled under the settlement were not thereby extinguished. The trustees of the settlement would then hold the *money* on trust on the same terms as the settlement. So that if X held the land for life with remainder to Y before the sale, after the sale, X held a life interest in the proceeds of the sale and Y was entitled to the capital on the death of X.[18] This process whereby the purchaser takes free from the interests under the settlement is known as overreaching.[19] Perceptions of wealth had changed. Land was no longer seen land as synonymous with wealth, status and dynastic ambition. Beneficiaries under settlements became equally happy to have their inheritance in the form of money.[20]

It is now not possible to create new settlements for the purposes of the Settled Land Act 1925.[21] All successive ownership must take effect as a "trust of land".[22] Existing settlements remain valid.[23]

(3) Trusts for sale

During the nineteenth century successive and concurrent interests in land were also created under "trusts for sale". A trust for sale is where land was held by trustees for the sole purpose of selling it in order to make a fund of money. This, for example, provided inheritance for younger sons and daughters, or could be used to pay debts that had been incurred by the deceased's estate. Where land was held on trust for sale the trustees were under a duty to sell the land. Because of this the beneficial interests under a trust for sale were regarded by the courts as personal property rather than real property. This is known as the doctrine of conversion. As the trustees were under a legal obligation to sell the land the courts "regarded as done that which ought to be done" and viewed the beneficiaries' interests as interests in money (personal

---

16   This structure was a change from the Settled Land Act 1882 which did not vest the fee simple in the tenant for life. But it gave him powers to deal with the land. These powers would ensure that the purchaser would take the land free from the interests under the settlement: C. Harpum [1990] C.L.J. 277.

17   Law of Property Act 1925 s.2(1)(i). A settlement would usually have "trustees of the settlement". Their role was to receive the money that arose when the tenant for life dealt with the land in accordance with the Act.

18   Baker, *An Introduction to English Legal History* (1979) "strict settlements".

19   The use of overreaching was a cornerstone of the 1925 property legislation. We will consider it in the chapters on Land Transfer Law.

20   P.Birks "Before we begin: Five keys to Land Law" in *Land Law Themes and Perspectives*, Ch.18.

21   Trusts of Land and Appointment of Trustees Act 1996 s.2(1).

22   Trusts of Land and Appointment of Trustees Act 1996 Sch.1, para.5.

23   s.2(2)(a).

property). They were still property rights that could affect a purchaser of the land.[24] The rules of the 1925 legislation enabled the purchaser to take free from them provided he paid the purchase money to two trustees or a trust corporation.[25]

> **Law Reform**
> We have already seen that a trust is imposed in all cases of co-ownership. The type of trust imposed in 1925 was a trust for sale. Our modern system of owner occupation showed the strict settlement and the trust for sale to be outdated. All successive and concurrent ownership now takes effect as a Trust of Land and is subject to the statutory regulation laid down by the Trusts of Land and Appointment of Trustees Act 1996. Following the Trusts of Land and Appointment of Trustees Act 1996 s.2(1) it is no longer possible to create new settlements for the purposes of the Settled Land Act 1925.

2 The joint tenancy and the tenancy in common

A. CO-OWNERSHIP AND UNITY OF POSSESSION

The law of co-ownership applies where more than one person owns land at the same time. Co-owners have what is known as "unity of possession". Without this there cannot be co-ownership.[26] We think of possession in terms of the right to exclude others. Unity of possession therefore means that one co-owner cannot exclude the other, but together they can exclude the whole world.[27] Let's say that Andy and Rachel are co-owners of a house. They do not have different rights to possess different sections of their house. Each has the right to possess the whole, and nothing separately. They do not have the right to exclude each other. But together they can exclude everyone else. The idea of "possession" is not the same as "occupation", which describes what someone is doing with the land *in fact*. We might say therefore that possession confers a right of occupation.

---

24 G.Spence, *The Equitable Jurisdiction of the Court of Chancery* (1846–1849) Vol II, pp.380–1; also Harpum, "Overreaching, Trustees' Powers and Reform of the 1925 Legislation" [1990] C.L.J. 277, pp.283–5; J.S.Anderson, "The Proper, Narrow Scope of Equitable Conversion in Land Law" (1984) 100 L.Q.R. 86, pp.89–90.
25 "Overreaching": Law of Property Act 1925 s.2(1)(ii), and s.27 (prior to its amendment by Trusts of Land and Appointment of Trustees Act 1996).
26 R.Smith, *Plural Ownership*, p.22.
27 Above, p.28; *Wiseman v Simpson* [1988] 1 W.L.R. 35.

> **The Inheritance Issue**
> What we need to do is to look at the nature of co-ownership. For example, what are Andy and Rachel entitled to? What happens when one of them dies? Does their interest pass to the other co-owner or can they leave it to their relatives in their will? This depends on the *form* of co-ownership by which Andy and Rachel own their house.

B. THE JOINT TENANCY AND THE TENANCY IN COMMON

The two most important forms of co-ownership are the joint tenancy and the tenancy in common.[28] The consequences that flow from the joint tenancy for the inheritance issue are different from those flowing from the tenancy in common.

C. THE JOINT TENANCY

The essence of a joint tenancy is that the co-owners *together own the whole* estate, e.g. the fee simple. Separately they own nothing.[29] This is unity of *ownership* not just unity of possession.

The right of survivorship (ius accrescendi): Where one joint tenant dies, as far as the co-owned property is concerned, he does not die owning a distinct and separate interest in the co-owned property. He was only part of a group that together owned the whole estate. This means that he has no separate interest that he can leave by will on his death or that can pass under the rules of intestacy. The surviving co-owner(s) will continue to own the whole of the estate: When a joint tenant dies he merely leaves the other remaining joint tenants owning the whole. When there is only one person left, that person is absolutely entitled to the whole. In the joint tenancy there is something of the "winner takes all"! The longest living co-owner gets the whole estate.

> **Example one:** John and Mary buy a house together and it is conveyed to them "as joint tenants". Mary dies. So John, by right of survivorship, is regarded as the absolute owner of the house.
>
> **Example two:** In 1991, Jim, Peter and David purchase "Barnacle House" as joint tenants. In 1998 Peter dies. Jim and David continue to own the whole together. David dies in 2008, which means that Jim, on David's death, becomes solely and absolutely entitled to the fee simple of Barnacle House.

---

28 Note that the word tenancy is used here in a special sense: a derivative of tenure meaning to hold. It has nothing to do with tenant in a landlord and tenant sense.

29 Stephens, *Commentaries* (1858); *A.G. Securities v Vaughan* [1990] 1 A.C. 417.

Fragment from a typical problem question

In 1991, Jim, Peter and David together buy Barnacle House. (Many events happen now, which you will know how to interpret after this Chapter).

In 1998 Peter dies. His will leaves "my interest in Barnacle House to Melissa". Advise Melissa, who is claiming that she has an interest in Barnacle House.

LECTURER: What do you think?

STUDENT: I think that if they are joint tenants Melissa cannot have any share in the land.

LECTURER: This is a fair answer. However, you need to explain how you got there (or your "working out") a little more carefully.

For example, if at the time of Peter's death the co-owners held as joint tenants then the provision in the will can have no effect. Peter was one of a number of co-owners who were together regarded as owning the whole estate. Separately he owned nothing, so he had nothing to leave by will.

Much of what we now study under the principles of co-ownership is dedicated to determining how we can tell whether the parties are joint tenants or tenants in common, and when either may come into existence.

(1) The inheritance issue where it is uncertain who dies first

John and Mary are co-owners of their house. They hold as joint tenants. If it is uncertain who dies first, for example if they are both involved in a road traffic accident, there may be a problem. The law must be able to determine who died last because that person will have become entitled absolutely to the house. The house will pass under the will or intestacy of the one who died last. Section 184 of the Law of Property Act 1925 provides that where two or more persons have died in circumstances that make it uncertain who survived whom it is presumed that the younger person survived the older one. Thus, in our example, if John is younger than Mary, he will be presumed to have survived Mary and the house will pass under his will.

D. THE TENANCY IN COMMON

If co-owners hold as tenants in common the consequence on the death of a co-owner is very different. Each tenant in common is seen as having a separate, identifiable share of the property.

But it is not yet a share that has been realised or "divided". In the Law of Property Act 1925 you will see the interest of a tenant in common referred to as an "undivided share" in land.[30]

(1) No unity of interest

With a tenancy in common each co-owner has a separate interest. The co-owners do not own the whole together. Accordingly, survivorship does not apply. Just like any other property therefore, this share can be left by will or can pass under the intestacy rules.

> **For example, Jim, Peter and David co-own "Barnacle House" as tenants in common. In 1998 Peter dies. His will leaves "my interest in Barnacle House to Melissa". Melissa takes under the will. She would then have an interest in the house. If he died intestate his next of kin would take his interest.**

E. THE CHARACTERISTICS OF THE JOINT TENANCY: THE FOUR UNITIES

In order for a joint tenancy to come into being, the "four unities" must be present.[31] They describe the principle that together the co-owners own the whole estate.[32] It is necessary to establish that the four unities exist in order for there to be a joint tenancy. For a tenancy in common, where survivorship does not apply, there does not have to be unity of interest, time or title. The only unity required is that of possession: the minimum requirement for co-ownership.

(1) Unity of possession

This idea is described above.[33] Together the co-owners are entitled to possess the land. Together they can exclude the whole world but they cannot exclude each other.[34]

(2) Unity of interest

For a joint tenancy there must be unity of interest. There must be an interest that the co-owners all own together, e.g. the fee simple estate. If John owned a life interest and Mary the freehold, these are different interests.[35] So there is no "whole" to be owned by both. Also, there is no unity of interest where the co-owners hold distinct proportions of the interest, e.g. 70 per cent and 30 per cent.[36] If it can be identified that the co-owners have distinct shares of the interest in this way, either expressly or impliedly, each owns a particular share. It cannot therefore be said that together the co-owners own the whole of the interest and individually, nothing.

---

30   e.g. s.34(1): The subheading refers to the difference between the tenancy in common and the joint tenancy as "Undivided Shares and Joint Ownership".
31   *A.G. Securities v Vaughan* [1990] 1 A.C. 417.
32   Smith, *Plural Ownership*, p.27.
33   Above section 2A, p.226.
34   *A.G. Securities v Vaughan* [1990] 1 A.C. 417.
35   *Wiscot's Case* (1599) 2 Co. Rep. 60b; Smith, *Plural Ownership*, p.28.
36   *Bull v Bull* [1955] 1 Q.B. 234; *Williams & Glyn's Bank v Boland* [1981] A.C. 487 although the point was implicit in both cases.

(a) The Building Block of the joint tenancy

The idea of unity of interest is vitally important to the joint tenancy, so much so that we can hold it against the judgments in co-ownership cases and understand them on a deeper level. This is why I call unity of interest the Building Block of the joint tenancy. We will be using it to hold against the cases and see why a judge in one case recognised a joint tenancy and a judge in another, a tenancy in common.

> **Unity of Interest: The BUILDING BLOCK of the Joint Tenancy**
> Each owns the whole interest together. None of the co-owners has separate and identifiable shares. SURVIVORSHIP: is the necessary by-product of unity of interest. When one joint tenant dies he does not die owning anything separate that he can leave by will. When he dies the remaining co-owners own the whole of the estate together.

(3) Unity of title

If A, B and C co-own land they can only be joint tenants if they all became owners of the interest in land together through the same deed of conveyance or act of adverse possession. If one year later C sells his share to X, X cannot be a joint tenant because he has not derived his interest from the same source as A and B derived theirs. The sale by C is perfectly valid. But X takes as a tenant in common in relation to A and B. And X has a separate interest that he can leave by will.

(4) Unity of time

The interests of the co-owners must all vest at the same time. Thus, A, B and C, in order to be joint tenants, must all take their interests in the land at the same time.

F. IDENTIFYING WHETHER CO-OWNERS ARE JOINT TENANTS OR TENANTS IN COMMON

Identifying how co-owners hold the property, whether as joint tenants or as tenants in common, is far from being a legal technicality. It profoundly affects people's lives and how their property is distributed. On the death of a co-owner, the question of who is entitled to the property will depend on how the property was held, joint tenancy or tenancy in common.

For example: John and Mary are longstanding friends, they buy a house together: "Broadacres", and live there contentedly all their lives.

Mary has made a will leaving all her property to her cousin Fred. But does the will include half of Broadacres? As you know it can only do so if John and Mary are tenants in common. Doubtless Mary has not thought about this.

Last Will and Testament: Mary
Being of sound mind and body I hereby leave all my property to my dear cousin Fred.

In 2010 she dies (R.I.P. Mary). But there is a distressing property dispute in her wake: by virtue of Mary's will Fred is claiming that he is entitled to Mary's share of the house. John does not particularly want to sell the house or to give half of its value to Fred in order to "buy him out". The issue came as a shock to him on Mary's death. This is a particularly distressing time for him. People in this type of situation need some form of stability.

This situation is far from uncommon in the law reports. What the judge must do is to identify the type of co-ownership as this is crucial to the question of ownership of the house on Mary's death. If the judge identifies that John and Mary held as joint tenants, John would become absolute owner of the house under the right of survivorship. Mary is not in law regarded as having any separate share that she could leave by will. On the other hand, if the judge concludes that John and Mary held as tenants in common, then Mary would be regarded as owning a distinct interest in the house that she *could* leave by will to whomsoever she pleases (or it would pass by the intestacy rules). This would mean that John would have to buy Fred out.

IN THE HIGH COURT OF JUSTICE: CHANCERY DIVISION
Between:
FRED: Appellant
- and –
JOHN: Respondent

For the Appellant: Argues that John and Mary held as tenants in common, so that the provision in the will can take effect as a gift to him. He argues that John will have to "buy him out".

For the Respondent: Argues that they held the property as joint tenants so that when Mary died John got the whole of the house by right of survivorship. He wants to stay in occupation and doesn't want to "buy Fred out".

G. CRITICAL THINKING ABOUT THE PRINCIPLES OF CO-OWNERSHIP

LECTURER: So we can see how important it is for the law to offer the right way of determining whether co-owners such as John and Mary held as joint tenants or tenants in common.

Neither John nor Mary should have any "nasty surprises" on either's death. This is a traumatic enough time without having to worry about ownership disputes.

We are often asked to construct an argument about whether the rules of co-ownership are good or bad, fair or unfair. If the rule does not support the basic policies of the Building Blocks we can legitimately conclude that it is bad law.

STUDENT: I think that BUILDING BLOCK NO 7 is particularly important in the context of co-ownership.

BUILDING BLOCK NO 7: Land Law is "facilitative": the Law should give effect to people's reasonable expectations or intentions
Hold the rules of co-ownership against the policy in this Building Block and consider the extent to which the rule produces the result that people would expect in a particular situation. We can legitimately say that the rule is good or bad fair or unfair accordingly.

LECTURER: So if the reasonable expectation of the type of situation in question is that the survivor will get the whole of the property on the death of the other, and the rules of law provide for a tenancy in common, then the law is bad.

STUDENT: With John and Mary's example in mind I think that BUILDING BLOCK NO 6 is also important in constructing an argument about whether the law is good or bad.

BUILDING BLOCK NO 6: The Need for Certainty and Predictability in Land Law Rules
It is similarly important that the *law itself* is sufficiently clear on the question of how a joint tenancy or tenancy in common comes into being, or how the former is turned into the latter. Lawyers must be able to advise people like John and Mary with certainty as to who will own the property after one of the co-owners dies. It should not be necessary, particularly in this type of situation, to go to court to determine the legal outcome of the situation. If the law is uncertain this provides evidence for an argument that the rules of co-ownership are not good and fair law.

---

3 Identifying whether there is a joint tenancy or a tenancy in common

Before we begin to learn how the law determines whether there is a joint tenancy or a tenancy in common it is important to remember that there is a trust in all cases of co-ownership.[37] This

---

37   Law of Property Act 1925 s.34–36.

means it is necessary to deal with legal and equitable title separately. How can we tell which of the co-owners are the trustees and which are the beneficiaries? The trustees are the persons to whom the legal title has been conveyed. So we must look at the conveyance. For example: Alan, Barry, Claire, Daniel and Ernie decide to purchase a house together. They decide that the house will be conveyed into the names of Alan, Barry and Claire, because all agree that those three are better placed to manage the house. When the house is conveyed to Alan Barry and Claire the parties create an express trust, i.e. it is stated that they should hold the house on trust for themselves and Daniel and Ernie as Example 1. Where there is no express trust and land is conveyed to more than one person as co-owners, they hold on trust for themselves.[38] So if land is conveyed jointly to Ian, Martin and Vanessa, there will be the statutory trust, as illustrated in Example 2.

Example 1.

CONVEYANCE: "To A, B and C for themselves and D and E in equity":

LEGAL TITLE   **A B C**

EQUITABLE INTEREST   **A B C D E**

Example 2.

CONVEYANCE: "To I, M and V" (no trust mentioned):

LEGAL TITLE   **I M V**

EQUITABLE (or "beneficial") INTEREST I M V

---

(1) The working of the statutory trust[39]

As part of a structure that was designed to simplify the transfer of co-owned land, the Law of Property Act 1925 provides that where there is more than one person holding the *legal estate* they will always be joint tenants.[40] It can never be split up and turned into a tenancy in common: "severance".[41] Thus, when one trustee dies, he will drop out of the picture leaving the remaining owning the whole of the legal estate. This is true regardless of how the equitable estate is held, which may well be a tenancy in common. There are important conveyancing reasons for the imposition of a joint tenancy on the legal estate which we will consider in the next chapter. For now all we need to know is that when we are determining whether a joint tenancy or a tenancy in common exists, it is the *equitable/beneficial interest* with which we are concerned.

The equitable interest: can be held as either a joint tenancy or a tenancy in common. This may seem annoyingly technical but just remember that the equitable interest is the real ownership of the land. The land is registered in the name of the trustees and they have to manage the land—but it is the beneficiaries who are entitled to the profits and value of the land. Let's go back to the John and Mary example above.

---

38   Law of Property Act 1925 ss.34–36.
39   We will consider how the statutory trust works and is regulated in greater detail in the next Chapter.
40   Law of Property Act 1925 s.1(6).
41   Law of Property Act 1925 36(2); in section 4 below we will consider the law of severance.

LEGAL ESTATE: John, Mary (joint tenancy imposed by Law of Property Act 1925)

EQUITABLE (OR BENEFICIAL) INTEREST: **John, Mary (can be joint tenancy or tenancy in common)**

So when we are looking at what type of co-ownership exists, and whether a deceased co-owner's share passes to the other co-owners or can be left by will or intestacy, it is the equitable or "beneficial" interest with which we are concerned.

A. HOW TO DETERMINE THE NATURE OF THE PARTIES' CO-OWNERSHIP: JOINT TENANCY OR TENANCY IN COMMON?

We approach the question of the form of the co-ownership in two stages: firstly, we consider whether there is a joint tenancy or a tenancy in common *at the time of the purchase of the property*. This is determined by the co-owners' intentions or the testator's intentions (if the co-ownership arises under a will). Intention is determined by looking at the instrument creating the co-ownership, such as a conveyance of a house or a will. We look at surrounding circumstances and if this does not yield a result there is a default presumption of a joint tenancy unless one of the equitable presumptions of a tenancy in common applies. The four unities must be present in order for a joint tenancy to exist. Secondly, the law allows co-owners to change the nature of their co-ownership of the beneficial interest *after the acquisition of the property*. Even if a joint tenancy is set up originally there are several ways in which co-owners can break it up and create a tenancy in common instead. So we need to know whether an initial joint tenancy has been turned into a tenancy in common by subsequent actions. This is known as "severance". We will look at severance in section 4 below.

(1) The instrument creating the co-ownership (conveyance or will)

(a) Express declaration in the conveyance or will is conclusive

If co-ownership is expressly created by a document, e.g. a conveyance or a will, and there is an express declaration as to how the equitable interest is held then the courts will give effect to it, unless there is fraud or mistake.[42] So if the conveyance to the co-owners provides that they take as equitable (or beneficial) joint tenants then they will be joint tenants, but the declaration must

---

42   *Goodman v Gallant* [1986] Fam. 106.

refer to the *equitable* interest. An express declaration in the conveyance or will is absolutely conclusive of the matter.[43]

> **Example**
> I leave my land "Blackhill Farm" to my dear sons Chris and Ali to hold unto themselves as joint tenants in law and in equity.
>
> A conveyance of land: "to A, B and C, to hold at law for themselves in equity as joint tenants".
>
> In a perfect world all co-owners would expressly declare how they hold the property—*but alas, we do not live in a perfect world!*

In *Goodman v Gallant*[44] a wife owned a half share of her matrimonial home. When she was divorced from her husband she and her new partner bought her former husband's share of the house. Therefore, she had contributed 75 per cent of the value of the house. When the house was transferred to herself and her new partner, the conveyance expressly declared that they took as joint tenants. This was conclusive of the matter. There was a joint tenancy, even though the parties had contributed in unequal proportions to the purchase of the house.

An express declaration that the co-owners will hold as joint tenants has a surprising consequence that is no doubt alarming to the person who makes the major contribution to the purchase price. If joint tenants break up the joint tenancy and sell and split the proceeds then they will be entitled only to equal shares and not shares in proportion to their original contribution. This was the result in *Goodman v Gallant*.[45] Where they have contributed in unequal shares this might seem somewhat unfair. But it works like this: when a joint tenancy is created they are each deemed to own the whole together; no separate shares are recognised. So that when a joint tenancy is broken up then the only thing the law can do is distribute equally.[46] This principle holds good even if the parties intended different shares. Indeed, in *Singla (Brown's Trustee in Bankruptcy) v Brown*[47] co-owners had intended one of them to own a 1 per cent interest. The house was conveyed to them as joint tenants. When the joint tenancy was severed Thomas Ivory J. held that they had equal shares.

---

43 For the somewhat controversial view that beneficial interests expressly declared can thereafter be varied under the doctrine of proprietary estoppel see *Clarke v Meadus* [2010] EWHC 3117, relying on an observation of Baroness Hale in *Stack v Dowden* [2007] UKHL 17: see Pawlowski [2011] Conv. 245.
44 [1986] Fam. 106.
45 [1986] Fam. 106.
46 *Nielson-Jones v Fedden* [1975] Ch. 222, p.228, per Walton J.
47 [2008] 2 W.L.R. 283.

LECTURER: Consider the following extract all about the equal share trap: L.Tee, "Co-ownership and trusts" in *Land Law Issues, Debates, Policy*[48]:

"A further objection to beneficial joint tenancy is perhaps less weighty, but can still cause distress. This is that upon severance, the couple will automatically hold equal shares, whatever their original contributions. No doubt this is also explained to couples at the start, but . . . no doubt many couples will not fully understand the implications. It has been suggested that this trap could be circumvented by creating an express trust to provide that, in the case of severance, the respective shares should be other than equal. Whether this would be acceptable to a court without legislation is unclear – the possibility seems to undermine the theoretical basis of joint tenancy as two (or more) identical interests. But in the meantime, and pending any decision, caselaw provides examples of the annoyance felt when this particular trap is sprung on the unwary major contributor to the purchase."

LECTURER: Why would "an express trust to provide that, in the case of severance, the respective shares should be other than equal" undermine the nature of the joint tenancy?

STUDENT: A joint tenancy does not recognise separate shares: all the co-owners own the whole together. So there is no basis from which to say the law should recognise the unequal contributions.

LECTURER: Is *Goodman v Gallant* good law in this respect? Hold what you have learned about this rule against our Building Blocks. If the rule supports or undermines any of the fundamental ideas behind Land Law contained in our Building Blocks we may legitimately argue that the law is good or bad accordingly.[49]

STUDENT: Well, I would firstly use BUILDING BLOCK NO 7: The policy that Land Law should give effect to the co-owners' intentions or reasonable expectations. Land Law should bring about the consequences that most people in that situation would expect. In this context we can say that *Goodman v Gallant* does *not* allow for the legal consequences that most people would expect in this situation. Most people would expect the major contributor to own a proportionate share of the house.

> **BUILDING BLOCK NO 7: Land Law is "facilitative" and should give effect to the parties' intentions or reasonable expectations**
> In this context we can say that if the rules of co-ownership fail significantly to reflect the parties' intentions or reasonable expectations with regard to what should happen to the co-owned property, then those rules are bad law.

LECTURER: And doubtless they would not understand the technical explanation for why the parties would always obtain equal shares on the break-up of a joint tenancy, i.e. coming

---

48   L.Tee (ed.) (Willan Publishing, 2002), p.132, at pp.137–8 (footnotes omitted).
49   For the full text of our Building Blocks together with instructions on how to use them to construct a convincing argument, see Chapter 1.

from the idea of unity of interest. Therefore, the law would not even make sense to most domestic co-owners.

STUDENT: It is not what they would expect the law to do. So unless parties were made aware of this consequence at the time of the conveyance to themselves as joint tenants (and even then, as Tee points out, this might not be effective), then the law is not good. Tee also puts forward the view in the extract that this would come as a surprise to most couples. She shows that the law relating to joint tenancies fails in a significant respect to give effect to co-owner's reasonable expectations. This is a significant criticism of the law on the basis of BUILDING BLOCK NO 7.

> Note how our Student used Tee's observation in the extract to strengthen the reason for the conclusion by showing that the criticism applies more widely than in the context of one case (which would not be much of a problem if the issue were not typical of most cases.)

(2) Words of severance

The courts will infer a tenancy in common from any words in the conveyance or will that indicate *separation* of interest: "words of severance". For example, the conveyance might include words such as "to A and B *equally*", "to be *divided between* A and B", "to *divide* amongst", "respectively", "to share",[50] etc. Such expressions will give rise to a tenancy in common because they show that the intentions of the testator or those of the parties to a conveyance cannot be to create a beneficial joint tenancy. Words of severance are inconsistent with the nature of a joint tenancy "that each owns the whole".[51]

> Words of severance are expressions that are inconsistent with the *nature* of the joint tenancy, that being that together all the co-owners own the whole—joint tenants do not hold in separate shares.

> **Unity of Interest: The BUILDING BLOCK of the Joint Tenancy**
> Each owns the whole interest together. None of the co-owners has separate and identifiable shares. Words of severance indicate separate shares. SURVIVORSHIP: is the necessary by-product of unity of interest. Because the co-owners together own the whole of the interest and separately own nothing when one dies he does not die owning any separate interest that he can leave by will. Words of severance show that there are separate interests to leave by will.

---

50   *Robertson v Fraser* (1870–71) L.R. 6 Ch. App. 696.
51   Smith, *Plural Ownership*, p.31.

(3) Circumstances in which the will was made or the conveyance executed

The courts may look at the circumstances surrounding the making of the will or conveyance in order to ascertain whether a joint tenancy or a tenancy in common was intended.[52] This may be the case even where there are words of severance.

LECTURER: Let's try an example. Mr Bennett makes the following will: "I leave my house, Longbourn, to my beloved daughters Jane, Elizabeth, Mary, Kitty and Lydia that they might continue to live in family harmony for the rest of their lives".[53] The sisters are middle-aged and all live at Longbourn.

STUDENT: The father has given no express declaration as to whether his daughters are to take as joint tenants or tenants in common under the will. So *Goodman v Gallant* cannot apply. There are no words of severance indicating that the father intended his daughters to have separate interests in Longbourn.

LECTURER: But what inference can the court make about Mr Bennett's *likely* intentions here, from the surrounding circumstances of the case? The question we are really asking is whether the father intended his daughters each to have a separate interest that they can leave by will or whether he intended survivorship to operate. The court will look at the consequences of the joint tenancy and the tenancy in common and determine which consequences the circumstances of the case show to be the intended ones.

> Do the circumstances of the case reveal that the consequences described here were the likely intention of Mr Bennett?

> **Unity of Interest: The BUILDING BLOCK of the Joint Tenancy**
> Each owns the whole interest together. None of the co-owners has separate and identifiable shares. SURVIVORSHIP operates with a joint tenancy. One co-owner dies leaving the remaining co-owner(s) owning the whole.

Did Mr Bennett intend these consequences? Or did he intend his daughters to have separate interests?

STUDENT: Because Mr Bennett said that he intended his daughters to "continue to live in family harmony", and because all the daughters are living at Longbourn, one likely inference the court might make is that Mr Bennett intended for survivorship to operate

LECTURER: Why?

STUDENT: Because it works so that when one co-owner dies she just drops out of the picture leaving the other daughters "owning the whole together". This is likely to be more conducive

---

52   R.Smith, *Plural Ownership*.

53   An example given by Smith (changed in details here), *Plural Ownership*, p.32, citing *Clerk v Clerk* (1694) 2 Vern. 323 in which a joint tenancy was found despite words of severance.

to the daughters living together happily than would be the case if, when one daughter dies, her interest in Longbourn passes to whoever inherits her property by will or intestacy (which may not be her sisters). This would be the effect of a tenancy in common.

LECTURER: Well done! This is exactly how the courts would look at the surrounding circumstances of the case in order to determine the intentions of the person(s) setting up the co-ownership.

(4) Inconsistent wording in a conveyance

In *Joyce v Barker Bros (Builders) Ltd*[54] property was conveyed to a couple "in fee simple as beneficial joint tenants in equal shares". Vinelott J. held that the conveyance made no sense as it stood. So applying a somewhat mechanical rule of construction he held that where a document contains contradictory expressions, here "joint tenants" (indicating naturally a joint tenancy) and "equal shares" (indicating separate and distinct shares: a tenancy in common), the earlier provision will prevail.[55] *Joyce v Barker Bros* was distinguished in *Martin v Martin*.[56] Mrs Martin and her son and daughter-in-law purchased a property in which to live together. It was conveyed to all three "upon trust. . . for themselves as beneficial joint tenants in common in equal shares". It was held that the words "in equal shares" either constituted words that severed the joint tenancy created by the earlier inconsistent provision, or "provided a controlling context for the word 'joint' and so created a tenancy in common". Thus, Mrs Martin's share passed to her estate when she died. Survivorship did not apply. Millett J. reasoned purposively and criticised the mechanical rule whereby the earlier inconsistent provision would prevail. He referred "to equity's preference for a tenancy in common".[57] This places greater emphasis on what he thought to be the parties' intentions from the conveyance.

(5) The default presumption of an equitable joint tenancy

Remember that we are looking at how we identify whether co-owners of property hold as joint tenants or as tenants in common. We have seen that the courts seek to ascertain the intentions of the person(s) setting up the co-ownership by examining the conveyance or will. If there is an express declaration of how the beneficial interest is held then this will be conclusive. The courts will also seek to identify any words of severance and will look at the disposition as a whole and its surrounding circumstances. However, if there is no indication from the conveyance or will whether the parties hold as beneficial joint tenants or tenants in common, and the land is transferred into two or more people's names, there is a presumption that they are to be joint tenants in equity[58]— unless one of the following equitable presumptions of a tenancy in common applies.

(6) The equitable presumptions of a tenancy in common

In the absence of an express declaration in the conveyance or any further evidence of intention, there are situations in which equity will presume that the parties intended to create a tenancy in common and not a joint tenancy. The list of situations is not closed.[59]

---

54 (1980) 40 P. & C.R. 512.
55 *Forbes v Git* [1922] 1 A.C. 256; [1987] Conv. 405.
56 (1987) 54 P. & C.R. 238.
57 (1987) 54 P. & C.R. 238: J.E.A. "What's Mine is Mine and What's Yours is Ours" [1987] Conv. 405.
58 Confirmed in *Stack v Dowden* [2007] UKHL 17.
59 *Malayan Credit Ltd v Jack Chia-MPH Ltd* [1986] A.C. 549.

> **What is a "presumption"?** This means that the court will hold that there is a tenancy in common unless it is proven that the parties intended a joint tenancy. A presumption merely reverses the burden of proof.

Generically speaking the situations in which equity will presume a tenancy in common are ones in which survivorship seems particularly unfair,[60] e.g. where there is a business relationship between the co-owners equity presumes it is unlikely that they would intend their share to go to the other co-owner when they died. They would intend it to go to their families or be otherwise passed under their will.

(a) Unequal contributions to the purchase of land

Equity considers that survivorship would be unfair in circumstances where one party has contributed more than another to the purchase of the land. The argument runs that they should have an interest that they can dispose of by will. Thus, where co-owners have contributed to the purchase in unequal amounts and this has given rise to unequal shares equity will presume that their intention is to take as tenants in common.[61]

> **The relationship between this principle and express declarations**
> Remember that where there is an express declaration in the conveyance or will that the co-owners are to take as beneficial joint tenants, there will be a joint tenancy irrespective of unequal contribution to the purchase: *Goodman v Gallant* [1986] Fam. 106.

Where the house is registered in the co-owners' joint names in a domestic situation, it was held by the House of Lords there is a presumption that because the couple put the house in joint names, they intended equal shares.[62] Baroness Hale considered that this also meant that they intended to own the interest in the house jointly, i.e. as a joint tenancy and not in separate shares. This was intended to reflect the reality of modern home ownership, where couples typically share the running of the household and contribute what they can when they can.[63] Although this is a strong presumption, it can be rebutted with evidence that shows the parties intended to keep separate interests in the house.[64] However, more than unequal contributions must be shown.

---

60   *Burgess v Rawnsley* [1975] Ch. 429, p.440, per Lord Denning M.R.
61   *Lake v Gibson* (1729) 1 Eq. Cas. Ab. 290; *Walker v Hall* [1984] 5 F.L.R. 126.
62   *Stack v Dowden* [2007] UKHL 17.
63   *Laskar v Laskar* [2008] EWCA Civ. 347; [2008] 1 W.L.R. 2695 (purchase by mother and daughter) confirmed that the presumption of a joint tenancy only operates where property is purchased for domestic purposes and not for commercial reasons, e.g. as an investment.
64   As was the case on the facts of *Stack* itself. For a detailed consideration of the type of evidence that might suffice to rebut this presumption see Chapter 3.

Where the property is registered in the sole name of one of the co-owners, but another has acquired an equitable interest under a common intention constructive trust, i.e. where there is no express declaration of trust,[65] it is rare for there to be a beneficial joint tenancy.[66]

(b) Business partnerships

Equity will presume a tenancy in common where property is acquired by business partners, i.e. the property is co-owned by business partners, as established in *Lake v Craddock*.[67] The court will hold that the co-owners are tenants in common. For this presumption to apply, the property must have been acquired for commercial purposes.[68] The reason that Equity presumes a tenancy in common in this situation is that the most likely expectation of business partners when they buy property together is that the right of survivorship inherent in the joint tenancy would not apply. The business partners would generally expect their share of the co-owned premises to pass to their family under their will, and not go to their business partner.

BUILDING BLOCK NO 7: Land Law is "facilitative": the rules of land law should give effect to the parties' intentions or reasonable expectations

Can you see that the law in this section reflects the principle that Land Law should give effect to peoples' intentions and reasonable expectations with regard to co-owned property? Without knowing anything about the law it is likely that most business partners who co-own property together would expect and want to be able to leave their share of the co-owned business premises to their families by will. They have worked hard and put their hard-earned money into buying the business premises, and presumably this is where they work. Most business owners would expect that when they died this work and financial investment would benefit their families and not their business partner. Survivorship in this context would operate in an unjust way to the co-owners and their families.

But this is only a presumption. It is not absolute. If there is evidence that the parties intended a joint tenancy and not a tenancy in common then this will be enough to displace the equitable presumption. In the diagram below we consider the type of evidence required.

---

65   *Stack v Dowden* [2007] 2 A.C. 432, p.458, per Baroness Hale.

66   But see *HSBC Bank Plc v Dyche* [2010] 2 P. &. C.R. 4, which concerned very different circumstances. There was a common understanding that a house would be reconveyed to the claimants jointly when they paid off a loan. When this did not happen they acquired a beneficial interest under the principles of the common intention constructive trust, see Chapter 3. H.H. Judge Purle QC held that the legal owner held the house on trust for both of them as beneficial joint tenants.

67   (1732) 3 P.Wms. 158.

68   *Malayan Credit Ltd v Jack Chia-MPH Ltd* [1986] A.C. 549, PC, pp.559–60, per Lord Brightman.

> **Do the circumstances of the case reveal that the intentions of the parties are consistent with holding as joint tenants?**

> **Unity of interest: The BUILDING BLOCK of the Joint Tenancy:**
> Each owns the whole interest together. None of the co-owners has separate and identifiable shares. SURVIVORSHIP operates with a joint tenancy. One co-owner dies leaving the remaining co-owner(s) owning the whole. Do the parties' intentions show that they want these legal consequences?

(i) The equitable presumption applies where the co-owners have separate businesses

In *Malayan Credit Ltd v Jack Chia-MPH Ltd*[69] the co-owners were not business partners but jointly purchased property in order to run separate businesses from that property. In this situation the law that applies to business partnerships had to be developed to cover this situation. Did the equitable presumption of a tenancy in common apply or not?

   THE FACTS: The parties had together purchased a lease of business premises, so they were co-owners of the lease. But they ran separate businesses. They were not partners in the same business and were using the premises for their separate business purposes. There was no express declaration in the conveyance and so the question was whether they held the property as joint tenants or tenants in common. Did the equitable presumption of a tenancy in common apply here?

   THE CONCLUSION: For the presumption to apply it did not matter that the co-owners ran separate businesses. Lord Brightman held that the equitable presumption of a tenancy in common applied to this situation.

> The facts and conclusion of a case do not tell us very much. To understand the principles fully, and to apply them to a problem, or to create an argument about them, we need to know the *reasoning*. For this purpose we need to examine the judgment in the case.

LECTURER: We are going to look at an extract from the judgment of Lord Brightman in the Privy Council. Look carefully at the reasoning, asking *what factors were so important to the judge that they led him to his conclusion?* OR: *what factors is the judge assuming would have to have been different in order for him to come to a different conclusion?*

   LORD BRIGHTMAN: "The argument is that, in the absence of an express agreement, persons who take as joint tenants at law hold as tenants in common in equity only in three classes of case: first, where they have provided the purchase money in unequal

---

69   [1986] A.C. 549, PC.

shares; in this case they hold the beneficial interest in similar shares: secondly where the grant consists of a security for a loan and the grantees were equal or unequal contributors to the loan; again they would hold the beneficial interest in the same shares; and thirdly, where they are partners and the subject matter of the grant is partnership property . . . The plaintiff contends that the instant case falls into none of these three categories. Therefore it is said that the lessees hold as joint tenants in equity as well as at law, with the result that either party was at liberty to sever the joint tenancy and thus ensure that the beneficial interest was thereafter held in equal shares . . .

The matter came before the High Court . . . The trial judge held that as the premises were disproportionately divided between the parties, there was a tenancy in common in unequal shares . . . He said that he was fortified in this view by the fact that the stamp duty was paid in unequal shares, as also the rent. The Court of Appeal reversed the trial judge, holding that there was a joint tenancy which, on later severance, became a tenancy in common in equal shares . . .

It seems to their Lordships that where premises are held by two persons as joint tenants at law for their several business purposes, it is improbable that they would intend to hold as joint tenants in equity. Suppose that an accountant and an architect take a lease of premises containing four rooms, that the accountant uses two rooms, and that the architect uses two rooms. It is scarcely to be supposed that they intend that if, for example, the accountant dies first without having gone through the formalities of a severance, the beneficial interest in the entire premises is to survive to the architect. Their Lordships do not accept that the cases in which joint tenants at law will be presumed to hold as tenants in common in equity are as rigidly circumscribed as the plaintiff asserts. Such cases are not necessarily limited to purchasers who contribute unequally, to co-mortgagees and to partners. There are other circumstances in which equity may infer that the beneficial interest is intended to be held by the grantees as tenants in common. In the opinion of their Lordships, one such case is where the grantees hold the premises for their several individual business purposes . . ."

LECTURER: Can you see how the reasoning in this paragraph above is based on one of our Building Blocks? It provides a basis for the reasoning that the equitable presumption of a tenancy in common should be extended to cases where co-owners hold property, using it for their separate businesses. Lord Brightman concludes this because this would be most people's likely intentions or expectations in the circumstances.

BUILDING BLOCK NO 7: Land Law is "facilitative": the rules of land law should give effect to the parties' intentions or reasonable expectations

Thus, the judge's reasoning is consistent with the principle that Land Law should give effect to the owner's intentions and reasonable expectations with regard to co-owned property. Lord Brightman's reasoning gives an illustration of how the Land Law judges think this principle of giving effect to intentions is important.

STUDENT: So this case presented the judge with a novel set of facts that were not precisely covered by any rule. The judge re-invented the rule and said that from now on it would extend to separate businesses.

LECTURER: In short this is an example of judges making the law. And here, he extended the equitable presumption of a tenancy in common to this type of situation because he thought that it would make better law. He justified this on the basis of our BUILDING BLOCK NO 7.

LECTURER: Lord Brightman now goes on to apply all of the law in this area (including the equitable presumption applicable to business partners) in order to conclude that the co-owners were not joint tenants (as the Court of Appeal had held) but tenants in common.

> **BUILDING BLOCKS:** So if you are arguing a case and it is uncertain whether the particular rule applies to the set of facts you are arguing about, it is well worth trying to persuade the judge that the interpretation you are arguing for will support a fundamental policy of Land Law (one or more of our Building Blocks).

LORD BRIGHTMAN'S JUDGMENT CONTINUES: "There are features in the instant case which appear to their Lordships to point unmistakably towards a tenancy in common in equity, and furthermore towards a tenancy in common in unequal shares: (1) the lease was clearly taken to serve the separate commercial interests of the defendant and the plaintiff.[70] (2) Prior to the grant of the lease the parties had settled between themselves what space they would respectively occupy when the lease came to be granted.[71] This was roughly 62 per cent to the defendant and 38 per cent to the plaintiff. (3) Prior to the grant of the lease, the parties had made meticulous measurements of their respective allotted areas, and divided their liability for the rent and service charge in unequal shares in accordance with the respective areas that they would occupy.[72] (4) Prior to the grant of the lease, the plaintiff was invoiced for its due share of the deposit which was to be paid to the landlord as security under the terms of the lease, the apportionment being made in unequal shares in the like manner. This deposit was a sum which was not to be refundable by the landlord until the termination of the lease . . . (5) After the grant of the lease, the defendant and the plaintiff paid the stamp duty and the survey fees in the same unequal shares. (6) As from the grant of the lease, the rent and service charges were paid in the same unequal shares.

With great respect to the Court of Appeal, their Lordships feel unable to support their conclusion that the parties are [beneficial joint tenants]."

---

70   Here his lordship is relating the facts to the equitable presumption of a tenancy in common in cases of business co-owners. There is a clear intention for separate shares. To learn more about this finding of intention relate what Lord Brightman says back to the "accountant and architect" example earlier in this judgment.

71   Showing a clear intention to have separate interests. Here his lordship is looking at the intentions of the parties from "surrounding circumstances"—see above in this Chapter, section 3, p.238.

72   Looking at unequal contributions, and showing an intention to own separate shares—an intention that survivorship would be inappropriate.

LECTURER: To understand Lord Brightman's reasoning we must go right back to the essence of the joint tenancy: *unity of interest*.

Unity of Interest: The BUILDING BLOCK of the Joint Tenancy

Each owns the whole interest together. None of the co-owners has separate and identifiable shares. This describes the idea of unity of *ownership*. Each owns the same interest in the property together; separately they own nothing. Survivorship is the necessary by-product of unity of interest. Because the co-owners together own the whole of the interest and separately own nothing, when one dies he does not die owning anything separate and identifiable that he can leave by will.

Lord Brightman reasoned that the parties held as tenants in common because points (2)–(6) showed they had wanted separate shares and not a joint interest. He deduced from this conduct that this was the result that the parties had intended. Hold this against our Unity of Interest: The BUILDING BLOCK of the Joint Tenancy. What was Lord Brightman actually saying here?

STUDENT: That the features of the case were inconsistent with the nature of the joint tenancy.

LECTURER: OK then, how were the parties acting that showed inconsistency with *unity of interest*?

STUDENT: They divided up the space and considered this to determine their separate liability under the lease. They allocate separate rent payments. They also did this with the security deposit, stamp duty and service charges. This showed two people acting in a way that showed they wished to keep their obligations and entitlements *separate*.

LECTURER: Very good reasoning. It is worth noting here that this shows the high regard that the courts have to the parties' intentions. Thus, if we change the *Malayan Credit* facts around a little: Even though the parties had two separate businesses, if their conduct showed that they intended to be joint owners with unity of interest, this equitable presumption would have been displaced. The presumptions give way to evidence of actual intention. Consider this example problem question:

Jane, Elizabeth, Mary, Kitty and Lydia were left the family home "Longbourn" in the will of their late father: Mr Bennett. Mr Bennett's will provided that "My house I leave to my beloved daughters. May it enable you to continue to live in family harmony for the rest of your lives and provide a base from which to run the family business". The daughters are all middle-aged and reside at Longbourn. Elizabeth has recently died leaving all her property, real and personal, to her cousin William Collins. Advise William Collins, who is claiming an interest in Longbourn.

Let's incorporate all the principles we have so far discussed. We can start from the fact that Mr Bennett has not expressly declared whether his daughters are to take as joint tenants or tenants in common. So . . . then what will the courts look at?

STUDENT: Words of severance—but there seem to be no such words here. The will is looked at in the light of surrounding circumstances. Thus, the fact that Mr Bennett wishes his daughters to continue living there until they die suggests that survivorship is the most likely intention. The circumstances of the daughters, i.e. they are close, shows that Mr Bennett's actual intention is for survivorship to operate.

LECTURER: So how does this relate to Mr Bennett's reference to Longbourn being used for the "family business"? How does this relate to the principles in *Malayan Credit Ltd v Jack Chia-MPH Ltd*?

STUDENT: Lord Brightman's reasoning would not preclude a tenancy in common where it was members of the same family running a business from co-owned property and without further evidence this fact might invoke the equitable presumption that a tenancy in common exists. However, with this situation, as may be the case with many family businesses, not only is the intention likely to be that the family partners intend survivorship, but we have proved by looking at the will and its surrounding circumstances that Mr Bennett *really did intend* that his daughters took as joint tenants.

LECTURER: So the actual intentions will prevail and the daughters will be held to be joint tenants of Longbourn. So what's your advice to William Collins? Always state the legal consequences.

STUDENT: The remaining sisters take by survivorship—William Collins has no interest.

(c) Mortgagees

As we have seen a mortgage is an interest in property. It is security for a loan of money. The security gives the lender certain rights over the borrower's property, e.g. in the case of a legal mortgage of land the lender can take possession of mortgaged property and sell it in order to recoup its investment should the borrower default on the terms of the loan agreement.[73] Where two or more persons advance money and take a mortgage in return, they are co-owners of this security. There is an equitable presumption that they take their security as tenants in common.[74] Thus, whether the lenders who granted the security (mortgagees) were "equal or unequal contributors to the loan . . . they would hold the beneficial interest in the same shares".[75]

---

73   *Four-Maids Ltd v Dudley Marshall (Properties) Ltd* [1957] Ch 317; Law of Property Act 1925 ss.85, 101, 103, 109.
74   *Morley v Bird* (1798) 3 Ves. 628; *Re Jackson* (1887) 34 Ch. D 732.
75   *Malayan Credit Ltd v Jack Chia-MPH Ltd* [1986] A.C. 549 PC, p.559, per Lord Brightman.

MAP of the principles: Ascertaining whether co-ownership is a joint tenancy or a tenancy in common.

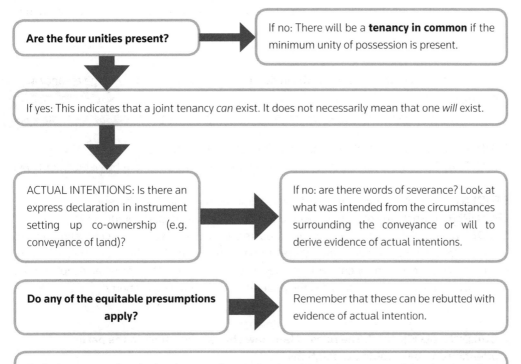

Are the four unities present?

If no: There will be a **tenancy in common** if the minimum unity of possession is present.

If yes: This indicates that a joint tenancy *can* exist. It does not necessarily mean that one *will* exist.

ACTUAL INTENTIONS: Is there an express declaration in instrument setting up co-ownership (e.g. conveyance of land)?

If no: are there words of severance? Look at what was intended from the circumstances surrounding the conveyance or will to derive evidence of actual intentions.

Do any of the equitable presumptions apply?

Remember that these can be rebutted with evidence of actual intention.

Default presumption: In the absence of any indication of intentions, or any of the situations that trigger the equitable presumptions of a tenancy in common, there is a presumption that if the four unities are present then a beneficial joint tenancy will arise. How strong is this presumption? How likely is it to arise, given all the circumstances above?

(7) Critical Thinking exercises: problem solving and Building Blocks

(a) A joint tenancy or a tenancy in common?

In *Martin v Martin*[76] Millet J. referred "to equity's preference for a tenancy in common".[77] *Megarry & Wade* observes that "equity . . . preferred the certainty and equality of a tenancy in common to the chance of 'all or nothing' which arose from the right of survivorship".[78] "Survivorship is looked upon as odious in equity".[79] In *Burgess v Rawnsley*[80] Lord Denning M.R. stated that "[t]he

---

76   (1987) 54 P. & C.R. 238.
77   (1987) 54 P. & C.R. 238; J.E.A. "What's Mine is Mine and What's Yours is Ours" [1987] Conv. 405.
78   *Megarry & Wade the Law of Real Property*, para.13–021.
79   *Megarry & Wade*, above, para.13–021, citing *R v Williams* (1735) Bunb. 342, *Re Woolley* [1903] 2 Ch. 206.
80   [1975] Ch. 429.

thing to remember today is that equity leans against joint tenants and favours tenancies in common".[81] Smith observes that "a tenancy in common is to be preferred as a 'usable interest' . . . Where members of a family are involved . . . then survivorship can make sense. In most other contexts, it will be indefensible.[82] The result was that equity implied a tenancy in common in certain types of cases".[83]

> So as a method of owning property which do we prefer: the joint tenancy or the tenancy in common?

STUDENT: I would like to feel that I had a definite share in the house.

LECTURER: So it may be important to you that you can leave this share by will to your loved ones?

STUDENT: Yes, that you have nothing if you die first seems unfair: It's arbitrary.

LECTURER: In what type of situation would this unfairness seem particularly acute?

STUDENT: If I were buying a house with friends from university. I would want my share to go to my relatives if I died before the others. If I had not just studied this, this is what I would probably expect to happen. So tenancies in common give effect to what people would expect in this situation and so it is the preferable way of holding property.

> **BUILDING BLOCK NO 7: The rules of land law should give effect to the parties' intentions or reasonable expectations**
>
> In allowing rules that recognise a tenancy in common to exist the rules of co-ownership reflect the parties' reasonable expectations with regard to what should happen to the co-owned property.

But in this type of situation equity does not presume a tenancy in common, unless my friends and I contributed in unequal proportions to the purchase and this gave rise to unequal shares.

LECTURER: So you would have to make your intentions clear in the conveyance of the property.

STUDENT: Yes, but most people would not know to do this. So on BUILDING BLOCK NO 7 the law is not good and fair.

LECTURER: They would be legally advised in a house purchase? This means that the parties would have a chance to understand how to express their intentions correctly and get the result they expect.

---

81   Equity leans against joint tenancies: *Kinch v Bullard* [1999] 1 W.L.R. 423, p.430, per Neuberger J.
82   See M.P.Thompson [1987] Conv. 29; A.M.Prichard [1987] Conv. 273; Thompson [1987] Conv. 275.
83   Smith, *Plural Ownership*, p.33.

LECTURER: See what we are doing here? Don't forget to argue *imaginatively* ask questions and interrogate this Building Block to see whether in the actual situation the law is unfair.

Do you think that there may be situations in which the co-owners may have the opposite expectation: that the surviving co-owner will own the whole of the house if the other dies? I want you to consider how the law of co-ownership may apply in the owner occupation context.

Owner occupation

The social context of Land Law has changed. At the time of the 1925 legislation most people rented the houses in which they lived. When lawyers talked of co-ownership of land and whether there was a joint tenancy or a tenancy in common it was usually in the context of inheritance and investment. At the time the tenancy in common was the preferred form of co-ownership: J.S.Anderson, *Lawyers and the Making of English Land Law* 1832–1940, pp. 287, 290.

However, there was a change in the way people held property that took place later in the century: from rented accommodation to owner occupation. Therefore the law of co-ownership determines how couples and other domestic occupiers hold their house: Joint tenants or tenants in common.

STUDENT: Where a couple buy a house and perhaps raise a family. If one of the couple dies most people would probably expect that the surviving partner would then own the whole house.

LECTURER: And if they were to find out that this was not the case, what kind of an impact might it have?

STUDENT: If the deceased partner's share passed under her will or under the rules of intestacy, to someone else, that person will then claim an interest in the house. This is probably not what people would generally expect and it would be a terrible shock. A bit like our John and Mary example (p.230 above).

LECTURER: Are there ways in which these expectations could be managed by legal advisers? A lawyer could easily explain to the co-owners the implications of their choice of joint tenancy or tenancy in common.

STUDENT: Not really. The partners may have been advised by lawyers at the outset of the purchase but they may not remember this, or understand it. They are very technical legal concepts. In the extract from the article that we studied when talking about the "equal share trap" of the joint tenancy (p.236 above) L.Tee observes that "No doubt this is also explained to couples at the start, but again – no doubt many couples will not fully understand the implications".[84]

---

84   L.Tee, "Co-ownership and trusts" in *Land Law Issues, Debates, Policy*, p.132, at pp.137-8 (footnotes omitted).

LECTURER: Our STUDENT is now beginning to use academic authority to lend weight to the evidence for the argument and has now picked up on the fact that we need to ask questions before we can definitely say that a Building Block is supported or undermined.

LECTURER: So in a domestic situation, if the law provides for a "default" joint tenancy then we can say it is good law because it supports BUILDING BLOCK NO 7.

BUILDING BLOCK NO 7: The rules of land law should give effect to the parties' intentions or reasonable expectations

In allowing rules that recognise a joint tenancy in the absence of any express declaration of intent the rules of co-ownership would reflect domestic co-owners' reasonable expectations with regard to what should happen to the co-owned property. It would therefore be good law.

Does the law have this effect?

STUDENT: Well, if there are no words of severance there will be a joint tenancy because this is the "default" presumption in the absence of any other indication of their intentions. This is true in a domestic situation even where the partners contributed to the purchase in unequal amounts: *Stack v Dowden*, see p.240 above.

LECTURER: Here is a chart of our argument:

PREMISE ONE: The law is good if it gives effect to people's reasonable expectations about what will happen to their property.

PREMISE TWO: The joint tenancy would accord with peoples' expectations in this type of domestic situation.

PREMISE THREE: In order to be fair the law needs to make this a default presumption because the parties cannot be expected to fully appreciate legal consequences.

PREMISE FOUR: This is what the law mainly does in this type of situation.

CONCLUSION: The law is good and fair.

Can you see that PREMISE THREE weakens the argument if it is in fact established that parties can be expected to rely on legal advice at the outset of the purchase? It weakens the need for the law simply to impose a joint tenancy in domestic situations if the parties themselves can be relied upon to choose the type of co-ownership in an informed way.

LECTURER: In the light of your argument that most domestic co-owners would expect their share to go to the other co-owner on their death (survivorship) AND that they may well still hold this view even where they were initially advised of the consequences, hold the law against BUILDING BLOCK NO 1: Residential Security. Is the law good or bad according to this Building Block?

> **BUILDING BLOCK NO 1: Residential Security**
> Residential security is now a main purpose behind the ownership of land in this country. When we look at the rules of co-ownership we can say that they are good or bad depending on the extent to which they protect someone's right to continue living in the home.

STUDENT: In the owner occupation context, where people buy residential property in order to live there with their families, the joint tenancy better protects residential security. Where one co-owner dies the other becomes automatically entitled to the whole of the property by survivorship. But if there is a tenancy in common, one of the co-owners may leave his share to someone in his will and that person may seek to sell the house when he inherits the share. This undermines the surviving co-owner's residential security.

LECTURER: And if what you have argued above is correct, this means that the law is good and fair on the basis of BUILDING BLOCK NO 1 as well. Indeed, Lord Denning in *Bedson v Bedson*[85] argued unsuccessfully for a form of indestructible joint tenancy in the matrimonial context.

However now consider the opposite point of view.

> **L.Tee, "Co-ownership and trusts"** in *Land Law Issues, Debates, Policy,* **p.137**
> "It seems to be a common, and perfectly understandable, misconception that one can leave one's 'half' of the house by will . . . .. This issue seems particularly worrying now, in view of the rise in the divorce rate and the increase in serial cohabitation. . . . In the context of such familial instability, it seems increasingly inappropriate that property should automatically pass in accordance with a half understood agreement, possibly made many years previously, rather than as the deceased subsequently intended." (Footnotes omitted).

LECTURER: So when a marriage or cohabitation has broken up, the joint tenancy might operate unfairly. The partners might think that they can leave their share by will, e.g. to a new partner, which they cannot do in a joint tenancy. The joint tenancy also has the potential to operate unfairly where one of the couple dies before having made arrangements for the

---

85   [1965] 2 Q.B. 666.

house. This will mean that their former spouse or partner will then own the whole of the house. This is unlikely to represent the deceased co-owner's intentions, particularly if they have a new family.

STUDENT: So the law ought to recognise a tenancy in common. This would truly give effect to the parties' intentions.

LECTURER: These are at least some of the issues that arise in the context of the principles of co-ownership. They become particularly relevant when we look at the law of severance.[86]

(b) Problem solving—stringing the principles together

> In 1990, Alan, Brian, Claire and David purchased a large Victorian terraced house from which they intended to run a doctor's practice. They contributed in unequal proportions to the purchase price and the house was conveyed "to all of them as joint tenants in law and in equity".
>
> Brian dies and his will leaves all his property to his aunt Patricia. Does Patricia have any claim to the house?

LECTURER: Ok, let's have a look at this one.

STUDENT: I think it is a joint tenancy. Is this a good starting point for solving the problem?

LECTURER: I'm afraid not. What you have expressed is a conclusion. If anything it is a finishing point. Legal problems are answered by your telling me *how you arrived at your particular conclusion*. You have to give me the *reasons* for your conclusion: show your "working out"! This will often involve stating the principles from the cases and applying or distinguishing them.

STUDENT: When a co-ownership situation is set up the court will look at the document that establishes the co-ownership, here the 1990 conveyance, in order to determine the parties' intentions as to whether they hold the Victorian house as equitable joint tenants or tenants in common: I say "equitable" because all co-ownership takes effect under a trust and the legal estate must be a joint tenancy (Law of Property Act 1925 ss.34–35).

LECTURER: Good, and what are the legal principles that apply to this conveyance?

STUDENT: There are unequal contributions and they are business partners—two situations in which equity presumes a tenancy in common. And the house was conveyed "to all of them as joint tenants in law and in equity".

LECTURER: Unfortunately you have lapsed into just repeating the facts of the question. You have to take the bull by the horns and apply the legal principles to arrive at a conclusion. Remember what it is that you are doing. You are *solving a legal problem*. This is all about predicting a legal outcome for the parties involved—it's all about the legal consequences for the parties. Try stating these first and allow those to lead you to the principles of law.

---

86 Should the beneficial joint tenancy be abolished? For further argument see "Yes": M.P.Thompson [1987] Conv. 29; "No": A.M.Prichard [1987] Conv. 273; Thompson [1987] Conv. 275 (reply).

STUDENT: Well, Patricia can only claim an interest in the Victorian house if the law allows the provision in Brian's will to take effect. If Brian has died a joint tenant of the house the provision in the will is null and void. Patricia will have no claim on the house.

LECTURER: Good, now what?

STUDENT: The very first principle is that if there is an express declaration in the conveyance of the land to the co-owners (or the will if it is an "inheritance" co-ownership) then this declaration is conclusive in the absence of fraud or mistake: *Goodman v Gallant*.[87]

LECTURER: And how does this relate to the equitable presumptions of a tenancy in common. Two are potentially relevant here: where co-owners contribute in unequal proportions and where they are business partners.

STUDENT: An express declaration is conclusive evidence of a joint tenancy in this case: *Goodman v Gallant*. The equitable presumptions are rebutted by this evidence of the parties' actual intention. Therefore Brian died as a joint tenant and Patricia cannot claim an interest in the house.

LECTURER: Very good!

(8) Guidance on legal reasoning—applying and distinguishing cases

How do we use past cases to give us answers to present legal problems? Firstly we identify the nature of the legal problem by stating the legal consequences of the rules to the parties—the way we did in the dialogue above. Then we ask what *are the precedent cases nearest to this problem?* What conclusion did the judge come to and why?

At this point we have reached the stage whereby we can use the precedent case to help us predict a solution to the problem (which is the whole point of the exercise). To give rise to the *same conclusion* as the precedent case the problem facts must have *materially similar properties* to the precedent case,[88] or, as we may put it, the same significant features as that case. The significant features of the precedent case are identified by reading the relevant judgment and asking questions like: *what would have to have been different about the case for the judge to decide it the other way?*

APPLYING: If the same material properties are present then we come to the same decision as the precedent case upon which we are relying. We "apply" it. To use our problem example above: we "applied" *Goodman v Gallant*.

DISTINGUISHING: But if the material features are not the same then we "distinguish" the precedent case. We then come to the opposite conclusion. Here we are saying, in effect, that whilst this is the rule that should apply, the *result* would be different in our problem case because the case itself is different and justifies a different result. We "distinguish" the precedent case.

---

87   [1986] Fam. 106.

88   Expression and idea: Schauer, *Thinking Like a Lawyer* (Harvard University Press, 2009), Ch.5, "The Use and Abuse of Analogies".

> Let's say that our problem above had these features instead: in 1990, Alan, Brian, Claire and David purchased a large Victorian terraced house from which they intended to run a doctor's practice. They contributed in unequal proportions to the purchase price and the house was conveyed "to all of them on trust to hold jointly in common". Brian dies and his will leaves all his property to his aunt Patricia. Does Patricia have any claim to the house?

I might offer the following piece of legal reasoning to justify my conclusion that the court would have to look deeper into the intentions of Alan, Brian, Claire and David, and not simply rely on the 1990 conveyance, before we could say whether they took as joint tenants or tenants in common.

Identification of problem	Patricia will only be able to take under the will if she can establish that Brian was a tenant in common. Joint tenancies operate by right of survivorship. As to the effect of the wording in the conveyance, it was held in *Goodman v Gallant* that a declaration in the conveyance or will is conclusive of the matter, so that a stipulation that co-owners hold "as joint tenants in law and equity" as in that case, will mean that the parties are joint tenants.
Identification of a precedent case which is quite near in facts to the problem	Our case is materially different because of the hopeless ambiguity of the 1990 conveyance: the wording "jointly" leads one in the direction of the joint tenancy and the words "in common" lead in the opposite direction. Consequently there is no unambiguous express declaration to which a court could give effect. The court
Goodman v Gallant distinguished – materially different	would therefore have regard to the parties' business relationship and their unequal contributions and apply the equitable presumptions of a tenancy in common.

Judges apply and distinguish precedent cases all the time. This is the system on which English Law is based. Judges don't always say that this is what they are doing expressly, e.g. many a judge may remark of this situation that *Goodman v Gallant* is "unhelpful in the present case", and then state why in similar terms.

Use of the facts of past cases

Have you noticed that the only time we refer to "case facts" is when we use them to better help us articulate the *reason* for the decision in that case or to apply or distinguish it? Students will often simply recite case facts without quite knowing why they are doing it. They will often ask *how much should we include of the facts of cases?* Once you properly grasp the process of legal reasoning you will use only those facts that you need to help you articulate the rules and, for the next stage, to apply and distinguish the selected precedent cases.

Severance[89]

A. INTRODUCTION

What is severance? Even if we have identified that a beneficial joint tenancy existed at the time at which the co-ownership was created, it can be broken up and turned into a tenancy in common by the subsequent actions of one or all of the co-owners. So when we are looking at how the property of the co-owners devolves on their death, you also have to consider whether the situation has changed between the initial setting up of the co-ownership and the death of the relevant co-owner.

The law identifies several grounds on which a beneficial joint tenancy may be held to have been severed, e.g. one co-owner may sever his interest by "notice in writing". A joint tenancy may also be severed by "mutual agreement" of all the co-owners, and by a "course of conduct" that involves all the co-owners. *How do we know whether a joint tenancy has been severed on these grounds?* Although there are identified criteria that must be fulfilled the courts will essentially be looking for an act or intention inconsistent with the very nature of the joint tenancy: *unity of interest*.[90]

> **The law of severance is basically about showing an act or intention inconsistent with this.**

> **Unity of Interest: The BUILDING BLOCK of the Joint Tenancy**
> Unity of interest describes the idea of unity of *ownership*. All of the co-owners together own the whole of the interest in the property together; separately they are taken to own nothing. SURVIVORSHIP: This is the by-product of unity of interest. The nature of severance is that the act or intentions of the co-owner(s) establish that they want separate interests to leave by will—they no longer intend for survivorship to operate.

There are two points to note initially. Firstly, a joint tenant cannot sever by his will. The reason for this is that a will only takes effect on death, and by the time the joint tenant has died, he has died not owning anything separate.[91] Thus, he has nothing to leave by will. Therefore severance must take place before the death of the relevant co-owner. Secondly, the 1925 legislation provides that the legal estate, where held by more than one person, must be held on a joint tenancy and can never be severed.[92]

---

89   See further: Tee, "Co-Ownership" in *Land Law: Issues Debates Policy*; also Tee [1995] Conv. 105; Thompson [1987] Conv. 275; [1987] Conv. 29.

90   See R.Smith, *Plural Ownership*, Ch.4, where the author shows that actions and intentions must be inconsistent with the idea of unity of interest. See section 2 in this chapter above for an explanation of unity of interest.

91   *Carr v Isard* [2006] EWHC 2095 (Ch), para.10.

92   Law of Property Act 1925 ss.1(6); 36(2).

(1) The consequences of severance

How the land is held after severance depends on the method by which the joint tenancy has been severed. Let us say that A, B and C hold as joint tenants. If A *alone* severs her interest, she now has an identified share that she can leave by will or intestacy. But no more of the interest will accrue to her by survivorship on the deaths of B or C. However, B and C remain as joint tenants between each other: they "each own the whole" of what is left. Survivorship operates between B and C.

A's unilateral severance

This is the position before any relevant death. A has severed her beneficial interest so as to make her a tenant in common in relation to the others. B and C remain joint tenants in relation to each other

LEGAL ESTATE (always a Joint Tenancy)   A B C

EQUITABLE INTEREST   A │ B C

If there are only two joint tenants to begin with (e.g. A and B) and one unilaterally severs their interest both will henceforth be tenants in common with separate interests

---

If B dies, A and C will hold the legal estate as joint tenants for themselves in the following shares: A (one third of the beneficial interest) and C (two thirds of the beneficial interest). B's share has accrued to C by survivorship in which A no longer has any part. The legal estate is always held as a joint tenancy so whenever a joint tenant dies he or she drops out of the picture and the others hold the estate together by virtue of survivorship.

If A, B and C sever together they all become tenants in common in relation to each other. All have separate beneficial shares they can leave by will. Survivorship does not operate. Once the joint tenancy is severed the new tenants in common take in equal shares irrespective of what contribution was made originally.[93]

Where joint tenants sever together

LEGAL ESTATE (always a Joint Tenancy)   A   B   C

EQUITABLE ESTATE   A │ B │ C

---

93   *Goodman v Gallant* [1986] Fam. 106.

(2) How can we say whether the law of severance is good or bad law?[94]

Before we can say whether any rules of law are good or bad fair or unfair we need to see them in the context in which they operate. When the courts apply the rules that determine whether the joint tenants have severed the beneficial joint tenancy or not, they are making important decisions as to who should get the co-owned property after the death of a co-owner. When one co-owner dies, if the court finds that the joint tenancy has been severed, the deceased co-owner's share passes by their will or under the rules of intestacy. This might be in accordance with the co-owners' expectations. It might not. If the court finds that the joint tenancy has not been severed then the remaining co-owner(s) will get the deceased co-owner's share by survivorship. Again this may or may not reflect the wishes of either the deceased or the surviving co-owners.

> **Example:** *Gore and Snell v Carpenter* (1990) 60 P. & C.R. 456
> A married couple, Mr and Mrs Carpenter, co-owned property on a beneficial joint tenancy. They were divorcing and negotiating for a separation of their assets. The husband had formed a new relationship and clearly wanted his share in the property he co-owned with his wife to go to his new partner Mrs Snell (he made a will to this effect). The husband died and Mrs Snell claimed a half share of the co-owned property. The court held that at the time of his death, the joint tenancy had not been severed and Mr Carpenter's estranged wife became the absolute owner of the co-owned property by right of survivorship.

We use our Building Blocks to determine whether the law of severance is good or bad law. If the law can broadly be said to support the policies in the Building Blocks then we can legitimately conclude that it is good law.

> **BUILDING BLOCK NO 7:** The rules of Land Law should give effect to the parties'
> intentions or reasonable expectations
> So therefore we might say that the law of severance is good if, taking all the rules into account and the many different human situations to which they apply, they give broad effect to what most co-owners would expect to happen to their share in a particular situation. *Is Gore and Snell v Carpenter good and fair law—what are your initial impressions?*

And it is not just by looking at people's general expectations and wishes regarding co-owned property that we can say whether the law is good or bad. A finding of a joint tenancy (i.e. if the court finds that severance has *not* occurred) means that the surviving co-owner will, on the death of the other, become absolutely entitled to the property by right of survivorship. If the

---

94   On the ideas in this section see M.P.Thompson [1987] Conv. 29 and 275.

court finds that there *has* been a severance, the deceased co-owner will have died as a tenant in common. Thus, the remaining co-owner will not be absolutely entitled to the property. The survivor will then have to contend with someone else who claims an interest in what may well be their family home. *Which consequence better protects the remaining co-owner's residential security—the finding of no severance or the finding of a severance?* Might it be fair if the courts apply the rules restrictively?

> **BUILDING BLOCK NO 1: Residential Security**
> Residential security is now a main purpose behind the ownership of land in this country. We can say that the rules of co-ownership are good or bad depending on the extent to which they protect someone's residential security.

The law has the onerous task of deciding who owns people's homes and business premises. For such an important task we can only say the law is good and fair if it provides certainty and predictability.

> **BUILDING BLOCK NO 6: The Need for Certainty and Predictability in Land Law Rules**
> If the rules are clear as to how they will apply in future cases, i.e. if they allow people to predict the outcome of their actions and of particular situations then those rules are good law.

The law of co-ownership must allow people to know where they stand in respect of co-owned property, i.e. are they going to inherit all by survivorship or (if severance has occurred) may someone else be claiming an interest in the house on the death of a fellow co-owner? People must be able to predict what is going to happen to the property on the death of their co-owner(s) and order their affairs accordingly. If not you are fully justified in saying that the law is not good. Any law that allows a co-owner to sever his or her share *secretly* would be a problem here. *Can you think of why?*

B. SEVERANCE OF A JOINT TENANCY BY NOTICE IN WRITING[95]

Section 36(2) of the Law of Property Act 1925 provides that

"... where a legal estate (not being settled land) is vested in joint tenants beneficially, and any tenant desires to sever the joint tenancy in equity, he shall give to the other joint tenants

---

95   L.Tee, "Co-ownership and trusts" in *Land Law Issues, Debates, Policy*, p.132; R.Smith, *Plural Ownership*; L.Tee [1995] Conv. 105; M.Thompson [1987] Conv. 29 and 275; B.Crown (2001) 117 L.Q.R. 477.

a notice in writing of such desire or do such other acts or things as would, in the case of personal estate, have been effectual to sever the tenancy in equity".

Where one joint tenant gives notice to the other joint tenant(s) in writing of his desire to sever the beneficial joint tenancy, then this will be effective to sever. The effect of severance under this head is that the party serving the notice severs his own interest and becomes a tenant in common with his own separate and distinct interest that he can then leave by will.[96] However, he loses his right of survivorship. The others, if more than one, remain as joint tenants and retain survivorship as between themselves (see the previous section).

(1) How might we argue whether section 36(2) is good law?

The intention of Parliament behind s.36(2) was probably to introduce an easy method of severance. The section is clear that notice must be given to all the other joint tenants. Thus severance would not occur behind the back of other co-owner(s). Otherwise, there would be a nasty shock to the other co-owner(s) on the death of the person severing, when the other co-owners probably expect survivorship to operate. We might say therefore that this is good law on the basis of BUILDING BLOCK NO 6.

> **BUILDING BLOCK NO 6: The Need for Certainty and Predictability in Land Law Rules**
> The law of co-ownership must allow people to know where they stand in respect of co-owned property, i.e. are they going to inherit all by survivorship or (if severance has occurred) may someone else be claiming an interest in the house on the death of a co-owner? Any law that allows a co-owner to sever his or her share secretly would be a problem here.

Indeed, if a couple are married or living together and beneficial joint tenants of the family home, if one severs secretly it potentially undermines the residential security of the other and gives that other no opportunity to order their affairs.[97] We can thus say that s.36(2) fulfills a valuable function. The extent to which s.36(2) achieves these aims depends on how readily the courts will say that a document amounts to "a notice in writing" to sever. Will the parties really understand that this is the legal effect of the document?[98]

(2) How and to whom must the notice be "given"?

As we have seen where one joint tenant gives notice to the other joint tenant(s) in writing of his desire to sever the beneficial joint tenancy, then this will be effective to sever his interest. *To whom must the notice be given?* It is clear from the language of s.36(2) that if there is more

---

96   The position on the legal estate remains unchanged because the Law of Property Act s.36(2) provides that the legal estate can never be severed and must always be held as a joint tenancy.

97   By contrast Smith sees little harm in allowing the other co-owner to be surprised by the severance: "Although the idea of taking the other party by surprise when they expect survivorship to operate is unappealing, what harm does it do?", Smith, above p.51.

98   Smith, *Plural Ownership*, p.53.

than one other co-owner then the severing co-owner must give notice in writing to all of them and not just one.

A notice in writing is sufficiently served if it is left at the last-known place of abode or business of the other co-owner(s).[99] The letter must arrive at the premises on the address, e.g. by being posted through the letterbox.[100] It is not necessary for the addressee to receive it.[101] A notice is also sufficiently served if it is sent by registered letter or recorded delivery addressed by name and sent to the last known address of the co-owner. "[S]ervice shall be deemed to be made at the time at which the registered letter would in the ordinary course be delivered."[102] This is intended to be an additional provision. It is not a requirement for service to take place by recorded delivery.[103] However, if a co-owner chooses to send the notice by recorded delivery, it is sufficient that the letter is signed for and not returned undelivered. Again, it does not need to have been received by the addressee. In *Re 88 Berkeley Road NW9*[104] it was the sending co-owner herself who signed for the letter. The addressee did not receive it. This was sufficient to sever the joint tenancy.

In *Kinch v Bullard*[105] a husband and wife were divorcing. The wife was terminally ill and wanted to sever the beneficial joint tenancy of their matrimonial home, so that her half of the property would not pass by survivorship to her estranged husband on her death. She sent a notice of severance to the husband at the matrimonial home. However, she intercepted the letter and destroyed it because she changed her mind about the severance. The husband had in the meantime suffered a serious heart attack and in all probability would predecease the wife. She changed her mind

"presumably because she had come to the conclusion that, in view of his serious heart attack [the husband] was likely to predecease her, and that it would therefore be she, rather than he, who would benefit if the tenancy was not severed."[106]

It was held that severance had taken place and that the husband's estate was entitled to half the proceeds of sale. The essential principle here is that the notice does not need to be received by the other co-owner(s).

LECTURER: The wife's argument had been that because she had changed her mind at the time when the notice was delivered, she did not fulfil the criteria of s.36(2):

---

99   Law of Property Act 1925 s.196(3).
100   *Holwell Securities Ltd v Hughes* [1974] 1 W.L.R. 155; *Kinch v Bullard* [1999] 1 W.L.R. 423, p.429 per Neuberger J.
101   *Kinch v Bullard* [1999] 1 W.L.R. 423.
102   s.196(4), unless the letter is returned undelivered: *Kinch v Bullard* [1999] 1 W.L.R. 423, p.427 per Neuberger J.
103   *Kinch v Bullard* [1999] 1 W.L.R. 423, p.427 per Neuberger J.
104   [1971] Ch. 648; also *Wandsworth London Borough Council v Attwell* (1995) 94 L.G.R. 419; *Newborough (Lord) v Jones* [1975] Ch. 90; *Van Haarlam v Kasner* (1992) 64 P. & C.R. 214—addressee in prison at the time of service.
105   [1999] 1 W.L.R. 423.
106   *Kinch v Bullard* [1999] 1 W.L.R. 423, per Neuberger J.

NEUBERGER J. "[The wife argued that] the fact that [she] changed her mind and no longer 'desired to sever the joint tenancy' by the time that the notice might otherwise have been said to have been 'given' (i.e. by the time that the notice arrived at the property) meant that the notice was ineffective to effect such severance. This argument is based on the language of section 36(2). Assuming that the notice was validly 'given' pursuant to section 196(3), the giving of the notice only occurred when it was actually delivered to the property, and at that time [the wife] no longer 'desired to sever the joint tenancy.'"

LECTURER: Neuberger J. did not like this argument, and in his reasoning against it he said that it would make the law too uncertain. So we can follow his judgment with BUILDING BLOCK NO 6: The Need for Certainty and Predictability in Land Law Rules.

BUILDING BLOCK NO 6: The Need for Certainty and Predictability in Land Law Rules
The law of co-ownership must allow people to know where they stand in respect of co-owned property.

NEUBERGER J. "In my judgment. . . [the wife's] argument is not correct. The function of the relevant part of section 36(2) is to instruct any joint tenant who desires to sever the joint tenancy how to do it: he is to give the appropriate notice (or do such other things as are prescribed by the section). Clear words would be required, in my judgment, before a provision such as section 36(2) could be construed as requiring the court to inquire into the state of mind of the sender of the notice. Once the sender has served the requisite notice, the deed is done and cannot be undone . . ."

"I reach this conclusion based on the proper construction of section 36(2). However, it appears to me that it is also correct as a matter of policy. If it were possible for a notice of severance or any other notice to be ineffective because, between the sender putting it in the post and the addressee receiving it, the sender changed his mind, it would be inconvenient and potentially unfair. The addressee would not be able to rely confidently upon a notice after it had been received, because he might subsequently be faced with the argument that the sender had changed his mind after sending it and before its receipt. Further, as I have already mentioned, it is scarcely realistic to think that the legislature intended that the court could be required to inquire into the state of mind of the sender of the notice in order to decide whether the notice was valid . . . [. . .] if the court starts implying exceptions into the clear and simple statutory procedure, confusion and uncertainty could result."

LECTURER: Can you see how Neuberger J. reasoned on the basis that the law should be predictable and clear?

STUDENT: He thought that the wife's argument would make it impossible for the courts, lawyers, and the other co-owners to predict when severance had taken place.

LECTURER: Neuberger J. later in his judgment says that certainty is particularly important with a statutory provision "intended to have practical consequences". What did he mean?

STUDENT: That the issue of severance determines whether the surviving co-owner will own the whole of the property or whether the deceased co-owner's estate will be able to claim half by way of will or intestacy.

LECTURER: This is a big consequence likely to have dramatic personal effect. Can you say why?

STUDENT: If severance has taken place and someone else can claim a share in the property then that person may try to obtain a sale of the house. This means that the surviving co-owner's residential security is threatened.

LECTURER: This would be far less of a problem were that co-owner to have known in advance and been able to order their affairs accordingly—which is what s.36(2) is all about.

Neuberger J. then reveals a potential exception to the rule that a notice is deemed to be served when it is delivered. He said that a statute (here s.36(2)) could not be relied upon to perpetrate a fraud. Thus, if a person sends a notice of severance, *and that same person* intercepts it, and claims that severance has taken effect by virtue of s.36(2) then they will be unable to rely on s.36 and the notice will be of no effect. The joint tenancy and right of survivorship will remain intact. This exception was discussed obiter and it may be unclear as to how it would apply in the future.

(3) What does a "notice in writing" actually have to say?

The notice does not have to be worded in any particular technical form and "severance" does not have to be referred to directly. There is no prescribed form of document: any form of writing may suffice. Indeed statements made in the context of court proceedings or communications between the parties have been held to amount to a notice in writing for the purposes of s.36(2).[107] Section 36(2) does not require a signature.[108] So what are we looking for? When we see some document, in whatever form, be it a letter, email, court documents etc, given by one joint tenant to all the others, what must be *in* that document so that we recognise it as evidencing "a desire to sever the joint tenancy" for the purposes of s.36(2)?

The notice must show an *immediate intention* to sever the joint tenancy. We now need to determine what this means. In *Wallbank v Price*[109] a written declaration by one of two beneficial joint tenants that her daughters would hereafter have her "half share" of a co-owned house, operated as a "notice in writing" for the purposes of s.36(2).

> "The statement that [the defendant] had a 'half share' to be dealt with is, in my judgment, inconsistent with the continuing existence of a joint tenancy in equity. The creation of a 'half share' is the inevitable consequence of the severance of a joint tenancy in equity where there are two joint tenants."[110]

---

107   *Burgess v Rawnsley* [1975] Ch. 429.
108   *Re Draper's Conveyance* [1969] 1 Ch. 486, per Plowman J.
109   [2007] EWHC 3001 (Ch).
110   Per Lewison J., para.49.

In *Re Draper's Conveyance*[111] a husband and wife were joint tenants of their matrimonial home. The wife started divorce proceedings. She issued a supporting statement ("affidavit") in the court proceedings in which she requested a sale of the house and an equal division of the proceeds of sale. Plowman J. held that this statement was sufficient as a notice in writing to sever the joint tenancy.

LECTURER But why? Remember that it is the reasoning in the case that will help you construct your arguments.

THE REASONING: PLOWMAN J.: "It seems to me that that summons, coupled with the affidavit in support of it, clearly evinced an intention on the part of the wife that she wished the property to be sold and the proceeds distributed a half to her and a half to the husband . . . it seems to me that that is wholly inconsistent with the notion that a beneficial joint tenancy in that property is to continue."

The wife's request in the divorce petition was direct and immediate. She wanted "half and half". As you see from the quotation from the judgment, Plowman J. concluded that the intention to have the property immediately divided was inconsistent with the nature of a joint tenancy. This is why the statement was sufficient to sever. The wife indicated directly in her divorce petition that she wanted a division of her and her husband's interests in the house. She wanted her interest to be separated from her former husband's. This is inconsistent with the nature of the joint tenancy—*unity of interest*—the idea that "together they own the whole house".

What the judge was looking for was an intention inconsistent with the essence of a joint tenancy.

Unity of Interest: The BUILDING BLOCK of the Joint Tenancy
Each owns the whole interest together with the others. None of the co-owners has separate and identifiable shares. This is the dominant feature of the joint tenancy. It describes the idea of unity of *ownership*. Each owns the same interest in the property together; separately they own nothing.

Now we have to consider why our next case is different from *Re Draper's Conveyance*. In *Harris v Goddard*[112] a husband and wife were beneficial joint tenants of their matrimonial home. The wife petitioned for divorce. The Matrimonial Causes Act 1973 gives a judge discretion to re-distribute property amongst the couple or to order one spouse to pay financial support to the other. In the petition the wife requested "a property transfer order or whatever order the court saw fit". Although a divorce petition could amount to a notice in writing, this one did not operate to sever the wife's beneficial joint tenancy of the matrimonial home.

---

111 [1969] 1 Ch. 486; Baker (1968) 84 L.Q.R. 462.
112 [1983] 3 All E.R. 242, CA.

THE REASONING: LAWTON L.J. "When a notice in writing of a desire to sever is served pursuant to s.36(2) it takes effect forthwith. It follows that a desire to sever must evince an intention to bring about the wanted result immediately. A notice in writing which expresses a desire to bring about the wanted result at some time in the future is not, in my judgment, a notice in writing within s.36(2). Further, the notice must be one which shows an intent to bring about the consequences set out in s.36(2), namely that the [interests in the house should be divided up] . . . [113] Paragraph 3 of the [wife's] petition does no more than invite the court to consider at some future time whether to exercise its jurisdiction under s.24 of the 1973 Act or, if it does, to do so in one or more . . . different ways".

LECTURER: So taking these two cases together, we need to determine what the rules are.

STUDENT: The notice, whatever documentary form it takes, must express an intention to sever the joint tenancy immediately. This was true in *Re Draper's* but not in *Harris v Goddard*, in which the wife's petition was vague and speculative.

LECTURER: And secondly, what has the sender of the notice got to *intend*: How was *Re Draper's* different from *Harris v Goddard* on this point?

STUDENT: In *Re Draper's* the wife wanted the interests in the house divided up. This was clear. In *Harris v Goddard*, the wife was insufficiently specific as to what she wanted the court to

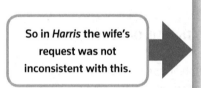

So in *Harris* the wife's request was not inconsistent with this.

Unity of Interest: The BUILDING BLOCK of the Joint Tenancy:

Each owns the whole interest together with the others. None of the co-owners has separate and identifiable shares. This is the dominant feature of the joint tenancy. It describes the idea of unity of *ownership*. Each owns the same interest in the property together; separately they own nothing.

do with the property—so the court was unable to infer that she wanted separate interests in the property she co-owned with her husband: the requirement for severance.

(4) The issue of whether proceedings need to be irrevocable

In *Nielson-Jones v Fedden*[114] Walton J. had said that the notice must be irrevocable. Because court proceedings, including divorce, are revocable (i.e. they can be stopped), he considered that *Re Draper's Conveyance*[115] was wrongly decided. The Court of Appeal in *Burgess v Rawnsley*[116] and in *Harris v Goddard* declined to accept this view and considered that the wife's divorce petition could amount to an effective "notice in writing".

113   See also *Gore and Snell v Carpenter* (1990) 60 P. & C.R. 456, p.462.
114   [1975] Ch 222.
115   [1969] 1 Ch 486.
116   [1975] Ch 429, p.447, per Sir John Pennycuick.

As far as concerns other documents, in *Pudner v Pudner*, Chadwick L.J. considered that the draft of a will might be sufficient.[117] Note however that we are not saying that a joint tenancy can be severed by the operation of a will on the death of the other joint tenant, but that a will, as a document, might contain sufficient evidence of an intention to sever to satisfy section 36(2) so that if it were shown to the other joint tenant(s) it might operate as a notice in writing.

(5) Critical Thinking

> Of *Re Draper's Conveyance* and *Harris v Goddard*, Smith observes: "Whilst the absence of technicalities is to be applauded . . . [o]ne suspects that the lawyers drafting the court applications in these cases paid no attention at all to severance and that the differing results were entirely accidental" (*Plural Ownership*, p.53). *Is this a good thing?* Hold Smith's observation against our Building Blocks and see whether it supports or undermines any of their policies and principles.

BUILDING BLOCK NO 6: The Need for Certainty and Predictability in Land Law Rules:
The law of co-ownership must allow people to know where they stand in respect of co-owned property, i.e. are they going to inherit all by survivorship or (if severance has occurred) may someone else be claiming an interest in the house on the death of a co-owner? The law must allow solicitors to be able to advise their clients about the consequences of their actions.

BUILDING BLOCK NO 7: The rules of Land Law should give effect to the parties' intentions or reasonable expectations:
Land Law is "facilitative" (P.Birks) We can say that if the rules of co-ownership fail significantly to reflect most peoples' reasonable expectations with regard to what should happen to the property in a particular situation, then those rules are bad law.

LECTURER: In his observation what is Smith actually saying?
STUDENT: That severance can be the accidental consequence of the drafting of certain documents such as the divorce petitions in these cases. The purpose of the documents was not to sever the couple's joint tenancy. The documents had another purpose.
LECTURER: So does severance happen contrary to the intentions of the severing co-owner?
STUDENT: Not really. Severance in the context of divorce *is* what most people would expect. In *Re Draper's Conveyance* the couple were divorcing and negotiating for a separation of their

---

117   [2006] EWCA Civ 250 CA.

assets. This seems the most natural situation from which to derive a severance of their joint tenancy. It would mean they would have a separate interest in the home and were either to die before negotiations were complete, survivorship has the potential to operate unfairly. People's expectations in this type of situation may well be that they have their own separate share in the house.[118]

LECTURER: So the law to an extent supports BUILDING BLOCK NO 7. Although you have argued that accidental severance works no hardship, at least in divorce cases, severance *is* a bit of a lottery depending on how the courts construe the divorce documents. This surely reflects no credit on the legal system?

STUDENT: If one co-owner dies before they have fully separated their property, then it may not be clear to even the lawyers whether the documents that the parties have exchanged will be sufficient to sever the joint tenancy. This unpredictability is a serious criticism given that severance determines that survivorship no longer operates and the remaining co-owner may face the possibility that someone else may be claiming a share in the house.

(6) Problem solving—fitting it all together

> In 1990, Alan, Brian, Claire and David purchased a large Victorian terraced house from which they intended to run a doctor's practice. They contributed in unequal proportions to the purchase price and the house was conveyed "to all of them as joint tenants in law and in equity".
>
>   Brian becomes disillusioned with being a doctor and wants to go off on a world cruise. He writes to Claire and says that he would like at sometime in the future for the others to buy his share of the house. He has no further use for it. He asks Claire to show the letter to all the others. Brian dies and his will leaves all his property to his aunt Patricia. Advise all parties.

LECTURER: So what do you think of this one?

STUDENT: I think the letter that Brian writes to Claire could amount to a notice in writing but the problem is that he has not shown it to all the others.

LECTURER: Hang on—just slow down a minute. You have started in the middle. The judges whose judgments you have read all proceed on the same basis in order to solve the dispute before them. They present a legal account of the problem. Firstly then, there is only one possible way in which Patricia could have a claim to a share in the co-owned property and that is if Brian died a tenant in common. In essence *that* is the legal problem.

STUDENT: Oh yes, a joint tenancy works by right of survivorship. They all own the whole together so that if one dies there is only one less owing the whole. Patricia would not be able to claim any interest in the house.

---

118   M.P.Thompson [1987] Conv. 29.

LECTURER: Remember to cite legal authority for the principles you are using to solve the problem.

STUDENT: OK so before considering any question of severance we must consider how the co-owners elected to hold the property at the time of the creation of the co-ownership: the conveyance. There is an unequivocal express declaration that the parties hold as joint tenants and this is conclusive of the matter: *Goodman v Gallant*.

LECTURER: Good. So we are saying that unless Brian has subsequently severed his beneficial interest, the other co-owners take by right of survivorship. Patricia would get nothing. So now we can consider the "notice in writing" ground.

STUDENT: Section 36(2) of the Law of Property Act 1925 provides that an equitable joint tenant can sever their interest, thereby creating a tenancy in common, by giving notice in writing. However, the statute says that the notice must be sent to "all" the joint tenants, which means Alan, Claire and David. There is a doubt here as to whether this requirement is satisfied because he only writes to Claire, asking her to show the letter to the others. On a literal interpretation of s.36 this would not suffice. Also by reference to the service methods identified in the Act, these are all specific as to the fact that the letter should be addressed to the joint tenants concerned. The Act also implies strongly that Brian would have to *himself* give to the others the notice.

LECTURER: Even on a "purposive" interpretation of the statute (where we take into account the policy behind the Act), the idea of the statutory method of severance was to provide a *transparent* method of severance, so that the other joint tenants would be aware of the severance. Thus, if Claire forgot to show the letter to the others, they would not know about the severance.

LECTURER: Now move on to the question of whether Brian's letter displays the type of content that will bring about a severance. *Re Draper's Conveyance* held that the notice must display an intention to bring about the consequences of severance *immediately*.

<table>
<tr><td>

The intention displayed in Brian's letter must be inconsistent with the *essence* of a joint tenancy

</td><td>

Unity of Interest: The BUILDING BLOCK of the Joint Tenancy
Each owns the whole interest together with the others. None of the co-owners has separate and identifiable shares.

</td></tr>
</table>

STUDENT selects a relevant precedent case with similar facts and articulates the judge's reason for the decision

STUDENT: Brian's letter does demonstrate some intention that he wants a separate interest in the house. He shows that he wishes his share to be separated off. Just like the wife in *Re Draper's Conveyance*, who stated in her divorce petition that she wanted a half share of the matrimonial home. This was held sufficient to sever. However, the relevant document in that case

> **And "distinguishes" it because the problem facts are substantially different**

> **And comes to the opposite conclusion**

showed that the wife wanted separate interests immediately. The major problem here is that because Brian describes his desire in future speculative terms, i.e. "he would like at sometime in the future for the others to buy his share of the house", this does not demonstrate a desire to bring about separate interests *immediately*. Thus, on the authority of *Re Draper's Conveyance* this is insufficient to satisfy the requirements of s.36(2) for a severance by notice in writing.

LECTURER: So our case looks more like *Harris v Goddard*. What was that one about?

STUDENT: It was held that the wife did not show immediate intention to sever—her request was purely speculative.

LECTURER: Good, but don't forget to state the legal consequences for the co-owners and Patricia. After all this is what *solving* a legal problem is all about.

STUDENT: Because Brian's letter was insufficient to sever he died as a joint tenant. Thus, because of the right of survivorship Patricia has no interest in the house.

C. SEVERANCE BY AN ACT OF A CO-OWNER OPERATING ON THEIR OWN SHARE

In addition to the statutory ground under s.36(2) the case of *Williams v Hensman*[119] articulated that a beneficial joint tenancy can be severed in three ways: firstly, by "an act of any one of the persons interested operating upon his own share"; secondly, by mutual agreement and thirdly, by a course of dealing. We will consider each of these in turn.

The first of these common law methods of severing a beneficial joint tenancy is where one co-owner deals with his own share in a recognised way, e.g. if a co-owner sells his share to another: "alienates" it. He is then acting or "operating" on his own share.[120] Traditionally it is said that this method severs a joint tenancy because it destroys one of the four unities:

> "The properties of a joint estate are derived from its unity, which is fourfold; the unity of interest, the unity of title, the unity of time, and the unity of possession . . . an estate in joint tenancy may be severed and destroyed . . . by destroying any of its constituent unities."[121]

For example, A, B and C are co-owners of Broadacres. A sells his share to X. Note that this operates only as a sale of A's equitable (or beneficial) interest. X can only take as a tenant in common. The traditional explanation is that because X did not derive title from the same source as B and C there

---

119 (1861) 1 John & H. 546, per Page-Wood V.C., p.546.
120 *Nielson-Jones v Fedden* [1975] Ch. 222.
121 *Blackstone's Commentaries*, 8th edn (1778), Vol II, pp.180, p.185.

is no unity of title and there cannot therefore be a joint tenancy. However, this is a unilateral method of severance and B and C remain as beneficial joint tenants as between themselves. B and C enjoy the right of survivorship, X does not—but X does have a separate interest that he can leave by will. In the event that there are only two joint tenants to begin with (e.g. A and B) and A unilaterally severs by selling her interest, both are henceforth tenants in common.

In one sense however, holding that a sale of a joint tenant's interest affects a severance is illogical. Joint tenants "own the whole together". They do not own anything separate that they can sell individually. However, it is said that the sale of the co-owner's share brings about the severance and the sale simultaneously.[122] *Megarry and Wade* observes that "At common law, the alienation of property was favoured against the right of survivorship".[123]

(1) What "act" will suffice to sever?

The ground extends to a contract for the sale of a co-owner's interest.[124] Where a co-owner mortgages his beneficial share, this will also sever his interest. In *First National Securities Ltd v Hegerty*[125] there were two joint tenants of the legal estate. They held for each other as beneficial joint tenants. One forged his co-owner's signature on a mortgage of the estate. The mortgage could not take effect against the legal estate, because one of the legal owners had not properly given her consent. However, it was held that he had mortgaged his share of the equitable interest. This severed the beneficial joint tenancy. Henceforth he was a tenant in common of his beneficial share.[126]

There is authority for the proposition that where a co-owner unilaterally grants a lease of his share, this will operate to sever his interest. It may create a "partial severance" whereby the joint tenancy is restored when the lease comes to an end.[127] A sale of a share by one co-owner to one of the other co-owners also brings about a severance of that share. So if A,B and C are joint tenants and A acquires C's interest, A is a joint tenant with B in relation to A's original share and a tenant in common of the share acquired from C in relation to B, with whom he has no unity of title. The position may be different where there are only two co-owners (A and B) where the release of A's beneficial share to B would end the equitable co-ownership, although both would remain on the legal title unless there was a transfer into the sole name of B.[128]

If a joint tenant is declared bankrupt by the court his property automatically vests in the trustee in bankruptcy. If he is a beneficial joint tenant in relation to any property the act of bankruptcy severs his interest.[129] This is "an involuntary form of alienation".[130]

---

122   Crown (2001) 117 L.Q.R. 477.
123   C.Harpum, *Megarry and Wade, Law of Real Property*, 6th edn (London: Sweet & Maxwell, 1999), p.492.
124   *Burgess v Rawnsley* [1975] Ch. 429, p.446, per Sir John Pennycuick; *Wilson v Bell* (1843) 5 Ir. Eq. R. 501, p.507.
125   [1985] Q.B. 850.
126   Also *Ahmed v Kendrick* (1988) 56 P. & C.R. 120; *Bank of Ireland Home Mortgages Ltd v Bell* [2001] 2 All E.R. 920; [2001] 2 F.L.R. 809; *Mortgage Corporation v Shaire* [2000] 1 F.L.R. 973.
127   Fox [2000] Conv. 208; Crown (2001) 117 L.Q.R. 477; Nield [2001] Conv. 462.
128   In *Gore & Snell v Carpenter* Blackett-Ord J. indicated obiter that releasing a share to another co-owner would not count as an "act of a co-owner operating on his own share" (1990) 60 P. & C.R. 456, p.461.
129   *Re Gorman* [1990] 1 W.L.R. 616.
130   *Megarry and Wade Law of Real Property*, 7th edn (2008), para.13–046.

In *Hawkesley v May*[131] Havers J. held that an oral declaration by one joint tenant to the other(s) that he wishes for a separate interest was sufficient to sever a joint tenancy. Although the property was personalty in that case, in *Re Draper's Conveyance*[132] Plowman J. indicated that a unilateral declaration of intention to sever would be sufficient in cases of co-ownership of land. Lord Denning M.R. in *Burgess v Rawnsley*[133] thought similarly. The point was not supported by Sir John Pennycuick in that case,[134] and is now thought to be wrong.[135] In *Nielson-Jones v Fedden*[136] Walton J. said that an oral unilateral declaration of intent is insufficient and criticised *Re Draper's Conveyance*.[137] It seems correct to suggest that the only unilateral action of a co-owner that will sever a joint tenancy is a "notice in writing" for the purposes of s.36(2) or one of the acts described above.[138]

D. SEVERANCE BY MUTUAL AGREEMENT OF THE CO-OWNERS

A beneficial joint tenancy can be severed where there is a mutual agreement between co-owners to sever their interests. This is one of the two methods that allows severance on the basis that equity leans against joint tenancies. An agreement to sever a beneficial joint tenancy can be derived from statements that are entirely oral.[139] The agreement does not need to be in writing or specifically enforceable.[140] So here is something of an exception to the usual high degree of formality for dealing with interests in land. Agreement of all the joint tenants is necessary. Severance cannot be affected behind the backs of any of the co-owners.[141] The agreement does not need to be express and can be spelt out of a variety of factual circumstances.[142] The effect of severance by mutual agreement is that *all* the co-owners will afterwards hold as beneficial tenants in common.

(1) Precedent cases on mutual agreement

In *Burgess v Rawnsley*[143] Mrs Rawnsley and Mr Honick met at a scripture rally and began a friendship. They purchased a house as joint tenants in law and in equity. Mr Honick had intended that Mrs Rawnsley would become his wife and the house would be their matrimonial home. Mrs Rawnsley did not share this perception and had intended to occupy the first floor with

---

131   [1956] 1 Q.B. 304.
132   [1969] 1 Ch. 486.
133   [1975] Ch. 429.
134   "An uncommunicated declaration by one party to the other, or indeed a mere verbal notice by one party to the other clearly cannot operate as a severance": [1975] Ch. 429, p.448, per Sir John Pennycuick; also *Gore & Snell v Carpenter* (1990) 60 P. & C.R. 456, per Blackett-Ord J., p.462.
135   *Megarry and Wade Law of Real Property*, para.13–041.
136   [1975] Ch 222, p.230.
137   Also *Partriche v Plowlet* (1740) 2 Atk. 54, per Lord Hardwicke L.C.
138   See L.Tee, "Co-ownership and trusts" in *Land Law Issues, Debates, Policy*, p.132, at p.141.
139   *Burgess v Rawnsley* [1975] Ch. 429, p.441 per Browne L.J.
140   *Burgess v Rawnsley*, above p.446, per Sir John Pennycuick.
141   *Williams v Hensman* (1861) 1 John & H. 546, per Page-Wood V.C., p.546.
142   *Burgess v Rawnsley* [1975] Ch. 429, p.444 per Browne L.J. *Barracks v Barracks* [2005] EWHC 3077, para.18.
143   [1975] Ch. 429.

Mr Honick occupying the ground floor. Once this misunderstanding about their relationship had come to light they orally agreed that Mrs Rawnsley would sell her interest to Mr Honick for £750. But then she asked for more money and negotiations broke down. Then Mr Honick died. The executors of his will claimed that severance had take place and consequently Mr Honick's half of the house fell to be distributed under the terms of his will. Mrs Rawnsley claimed to be entitled to the whole of the ownership of the house by survivorship. The Court of Appeal held that there was severance because Mr Honick and Mrs Rawnsley had reached an agreement for a sale of her share to him for £750. This was enough to establish a "mutual agreement" to sever their interests.

But *why* and *how*? Mr Honick and Mrs Rawnsley did not agree specifically to sever the joint tenancy. No mention was made of severance.[144] However, as Sir John Pennycuick observed this ground applies "whether the agreement between the two joint tenants is expressly to sever or is to deal with the property in a manner which involves severance."[145]

> What had Mr Honick and Mrs Rawnsley done that "involved severance"? The judges are looking for some agreement between the co-owners in relation to the co-owned property that discloses an intention that is inconsistent with their still wanting unity of interest.

Unity of Interest: The BUILDING BLOCK of the Joint Tenancy
Each owns the whole interest together with the others. None of the co-owners has separate and identifiable shares. Each owns the same interest in the property together; separately they own nothing.

SURVIVORSHIP: This is the by-product of unity of interest. Because the co-owners together own the whole of the interest and separately own nothing when one dies he does not die owning anything separate that he can leave by will. If the agreement establishes that the parties either mutually intend that survivorship should no longer operate or intend separate interests, then this should be sufficient to establish severance by mutual agreement: R.Smith, *Plural Ownership*, p.74

LECTURER: How was Mr Honick and Mrs Rawnsley's agreement inconsistent with their wanting to continue with unity of interest? Survivorship operates in a joint tenancy: Is there anything that the parties agreed to in relation to the property that was inconsistent with survivorship?[146]

---

144 In *Szabo v Boros* [2002] W.T.L.R. 1389 the Court of Appeal, British Columbia held that there was no express act required to establish "mutual agreement".
145 The courts look at what the co-owners subjectively agreed to do with the property and determine whether this is consistent with survivorship: Conway [2009] Conv. 67, commenting on the Australian decision *Saleeba v Wilke* [2007] QSC 29.
146 The mutual agreement to dispose of property must be unequivocally inconsistent with a joint tenancy continuing: *Carr v Isard* [2006] EWHC 2095 (Ch).

STUDENT: The reason is that they were negotiating for one to buy the other's share, i.e. showing that their intention was to own separate shares and not to "own the whole together".

LECTURER: And what if the facts were slightly different. Let's say that Mr Honick and Mrs Rawnsley got married and lived happily ever after. But because they were a couple who met later in their lives (this was true of the actual facts) Mr Honick had a desire to make sure that his daughter was provided for. So he and Mrs Rawnsley, who had similar intentions, sat down and agreed that Mr Honick would make a will leaving his share of the house to his daughter. This he did. They fall out—he dies and Mr Rawnsley claims to own the house by survivorship. Would this conduct be sufficient to establish severance by mutual agreement?

STUDENT: The parties have "mutually agreed" that survivorship should not operate. Although they do not even mention "severance" and probably do not even know about it, they have dealt "with the property in a manner which involves severance". Regarding the Unity of Interest BUILDING BLOCK their agreement "involves severance" because the couple are showing that they do not want survivorship to operate.

LECTURER: If joint tenants make mutual wills (i.e. wills that are executed as a result of an agreement for both to dispose of their property in a particular way), in a manner that is inconsistent with the operation of the right of survivorship, then this would operate to sever their beneficial joint tenancy.[147] Remember that we are not saying that it is *the will* that can sever, this it cannot do.[148]

Now we need to consider how this next case is different. Let's see how we would "distinguish" it from *Burgess v Rawnsley*. In *Nielson-Jones v Fedden*[149] a husband and wife were joint tenants of their matrimonial home. They were contemplating divorce and negotiating to separate their property. The husband was living in the matrimonial home and the wife elsewhere.

> *Nielson-Jones v Fedden*— **a mutual agreement?**
>
> **MATERIAL FACTS:** The wife suggested that the matrimonial home should be sold and that the proceeds of sale should be used to buy a smaller house where the husband should live and be able to see the children. Both signed a memorandum to this effect. A purchaser was found and the husband and wife each received £200 from the deposit paid.
>
> **THE LEGAL ARGUMENTS:** The husband died before completion of the sale and the parties never finished their negotiations. Did the parties' negotiations and other actions mean that the joint tenancy had been severed by mutual agreement? Was the wife entitled to the whole of the proceeds of sale by survivorship or did she hold them on trust for herself and her husband's estate in equal shares?
>
> **THE CONCLUSION:** It was held that none of this conduct disclosed a "mutual agreement" to sever the joint tenancy.

---

147 *Re Wilford's Estate* (1879) LR 11 Ch.D. 267; *Walker v Gaskill* [1914] P. 192.
148 *Carr v Isard* [2006] EWHC 2095 (Ch), para.10. A will does not sever of itself.
149 [1975] Ch. 222.

Why? What was so different about this case? To identify the steps in the reasoning read the extract from the judgment of Walton J. and keep asking the questions *what were the factors about this case that were so important to the judge that they led him to the conclusion he came to?* OR: *What would have to have been different for the judge to come to a different conclusion?*[150]

THE REASONING: WALTON J. "[A]ll the memorandum does . . . is in my opinion, to agree that the requisite amount of the proceeds of sale should be made available to [the husband] for the purpose of purchasing a new house, but without any agreement as to the ownership of the new house, basically because, I think, the [wife], at any rate, never thought about the matter. She was simply concerned with the money being made available to [the husband], not with the question of ownership of the money . . .

[Can the memorandum] be read as a severance of their joint beneficial interests: an agreement to the effect that each of them thereafter is to be solely entitled to his and her respective one half share in [the sale] proceeds? With the best will in the world, I find myself wholly unable to give the memorandum such a construction . . . It appears to me that the memorandum is dealing solely with the use by [the husband] of the whole of the proceeds of sale, and that, qua ownership, use is wholly ambiguous: hence, it cannot be implied from the fact that [the husband] was to have the use of the whole of the money either that the title thereto was assigned to him or that he was entitled to have his own half absolutely, and [the wife] her own half share absolutely.

[I]s it possible from the correspondence, more particularly from the determination therein manifested by both parties that their respective financial affairs were going to be kept separate, whether or not coupled with the fact that they were both negotiating as to what precise share of the proceeds of sale each should take, and whether or not coupled with the actual distributions out of the deposit paid by the purchaser [of the matrimonial home], to say.. that there was a sufficient course of conduct by [husband and wife] as to lead to the implication of an agreement to sever, and hence a severance? . . .

It appears to me that when parties are negotiating to reach an agreement, and never do reach any final agreement, it is quite impossible to say that they have reached any agreement at all. Certainly it is not possible to say that they have reached an agreement to sever merely because they have, in the course of those negotiations, reached an interim agreement for the distribution of comparatively small sums of money. It will be borne in mind that the total amount of the deposit was £1,000 . . . Had the whole of that £1,000 been distributed equally between [husband and wife], this would at least have been consistent with an agreement that they should take the whole of the proceeds of sale in equal shares. But a distribution of part of that £1,000 only . . . appears to me to point away from any such agreement having been reached, rather than to the reaching of any such agreement."

---

150   Adapted from critical thinking questions identified by L.Elder, *I Think Critically Therefore I Am* Times Higher Education Supplement (August 2009).

LECTURER: What do you think? Was this the correct decision?

STUDENT: The parties were talking about what should happen to the sale proceeds only in the context of providing the husband with a place to *live*. They left out the question of *ownership* of the sale proceeds altogether, so no one could say whether they had agreed to hold the proceeds separately or jointly. Neither did their agreement show that they no longer wanted survivorship to operate. Furthermore, because the couple had not reached a *final* agreement about what was to happen to the proceeds of sale Walton J. held that it was not possible to establish a "mutual agreement" to sever.

> Walton J concluded that severance had not take place. Is this correct? Is it correct that the parties' agreement was not inconsistent with the idea of a joint tenancy?

Unity of Interest: The BUILDING BLOCK of the Joint Tenancy

Each owns the whole interest together with the others. None of the co-owners has separate and identifiable shares. For there to be a mutual agreement to sever there must be an agreement between the parties about the property which is inconsistent with the idea that they should *continue* to own the whole. SURVIVORSHIP: is the by-product of unity of interest. Because the co-owners together own the whole of the interest and separately own nothing when one dies he does not die owning anything separate that he can leave by will. If the agreement establishes that the parties mutually intend that survivorship should no longer operate, this should be sufficient to establish severance by mutual agreement.

(2) Mutual agreement and co-owners who are negotiating to split their property on divorce or separation[151]

From *Nielson-Jones v Fedden* it is clear that judges are unwilling to find a mutual agreement where the parties are negotiating a separation of their property on divorce. Indeed, in *Gore & Snell v Carpenter*[152] a husband and wife were joint tenants of two houses. They were divorcing and negotiating for a separation of their assets. The husband wrote to the wife proposing that she have one house and he the other. However, although she agreed "in principle" she said that a number of details had to be sorted out first. Thus, there was no severance by mutual agreement.

---

151   For example, L.Barnes, (2011) 108 Fam. Law 13 considers severance in this context.
152   (1990) 60 P. & C.R. 456.

"The correspondence does not, in my judgment, show any such mutual agreement. . . . Afterwards, when the discussion ranged more over the proposal that each party should take one house and that there should be a financial settlement, again there was no agreement reached. They were very near it – it was an agreement in principle – but I think each party reserved their rights and when the divorce proceedings had come on, if they had come on, it would have been open to them to have argued for some other provision."[153]

LECTURER: This shows that the courts are reluctant to infer severance when co-owners are divorcing and negotiating a separation of assets. Is this good law? Should the position be any different? Let's critically evaluate *Nielson-Jones v Fedden* and *Gore and Snell v Carpenter*. We will construct an argument using our Building Blocks about whether the law is good or bad fair or unfair. We have to determine whether that case supports or undermines any of the policies and principles contained in our Building Blocks.

> Do you think this was too restrictive an application of the law? Should the judges have recognised that the joint tenancies had been severed? Remember that the rules as to whether severance has occurred determine whether the deceased co-owner's part of the property passes by will or intestacy to persons whom he, presumably, would rather get his share, or whether the surviving co-owner is entitled to the whole by survivorship.

STUDENT: The judges in both cases found that severance had not occurred. It is at least strongly arguable that this goes against BUILDING BLOCK NO 7. The parties were separating and it is likely that they would expect to have separate shares for them to leave by will.

> **BUILDING BLOCK NO 7: The rules of Land Law should give effect to the parties' intentions or reasonable expectations**
> Land Law is "facilitative" (P.Birks) We can say that if the rules of co-ownership fail significantly to reflect most peoples' reasonable expectations with regard to what should happen to the property in a particular situation, then those rules are bad law.

This is like the argument we had about *Re Draper's Conveyance, Harris v Goddard* in the context of divorce petitions operating as a "notice in writing" to sever (above).

LECTURER: A fair solution does appear to be to ensure that a divorcing (or separating) couple have separate shares that can then be passed on to new partners and families if the co-owner dies prematurely.[154]

---

153   Above per Blackett-Ord J.
154   M.P.Thompson [1987] Conv. 29.

STUDENT: Probably the last thing a divorcing spouse would want on their death is for their estranged spouse to get their share in the house as well.[155] Thus, neither *Nielson-Jones v Fedden* nor *Gore and Snell v Carpenter* give effect to the parties' intentions and reasonable expectations and is therefore not good law.

STUDENT: Also if parties are negotiating for separate shares in any case then it is clear that this is what they intend. I don't see why the law could not give effect to this. Why does there need to be a dogged insistence on a "final agreement"?[156]

LECTURER: What about BUILDING BLOCK NO 6?

STUDENT: I felt that a strong point about both judgments was that they provide law that is certain and clear. Unless the parties have reached a definite and final agreement there will be survivorship. This means that the parties and many like them can be advised very definitely as to the consequences of their actions. Severance is less likely to happen accidentally.

Thus, on BUILDING BLOCK NO 6 *Nielson-Jones v Fedden* and *Gore and Snell v Carpenter* is good and fair law.

BUILDING BLOCK NO 6: The Need for Certainty and Predictability in Land Law Rules

The law of co-ownership must allow people to know where they stand in respect of co-owned property, i.e. are they going to inherit all by survivorship or (if severance has occurred) may someone else be claiming an interest in the house on the death of a co-owner? The law must allow solicitors to be able to advise their clients about the consequences of their actions.

LECTURER: You are building a good argument here. If you want to make it stronger make sure that you treat the Building Blocks as a starting point in your construction. Go and look up some of the articles cited in the footnotes and see if their arguments will take yours any further.

E. SEVERANCE OF A JOINT TENANCY BY COURSE OF CONDUCT

The final method of severance articulated in the case of *Williams v Hensman*[157] is where the parties have undertaken a course of conduct that shows that the interests of all were mutually treated as separate and distinct shares in the land.

---

155   See L.Tee, "Co-ownership and trusts" in *Land Law Issues, Debates, Policy*, p.132; M.P.Thompson [1987] Conv. 29; M.P.Thompson *Modern Land Law*, 4th edn (Oxford University Press, 2009).

156   R.Smith, *Plural Ownership*.

157   (1861) 1 John. & H. 546.

"And, in the third place, there may be a severance by any course of dealing sufficient to intimate that the interests of all were mutually treated as constituting a tenancy in common. When the severance depends on an inference of this kind without any express act of severance, it will not suffice to rely on an intention, with respect to the particular share, declared only behind the backs of the other persons interested. You must find in this class of cases a course of dealing by which the shares of all the parties to the contest have been affected."[158]

Like the "mutual agreement" head, this head looks to the intentions of the parties. In order to recognise a severance the courts are looking to determine that the co-owners have treated themselves as owning separate shares. As we can see from the extract immediately above all the co-owners must be involved in treating their interests as a tenancy in common. An uncommunicated declaration by one co-owner behind the backs of the others is insufficient to sever. All joint tenants must be aware of the common intention; there must be a shared understanding.[159]

> The co-owners' mutual conduct must show that they are treating themselves as holding the land differently from this.

> **Unity of Interest: The BUILDING BLOCK of the Joint Tenancy**
> Each owns the whole interest together. None of the co-owners have separate and identifiable shares. Is there a course of mutual dealing by all the co-owners that is inconsistent with this? Is there anything about the parties' mutual conduct that shows they no longer intend survivorship to operate?

In *Re Denny*,[160] on the distribution of an estate, three sisters signed final accounts giving them separate and distinct shares in the estate. This was held to be a course of conduct by which they mutually treated themselves as owning separate shares. Their original joint tenancy was severed accordingly. Similarly in *Flannigan v Wotherspoon*[161] a property was co-owned by two sisters as joint tenants. It was held that severance of the joint tenancy had taken place where the sisters had agreed to sell the property and to divide the proceeds between them.

LECTURER: Were these cases correctly decided? You can form a valid opinion by holding them against our Building Blocks in the way shown above.

---

158   *Williams v Hensman* (1861) 1 John & H. 546, p.557 per Sir William Page Wood V.-C.
159   Confirmed in *Carr v Isard* [2006] EWHC 2095 (Ch), para.21.
160   (1947) 177 L.T. 291, Jenkins J.
161   [1953] 1 D.L.R. 768.

STUDENT: I think the cases were correctly decided because the sisters (in both cases) treated themselves as owning separate shares—they divided up the proceeds of sale in *Flannigan* and sign the accounts to this effect in *Re Denny*. This showed that they did not wish survivorship to operate and that they wanted separate shares.

Had the husband and wife in *Nielson-Jones v Fedden*[162] divided the proceeds of sale between them this would have been held to sever on this ground. If you remember in that case the husband and wife had agreed that their former matrimonial home should be sold and the proceeds used to buy a house in which the husband could live. This was held not to be an agreement that the couple had decided to separate their shares and own half the proceeds each. They found a purchaser and each took £200 from the total deposit of £1000. Walton J. intimated that had they split the whole deposit equally then this may have shown that they were treating themselves as owning distinctly separate shares. Had this been the case, it would have been a relevant "course of dealing" so as to sever their joint tenancy.

> "Had the whole of that £1,000 been distributed equally between [husband and wife], this would at least have been consistent with an agreement that they should take the whole of the proceeds of sale in equal shares."

In *Greenfield v Greenfield*[163] two brothers owned a house over a long period of time as joint tenants. They restructured the accommodation into two maisonettes so that each could live in a maisonette with their family. It was held that merely changing the accommodation within the house did not show an intention to change the joint tenancy into a tenancy in common.

LECTURER: Do you think that the judge made the correct decision in this case? Do you agree that the brothers' mutual conduct failed to show an intention to sever?

> In order to sever, the brothers' conduct would have to have been inconsistent with this.

Unity of Interest: The BUILDING BLOCK of the Joint Tenancy
Each owns the whole interest together. None of the co-owners have separate and identifiable shares. Is there a course of mutual dealing by all the co-owners that is inconsistent with this?

STUDENT: All the brothers in *Greenfield* did was to convert the house into two separate spaces. This does not have any bearing on how they *owned* the house: joint tenants or otherwise. A change of use does not show that co-owners intend to change the way they own the house.

---

162   [1975] Ch. 222.
163   (1979) 38 P. & C.R. 570.

There was nothing about their conduct that showed they no longer wanted to "own the whole together" and that they henceforth wanted separate shares.

Judges have recognised in principle that co-owners' negotiations, e.g. on divorce or separation, could amount to a relevant "course of conduct" for the purposes of severance. In *Burgess v Rawnsley*[164] Sir John Pennycuick stated:

"I do not doubt myself that where one tenant negotiates with another for some rearrangement of interests, it may be possible to infer from the particular facts ... a common intention to sever, even though the negotiations break down. Whether such an inference can be drawn must, I think, depend upon the particular facts."[165]

That notwithstanding, as with the mutual agreement ground, negotiations for separation of assets, e.g. on divorce or partnership break-up have rarely been held as a sufficient course of dealing to sever, in the absence of a definite and final agreement as to the distribution of assets. In *Gore & Snell v Carpenter*[166] negotiations between a husband and wife who owned two houses on joint tenancy, including a suggestion that the joint tenancies should be severed, and that the husband should have one house and the wife the other, were held not to amount to a course of conduct. Blackett-Ord J. reasoned as follows:

"There were negotiations, as I have said, but negotiations are not the same thing as a course of dealing. A course of dealing is where over the years the parties have dealt with their interests in the property on the footing that they are interests in common and are not joint ... But in the present case there were simply negotiations between the husband and the wife and again there was no finality and there was no mutuality. For severance to be effected by a course of dealing all the joint tenants must be concerned in such a course and in the present case there is no evidence that [the wife] was committing herself to accepting a tenancy in common prior to the property division which would have been made in the divorce proceedings."

(1) The difference between mutual agreement and course of conduct

It will be apparent that there is a great deal of overlap between these two grounds of severance. Indeed in many cases, such as *Flannigan v Wotherspoon* the same conclusion would have been reached on the mutual agreement ground. One possible difference exists in the fact that in order to establish a relevant course of conduct it is not necessary for any agreement to have

---

164 [1975] Ch.429, p.443.

165 The rather slender (though accepted) evidence in that case of an agreement by Mr Honick and Mrs Rawnsley to buy/sell her share for £750, which she then went back on, fell far short of establishing a course of conduct. "In the present case the negotiations between Mr Honick and Mrs Rawnsley, if they can be properly described as negotiations at all, fall, it seems to me, far short of warranting an inference. One could not ascribe to joint tenants an intention to sever merely because one offers to buy out the other for £X and the other makes a counter offer of £Y": [1975] Ch.429, p.447, per Sir John Pennycuick.

166 (1990) 60 P. & C.R. 456.

been reached. It is sufficient that the parties treated themselves as having separate interests, provided of course that there is a shared understanding between them. Another difference exists in the fact that with the "course of conduct" ground, common intention to sever is inferred objectively from the parties' conduct, unlike the "mutual agreement" ground which looks at what the parties subjectively agreed to do with the property.[167]

(2) Reform of the law of severance: the Law Commission

The Law Commission has proposed reform of the law of severance, to abolish mutual agreement and course of conduct as methods of severance and to allow a joint tenant to sever by will.[168]

LECTURER: It aims to abolish the informal methods of severance: mutual agreement and course of conduct. Is the law in these areas really so bad?

STUDENT: I think that agreements and conduct can arise informally, as was probably the case in *Burgess v Rawnsley*. People do not always go about their affairs formally and may not think to serve a notice in writing. Therefore, the informal grounds of severance give effect to the intentions of the parties without the need for formality. In this sense they are good law on the basis of BUILDING BLOCK NO 7.

LECTURER: Do you think that allowing their joint tenancy to be severed by making an express provision in their will should fill this gap.

STUDENT: Not really because not everyone will go through the formality of making a will.

LECTURER: But is the law relating to mutual agreement and course of conduct good law anyway. Would we miss it?

STUDENT: The courts have given a very restrictive interpretation of what agreement or conduct satisfies these grounds. Couples who are divorcing and separating their assets are likely to want separate interests. Yet the law does not reflect this. It requires the parties to have reached a final agreement about what should be done with the co-owned property before an informal severance will be recognised. So looking at the matter further, the law itself does not give effect to the reasonable expectations of co-owners. It is not good law.

> **BUILDING BLOCK NO 7: The rules of Land Law should give effect to the parties' intentions or reasonable expectations.**

LECTURER: But at least allowing severance by will might have averted what may have been a potential injustice in *Gore and Snell v Carpenter*. The husband had made a will in favour of Mrs Snell and this would have severed the joint tenancy allowing her to take under the will.

---

167   Conway [2009] Conv. 67, commenting on the Australian decision *Saleeba v Wilke* [2007] QSC 29.
168   Working Paper No.94 (1985). For comment see L.Tee [1995] Conv. 105, some of which form the basis of arguments in this dialogue.

STUDENT: There is also probably much uncertainty that surrounds the informal grounds of severance,[169] i.e. when they have been effectively established, what conduct suffices etc. For doctrines that have such important consequences there should be certainty and predictability.

BUILDING BLOCK NO 6: The Need for Certainty and Predictability in Land Law Rules

---

LECTURER: Let's create an argument about the latter part of this proposal: that severance should be allowed by will. This might have averted an injustice in cases such as *Gore and Snell v Carpenter*. How?

STUDENT: The husband had made a will in favour of Mrs Snell and this would have severed the joint tenancy allowing her to take under the will. So as we have already said, if the Law Commission's proposal became law and severance by will was allowed this would be good law in accordance with BUILDING BLOCK NO 7.

LECTURER: But can you see that in accordance with one of our other Building Blocks it might be unfair if the law *did* allow severance by will?

STUDENT: On the basis of BUILDING BLOCK NO 6—it would be bad law.

BUILDING BLOCK NO 6: The Need for Certainty and Predictability in Land Law Rules:

The law of co-ownership must allow people to know where they stand in respect of co-owned property, i.e. are they going to inherit all by survivorship or (if severance has occurred) may someone else be claiming an interest in the house on the death of a co-owner? Any law that allowed a co-owner to sever their share secretly would be a problem here.

STUDENT: Allowing severance by will is allowing severance to take place in secret. A co-owner can make a will behind the back of the other and the surviving co-owner will be unaware of the severance until the will was disclosed on death.

LECTURER: What other Building Block might be relevant here?

STUDENT: Allowing severance by will might threaten the residential security of the surviving co-owner, as they would not know that the beneficiary under the will would be claiming an interest in their home and may want the property sold.

BUILDING BLOCK NO 1: Residential Security

Rules of Land Law should give protection to people's residential security and can be said to be good or bad accordingly.

---

169   L.Tee, "Severance Revisited" [1995] Conv. 105.

LECTURER: The co-owner who wishes to leave his share to his new partner could always serve a notice in writing. Why would this be the fairest approach?

STUDENT: It would have the added advantage of ensuring that the other co-owner is aware of the severance.

LECTURER: Good, you have conducted this analysis very well. There are of course other points you could make and develop, but I think ultimately you are concluding that the Law Commission's suggestion for severance by will, would not make good law.

F. SEVERANCE OF A JOINT TENANCY BY OPERATION OF THE FORFEITURE RULE

Survivorship will not operate where one joint tenant has unlawfully killed another. This is known as the forfeiture rule. It is "a rule of public policy which in certain circumstances precludes a person . . . from acquiring a benefit in consequence of the killing".[170] This includes "aiding and abetting" and "counselling or procuring" the death of another.[171] So if Katie and Sampson are joint tenants of a house and Katie murders Sampson, under the forfeiture rule she will not be able to acquire Sampson's share of the house by right of survivorship. The law holds that the deceased co-owner's share is severed and passes to whoever is entitled under his will or under the intestacy rules.[172] In *Dunbar v Plant*[173] the forfeiture rule applied where one joint tenant helped the other to commit suicide.

(1) The court has power to modify the effects of the rule

In all cases other than murder[174] the court has power to modify the effects of the forfeiture rule and allow survivorship to operate if the justice of the case requires it "having regard to the conduct of the offender and of the deceased and to such other circumstances as appear to the court to be material".[175] In *Re K*[176] a wife killed her husband. The court modified the rule and permitted a wife to take co-owned property by right of survivorship. The deceased had inflicted severe domestic violence on her. In *Dunbar v Plant*[177] the court also allowed survivorship to operate because of the circumstances of the case.

---

170   Forfeiture Act 1982 s.1(1).
171   Forfeiture Act 1982 s.1(2); *Dunbar v Plant* [1998] Ch. 412.
172   If there are more than two joint tenants there is Commonwealth authority for the proposition that the deceased co-owner's share is held by the legal owners on constructive trust for the innocent joint tenant, otherwise they would lose out. If the deceased's interest were severed the innocent joint tenant would lose what he would have gained by survivorship: *Rasmanis v Jurewitsch* (1970) 70 S.R. (NSW) 407. Jackson, Pearce and Stevens, *Land Law*, 4th edn (London: Sweet & Maxwell, 2008), Ch.12; *Megarry and Wade Law of Real Property*, para.13–049.
173   [1998] Ch. 412.
174   Forfeiture Act 1982 s.5.
175   s.2(2).
176   [1985] Ch. 85.
177   [1998] Ch. 412 (above).

Chapter 5

Statutory Regulation of Co-ownership: Trusts of Land

CHAPTER OVERVIEW

In this chapter you will find:

- An introduction to the Trust of Land and the principles that regulate co-ownership
- The method by which the law resolves disputes between co-owners
- Full case extracts and instructions on legal reasoning
- Constructed argument about the cases using Building Blocks.

The Statutory Trust

1

The Law of Property Act 1925 ss.34–36 lays down a scheme for co-ownership of land. Wherever land is conveyed, or left by will, to more than one person (either as joint tenants or tenants in common), the co-ownership takes effect under a trust, even though the parties do not provided for a trust expressly.

Example

Land is conveyed "to Abby, Claire and Michael". They will hold the land on the statutory trust as follows:

LEGAL ESTATE

Abby, Claire, Michael
———————————————

EQUITABLE (or "beneficial") INTEREST   **Abby, Claire, Michael**

Of course the parties are free to impose a different trust: such as the land is conveyed to Abby and Claire to hold for the benefit of themselves and Michael. And they may provide expressly that they hold the shares of the beneficial ownership in whatever proportions they please.[1]

A. WHY DID THE 1925 DRAFTSMAN IMPOSE A TRUST IN ALL CASES OF CO-OWNERSHIP OF LAND?

At the time of the 1925 legislation the tenancy in common was the preferred form of co-ownership.[2] As you now know, where land is held as a tenancy in common the co-owners have distinct and identifiable shares that they can leave by will to their families or that will pass under the rules of intestacy. Tenancies in common were perceived by the 1925 reformers to cause a problem for the management and sale of land. For example, land would be left to persons in a will as tenants in common. Every time one of the tenants in common died, he could leave his share by will, and often did, to more than one person. Thus, title would "fragment", i.e. on each death more and more people would become co-owners of the land with distinct and identifiable shares. Interests in land, as you know, are property rights that potentially bind third party purchasers of the land and mortgage lenders lending money on the security of the land. This made title to the land unmanageable and very difficult to sell because the purchaser or mortgage lender would have to obtain the consent of all the owners of the separate fragments in order to be sure of taking a good title. It was quite possible that co-ownership like this could render land economically stagnant. In 1920, Sir Claud Schuster, Permanent Secretary of the Lord Chancellor's Office, made this observation:

> "I have the misery to be the owner of an undivided share [a tenant in common] in a block of buildings in Manchester which is already owned in forty sections and will on the occasion of the next death run into hundreds. The difficulty of managing the property and dealing with the tenants is immense. It is almost a commercial impossibility to effect necessary improvements, and the lawyers' bill year by year swallows up an enormous proportion of the gross rental".[3]

B. THE 1925 RADICAL SOLUTION: A TRUST IN ALL CASES OF CO-OWNERSHIP

The Law of Property Act imposes a trust in all cases of co-ownership.[4] This solved the fragmentation of title problem: but *how*? Before we consider this we need to remind ourselves

---

1   If they expressly declare that they hold the beneficial interest in unequal shares of whatever proportions this will necessarily result in a beneficial tenancy in common.

2   J.S.Anderson, *Lawyers and the Making of English Land Law* 1832–1940 (Oxford: Clarendon Press, 1992), p.287.

3   Quoted in J.S.Anderson, *Lawyers and the Making of English Land Law* 1832–1940, p.290. Arthur Underhill, a conveyancing barrister made a similar observation: (1920) 37 L.Q.R. 107 quoted above p.288.

4   Law of Property Act 1925 ss.34 and 36.

what a trust *is*. If you remember, a trust is a device whereby trustees are the legal owners of property but they are holding it for the benefit of others: the beneficiaries. It is the beneficiaries that effectively own the land. They are entitled to the profit from the land and to live there. There is nothing to stop a trustee from also being a beneficiary, so that A and B might hold the land for the benefit of themselves and C and D. Consider this example:

City of London Building Society v Flegg **[1988] A.C. 54**

A couple, Mr and Mrs Maxwell-Browne, and the wife's parents, Mr and Mrs Flegg, decided they wanted to pool their resources so that they could buy a much bigger house together. The couple raised their part of the purchase by way of mortgage and Mr and Mrs Flegg sold their current house to pay for their part of the purchase. They all decided that the property they bought together should be conveyed into the sole names of Mr and Mrs Maxwell-Browne. They held Bleak House on trust for themselves and Mr and Mrs Flegg in equity:

LEGAL TITLE

Mr M-B Mrs M-B

EQUITABLE (or "beneficial") INTEREST   **Mr M-B Mrs M-B Mr F Mrs F**

The 1925 draftsman imposed a trust in all cases where land is co-owned. The trustees deal with the legal title on behalf of all the co-owners. The trustees can sell the land to the purchaser, lease it to a tenant or mortgage it to a bank, without the purchaser, tenant or lender having to get the permission of all the co-owners.[5]

However, by itself the trust device was useless to solve the fragmentation of title problem. Equitable interests in land are also property rights that potentially bind purchasers. *How* would the purchaser obtain a good title from the trustee? And as to the problem of tenancies in common causing fragmentation of the title, what's to stop this happening with the legal estate that the trustees are holding? One could die leaving his share to his four daughters etc. Within a matter of years the number of trustees would have multiplied and any purchaser would have to obtain just as many consents to the transaction as before. The trust device by itself would not solve the fragmentation of title problem. Thus, the draftsman of the 1925 legislation employed two further mechanisms.

(1) Overreaching

Overreaching is a device that allows a purchaser or mortgage lender to take a good title from trustees of land free from the claims of the equitable co-owners. He does not have to make any

---

5   The question of whether the purchaser takes a title clear from the equitable interests is something we will consider later in this chapter and in the next chapters on Land Transfer Law.

enquiries as to the beneficial interests. He can simply take free from them. All he needs to do is to fulfil certain procedural requirements in dealing with the trustees.[6] The trustees have these overreaching powers to convey legal title to the land free from the equitable interests of the other co-owners under the trust. We will examine these later in this chapter and in the Chapters on Land Transfer Law.

(2) Maximum number of trustees who will always hold the legal estate on a joint tenancy

> The Law of Property Act 1925 imposes a maximum number of trustees: four—and those trustees will always hold the legal estate as a joint tenancy.

Remember in the previous chapter that I told you that the legal estate would always be held on a joint tenancy: by the authority of s:1(6) of the Law of Property Act 1925? I asked you to suspend your disbelief as to *why*. You will now understand why. It means that the legal estate *cannot* fragment. A joint tenancy operates by right of survivorship so that if one joint tenant dies he drops out of the picture. He does not have any separate interest that he can leave by will or that can be inherited under the rules of intestacy. The Law of Property Act 1925 also provided that the legal estate can never be severed and turned into a tenancy in common.[7] This means that there is always an identifiable and diminishing number of trustees holding the legal estate. The purchaser deals with these people. More can be appointed and if there is ever a situation where there are no trustees, the court will appoint some.[8] The Law of Property Act 1925 and the Trustee Act 1925 provides that a maximum number of four trustees can hold the legal estate.[9] Thus a purchaser or mortgage lender will only have to find four people. These trustees will hold the legal estate to the land on trust for the other co-owners as beneficiaries.

The *equitable* interests under the trust can be held either as a joint tenancy or a tenancy in common, and the interests can be severed to create a tenancy in common. Thus it is in the context of the equitable interests that we consider firstly whether the co-owners hold as joint tenants or tenants in common and then, after the conveyance or will takes effect, whether the joint tenancy of the equitable interest has been severed. So make sure you deal with the legal title and the equitable interest separately.

---

6   Law of Property Act 1925 ss.2 and 27 concern the trustees' overreaching powers.
7   Law of Property Act 1925 s.36(2).
8   Under the equitable principle that *a trust will never fail for want of a trustee*.
9   Law of Property Act 1925 ss.34(2); Trustee Act 1925 s.34(2).

> **Example: the statutory trust**
>
> A house is conveyed to Alan, Clive and Martin. Let us say that there is wording in the original conveyance of the house that indicates that they hold in equity as tenants in common. Let us also say that Clive dies "leaving all his estate" to his cousin John. The will cannot take effect in relation to the legal estate. Survivorship applies as it is a joint tenancy. Thus, in relation to the legal estate Clive dies leaving Alan and Martin owning the whole by survivorship. As far as the equitable interest is concerned, it is a tenancy in common so Clive had a defined share to leave by will, and the gift to John will thus take effect. So after Clive's death the situation will be as follows
>
> LEGAL ESTATE [always a joint tenancy]
>
> **Alan   ~~Clive~~   Martin**
>
> EQUITABLE INTEREST [tenants in common]   **Alan ┃ John ┃ Martin**
>
> Alan and Martin are holding the house on trust for themselves and John.

(a) How do we know who will be the four trustees?

The Law of Property Act 1925 provides that the trustees are the first four people of full age and competence named in the conveyance.[10] A minor cannot hold a legal estate in land.[11] Let's look at an example, five doctors wanted to set up a local practice and were buying premises for a surgery. The surgery was conveyed to A, B, C, D and E. It is co-ownership so there would be a trust. Only A, B, C, and D could be trustees (they are the first four of full age named). They would hold the legal estate for A, B, C, D and E, who would have equitable interests under the trust.

> **Summary**
> So we have a statutory co-ownership trust managed by a limited number of trustees with overreaching powers. Together these provisions solved the fragmentation of title problem. However, in the chapters on Land Transfer Law we will consider how effective this device is in modern co-ownership situations, where the possibility of fraudulent trustees has already caused some injustice.

(3) The statutory trust in modern context

As we have seen in several contexts that we have studied so far the social phenomenon of owner occupation changed the landscape of Land Law. People co-own houses usually in order to live in them and joint tenancies are more common. Thus, the statutory trust, imposed by the Law of Property Act 1925, looks slightly odd. For example, a couple buy a house as a home and it is conveyed into their joint names. They hold legal title to the house on trust for each other.

---

10   Law of Property Act 1925 ss.34(2).
11   Law of Property Act 1925 s.1(6).

Example

Land is conveyed "to Abby and Michael in equal shares". They will hold the land on the statutory trust as follows:

LEGAL ESTATE [always a joint tenancy]

Abby Michael

━━━━━━━━━━━━━━

EQUITABLE INTEREST   **Abby Michael**

C. THE TRUSTS OF LAND AND APPOINTMENT OF TRUSTEES ACT 1996

The Law of Property Act 1925 also provided that all co-ownership was deemed to create not only a *trust* but a trust *for sale*. A trust for sale is a type of trust that gained popularity in the nineteenth century. For example, land would be left to trustees in a will, expressly to be sold, in order to provide a fund of money, e.g. to pay the costs of administering the estate, to pay debts, or to provide an inheritance for people who were not direct heirs.[12] Where land was held on trust for sale the trustees were under a duty to sell the land. Because of this the beneficial interests under a trust for sale were regarded by the courts as personal property rather than real property. This is known as the "doctrine of conversion". As the trustees were under a legal obligation to sell the land the courts "regarded as done that which ought to be done" and viewed the beneficiaries' interests as interests in money (personal property).[13] Under the Law of Property Act 1925 trustees for sale were given powers to postpone sale and to manage the land, e.g. lease and mortgage it.[14] But the default position, if the trustees were not unanimous in wanting to postpone sale of the land, was that they were under a duty to sell.[15] With the phenomenal increase in people owning the houses in which they lived, the statutory trust for sale, with its duty on the trustees to sell the land and its notional regard of the beneficial interests as interests in personal property, was looking increasingly outdated and unreal.[16] In *Williams & Glyn's Bank v Boland* it was observed that co-owners bought a house in order to *live in it*. Imposing a trust *for sale* onto this situation was unreal. The co-owners would not

---

12   G.Spence, *The Equitable Jurisdiction of the Court of Chancery* (1846–1849), Vol II, p.380.

13   They were still property rights that could affect a purchaser of the land: G.Spence, *The Equitable Jurisdiction of the Court of Chancery* (1846–1849) Vol II, pp.380–1. The doctrine of conversion did not aid the conveyancing purposes of the Law of Property Act 1925. For this, overreaching powers were needed: Harpum, "Overreaching, Trustees' Powers and Reform of the 1925 Legislation" [1990] C.L.J. 277, pp.283–5; J.S.Anderson, "The Proper, Narrow Scope of Equitable Conversion in Land Law" (1984) 100 L.Q.R. 86, pp.89–90.

14   Law of Property Act 1925 s.28.

15   *Re Mayo* [1943] Ch. 302.

16   See comments made in *Bull v Bull* [1955] 1 Q.B. 274.

conceivably imagine that the legal owner(s) were under a duty to sell the land that they had bought to live in![17] It was time for a change.[18]

(1) The Trusts of Land and Appointment of Trustees Act 1996—The New "Trust of Land"[19]

Under the Trusts of Land and Appointment of Trustees Act 1996 (TLATA 1996), co-ownership still takes effect under a trust, but no longer a trust for sale. The 1996 Act provides that all concurrent and successive ownership takes effect as a Trust of Land.[20] A trust of land is defined as "any trust of property which consists of or includes land".[21] It extends to all types of trust, express, implied, resulting, constructive[22] and bare trusts.[23] Thus, all co-ownership takes effect as a trust of land. This new trust of land does not impose a duty to sell on the trustees. It is still possible to *expressly* create a trust for sale but the trustees have a statutory non-excludable power to postpone sale.[24]

(2) Successive ownership and the Trusts of Land and Appointment of Trustees Act 1996

Since TLATA 1996 came into force it has not been possible to create new settlements under the Settled Land Act.[25] However, any settlements which were still in existence on January 1, 1997 continue until the settlement comes to an end. Where there is an attempt to create a settlement this takes effect as a declaration of a trust of land.[26]

(3) Trusts of land constructed in the same way

The new trust of land is structured in the same way, i.e. there must be no more than four trustees, the legal estate must be held as a joint tenancy and the legal estate can never be severed.[27]

---

17 [1981] A.C. 487, HL; [1979] Ch. 312, CA. The courts found ways around this duty on the trustees to sell the land. For example, where there was a dispute as to what should be done with the land, the courts would no longer automatically order sale but would postpone sale of the house if there was another additional ("collateral") purpose for acquiring the land, such as a home for one or both of the parties. For example see *Jones v Challenger* [1961] 1 Q.B. 176; *Re Buchanan-Wollaston's Conveyance* [1939] Ch. 738.

18 See the Law Commission, *Transfer of Land; Trusts of Land* (Law Com No.181, 1989).

19 See J.MacKenzie, A.Walker, P.Walton, *A Guide to the Trusts of Land and Appointment of Trustees Act 1996* (Old Bailey press, Law in Practice Series 1998); L.M.Clements, "The Changing Face of Trusts: The Trusts of Land and Appointment of Trustees Act 1996" [1998] M.L.R. 56.

20 ss.2, 4 and 5; s.3 abolishes the doctrine of conversion.

21 s.1(1)(a).

22 For example the common intention constructive trust in *Stack v Dowden* [2007] UKHL 17.

23 TLATA 1996 s.1(2)(a).

24 TLATA 1996 s.4.

25 s.2. For successive ownership and the Settled Land Act 1925 see Chapter 4 section 1E.

26 s.2, Sch.1.

27 Law of Property Act 1925 ss.1(6) and 36(2).

The Statutory Scheme for Regulation of Trusts of Land

The Trusts of Land and Appointment of Trustees Act 1996 provides a scheme of regulation that applies to all trusts of land, express, statutory or implied.[28] This scheme lays down the powers that trustees have to deal with the land. It also provides a system of dispute resolution. For instance where co-owners disagree as to what should happen to the land the Act provides a way of determining *whose voice will prevail*.

Let's consider an example: Adam, Brian, Cully, David and Eric are all veterinary surgeons who want to buy premises so that they can set up a vet's practice. They purchase "Herriot House". It is agreed between them that Adam, Brian and Cully will hold title to the property and so Herriot House is conveyed into the names of those three. They hold the land on trust for themselves and David and Eric. This would be the case either because David and Eric contributed to the purchase price or because the conveyance expressly provided that they held interests.

Co-ownership of Herriot House
LEGAL TITLE [joint tenancy]

Adam Brian Cully

▬▬▬▬▬▬▬▬▬▬▬▬▬▬▬▬

EQUITABLE TITLE   **Adam Brian Cully David Eric**

As a trust is imposed in all cases of co-ownership, we will need to know how that trust works. We already know how to identify who the trustees are. They are the persons who are holding legal title. What powers do they have? Can they do anything they like with the land? What about the people who are not on the legal title, David and Eric in our example? Can their voice be heard? After all, they may have paid just as much as the trustees towards the property and be equal partners in every other sense.

A. POWERS OF TRUSTEES OF LAND

What if Adam, Brian and Cully want to raise money in order to refurbish the surgery? Can they grant a mortgage on Herriot House without asking David and Eric?

---

28   For a useful account see R.Smith, *Plural Ownership* (Oxford University Press, 2005).

> **Section 6 General powers of trustees**
> **(1) For the purpose of exercising their functions as trustees, the trustees of land have**
> **. . . . all the powers of an absolute owner.**

So the answer is that Adam, Brian and Cully have the power to mortgage Herriot House because they have all the powers that they would have if they were the absolute owners[29]: an absolute owner can create a mortgage over land that he owns. As far as the rights of the beneficiaries are concerned, in our example, David and Eric, we note that s.6 provides that trustees have these powers "for the purpose of exercising their functions as trustees". This means that whenever they are exercising any of their powers, such as the power to grant a mortgage, they must act *as trustees*, that is, as someone responsible for holding property for the benefit of another. In equity a trustee is under a strict duty to put the interests of the trust before their own personal interest.[30] Section 6(6) of the Trusts of Land and Appointment of Trustees Act 1996 provides that "[t]he powers conferred by this section shall not be exercised in contravention of . . . any rule of law or equity". Section 6(5) provides that the trustees, when exercising their powers, must "have regard to the rights of the beneficiaries".

> **So, before Adam, Brian and Cully execute a mortgage on Herriot House in return for a**
> **loan to refurbish the surgery, they must, before doing so, act solely in the best interests**
> **of the trust, i.e. the provision of a vet's surgery and it's management for business**
> **purposes. They must have regard to the rights of David and Eric. This may take the form**
> **of considering whether a mortgage, in the current financial climate, is in the best**
> **interests of all of the vets. It might be the case that the practice cannot sustain the**
> **financial commitment in the short term.**

(1) The power to convey the land to the beneficiaries, if absolutely entitled

Under s.6(2) trustees have the power to convey the land to the beneficiaries even if they have not requested this. Before the trustees can do this the beneficiaries must be absolutely entitled, of full age, and of legal capacity.[31] For example, the beneficiaries would not be absolutely entitled where it is in the trustees' discretion who gets the property and they have yet to make such an appointment[32] or where there is someone else with a life interest outstanding under the trust of land.[33] If the trustees exercise this power the beneficiaries will have to do whatever

29   The broader s.6 powers replaced the old s.28 powers under the Law of Property Act 1925, which were "complex, disjointed and limited": J.MacKenzie, A.Walker, P.Walton, *A Guide to the Trusts of Land and Appointment of Trustees Act 1996* (Old Bailey press, Law in Practice Series 1998), p.31.
30   For example *Boardman v Phipps* [1967] 2 A.C. 46. A discussion of these duties is beyond the scope of this book.
31   s.6(2).
32   Known as a "discretionary trust".
33   See the commentary on the Act by J.MacKenzie, A.Walker, P.Walton, *A Guide to the Trusts of Land and Appointment of Trustees Act 1996* (1998), p.33.

is necessary to ensure that the legal title is vested in them,[34] e.g. they must ensure that title is registered in their name at the Land Registry. The thinking behind this is that it allows trustees to terminate the trust and be discharged from their duties when the beneficiaries are absolutely entitled to the trust property.[35] Indeed under ordinary principles of trust law when beneficiaries under a trust are together absolutely entitled to the trust property and they are of full age they can require the trustees to vest the property in them.[36] Section 6(2) just takes the principle one stage further and allows the trustees to take the initiative and convey the land to the beneficiaries, whether they have required them to do so or not.

(2) The power to purchase land for occupation

Trustees can purchase land for occupation by a beneficiary,[37] which is something they could not do under the old law.[38]

(3) The power to partition the land

The trustees can partition the land amongst beneficiaries entitled, provided the beneficiaries are holding the land as tenants in common, not joint tenants, and are absolutely entitled.[39] To "partition" effectively means to destroy unity of possession, and therefore the co-ownership, so that each beneficiary becomes "sole tenant of the piece of land allotted to him".[40] The beneficiaries will henceforth be able to have exclusive possession of their part of the land and be able to exclude the others from that part.[41] The trustees must obtain the consent of the beneficiaries to a partition. An outright sale of the land or a conveyance of the land to the beneficiaries is much more likely to be used as a way of bringing a trust to an end.[42]

(4) Delegation to a beneficiary of full age

Trustees can, by power of attorney, "delegate to any beneficiary or beneficiaries of full age and beneficially entitled to an interest in possession in land, any of their functions as trustees which relate to the land".[43] If a power is so delegated to a beneficiary that beneficiary is in the same position as a trustee in relation to the exercise of that function. So, for example, he will need to have regard to the interests of other beneficiaries when exercising that function.

For example, let's say that a farm is held on trust by three trustees for Simon for life and remainder to his son Derek, under the terms of their father's will. Simon is of full age. He works

---

34   TLATA 1996 s.6(2)(a).
35   J.MacKenzie, A.Walker, P.Walton, above, p.33.
36   *Saunders v Vautier* (1841) Cr. Ph. 240; J.MacKenzie, A.Walker, P.Walton, above p.33.
37   TLATA 1996 s.6(3); Trustee Act 2000 s.8(1)(b). They can also purchase land "as an investment" or "for any other reason": Trustee Act 2000 s.8(1).
38   *Re Power* [1947] Ch. 572.
39   TLATA 1996 s.7.
40   Harpum, Bridge and Dixon, *Megarry and Wade Law of Real Property*, 7th edn (London: Sweet & Maxwell, 2008), para.13–101. This is a transaction that must be by deed under s.52 of the Law of Property Act 1925: ibid.
41   For "unity of possession", the basic requirement of co-ownership, see Chapter 4, section 2.
42   J.MacKenzie, A.Walker, P.Walton, *A Guide to the Trusts of Land and Appointment of Trustees Act 1996* (1998), p.36. Although a conveyance of land to (say) three beneficiaries would create a new trust of land whereby they would hold on trust for themselves.
43   TLATA 1996 s.9. "Functions" appears to mean trustees wide powers under the 1996 Act. See J.MacKenzie, A.Walker, P.Walton, above, p.42.

and manages the farm and he lives there at the farmhouse. It is obviously more convenient for Simon to have some powers of management, e.g. he may wish to rent out one of the farm cottages, and therefore must have leasing powers. He may also need to raise money on the security of the farm, in order to fund developments. He would thus need mortgaging powers. He is a beneficiary and he has the immediate right to enjoy the land, i.e. his is an interest *in possession*. So the three trustees can, by power of attorney, delegate any of their wide s.6 functions, including leasing and mortgaging powers.

As far as a person dealing with the beneficiary is concerned, they can assume that the delegation is a proper one under s.9 and the transaction will be valid if he deals in good faith with the beneficiary and does not have knowledge at the time of the transaction that the delegation was improper.[44]

(5) Trustees powers can be excluded and restricted

Trustees' powers under ss.6 and 7 can be excluded or restricted by the disposition creating the trust, such as a conveyance of land.[45]

Let's return to our example with the vets. Remember that Adam, Brian, Cully, David and Eric purchased "Herriot House" in order to start a vet's practice. Adam, Brian and Cully hold title to the property for themselves and David and Eric in equity. If, prior to the purchase of Herriot House, David and Eric were concerned to stop Adam, Brian and Cully from mortgaging Herriot House and getting the practice into debt, they could, prior to the conveyance, insist that their power to mortgage is excluded.

(6) The exercise of the trustees' powers can be made subject to obtaining consent

If the disposition creating the co-ownership "makes provision requiring any consent to be obtained to the exercise of any the trustees' powers" contained in ss.6 and 7, "the power may not be exercised without that consent".[46] So if the instrument setting up the co-ownership trust provided that someone's consent was needed before the trustees could sell, lease, mortgage, or exercise any of their other powers under ss.6 or 7, then the trustees would be in breach of trust and liable to the beneficiaries if they did not obtain that consent.

What about the purchaser from the trustees? Section 10(1) provides that where more than two persons' consent is required to a transaction, "the consent of any two of them . . . is sufficient in favour of a purchaser".[47] For example, if three consents are required before the trustees can sell the land, and the purchaser only makes sure that two of them have been obtained, then this is sufficient. He will take a clear title and not have to give effect to the interests of the beneficiaries.

---

44 TLATA 1996 s.9(2).
45 s.8(1). This ability to exclude or restrict "does not apply in the case of charitable, ecclesiastical or public trusts": s.8(3).
46 s.8(2).
47 The definition of purchaser is broad and includes a mortgage lender and lessee.

Returning to Herriot House, let's say that the conveyance to Adam, Brian and Cully expressly states that they cannot grant a mortgage on Herriot House without first obtaining Eric, Brian and David's consent. The mortgage lender only has to make sure that the trustees have obtained two of these consents and the lender will take its mortgage of Herriot House free from the interests of the beneficiaries.

(7) Beneficiaries' rights to be consulted before the trustees deal with the land

"The trustees of land shall, in exercising their functions relating to the land subject to the trust . . . so far as practicable, consult the beneficiaries of full age and beneficially entitled to an interest in possession in the land".[48] Thus beneficiaries under a trust of land have a right to be consulted if the trustees propose to deal with the land as permitted by the 1996 Act. This applies to trusts that were created or came into existence *after* January 1997, when TLATA 1996 came into force. This right of consultation can be expressly excluded in the instrument setting up the co-ownership trust, e.g. a conveyance.[49] Only beneficiaries entitled to an interest *in possession* are required to be consulted. Thus, if land is left in trust to A for life, remainder to B, B does not have a right to the immediate enjoyment of the land (an interest *in possession*). Thus, he does not have the right to be consulted if the trustees intend to deal with the land. However, A does. The right of consultation only applies where the beneficiaries are of full age.

> Returning to our example with the vets, Adam, Brian and Cully are holding Herriot House for themselves and David and Eric beneficially. They are all beneficially entitled to an interest in possession and are of full age. Consequently if Adam, Brian and Cully were considering dealing with the land in some way, they must consult with David and Eric before doing so. Otherwise, if the transaction damages the value of the property or the interests of David and Eric, the latter two may sue Adam Brian and Cully for breach of trust.

However, the trustees are only under an obligation to consult the beneficiaries *as far as is practicable*. "What is practicable depends upon the circumstances of the trust and the beneficiaries."[50] If a beneficiary is not contactable with reasonable effort, it might be that the trustees are not required to consult him.[51] For example, if David was travelling and it was not easy to contact him, the trustees may not be required to consult him. However, this does engender an amount of uncertainty in the law.

---

48   TLATA 1996 s.11.
49   s.11(2)(a).
50   J.MacKenzie, A.Walker, P.Walton, *A Guide to the Trusts of Land and Appointment of Trustees Act 1996*, p.49. For criticism of these qualified provisions and their effect see R.Smith, *Plural Ownership*, pp.148–152.
51   See for example Smith, *Plural Ownership*, p.150.

Once the trustees have consulted with relevant beneficiaries they must give effect to their wishes.[52] If there is a number of beneficiaries and there is not one consistent view about what the trustees should do with the property, the trustees must give effect to the wishes "of the majority (according to the value of their combined interests)".[53] Consequently, the consultation process will become useless in resolving a dispute between co-owners where there are only two holding on trust for each other in equal shares.[54] Here a court application with be necessary.[55] This will encompass many co-ownership situations with spouses and couples disputing over whether and when to sell the matrimonial home.

The trustees are only required to give effect to the wishes of the beneficiaries "so far as consistent with the general interest of the trust".[56]

> If Adam and Brian were the trustees of Herriot House, holding for themselves and Cully, David and Eric in equity, and they wished to take out a loan to update the surgery at Herriot House and in return to grant a mortgage over the property to the bank, they would need to consult with Cully, David and Eric.
>
> Let's say that all three objected to the mortgage. The vet's practice was not sufficiently profitable to support the loan repayments and the bank was demanding a high rate of interest. In addition to this the refurbishments were not necessary at this time. Here, if Adam and Brian still went ahead with the mortgage it is strongly arguable that it is not in the general interests of the trust. Thus, as they have not given effect to the wishes of the majority, they will be in breach of trust.

(8) The position of purchasers vis-à-vis the trust beneficiaries: overreaching

Beneficial interests under a trust are "property rights" that are capable of binding all future purchasers and mortgage lenders. The statutory overreaching provisions laid down in s.2 of the Law of Property Act 1925 state that a purchaser of a legal estate in land, which includes a mortgage lender, shall not be concerned with the equitable interests under a trust of land. The exact wording states that "[a] conveyance to a purchaser of a legal estate in land shall *overreach* [an] equitable interest".[57] Although not all equitable interests can be overreached, equitable interests under a trust *can be*.[58]

---

52   s.11(1)(b).
53   s.11(1)(b).
54   Smith, *Plural Ownership*, p.151.
55   Under s.14 (see below).
56   s.11(1)(b).
57   Emphasis mine.
58   See the chapters on Land Transfer Law.

As we see in the chapters on Land Transfer Law, s.2 is not just a helpful occasional little provision tucked away in the Law of Property Act 1925; it is a cornerstone of the 1925 scheme for making land subject to co-ownership easier to transfer to a purchaser.[59]

> *The 1925 draftsman's scheme*
> **Section 1: *Estates and Interests*:**
> **Limit the number of legal estates and interests that bind a purchaser automatically; Make all other interests equitable only.**
>
> **Section 34–36: *Co-ownership provisions*:**
> **Vest the legal estate in a small number of persons capable of dealing with it.**
>
> **Section 2: *Overreaching*:**
> **And then lay down a system that made it very easy for the persons holding the legal estate to convey it to purchasers free from the equitable interests under the trust.**

The statutory condition for overreaching is that the purchase money or mortgage advance must be paid to two or more trustees or a trust corporation.[60] Even though the equitable interest is then no longer enforceable against the land in the hands of the purchaser/mortgage lender, the beneficiaries can claim their interests out of the purchase money/mortgage advance in the hands of the trustees.[61]

It is very clear that when everything is "properly done" by the trustees a purchaser or mortgage lender need not be concerned with the property rights of the beneficiaries. His interest will take priority. But even where the purchaser pays the purchase money to two trustees, does overreaching "work" when everything is *not* properly done? What if the trustees deal with the land in a way that is beyond their powers entirely, an *ultra vires* disposition? Or what if they exercise their powers improperly? Indeed, s.6(6) of TLATA 1996 provides that "[t]he powers conferred by this section shall not be exercised in contravention of . . . any rule of law or equity". Section 6(5) provides that the trustees, when exercising their powers, must "have regard to the rights of the beneficiaries". Let's say that the trustees have not consulted the beneficiaries in accordance with their s.11 duty or have executed a mortgage preferring their own interests over those of the beneficiaries, thus disregarding the interests of the beneficiaries.

---

59   Harpum, *Overreaching, Trustees' Powers and Reform of the 1925 Legislation* [1990] C.L.J. 277; J.S. Anderson, *Lawyers and the Making of English Land Law 1832–1940*, two very helpful works that identify this scheme.

60   Law of Property Act 1925 ss.2 and 27.

61   See for example, B. Cherry, *The New Property Acts – Lectures to the Law Society* (1926). If these "capital money requirements" are not met, the beneficial interests remain capable of binding a purchaser or mortgage lender. The rules which then determine whether beneficial interests will bind a purchaser depend on whether title to the land is registered.

Whether the transaction is *ultra vires* or simply improper, our question is whether that transaction will overreach the interests of the beneficiaries or whether the beneficiaries can enforce their property rights against the innocent purchaser or lender. If overreaching does not take place this means that a mortgagee may not be able to enforce his security by taking possession of the house. In the case of a sale, the purchaser may have to concede that the beneficiaries have a prior right to a share in the land. Clearly this is an important question.

There is substantial support for the proposition that a conveyance beyond the powers of trustees will not overreach the beneficial interests.[62] So far so good. But if this is true a further question arises: Does the contravention of a consultation requirement or trustees' breach of ss.6(5) and 6(6) *mean that the disposition is beyond the trustees' powers, i.e. ultra vires?* It could readily be seen as an "internal matter" only. One for which the beneficiaries can sue the trustees for breach of trust but which would not affect the purchaser.[63]

(a) Unregistered title
Where title to the land is unregistered, s.16 of the Trusts of Land and Appointment of Trustees Act 1996 introduces considerable purchaser protection, whether necessary or not. Section 16(1) provides that a purchaser or mortgage lender can take free from the interests of the beneficiaries even if the trustees have not complied with s.6(5). The same is true of contraventions of s.6(6), unless the purchaser has actual notice of the trustees' misconduct. Where the trustees powers have been limited under s.8 "the limitation does not invalidate any conveyance by the trustees to a purchaser who has no actual notice of the limitation".[64]

(b) Registered title
Registered land was left out of this protection, probably because its system of purchaser protection is much more comprehensive and designed in such a way that the default position is that the purchaser takes free. So unless there is an entry on the register that states that consents, consultation, or compliance with the ss.6(5) and 6(6) is necessary then the purchaser will take free.[65] This is in pursuance of a policy to keep trusts off the face of the land register.[66] Ferris and Battersby argue against this, stating that the omission of registered land from the protection offered purchasers under TLATA 1996 s.16 was significant. Any disposition that contravenes the consultation requirement or ss.6(5) or 6(6) is *ultra vires* and therefore that such a disposition (if the land is registered) will *not* overreach the interests of the beneficiaries.[67] The point does not

---

62 C.Harpum, "Overreaching, Trustees' Powers and Reform of the 1925 Legislation" [1990] C.L.J. 277 and judicial support: *State Bank of India v Sood* [1997] Ch. 276; for a counter-argument N.Jackson, "Overreaching and the Rationale of the Law of Property Act 1925" Nottingham Law Journal (Winter 2006); N.Jackson, "Overreaching and Unauthorised Dispositions of Registered Land" [2007] Conv. 120. For judicial support that an *ultra vires* disposition *will* have overreaching effect see *National Westminster Bank v Malhan* [2004] EWHC Civ 847.

63 See the argument advanced by M.Thompson, *Modern Land Law*, 4th edn (Oxford University Press, 2009), pp.274–276.

64 TLATA 1996 s.16(3)(b).

65 The relevant entry would be by way of a "restriction".

66 As we see in Chapter 8.

67 G.Ferris and G.Battersby [1998] Conv. 168; for a counter-argument N.Jackson [2007] Conv. 120.

have conclusive authority. As if to stamp out any further possibility of this ultra vires argument arising in the future, s.26 of the Land Registration Act 2002 provides that any limitation that may otherwise affect the validity of the disposition—will not affect a purchaser.[68] The effect of this provision is that *any* disposition, whether beyond the trustees powers or simply improper, will not affect the purchaser or mortgagee on the other end of the transaction.

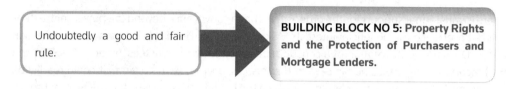

Undoubtedly a good and fair rule.

BUILDING BLOCK NO 5: Property Rights and the Protection of Purchasers and Mortgage Lenders.

B. RIGHTS OF THE BENEFICIARIES

(1) A right of occupation

> **Trusts of Land and Appointment of Trustees Act 1996 s.12: The Right to Occupy**
> "12(1) A beneficiary who is beneficially entitled to an interest in possession in land subject to a trust of land is entitled by reason of his interest to occupy the land at any time if at that time-
> (a) the purposes of the trust include making the land available for his occupation . . . or
> (b) the land is held by the trustees so as to be so available.
> (2) Subsection (1) does not confer on a beneficiary a right to occupy land if it is either unavailable or unsuitable for occupation by him."

Thus a trust beneficiary with an interest in possession has a right to occupy the property.[69] At the time at which the beneficiary wishes to occupy the land the purpose of the trust must include allowing him to occupy, or at least the land must be available for this purpose. Where property is purchased as a family home the purpose will be to occupy the house.[70] By contrast, a property purchased solely for commercial purposes, or for its rental income, or was left in a will in order to be sold and the proceeds divided,[71] may exclude the s.12 right of occupation.

---

68   Unless the limitation is first registered as a "restriction" against the title. Again the meaning of "purchaser" is very broad and includes, amongst other things, a mortgage lender.
69   Under the old law the beneficiary under the old-style "trust for sale" had a right to occupy the land if this was the purpose of acquiring the house: *Bull v Bull* [1955] 1 Q.B. 234: Thompson, *Modern Land Law*, pp.353–4.
70   See for example, *Bull v Bull* [1955] 1 Q.B. 234 and *Williams & Glyn's Bank Ltd v Boland* [1981] A.C. 487.
71   *Barclay v Barclay* [1970] 2 Q.B. 677.

If the land is either unavailable or unsuitable for occupation then the beneficiary has no right of occupation under s.12. The courts have taken a common sense approach and stated that "'suitability' for this purpose must involve a consideration not only of the general nature and physical characteristics of the particular property but also a consideration of the personal characteristics, circumstances and requirements of the particular beneficiary".[72]

(a) Regulation and restriction of the section 12 right of occupation

As you remember from when we studied the nature of co-ownership, co-owners cannot exclude each other from possession of the land. However, there are many situations in which trustees will need to regulate the occupation of co-owned property. Under s.13(1) of the Trusts of Land and Appointment of Trustees Act 1996 "[w]here two or more beneficiaries are . . . entitled under section 12 to occupy land, the trustees of land may exclude or restrict the entitlement of any one or more (but not all) of them".

> Returning to our example with the vets, let's say that Herriot House comprises a surgery on the ground floor and living accommodation for two people on the first floor. It is more convenient for Adam and Brian to live on the premises because the others already have accommodation nearby. Thus, Adam and Brian can effectively exclude the others (Cully, David and Eric) from occupying the living accommodation at Herriot House.

As a general principle of trusts law trustees must act unanimously, and this applies to the exercise of their s.13 power to exclude or restrict rights of occupation. Thus, if one of the trustees does not agree to the exclusion, a court application will be necessary under s.14.[73]

Trustees cannot exclude all beneficiaries at once, but the division of premises into two parts to be occupied exclusively by one co-owner in each part was held to be acceptable in *Rodway v Landy*.[74] The property in question was a doctor's surgery and both co-owners were doctors. Physically partitioning the surgery meant that each doctor was excluded from the other doctor's section of the surgery. The court held that this was a valid exercise of the s.13 power.

(b) Duty to act reasonably

In exercising this power to exclude or restrict the occupation of one or more beneficiaries, trustees must act reasonably. They cannot unreasonably exclude any beneficiary or restrict any beneficiary's right to occupy to an unreasonable extent.[75] The criteria to which the trustees must

---

72 *Chan v Leung* [2003] 1 F.L.R. 23, per Jonathan Parker L.J.
73 See below.
74 [2001] EWCA Civ 471.
75 TLATA 1996 s.13(2).

have regard when they are considering exercising their powers to exclude or restrict the right to occupy include "(a) the intentions of the person or persons (if any) who created the trust, (b) the purposes for which the land is held, and (c) the circumstances and wishes of each of the beneficiaries who is . . . entitled to occupy the land under section 12".[76]

> When our vets initially purchased the property it comprised only of a vet's surgery. The co-owners' intentions on setting up the co-ownership trust were to use the land purely for business purposes. A year later and the vets restructure the accommodation so as to provide living space on the first floor. Thus, Adam and Brian can restrict the occupation of Cully, David and Eric and allow Adam and Brian to occupy the first floor. Is this a reasonable exercise of their powers under s.13?

Criterion (a) concentrates on the vets' intentions when the co-ownership was set up, so will not take account of a change of purpose and use of the property. On the other hand (b) will and it is likely that having regard to the fact that the purpose of the vets' co-ownership now includes the provision of limited living space the trustees' regulation of the occupation of Herriot House is likely to be considered reasonable. The trustees clearly should have regard to factors such as the size and nature of the premises.

In regulating the occupation of trust property the trustees must also have regard to the "the circumstances and wishes of each of the beneficiaries who is . . . entitled to occupy". For example, a small house, suitable for the occupation of two, is left on trust to four adult siblings in a will. Two of them are married and have independent means and each wish to use the house as a matrimonial home. The other two are studying at university nearby, have limited means, and wish to occupy the house. The trustees allow the two students to occupy the house and exclude the two married ones. This is clearly reasonable considering all the beneficiaries' circumstances.[77]

(c) Where the relevant beneficiary is already in occupation

Trustees may not prevent a beneficiary from occupying the property if he is already in occupation or restrict his occupation in such a way that is likely to result in that person ceasing to occupy the land, unless the trustees obtain either that beneficiary's consent or court approval.[78] Thus, the s.13 power is unlikely to be applicable in cases where a marriage or cohabitation has broken down, as both partners will already be living in the property. Furthermore, where both partners are trustees,

---

76   TLATA 1996 s.13(4).
77   Although the excluded beneficiaries may apply to the court under s.14 for an order of sale of the house, for which the courts will consider similar factors. See below.
78   TLATA 1996 s.13(7).

as is often the case, they are unlikely to agree to the exclusion or restriction of the occupation of one of them. Thus, they will need to make a court application to resolve the dispute.[79]

(d) Trustees may impose reasonable conditions on occupying beneficiaries

Section 13(3) provides that "[t]he trustees of land may from time to time impose reasonable conditions on any beneficiary in relation to his occupation of land by reason of his entitlement under section 12". Under s.13(5) this includes "conditions requiring him . . . to pay any outgoings or expenses in respect of the land, or . . . to assume any other obligation in relation to the land or to any activity which is or is proposed to be conducted there". An occupying beneficiary may be required to "make payments by way of compensation to the beneficiary whose entitlement has been excluded or restricted".[80] He may also be required to "forgo any payment or other benefit to which he would otherwise be entitled under the trust so as to benefit that beneficiary".[81]

The old law was unclear as to when an occupying beneficiary could be required to pay the other compensation.[82] Thus, s.13(6)

> "is likely to be useful in domestic arrangements where a relationship ends but in which a parent and children must remain in the premises. It may assist advisers in reaching an appropriate settlement of property disputes".[83]

This is one of the trustees' functions so it can be reviewed by the court under s.14.[84] This will be particularly relevant in the situation of the breakdown of a marriage or co-habitation where the house in not sold immediately and where only one partner remains in occupation. Although it is unlikely that both will agree on the payment of an occupational rent by the occupying partner to the excluded partner, the court can impose such a requirement. In *Stack v Dowden*[85] not surprisingly, the former co-habitants, who were the co-trustees, could not agree as to the payment of an occupational rent. In determining the outcome, the courts will have regard to the criteria in s.15.[86]

---

79   For further detail see Jackson, Pearce and Stevens, *Land Law*, 4th edn (London: Sweet & Maxwell, 2008), Ch.13.

80   TLATA 1996 s.13(6)(a).

81   s.13(6)(b).

82   *Dennis v McDonald* [1982] Fam. 63; also *Chhokar v Chhokar* [1984] F.L.R. 313.

83   J.MacKenzie, A.Walker, P.Walton, *A Guide to the Trusts of Land and Appointment of Trustees Act 1996*, p.59.

84   See *Stack v Dowden* [2007] UKHL 17; *Murphy v Gooch* [2007] EWCA Civ 603.

85   [2007] UKHL 17.

86   *Stack v Dowden* [2007] UKHL 17; *Murphy v Gooch* [2007] EWCA Civ 603; also, Thompson, *Modern Land Law*, p.360–1. We will consider dispute resolution and the s.15 criteria immediately below.

3 How TLATA 1996 resolves disputes between co-owners

A. DISPUTE RESOLUTION

Co-owners may fall out and one may want the property sold; the other may wish to remain in occupation. There may be a creditor of one of the co-owners involved, who wants the property sold in order to pay off that co-owner's debts. The different voices of the co-owners want different things. The law must determine *whose voice shall prevail*.[87] The dispute resolution mechanism under the Law of Property Act 1925[88] was replaced by ss.14 and 15 of the Trusts of Land and Appointment of Trustees Act 1996.

> **Herriot House—the story so far**
> Adam, Brian, Cully, David and Eric together bought Herriot House in order to run a veterinary practice. It was conveyed to Adam, Brian and Cully to hold for themselves and David and Eric in equity. Since the five vets bought the house and started the practice, Cully and David wish to go and live in Australia together. They want Herriot House sold and the proceeds distributed between the co-owners. This will enable them to start their new life. However, Adam, Brian and Eric want to carry on running their veterinary practice at Herriot House. So they do not wish the property to be sold. The parties have seriously fallen out and are getting nowhere with negotiations and compromise. Deadlock—how can their dispute be resolved?

(1) The powers of the court

The court has wide powers to decide what is to happen to the property. Under s.14 the court can make any order it thinks fit in relation "to the exercise by the trustees of any of their functions (including an order relieving them of any obligation to obtain the consent of, or to consult, any person in connection with the exercise of any of their functions)".[89] Basically therefore, anything the trustees have power to do with the property, the court can review. For instance, a decision to sell, mortgage or lease the land is challengeable under s.14, as is the trustees' decision not to sell the trust property.[90] A dispute about the exclusion or restriction of one of the co-owners can be resolved by the court, as can the question of the payment of occupational rent. As noted above this is particularly useful in situations where a cohabitation has broken up and one of the co-owners has left. The court can require the beneficiary in occupation to pay an occupational rent.[91] The court can make an order for partition of the land because this is one of the trustees'

---

87   *Re Buchanan-Wollaston's Conveyance* [1939] Ch. 738, p.747 per Sir Wilfrid Greene M.R.
88   s.30.
89   TLATA 1996 s.14(2)(a).
90   Smith, *Plural Ownership*, p.149, citing the Law Commission report behind TLATA 1996: Law Com. No.181, para.12.6.
91   *Stack v Dowden* [2007] UKHL 17; *Murphy v Gooch* [2007] EWCA Civ 603.

powers.[92] If a proposed transaction with the land requires consent the court has power to dispense with this.[93] The same applies with the trustees' obligation to consult with the beneficiaries under s.11. Thus, anything the trustees have power to do, can be challenged by an interested party under s.14 and the court can order accordingly. In *Hopper v Hopper*[94] the court could not make an order for compulsory purchase of a beneficiary's interest because the trustees have no such power. The court cannot under s.14 "make any order as to the appointment or removal of trustees".[95]

Under this section a person may also apply to the court for a declaration as to the nature or extent of his or her interest in the property.[96] For example, a person who has made a contribution to the purchase of the home may apply to the court to determine firstly whether they have an interest in the house and secondly, the extent of that interest. Thus, a cohabitee wishing to establish an interest in the home under a common intention constructive trust will make the initial application to the court under s.14.[97]

(2) Who may make an application to the court under section 14?

Section 14(1) provides that "any person who is a trustee of land or has an interest in property subject to a trust of land may make an application to court for an order" in respect of trust property. This includes a mortgagee or chargee, i.e. a secured creditor of any beneficiary.[98] Also, a creditor can make an application for sale of co-owned property where one of the co-owners has incurred a debt and the creditor obtains a "charging order" over his beneficial interest in the property.[99]

> So any of our five vets may apply to the court under s.14 and the court has a wide discretion to make any order in relation to Herriot House. It may order sale so that Cully and David can get their money in order to go to Australia. It may decline to make any order and prevent the land from being sold, so that Adam, Brian and Eric can carry on running the practice. If it declines sale and Cully and David no longer occupy the house or run the practice, the court might order compensation to be paid to them by the others who remain in occupation.

(3) How will the court determine what to do with co-owned property?

How does the court decide how to exercise its discretion in what should be done with co-owned property? How will the court decide the future of Herriot House? In any application under s.14, the court must have regard to the matters contained in s.15.

---

92   *Atkinson v Atkinson* June 30, 2010, unreported (Westlaw).
93   *Atkinson v Atkinson* above.
94   [2008] EWHC 228.
95   TLATA 1996 s.14(3).
96   TLATA 1996 s.14(2)(b).
97   See for example *Stack v Dowden* [2007] UKHL 17.
98   *Mortgage Corporation v Shaire* [2001] Ch. 743.
99   *Lloyds Bank Plc v Byrne and Byrne* [1993] 1 F.L.R. 369.

> **Section 15 Matters relevant in determining applications**
> "(1) The matters to which the court is to have regard in determining an application for an order under section 14 include–
>   (a)   the intentions of the person(s) (if any) who created the trust,
>   (b)   the purposes for which the property subject to the trust is held,
>   (c)   the welfare of any minor who occupies or might reasonably be expected to occupy any land subject to the trust as his home, and
>   (d)   the interests of any secured creditor of any beneficiary . .
> (3) In the case of any other application, other than one relating to the [section 13 power to exclude or restrict the right to occupy] . . . the matters to which the court is to have regard also include the circumstances and wishes of any beneficiaries of full age and entitled to an interest in possession in property subject to the trust or (in case of dispute) of the majority (according to the value of their combined interests)."

Parliament's intention behind the s.15 factors under the Trusts of Land and Appointment of Trustees Act 1996 was to provide guidelines on how to resolve disputes regarding co-owned property. Under the old dispute resolution mechanism, s.30 of the Law of Property Act 1925, case law had provided such guidance. The Law Commission report prior to the enactment of the Trusts of Land and Appointment of Trustees Act 1996 stated that one of the purposes of s.15 was to put this law "on a statutory footing".[100] Thus, much of the case law prior to 1996 on dispute resolution remains relevant.

(4) Cases involving bankruptcy

Where one of the co-owners is bankrupt his property vests in the trustee in bankruptcy. This includes the bankrupt's share of co-owned property, i.e. his beneficial share. Thus, in such cases a trustee in bankruptcy will usually apply to the court under s.14 for a sale of the property, in order that the proceeds of the bankrupt's share can be used to pay off his creditors. In such cases of bankruptcy the s.15 criteria do not apply to determine whether the court will order sale of the property.[101] Instead the courts must consider the criteria contained in s.335A of the Insolvency Act 1986. We will consider this law in a section below.

(5) A "balancing exercise" weighing all section 15 (and other) factors

In most of these cases there is more than one of these criteria that is relevant. In *MIA Holman v Howes*[102] it was reasoned that there is not one of these factors that has automatic priority. The courts should conduct a balancing exercise considering all factors that weigh against and

---

100   Law Commission Report No. 181, *Transfer of Land: Trusts of Land* (1989), para. 12.9; also J.MacKenzie, A.Walker, P.Walton, *A Guide to the Trusts of Land and Appointment of Trustees Act 1996* (1998); B.McFarlane, N.Hopkins, S.Nield, *Land Law Text, Cases and Materials* (Oxford University Press, 2009), p.633.
101   TLATA 1996 s.15(4); Insolvency Act 1986 s.335A.
102   [2005] EWHC 2824 (Ch), affirmed on appeal [2007] Fam. Law 987.

in favour of sale, making an order accordingly.[103] We see that the courts are to consider factors (a)–(d) above, but they must also have regard to "the circumstances and wishes of any beneficiaries of full age and entitled to an interest in possession in property subject to the trust".[104] For example, in *Edwards v Lloyds TSB Bank Plc*[105] Park J. considered the wishes of the co-owner remaining in occupation after her husband had left the house. These and other factors were weighed against a secured creditor of the husband and the court postponed sale for five years.

It is important to note that the factors contained in s.15 are not exclusive of other considerations.[106] Other factors may also be relevant, such as the health of one of the beneficiaries.[107] In *Bank of Ireland Home Mortgages Ltd v Bell*[108] the ill-health of an occupying beneficiary was considered to be a reason for a short postponement of sale rather than as grounds for refusing it, primarily because the factors in favour of sale were so overwhelming.

> Cully and David want Herriot House to be sold so that they can go to Australia. Adam, Brian and Eric want to continue to occupy the house and run the vet's practice. Referring to s.15(1)(a) and (b), the original purpose of buying Herriot House was indeed to run the practice. So they will argue that this factor should prevail and premises should not be sold because that purpose is still capable of being carried out. Referring to s.15(3), if all of our vets have the same size interests, Adam, Brian and Eric's wishes will carry greater weight over Cully and David's. Again this would weigh in favour of non-sale. However, this is only one factor to consider: *MIA Holman v Howes* [2005] EWHC 2824.

(6) Critical Thinking: understanding how judges approach a section 14 application

LECTURER: We are going to look at a s.14 application for sale of a house. Here we will see how the judge approached the question of "whose voice should prevail".

THE FACTS: In *MIA Holman v Howes*[109] a husband and wife were estranged and were attempting reconciliation. They purchased a house together, using in the main the wife's savings. The purpose of their buying the house was to provide a home and security for the wife should their attempt at reconciliation fail. The husband gave his wife assurances that he would not seek a sale of the house.[110] The reconciliation failed. The wife wished to remain in occupation and the husband wanted a sale.

---

103   *MIA Holman v Howes* [2005] EWHC 2824 (Ch).
104   TLATA 1996 s.15(3).
105   [2004] EWHC 1745; [2005] 1 F.C.R. 139.
106   *Edwards v Lloyds TSB Bank Plc* [2004] EWHC 1745; [2005] 1 F.C.R. 139, per Park J.
107   R.Smith, *Plural Ownership*, p.159.
108   [2001] 2 F.L.R. 809, CA, per Peter Gibson L.J.
109   [2005] EWHC 2824 (Ch), affirmed on appeal [2007] EWCA Civ 877.
110   para.56.

CONCLUSION: The judge at first instance refused to order sale, and this was affirmed by the Court of Appeal. However, to understand the balancing exercise, we need to know the reasoning of the judge:

THE REASONING: MR ALAN STEINFELD QC: "The [husband] seeks an immediate sale of the property . . . The claimant is not prepared to agree to such sale but wishes, instead, to remain living at the property. Again I do not find this surprising. The claimant has lived at the property since it was purchased in 1979 and it would plainly be a hardship to her if she was forced to vacate it.

The question of whether or not the Court should direct the sale of land held on trust is now governed by sections 14 and 15 of the 1996 Act, which altered the previous law, see *Mortgage Corporation v Shaire* [2001] Ch 743, *per* Neuberger J. As he put it there:

> '. . . section 15 has changed the law. As a result of section 15, the court has greater flexibility than heretofore, as to how it exercises its jurisdiction on an application for an order for sale on facts such as those in *In re Citro* and *Lloyds Bank plc v Byrne & Byrne*. There are certain factors which must be taken into account: see section 15(1) and, subject to the next point, section 15(3). There may be other factors in a particular case which the court can, indeed should, take into account. Once the relevant factors to be taken into account have been identified it is a matter for the court as to what weight to give to each factor in a particular case.'"

LECTURER: So here we can see that the judge is outlining the "balancing exercise" to be undertaken in s.15.

STUDENT: The judge mentions two cases, having stated that the court now has greater flexibility than before. What does this mean?

LECTURER: The two cases concerned secured creditors of one of the co-owners and held that their interests and wishes (for sale) would have virtually automatic priority over any family wishing to remain in occupation. We will consider cases on this later. As you know *Holman v Howes* was a dispute between a husband and wife, there was no creditor involved. The judge was simply pointing out that the court has flexibility to weigh the differing interests and order the outcome that the judge thinks fit in that case.

MR ALAN STEINFELD QC CONTINUES: "Under section 14(2) on an application for an order under that section, which includes an order relating to the exercise by the trustees of any of their functions (and as such would therefore include an order relating to the trustees' power of sale) the court may make any such order as it thinks fit. Under section 15(1) and (3) various matters are set out to which the court is to have regard in determining an application for order under section 14.

It seems to me that for present purposes I can deal with (a) and (b) together. It is plain on the evidence that the primary intention for which the property was purchased was to provide a home for the parties and their daughter with the hope that the parties would be reconciled and would remarry. It was, however, recognised by both parties . . . that it was quite possible that the relationship would not be restored. The defendant was concerned to encourage the claimant to a large extent against her inclination to give it a try . . .

But clearly assurances of some kind were given to the [wife] . . . . they must have been assurances that come what may [she] was to be entitled to stay in the property for so long as she wished. The witnesses all talk about the defendant having assured the claimant that, if the reconciliation did not work out and he left the property, he would not make any "claim" on it . . . in the sense of seeking to have the property sold without the [wife's] consent. In other words the [wife] was indeed to be secure in the property for so long as she wished . . .

I . . . hold that for the purpose of section 15(1)(b) the purpose for which the property is held is to provide a home for the claimant for so long as she desires it."

LECTURER: Under s.15(1)(a) the judge is required to consider "the intentions of the person(s) (if any) who created the trust" and s.15(1)(b) the purposes for which the property subject to the trust is held". Here the husband and wife bought the house together and thus set up the statutory co-ownership trust. Their purpose in doing so was to provide security for the wife should the reconciliation fail. This is the same as s.15(1)(b) so there was no need to consider them separately. Can you think of any circumstances in which a judge might need to give separate consideration to (a) and (b)?

STUDENT: It might be that a father has left property to his three adult daughters in his will with the intention that they should live together "in family harmony". These intentions will be considered under s.15(1)(a). If, ten years later, two of them are married and living elsewhere and only one of them is continuing in occupation, the purposes for holding the property have changed.

LECTURER: Good. And s.15(1)(b) will give the judge greater flexibility to consider the *current* purposes for which the property is held. Can you say that the law considered so far is good or bad fair or unfair using any of our Building Blocks?

STUDENT: I would say that the requirement for the judge to consider the purposes for which the property was bought in the first place, and the purpose for which it is currently used, before any order is made, gives due weight to the co-owners' intentions. Thus it is good and fair on BUILDING BLOCK NO 7.

BUILDING BLOCK NO 7: Land Law is "Facilitative" and should give effect to the parties' intentions or reasonable expectations

If a rule of law supports or undermines one of the essential principles in our Building Blocks then we can legitimately say that the rule is good or bad accordingly. Peter Birks argues that giving effect to what people want to achieve through ownership of land is one of the important functions of Land Law: Land Law is "facilitative": "Before we begin: Five keys to land law" in *Land Law Themes and Perspectives*, Ch.18, p.457.

As this is one of the primary *aims and purposes* of Land Law the rules should enable people to acquire land and to achieve what they intend to achieve by owning the land.

MR ALAN STEINFELD QC CONTINUES: "[U]nder section 15(3) I must also have regard to the 'circumstances and wishes' of each of the beneficiaries who is entitled to an interest in possession in the relevant property. That would include the [husband] himself. The defendant says he wishes the land to be sold in order to pay off his liabilities, in particular his liabilities to the Inland Revenue . . . However, he conceded in his evidence that it is not essential for the property to be sold for this purpose. He has sufficient assets of his own . . . His evidence was essentially that he would like, if possible, to have additional money to support himself in his retirement.

Weighing up the factors, as I am enjoined by section 15 to do, it seems to me that it would not be right to order an immediate sale of the property . . . I do not see why given the assurances that in my judgment she in substance received at the time when the property was purchased that she would not be evicted from the property save with her consent, the court should so direct.

As regards the desire of the defendant to realise his interest in the property, delaying the sale of the property obviously means that he will be unable by a sale to realise his interest and so pay off his debts and leave himself with a lump sum for his retirement. On the other hand he does have other property . . . which I assume has substantially increased in value since its purchase and which at the moment he holds purely as an investment property. Furthermore he has inherited substantial sums from his father's estate. He is entitled to a . . . pension, appears to be living in rent free accommodation and when he retired he received a lump sum payment in respect of his pension.

Accordingly pursuant to the . . . application under section 14 of the 1996 Act . . . I direct that the property should not for the time being be sold without the consent of the claimant . . . I say 'for the time being' because it is conceivable that circumstances could arise in the future which would make the sale of the property more compelling than it appears to me at the moment."

LECTURER: So ultimately the judge refused to order sale. He refused because the husband had assured the wife that her security would be protected and that he would not press for a sale. Can you say whether the s.14 and 15 law protects or undermines any of our Building Blocks?

STUDENT: Where needed, as was the case in *Holman v Howes*, it gives the judge the ability to safeguard a person's residential security. On the basis of BUILDING BLOCK NO 1: Residential Security, this is good law.[111]

BUILDING BLOCK NO 1: Residential Security

We can legitimately say that where the rules operate in the context of owner occupation of property, they are good and fair if they give effective protection to people's residential security. Land Law now operates in the context of owner occupation and its rules should give effect to the purposes for which people buy and use houses. The rules of Land Law do not exist in a vacuum.

---

111   For the full text of our Building Blocks and instructions on how to use them to build an argument see Chapter 1.

LECTURER: The husband in this case wanted the house sold in order that he could pay off some debts, in particular one to the Inland Revenue, and have a lump sum for his retirement. The judge did not seem to think that this weighed very strongly, i.e. he did not seem willing to order sale on the strength of it. Why not?

STUDENT: Well, he had substantial additional property and money, e.g. his inheritance and his pension, and appeared therefore to have little need to realise his share in the house.

LECTURER: Indeed. Because of conflicting interests and purposes connected with human beings' ownership of land, it must be recognised that land is not always a fluid investment.[112]

> Ormrod L.J. in *Browne v Pritchard* [1975] 1 W.L.R. 1366 said that buying a share in the home "is the least liquid investment that one can possibly make".

About *Browne v Pritchard*, Smith observes that "It seems odd if one of the parties enjoys the luxury of the former family home, whilst the other, deprived of capital resources, has to accept inferior accommodation".[113] What do you think about this?

STUDENT: It will often be the case that co-owners have a substantial amount of money tied up in the house. If a relationship has broken down and one party cannot live in the house, that person's money is effectively tied up. This might be a real hardship for some co-owners.

LECTURER: Remember that under s.13 of TLATA 1996 the trustee co-owners can require compensation to be paid to co-owners excluded from occupation. As this is a function of the trustees the court can order compensation to be paid.

STUDENT: But this is unlikely to be a capital sum that the co-owner has invested in the house. Thus, they may not be able to buy another house. However, I still think that Smith's comment is unduly simplistic remark given the number of complex factors at work here. These cases are an unfortunate consequence of serial marriage and cohabitation taking place in the context of owner-occupation. Residential security of more vulnerable parties and the fact that the home is often an expression and source of personal identity are both powerful psychological needs of the person seeking to remain in the house.

LECTURER: So this "weighing exercise" required by s.15 gives effect to the needs of society, perhaps its more vulnerable members. It does not simply treat land as a commercial commodity.

STUDENT: I would use BUILDING BLOCKS NO 1 and 3 as evidence for my argument that the law as it was applied in *Holman v Howes* and *Browne v Pritchard* is good in this respect.

BUILDING BLOCK NO 3: Property and Identity
Rules are good if they take proper account of the fact that people may gain a sense of value and worth from ownership of their homes.

---

112   Smith, *Plural Ownership*, p.164. The quotation from *Browne v Pritchard* [1975] 1 W.L.R. 1366 is from here.
113   *Plural Ownership*, p.164.

B. SECTION 15 FACTORS

So we have seen above that before making an order under s.14 in relation to co-owned property the court will weigh in the balance the s.15 criteria. We will now consider each of these factors in turn.

(1) The intentions of the person who created the trust

In *Re Buchanan-Wollaston's Conveyance*[114] four neighbouring house owners, who lived on the coast, jointly purchased a strip of land in front of their houses. They agreed by contract in the conveyance that the purpose of their purchase was to stop the land from being built upon. They agreed that they would all have to be unanimous if the land were to be sold. One of the co-owners wanted to sell the land and applied to the court for an order accordingly.[115] The court refused to order sale because it went against the co-owners' original intentions as expressed in the contract.

It is important to realise however that it is not necessary for the co-owners' intentions to be put into a contract. Under s.15(1)(a) the court will attempt to ascertain what those intentions were when the co-ownership was set up, no formal agreement is necessary.

(2) The purposes for which the property is held[116]

The courts will also consider the purpose for which the property is held, for example, the provision of a matrimonial home or a home for children, giving a home to an elderly parent. Although there is some overlap here with (a) above, e.g. *Re-Buchanan-Wollaston's Conveyance* could be considered on either ground, they may be considered as separate grounds where the purpose of the co-ownership has changed from that operating at the start. In many cases, the intentions of the persons setting up the co-ownership trust and the purposes for which the land is held will be the same.

As we have seen in *MIA Holman v Howes*[117] the court refused sale of a house owned jointly by a husband and wife on the ground that the purpose of a house purchase was to provide a wife with residential security should an attempted reconciliation fail. Also in *Jones (A.E.) v Jones (F.W.)*[118] a father and son purchased a house, the father providing the larger part of the purchase price. The purpose was to provide the son with a house to live in. The father died and the son's step-mother, who had inherited the father's interest, wanted the house sold. Sale was not ordered because it would defeat the purpose of providing the son with a home for life.[119]

---

114   [1939] Ch 738.
115   The case was decided under the old dispute resolution provision: Law of Property Act 1925 s.30.
116   This search for the purpose of the trust was created by the courts under the old dispute resolution provision, s.30 of the Law of Property Act 1925. At this point trustees were under a duty to sell the land. Thus, when disputes arose as to whether co-owned houses were to be sold or retained, the courts held that where there was another purpose behind the ownership of the house, the courts would not order sale.
117   [2005] EWHC 2824 (Ch), affirmed on appeal [2007] Fam. Law 987.
118   [1977] 1 W.L.R. 438.
119   See Jackson, Pearce and Stevens, *Land Law*, Ch.13.

Many disputes as to whether a house should be sold arise in the context of the breakdown of a cohabiting relationship. The usual situation is that one party wants the house sold, the other wishes to remain in occupation. Where the relationship has broken down the court will hold that although the purpose of buying the house was to provide a home for the couple, that purpose is dead when the couple's relationship breaks down. In such cases sale will usually be ordered because the purpose of providing a home for the *couple* has come to an end. In *Jones v. Challenger*[120] a husband and wife jointly bought a house, the purpose of which was to provide a matrimonial home. The wife had left the husband and she sought a sale of the house. He wished to remain in occupation. Devlin L.J. reasoned that

> "In the case we have to consider, the house was acquired as the matrimonial home. That was the purpose of the joint tenancy and, for so long as that purpose was still alive, I think that the right test to be applied would be that in *Re Buchanan-Wollaston's Conveyance* [1939] Ch 738. But with the end of the marriage, that purpose was dissolved and the [house should be sold]."

However, the court may not order sale where there is an additional purpose, beyond that of providing a home for the *couple* to live in as their matrimonial home, e.g. the provision of a home for children (see below).

(a) Critical thinking and problem solving
LECTURER: Let's apply the principles we have studied so far to our Herriot House problem.

Remember that Cully and David want Herriot House to be sold so that they can go to Australia. Adam, Brian and Eric want to continue to occupy the house and run the vet's practice.
Discuss Cully and David's likelihood of obtaining an order for sale under ss.14 and 15.

STUDENT: Referring to s.15(1)(a) and (b), it might be argued on behalf of Adam, Brian and Eric that the purpose of the co-ownership of the House was to run a vets practice and that is still capable of being carried out. Thus, the court should not order sale.

LECTURER: This was the primary purpose of purchasing Herriot House, as was the situation in *Holman v Howes* and *Re Buchanan-Wollaston's Conveyance*. Don't forget to cite your cases in support of your argument. Can you think of some counter-arguments for Cully and David along the lines of *Jones v Challenger*? Try to emulate the way in which the judges consider the issues.

---

120   [1961] 1 Q.B. 176.

STUDENT: Well, with only three vets remaining the nature and structure of the practice may have changed. The business model of the practice may have to change significantly as a result of two partners leaving. What evidence do you think the court may require before ordering sale?

LECTURER: The court may require evidence that it would be possible to purchase alternative premises before ordering sale, e.g. is there anything in the same area, perhaps more modestly priced, that will enable them to retain their client base?

STUDENT: And if there is not, and the remaining three vets are continuing to run the practice successfully, the court may consider this as an additional factor: they would have to build the business up again from scratch. This may weigh against sale.

(3) The welfare of any minor in occupation or who might reasonably be expected to occupy the property as his home

Before making any order the court must now expressly consider the welfare of any minor in occupation or who might reasonably be expected to occupy the property as his home. In *Re Evers Trust*[121] a cohabiting couple broke up. The man left and sought a sale of their jointly owned house. Sale was refused because a child was occupying the home. The Court of Appeal stated that the man was at liberty to apply for an order for sale in the future should the parties' circumstances change. So a sale may not be ordered even though a relationship has broken down where there are young children.[122] In *Edwards v Lloyds TSB Bank Plc*[123] Park J. postponed sale of the family home for five years against a secured creditor, even though the husband had left, because the purpose of having the house was to provide a home for children. Park J. also indicated that the court may still consider their need for a home even when children have come of age: for example if they are in further or higher education and are still "in practice" dependent on one or both of their parents for the provision of a home.[124]

However, a child's interests will not automatically prevail.[125] It is just one of the factors that the courts must weigh, where appropriate, in deciding what order to make in relation to co-owned property.

(4) The interests of any secured creditor of any beneficiary

At this point we leave our vets to their argument on what should be done with Herriot House. Here we are going to think critically about the way in which the courts prioritise competing interests, such as the wishes of a family to remain in occupation of the trust property, against the interest of a creditor who wants the house sold in order to get their money back.

---

121   [1980] 1 W.L.R. 1327.

122   *Dennis v McDonald* [1982] Fam. 63.

123   [2004] EWHC 1745; [2005] 1 F.C.R. 139.

124   *Edwards v Lloyds TSB Bank Plc* above.

125   See for example, *Bank of Home Mortgages v Bell* [2001] 2 F.L.R. 809, where the child had almost come of age and sale was ordered in favour of a secured creditor: "But the son at the time of the trial was not far short of 18 and therefore that should only have been a very slight consideration", per Peter Gibson L.J.

How does such a dispute arise?

Two co-owners hold the legal estate on trust for each other. One co-owner may have borrowed money from a bank, without the knowledge of the other co-owner, and the bank has a charge on the co-owner's *equitable* interest as security. The bank has an equitable charge. Thus, in the event that the co-owner defaults under the loan agreement, the secured creditor may apply to the court under s.14 for an order of sale of the co-owned property. The creditor will want the house sold in order to get his money back. The other co-owner will want to remain in occupation.

(a) An explanation of context

Where there is a mortgage of the *legal* estate in land the mortgagee has the right of possession immediately and a power to sell the house. The power of sale becomes exercisable on the borrower's default under the terms of the mortgage.[126] Thus, a *legal* mortgagee/chargee has remedies at its fingertips to enforce its security and would not use the TLATA 1996 dispute resolution mechanism in order to enforce a sale. A legal mortgagee can only be prevented from taking possession and selling the house by an occupier who has acquired a beneficial interest under a trust which takes priority over the lender's interest, as in *Williams & Glyn's Bank Ltd v Boland*.[127] The difference with the situation under discussion here and the *Boland* case is that in *Boland* the husband was the sole legal owner, the wife having acquired a beneficial interest by contributing to the purchase. Thus, he had full powers to mortgage the legal estate and the bank accordingly acquired a legal mortgage. In the type of case we are discussing here, both partners hold the legal estate jointly and one of the co-owners has mortgaged their equitable interest only. A bank with an equitable mortgage will not have the remedies of possession and sale. It will need to bring a TLATA s.14 claim for an order of sale.

It is not common for a single co-owner to bring about this situation deliberately, i.e. a mortgage over his equitable interest only. In most cases today the mortgage of a single co-owner's interest arises as a result of a failed mortgage of the whole legal estate.[128] For example, let's say A and B are joint owners of "Broadacres". This co-ownership takes effect under the statutory trust of land: they will hold on trust for each other. A mortgage is granted in favour of the Crunchy Bank. However, although the deed purports to have been executed by A and B, A has forged B's signature on the mortgage deed. The mortgage cannot take effect against the legal estate in Broadacres, because B, who is a co-owner of the legal estate, has not consented to it. It takes effect against A's equitable interest only.[129] The Crunchy Bank does however have an equitable mortgage and is an interested party with locus standi to apply for an order of sale under s.14.

---

126   Law of Property Act 1925, ss.101–103.

127   [1981] A.C. 487.

128   Crown (2001) 117 L.Q.R. 477.

129   Forgery: mortgage valid against forger's equitable share of the house: *Mortgage Corporation Ltd v Shaire and Others* [2000] 1 F.L.R. 973, p.985 per Neuberger J.; *Thames Guaranty Ltd v Campbell and Others* [1985] 1 Q.B. 210; *Ahmed v Kendrick* [1988] 2 F.L.R. 22.

The same principle applies where the borrower has exerted undue influence over their co-owner in order to get their consent to the transaction so that the mortgage is unenforceable against that co-owner.[130]

(b) Section 15(1)(d) in the context of the family home

The courts under s.15 of the 1996 Act will have to weigh the interests of a secured creditor of any beneficiary against the desire of other co-owners, such as spouses with children, to remain in occupation of the house. They may have known nothing about the mortgage or debt. Thus, the contest is essentially between two innocent parties. A spouse may not want to move out of an area in which they have lived all their lives, children may be settled at the local school and be at a crucial time in their education, and they may be unable to afford another house if the property is sold.

(c) Whose voice shall prevail: the family's or the creditor's?

LECTURER: Although this dispute is technically different from the one we encountered in *Williams & Glyn's Bank Ltd v Boland*, the law must balance the same policy considerations. Can you remember why it is important for banks who lend money on the security of the family home to be able to get their money back?

STUDENT: If the banks cannot be sure that they can sell houses in order to recoup their money, they may become reluctant to lend to small businesses in the future or to families in order to help them purchase a home. This could have a detrimental effect on our economy.

BUILDING BLOCK NO 5: Property Rights and the Protection of Purchasers and Mortgage Lenders

We can argue that a development of a rule in a case or statute is good or bad fair or unfair, depending on the extent to which it gives the lender ready access to its security, i.e. the law must not unduly impede sales of the family home where a creditor is involved.

LECTURER: But the other co-owner has a case that is at times equally compelling. In the situation in which these equitable mortgages arise, why is the other co-owner's case particularly compelling?

STUDENT: Because they have been the victims of fraud. Their partner has forged their signature on the mortgage.

LECTURER: The innocent co-owner is threatened with the loss of their home. Which of our other Building Blocks do you think is relevant?

STUDENT: BUILDING BLOCK NO 1: Residential Security.

---

130   *First National Bank Plc v Achampong* [2003] EWCA Civ 487; [2004] 1 F.C.R. 18.

BUILDING BLOCK NO 1: Residential Security

We can legitimately say that where the rules operate in the context of owner occupation of property, they are good and fair if they give adequate protection to people's residential security. People have built their life around the family home and maybe they cannot be readily uprooted. Perhaps there are children at a particular school and a sale would be disruptive to their education.

STUDENT: Even though it is important that the lender receives their money back, we might argue that the law should not order sale unless there is no other possible alternative. Maybe they should even give priority to residential security. I remember one of the Law Lords in *Boland* made an observation that families living in the home should always be within the contemplation of bank managers when they lend money on the security of the home.

(d) The position regarding creditors pre-TLATA 1996

Where a co-owner charges their beneficial interest to a bank, this was said to change the basis on which the parties co-own the house. It changed the "purpose" for which the property is held for s.15(1)(b). The purpose of owning the house solely as a matrimonial home had ceased to exist.[131] Following the approach taken in bankruptcy cases, *Lloyds Bank Plc v Byrne*[132] held that the interests of creditors would prevail unless there were exceptional circumstances. The courts would order a sale of the house to ensure that the creditor got its money back.

(e) Has the TLATA 1996 changed the law in respect of disputes between co-owners and creditors?

(i) Case study 1: Mortgage Corporation Ltd v Shaire

The first indication that TLATA 1996 had changed this position came in *Mortgage Corporation Ltd v Shaire*.[133] We will study the case and its reasoning.

> **THE FACTS:** A couple, Mrs Shaire and Mr Fox, were co-owners of their family home. Mrs Shaire had a 75 per cent share of the house and Mr Fox a 25 per cent share. The house had been Mrs Shaire's matrimonial home, which she had co-owned in equal shares with her former husband. When Mrs Shaire began a relationship with Mr Fox, her former husband transferred his interest in the house to Mrs Share and Mr Fox, as part of a divorce settlement. Mr Fox later died. It came to light that he had forged Mrs Shaire's signature on a mortgage of the house in favour of the Mortgage Corporation, a fact that she had not known. Thus, the mortgage took effect against

---

131   *Mortgage Corporation Ltd v Shaire and Others* [2000] 1 F.L.R. 973, p.992 per Neuberger J.; *Barclays Bank Plc v Hendricks and Another* [1996] 1 F.L.R. 258, p.263 per Laddie J.; *Banker's Trust Co v Namadar* [1997] E.G. 20.

132   (1991) 23 H.L.R. 472.

133   [2000] 1 F.L.R. 973; [2001] 4 All E.R. 364. O.Radley-Gardner, "Section 15 of TLATA, or, the Importance of Being Earners" [2003] 5 *Web Journal of Current Legal Issues* 1-7; "Chargees and Family Property" [2001] 1 W.J.C.L.I.; Probert [2002] Conv. 61; S.Pascoe, "Section 15 of the Trusts of Land and Appointment of Trustees Act 1996—A Change in the Law?" [2000] Conv. 315.

Mr Fox's beneficial interest only. The Mortgage Corporation, as "a secured creditor of a beneficiary" made an application under s.14 of the 1996 Act for an order that the house should be sold. Not surprisingly Mrs Shaire wished to remain in occupation.

CONCLUSION: Neuberger J. refused to order sale provided that Mrs Shaire could pay some interest to the Mortgage Corporation in respect of the money outstanding.

Let's now examine an extract from Neuberger J.'s reasoning and see the way in which he approaches this TLATA claim.

How to identify a chain of reasoning

First we identify what the judge is reasoning about. You need to identify their conclusion. To identify a judge's reasoning it is helpful to ask questions like: *what were the factors that were so important to the judge that they led him to that particular conclusion?* OR: *What would have to have been different about the facts for the judge to come to another conclusion?* L.Elder, "I Think Critically Therefore I Am" *THES* (August 2009).

THE REASONING: NEUBERGER J: "The question here is ought I to make an order for sale of the house and, if not, what order ought I to make? Until the 1996 Act came into force on 1 January 1997, property owned by more than one person, not held on a strict settlement, was held on trust for sale, and s.30 of the Law of Property Act 1925 applied. In that connection the law had developed in the following way. In *Re Citro (Domenico) (A Bankrupt); Re Citro (Carmine) (A Bankrupt)* [1991] Ch 142 . . . Nourse LJ said this:

> 'Where a spouse who has a beneficial interest in the matrimonial home has become bankrupt under debts which cannot be paid without the realisation of that interest, the voice of the creditors will usually prevail over the voice of the other spouse and a sale of the property ordered within the short period. The voice of the other spouse will only prevail in exceptional circumstances. No distinction is to be made between a case where the property is still being enjoyed as a matrimonial home and one where it is not.
>
> What then are exceptional circumstances? As the cases show, it is not uncommon for a wife with young children to be faced with eviction in circumstances where the realisation of her beneficial interest will not produce enough to buy a comparable home in the same neighbourhood, or indeed elsewhere; and, if she has to move elsewhere, there may be problems over schooling and so forth. Such circumstances, while engendering a natural sympathy in all who hear of them, cannot be described as exceptional. They are the melancholy consequences of debt and improvidence with which every civilised society has been familiar.'

In *Lloyds Bank Plc v Byrne and Byrne* [1993] 1 FLR 369, the Court of Appeal had to consider a number of grounds advanced for distinguishing between a case (such as *Citro*) where the trustee in bankruptcy of one of the owners of a beneficial interest in the property wanted to sell, and a case (such as *Byrne*) where a mortgagee or chargee of the one of the parties' beneficial interests wished to sell . . . . [It came to the conclusion that] there was, in relation to trusts for sale and before the 1996 Act came into force, no difference between the two types of case considered in *Citro* and *Byrne*. The normal rule in such cases was that, save in exceptional circumstances, the wish of the person wanting the sale . . . would prevail, and that the interests of children and families in occupation would be unlikely to prevail . . .

However, trusts for sale and s.30 have now been effectively replaced by the 1996 Act. Section 1 of the 1996 Act has the effect of rendering trusts for sale obsolete . . . and replacing them with the less arcane and simpler trusts of land. [Neuberger J set out ss.14 and 15] . . .

To my mind, for a number of reasons, [counsel] is correct in his submission, on behalf of Mrs Shaire, that s.15 has changed the law . . . [I]t is hard to reconcile the contention that Parliament intended to confirm the law as laid down in *Byrne* with the fact that, while the interest of a chargee [mortgagee] is one of the four specified factors to be taken into account in s.15(1)(d), there is no suggestion that it is to be given any more importance than the interests of the children residing in the house: see s.15(1)(c) . . . [. . .]

. . . [T]he Law Commission report which gave rise to the 1996 Act, *Transfer of Land, Trusts of Land*, Law Com No 181 (1989) tends to support this view as well . . . In para 12.9 of the report the Law Commission describe the aim as being to 'consolidate *and rationalise*' (emphasis added) the current approach. When commenting on the proposed equivalents of what are now s.15(1) and s.15(3) the Law Commission said this . . .

'Clearly, the terms of these guidelines may influence the exercise of the discretion in some way. For example, it may be that the courts' approach to creditors' interests will be altered by the framing of the guideline as to the welfare of children. If the welfare of children is seen as a factor to be considered independently of the beneficiaries' holdings, the court may be less ready to order the sale of the home than they are at present.'

Finally, at para 13.6 the Law Commission said this:

'Within the new system, beneficiaries will be in a comparatively better position than beneficiaries of current trusts of land. For example, given that the terms governing applications . . . will be less restrictive than they are at present, beneficiaries will have greater scope to challenge the decisions of the trustees and generally influence the management of the trust land.'

[T]o put it at its lowest, it does not seem to me unlikely that the legislature intended to relax the fetters on the way in which the court exercised its discretion in cases such as *Citro* and *Byrne*, and so as to tip the balance somewhat more in favour of families and against banks and other chargees . . . there were indications of judicial dissatisfaction with the state of the law at that time . . . which suggests a desire for a new approach.

All these factors, to my mind, when taken together point very strongly to the conclusion that s.15 has changed the law. As a result of s.15, the court has greater flexibility than heretofore as to how it exercises its jurisdiction on an application for an order for sale on facts such as those in *Citro* and *Byrne*. [. . .]

Bearing in mind these conclusions as to the effect of the 1996 Act, ought I to make an order for sale? [. . .] So far as s.15(1)(a) is concerned, the house was acquired in 1987 as a home for Mr Fox, Mrs Share and Adam [her son who was of age], and Mrs Shaire and Adam still live there and still want to live there . . . Mr Fox changed the basis on which he held his interest when, albeit unknown to Mrs Shaire, he charged that interest first to FNB and then to TMC for a large sum to assist his business. [. . .]

It is difficult to say for what purposes the house is held. So far as Mrs Shaire is concerned it is held for her to live in. So far as TMC is concerned . . . it is naturally anxious to sell to realise as much as it can from the mess it has got into through Mr Fox's dishonesty. [. . .]

Section 15(1)(c) does not apply. Section 15(1)(d), concerned, as it is, with the interests of any secured creditor of any beneficiary, requires one to have regard to TMC's interest, which I have already described.

As to s.15(3), the majority of the beneficial interest is held . . . by Mrs Shaire and she obviously wishes to remain in occupation.

Having gone through the statutory required factors, I stand back to look at the position of the two parties. TMC do not want to be tied into a 25% equity in a property producing no income and with no certainty as to when it will be released. Mrs Shaire is 48 and there is no reason to think that she will sell in the foreseeable future. TMC will also have no control over the state of the house or whether it is properly insured . . . TMC point out that Mrs Shaire does not appear to need a house with three bedrooms, as she lives there alone with her son. [. . .]

To my mind, for Mrs Shaire to have to leave her home of nearly a quarter of a century would be a real and significant hardship but not an enormous one. She would have a substantial sum that she could put towards a smaller home . . . On the other hand, I have no evidence as to what properties might be available for the sort of money which she would be able to pay. For TMC to be locked into a quarter of the equity in a property would be a significant disadvantage unless they had a proper return and a proper protection so far as insurance and repair is concerned.

   . . . [I]f . . . Mrs Shaire can really pay a proper return, it would be right to refuse to make an order for possession and sale primarily because Mrs Shaire has a valid interest in remaining in the house and has a 75% interest in it, and because TMC is ultimately in the business of lending money on property in return for being paid interest."

LECTURER: On what basis did Neuberger J. make his decision? How did he describe the strength of Mrs Shaire's claim?

STUDENT: He said that the purpose of the house was to provide her with a home (referring to the factor in ss.15(1)(a) and (b)) and that it would be a significant hardship for her to leave the home in which she had spent nearly 25 years. I think the judge was also influenced by the fact that Mrs Share did not know about Mr Fox's fraudulent mortgages.

LECTURER: And how did Neuberger J. describe the secured creditor's interest in sale of the house.

STUDENT: That the court is required to consider their interests in getting their money back under s.15(1)(c). But he also thought that there is more than one way of achieving this. The creditor should not be able to get the whole amount back, because Mrs Shaire's claim to residential security was stronger, but sale would be ordered unless Mrs Shaire could pay the bank a "proper return" on the loan.

LECTURER: Good. So the interests of the family prevail unless it is really a case of last resort, i.e. sale is the only way a creditor is going to get its money back. How would this case have been decided *before* the Trusts of Land and Appointment of Trustees Act 1996?

STUDENT: Neuberger J. suggests that sale would have been ordered. Ordinary hardship, even if severe—as in the case of *Citro*—would not allow the court to refuse sale. Thus, Mrs Shaire would have been in a worse situation under the old law.

LECTURER: So how did Neuberger J. come to the conclusion that TLATA 1996 had changed the law?

STUDENT: By looking at the intentions of parliament in enacting TLATA 1996 (through the Law Commission reports). He said that the interests of creditors were now not intended to prevail automatically but were one of a number of factors to be considered. Parliament had intended to offer greater protection to the family in occupation.

LECTURER: So TLATA 1996 did change the law and this is good and fair because it strikes a better balance between competing aims and interests of Land Law, not just giving automatic priority to one of them.

The post-TLATA 1996 approach as identified in *Mortgage Corporation v Shaire*

BUILDING BLOCK NO 1:
Residential Security

BUILDING BLOCK NO 5: The
Protection of Purchasers and
Mortgage Lenders

=

Equal weighting
OUTCOME: Sale not ordered unless a last resort

(ii) Case study 2 – Bank of Ireland Home Mortgages Ltd v Bell[134]

THE FACTS: In *Bank of Ireland Home Mortgages Ltd v Bell*[135] a husband and wife were joint owners of their family home. The husband forged the wife's signature on a mortgage of the legal estate in order to secure a loan of £150,000. Because of the forgery, the mortgage took effect against the husband's equitable interest in the property. The bank commenced proceedings under section 14 for an order of sale of the property. By the time of the proceedings the debt had mounted to £300,000 and was considerably greater than the value of the house. Mrs Bell was paying the bank no interest on the loan.

CONCLUSION AT FIRST INSTANCE: The judge held that there should be no order of sale on the basis that "the property was purchased as the family home; second, that it was now occupied by Mrs Bell and her son; and third, that she was in poor health".[136]

CONCLUSION ON APPEAL: The Court of Appeal overturned the judge's decision and ordered sale of the house.[137]

LECTURER: So now we need to consider the Court of Appeal's grounds for overturning the first instance judge's decision. Look at the extract from the judgment of Peter Gibson L.J. and ask: *What were the factors that were so important to Peter Gibson L.J. that they led him to the conclusion that he reached about the sale of the house?* Does this case differ from *Mortgage Corporation v Shaire*? Is there any way these two can be reconciled?

THE REASONING: PETER GIBSON L.J. "The refusal to order sale was made in the exercise of the discretion conferred on the judge by section 14 Trusts of Land and Appointment of Trustees Act 1996. [The judge then listed the s.15 factors to which the court must have regard when exercising its discretion] . . .

---

134   Probert [2002] Conv. 61.
135   [2001] 2 F.L.R. 809, CA.
136   [2001] 2 F.L.R. 809, CA, per Peter Gibson L.J., summarising the reasons of the first instance judge.
137   See also *First National Bank Plc v Achampong* [2003] EWCA Civ 487; [2004] 1 F.C.R. 18.

On well-established principles, this court can only interfere with the exercise by the judge of his discretion if he erred, such as by taking into account irrelevant considerations or leaving out of account relevant considerations or otherwise being plainly wrong in his conclusion . . .

In my judgment, the judge did err in the exercise of his discretion . . .

[Considering s.15(1)(d)] the judge does not mention the fact that the debt was at the time of the trial some £300,000, and increasing daily, no payment of either capital or interest having been received from Mr Bell (or Mrs Bell for that matter) [for eight years]. Mrs Bell's beneficial interest is only about 10 per cent at the very most . . . and there is no equity in the property which would be realised for her on a sale of the property. In effect, therefore, the bank would take all the proceeds on a sale.

> **This means that the house was worth less than the debt to the bank: we call this "negative equity".**

That is a most material consideration to which the judge should have given great weight . . .

Second, the judge referred to the property being purchased as a family home . . . Let me assume that the judge thereby had regard to section 15(1)(a), the intentions of the persons creating the trust. But that purpose ceased to be operative once Mr Bell left the family . . . Therefore that purpose is not a matter to which the judge could properly have regard.

Third, the judge referred to the occupation of the property by Mrs Bell and her son. Let me assume that thereby the judge was referring to section 15(1)(b), the purposes for which the property is held. But that is not an operative purpose of the trust since the departure of Mr Bell. The reference to the son may also be a reflection of section 15(1)(c), the welfare of a minor occupying the property. But the son at the time of the trial was not far short of 18 and therefore that should only have been a very slight consideration.

Fourth, the judge referred to Mrs Bell's poor health. At the time of the trial she was facing an operation. I accept that the judge could properly have regard to this, but it would provide a reason for postponing a sale rather than refusing a sale. [. . .]

Prior to the 1996 Act the courts under section 30 of the Law of Property Act 1925 would order the sale of a matrimonial home at the request of the trustee in bankruptcy of a spouse or at the request of the creditor chargee of a spouse, considering that the creditors' interest should prevail over that of the other spouse and the spouse's family save in exceptional circumstances. The 1996 Act, by requiring the court to have regard to the particular matters specified in section 15, appears to me to have given scope for some change in the court's practice. Nevertheless, a powerful consideration is and ought to be whether the creditor is receiving proper recompense for being kept out of his money, repayment of which is overdue . . . In the present case it is plain that by refusing sale the judge has condemned the bank to go on waiting for its money with no prospect of recovery from Mr and Mrs Bell and with the debt increasing all the time, that debt already exceeding what could be realised on a sale. That seems to me to be very unfair to the bank. [. . .]

In my judgment, therefore, the judge took into account irrelevant considerations and left out of account material considerations. I have to say that in refusing sale he seems to me to have been plainly wrong. That means that, if my Lord agrees, this court can substitute its own discretion for that of the judge . . . It seems plain to me, for the reasons already given, that a sale should be ordered . . . Mrs Bell should be permitted to put in evidence related to the timing of the sale, including, if she thinks it material, evidence about her health, and the bank should have the opportunity to reply to such evidence."

LECTURER: It seemed like the judge at first instance had taken a very "family-oriented" approach. How did Peter Gibson L.J. assess the claim of Mrs Bell and her son?

STUDENT: Well, he said that the purpose to provide a family home (considering s.15(1)(a) and (b)) had ceased to exist when Mr Bell left and the marriage broke up. This is in line with cases like *Jones v Challenger* but conflicted in this respect with *Mortgage Corporation v Shaire*. In that case the judge said that the purpose was to provide her with a home, irrespective of the fact that her partner had died (although perhaps that was a distinguishing feature).

Peter Gibson L.J. also held that the interests of Mrs Bell's son (under s.15(1)(c)) were not of much consideration here because he was nearly 18—which I agree with.

LECTURER: So there was not much, according to the judge, to weigh *against* sale. How did Peter Gibson L.J. assess the claim of the bank?

STUDENT: This seemed to be more compelling. The house was worth less than the debt to the bank.

LECTURER: Which showed that the bank was in trouble—It could not get all of its money back in any case and because the debt was mounting the bank could get less and less of its money as time passed. In this situation we say that the bank's security is "vulnerable", i.e. as time goes by the sale of the house is less likely to pay off the loan or a significant amount of it.

STUDENT: The other factors that Peter Gibson L.J. thought to be relevant were that Mrs Bell only had a 10 per cent interest in the house and she had not paid any money to the bank for eight years.

LECTURER: Good. Do you think that this case shows a return to the pre-TLATA 1996 approach, i.e. to award sale in all but exceptional circumstances?

STUDENT: Superficially it looks like it—a very pro-bank decision. However, on closer examination Peter Gibson L.J. still conducted a "weighing exercise", i.e. balancing all the factors in s.15(1) and (3). He did not therefore return to the old law which ordered sale in all but exceptional circumstances. It's just that there was not much to "weigh" against sale.

LECTURER: But the Court of Appeal decision in *Bell* does show the limit of the post-TLATA 1996 approach as far as concerns its willingness to protect residential security and the interests of the family. Can you identify what that limit is?

STUDENT: *The bank must have some prospect of getting some return on its loan investment and the house must be adequate security for the loan.*

(iii) Case study 3: Edwards v Lloyds TSB Bank Plc

THE FACTS: In *Edwards v Lloyds TSB Bank Plc*[138] a husband and wife were joint owners of their matrimonial home. They separated and the husband moved out. At this time he took out an overdraft facility with the bank in order to finance his company. The bank wanted the house as security, i.e. in case the husband could not pay off the overdraft the bank would be able to sell the house. The husband forged his wife's signature on a mortgage of their home, so the mortgage took effect against his equitable interest only. The husband's business failed and the bank applied for order of sale under s.14. Sale was postponed. *Why?*

THE REASONING: PARK J: "The company obviously failed and the bank is still owed money. I assume that there has never been any prospect of recovering anything from the company itself. The husband is liable on his personal guarantee [to repay the overdraft] . . . plus interest and costs, but he cannot be traced and any claim against him based on his personal covenant is presumed to be worthless. That leaves the bank with whatever rights against the house which it may have under the mortgage deed . . ."

LECTURER: I have included this passage to show you why banks need mortgages. They have the loan contract with the husband, as here, but there is little point in suing him for breach of contract if he fails to make the repayments because *he has no money*. So the bank will have rights over the home in order that it might be sold. This gives them a "second bite of the cherry" at getting their money back.

PARK J. CONTINUES: "The correct position is that, although the deed did not create a legal mortgage of the entire ownership interest in the house, it did create an equitable mortgage of the husband's 50% beneficial (or equitable) interest in the house . . .

The bank . . . has an equitable charge over a 50% . . . share . . . and it seeks an order for the entirety to be sold . . . [T]he matter is governed by ss.14 and 15 of the Trusts of Land and Appointment of Trustees Act 1996 . . .

It is common ground that one of the orders which the court can make is an order for the house to be sold, but it is no longer the case that, because the house is held on trust for sale, the law begins with a presumption that an order for sale should be made unless the court directs a postponement. Section 15(1) sets out a non-exclusive list of four factors to which the court is to have regard in determining an application under s.14 . . . By way of comment on those factors, the original intention was no doubt to provide a matrimonial home for the husband, Mrs Edwards and their children. In part that purpose has gone, because the marriage is over and the

138   [2004] EWHC 1745; [2005] 1 F.C.R. 139. This case discusses *First National Bank Plc v Achampong* [2003] EWCA Civ 487; [2004] 1 F.C.R. 18, which is well worth your looking at.

husband is no longer living in the house, but in part the purpose still survives, because the house is still the home for Mrs Edwards and the two children of the former marriage. A further factor, (c), is the welfare of any minor who occupies the property as his home. The two children are still minors, and they live in the house, so this factor is certainly relevant. Factor (d) is also relevant: 'the interests of any secured creditor of any beneficiary'. That brings into the evaluation the interests of the bank. Subsection (3) states that the court is also to have regard to the circumstances and wishes of any beneficiary of full age entitled to an interest in possession in the property. In this case that means that the court is to have regard to the circumstances and wishes of Mrs Edwards. Her wish is that the house should not be sold.

I was referred to three recent decisions which considered the application of ss.14 and 15 in cases having some similarities to the case before me: *The Mortgage Corporation v Shaire* . . . *Bank of Ireland Home Mortgages Ltd v Bell* and *First National Bank plc v Achampong* . . . In the first of those cases Neuberger J said that, in his opinion, ss.14 and 15 had to some extent changed the law. The court has a greater flexibility as to how it exercises its jurisdiction on an application for an order for sale. Having taken into account the factors identified in s.15 and such other factors as arose, 'it is a matter for the court as to what weight to give to each factor in a particular case'. All three cases bring out the point that, if there is a creditor of a husband or wife and the creditor's interest is to be taken into account (as the bank's interest is in this case), it is unsatisfactory for the court simply to say that it declines to make any order for sale. In the Bank of Ireland case the Court of Appeal, reversing the decision of the first instance judge, said: 'In the present case it is plain that by refusing sale the judge has condemned the bank to go on waiting for its money with no prospect of recovery from Mr and Mrs Bell and with the debt increasing all the time, that debt already exceeding what could be realised on a sale.' There are observations to a similar effect in the Achampong case. In *The Mortgage Corporation v Shaire* Neuberger J left it to the parties to try to agree terms between themselves, but he made it clear that, if Mrs Shaire would not agree to something which gave the bank a realistic prospect of recovering at least some of its money, he would simply make an order for sale."

LECTURER: This paragraph shows the limit that we identified earlier on the courts' protection of the family and other co-owners wishing to remain in occupation. Can you identify what that is?

STUDENT: Sale will not be refused unless the bank's security is relatively safe and they can recover at least some of their money.

PARK J. CONTINUES: "In this case the bank has applied for an order for sale, and Mrs Edwards has opposed the application. I must weigh up the various factors which are relevant and do the best I can to reach a balanced conclusion. I mention now two particular points on the facts of this case which were (I believe) not present in any of the three cases to which I was referred. First, if the house was sold now it is hard to see how Mrs Edwards could find the money to buy another smaller one. In the other cases it appears to have been different . . . In the present case, in contrast, the house is a two-bedroom house in which Mrs Edwards already has to share a bedroom with her daughter. The house is obviously at the lower end of the range of prices for houses in the area where she lives. If there was a sale and the husband's debt to the bank was taken out of half of the net proceeds before the balance was available to Mrs Edwards, I very much doubt that she would be able to find another house which she could afford to buy and which would be adequate to accommodate her and her children."

LECTURER: Do you think that this is quite a novel consideration?

STUDENT: It was a point that was raised in *Shaire*—Neuberger J. said that she would have a substantial sum with which to buy alternative accommodation. Here the fact that Mrs Edwards could not afford a house in the area for her share of the sale proceeds seemed to weigh heavily against sale, although Mrs Bell was clearly in the same position.

PARK J. CONTINUES: Second, whereas in the other three cases it appears that the debt owed to the bank already exceeded the value of the interest over which the bank had an equitable charge [i.e. the value of the husband's interest], in the present case that is not so. On the figures . . . the value of the bank's security (a 50% interest in the house) would be (if the entirety were sold) about £70,000. The husband's debt to the bank (£15,000 plus interest plus costs) is unlikely at present to be more than £40,000. It is true that interest is not currently being paid to the bank on the debt owed to it, but interest continues to accrue on the debt, and now and for some time to come the security will be sufficient to cover the increasing amount of the debt."

LECTURER: How does Park J. assess the claim of the bank here?

STUDENT: The bank's security was not in danger. The value of the house will easily cover it. The interest will be added to the debt and when the house is sold in the future the bank will have its money. The only potential problem for the bank is that it is not getting any immediate return on the loan.

PARK J. CONTINUES: "In the circumstances I do not want to order an immediate sale, because I believe that that would be unacceptably severe in its consequences upon Mrs Edwards and her children. But equally I believe that I should make some order which, admittedly later rather than sooner, should enable the bank to recover its debt with accrued interest upon it. I intend to make an order along the following lines.

i)   There be no order for an immediate sale of the house.

ii)   However, there be an order for a postponed sale of the house.

iii) . . . the sale should be postponed for five years. My thinking behind that period is that Mrs Edwards' younger child, her daughter, is now 13. In five years time she will not be a minor, and her interests will not be a factor which the court is required to take into account under factor (c) in section 15. Further, it seems possible that by then it will no longer be in practice incumbent on Mrs Edwards to provide a home at her expense for her son and daughter.

iv) Either party may at any time apply to the court for my present order, and in particular the five years period prescribed in it, to be reviewed and, if the court thinks fit, varied. The main contingency which I have in mind is that at the end of the five years period either Mrs Edwards' son or her daughter or both of them may still be in full time education and in practice dependent on their mother for the provision of a home. If that happens Mrs Edwards may wish to apply for the period to be extended."

LECTURER: And this is the last case we consider in relation to TLATA 1996 claims and s.15. Let's critically evaluate the law.

STUDENT: *Edwards* definitely confirms that the courts do not give automatic priority to secured creditors who want sale of the co-owned family home. It also confirms that there is a limit to the protection of families: i.e. the creditor's security must be "safe".[139]

LECTURER: Is there anything about this case that seemed novel?

STUDENT: It does extend protection to co-owners in occupation in the sense that it is not considered necessary that the remaining co-owner pay some interest to the lender in the immediate future. And the court will consider that children may need a home even when they are of age, if they are in full time education.

LECTURER: So is the law good and fair?

STUDENT: We have already used our Building Blocks to show why it is important that the law protects creditors in this way: BUILDING BLOCK NO 5: The Protection of Purchasers and Mortgage Lenders. We can see that the courts do attempt to ensure that sale is an absolute last resort, thus giving greater protection to the important social need of residential security: BUILDING BLOCK NO 1.

Further research

LECTURER: Your answer will be significantly better if you can show that the academic articles *also* thought our Building Blocks were being supported or undermined and how they may have been out of balance so as to require a change. This would make your answer significantly better because much has in fact been said about these issues and you are showing that you are aware of it. For example:

S.Pascoe, "Section 15 of the Trusts of Land and Appointment of Trustees Act 1996 – A Change in the Law?" [2000] Conv. 315;
O.Radley-Gardner, "Section 15 of TLATA, or, the Importance of Being Earners" [2003] 5 *Web Journal of Current Legal Issues* 1–7;
M.P.Thompson, "Secured Creditors and Sales" [2000] Conv. 329–336.

---

139   For example Probert [2002] Conv. 61.

And finally it is worth considering the most recent applications of s.15. In *Edwards v Bank of Scotland Plc*[140] an estranged husband and wife owned substantial property as tenants in common. The wife forged the husband's signature on a mortgage to the bank (so it took effect against her equitable interest). In ordering sale on the application of the lender the court took into consideration the factor that the creditor was being kept out of their money. It also took into consideration the circumstances of the beneficiaries, as required under s.15(3). The fact that the husband's beneficial interest was amply sufficient for the purchase of another property meant that all the factors weighed in favour of sale. Indeed, similar factors were relevant in *C Putnam & Sons v Taylor*,[141] in which sale was ordered because there would be sufficient equity in the house to enable the couple to purchase a smaller house, and that it would be unfair to keep the creditor from their money. Sale was postponed for seven months so that the couple could sell the house themselves and find alternative accommodation.

LECTURER: How do you think the approach in these recent cases differs from the pre-TLATA law?

STUDENT: As we have seen, under the old law the court would order sale at the request of a secured creditor of any beneficiary unless there were exceptional circumstances. Now, it seems important to the courts that these interests are balanced and they are routinely considering factors such as whether the other co-owners would be able to purchase alternative accommodation with what remains of the net sale proceeds.

LECTURER: We note also that the court would order a short postponement to enable the co-owners to find alternative accommodate and even conduct the sale themselves. On which of our Building Blocks might we say that *this is good law*?

STUDENT: The s.15 factors expressly allow courts to consider and resolve issues surrounding the residential security of the other co-owners. Creditors' interests are not given automatic priority. The law is good on the basis of BUILDING BLOCK NO 1.

BUILDING BLOCK NO 1: Residential Security

We can say that Land Law rules are good and fair if they give protection to people's residential security. Many people now co-own land in order to provide themselves with a home and the rules of Land Law should recognise and support the purposes behind land ownership in this country.

---

(5) Sections 14 and 15 of TLATA 1996 and the court's matrimonial jurisdiction

As far as divorcing spouses are concerned, it is preferable for any dispute about sale of the former matrimonial home to be resolved in an application for ancillary relief under the

---

140   [2010] EWHC 652 (Ch).
141   [2009] EWHC 317 (Ch).

Matrimonial Causes Act 1973, where the court can see the "whole picture".[142] However, exceptionally such disputes may be resolved by an application of one of the spouses under s.14 of the Trusts of Land and Appointment of Trustees Act 1996. In *Miller Smith v Miller Smith*[143] the court ordered sale under s.14 because of the cost involved in the husband maintaining the property and the likely delay of ancillary relief proceedings.[144]

(6) Cases where a co-owner of land is bankrupt

It may be the case that a co-owner of a house is declared bankrupt. This is a legal state in which the property of the bankrupt including his share of co-owned land is vested in the trustee in bankruptcy. This legal state of bankruptcy has the effect of severing a beneficial joint tenancy so that the trustee in bankruptcy holds as a tenant in common in relation to the other joint tenants. A trustee in bankruptcy "is under a statutory duty to realise the assets of the bankrupt" in order that the bankrupt's creditors are, as far as possible, paid.[145] A trustee in bankruptcy may make an application to the court under s.14 of the Trusts of Land and Appointment of Trustees Act 1996 requesting that the whole of the co-owned house be sold in order to realise the share of the bankrupt co-owner.

Thus, in a way not dissimilar to the position of secured creditors under s.15(1)(d), there is a conflict of policy interests. The same Building Blocks will be relevant. The bankrupt's family or any other co-owners will want to remain in occupation of the house, and may not even have been aware of their co-owner's debts. On the other hand, the trustee in bankruptcy, in pursuance of his statutory duty to the bankrupt co-owner's creditors, will want sale of the house.

(a) Whose voice will prevail?

A trustee in bankruptcy may make an application to the court under s.14 of the Trusts of Land and Appointment of Trustees Act 1996 for an order in relation to co-owned property.[146] As we have seen, under s.14, the court may make any order it thinks fit. However, whereas in disputes that involve secured creditors and other co-owners wanting sale, the court must have regard to the s.15 criteria, where the dispute involves a trustee in bankruptcy making the application, s.15 does not apply.[147] The relevant legislation governing disputes in bankruptcy cases is the Insolvency Act 1986.

(b) The Insolvency Act 1986 section 335A

For the first year after bankruptcy s.335A(2) of the Insolvency Act 1986 provides that on application for sale by the trustee in bankruptcy under s.14 "the court shall make such order as

---

142   *Miller Smith v Miller Smith* [2009] EWCA Civ 1297.
143   [2009] EWCA Civ 1297.
144   For fuller consideration see K.Hamilton *Sale or Stay?* (2010) 94(Mar) Fam. L.J. 11–13.
145   *Lloyds Bank Plc v Byrne and Byrne* [1993] 1 F.L.R. 369, p.372, per Parker L.J.; *Mortgage Corporation v Shaire and Others* [2000] 1 F.L.R. 973, p.986, per Neuberger J.; *Barrett v Barrett* [2008] EWHC 1061 (Ch).
146   He is an "interested party" for the purposes of s.14(1).
147   Trusts of Land and Appointment of Trustees Act 1996 s.15(4); Insolvency Act 1986 s.335A(1). Thus any change in the law brought about by s.15, as considered in *Mortgage Corporation v Shaire* [2000] 1 F.L.R. 973, does not apply in cases of bankruptcy.

it thinks just and reasonable having regard to . . . the interests of the bankrupt's creditors and all the circumstances of the case other than the needs of the bankrupt". Where the application concerns "a dwelling house which is or has been the home of the [bankrupt or the bankrupt's spouse or civil partner or former spouse or former civil partner]" the court must have regard, to:

"(i)   the conduct of the [spouse, civil partner, former spouse or former civil partner], so far as contributing to the bankruptcy,

(ii)   the needs and financial resources of the [spouse, civil partner, former spouse or former civil partner], and

(iii)   the needs of any children; and
         all the circumstances of the case other than the needs of the bankrupt."[148]

Section 335A(3) provides that if the application under s.14 is made after the first year after bankruptcy "the court shall assume, unless the circumstances of the case are exceptional, that the interests of the bankrupt's creditors outweigh all other considerations". Thus, after the first year of bankruptcy sale will be ordered unless the circumstances of the case are exceptional.

(c) What counts as "exceptional circumstances"[149]

This has been interpreted narrowly to mean not just "severe" but "unusual" or "uncommon". In *Re Citro (Domenico) (A Bankrupt); Re Citro (Carmine) (A Bankrupt)*,[150] it was held that if the debts of the bankrupt can only be paid by a sale of the house then it should be sold unless circumstances are exceptional. A wife facing eviction, and the possibility that "the realisation of her beneficial interest will not produce enough to buy a comparable home in the same neighbourhood, or indeed elsewhere", and disruption to a child's schooling, was thought to be unfortunate but not "exceptional". This was part of the ordinary and "melancholy consequences of debt and improvidence with which every civilised society has been familiar".[151]

The courts had taken an apparently more lenient approach and held the interests of the wife and young children to prevail over the bankrupt's creditors, in the earlier case of *Re Holliday*.[152] The husband did have debts but this was a voluntary bankruptcy, thought to be an attempt to avoid having to transfer the house to his wife as part of a divorce settlement. It is suggested that *Citro* is the standard approach. Sale was not ordered immediately in *Re Raval (A Bankrupt)*,[153] where the bankrupt's spouse had paranoid schizophrenia,[154] and *Re Bremner*[155] in which the bankrupt only had six months to live and his wife needed to care for him. These cases illustrate

---

148   Insolvency Act 1986 s.335A(2).
149   D.Brown, "Insolvency and the Matrimonial Home—Sins of the Fathers: *In Re Citro (A Bankrupt)*" (1992) 55 M.L.R. 284; also M. Pawlowski, "Insolvency—Ordering a Sale of the Family Home" [2007] Conv. 78–87.
150   [1991] Ch. 142; [1990] 3 All E.R. 952 CA, the law prior to s.335A was very similar.
151   [1991] Ch. 142, per Nourse L.J. For the same approach see *Re Lowrie* [1981] 3 All E.R. 353 and *Re Bailey* [1977] 1 W.L.R. 278.
152   [1981] Ch. 405.
153   [1998] 2 F.L.R. 718.
154   See also *Everitt v Budhram* (2009) in which sale was postponed for an additional year because the bankrupt's wife was mentally ill.
155   [1999] 1 F.L.R. 912.

just how unusual the circumstances of the case must be before the interests of the bankrupt's creditors for sale will not automatically prevail.[156] In *Barca v Mears*[157] the bankrupt's son had special educational needs and he was looking after him at the home for most of the week. This was held to be insufficiently unusual to qualify as "exceptional circumstances". Arguments have been considered as to whether the courts' interpretation of the "exceptional circumstances" test is contrary to art.8 of the Human Rights Act 1998.[158] Article 8(1) guarantees that "[e]veryone has the right to respect for his private and family life, his home and his correspondence". The argument runs that the courts are obliged by this provision to interpret the "exceptional circumstances" test in a broader way, for example, by refusing sale when circumstances are severe but not unusual.[159] However, the general weight of opinion in the cases is that the test as currently interpreted is compliant with art.8.[160]

As far as the s.15 criteria are concerned, the courts have indicated that the balance they are required to consider between the interests of beneficiaries and those of creditors is already compliant with art.8 of the European Convention on Human Rights.[161]

---

156   Also *Claughton v Charalambous* [1999] 1 F.L.R. 740 (sale postponed because bankrupt's wife seriously ill).
157   [2004] EWHC 2170; [2005] 1 P. & C.R. DG7.
158   *Barca v Mears* [2004] EWHC 2170.
159   Dixon [2005] Conv. 161.
160   *Nicholls v Lan* [2007] 1 FLR 744; *Donoghue v Ingram* [2006] EWHC 282; also Jackson, Pearce and Stevens, *Land Law*, Ch.13.
161   *National Westminster Bank Plc v Rushmer* [2010] EWHC 554.

Chapter 6

Land Transfer Law (1): General Principles

CHAPTER OVERVIEW

In this chapter you will find:

- An introduction to the issues of conveyancing
- The reasons why it is so important for a purchaser to prove good title
- Instructions on how to think critically about land transfer law
- The reasons behind the 1925 legislative reform.

Introduction: issues involved in a Land Transfer System

1

A. VISITING AN ESTATE AGENTS

It would be very unusual for land/houses to stay in the same ownership for any great length of time. We moderns are used to walking down the high street of a town or city and passing several estate agents' windows. We may see several people looking in: a nervous first time buyer, who is wondering whether they have enough deposit saved to buy a two-bedroomed apartment.

What is it going to be like to live with a mortgage as well as a dog?

There is a couple at a desk behind which sits an "independent mortgage adviser". He tells them how much it will cost per month to purchase the four bedroomed house on the new housing estate. They think it will be a good investment for their future and will provide room for their growing young family. He is advising them to take advantage of an offer of a low fixed interest rate for the first two years from the X Bank.

> Just coming out, clutching a stack of leaflets and looking hopeful is an elderly couple who have taken a decision to downsize. They are looking for a bungalow.

Each month, estate agents and other property professionals keep us informed of the statistics: average house prices (which you can now see at the Land Registry), whether sales are up or down etc. Like it or not, buying houses (land) has become deeply entwined with our lives. The property market is a massive factor in local, national, and, as we have recently seen, global, economy.

B. OWNER OCCUPATION AND THE BANKS' INVOLVEMENT IN THE HOUSE-BUYING PROCESS

This state of affairs, whereby a significant proportion of the population *buys* (rather than rents) the house in which they live, is, as we have seen, a relatively new phenomenon. Successive governments in the 1980s pressed the policy of owner occupation. In pursuance of this policy, they sold off a good deal of council housing stock, and introduced the "right to buy" legislation, under which a council tenant would be given a discount when they purchased their council house.[1] Thus, houses are changing hands much more frequently. But as we have also seen, there is another key player in the housing market: the institutional lender. The drive towards owner occupation, as the governmental policies understood, depends on the ready availability of "mortgage finance".

> **The banks' involvement**
> Most people do not have the cash available to buy a house outright. They have to borrow money from a bank or building society in order to finance their purchase. They put down a deposit and borrow the rest. The bank then takes a mortgage on the house. A mortgage is an interest in the property: a security for the loan, which means that the bank, if the borrower fails to pay the loan instalments, can have a second bite at the cherry of getting its money back by repossessing the house and selling it.

---

1   Legislation passed in the 70s (the Administration of Justice Acts 1970–3) brought the law up to date with this modern socio-economic phenomenon. Previously many people rented the houses in which they lived, and in order to protect residential security, parliament passed a series of Rent Acts throughout the twentieth century. These fixed rents, and gave security of occupation. Also, the Law of Property Act 1925 ensured proper procedure for landlords to comply with if they wanted to evict the tenant. The courts interpreted the provisions to give tenants extensive "relief" from this forfeiture process. These relief provisions are still used in full force today in respect of many tenancies. The Administration of Justice Acts 1970–3 give owner occupiers the same level of protection from eviction in cases of mortgage repossessions.

C. THE BUYER MUST BE ABLE TO PROVE THAT THE SELLER OWNS THE ESTATE IN THE LAND

So we now understand *one* need for a solid and secure system of transferring ownership of land from one owner to another. It is important that the new owner gets what they pay for. Therefore one need that Land Transfer Law must provide for is the need to be able to prove that the seller owns what they say they own.

> **What are people actually buying in our "visit to the estate agents"?**
> It is important to see beyond the technicalities in this chapter to the real-life human drama beneath. What people are actually buying when they buy land or a house is an "estate" in that land. But as we saw in Chapter 2, this is practically indistinguishable from actual ownership of the land. Remember this and you will learn to see beyond the technicalities.

(1) The need for proof of title

STUDENT: I can't quite see why there is a need for the seller to prove that he owns the land.

LECTURER: If I buy something on eBay I pay my money and they send me the goods. But the seller might not actually have the goods, and I am defrauded. Or the seller himself might have purchased accidentally goods that were stolen—which were not *his* to sell.

STUDENT: So when you are buying land you have to make sure that the seller owns it, as he says he does. How is this proven?

LECTURER: You need documentary proof of ownership, or "title".

LECTURER: If you remember from Chapter 3 the way in which an estate in land (ownership of it) is transferred to a buyer is by the execution of a "deed of transfer", or deed of "conveyance". Section 52 of the Law of Property Act 1925 requires that legal estates and interests in land must be created by deed. So the "title deeds" to the house gives the buyer a way of proving that the seller owns the land. The buyer must examine all the documents in the seller's possession to make sure that the land was properly transferred to him, and that it had been properly transferred to the person who sold it to him, and so forth. We call this a "chain" of ownership or title. The system of registration of title has a different way of proving ownership—the would-be purchaser simply looks at the land register to ascertain that the seller has title to sell.

STUDENT: But in the old system how would title ever be proved properly? Land has been around forever. Do you mean that the purchaser would have to check right back to the Doomsday Book? This would cost a fortune in conveyancing fees!

> So an efficient system of land transfer must give the buyer a fairly inexpensive and reliable way of proving that the seller owns what he says he owns, or, we might say, has the power to transfer the land to the buyer. As you can see, the system of Registered Land has done this.

D. THE NEED FOR A SYSTEM OF "PRIORITY"

In Chapter 1 we saw that many different rights can exist in relation to the same land/house. For example, a person may acquire a beneficial interest under a trust and this will give them a share of the ownership of the house as a co-owner: as we have seen, it is possible for a person to acquire a share of the ownership of a house by contributing to the purchase price.

> Look back to *Williams & Glyn's Bank v Boland* in Chapter 1 (Chapter 1 section 3: Constructing an argument with the Building Blocks)

It is also possible for a person to acquire an interest in land where the legal owner makes a promise that they will acquire a share, and they rely on this to their detriment.[2] It may be that the legal owner creates a trust, whereby he holds the house for himself and another. For example, if a couple are newly married and they move into a house already owned by the wife, she may decide to execute a document providing that her new husband should have a half-share of the house. There may be a situation like our Herriot House example in Chapter 5, where property is purchased by five persons but conveyed into the names of three of them. The conveyance then provides that they hold the property for themselves and for the others. Whichever way, it is possible that a person, whose name is not on the legal title to the land, may nonetheless have a share of its ownership.[3] And the form which this share will take is that of an interest under a trust: what we call a *beneficial* interest.[4]

There are also many different types of smaller rights that can exist over someone else's land, such as restrictive covenants and easements.

(1) The need for a system of "priority" for these interests

A key factor in understanding the proper functioning of a Land Transfer system is to understand that all these rights in land are *property rights*.

> **BUILDING BLOCK NO 5: Property Rights and the Protection of Purchasers and Mortgage Lenders**
>
> In Chapter 1 we saw that a fundamental principle of Land Law was this idea that rights in land are property rights. Turn back to this Building Block. What is a "property right"? Can you contrast it with another type of right? What are the dangers for purchasers and mortgage lenders posed by property rights in the land they are buying or taking as security?

---

2   Remember *Gillett v Holt* [2001] Ch. 210 from Chapter 2?

3   It is becoming increasingly common for married couples and cohabiting couples to put the house in joint names legally: *Stack v Dowden* [2007] 2 A.C. 432.

4   Strictly speaking interests that arise by virtue of the doctrine of proprietary estoppel, as in *Gillett v Holt* [2001] Ch. 210 at the end of Chapter 2, are not interests under a trust, although they can be given effect to in that way.

Property rights are enforced against the *land itself*. Technically you are saying "I have a right in that land—you must let me exercise it". The right is asserted against the land itself and not against the owner for the time being of that land. This means that any future owner of the land will have to give effect to the right. It does not matter who owns the land. It might have been sold several times over. Parliament and judges have to bear this concept in mind when creating and interpreting a system of Land Transfer Law. Its rules must determine whether a prior interest in the land, such as a beneficial interest or a restrictive covenant, will bind a future purchaser or mortgage lender when he purchases the land.

And so, we need to understand that a primary function of Land Transfer Law is to lay down a system of "priority rules" that determine whether the purchaser or the person with the prior right has the first claim to the land. We looked at "priority rules" when we studied *Williams & Glyn's Bank v Boland* in Chapter 1.

> **It's all a question of** *priority*
> So a recurrent question in Land Transfer Law is: *when the land/house is sold whose interest has priority—the purchaser's/mortgage lender's or the person who owns the prior right?*

E. CRITICAL THINKING ABOUT LAND TRANSFER LAW

How does this relate to our Building Blocks? When we are constructing our arguments about whether Land Transfer Law is good or bad fair or unfair we need to bear in mind that without mortgage finance, our system of owner occupation would probably fail.

> **BUILDING BLOCK NO 5: Property Rights and the Protection of Purchasers and Mortgage Lenders**
> We can argue that a development of a rule in a case or statute is good or bad fair or unfair, depending on the extent to which it supports or undermines the idea that rules of Land Transfer Law should protect a purchaser or mortgage lender from being bound by prior property rights in the land. This is the policy behind the 1925 property legislation. A rule is good if when applied in future cases it would mean that mortgage lenders are not bound by prior rights that were difficult to discover. Banks and building societies often lend to small businesses on the security of family homes. If they cannot be sure that they will be able to take possession and sell a house in order to recoup their money in the event of the borrower's default on the loan repayments, i.e. that someone does not have a prior right to possession (such as Mrs Boland), then they may become reluctant to lend money. This will affect our economy. They may also become reluctant to lend money to residential house purchasers.

Yet on the other hand, the need for residential security and the rise of the owner occupation phenomenon, suggests strongly that this is a factor in deciding whether the rules are good and fair.

> **BUILDING BLOCK NO 1: Residential Security**
>
> We can say that Land Transfer Law is good if it ensures that people's residential security is protected. People with prior rights in the land, such as Mrs Boland, should not have those rights destroyed when the land is mortgaged by the legal owner: See e.g. Gray and Symes, *Real Property and Real People* (1981). We might equally say that when people buy a home in order to live there it is not right that they should be bound by someone else's prior right in that house: See e.g. *In Re Sharpe* [1980] 1 All E.R. 198. Construct a basic argument to show how the existence of some smaller rights in land might be damaging to purchasers like the ones identified in our "visit to the estate agents".

So the law must strike a balance between these opposing policy interests.[5] We also need to ask whether the rules reflect ideas of moral justice: BUILDING BLOCK NO 2: Ideas of Justice, and whether the rules produce certainty and predictability: BUILDING BLOCK NO 6.[6] Part of knowing whether the rules undermine these Building Blocks is learning how to ask questions and cross examine the Building Blocks, i.e. how to *argue imaginatively*. Just because an occupier is evicted by an institutional lender this does not justify our saying that the rules are unfair.[7] For example, if the occupier had legitimate ways in which to protect themselves against such a happening we can argue that the rule allowing eviction is not unfair. The way in which to develop the ability to ask questions is to read carefully the arguments of others in articles. Reading a couple of articles, relevant passages in books, Law Commission reports, and longer extracts from full judgments in cases, will suffice. Your aim is to identify the kinds of question that land transfer lawyers (or "conveyancers") ask about the system.

There are a number of extracts from such sources throughout these next chapters on Land Transfer Law. There are also LECTURER and STUDENT dialogues to help you ask questions and construct argument.

---

5   Gray calls this the balance between "alienability" and "fragmentation" or between "exchange value" and "use value": K. Gray, *Elements of Land Law*, 2nd edn (London: Butterworths, 1993).
6   For the full text of our Building Blocks and information on how to use them to construct an argument, see Chapter 1.
7   Chapter 1 contains instructions on how to ask questions about whether the policies and principles of Land Law are supported or undermined by various situations.

The mechanics and the pre-1925 position of Land Transfer Law

2

A. PROBLEMS FOR PURCHASERS OF THE ESTATE

So now let's look at problems that faced purchasers and mortgage lenders prior to the enactment of the 1925 property legislation. Many different estates and interests were able to co-exist in relation to the same piece of land. This made it difficult for a purchaser to buy land. For example, in the nineteenth century it was common to find land tied up for generations. Land was left to A for life, remainder to B in fee tail, and then remainder to C in fee simple. A, B and C all had estates in the land. Three separate estates with three separate owners existed in relation to the same plot of land: the life interest, the fee tail, and the fee simple. A purchaser would want the absolute fee simple estate, not these limited rights, because it is only the fee simple that would give him unrestricted ownership of the land. If he purchased A's interest, he could only enjoy the land for the length of A's life. If he purchased B's fee tail, this again would be a limited interest. If he purchased C's interest, it might never fall into possession, as B might have heirs. Another way of looking at the purchaser's problem is that he would have to piece together an unrestricted ownership by obtaining all the more limited estates that existed in relation to the land.[8]

Fragmentation of title and co-ownership[9]: Another conveyancing problem, far more relevant for our purposes, was "fragmentation of title". Prior to the 1925 legislation the legal fee simple estate might be held by many people at the same time in separate shares. You will remember that these are called "tenancies in common".

> If you remember from Chapter 4 section 2, The Principles of Co-ownership, a tenancy in common is a way in which co-owners hold land. It means that they each have a separate and identifiable interest in the land which they can leave to anyone they like by will, or it will pass under the rules of intestacy. Unlike the joint tenancy, the other way of co-owning land, the share of one co-owner does not pass to the remaining co-owners when he dies.

---

8   Prior to the 1925 legislation, two devices had been used to give to the purchaser the full and unrestricted fee simple estate: 1. The process known as "barring the entail", whereby the land was conveyed to the purchaser in such a way as to preclude the claim of the person entitled to the entail. The purchaser thus gained an unencumbered fee simple estate. 2. The person who had the life interest that was currently in possession of land, the "tenant for life" was given powers of disposition. This would enable him to convey the fee simple to a purchaser: see the Settled Land Act 1882. Thus, it might be argued that the 1925 reforms did not achieve anything radical in terms of protecting a purchaser from these fragmented settled estates: George Osborne Morgan, *Land Law Reform in England* (1888). The Settled Land Act 1925 went one step further by vesting the whole fee simple in the tenant for life, endowing him with powers of disposition, and then rendering void any disposition that was beyond these powers: J.S.Anderson, *Lawyers and the Making of English Land Law 1832–1940* (Oxford: Clarendon Press 1992); C.Harpum, "Overreaching, Trustees' Powers and Reform of the 1925 Legislation" [1990] C.L.J. 277. We looked at the 1925 land transfer reforms in the context of successive ownership and the Settled Land Act 1925 in Chapter 4, p.223. Because of the declining importance of strict settlements after the Trusts of Land and Appointment of Trustees Act 1996 I do not propose to cover the matter any further in these chapters on land transfer.

9   C.Harpum [1990] C.L.J. 277.

These separate interests in the same land would be left to many different people in the co-owners' wills. So if a purchaser wanted to buy the land, or take a lease, or its owners wanted to create a mortgage, the purchaser or mortgagee had to track down all the people who owned the different fragments of the estate and obtain their permission to the transaction.[10] In some cases title was almost impossible to discover.[11]

B. HOW LEGAL AND EQUITABLE RIGHTS IN THE ESTATE BIND A PURCHASER

Furthermore, property rights in land would bind purchasers or mortgage lenders in different ways, depending on whether the right was legal or equitable. We will now examine these briefly to see how they made life difficult for purchasers.

> **The need to relate back to ideas about "equity" in Chapter 2**
> Before you can understand how legal and equitable rights have to be accommodated within a system of Land Transfer you must have a thorough grounding in the knowledge of English Law's peculiar development of two sets of rules. Re-visit the section in Chapter 2 on what equity *is* and how it works.

(1) How legal property rights in the estate bind a purchaser

Where a property right was recognised by ordinary Land Law, the common law, for example, a lease, an easement, or a mortgage on the land, it was recognised as a right that "bound the whole world". A legal right is a right *in rem*, which means that it is a right in the land itself. This means that anyone buying the land, receiving it as a gift, or coming by it any other way, will automatically be bound by that interest.

> **Although this rule is not relevant in the system of Registered Land it is important that we understand how it works**

For example, if Alison is the owner of the freehold of a house and grants a lease to Matthew, he then has a legal right in the land. If Alison sold the house to Derek, the latter would have to give effect to Matthew's lease. It binds any person who comes into possession of the house from Alison, whether as a gift or as a purchase. It is irrelevant whether Derek knew about the lease or not. Similarly, if Manpreet was the owner of Broadacres and granted a right of way (an easement) for 30 years by deed to Jonathan, he would have a legal right in Broadacres. He could then

---

10   You may remember from Chapter 5 that it was this problem of fragmentation of ownership that led to the rule that a legal estate in land could only be held as a joint tenancy (which operates by right of survivorship and no share can be left to anyone in a will), and there could only be a maximum of four people holding the legal estate.

11   A.Underhill (1920) 37 L.Q.R. 197; J.S.Anderson, *Lawyers and the Making of English Land Law 1832–1940*, p.288.

enforce that right of way against any purchaser of Broadacres from Manpreet. Jonathan's right is a right in the land itself.

(2) Equitable property rights bind the whole world *except* "Equity's Darling"

> Although this rule has been substantially modified by the 1925 legislation, and is not relevant at all in the system of Registered Land, it is important that we understand how it works.

Equity has an important principle at its centre. Many of its rules were formulated on the basis that the defendant should act *in good conscience*. Thus it is said that equity "operates on the conscience of the individual". For example, Frank is the freehold owner of Blueacre. He inherited it from his sister and in accordance with the terms of her will, he is holding the house on trust for his grandchildren. Thus, the grandchildren have an equitable interest in the land. Frank also owns Redacre and has entered into a restrictive covenant with his neighbour, Asif, promising not to build any more than one house on Redacre. As we saw in Chapter 2 a restrictive covenant is also an equitable interest. Frank then sells both houses and leaves the country with the proceeds of sale. The new owner of Redacre starts to build a housing estate on the land. The new owner of Blueacre refuses to recognise the grandchildren's rights. The grandchildren and the neighbour have causes of action against Frank, for breach of trust and contract respectively. But they are unlikely to find him.[12] Our question concerns the extent to which the grandchildren and Asif can enforce their rights against the new owners of Blueacre and Redacre respectively. Can the grandchildren force the new legal owners of Blueacre to hold it for them on trust? Can Asif force the new owner of Redacre to stop building on the land and demolish the existing structures? So we ask: when will equitable rights bind a purchaser?

The rule that applied here is the so-called "Equity's Darling" rule. Equitable rights will bind the whole world, meaning every new transferee of the land *except* Equity's Darling. Thus, if the new purchasers of Blueacre and Redacre can establish that they are Equity's Darling then they will take free from the rights of the grandchildren and Asif.

> **The Equity's Darling rule (doctrine of notice): a conscience-based doctrine**
> Predictably, the doctrine that was established by equity to tell us when equitable rights would bind a purchaser is designed to make him take the house/land subject to the right only if he had a bad conscience when he undertook the transaction.

---

12   This is a common context of a land transfer dispute. The owners of rights will seek to enforce them against the land because it provides them with a more effective remedy.

(3) Who is Equity's Darling? The bona fide purchaser of a legal estate for value without notice

Prior to 1925 it was the doctrine of notice that determined whether equitable rights in land would bind a purchaser of that land. Its principles are illustrated by *Pilcher v Rawlins*.[13] The plaintiffs had an equitable mortgage over certain property. The owner of the property then conveyed the property to X. This was a conveyance of the legal estate.[14] However, when conveying the property the owner had concealed the fact that there was a prior equitable mortgage on the land. The plaintiffs claimed that their equitable mortgage took priority over the later conveyance of the legal estate in the land to X, or, in alternative language, X was bound by their right and had to give effect to it.

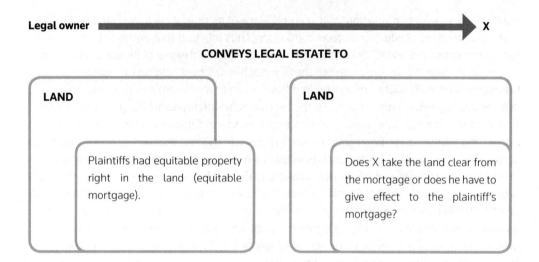

Lord Hatherley L.C. held that X took free from the plaintiff's equitable mortgage because X was a bona fide purchaser of a legal estate for value without notice of the mortgage. He was "Equity's Darling". The reason was that because he did not know about the prior existence of the mortgage, X's conscience was clear when he took a transfer of the land. Lord Hatherley L.C. observed that upon establishing "the plea of purchase without notice . . . . equity declines all interference with the purchaser, having, as is said, no ground on which it can affect his conscience". Sir W.M.James L.J. observed that

"a purchaser, when he has once put in [the plea of bona fide purchaser], may be interrogated and tested to any extent as to the valuable consideration which he has given . . . and also

---

13   (1871–72) L.R. 7 Ch. App. 259.
14   This way was the pre-1925 way of creating a mortgage in the property, the land itself would be conveyed to the lender as security for a loan. This was why the conveyance took place in this case. The precise question was whether the second lender was bound first to give effect to the first mortgage.

the presence or the absence of notice; but when once he has gone through that ordeal, and has satisfied the terms of the plea of purchase for valuable consideration without notice, then, according to my judgment, this Court has no jurisdiction whatever to do anything more than to let him depart in possession of that legal estate".

Maitland explains that equity will not make a purchaser take land subject to a prior equitable right where he has bought that land in good faith and with no prior knowledge of the equitable right. He has purchased a legal estate and equity will not interfere with that right unless his conscience is affected.

> "How could it be otherwise? A purchaser in good faith has obtained a legal right. In a court of law that right is his: the law of the land gives it him. On what ground of equity are you going to take it from him? He has not himself undertaken any obligation . . . . he has done no wrong, he has acted honestly and with diligence. Equity cannot touch him."
>
> F.W.Maitland, *Lectures in Equity* (1936), pp.114–5

(4) The doctrine of notice ("Equity's Darling rule") in detail

Under the doctrine of notice a purchaser will take free from a prior equitable property right in the land if he can establish that he is a *bona fide purchaser of a legal estate for value without notice.*

"**Bona fide**": This means that the purchaser must act in "good faith". There is no specific example in this context, but using other contexts, it might be said that the purchaser must be purchasing the land for genuine reasons, which, here, may mean that he is not purchasing the land in collusion with the vendor in order deliberately to defeat someone's earlier right.[15]

"**Purchaser for value**": A person who purchases the legal estate in land must give value for it. But, as with the law of contract, the consideration that the purchaser gives for the estate does not have to be adequate.[16] But some value must be given. Otherwise, the purchaser is deemed to be a "volunteer" and under this doctrine must take subject to any prior equitable rights.[17]

"**Of a Legal Estate**": Clearly this would include a freehold and a leasehold estate in land. It also includes a mortgage.[18] The purchaser must have bought a *legal* estate, such as a properly executed freehold of leasehold, or a legal mortgage. If any of the formalities are defective, the

---

15   In the context of the duty of good faith associated with the exercise of the mortgagee's right to possess and sell the mortgaged property, see *Meretz Investment NV v ACP Ltd* [2007] EWCA Civ 1303; also *Quennell v Maltby* [1979] 1 W.L.R. 318.

16   M.Thompson, *Modern Land Law*, 4th edn (Oxford University Press, 2009) p.49.

17   *Kettlewell v Watson* (1882) L.R. 21 Ch. D. 685, p.709.

18   *Kingsnorth Finance Co Ltd v Tizard* [1986] 1 W.L.R. 783.

purchaser will not get a legal estate.[19] Only a purchaser of a legal estate can claim to be Equity's Darling.[20]

"**Without Notice**": In order to take a legal estate in land free from a prior equitable right the purchaser must not have notice of the right. This "doctrine of notice" is in three parts. A purchaser with, actual, constructive, or imputed notice, of a prior equitable right will take the estate subject to that right.

(a) Actual notice
Actual notice is where "the rights have been brought directly to the attention of the [purchaser] such that she does know of the existence and nature of those rights".[21] For example, if when Frank sold Blueacre the purchaser actually knew that Frank was holding the house on trust for his grandchildren, then the purchaser would take subject to the rights of the grandchildren.

(b) Constructive notice
As Maitland puts it, if the law takes the step of subjecting a purchaser to rights that he knows about, "another is inevitable. If we stop here purchasers will take care not to know of the trust [or other right] . . . they will shut their eyes. . . . It is not enough that you should be honest, it is required of you that you should also be diligent".[22] Thus, a purchaser will take subject to equitable property rights that he *would have known about* had he inspected the land and investigated the title documents. This is known as "constructive notice." A purchaser must "make all such investigations of his vendor's title as a prudent purchaser would have made."[23]

(i) The purchaser must inspect the title documents
A purchaser is required to inspect the title documents to the property, to make sure that there are no equitable rights, such as express trusts or restrictive covenants which exist in relation to the land.[24] The Law of Property Act 1969 provides that he must look back 15 years.[25] This means that a purchaser will take the land subject to an equitable interest, such as a restrictive covenant, if it could have been found recorded on the deeds of conveyance to the land. Whenever the land was transferred from seller to buyer there would have been such a deed. A purchaser must establish that the right was not disclosed by the deeds in the last 15 years.[26] If there was a deed of conveyance 12 years ago and one 17 years ago, the purchaser would have to go back and

---

19   Law of Property Act 1925 s.52.
20   *McCarthy & Stone Ltd v Julian S. Hodge & Co Ltd* [1971] 1 W.L.R. 1547.
21   A.Hudson, *Equity and Trusts*, 6th edn (Routledge-Cavendish, 2009), p.1110.
22   F.W.Maitland, *Lectures in Equity* (1936), pp.113–4; *Kettlewell v Watson* (1882) L.R. 21 Ch. D. 685.
23   Maitland, above pp.113–4.
24   Not all equitable interests have been formally created and noted on the deeds of conveyance. For example, a spouse who has contributed to the purchase price of her family home will have informally acquired an equitable interest under a resulting or constructive trust. These interests arise without any writing at all and therefore cannot be discovered by a purchaser or mortgage lender by inspecting the title deeds. They must be discovered by inspecting the land, looking for signs of occupation, and asking questions: *Kingsnorth Finance Co Ltd v Tizard* [1986] 1 W.L.R. 783 (see below).
25   Law of Property Act 1969 s.23.
26   *In re Nisbet and Potts' Contract* [1906] 1 Ch. 386. The statutory period applicable at this time was 40 years.

examine the latter to make sure there were no equitable rights mentioned therein. A purchaser is entitled to take the documents at face value and is not obliged to ask whether there is anything that must be rectified.[27]

(ii) The purchaser must inspect the land itself

According to the doctrine of notice, a purchaser would have to make inquiries to see if there was anyone other than the person selling the legal estate able to assert rights against the land. It was common at the time of the 1925 legislation for someone other than the seller to be in occupation, under a tenancy for example, and for the seller to live somewhere else. Thus, the courts established that the purchaser could not just rely on the word of the seller that no one had any equitable rights that might bind him once he had bought the land.[28] The purchaser had to inquire of persons in occupation of the land.

In *Hunt v Luck*[29] the freehold owner was not in occupation of the land, his tenants were. Those tenants had rights in the land. The owner mortgaged the land and the question was whether the lender, as a purchaser of a legal estate for value, took his estate subject to the rights of the tenants. Vaughan Williams L.J. held that if the purchaser knows that the vendor is not in occupation himself but someone else is, he must make inquiries of those persons in occupation to see what rights they have. If the purchaser chooses not to do this, he will not be able to take the land free from any rights the occupiers may have. The purchaser would not have made sufficient inspections and inquiries to be able to assert that he was a purchaser without constructive notice.[30] Thus, to return to our example: Frank is holding Blueacre on trust for his grandchildren. If, when the purchaser of Blueacre went to inspect the house, any of Frank's grandchildren were adult[31] and in occupation of the house, the purchaser would be deemed to have constructive notice of their equitable interests under the trust.

(c) Imputed notice

The knowledge of the purchaser's agent, e.g. solicitor or surveyor, is attributed to the purchaser himself. This means that if his solicitor is aware of someone with an equitable right in the land, the purchaser will take subject to that right, even though he did not know of it himself.[32] Thus, if in our Redacre example, the solicitor acting for the purchaser of Redacre was well aware that Frank had granted the benefit of a restrictive covenant to Asif, this notice would be "imputed" to the purchaser. He would take subject to Asif's rights under the covenant.

---

27 *Smith v Jones* [1954] 1 W.L.R. 1089, a purchaser was not obliged to inquire into a tenant's right to rectify a lease: E.H.Burn, *Maudsley & Burn's Land Law Cases and Materials*, 8th edn (Oxford University Press, 2004), pp.47–49.
28 For a later manifestation of this principle see *Hodgson v Marks* [1971] Ch. 892.
29 *Hunt v Luck* [1902] 1 Ch. 428.
30 *Hunt v Luck*, above pp.432–3; *Barnhart v Greenshields* (1853) 9 Moo. P.C. 18; *Taylor v Stibbert* (1794) 2 Ves. Jun. 437; *Daniels v Davison* (1809) 16 Ves. Jun. 249; *Allen v Anthony* (1816) 1 Mer. 282.
31 For this principle it is necessary that the owner of the equitable interest is of full age, otherwise they could not answer the purchaser's enquiries about their interest.
32 *Kettlewell v Watson* (1882) L.R. 21 Ch. D. 685.

(5) Law of Property Act 1925 section 199

Section 199 of the Law of Property Act 1925 puts the doctrine of notice on a statutory footing.[33] The provision was intended, if anything, to restrict the doctrine of notice.[34]

> **"199 Restrictions on constructive notice**
>
> (1) A purchaser shall not be prejudicially affected by notice of . . .
>
>   (ii) any other instrument or matter or any fact or thing unless-
>
>   (a) it is within his own knowledge, or would have come to his knowledge if such inquiries and inspections had been made as ought reasonably to have been made by him; or
>
>   (b) . . . it has come to the knowledge of his. . . agent [e.g. solicitor], as such, or would have come to the knowledge of his solicitor or other agent, as such, if such inquiries and inspections had been made as ought reasonably to have been made by the solicitor or other agent."

(6) The effect of the doctrine of notice

If a purchaser has acquired a legal estate in the land for value and without notice of a prior equitable right, then this means that the right ceases to exist as an interest in the land. The right has been extinguished forever and cannot be revived against anyone who later purchases the land.[35] This is the case even if the purchaser later transfers the land to a person who knows full well that there was an equitable right in the land. So, if the purchaser of Blueacre is a bona fide purchaser and does not have any of the forms of notice identified above, then the grandchildren's rights cease to exist. They will of course have a personal remedy against Frank, and will be able to assert that he holds on trust for them any property that Frank acquired in exchange for the land (e.g. money). But they will not be able to claim against the purchaser of Blueacre. If that purchaser of Blueacre then sells the land to Mr and Mrs Chandi, who know full well that the house was originally held on trust by Frank, the rights of the grandchildren against the land have been extinguished and cannot be revived by the later purchaser's, Mr and Mrs Chandi's, notice. As Fry J. observed in *Kettlewell v Watson*[36]:

> "a *bona fide* purchaser for value without notice may deal as he will with the estate which he has acquired, that he has a right to have the whole world as purchasers from him, and that he has a right, therefore, to convey, even to a person cognizant of the infirmity of his title".

(7) Problems associated with the doctrine of notice

The original idea behind the doctrine of notice was that an honest and diligent purchaser would be able to take the land free from equitable rights. His conscience would be clear, and thus, so

---

33   Re-enacting Conveyancing Act 1882 s.3(1).
34   M.Thompson, *Modern Land Law*, p.55.
35   *Wilkes v Spooner* [1911] 2 K.B. 473.
36   (1882) L.R. 21 Ch. D. 685.

would his title. However, time and again judges of conveyancing disputes would remark about the length to which the courts had taken the doctrine of notice. The standard of diligence required of a purchaser, before he could be "Equity's Darling" was very high indeed. Ordinary purchasers would not be capable of knowing what to look for and how to prevent themselves being "fixed with notice" of adverse equitable rights. The whole conveyancing process of making sure that the seller had a good title and that no one was claiming prior equitable rights, took a great deal of time and legal skill. The process was therefore expensive. Fry J. in *Kettlewell v Watson*[37] commented that:

"In this case a piece of land of about four acres has been subdivided into numerous parcels, which have been purchased, for small sums of money, by various persons, many of whom are now before the Court as litigants in this very expensive and elaborate litigation. Such purchasers are exposed to this difficulty, that they must either expend a large sum of money in investigating the title, according to the regular forms of conveyancing, or they must run the risk (which they might even not escape by that investigation) of finding themselves involved in a very heavy litigation."

Although a prudent purchaser would investigate his seller's title anyway, not the least because he needed to make sure that he had a legal estate to sell, and to ascertain that there were no legal rights on the land, such as tenancies, as these would bind him anyway,[38] Maitland comments that the courts had stretched the doctrine of notice far beyond what an ordinary purchaser *would* be able to do, and what was usual for him to do when ascertaining his vendor's title.

"[I]n reading some of the cases about constructive notice we may be inclined to say that equity demanded not the care of the most prudent father of a family but the care of the most prudent solicitor of a family aided by the skill of the most expert conveyancer."[39]

(a) Conveyancing with trusts

Conveyancing where there was a trust, as in our Blueacre example with Frank holding the estate on trust for his grandchildren, was especially difficult. It would be the trustees who would convey legal title to the land to the purchaser, because it was trustees who held legal title. However, as far as the equitable interests under the trust were concerned, as against a purchaser, "equitable interests were almost as well protected as legal interests".[40] The doctrine of constructive notice was the single most significant problem that the 1925 land transfer reforms were designed to overcome.[41] The way that the courts had stretched the doctrine meant that it only required the

---

37 (1882) L.R. 21 Ch. D. 685, pp.701–2.

38 F.W.Maitland, *Lectures in Equity* (1936), p.119.

39 Maitland, above p.119; Similarly, in *Pilcher v Rawlins* Lord Hatherley L.C. thought that the cases on the doctrine of notice had "undoubtedly have gone very far . . . I confess that the extent to which this doctrine has been carried was not wholly satisfactory to me": (1871–72) L.R. 7 Ch. App. 259, p.266.

40 (2006) 69 M.L.R. 214, p.217: J.S.Anderson, *Lawyers and the Making of English Land Law 1832–1940*, pp.268–9.

41 The following is taken from a paragraph in another article by the current author: (2006) 69 M.L.R. 214. I reproduce the references as reproduced there.

merest mention of the existence of a trust in one deed of conveyance in the chain of title, and the purchaser would be fixed with notice of the beneficiaries' equitable rights.[42] The purchaser then had to make exhaustive, difficult and sometimes inappropriately personal inquiries into the trust. Unless he did this a purchaser would have notice of all the equitable interests under the trust, which often represented a considerable part of the value of the land.[43] So what type of inquiry did he have to make? The purchaser had to make sure that the trustees had been properly appointed and had the requisite powers to make the transfer.[44] He had to ensure that the trustees had obtained any consent to the transaction that was required by the trust, if any, and, where the purpose of the trust was to sell the land and make a fund of money for paying debts and other charges, he had to ensure that the proceeds of sale were properly applied to these purposes.[45] Thus, the purchaser had to inquire into the mechanics of the trust, which was often time-consuming and not the kind of inquiry that it was easy for an outsider to the trust to make.

> **Conveyancing with trusts was like getting caught in a spider's web**
> All in all it seemed that once there was a trust mentioned in the chain of title, the purchaser had to ask questions and the more information he obtained about the trust—the more inquiries he had to make.

Legal questions would go back and forth between the lawyers for the seller and the purchaser. Conveyancing that involved a trust would be hugely time-consuming and correspondingly expensive, as Lord Haldane observed in his *Real Property and Conveyancing Bill*.[46] Land Registrar Brickdale thought that "One of the evils afflicting traditional conveyancing . . . was the ever-present possibility that a purchaser might find himself 'fixed with notice'—a process which he seems to have thought rather like pig-sticking in its gleeful brutality to the innocent and vulnerable".[47]

C. THE WINDS OF CHANGE

The idea behind the 1925 land transfer reforms, which culminated in the property legislation of 1925, was to change the rules so that conveyancing became quicker and cheaper. Liberal

---

42   C.Harpum, "Overreaching, Trustees' Powers and Reform of the 1925 Legislation" [1990] C.L.J. 277.

43   Anderson, above pp.266–280. *In re Soden and Alexander's Contract* [1918] 2 Ch. 258 made reference to this difficulty and approved the practice whereby deeds would actually suppress the existence of a trust in order that the purchaser would not be fixed with notice of the equitable interests under the trust: Harpum, above, p.283; Anderson, "The 1925 Property Legislation: Setting Contexts" in S.Bright and J.Dewar (eds), *Land Law Themes and Perspectives* (Oxford University Press, 1998), pp.107, 111–3.

44   Anderson, above pp.266–280; Harpum, above p.283; Anderson, "The 1925 Property Legislation: Setting Contexts" in S.Bright and J.Dewar (eds), *Land Law Themes and Perspectives* (1998), pp.107, 111–3.

45   G.Spence, *The Equitable Jurisdiction of the Court of Chancery* (1846–1849), Vol II, p.380; Maitland, *Equity* (1936), Lecture 10 and reviser's comments, pp.209–12; Harpum, above pp.283–5.

46   The *Real Property and Conveyancing Bills 1913–1915* were the forerunners of much of the 1925 property legislation that we have today. They were, however, different in important respects: see Anderson, *Lawyers and the Making of English Land Law 1832–1940*.

47   J.S.Anderson, *Lawyers and the Making of English Land Law 1832–1940*, p.266, citing Brickdale's evidence to the *Royal Commission on the Land Transfer Acts* (1909) "Minutes of Evidence" (1909) H.C.P. xxvii 733, para.1984–2004.

politicians wanted to make sure that land could be divided up and sold to ordinary people in small plots, which "would do much to foster the good of society in general by instilling in an individual a sense of identity and security".[48] George Osborne Morgan concluded that the doctrine of constructive notice was a problem,[49] and that "the first step towards bringing small properties within reach of the poorer classes is to make sales easy and transfers cheap".[50]

(1) Summary

The conveyancing difficulties considered in this chapter were an essential force behind the fundamental restructure of Land Law undertaken by the so-called "1925 Property Legislation". The problems with land transfer centred on the disproportionate costs that were associated with the ordinary purchase of land. It was because of the "fragmentation of title" associated with tenancies in common and the degree of diligence and skill required by the doctrine of constructive notice in order for a purchaser to take free from equitable interests, that the most ordinary of transactions with land gave rise to huge legal costs. Something needed to be done. Land Law needed a scheme of land transfer that enabled a purchaser to acquire title to land *easily* and above all: *cheaply*.

---

48   Jackson, (2006) 69 M.L.R. 214, p.218, referring to George Osborne Morgan's pamphlet, *Land Law Reform in England* (1880), pp.8, 21–23.
49   *Land Law Reform in England* (1880), pp.15–23.
50   Above, p.22, quoted (2006) 69 M.L.R. 214, p.218.

Chapter 7

Land Transfer Law (2): The 1925 Legislation

CHAPTER OVERVIEW

In this chapter you will find:

- An introduction to the draftsman of the 1925 legislation and what he intended to achieve
- The 1925 scheme for simplifying conveyancing
- The principles of land transfer where title to land is unregistered
- Full extracts from cases and instructions on how to think like a land lawyer
- Constructed argument using Building Blocks.

The 1925 Legislation

1

The 1925 legislation restructured land transfer law. It was designed to make conveyancing easier and cheaper. One important idea behind the legislation was to pave the way for a system of compulsory registration of title, where title to the land would be registered and held at the Land Registry.[1] This was laid down by the Land Registration Act 1925. This system would gradually supersede the old system of conveyancing by examining the title deeds (which has become known as "unregistered land").

But as we saw in the previous chapter, Land Law was in such a tangle, and conveyancing so difficult, that before any new registration system could be introduced, it was necessary to reform the basic principles. Titles to land had to be simplified so that there was something clear and coherent to register and keep at the Land Registry.[2] Since the enactment of the Land Registration Act 2002, which repealed the Land Registration Act 1925 in its entirety, there has been a strong drive to get all land in England and Wales on the central Land Register. When this has finally happened, we can consign the old unregistered land rules to history. But because it has not

---

1 Today the system of registration of title is by far the dominant system of land holding. We study registered land in the next Chapter.
2 *Royal Commission on the Land Transfer Acts*, Second and Final Report (1911).

happened yet, we need to know how title is transferred in the old way. We will first consider the general principles of the 1925 legislative reform.

> **The 1925 Property Legislation and its Author: Sir Benjamin Lennard Cherry (1869–1932), lawyer and parliamentary draftsman**
>
> "Cherry practised as a conveyancer and draftsman of parliamentary Bills. [He] was the main author of the Birkenhead property legislation, consisting of the Law of Property Act of 1925 and six ancillary statutes. . . . It revolutionized land law, and was at that time the largest single body of legislation which had ever been placed on the British statute book. . . . Professor D. Hughes Parry said of the revolutionary Birkenhead Acts, named after the lord chancellor of the time, that Cherry nursed them jealously and defended them wholeheartedly, as if they were his children, adding that he took endless pains in lectures, textbooks, and articles to make their effect generally known and he won over the solicitors of the country, who had profited greatly from the complexities of old-style conveyancing, to a sympathetic administration of the new law. Viscount Haldane, one of five lord chancellors associated with the prelude to and creation of the Birkenhead Property Acts . . . said of Cherry that he was master of the new oceans on which, as a result, practitioners had been called to embark (*New Property Acts*, v). Wolstenholme, himself a great reformer and conveyancer, had already suggested making land transferable, like stocks and shares, free from trusts and settlements and Cherry called him 'the originator of the germ'" (*Wolstenholme and Cherry*).
>
> Oxford Dictionary of National Biography: In Association with the British Academy: From the Earliest Times to the Year 2000 by H.C.G Matthew and Brian Harrison (2004); 210 words from the entry on Sir Benjamin Lennard Cherry by Francis Bennion, by permission of Oxford University Press.

A. AN OUTLINE OF THE 1925 SCHEME: ESTATES-BASED CONVEYANCING[3]

In the last chapter we saw that the law allowed many people to own many different estates and interests in the same piece of land. They were all legal and they all would bind a purchaser automatically. For example, if A owned a life interest in the land, B, a fee tail, and C a fee simple in remainder (a typical settlement), how could a purchaser make sure that he obtained the absolute fee simple in possession? He did not want to have to give effect to a stranger's interest first. He wanted the totality of the ownership of the land. We also saw that at the time of the 1925 legislation, where the fee simple estate in land was owned by than one person the preferred form of co-ownership was the tenancy in common.[4] Each tenant in common had a separate share that they could leave it by will to several people—who would then each own a smaller share of the estate. Every time a co-owner died the legal estate would split up (or "fragment") into more and

---

3   See for example, P.Sparkes, *A New Land Law* (Hart, 1999).
4   See Chapter 6.

more shares. Before buying the land a purchaser had to make sure that the owner of each separate share of the estate consented to the sale. In one example given prior to the enactment of the 1925 legislation, there were more than 40 co-owners of a block of buildings, all having separate shares, and all having to give consent to a sale.[5] This problem is often referred to as "title fragmentation",[6] must have been the bain of the life of many a person wanting to purchase land.

As we saw in the previous chapter the other significant problem was the lengths to which the courts had take the doctrine of constructive notice. So what did the draftsman do about these conveyancing problems?[7]

Benjamin Cherry's scheme for reform
(i) Limit the number of legal estates and interests, because they bind a purchaser automatically, and make all the rest equitable only;
(ii) Make sure the ownership of the legal fee simple estate can't be fragmented up and put it in the hands of a small number of people capable looking after it and able to transact with the estate and convey good title to a purchaser/mortgage lender;
(iii) Introduce quick and cheap ways for the owner(s) to transfer the estate to a purchaser free from equitable interests and from the gleefully brutal effects of the doctrine of notice.

(1) Limit the number of legal estates and interests

The 1925 draftsman, Benjamin Cherry, limited the number of legal estates that could bind the whole world to TWO: Fee Simple Absolute in Possession (freehold) and the Term of Years Absolute (leasehold). All the others would henceforth be equitable interests only. As we shall see, he then introduced a quick and easy system of making sure that the purchaser (or mortgage lender) of the legal estate would take free from equitable interests.

And here it is in black and white →

Law of Property Act 1925

"1. Legal estates and equitable interests

(1) The only estates in land which are capable of subsisting or of being conveyed or created at law are-

(a) An estate in fee simple absolute in possession;

(b) A term of years absolute

(3) All other estates, interests, and charges in or over land take effect as equitable interests."

---

5   J.S.Anderson, *Lawyers and the Making of English Land Law 1932–1940* (Oxford: Clarendon Press, 1992), p.290. The example continued that on the next death the number of co-owners would exceed 100.

6   For example, Harpum, [1990] C.L.J. 277; M.P.Thompson, *Modern Land Law*, 4th edn (Oxford University Press, 2009).

7   See for example, Harpum, "Overreaching, Trustees' Powers and Reform of the 1925 Legislation" [1990] C.L.J. 277.

So only two estates can now exist as legal estates: the freehold (fee simple absolute in possession) and the leasehold (term of years absolute). All other estates have been reclassified as equitable interests. Thus, a purchaser could deal with the seller of the fee simple estate in the confidence that all other estates and interests would be equitable, and that there was an easy system laid down for making sure that he was not bound by these equitable interests.

However it is important to note that s.1 says that the freehold and leasehold are *capable* of being legal estates. This means that they still have to comply with the required formalities before they *are* actually legal estates.

> **LECTURER:** Revisit Chapter 3 section 2A, p.119, and look at the formalities required for the creation of legal estates and interests in land.

The Law of Property Act 1925 also limited the number of rights in land that are capable of existing as legal interests (smaller rights). All others were deemed to be equitable only. Thus, a purchaser of the fee simple would only have to look for a few types of interest that he knew would bind him automatically. The Law of Property Act 1925, as we shall see later in this section, then provided a means by which a purchaser could easily and cheaply take the land free from equitable interests without having to make exhaustive enquiries about their existence.

Law of Property Act 1925

> **And here it is in black and white**

"1. Legal estates and equitable interests

(1) . . . . . (as above)

(2) The only interests or charges in or over land which are capable of subsisting or of being conveyed or created at law are-

    (a) An easement, right, or privilege in or over land for an interest equivalent to an estate in fee simple absolute in possession or a term of years absolute;

    (b) a rentcharge. . .

    (c) A charge by way of legal mortgage;

    (e) Rights of entry exercisable over or in respect of a legal term of years absolute. . .

(3) All other estates, interests, and charges in or over land take effect as equitable interests."

LECTURER: Before going any further—we need to consolidate what we have learned by a game of identification. Tell me whether the following estates and interests in land are legal or equitable. What about a fee simple?[8]

---

8   For further details see Chapter 2 section 3.

STUDENT: It's capable of being a legal estate (s.1(1)(a)), and will be, provided there is a deed (s.52 LPA 1925).

LECTURER: Excellent. This is correct, provided of course that it is a fee simple absolute *in possession*.

> **Estates in Land**
> To make sure you fully "get" the meaning of s.1, go back to the section on estates in land in Chapter 2 section 3 and look at what "in possession" means and the terms that have the contrary meaning.

LECTURER: What about a lease for a two year term?

STUDENT: A legal estate, but it doesn't require a deed because it falls within the s.54(2) exception, or at least it will do if there is no premium to be paid and the lease is for the best market rent obtainable.

> **We will look at this exception to the formality requirement when we study leases.**

LECTURER: OK then, what about a right of way granted by Harry to Vanessa, until Harry moves out of No 35 Elm Close.

STUDENT: Legal under s.1(2).

LECTURER: No.

STUDENT: But a right of way is an easement and that falls into s.1(2)(a).

LECTURER: I don't doubt it . . . but read the rest of the provision.

STUDENT: An easement "for an interest equivalent to an estate in fee simple absolute in possession or a term of years absolute". Oh, this refers to the length of time that the right must be for. The right of way Harry grants is not for an indefinite length of time (fee simple), nor for a set term of years. The right is not in the list of legal interests, so if anything it will be equitable: s.1(3).

LECTURER: A restrictive covenant?

STUDENT: Equitable—it's not in the list of legal interests: s.1(3).

> **Can you do this?**

LECTURER: A beneficial interest under a trust?

STUDENT: Equitable—not in the s.1(2) list.

LECTURER: Good, I think you've got the hang of this now.

(a) Legal estates and interests bind the whole world where title to the land is unregistered

If a person can show that he is owner of a legal interest, such as an easement, then, where the land is unregistered, that interest automatically binds every subsequent purchaser of the land over which he has the right. If a person can show entitlement to one of the two legal estates, the fee simple absolute in possession or the term of years absolute, then that person will be able to assert his prior right to that estate against *anyone*.

For example, if Derek was the owner of the fee simple to Freeacre and Matthew forges a document, purporting to be a deed of conveyance, transferring the legal estate in Freeacre to Peter, then Derek will be able to claim the land back. It does not matter how innocent Peter is. Legal estates and interests bind the whole world.[9] This shows us one of the vital reasons why a purchaser of a legal estate in land, must establish that the seller *owns what he says he owns*.[10] And we have seen that the way in which this is done is by proving an unbroken chain of transfers (or "conveyances") of the land to the current seller. Where title to the land is registered, the Land Registration Act 2002 lays down its own rules for when an estate or interest binds a purchaser. We will consider these rules in Chapter 8.

(b) How does the purchaser prove that the seller owns the legal estate?

Where title is unregistered, the seller of the estate must show an unbroken chain of transfers from previous owners to himself for a period of 15 years.[11] There may not be a conveyance at exactly the 15 year point so the purchaser would have to go back to the first conveyance made before then, e.g. 17 years. We call this establishing "good root of title".

(2) Problems with legal co-ownership of the estate

As we saw above, where land was co-owned this could create problems. So Benjamin Cherry, the 1925 draftsman, imposed a statutory trust whenever land is conveyed or left by will to more than one person.

> **A trust**
> Remember that a trust is a device whereby property is owned legally by "trustees". However, they hold the property for the beneficiaries in equity: See Chapters 2 (section 3) and 4 (section 1C, p.220). The equitable interest is the real ownership of the land.

The legal estate cannot be held by more than four persons or "trustees" and if land is conveyed to 10 people, the Law of Property Act 1925 provides that the legal estate will be held for the first four of full age named.[12] They are deemed to hold the estate on trust for themselves and the other co-owners in equity.[13] They will hold the legal estate on a *joint tenancy*, which operates by right of survivorship.[14]

---

9   F.W. Maitland, *Lectures in Equity* (1936).
10   R. Smith, *Property Law*, 2nd edn (Longman, 2003)
11   Law of Property Act 1969 s.23.
12   Law of Property Act 1925 s.34(2).
13   Law of Property Act 1925 ss.34–36.
14   s.1(6).

> **The legal estate cannot be fragmented**
> The legal estate cannot therefore be held in separate shares that can be left by will or otherwise pass on the death of a co-owner through the rules of intestacy. As the joint tenancy operates by right of survivorship, the Law of Property Act 1925 thus ensures that there is an ever diminishing number of trustees holding the legal title: it is absolute and indestructible, i.e. incapable of being fragmented.

But what about the other co-owners? Those four owners (or fewer) of the legal estate are deemed to hold it on trust for themselves and all the other co-owners.

The Law of Property Act 1925, by vesting title in a small and diminishing number of trustees, and, as we shall see below, by giving them the power to convey the fee simple to a purchaser or mortgage lender free from all equitable interests in the land, provided a quick and easy method of dealing with co-owned land.[15] The trustees would hold the proceeds of sale on trust for the other co-owners.[16] It is less common now to find land owned by so many people. A typical situation of co-ownership arises where land is conveyed to a husband and wife, and the automatic statutory trust means that they are holding on trust for each other. Trusts can also arise impliedly where one person contributes to the purchase of property which is put into the name of another.

(3) Transferring the legal estate to a purchaser free from equitable interests

The rationale of reducing the number of legal estates and interests that could exist was to limit the possibility that purchasers of the fee simple would be bound by legal interests in that land. Remember that where title to the land is unregistered legal estates bind the whole world. The draftsman made all other interests equitable only: s.1(3) Law of Property Act 1925. But this simple act of reclassifying interests as equitable instead of legal would be unlikely to achieve much protection for the purchaser. The way that the courts had interpreted the doctrine of notice meant that a purchaser would nearly always be fixed with notice of, and therefore be bound by, equitable rights. Whatever the conscience-based origin of the rule, the courts had ensured that equitable rights were almost as well protected as legal rights.[17]

---

15   A "purchaser" is defined broadly under the Law of Property Act 1925 and includes a mortgagee and lessee: s.205(1)(xxi).
16   Evidence before the Royal Commission called this "registration without a register". It achieved the same purpose of ensuring that the purchaser need only deal with a limited number of owners of the legal estate, and could disregard equitable interests: *Royal Commission on the Land Transfer Acts* (1909) and (1911), both the "Minutes of Evidence" and the "Second and Final Report" in 1911.
17   Murphy, Roberts and Flessas, *Understanding Property Law*, 4th edn (London: Sweet & Maxwell, 2004); Maitland, *Lectures in Equity* (1936); J.S.Anderson, *Lawyers and the Making of English Land Law*, pp.268–9: Jackson, (2006) 69 M.L.R. 214.

> **The problems associated with the Doctrine of Notice**
> To make sure you have the foundations of the 1925 legislative reforms fully in place go back to the previous Chapter: Land Transfer Law (1) and consider what were the problems that the doctrine of notice caused.

B. THE "CURTAIN" BETWEEN THE PERSON WHO CAN SELL THE LEGAL ESTATE AND THE EQUITABLE RIGHTS OF OTHERS

> Benjamin Cherry, the 1925 draftsman, declared war on the doctrine of notice!

The aim of the provisions of the 1925 legislation is to draw a metaphorical "curtain" over the legal estate, shielding the purchaser from all equitable interests in the land. In more prosaic terms, the idea was to ensure that the purchaser could deal with the person offering the legal estate for sale without having to make difficult inquiries to ensure that he took the land free from equitable interests. Henceforth it would be irrelevant whether the purchaser had notice of any equitable interest, or whether it was mentioned in the title deeds. He could buy the legal estate in the knowledge that all of this was irrelevant.[18] It seems that Benjamin Cherry wanted to legislate the doctrine of notice out of existence.[19]

> **Close up your eyes and draw the curtain close**
> "From what has been stated the reader will no doubt have grasped the great and salient fact that. . . . a *bona-fide* purchaser or lessee may, in the words of Shakespeare, 'Close up his eyes and draw the curtain close' – in other words, deal with the owner of the legal estate without troubling himself with the equities of third parties, even if he had notice of them"
>
> A.Underhill, *A Concise Explanation of Lord Birkenhead's Act (The Law of Property Act, 1922 in Plain Language)"* (1922), p.91.

---

18   B. Cherry, *The New Property Acts – Lectures to the Law Society* (1926).

19   J.S. Anderson, *Lawyers and the Making of English Land Law*; see also Haldane's *Real Property and Conveyancing Bills 1913–1915*, the forerunners of the 1922–1925 property legislation. Those Bills were based on these same principles.

BUILDING BLOCK NO 5: Property Rights and the Protection of Purchasers and Mortgage Lenders

This was good news for the purchaser and mortgage lender. As we saw in Chapter 1 it is an important aim of Land Law to ensure that a purchaser can buy land, or a mortgage lender take its security on land, free from prior rights in the land. This is vital for our system of owner occupation and for the economy. Thus, when we hold Benjamin Cherry's curtain up against this Building Block we can see that it supports it. Thus, it is good and fair law.

However, on its own, Benjamin Cherry's curtain would make for poor protection for equitable interest in the land.

Making Friends with the Building Block

When we look at Cherry's way of dealing with equitable interests, we will see that it was good news for the purchaser, because (assuming all went to plan) he would not have to worry about the doctrine of notice. But on its own it would make for poor protection for equitable interests. Look back at BUILDING BLOCK NO 5 in Chapter 1 and then answer the following:

If the purchaser's life was made easier, who might be at the other end complaining?

If equitable interests were prevented from binding a purchaser why might this be a problem?

Now give as detailed an EXAMPLE as you can to illustrate problems that might exist if an equitable interest (for example a beneficial interest under a trust or a restrictive covenant) was destroyed on the transfer of land to a purchaser.

So our 1925 draftsman, Benjamin Cherry, had to strike a balance between offering significant protection to purchasers of the legal estate, and equitable interests, the owners of which would not want to see their rights destroyed when the land was transferred to the purchaser.[20] In the next section we will consider the rules of priority that apply where title to the land is unregistered. In Chapter 8 we will consider the rules that apply in registered land law.

---

20   K. Gray, *Elements of Land Law*, 2nd edn (London: Butterworths, 1993).

C. THE RULES OF PRIORITY OF INTERESTS WHERE TITLE TO LAND IS UNREGISTERED

(1) Certain types of equitable interest can be registered as land charges

Benjamin Cherry considered it important to find a way for certain types of equitable interest to bind future purchasers of the land. For example, one interest that falls into this class is a restrictive covenant. If you have the benefit of a landowner's covenant not to build on his land, this is very valuable to you. It can help maintain the character of a neighbourhood by preventing the building of dense housing. It can maintain peace and quiet, which can be very important to a neighbouring landowner. The person who covenants not to build can still be liable to pay damages, if they can be found. But unless the covenant can be made to bind the land, it cannot be enforced against subsequent purchasers. If you were the owner of a restrictive covenant would you be happy with a monetary payment instead from the person who granted you the right? Or would you want to be able to enforce the right against every future purchaser of the land, and thus be able to stop any building?

Accordingly, the 1925 draftsman introduced a means by which particular types of equitable interest could be made to bind the land and subsequent purchasers. But it was not by reliance on the doctrine of notice. It was a simple mechanism by which the owner of certain types of equitable interest in land, such as a restrictive covenant or equitable easement, would have to register it first, as a "Land Charge". This gave the owner of that interest a mechanism to make sure his interest would bind a purchaser. The Land Charges Act 1972[21] lays down the simple rule that if the owner of an equitable interest that is a "Land Charge" registers that right prior to the land being sold, any future purchaser of the land will be bound by that right.[22] If he does not register his right prior to a sale, the purchaser will not be bound by it. Whether or not the purchaser has notice of the interest is irrelevant.[23] Thus, the protection of an equitable interest against a purchaser, for the first time, required positive action on the part of the owner of that interest. He could no longer remain passively reliant on the doctrine of notice.

> **Land Charges Registration REPLACES the Doctrine of Notice**
> The salient feature of land charges registration is that the doctrine of notice does not apply to any of the interests that are registrable. It does not matter whether the purchaser had any notice of the right in question or whether he ought to have been able to find out about the right. This is a system of prioritising equitable interests that, for the first time, had no relation whatsoever to the purchaser's conscience.

---

21   This replaces the Land Charges Act 1925, which enacted this system.
22   Remember that the word "purchaser" includes a mortgagee or lessee: Law of Property Act 1925 s.205(1)(xxi).
23   Law of Property Act s.199(1).

(a) What interests are registrable as land charges?

It is important to note that not all equitable interests can be registered as land charges, only a selected few. The 1925 draftsman made a "judgement call" and identified those interests where he thought that the owner of the interest would need his interest to be enforced against the land itself, and would not be content with a monetary payment,[24] a restrictive covenant for example.

(b) How does the land charges system work?

Now we will look at the rules with the precision of a lawyer: so when we are advising a purchaser in an unregistered land transaction as to whether he is bound by any equitable interests, the first thing we need to do is to consider whether a given interest is a registrable land charge: *is the type of interest you are considering in the list of land charges in the Land Charges Act 1972*? If no, we simply go on to something else. If yes, we then ask, *has the interest been registered*? Then we give advice to the purchaser depending on whether the interest has been registered. *We state the effect of registration/non-registration and the irrelevance of notice doctrine.*

LAW IN ACTION: (the 1925 Land Charges Act was replaced with the following provisions):

> **The lawyer's questions**

Land Charges Act 1972

2. The register of land charges

A Class A land charge: A charge can be put on the land to secure repayment where a statutory payment has been made.

> Types of interest that can be registered: *is mine in the list?*

A Class B land charge is a charge created by a statute (not being a local land charge). It can be registered in order to recover costs and expenses. For example, a charge may be registered in order to recover legal aid.

Class C land charges: This is by far the most important category.

Class C(i): A puisne (pronounced "puny") mortgage

This is a legal mortgage. As it is a legal interest this is the one exception to the rule that, in unregistered land, legal interests bind the whole world. This type must be registered before it binds the land. When a mortgage of unregistered land is created it is usual for the lender to retain the title deeds to the property. If a second legal mortgage is created, the first lender

> A second legal mortgage of Blackacre? The lender does not have the title deeds: see Class C(i).

---

24   B. Cherry, *The New Property Acts – Lectures to the Law Society* (1926).

will have the title deeds, so any lender after this who is thinking of lending money on the security of the land will know that the land is already subject to a first mortgage. However, there is no way of alerting future lenders to the fact that there might be a *second* mortgage, or a third, because later lenders do not have the title deeds. A puisne mortgage is a "mortgage which is not protected by a deposit of documents" and it must be registered before the lender can claim that his mortgage takes priority over a later transaction.

> A right granted by James to Sophie to purchase his farm for £30,000, within 10 years? Class C(iv) estate contract.

Class C(ii): A limited owner's charge: for example, if a person with a limited interest in the estate, someone with a life interest under a settlement, pays a liability due on the estate, he can secure repayment by registering this charge against the land.

Class C(iii): A general equitable charge: this is a "residual" category of charge. For example, the so-called "unpaid vendor's lien". This is where a purchaser buys land but fails to pay over the full purchase money. The seller can register a charge against the land to claim the remainder.

> Jack owns "Heath Green" and formally agrees that if he sells it, he will give Dominic first refusal: Class C(iv).

Class C(iv): An estate contract. This is a very important category. An estate contract is defined as "a contract by an estate owner . . . to convey or create a legal estate." For example, if Simon contracts to sell Redacre to John, the latter has more than just a contractual promise. It can be enforced against the land. It is an interest in the land itself. This category includes:

> An *"option to purchase"*: This is where the owner of an estate grants to someone a right to purchase land within a particular timeframe.

> A *"right of pre-emption"*: This is a right to have the first opportunity to buy land, if (but only if) the owner should decide to sell.

> A covenant entered into by Usha not to build on her large back garden? Class D(ii).

Class D land charges:

Class D(i) An Inland Revenue Charge: HMRC can take a charge on someone's land to secure the payment of unpaid inheritance tax.

> A restrictive covenant created in 1920? Doctrine of notice applies: see D(ii).

Class D(ii): A restrictive covenant: we have already considered this type of interest. To be registrable as a land charge it has to have been created on or after January 1, 1926. If the restrictive covenant is created before this date then the doctrine of notice determines whether it binds a purchaser.

Class D(iii): An equitable easement: again, we have already looked at this type of interest. The important thing to remember is that for an easement to be registrable as a Land Charge it must be equitable. Also it must have been created on or after January 1, 1926.

> A right of way for the life of X over Redacre? Class D(iii)

Class E land charge: "An annuity created before 1st January 1926 and not registered in the register of annuities."

Class F land charge: A spouse or civil partner's right to occupy the matrimonial or family home. See immediately below.

> Mr and Mrs Peters are married. Mrs P is the sole legal and beneficial owner of their home. Mr P has a statutory right of occupation.

(c) The "Class F" land charge

In a series of cases from 1949 onwards, the Court of Appeal sought to give protection to wives who had been deserted by their husbands. It created the "deserted wife's equity" which gave her the right to stay in occupation of the family home, so that the husband could not evict her.[25] The Court of Appeal even held that the deserted wife's equity was a form of property right that not only bound the husband but bound purchasers of the house from the husband. The House of Lords in *National Provincial Bank Ltd v Ainsworth*[26] held that the wife's "equity" to remain in the home was not a property right in the land. It was a mere personal obligation that she could assert against her husband alone.

Shortly after *Ainsworth* parliament passed the Matrimonial Homes Act 1967, which gave to spouses a statutory right not to be excluded from the family home or to enter back into occupation of it. This was eventually consolidated into the Family Law Act 1996, which now extends rights of occupation in the family home to same-sex partners who have registered a "civil partnership".[27] These rights are called rights of occupation or "home rights". The right does not extend to unmarried cohabitees. Although the statutory right of occupation remains a personal right, it can be protected against purchasers and mortgage lenders by registering it as a notice (in registered land)[28] and as a *Class F land charge* (in unregistered land). Section 4(8) of the Land Charges Act 1972 provides that "[a] land charge of Class F shall be void as against a purchaser of the land charged with it. . . unless the land charge is registered. . . before the

---

25   For example, *Bendall v McWhirter* [1952] 2 Q.B. 466; *Street v Denham* [1954] 1 W.L.R. 624; *Gurasz v Gurasz* [1970] P.11: Thompson, *Modern Land Law*, pp.80–83.

26   [1965] A.C. 1175.

27   Civil Partnership Act 2004 Sch.9.

28   We consider the rules that apply to registered land in the next chapter.

completion of the purchase". The court has power to regulate these "home rights",[29] and in doing so must take into account "all the circumstances" including the housing needs and resources of the parties and of any relevant child, their financial resources, "the health, safety or well-being of the parties and any relevant child, and the conduct of the parties in relation to each other and otherwise".[30] In *Kaur v Gill*[31] the court considered the position of the purchaser, and held that a purchaser was not bound by a right of occupation where it had been registered as a notice on the land register. The purchaser's solicitor had conducted an inadequate search. The court took into account the position of the purchaser, who was blind and had bought the house for its convenience to him.[32]

(d) The effect of registration of a land charge: the purchaser is bound by the right

The lawyer's questions	**Law of Property Act 1925 s.198: effect of registration under the Land Charges Act**

Ok. The interest is in the list: has it been registered in the Land Charges Register?

If yes

If the owner of an interest in land which falls within any of the above classes, registers that right in the Land Charges Register then *that interest will bind every subsequent purchaser of the land.* Thus, if John has the benefit of a restrictive covenant over his neighbour's land, preventing the neighbour from building on it, or has entered into a contract with his neighbour to buy his property, an estate contract, then if he registers that right as a land charge, any purchaser of his neighbour's land will have to give effect to John's right. Technically the way in which this is achieved is that "registration . . . . shall be deemed to constitute actual notice [of the right] to all persons and for all purposes connected with the land".

(e) The effect of non-registration of a land charge: the purchaser is not bound

The lawyer's questions

Land Charges Act 1972 s.4: effect of failure to register a land charge and protection of purchasers

Ok. The interest is in the list: has it been registered in the Land Charges Register?

An interest that falls within Classes A, B, C(i), C(ii), C(iii) "shall be void as against a purchaser of the land . . . unless the land charge is registered . . . before the completion of the purchase". An estate contract and an interest that falls within Class D "shall be void as against a purchaser for money or money's worth . . . of a legal estate in the land charged with

---

29   Family Law Act 1996 s.33.
30   s.33(6).
31   [1988] 2 F.L.R. 328.
32   Jackson, Pearce and Stevens, *Land Law*, 4th edn (London: Sweet & Maxwell, 2008), para.20–054.

it, unless the land charge is registered". The difference between these two provisions seems to be insignificant. ***If the owner of an interest that can be registered as a Land Charge fails to register it in the Register of land charges, a purchaser will not be bound by it.***

If no

(f) The doctrine of notice is irrelevant to land charges

"Law of Property Act 1925, s.199: restrictions on constructive notice

(1) A purchaser shall not be prejudicially affected by notice of –

(i) Any [interest] capable of registration under the provisions of the Land Charges Act . . . which is void or not enforceable as against him under that Act . . . by reason of the non-registration thereof."

> If the interest is in the list of land charges but has not been registered it will not bind a purchaser, whether he has notice of the interest or not

(g) Cases on the land charges system

Having interpreted the statute to conclude whether or not your client or advisee's right will bind a purchaser, you must cite any relevant case law that has interpreted the legislation. Here we get to see the land charges system as it plays out in real life.

In *Hollington Brothers Ltd v Rhodes*[33] the plaintiffs had entered into negotiations for a lease of a block of offices with Rhodes, who then sold the block to Daymar Estates Ltd. The block was sold "subject to . . . such leases and tenancies as may affect the premises". Daymar Estates, on acquiring the block of offices, gave notice to the plaintiffs to quit the premises. Although the action failed on the basis that there was no contract for a lease between the plaintiffs and the defendants, Harman J. said that even if there were, such a contract is a contract for the grant of an interest in land (a lease). Thus it is an "estate contract" that would not have bound Daymar Estates Ltd, notwithstanding the fact that they knew about the existence of the right. Because the plaintiffs had not registered their right as a Class C(iv) land charge, Daymar Estates, as purchasers of the office block, took free from it. Commenting on the purpose of the legislation, Harman J. said:

> "[I]t appears at first glance wrong that a purchaser, who knows perfectly well of rights and is expressed to take subject to them, should be able to ignore them. . .The fact is that it was the policy of the framers of the legislation of 1925 to get rid of equitable rights of this kind unless registered. . . . There is, after all, no great hardship in this. The plaintiffs could, at any time until the completion of the [sale] to Daymar Estates Ltd have preserved their rights by registration."[34]

---

33 [1951] 2 All E.R. 578.
34 [1951] 2 All E.R. 578, p.580; Also, *Wright v Dean* [1948] Ch. 686; *Sharp v Coates* [1949] 1 K.B. 285: H.W.R.Wade, "Land Charge Registration Reviewed" [1956] C.L.J. 216, p.227.

(h) Case study 1[35]: Midland Bank Trust Co Ltd v Green[36] and Critical Thinking

The leading case that demonstrates the effect of failure to register a land charge is the House of Lords decision in *Midland Bank Trust Co Ltd v Green*.

> **THE FACTS:** A father, Walter, was the owner of several farms. His son, Geoffrey, operated one of the farms: "Gravel Hill Farm". In 1961 Walter granted to Geoffrey an option to purchase Gravel Hill Farm during a period of 10 years on very advantageous terms. A solicitor properly drew up the option but failed to register it as a land charge. Title to Gravel Hill Farm was unregistered so the Land Charges registration system applied. In 1967, after an apparent change of heart, Walter no longer wished Geoffrey to be able to purchase Gravel Hill Farm, so he took advice from a different solicitor on what could be done. That solicitor told Walter that Geoffrey's option to purchase had not been registered as a land charge so the way to defeat the option was to arrange a sale. So in 1967, Walter sold the farm, then worth £40,000, to his wife Evelyne, Geoffrey's mother, for £500.

> **THE LEGAL QUESTIONS:** The question was whether, after the sale of Gravel Hill Farm to Evelyne, she was bound to give effect to Geoffrey's option to purchase. An option to purchase is an "estate contract" and so registrable as a Class C(iv) land charge. Geoffrey had not registered his option. It was held that according to what is now s.4 of the Land Charges Act 1972, the option was void and could not be enforced against Evelyne. Geoffrey argued unsuccessfully that: firstly, Evelyne was not a "purchaser for money or money's worth", having paid inadequate consideration for Gravel Hill Farm; and secondly, that there was a requirement in the Land Charges Act that a purchaser should act in good faith, and Evelyne had not. We will now examine the House of Lords' reasoning:

> **THE REASONING: LORD WILBERFORCE:** "The option was, in legal terms, an estate contract and so a [land] charge, class C. . . The correct and statutory method for protection of such an option is by means of entering it in the Register of Land Charges. . . If so registered, the option would have been enforceable, not only (contractually) against Walter, but against any purchaser of the farm. . . [. . .]
>
> Thus the case appears to be a plain one. The 'estate contract' which by definition. . . includes an option to purchase, was entered into after January 1, 1926; Evelyne took an interest (in fee simple) in the land 'for valuable consideration' – so was a 'purchaser': she was a 'purchaser' for money – namely £500: the option was not registered before the completion of the purchase. It is therefore void as against her.
>
> In my opinion this appearance is also the reality. The case is plain: the Act is clear and definite. Intended as it was to provide a simple and understandable

---

35   For some ideas in this section see J. Stevens, "Is Justice a Priority in Priorities?—The Re-introduction of Morality to Registered Conveyancing", in *Property and Protection*, eds F. Meisel and P. Cook (Oxford: Hart Publishing, 2000) p. 177.

36   [1981] A.C. 513.

system for the protection of title to land, it should not be read down or glossed: to do so would destroy the usefulness of the Act. Any temptation to remould the Act to meet the facts of the present case, on the supposition that it is a hard one and that justice requires it, is, for me at least, removed by the consideration that the Act itself provides a simple and effective protection for persons in Geoffrey's position – viz – by registration.

[Geoffrey] submitted two arguments as to the interpretation of [the Act]: the one sought to introduce into it a requirement that the purchaser should be 'in good faith'; the other related to the words 'in money or money's worth.'. . . [I]t would be a mistake to suppose that the requirement of good faith extended only to the matter of notice. . . Equity still retained its interest in and power over the purchaser's conscience. . . But did this requirement, or test, pass into the property legislation of 1925? [. . .]

My Lords, I recognise that the inquiring mind may put the question: why should there be an omission of the requirement of good faith in this particular context? I do not think there should be much doubt about the answer. Addition of a requirement that the purchaser should be in good faith would bring with it the necessity of inquiring into the purchaser's motives and state of mind. The present case is a good example of the difficulties which would exist. If the position was simply that the purchaser had notice of the option, and decided nevertheless to buy the land, relying on the absence of notification, nobody could contend that she would be lacking in good faith. She would merely be taking advantage of a situation, which the law has provided, and the addition of a profit motive could not create an absence of good faith. But suppose. . . the purchaser's motive is to defeat the option, does this make any difference? Any advantage to oneself seems necessarily to involve a disadvantage for another: to make the validity of the purchase depend upon which aspect of the transaction was prevalent in the purchaser's mind seems to create distinctions equally difficult to analyse in law as to establish in fact: avarice and malice may be distinct sins, but in human conduct they are liable to be intertwined. The problem becomes even more acute if one supposes a mixture of motives. [. . .]

My Lords, I can deal more shortly with [Geoffrey's] second argument. It relates to the consideration for the purchase. The argument is that the protection [of the Land Charges Act 1972] does not extend to a purchaser who has provided only a nominal consideration and that £500 is nominal. . . . The word 'purchaser', by definition [of the Land Charges Act], means one who provides valuable consideration – a term of art which precludes any inquiry as to adequacy. . . There is nothing here which suggests, or admits of, the introduction of a further requirement that the money must not be nominal."

LECTURER: Before we "critically evaluate" Lord Wilberforce's judgment in *Midland Bank v Green* I would like us to consider the following extract from an article by H.W.R.Wade.

"Land Charge Registration Reviewed" [1956] C.L.J. 216, p.227

"The policy of 1925 was to abandon the equitable principle of notice in favour of the mechanical principle of registration. This was a shift from a moral to an a-moral basis. Its justification was that the doctrines of constructive and imputed notice had been over-refined. . . But those difficulties could be avoided without the defiance of ethics which occurs when a purchaser with *actual* notice is allowed to disregard a third party's rights. This is putting an unreasonable penalty on the venial fault of non-registration. . . Between the two extremes of making all notice relevant, or all notice irrelevant, lies the middle road of making actual notice relevant, but not constructive notice. The benefits of registration can be obtained, and unconscionable results also avoided, by providing that an unregistered charge shall be void against a purchaser provided that he. . . had not actual notice of it.

But there is one case where even constructive notice ought to be respected: where the owner of the [interest] is in possession of the land [like Geoffrey Green in *Midland Bank v Green*]. They can, it is true, protect themselves by registration. But in practice they will often fail to register, quite excusably. Take the case of a tenant who is let into possession under an agreement for a lease [NB not an actual lease but a contract for one. This is an "estate contract"]. Under the old law he was safe, for no later purchaser could secure the legal estate from the landlord without at least constructive notice of the tenant's interest. But today, unless he registers an estate contract, the tenant will *be defeated by any later purchaser of a legal estate.* [Citing *Hollington Brothers v Rhodes*]."

LECTURER: Do we agree with Wade's argument? When we are thinking critically, or creating an argument about something our Building Blocks provide evidence for our conclusions. We hold up the reasoning in these extracts, and what we already know about the land transfer system, and see whether it furthers or undermines any of the principles in the Building Blocks. We can say the author or judge reaches a good conclusion if it furthers the Building Blocks, but not if it undermines them.

Firstly, what argument is Wade actually putting forward?

STUDENT: He concludes that the land charges legislation is not good because it goes too far in the direction of protecting a purchaser of unregistered land. The land charges system unjustifiably penalises someone who does not register their right. There should be a better balance struck leaning more towards protecting smaller rights, such as Geoffrey's in *Midland Bank v Green* (above).

LECTURER: To support this conclusion, Wade advances the following premises or reasons.

    i)   The legislation is amoral because it allows a purchaser who knows about a pre-existing right belonging to a claimant to be able to ignore and take free from it merely because the owner of the right did not register it as a land charge (*assuming that it would be immoral for a purchaser to ignore a prior right when he knew about it*).

    ii)   It is not always reasonable to expect people to register their rights, particularly when they are in possession of the land.

iii) The purchaser in any case does not need the protection of the legislation if he already knows about the right.

So let's hold up Wade's reasoning and the reasoning in *Midland Bank v Green*, against the Building Blocks, and against what we already know about Benjamin Cherry's land transfer system, and see whether we think the arguments are supportable. But remember that we have to cross examine the evidence contained in our Building Blocks carefully.

STUDENT: The rules of the 1925 legislation, of which the land charges system is a part, were intended to make conveyancing cheaper and easier, as both Wade and Lord Wilberforce in *Midland Bank v Green* observe. If the rules achieve this they are good and fair law in accordance with BUILDING BLOCK NO 5.

BUILDING BLOCK NO 5: Property Rights and the Protection of Purchasers and Mortgage Lenders

We can argue that a development of a rule in a case or statute is good or bad fair or unfair, depending on the extent to which it supports or undermines the idea that rules of Land Law should protect a purchaser or mortgage lender from being bound by prior interests in the land. We have now observed a great deal about the policy behind Benjamin Cherry's 1925 property legislation. Conveyancing was complex and expensive, largely because of the doctrine of constructive notice. A purchaser should be able to take land free from prior equitable rights quickly and easily. Land is an important purchase, both for residential and commercial purposes. Therefore the law should ensure that purchasers can acquire a "good title" free from equitable rights that they could not readily have discovered. Thus, rules of Land Law are good if they support this policy. Banks and building societies often lend to small businesses on the security of family homes. If they cannot be sure of their security, i.e. if the rules recognise rights that will bind them and stop them from selling the house if the borrower defaults, then they may become reluctant to lend money. This will affect our economy.

STUDENT: The land charges system provides an easy way for a purchaser to take free from prior equitable rights in the land, such as Geoffrey's. If he does not register his right the purchaser is not bound by it. This obviously supports BUILDING BLOCK NO 5 and we can say that it is good law accordingly. Lord Wilberforce makes these kinds of observation in *Midland Bank v Green*.

"Intended as it was to provide a simple and understandable system for the protection of title to land, [the Act] should not be read down or glossed: to do so would destroy the usefulness of the Act."

LECTURER: What if *Midland Bank v Green* had been decided the other way? How would it have undermined BUILDING BLOCK NO 5?

STUDENT: Well, if Lord Wilberforce had said that it was necessary to determine whether the purchaser was in good faith when they purchased the land, and held that purchasing land in order to defeat someone's prior right was "bad faith", then this could introduce problems of uncertainty into the law. How could you define what is a "genuine purchase"? Thus, purchasers would not be able to predict in advance whether they would acquire a "good title" free from equitable property rights, because the rule would be inherently uncertain. We can say therefore that the decision of the House of Lords in *Midland Bank v Green* is good law on the basis of BUIDING BLOCK NO 6.

BUILDING BLOCK NO 6: The Need for Certainty and Predictability in Land Law Rules

If the rules are clear as to how they will apply in future cases, i.e. if they allow people (e.g. purchasers or occupiers) to predict the outcome of their actions then they are good law. Atiyah says that this is particularly important where people have strong expectations that their rights will be protected. This is the case with property because people attach so much importance to it.

LECTURER: At the moment we are disagreeing with Wade's argument. We are saying that the Land Charges system is actually good and fair law. Now we need to consider some of his arguments more explicitly. There is undeniably a tension here. Do you think that the legislation goes too far in the direction of protecting the purchaser?

STUDENT: Wade makes the point that not every person could be expected to register their right, particularly if they are in occupation of the land. However, most rights registrable as land charges are all ones that come into being commercially, i.e. as a result of a bargain between the parties (with the possible exception of the right of occupation or home rights under the Family Law Act 1996). This detracts from Wade's point. If a right comes into being formally like this, its owner can be expected to register it. The parties will probably be legally advised. After all, in *Midland Bank v Green*, it was only because of the negligence of the solicitor that Geoffrey's estate contract was not registered.

LECTURER: But even so—allowing for human error, the loss of the right does seem a heavy price to pay (as Wade says).

STUDENT: I suppose it depends largely on whether there is anything to say on the other side of the argument. Does the purchaser actually *need* the law to protect him to this extent? The original purpose of the legislation was to protect purchasers from having to make extensive enquiries about interests—to stop them from being bound by right that they *could not have discovered*. The problem was essentially with the extent to which the courts had interpreted the doctrine of constructive notice. Actual notice, where a purchaser was made to take subject to interests that he was informed about, did not cause a problem.

Note that our STUDENT is asking questions and cross examining the evidence in BUILDING BLOCK NO 5: see Chapter 1 for advice on how to do this. The STUDENT is saying that equitable rights should only be easily overridden where a purchaser *needs* to be protected.

LECTURER: But if we said that a purchaser would be bound by interests of the land charge type, even though they had not been registered, *if he had actual notice of them* would this make a workable rule? Wade does not seem to consider this point.

BUILDING BLOCK NO 6: The Need for Certainty and Predictability in Land Law Rules
See above.

STUDENT: A rule that said that a purchaser would have to take subject to interests that he had actual notice of, is sufficiently clear as to future operation. Judges in both the cases we examined had little difficulty in knowing whether the purchasers had actual notice of the right: both did. It is unlikely to lead to extensive litigation, as the few cases that we have examined show.[37]

LECTURER: Indeed there is a comparable rule under the Law of Property Act 1969 s.25 which allows a purchaser to be paid compensation if he is subjected to a registered land charge because the name of the relevant estate owner (i.e. the means by which a purchaser would conduct a search of the land charges register) is hidden behind good root of title. A purchaser will be entitled to compensation *unless he has actual knowledge of the right*.

In *Midland Bank v Green*, Lord Wilberforce seems adamant that Geoffrey Green suffered no injustice. He could have registered his right. Is it really immoral for a purchaser with prior knowledge of a right to take the land free from that right, if it remained unregistered? Let's measure *Midland Bank v Green* against our ideas of moral justice in BUILDING BLOCK NO 2.

BUILDING BLOCK NO 2: Ideas of Justice
Rules are good and fair if they take account of moral justice: Every person should be accorded the freedom of their will and autonomous choice. Thus, if people deal with each other and with their property in a way that violates the will of another then the law should offer that other some remedy. We may legitimately say that Land Law is bad if it does not do so.

STUDENT: I think this provides evidence for the conclusion that *Midland Bank v Green* is not unjust. The fact that Geoffrey knew that he possessed the right and could have taken steps to protect it, shows that his parents had no influence over his affairs. There was in no sense an act of reliance on Geoffrey's part, e.g. if he had held back from registering his right because his parents had promised that they would honour it, this may have been different.

---

37   J.Stevens, above, fn.35.

(i) How are land charges registered?

The interest that is intended to bind the land must be registered against the name of the person who owns the land.[38] The registration must also describe the property affected, as there may be more than one landowner of the same name.[39] The Land Charges register comprises only a list of names of land owners, and charges registered against their names. There is no "reference to any map or plan. . . . [T]he title deeds reveal the names of the various estate owners, and searches are made against all of them. All registered charges can thus be brought to light".[40] There are two problems with a name register in contrast with a register that identifies the land and documents the interests affecting that land.

Firstly, a purchaser must search under the correct form of the name. A sight mistake in spelling or form and the search will not reveal the interests that are registered against that person. In *Diligent Finance Co Ltd v Alleyne*[41] a wife attempted to register a Class F land charge against her husband's name, to protect her right to occupy the family home. The registration was held to be ineffective because she failed to include his middle name. Thus, when a potential lender searched against the correct name and got a clear result, it was held that they could rely on the search.[42] But in *Oak Co-operative Building Society v Blackburn*[43] the owner of an estate contract registered it against the name of the owner of the house. Although she registered against a technically incorrect version of the owner's name, he was known by this name locally. The owner mortgaged the property. The lender searched against an incorrect name and was bound by the estate contract. The land charge was registered under an approximation of the right name and the lender had not searched under the correct name at all.[44]

Secondly, what if an interest is registered against the name of a person who owned the land more than 15 years ago and that name has not been mentioned in the deeds since? It might be that the land has changed hands five times in the last 30 years. We know that a purchaser must search back at least 15 years in order to ascertain that the land properly passed to the hands of the current seller through an unbroken chain of transactions and transfers. But before this, a land charge might have been registered against the name of an owner that sold the land more than 15 years ago, so that his name will not be on the deeds in the last 15 years of transactions. Because a purchaser only has to search back 15 years in order to ascertain good root of title, and the corresponding rule is that he is not entitled to see any more of the deeds than would disclose this root, he has no means by which to discover a land charge that will bind him.[45] The only effective remedy for this problem is to construct a system which included maps of the land affected and to re-register all land charges against the land itself. This was deemed to be

---

38   Land Charges Act 1972 s.3(1): "A land charge shall be registered in the name of the estate owner whose estate is intended to be affected".
39   Thompson, *Modern Land Law*, p.83.
40   H.W.R.Wade, "Land Charge Registration Reviewed" [1956] C.L.J. 216, p.218.
41   (1972) 23 P. & C.R. 346.
42   Thompson, *Modern Land Law*, p.83.
43   [1968] Ch. 730.
44   Thompson, above, pp.83–4.
45   Wade, above, p.218.

impractical.[46] Thus, the Law of Property Act 1969 s.25 allows for compensation to be paid to a purchaser who has suffered loss by being bound by a land charge in such circumstances, provided that the purchaser does not have actual knowledge of the relevant charge.

(j) Land Charges Registration—only ever a temporary solution

Critics were not slow to point out that Benjamin Cherry's land charges registration scheme had "the outward appearance of an exact science, subject to rigid principles and precisely detailed rules", but that "the detailed rules go radically wrong at a number of points".[47] The system of registration of Land Charges was inherently flawed because it extended on a massive scale a system that could only cope with registration of a very limited number of charges on the land.

> "Lord Birkenhead and Sir Benjamin Cherry appear to have succeeded in creating the conveyancing equivalent of a Frankenstein's monster, which with the passing years would become not only more dangerous but also more difficult to kill".[48]

The scheme of land charges registration operates only in the context of unregistered conveyancing. As it became apparent that Benjamin Cherry had been over-ambitious in laying down the system of land charges, critics consoled themselves with the thought that it would soon cease to operate.[49] In 1956 Wade observed that the real answer lay in ensuring that all titles to land were registered.[50]

> Some students feel the need to clarify why we are talking about "land charges registration" at all in the context of "unregistered land". If you are one of these, just remember that the system of registration of title is a whole system of land transfer whereby the title to that land and all third party rights are registered centrally at the Land Registry. The system of land charges registration is a limited system of ensuring that a purchaser of unregistered land can be bound by some (but not all) equitable interests.

(2) Equitable rights that are "overreached" on sale on payment of purchase money to two trustees[51]

Remember that the idea of the 1925 legislation was to draw a metaphorical "curtain" between the owner of the legal estate and anyone with an equitable interest, so that a purchaser transacting with the legal owner would not be affected by equitable interests, *whether he had*

---

46   H.W.R.Wade, "Land Charge Registration Reviewed" [1956] C.L.J. 216.

47   Wade, above, pp.216–7.

48   H.W.R.Wade, above, p.216.

49   H.W.R.Wade, above, pp.219–220.

50   Above, p.219; All details of the ownership of the land, the map, the owners, the interests, are recorded centrally at the Land Registry. This is a wholly self-contained system of land transfer that we examine in the next chapter.

51   C.Harpum, "Overreaching, Trustees' Powers and Reform of the 1925 Legislation" [1990] C.L.J. 277; D.Fox, "Overreaching" in P.Birks and A.Pretto-Sakmann (eds), *Breach of Trust* (Hart Publishing, 2002), p.95.

notice thereof or not. The purchaser would pay the purchase money to the owner of the legal estate and take free from the equitable interest. This is a process known as "overreaching". The equitable interest is "overreached". Benjamin Cherry's idea behind his 1925 legislation was that if an equitable interest was not of the land charge-type, a purchaser would be able to take free from it automatically, whether he had notice of it or not. That would be all other equitable interests – simply overreached or overridden on a sale, lease or mortgage of the land.[52] The equitable interest cannot then be enforced against the land in the hands of the purchaser.

As we have seen, the 1925 draftsman made a "judgement call" and identified those interests where he thought that the owner of the interest would need to enforce it against the land itself, binding subsequent purchasers; that the owner of that type of interest would not be content with a monetary payment.[53] The reformers considered that other types of equitable interest did not need to be enforced against the land. The owners of those rights would be content with a claim against the proceeds of sale.[54] If we look at the main types of interest that were not identified as land charges, we can see that Benjamin Cherry's assumption at the time of the 1925 legislation was a perfectly reasonable one:

Beneficial interests under a trust of land (co-ownership): At the time of the 1925 legislation, trust beneficiaries did not want to occupy houses and land. It was held usually for the purposes of investment. Land was often left by will to trustees for a number of beneficiaries, e.g. children or grandchildren, to provide them with an income. So all parties would be equally content if the land was sold by the trustees and the *money* held by them on trust instead.

Settlements: Settlements were used as a way of keeping land in the family. Land would be left (e.g. in a will or upon a marriage) to the son for life, then to his son, and so on down the generational line. By the end of the nineteenth century, land, as a means of wealth, had lost its attraction for the gentry. So if the land was sold the family would usually be content with a settlement of money instead.[55]

(a) Which equitable interests are "overreachable"?

Benjamin Cherry, the draftsman of the 1925 property legislation, would have liked the "curtain" to have been universal, i.e. to apply to every single other interest that was not a registrable land charge so that a purchaser would not be concerned with *any* other equitable interest.[56] But when the universal curtain provisions were introduced into parliament as part of the Law of Property Bill in 1920, Viscount Cave[57] and others objected. So when Benjamin Cherry finally

---

52   A "conveyance of a legal estate": Law of Property Act 1925 s.2, s.205(1)(ii).

53   J.S.Anderson, *Lawyers and the Making of English Land Law 1832–1940*.

54   A.Underhill, *A Concise Explanation of Lord Birkenhead's Act (The Law of Property Act, 1922 in Plain Language)* (1922), pp.78–91.

55   Baker, *An Introduction to English Legal History* (London: Butterworths, 1979): "Strict Settlements".

56   Technically the "universal curtain" was brought about by deeming that all equitable interests arise under a trust for sale or settlement and then providing that the trustees could overreach them: Law of Property Bill 1920, clauses 3 and 4; J.S.Anderson, *Lawyers and the Making of English Land Law 1832–1940*, pp.295–302. Expression "universal curtain": Anderson, above, p.297.

57   "[A] Law Lord and sometime senior Conservative politician": Anderson, above p.297.

saw his 1925 Legislation enacted into law,[58] the rights that fell within his category of "overreachable rights", were fewer, but still included equitable interests under a trust of land and settlements.[59]

(b) Protection for beneficiaries: the Two-Trustee Rule

There was a safeguard introduced in 1925 for the protection of beneficiaries. At the time of the 1925 legislation there was evidence of fraud on the part of trustees. It is the trustees that hold legal title to the property. They have much power. They have all the powers of an absolute owner.[60] But the nature of the trust is that the trustee must look after the property for the benefit of the beneficiary. And if they sell the land, which as legal owners they have the power to do, equity provides that they hold the proceeds of sale for the beneficiaries. Trustees might commit fraud however. They might sell the land and abscond with the proceeds of sale. In 1925, evidence suggested that fraud usually only occurred where there was only one trustee looking after the land.[61] Sections 2 and 27 of the Law of Property Act 1925 introduce a requirement for a would-be purchaser from trustees, or a mortgage lender loaning money to them: Before they can take the land free from equitable interests under a trust of that land, they must pay any purchase or mortgage money arising under the transaction, to two trustees or a trust corporation. If purchase money or mortgage advance is paid to one trustee only, the beneficiaries can still potentially enforce their interests against the land in the hands of the purchaser.[62]

(c) Overreaching in application

A purchaser or mortgage lender will take free from equitable interests *whether he had notice thereof or not*, provided that:

- The interest is of an overreachable kind (trusts and interests under settlements are overreachable);
- Overreaching occurs on a "conveyance of a legal estate" to a purchaser: this is a sale, lease or mortgage of one of the two legal estates. Usually we are looking at an outright sale or a mortgage of the fee simple (freehold).
- The purchase money or mortgage advance must be paid to at least two trustees or a trust corporation.[63]

---

58   How different now! The amended Bill became the Law of Property Bill 1921, which was enacted as the Law of Property Act 1922. This was then consolidated into the Law of Property Act 1925 that we know today. It was no longer the case that all equitable interests were deemed to arise under a trust, e.g. estoppel rights, and not all co-ownership rights technically arose under the statutory trust with overreaching powers, e.g. informal beneficial interests. But the gap was plugged judicially: *Bull v Bull* [1955] 1 Q.B. 234; *Williams & Glyn's Bank v Boland* [1981] A.C. 487; J.S.Anderson, *Lawyers and the Making of English Land Law 1832–1940*, p.330–1; see now the Trusts of Land and Appointment of Trustees Act 1996.

59   Anderson, above.

60   The Trusts of Land and Appointment of Trustees Act 1996 s.6. They are not regarded as absolute owners in law. They have these powers "for the purpose of exercising their functions *as trustees*" Thus, they must continue to look after the land, or proceeds of sale, for the beneficiaries: See Chapter 5 section 2.

61   "It had been a commonplace that trustee fraud virtually only arose where a single trustee had the title": Anderson, above, p.292.

62   As was the case in *Williams & Glyn's Bank v Boland* [1981] A.C. 487.

63   Law of Property Act 1925 ss.2 and 27.

So let's consider a problem so as to practice applying the overreaching provisions. Mrs X had contributed financially to the purchase of her family's home. The house was transferred into Mr X's and his brother's name, not hers. We know that by virtue of her contribution, Mrs X has an interest in the house under a trust. Mr X and his brother hold the house on trust, partly for her and partly for themselves. The next thing she discovers is that Mr X and his brother have mortgaged the house in return for a loan to support their ailing business, which they are empowered to do being the legal owners.[64] The building society is now claiming possession of the house, because Mr X and his brother have defaulted on the loan repayments. The building society wishes to evict Mrs X so that it can sell the house with vacant possession in order to get its money back. Mrs X argues that she has an interest under a trust, because of her contribution to the purchase of the house. Her interest was in existence first and she knew nothing about the mortgage. She resists the bank's claim to possession and argues that she has a right to stay in the house. The bank argues that the mortgage granted to it by Mr X and his brother, *overreached* Mrs X's equitable interest. They will accordingly be able to take possession of the house and sell it to recover their money, evicting Mrs X.

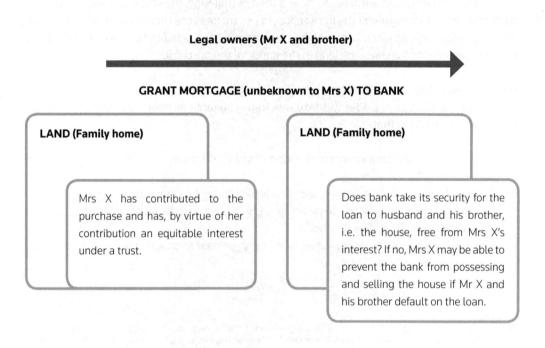

Legal owners (Mr X and brother)

GRANT MORTGAGE (unbeknown to Mrs X) TO BANK

LAND (Family home)

Mrs X has contributed to the purchase and has, by virtue of her contribution an equitable interest under a trust.

LAND (Family home)

Does bank take its security for the loan to husband and his brother, i.e. the house, free from Mrs X's interest? If no, Mrs X may be able to prevent the bank from possessing and selling the house if Mr X and his brother default on the loan.

OUR LEGAL QUESTION: Does Mrs X's equitable interest have priority over the bank's mortgage, or can the bank evict Mrs X and sell the house? We need to apply Benjamin Cherry's overreaching provisions as laid down in s.2 of the Law of Property Act 1925.

---

64   Similar facts to *National Westminster Bank Plc v Malhan* [2004] EWHC 847 (Ch). On a different point A. Morritt V.C. held that a mortgage that was beyond the powers of the trustees would still overreach the beneficial interests.

> **Law of Property Act 1925 s.2 – the overreaching provisions**
> **s.2(1) Conveyances overreaching certain equitable interests**
> "A conveyance to a purchaser of a legal estate in land shall overreach any equitable interest or power affecting that estate, whether or not he has notice thereof, if-"
> The interest is overreachable: interests that are overreachable include beneficial interests under a trust of land and settlements; and-
>
> **Law of Property Act 1925 s.27**
> "(2) A purchaser of a legal estate from trustees of land shall not be concerned with the trusts affecting the land" provided that he pays the purchase money or mortgage loan money, to no fewer than two trustees or a trust corporation.

The Lawyers' Questions

Does Mrs X have an interest that can be overreached? Yes, see LPA 1925 s.2.

Is a mortgage a "conveyance of a legal estate"? Yes: LPA 1925, s.205(1)(ii). Is a mortgagee a "purchaser"? Yes: LPA 1925 s.205(1)(xxi).

Did the bank pay the mortgage advance to two trustees or a trust corporation as required by LPA 1925 s.27? Yes. They paid the loan money to Mr X and his brother who were holding the legal estate on trust for themselves and Mrs X.

We could provide an answer to the problem in something like the following way: the effect of my answer on the issues raised in the problem is that Mrs X's equitable interest under the trust was overreached by the mortgage. The reason is that under s.2 of the Law of Property Act 1925, where the mortgage advance is, as here, paid to two or more trustees (the brothers in our case) the lender will take its interest in the land, the mortgage, free from Mrs X's equitable interest. The effect of this is that Mrs X will not be able to resist the lender's claim to possession of the house. The bank's interest takes priority.

Overreaching applies in the same way in the system of title registration, which we study in the next chapter, so all the same cases and statutory provisions apply.[65] We will study the cases in

---

65   For an argument to the contrary see Jackson (2006) 69 M.L.R. 114.

more depth when we look at the system of registration of title. As most titles to land are now registered, the courts usually have to deal with overreaching in that context.

(d) Cases on overreaching

When we are providing a legal solution to a particular problem, in order to show that our conclusion that "X takes subject to the right", or "Y is unable to enforce her right against the purchaser of land", we must show that our conclusion is supported by reasoning in the cases: not the facts, not the conclusion, but the *reasoning*. Knowing how the cases applied the overreaching rules and understanding what was said about the rules and "the policy of 1925" will also help us to critically evaluate the overreaching provisions. The leading case on overreaching is the House of Lords decision in *City of London Building Society v Flegg*.[66]

> **THE FACTS:** Mr and Mrs Flegg and their daughter and son-in-law, Mr and Mrs Maxwell-Browne, together purchased Bleak House. Mr and Mrs Flegg sold their bungalow in order to contribute to the purchase of the house. Mr and Mrs Maxwell-Browne borrowed money to fund their contribution to the purchase, and granted the lender a mortgage on Bleak House. Although when the parties bought the house their lawyer advised the Fleggs that the house should be transferred into all four names, the Fleggs acted against this advice.[67] The house was transferred into the two names of Mr and Mrs Maxwell-Browne. They held legal title to Bleak House on trust for themselves and Mr and Mrs Flegg. Thus, Mr and Mrs Flegg had an equitable interest in the house. Subsequently, and unbeknown to Mr and Mrs Flegg, the Maxwell-Brownes borrowed a larger sum of money from the City of London Building Society, who took a mortgage on Bleak House. The Maxwell-Brownes, who were now in considerable financial difficulty, defaulted on the loan repayments. The building society commenced these proceedings for possession of Bleak House against Mr and Mrs Flegg.

> **THE CONCLUSION:** The House of Lords held that the bank was entitled to repossess the property. The mortgage, as a conveyance of a legal estate made by two trustees Mr and Mrs Maxwell-Brown, overreached the Fleggs' beneficial interest under ss.2 and 27 of the Law of Property Act 1925. The building society therefore took their interest in Bleak House free from the Fleggs' equitable interest under the trust.

LECTURER: Let's just comment briefly here on whether we think that the overreaching provisions are good and fair law.

---

66   [1988] 1 A.C. 54; R.Smith (1987) 103 L.Q.R. 520; W.Swadling (1987) Conv. 451; C.Harpum [1987] C.L.J. 392, [1990] C.L.J. 277; (1988) 51 M.L.R. 365.

67   The reason that the Fleggs did not wish the house to be registered in their names was that they erroneously thought that this would make them liable under the mortgage granted by Mr and Mrs Maxwell-Browne.

STUDENT: They are certainly good law when we hold overreaching against BUILDING BLOCK NO 5. The lender in *Flegg* simply took free from the equitable interests of the Fleggs without having to make difficult enquiries. It certainly furthers the policy of making transfers of land easy and cheap.

> **BUILDING BLOCK NO 5: Property Rights and the Protection of Purchasers and Mortgage Lenders**

LECTURER: But it was a close run thing for the bank. What is the distinguishing feature between *Flegg* and *Williams & Glyn's Bank Ltd v Boland* in which the bank *did not* take free from Mrs Boland's equitable interest?

STUDENT: In *Boland* Mr Boland was the sole legal owner holding on trust for himself and his wife. Therefore, the mortgage did not fulfil the requirements for overreaching to take place, i.e. the mortgage money was paid to a sole trustee and not to "two or more trustees" as required by s.2 of the Law of Property Act 1925.

LECTURER: Isn't this a bit of a lottery?

STUDENT: How would the bank know whether there was an equitable interest so that it could insist that a second trustee be appointed?

LECTURER: Benjamin Cherry had simply thought that all trusts would be expressly created and thus apparent from the "face" of the title deeds.[68]

STUDENT: So with informal trusts like *Boland*, I would guess a fairly common situation, a mortgagee from the sole legal owner would not know whether that legal owner was in fact holding on informal trust for someone else. So Benjamin Cherry's two-trustee rule actually *undermines* BUILDING BLOCK NO 5.

LECTURER: What about the overreaching provisions in general? Are they good and fair law?

STUDENT: I think that overreaching undermines BUILDING BLOCK NO 1: Residential Security. In cases like *Flegg* the owners of the equitable interests are occupiers and entirely innocent—they know nothing about the mortgage and through overreaching are being threatened with the loss of their homes.

LECTURER: This was another situation that Benjamin Cherry did not foresee. For the moment however, we will leave our arguments on overreaching. We will need to consider the topic in more detail in the next chapter on registered land.

---

68   Harpum, "Overreaching, Trustees' Powers and Reform of the 1925 Legislation" [1990] C.L.J. 277.

(3) Land transfer where title is unregistered: summary

DOES THE SELLER OWN WHAT HE SAYS HE OWNS? Purchaser must make sure that the vendor can sell a "good title", proving an unbroken chain of transfers of the land to the current seller going back 15 years.

WHAT INTERESTS WILL BIND THE PURCHASER after he has bought the land?

LEGAL INTERESTS: LPA 1925 s.1(2), bind the whole world. They will bind any purchaser of the land.

EQUITABLE INTERESTS: LPA 1925 s1(3)—any interest not in the s.1(1) and 1(2) list of legal estates and interests, will bind a purchaser or not in accordance with the following rules.

Is it a land charge?
Is the interest in the list of "land charges"? If registered against the name of the land owner it binds. If not, it doesn't. Purchaser's notice is irrelevant: *MB v Green*; LCA 1972.

Overreaching
If the interest is not in the list of land charges is the interest overreachable? If so, in order to overreach it the purchaser or lender must pay the purchase/ mortgage money to two trustees: LPA 1925 ss.2 and 27.

BUT THIS DOES NOT COVER EVERY POSSIBLE SCENARIO: Do any interests fall between the cracks of land charges and overreaching? What happens if an equitable interest under a trust has not been overreached because the purchase money or mortgage advance was paid to only one trustee?

The doctrine of notice
Where title to land is unregistered there is a residual role for the doctrine of notice. For example, if an equitable interest is capable of being overreached, but has not been overreached because there is only one trustee—then the doctrine of notice applies.

Before we go any further, go back to the section on the doctrine of notice or the "Equity's Darling rule" in the previous chapter and remind yourself how it works.

(4) Where title to land is unregistered there is a residual role for the doctrine of notice

It seems reasonably apparent that the 1925 draftsman's intention was that the doctrine of notice would not have much role to play in land transfer law.[69] With unregistered land law, his intention was to ensure as far as possible that all equitable interests would either be registrable land charges or be overreachable. In registered land law the doctrine of notice has no application whatsoever. However, in unregistered land law the doctrine still has a residual role to play.

(a) The economic emancipation of women and the socio-economic phenomenon of "owner occupation"

> "When the questions changed, as they did when owner-occupation combined with the economic emancipation of women to fuse the new social forms of co-ownership, Cherry's Acts were hopelessly inadequate."
>
> J.S.Anderson, *Lawyers and the Making of English Land Law 1832–1940*, p.331

When women started to go out to work more often, they gained financial power to contribute to the purchase of their home.[70] But the house would often have been put in the name of the husband or partner alone. However, because the wife or cohabitee contributed to the purchase price this gave her an interest in the house under a trust. When cases concerning these informal trusts come before the court the context is usually as follows: unbeknown to the wife or partner with the equitable interest, the legal owner has mortgaged the house to a bank or building society. He is the sole legal owner and so has power to mortgage the house. The issue arises if the legal owner, the borrower, defaults on the loan repayments. The building society will then seek to repossess the house. It is at this point that the wife or partner asserts that their equitable trust interest takes priority over the lender's mortgage.

The type of interest that the wife or other partner will have in these cases is a beneficial interest under a trust of land. These interests are overreachable. But often in such cases there is one person only holding the legal title to the land on trust. In our example: the husband. Thus, because of the two trustee rule, the wife's interest has not been overreached. In such cases the question of whether a purchaser or mortgage lender takes subject to the equitable right of the beneficiary or free from it, is determined by applying the *doctrine of notice*.

---

69   B.Cherry, *The New Property Acts* (1926), Lectures to the Law Society. In this work, Benjamin Cherry acknowledged a limited role for the doctrine of notice in the context of trusts, and that these interests would sometimes arise where there is only one trustee (secret trusts). But at this time no one could have foreseen the development of trusts in the context of owner occupation.

70   Also Thompson, *Modern Land Law*, pp.54–8.

If you remember, if someone other than the seller or mortgagor is occupying the property, a purchaser or mortgage lender must make enquiries about any rights that occupier may have. Otherwise they will be fixed with constructive notice of the rights of the occupier. This is now on a statutory basis by virtue of s.199 of the Law of Property Act 1925.

Earlier cases held that the occupation of a wife could not amount to notice of her rights to the purchaser. Firstly, she occupied the property as a wife and not as someone who was able to assert a separate interest in the house. One case held that she occupied as a "shadow of the occupation of her husband".[71] In *Williams & Glyn's Bank v Boland*[72] these cases were regarded as "heavily obsolete". Secondly, whenever anyone was in occupation *at the same time* as the legal owner then this would not give constructive notice of the occupier's rights. Their occupation would not be *inconsistent* with the title offered by the vendor. The sense of the cases was that there was nothing to alert a purchaser to the fact that someone other than the vendor could claim a right in the house. Thus, it would not be reasonable to expect the purchaser to inquire about the rights of such occupiers.[73] Thus, the purchaser or mortgage lender would *never* have notice of a wife's or cohabitee's rights and could purchase or take the house as security, free from her equitable interest.[74] These cases are no longer good law, as held in *Hodgson v Marks*,[75] and in *Williams & Glyn's Bank v Boland*.[76]

(b) Case study 2: Kingsnorth Finance Co Ltd v Tizard[77]

THE FACTS (from the report): Mrs Tizard had contributed financially to the purchase of her matrimonial home. The property was in the name of her husband. Their marriage broke down. At this time he took out a loan behind her back from Kingsnorth Finance and defaulted. Kingsnorth brought an action for possession of the house and Mrs Tizard claimed a beneficial interest. The whole question was whether Kingsnorth were fixed with notice of Mrs Tizard's beneficial interest. If so, her right would take priority and they would be unable to take possession of the house. Kingsnorth did not have actual notice of her interest so the question was whether under s.199 of the Law of Property Act 1925, they had made such inspections of the property as ought reasonably to have been made. At the time the inspections were made Mrs Tizard did not sleep at the house although she returned each day to care for the couple's children. Mr Tizard had described himself as "single" on the loan application form. When Kingsnorth's surveyor inspected the property Mr Tizard told him that he was separated and his wife was no longer living there.

---

71   *Bird v Syme-Thompson* [1979] 1 W.L.R. 440; Thompson, *Modern Land Law* p.55, n.101.
72   [1981] A.C. 487, per Lord Wilberforce.
73   M.Thompson, *Modern Land Law*, p.55.
74   *Caunce v Caunce* [1969] 1 W.L.R. 286; *Bird v Syme-Thompson* [1979] 1 W.L.R. 440.
75   [1971] Ch. 892.
76   [1981] A.C. 487.
77   [1986] 1 W.L.R. 783.

THE CONCLUSION: It was held that Kingsnorth Finance Co Ltd were fixed with constructive notice of Mrs Tizard's interest.

Read the following extract from the judgment of Judge John Finlay Q.C. and identify *why* the wife won the case. This is what will tell us about the working of the doctrine of notice. This is the material that we need to hold against our Building Blocks in order to create a convincing argument. We identify the reasons for the judge's decision by asking questions like: *what were the factors that were so important to the judge that they led him to decide what he did AND WHY?* OR *What factors would have to have been different before the judge would have decided the case in favour of Kingsnorth Finance Co Ltd?*

THE REASONING: JUDGE JOHN FINLAY QC: "Mrs Tizard was, in my judgment, in occupation of [the house] notwithstanding that Mr Tizard was living there also; and notwithstanding the fact that on numerous occasions she slept elsewhere. The 'physical presence' to which Lord Wilberforce refers [*Williams & Glyn's Bank v Boland*] does not connote continuous and uninterrupted presence; such a notion would be absurd. Nor, indeed do I consider that the requisite 'presence' is negatived by regular and repeated absence. I find that Mrs Tizard was in [the house] virtually every day for some part of the day; that her life and activities were based on her presence, interrupted though it was, in [the house]; there she prepared herself for work; there she cared for her children; there she looked after the house . . .

[I]n the case of unregistered land . . . the circumstances must be such that she would have been found had proper inspections, inquiries and searches been made. [. . .]

[Kingsnorth Finance Co Ltd had] the knowledge . . . [that] contrary to what he had said in his application, [Mr Tizard] was married. That put them on notice that further inquiries were necessary; the inquiries which in these circumstances ought reasonably to have been made by [Kingsnorth Finance Co Ltd] would, in my judgment, have been such as to have apprised them of the fact that Mrs Tizard claimed a beneficial interest in the property; and accordingly, they would have had notice of such equitable rights as she had and the mortgage in these circumstances takes effect subject to these right. [. . .]

On the balance of probabilities, I find that the reason [the surveyor] did not find Mrs Tizard in the house was that Mr Tizard had arranged matters to achieve that result. He told Mrs Tizard that on a particular Sunday, and I find in fact that it was the Sunday that [the surveyor] did inspect, he was going to entertain friends to lunch and would she take the children out for the day. She did; and having regard to the manner in which I find that the signs of her occupation were temporarily eliminated by Mr Tizard, the reasonable inference is that he made this request so that [the surveyor] could inspect and find no evidence of Mrs Tizard's occupation. [. . .]

> . . . Mr Tizard appears to have been minded to conceal the true facts; he did not do so completely; [Kingsnorth] . . . had information which should have alerted them to the fact that the full facts were not in their possession and that they should make further inspections or inquiries; they did not do so; and in these circumstances I find that they are fixed with notice of the equitable interest of Mrs Tizard . . . In the circumstances of the present case I am not satisfied that the pre-arranged inspection on a Sunday afternoon fell within the category of 'such inspections which ought reasonably to have been made'."[78]

LECTURER: So what was Finlay J.'s conclusion?

STUDENT: That Kingsnorth Finance did not make proper enquiries about the existence of Mrs Tizard.

LECTURER: But what was the *legal effect* of this finding of the judge's? Remember to state the consequences for the parties.

STUDENT: That Kingsnorth were purchasers with constructive notice and took their mortgage in the house subject to Mrs Tizard's rights, according to s.199 of the Law of Property Act 1925. She had an equitable interest under a trust. Thus the bank could not take possession of the house and sell it because the wife had the prior claim to possession.

LECTURER: Good. In *Tizard* itself, Mrs Tizard was quite happy for the house to be sold (which is not usually the case in such disputes). The effect of the decision that Kingsnorth took their interest in the house, the mortgage, subject to her rights meant that when the house was sold, Mrs Tizard could have her share out of the proceeds of sale *before* the bank took their loan money. The order of priority could be very significant if the proceeds of the sale of the house would not cover both the wife's and the bank's claims.

What was Finlay J.'s reasoning?

STUDENT: Once the surveyor knew that Mr Tizard was married, they should have made further inquiries into whether his wife claimed a beneficial interest in the house. A pre-arranged inspection on a Sunday afternoon was insufficient for these purposes. It is quite clear that had Kingsnorth made a more thorough inspection and still not found evidence of Mrs Tizard's rights in the house, then they would have taken free from those rights (answering the question: *what factors would have to have been different before the judge would have decided the case in favour of Kingsnorth Finance Co Ltd?*) He considered that their inspection was deficient because it was pre-arranged on a Sunday afternoon.

LECTURER: So now we reach a point where we can critically evaluate the decision in *Tizard*. We can create an argument about it. Do we think it was a fair decision? Hold the reasoning against our Building Blocks in order to determine whether it furthers or undermines any of the policies and principles contained therein. This will give you the evidence for your argument. We will remember to cross examine the evidence in the Building Blocks. There are instructions on how to do this in Chapter 1.

---

78   Compare *Midland Bank Ltd v Farmpride Hatcheries Ltd* (1980) 260 E.G. 493 in which the occupier deliberately concealed their right, and there was no further evidence of it. Thus, the lender was not fixed with notice of the right and took free from it: E.H.Burn, *Maudsley & Burn's Land Law Cases and Materials*, pp.28–9. Also compare *Le Foe v Le Foe* [2001] 2 F.L.R. 970, in which it was considered obiter that a surveyor acting for a lender was not required to look for signs of occupation. His purpose was to determine that the house was worth sufficient to pay the debt in the event of a forced sale: see M.Thompson, *Modern Land Law*, p.58.

STUDENT: First, I would take BUILDING BLOCK NO 2: Ideas of Justice. Ownership of property, here a house, gives the owner a great deal of power. It means that the owner of property can sell it and mortgage it.

BUILDING BLOCK NO 2: Ideas of Justice

Rules are good and fair if they take account of moral justice: every person should be accorded the freedom of their will and autonomous choice. However, Land Law should decide its rules to guard against the potential for the legal owner to deal with the land in a way that dramatically affects the life of the other spouse: "domination-potential": Harris, *Property and Justice*, p.273.

In our modern culture of owner occupation, the family's well-being may depend on stable and continued residence in a house. Thus, where the legal ownership of the house is in the name of only one member of the family, here Mr Tizard, there is the potential for abuse of the power that goes with ownership: "domination-potential". Mr Tizard can mortgage the house without Mrs Tizard knowing, run off with the proceeds, and leave Mrs Tizard and her children to face a surprise eviction. The law ought to give her some protection against this insecurity. Thus, in this respect I would conclude that by giving a broad interpretation of the circumstances in which banks etc. are fixed with constructive notice, *Tizard* is good law.[79]

LECTURER: This also suggests that the law as seen in *Kingsnorth Finance v Tizard* is good and fair law because it gives adequate protection to the family's need for residential security.

STUDENT: Yes. The broad interpretation of what a purchaser/ mortgagee must do before they can be said to have made a "reasonable inspection" of the land in order to take free from the occupier's rights, clearly gives generous protection to the interests of family members. This enables them to stay in occupation and resist the claim of the bank for repossession. Although Mrs Tizard herself was not actually living at the property, I am thinking of all the other Mrs Tizards in the future. In the context of owner occupation this type of dispute appears quite frequently.

BUILDING BLOCK NO 1: Residential Security

We can legitimately say that where the rules operate in the context of owner occupation of property, they are good and fair if they give effective protection to people's residential security. Land Law now operates in the context of owner occupation. Land Law rules should give effect to the purposes for which people buy and use land/houses.

---

79   For this conclusion see Harris, *Property and Justice* (Oxford: Clarendon Press, 1996), p.273.

LECTURER: But let's test the strength of the claim that because *Tizard* gave priority to residential security it is good and fair law: We will cross examine the evidence in BUILDING BLOCK NO 1. Is there anything that wives/non-owning partners could do in this type of situation to protect their interest in the house: to equalise power so to speak?

STUDENT: Looking at the unregistered land rules that we have considered the only way of making sure that an equitable interest in land will bind a purchaser/mortgage lender is by registering it as a land charge. An equitable interest under a trust is not in the list of land charges.

LECTURER: But if it were, would this be an effective way in which future Mrs Tizards and Mrs Bolands could protect their equitable rights from being destroyed? Could people in this position be reasonably expected to take such a step?

STUDENT: As she has gained her interest entirely informally, i.e. by contributing to the purchase price, she may not even be aware that she *has* a right in the house. So it is not reasonable for the law to expect her to register her right, even if the law permitted it.

LECTURER: So this class of litigant as a whole is still likely to need the law's protection against the bank.

STUDENT: Just "thinking outside the box": why should a house ever be put in the name of one of the couple and not both?

LECTURER: It is more usual today to find the house in both names.

STUDENT: So if we can expect people to insist on the house being in joint names, this would equalise power between the couple. The legal owner could not then execute a mortgage on the house on their own. This means that there is less justification for saying that the law should make it harder, as it did in *Tizard*, for a bank to repossess a house, where the house was in the husband's (or other partner's) name only.

LECTURER: But is it legitimate to have this expectation that couples should put their house in joint names?

STUDENT: It seems that because family feeling and emotion is mixed up with ownership of the house, that we could never really say that it is up to the parties to protect their interests and that the law should not protect them against adverse consequences.

LECTURER: So let's see what other class of litigant is affected by decisions such as *Tizard*. Who is the other innocent party in all this?

STUDENT: Banks.

LECTURER: If they are bound by prior equitable rights in the land then they will be unable to sell the house in order to recoup their investment if the legal owner defaults on the loan repayments.

STUDENT: Looking at BUILDING BLOCK NO 5: Property Rights and Protection of Purchasers and Mortgage Lenders, there is certainly an argument that *Tizard* is not a good development of law. This was a very broad interpretation of the doctrine of notice. When thinking about how the case will lay down guidance to lenders in the future about how to make sure that they are not bound by the equitable interests of other members of the family, it seems to be the case that they will be unable to go to the house just once. They may have to repeatedly inspect the house and ask many quite difficult questions if they are not to be fixed with constructive notice of equitable rights.

LECTURER: This might add to the cost of taking out a loan?

STUDENT: I was thinking more about the uncertainty whether a bank will be able to enforce its security by selling the family home.

BUILDING BLOCK NO 6: The Need for Certainty and Predictability in Land Law Rules

---

LECTURER: This is where it is vital to look at the whole picture and make sure we know how *Tizard* relates to other rules of Land Law. What about overreaching?

STUDENT: Mrs Tizard's equitable interest was a beneficial interest under a trust so it would have been overreached if the mortgage loan had been paid to two legal owners instead of just Mr Tizard: Law of Property Act 1925 ss.2 and 27. So any lender might simply insist on the appointment of a second trustee.

LECTURER: Now let's consider the arguments in an article— see if it adds to our argument about *Tizard*. Thompson observed that the decision may "increase the transaction cost of conveyancing"[80]:

"With respect, this seems to go too far. Suppose [the surveyor] had asked where the mother of the children was and had been told that she was dead or that she had left years ago and her present whereabouts, or even whether she was still alive, was unknown. What then is he supposed to do? Clearly, an inspection of the property should take place. If the mortgagor [borrower, Mr Tizard] says this can take place at the weekend, can it really be supposed that the mortgagee's agent must insist on calling at an alternative, unannounced time to check whether the mortgagor is lying? Similarly must he insist upon rifling through drawers and cupboards, inevitably causing offence? It is submitted that such behaviour goes far beyond what are reasonable inquiries."

LECTURER: It is interesting to note that the argument in this article is based entirely on BUILDING BLOCK NO 5: Property Rights and Protection of Purchasers and Mortgage Lenders.

STUDENT: This article concludes that the conduct now required by lenders to make sure they are not "fixed with notice" of the rights of beneficiaries, may make it difficult to obtain loan finance on the security of the matrimonial home.

LECTURER: Or the cost of borrowing increases?

---

80   M.Thompson, "The Purchaser as Private Detective" [1986] Conv. 283.

(5) The mortgagee's "escape route"[81]

(a) Appoint a second trustee

Of course a mortgage lender or other purchaser may adopt the simple expedient of ensuring that a second trustee is appointed. In this way the equitable rights under any trust of the land will be overreached.[82] The mortgage lender or purchaser will thus take free from those rights.

> **Overreaching**
> If you have any difficulty in understanding this statement, go back to the section above on overreaching. How does it work? What difference does it make to the priority of equitable interests on a mortgage or sale of the land subject to a trust?

(b) A mortgage lender will never be bound by an equitable interest where the mortgage is used to acquire the house

In *Abbey National Building Society v Cann*[83] Mrs Cann had a beneficial interest under a trust that arose through her contribution to the purchase of a house. The house was put in the name of her son. The son sold this house and purchased another with the aid of a loan from the Abbey National. A mortgage was executed on the house. Where a mortgage is used in order to buy a house the deed of transfer in return for payment of money to the seller, and the execution of the mortgage deed in favour of the bank happen on the same day. It is essentially the bank's money that has financed the transaction. And this is what happened in *Cann*. Mrs Cann argued that the legal estate in the house (that was transferred by the deed) vested in her son a fraction of before the creation of the bank's mortgage. Thus, her interest in the house existed before the bank's mortgage. Consequently, because she was in occupation the mortgage took effect subject to her right.[84] The House of Lords rejected Mrs Cann's argument, holding that for all purposes the transfer of the legal estate and the execution of the mortgage are taken to happen at the same time.

The case is useful in that it meant that whenever a mortgage is needed to *acquire* a house, the lender's interest will always have priority over anyone claiming a beneficial interest in the house through their contribution to its purchase. This seems the fairest approach as in these cases the house could not have been acquired without the lender's money.

---

81   M.Thompson [1986] Conv. 283.
82   *City of London Building Society v Flegg* [1988] A.C. 54.
83   [1991] 1 A.C. 56.
84   As this was registered land, she need only prove that she was in occupation and not that the building society had notice of her rights.

(c) Express and implied consent

If Mrs Tizard had expressly consented to granting a mortgage this would have postponed her interest to that of the lender. The lender's mortgage would have priority over her rights. The law will deem an equitable co-owner to have consented *impliedly* to the mortgage where she knew about the mortgage or knew that the house could not have been purchased without a mortgage being granted.[85] We will consider this principle in more detail in the next Chapter on the system of registration of title to land.

[85] *Bristol and West Building Society v Henning* [1985] 2 All E.R. 606; *Equity and Law Home Loans Ltd v Prestidge* [1992] 1 W.L.R. 137; M.Thompson [1986] Conv. 57; (1986) 49 M.L.R. 245.

Chapter 8

Land Transfer Law (3): Registration of Title to Land

CHAPTER OVERVIEW

In this chapter you will find:

- The structure of registered Land Law and the Land Registration Act 2002
- The priority rule
- The ways in which third party rights are protected
- The principle of overreaching
- The rules for altering the land register
- Constructed argument throughout using Building Blocks.

An overview of the basic principles of title registration

1

In the previous chapter we saw that the idea behind the reforms of 1925 in relation to unregistered conveyancing was to make land easy to transfer from seller to buyer. The Land Registration Act 1925[1] established a parallel system of land transfer, with the same aim. The Land Registration Act 2002 repeals and replaces the 1925 Act in its entirety. Title to the land is registered centrally at the Land Registry. The land register records all dealings in relation to that land, that is, the details of the owner and of any interests that exist in relation to the land.[2] So how does this system of registration of title to land actually work? We must never forget that an essential function of land registration is to simplify conveyancing. Thus, firstly we need to recall our two essential questions to which a good land transfer system must provide some answer (see Land Transfer Law (1): General Principles):

---

1   And its forerunners the Land Transfer Acts of 1875 and 1897.
2   There had been prior attempts to introduce such a system: Transfer of Land Act 1862 which failed because it required the registration of every dealing with the land and thus became too complicated (George Osborne Morgan, *Land Law Reform in England* (1880), pp.12–3; J.S.Anderson, *Lawyers and the Making of English Land Law 1832–1940* (Oxford: Clarendon Press, 1992), pp.114–5).

> **The two essential principles a good land transfer system must address:**
> 1. How does the buyer prove that the seller owns what he says he owns?
> 2. What are the rights in land that will bind a purchaser after he has completed the transaction?

Now we need to consider how the system of registration of title to land provides answers to these questions.

A. THE GENERAL PRINCIPLES

One objective behind the system of central registration of title was to remove the need for solicitors to re-examine the title deeds every time the land was sold. Where land is unregistered, in order to prove that the seller owned what he claimed to own, the purchaser's solicitor must examine the deeds of conveyance in order to establish "good root of title", i.e. that there is an unbroken chain of transactions going back 15 years and ending with a transfer to the current seller. This was time-consuming and wasteful of effort, because it required title to be proved in this same way every time there was a sale of the land.[3] In the system of land registration, the registrar examines the title deeds once and for all when the land is first submitted for registration. He records the ownership of the land and any interest existing in relation to that land, on a separate three-part register. Every subsequent purchaser needs only to look at the register to ascertain the ownership of the land.

When land is sold it must be submitted for registration at the land registry. The Land Registrar awards the title submitted by the applicant a "class" of title. The freehold estate, the fee simple absolute in possession, can be awarded three possible classes of title: absolute, qualified and possessory. We will consider these grades of title when we look at "first registrations" below.

(1) The land register is a "once and for all" record of ownership

Once title to the land and any interests in the land are recorded on the land register, this operates as a "once and for all" record of the ownership of the land. Thus, where a purchaser is buying registered land, his solicitor no longer has to examine the dusty title deeds. He merely examines the register of title at the Land Registry.[4]

---

3   George Osborne Morgan, *Land Law Reform in England* (1880), p.6–7; Jackson (2006) 69 M.L.R. 214, p.224.
4   The land register will also contain a map of the land in question.

(2) Substantive registration—a "statutory proprietorship"

But how does the Land Register tell a purchaser that his seller has the ability to transfer a good title to him, i.e. one that he is entitled to sell? How does it tell the purchaser what interests in the land, e.g. restrictive covenants or estate contracts, will bind him after the sale? In this section we will see how the system of registration of title to land provides comprehensive answers to these questions. In later sections we will explore the detail of the system.

The original idea behind the creation of the registered land system in this country was to create a new law, or form of ownership. In relation to the earlier registration statutes[5] Hogg observes:

"No suggestion appears to have been made to the effect that the [registered land system], was intended to confer, or could be construed as to confer, anything but actual ownership on registered proprietors, an ownership which was to be as efficacious for all purposes as the old legal estate".[6]

> **Statutory ownership**
> Section 58(1) of the Land Registration Act 2002 provides that "If, on the entry of a person in the register as the proprietor of a legal estate, the legal estate would not otherwise be vested in him, it shall be deemed to be vested in him as a result of the registration".

It is quite clear that s.58[7] confers on a person registered as proprietor of a legal estate, a statutory ownership. *But what is the quality of this ownership?* The originators of the registered land system wished to obliterate the language of "legal" and "equitable".[8] The type of ownership conferred is novel. However, it is subject to another's right to have the register "altered" in their favour. For example, if A forges a transfer of B's land to himself and then obtains a registration of that land in his name, the register may be altered in favour of B so that A's registration may be cancelled.[9] It appears that the system envisages that B's rights to the land, under ordinary

---

5   The Land Transfer Acts 1875 and 1897.

6   J.E.Hogg, *A Treatise on the Law Relating to Ownership and Incumbrance of Registered Land and Interests Therein* (1906), p.31.

7   And its predecessor Land Registration Act 1925 s.69.

8   "The language of the 1875 Act throughout, in using the expressions 'fee simple', 'estate', etc., without the addition of 'legal' or 'equitable', and avoiding the use of 'legal' or 'at law' otherwise than in the general sense of 'valid' or 'lawful' as applied to estates in land when once placed on the register, agrees with what appears to have been the intention of the [Royal Commission of 1870] – to place the 'legal estate' in its technical sense in abeyance altogether for practical purposes": J.E.Hogg, *A Treatise on the Law Relating to Ownership and Incumbrance of Registered Land and Interests Therein* (1906), p.23.

9   The provisions for alteration of the Land Register are discussed below in section 9 of this Chapter.

unregistered land principles their "legal" ownership, is demoted, albeit temporarily,[10] to the statutory ownership.[11]

There are other provisions in the Land Registration Act 2002 that help us to answer the question, *what is the quality of the statutory ownership?* The statute confers on the registered proprietor of an estate all the powers of transfer and creation of interests that an absolute owner under the ordinary law would have.[12] In this way the statute deems that he has a good title to transfer or the ability to create the interest he is purporting to create, e.g. a transfer of the fee simple or creation of a lease or a mortgage. Section 23 of the Land Registration Act 2002[13] provides that "[o]wner's powers in relation to a registered estate consist of power to make a disposition of any kind permitted by the general law". Thus, the owner of registered land can make any disposition that the general law permits, e.g. sale, lease, mortgage, creation of easements and covenants etc. The only exception is that a registered proprietor cannot create a mortgage by virtue of the old device of granting a long lease that ceases on redemption of the mortgage.[14]

Naturally, as we have seen in the previous two chapters, the quality of someone's ownership depends largely on what other interests in the land can be enforced against them: thus a purchaser is also interested in what interests will bind him following a transfer of land. A cornerstone of the land registration system therefore is that it deems that a purchaser for valuable consideration, when registered as proprietor, takes that land free from most pre-existing property rights. We refer to this as "the priority rule".[15]

And thus, by a fiction of ownership created by the statute, the purchaser of registered land knows that his seller has the ability to transfer title and has the ability to transfer it to him free from most prior interests in the land. Thus we have a system, not of "registration *of* title", but of "title *by* registration".[16] Such is the effect of what we call "substantive registration".[17] The estates and interests that must be substantively registered, i.e. with a title in their own right, and which

---

10   It seems correct to state that any rights that have been "demoted" in this way are given effect to through the explicit provisions to alter the register in the circumstances therein specified, and not otherwise: Hogg, above pp.95–99.

11   Hogg, above pp.95–99; It is submitted that this is a preferable explanation for the operation of the statutory ownership conferred by s.58 than that offered by the Court of Appeal in *Malory Enterprises Ltd v Cheshire Homes (UK) Ltd* [2002] EWCA Civ 151, on the similar s.69 of the 1925 Act. This refers to the fact that s.69 (now 58) confers only "bare legal title" and not "equitable title"; It is not correct in registered land law to speak in these terms. According to the framers of the system this statutory ownership provision may sometimes confer what we know as full ownership, but it was clearly intended that it would not always do so, i.e. the ownership of a fraudulently registered proprietor would not obliterate a claim by the "true" owner under the jurisdiction to alter the register; also commenting on *Malory* see A. Hill-Smith, [2009] Conv. 127. We will consider the extent to which the courts have taken notice of these principles when we look at "alteration of the land register" below. In relation to the effect of substantive registration under the 2002 Act, see C.Harpum, S.Bridge and M.Dixon, *Megarry and Wade Law of Real Property*, 7th edn (London: Sweet & Maxwell, 2008), paras 7–115–7–117.

12   Land Registration Act 2002 s.23.

13   This Act repealed and replaced the Land Registration Act 1925 in its entirety.

14   Law of Property Act 1925 ss.85–6.

15   Land Registration Act 2002 ss.29–30. For first registrations, priority is largely determined prior to application.

16   A.Pottage, "The Originality of Registration", referred to by C.Harpum, keynote address to Conference on the Land Registration Bill 2001.

17   It has been referred to as the "statutory magic", e.g. Slade L.J. in *Argyle Building Society v Hammond* (1984) 49 P. & C.R. 148, p.153: E.H.Burn, *Maudsley & Burn's Land Law Cases and Materials*, 8th edn (Oxfod University Press, 2004), p.106.

have this effect are contained in s.4 of the Land Registration Act 2002 (for first time registrations) and s.27 (for the transfer or creation of estates/interests of a title that is already registered.)

(3) Substantive registration and co-ownership/trusts

A key issue that we have been exploring in these chapters is the position of trustees. Land may have been conveyed to A and B, to hold on trust for themselves and C and D, or there may be a sole legal owner who is holding on trust for themselves and another, e.g. a cohabitee who has contributed to the purchase price.[18] Under ordinary principles if the trustees sell or mortgage the land, equitable interests under a trust are property rights that potentially bind future purchasers/mortgage lenders of the land. Thus, because all co-ownership in one way or another arises under a trust[19] it is vital that registered land law deals with the question of how trustees convey a good title to a purchaser, i.e. *how does a trustee(s) prove to a buyer/mortgagee that he has the ability to convey the title to the land free from the equitable interests under the trust?*

BUILDING BLOCK NO 5: Property Rights and the Protection of Purchasers and Mortgage Lenders

It is imperative that registered land offers a way of ensuring that purchasers are not bound by the equitable interests under a trust.

In the registered land system trustees are registered as the owners of the estate in the sense discussed above. There is "no separate form of fiduciary proprietorship" applicable only to trustees.[20] And the trust is kept off the face of the register.[21] Trustees have the same powers of transaction and the same powers to convey land to a purchaser or mortgage lender free from most pre-existing interests in the land.[22] There are sections that emphasise that vis a purchaser, trustees are to be treated as absolute owners with full ability to transfer title, for example, s.78 of the Land Registration Act 2002[23] provides that "the registrar shall not be affected with notice of a trust",[24] so the equitable interests cannot obtain a foothold in the title of the new purchaser.[25] Section 26 provides that "a person's right to exercise owner's powers in relation to a registered estate or charge is to be taken to be free from any limitation affecting the validity of a disposition". This is true unless the limitation has been entered on the register or imposed by the Land

---

18   As in *Williams & Glyn's Bank Ltd v Boland* [1981] A.C. 487.
19   This is explained in Chapters 4 and 5.
20   (2006) 69 M.L.R. 114, pp.223–4—an earlier article by the author of this book.
21   There is nothing explicitly in the Land Registration Act 2002 to this effect, but it is implicit from the structure of the system. The corresponding provision of the (now repealed) Land Registration Act 1925 was s.94(1).
22   The priority rule under ss.29–30.
23   The statute that regulates registration of title to land.
24   This re-enacts the similar total abolition of the doctrine of notice from registered land transactions in relation to trusts contained in the Land Registration Act 1925 s.74.
25   It was only through the doctrine of notice that an equitable interest under a trust could ever bind a purchaser or mortgage lender anyway: F.W.Maitland, *Lectures in Equity* (1936). See Chapter 6.

Registration Act 2002 itself.[26] Thus even if the trustees are making the transfer in breach of trust, or have no authority to make the transaction because their statutory trustees' functions have been limited,[27] the purchaser is still on safe ground. He takes a good title. For all purposes of transfer to a purchaser the equitable interests under the trust "are behind the impenetrable curtain of the register book".[28] There is only one circumstance in which a trust beneficiary's interest can bind a purchaser or mortgage lender, and this we saw in *Williams & Glyn's Bank Ltd v Boland*.[29] We will examine this fully below. But the fact of a beneficial interest binding registered land in this way was not envisaged by the original framers of the system. It was in effect judicial creativity in response to our trend of owner occupation.

It is important to note that trustees still have to hold the land for the beneficiaries; they cannot escape their own obligations. This was implicit under the Land Registration Act 1925,[30] but has been made explicit under the 2002 Act.[31] Indeed, under s.26 a disposition is to be taken as free from limitations, e.g. on the powers of the trustees, *only* for the purpose of allowing a purchaser to take a good title.[32] This gives huge responsibility to the trustees to execute only proper transfers and to look after the proceeds of its sale for the beneficiaries.

BUILDING BLOCK NO 2: Ideas of Justice

As we saw in Chapter 7 when we considered *City of London Building Society v Flegg* this responsibility was misplaced. It may well affect our ideas of justice in relation to the registered land system.

However, trust beneficiaries can enter "restrictions" to ensure that their interests are properly dealt with.[33]

So all in all, the system of registration of title to land confers statutory ownership – a title that is good against the whole world and which the registered proprietor can transfer to any buyer. As Lord Watson observed in *Gibbs v Messer*,

---

26   Land Registration Act 2002 s.26(2).
27   Under s.8 of the Trusts of Land and Appointment of Trustees Act 1996.
28   T.B.F.Ruoff, *An Englishman Looks at the Torrens System* (1957), p.30, footnotes omitted; also J.E.Hogg, *A Treatise on the Law Relating to Ownership and Incumbrance of Registered Land and Interests Therein* (1906), pp.8–12.
29   [1981] A.C. 487.
30   "Equitable interests and trusts cannot, consistently with the objects to be attained by registration of title, bind or affect the ownership of a registered proprietor, unless such interests are of his own creation". *Commission on Registration of Title*, Report, (1857) H.C.P. xxi 245, para.50, 30, quoted J.E.Hogg, *A Treatise on the Law Relating to Ownership and Incumbrance of Registered Land and Interests Therein* (1906), p.9; also T.B.F.Ruoff, *An Englishman Looks at the Torrens System* (1957), p.30.
31   Land Registration Act 2002 s.11(3) and (5).
32   If the disposition is unlawfully made, e.g. it is one that is made in breach of trust, or *ultra vires*, the trustees are still liable to the beneficiaries: "This section has effect only for the purpose of preventing the title of a disponees being questioned (and so does not affect the lawfulness of a disposition)". It is not to be supposed that s.26 is restricted to the example given.
33   We will consider the "restrictions" method of regulating dealings with registered land below.

"Every one who purchases . . . from a registered proprietor . . . shall thereby acquire an indefeasible right, notwithstanding the infirmity of his author's title".[34]

> **The curtain principle**
> If you remember from the previous chapters, the draftsman of the 1925 legislation, Benjamin Cherry, was the most ardent proponent of the idea that between the legal owner and the equitable interests in the land, a "curtain" should be drawn. A purchaser should be able to deal with the legal owner without having to investigate equitable interests, i.e. what was behind the curtain. Substantive registration is the ultimate curtain provision.

(4) Alteration and rectification of the Land Register and the "insurance principle"

Because of the effect of substantive registration it is vital to have a mechanism by which the register can be altered if, for example, a mistake has been made. Schedule 4 of the Land Registration Act 2002 makes provision for the court or the registrar to alter the register in order, for example, to bring it up to date or to correct a mistake.[35] The state guarantees each registered title. If the land register is altered, or even where the register is not altered, and this causes loss, a person may be entitled to an indemnity payment from the state.[36] Alteration is not automatic. Case law has shown that it is possible that where title is gained through registration under a forged disposition, title may never be altered.

(5) Registration of title to land is compulsory

Registering title to land is not optional. It is compulsory. Land Registration operates in geographical districts, with each district having its own Land Registry. Following the 1925 Act, the idea was to extend compulsory registration gradually, district by district. The process took longer than the reformers imagined and the last compulsory registration order was made in 1989! More than 90 percent of all titles to land are now registered.[37]

---

34 [1891] A.C. 254; Quoted J.E.Hogg, *A Treatise on the Law Relating to Ownership and Incumbrance of Registered Land and Interests Therein* (1906), p.38. References: Jackson (2006) 69 M.L.R. 214, p.226.

35 Sch.4, para. 2.

36 Land Registration Act 2002 sch.8. We will consider alteration and rectification below in this chapter.

37 R.Smith, "The role of registration in modern land law" in L. Tee (ed.) *Land Law Issues, Debates, Policy* (Willian Publishing, 2002) p.30.

Compulsory registration—Land Registration Act 2002 ss.4 and 27
It works like this: on the occurrence of certain dealings with the land, for example, the transfer of the fee simple estate or a leasehold estate granted for a term of more than seven years, the transaction *must be completed by substantive registration*. Most legal mortgages ("charges") are also substantively registrable. The significance of this, as we shall see later, is that the mortgage lender will get the same protection from prior rights in the land as a purchaser of that legal estate. The new owner of the estate or charge must be registered as proprietor of the estate or interest.

And they gain *title by registration* in the way described above.

Compulsory substantive registration is dealt with in two categories in the Land Registration Act 2002.

"First Registrations"—Land Registration Act 2002 s.4
If the title to the land has not previously been registered, then the estate transferred or created must be registered. We call these "First Registrations".

"Registrable Dispositions"—Land Registration Act 2002 s.27
If title to the land is already registered, there are certain dealings with that title which *must* be substantively registered. We call these "Registrable Dispositions".

B. RIGHTS IN LAND THAT WILL BIND A REGISTERED PROPRIETOR FOR VALUABLE CONSIDERATION AFTER COMPLETING THE TRANSACTION

(1) The registered land priority rule—the mirror principle

As we saw above, when a person, such as a purchaser or mortgage lender is registered as proprietor of an absolute estate[38] or charge they take this estate or charge free from all other property rights that exist in relation to that land, e.g. beneficial interests under a trust, restrictive covenants etc.[39] However, there are two principal exceptions. The first is that a purchaser *will* take subject to interests that are registered against the title.

---

38   For classes of title other than "absolute" there are certain reservations: Land Registration Act 2002 s.11(6)–(7).
39   Land Registration Act 2002 ss.11, 12, 29 and 30.

(a) Interests that are registered against the title

A purchaser of a registered estate is bound by any interest that is registered against the title. However, as with unregistered land, only certain types of interest can be made to bind the land in this way, e.g. restrictive covenants, estate contracts. The idea was to ensure that the same types of interest that could be made to bind unregistered land as land charges could be made to bind the land in registered land. Beneficial interests under a trust cannot be registered so as to bind the title of a subsequent registered proprietor in this way.[40]

(b) Interests which override first registrations or registered dispositions

The second exception is where the interest falls into the class of "overriding interests".[41] Overriding interests will bind a purchaser automatically, even though that interest remains unregistered against the title. The types of interest that can bind as overriding interests are contained in Sch.1 (unregistered interests that override first registrations) and Sch.3 (unregistered interests that override registrable dispositions) of the Land Registration Act 2002. The idea of having a class of interest that will bind a purchaser automatically is to protect certain interests from being destroyed on a transfer of registered land, i.e. where the owner of the interest cannot reasonably be expected to register it against the title. One important category of overriding interest, the rights of persons in actual occupation, includes beneficial interests under a trust: provided they belong to a person in occupation. This is the single instance in which such interests can bind a purchaser or mortgage lender once they are registered as proprietor of their estate or charge. This was how Mrs Boland's interest was held to bind the bank in *Williams & Glyn's v Boland*.

> **The priority rule—a summary**
> Apart from these two exceptions, the purchaser, when registered as proprietor of an absolute estate, takes free from all other interests in the land. The purchaser or mortgage lender may thus transact with the owner of the legal estate or other interest safe in the knowledge that he will take it free from all interests, unless they are registered against the title to the estate or overriding.
>
> The registered land priority rule leaves no room whatsoever for the doctrine of notice. Indeed, it has become something of an article of faith of land registration that the doctrine of notice has no application whatsoever: *Williams & Glyn's Bank v Boland*.

LECTURER: Consider the Critical Thinking Exercise on *Boland* in Chapter 1 (section 4). How does the above relate to the way Lord Wilberforce described this system of rules and how it works?

---

40   Land Registration Act 2002 s.33.
41   The term "overriding interest" was used in the 1925 Act and has been replaced by the term "interests which override". There is no substantive difference in meaning so in this chapter, for ease of reference, I often use the former expression.

STUDENT: Lord Wilberforce said that the aim of the system of registration of title to land is to simplify conveyancing, i.e. so that a purchaser or mortgage lender will know exactly whether they are going to take a good title and exactly what interests will bind them simply by looking at the land register.

LECTURER: And this is known as the "mirror principle", i.e. the land register *reflects* the title that the purchaser will take once he is registered as the owner. The idea is that he should not have to make many additional inquiries about interests that may bind him, inspections of the land, and inquiries as to whether his seller actually owns the title he is selling. He gets precisely what it says he gets on the land register. So let's verify this. Look back over the work we have done so far in this chapter and see if you can confirm what Lord Wilberforce says.

STUDENT: The very first thing we studied in this chapter was how land registration creates a "statutory proprietorship". The person who is registered as proprietor is deemed for all purposes of transfer to a purchaser/mortgagee to have the ability to sell the title/deal with it. He is deemed to be the owner. This is conclusive, i.e. the purchaser doesn't need to make any further enquiries as to whether the seller owns what he says he owns. Section 58 even provides that a person who is registered as the owner is deemed to *be* the owner even if under ordinary unregistered land principles he would not have acquired the estate. And s.26 provides that a registered owner is deemed to be able to transfer/deal with the land, even if the reality is that his powers of transaction are in some way limited. Thus, a purchaser is protected against a transfer that is improper, such as one that is beyond the powers of trustees.

LECTURER: Unless of course the limitation on the power of the registered proprietor is entered on the register of title.

STUDENT: Then it will be clear on the face of the register that the seller cannot make good title. This is a fact that supports the mirror principle. It again makes the register conclusive as to what a seller can and cannot do with the land. So the purchaser can ascertain as much merely by examining the land register. So far, Lord Wilberforce is right!

LECTURER: So the land register *is* really a mirror of ownership—precisely because it *creates* that ownership. Good, now what about the interests that bind a purchaser? Is the land register a "mirror" here as well?

STUDENT: What we have studied immediately above says that a purchaser, when he is registered as proprietor of the estate or charge, takes the estate free from all prior interests. However he is bound by interests that are registered against the title.

LECTURER: So up to now is the land register a "mirror" of the interests that will bind a purchaser? It is conclusive evidence of the interests that will affect his title?

STUDENT: Yes, he just needs to look at the register in order to ascertain the interests that will bind him once he is registered as proprietor. The land register is a mirror so far. This is exactly what Lord Wilberforce was saying in *Williams & Glyn's Bank v Boland*.

LECTURER: Can you create an argument about whether these principles examined so far create good or bad law? We use our Building Blocks as evidence for a conclusion. We can legitimately say that rules are good or bad fair or unfair depending on the extent to which they support or undermine the fundamentals of Land Law as identified in our Building Blocks.

STUDENT: I would definitely start with BUILDING BLOCK NO 5.

BUILDING BLOCK NO 5: Property Rights and the Protection of Purchasers and Mortgage Lenders

We can argue that a development of a rule in a case or statute is good or bad fair or unfair, depending on the extent to which it supports or undermines the idea that rules of Land Law should protect a purchaser or mortgage lender from being bound by prior interests in the land. This is the policy behind the 1925 property legislation. A rule of Land Law is good if when applied in future cases it would not make life difficult for purchasers buying land, i.e. the rule would not mean that the land, when it is transferred to them, will be bound by rights that a purchaser or mortgage lender could not have found out about in advance.

Land is one of the most important investments ordinary people will make. They buy houses in order to live in them. Because of these factors they should be able to acquire a good title fairly easily. If a purchaser is bound by a prior right it may devalue their purchase, which consequence is severe. Banks and building societies often lend to small businesses on the security of family homes. Lenders must be sure of their security, i.e. sure that the law will not recognise rights that will bind them and stop them from selling the house if the borrower defaults—as in *Boland*. If they cannot be sure of their security then they may become reluctant to lend money. This will affect our economy.

I think that the principles we have examined so far give ample support to the policy in BUILDING BLOCK NO 5. The register mainly provides conclusive evidence that a seller or borrower is able to transfer good title. The only interests that will bind a purchaser or mortgage lender, when they are registered as proprietor are ones that have been registered. Thus, all a purchaser needs to do is to look at the land register.

LECTURER: But what about the exception known as "overriding interests"? What are these?

STUDENT: There are certain interests that do not have to be registered before they will bind a person who is purchases an estate or charge and is then registered as proprietor. These are called "interests which override" or overriding interests.

LECTURER: And this is what Lord Wilberforce said that Mrs Boland had to prove before her beneficial interest that she acquired through contribution to the purchase price could be said to bind the bank who took a later charge (mortgage) over the house (see Chapter 1, section 4). She did!

Hold this Building block against what you have just read (and already know) about the decision in *Boland*. Can you understand why banks objected to the decision in *Boland*? Make an argument on this Building Block for the conclusion that banks were justified in objecting to the decision.

BUILDING BLOCK NO 5:
Property Rights and the Protection of Purchasers and Mortgage Lenders
Rules are good if they allow purchasers to know what rights are going to bind them after a transfer of the title.

(2) The mirror principle: conclusiveness

Thus, the "mirror principle" articulates one of the fundamental principles of registered land law: The idea is that apart from overriding interests, the registered title to the land held at the Land Registry should *reflect* accurately the ownership of the estate and all the interests in it that will bind a purchaser. The land register should be a "mirror" of the actual state of the title to the land. The purchaser should have no nasty surprises, i.e. interests that are not noted on the title and that still bind him.

> **The Law Commission refer to this as the aim to make sure that the land register is as far as possible *conclusive as to priorities*.**
> **"The fundamental objective of the [2002 Act] is that . . . the register should be a complete and accurate reflection of the state of the title of the land at any given time, so that it is possible to investigate title to land. . . with the absolute minimum of additional enquiries and inspections":**
>
> Law Commission, *Land Registration for the Twenty-First Century—A Conveyancing Revolution* (2001) Law Com No.271, paras.1.5–1.6.

(3) Overriding interests

Overriding interests are the "crack in the mirror" of the register of title because they do not need to be registered in order to bind the purchaser or mortgage lender once he is registered as proprietor of the estate or charge. The register is not therefore a completely accurate reflection of the rights that will bind a purchaser. Thus the existence of overriding interests is the major defect in the system.[42]

But the land register was never intended to be a perfect mirror of title. The land registration system had to accommodate certain rights that people could not normally be expected to

---

42   Dworkin, "Registered Land Reform" (1961) 24 M.L.R. 135; Law Commission, *Land Registration for the Twenty-First Century, A Conveyancing Revolution* (Law Com No. 271), para. 8.6; Jackson, "Title by Registration and Concealed Overriding Interests" (2003) 119 L.Q.R. 660, p.661.

register, for example, rights to sewers and drains, or the rights that belong to someone in possession of the land.[43] In its reports prior to the Land Registration Act 2002, the Law Commission observed that certain interests are vulnerable to being destroyed if they were not given automatic protection in the event that the land is sold or otherwise dealt with. The rights that the Law Commission had in mind when drafting the 2002 Act were equitable rights belonging to spouses and partners who had contributed to the purchase of the house, such as the right belonging to Mrs Boland in *Williams & Glyn's Bank v Boland*.[44] They could not be expected to register them because in all probability, they are unaware that they have such rights. They should be permitted to bind a purchaser.[45] However, these interests could potentially quite severely devalue the title of the purchaser.

> **A beneficial interest under a trust will only be capable of falling within the category of overriding interests in certain circumstances which we will consider below.**

LECTURER: Is this good law?

STUDENT: The law says that a purchaser or mortgage lender will be bound by an overriding interest even though the interest is not registered. So the law ensures that people who have these informally created interests, such as Mrs Boland, will simply be able to stay in occupation and have their rights protected! Because of this, the purchaser or bank will be unable to evict her. She has the prior right to possession. So the existence of "overriding interests" is good law on the evidence of BUILDING BLOCK NO 1 and NO 3.

> **BUILDING BLOCK NO 1: Residential Security**
> We can legitimately say that where the rules operate in the context of owner occupation of property, they are good and fair if they give effective protection to people's residential security. Land Law now operates in the context of owner occupation and its rules should give effect to the purposes for which people buy land.

> **BUILDING BLOCK NO 3: Property and Identity**
> Rules are good if they take proper account of the fact that people gain a sense of value and worth from ownership of land, particularly in the context of owner occupation. Thus, Land Law rules should not deprive people of that possession without adequate safeguard. The provision for "overriding interests" provides such safeguard.

---

43   Anderson, *Lawyers and the Making of English Land Law 1832–1940*, pp.277–8.
44   [1981] A.C. 487.
45   Per Lord Oliver in *Abbey National Building Society v Cann* [1991] 1 A.C. 56, p.78. Law Commission, *Land Registration for the Twenty-First Century, A Conveyancing Revolution* (2001, Law Com No 271).

2

The rationale of the Land Registration Act 2002

The Land Registration Act 2002 originated from a project of the Joint Working Group of the Law Commission and HM Land Registry. This resulted in two Reports prior to the Land Registration Act 2002: *Land Registration for the Twenty-First Century*.[46] The Land Registration Act 2002, which came into force on October 13, 2003, repealed the Land Registration Act 1925 in its entirety.

A. THE LEGAL OBJECTIVES OF THE LAND REGISTRATION ACT 2002

> **Land Register should be "as far as possible conclusive as to priorities"**
> "The fundamental objective of the [Act] is that . . . the register should be a complete and accurate reflection of the state of the title of the land at any given time, so that it is possible to investigate title to land . . . with the absolute minimum of additional enquiries and inspections": Law Com No.271, paras 1.5–1.6.

A purchaser should be able to ascertain the rights that will bind him by looking at the register alone. The 2002 Act achieves its aim firstly, by the introduction of a system of "e-conveyancing", whereby title is investigated on line, and secondly, by making substantive reforms of registered land law. The Law Commission acknowledged the need to retain a category of overriding interests.

(1) Electronic conveyancing and the "registration gap"

The 2002 Act makes provision for the future introduction of a system of electronic conveyancing.[47] The Land Registry is working towards this but it has yet to be fully implemented. The idea is that a purchaser or mortgage lender will be able to investigate title to the land by looking at an online register. The other facet of electronic conveyancing is that the estate in land will be transferred from seller to buyer entirely electronically. This will abolish the current two-stage system of conveyancing, whereby there is a gap of time between execution of the deed of transfer to the purchaser and his registration as proprietor of the estate. A problem currently arises in this two-stage system because it is only at the point of *registration* that the purchaser gains the protection of substantive registration and takes free from prior rights in the land. This means an overriding interest could arise after execution of the deed but before registration. In short, he could be bound by an overriding interest that he could not have discovered. It is also

---

46   Law Com No.254 (the Consultative Document) and the Final Report: *Land Registration for the Twenty-First Century–A Conveyancing Revolution* (Law Com No. 271, 2001).
47   Land Registration Act 2002 ss.92 and 93. Sch.5.

possible for an interest to be expressly created and then registered against the title in this "registration gap". There were legal solutions under the 1925 Act.[48]

The major significance of electronic conveyancing is that it will eliminate this "registration gap". Transactions in land will be conducted entirely online. The document of transfer or creation of an interest will be executed online and at the same time the transaction will be registered at the Land Registry.[49] Section 91 of the Land Registration Act 2002 allows a document that creates a disposition of a registered estate or charge, a disposition of an interest that is to be protected as a notice in the register, or a disposition which triggers compulsory registration, to take electronic form. Section 93 gives the power to require that document to be in electronic form and to be simultaneously registered before it can take effect.

(2) Reforms of substantive registered land law

The aim of the Land Registration Act 2002 is to make the land register "as far as possible conclusive as to priorities", i.e. it will "mirror" more accurately all the dealings that have occurred in relation to the land so that a purchaser will have a better idea of the rights and interests that will bind him after a transfer of the land. The Act contains provisions to bring more estates and interests onto the register.

(a) Provisions for compulsory and voluntary first registration

Where land is unregistered it only becomes compulsory to register the title on the occurrence of certain dealings. As we shall see the 2002 Act introduces new provisions for compulsory and voluntary first registration.

(b) Making many more leasehold estates registrable

The 2002 Act reduced the length of leases that are compulsorily registrable as estates in their own right, from terms greater than 21 years to terms greater than seven years. Power is given to the Lord Chancellor to reduce the length of registrable leases yet further.[50] Commenting on the 1925 Act the Law Commission observes that:

> "At present, most business leases – the most common form of commercial dealing with land – are granted for periods of less than 21 years and are therefore incapable of registration. We can see no justification for excluding such leases from the benefits of land registration and, in particular, electronic conveyancing."[51]

---

48   In practice the purchaser's position is protected by what is called a "priority search", i.e. when a prospective purchaser makes an official search of the register of title he is accorded priority for a certain period. See now Land Registration Act 2002 s.72(6). As far as overriding interests were concerned, the House of Lords held that the relevant time for establishing "actual occupation" for the purposes of one important category of overriding interest (the rights of persons in actual occupation (now Land Registration Act 2002 Sch.3(2)) is the time of execution of the deed and not registration: *Abbey National Building Society v Cann* [1991] 1 A.C. 56; This avoided "conveyancing absurdity": *Lloyds Bank v Rosset* [1989] Ch.350; also *Brown & Root Technology Ltd v Sun Alliance and London Assurance Co* [2000] 2 W.L.R. 566.

49   Law Com No.271, para.2.1(2).

50   Land Registration Act 2002 s.118.

51   Law Com No.271, para.2.6.

Reducing the length of compulsorily registrable leases furthers the 2002 Act's aim to ensure that the land register is as far as possible "conclusive as to priorities". Under the Land Registration Act 1925, legal lease of less than 21 years were overriding interests, which meant that a purchaser of the freehold estate would be bound by such a lease when it was not registered. Now, leases granted for a period of more than seven years *must be registered* before they can bind a purchaser of the freehold.

(c) The Land Registration Act 2002 permits the registration of Crown land

Under the Land Registration Act 1925 Crown land was not registrable. This is because the Act only permitted "estates" to be registered. The Crown owns land outright, as we saw in Chapter 2. It does not hold land by virtue of an estate.[52] The 2002 Act provides that Her Majesty the Queen "may grant an estate in fee simple absolute in possession out of demesne land to Herself".[53] Then the Queen can register her land.

(d) Narrowing the scope of the categories of "overriding interests"

You will remember that overriding interests are those rights that will bind a purchaser automatically, even though they are not registered. They are, in effect, the "crack in the mirror" of title registration, although we also saw that such a category is necessary as the owner of such interests could not be expected to protect them through registration. A balance must be struck.

In its final report prior to the Land Registration Act 2002, the Law Commission observed that we live in a "culture of registration" and it is not acceptable for so many interests to be created off the register and still bind a purchaser.[54] The Law Commission acknowledged that there are large numbers of overriding interests that exist in relation to land, the owners of which may not appreciate the need to register their rights. Consequently, if the land registration system was to require that all interests must be registered in order to bind a transferee of the estate, these persons would probably lose their property rights as unprotected interests. The Law Commission thought that this could amount to the state effectively taking away property for the purposes of s.1 of the Human Rights Act 1998.[55]

". . . it is unreasonable to expect all encumbrancers to register their rights, particularly where those rights arise informally, under (say) a constructive trust or by estoppel. The law pragmatically recognises that some rights can be created informally, and to require their registration would defeat the sound policy that underlies their recognition. Furthermore, when people occupy land they are often unlikely to appreciate the need to take the formal step of registering any rights that they have in it. They will probably regard their occupation as the only necessary protection."[56]

---

52   Law Com No.271, para.2.7.
53   Land Registration Act 2002 s.79(1). "Demesne" is the way of describing land held outright by the Crown.
54   Law Com No.271, paras 8.74–8.88.
55   Law Com No 271, para.8.74. The peaceful enjoyment of possessions.
56   Law Com No.254, *Land Registration for the Twenty-First Century: A Consultative Document*, para.4.17; Law Com No.271, para.8.53.

(e) Critical Thinking—BUILDING BLOCK NO 8: Statutory rules should give effect to the purpose behind their enactment

Do the rules achieve the purpose behind the 2002 Act?

The 2002 Act narrowed the scope for interests in land to take effect as overriding interests, as we will see below. The basic principle underlying the changes to overriding interests is that interests should be overriding *only* where protection against purchasers is needed but it is not reasonable to expect the interest to be noted on the register. The balancing principle is that a purchaser should not be bound by rights which he could not have discovered or of which he was not actually aware: Law Com No.271, paras 8.74–8.88. The rules that determine when interests can be overriding are drafted to reflect this balance.

BUILDING BLOCK NO 1:

Residential Security

We live in a culture where rights in the family home come into being informally. The owner of that right (for example Mrs Boland in *Williams & Glyn's Bank v Boland*) may not appreciate that they have got a right, let alone the need to protect it by registering it! If their interest is not permitted to bind purchasers and mortgage lenders, where unbeknown to them the legal owner has mortgaged the house, then they can be evicted.

BUILDING BLOCK NO 5: Property

Rights and the Protection of Purchasers and Mortgage Lenders

But a balance must be struck. Look back at this Building Block in Chapter 1 and see how damaging it can be for a purchaser to have to take subject to rights such as those belonging to a Mrs Boland. Look at the specific policy that relates to lenders such as banks and building societies, and their need to be able to sell the house with vacant possession so that they can get their investment back.

This information will help you to formulate a way of evaluating the rules. It is always legitimate to criticise statutory rules on the basis that they do not "do what it says on the tin", i.e. achieve the intentions of Parliament behind their enactment. We will use this form of analysis when we study the rules of the Land Registration Act 2002.

> **BUILDING BLOCK NO 8: Statutory rules should give effect to the purpose behind their enactment**
> This reasoning of the Law Commission behind the Land Registration Act 2002 is invaluable as it tells us the intentions of parliament behind the rules. If the rules do not achieve these purposes we may legitimately say that they are not good law. Also, the courts will take parliament's intentions behind the 2002 into account when they are interpreting its rules. So where the meaning of a rule is unclear we can offer a "policy-consistent" interpretation.

(f) Reform of the doctrine of adverse possession in relation to registered land

Prior to the 2002 Act, the doctrine of adverse possession operated in the same way, whether title to the land was registered or unregistered. Many claims to land are made under this doctrine. It is now more difficult for a squatter to assert a claim to registered land.[57] We examined these reforms in Chapter 3.

3 Where title to land is registered for the first time

We now proceed to examine the provisions of the Land Registration Act 2002 in detail. We will start by looking at the law that applies where land that is previously unregistered is registered for the first time. Registration of title to land is compulsory. However, it only becomes compulsory to register the title on the occurrence of certain dealings with it, the most obvious one being a sale of that land. The Land Registration Act 1997 considerably extended the dealings with land that trigger compulsory registration.[58] Section 4 of the Land Registration Act 2002 largely codified this, but added some new triggers.[59] These compulsory registration triggers are contained in s.4 of the Land Registration Act 2002.

A. DEALINGS WITH UNREGISTERED LAND WHICH TRIGGER COMPULSORY FIRST REGISTRATION

(1) Transfers of unregistered freehold and leasehold estates

Where there is a transfer for valuable consideration or by gift[60] of a freehold estate in land or the transfer for valuable consideration or by gift of a lease with more than seven years left to run, the

---

57 Land Registration Act 2002 Sch.6, Part 9, ss.96–98.
58 Land Registration Act 1997 ss.123 and 123A.
59 C.Harpum and J.Bignell, *Registered Land: Law and Practice under the Land Registration Act 2002* (Jorden Publishing 2004), para.2.8.
60 Which includes the situation in which land is left as a gift by will. The assent of the personal representatives of the deceased will trigger compulsory first registration: s.4(1)(ii).

purchaser or donee must register the title to that freehold or lease.[61] You will see that this category includes the "large ownership rights", the freehold and leasehold estates. Thus, where one of our "visitors to the estate agents" in Chapter 6 purchases a freehold house, title to which is unregistered, it is compulsory for him to register his ownership once it has been transferred to him.

(2) The grant of a lease out of an unregistered legal estate for a term greater than seven years

Where a lease is granted for a term of more than seven years from the date of the grant, and "for valuable or other consideration [or] by way of gift" the grantee must register the lease.[62]

(3) Certain other leases

There are other types of lease granted out of a freehold or leasehold estate[63] that must be registered, this time irrespective of their length, for example, a lease that takes effect in possession after the end of the period of three months beginning with the date of the grant.[64] This is the so-called "reversionary lease". The tenant is granted the lease immediately, but it takes effect in the future. The idea behind requiring the registration of these leases is that legal leases granted for a period of seven years or less are overriding interests, which means they bind a purchaser irrespective of registration. Thus, unless reversionary leases were required to be registered, a purchaser of the freehold would be bound by a lease that was not on the register and was almost impossible to discover when inspecting the land, the tenant not yet being in possession.[65]

(4) A first protected legal mortgage of an unregistered estate

For example, David is the owner of the freehold of Blackacre, which is unregistered land. David takes out a loan and grants a first mortgage on the estate to the Bradgate Bank. That mortgage must be registered. The requirement works slightly differently from the other compulsory registration requirements. A first protected legal mortgage of an unregistered legal estate triggers first registration of the mortgaged estate.[66] Thus, upon the grant of the mortgage, David is required to register his freehold estate in Blackacre. When the estate becomes registered the mortgage is registered against the title and the mortgagee registered as proprietor of the charge. The mortgage is a registered estate with protection of the special rule of priority

61   Land Registration Act 2002 s.4(1)(a)(i) and (ii).
62   s.4(1)(c)(i) and (ii).
63   In order to trigger compulsory first registration they must be granted out of an unregistered legal freehold or leasehold estate. If the latter, the lease must have more than seven years left to run: Land Registration Act 2002 s.4(2).
64   Land Registration Act 2002 s.4(1)(d).
65   Law Commission, *Land Registration for the Twenty-First Century – A Conveyancing Revolution* (Law Com No. 271).
66   s.4(1)(g), provided that estate is an unregistered legal freehold or leasehold estate. If the latter, the lease must have more than seven years left to run: Land Registration Act 2002 s.4(2).

discussed above.[67] "First protected" means that the mortgage is to take effect as a mortgage protected by deposit of the title documents of the mortgaged estate with the lender and the mortgage ranks first in priority above any other mortgages on the estate that exist at the time of creation.[68]

B. THE DUTY TO APPLY FOR FIRST REGISTRATION OF TITLE

Upon the occurrence of any of these compulsory registration dispositions, the transferee or grantee of the estate or interest is under a duty to apply for it to be registered.[69] The exception is the first legal mortgage, where it is the *grantor* of the mortgage (the borrower) who must apply for the mortgaged estate itself to be registered.[70]

> **Effect of non-compliance with registration requirement**
> The effect of non-compliance with this duty is that "the transfer, grant or creation becomes void as regards the transfer, grant or creation of a legal estate": Land Registration Act 2002 s.7(1).

> **Legal consequence**
> In cases where there is a transfer of a registrable estate and the transferee fails to apply for first registration, "the title to the legal estate reverts to the transferor who holds it on bare trust for the transferee": Land Registration Act 2002, s.7(2)(a). In cases of the grant of a registrable estate or interest "the grant or creation has effect as a contract made for valuable consideration to grant or create the legal estate concerned": s.7(2)(b).

C. VOLUNTARY FIRST REGISTRATION: WHEN TITLE *MAY* BE REGISTERED FOR THE FIRST TIME

Certain estates and interests in land may be registered even when there are no dealings with them. Section 3 of the Land Registration Act 2002 contains provision for voluntary first

---

67 C.Harpum and J.Bignell, *Registered Land: Law and Practice under the Land Registration Act 2002*, para 2.19. Where a lease is granted out of unregistered land it is not similarly compulsory to register the landlord's title to the freehold.
68 Land Registration Act 2002 s.4(8)(a) and (b); C.Harpum and J.Bignell, above para 2.19.
69 Land Registration Act 2002 s.6(1). Registration must be applied for within two months: s.6(4).
70 Land Registration Act 2002 s.6(2); also, Stevens and Pearce, *Land Law*, 3rd edn (London: Sweet & Maxwell, 2004), p.74.

registration. A person may "apply to the registrar to be registered as the proprietor of an unregistered legal estate".[71] A fee simple estate, and a leasehold estate "granted for a term of which more than seven years are unexpired" may be registered. A discontinuous (or "timeshare") lease may be voluntarily registered irrespective of its length.[72] Rentcharges may be voluntarily registered[73] as may a profit à prendre in gross (e.g. fishing rights over another's land), and franchises,[74] (e.g. the right to hold a fair or market). These can be valuable rights.[75]

> **These provisions for voluntary first registration are novel. Are they good law?**

> **BUILDING BLOCK NO 8: Statutory rules should give effect to the purpose behind their enactment**
> The intention of Parliament was to ensure that the Land Register was, as far as possible "conclusive as to priorities". If the rules do not achieve these purposes we may legitimately say that they are not good law.

D. CLASSES OF TITLE AWARDED ON FIRST REGISTRATION

When title to an estate is submitted for registration, the registrar will conduct a "once and for all" examination of title.[76] It will be given a class of title: the freehold estate, the fee simple absolute in possession, can be awarded three possible classes of title: absolute, qualified and possessory. The grade awarded depends on the extent to which the registrar is satisfied that person applying for first registration is entitled to the ownership of the estate.

A person may be registered with title absolute "if the registrar is of the opinion that the person's title to the estate is such as a willing buyer could properly be advised by a competent professional adviser to accept".[77] "Qualified" title may be awarded where either the title presented for registration is subject to certain reservations that may cause the title to be disturbed, e.g. the

---

71   s.3(2).
72   s.3(4).
73   s.3(1)(b).
74   s.3(1)(c) and (d).
75   C.Harpum and J.Bignell, above para.2.6.
76   It is possible for titles to be upgraded: Land Registration Act 2002, Part 6.
77   Land Registration Act 2002 s.9(2).

transfer to the person making it was a breach of trust,[78] or "the person's title to the estate has been established only for a limited period".[79] A "possessory" title will be awarded if the registrar cannot award the estate any other class of title and the applicant is in "actual possession of the land, or in receipt of the rents and profits of the land".[80] This is the weakest claim to ownership and may be disturbed in the future by a better claimant, e.g. one who can establish a better documentary claim to the estate.

Similar classes of title apply to the leasehold estate, the term of years absolute, with one addition. The registrar will award title absolute if, in addition to being "of the opinion that the person's title to the estate is such as a willing buyer could properly be advised by a competent professional adviser to accept", he "approves the lessor's title to grant the lease",[81] i.e. he can establish the landlord's ownership of the freehold estate because it is registered. Otherwise, "good leasehold" title may be awarded.

E. THE EFFECT OF FIRST REGISTRATION: THE PRIORITY RULE

On first substantive registration as proprietor of the estate or interest the estate becomes vested in the new registered proprietor, together with all interests that benefit the estate, for example, a right of way over a neighbour's garden.[82] When title to an estate, interest, or charge is submitted for first registration, the interests that bind the estate will have already been determined under the rules of unregistered conveyancing.[83] The rule that declares the interests that will bind the estate of the first registered proprietor is contained in ss.11 and 12 of the Land Registration Act 2002.[84] Section 11 provides that a person once registered as proprietor of an absolute estate takes the estate free from all prior estates and interests in the land, except:

(1) Interests which are the subject of an entry in the register in relation to the estate[85]

The registrar will have examined the title submitted for registration and where it is evident that an interest affects that title, such as an easement, they will enter a "notice" on the register that protects the priority of that interest.[86] The new registered proprietor will be bound by the interest, e.g. the easement. If the estate is, under unregistered land principles, bound by (e.g.) an estate

---

78   C.Harpum and J.Bignell, above, p.39.
79   s.9(4).
80   s.9(5).
81   s.10(2).
82   Land Registration Act 2002 s.11(3).
83   C.Harpum and J.Bignell, *Registered Land: Law and Practice under the Land Registration Act 2002*, para.4.1.
84   Section 11 states the priority rule that affects freehold estates. Section 12 states the same rule for leasehold estates.
85   Land Registration Act 2002 s.11(4)(a).
86   We will consider below the different entries on the land register that can protect smaller rights in land from being destroyed on a sale or mortgage.

contract because it is registered as a land charge under the Land Charges Act 1972, the land registrar will enter the estate contract as a "notice" on the register of title, which protects its priority over the estate of the new registered proprietor. He will have to give effect to it.

(2) Overriding interests which fall within any of the paragraphs of Schedule 1[87]

A person when they are registered as first proprietor of an estate or charge takes that estate subject to any overriding interests that subsist in relation to the land. An overriding interest is an interest in land that will bind a registered proprietor even though that interest is not registered. The overriding interests that bind on first registration of title are listed in Sch.1 of the Land Registration Act 2002. We will consider the application of Sch.1 as part of the Critical Thinking exercise immediately below.

(3) Interests acquired under the Limitation Act 1980 of which the proprietor has notice[88]

This means that a first registered proprietor will take the land subject to any rights acquired under the doctrine of adverse possession of which he has notice.[89] The Land Registration Act 2002 abolishes squatters' rights as a category of overriding interest. So they will not automatically bind a first registered proprietor.[90] Instead, a first registered proprietor will only take subject to the rights of a squatter if he has notice of them. The Act does not say "knowledge", so presumably the purchaser will be bound by the rights of a squatter where he knew or ought to have known of their existence, e.g. the squatter is in occupation of the land and his rights could have been discovered by inspection.

(4) Overriding interests that bind on first registration—Critical Thinking

You will remember that an overriding interest is an interest in land that will bind a registered proprietor even though that interest is not registered. Land registration is intended as we have seen to affect a statutory ownership of the title whereby it is transparent from the face of the register which interests will bind a purchaser and which will not. Overriding interests are the crack in this mirror of title.

(a) Schedule 1 provides that the interests which override first registration are as follows:

Paragraph 1: A lease granted for a term not exceeding seven years from the date of the grant. This paragraph of overriding interest excludes other leases of any length that are required to be registered under s.4, for example "reversionary leases". These leases are particularly difficult for a purchaser to discover when he inspects the land, as the tenant will not be in possession.

---

87   Land Registration Act 2002 s.11(4)(b).
88   s.11(4)(c).
89   See Chapter 3, section 3D.
90   The 2002 Act severely curtails the way the doctrine itself operates in relation to titles that are already registered: see Sch.6. So it is unnecessary to have a corresponding provision that applies to transfers of land that are already registered under s.29 and 30.

Paragraph 2: An interest belonging to a person in actual occupation, so far as relating to land of which he is in actual occupation, except for an interest under a settlement under the Settled Land Act 1925. This is a common overriding interest, and is the one that Mrs Boland successfully established against the bank in *Williams & Glyn's Bank v Boland*.[91] In order to establish an overriding interest under this paragraph, it is necessary to prove: 1. An interest in the relevant land. As you see, equitable interests that exist where land is held in settlements cannot be protected as overriding under this paragraph. Equitable interests under a trust of land can be so protected. Indeed, as we saw in *Boland*, the interest to which Mrs Boland was entitled was an interest under a trust. 2. The claimant must also establish that they are in actual occupation of the land.[92]

Paragraph 3: A legal easement or profit à prendre: In order to be overriding, the easement must be legal, so it must fall within s.1(2) of the Law of Property Act 1925. Any legal easement will fall within this paragraph, irrespective of whether it has been expressly granted by deed or arises by implication of law.[93] Thus, a legal easement over unregistered land will bind a transferee of that land when he is registered as proprietor of the estate, even though the easement has not been registered.

(b) Other overriding interests that fall within Schedule 1

The interests we have just discussed are the most common overriding interests. In its report prior to the 2002 Act, the Law Commission stated that the aim of the 2002 Act would be to narrow the scope of these three categories of overriding interest, and to phase out others altogether. There are other rights that exist as overriding interests that bind first registered proprietors of an estate in land including a customary right, a public right, a local land charge, certain mineral rights. The following rights will override the estate of a first registered proprietor but will cease to be overriding 10 years after the coming into force of the 2002 Act, i.e. October 13, 2013:[94] a franchise; a manorial right; a right to rent from land which was reserved to the Crown on the granting of any freehold estate; the liability to repair an embankment or sea or river wall; a right to payment in lieu of tithe; a right in respect of the repair of a church chancel.[95]

---

91   [1981] A.C. 487.
92   We will consider the meaning of "actual occupation" below in relation to Sch.3: *Interests which override registered dispositions*. This provision is broader than the corresponding provision in Sch.3.
93   Cf. the position regarding Sch.3 and interests which override registered dispositions: see below under consideration of Sch.3 para.3.
94   Land Registration Act 2002 s.117(1).
95   Certain land in the vicinity of a church is subject to the obligation to repair the church chancel; where the owner of the land is deemed to be a "lay rector". This is a right in the land itself that can be enforced against any future owners of that land. In *Aston Cantlow and Wilmcote with Billesley PCC v Wallbank* [2002] Ch. 51, a couple had been given a house. The conveyance expressly declared the existence of the obligation to repair the local church's chancel. When the church submitted the bill, the couple objected, claiming, *inter alia*, that the existence of the obligation contravened the Human Rights Act. The Court of Appeal upheld this claim, but on appeal in *Aston Cantlow and Wilmcote with Billesley P.C.C. v Wallbank* [2003] 3 W.L.R. 283, the House of Lords overturned the decision, holding the couple subject to the obligation. Under the Land Registration Act 2002, the obligation to repair, which is potentially very onerous indeed, is an overriding interest that binds land irrespective of registration, here, until October 13, 2013, when it will have to be registered: Land Registration Act 2002 s.117.

LECTURER: Let's work through a problem on the priority rule for first registrations.

> V sells the freehold estate in Yellowacre to P. Title is unregistered. Upon completion of the purchase P submits the estate to be registered at the Land Registry. Weeks later P is faced with several people claiming rights in his estate that bind him.
>
> Roger claims that V had granted him a lease by deed for five years; Z, P's neighbour claims a right for life to walk over the land to get to his house; Billy claims an option to purchase (an "estate contract"). Advise P.

LECTURER: First of all tell me about the estate that P acquires.

STUDENT: When he is registered as proprietor, the freehold estate in Yellowacre vested in P: LRA 2002 s.11.

LECTURER: So we turn to our next important question: what are the interests in Yellowacre that will bind P once he is registered as proprietor? Remember in your answer to outline the nature of the problem, i.e. this is a priorities dispute.

STUDENT: I see we have quite a few people claiming prior rights in the land, e.g. Roger is arguing that his five year lease has priority over P's newly registered estate, so that P will be unable to evict him; P's neighbour is claiming a right for life to walk across the land. Billy is claiming an option to purchase the land which, if it binds P's title, will be enforceable and Billy will be able to purchase the land from P.

LECTURER: Good, you stated the nature of the problem. Now let's see if we can predict a solution by applying the relevant law.

STUDENT: The interests that bind Yellowacre will already have been determined by the unregistered land rules when the estate was transferred by deed to P. We need to apply these rules, and the priority rule in s.11 of the Land Registration Act 2002. Then we consider whether any of the interests automatically override P's estate under Sch.1.

Concerning Roger: under the unregistered land rules Roger has a legal leasehold estate which is binding on P. It is a legal estate so it binds the whole world. This is reflected in Sch.1 para.1 which provides that a lease of seven years or less is an overriding interest under Sch.1 para.1. Thus, P is bound by the lease.

LECTURER: What about Z's easement? Did it bind P when Yellowacre was transferred to him as unregistered land?

STUDENT: If it is a legal interest then it binds the whole world. And this is reflected in Sch.1 para.3, which provides that legal easements are overriding interests. P would be bound by the easement.

LECTURER: Just a minute—is it a legal interest?

STUDENT: No—because it is "for life" and thus cannot be a legal easement under s.1(2) of the Law of Property Act 1925, which requires the easement to be of perpetual duration or a length "equivalent to a term of years". "For life" is neither of these. Therefore it is an equitable easement.

LECTURER: So it does not bind the whole world. But how are equitable interests protected according to the unregistered land rules?

STUDENT: Ah! I remember—an equitable easement is a registrable land charge. Thus, unless Z registered it as a land charge it will be void against P's estate: Land Charges Act 1972 s.4. Thus the registrar would not register this interest as binding P's registered estate.

LECTURER: And it is not an overriding interest under Sch.1 para.1 because it is equitable.

STUDENT: And exactly the same applies to Billy's estate contract. When Yellowacre was transferred by deed to P as unregistered land, we note that an estate contract is a registrable land charge under the Land Charges Act 1972. Thus, it is void if Billy has not registered it. Thus, when P submits his title for first registration the registrar cannot register the estate contract as binding the title.

F. THE EFFECT OF FIRST REGISTRATION WITH "QUALIFIED" OR "POSSESSORY" TITLE

If the proprietor is registered with "qualified" title the effect of his registration as proprietor is the same as if he had been registered with absolute title. However, it is unlike in this respect: with qualified titles there are identified defects in title and the new registered proprietor will be subject to these defects. He may be bound by estates, rights or interests that have priority to his own.[96] Registration with a possessory title is subject to "the enforcement of any estate, right or interest adverse to, or in derogation of, the proprietor's title subsisting at the time of registration or then capable of arising".[97]

G. CAUTIONS AGAINST FIRST REGISTRATION

Where land is unregistered, there is obviously no registered title against which to register the existence of an interest in the land that you do not wish to be destroyed by the statutory proprietorship effect of first substantive registration, or register any concern that you may have that you have a better claim to the estate. So how can a person protect an interest or claim in that land from being unenforceable once title to the estate is registered for the first time? The Land Registrar keeps a separate register of "cautions against first registration".[98] The owner of an estate or interest in unregistered land who, e.g., may wish to oppose an application for first registration[99] may apply to register a caution against first registration of the estate.[100] Where there is an application to register the land for the first time, "the registrar must give the cautioner

---

96   Land Registration Act 2002 s.11(6).

97   s.11(7).

98   Land Registration Act 2002 s.19(1).

99   For example, "he has some claim to the land himself": C.Harpum and J.Bignell, *Registered Land: Law and Practice under the Land Registration Act 2002*, paras.5.1, 5.4.

100   Land Registration Act 2002 s.15(1). It is not possible to register a caution against your own estate and thereby impede its first registration: s.15(3).

notice of the application and of his right to object to it".[101] A caution against first registration does not guarantee the priority of an interest, i.e. that it will bind the land when that land is registered.[102] But on first registration of the estate to which the interest relates, the Land Registrar may register the interest against the title. In this way the interest will bind the land.

> **Cautions against first registration**
> A person with an easement over unregistered land may apply to register a caution against first registration of that land. When there is an application for first registration of the land over which the easement is claimed, the Registrar, if satisfied as to the validity of the claim, may register the easement against the title, when he registers title to the estate for the first time.

The person applying for first registration of the land may apply to have the caution cancelled.[103]

H. DUTY TO DISCLOSE UNREGISTERED INTERESTS

There is a duty on persons applying for first registration of an estate or charge to disclose to the registrar information about any unregistered interest that overrides his title under schedule 1.[104] Thus, the registrar will be able to register that interest, if appropriate, and it will never again be an overriding interest.[105] The aim of this provision is to make the land register a more accurate reflection of interests in that land.[106]

I. MULTIPLE ESTATES AND MULTIPLE TITLES

As you will appreciate by now there are many different estates and interests that can exist in relation to land. Some of these are registrable with title in their own right. Thus, there may be more than one title that exists in relation to a plot of land. For example, Fred has registered his freehold estate. He grants a 10-year lease to Vanessa, who registers her leasehold estate. Both have title in their own right. Both, when registered as proprietor, take the estate free from all other estates and interests that exist in relation to the land except overriding interests and interests entered on the register. As well as substantively registering the lease, what the Land Registrar will do in this situation is to enter the lease as a notice on the register of title to the freehold estate. It will then bind subsequent purchasers of the freehold.

---

101   s.16(1).
102   s.16(3).
103   s.18(1).
104   Land Registration Act 2002 s.71(a).
105   s.29(3).
106   The duty applies to interests "within the actual knowledge of the applicant; and [which] affect the estate to which registration applies": Land Registration Rules 2003, rr. 28 and 57(1): C.Harpum and J.Bignell, *Registered Land: Law and Practice under the Land Registration Act 2002*, paras 4.19 and 11.19.

4

Transactions with land already registered: registrable dispositions

A. AN OUTLINE AND A SIMPLE TRANSACTION

In the last section we examined the rules that apply where land is unregistered and is then brought onto the register for the first time. But what about the situation where land is already registered? How is registered land transferred from one person to another? What property rights will bind a purchaser or a lender taking a mortgage of a registered house as security?

Where title to an estate in land is already registered, certain important transactions with, or "dispositions" of, that title, e.g. sale or mortgage, *must be registered*. We call these "registrable dispositions". Broadly speaking, they are the larger ownership rights and are registered with title in their own right.[107] The list of registrable dispositions is found in s.27 of the Land Registration Act 2002.

> **Transfer of the freehold of No.53 Belbury Street**
> Mark and Jane pay a visit to the local estate agents. They are first-time buyers looking for a modest terraced house. After viewing several houses they decide to buy No.53 Belbury Street, Edgestow, title to which is registered. So they have to make sure the seller owns the house and has the ability to transfer it to them. It is a straightforward matter of searching the land register to make sure title is registered to the seller and that there are no restrictions on his ability to sell. Mark and Jane complete their purchase. The house is freehold, a transfer of which is a "registrable disposition". In fact it is possibly one of the commonest forms of transaction with a registered estate. Because it is a registrable disposition, Mark and Jane *must* be registered as the new proprietors. Once registered as proprietors ("owners") of the freehold of No.53 Belbury Street they gain full ownership of the house—the statutory proprietorship effect of substantive registration.

Whilst in the process of buying No.53 Belbury Street, Mark and Jane's solicitor will have investigated the issue of what property rights would bind Mark and Jane's new registered title to the house. What if a neighbour claims an easement or the benefit of a restrictive covenant? What if the seller's mother had contributed to his purchase and is now claiming that she is entitled to live in the house? The rule that tells Mark and Jane what interests bind *registered dispositions* such as theirs is contained in s.29 and 30 of the Land Registration Act 2002.

---

107   One exception being an easement, which is a registrable disposition.

> And so our structure here is to consider firstly the question of title: what titles must be registered so as to vest full ownership in the new proprietor(s)?: s.27.
>
> And secondly, what interests will bind these titles? We need to know the "priority rule" that applies to these transactions: s.29 and 30.

B. REGISTRABLE DISPOSITIONS: SECTION 27

(1) A transfer of a registered estate[108]

A "registered estate" is a legal estate the title to which is entered in the register.[109] For example, Broadacres is land that is already registered. X is the registered proprietor of the freehold estate, which he sells and transfers to Y, Y must register this transfer. Y will be entered as the proprietor in place of X.[110] This is an everyday transaction with registered land.

> Most of the visitors to the estate agents at the beginning of Chapter 6 will be involved in this sort of transaction. This was what Mark and Jane did in our above example.

A transfer of a leasehold estate also falls into this category: it is a legal estate. If it is registered and then transferred then this transfer must be registered. For example, Jake is the registered proprietor of a 25 year lease of a shop and he sells this lease to The Travel Company. The Company must register the transfer of the lease into its name.

(2) The grant of a lease for a term of more than seven years[111]

A lease granted out of a registered estate for a term greater than seven years from the date of the grant *must be registered.* So taking our first example above, if Y then grants a 10 year lease of a cottage on Broadacres to Z, Z must register his lease with title in its own right. The registrar must also enter Z's lease as a notice on the title to the freehold.[112] The lease will then bind future purchasers of the freehold.

Under the Land Registration Act 1925 leases were required to be registered only when they were granted for a term greater than 21 years.

LECTURER: The rule is that a lease which is granted for a term of over seven years, rather than 21, must be registered before it can have legal effect. Is this rule good law? Hold it against BUILDING BLOCK NO 8 in which we say that a rule is good law if it gives effect to the intentions of parliament behind the enactment of that rule.

---

108   Land Registration Act 2002 s.27(2)(a).
109   s.132(1) not including a charge.
110   Sch.2 para.2.
111   Land Registration Act 2002 s.27(2)(b).
112   s.38; Sch.2, para.3.

> **BUILDING BLOCK NO 8: Statutory rules should give effect to the purpose behind their enactment**
> The main objective of the Land Registration Act 2002 is that the land register should be as far as possible "conclusive", i.e. it should have all the information that a purchaser needs about the interests that will bind them after the transfer. *Does this rule achieve this aim?*

STUDENT: Under the Land Registration Act 1925, legal leases of 21 years or less were overriding interests, which meant that when the landlord sold the freehold estate, and the purchaser registered his estate, that purchaser would be bound by any lease of the land for a term of 21 years or less, even though it was not registered. Purchasers of registered land would have to undertake many more inspections and enquiries to make sure that they were not bound by leases.

Under the new rule all leases granted for a term of over seven years must be registered before they can bind a purchaser of the freehold estate.

LECTURER: So hold this against BUILDING BLOCK NO 8. Is it good law? Bear in mind that the Law Commission observed that "most business leases—the most common form of commercial dealing with land—are granted for periods of less than 21 years".[113]

STUDENT: So many leases were created that would bind purchasers of the freehold even though they were not registered. The new rule means that the title at the land registry will be a more accurate reflection of the estates and interests that will bind a purchaser, because all leases over seven years must be registered. On the basis of BUILDING BLOCK NO 8 reducing the length of registrable leases is a good rule.

LECTURER: And what about our other Building Blocks?

STUDENT: I think that the new rule supports the policy in BUILDING BLOCK NO 5. It helps to ensure that purchasers are not bound by interests in the land which they could not have readily discovered. Now there are many more leases that must be registered before they will bind such purchasers of the freehold estate.

> **BUILDING BLOCK NO 5: Property Rights and the Protection of Purchasers and Mortgage Lenders**
> Both categories of litigant, purchasers and mortgage lenders must have a safe and fairly inexpensive way of ensuring that land can be transferred to them, or offered as security for a loan. It is important that they are not bound by prior rights such as leases unless they could be made aware of this in advance. See this Building Block in Chapter 1.

---

113   Law Com No.271, para.2.6.

Power is given to the Lord Chancellor to reduce the length of registrable leases yet further.[114]

(3) Other types of lease[115]

Certain other types of lease (of whatever length) granted out of a registered estate are registrable dispositions, for example, a timeshare lease (otherwise known as a "discontinuous lease")[116] and a lease that is granted to take effect in possession after the end of the period of three months beginning with the date of the grant (otherwise known as a "reversionary lease").[117]

> **A reversionary lease**
> An example of a reversionary lease is where two students are granted a lease of a studio flat in March but they do not have possession until October.

The thinking behind making these reversionary leases registrable is that they would otherwise be overriding interests, binding purchasers of the freehold title even though they had not been registered. This would be problematic for a purchaser because the tenant would not be in possession so that the purchaser would be unable to discover an interest that would bind him automatically.[118] Thus, these leases must be registered with title in their own right as *registrable dispositions*. The registrar must also enter the lease as a notice on the title to the freehold.[119] The lease will then bind future purchasers of the freehold.

(4) The grant of a lease of a registered franchise or manor

These are dispositions that must be registered with title in their own right. The registrar must also make an entry of the right as a notice on the register in respect of that interest.[120]

(5) Express grant or reservation of a legal easement[121]

The express grant or reservation of any easement or profit à prendre provided they are capable of being legal under s.1(2)(a) of the Law of Property Act 1925. Thus, if Y grants a right of way over his freehold estate to C, C must register this easement.

> The registrar must register C's land as having the benefit of the easement (if C's land is registered). And the burden of the easement must be registered against Y's freehold title: Land Registration Act 2002, Sch.2, para.7 Thus, subsequent dealings with Y's freehold title (e.g. a sale of it) will be bound by the easement.

---

114   Land Registration Act 2002 s.118.
115   Land Registration Act 2002 s.27(2)(b)(ii) and (iii).
116   "Discontinuous leases are becoming more common, as they are sometimes used in the growing practice of time-sharing in holiday homes, as where a lump sum is paid for the right to occupy a cottage for one week in each year for 80 years": C.Harpum, S.Bridge, M.Dixon, *Megarry & Wade The Law of Real Property*, para.17–055.
117   Leases covered by particular provisions of the Housing Act 1985 are also registrable dispositions: s.27(2)(b)(iv) and (v).
118   Law Commission, *Land Registration for the Twenty-First Century – A Conveyancing Revolution* Law Com No.271.
119   s.38; Sch.2, para.3.
120   s.38; Sch.2, para.4.
121   Land Registration Act 2002 s.27(2)(d).

Under the Land Registration Act 1925, easements legal or equitable, expressly granted or impliedly granted were all capable of being overriding interests. Thus, there were many easements that could potentially bind a purchaser that could not readily be discovered by inspection of the land. The thinking behind this provision of the 2002 Act was that expressly granted easements do not require protection as overriding interests. If a person is granted an interest in land it is reasonable to expect them to register their right to protect it against sale of the land.[122] Correspondingly, expressly granted easements are registrable dispositions and not overriding interests.[123]

LECTURER: I want you to consider whether you think that it is good law to include other types of lease and expressly granted legal easements in the category of registrable dispositions. Bear in mind that under the old law, the Land Registration Act 1925, these interests were all overriding interests. What was the consequence of this?

STUDENT: If they were overriding it means that they would bind a purchaser, he or she would have to give effect to that interest, even though it was not registered.

LECTURER: Is this good law?

STUDENT: Well, again it meant that there would be many transactions with the land that would take place "off the register". I would firstly use BUILDING BLOCK NO 5 as evidence for my conclusion that this is not good law.

> **BUILDING BLOCK NO 5: Property Rights and the Protection of Purchasers and Mortgage Lenders**

Purchasers and mortgage lenders need to be able to identify by looking at the register those rights that will bind them following a transfer of the estate.

LECTURER: Otherwise we may legitimately say that the system creates bad law?

STUDENT: Yes, in our system of owner occupation people need to know that the land they are buying is not going to be devalued by people claiming interests in it. When a bank or building society takes a mortgage over property, they need to be sure that they can realise their security by selling the house, otherwise they may become reluctant to lend money on the security of land in the future. Someone claiming a lease that could not have been discovered by inspection of the land may prevent them from selling land.

STUDENT: Requiring the substantive registration of some types of lease (of whatever length they are) and expressly granted legal easement means that the register will be a more accurate reflection of the dealings with the land. So I would also use our new BUILDING BLOCK NO 8 to justify my conclusion that the rules of "registrable dispositions" are good law.

---

122   And when electronic conveyancing comes into effect the express grant of an easement will be simultaneously registered. See section 2 of this chapter.

123   Law Commission, above, para.8.71.

LECTURER: The land register will now be a better "mirror" of the state of the ownership and interests in that land.

(6) The express grant or reservation of a rentcharge or right of entry under a lease or rentcharge[124]

These are dispositions that must be registered with title in their own right. The registrar must also make an entry of the right as a notice on the register in respect of that interest.[125]

(7) The grant of a legal charge (mortgage)[126]

If Y wants to raise money to start a business, and in return for a loan grants Floyds TSB a mortgage or as we say "charge" of his freehold estate, Floyds must "be entered in the register as the proprietor [owner] of the charge".[127] A transfer of a charge and the grant of a "sub-charge" are both also registrable dispositions.[128]

> So let's say that when Mark and Jane purchased No.53 Belbury Street they needed a mortgage in order to do so. They borrowed 85 per cent of the purchase price from the Wither & Co Bank Plc and paid 15 per cent themselves. They granted Wither & Co Bank a mortgage ("charge") which, as you know, gives the bank rights over their freehold interest in No.53 Belbury Street. Mark and Jane must register the transfer of the house, and the Wither & Co Bank Plc must be registered as proprietor of the charge. The charge will be registered against Mark and Jane's freehold title of No.53 Belbury Street.

C. REGISTRABLE DISPOSITIONS: THE DUTY TO REGISTER AND THE EFFECT OF REGISTRATION AND CONSEQUENCES OF NON-REGISTRATION

These transactions with registered land cannot take effect as legal estates or interests until the registration requirement is met.[129] The disposition will however, take effect as an equitable interest.

(1) Title by registration: the registered proprietor's powers of disposition

So when Mark and Jane are registered as proprietors of the freehold estate in No 53 Belbury Street in accordance with the requirements of s.27 and Sch.2 they are deemed by the statute to be the

---

124 Land Registration Act 2002 s.27(2)(e).
125 s.38; Sch.2, para.6 and 7.
126 s.27(2)(f).
127 Land Registration Act 2002 Sch.2 para.8.
128 s.27(2)(3).
129 s.27(1).

absolute owner for all purposes of transfer and other transaction with that estate. A registered proprietor has the "power to make a disposition of any kind permitted by the general law".[130]

A registered proprietor cannot create a mortgage by grant of a lease to the lender that ceases on redemption of the mortgage. This is one of the two ways of creating a mortgage under the Law of Property Act 1925.[131] In registered land it is only possible to create a mortgage by "a charge by deed expressed to be by way of legal mortgage". As you know, this is a collection of rights granted to the lender that gives them security for a loan, e.g. it gives a power of sale and the right of possession of the land. As the Land Registration Act 2002 shows, it is more accurate to refer to this as a "charge".

D. REGISTRABLE DISPOSITIONS: THE PRIORITY RULE (SECTIONS 29 AND 30)

A person who is buying land that is already registered, or a lender taking a mortgage on registered land as security for a loan, will need to know what prior rights in that land, e.g. restrictive covenants or beneficial interests under a trust, will bind him once he is registered as the new proprietor of the estate.

> This is the second issue that any good land transfer system should address. Mark and Jane, when they were thinking about buying No.53 Belbury Street needed to know what rights already existed in relation to that land. This is because, if they found their title "bound" by these interests, someone else would have certain prior claims. If someone can assert a beneficial interest under a trust, e.g. if their seller had been holding No.53 on trust for herself and her partner because her partner had contributed to the purchase, the partner may be able to establish a claim to part ownership of Mark and Jane's new house.

> **We need to know what interests in the land bind proprietors such as Mark and Jane (we say "have priority" over their registered disposition) and which ones do not (meaning they are not affected by them).**

---

130   Land Registration Act 2002 s.23(1). Similarly, the registered proprietor of a charge has "power to make a disposition of any kind permitted by the general law", with some exceptions: see s.23(2)(a) and (b).
131   Law of Property Act 1925 s.85(1).

Where a purchaser or mortgage lender, or other person, has given "valuable consideration" for their estate in the land,[132] they can claim the benefit of the priority rule contained in s. 29 and 30 of the Land Registration Act 2002.[133] This priority rule applies to registered dispositions *at the point at which that transaction is registered*. When a person, such as Mark and Jane, is registered as proprietor (owner) of the estate, interest or charge they take their estate free from all other prior interests in that land.[134] (This is subject to the exceptions we consider below). Indeed, a bank or building society that has lent money to the owner of a registered estate, such as Mr Boland in *Williams & Glyn's Bank v Boland*,[135] and been granted a charge over the estate, will, when it is registered as proprietor of the charge, take it free from all pre-existing interests in the land (subject to the exceptions we consider below). *Is this good law?*

> **BUILDING BLOCK NO 5: Property Rights and the Protection of Purchasers and Mortgage Lenders**
>
> When a bank or building society takes a mortgage over property, they need to be sure that they can realise their security by selling the house, otherwise they may become reluctant to lend money on the security of land in the future. Someone claiming a prior right that could not have been discovered by inspection of the land may prevent them from selling it in order to realise their security.

There are exceptions. Under the priority rule laid down by s.29 and 30 a purchaser or mortgage lender will take their estate or interest in the land *subject to*: 1) an interest that is a registered charge or the subject of a notice in the register; 2) overriding interests listed in Sch.3; 3) Interests that appear from the register to be excepted from the effect of registration, and 4) certain leasehold covenants (in the case of a disposition of a leasehold estate). We are concerned primarily with the first two of these exceptions.

The time at which the purchaser or mortgagee takes free from prior rights in the land is the time of his registration as proprietor of the estate or charge.[136] The s.29 and 30 priority rule is conclusive. It is of no relevance whatsoever that the registered disponee may have had notice of any prior rights. The doctrine of notice has no relevance in registered land.

(1) Interests which have priority over registered dispositions

(a) A registered charge or the subject of a notice in the register

Where an interest is entered as a "notice" on the land register, its priority is protected. This means that all subsequent dealings with the title will take effect subject to that interest.

---

132   We consider the requirement for valuable consideration below.
133   Section 29 applies this rule to estates and s.30 to charges.
134   ss.29 and 30 avoid use of the word "purchaser", probably because of the connotations of "good faith" that attend the definition of the word in the Law of Property Act 1925.
135   [1981] 1 A.C. 487.
136   Land Registration Act 2002 ss.29(1) and 30(1).

> If on conducting a search of the register, Jane and Mark's solicitor had seen that there was a restrictive covenant registered against the title preventing the land from being used for anything other than residential purposes, the solicitor would advise Mark and Jane that this interest would bind them on becoming the registered owners.

Not all interests in land can be registered as a "notice". Broadly, it is intended that those same interests that could be made to bind the land where title is unregistered (through the land charges system) could be registered by way of "notices" and thus be made to bind title in registered land, e.g. restrictive covenants, estate contracts, equitable easements. We will consider the "notice" as a mechanism for protecting smaller rights in land below.

(b) Overriding interests listed in Schedule 3

If you remember from the previous sections in this chapter overriding interests are those rights that will bind a purchaser automatically, even though they are not registered. If the land register is supposed to be a mirror of the state of the title, i.e. the interests that are going to bind a purchaser following a sale, then overriding interests are the *crack in the mirror*. The interests that override registered dispositions are contained in Sch.3.

> Thus, if Elwin is the registered owner of "The Priory" and he wishes to borrow £100,000 on the security of the house in order to expand his business, the lender, when registered as proprietor of a charge, must make enquiries and inspect the land to ensure there are no overriding interests of the type listed in Sch.3. Otherwise they will take subject to them.

The existence of a category of overriding interests in a land transfer system based on conferring ownership through the land register is unsatisfactory.

BUILDING BLOCK NO 5: Property Rights and the Protection of Purchasers and Mortgage Lenders
When a bank or building society takes a mortgage over property, they need to be sure that they can realise their security by selling the house, otherwise they may become reluctant to lend money on the security of land in the future. Someone claiming a prior right that could not have been discovered by inspection of the land may prevent them from selling it in order to realise their security.

We will consider the overriding interests that fall within Sch.3 in detail in section 7 below in this chapter.

(c) Interests that appear from the register to be excepted from the effect of registration

Where an estate has been registered with other than title absolute it may be the case that there are defects in the title. They take priority over a registered disposition of the estate.[137]

(d) Covenants affecting leasehold estates

In cases of a disposition of a leasehold estate the purchaser of the lease takes the lease subject to the burden of any covenants that affect the lease, e.g. if the tenant is restricted from using the land in a particular way.[138]

(2) Sections 29 and 30 only apply where there has been valuable consideration

In order for this priority rule to operate, valuable consideration must have been given for the estate, interest or charge. The Act defines "valuable consideration" as not including "marriage consideration or a nominal consideration in money".[139] The Act does not indicate what would amount to nominal rather than valuable consideration. In the unregistered land case of *Midland Bank Trust Co Ltd v Green*,[140] £500 was not a nominal consideration for a £40,000 estate.

If the priority rule in s.29 and 30 does not apply, e.g. because there has been no consideration for the disposition, the prior property rights that will bind a person taking the estate is determined by the ordinary "first in time" rule. An interest that has been created over the land, such as a beneficial interest or a restrictive covenant, *before* the transfer of the land, will bind the transferee. It makes no difference whether the prior right has been registered.[141]

(3) Where the transfer of land has been forged

Another example of a situation in which the s.29 and 30 priority rule would not apply is where the transfer of the registered land, or other disposition, has been forged. In *Malory Enterprises Ltd v Cheshire Homes (UK) Ltd*.[142] A was registered proprietor of land. B fraudulently obtained the land certificate in his own name.[143] B then forged a transfer of the land to C, who was registered as proprietor.[144] In the Court of Appeal, Arden L.J. held that the forged transfer was not a "disposition". So it did not have the protection of the priority rule that ordinarily protected purchasers for valuable consideration. Although decided under the Land Registration Act 1925 it is thought that the effect of a forged transfer is the same under the 2002 Act. "A purported disposition which is of no legal effect, such as a forged transfer, will not constitute a registered disposition".[145] Thus, even if an innocent person buys land under a forged transfer, he will take the land subject to all interests

---

137   By virtue of ss.29(2)(a)(iii) and 30(2)(a)(iii).
138   s.29(2)(b): C.Harpum and J.Bignell, *Registered Land: Law and Practice under the Land Registration Act 2002*, para.9.8.
139   s.132(1).
140   [1981] A.C. 513.
141   Land Registration Act 2002 s.28; For further consideration of this rule: *Halifax Plc v Curry Popeck* [2009] 1 P. & C.R. DG3.
142   [2002] Ch. 216.
143   Land Certificates are no longer relevant as a way of proving title under the 2002 Act.
144   I am grateful to Thompson, *Modern Land Law*, 4th edn (Oxford University Press, 2009), p.148 for these simplified facts.
145   C.Harpum, S.Bridge, M.Dixon, *Megarry & Wade The Law of Real Property*, para.7–61, citing *Malory Enterprises Ltd v Cheshire Homes (UK) Ltd* [2002] Ch. 216.

that existed in relation to the estate when he was registered as proprietor, e.g. the rights of the true owner of the estate.[146] Given that C was entirely innocent this seems a difficult decision. It does not fit easily within the distinct structure of registered land law which confers ownership on all registered proprietors subject only to the rules for altering the register.

(4) Priority over subsequent transactions

As well as gaining substantial immunity from prior rights in the land, registered dispositions also have priority over any later dealings with the land. For example, when a registrable lease or easement is registered under s.27 the Land Registrar will also register the lease or easement against the title to the freehold estate. Thus, if there follows a sale of that freehold, the purchaser will be bound by the easement or lease.

5   The protection of smaller rights in land

This is where we look at how the Land Registration Act 2002 gives protection to other rights (or minor interests) in land from being destroyed on a registrable disposition.

> **BUILDING BLOCK NO 5: Property Rights and the Protection of Purchasers and Mortgage Lenders**
>
> Read right through BUILDING BLOCK NO 5 in Chapter 1 very carefully. Having become familiar with our Building Blocks I think that you probably suspect that a relentless insistence on "title by registration" might not be the whole story. You will see that although purchasers need protection from being bound by prior rights in the land, the owners of those prior rights need protection too. A balance must be struck.

If all other property rights were prevented from binding a purchaser or mortgage lender, then this too will be unjust. For example, what would be the position of a tenant under a lease for a shorter term; or the neighbour if restrictive covenants were unenforceable against the land itself; or beneficial interests under a trust of land if the mortgage takes priority and the beneficiary cannot enforce her interest against the land so as to remain in occupation (revisit Mrs Boland in *Williams & Glyn's Bank v Boland*,[147] or Mr and Mrs Flegg in *City of London Building Society v Flegg*,[148] and the mother in *Re Sharpe*,[149])? These other interests need protection in precisely the opposite sense.

---

146   ibid.
147   [1981] A.C. 487.
148   [1988] A.C. 54.
149   [1980] 1 W.L.R. 219.

> **Meet "notices" "restrictions" and "overriding interests".**

We need to bear in mind throughout the question of whether these mechanisms strike a good balance between BUILDING BLOCK NO 5 and our other Building Blocks, for instance:

BUILDING BLOCK NO 1: Residential Security	**BUILDING BLOCK NO 2:** Ideas of Justice
BUILDING BLOCK NO 3: Property and Identity	**BUILDING BLOCK NO 6:** The Need for Certainty and Predictability in Land Law Rules

(1) Background: notices and restrictions

When we studied the system of unregistered land, we saw that certain rights can be made to bind the land itself in the hands of a purchaser where the owner of that right has registered it as a land charge.[150] In this way the purchaser or mortgage lender would have a ready means of ascertaining their existence. However, the types of right that could be made to bind the land in this way were limited, i.e. it applied to estate contracts, restrictive covenants etc. but not to beneficial interests under a trust.

In the system of registered land, these same types of right (and others) can also be made to bind the land. The Land Charges Act 1972 does not apply. The owner of the interest must apply to enter that interest as a "notice" on the Land Register, i.e. the register of title.

As far as concerns beneficial interests under trusts, the idea in registered land is again that these interests cannot be made to bind the land. But the registered land system gives trusts some protection through the mechanism of a "restriction". This is also an entry on the register of title. But it does not ensure that anyone dealing with the land in the future is bound by the beneficial interest. It "restricts" the way in which the land can be dealt with. For example, a restriction can be entered on the register which states that the trustees do not have power to execute a second mortgage on the property.

We will now examine the operation of "notices" and "restrictions" in turn.

---

150   *Midland Bank Trust Co Ltd v Green* [1981] A.C. 513.

A. NOTICES

A "notice" is an entry on the register of title that discloses a right that will bind title to the land. For example, the owner of the benefit of a restrictive covenant, that can prevent her neighbour from building on his land, can apply to the Land Registrar to register the burden of the covenant against the registered title to her neighbour's land. The Land Registrar will enter a "notice" on the charges register of her neighbour's title containing the details of the right.[151] The effect of registering a notice is that from this point onwards every purchaser of her neighbour's registered estate in the land will be bound by the covenant. It guarantees the priority of the right over any subsequent transfer or other dealing with the land.[152] This you will remember from our "priority rule" that applies to registered dispositions.

> **The Priority Rule: ss.29 and 30**
> This is the rule that protects purchasers and mortgage lenders when they are registered as proprietor of a registered estate or charge. It says that they take the estate free from all prior interests in that land, such as restrictive covenants etc, EXCEPT where the interest is:
> - A registered charge or the **subject of a notice in the register;**
> - An overriding interest in Sch.3, etc.

(1) Excluded interests: interests that *cannot* be protected by registering a notice

Many rights are registrable in this way, so as to protect them from being destroyed on a transfer of the registered estate. For example, an estate contract,[153] and a Family Law Act 1996 right of occupation.[154] However, certain rights can never be protected by way of a notice. Section 33 of the Land Registration Act 2002 contains a list of "excluded interests".

(a) Beneficial interests under a trust

It will not surprise you to learn that beneficial interests under a trust of land, and interests under a settlement of land, cannot be made to bind the land in the hands of a transferee or mortgagee of that land. Such rights cannot be registered as a notice.[155]

---

151   Land Registration Act 2002 s.32(1).
152   Land Registration Act 2002 s.32(3).
153   *Lombatieres v Mornington Estates (UK)* [2004] EWHC 825.
154   Family Law Act 1996 s.31(10).
155   Land Registration Act 2002 s.33(a)(i) and (ii). But as we shall see later, other provisions of the Land Registration Act 1925, and now the Land Registration Act 2002, have been interpreted to give protection to beneficial interests under a trust of land so as to make them bind the land in the hands of a purchaser or mortgage lender as *overriding interests*. This came about through *Williams & Glyn's Bank v Boland* [1981] A.C. 487.

(b) Short leases

Other excluded interests include a lease that "is granted for a term of years of three years or less from the date of the grant" and not one of the leases that are required to be registered with title in their own right as a "registrable disposition".[156] A legal lease granted for a term of seven years or less is an overriding interest under Sch.3. There is power to reduce the length of registrable leases further and it is anticipated that leases granted for terms exceeding three years will be registrable dispositions. Thus, only leases for terms of three years or less will be overriding and incapable of registration. When this happens these provisions will look much tidier!

There are other interests that cannot be registered as a notice, a restrictive covenant under a lease (not a freehold one) and an interest in a coal mine.[157]

(2) Procedures for entering a notice on the land register in respect of an interest: agreed and unilateral notices

Section 34(1) provides that "[a] person who claims to be entitled to the benefit of an interest affecting a registered estate or charge may, if the interest is not excluded by section 33, apply to the registrar for the entry in the register of a notice in respect of the interest". An agreed notice may be entered if the registered proprietor of the estate subject to the interest consents to the entry of a notice against his estate and the land registrar "is satisfied as to the validity of the applicant's claim".[158] A unilateral notice can be entered without the consent of the registered proprietor of the estate.[159] The registrar must give notice of the entry to the proprietor.[160] The registered proprietor may apply to the registrar for the notice to be cancelled,[161] but where such an application is made the registrar must notify the person entitled to the interest protected by the notice, and inform him that the notice will be cancelled unless he objects.[162] If they do not object within a certain time period, the notice will be cancelled.[163]

(3) Duty to disclose unregistered interests that may bind title

When a person is applying to be registered as proprietor of an estate or interest under s.27 then they must disclose to the registrar any information they have about an interest in the land that would be overriding under Sch.3. If the interest is of a type that can be registered as a notice, the Registrar will enter it on the register. That interest, once it has been so registered ceases to be overriding and can never be so again.[164]

---

156 Land Registration Act 2002 s.33(b)(i) and (ii).
157 s.33(c) and (e).
158 s.34(3)(a), (b) and (c).
159 Because of the potentially hostile nature and effect of registering a unilateral notice, there is a requirement that a person must not exercise the right to register a notice without reasonable cause: Land Registration Act 2002 s.77(1)(b). In *Fitzroy Development Ltd v Fitsrovia Properties Ltd* [2011] EWHC 1849 (Ch), it was held that a "reasonably arguable case" would satisfy this requirement.
160 s.35(1)(a) and (b).
161 s.36(1)(a) and (b).
162 s.36(2) and (3).
163 s.36(3).
164 s.29(3).

LECTURER: Is this duty of disclosure good and fair law? Remember that in order to create an argument about whether a rule is good or bad law we need evidence for our conclusion. We get our evidence from our Building Blocks. We can say that a rule is good or bad fair or unfair depending on the extent to which it supports or undermines the policy or principle in the Building Block.

STUDENT: I would argue that this duty of disclosure is good law on the basis of BUILDING BLOCK NO 5 because it reduces the number of overriding interests that can bind a purchaser or mortgage lender. Overriding interests are dangerous to purchasers because they are interests that will bind the land even though they are not registered. This duty of disclose ensures that as many interests as possible are registered—providing a readily available source of information to future purchasers and mortgage lenders.

BUILDING BLOCK NO 5: Property Rights and the Protection of Purchasers and Mortgage Lenders

Because of the importance of land in society there is a need to ensure that it is transferred easily.

LECTURER: What about our new Building Block? A statutory rule should not exist in a vacuum. So we may say that this duty to disclose unregistered interests is good law if it fulfils the aims of parliament behind the Land Registration Act 2002.

BUILDING BLOCK NO 8: Statutory rules should give effect to the purpose behind their enactment

The main objective of the Land Registration Act 2002 is that the land register should be as far as possible "conclusive", i.e. it should have all the information that a purchaser needs about whether they will acquire a good title and about the interests that will bind them on registration.

"The fundamental objective of the [Act] is that . . . the register should be [as far as possible] a complete and accurate reflection of the state of the title of the land at any given time": Law Com No.271, paras 1.5–1.6

STUDENT: I think that imposing a positive duty on people to give any information they have on interests in the land will enable the registrar to register those interests on the title. It will make the land register more conclusive. Thus, the duty of disclosure is good law in accordance with BUILDING BLOCK NO 8. This is a positive drive to make the land register reflect the interests that bind the title to the land.

(4) Validity of interests protected by a notice

You will remember that when a purchaser is registered as proprietor of an absolute estate it is the *act of registration* itself that gives him ownership of that estate. He becomes the owner of it when his name is entered as proprietor. This is true even if he was not entitled to the estate prior to his registration. The same is *not* true of registration of notices. The entry of a notice on the land register does not confer validity on the interest. If a person who registers a notice was not entitled to the interest he claims to have, the registration will not give him that interest. But registration of a notice "does mean that the priority of the interest, if valid, is protected".[165]

B. RESTRICTIONS

A restriction is an entry on the register that instructs the land registrar not to register any further disposition with that land, such as a transfer of the fee simple estate or a mortgage of that estate, *without complying with the terms of the restriction*.[166] The entry of a restriction does not give *priority* to the interest protected by the restriction in the way that a notice does, i.e. a restriction does not ensure that the interest binds a purchaser. The idea of the restriction is to give the ability to control how land is dealt with. Restrictions apply in particular to trusts. For example:

> **Celia holds Blackacre on trust for Alan and Brando. It is an express trust established by their uncle and the trust instrument provides that Brando's consent is required before the land can be sold. Brando might apply to enter a restriction on the land register to this effect, so that the registrar would be unable to register a transfer of the land from Celia to another person, unless Brando had consented.**

(1) Critical Thinking about restrictions and cross examining the evidence

LECTURER: Let's think about how the trust beneficiaries in this next case could have used "restrictions" as a means of protecting their interests. We studied *City of London Building Society v Flegg* in the previous chapter. What happened in the case?

STUDENT: Mr and Mrs Flegg and their daughter and son-in-law, Mr and Mrs Maxwell-Browne purchased a house together. The house was registered land. Mr and Mrs Flegg contributed to the purchase price. They chose not to be registered as proprietors, so Mr and Mrs Maxwell-Browne were the only two out of the four who were registered. However, the Fleggs did have a beneficial interest under a trust and the Maxwell-Brownes were holding title to the house on trust for themselves and the Fleggs. Sometime later the Maxwell-Brownes borrowed a significant sum and executed a mortgage over the house.

---

165   s.32(3).
166   s.41(1). Section 40(1) defines a restriction as "an entry in the register regulating the circumstances in which a disposition of a registered estate or charge may be the subject of an entry in the register".

LECTURER: Could they do this?

STUDENT: The house was registered land and, when Mr and Mrs Maxwell-Browne were registered as proprietors of the estate they were deemed to have all the powers of an absolute owner: Land Registration Act 2002 s.23.[167]

LECTURER: So this included the execution of a charge in favour of the City of London Building Society?

STUDENT: Yes.

LECTURER: What happened then?

STUDENT: The Maxwell-Brownes got themselves into a financial pickle and defaulted on the loan repayments. The building society brought an action for possession, which the Fleggs defended by claiming that their prior interest in the land amounted to an "overriding interest" that bound all purchasers and mortgage lenders [(we shall see why and how when we look at Sch.3)]. The House of Lords held that the Fleggs did *not* have an overriding interest. The Building Society had taken their mortgage free from the Flegg's beneficial interest. As we studied in the previous chapter, because the mortgage was "a conveyance of a legal estate" and the lender paid the mortgage loan money to *two trustees* (the Maxwell-Brownes), they took their interest in the land, the mortgage, free and clear from the Flegg's interest.

LECTURER: We say that the mortgage had, because of this, "overreached" their interest.[168] The 1925 legislation introduced "overreaching" as a way of making sure that purchasers could quickly and easily get a good title to the land, free from beneficial interests under trusts, by taking the simple expedient of paying the purchase money to two trustees or a trust corporation.[169] Overreaching applies in the same way in registered land law and we consider it in detail below.

BUILDING BLOCK NO 5: Property Rights and the Protection of Purchasers and Mortgage Lenders

Although the decision of the House of Lords in this case supported our BUILDING BLOCK NO 5: Property Rights and the Protection of Purchasers and Mortgage Lenders, it caused significant problems for our other BUILDING BLOCKS, e.g. NO 1: Residential Security, NO 2: Ideas of Justice, and NO 3: Property and Identity. It meant that the Fleggs lost their home, and with it their residential security. So we could say that the case is bad law in this respect.

Let's see what the Fleggs could have done about the situation themselves.

---

167   The provision at the time was Land Registration Act 1925 s.18.
168   This "overreaching" rule is contained in Law of Property Act 1925 ss.2 and 27.
169   There was only a single trustee in *Williams & Glyn's Bank Ltd v Boland* [1981] A.C. 487, which is why there was a different result in that case.

LECTURER: I want you to imagine that you are the solicitor advising the Fleggs and Maxwell-Brownes prior to their purchase of the house. How can you use all that you know about the land registration system to produce a better outcome?

STUDENT: Firstly, when the co-ownership trust is set up I would make it a condition of the purchase that the Maxwell-Brownes, the trustees, must get the Fleggs' consent to any further mortgages on the estate.

LECTURER: And how would you need to give effect to this at the land registry?

STUDENT: By applying to enter a restriction against the Maxwell-Brownes' registere proprietorship of the estate that they have no power to mortgage the title unless the Fleggs give their consent.

LECTURER: What is the effect of this?

STUDENT: The registrar will be unable to register any further mortgages (charges) against the title unless the Fleggs consent.

LECTURER: And this would effectively veto the transaction. You could alternatively advise that the Maxwell-Browne's powers as trustees should be restricted and their power to execute further mortgages taken away: under the Trusts of Land and Appointment of Trustees Act 1996 s.8 (see Chapter 5).

STUDENT: And then I would apply to enter a restriction to this effect at the same time as applying for the Maxwell-Brownes' registration as proprietors of the title to the house. Then the City of London Building Society would have seen by looking at the title that their would-be borrowers did not have the power to grant them security for the loan.

LECTURER: And so your restriction would have vetoed the transaction. Well done! I see you are getting the hang of restrictions nicely.

> **Building Blocks, Critical Thinking about registered land and cross examining the evidence in the Building Blocks:** When you are considering whether you think that the rules of registered land law support or undermine our Building Blocks, we need to know to what extent it is *justifiable* to say that a rule undermines, e.g. residential security or purchaser protection. This will depend on what other protection is available. So it is part of valid argument construction to say that where other protection is available then the law does not need to provide it. So part of argument construction is to *get creative* and think about ways in which people with interests in land and purchasers of that land or mortgage lenders, can protect themselves.

(2) What interests can be protected by restrictions?

The registrar cannot enter a restriction to protect the priority of a right or claim in relation to a registered estate or charge that is capable of being protected by a notice.[170] In 1925, one

---

170 Land Registration Act 2002 s.42(1)(c) and 42(2). And thus, the regimes of notices and restrictions are mutually exclusive.

important intention behind the restriction was to give trust beneficiaries,[171] and people with equitable interests under a settlement, some means to protect their interests, if not by ensuring that their interest bound the land in the hand of the purchaser or mortgage lender, at least by giving them the ability to control the way in which the estate in land was dealt with in the future, as we have seen in our dialogue above.[172] In 1925 trusts largely arose expressly, where the beneficiaries were well aware of their interests and well capable of protecting them by restrictions.[173]

(3) The circumstances in which a restriction can be entered

(a) To prevent invalidity or unlawfulness of a disposition

When can a restriction be used? The land registrar may enter a restriction in one of three circumstances, two of which are particularly relevant in the context of trusts.[174] Firstly, a restriction can be entered on the Land Register to prevent "invalidity or unlawfulness in relation to dispositions of a registered estate or charge".[175] For example, if the estate is held on trust and the trustees' powers are limited,[176] as in the example above, then a restriction can be entered on the register. The effect of the restriction would be that no transaction that is outside the powers of the trustees can be registered. The restriction would stipulate what transactions the trustees are not empowered to undertake. Where someone is required to consent to dealings with the land, so that failure to obtain consent would be a breach of trust and thus unlawful, the restriction would stipulate that no dealing with the land can take place unless the consent of *N* is obtained.[177]

(b) To secure overreaching

Secondly, the registrar may enter a restriction in order to make sure "that interests which are capable of being overreached on a disposition of a registered estate or charge are overreached".[178] To understand the nature and importance of such a restriction we need to consider some background.

In registered land, equitable (or "beneficial") interests under a trust are capable of being overriding interests under Sch.3 para.2[179] of the Land Registration Act 2002. Whenever the

---

171   Carried through to the 2002 Act.

172   J.E.Hogg, *A Treatise on the Law Relating to Ownership and Incumbrance of Registered Land and Interests Therein* (1906), p.207–230. "The intention behind these restrictions was to ensure that the land was dealt with in accordance with the terms of the trust or settlement. The nature of the beneficiary's interest changed from a proprietary right to a mere restriction or 'restraint on alienation' ": Jackson, "Overreaching in Registered Land Law" (2006) 69 M.L.R. 214, p.228, referring to Hogg, above p.7.

173   J.S.Anderson, *Lawyers and the Making of English Land Law 1832–1940.*

174   Although the provisions are not limited to the context of trusts.

175   s.42(1)(a). "An entry might also be made to prevent a breach of contract": C.Harpum and J.Bignell, *Registered Land: Law and Practice under the Land Registration Act 2002*, para.10.56.

176   This would also apply where there was a corporation with restricted powers: C.Harpum and J.Bignell, above para.10.56.

177   C.Harpum and J.Bignell, above para.10.56.

178   Land Registration Act 2002 s.42(1)(b).

179   But only in certain circumstances that we will study below.

trustee, such as Mr Boland in *Williams & Glyn's Bank Ltd v Boland*, deals with the land, e.g. mortgages it, the lender will, when he is registered as proprietor of the charge, take free from all interests in the land *except registered interests and overriding interests*. As we saw in *Boland* this meant that the lender had to give effect to Mrs Boland's interest and it could not repossess and sell the house when Mr Boland defaulted on the payments. The situation is perhaps even more difficult where *transfers* of the registered estate are concerned. Imagine that Mr Boland had been selling the house and it was Mark and Jane who were buying it. They would not want to discover that Mrs Boland had a claim to half the value of their house when they first moved in! Yet this would be the effect because registered dispositions take effect subject to overriding interests and Mrs Boland's trust interest was overriding.[180]

But as we shall see below a trust interest will not bind the title as overriding where it has been "overreached".[181] If you remember from Land Transfer Law (2) we considered "overreaching". As you saw from our dialogue above, this is where a purchaser or mortgage lender *who pays the purchase money to two trustees* or a trust corporation takes free from the beneficial/equitable interests under the trust. The overreaching provisions are contained in s.2 and 27 of the Law of Property Act 1925. It is a quick and simple way for a purchaser or mortgage lender to take free from beneficial interests, such as those belonging to Mr and Mrs Flegg. They do not have to make any inquiries and it does not matter that they have notice of the trust. Overreaching applies in registered land law.

Is overreaching good and fair law?	We have seen that overreaching is good law from the perspective of **BUILDING BLOCK NO 5: Property Rights and the Protection of Purchasers and Mortgage Lenders.**

However, it is not self-evident from the face of the land register that a trust exists, so how will a purchaser or mortgage lender *know* when there are beneficial interests that potentially bind him, and thus know when to make sure he pays the purchase/mortgage money to two trustees? A restriction may be entered as follows:

"No disposition by a sole proprietor of the registered estate (except a trust corporation) under which capital money arises is to be registered unless authorised by an order of the court."[182]

Such a restriction would protect purchasers and mortgage lenders where there is an express or statutory trust of land. It would ensure overreaching.

---

180   Fortunately it does not happen very often with sales, but note *Re Sharpe* [1980] 1 W.L.R. 219. I am indebted to Professor Mark Thompson for this observation.
181   *City of London Building Society v Flegg* [1988] A.C. 54.
182   Land Registration Rules 2003 Sch.4: Harpum and Bignell, above p.126.

In the situation where two or more people are registered as owners of the estate, they will hold on trust of land for each other. If one then severs the joint tenancy in equity, or they are already holding as tenants in common in equity, and then that co-owner dies, their estate will inherit their beneficial interest. The legal estate is always held as a joint tenancy which means that each time a co-owner dies he will drop out of the picture. Consequently, there will be a hidden trust not apparent on the register of title with possibly only one trustee. In this situation, i.e. when two or more persons are registered as proprietors of a registered estate, the registrar is *obliged* to enter a restriction that ensures that overreaching takes place.[183]

> **BUILDING BLOCK NO 5: Property Rights and the Protection of Purchasers and Mortgage Lenders**
> Is this good law?

6 The structure and organisation of the Land Register

The Land Register is divided into three parts: the Property Register, the Proprietorship Register, and the Charges Register.

The Property Register gives details about the land. It includes a map.

The Proprietorship Register has all the details of the person who owns the registered estate: the registered proprietor. It includes details, if any, of what he can and cannot do with the land. Restrictions are entered in the proprietorship register.

The Charges Register contains details of the interests that bind the estate, e.g. any restrictive covenants, easements or estate contracts. It is thus in the charges register that notices are entered.

7 Overriding Interests—Schedule 3

As we have already seen an overriding interest is an interest that will bind a purchaser or mortgage lender even though the interest is not entered on the land register. All transactions

---

183   Land Registration Act 2002 s.44(1). See later in this Chapter for a further consideration of overreaching.

with registered titles ("registrable dispositions") take effect subject to the overriding interests contained within Sch.3. Recall the priority rule that applies to registered dispositions.

> **Transactions with registered land—The Priority Rule, ss.29 and 30**
> A purchaser, including a mortgage lender, when registered as proprietor of a registered estate or charge, takes the estate free from all prior property rights in that land, EXCEPT where the interest is:
> - A registered charge or the subject of a notice in the register;
> - An **overriding interest** that falls within any of the paragraphs of Sch.3.
>
> There are two other exceptions discussed in section 4 of this Chapter.

Because overriding interests are those rights that will bind a purchaser automatically, even though they are not registered, they are the "crack in the mirror" of title registration. The land register will never provide fully "conclusive" evidence as to the interests that will bind a purchaser whilst there is such a category of overriding interest. There will always be additional inquiries and inspections that need to be made by a purchaser or mortgage lender.

> The existence of overriding interests means that a purchaser cannot ascertain title from the register alone. So their existence can be seen as a defect in registered land law.

> **BUILDING BLOCK NO 5:**
> **Property Rights and the Protection of Purchasers and Mortgage Lenders**
> Rules are good if they allow purchasers to know what rights are going to bind them after a transfer of the title.

Although the Law Commission observed that we live in a "culture of registration" and it is not acceptable for so many interests to be created off the register and still bind a purchaser,[184] it did not consider that it was justifiable to eliminate overriding interests altogether, i.e. to make the land register an *entirely accurate* mirror of the state of the title at any given time. Many overriding interests arise informally and their owners may not appreciate the need to register them in order to make sure they bind a purchaser.

> ". . . it is unreasonable to expect all encumbrancers to register their rights, particularly where those rights arise informally, under (say) a constructive trust or by estoppel . . . Furthermore, when people occupy land they are often unlikely to appreciate the need to take the formal step of registering any rights that they have in it."[185]

184　Law Com No.271, *Land Registration for the Twenty-First Century – A Conveyancing Revolution*, paras 8.74–8.88.
185　Law Com No.254, para.4.17; Law Com No.271, paras.8.53 and 8.74.

So already we see that the registered land system must affect a compromise between our BUILDING BLOCK NO 5 and BUILDING BLOCK NO 1.

> **BUILDING BLOCK NO 5: Property Rights and the Protection of Purchasers and Mortgage Lenders:** It is important that purchasers are not bound by too many unregistered interests that are difficult to discover.

> **BUILDING BLOCK NO 1: Residential Security:** Yet spouses, cohabitees and family members may have interests in the home of which they are unaware. If these rights are not protected without requiring them to be registered these people may end up losing their home should the legal owner mortgage the house.

A. OVERRIDING INTERESTS THAT BIND REGISTERED DISPOSITIONS

(1) Schedule 3, paragraph 1: Leasehold estates in land

Leases of seven years or less will bind a purchaser even though they are not registered. The Law Commission considered that some protection was required for these leases because it is not reasonable to expect the tenant to register them. There are exceptions, for example, a lease that is granted to take effect in possession three months or more from the date of the grant ("reversionary leases") and a discontinuous lease, e.g. a lease to give effect to a timeshare arrangement. These are registrable dispositions must be registered before they bind purchasers, as we have seen.[186] The reason why these leases are exceptions and do not take effect as overriding is that the tenant will not be in occupation of the premises. Thus, when a purchaser goes to inspect the land he will not have a ready means of ascertaining the existence of the lease.[187]

LECTURER: Is the law in this paragraph good or bad law?

STUDENT: I think it is good law (holding it against BUILDING BLOCK NO 8) because although leases of seven years or less will bind a purchaser of the landlord's freehold title, even though it is not registered, the lease could easily be discovered by potential purchasers because they will see the tenant when they inspect the land prior to the purchase.

LECTURER: So the law fulfils parliament's objectives?

STUDENT: Yes I think it does. Leases that the purchaser could only discover by making more than the "minimum of additional enquiries", i.e. reversionary and discontinuous leases

---

186   Land Registration Act 2002 s.27(2).
187   Law Commission, *Land Registration for the Twenty-First Century—A Conveyancing Revolution* Law Com No.271.

(where the tenant will not be in occupation, or only in occupation for a few weeks per year), will not bind the purchaser unless they are registered. They will then be able to find out about them easily by looking at the register.

BUILDING BLOCK NO 8: Statutory rules should give effect to the purpose behind their enactment

Remember that we can criticise a statutory rule, i.e. we can say that it is a good or bad rule, on the basis of whether it achieves parliament's objectives behind its enactment. Remember that the Law Commission stated that "The fundamental objective of the [Act] is that . . . the register should be a complete and accurate reflection of the state of the title of the land at any given time, so that it is possible to investigate title to land . . . with the absolute minimum of additional enquiries and inspections": Law Com No.271, paras.1.5–1.6.

---

(2) Schedule 3 paragraph 2: The rights of persons in actual occupation

Because there is so much to consider in relation to this overriding interest we will consider it in a separate section below. Mrs Boland fell into this category, or its predecessor, s.70(1)(g) of the Land Registration Act 1925, when it was held that the interest she had acquired by contributing to the purchase price bound a later mortgage lender.

(3) Schedule 3 paragraph 3: Legal easements and profits à prendre

An easement is a limited right to do something on land belonging to another, for example, a right to walk over land, to store things on land, rights of drainage, a right to park a car, etc. A profit à prendre is the right to take something from land belonging to another, e.g. fish.

Legal easements and profits are overriding interests except in the following circumstances

Schedule 3(1) A legal easement or profit à prendre . . . which at the time of the disposition-

(a) is not within the actual knowledge of the person to whom the disposition is made, and

(b) would not have been obvious on a reasonably careful inspection of the land over which the easement or profit is exercisable.

(2) The exception in sub-paragraph (1) does not apply if the person entitled to the easement or profit proves that it has been exercised in the period of one year ending with the day of the disposition.

Under Sch.3 para.3 only *legal* easements are capable of overriding registered dispositions.[188] Furthermore, expressly granted easements are registrable dispositions and not overriding interests. In order to be overriding an easement must come into being by *implied* grant or prescription. This means that the easement has not been granted expressly but has arisen by operation of law in certain circumstances, like implied terms within a contract, or where the right has been exercised over a long period of time.[189] Although the 2002 Act does not say so directly, a cumulative effect of the provisions of the Act and the logic of land registration means that expressly granted easements and profits cannot be overriding under Sch.3.[190]

(a) The new "reasonably careful inspection" test

Schedule 3 para.3 includes a reasonable inspection defence so that a purchaser of registered land will not be bound by an easement or profit that was not obvious on a reasonably careful inspection of the land. But he will be bound if he had actual knowledge of the right. This is not intended to reintroduce the unregistered land doctrine of notice into registered land. The new registered land test derives from *Yandle & Sons v Sutton, Young & Same*: the easement or profit must be visible "to the eye, or by necessary implication from something which is visible to the eye".[191] In short, in order to bind as an overriding interest, the easement must have been obvious to a hypothetical purchaser conducting a reasonably careful inspection of the land prior to purchase.

The easement does not have to be obvious on a reasonably careful inspection where the right has been exercised within one year prior to the registered disposition. This is designed for invisible rights that need preservation, such as rights of drainage.[192] Thus the purchaser will take subject to such rights anyway, whether they are obvious or not.

LECTURER: This is a big change in the law. Under the Land Registration Act 1925 *all* easements and profits were overriding, whether legal or equitable, whether created expressly or coming into being impliedly, whether discoverable by a purchaser or not.[193] Do you think that this is good law? We get the evidence for our conclusion from our Building Blocks. To what extent does the law support or undermine the policies and principles contained in the Building Blocks?

STUDENT: I would firstly take our BUILDING BLOCK NO 5: Property Rights and the Protection of Purchasers.

---

188   Under the 1925 Act equitable easements could also be overriding.

189   We will consider easements in a separate chapter below.

190   Firstly expressly granted *legal* easements and profits are registrable dispositions and so do not operate at law until the registration requirement is met: s.27(1). Thus, they are not *legal* easements and profits until they are registered. The land registrar is under a duty to enter a notice in the register of title to the burdened estate in respect of the interest in question: easements (Sch.2(7)); Profits (Sch.2(6)). Once the interest is registered as a notice it can never fall within Sch.3 para.3: s.29(3) (registered estates); s.30(3) (registered charges). Once electronic conveyancing comes fully into effect, an expressly created interest, such as an easement or profit, cannot come into being *at all* unless it is created online and simultaneously registered.

191   Per Sargant J. [1922] 2 Ch. 199, p.210.

192   Law Com No.271, paras 8.69–8.70.

193   *Celsteel Ltd v Alton House Holdings Ltd (No.1)* [1986] 1 W.L.R. 512.

> **BUILDING BLOCK NO 5: Property Rights and the Protection of Purchasers and Mortgage Lenders**
> It is important for a purchaser to have a ready means of ascertaining what rights will bind him following a registered transfer.

Firstly, Sch.3(3) greatly reduces the number of easements and profits capable of binding a purchaser as overriding interests. For example, expressly created easements must be registered. The 2002 Act also introduces the "reasonable inspection defence" which means that a purchaser will not be bound by an easement or profit if that right was undiscoverable.

LECTURER: So we can say that Sch.3 para.3 is good law on the basis of BUILDING BLOCK NO 5. But what about any of our other Building Blocks?

STUDENT: I would argue that it is good law because it give effect to parliament's intentions behind the 2002 Act, to make the land register as far as possible conclusive as to the interests that will bind a purchaser—with only the minimum additional enquiries and inspections: Law Com No.271, paras. 1.5–1.6.

> **BUILDING BLOCK NO 8: Statutory rules should give effect to the purpose behind their enactment**
> We can say that a rule is a good or bad fair or unfair on the basis of whether it achieves parliament's objectives behind its enactment. Rules should not exist for their own sake.

(4) Schedule 3, paragraphs 4–16

Other rights will override a registered disposition under Sch.3: 4. A customary right; 5. A public right; 6. A local land charge; Paragraphs 7–9 contain certain mineral rights; 10. A franchise; 11. A manorial right; 12. A right to rent from land which was reserved to the Crown on the granting of any freehold estate; 13. The liability to repair an embankment or sea or river wall; 14. A right to payment in lieu of tithe, and 16. A right in respect of the repair of a church chancel. The position relating to these interests is the same as it is in relation to interests that override first registration. Paragraphs 10–14 and 16 will cease to be overriding on October 13, 2013, 10 years after the Act came into force.[194]

(5) Duty to disclose unregistered interests

As we have seen there is a duty on a person applying to register a registrable disposition to disclose to the registrar information about any unregistered interest that overrides his title under Sch.3.[195] Thus, the registrar will be able to register that interest, if appropriate,

---

194 Land Registration Act 2002, s.117: Harpum and Bignell, *Registered Land: Law and Practice under the Land Registration Act 2002*, para.11.2.
195 Land Registration Act 2002 s.71(b).

and it will never again be an overriding interest.[196] The duty applies to interests "within the actual knowledge of the applicant; and [which] affect the estate to which registration applies".[197]

B. THE RIGHTS OF PERSONS IN ACTUAL OCCUPATION: SCHEDULE 3 PARAGRAPH 2 (MRS BOLAND'S CATEGORY)

Where a person has a property right in the land, such as a beneficial interest under a trust, and is in actual occupation of the property, then their right may override a registered transaction with the estate, such as a sale or a mortgage, even though that right is not registered. This is the overriding interest that Mrs Boland established which prevented the bank from repossessing the house in *Williams & Glyn's Bank Ltd v Boland*.[198]

> Schedule 3 para.2 protects as an overriding interest:
> "2. An interest belonging at the time of the disposition to a person in actual occupation, so far as relating to land of which he is in actual occupation, except for –
> (a) an interest under a settlement . . .
> (b) an interest of a person of whom inquiry was made before the disposition and who failed to disclose the right when he could reasonably have been expected to do so;
> (c) an interest –
>   (i) which belongs to a person whose occupation would not have been obvious on a reasonably careful inspection of the land at the time of the disposition, and
>   (ii) of which the person to whom the disposition is made does not have actual knowledge at that time.
> (d) a leasehold estate in land granted to take effect in possession after the end of the period of three months beginning with the date of the grant and which has not taken effect in possession at the time of the disposition."

(1) Schedule 3, paragraph 2

Schedule 3 para.2 has family roots that run deep in land transfer law. The provision it replaces, s.70(1)(g) of the Land Registration Act 1925, was designed to preserve as against a purchaser, the rights of persons in occupation or physical possession of land. In unregistered land, it was the occupation of the person with the right that fixed a purchaser with notice of their rights.[199] This category of overriding interest was designed to preserve this rule in the context of registered land.[200]

---

196   s.29(3).
197   Land Registration Rules 2003, rules 28 and 57(1): C.Harpum and J.Bignell, above paras. 4.19 and 11.19.
198   [1981] A.C. 487.
199   *Hunt v Luck* [1901] 1 Ch. 428.
200   It did not do so exactly. There are differences, but they do not concern us here.

From the occupier's point of view, their rights are not easily accommodated in the registered land system. They tend to belong to people who could not be expected to register their rights. Therefore, they need the system to prevent their rights from being destroyed when a purchaser of the house, or mortgage lender, registers their estate or charge. Lord Denning M.R., in *Strand Securities Ltd v Caswell*[201] said that the purpose of this category of overriding interest was "to protect a person in actual occupation from having his rights lost in the welter of registration".

Section 70(1)(g), the provision which Sch.3(2) replaces, was not *at its inception* designed to accommodate the vast number of informal co-ownership rights that could potentially belong to someone in occupation of a house. At the time of the Land Registration Act 1925 the reformers envisaged that only a small number of rights would fall within this category, cellars and drains in the ownership of a neighbour or local authority for example, or tenants in occupation under a lease.[202]

(2) Case study 1: Williams & Glyn's Bank Ltd v Boland

In order to establish an overriding interest under Sch.3(2) of the Land Registration Act 2002, a person must firstly show that they have an interest in the land and secondly show that they are in "actual occupation".

> **THE FACTS** We will look at *Boland* again. If you remember, when Mr and Mrs Boland bought their home the house was registered in the husband's name only. Mrs Boland had contributed to its purchase and thereby acquired a beneficial interest under a trust. In order to expand his business, Mr Boland borrowed large sums of money from the Williams & Glyn's Bank. In return he executed a legal charge on the home. Mrs Boland was unaware of the mortgage. Mr Boland's business failed and he defaulted on the loan repayments.
>
> **THE LEGAL QUESTION:** When the bank registered its charge over the house, was it subject to Mrs Boland's prior interest in the house? Did Mrs Boland's right amount to an overriding interest? This would stop them from taking possession of the house and evicting Mrs Boland.

"The bank did not make any inquiries of [Mrs Boland]. They simply took a charge on [the] matrimonial home to secure the indebtedness. Later on the business failed. The company became insolvent and was put into liquidation. . . . there remain[ed] £32,500 owing. The bank [then came down] on Mr Boland for that sum. They claim[ed] possession of the matrimonial home . . . The wife resists by reason of her half-share in the house."[203]

---

201   [1965] Ch. 958, p.979.
202   Registrar Brickdale, *Royal Commission on the Land Transfer Acts* (1909) Minutes of Evidence, H.C.P. xxvii. 733, quoted in J.S.Anderson, *Lawyers and the Making of English Land Law 1832–1940* from p.277.
203   Per Lord Denning M.R. in the Court of Appeal [1979] 1 Ch 312, pp.327–8.

CONCLUSION: It was held that the Williams & Glyn's bank took subject to Mrs Boland's equitable interest in the house. She had an overriding interest, subject to which their registered charge took effect. We will look at the reasoning in the case to see how and why this came about.

LECTURER: The first issue was that it was necessary for Mrs Boland to prove that she had an interest in the house. Without this, she could not establish an "overriding interest".

THE REASONING LORD DENNING M.R.[204]: "In former times the house was usually conveyed into the name of the husband alone. He was the one who went out to work, earned the money, paid the deposit and the mortgage instalments. But when the wife went out to work, things changed. Her earnings . . . went into the family pool. Out of it the outgoings were paid including the deposit and the mortgage instalments. The conveyancers in the old days would have held that the wife gained no interest whatever in the house by reason of her contributions . . . Nor, if it was sold, did she have any share in the proceeds of sale . . .

It was in *Gissing v Gissing* [1971] AC 886 when the House held that, in these cases of the matrimonial home, a wife, who contributes in money or money's worth, does obtain a proprietary interest. It is done by way of a trust imposed on the husband. Even though the house is taken in the husband's name alone, the law imposes a trust upon him by which he holds the legal estate in trust for them both jointly . . . [. . .]

The next problem is to place this trust concept into the conveyancing structure erected by the property legislation of 1925 . . . No doubt the framers of the statute had in mind the case where the legal estate was vested in *two* persons. They became trustees . . . and could together "overreach" any equitable interests. They could sell the land so as to give a good title to the purchaser free of any equitable interests . . . section 2(1)(ii) and (2) and section 27(2) of the Law of Property Act 1925."

LECTURER: We will consider "overreaching" in a later section in this Chapter. But if you wish to understand what Lord Denning M.R. is saying, refer back to Land Transfer Law (2) in which we consider the structure of the 1925 legislation.

LORD DENNING M.R. CONTINUES: "But the framers of the statutes did not. . . think of the cases where the legal estate is vested in one person on trust for two or more persons jointly as beneficial owners: and then that one single person sells the land to a purchaser who pays him the full price. Does the purchaser take free of any of the equitable interests? [. . .]

Once it is held that the wife has an equitable interest in the land – it is easy to apply the provisions of the Land Registration Act 1925. . ."

---

204 Court of Appeal [1979] 1 Ch. 312. The decision and reasoning of the Court of Appeal was upheld by the House of Lords: [1981] A.C. 487.

LECTURER: This case was decided on the basis of the provisions of the 1925 Act, which was repealed in its entirety by the Land Registration Act 2002. *Boland* was applying s.70(1)(g) of the 1925 Act, which was replaced by Sch.3 para.2 of the 2002 Act, the provision we are considering in this section. The basic principles discussed in this case are the same and still good law under the 2002 Act.

So it has been established that Mrs Boland has an interest in the home: an interest under a trust by virtue of her contribution to the purchase. The second point which must be proven before a claimant can establish an overriding interest falling within this category is that she was in *actual occupation*.

LORD DENNING M.R. CONTINUES: "[Her interest may be] an 'overriding interest' if it comes within section 70(1)(g) . . . . The wife clearly has rights . . . The only question is whether she is herself a person 'in actual occupation' . . .

In *Caunce v Caunce* [1969] 1 W.L.R. 286 Stamp J. seems to have held that, when a wife was living in the matrimonial home with her husband, it was the husband alone who was in actual occupation of it. The wife was not. Stamp J. said that she: '. . . was not in apparent occupation or possession. She was there ostensibly, because she was the wife, and her presence there was wholly consistent with the title offered by the husband to the bank.'

This was followed by Templeman J in *Bird v Syme-Thomson* [1979] 1 W.L.R. 440, when he said . . . 'In my judgment, when a mortgagor is in actual occupation of the matrimonial home, it cannot be said that his wife also is in actual occupation.' He followed it also in the present case when he said: 'actual occupation for the purposes of section 70(1)(g) does not include the position of the wife of the legal owner who is in occupation.' Any other view, he said, would lead to chaos."

LECTURER: Can you think of why Templeman J. might have thought it would lead to chaos? Use reasoning based on BUILDING BLOCK NO 5.

BUILDING BLOCK NO 5: Property Rights and the Protection of Purchasers and Mortgage Lenders

We can argue that a development of a rule in a case or statute is good or bad fair or unfair, depending on the extent to which it supports or undermines the idea that rules of Land Law should protect a purchaser or mortgage lender from being bound by prior interests in the land. This is the policy behind the 1925 property legislation. Banks and building societies often lend to small businesses on the security of family homes. Banks must be sure of their security. If the courts recognise too many rights that will bind them and stop them from selling the house if the borrower defaults, then they may become reluctant to lend money. This will affect our economy.

STUDENT: I think he was foreseeing a problem that could occur because many houses must be registered in one of the spouses' names alone. And it may be common that this sole legal owner mortgages the house. In such cases the other spouse, cohabitee or family member may often have contributed to the purchase and thereby acquired an interest in the house.

LECTURER: Therefore? Relate the point you make to the argument.

STUDENT: Templeman J. was reluctant to accept that such people, particularly wives in this case, could establish that they were "in actual occupation" because it is this factor which ensures that their interest will bind the bank as an overriding interest under (now) Sch.3(2). So he was saying that this would make bad law on the basis of BUILDING BLOCK NO 5 because it would lead to a vastly larger number of overriding interests.[205]

LECTURER: Good. Now listen to what Lord Denning M.R. says about the other side of the argument.

> **LORD DENNING M.R. CONTINUES:** "I profoundly disagree. Such statements would have been true a hundred years ago when the law regarded husband and wife as one: and the husband as that one. But they are not true today. . . Most wives now are joint owners of the matrimonial home – in law or in equity – with their husbands. They go out to work just as their husbands do. Their earnings go to build up the home just as much as their husband's earnings. Visit the home and you will find that she is in personal occupation of it just as much as he is. She eats there and sleeps there just as he does . . . These instances all show that 'actual occupation' is matter of fact, not matter of law." . . .

LECTURER: And so Lord Denning M.R. concluded that Mrs Boland was "in actual occupation" and therefore had an overriding interest. Because of this, her beneficial interest in the land was binding on the Williams & Glyn's Bank. And the law is now clear: "actual occupation" for the purpose of establishing an overriding interest under Sch.3(2) is a simple matter of fact: *is the person claiming the interest there or not?*

In common with many judges, Lord Denning now seeks to justify his decision on policy grounds. Can you see which of our Building Blocks is relevant?

> **LORD DENNING M.R. CONTINUES:** "I see no reason why this should cause any difficulty to conveyancers. Nor should it impair the proper conduct of businesses. Anyone who lends money on the security of a matrimonial home nowadays ought to realise that the wife may have a share in it . . . It seems to me utterly wrong that a lender should turn a blind eye to the wife's interest or the possibility of it – and afterwards seek to turn her and the family out – on the plea that he did not know she was in actual occupation. If a bank is to do its duty, in the society in which we live, it should recognise the integrity of the matrimonial home. It should not destroy it by disregarding the wife's interest in it – simply to ensure that it is paid the husband's debt in full . . . We should not give monied might priority over social justice."

---

205   There are limitations introduced by Sch.3(2) which we consider below.

The two other Court of Appeal judges agreed with Lord Denning M.R. and the House of Lords upheld the decision when the bank appealed.

LECTURER: And so a shy provision in the Land Registration Act 1925 designed to accommodate small tenancies, cellars and drains, suddenly gained prominence: it was the way in which the land registration system now gives protection to the residential security of spouses, cohabitants and other family members who have an interest in the home.

So why did Lord Denning MR think it "utterly wrong" to protect the bank's interest in this sort of case?

STUDENT: The implication appears to be that banks could make more enquiries when they are lending money to a sole legal owner, to investigate whether there is anyone else in occupation who might be able to claim an interest in the land.

LECTURER: Why?

STUDENT: Because the people who might claim an overriding interest live in the property as their home. They are threatened with the loss of that home through the repossession process. Effectively, *Boland* is good law on the basis of BUILDING BLOCK NO 1.

BUILDING BLOCK NO 1: Residential Security

Rules are good and fair if they give protection to people's residential security. Land Law now operates in the context of owner occupation and its rules should give effect to the purposes for which people buy houses. People place a good deal of importance on land ownership and the law should protect this. When people are using land ownership to create a home this is a significant part of their lives.

The main law that we take forward from *Boland* is that in order to establish an overriding interest for the purposes of Sch.3 para.2, the claimant must 1) have an interest in land and 2) be in "actual occupation", which is a question of fact—someone either occupies or they do not. We will now consider each of these elements in detail.

(3) The claimant must establish that they have an interest in land

In order to establish an overriding interest under Sch.3 para.2 the claimant must firstly prove that they have an interest in the land: a property right. *So what interests will count for this purpose?* We have seen from *Boland* that an equitable interest under a trust will fall within this category. Other examples of rights that have been protected as overriding under this provision are estate contracts, for example, an option to purchase land.[206] Schedule 3(2) includes a right

---

206 *Kling v Keston Properties Ltd* (1985) 49 P. & C.R. 212; *Woolwich Equitable Building Society Ltd v Marshall* [1952] Ch. 1.

of pre-emption, which is the right granted to a person to be offered the property if the owner should decide to sell it: a right of "first refusal". There was some doubt as to whether this was a property interest from the point of creation to the point at which the owner decided to sell. The Land Registration Act 2002 s.115 provides that a right of pre-emption is to be regarded as a property right capable of binding successors in title. The Land Registration Act 2002 s.116 provides that the equity that arises under the doctrine of proprietary estoppel is an interest capable of binding successors in title. For our purposes this means that it is capable of being overriding, if the other requirements of Sch.3(2) are met. Thus, in *Gillett v Holt*,[207] which we considered in our Critical Thinking Exercise at the end of Chapter 2, if Mr Holt had sold the farm to a purchaser, Mr Gillett could have claimed an overriding interest as he occupied the farm.[208] Section 116 also provides that a "mere equity" is an interest capable of binding successors in title. Accordingly the right to set aside a transaction on the ground of undue influence, which is a "mere equity", has been held to amount to an interest in land for the purposes of establishing an overriding interest within Sch.3(2).[209] A right to rectify a contract and conveyance was an interest for these purposes in *Blacklocks v LB Developments (Godalming) Ltd*,[210] as was a right to rectify the land register in *Malory Enterprises Ltd v Cheshire Homes (UK) Ltd*.[211]

Finally, where a vendor sells land and is not paid by the purchaser, he retains a right to be paid, that is an interest in the land itself. This is known as an "unpaid vendor's lien" and is capable of being an overriding interest if the vendor remains in occupation.[212]

(a) What is not capable of falling within Schedule 3 paragraph 2?

As we have seen, it is necessary for the claimant to have an interest in land. The House of Lords in *National Provincial Bank Ltd v Ainsworth*[213] held that the "deserted wife's equity" was not a property right in the land. It was a mere personal obligation that she could assert against her husband alone. There was no interest in land capable of taking effect as overriding. Indeed, it is now on a statutory basis that a spouse's or civil partner's statutory right to occupy the family home cannot be an overriding interest, either for the purposes of Sch.1 or 3.[214] Interests under a settlement under the Settled Land Act 1925 are expressly excluded by the Land Registration Act 2002 from being overriding under this paragraph.[215] This replicates the position under the 1925 Act. Reversionary leases of the type mentioned in Sch.3(2)(d) are excluded from being overriding.

(4) The claimant must establish that they are "in actual occupation"

If you look back at Sch.3 para.2, it protects as overriding *only* the rights of those *belonging to persons in actual occupation*. It is the actual occupation of the owner of the right that gives their

---

207   [2000] 2 All E.R. 298.
208   This is subject to the other rules in Sch.3 para.2.
209   *Thompson v Foy* [2009] EWHC 1076 (Ch), paras.118 and 134–138, per Lewison J.
210   [1982] Ch. 183.
211   [2002] Ch. 216.
212   *London and Cheshire Insurance Co Ltd v Laplagrene Property Co Ltd* [1971] Ch. 499.
213   [1965] A.C. 1175.
214   Family Law Act 1996 s.31(10)(b).
215   Land Registration Act 2002 Sch.3, para.2(a).

interest its status as an "overriding interest", and means that the interest will bind a purchaser or mortgage lender after a transaction with a registered estate.

> **The 2002 Act, like its predecessor the Land Registration Act 2002, does not define the words "actual occupation". We need to look to the cases for the meaning of the words. Thus the pre-1925 case law on the meaning of "actual occupation" is still good law.**

(a) A question of fact

Boland (in the extract above) tells us that the question of whether a person is in actual occupation is a question of fact. What is required is some form of physical presence, as seen in the word "actual".[216] There is no special doctrine that decides whether or not a person can be deemed to be in occupation. There is an exception to this in the case of minor children with an interest in the land. They occupy property as shadows of occupation of their parents.[217] Thus, children are unable to establish an overriding interest under Sch.3 para.2. One reason could be that it would not be possible for a purchaser to make any inquiries of a child as to any rights they may have. Occupation does not need to be exclusive. It can be shared.[218] An employee or agent can "occupy" on behalf of his employer or principal,[219] e.g. builders working at the property.

In *Abbey National Building Society v Cann*[220] Lord Oliver held that actual occupation involves "some degree of permanence and continuity which would rule out mere fleeting presence".[221] It was held that the actions of a person preparing to occupy a house 35 minutes prior to completion of a purchase, moving in belongings and laying carpets, were not sufficient to establish actual occupation.

(b) Actual occupation or not?

In one sense *Boland* was an easy case. Mrs Boland was physically resident. There was no doubt that she occupied the house. But what facts will establish actual occupation in more borderline cases? There will be many that are on the "fuzzy edges"[222] of the rule.

(i) *Actual occupation not destroyed by temporary absence: symbolic occupation*

An example of a case of the fuzzy edges of the "actual occupation" rule is *Chhokar v Chhokar*.[223] In this case a matrimonial home was registered in the sole name of the husband. He held the

---

216   *Williams & Glyn's Bank Ltd v Boland* [1981] A.C. 487, p.504 per Lord Wilberforce.
217   *Hypo-Mortgage Services Ltd v Robinson* [1997] 2 F.C.R. 422, per Nourse L.J.
218   *Hodgson v Marks* [1971] Ch. 892, p.912, per Ungoed-Thomas J.
219   *Abbey National Building Society v Cann* [1991] 1 A.C. 56, p.93 per Lord Oliver; *Strand Securities Ltd v Caswell* [1965] Ch. 958 p.984 per Russell L.J. Although this does not apply to a licensee who is in occupation. It will not be accepted as the occupation of the licensor: ibid., p.981 per Lord Denning M.R.
220   [1991] 1 A.C. 56.
221   [1991] 1 A.C. 56, pp.93–94.
222   F.Schauer, *Thinking Like a Lawyer* (Harvard University Press, 2009), p.24 "The Generality of Rules".
223   [1984] F.L.R. 313.

house on trust for himself and his wife, because she had contributed to the purchase price. The husband and an accomplice (Mr Parmar) tried to evict her from the matrimonial home and destroy her interest in it, by arranging a sale of the house to Mr Parmar at significantly under market value. They arranged the timing of the completion of the sale for when Mrs Chhokar was in hospital giving birth to the couple's second child. When she returned to the house, Mr Parmar had changed the locks. When she attempted to continue living in the house, he assaulted her and vandalised the house. Ewbank J. held[224] that

"The wife on that date was not in the house because [Mr Parmar] had put her out, but some of her furniture was there. I have to consider whether she was in actual occupation on the [relevant day of completion of the transaction]. I have no difficulty in deciding that she was in actual occupation. Her interest, accordingly, in the house is an overriding interest".

Thus, a person can establish "actual occupation" even though they are not physically present, provided that there is some indication of presence, such as furniture.[225] So it is clear that "actual occupation" is defined to reflect a commonsense approach to the way we live. We are not in our houses 24/7. We take holidays, and pay visits. It would be nonsensical to suppose that an overriding interest would be lost because of such temporary absence. It was held in *Hoggert v Hoggert*[226] that a person seeking to establish actual occupation on the basis of this symbolic occupation principle must manifest a continuing intention to occupy.[227]

However, absence for an extended period may mean that any possessions left in the house will not signify "actual occupation".[228]

(ii) Critical thinking on Chhokar v Chhokar

LECTURER: What would have been the position in unregistered land? Would Mr Parmar have taken free from or subject to Mrs Chhokar's interest?

STUDENT: Subject to it, because he had actual notice of her rights.

LECTURER: That's correct. And in registered land?

STUDENT: It is actual occupation that gives the right overriding status. So everything depends on that.

LECTURER: That's right. Now make an argument about whether the case creates good law.

STUDENT: I think we can use BUILDING BLOCK NO 2 to make an argument.

---

224 Affirmed by Cumming-Bruce L.J. in the Court of Appeal.
225 Also *Hoggett v Hoggett* (1979) 39 P. & C.R. 121; *Bhullar v McArdle* [2001] EWCA Civ 510 (tidying away garden waste and composting was not actual occupation).
226 (1980) 39 P. & C.R. 121. This was confirmed and applied in *Thompson v Foy* [2009] EWHC 1076 (Ch.)
227 For a modern application of the symbolic occupation principle see *Thompson v Foy* [2009] EWHC 1076 (Ch), paras.129–130 per Lewison J.
228 *Stockholm Finance Ltd v Garden Holdings Ltd* [1995] N.P.C. 162.

BUILDING BLOCK NO 2: Ideas of Justice

Rules are good and fair if they take account of moral justice: every person should be accorded the freedom of their will and autonomous choice. Thus, if people deal with each other and with their property in a way that violates the will of another then the law should offer that other some remedy. Land Law should decide its rules to guard against the potential for the legal owner, e.g. the husband, to deal with the land in a way that dramatically affects the life of the other spouse, e.g. by mortgaging the house behind her back and then defaulting on the repayments: "domination-potential": Harris, *Property and Justice*, p.273.

STUDENT: I think that this case averted a profound injustice. Mr Chhokar was the sole registered proprietor of the house and he had abused the power that comes with this statutory ownership. He attempted to dominate the way in which the wife could live in a particularly ugly way. He did not respect the will and autonomous choice of his wife. Thus the law is good because it stepped in and undid the effects of the husband's unconscionable behaviour.

LECTURER: The purchaser had behaved immorally, changing the locks and violently evicting the wife.

STUDENT: It is nice to see that the law drew the line and protected the trust and confidence that family members often have in each other.

In *Chhokar v Chhokar* [1984] F.L.R. 313, p.330, Cumming-Bruce L.J. commented that "it is not easy to find language which, with becoming moderation, describes the moral turpitude of every step taken by Mr Parmar [the purchaser] throughout this transaction".

We can also see that, by recognising that wives have overriding interests in these circumstances, even though they were not physically resident at the time of the purchase, the law gives protection to people's residential security by ensuring that the purchaser or mortgage lender takes subject to their rights. *Chhokar v Chhokar* is therefore good and fair law on the basis of BUILDING BLOCK NO 1.

BUILDING BLOCK NO 1: Residential Security

Rules are good and fair if they give protection to people's residential security. Land Law now operates in the context of owner occupation. Therefore its rules should give effect to the purposes for which people buy houses.

STUDENT: I do have a problem with this case though. It achieved a good and fair result but the registered land method of deciding priority does seem somewhat arbitrary. The judge achieved justice in this case but what if the husband had got rid of the furniture?

LECTURER: Or involved a third accomplice and insisted they were appointed as the second "trustee" to receive the proceeds of sale? Or what if the husband had removed all traces of occupation, but that the purchaser was entirely innocent of all knowledge of this? Should the purchaser take free from the occupier's interest in these circumstances?

> Keep these situations in your mind as you work through the rest of this Chapter. See if you think the law makes adequate provision for them.

Can you make an argument for or against *Chhokar v Chhokar* on the basis of BUILDING BLOCK NO 6?

> **BUILDING BLOCK NO 6: The Need for Certainty and Predictability in Land Law rules**
> If the rules are clear as to how they will apply in future cases, i.e. if they allow people (e.g. purchasers or occupiers) to predict the outcome of their actions then they are good law. Purchasers and mortgage lenders need to predict in advance the types of inspections they will need to make in order to take free from an occupier's right. Does *Chhokar v Chhokar* offer a workable rule?

STUDENT: We could criticise of the rule on the same basis that we did about *Kingsnorth Finance Co Ltd v Tizard*[229] (see Chapter 7 Land Transfer Law (2) p.380). In order to discover an occupier the bank or building society may be involved in some difficult inspections of the land. It is unclear from *Chhokar v Chhokar* what type of furniture will be sufficient to establish "actual occupation".

LECTURER: So it is unclear how the courts will interpret this "constructive occupation" rule? What consequences might this have?

STUDENT: Future purchasers and mortgage lenders will be uncertain as to what they have to look for in order to establish whether anyone is in actual occupation.

> The Land Registration Act 2002 adds some purchaser protection that may make the position of the purchaser easier in this type of situation. We will consider this below.

LECTURER: Therefore, *Chhokar* may also be bad law when we consider BUILDING BLOCK NO 5. What if the purchaser in *Chhokar* had been entirely innocent of the husband's misconduct?

---

229 [1986] 1 W.L.R. 783.

> **BUILDING BLOCK NO 5:** **Property Rights and the Protection of Purchasers and Mortgage Lenders**
> Lenders need to be sure of their security. Otherwise they may be reluctant to lend money. This would be problematic for the economy and small businesses, and for people wanting to buy homes.

STUDENT: I stil think that Sch. 3(2) should protect the rights of people whose rights are vulnerable to being destroyed by the purchase or mortgage. They probably don't even appreciate that they have interests in the land that need to be protected.

A modern case to apply the symbolic occupation principle under the 2002 Act is *Link Lending v Bustard*,[230] in which we see that the justice reasons for finding the claimant in occupation are equally as compelling as *Chhokar v Chhokar*. The lender was attempting to enforce a legal charge that had been dishonestly executed over the home of the defendant. She had an equitable interest and the only question here was whether she was in "actual occupation": she had been detained in a residential care unit for the previous year, due to her severe mental condition. So she had not been in physical residence. It was argued for the bank that her occupation was insufficiently permanent. Mummery L.J. considered that

"The degree of permanence and continuity of presence of the person concerned, the intentions and wishes of that person, the length of absence from the property and the reason for it and the nature of the property and personal circumstances of the person are among the relevant factors."

The defendant's absence had been involuntary, due to her mental condition. Her furniture was still present at the property, she intended to return and she made weekly supervised visits to the property. The Court of Appeal upheld the judge's finding that she was in "actual occupation" and her interest consequently bound the lender as overriding under Sch. 3(2).[231]

(iii) Actual occupation and derelict property
The facts that will establish "actual occupation" will depend on the nature of the property and what it is used for. In *Lloyds Bank Plc v Rosset*[232] the question arose as to whether "actual occupation" could be established of a semi-derelict house undergoing renovation. This case concerned what was to be Mr and Mrs Rosset's family home. The house was registered in Mr Rosset's sole name, but Mrs Rosset claimed a beneficial interest. Unbeknown to Mrs Rosset, her husband had mortgaged the house in order to fund the cost of the renovations. By a 2:1 decision[233] it was held that she was in actual occupation because builders were working at the

---

230 [2010] EWCA Civ 424; [2010] 2 P. & C.R. DG 15. Also reported as *Link Lending Ltd v Hussein*.
231 Whether or not Mrs Bustard's occupation could have been discovered on a reasonably careful inspection did not appear to be an issue. This is a requirement of Sch.3(2) which we consider below in this section.
232 [1989] Ch. 350.
233 Purchas and Nicholls L.JJ. in the majority, Mustill L.J. in the minority.

property every day. Her interest therefore bound the bank.[234] Similarly *Malory Enterprises v Cheshire Homes*[235] concerned derelict land. The claimants boarded up the buildings and erected steel fences on the boundary. This was sufficient to establish actual occupation. *Rosset* was relied upon in *Thomas v Clydesdale Bank Plc*,[236] in which it was held that actual occupation could be established by the presence of builders and interior designers and the almost daily presence of the claimant.

(iv) Case study 2: Lloyds Bank Plc v Rosset

Now we will look at how the judges come to some of these decisions. Essentially rules are made of words, and words are "open-textured".[237] The words "actual occupation" are insufficiently precise to indicate to a judge one clear meaning for every possible set of facts that could come before the court. So how do judges arrive at their conclusions? They consider how the rule *should* apply and what it was designed to do.

> **This is where judges perceive our BUILDING BLOCKS as *part of the law itself*.**

Let us consider the reasoning of the three Lord Justices of Appeal in *Lloyds Bank Plc v Rosset*.[238] The question of whether one could "actually occupy" property without living there was novel. The statutory language, which was in this respect the same as the 2002 Act, did not cover this situation. There was nothing in the statute to give a "yes" or a "no" answer. Look carefully at the following extracts and see how the judges based their reasoning on our Building Blocks.

> **NICHOLLS L.J.:** "Given that in today's society, property is used for a variety of purposes, it would 'defeat the purpose intended to be achieved by' overriding interests if 'in every day speech actual occupation of a house can never exist short of residence'. 'I accept that in ordinary speech one normally does equate occupation in relation to a house with living there . . . That is the normal position, with a house which is fit for living in. But that does not provide the answer in the present case, where the house was semi-derelict. If, day after day, workmen are actively building a house on a lot of land, or actively and substantially renovating a semi-derelict house, it would be contrary to the principle underlying paragraph (g) [now schedule 3(2)] if a would be purchaser or mortgagee were entitled to treat that site as currently devoid of an occupant for the purpose of [establishing an overriding interest] . . . In my view, the test of residence propounded by the bank is too narrow. As the judge observed, what constitutes occupation will depend upon the nature and state of the property in question."[239]

---

234 The decision in *Rosset* was overturned by the House of Lords on the point of whether Mrs Rosset could establish an interest in the house: [1991] 1 A.C. 107. Thus, the point on whether that interest was overriding, and the meaning of actual occupation, was not considered by the House.

235 [2002] Ch. 216.

236 [2010] EWHC 2755 (QB).

237 H.L.A.Hart, *The Concept of Law* 2nd can (Oxford: Clarendon Press, 1997), pp.127–8.

238 [1989] Ch. 350.

239 *Lloyds Bank Plc v Rosset* [1989] Ch. 350, p.377.

LECTURER: So what construction of the statute did Nicholls L.J. arrive at?

STUDENT: That one could "actually occupy" semi-derelict property. Mrs Rosset showed her actual occupation because she had builders who were working at the property renovating it. Someone was clearly employing the builders and able to answer any inquiries that a purchaser or mortgage lender may make.

LECTURER: And why did he reach this conclusion?

STUDENT: To require the *physical residence* of the person claiming "actual occupation" would be "contrary to the principle" underlying this type of overriding interest. This is because it would exclude many people like Mrs Rosset from establishing an overriding interest. These people need protection for their interests against banks and building societies.

> **BUILDING BLOCK NO 8: Statutory rules should give effect to the purpose behind their enactment**
> If you remember overriding interests are supposed to protect people who would not readily appreciate the need to register their rights.

LECTURER: Now consider the position of the other judges.

> **PURCHAS L.J.** [Came to the same conclusion as Nicholls L.J.] observed: ([1989] Ch. 350, p.406) "Misleading or deceptive husbands will exist in financial matters quite apart from the breakdown of a marriage and should therefore, be within the contemplation in any event of bank managers and others in a like position."

> **BUILDING BLOCK NO 2: Ideas of Justice**
> The law should protect against the domination-potential of being the sole legal owner as the husband was in *Rosset*. He has the power to mortgage the house and undermine the wife's, or other occupier's interest: Harris, *Property and Justice*.

> **MUSTILL L.J.** ([1989] Ch. 350, p.398) was in the minority deciding that actual occupation of a semi-derelict house in the process of renovation *could not* be established. He observed: "Nobody who arrived on the site to make inquiries about possible interests adverse to those of the person with paper title . . . would imagine that masons and plasterers working on the fabric, with vans parked outside bearing names which were obviously those of tradesmen rather than people who might have adverse claims to the property, could be in occupation of the site, in any relevant sense, rather than coming and going to work upon it".

LECTURER: What was Mustill L.J.'s interpretation of the statute?

STUDENT: That Mrs Rosset could not be in actual occupation because she was not in residence herself. Thus she would be unable to establish an overriding interest and the bank would be able to take possession of the house.

LECTURER: On what basis did Mustill L.J. justify this interpretation?

STUDENT: The bank, when its representative arrived to make an inspection of the property, would not be able to tell that there was another person claiming an interest against the land. The idea is that a person's occupation of the property would indicate to a purchaser or mortgage lender that someone other than the vendor or borrower might claim an adverse interest. There was no indication of Mrs Rosset here—and so no-one of whom the bank could make inquiries.

LECTURER: So BUILDING BLOCK NO 5 provided a strong justification for Mustill L.J.'s construction of the statute.

BUILDING BLOCK NO 5: Property Rights and the Protection of Purchasers and Mortgage Lenders

A rule is good or bad fair or unfair, depending on the extent to which it supports or undermines the idea that rules of Land Law should protect a purchaser or mortgage lender from being bound by prior interests in the land. This is the policy behind the 1925 property legislation. Banks and building societies often lend to small businesses on the security of family homes. They must be sure of their security, so the court should not recognise too many rights that will bind them and stop them from selling the house if the borrower defaults. Otherwise they may become reluctant to lend money. This will affect our economy.

(v) The facts necessary to establish actual occupation depend on the nature of the property

In *Link Lending v Bustard*,[240] the Court of Appeal confirmed that the facts necessary to establish actual occupation depend on the nature of the property.[241] For example, actual occupation of a garage has been established by the presence of a car. In *Kling v Keston Properties*[242] the claimant was a tenant of a flat in Chelsea, and also of a garage in the grounds. He was granted a right of pre-emption or "first refusal" to buy the garage. The claimant did not register his right. In breach of the right, the owners granted a 99-year lease to another, who registered the lease.

Whose interest has priority?

The dispute: The claimant wrote to the purchaser of the lease formally exercising his right to purchase the garage on the same terms from her. She wrote back "purportedly terminating the plaintiff's licence to occupy the garage".

---

240   [2010] EWCA Civ 424; [2010] 2 P. & C.R. DG 15.
241   See also *Thomas v Clydesdale Bank Plc* [2010] EWHC 2755 (QB).
242   (1989) 49 P. & C.R. 212.

Vinelott J. held that the claimant had an interest in the garage, the right of pre-emption, and was in actual occupation because he regularly parked his car in the garage. Thus, his right bound the purchaser of the garage.

(c) A person does not need to occupy by virtue of the interest they are claiming as overriding

In *Webb v Pollmount*[243] the occupier was a tenant, occupying under a lease, with an option to purchase the property. It was held that his option was overriding. It did not matter that his occupation was by virtue of the lease and not the interest he claimed as overriding.

(5) When must the claimant prove they are in actual occupation?

A claimant must prove that they are in actual occupation at the time of completion of the transaction. This was decided by the House of Lords in *Abbey National Building Society v Cann*.[244] If you remember conveyancing at present takes place in two stages: completion of the transaction: 1. where the purchase money is paid and the deed of transfer executed; and where the mortgage loan is paid over and the mortgage deed executed, and then 2. registration of the transaction a few weeks later. Although the time for determining whether a purchaser is affected by an overriding interest is at the time he *registers* his disposition,[245] a purchaser or mortgagee will inspect the land prior to completion not after. Thus, it would be a "conveyancing absurdity" for a person to be able to enter into occupation *after* completion of the transaction, but *before* the purchaser or mortgagee has registered it, and then be able to claim an overriding interest.[246] Thus, the relevant time for a person to prove actual occupation is upon completion of the transaction, not registration. This is also the effect of the provisions of the Land Registration Act 2002.[247]

However, apart from the question of actual occupation the relevant date for determining whether a purchaser or mortgage lender takes subject to overriding interests is the date of registration of the disposition.[248]

> When electronic conveyancing comes into force this will cease to matter, as the completion of the transaction and its registration will happen simultaneously.

(6) An interest of a person in actual occupation can only be overriding "so far as relating to land of which he is in actual occupation"

As with interests belonging to occupiers that override first registrations, Sch.3 para.2 of the Land Registration Act 2002 provides that a person can only assert an overriding interest in

---

243   [1966] Ch. 58.
244   [1991] 1 A.C. 56, confirming the decision of the Court of Appeal in *Lloyds Bank Plc v Rosset* [1989] Ch. 350.
245   Land Registration Act 2002 ss.29 and 30.
246   [1991] 1 A.C. 56, p.88, per Lord Oliver.
247   The decision in *Thompson v Foy* [2009] EWHC 1976 that actual occupation must be proven also at the time of registration, is clearly wrong.
248   Land Registration Act 2002 s.29(1).

relation to the part of the land they are actually occupying. So if a person has an option to purchase a whole estate but is only occupying a cottage on part of that estate, a purchaser will only be bound by his option to purchase the cottage. Of course he could register the option as a notice against the title to the estate and then it would be fully exercisable over the whole estate. The 2002 Act thus overrules the decision in *Ferrishurst Ltd v Wallcite Ltd*[249] to the contrary, where a person who was only in actual occupation of part of the land could enforce rights that he had over the whole of the land. In *Ferrishurst*, Robert Walker L.J. had commented that "the burden on a purchaser to make inquiries is now heavier than before".[250]

Thompson v Foy[251] is a recent application of this provision of the 2002 Act. In this case a cottage had been extended to provide an entirely separate dwelling for the claimant's daughter and her husband. It was held that the claimant could only establish an overriding interest in relation to the land she occupied, i.e. the cottage and not the extension.

LECTURER: Which one of our Building Blocks does this new law support?
STUDENT: Firstly I would say that it is good law on the basis of BUILDING BLOCK NO 8:

> **BUILDING BLOCK NO 8: Statutory rules should give effect to the purpose behind their enactment**
> We can criticise a statutory rule, i.e. we can say that it is a good or bad rule, on the basis of whether it achieves parliament's objectives behind its enactment.
>
> Remember that the Law Commission stated that "The fundamental objective of the [Act] is that . . . the register should be a complete and accurate reflection of the state of the title of the land at any given time, so that it is possible to investigate title to land . . . with the absolute minimum of additional enquiries and inspections": Law Com No.271, paras.1.5–1.6.

LECTURER: Good, it is not easy for a purchaser or mortgage lender to understand when undertaking an inspection of a large title that a person who is in occupation of part of it may nonetheless be able to assert rights to the whole of the title. So a person is only able to claim that his right binds as overriding to the extent of the area occupied. This is good law as it minimises the type and extent of enquiries that a purchaser needs to make. It is also good law on the basis of BUILDING BLOCK NO 5.

---

249   [1999] Ch. 355.
250   [1999] Ch. 355: Law Commission, *Land Registration for the Twenty-First Century—A Conveyancing Revolution* Law Com No.271, para.8.57.
251   [2009] EWHC 1076 (Ch), para.129, per Lewison J.

> **BUILDING BLOCK NO 5: Property Rights and the Protection of Purchasers and Mortgage Lenders.**

(7) The "reasonably careful inspection" test and the relevance of the registered disponee's "actual knowledge" of the interest

Under the Land Registration Act 1925 an interest would be overriding simply by virtue of actual occupation, whether the purchaser could have discovered the occupier or not. In *Kling v Keston Properties* Vinelott J. observed that

> "It is quite clear that there can be cases where a purchaser may make the most searching inquiries without discovering that the land in question is in the actual occupation of a third party. It is disquieting that the system of land registration which is being steadily extended should be so framed that a person acquiring an interest in registered land may find his interest subject to an option or right of pre-emption which has not been registered and notwithstanding that there is no person other than the vendor in apparent occupation of the property and that careful inspection and inquiry has failed to reveal anything which might give the purchaser any reason to suspect that someone other than the vendor had any interest in or rights over the property".[252]

Consequently the Land Registration Act 2002 introduces a requirement that a person's occupation must have been "obvious on a reasonably careful inspection of the land at the time of the disposition". Otherwise, that person will be unable to assert an overriding interest under sch.3 para.2.[253] Note that it is the *occupation* and not the occupier's *interest* that must be discoverable. The question is hypothetical, i.e. what would have been obvious on a reasonably careful inspection.[254] This provision is part of the 2002 Act's aim to reduce the opportunities for interests to override a registered disposition.

(a) What is "obvious on a reasonably careful inspection"?

There have been concerns that the 2002 Act's "reasonably careful inspection" defence will re-introduce into registered land all the difficulties associated with the doctrine of constructive notice. [255]

> Revisit the section on constructive notice above (Land Transfer Law (1) section 2B) and see whether you think the new "reasonably careful inspection" test is the same as constructive notice. You need to identify the elements of constructive notice and the elements of this new test and compare them.

---

252 (1985) 49 P. & C.R. 212, pp.221–2.
253 Sch.3(2)(c)(i).
254 See *Thompson v Foy* [2009] EWHC 1076 (Ch), para.132 per Lewison J.
255 Emmet and Farrand, *Title*, commenting on the "reasonably careful inspection" test in the 2002 Act, quoted, Thompson, *Modern Land Law*, p.131.

The Law Commission, in its report prior to the 2002 Act, showed that the new test will have no such effect.[256] The "reasonably careful inspection" requirement is a "less demanding test" for a purchaser to satisfy, modelled on the legal test that determines the extent of a seller's contractual duty to a purchaser to disclose defects in his own title,[257] e.g. someone with a right that would bind him or a limitation on the use of the land. The seller only has a duty to disclose latent defects; matters that are within his exclusive knowledge. If a defect is patent the purchaser could have seen it for himself and takes the title subject to the defect with no comeback against the seller.[258] A "patent" defect is something that "arises either to the eye, or by necessary implication from something which is visible to the eye".[259] Thus, the test in the 2002 Act is purely and simply whether the *occupation* is discoverable in this sense.[260] It does not mean that the purchaser must pursue all inquiries to ascertain whether anyone can claim an adverse interest. The idea is that the purchaser or lender would be able to ensure that he was not bound by any interest of the occupier, either by obtaining a waiver or by requiring them to join the transaction.[261]

Thus, in order to establish an overriding interest under Sch.3(2) an occupier now must introduce evidence to show that his occupation would have been obvious, either in plain view that the occupier was there, or as a necessary implication from what was visible at the premises. Cases such as *Boland*, where the occupier was physically resident, would not cause a problem. But in borderline cases it is not at all clear what the courts would deem to be "obvious" in this sense. Female possessions in a house in the sole name of a man may "by necessary implication" lead to the conclusion that a woman lived there.

There is little case law on the requirement that occupation must be obvious on a reasonably careful inspection. In *Thomas v Clydesdale Bank Plc*[262] it was held that there must be obvious, visible signs of the occupation on which the claimant relies. The presence of builders and interior designers at a property undergoing renovation, in addition to the daily presence of the person claiming occupation, was held to be sufficient. Once there were visible signs of occupation, it was also thought that in order to ascertain the permanence of someone's occupation, the purchaser or lender may be required to make some enquiries relating to the occupiers intentions, wishes and circumstances.[263]

---

256 Law Com No.254, paras 5.71–5.73.
257 Law Com No.271, para.8.62(1).
258 The reason is that a purchaser is no longer relying on matters that are within the exclusive knowledge and control of the seller: *Peyman v Lanjani* [1985] Ch. 457, p.496 per Slade L.J. C.Harpum, "Selling Without Title: a Vendor's Duty of Disclosure?" (1992) 108 L.Q.R. 280.
259 *Yandle & Sons v Sutton, Young & Same* [1922] 2 Ch. 199, per Sargant J., p.210: Law Com No.271, para.8.62(1).
260 Law Com No.271, para.8.62.
261 For consideration of the 2002 Act's "reasonably careful inspection" test see N.Jackson (2003) 119 L.Q.R. 660.
262 [2010] EWHC 2755 (QB); Bogusz [2011] Conv. 268.
263 *Thomas v Clydesdale Bank Plc* [2010] EWHC 2755 (QB), para.38.

(b) Critical Thinking: the reasonably careful inspection

LECTURER: What do you think is the point being made by the detractors of the "reasonably careful inspection" test?

STUDENT: If it is *really* going to re-introduce the doctrine of constructive notice, I remember from the previous two chapters that this caused extensive cost and litigation. Purchasers would either have to spend disproportionate sums on legal costs or risk being bound by an adverse interest (see Chapter 6 section 2B, p.344).

A modern application of the doctrine of constructive notice was *Kingsnorth Finance v Tizard* (see the previous Chapter, p.380) in which a mortgagee was bound because he knew about the borrower's married status so should have enquired about whether his wife had a beneficial interest in the house. Finlay J. also said that an isolated inspection of the property, pre-arranged on a Sunday afternoon, was not sufficient to satisfy the requirement of a reasonable inspection.

LECTURER: And do you think that the 2002 Act's "reasonably careful inspection" test is the same?

STUDENT: No. From what was said above it is clear that a purchaser will not have to make the type of enquiry that would reveal that the occupier claimed an interest in the land. The only enquiries necessary are ones that are aimed at establishing the type and permanence of the claimant's occupation. And to begin with, there must be visible signs of occupation.

As to what is a "reasonably careful" inspection, in order to ascertain these signs, it might be the case that a judge could consider that a pre-arranged inspection with the vendor/borrower might not be sufficient to discover who is in *occupation* and that misleading and deceptive husbands (and wives and other partners!) ought to be within the contemplation of banks and building societies lending money on the security of houses.[264] So they might impose quite high standards of what could be expected, i.e. that banks should anticipate that borrowers might attempt to hide all traces of occupiers and so should make a second inspection, e.g. unannounced.

LECTURER: And so? . . . . This is not the same as the doctrine of constructive notice that you have just outlined.

STUDENT: No, the purpose of that doctrine is that a purchaser/mortgagee must pursue all reasonable enquiries in order to discover *any adverse interests*. The purpose of the 2002 Act's test is only to discover *visible signs of occupation*. This is a much narrower and restricted enquiry.

> **LECTURER:** But to get some idea of how the 2002 Act's "reasonably careful inspection" test will *really* work in practice go back and consider the cases of *Lloyds Bank v Rosset, Kling v Keston Properties* and *Chhokar v Chhokar* (earlier in this section). Imagine that the same set of facts came before a judge under the Land Registration Act 2002. How would the case be decided today?

---

264 Per Lord Scarman, *Williams & Glyn's Bank Ltd v Boland* [1981] A.C. 487.

LECTURER: Let's move on now to consider the *purpose* of the "reasonable inspection" requirement. The 2002 Act is intended to reflect a compromise? What is this compromise?

STUDENT: Between people such as Mrs Boland and Mrs Rosset who need their rights protecting because they cannot be expected to register them, and purchasers and mortgage lenders who need to be able to take a good title free from these rights. So the Act is saying that it is fair to allow purchasers to be bound by overriding interests where they had opportunity enough to find out about the occupier and make enquiries, but where the purchaser has no such opportunity then he should not be bound by the occupier's interest.

So this is good law on the basis of BUILDING BLOCK NO 5.

BUILDING BLOCK NO 5: Property Rights and the Protection of Purchasers and Mortgage Lenders

We may say that the law is good if it prevents purchasers and mortgage lenders from being too readily bound by prior rights in the land.

LECTURER: How effective do you think the "reasonably careful inspection" test will be?

STUDENT: It depends on what the courts consider to be a "reasonably careful inspection".

LECTURER: Well apply the analysis on judicial reasoning that we conducted in relation to *Lloyds Bank Plc v Rosset* (above).

STUDENT: What the courts consider to be a "reasonably careful inspection" may depend on the nature of the purchaser, e.g. with ordinary residential purchasers the court may think that this requirement is satisfied very easily. People who are buying a house in which to live will not be likely to understand the significance of finding another person in occupation. If the courts gave a strict interpretation of what a purchaser could have discovered in this situation, e.g. there were traces of someone else's belongings in the property so their occupation is held to be visible, the purchaser may end by being bound by what is *in reality* not discoverable to them at all!

LECTURER: Because he did not appreciate what he was looking at?

STUDENT: Yes.

LECTURER: So because the words "reasonably careful inspection" are capable of a variety of shades of meaning and interpretation we are in the same position in which the Court of Appeal found itself in *Lloyds Bank Plc v Rosset*. Will any of our Building Blocks underpin judicial constructions of the reasonably careful inspection defence?

STUDENT: A strong possibility is that a judge might reason on the basis of BUILDING BLOCK NO 8—a little like Mustill L.J. did in *Rosset*.

LECTURER: So what would be the argument here?

STUDENT: A judge might adopt a restrictive interpretation of what could ordinarily be discovered on a reasonably careful inspection based on the idea that it was the intention of the 2002 Act to reduce the scope of purchaser enquiries prior to purchase of land.

BUILDING BLOCK NO 8: Statutory rules should give effect to the purpose behind their enactment

We can criticise a statutory rule, i.e. we can say that it is a good or bad rule, on the basis of whether it achieves parliament's objectives behind its enactment.

Remember that the Law Commission stated that "The fundamental objective of the [Act] is that . . . the register should be a complete and accurate reflection of the state of the title of the land at any given time, so that it is possible to investigate title to land . . . with the absolute minimum of additional enquiries and inspections": Law Com No.271, paras.1.5–1.6.

LECTURER: This would be a very typical judicial interpretation of a statute. And it also promotes BUILDING BLOCK NO 5: Property Rights and the Protection of Purchasers and Mortgage Lenders.

STUDENT: Certainly it helps to make the land register more "conclusive as to priorities" by ensuring that purchasers and mortgage lenders are not bound by rights that they could not have found out about in advance of the purchase/mortgage.

LECTURER: But is this really the end of the story? What other factors might be in a judge's mind?

STUDENT: A judge might also interpret the meaning of "a reasonably careful inspection" very widely in order to give protection to an occupier. What if a sole registered proprietor, such as Mr Chhokar in *Chhokar v Chhokar* had removed all traces of his wife's belongings and arranged to mortgage the house behind her back?

LECTURER: So you are saying that the judge might adopt a very broad view of what the lender could have discovered in order to protect the wife in this case from a harmful exercise of the power that arose from her husband's legal ownership of the house.

BUILDING BLOCK NO 2: Ideas of Justice

The law should protect against the domination-potential that arises as a result of being the sole legal owner as the husband was in *Chhokar*. He has the power to mortgage the house and undermine the wife's, or other occupier's interest: Harris, *Property and Justice*, p.273.

(c) Where the purchaser has actual knowledge of the occupier's interest then they cannot rely on the reasonable inspection defence[265]

The only circumstance in which a purchaser or mortgage lender *will* take subject to an interest belonging to an occupier whose occupation was not obvious on a reasonably careful inspection

---

265   Land Registration Act 2002 Sch.3, para.2(c)(ii).

of the land is where the purchaser or lender has actual knowledge of the occupier's interest. Thus, if a purchaser knew that the claimant had an interest in the property, he would take subject to her interest, whether her occupation was discoverable or not.

LECTURER: Go back and consider the facts of *Chhokar v Chhokar*. How would this case be decided under this rule?

STUDENT: Well, in that case the husband arranged to sell the house to an accomplice at an undervalue in order to defeat the wife's rights in the house. The purchaser knew about the wife's rights. So they would be overriding, even if her occupation was not discoverable.

But what facts will suffice to establish actual knowledge? If you look over Chapter 6 it is clear that actual knowledge was usually established where the interest concerned was in some formal document that the purchaser had. However, the types of interest belonging to modern day occupiers are often established entirely informally, i.e. by contribution to the purchase of the house. Thus, in *Thomas v Clydesdale Bank Plc*[266] it was held that "actual knowledge of the facts that give rise to the interest" is sufficient.

> "I consider that the question of actual knowledge under paragraph 2(c)(ii) has to be construed in the context of the type of interest which is being dealt with. Where an interest belongs to somebody in actual occupation, very often the scope and extent of that interest will depend on the legal analysis of a number of facts and will rarely be ascertainable from a legal document."[267]

Thus, in this case, the occupier claimed a beneficial interest under a trust. She had a prospect of establishing that the bank had actual knowledge of her interest because they knew that the legal owner had a new partner, that she would contribute £100,000 to the purchase, and that the property was intended to be their family home.[268]

(8) Inquiry and disclosure

Once a purchaser discovers a person other than the vendor or mortgagor in occupation they are then in a position to be able to inquire as to that person's rights and to determine whether he takes free from, or subject to, those rights.[269] The usual reason a purchaser or mortgage lender will inquire as to the rights of an occupier is to make sure that they either sign a waiver, postponing any rights they may have to those of the lender,[270] or to have the occupier join the transaction, which would automatically postpone their rights to the lender.

---

266 [2010] EWHC 2755.
267 para.48.
268 paras 49–50.
269 *Hodgson v Marks* [1971] Ch. 892, pp.913–4, per Ungoed-Thomas J.
270 *Winkworth v Edward Baron Developments Ltd* [1986] 1 W.L.R. 1512.

Thus under Sch.3 para.2 an interest belonging to a person in occupation will not be overriding where inquiry was made of that person before the disposition and they failed to disclose their right when they could reasonably have been expected to do so.[271]

> The idea behind this provision, which substantially replicates the same provision under the 1925 Act, is that the rights of an occupier will not bind a purchaser if he asks the occupier if they have any rights and the occupier does not reveal the right to the purchaser.

If the occupier reveals their rights then the purchaser can choose either to abort the transaction or to obtain a waiver from the occupier to the effect that their rights will not bind him. If the purchaser does not inquire of any person in occupation, if they have rights, he risks taking subject to those rights.[272] As Lord Denning M.R. observed in *Williams & Glyn's Bank v Boland*,[273]

> "[o]nce it is found that a wife is in actual occupation, then it is clear that . . . a purchaser or lender would be well advised to make inquiry of the wife. If she then discloses her rights, he takes subject to them. If she does not disclose them, he takes free of them."

It is not possible to obtain enforceable consent from minor children that their interests would not take priority over a purchaser's. This is probably why a minor child's occupation is only regarded as a "shadow" of the occupation of their parents, so that their rights will be unable to take effect as overriding.[274]

It is self-evident from Sch.3(2) that the purchaser must make inquiries *of the occupier* himself, and not simply ask the vendor whether any other person may be able to claim a right in the land. In *Hodgson v Marks*[275] Mrs Hodgson was the sole owner of her house. Her lodger, Evans, gained her trust and she transferred the house to him on the understanding that he would hold it for her. Thus, she retained the beneficial interest of the house.[276] Evans sold the house, without her consent, to Mr Marks—who then mortgaged it. Mr Marks took subject to her rights, because he made no inquiry at all of her. Her interest also overrode the mortgage:

> "As to the defendant building society it is plain that it made no inquiries on the spot save as to repairs; it relied on Mr Marks, who lied to it; and I waste no tears on it."[277]

---

271   Land Registration Act 2002, Sch.3, para.2(b).
272   *Winkworth v Edward Baron Developments Ltd* [1986] 1 W.L.R. 1512.
273   [1979] 1 Ch. 312, p.332.
274   *Hypo-Mortgage Services Ltd v Robinson* [1997] 2 F.L.R. 71.
275   [1971] Ch. 892.
276   [1971] Ch. 892, p.908 per Ungoed-Thomas J., under the doctrine of *Rochefoucauld v Boustead* [1897] 1 Ch. 196; *In re Duke of Marlborough* [1894] 2 Ch. 133.
277   [1971] Ch. 892, p.932, per Russell L.J.

In order to prevent a right from gaining overriding status, the purchaser must make inquiries of the occupier that are directed at ascertaining what rights they would have in the event that the purchaser went ahead with the contemplated transaction. It would be sufficient for a purchaser to make general inquiries as to rights that an occupier may have in relation to land.[278]

The 2002 Act makes one change, namely that rights will only fail to attain overriding status if the occupier failed to disclose their right when they could reasonably have been expected to do so. Thus it must be reasonable in the circumstances to expect the occupier to disclose their rights. For example where a spouse or cohabitee does not know they have an interest in the land, they will be unable to disclose it.

C. OTHER CIRCUMSTANCES IN WHICH PRIORITY IS POSTPONED TO THE LENDER

Rights will not be overriding where the priority of the interest has been expressly or impliedly postponed to the lender, or where the mortgage is required to *acquire* the property.

(1) Express consent to the mortgage

If a house is purchased with the aid of a mortgage, and an equitable co-owner expressly consents to the mortgage, their interests will not bind the bank.[279] Thus, if Mrs Boland had expressly consented to granting a mortgage this would have postponed her interest to that of the lender. Thus, it became the practice for banks to obtain waivers from adults in occupation. This would give priority to the lender.[280]

(2) Implied consent to the mortgage[281]

The law will deem an equitable co-owner to have consented to the mortgage where they knew about the mortgage or knew that the house could not have been purchased *without* a mortgage being granted. In *Bristol and West Building Society v Henning*[282] a house was in the sole name of one partner, Mr Henning. The other partner had an equitable interest in the house by virtue of her contribution to the purchase and the couple intended that they should jointly own the house. Most of the purchase price was financed by mortgage, which again was obtained in the sole name of Mr Henning. His partner claimed that her equitable interest took priority over the bank's mortgage. However, because she knew that Mr Henning had granted a mortgage in order to purchase the new house, and the fact that she had benefited from the mortgage, she was impliedly taken to have consented to the priority of the lender's rights over her own equitable interest.[283] This principle was taken further in *Equity and Law Home Loans Ltd v Prestidge*.[284]

---

278   *Winkworth v Edward Baron Developments Ltd* [1986] 1 W.L.R. 1512; Stevens and Pearce, *Land Law*, pp.114–5.
279   *Abbey National Building Society v Cann* [1991] 1 A.C. 56, p.89, per Lord Oliver.
280   *Woolwich Building Society v Dickman* [1996] 3 All E.R. 254.
281   See M.Thompson [1986] Conv. 57; (1986) 49 M.L.R. 245.
282   [1985] 2 All E.R. 606.
283   Also *Paddington Building Society v Mendelsohn* (1985) 50 P & C.R. 244.
284   [1992] 1 W.L.R. 137.

Where an equitable co-owner is taken to have impliedly consented to a mortgage, and that mortgage is subsequently discharged by a loan from another lender, the second lender's rights will have priority over the equitable co-owner's rights to the same amount of the first mortgage. The second lender "steps into the shoes" of the first. This is known as "subrogation".[285] In principle the second lender should be in no worse position than the first, as it is the second lender's money that has paid off the first loan.[286]

(3) Mortgage is required to *acquire* the property

The effect of the ruling in *Abbey National Building Society v Cann*[287] is that where a house is *initially acquired* with the aid of a mortgage, that mortgage will always have priority over any equitable co-ownership rights. A house was purchased in the sole name of Mr Cann. His mother contributed to the purchase price and thus had an equitable interest. A mortgage had been required in order to finance the purchase. Mr Cann defaulted on the repayments and Mrs Cann claimed an overriding interest by virtue of being in occupation. She argued that there was a tiny moment of time in which the legal estate of the house vested in Mr Cann unencumbered by the mortgage. Her interest took effect against the estate in this time and was therefore overriding. The argument failed. In cases where a mortgage is required in order to purchase a house it was held that there was no moment in time where the borrower acquired the legal estate unencumbered by the mortgage.[288]

(4) Occupational overriding interests and sections 14 and 15 of the Trusts of Land and Appointment of Trustees Act 1996

Even if a lender does not have priority over the rights of an equitable co-owner, the lender still has jurisdiction to apply for an order of sale under ss.14 and 15 of the Trusts of Land and Appointment of Trustees Act 1996.[289] As we have seen in Chapter 5, sale is not automatic. Under s.15 the court must consider various factors, such as the purpose of the house and the welfare of any minor child in occupation. If sale is ordered, the occupier with the overriding interest will be entitled to have their interest satisfied out of the proceeds of sale *before* the lender can claim any balance to discharge the mortgage debt. The order of priority of interests will be significant where the house is not likely to sell at a price sufficient to satisfy both.

D. OVERREACHING

(1) What is overreaching?[290]

As we saw in the previous chapter, where an equitable interest has been overreached on a sale or mortgage it means that the purchaser or mortgage lender can simply take the estate he has

285 *Mortgage Corporation Ltd v Shaire* [2000] 1 F.L.R. 973.
286 See *Castle Phillips Finance v Piddington* [1995] 1 F.L.R. 783: C.Harpum, S.Bridge, M.Dixon, *Megarry & Wade The Law of Real Property*, para.13–106. *Prestidge* was explained as based on the principle of estoppel: ibid.
287 [1991] 1 A.C. 56.
288 For a modern application of this principle to the Land Registration Act 2002 see *Re North East Property Buyers Litigation* [2010] EWHC 2991 (Ch). It applied to a right reserved by a vendor on the same day as a charge.
289 *Skipton Building Society v Clayton* (1993) 66 P. & C.R. 223.
290 C.Harpum [1990] C.L.J. 277; G.Ferris and G.Battersby [1998] Conv. 168.

purchased or charge he has been granted, free from a prior equitable interest. Thus, if a mortgage overreaches an occupier's beneficial interest under a trust, the lender takes free from that interest. It can take possession and sell the house in order to realise its security.

> **s.2 Law of Property Act 1925 Conveyances overreaching certain equitable interests and powers**
>
> "(1) A conveyance to a purchaser of a legal estate in land shall overreach any equitable interest or power affecting that estate, whether or not he has notice thereof, if
> . . . . (ii) the conveyance is made by trustees of land and the equitable interest or power is at the date of the conveyance capable of being overreached by such trustees . . . . and the requirements of section 27 of this Act respecting the payment of capital money arising on such a conveyance are complied with."

We see from this four things: Firstly, overreaching takes effect on a "conveyance of a legal estate", this includes a sale, lease and a mortgage.[291] Secondly, the conveyance must be made to a *purchaser*, which means "a person who acquires an interest in or charge on property for money or money's worth . . . . . and includes a chargee by way of legal mortgage".[292] Thirdly, not all equitable interests can be overreached. The types of interest registrable as land charges in unregistered land,[293] broadly comparable to those registrable as "notices" under the Land Registration Act 2002, are expressly excluded from overreaching.[294] Equitable interests under a trust are overreachable, as are interests under a settlement. Fourthly, any purchase money or mortgage advance that arises under the conveyance (called "capital money") must be paid to at least two trustees or a trust corporation.[295] This is the "capital money requirement". Thus if in any of the cases involving beneficial interests that we have examined in this chapter, for example: *Williams & Glyn's Bank v Boland, Chhokar v Chhokar*, the mortgage had been executed by two legal owners holding on trust rather than a sole legal owner holding on trust, the lender would have been able to take free from the occupiers' interests.

Overreaching ensures that the purchaser or mortgage lender takes free from an equitable interest that might otherwise have bound him and devalued his estate, e.g. an occupier's interest under a trust. If a mortgage overreaches a beneficial interest under a trust, the lender can then sell the estate with vacant possession, evicting the beneficiaries. Overreaching applies in the same way whether title is registered or unregistered, so all the same cases and statutory provisions apply.[296]

---

291   Law of Property Act 1925, s.205(1)(ii). The conveyance must not be a sham: *HSBC Bank Plc v Dyche* [2009] EWHC 2954 (Ch).
292   Law of Property Act 1925 s.205(1)(xxi).
293   For example, estate contracts, equitable easements, restrictive covenants.
294   Law of Property Act 1925 s.2(3).
295   Law of Property Act 1925 s.27. For a modern application of this rule see *HSBC Bank Plc v Dyche* [2009] EWHC 2954 (Ch).
296   For an argument to the contrary see N.Jackson (2006) 69 M.L.R. 114.

> **Example**
>
> Mrs X had contributed financially to the purchase of her family's home. The house was transferred and registered in her husband's and his brother's name. We know that by virtue of her contribution, her husband and his brother hold the house on trust, partly for her and partly for themselves. Her husband and his brother then mortgage the house, which they are empowered to do, being the registered proprietors. The building society, which lent them the money, is now claiming possession of the house, because the brothers have defaulted on the loan repayments. Mrs X resists the bank's claim to possession and argues that she has an overriding interest because she is in actual occupation.
>
> For an overriding interest it is necessary that Mrs X establishes 1. an interest in land and 2. actual occupation. Because overreaching means that her interest cannot be enforced against the land, *she falls at the first hurdle!* She no longer has any interest in the land.

What then happens to a beneficial interest that has been overreached? The answer is that it is not defeated entirely but takes effect against any money or substitute property received by the trustees in exchange for the estate or charge created by the conveyance.[297] The trustees hold these proceeds on the same trusts as they were holding the land. Overreaching affects a displacement of the beneficial interest[298]

(2) Cases on overreaching

The leading case on overreaching is the House of Lords decision in *City of London Building Society v Flegg.*[299] Mr and Mrs Flegg and their daughter and son-in-law, Mr and Mrs Maxwell-Brown, together purchased "Bleak House". Mr and Mrs Flegg sold their property in order to contribute to the purchase of the house. Mr and Mrs Maxwell-Brown borrowed money to fund their contribution to the purchase, and granted the lender a mortgage on Bleak house. Although when the parties bought the house their lawyer advised the Fleggs that the house should be transferred into all four names, the Fleggs acted against this advice. The house was transferred into the two names of Mr and Mrs Maxwell-Brown. They held legal title to Bleak House on trust for themselves and Mr and Mrs Flegg. Thus, Mr and Mrs Flegg had an equitable interest in the house. Subsequently, and unbeknown to Mr and Mrs Flegg, the Maxwell-Browns borrowed a larger sum of money from the City of London Building Society, who took a mortgage on Bleak House. The Maxwell-Browns, who were now in considerable financial difficulty, defaulted on the loan repayments. The building society commenced these proceedings for possession of Bleak House against Mr and Mrs Flegg.

---

297   This is not entirely correct in relation to mortgages where the beneficial interests take effect against what we call the "equity of redemption" in the land, i.e. the right to pay off the loan and get back the land unencumbered.

298   Sir Benjamin Cherry, D.Hughes Parry and J.R. Perceval Maxwell (eds), *Wolstenholme and Cherry's Conveyancing Statutes*, 12th edn (London: Stevens & Sons, 1932), p.232.

299   [1988] 1 A.C. 54; R.Smith (1987) 103 L.Q.R. 520; W.Swadling (1987) Conv. 451.

(a) Case study 3: House of Lords, City of London Building Society v Flegg[300]

THE COURT OF APPEAL: held that the Fleggs had an overriding interest by virtue of their actual occupation of Bleak House. Thus, their interest bound the bank and it could not repossess and sell the house.

THE HOUSE OF LORDS: overturned this decision. The mortgage, as a conveyance made by two trustees, Mr and Mrs Maxwell-Brown, overreached the Fleggs' beneficial interest under the trust. The building society therefore took their interest in Bleak House free from the Fleggs' equitable interest under the trust. They could repossess and sell the house.

THE REASONING: LORD TEMPLEMAN: "One of the main objects of the legislation of 1925 was to effect a compromise between on the one hand the interests of the public in securing that land held in trust is freely marketable and, on the other hand, the interests of the beneficiaries in preserving their rights under the trusts . . . By the Law of Property Act 1925 trustees . . . may convey land held on trust . . . discharged from the trusts . . . the only protection of the beneficiaries is that capital money must be paid to at least two trustees or a trust corporation . . . [S]ection 70 of the Land Registration Act 1925 [now replaced by schedule 3(2) Land Registration Act 2002] cannot have been intended to frustrate this compromise and to subject the purchaser to some beneficial interests but not others depending on the waywardness of actual occupation. The Court of Appeal took a different view, largely in reliance on the decision of this House in *Williams & Glyn's Bank Ltd v Boland* [1981] A.C. 487. In that case the sole proprietor of registered land held the land as sole trustee . . . for himself and his wife as tenants in common. This House held that the wife's beneficial interest coupled with actual possession by her constituted an overriding interest and that a mortgagee from the husband . . . took subject to the wife's overriding interest. But in that case the interest of the wife was not overreached . . . because the mortgagee advanced capital moneys to a sole trustee. If the wife's interest had been overreached by the mortgagee advancing capital money to two trustees there would have been nothing to justify the wife in remaining in occupation against the mortgagee. There must be a combination of an interest which justifies continuing occupation plus actual occupation to constitute an overriding interest. Actual occupation is not an interest in itself . . . .

For these reasons . . . I would allow this appeal and restore the order of [the judge] who ordered the respondents to deliver up Bleak House to the [building society]."

LECTURER: Why could Mr and Mrs Flegg not stay in possession of the house?

STUDENT: Because their interest in the house, their beneficial interest under a trust, was overreached by the mortgage executed by the two registered proprietors: Mr and Mrs Maxwell-Browne.

---

300 [1988] 1 A.C. 54.

LECTURER: But what is overreaching and how did it work in this case?

STUDENT: When the Maxwell-Brownes' executed a mortgage over Bleak House this was a "conveyance of a legal estate". The interest of the Fleggs was overreachable. It was a beneficial interest under a trust. So the effect of the conveyance was that the building society took their mortgage free from the Fleggs' interest. The Fleggs' beneficial interest was no longer in the land itself but existed in the money paid to the Maxwell-Brownes by the building society. It was unfortunate that they no longer had this money and had committed blatant and fraudulent breaches of trust.

LECTURER: Very good. Where what Lord Templeman (and the Law of Property Act) calls "capital money" arises, i.e. a house is sold, exchanged, or mortgaged in return for a loan of money, this money or substitute property must be paid to two trustees or a trust corporation. We will look below at the overreaching effect of a disposition where no capital money arises.

Now let's consider whether we think that overreaching is good or bad law. Hold the rules against our Building Blocks and say whether you think that they support or undermine the principles contained in the Building Blocks.

STUDENT: I think that there are many of our Building Blocks that will apply. On the basis of BUILDING BLOCK NO 2 overreaching is bad law. It permitted Mr and Mrs Maxwell-Browne to use their powers as the legal owners of Bleak House to render their parents homeless and to take away from them a substantial asset. The law should offer some protection against this kind of abuse of power.

BUILDING BLOCK NO 2: Ideas of Justice

Does overreaching, and how it arises, permit any violations of our ideas of justice?

LECTURER: But could we cross examine this Building Block. *Could the Fleggs have done anything to protect their own interests?* If so, it makes the case for the automatic protection of their interest less compelling.

STUDENT: So we must consider what means are available to them to protect their interest in Bleak House. They could have used "restrictions" to prevent the unlawful conduct of the registered proprietors: Land Registration Act 2002 s.42(1)(a).

LECTURER: How do you reach this conclusion?

STUDENT: They could have been advised, when all four first purchased Bleak House, to restrict Mr and Mrs Maxwell-Browne's powers of disposition so that they could not grant any more mortgages over the house. Then they could have applied to register a restriction against the title, in the Proprietorship Register, to this effect. This would mean that the registrar could not register any more mortgages—which would put off any lender because Bleak House could not be used as security for a loan.

LECTURER: So arguably the case does not undermine BUILDING BLOCK NO 2 as much as we first thought. In any case I think we can say that overreaching is good law on the basis of another of our Building Blocks.

STUDENT: BUILDING BLOCK NO 5.

> **BUILDING BLOCK NO 5: Property Rights and the Protection of Purchasers and Mortgage Lenders**
> The overreaching provisions allow a purchaser to take free from beneficial interests under a trust: quickly and easily.

LECTURER: As you see Lord Templeman in *City of London Building Society v Flegg* justified overreaching very strongly on the basis of BUILDING BLOCK NO 5. Can you say how?

STUDENT: He said that land should be freely marketable and a purchaser or mortgage lender should be able to rely on overreaching to take free from the beneficial interests and so obtain a clear title. This is as important for residential purchasers as it is for mortgage lenders. Without overreaching a purchaser or mortgage lender would have to make many more enquiries.

LECTURER: But is this premise for the argument is sound? You cite the idea that the 1925 policy is that a purchaser should take a good title without having to trouble himself with too many enquiries. You do not say what this means or challenge it. It is the weak point in your argument as it is a very lightweight bridge to drive your rather heavy conclusion across: that overreaching is good law. And we shall see later that there are points to be made against it. Let's unpack this idea of inquiry a bit more. If there is still a reasonable degree of protection given to the purchaser and the enquiries he must make are not onerous, then the conclusion that overreaching and *Flegg* is bad law would follow.

In 1925 what were the kinds of enquiry that a purchaser had to make when conveyancing with trusts?

> **So let's consider the idea of enquiry a bit more to see whether reform could be made.**

STUDENT: Prior to 1925, land was difficult to transfer and purchasers would often have to make exhaustive enquiries before they could get a good title. The way in which the courts interpreted the doctrine of constructive notice meant that purchasers would be put on notice of a trust if there was the merest mention of one anywhere in the chain of title deeds. They had to find out whether the trustees conveying the land were properly appointed, whether they had the power to make the transfer, whether the purchase money was properly applied. All this meant many enquiries.

LECTURER: And what was the consequence? What was the problem all these enquiries caused?

STUDENT: It cost money and took a great deal of time. The process of conveyancing was expensive. So overreaching was used to make these enquiries unnecessary. Where capital money arose under the transaction all the purchaser had to do was pay the purchase money to two trustees and he would take free from the beneficial interests.

LECTURER: This policy reason justifies the conclusion that overreaching still has an important function and we should think twice about reforming it?

STUDENT: Yes.

LECTURER: I feel it should be qualified in some way. It's too "black and white". You have to subject the idea of purchaser enquiries to a little cross-examination. Let's imagine that your idea of enquiry is in the dock. What questions would you ask it? Cross-examine it and see whether it justifies overreaching today. To help you out I will answer your questions on its behalf.

STUDENT: Are you still relevant today, i.e. without overreaching would a purchaser/ mortgage lender still have the same sorts of problem with enquiries?

LECTURER: Not in the same way. A purchaser would only be affected by the trust if the beneficiary was in actual occupation. Enquiries about the trustees' powers etc will no longer be relevant: s.26.

STUDENT: So is it easier for purchasers to find out about the beneficial interests?

LECTURER: Now you can fill in the gaps! What does LRA 2002 Sch.3(2) tell us about the extent to which a purchaser needs to enquire into equitable interests?

STUDENT: That an interest belonging to a person in actual occupation cannot bind as overriding unless it was within the actual knowledge of a purchaser or occupation could have been discovered on a reasonably careful inspection of the land. So a purchaser or mortgage lender must inspect the land "reasonably carefully" and if someone is in obvious occupation they must ask them about their rights, preferably obtaining a waiver.

LECTURER: So it may be arguable that enquiries now are less onerous than they were. Is this what you are arguing?

STUDENT: Yes.

LECTURER: And what does this mean for our overreaching argument?

STUDENT: That overreaching is less justifiable on the basis of 1925 policy of purchaser protection than I thought!

LECTURER: So if there are other things we can say about why overreaching might not be good law we are well justified in saying that ss.2 and 27 of the Law of Property Act 1925 ought to be reformed, at least to protect trust beneficiaries in occupation such as the *Fleggs*.[301]

At the time of the 1925 legislation, people did not want to occupy land. It was held usually for the purposes of investment. Land was often left by will to trustees for a number of beneficiaries, e.g. children or grandchildren, to provide them with an income. So all parties would be equally content if the land was sold by the trustees and the money held by them on trust instead.

What is the position now?

STUDENT: In our system of owner occupation people buy land for the purposes of occupation. Beneficiaries will not be equally content with an interest in the proceeds of sale or mortgage. If their interest is overreached by a sale or mortgage, they will not be able to remain in occupation. Thus, on the basis of BUILDING BLOCK NO 1 we can say that the overreaching rules are bad law.

---

301 See the arguments against overreaching in J.Stevens, "Is Justice a Priority in Priorities? The Re-introduction of Morality to Registered Conveyancing" in F.Meisel and P.Cook (eds), *Property and Protection* (Hart Publishing, 2000), p.177.

> **BUILDING BLOCK NO 1: Residential Security**
> Do the overreaching rules give adequate protection to Residential Security?

LECTURER: Also, the typical context in which the overreaching rules are considered now is when there has been a mortgage and the legal owners, the "two trustees", have defaulted on the payments due under a loan. So although the mortgage was a breach of trust and the beneficiaries can sue the trustees, the trustees (as in the case of the Maxwell-Browns) will no longer have any money with which to compensate the beneficiaries. In cases like *Flegg* it means that the beneficiaries have really and truly lost everything.

Following the decision in *Flegg*, the Law Commission proposed the reform that beneficiaries in occupation of the land, such as the Fleggs, should be required to consent to the overreaching of their interests.[302] However, the proposed reforms were never enacted into law.

> "First, the exclusively financial protection given by the 1925 legislation is no longer appropriate for occupiers of their own homes; their real concern is often with the enjoyment of the property itself which will be lost after overreaching. Secondly, as the general understanding of many of the beneficiaries with whom we are concerned is that they are joint owners, they should have appropriate ownership rights. There is scant justification for the law giving preference to the wishes of one joint owner over those of another, simply because the former was constituted trustee of the legal estate. Thirdly, it is unsatisfactory that the consequences which a sale visits upon a beneficiary in occupation are different depending whether the legal estate happens to have been vested in one, or in more than one, person."

(3) It is not necessary for capital money to arise under the transaction before overreaching can take effect

In *State Bank of India v Sood*[303] the question of overreaching arose in the context of a mortgage of land by trustees holding for several beneficiaries. The mortgage had been executed over the land in order to secure an overdraft facility. Thus, strictly speaking no "capital money" arose at all in the transaction. The trustees received no money so the question in the case was whether this precluded overreaching. Peter Gibson L.J. in the Court of Appeal held that it was not necessary for capital money to arise in order for overreaching to take effect.

> "I accept that a novel and important point of law is raised by this appeal. Lending institutions regularly take security from businessmen in the form of a legal charge on property (which very frequently means that the matrimonial home is charged) to secure existing and future

---

302   The Law Commission, *Transfer of Land, Overreaching: Beneficiaries in Occupation* (Law Com No.188 (1989)), para.3.5. Footnotes are omitted.
303   [1997] Ch. 276.

indebtedness, and very commonly that property will be registered land held by two registered proprietors on trust . . . with no restriction registered in respect of their power to transfer or mortgage that property. It was not suggested that it had ever been the practice of mortgagees to make enquiries of occupiers of the property as to any claimed rights."[304]

(4) Certain interests that arise under the doctrine of proprietary estoppel are overreachable

In *Birmingham Midshires Mortgage Services Ltd v Sabherwal*[305] Mrs Sabherwal claimed an interest in the house under the doctrine of proprietary estoppel.[306] As you know these rights arise on similar grounds to rights under a constructive trust.[307] They are not, strictly speaking, interests under a trust. So one question was whether Mrs Sabherwal's interest was capable of being overreached. The court held that the interest was overreachable.

This depends on the type of estoppel right in question. If the right is by way of an estoppel easement[308] or right of such a nature then it will not be overreachable. Rights that arise in the same or similar context to "family-type" rights, such as interests in a house acquired under the doctrine of resulting or constructive trust, were overreachable.[309] Trusts have always been overreachable and there is no reason why a right acquired in very similar circumstances should not also be overreachable.

A purchaser or mortgage lender's personal liability

8

A. THE LAND REGISTRATION ACT 2002 CANNOT BE USED AS AN INSTRUMENT OF FRAUD

In previous sections we have considered the rules that decide which interests in land have priority over the estate or interest of the registered proprietor of a registrable estate, interest or charge. It remains the case that no legal form, even the well-protected *registrable disposition*, can remain standing where fraud is established. A statute cannot be used as an engine of fraud.[310]

---

304   [1997] Ch. 276, p.285.

305   (2000) 80 P. & C.R. 256; C.Harpum (2000) 116 L.Q.R. 341.

306   See *Gillett v Holt* [2001] Ch.210.

307   See Chapter 3.

308   For example *ER Ives Investment Ltd v High* [1967] 2 Q.B. 379.

309   See also *Sommer v Sweet* [2005] EWCA Civ 227, which confirmed this analysis.

310   This doctrine, the rule in *Rochefoucauld v Boustead* [1897] 1 Ch. 196, which we considered in Chapter 3 was applied directly in the context of registered land in *Lyus v Prowsa Developments* [1982] 1 W.L.R. 1044.

> **Example**
> A is the registered proprietor of an estate and has granted X an option to purchase the estate on favourable terms. A sells the estate to B. Under s.29 of the Land Registration Act 2002, as you know, when registered as proprietor of the estate B takes the estate free from all prior interests in the land that are not either registered against the title or overriding interests. However, if X can establish that B purchased the land and committed a "fraud" in attempting to use s.29 to take free from X's estate contract, then the judge will set aside s.29 and make B take his registered estate subject to X's option.

B. THE FRAUD DOCTRINE

The rule was applied in *Rochefoucauld v Boustead*.[311] The plaintiff owned estates in Ceylon and entered into an oral agreement with the defendant. He was to take a transfer of the estates and hold them on trust for the plaintiff. After conveyance of the estates to the defendant, he denied that the plaintiff had any claim to the estate. The arrangement had not been put in writing, and under the Statute of Frauds 1677, was void. It was held that the defendant could not plead the statute in order to allow him to defeat the plaintiff's right and keep the land for himself. Lindley L.J. observed that

> "The Statute of Frauds does not prevent the proof of a fraud; and . . . it is a fraud on the part of a person to whom land is conveyed as a trustee, and who knows it was so conveyed, to deny the trust and claim the land himself."[312]

Rochefoucauld was applied in *Bannister v Bannister*.[313] In this case the defendant owned two adjacent cottages. She agreed to sell them at a reduced price to her brother-in-law. He orally undertook to allow her to live in one of the cottages rent free for as long as she wished. And because of this he obtained the cottages at "a bargain price". The conveyance of the cottages to her brother-in-law did not contain the terms of the oral understanding. The agreement required writing in order to be enforceable. After the transfer he attempted to evict the claimant. However, Scott L.J. dismissing the claim for possession (on appeal by the brother in law) stated that

> "[A] constructive trust is raised against a person who insists on the absolute character of a conveyance to himself for the purpose of defeating the beneficial interest, which, according to the true bargain, was to belong to another."[314]

---

311   [1897] 1 Ch. 196. See also *In re Duke of Marlborough* [1894] 2 Ch. 133; *Lincoln v Wright* 4 De. G. & J. 16; *Haigh v Kaye* L.R. 7 Ch. 469; *Heard v Pilley* L.R. 4 Ch. 548.

312   [1897] 1 Ch. 196, p.206, per Lindley L.J. The rule does not require fraudulent intent at the time of the conveyance. It is enough "when the absolute quality of the conveyance is set up for the purpose of defeating the beneficial interest": *Bannister v Bannister* [1948] 2 All E.R. 133.

313   [1948] 2 All E.R. 133.

314   [1948] 2 All E.R. 133, p.136.

It was considered material that the defendant would not have sold the cottages at a reduced price to her brother-in-law *but for* his undertaking.[315] The conveyance was not made voluntarily, but under the influence of the undertaking.[316]

A similar case applying the fraud doctrine is *Pallant v Morgan*.[317] The agents of two neighbouring landowners were both intending to bid for property in an auction. They entered into an agreement immediately before the auction that the plaintiff's agent should not bid and that the defendant would acquire the land and divide it between himself and the plaintiff. The defendant's agent obtained the property as agreed and refused to honour the agreement. The agreement would have otherwise failed for lack of certainty. However, Harman J. refused to allow the defendant to plead this rule of law and held that the defendant held the property on trust for them jointly.[318] Harman J. held that it would be fraudulent for the defendant to retain the whole of the property in denial of the agreement. The finding of fact that appeared material to the judge's decision was that the defendant's agent's conduct influenced the plaintiff's agent's action not to bid at the auction: "I do not think he would have acted in the way he did unless he at least thought he had reached such an agreement".[319]

C. THE BASIS OF THE FINDING OF "FRAUD"—CONTROL, INFLUENCE AND BUILDING BLOCK NO 2: IDEAS OF JUSTICE

Story observes: "If the means of personal control are given, they must be always restrained to purposes of good faith and personal good". This appears to spell out the basis of the fraud doctrine.[320] In each of the above cases the material finding appeared to be that the legal owner, e.g. the brother-in-law in *Bannister*, the defendant's agent in *Pallant v Morgan*, and the transferee of the Ceylon estates in *Rochefoucauld* all acquired an ascendancy over the affairs of another by influence, e.g. a promise that the claimant could live in one of the cottages for life, or that property would be acquired effectively for a *joint* venture, or that *in reality* they would hold the land in trust for the claimant. Influence was demonstrated by the fact that the claimant had relied on this and the defendants had effective control over the situation once the conveyance had been made. They could now profit personally from that control.

---

315 "She would not have sold the two cottages to the plaintiff . . . if the plaintiff had not agreed to let her stay in No.30 as long as she liked rent free": above, p.134. It was found that the defendant sold the cottages at a price that was three-eighths below the contemporary market value, above, p.134, "and that, but for this undertaking, the defendant would not have sold the two cottages to the plaintiff at what, on the uncontradicted evidence of value, he rightly described as 'a bargain price' ": above, p.135.

316 See also, Gray and Gray, *Elements of Land Law*, 3rd edn (London: Butterworths, 2001), pp.705–6.

317 [1952] Ch. 43, applying *Chattock v Muller* 8 Ch.D. 177.

318 [1952] Ch. 43, p.47.

319 [1952] Ch. 43, p.47. The headnote describes this as "the true view" of the situation. In the similar fact case of *Banner Homes Group Plc v Luff Developments Ltd* [2000] 2 W.L.R. 772, the Court of Appeal reached the same result on the basis that it was "inequitable for the acquiring party to retain the property for himself in a manner inconsistent with the arrangement or understanding on which the non-acquiring party has acted" (pp.794–5): Gray and Gray, *Elements of Land Law*, p.709.

320 Story, *Commentaries on Equity Jurisprudence* (1834, first English ed. 1884, repr. 1988), para.308.

D. WHAT CONSTITUTES A "FRAUD" IN A LAND REGISTRATION CONTEXT?

In *Lyus v Prowsa Developments Ltd*[321] the fraud doctrine was applied to land registration. Development land was owned subject to a mortgage. The owners then entered into a contract to build a house on one of the plots for the claimants (an estate contract). The owners went insolvent and the mortgagees under their power of sale sold the estate to Prowsa Developments. Although the mortgagees had the power to transfer the estate free from the claimant's estate contract, which was in fact registered, because their mortgage had been granted prior to the estate contract and thus took priority over it, the estate was conveyed to Prowsa Developments expressly "subject to" the estate contract. Applying *Midland Bank Trust Co v Green*[322] Dillon J reasoned that it is not fraud to rely upon one's strict legal right to take free from an interest.[323] However, where the purchaser genuinely agrees to give effect to the prior interest in the land he thereby confers a fresh right on the interest-holder. Dillon J. distinguished *Miles v Bull (No.2)*[324] on the basis that a "subject to" clause in that case was inserted routinely for the protection of the vendor, e.g. to ensure compliance with his duty of disclosure, rather than with any intention on either part of binding the purchaser.[325] *Lyus* was approved by Fox L.J. in *Ashburn Anstalt v Arnold*.[326] If fraud is established in this way the law imposes a constructive trust on the purchaser to hold his registered disposition subject to the rights of the claimant.

Fraud may be recognised where a purchaser has given representations that he will give effect to the rights of the claimant and this has induced "a false sense of security as to the purchaser's intention".[327]

> So if B in our example had told X "don't worry about registering your right—I will make sure you can exercise your option" and X, not being particularly familiar with either commerce or land registration, relied on this and took no further action, then B may have to abide by that representation. The title to B's estate would be held to be bound by X's option.

LECTURER: What do you think of *Lyus v Prowsa Developments*?

STUDENT: I am glad that the purchasers were made to take the estate subject to the claimants' right.

LECTURER: But let's look a little closer. What we need to do is measure the facts of the case against our articulated idea of fraud above.

---

321   [1982] 1 W.L.R. 1044.
322   [1981] A.C. 513.
323   [1982] 1 W.L.R. 1044, p.1054, per Dillon J.
324   [1969] 3 All E.R. 1585.
325   Also *Hollington Bros. Ltd v Rhodes* (1951) 2 T.L.R. 691.
326   [1989] Ch. 1.
327   Gray and Gray, *Elements of Land Law*, p.1066 quoting *Holt, Renfrew & Co Ltd v Henry Singer Ltd* (1982) 135 D.L.R. (3d) 391, p.410; also *Loke Yew v Port Swettenham Rubber Co Ltd* [1913] A.C. 491.

> **The point at which the law intervenes**
>
> In each of the above cases the material finding appeared to be that the legal owner, e.g. the brother-in-law in *Bannister*, the defendant's agent in *Pallant v Morgan*, and the transferee of the Ceylon estates in *Rochefoucauld* all acquired an ascendancy over the affairs of another by influence, e.g. a promise that the claimant could live in one of the cottages for life, or that property would be acquired effectively for a *joint* venture, or that *in reality* they would hold the land in trust for the claimant. Influence was demonstrated by the fact that the claimant had relied on this and the defendants now had effective control over the situation, and could profit personally from that control. The law then intervened at this point to stop the defendants, the legal owners, from taking advantage of this control.

LECTURER: So we need to look for the element of reliance that shows that the conveyance to the purchasers was influenced by the purchaser's undertaking that they would give effect to the claimant's estate contract.

STUDENT: The claimants themselves have not lost anything. The mortgagee had priority to their estate contract in any case and could convey the estate to a purchaser free from it. It is also true that the claimants themselves did not rely on the word of the purchaser.[328]

LECTURER: No, but in the same sense, a beneficiary does not rely on the word of his chosen trustee when an express trust is first created. Remember that it is the *settlor* who conveys the property to the trustee and exacts the representation that the latter will hold it for another. It is the settlor who places reliance in his trustee.[329] And once the conveyance is complete the trustee has the power to abuse the trust and keep the property. But the courts hold him to it because, as Lord Nottingham once articulated, to do otherwise would allow "manifest fraud" if the settlor's wishes were not carried out.[330] The courts have never had any difficulty here about deciding that a trustee holds for a *third party*.[331] Can you draw a parallel here?

STUDENT: So maybe it is not so much what the claimants have lost but what the defendants' gained and how they gained it.

LECTURER: I would say so yes.

STUDENT: They promised to take subject to the claimant's rights and we can say that the conveyance was exacted on that basis. The selling mortgagees clearly stipulated for this and the purchasers agreed. So the conveyance was made in reliance on the defendants' representation that they would give effect to the claimant's estate contract.

---

328 Another valid question that has arisen is whether the rule in *Rochefoucauld* should be applied to force a transferee to hold on trust, not for the transferor (as in *Rochefoucauld* and *Bannister v Bannister*) but for a third party: T.Youdan, [1984] C.L.J. 306; Feltham [1987] Conv. 246; Youdan [1988] Conv. 267. See M.P.Thompson [1985] C.L.J. 280.

329 That this is the true nature of the trust see F.W.Maitland, *Lectures in Equity* (1936), pp.43–4.

330 *Mildmay & Duckett's Case*, cited and quoted by Yale, "The Revival of Equitable Estates in the Seventeenth Century: An explanation by Lord Nottingham" [1957] C.L.J. 72.

331 See the views of M.P.Thompson [1985] C.L.J. 280.

> **The relevance of undervalue**
> It is not necessary that the conveyance is made at an undervalue but this may provide evidence that the transferor was influenced by the purchaser's representation. It was a significant factor in *Bannister v Bannister*: see Gray and Gray, *Elements of Land Law*, pp.1065–6.

LECTURER: Remember the factor that we are looking for is *ascendency*, i.e. that the defendant has influenced the actions of the transferor—has now, because of this influence effective control over the interests of the transferor/claimant. Let's look at BUILDING BLOCK NO 2 and see whether we can ask some questions about this idea and how it applies to *Lyus v Prowsa Developments*.

> **BUILDING BLOCK NO 2: Ideas of Justice**
> Rules are good and fair if they take account of the idea that every person should be accorded the freedom of their will and autonomous choice. Thus, if people deal with each other and with their property in a way that violates the will of another then the law should offer that other some remedy.

STUDENT: I think that the idea of fraud, as we have articulated above, *itself* reflects these notions of moral justice. In *Bannister v Bannister*, the brother-in-law made a representation that if the defendant conveyed the cottages to him she could live in one of the cottages for her lifetime. She relied on this and made the conveyance. She could do nothing once the conveyance had been made. He had ascendancy over her will—she wouldn't have made the conveyance *but for* the representation—and he was not permitted to profit from the control that he had thus gained from being the absolute legal owner. We can legitimately say that this is good law on the basis of BUILDING BLOCK NO 2.

LECTURER: And the same observations may be made of *Rochefoucauld v Boustead* and *Pallant v Morgan*, e.g. the plaintiff's agent in the latter case refrained from bidding at an auction in his principal's interest on the basis of a representation that the defendant's agent would acquire the property for them jointly.

Do you think *Lyus v Prowsa Developments* has the same features as these cases?

STUDENT: Well there is a simple way of protecting an estate contract from being destroyed on a transfer, i.e. by registering it as a notice. In many cases I feel that it would be difficult to establish that the purchaser, by their representations, had gained the necessary influence over a claimant's affairs, whether or not they themselves were the transferor, where they could have taken this simple expedient to look after their own interest. Estate contracts are not like trusts, they are created formally and it is thus reasonable to expect the claimant to register their right.

LECTURER: Although on the unusual facts of *Lyus* registration of the estate contract would have made no difference because the selling mortgagee acquired their interest first and could thus sell free from subsequent rights. But I agree that in most cases that involve unregistered rights such as estate contracts, the necessary element of influence may be lacking. Thus, it would be an improper application of the fraud doctrine.

> "The mortgagee says to the execution creditor, 'You are not prejudiced, for you knew of my security.' The execution creditor replies, 'I knew that you had a security, but you knew the law as well as I.'"
>
> Per James L.J. in *Edwards v Edwards* 2 Ch.D. 291, quoted by Lord Cozens-Hardy M.R. in *In re Monolithic Building Company, Tacon v The Company* [1915] 1 Ch. 643, p.666.

E. A BROADER APPROACH?

There are a number of commonwealth authorities cited by Gray and Gray, which purport to apply the fraud doctrine in much broader circumstances, e.g. where there are certain "irregularities" within a transfer then this might invalidate it on the fraud ground. A purchaser has been held to take subject to an interest that he would otherwise take free from, for example, *Efstratiou, Glantschnig and Petrovic v Glantschnig*[332] in which

> "with inordinate speed, a disaffected husband transferred his registered title in the matrimonial home to a friend [the purpose being] . . . to defeat the unprotected equitable rights of the transferor's wife as a beneficiary behind a trust".[333]

However, these cases are broader and out of line with the cases applying the fraud doctrine over centuries. It is submitted that these cases might be better described as the application of a criteria that a purchaser must act "in good faith". Indeed *Efstratiou* resembles the way in which Lord Wilberforce defined "good faith" in *Midland Bank Trust Co v Green*.[334] It must be noted however, that "bad faith" and "fraud" are two entirely different bases for liability. Indeed, Lord Wilberforce stated that there is no place for a requirement of "good faith" in the Land Charges Act 1972 (unregistered land) but confirmed the view that once fraud was established any statute could be set aside. It is clear from the terms of ss.29 and 30 of the Land Registration Act 2002 that a purchaser, or other registered disponee, who gives valuable consideration does not have to act "in good faith".[335] The fraud doctrine in the narrow sense as defined above, is however, preserved.[336]

---

332   [1972] N.Z.L.R. 594 (NZCA), see Gray and Gray, above, p.1063.

333   Footnotes omitted.

334   [1981] A.C. 513.

335   See Cooke and O'Connor, "Purchaser Liability to Third Parties in the English Land Registration System: A Comparative Perspective" (2004) 120 L.Q.R. 640.

336   Law Commission *Land Registration for the Twenty-First Century* (Law Com. No.254, 1998) and Law Commission, *Land Registration for the Twenty-First Century – A Conveyancing Revolution* (Law Com. No.271, 2001), para.4.11.

In any case, such cases as *Efstratiou* are well catered-for under the Land Registration Act 2002. The wife could have established an overriding interest under Sch.3(2)[337] and, had the husband appointed a second trustee, the purchaser was clearly aware that his seller was holding the house on trust for his wife. Thus, he would arguably be liable as what we call an "intermeddler". A detailed description of this basis of personal liability properly belongs in a book on Equity and Trusts. But briefly: there are two doctrines by which an intermeddler is personally liable to the beneficiaries: the doctrine of recipient liability and the doctrine of dishonest assistance in a breach of trust. The doctrine of recipient liability requires the purchaser to have knowledge of a breach of trust, and the knowledge must be of such a nature as to make it unconscionable for the recipient to retain the benefit of the receipt, i.e. the house. In such cases the purchaser holds the property on constructive trust for the beneficiary.[338]

F. CRITICAL THINKING: A COACH AND HORSES OR A WELCOME MORAL ELEMENT?

There have been fears that at its very worst this "fraud" doctrine could drive a coach and horses through the logic of land registration, i.e. that a purchaser, when registered as proprietor, takes free from all unregistered rights with the exception of overriding interests.[339] However, it must be remembered that this constructive trust is imposed on the *conscience of the purchaser*. It is not a case of a property right surviving a transaction with the land so that it binds all future purchasers, or of the purchaser taking subject to a right of which he has notice. This is personal liability. *This particular purchaser* has a bad conscience so that the claimant has a right against *his* registered estate.[340] In one sense it is refreshing to see an element of conscience and morality in a system of conveyancing that is essentially amoral.[341]

LECTURER: So if in this final section we take a little bit of licence for a moment. Do you think that the fraud doctrine has any scope to operate at all in the context of land registration?

STUDENT: In most cases involving expressly created rights that can be protected through registration as a notice they come into being expressly. It is reasonable to expect a claimant

---

337 See e.g. Cooke and O'Connor, above.

338 *Bank of Credit and Commerce International (Overseas) Ltd v Akindele* [2001] Ch. 437. For comment on the intermeddling doctrines in the context of land registration, see Cooke and O'Connor, "Purchaser Liability to Third Parties in the English Land Registration System: A Comparative Perspective" (2004) 120 L.Q.R. 640, suggesting that the concept should be applied restrictively. Again this is a species of personal liability that is preserved under the Land Registration Act 2002: Law Commission, *Land Registration for the Twenty-First Century – A Conveyancing Revolution* (Law Com. No.271, 2001).

339 Kenny, "Constructive Trusts of Registered Land" (1983) 46 M.L.R. 96; Harpum, "Constructive Trusts and Registered Land" [1983] C.L.J. 54.

340 See *Creque v Penn* [2007] UKPC 44.

341 Wade argues that "[t]he policy of 1925 was to abandon the equitable principle of notice in favour of the mechanical principle of registration. This was a shift from a moral to an amoral basis": "Land Charges Registration Reviewed" [1956] C.L.J. 216, p.277; also J.Stevens, "Is Justice a Priority in Priorities? Law Reform and the Re-introduction of Morality to Registered Conveyancing" in *Property and Protection*, p.177.

to protect their own interests. Therefore, it could only rarely be established that a transferor was legitimately reliant on a representation made by a purchaser to respect the rights of the third party. That third party could have acted in their own interests to make sure the purchaser took subject to their rights.

LECTURER: In any case, following the introduction of electronic conveyancing an expressly created interest will have to be created electronically and simultaneously registered. After this point the fraud doctrine will be unlikely to apply to expressly created interests outside of the unusual facts of *Lyus v Prowsa Developments*. The same argument would apply to substantively registrable leases, easements and profits.

What about other interests?

STUDENT: Well, leases of seven years or less are overriding, as are impliedly granted easements and profits.

LECTURER: What about trusts?

STUDENT: They are protected as overriding interests where the beneficiary is in actual and discoverable occupation. I think this will cover a significant number of cases. It is possible that the fraud doctrine might apply where either the interest would otherwise be overreached, or where the beneficiary is not in occupation. However, where the purchaser has knowledge that the transfer is in breach of trust to such a degree that makes it unconscionable to take free from the trust, which may well be the case if they have promised to take the estate "subject to" the trust, then they will be personally liable under the doctrine of "recipient liability" (see above).

LECTURER: So not only will the land registration system reduce the possibility of cases like *Lyus* arising, but, with almost all other interests in land they are either overriding or a purchaser will have personal liability under the "recipient liability" doctrine.

STUDENT: Registered land has its bases covered already!

Alteration of the land register

9

Because of the effect of substantive registration with absolute title, i.e. to vest ownership of the estate, interest or charge in the registered proprietor, irrespective of whether they were so entitled under the principles of unregistered land law,[342] there must be some provision made for altering the register in order, e.g. to correct mistakes. In order to make the land register more conclusive Sch.4 provides that where there are grounds for alteration,[343] it must be done unless there are exceptional circumstances which justify an alteration not being made.[344] Where alteration of the register amounts to what the 2002 Act defines as "rectification" then in order

---

342   *Re 139 High Street, Deptford* [1951] Ch. 884.
343   Land Registration Act 2002 s.65.
344   Sch.4(3)(3) and 6(3); Law Commission, *Land Registration for the Twenty-First Century* (Law Com. No.254, 1998).

not to disturb the title of a registered proprietor in possession of the land Sch.4 makes it more difficult to alter the register in a way that affects his title without his consent.[345] A person suffering loss as a result of rectification or non-rectification may be entitled to an indemnity payment.[346]

A. GROUNDS FOR ALTERATION OF THE LAND REGISTER

Schedule 4(2) provides that "the court may make an order for alteration of the register for the purpose of (a) correcting a mistake, (b) bringing the register up to date, or (c) giving effect to any estate, right or interest excepted from the effect of registration". If the court has power to make such an order "it must do so, unless there are exceptional circumstances which justify its not doing so".[347] Schedule 4(5) provides that "the registrar may alter the register for the purpose of (a) correcting a mistake, (b) bringing the register up to date, (c) giving effect to any estate, right or interest excepted from the effect of registration, or (d) removing a superfluous entry". If the registrar has power to make such an alteration he must do so "unless there are exceptional circumstances which justify not making the alteration".[348]

(1) Mistake

The register may be altered to correct a mistake. Examples of a mistaken registration would be: where a person is registered as proprietor of land to which he is not entitled[349]; where a person is registered as proprietor under a forged transfer of the land[350]; where a interest, e.g. a restrictive covenant, that was binding on the title, had by mistake not been entered on the register[351]; or conversely, where an interest had been entered as a notice, but the interest itself was invalid.[352] "Mistake" has been interpreted broadly.[353] The ground does not just apply to mistakes of a procedural nature. The mistake does not have to have been made by the Land Registry. In *Cygnet Healthcare v Greenswan Consultants Ltd*[354] the parties to the conveyance had mistakenly failed to create an interest. The estate was then registered without it.[355]

---

345 Sch.4(3)(2) and (6)(2); Law Com. No.254, 1998.

346 Land Registration Act 2002 Sch.8.

347 Sch.4(3)(3). This duty applies whether to a rectification (para.3(3)) or to an ordinary alteration: Land Registration Rules 2003, r.126. No similar rules were made regarding ordinary alteration by the registrar, see below.

348 Sch.4(6)(3).

349 *Chowood Ltd v Lyall (No. 2)* [1930] 2 Ch. 156. In *Baxter v Mannion* [2010] EWHC 573 (Ch); [2010] 1 W.L.R. 1965, affirmed on appeal [2011] EWCA Civ 1120, the register was altered against someone who was never entitled to be registered as proprietor.

350 *Norwich and Peterborough Building Society v Steed* [1993] Ch. 116. *Barclays Bank Plc v Guy* [2008] EWCA Civ 452—where land is mistakenly registered and then sold on, this has not been regarded as a "mistaken registration". Thus, there was no alteration.

351 *Rees v Peters* [2011] EWCA Civ 836; [2011] 2 P. & C.R. 18.

352 For further elaboration see Harpum, Bridge, Dixon, *Megarry & Wade Law of Real Property*, para.7–133.

353 *Baxter v Mannion* [2010] EWHC 573 (Ch); [2010] 1 W.L.R. 1965, affirmed on appeal [2011] EWCA Civ 1120. A person was registered as proprietor on the basis of adverse possession but could not establish the required period of possession for that doctrine. The register was rectified against them. This was the correction of a mistake.

354 [2009] EWHC 1318.

355 See Dixon, *Modern Land Law*, 7th edn (Routledge, 2010), p.85.

Although where a person is registered under a forged transfer this can amount to a "mistaken registration" the position was different in *Barclays Bank Plc v Guy*[356] in which the proprietor had signed a deed of transfer but it was released and registered prematurely, and possibly fraudulently, without the owner's authority. Because of the deed and the fact it was signed when the transfer was registered, the new proprietor was entitled to the full effect of s.58 and to exercise owners powers. He executed a charge to secure a large sum and the charge was held to be perfectly valid and genuine.[357] Thus, there was no "mistaken" registration of the charge. The reason was that the original fraudulent transfer was voidable not void and the transfer had not been set aside at the time of the charge. The chargee was entitled to rely on the full effects of registration. It was thought that even if the chargee had known that there may be problems with the title this would not provide grounds for alteration.

(2) Bringing the register up to date

It may be necessary to update the register, for example where the court determines that a person is entitled to an interest in the land.[358]

(3) Giving effect to any estate, right or interest excepted from the effect of registration

Where a person is registered with a title less than absolute, i.e. qualified or possessory, he takes subject to certain unregistered interests and identified defects in title. These may be entered on the register under this ground. For example, qualified title may be awarded if, on application for first registration, the "root of title" established is less than 15 years.[359] It may transpire that had title been established for the full 15 years there would be an interest that binds the land. The register can be altered to reflect this position.

(4) Removing a superfluous entry

In *Stein v Stein*[360] a restriction was removed on this ground. Another example would be the removal of a lease that has come to an end.

B. WHAT AMOUNTS TO "EXCEPTIONAL CIRCUMSTANCES"?

Under the jurisdiction to alter the register there is an obligation to do so "unless there are exceptional circumstances".[361] This is a question of fact. In *Derbyshire County Council v Fallon*,[362] the proprietors were mistakenly registered with part of the Council's land. However, because they had already built on the land, no alteration was made. These were exceptional circumstances.

---

356 [2008] EWHC 893 (Ch).
357 See also the Court of Appeal *Guy v Barclays Bank Plc* [2010] EWCA Civ 1396; [2011] 1 W.L.R. 681.
358 ibid.
359 *Megarry & Wade The Law of Real Property* above, para.7–035.
360 [2004] EWHC 3212.
361 Land Registration Act 2002, Sch.4(3)(3) and 4(6)(3). Where the land register is altered pursuant to a court order, this rule applies whether the alteration amounts to rectification or not: Sch.4(3)(1) (rectifications), Land Registration Rules 2003, r.126 (ordinary alterations), but where the alteration is made otherwise than pursuant to a court order, the rule applies only to rectifications. For the distinction between "alteration" and "rectification" see immediately below.
362 [2007] EWHC 1326.

C. WHERE AN ALTERATION AMOUNTS TO "RECTIFICATION"

The Land Registration Act 2002 draws a distinction between alterations that do and don't amount to "rectification". Where alteration of the register amounts to what the 2002 Act defines as "rectification" then a person suffering loss as a result of rectification or non-rectification may be entitled to an indemnity payment.[363] It is also *rectification* that triggers the protection against alteration of the register given to the registered proprietor in possession.[364] Schedule 4(1) defines "rectification" as "alteration which (a) involves the correction of a mistake, and (b) prejudicially affects the title of a registered proprietor." We have examined what amounts to a mistaken registration above. Part (b) means that the registered proprietor would suffer some loss if the register were altered, e.g. the registrar may change the register to allocate part of the land to a neighbour because it was mistakenly registered to the wrong title.[365] There is no prejudice where title is altered to give effect to an interest that already bound that title, i.e. an overriding interest.[366]

(1) A person registered as proprietor under a forged transfer

A person who is an innocent victim of a forged transfer of land, subsequently registered, may face the possibility that the register will be altered against him on the application of the person originally entitled *but for* the registration, or by order of the court. Where a person is registered as proprietor under a forged transfer, this is a mistaken registration,[367] so alteration is a possibility. So what we need to know is whether such an alteration amounts to a "rectification" first, for the protection that is applied to registered proprietors when in possession of the land, and secondly, so as to ascertain whether the mistakenly registered proprietor would be entitled to an indemnity payment if the register were rectified against him.

Therefore if a person has been registered as proprietor under such a transfer, our question is whether any alteration of the register in favour of the person who would otherwise be the true owner would "prejudicially affect the title" of the registered proprietor. If he acquires full ownership through registration, the intended effect of substantive registration since at least 1857,[368] something would be taken away from him and he would thus suffer loss.[369] However, if the view in *Malory Enterprises Ltd v Cheshire Homes (UK) Ltd*[370] were accepted, i.e. that a forged transfer is not a "disposition" resulting in priority protection,[371] then the registered proprietor

---

363   Land Registration Act 2002, Sch.8.
364   Land Registration Act 2002, Sch.4(3)(1) and 4(6)(1).
365   *Re 139 Deptford High Street* [1951] Ch. 884.
366   *Re Chowood's Registered Land* [1933] Ch.574.
367   See for example Harpum, Bridge, Dixon, *Megarry & Wade Law of Real Property*, para.7.133.
368   See section 1 in this Chapter above.
369   Thompson, *Modern Land Law*, p.157 also takes this point.
370   [2002] Ch. 216.
371   The position appears to be different where the person registered as proprietor as a result of the fraud then deals with the land. In *Guy v Barclays Bank Plc* [2010] EWCA Civ 1396; [2011] 1 W.L.R. 681, a registered estate was transferred without the authority of the proprietor. The new registered proprietor then executed a charge on the land. Rectification of the register was refused. The charge, having been executed by a registered proprietor with the statutory powers was "valid and genuine".

takes subject to the claims of the "true" owner in any case. He thus suffers no "prejudice" or loss if the register were altered to reflect these claims. At least as far as indemnities are concerned Sch.8(1)(2)(b) provides that "the proprietor of a registered estate or charge claiming in good faith under a forged disposition is, where the register is rectified, to be regarded as having suffered loss by reason of such rectification as if the disposition had not been forged". Thus, a person registered as proprietor under a forged transfer is entitled to be indemnified by the registrar. Arguably however, such a person may not be regarded as suffering loss for the purposes of the protection afforded to a "proprietor in possession".[372]

D. ALTERATION AGAINST A PROPRIETOR IN POSSESSION: CRITICAL THINKING

We have seen above that the provisions that allow for the land register to be altered reflect the idea that the register should be as accurate as possible. It should reflect the state of the title and interests against that title with accuracy. Thus, alterations should be made unless there are "exceptional circumstances".

> **BUILDING BLOCK NO 8: Statutory rules should give effect to the purpose behind their enactment**
> We can criticise a statutory rule, i.e. we can say that it is a good or bad rule, on the basis of whether it achieves parliament's objectives behind its enactment.

> Remember that the Law Commission stated that "The fundamental objective of the [Act] is that . . . the register should be a complete and accurate reflection of the state of the title of the land at any given time, so that it is possible to investigate title to land . . . with the absolute minimum of additional enquiries and inspections": Law Com No.271, paras 1.5–1.6.

LECTURER: So far then is Sch.4 good law?

STUDENT: Yes, because a registered proprietor gets full ownership through *being registered as proprietor*, there must be some way of correcting the land register, e.g. because he may have been registered as proprietor by mistake, or with more land than (under ordinary principles) he is entitled to. Also, the register of title may be out of date, e.g. an interest may be registered that is no longer valid. So the register will not accurately reflect the interests that bind the title.

---

372   See below.

LECTURER: So is Sch.4 good law? Make sure you relate your observations to the question.

STUDENT: Yes, because it allows the court and the registrar to make changes to the land register in order to make it more accurate. And there is a duty to make these changes in the absence of "exceptional circumstances". This law supports BUILDING BLOCK NO 8 – It achieves parliament's objectives behind the enactment of the Land Registration Act 2002, as revealed in the statement of the Law Commission.

LECTURER: But I want you to think now about who might be *adversely* affected by alteration of the register.

STUDENT: Well, the absolute worst case scenario is where someone is a registered proprietor and his title is altered he may find that he no longer owns part or even the whole of the land.

LECTURER: This might be particularly difficult for a registered proprietor who has been in possession of the land for some time.

STUDENT: Looking at BUILDING BLOCK NO 1 the law should give some protection to a person in possession of the land.

BUILDING BLOCK NO 1: Residential Security

Land Law rules should protect a person's residential security. The expectation of continued stability is strong within a person. Atiyah considers that "[e]xpectations based on, and allied with, physical possession, seemed, in a stable society, to be the most natural type of expectation to be protected": P.S.Atiyah, *The Rise and Fall of Freedom of Contract*, p.109.

Accordingly, where the alteration affects the title of a proprietor in possession it should not be made without the consent of that proprietor unless "he has by fraud or lack of proper care caused or substantially contributed to the mistake, or it would for any other reason be unjust for the alteration not to be made".[373] However, this protection applies only where an alteration amounts to "rectification" under Sch.4(1),[374] i.e. it "involves the correction of a mistake, and prejudicially affects the title of a registered proprietor".[375]

> Section 131 defines a "proprietor in possession". "Land is in the possession of the proprietor of a registered estate in land if it is physically in his possession". In the case of (a) landlord and tenant; (b) mortgagor and mortgagee; (c) licensor and licensee; (d) trustee and beneficiary, "the possession of the second-mentioned person is to be treated . . . as the possession of the first-mentioned person".

---

373   Land Registration Act 2002, Sch.4(3)(2) and 4(6)(2).
374   Sch.4(3)(1) and 4(6)(1).
375   See *Sainsbury's Supermarkets Ltd v Olympia Homes Ltd* [2005] EWHC 1235.

Thus, where a registered proprietor is in possession of the land, the register of his title will not be altered unless either of the two grounds above apply. Thus, the circumstances in which the register may be altered are restricted.

(1) Where a registered proprietor has contributed to the mistaken registration

Where a registered proprietor has himself contributed to the mistaken registration through fraud or lack of proper care the register can be altered against him. "Lack of proper care" might mean that he has not exercised the proper degree of diligence in investigating the land included or not included in the title. If a person has become registered proprietor through his own fraud, then the title can be altered against him.

(2) Or it would for any other reason be unjust for the alteration not to be made

What would be "unjust" is a question of fact. In *Sainsbury's Supermarkets Ltd v Olympia Homes Ltd*,[376] the claimants had an option to acquire land to provide a roundabout for one of their stores. The land was unregistered and was sold to Olympia in circumstances whereby they became equitable and not legal owners. Thus, although Sainsbury's had not registered their option as a land charge it was still binding on Olympia. Olympia were mistakenly registered as first proprietors of the *legal* estate, which by s.11 of the Land Registration Act 2002 meant they took free from the option, and they were in possession of the land. It was held unjust not to rectify the register to give effect to Sainsbury's option. Olympia purchased the land on the basis that they would allow Sainsbury's to build a roundabout. Mann J. stated that "[w]ere the register not to be rectified then [Olympia] would have acquired a windfall which would be potentially very significant indeed".

In one case it was held unjust *to rectify* the register where a transfer had been obtained by fraud and transferred to a purchaser, who was registered as proprietor. The registered proprietor had been in possession for a considerable amount of time and had been unaware of the fraud.[377] In *Rees v Peters*,[378] it was held that it was unjust not to order the register to be rectified to give effect to a restrictive covenant that had been mistakenly omitted from the register. The reason was that the registered proprietor had actual notice of the covenant at all times. This seems quite a remarkable decision given that it is an article of faith of the land registration system that the doctrine of notice has no relevance.[379]

---

376   [2005] EWHC 1235; Dixon [2005] Conv. 447.
377   *Pinto v Lim* [2005] EWHC 630.
378   [2011] EWCA Civ 836; [2011] 2 P. & C.R. 18.
379   In *Baxter v Mannion* [2010] EWHC 573 (Ch); [2010] 1 W.L.R. 1965, affirmed on appeal [2011] EWCA Civ 1120, the register was altered against someone who was never entitled to be registered as proprietor. It was unjust not to rectify the register in such circumstances.

10 Indemnity

A person who suffers loss where the register is altered may be entitled to an indemnity. This reflects the "insurance principle" of registered land law. The state guarantees title to registered land. Thus, if a title is registered and it needs to be rectified and this causes someone to suffer loss, they are entitled to compensation from public funds. The claimant must have suffered "loss". This will not be the case if the register is altered to give effect to an overriding interest, as he takes his title subject to overriding interests in any case under ss.11 and 29.[380] As far as forged transfers are concerned, Sch.8(1)(2)(b) provides that the proprietor of a registered estate or charge claiming in good faith under a forged disposition is, where the register is rectified, to be regarded as having suffered loss by reason of such rectification as if the disposition had not been forged".

A. THE GROUNDS FOR AN INDEMNITY PAYMENT

The grounds on which a person suffering loss is entitled to be indemnified are contained in Sch.8 of the Land Registration Act 2002.

(1) Rectification of the register

If loss is caused by rectification, in the narrow sense defined above, then the person suffering loss is entitled to be indemnified.[381] For example, a person who is registered as proprietor under a forged disposition will be entitled to an indemnity payment where the register is rectified and his name deleted as proprietor.

(2) A mistake whose correction would involve rectification of the register

This ground covers the situation where there is a mistaken registration but the register is *not* rectified.[382] A person suffering loss as a result may claim an indemnity. For example, an option to purchase was binding on the registered proprietor when the land was transferred to him but the option had been mistakenly left off the register so the proprietor took free from it. If the register was not rectified the person claiming the benefit of the option is entitled to an indemnity payment.

(3) Other grounds for obtaining an indemnity payment

An indemnity can be claimed for loss resulting from "a mistake in an official search and a mistake in an official copy,[383] and a mistake in a document kept by the registrar which is not an original and is referred to in the register".[384]

---

380 *Re Chowood's Registered Land* [1933] Ch.574.
381 Land Registration Act 2002 Sch.8(1)(a).
382 Sch.8(1)(b).
383 A person can make an "official copy" of documents held at the land registry that are part of a registered title, such as leases and charges, or documents relating to an application for registration etc: Harpum, Bridge, Dixon, *Megarry & Wade Law of Real Property*, para.7.120. If there is a mistake in these documents and a person suffers loss by reason of that mistake then they can obtain an indemnity payment.
384 Land Registration Act 2002 Sch.8(1)(c), (d) and (e).

B. IF LOSS IS SUFFERED BY THE CLAIMANT'S OWN FRAUD OR LACK OF PROPER CARE

A person is not entitled to an indemnity for loss where that loss was suffered "wholly or partly as a result of his own fraud, or wholly as a result of his own lack of proper care".[385] It may be the case that the loss was caused only partly by the claimant's lack of care, in which case the indemnity payment will be reduced accordingly. Schedule 8(5)(2) provides that "where any loss is suffered by a claimant partly as a result of his own lack of proper care, any indemnity payable to him is to be reduced to such extent as if fair having regard to his share in the responsibility for the loss".

C. AMOUNT OF INDEMNITY

Compensation is payable in respect of "loss" suffered as a result of rectification or non-rectification. In respect of the value of an indemnity for the loss of an estate, interest or charge, the indemnity payment will not exceed the value of the estate, interest or charge as it stood immediately before rectification.[386] Thus, if a person is mistakenly registered as proprietor of land he has purchased in good faith and the register is rectified against him then he is entitled to be compensated for the value of the land immediately before rectification of the register.[387] Where a person suffers loss as a result of the register *not* being rectified, e.g. the person who was originally entitled to the land if the register were not rectified in the immediate above example, then the amount of compensation will be the value of the land "at the time when the mistake which caused the loss was made".[388]

Database of reports and articles for independent research

The Land Registration Act 2002 was enacted following an extensive review of the law and recommendations for reform, made by the Law Commission and the Land Registry.

The Final Report: Law Commission, *Land Registration for the Twenty-First Century, A Conveyancing Revolution* (Law Com No.271, 2001).

The Law Commission's earlier Consultation Document on land registration is *Land Registration for the Twenty-First Century, A Consultative Document* (Law Com No.254, 1998).

---

385 Sch.8(5).
386 Sch.8(6).
387 Sch.8(6)(a).
388 Sch.8(6)(b).

M.Dixon, "The Reform of Property Law and the Land Registration Act 2002: A Risk Assessment" [2003] Conv. 136.

R.Smith, "The role of registration in modern land law" in L. Tee (ed.) *Land Law Issues, Debates, Policy* (Willan Publishing, 2002).

N.Jackson, "Title by Registration and Concealed Overriding Interests—The Cause and Effect of Antipathy to Documentary Proof" (2003) 119 L.Q.R. 660.

J.Stevens, "Is Justice a Priority in Priorities? The Re-introduction of Morality to Registered Conveyancing" in F.Meisel and P.Cook (eds), *Property and Protection* (Oxford: Hart Publishing, 2000).

C.Harpum, "Overreaching, Trustees' Powers and Reform of the 1925 Legislation" [1990] C.L.J. 277.

N.Jackson, "Overreaching in Registered Land Law" (2006) 69 M.L.R. 214.

Chapter 9

The Leasehold Estate

CHAPTER OVERVIEW

In this chapter you will find:

- The essential characteristics of a lease
- Full extracts from judgments and instructions on how to solve problems like a land lawyer
- The principles by which leases are created.

Introduction

1

In this chapter on leases we will be working on the skill of reading cases, extracting legal reasoning, and solving legal problems. As a lease is essentially ownership of the land *for a time* we will use BUILDING BLOCK NO 4: Ideas of Ownership, to evaluate whether the judge in a case correctly or incorrectly identifies a lease as existing on the facts of a case. We will also use our Building Blocks to construct an argument about the law. We will hold the rules against the ideas in the Building Blocks, for example BUILDING BLOCK NO 6: The Need for Certainty and Predictability in Land Law Rules, and consider whether the rules support or undermine our Building Blocks. For the full text of Building Blocks and instructions on how to use them to construct an argument see Chapter 1.

A. A "LEASE"[1]—OWNERSHIP OF THE LAND FOR A TIME

A lease is not a limited right in land, for example, to walk over another's land for one particular purpose such as access: an easement. The idea of a lease is to confer nothing less than *ownership/possession*[2] of the land for a specified period of time.

(1) What is ownership?

> **BUILDING BLOCK NO 4: Ideas of Ownership**
>
> "Ownership itself is a set of open-ended use privileges and open-ended powers to control the use made by others of the property. . . . It is simply not possible to list all the potential uses which the owner may make of the property – she can live on it, use it for growing crops, climb trees on it, and so on": S.Bright, "Of Estates and Interests: A Tale of Ownership and Property Rights" in *Land Law Themes and Perspectives*, p.529. An owner can sell his interest in the land, can leave it by will, give it away, and destroy it. The owner has a "stake" in the land, i.e. they can include or exclude anyone they please: *Marchant v Charters* [1977] 1 W.L.R. 1181, p. 1185 per Lord Denning M.R. The key factor of possession/ownership is *control* over the premises without interference from others: Gray & Gray, *Land Law Core Text*, p.90.

To know what a lease *is*, we must understand properly this idea of *ownership*. We should avoid confusion with the term "occupation", which is used to describe the fact that a person is living there or using the land. This does not necessary mean that they have a "stake" in it, in the sense described. Just because someone occupies land under a contract with the freehold owner does not necessarily mean that the occupier has a lease.

(2) A lease compared to more limited rights in land

A right of ownership such as a lease is very different from a more limited right in the land such as an easement or a restrictive covenant. Such rights are not *exclusive*, i.e. the person entitled to exercise the right cannot exclude anyone else from lawfully doing so.[3] Furthermore, smaller rights such as easements and restrictive covenants concern one purpose only, for example the right to gain access over another's land, or the right to prevent another from building on his land.

---

1   Throughout this Chapter the terms "tenancy" and "lease" are used interchangeably. Another name for a lease is *demise*.
2   Although it may be important in certain contexts to draw a distinction between *possession* and *ownership*, for our purposes here the qualities associated with possession are ostensibly the same as the qualities associated with ownership. They were treated as such by the House of Lords in the leading landlord and tenant decision of *Street v Mountford* [1985] A.C. 809. For a useful argument on this see Harris, *Property and Justice* (Oxford: Clarendon Press, 1996), p.81.
3   S.Bright, "Of Estates and Interests: A Tale of Ownership and Property Rights" in *Land Law Themes and Perspectives* (Oxford University Press, 1998), p.538.

> "[i]t is the open-endedness of the use privileges that ownership brings that sets estates [such as leases] . . . apart from other . . . interests in land".
>
> S.Bright, "Of Estates and Interests: A Tale of Ownership and Property Rights" in *Land Law Themes and Perspectives*, p.534.

(3) A lease is an estate in land of limited duration

The lease is ownership of the land *for a time*. Its time is limited. The person who owns the freehold estate in the land (the "landlord" or "lessor") has parted with their control over the land for the length of the lease. But they continue owning the freehold estate. They have carved the lease out of their freehold. This is a common way of exploiting the commercial value of land.[4] During the lease the freehold owner has the right to have the land back after the lease has come to an end ("expires" or, as we often say, "determines"). We call this the "freehold reversion".

Landlord/lessor	Person who has granted the lease out of their freehold estate.[5]
Freehold reversion	The right to have the possession of the land back at the end of the lease.

(4) The varied extent of the leasehold arrangement

The leasehold estate, creating the relationship between landlord and tenant, arises in many different and varied circumstances. A lease can be granted for any time period. It is a highly useful legal arrangement. As Bridge observes:

> "Residential accommodation such as bed-sits are frequently let on 'periodic tenancy', where the tenant pays rent on a periodic basis and the landlord-tenant relationship continues until either party determines it by serving written notice on the other."[6]

Example
Mr Colman is the freehold owner of a house. He grants a month-by-month tenancy to Alison [a periodic tenancy]. Either party can end the tenancy by giving one month's notice to the other.

---

4   Stevens and Pearce, *Land Law* 3rd edn (London: Sweet & Maxwell, 2004), p.157; P.Birks, "Before we begin: Five keys to land law" in *Land Law Themes and Perspectives*, Ch.18, p.462.
5   Or out of a longer leasehold than the one they grant.
6   S.Bridge, "Leases – contract, property and status" in L. Tee (ed.) *Land Law, Issues Debates Policy*, (Willan Publishing, 2002), p.98.

"Commercial property, such as offices, shops and garages, is more likely to be let on a 'fixed-term tenancy' for five, or ten, or fifteen years. The rent may be subject to review pursuant to a preordained procedure at defined intervals during the lease."[7]

> **Example**
> Adam, Brian, Cully and David want to start a vets practice and require offices. They lease offices Nos 3–5 Octavian Street, Derby for a term of seven years. Their landlord, Mr Browne, will want to make sure that he gets the full commercial value out of the land, so he includes a clause for the rent to be reviewed every year.

"Then there is the 'long lease', used principally in relation to developments of houses or flats, which involves the grant of a lease for hundreds, sometimes thousands, of years, in consideration of the payment of a capital sum known as a premium and a 'ground-rent'. These leasehold interests are conceptually much closer to freeholds (the so-called 'fee simple absolute in possession') than periodic tenancies, and they are traded on the housing market in much the same way."[8]

> **Example**
> Joanna wants to buy a home in the centre of Manchester. She likes a contemporary flat in a stylish block. It is priced £250,000. The flat is not freehold it is "leasehold" (very common in the purchase of flats) on a lease of 999 years. This is practically speaking indistinguishable from full freehold ownership and the flat sale to Joanna goes through in the normal way.

(5) A lease is an estate in the land itself and therefore a property right

A lease is a property right. It is an estate in the land itself.[9] The consequence of being an estate in the land is that the lease is capable of binding third parties who later come to own the freehold, e.g. if the landlord sells his freehold reversion.[10] Thus, if I have a six month lease and my landlord sells the house to a third party, I can potentially enforce the lease against the purchaser.

An important privilege of ownership is that the owner can sell or give away his property. Thus, a lease can be sold by the tenant, bought by another, or, if desired, given away. It is *property*. When a lease is transferred to another we call this "assignment". This does not affect the landlord's freehold reversion, which he still owns. The freehold reversion can also be bought and sold. For

---

7   ibid.
8   S.Bridge "Leases—contract, property and status" in *Land Law, Issues Debates Policy*, p. 98.
9   *Street v Mountford* [1985] A.C. 809.
10   You considered the circumstances in which a lease will bind purchasers of the land in Chapter 6, 7 and 8 on Land Transfer Law.

example, it has become an accepted term of modern life that a council tenant may have the "right to buy" his or her council house. In Land Law terms, the tenant already has ownership of the house for a time: the tenancy. But the "right to buy" means that the tenant can purchase the freehold reversion from the council.

| The tenant "assigns" the lease. | The tenant transfers all his rights under the lease, i.e. to own the land for a defined period, to another. |

| Landlord sells and assigns the freehold reversion. | The landlord transfers his freehold rights in the land, i.e. the right to have the land back at the end of the lease, to another. |

Alternatively the tenant can "sublet". This means that he does not part with his leasehold estate in the land. He grants or carves another lease out of it to another. This is a way in which the tenant can exploit the value of his lease without parting with it altogether. He has what we call the "head lease". The "sub-lease" will be for a shorter period of time. For example, a tenant owning a 99-year lease might grant a lease to another for 25 years. The ability to grant and create interests in the land is, again, one of the characteristics of ownership of an estate in the land.

| Sublet. | The tenant creates a shorter lease out of his own longer leasehold interest. |

(6) A lease distinguished from a licence

A lease is often contrasted favourably with a "licence" for someone to occupy land. A licence is defined as "permission" to occupy. It does not confer any right in the land itself, any *ownership*, but is sufficient to prevent the occupier from being classified as a trespasser: "The licence does not create an estate in the land to which it relates but only makes an act lawful which would otherwise be unlawful".[11] A licence is a purely personal right between the owner of land and an occupier. As a personal right it is enforceable only between the original parties (owner and occupier). If the owner sells the land the new owner is not bound to allow the occupier to continue to use the land.[12] Licences can be expressly created by the parties, for example by means of a contract. They can come into being impliedly, and by statute, for example where people such as the police or utilities personnel require access to premises.

---

11   *Street v Mountford* [1985] A.C. 809, per Lord Templeman.
12   *Clore v Theatrical Properties Ltd and Westby & Co Ltd* [1936] 3 All E.R. 483.

(7) The Law of Property Act 1925 defines a lease: term of years absolute

A lease is one of the only two estates capable of existing as a legal estate under s.1(1) of the Law of Property Act 1925. Section 205(1)(xxvii) defines a lease as a "term of years absolute". A lease must be created for a specified period of time: It must be a "term of years". This "includes a term for less than a year".[13] The mischief of the legislation is that a lease must exist for a defined period. Otherwise it could become confused with the freehold estate, which is of indefinite length.[14] The definition also includes "periodic tenancies" which are leases that although having no set duration at the outset, take effect from period to period,[15] e.g. week after week or month after month, until either party gives notice to terminate the tenancy.[16] Both landlord and tenant must have the ability to terminate the periodic tenancy. Otherwise it will not amount to a definable "term".[17]

Although the statute says that the lease must be "absolute", it is not at all clear what this means. It certainly does not mean that the estate cannot be brought to an end by any condition.[18] A lease can still be "absolute" even though it may be ended by either party serving a notice on the other or by an action by the landlord for repossession of the premises, e.g. for non-payment of rent.[19]

A lease can be granted to take effect "in possession", i.e. entitling the tenant to immediate enjoyment of the land. Or it can be "reversionary", which means that it is granted to take effect in the future.[20] For example, a university student might enter into tenancy in May for her to take possession of a house at the start of term in September. Where this is the case the lease takes effect "in reversion", i.e. possession of the land by the tenant is delayed.[21] Under the definition of a lease in the Law of Property Act 1925 it is not necessary for rent to be paid.[22]

(8) A lease is both property and contract

As well as being an estate in land a lease is also a contract, i.e. it is an agreement for the use and enjoyment of land. The lease contract has terms and conditions like any other contract. These provide the "ground rules" of the tenancy.[23] Because of the importance of the property to both the landlord and the tenant, it is important that the terms or "covenants" of the contract effectually regulate its use. See example below for typical covenants under a lease.

---

13   Law of Property Act 1925 s.205(1)(xxvii).
14   *Prudential Assurance Co Ltd v London Residuary Body* [1992] 2 A.C. 386.
15   Law of Property Act 1925 s.205(1)(xxvii).
16   *Javad v Aqil* [1991] 1 W.L.R. 1007; Stevens and Pearce, *Land Law*, p.189.
17   *Prudential Assurance Co Ltd v London Residuary Body* [1992] 2 A.C. 386, per Lord Templeman.
18   Harpum, Bridge, Dixon, *Megarry & Wade Law of Real Property*, 7th edn (London: Sweet & Maxwell, 2008).
19   Law of Property Act 1925 s.205(1)(xxvii); Harpum, Bridge, Dixon, *Megarry & Wade Law of Real Property*. This is known as "forfeiture".
20   s.205(1)(xxvii).
21   This is called a "reversionary lease". But a lease that is granted to take effect more than 21 years into the future is void: Law of Property Act 1925 s.149(3). A reversionary lease of whatever length, where possession is postponed for more than three months, is a "registrable disposition" under the Land Registration Act 2002. This means it must be registered before it will bind a purchaser of the freehold. The reason is that if the tenant is not in possession of the land, the purchaser will find it difficult to discover the existence of the lease: Law Commission, *Land Registration for the Twenty-First Century* (1998) Law Com. No. 271.
22   s.205(1)(xxvii).
23   Expression: Gray and Gray 4th edn (Oxford University Press, 2006) *Core Text on Land Law*, p.537.

> **THE TENANT'S COVENANTS:**
> To pay rent;
> To keep the interior of the premises in good repair and condition throughout the Term;
> To make good all damages and breakages;
> Not to assign, sublet or part with possession of the premises without the prior consent of the landlord.

> **THE LANDLORD'S COVENANTS:**
> That the tenant shall peaceably hold and enjoy the premises without unlawful interruption;
> To insure the buildings;
> To keep the central heating system in repair and proper working order.

The tenant's covenants are very important to the landlord, e.g. they ensure that the leased property is taken care of, that the landlord has some degree of control over who his tenants are, and that rent is paid on time. This will not only enable the landlord to exploit the land for immediate financial gain but it will preserve the economic value of his freehold reversion. The landlord's covenants will, e.g. ensure that the tenant lives in a reasonably comfortable environment.[24]

B. TYPES OF LEASE

(1) Fixed term tenancies

This is where the duration of the tenancy is specified in advance, for example one month, one year, five years or ten years. It comes to an end on the expiry of that term. A clause can be included in the agreement which allows landlord or tenant the right to end the tenancy after a certain point prior to the expiry of the contractual term, e.g. six months into a 12 month tenancy. This is known as a "break clause".

(2) Periodic tenancies

Periodic tenancies have no fixed duration at the outset. This is a tenancy initially for one period, e.g. a week or a month, and which automatically continues for another period until either landlord or tenant serves notice that they no longer wish the tenancy to continue. Thus, if there is more than one tenant and one serves notice to end the tenancy then this will be sufficient to terminate a periodic tenancy. Such tenancies only continue into a new period where all parties consent. Where one serves notice therefore, the requisite consent to the continuation of the periodic tenancy is absent.[25]

Periodic tenancies can be weekly, monthly or yearly. This depends on how the rental payments are calculated. If the tenancy stipulated that rent is £500 per month, it will be a monthly periodic

---

24 Gray & Gray, above.
25 *Hammersmith and Fulham LBC v Monk* [1992] 1 A.C. 478.

tenancy. So even if the tenant pays that rent in weekly instalments the tenancy will still be a monthly periodic tenancy. The length of notice required by law to end a periodic tenancy is determined by the core period. Thus, to end a monthly periodic tenancy one month's notice must be given to expire at the end of the period.[26] A yearly tenancy requires six months notice.[27] Landlord and tenant can agree a different period of notice if they wish.[28] In the case of a dwelling house four weeks' notice must be given, unless both parties agree a shorter period.[29]

A periodic tenancy can come into being expressly, as a result of the parties creating one, or can be implied by law. For example, where the parties have attempted to create a fixed term lease that is void, e.g. for uncertainty of the term, an implied periodic tenancy may arise if the tenant enters into possession of the land and pays rent monthly.[30] The basis of the implication is the intention of the parties. Thus a periodic tenancy will not arise where there is evidence that there was no intention to create one.[31]

(3) Tenancies at will and tenancies at sufferance

A tenancy at will does not create an interest in the land. It is a personal arrangement between the landlord and the tenant. It will not bind a purchaser of the freehold reversion.[32] The tenancy at will is easy to terminate. It can be ended at any time. One may arise expressly or by implication, e.g. where a fixed term tenancy has come to an end and the tenant still holds the property with the consent of the landlord. In this situation if there is no intention to create a periodic tenancy the occupier is a tenant at will. A tenancy at sufferance is where the tenant holds the land at the end of a lease without either the approval or the disapproval of the landlord.

2 The essential characteristics of a lease

An arrangement between an owner and an occupier for the use of land must, in order to be a lease, conform to the essential *nature* of a lease, as discussed in section 1 above. You will remember that a lease is ownership of the land *for a time*. Thus, the agreement must grant rights in the nature of *ownership*. We call this "exclusive possession". And the lease must be for a certain and definable time period (or "term"). If either of these features (or "essential characteristics") is missing, the occupier cannot have an estate in land, the "term of years absolute" as defined by the Law of Property Act 1925.

---

26 *Javad v Aqil* [1991] 1 W.L.R. 1007.
27 *Prudential Assurance Co Ltd v London Residuary Body* [1992] 2 A.C. 386, per Lord Templeman.
28 Harpum, Bridge, Dixon, *Megarry & Wade Law of Real Property*, para.17–074.
29 Protection from Eviction Act 1977, s.5; Harpum, Bridge, Dixon, *Megarry & Wade Law of Real Property*, para.17–073.
30 *Prudential Assurance Co Ltd v London Residuary Body* [1992] 2 A.C. 386.
31 *Javad v Aqil* [1991] 1 W.L.R. 1007.
32 "Probably the best analysis of it is that it is a form of tenure but one that confers no estate": Harpum, Bridge, Dixon, above para.17–078.

> **Thus, the essential characteristics of a lease are:**
> **(a) The term of the lease must be certain.**
> **(b) The tenant must be granted exclusive possession.**

In *Street v Mountford*,[33] Lord Templeman defined the essential characteristics of a lease as "the grant of land for a term at a rent with exclusive possession".[34] The Law of Property Act 1925 does not provide that rent should be paid under a lease. Quite the contrary: s.205(1)(xxvii) provides that " 'Term of years absolute' means a term of years (taking effect either in possession or in reversion *whether or not at a rent*) . . ."

A. THE TERM OF THE LEASE MUST BE CERTAIN

(1) Introduction

Because a tenancy creates an interest in land, it is ownership of the land *for a time* the lease must be of certain duration.[35] There must be certainty as to when the lease begins and ends. Without this, an arrangement for the use and occupation of property cannot be a lease.[36] The date of the termination of the lease must be certain by the time the lease begins.[37]

LECTURER: Here is a fragment from a typical problem question that raises this issue of whether the term of the lease is sufficiently certain. Keep this problem in mind as we study the cases and we will refer back to it.

> Norman, who has just been released from prison, has been allowed to occupy a house "until he can find a job and can afford to buy a house".
>
> Discuss whether Norman has a lease. This will take you into the "term certain" cases that we will now consider. You should identify how the principles have been formed and why we have such rules. Then we will understand more about how to apply them to resolve this problem.

The term of a lease must be certain in two senses: It must be certain when the lease is to begin and when it is to end.[38] The lease must have a certain or ascertainable start date so that it is

---

33   [1985] A.C. 809.
34   [1985] A.C. 809.
35   *Mexfield Housing Co-operative Ltd v Berrisford* [2011] Ch. 244.
36   There would be nothing to distinguish a lease from the fee simple: *Prudential Assurance Co Ltd v London Residuary Body* [1992] 2 A.C. 386.
37   *Prudential Assurance Co Ltd v London Residuary Body* [1992] 2 A.C. 386. This "term certain" rule applies in the same way to equitable leases: *Mexfield Housing Co-operative Ltd v Berrisford* [2011] Ch. 244. We consider equitable leases below in this chapter.
38   *Say v Smith* (1563) 1 Plowd 269.

certain when the lease will begin.[39] A lease to start when war breaks out for example, was sufficient in *Swift v Macbean*.[40]

It must also be certain when the lease will terminate. In *Lace v Chantler*[41] the term of the lease agreed by the parties was for the duration of the war. It was held to be invalid. No one would know when the war would end.[42]

> "The question immediately arises whether a tenancy for the duration of the war creates a good leasehold interest. In my opinion, it does not. A term created by a leasehold tenancy agreement must be expressed either with certainty and specifically or by reference to something which can, at the time when the lease takes effect, be looked to as a certain ascertainment of what the term is meant to be."[43]

(2) The House of Lords' decision in Prudential Assurance Co Ltd v London Residuary Body

After some doubt about the existence of the requirement for a certain term,[44] the principle was reaffirmed by the House of Lords in *Prudential Assurance Co Ltd v London Residuary Body*.[45]

(a) Reading a case

LECTURER: Before we study *Prudential Assurance* we need to make sure that we can identify the separate elements of a case, and those elements that are relevant to helping us solve a legal problem, like Norman's lease in our example problem question above.

STUDENT: This is something I always seem to have difficulty with. There is so much information in a Law Report!

LECTURER: There are three parts to a case: the facts, the judge's conclusion, i.e. the result of the case, and the reasoning. It is in the reasoning that we find the rule and often, we also find helpful comments by the judge on how it should apply.

STUDENT: So this is the element we need in order to solve a problem.

LECTURER: Yes that's right. All too often law students attempt to predict the legal outcome of a scenario by merely comparing case facts and the judge's conclusion. For example, "in *Lace v Chantler* there was a lease for the duration of the war and this was held to be invalid. In our case, Norman has a lease 'until he can find a job and can afford to buy a house'. Therefore this too will be invalid".

Here, we have left out the important part: *why* the lease was held to be invalid, i.e. *what was the rule that the judge applied in order to come to his conclusion?* It is only an application

---

39 *Harvey v Pratt* [1965] 1 W.L.R. 1025.
40 [1942] 1 K.B. 375; Stevens and Pearce, *Land Law*, p. 177.
41 [1944] K.B. 368.
42 Parliament passed the Validation of Wartime Leases Act 1944 in order to overcome the inconvenience of this ruling invalidating many such wartime leases: s.1(1). Such leases took effect as a term of 10 years with a right to end the lease when the war ended.
43 [1944] K.B. 368, per Lord Greene M.R. p.370.
44 *Ashburn Anstalt v Arnold* [1989] Ch. 1.
45 [1992] 2 A.C. 386.

of this same rule to the facts of the problem that can adequately support any conclusion *you* come to about Norman's lease. Without this, call it what you like, but it is not a piece of legal reasoning. Now we will return to *Prudential Assurance*.

THE FACTS: The owner of a shop that fronted the Walworth Road sold part of this land to the London County Council including the strip of land in front of the shop. This was to enable them to widen the Walworth Road. The Council, as part of the sale of the land to them, granted a leaseback of the strip to the shop owner. Without this there would be no front from the shop to the road for his customers.[46] The lease was purportedly granted until the land was required by the Council for the purposes of widening the Walworth Road.

CONCLUSION: It was held that the term of the tenancy was uncertain. The tenancy of the strip of land was therefore void.

EXTRACT FROM THE JUDGE'S REASONING: *Prudential Assurance Co Ltd v London Residuary Body* [1992] 2 A.C. 386.

LORD TEMPLEMAN: "Over 60 years later Walworth Road has not been widened . . . and it does not appear that the road will ever be widened . . . The agreement purported to grant a term of uncertain duration which, if valid, now entitles the tenant to stay there for ever and a day [. . .]

A [lease] for years is a contract for the exclusive possession and profit of land for some determinate period. Such an estate is called a 'term' . . .

> 'Every estate which must expire at a period certain and prefixed, by whatever words created, is an estate for years. And therefore this estate is frequently called a term, *terminus*, because its duration or continuance is bounded, limited and determined: for every such estate must have a certain beginning, and certain end.'[47]

In *Say v Smith* (1563) 1 Plowd. 269 a lease for a certain term purported to add a term which was uncertain; the lease was held valid only as to the certain term . . . Anthony Brown J. is reported to have said at p. 272:

> 'every contract sufficient to make a lease for years ought to have certainty in three limitations, viz. in the commencement of the term, in the continuance of it, and in the end of it; so that all these ought to be known at the commencement of the lease, and words in a lease, which don't make this appear, are but babble . . . And these three are in effect but one matter, showing the certainty of the time for which the lessee shall have the land, and if any of these fail, it is not a good lease, for then there wants certainty.'

---

46   Facts from the judgment of Lord Browne-Wilkinson.
47   Quoting *Blackstone's Commentaries on the Laws of England*, 2nd edn (1766) Vol. II, p. 143.

The Law of Property Act 1925, taking up the same theme provided, by section 1(1), that:

> 'The only estates in land which are capable of subsisting or of being conveyed or created at law are – (a) An estate in fee simple absolute in possession; (b) A term of years absolute.' [. . .]

The term expressed to be granted by the agreement in the present case does not fall within this definition . . . When the agreement in the present case was made, it failed to grant an estate in the land . . .

My Lords, I consider that the principle in *Lace v Chantler* [1944] K.B. 368 [above] reaffirming 500 years of judicial acceptance of the requirement that a term must be certain applies to all leases and tenancy agreements . . .

A lease can be made for five years subject to the tenant's right to determine if the war ends before the expiry of five years. A lease can be made from year to year subject to a fetter on the right of the landlord to determine the lease before the expiry of five years unless the war ends. Both leases are valid because they create a determinable certain term of five years."

(3) Problem solving using Lord Templeman's reasoning

LECTURER: Now you have read the extract from Lord Templeman's judgment in *Prudential Assurance* we have to be able to use it to solve a problem. Let's remind ourselves of our problem.

> Norman, who has just been released from prison, has been allowed to occupy a house "until he can find a job and can afford to buy a house". Discuss whether Norman has a lease.

Firstly it is necessary to identify the legal issue and the consequence for the parties.

STUDENT: The legal issue in our problem is whether the clause "until he can find a job and can afford to buy a house" creates a sufficiently certain and ascertainable "term" for a lease to exist.

LECTURER: Now you need to be able to identify the reason *why* Lord Templeman came to the conclusion that the lease in that case was void. This will give us the precise detail of the rule that we need to solve our problem.

STUDENT: The reason that the lease failed in *Prudential Assurance* was because the council in the end did not want to widen the road so that the lease could go on indefinitely. The rule applied was that it must be clear when it will *begin* and *end*. Any term purporting to allow the lease to go on indefinitely will be void for uncertainty.

LECTURER: Good, but before we apply this rule to Norman's problem, let's try to understand where it came from.

STUDENT: Lord Templeman identifies that the Law of Property Act 1925 s.1(1) recognises the lease as an estate (or ownership) in the land: a "term of years".

LECTURER: And so it must be properly differentiated from the fee simple estate which is indefinite ownership.

LECTURER: Hence the need for a "bounded term". This is the very nature of a lease.

STUDENT: And this is what the quotation from Blackstone says.

LECTURER: Now you have identified the rule and how it works we need to determine the effect of the rule on Norman's lease, our example problem question above. If our facts are materially identical to those in *Prudential Assurance* then we must come to the same conclusion.

> This is what we call **applying** the law or precedent. It is an integral part of legal problem solving that allows us to make the necessary step from identifying what the problem is to solving it, i.e. predicting a legal outcome. In Law Degree Learning Outcomes in many Higher Education institutions this is what is meant when it is required that you show the ability to "apply the law to a factual scenario".

So you need to examine the same possibilities in our case (Norman's lease) that Lord Templeman examined in *Prudential Assurance*.

STUDENT: On the facts of our problem it is not possible to say when Norman might find a job or be able to buy a house. He might never be in a position to do this. Consequently the lease could last indefinitely and it is void.

LECTURER: Because our facts were materially identical to the facts in *Prudential Assurance* the rule in that case must lead us to come to the same conclusion, i.e. that the lease is void.

> **Distinguishing a case**
> But if our facts were materially different from *Prudential Assurance* we are justified in saying that the rule there applied should not void the lease. Here we would be "distinguishing" *Prudential Assurance*.

If you were the draftsperson of Norman's "lease", how could you turn it into a valid lease with a duration that is ascertainable at the outset?

STUDENT: It is like Lord Templeman states in the last paragraph; give the lease an arbitrary certain term (e.g. a term of three years or less may be appropriate here) with a provision that allows Norman to end the lease if he gets a job and buys a house.

LECTURER: Good! This would make the lease a "bounded" estate in the land, properly distinguishable from the indefinite fee simple for the purposes of s.1 of the Law of Property Act 1925. The lease would in any case, definitely end after a stipulated number of years.

> STUDENT writes: Norman is allowed to occupy the house for a term of three years. Neither party can give notice before this time. This is subject to Norman's right to terminate this agreement on one month's notice should he accept an offer of employment or enter into a binding contract to purchase other accommodation.

LECTURER: That's very good! This is likely to be as near as we can get to giving legal effect to the arrangement intended by the parties.

(4) The requirement for a certain term and periodic tenancies

Periodic tenancies must also satisfy this requirement for the term to be certain. It looks initially as if they would not be able to do this as they may continue until either party chooses to put an end to the tenancy. Therefore, the term cannot be ascertained *at the beginning of the tenancy*, which is the requirement of the rule in *Prudential Assurance*. However, it is considered that the term of a periodic tenancy is ascertainable because:

1. The parties agree to an initial period at the outset, e.g. one month or one year, and unless either gives notice under the agreement, they consent at the end of each period to a further period;
2. Once the lease is terminated by notice of either party, which means that there is no more consent to the continuance of the tenancy,[48] the length of the lease can be calculated.[49]

"A tenancy from year to year is saved from being uncertain because each party has power by notice to determine at the end of any year. The term continues until determined as if both parties made a new agreement at the end of each year for a new term for the ensuing year."[50]

Thus, a periodic tenancy satisfies the "term certain" requirement provided both landlord and tenant have the ability to terminate the tenancy.[51]

(5) Critical Thinking: Constructing an argument about the "term certain" rule

LECTURER: At least the rule in relation to periodic tenancies in (4) above, avoids the "mischief" behind the rule. The landlord and tenant both have the right to give notice and end the

---

48   *Hammersmith London Borough Council v Monk* [1992] 1 A.C. 478.
49   *Prudential Assurance Co Ltd v London Residuary Body* [1992] 2 A.C. 386; Harpum, Bridge, Dixon, *Megarry & Wade Law of Real Property*, para.6–018–6–019.
50   *Prudential Assurance Co Ltd v London Residuary Body* [1992] 2 A.C. 386; p.394 per Lord Templeman.
51   *Prudential Assurance Co Ltd v London Residuary Body* [1992] 2 A.C. 386. *Doe'd Warner v Browne* [1807] 8 East 165; *Cheshire Lines Committee v Lewis & Co* (1880) 50 L.J.Q.B. 121.

lease. Thus, it can never be confused with the perpetual fee simple estate. The lease cannot continue indefinitely irrespective of the will of the parties,[52] as could the fee simple.

But I would like you to consider whether the rule requiring a lease to have a fixed and ascertainable duration is a good and fair rule? Here I am asking you to construct an argument about the term certain rule. We cannot just say "yes" or "no". Neither will an ultimate conclusion of "yes" or "no" be of much value to your Land Law examiner. There is *no right answer*. We say that the rule is good or bad, fair or unfair, depending on the extent to which it supports or undermines our Building Blocks.[53] Let's look at one of our Building Blocks that might help us construct an argument.

> **BUILDING BLOCK NO 8: A rule should give effect to its underlying rationale/ statutory purpose**
> Rules should not exist for rules' sake (F.Schauer, *Thinking like a Lawyer*, pp. 13–17). They should be reflections of a particular purpose or objective, or of what the statute imposing the rule was designed to do. Otherwise it is not a good rule.

LECTURER: Another way of stating the idea in BUILDING BLOCK NO 8 is that a rule should Do What it Says on the Tin!

STUDENT: On BUILDING BLOCK NO 8 we can see that the term certain rule is good law. As Lord Templeman observed in *Prudential Assurance Co Ltd v London Residuary Body* a lease is an estate in land that is "bounded". It is of itself a *term*, i.e. ownership of the land *for a time*. It is thus an integral part of what a lease is to say that it must be for a duration that can be specified.

LECTURER: And what about the Law of Property Act 1925 definition of a lease?

STUDENT: A lease is a "term of years absolute". This shows that the lease by nature is of limited and precise duration. The rule in *Prudential Assurance*, requiring the term of a lease to be ascertainable in advance, and certain of duration, reflects this. On BUILDING BLOCK NO 8 therefore, we may say that *Prudential Assurance* is a good rule.

LECTURER: A lease is a derivative of the fee simple estate, which is *indefinite* ownership of the land. It should not become confused with it.[54] On the other hand, I want you to consider your argument in a deeper way. Lord Browne-Wilkinson in *Prudential Assurance*, although agreeing with Lord Templeman that the lease was void due to its uncertain term, failed to see any value in having the rule:

"This bizarre outcome results from the application of an ancient and technical rule of law which requires the maximum duration of a term of years to be ascertainable from the

---

52   Stevens and Pearce, *Land Law*, p.192.

53   See Chapter 1 for the full text of our Building Blocks and information on how to create an argument.

54   See Harpum, *Megarry & Wade Law of Real Property*, 6th edn (London: Sweet & Maxwell, 1999); Thompson, *Modern Land Law* 4th edn (Oxford University Press, 2009).

outset. No one has produced any satisfactory rationale for the genesis of this rule. No one has been able to point to any useful purpose that it serves at the present day."[55]

STUDENT: I think I agree with what Lord Browne-Wilkinson says here. On BUILDING BLOCK NO 8 because a lease is of limited duration *by nature* it is not necessary for its length to be ascertainable in advance, provided it *cannot continue indefinitely* and become confused with the fee simple estate. Provided the estate can be ended by both parties it is still possible to say that the estate thereby created is of bounded duration.

LECTURER: And so if the lease in the *Prudential* case had contained a term allowing either party to end it upon giving, e.g. two months notice, it could not go on indefinitely against the will of the parties, which is the essential idea of the fee simple. Such a lease should be valid. We can say that it is still of a "bounded" duration.

Do any of our other Building Blocks show whether the "term certain" rule is good or bad law? Remember that if we hold the rule against the Building Blocks and see that the rule supports or undermines the principles contained in the Building Blocks we may legitimately say that the rule is good or bad fair or unfair accordingly.

STUDENT: I would use BUILDING BLOCK NO 7[56] it is important for the rules of Land Law to give effect to the parties' intentions.

> **BUILDING BLOCK NO 7: Land Law is facilitative and should give effect to the intentions and reasonable expectations of the parties**
> Thus we can say that a rule is good or bad, fair or unfair depending on the extent to which a rule facilitates the achievement of the parties' intentions.

The shop owner and the Council entered into this agreement so that the shop owner could make sure that his shop fronted onto the Walworth road. Thus, the term certain rule defeated these intentions completely. The parties' lease was held void.

LECTURER: The tenant was left in a precarious position as there was no lease and there was no public front to the shop.

> Lord Browne-Wilkinson in *Prudential Assurance* makes the point that the rule, although having little intrinsic purpose, still managed to defeat the commercial intentions of the parties: p.397.

LECTURER: Can you think of a counter-argument? Could the parties have done anything themselves to ensure that the law would give effect to their intentions? After all, the law

---

55   *Prudential Assurance Co Ltd v London Residuary Body* [1992] 2 A.C. 386, p. 396 per Lord Browne-Wilkinson.

56   BUILDING BLOCK NO 7 is based on the idea of Peter Birks that Land Law is facilitative and that Land Law "can be seen as facilitating the achievement of goals which people routinely want to achieve". P. Birks "Before we begin: Five keys to land law" in *Land Law Themes and Perspectives*, Ch.18, p.457.

should not always be in the position of rescuing arrangements when the parties themselves were perfectly capable of protecting their own interests.

STUDENT: Well, they were commercial parties, presumably capable of taking necessary steps. It would have been quite easy for them to have created a determinable 20 year lease of the strip of land, for example, as Lord Templeman pointed out in the last part of the extract above.

The term certain rule was applied recently in the case of *Mexfield Housing Co-operative Ltd v Berrisford*.[57] In this case a tenancy agreement provided that it could not be terminated unless the tenant fell into arrears with her rent or otherwise committed a breach of the agreement. It was held void for uncertainty because the maximum duration could not be ascertained at the outset of the tenancy. However, the Court of Appeal indicated that parliament should consider changing the rule.[58]

(6) Tenancies "for life"

Section 149(6) of the Law of Property Act 1925 provides that the grant of a lease "for life" or until a person marries is not void. Instead it takes effect as a lease of 99 years with a provision allowing the lease to be brought to an end when the relevant person dies or gets married. Without this provision the lease would be void under the *Prudential Assurance* principle. How do you know when someone is going to get married or die?

B. THE TENANT MUST HAVE BEEN GRANTED EXCLUSIVE POSSESSION

(1) Introduction: exclusive possession is the right of control over land

The other essential characteristic of a lease is that the tenant must have been granted "exclusive possession" of the premises. This does not mean simply that the tenant *lives there*, for which we might use the word "occupation".[59] As we have seen in section 1 above a lease is ownership of the land for a time. And we know what ownership *looks like*:

> **BUILDING BLOCK NO 4: Ideas of Ownership**
> As Bright says ownership is "a set of open-ended use privileges and open-ended powers to control the use made by others of the property": "Of Estates and Interests", *Land Law Themes and Perspectives*, p.529. An owner has a "stake" in the land: *Marchant v Charters* [1977]. He can include or exclude anyone he pleases, even the landlord. Effectively this means that he has *control* over the land: Gray and Gray, *Land Law*, p.90.

---

57   [2011] Ch. 244.
58   A suggestion also made by the House of Lords in *Prudential Assurance*, per Lord Browne-Wilkinson, p. 397.
59   *Clore v Theatrical Properties Ltd and Westby & Co Ltd* [1936] 3 All E.R. 483.

Thus, we may say that ownership, or as it is called in a leasehold context, *exclusive possession*, means that the tenant can stand at the door and say of anyone "you can come in" and "you cannot".[60]

> **Exclusive possession gives the tenant the right to exclude all others from the property, even the landlord.**

The grant of a right to use the land without *possession* is a licence not a lease.[61] "An occupier of residential accommodation at a rent for a term is either a lodger or a tenant . . . A lodger is entitled to live in the premises but cannot call the place his own."[62]

(2) Background

The cases that determine whether the tenant has exclusive possession mainly arose in the context of the statutory regulation of residential tenancies by the Rent Acts. These Acts gave tenants under a residential lease significant protection against eviction by the landlord as well as the right to have a "fair rent" registered. Thus landlords could not charge market price. The Rent Acts applied only to leases and not licences. Licensees could be readily evicted and any amount charged as the licence fee. Thus, it was very important to be able to tell whether an arrangement for use of property created a lease or a licence.

Landlords would often attempt to create licences rather than leases in order to avoid the statutory protection. Thus, they would try to ensure that the agreement only granted use of the land and not *exclusive possession*, i.e. the right to exclude everyone from the property even the landlord. The Housing Act 1988 introduced new types of tenancy which no longer attracted protection from rent increases or the same security of tenure. Thus, landlords could now charge market rents for property and gain possession from the tenant much more readily.[63] The "lease/licence" distinction consequently decreased in importance.

However, it remains important to distinguish between a lease and a licence because a lease creates a property right, whereas a licence does not. If an occupier has a lease then a purchaser of the landlord's freehold reversion may be bound by that lease.[64]

(3) Problem solving in the context of the exclusive possession rule

LECTURER: When we are given a landlord and tenant problem it may require us to determine whether the tenant has been granted exclusive possession. For this we need to look carefully at the agreement between the parties and hold it against the principles in the cases we are

---

60   I am indebted to my colleague Dr Alwyn Jones of Leicester De Montfort Law School for this illustration.
61   See above in this Chapter, section 1A.
62   *Street v Mountford* [1985] A.C. 809, pp. 817–8, per Lord Templeman; also *Allan v Liverpool Overseers* (1874) L.R. 9 Q.B. 180, pp.191–192.
63   M.Thompson, *Modern Land Law*, p.368. The protection under the Rent Act 1977 still applies to tenancies granted before the coming into force of the Housing Act 1988.
64   Subject to the rules of land transfer which we considered in Chapters 6, 7 and 8.

about to consider. Here is a typical landlord and tenant problem that raises the issue of exclusive possession and the distinction between a lease and a licence.

Mr and Mrs Jamieson signed identical agreements with the freehold owner of a two bedroom cottage to be allowed to occupy the cottage for a term of twelve months for a monthly fee of two hundred and fifty pounds each. The agreement provides as follows:

- This contract shall be construed as creating a licence only and not a tenancy.
- The owner will retain a key to the cottage.
- The owner will clean the cottage twice every week.
- The owner has the right to allow others to occupy the cottage, including himself.

The owner never attempted to carry out the cleaning services. Discuss whether Mr and Mrs Jamieson have a lease or a licence.

LECTURER: In this situation our discussion will involve extracting and considering the definitions, principles and rules that tell us how we determine whether an occupier has been granted exclusive possession. We get these from the reasoning in the cases. We then apply this to the problem in order to determine whether Mr and Mrs Jamieson have been granted *exclusive possession* of the premises, and therefore have a lease, or whether this arrangement creates only a licence. We will return to this problem frequently in this section.

(4) How do the courts test whether an agreement for occupancy grants "exclusive possession"?

We need to be able to determine whether Mr and Mrs Jamieson have been granted a lease or a licence. The issue turns on whether they have been granted exclusive possession. The courts used to determine whether the tenant had exclusive possession by looking at the intentions of the parties derived from all the circumstances.[65] Thus, the courts allowed statements made by the parties to determine whether the agreement created a lease or a licence.[66] However, this test was open to abuse because it allowed landlords to avoid creating a tenancy by stating in the agreement that their intention was to grant a licence only and not a lease. This drove a "coach and horses" through the statutory protection for tenants given by the Rent Acts.[67]

The House of Lords went back to first principles in *Street v Mountford*,[68] in which it was held that in order to determine whether a tenant has been granted exclusive possession of the property the court looks objectively at the *substance of what was agreed*. So if the substance of the agreement is that an occupier is granted rights to exclude all including the landlord, and

---

65   E.H.Burn, *Maudsley & Burn's Land Law Cases and Materials* 8th edn (Oxford University Press, 2004), p.469.
66   For example of this approach *Somma v Hazlehurst* [1978] 1 W.L.R. 1014.
67   *Street v Mountford* [1985] A.C. 809.
68   [1985] A.C. 809.

otherwise reveals that the occupier has rights that look like ownership, then it does not matter that there are statements in the agreement to the effect that "a personal interest" or "licence" is granted. It will still be recognised as a lease.

(5) The decision of the House of Lords in Street v Mountford— reading cases

LECTURER: We are going to look at the leading case of *Street v Mountford*. It is not the facts of the case that are important for our purposes, nor Lord Templeman's conclusion. We need the actual reasoning in Lord Templeman's judgment to understand what qualities the courts look for in *exclusive possession*.

> **THE FACTS:** Mrs Mountford occupied a flat owned by Mr Street. Their agreement gave her exclusive possession but it said it was a licence and Mrs M had signed a declaration that she knew and accepted that the licence did not give her a tenancy protected by the Rent Acts.
>
> **THE CONCLUSION:** Because the agreement granted exclusive possession, the House of Lords held that it was not a licence, but a lease. The court should look objectively at the substance of what was agreed and not what the parties called the agreement.
>
> **EXTRACT FROM LORD TEMPLEMAN'S JUDGMENT:** *Street v Mountford* [1985] A.C. 809
>
> **THE REASONING: LORD TEMPLEMAN:** "[Mrs Mountford] seeks to reaffirm and re-establish the traditional view that an occupier of land for a term at a rent is a tenant providing the occupier is granted exclusive possession. It is conceded on behalf of Mr Street that the agreement . . . granted exclusive possession to Mrs Mountford. The traditional view that the grant of exclusive possession for a term at a rent creates a tenancy is consistent with the elevation of a tenancy into an estate in land. The tenant possessing exclusive possession is able to exercise the rights of an owner of land, which is in the real sense his land albeit temporarily and subject to certain restrictions. A tenant armed with exclusive possession can keep out strangers and keep out the landlord unless the landlord is exercising limited rights reserved to him by the tenancy agreement to enter and view and repair. A licensee lacking exclusive possession can in no sense call the land his own and cannot be said to own any estate in the land. The licence does not create an estate in the land to which it relates but only makes an act lawful which would otherwise be unlawful."

LECTURER: Compare this reasoning to our BUILDING BLOCK NO 4: Ideas of Ownership. Note how Lord Templeman's definition of exclusive possession conforms to what a tenancy *is*—ownership of the land for a time.

> **BUILDING BLOCK NO 4: Ideas of Ownership**
> As Bright says ownership is "a set of open-ended use privileges and open-ended powers to control the use made by others of the property . . . It is simply not possible to list all the potential uses which the owner may make of the property – she can live on it, use it for growing crops, climb trees on it, and so on": "Of Estates and Interests" *Land Law Themes and Perspectives*, p.529. An owner has a "stake" in the land: *Marchant v Charters* [1977]. He can leave it by will, give it away. He can include or exclude anyone he pleases, even the landlord. Effectively this means that he has *control* over the land: Gray and Gray, *Land Law*, p.90.

STUDENT: He is saying that in order to be a tenant, a lease being an estate in the land, the occupier must have been granted rights and privileges that do look exactly like ownership: our ideas in BUILDING BLOCK NO 4. He can in a real sense call the land his own and exclude anyone he pleases, including the landlord (who must thereafter reserve a right to enter and inspect). It is the tenant and not the landlord who has control over the premises. He can control the use made by others of the premises. This is how it must be with a lease.

LORD TEMPLEMAN CONTINUES: "On behalf of Mr Street his counsel . . . relies on recent authorities which, he submits, demonstrate that an occupier granted exclusive possession for a term at a rent may nevertheless be a licensee if, in the words of Slade L.J. in the present case [1985] 49 P. & C.R. 324, 332: 'there is manifested the clear intention of both parties that the rights granted are to be merely those of a personal right of occupation and not those of a tenant'. In the present case, it is submitted, the provisions of the agreement . . . manifest the clear intention of both parties that the rights granted are to be those of a personal nature and not those of a tenant.

My Lords, there is no doubt that the traditional distinction between a tenancy and a licence of land lay in the grant of land for a term at a rent with exclusive possession . . .

[. . .] 'It is not, however, a question of words but of substance. If the effect of the instrument is to give the holder an exclusive right of occupation of the land, though subject to certain reservations or to a restriction of the purposes for which it may be used, it is in law a [lease] of the land itself . . .' "[69]

LECTURER: How does the reasoning in this paragraph affect counsel's submission on behalf of Mr Street?

STUDENT: It's not looking good! It means that the provisions of the agreement between himself and Mrs Mountford, saying that it is not a tenancy for the purposes of the Rent Acts or that it is a licence, will be of no effect if the tenant in actuality has exclusive possession.

---

[69]   Quoting Lord Davey in *Glenwood Lumber Co Ltd v Phillips* [1904] A.C. 405, pp.408–409.

LECTURER: And Mr Street had conceded that she had! Lord Templeman now gives an example of other authorities that show substance takes precedence over words.

LORD TEMPLEMAN CONTINUES: "[I]n *Taylor v Caldwell* (1863) 3 B. & S. 826 . . . the defendant agreed to let the plaintiff have the use of the Surrey Gardens and Music Hall on four specified days giving a series of four concerts a day and night fetes at the gardens and hall on those days, and the plaintiff agreed to take the gardens, and the hall and to pay £100 for each day. Blackburn J. said, at p.832:

> 'The parties inaccurately call this a 'letting,' and the money to be paid a 'rent,' but the whole agreement is such as to show that the defendants were to retain the possession of the hall and gardens so that there was to be no [lease] of them, and that the contract was merely to give the plaintiffs the use of them on those days.'

That was a case where the court after considering the purpose of the grant, the terms of the grant and the surrounding circumstances came to the conclusion that the grantee was not entitled to exclusive possession but only to use the land for limited purposes and was therefore a licensee.

In the case of residential accommodation there is no difficulty in deciding whether the grant confers exclusive possession. An occupier of residential accommodation at a rent for a term is either a lodger or a tenant. The occupier is a lodger if the landlord provides attendance or services which require the landlord or his servants to exercise unrestricted access to and use of the premises. A lodger is entitled to live in the premises but cannot call the place his own . . .

If on the other hand residential accommodation is granted for a term at a rent with exclusive possession, the landlord providing neither attendance nor services, the grant is a tenancy; any express reservation to the landlord of limited rights to enter and view the state of the premises and to repair and maintain the premises only serves to emphasise the fact that the grantee is entitled to exclusive possession and is a tenant. In the present case it is conceded that Mrs Mountford is entitled to exclusive possession . . . Mr Street provided neither attendance nor services and only reserved the limited rights of inspection and maintenance and the like set forth in . . . the agreement. On the traditional view of the matter, Mrs Mountford not being a lodger must be a tenant. [. . .]"

LECTURER: Hold the reasoning that you have just read against BUILDING BLOCK NO 4: Ideas of Ownership. It is correct if it conforms to these ideas. For instance does the "music hall" case referred to by Lord Templeman accord with these ideas of ownership, i.e. the persons hiring the hall did not have rights that amounted to ownership it thus being correct that they were found to be licensees?

> **BUILDING BLOCK NO 4: Ideas of Ownership**
> An owner can make use of his land in a variety of ways. An owner has a real "stake" in the land. He can leave it by will, give it away. He can include or exclude anyone he pleases, even the landlord. Effectively this means that he has *control* over the land.

STUDENT: Lord Templeman seemed to be suggesting that the people hiring the premises only had limited use of it. They did not have overall control of the premises, i.e. who came and went, and what else happened on it etc. They could use it only for the purpose of their limited activity. Overall control remained with the owner. Thus, because a lease is ownership of land *for a time*, and having studied the fundamental ideas of ownership in BUILDING BLOCK NO 4, it was the correct decision that they were licensees and not tenants. My reasoning is that the arrangement for occupation in the "music hall" case did not confer rights akin to ownership.

LECTURER: What about Lord Templeman's "lodger" example?

STUDENT: The occupier will not be able to "call the place his own" if someone else has unlimited rights of access.

LECTURER: Where, as part of an agreement for occupation, services are provided (such as linen changing and meals) the owner will need to retain considerable access to the premises. What about these cases?

STUDENT: In such cases the occupier hasn't the necessary control over who comes and goes. On our ideas of ownership this is certainly the right criteria to apply to hold that someone is *not* a tenant—a lease being a right of *ownership of the land*.

    LORD TEMPLEMAN CONTINUES: "In the present case, the agreement dated 7 March 1983 professed an intention by both parties to create a licence and their belief that they had in fact created a licence. It was submitted on behalf of Mr Street that the court cannot in these circumstances decide that the agreement created a tenancy without interfering with the freedom of contract enjoyed by both parties. My Lords, Mr Street enjoyed freedom to offer Mrs Mountford the right to occupy the rooms comprised in the agreement on such lawful terms as Mr Street pleased. Mrs Mountford enjoyed freedom to negotiate with Mr Street to obtain different terms. Both parties enjoyed freedom to contract or not to contract and both parties exercised that freedom by contracting on the terms set forth in the written agreement and on no other terms. But the consequences in law of the agreement, once concluded, can only be determined by consideration of the effect of the agreement. If the agreement satisfied all the requirements of a tenancy, then the agreement produced a tenancy and the parties cannot alter the effect of the agreement by insisting that they only created a licence. The manufacture of a five-pronged implement for manual digging results in a fork even if the manufacturer, unfamiliar with the English language, insists that he intended to make and has made a spade. [. . .]"

> And so the matter of whether a lease or licence has been created is determined by looking at all the circumstances of the case in order to determine whether the substance of the agreement is such that exclusive possession has been granted. The parties cannot turn what would otherwise be a lease into a licence simply by calling it one.

LECTURER: Now let's apply this case to our problem question involving Mr and Mrs Jamieson. Bear in mind however that at this stage you will only have arguments for a part of the problem.

> Mr and Mrs Jamieson signed identical agreements with the freehold owner of a two bedroom cottage to be allowed to occupy the cottage for a term of twelve months for a monthly fee of two hundred and fifty pounds each. The agreement provides as follows:
>
> - This contract shall be construed as creating a licence only and not a tenancy.
> - The owner will retain a key to the cottage.
> - The owner will clean the cottage twice every week.
> - The owner has the right to allow others to occupy the cottage, including himself.
>
> The owner never attempted to carry out the cleaning services. Discuss whether Mr and Mrs Jamieson have a lease or a licence.

Remember that in order to construct a solution to a legal problem we must first state the *legal nature* of that problem. Try to do this.

STUDENT: The agreements contained a provision that they would be called licenses.

LECTURER: Here you are not stating the nature of the problem you are merely repeating the facts.

STUDENT: OK then, the problem is whether Mr and Mrs Jamieson's agreement for occupation of the cottage amounts to a lease. This will only be the case if exclusive possession has been granted. A specific problem here is whether the owner's inclusion of the term that the agreement is called a "licence" will actually make it one in law.

LECTURER: That's very good. Now that we *have* a problem we need to find the material to solve it from Lord Templeman's judgment in *Street v Mountford*.

> So the first step in legal problem solving is to state *what the legal problem actually is.*

STUDENT: Firstly, he states quite clearly at the end that simply calling an agreement a "licence" will not make it one. The whole matter hinges on whether Mr and Mrs Jamieson have been granted exclusive possession. It is only an occupier with exclusive possession that has a lease. Otherwise it is a licence. A lease is an estate in land and in a very real sense confers *ownership* of that land, albeit temporary and subject to certain restrictions (Lord Templeman).

LECTURER: And what did Lord Templeman say that exclusive possession meant?

STUDENT: The right to control who comes and goes: "A tenant armed with exclusive possession can keep out strangers and keep out the landlord". And we decide this by looking not at what the parties said in the agreement but the reality of the situation.

> The second step in legal problem solving is to give the principles that we need to use to solve the problem. Here we get these from the reasoning in the cases.

LECTURER: Now what you need to do is hold these principles against our problem. Can we say what the outcome would be?

STUDENT: The question is whether the reality of the situation is that Mr and Mrs Jamieson can exclude everyone from the two bedroomed cottage including the landlord. The two clauses allowing the owner to retain a key and introduce other occupiers may show that it is the owner who has unrestricted access and control rather than Mr and Mrs Jamieson.

LECTURER: By analogy with the "music hall" case and Lord Templeman's "lodger" illustration. However, we need to look at law after *Street v Mountford* before we can go any further with our problem solving here. But you could comment briefly on the effect of the "cleaning services" clause.

STUDENT: As the reasoning of Lord Templeman shows, if the owner requires fairly unrestricted access to the premises for cleaning it will be clear that he has retained possession and control not Mr and Mrs Jamieson. They will not have exclusive possession and consequently will only be licensees.

> The third step in legal problem solving is to hold the principles derived from the reasoning in the cases against the facts of a given scenario and determine the outcome.

> **LECTURER:** We will unpack this step in legal problem solving later in this chapter.

LECTURER: Before we can construct any more of our solution to this problem we must consider some further law that will help us.

(6) Defining exclusive possession post-Street v Mountford

As we saw from Lord Templeman's reasoning in *Street v Mountford*, an occupier has exclusive possession if he can exclude all including the landlord. Thus, where a landlord has reserved the right to enter and inspect, this shows evidence that the agreement was intended to grant exclusive possession. Otherwise, no such reservation would be necessary. However, if a landlord in reality has fairly broad access to the premises in order to provide services, such as providing meals and cleaning, then the occupier will be a lodger. The reason is that the access required in order to provide the services diminishes the tenant's control over the premises and he will thus not, in reality, be able to exclude the whole world including the landlord.

A good example of the rule that where the owner retains broad access the occupier will only be a lodger is *Abbeyfield (Harpenden) Society Ltd v Woods*. A man was the occupier of a room in a residential home for the elderly:

> "In this case there is, besides the one room, the provision of services, meals, a resident housekeeper, and such like. The whole arrangement was so personal in nature that the proper inference is that he was a licensee."[70]

Similarly in *Marchant v Charters*[71] an occupier was held to be a licensee rather than a tenant because he had a genuine right to services such as cleaning and fresh linen. The access required to provide these services meant that it was the landlord who retained possession and control over the flat.

(a) Sham clauses

We must beware of so-called "sham clauses". These are fictitious terms in the agreement introduced by a landlord in order to lead to the conclusion that there is no exclusive possession. Whilst tenancies were protected by the Rent Acts tenants under a lease enjoyed security from arbitrary eviction and they could register a fair rent for the property. This protection applied to tenancies and not licenses. Thus, landlords would use sham clauses to make it look like the agreement did not grant the occupier exclusive possession. Although tenancies created after the Housing Act 1988 no longer attract this statutory protection, a tenancy is a property right that will bind third party purchasers of the landlord's freehold reversion. It is in this sense preferable to a licence and makes it important to distinguish between them.

A legal problem scenario will often require you to detect sham clauses and comment on their legal effect. A "sham" or "pretence" was defined by Lord Donaldson in *Aslan v Murphy*[72]:

> "Quite apart from labelling, parties may succumb to the temptation to agree to pretend to have particular rights and duties which are not in fact any part of the true bargain. Prima facie, the parties must be taken to mean what they say, but given the pressures on both parties to pretend, albeit for different reasons, the courts would be acting unrealistically if they did not keep a weather eye open for pretences, taking due account of how the parties have acted in performance of their apparent bargain. . . It is the true rather than the apparent bargain which determines the question 'tenant or lodger?' "

If the court finds that a clause is a "sham" or "pretence" it will be disregarded. The court will look at the true nature of the bargain between the parties. In *Aslan v Murphy* the owner of a small basement room (4ft 3in by 12ft 6in) agreed to allow the defendant to occupy the room on the following terms: the occupier had to vacate the room between 10.30am and 12 noon every day. There was also a clause providing that the owner could introduce another occupier into the room. The agreement stated that it did not confer exclusive possession.

---

70   [1968] 1 W.L.R. 374, per Lord Denning quoted by Lord Templeman in *Street v Mountford* [1985] A.C. 809.
71   [1977] 1 W.L.R. 1181.
72   [1990] 1 W.L.R. 766, pp.771–2.

CONCLUSION AND REASONING: What we see here is a clear example of "sham" clauses. The owner did not appear to mind the occupier using the room during 10.30–12 noon, and no services were provided contrary to what was agreed, which revealed that the vacation clause was a sham designed for the purpose of showing that there was no exclusive possession. Similarly it was not practical for another person to occupy such a small room.[73] It was held that the substance of the agreement was that exclusive possession of the room had been granted. The tenant had effective control over who came and went. Thus, the agreement created a tenancy.

In *Marcou v De Silvaesa*[74] even though there were sham clauses, e.g. requiring the occupier to vacate the premises, the substance of the arrangement was still personal as it included a genuine right to services. There was no exclusive possession.

LECTURER: Let's return to our problem with Mr and Mrs Jamieson. If you remember they signed agreements with the freehold owner of a two bedroom cottage. The agreement provided as follows:

> - This contract shall be construed as creating a licence only and not a tenancy.
> - The owner will retain a key to the cottage.
> - The owner will clean the cottage twice every week
> - The owner has the right to allow others to occupy the cottage, including himself.
>
> The owner never attempted to carry out the cleaning services. Discuss whether Mr and Mrs Jamieson have a lease or a licence.

We have already looked at the first clause in relation to the law in *Street v Mountford*.[75] Let's have a look at the third and fourth clauses.

> Remember that the first step of solving a problem is to state the nature of the legal problem that has arisen, which often involves mentioning the rules in a broad sense, and state the consequences of the applicable rule to the parties.

| Identifies the legal issues that have arisen. | **STUDENT:** The broad issue is whether these two clauses show that Mr and Mrs Jamieson are licensees or tenants. The problem involves whether the third clause in this agreement is genuine. |

---

73 "Both provisions were wholly unrealistic and were clearly pretences": [1990] 1 W.L.R. 766, p.773, per Lord Donaldson.
74 (1986) 52 P. & C.R. 204.
75 [1985] A.C. 809.

> **Identifies the legal consequences of the rules.**

If it is it would show that Mr and Mrs Jamieson are only lodgers because the provision of cleaning services would give the landlord significant control over the premises. Thus, Mr and Mrs Jamieson would not have exclusive possession and would therefore be licensees and not tenants. Exactly the same could be said of the fourth clause if that were genuine.

LECTURER: Good, you identify the nature of the legal problem well, and state the consequences of the rules to the parties. So many students would have begun by telling me all about *Aslan v Murphy* and sham clauses, or simply by writing out the facts of the problem. What is the particular rule that may help Mr and Mrs Jamieson here?

STUDENT: It might be the case that the clause was inserted for the sole purpose of creating a licence rather than a lease: *Aslan v Murphy*. In which case the court will ignore the clause and look at the substance of the agreement, to see whether the reality is that exclusive possession has been granted. Looking at the quotation from Lord Donaldson in *Aslan v Murphy*, the courts will look at how the parties have actually behaved in the performance of their agreement.

LECTURER: And how would we demonstrate that the clause was pretence?

STUDENT: By the fact that services were never given, as in the case of *Aslan v Murphy*.

LLECTURER: What do you think might be the legal effect of the fourth clause?

STUDENT: This also looks like a sham clause because Mr and Mrs Jamieson have taken the cottage as a matrimonial home. It is not realistic to introduce another occupier into this situation. This observation of "sham" would be strengthened if the landlord had never attempted to exercise this "right", as in *Aslan v Murphy*. It is then arguable that the reality being that Mr and Mrs Jamieson can exclude all including the landlord, that they have a lease not a licence.

> Our STUDENT is taking the reasons for Lord Donaldson's decision in *Aslan v Murphy* and holding them up against our problem in order to predict an outcome.

LECTURER: Very good! Now we need to consider some more law that will help us to put flesh on these bones.

(7) The issue of exclusive possession where the landlord retains a key to the premises

It is perfectly normal in a tenancy agreement for the landlord to reserve the right to retain a key to the premises. After all they have an interest in making sure the property is maintained and invariably have the right/duty in the agreement to inspect and repair. Thus, the landlord's retention of a key does not of itself affect the issue of exclusive possession. It all depends *why* the owner sought to retain a key. In this respect let us consider the judgment in *Aslan v Murphy*.

CASE EXTRACT: *Aslan v Murphy* **[1990] 1 W.L.R. 766, p. 773.**

> **THE REASONING: LORD DONALDSON:** "Provisions as to keys are often relied upon in support of the contention that an occupier is a lodger rather than a tenant. . . Provisions as to keys, if not a pretence which they often are, do not have any magic in themselves. It is not a requirement of a tenancy that the occupier shall have exclusive possession of the keys to the property. What matters is what underlies the provisions as to keys. Why does the owner want a key, want to prevent keys being issued to the friends of the occupier or want to prevent the lock being changed?
>
> A landlord may well need a key in order that he may be able to enter quickly in the event of emergency: fire, burst pipes or whatever. He may need a key to enable him or those authorised by him to read meters or to do repairs which are his responsibility. None of these underlying reasons would of themselves indicate that the true bargain between the parties was such that the occupier was in law a lodger."

LECTURER: Does this reasoning fit with our BUILDING BLOCK NO 4: Ideas of Ownership? Is it correct to say that "[n]one of these underlying reasons would of themselves indicate that the true bargain between the parties was such that the occupier was in law a lodger"? It is saying that none of these ideas negate the fact that the occupier has exclusive possession, which we know, is ownership. Do they?

BUILDING BLOCK NO 4: Ideas of Ownership

An owner can include or exclude anyone they please. The key factor of possession is *control* over the premises without interference from others: Gray & Gray, *Land Law Core Text*, p.90.

> **LORD DONALDSON CONTINUES:** "On the other hand, if the true bargain is that the owner will provide genuine services which can only be provided by having keys, such as frequent cleaning, daily bed-making, the provision of clean linen at regular intervals and the like, there are materials from which it is possible to infer that the occupier is a lodger rather than a tenant. But the inference arises not from the provisions as to keys, but from the reason why those provisions formed part of the bargain."

LECTURER: In the examples Lord Donaldson gave in the paragraph immediately above why does the landlord's reason for the retention of a key to the premises *negate* the fact that the tenant has been granted exclusive possession? Are they inconsistent with BUILDING BLOCK NO 4: Ideas of Ownership?

STUDENT: I think that they are inconsistent with the idea of what ownership/possession *is*. Essentially if something gives "possession" it gives control over the land, particularly in relation to who comes and goes. If the landlord retains a key for the purposes of frequent access for cleaning and other services this shows that it is the landlord and not the lodger who has retained effective control over the premises.

LECTURER: The lodger is unable to "call the room his own": *Street v Mountford* per Lord Templeman. What about the contrasting examples in the preceding paragraph?

STUDENT: Where a landlord retains a key to the premises in order to undertake agreed inspections and repairs, or to enter in the event of an emergency, I agree that this does not negate exclusive possession. It does not cut down the tenant's control of the premises, over who comes and goes.

LECTURER: After all, the landlord is the owner of the freehold and he needs to make sure, within the confines of the agreement, that he can protect the value of the property. This does not detract from the tenant's ownership of the land as a leaseholder. Let's end by applying this legal reasoning to our problem involving Mr and Mrs Jamieson. If you remember they agreed with the owner of a two bedroom cottage that they would be allowed to occupy it for a year. The issue was whether this agreement created a lease or a licence. Other provisions of the agreement provided that:

- This contract shall be construed as creating a licence only and not a tenancy.
- The owner will retain a key to the cottage.
- The owner will clean the cottage twice every week.
- The owner has the right to allow others to occupy the cottage, including himself.

> Our STUDENT identifies issue and applicable principles.

STUDENT: The fact that the owner retains a key to the cottage does not, of itself, have any significance in determining exclusive possession: *Aslan v Murphy*. It all depends *why* the owner sought to retain a key.

Here, if the third and fourth clauses were genuine and the key was to be used for these purposes, it would show that Mr and Mrs Jamieson did not have control over who came and went from the cottage.

> Here, our STUDENT identifies further detail of principles at the same time as applying them, i.e. holding them against our problem to consider whether the principles have the same consequences to the parties that they did in *Aslan v Murphy*.

However, as I have argued these to be sham clauses, designed to negate exclusive possession, shown, e.g. by the fact that the owner never attempted to carry out the cleaning services (above), the court will disregard this and look to the reality of the agreement. As Mr and Mrs Jamieson are in reality likely to have exclusive possession, given the fact that it would be impractical to introduce another occupier into a marital situation, and there is no other obvious reason why the owner sought to retain a key, it is likely that the reasoning in *Aslan v Murphy* will produce the conclusion that Mr and Mrs Jamieson are tenants.

(8) Special considerations applicable to joint occupiers

It is often the case that people occupy property together, e.g. as a matrimonial home or with university friends. The question is whether they are regarded as separate individual licensees or tenants with joint exclusive possession and control of the land.[76] Whether they have exclusive possession depends on factors in addition to ones considered above.

(a) Joint tenancies and the four unities[77]

How do we determine whether the occupiers own a joint leasehold estate in the land? We look for the hallmarks of joint ownership. These are the elements that must be present in the reality of the occupiers' situation:

Unity of possession: First, the occupiers must all be entitled to possess the whole of the premises, i.e. they cannot exclude each other but together they can exclude the whole world, including the landlord. In practice it is often difficult to make such a determination without regard to the occupiers' relationship with each other. For instance, a clause designed to negate exclusive possession by allowing the landlord to introduce another occupier may be judged sham or genuine depending on whether the occupiers have the type of relationship that would make this clause unrealistic,[78] e.g. a cohabiting couple of a small property.

Unity of interest: The occupiers must have joint rights and obligations, e.g. each co-owner is jointly and severally liable for the full rent (although in practice each might pay their own share). This means that each occupier is not liable only for a particular share of the rent. Together they are responsible for the total rent and separately each of them is liable for the whole amount if the others default. Landlords have sometimes sought to avoid the creation of a tenancy by introducing a clause in the agreement to the effect that the occupiers are liable for two separate fees. These will be disregarded as sham clauses if the reality of the situation is that they have undertaken the obligation together. For this we might ask: if one occupier was given notice to quit would this effectively mean that both would leave?[79] This may be the case with a co-habiting couple. In this way we can see that the intended use of the property may also be relevant to the issue of whether the occupiers have been granted a joint tenancy or only separate licences.

An example relating to the above elements is *Somma v Hazelhurst*,[80] in which an unmarried couple occupied a bedsitting room as a quasi-matrimonial home. Each had separate agreements in which they agreed to pay an amount for the room. There was also a clause that provided that the landlord might introduce another occupier. The case was decided before *Street v Mountford* and it was held that the couple were licensees on the basis of what was stated in the agreement.

---

76   *A.G. Securities v Vaughan* [1990] 1 A.C. 417; *Antonaides v Villiers* [1990] 1 A.C. 417.
77   See M.Thompson, *Modern Land Law*, pp. 378–9 who considers the "four unities" in some detail, including some of the points raised here.
78   Thompson, above.
79   See the comment of Lord Templeman on *Somma v Hazelhurst* [1978] 1 W.L.R. 1014 in *Street v Mountford* [1985] 1 A.C. 809: "If the landlord had served notice on H to leave and had required S to share the room with a strange man, the notice would only have been a disguised notice to quit on both H and S". Also, Thompson takes this point, above.
80   [1978] 1 W.L.R. 1014.

However, the case was overruled in *Street*. You will remember that the House of Lords in *Street v Mountford* held that the parties cannot alter the nature of an agreement merely by calling it, for example "a personal interest only". The courts must look objectively at the reality of the situation. Lord Templeman commented on *Somma v Hazelhurst* that

> "The sham nature of this obligation would have been only slightly more obvious if [the couple] had been married or if the room had been furnished with a double bed instead of two single beds".[81]

In reality, no one else *could* be introduced. The room had been taken so that the couple could live *together*. If one was required to leave, both would leave.[82] This indicated that they had joint possession and control over the room, and had assumed joint liability for the rent. Thus, the couple had a joint interest and together, could exclude everyone including the landlord.

Unities of title and time: Thirdly, each tenant must have acquired their interest in the land at the same time and under the same title.[83] Thus, landlords have sometimes sought to avoid the creation of a tenancy by executing two separate agreements. Again the courts will attempt to ascertain the reality of the situation, i.e. whether in fact the occupiers have a joint agreement.[84]

(b) The four unities: the problem-solving skill of "distinguishing"

LECTURER: Let's return to our problem involving Mr and Mrs Jamieson.

> Mr and Mrs Jamieson signed identical agreements with the freehold owner of a two bedroom cottage to be allowed to occupy the cottage for a term of twelve months for a monthly fee of two hundred and fifty pounds each. One of the clauses was that the owner has the right to allow others to occupy the cottage, including himself.
>
> Discuss whether Mr and Mrs Jamieson have a lease or a licence.

Here we are going to learn about what lawyers call "distinguishing" cases. This is where we look at our precedent case, here *Somma v Hazelhurst* (as explained in *Street v Mountford*) and consider whether, when we apply its reasoning to our case, the result might be different. We

---

81   [1985] 1 A.C. 809, p.825, per Lord Templeman.
82   See comments above.
83   *A.G. Securities v Vaughan* [1990] 1 A.C. 417.
84   Also M. Thompson, *Modern Land Law*, p.379.

have to consider whether our facts are *so* different (what lawyers call "materially different") that a different conclusion is justified.

Distinguishing

But before we can "distinguish" a case we must be able to identify those facts of the precedent case that were regarded by the judge as important to the conclusion and WHY they were so important. When we are doing this we are identifying the *reasoning* that tells us how the rule should apply.

LECTURER: So in *Somma v Hazelhurst* (as criticised by Lord Templeman in *Street v Mountford*) what were the factors that were so important to Lord Templeman that they led him to the conclusion that there should have been a tenancy and not a licence?[85]

STUDENT: Applying the reasoning that Lord Templeman did to this case, the couple were tenants and not licensees because the reality of the situation was that they had exclusive possession. They had exclusive possession because although they had agreed to pay separately under two different agreements, this was a sham. The reality was that they took the room together as a quasi-matrimonial home. They had a joint interest. If one left, both would leave. Secondly the judge thought it important that the home was a *matrimonial* home and comprised one single room. Because of this the judge held that the clause allowing the owner to introduce another occupier was a sham. It was impractical in this situation.

The first step to applying or distinguishing a case is to identify its reasoning. Our STUDENT correctly identifies the reasons why Lord Templeman came to the conclusion that a lease and not a licence should have been found in *Somma v Hazelhurst* [1978] 1 W.L.R. 1014.

LECTURER: Right! You comprehend the reasoning well. Now our next stage of solving our legal problem is to consider whether our case is materially the same or whether it may be "distinguished", i.e. leading to the opposite conclusion that a licence has been created.

A case is distinguished if our facts are so different from the case's facts that we must come to a different conclusion. We are working with the same rules—the ones that our STUDENT identified from *Somma v Hazelhurst* [1978] 1 W.L.R. 1014 (as criticised in *Street*).

---

85   This is a reformulation of a useful question designed to ascertain an author's reasoning for their conclusion found in L.Elder, *I Think Critically Therefore I Am: Times Higher Education Supplement* (August 2008).

STUDENT: Although Mr and Mrs Jamieson have signed separate agreements and agreed to pay separate amounts of rent, this does not negate unity of title and interest if the reality is that they have taken a joint estate. These may be "shams" on the part of the landlord to make their agreement look like a licence rather than a lease. Looking therefore at the other provisions of the agreement, it may be argued that it is a joint interest because they have taken the cottage together and both either stay or leave together. Thus in effect they have joint responsibilities for the rent.

LECTURER: So far then, we are "on all fours" with *Somma v Hazelhurst*. If the case is indistinguishable from Mr and Mrs Jamieson's case then we must come to the conclusion that a lease has been granted: the same conclusion that Lord Templeman arrived at in his reasoning about *Somma v Hazelhurst*.

STUDENT: There is one possible distinguishing feature. Unlike *Somma v Hazelhurst* the house is not a single room it is a two bedroom cottage. So it would not be absolutely impractical for the landlord to introduce another occupier as per the final clause. If this was thought to be a genuine part of the bargain, Mr and Mrs Jamieson would not have the requisite degree of control. The landlord would retain exclusive possession because he would have ultimate control over who came and went.

LECTURER: So what you are saying is that it might be possible to *distinguish* our case of Mr and Mrs Jamieson from the precedent case of *Somma v Hazelhurst*? You are saying that the facts in that case, upon which the judge justified his conclusion, are materially different. In our case there is not the same sense of *impracticality* to the clause that says the landlord is able to introduce another occupier.

Is a counter-argument possible?

STUDENT: Yes, because Mr and Mrs Jamieson have obviously taken the cottage as a matrimonial home, this requires privacy, which shows the final clause to be a sham, particularly if the landlord has not attempted to carry it out.

LECTURER: Very good. Now let us consider together the reasoning in other cases that apply the "four unities".

(9) Joint occupiers cases

THE FACTS: The House of Lords applied these criteria in *Antonaides v Villiers*.[86] Similarly to the case we have just considered, a co-habiting couple occupied a one bedroom flat. Each one had an agreement titled a "licence agreement". There was a clause which provided that each occupier was liable for half the rent (trying to show that there was no "joint" liability), and the agreements gave the landlord the right to introduce another occupier, including himself, who would share the flat with them.

CONCLUSION: The House of Lords found that these provisions were shams and that the reality of the agreement was that the couple had been granted exclusive possession.

---

86   [1990] 1 A.C. 417. *Antonaides v Villiers* was decided in a joint appeal with *AG Securities v Vaughan*, considered below.

CASE EXTRACT from *Antonaides v Villiers* [1990] 1 A.C. 417.

LECTURER: Now we will examine Lord Oliver's reasoning in *Antonaides v Villiers*:

 LORD OLIVER: "The appellants in this appeal are a young couple who at all material times were living together as man and wife. In about November 1984 they learned from a letting agency that a flat was available . . . They inspected the flat together and were told that the rent would be £174 per month. They were given the choice of having the bedroom furnished with a double bed or two single beds and they chose a double bed. So, right from the inception, there was never any question but that the appellants were seeking to establish a joint home and they have, at all material times, been the sole occupants of the flat.

 There is equally no question but that the premises are not suitable for occupation by more than one couple, save on a very temporary basis . . . When it came to drawing up the contractual arrangements under which the appellants were to be let into possession, each was asked to and did sign a separate licence agreement . . . under which each assumed an individual, but not a joint, responsibility for payment of one half of the sum of £174 previously quoted as the rent.

 There is an air of total unreality about these documents read as separate and individual licences in the light of the circumstance that the appellants were together seeking a flat as a quasi-matrimonial home . . . It cannot realistically have been contemplated that the respondent would either himself use or occupy any part of the flat or put some other person in to share accommodation specifically adapted for the occupation by a couple living together. These clauses cannot be considered as seriously intended to have any practical operation or to serve any purpose apart from the purely technical one of seeking to avoid the ordinary legal consequences attendant upon letting the appellants into possession at a monthly rent. . .

 The conclusion seems to me irresistible that these two so-called licences, executed contemporaneously and entered into in the circumstances already outlined, have to be read together as constituting in reality one single transaction under which the appellants became joint occupiers. That of course does not conclude the case because the question still remains, what is the effect? [. . .]"

LECTURER: What concrete conclusion have we got so far?

STUDENT: These were not separate agreements because the reality of the situation was that the couple were seeking to set up a joint home. In reality there was joint liability for the rent. The couple have a joint interest of some description, but as yet it is still uncertain what rights are created: lease or licence.

 LORD OLIVER: ". . .nobody acquainted with the circumstances in which the parties had come together and with the physical lay-out and size of the premises could seriously have imagined that the clauses in the licence which, on the face of them, contemplate the respondent and an apparently limitless number of other persons moving in to share the whole of the available accommodation, including the bedroom with what, to all intents and purposes, was a married couple committed to paying £174 a month in advance, were anything other than a smoke-screen [. . .]"

STUDENT: The reality of the situation was that the landlord could not realistically exercise the clause in the agreement; no one in reality could share with this couple in their situation. This meant that *in effect* they had exclusive possession.

LECTURER: They had exclusive possession and therefore the agreement was a lease.

LORD OLIVER: "If the real transaction was, as the judge found one under which the appellants became joint tenants with exclusive possession, on the footing that the two agreements are to be construed together, then it would follow that they were together jointly and severally responsible for the whole rent. It would equally follow that they could effectively exclude the [landlord] and his nominees."[87]

LECTURER: Now let's draw everything together and apply all the cases and the principles above to the problem with Mr and Mrs Jamieson. You will need to incorporate all the problem solving skills we have learned so far.

> Mr and Mrs Jamieson signed identical agreements with the freehold owner of a two bedroom cottage to be allowed to occupy the cottage for a term of twelve months for a monthly fee of two hundred and fifty pounds each. The agreement provides that the owner has the right to allow others to occupy the cottage, including himself.

STUDENT: I argued previously with you that Mr and Mrs Jamieson's case is materially indistinguishable from *Somma v Hazelhurst*, which, according to Lord Templeman in *Street v Mountford*, created a tenancy. The reasoning was that the couple took the cottage as a matrimonial home where a degree of privacy would be expected. This, and the fact that the owner has not attempted to exercise his "right" to introduce another occupier would lead to the conclusion that the couple in reality have the right to exclude the whole world including the landlord.

LECTURER: Do you find the reasoning in *Antonaides v Villiers* helpful in adding to your argument?

> Our STUDENT will need to "apply" or "distinguish" this case as well. But before they can do that they must extract the reasons for the decision in *Antonaides v Villiers*.

STUDENT: It is much more helpful on the "joint interest" point than Lord Templeman was in *Street v Mountford*. In *Antonaides* the couple were joint tenants with exclusive possession

---

87   [1990] 1 A.C. 417; See also *Mikeover Ltd v Brady* [1989] 3 All E.R. 618, in which joint occupiers were held to be licensees and *Hadjiloucas v Crean* [1988] 1 W.L.R 1006, in which they were tenants.

because despite executing separate agreements and agreeing to pay rent separately, they had in effect, taken the premises as a joint home. If one left, both would leave. In reality, there was one single transaction under which both became jointly liable for rent and other obligations. Given the nature of the parties' relationship and the layout of the flat, the clause that the landlord could introduce another occupier was unrealistic. Thus, there was a joint tenancy with exclusive possession.

LECTURER: Now, the next stage of our legal problem solving is to consider whether Mr and Mrs Jamieson's case is "distinguishable" from *Villiers* or whether it is on "all fours" with it.

STUDENT: Definitely on all fours. As I argued before, the purpose for taking the house is that of a family home. This is clearly a joint purpose, so the fact that the landlord executed two separate agreements can be regarded as a sham. Because in reality they took the cottage together they may be seen as assuming joint liability for the rent and other obligations. The house itself may be larger and in theory admit another occupier, but, as I have argued above, the parties' relationship and the fact that they would expect privacy makes this look unreal.

LECTURER: As the final stage of legal problem solving you must state the legal consequence of your reasoning for the parties involved.

STUDENT: The consequence of the above is that Mr and Mrs Jamieson have a joint tenancy with exclusive possession. They are not, as it was made to appear, licensees.

Let's look at a real case with "distinguishing features" from *Antonaides v Villiers*.[88] In *A.G. Securities v Vaughan*[89] the question was whether an agreement for occupation of a four-bedroom flat granted exclusive possession to its occupiers so as to create a tenancy rather than a licence. Each agreement was described as a "licence". The occupiers signed separate agreements at different dates and each paid a different amount of rent. The occupiers did not know one another. They were selected by the owner and came at different times. Each time an occupier left the flat the landlord replaced him with another occupier. The House of Lords held that the occupiers were licensees.

Lord Templeman in this case held that the occupiers could not have a joint tenancy because if one died then the landlord would have the right to replace him. If you remember the principal incident of a joint tenancy is the "right of survivorship". This means that when one joint tenant dies then the remaining tenants have exclusive possession together, i.e. they can together exclude the whole world. Lord Templeman said that because the landlord would be able to replace the occupier who died, it could not therefore be a joint tenancy.

CASE EXTRACT: Lord Oliver in *A.G. Securities v Vaughan*

> **LORD OLIVER:** "To begin with the appeal concerns a substantial flat in a mansion block consisting of four bedrooms, a lounge, a sitting-room and usual offices. The trial

---

88   [1990] 1 A.C. 417.
89   [1990] 1 A.C. 417, House of Lords, decided in the same appeal as *Antoniades v Villiers*.

judge found, as a fact, that the premises could without difficulty provide residential accommodation for four persons. There is no question but that the agreements with which the appeal is concerned reflect the true bargain between the parties. It is the purpose and intention of both parties to each agreement that it should confer an individual right on the licensee named, that he should be liable only for the payment which he had undertaken, and that his agreement should be capable of termination without reference to the agreements with other persons occupying the flat. The judge found that the agreements were not shams and that each of the four occupants had arrived independently of one another and not as a group. His finding was that there was never a group of persons coming to the flat all together. . . The only questions are those of the effect of each agreement vis-a-vis the individual licensee and whether the agreements collectively had the effect of creating a joint tenancy among the occupants of the premises for the time being by virtue of their having between them exclusive possession of the premises.

Taking first, by way of example, the position of the first occupier to be let into the premises on the terms of one of these agreements, it is, in my judgment, quite unarguable, once any question of sham is out of the way, that he has an estate in the premises which entitles him to exclusive possession. His right, which is, by definition, a right to share use and occupation with such other persons not exceeding three in number as the licensor shall introduce from time to time, is clearly inconsistent with any exclusive possession in him alone even though he may be the only person in physical occupation at a particular time. He has no legal title which will permit him to exclude other persons to whom the licensor may choose to grant the privilege of entry. That must equally apply to the additional licensees who join him. None of them has individually nor have they collectively the right or power lawfully to exclude a further nominee of the licensor within the prescribed maximum. [. . .]

. . . if the licence agreement is what it purports to be, that is to say, merely an agreement for permissive enjoyment as the invitee of the landlord, then each shares the use of the premises with other invitees of the same landlord. The landlord is not excluded for he continues to enjoy the premises through his invitees . . . Each person is individually liable for the amount which he has agreed, which may differ in practice from the amounts paid by all or some of the others.

. . . For my part, I agree with the dissenting judgment of Sir George Waller in finding no unity of interest, no unity of title, certainly no unity of time and, as I think, no unity of possession. I find it impossible to say that the agreements entered into with the respondents created either individually or collectively a single tenancy either of the entire flat or of any part of it. I agree that the appeal should be allowed."

LECTURER: The first material finding was that the separate agreements between the landlord and the individual occupiers, and their separate liability for payment, were not "shams". After this what happened?

STUDENT: They did not come to the property together as a group. Each took separate liability for their payment. The amounts that each paid could vary. There was no joint liability for the whole amount, i.e. the landlord could not recover the whole amount from any one of the occupiers if the others defaulted. Furthermore, it looks like they couldn't possibly have a joint estate in the flat. For one thing the agreements were not executed at the same time.

LECTURER: So no unity of interest, time and title. But the crucial unities are really unity of possession and interest.

STUDENT: In the second paragraph Lord Oliver reasons that because of the landlord's ability to introduce other occupiers from time to time, e.g. when one of the four left, then the occupiers could not be said to have exclusive possession, either together as a whole or individually. It is the landlord that has possession not the occupiers: "The landlord is not excluded for he continues to enjoy the premises through his invitees" [3rd paragraph]. So because there is no exclusive possession there is no tenancy.

LECTURER: Let's check out this reasoning with BUILDING BLOCK NO 4: Ideas of Ownership, we know that a lease is ownership of land *for a time*. This means that Lord Oliver's reasoning is correct if it reflects underlying ideas of what a lease *is*. We say that it must show the features of *ownership*.

> **BUILDING BLOCK NO 4: Ideas of Ownership:**
> An owner can include or exclude anyone they please. The key factor of possession is *control* over the premises without interference from others: Gray & Gray, *Land Law Core Text*, p.90.

STUDENT: The occupiers had no control over who came and went. It was the landlord only who had this level of control. Thus, because the key feature of ownership is control over the territory, and this factor was absent in *AG Securities v Vaughan* then Lord Oliver was correct to say that the occupiers were only licensees and not tenants.

LECTURER: Well done – you have comprehended the reasoning well.

(10) Multiple occupiers with separate (rather than joint) tenancies

Lord Oliver in *A.G. Securities v Vaughan*[90] observed that it is possible for multiple occupiers of premises each to have separate individual tenancies with the landlord.

(11) Exceptions where a licence exists even though there is exclusive possession

In *Street v Mountford*[91] Lord Templeman identified that there are exceptions to the rule that a person granted exclusive possession has a lease: "an occupier who enjoys exclusive possession is not necessarily a tenant".[92] Occupancy may be attributable to some legal relationship other than that of landlord and tenant,[93] e.g. a trespasser or a mortgagee in possession. In such cases,

---

90   [1990] 1 A.C. 417, p.471.
91   [1985] A.C. 809.
92   [1985] A.C. 809.
93   Harpum, Bridge, Dixon, *Megarry & Wade Law of Real Property*, pp.745–746, citing *Drover v Prosser* [1904].

even though the occupier has exclusive possession, he will only be a licensee. We will consider two other exceptions identified by Lord Templeman.

(a) Service occupiers

Another exception is where an employee is occupying his employer's property for the better performance of his duties. In such cases even though the employee has exclusive possession a licence will come into being rather than a tenancy.[94] Lord Templeman in *Street v Mountford* observes: "The test is whether the servant requires the premises he occupies in order the better to perform his duties as a servant".[95] In *Facchini v Bryson*[96] an employee was allowed to occupy their employer's property. He was held not to be a service occupier as his occupation of the house was not necessary in order for him to better perform his duties. In *Murray Bull & Co Ltd v Murray*[97] an employee was held not to be a service occupier because he occupied his employer's property simply because it was more convenient and not for the better performance of his duties.

> The legal consequence of finding that an employee is a service occupier is that they cannot establish a tenancy, even if there is exclusive possession.

(b) Family arrangements or acts of friendship or generosity

Where a person is let into occupation of a room or premises out of generosity, friendship or as a family arrangement, this will not result in a tenancy even if exclusive possession is granted. The reason is that there is generally no intention to create a legal relationship.[98] Thus, where an owner allowed her brother to occupy her house free of rent, it was held that no tenancy had been created.[99]

C. WHY THE LEASE AND LICENCE DISTINCTION IS STILL IMPORTANT TODAY

Although the Rent Acts no longer regulate residential tenancies, the distinction between a lease and a licence remains important for another reason. A tenancy is a property right. As we know it is an estate in the land itself; it is one of the two estates in land capable of existing at law: the "term of years absolute". Consequently, a lease will bind third parties who later come to own the freehold, e.g. if the landlord sells his freehold reversion.[100] A licence is a purely

---

94   *Norris v Checkfield* [1991] 1 W.L.R. 1241.
95   Citing *Mayhew v Suttle* (1854) 4 El. & Bl. 347 and Mellor J in *Smith v Seghill Overseers* (1875) L.R. 10 Q.B. 422; See also *Facchini v Bryson* [1952] 1 T.L.R. 138.
96   [1952] 1 T.L.R. 138.
97   [1953] 1 Q.B. 211.
98   *Facchini v Bryson* [1952] 1 T.L.R. 138; *Street v Mountford* [1985] A.C. 809; *Cobb v Lane* [1952] 1 T.L.R. 1037. Of course it is open to the parties to establish as a matter of fact that such intention existed.
99   *Cobb v Lane* [1952] 1 T.L.R. 1037.
100   We considered the circumstances in which a lease will bind purchasers of the land in Chapters 6, 7 and 8 on Land Transfer Law.

personal right giving the occupier permission to use the premises. It does not confer on the occupier any interest in the land itself. Thus, if the owner sells the land the transferee is not bound to allow the occupier to continue to use the land.

> **I don't know about you but I would much rather have my residential security protected should my landlord sell the house!**

(1) The decision of the House of Lords in Bruton v London & Quadrant Housing Trust

The law that came from *Street v Mountford*[101] took a rather unusual turn following the House of Lords' decision in *Bruton v London & Quadrant Housing Trust*.[102]

The Trust entered into an agreement, which was called a "licence", with Mr Bruton for the occupation of one of a block of flats in Brixton. Mr Bruton sued the Trust for breach of repairing obligations. These obligations applied only to tenancies.[103] He argued that his "licence" agreement with the Trust created a tenancy on *Street v Mountford* principles. The House of Lords held that because Mr Bruton had exclusive possession for a certain term then he had a tenancy. The trust was liable to repair the flat.

You may think that there is nothing unusual in this. However, the difficulty with the decision in *Bruton* was that the Housing Trust granting the tenancy had itself only a licence to use the block of flats. It had no property right in the block of flats.

> **A maxim of property law is *nemo dat quod non habet*. It means no one can give that which he has not, i.e. no one can give a better title than he has:** Mozley & Whiteley's *Law Dictionary* (11th edn, 1993)

If the Trust did not own a property right it is difficult to imagine how it could grant a tenancy (itself a property right) of one of the flats. The House of Lords held that Mr Bruton's tenancy would not bind a third party, i.e. if the owner sold the block the tenancy would not bind the purchaser.[104] It was a so-called *non-proprietary* tenancy. It created a tenancy between the Trust and Mr Bruton only.

---

101   [1985] A.C. 809.
102   [2000] 1 A.C. 406.
103   Landlord and Tenant Act 1985 s.11. We study covenants in leases and repairing obligations in the next Chapter.
104   See *Kay v Lambeth L.B.C.* [2006] UKHL 10; [2006] 2 A.C. 465 in which the House of Lords confirmed that the *Bruton* tenancy will not bind third parties in the way of a property right.

CASE EXTRACT: *Bruton v London & Quadrant Housing Trust* **[2000] 1 A.C. 406**

LORD HOFFMANN: "The decision of this House in *Street v Mountford* [1985] A.C. 809 is authority for the proposition that a 'lease' or a 'tenancy' is a contractually binding agreement, not referable to any other relationship between the parties, by which one person gives another the right to exclusive occupation of land for a fixed or renewable period or periods of time, usually in return for a periodic payment in money. An agreement having these characteristics creates a relationship of landlord and tenant to which the common law or statute may then attach various incidents. The fact that the parties use language more appropriate to a different kind of agreement, such as a licence, is irrelevant if upon its true construction it has the identifying characteristics of a lease. . .

In this case, it seems to me that the agreement, construed against the relevant background, plainly gave Mr Bruton a right to exclusive possession. There is nothing to suggest that he was to share possession with the trust . . . The trust did not retain such control over the premises as was inconsistent with Mr Bruton having exclusive possession . . . The only rights which it reserved were for itself and the council to enter at certain times and for limited purposes. As Lord Templeman said in *Street v Mountford* [1985] A.C. 809, 818, such an express reservation 'only serves to emphasise the fact that the grantee is entitled to exclusive possession and is a tenant.'[. . .]

My Lords, in my opinion, that is the end of the matter. But the Court of Appeal did not stop at that point. In the leading majority judgment, Millett L.J. said. . . that an agreement could not be a lease unless it had a further characteristic, namely that it created a legal estate in the land which 'binds the whole world.' If, as is the case, the grantor [the Housing Trust] had no legal estate, the agreement could not create one and therefore did not qualify as a lease . . .

. . . I must respectfully differ. . . the term 'lease' or 'tenancy' describes a relationship between two parties who are designated landlord and tenant. It is not concerned with the question of whether the agreement creates an estate or other proprietary interest which may be binding upon third parties. A lease may, and usually does, create a proprietary interest called a leasehold estate or, technically, a 'term of years absolute.' This will depend upon whether the landlord had an interest out of which he could grant it. Nemo dat quod non habet [meaning: no one can give what they do not have]. But it is the fact that the agreement is a lease which creates the proprietary interest. It is putting the cart before the horse to say that whether the agreement is a lease depends upon whether it creates a proprietary interest."

LECTURER: This is very controversial! We will return to the property right point in a moment. For now I want you to imagine that you are faced with the question "Discuss whether you think the decision in *Bruton v London & Quadrant Housing Trust* is good law". Choose your Building Blocks.

STUDENT: My first one is this:

> **BUILDING BLOCK NO 1: Residential Security**
> Land Law should protect people's residential security.

I think that the decision in *Bruton* was good law because it protected Mr Bruton's residential security. The Trust were held to certain basic standard repairing obligations that they would not have been had the agreement been found to be a licence.

LECTURER: I think you have a fair argument up to a point but you need to add more colour. Once you have an idea in your mind about the arguments you want to pursue using Building Blocks study a couple of articles to see whether academic authors make similar points and can help you take your arguments any further. For instance, your point on repairing obligations was developed by S.Bridge in *Land Law Issues Debates Policy*, p.119. The author comments on Lord Hobhouse's judgment in *Bruton*:

> "As befits a commercial judge, he adopts what might be described as a 'contractual' approach. . . The existence of a contractual relationship of landlord and tenant sufficed to trigger the statutory implication of the repairing covenant. The housing trust had capacity to enter into the contractual agreement. . .. Indeed, on policy grounds. . . a landlord should not be able to escape statutory repairing obligations by denying that they had capacity to grant a tenancy."

STUDENT: So on BUILDING BLOCK NO 1 we might say that *Bruton* is good law, despite its technical problems.

LECTURER: In *Street v Mountford* Lord Templeman reasoned that the requirement for exclusive possession derives from the fact that a lease is an estate in the land itself. It is a right asserted not against the person but against the land itself. In effect it is a right to exclude the whole world from the land, including the landlord and any purchaser from him. This is further reinforced by the fact that Lord Templeman in *Street* derived the requirement from the idea of *ownership*. A lease is ownership of the land, albeit for a limited time and subject to certain restrictions, and this requires that the owner be able to exclude all comers.[105] This is where the requirement of exclusive possession came from. Can you say how *Bruton* cuts right across this?

STUDENT: Mr Bruton would not have been able to exclude a third party purchaser. His tenancy would not bind them. Also, the requirement for exclusive possession in *Street v Mountford* was derived directly from the fact that a tenancy *is* an estate in land which is a property right not (or not only) a contract.

LECTURER: It has been said that *Bruton* employed a "relative" view of exclusive possession, i.e. he could exclude the whole world and his landlord but not purchasers from him, i.e. persons with a better claim to the land. This is sufficient.[106] Are you convinced by this?

STUDENT: I still think that the idea that Lord Templeman had in mind in *Street v Mountford* when he defined exclusive possession was that the occupier had a stake in the room. I think

---

105   S.Bridge in *Land Law Issues Debates Policy* (2002), p.118, also S.Bright (2000) 116 L.Q.R. 7.
106   S.Bridge in *Land Law Issues Debates Policy* (2002), p.118; compare S.Bright (2000) 116 L.Q.R. 7.

that this phrase is meaningless unless he is able, not only to exclude his immediate landlord, but to assert his rights against purchasers and if he wishes to, sell his interest in the property to a third party. I find it difficult picturing the so-called non-proprietary tenancy.

LECTURER: So you disagree with Lord Hoffmann. It is not "putting the cart before the horse to say that whether the agreement is a lease depends upon whether it creates a proprietary interest".

STUDENT: I think the House of Lords was trying to have the cart without the horse![107]

LECTURER: In *Bruton*, Lord Hoffmann considers that a tenancy can be brought into being and it does not necessarily have to exist as an estate in land. *Megarry & Wade* considers that it is possible that "[a]lthough an estate cannot exist without tenure [here, a tenancy], there seems no reason why tenure should not exist without any estate".[108] However, according to these authors if there is no estate ("ownership") created by the tenure, there is no need to prove that the lease is for a certain term.[109] The tenure exists "unconnected with any estate or interest"[110] so there is no logic behind requiring that tenure to possess the characteristics of a lease *as an estate in land*, e.g. a "term certain" and "exclusive possession". Whatever it is, it is not ownership so there should be no need to show that the tenancy *looks like* ownership, i.e. confers the right to exclude the whole world.[111]

STUDENT: Is the *Bruton* tenancy an entirely new type of tenancy then? It is interesting though that the *Megarry & Wade* observation rather confirms our argument above that the whole point of proving exclusive possession for a term certain is to establish an estate (ownership) which *is* a property right.

LECTURER: So we *can* have a non-proprietary tenancy but it is not established by the *Street v Mountford* test, which was grafted onto the first principle that a lease exists *as an estate in land*.

Creation of Leases

A. LEGAL LEASES

In this section we are concerned with how leases come into being: how they are created. If you remember the Law of Property Act 1925 reclassified all estates and interests in land. This reclassification reduced the number of estates and interests capable of existing as *legal* estates

---

107   A point also taken by M. Lower, "The Bruton Tenancy" [2010] Conv. 38, p.53.

108   Harpum, Bridge and Dixon, *Megarry and Wade Law of Real Property*, para.17–078, although this observation was not made in the context of the *Bruton* tenancy. The observation is made in the context of the "tenancy at will".

109   The author considers this to be the consequence of tenure without ownership. "Tenure" means to hold land of someone else (you may remember from Chapter 2) and it is a purely personal relationship. The author does not make the argument in the context of exclusive possession.

110   *Megarry and Wade Law of Real Property*, above.

111   Note the comment made by M. Lower, "The Bruton Tenancy" [2010] Conv. 38, p.39: "The idea that the lease is an estate in land could be said to be central to understanding the concept of exclusive possession".

and interests.[112] A lease is one of them. All other estates and interests were reclassified as equitable.

> **Law of Property Act 1925 s.1. Legal estates and equitable interests**
> "(1) The only estates in land which are capable of subsisting or of being conveyed or created at law are-
> (a) An estate in fee simple absolute in possession;
> (b) A term of years absolute"

Legal estates have teeth. They bind purchasers automatically. The draftsman's intention was to limit the number of estates and interests that had this effect. The idea was to give the holder of the legal estate the powers to transfer that estate to a purchaser as free as possible from most equitable interests. Where title to land is registered a legal lease granted for a period greater than seven years must be registered with its own title in order to be legal. Its effect is then to bind every subsequent dealing with the freehold title. A legal lease granted for a period of seven years or less is an overriding interest that will bind purchasers irrespective of registration.

However, we must note the wording of the Law of Property Act 1925. It says that a lease is *capable* of being a legal estate in land. Something else must be done in order to make the lease legal. It must comply with the requisite formalities.

(1) An estate or interest in land that is capable of being "legal" must be created by deed

Let's say that Adam, Brian, Cully and David want to start a vets practice and require offices. They go and view offices Nos 3–5 Octavian Street, Derby. The owner of the premises, Mr Browne, who will be their landlord, shows them round and they decide that the premises will be suitable for their vet's practice. Now the process of negotiation begins. The vets and Mr Browne must agree on a term for the offices to be leased to the vets. Because their vets practice is new, they do not want to over commit themselves, so all parties agree on a term of four years. In order to exist as a legal estate the vets' lease must be granted by deed:

> **Law of Property Act 1925 s.52 Conveyances to be by deed**
>
> "(1) All conveyances of land or of any interest therein are void for the purpose of conveying or creating a legal estate unless made by deed."

---

112   s. 1(1) and 1(2).

> LEASE OF NOS 3–5
> OCTAVIAN STREET
>
> Signed as a deed in the presence of XXX as witness, who also signs.

The grant of the lease by Mr Browne to the vets is a conveyance of a legal estate. In order to be a legal lease, it must be made by deed: s.52

The lease of 3–5 Octavian Street to the vets, granted by Mr Browne, the freehold owner, must, in order to be recognised as a deed: say it's a deed, and be signed, witnessed and delivered: Law of Property (Miscellaneous Provisions) Act 1989 s.1.

If a contract is entered into between the prospective landlord and tenant prior to the granting of a legal lease it will need to comply with the formalities for contracts as discussed below. The assignment of a legal tenancy must also be made by deed.[113]

(2) The section 54(2) exception

Section 54(2) of the Law of Property Act 1925 provides an exception to the rule that a legal lease must be created by deed. A legal lease can be created without a deed or even orally ("by parol")

> **Law of Property Act 1925 s.54(2) Creation of interests in land by parol**
> **"(2) Nothing in the foregoing provisions of this Part of this Act shall affect the creation by parol of leases taking effect in possession for a term not exceeding three years (whether or not the lessee is given power to extend the term) at the best rent which can be reasonably obtained without taking a fine."**

There are three criteria that must be established in order for a legal lease to come into being without a deed. All three criteria must be established. The lease must take effect in possession. This means that the tenant's right to take possession of the land must start as soon as the lease comes into being, i.e. the lease is not granted on May 3 for the tenant to take possession of the premises on September 1.[114] The requirement that the lease is for a term not longer than three years includes periodic tenancies that run from period to period. The lease must be at a rent that represents market value for that property.[115] In *Fitzkriston LLP v Panayi*,[116] there was no deed and no valid legal parol tenancy because the rent paid under the agreement was not the best obtainable. And as you can see from s.54(2) there must be no "fine", which is a sum payable at the start of the tenancy.[117]

---

113   *Crago v Julian* [1992] 1 W.L.R. 372.
114   This would be a reversionary lease.
115   Clarke and Greer, *Land Law Directions*, 2nd edn (Oxford University Press, 2010) p.131.
116   [2008] EWCA Civ 283.
117   A fine is taken in order to reduce the rent: Harpum, Bridge, Dixon, *Megarry & Wade Law of Real Property*), para.17–034.

LECTURER: Could the vet's lease fall within the s.54(2) exception, making it legal without a deed?

STUDENT: No because the vets are taking the property for a term longer than three years (four years).

Even if parties fail to create a legal lease, because there is no deed and the s.54(2) exception does not apply, it is possible either that an equitable lease has arisen or circumstances have given rise to a periodic tenancy. You will remember that a periodic tenancy can come into being by implication if this can be construed as the intention of the parties.[118] For example, a periodic tenancy may arise where the tenant has entered into possession of the land and started paying rent. A periodic tenancy falls within the s.54(2) exception and can thus come into being without a deed.

STUDENT: So if our four vets had moved into Nos 3–5 Octavian Street and had started paying rent to Mr Browne then they would have an implied periodic tenancy. This would be legal under s.54(2).

LECTURER: That's quite correct. Remember that the implication is based on the intentions of Mr Browne and the vets.

B. EQUITABLE LEASES

There are some situations in which equity will hold a lease to exist, even where it is not possible for that lease to take effect as a legal estate.

(1) Where the lease is created out of an equitable interest in the land

Where the landlord herself only owns an equitable interest in the land, e.g. she holds only an equitable interest in the fee simple estate, any tenancy she creates out of this interest will necessarily be equitable.

(2) Leases which do not comply with compulsory registration

Where a lease must be registered at the Land Registry with its own title in order to take effect as a legal estate, failure to comply with the compulsory registration requirement has the effect that the lease takes effect in equity only.[119] Thus, in this situation, even though the lease has been granted by deed it will take effect as an equitable lease.[120]

---

118   *Prudential Assurance Co Ltd v London Residuary Body* [1992] 2 A.C. 386; *Walsh v Lonsdale* (1882) 21 Ch. D. 9.

119   Land Registration Act 2002 s.7(1) (where the registrable lease is granted out of unregistered land and therefore constitutes a "first registration") and s.27(1) (where the lease constitutes a "registrable disposition"). See Chapter 8 and in this Chapter below at section 3C.

120   For the circumstances in which equitable leases will bind a purchaser of the landlord's freehold reversion see below in this Chapter at section 3C.

(3) Where there is a specifically enforceable contract to grant a lease then equity sees as done that which ought to be done

If a lease has not been created by deed it cannot be a legal lease, unless the s.54(2) exception applies. However, the lease may take effect as an equitable lease if the parties enter into a valid contract to grant a lease.

Let's say that after negotiating the terms of the lease of Nos 3–5 Octavian Street, Derby, the lease is never granted in a way that satisfies the requirements of a deed. However, the parties enter into a contract, i.e. a promise to grant a lease in the future. All the terms of the lease are put into a document which the vets and Mr Browne sign. This is a contract between the parties for the granting of a lease; the terms on which the property is to be let. Under certain circumstances a contract for a lease can give rise to an equitable lease.

(a) The contract must comply with section 2(1) of the Law of Property (Miscellaneous Provisions) Act 1989

> **Section 2(1) of the Law of Property (Miscellaneous Provisions) Act 1989 Contracts for sale etc. of land to be made by signed writing**
>
> **"(1) A contract for the sale or other disposition of an interest in land can only be made in writing and only by incorporating all the terms which the parties have expressly agreed in one document or, where contracts are exchanged, in each."**

If the contract is to grant a lease taking effect in possession, for a term of three years or less, at the best rent without taking a fine,[121] then it does not have to comply with s. 2(1). It can come into being entirely orally.[122]

(b) The contract must be specifically enforceable

At common law the only remedy for breach of a contract to create a lease is damages. "Specific performance" is an equitable remedy for breach of contract. Instead of requiring the person in breach to pay damages, she is made to go through and perform what she promised to do under the contract. It comes from the principle that "equity looks on that as done which ought to be done" and the landlord and tenant are "treated as if the lease had been granted with proper formalities".[123]

> "A person entitled merely to damages has no rights in the land; but a person entitled to specific performance has the right to demand the land itself, and so in the eyes of equity such a person is the rightful occupant. Just as a purchaser becomes equitable owner under

---

121   "A contract to grant such a lease as is mentioned in section 54(2) of the Law of Property Act 1925": Law of Property (Miscellaneous Provisions) Act 1989 s.2(5)(a).

122   s.2(5)(a).

123   Harpum, Bridge, Dixon, *Megarry & Wade Law of Real Property*, para.17–041.

a contract for sale, so an intended lessee becomes equitable tenant under a contract for a lease."[124]

The equitable remedy of specific performance is discretionary. It is not always available. A tenant may not be able to obtain specific performance if she is in breach of one of the terms of the agreement[125]: one of equity's maxims is that "he who comes to equity must come with clean hands". Further, as another maxim of equity is that "equity will not assist a volunteer", the tenant must have given consideration (e.g. rent) before the agreement is specifically enforceable.

(c) Walsh v Lonsdale[126]

This case shows an example of a situation in which an equitable lease came into being. The would-be landlord and tenant entered into a contract to grant a seven year lease of a mill. One of the provisions of the agreement was that the tenant would pay one year's rent in advance. The lease was never executed by deed so could not create a legal estate. However, the tenant had entered into possession and paid rent so a legal periodic tenancy had arisen. The landlord demanded a year's rent under the terms of the original agreement. The tenant argued that under the periodic tenancy there was no obligation to pay rent in advance.

It was held that the tenant had to pay in advance in accordance with the terms of the contract. The landlord and tenant had entered into a contract to create a lease and this contract was specifically enforceable. Thus, "equity looks on that as done which ought to be done" and an equitable lease came into being on the terms of the original agreement. It was held that wherever there is a conflict between law (the legal periodic tenancy here which required no payment in advance) and equity (the terms of the equitable lease which did) *equity will prevail*.

C. IS IT BETTER TO HAVE A LEGAL LEASE THAN AN EQUITABLE LEASE? LEASES AND LAND TRANSFER

(1) Priority where title to the land is unregistered

Owning a legal estate or interest in *unregistered* land is good because it means that your estate or interest will never be destroyed on a transfer of the land to a third party. Equitable leases in unregistered land must be registered as a Class C(iv) land charge in order to bind a purchaser of a legal estate in the land for money or money's worth.[127]

(2) Priority where title to the land is registered

The system of registration of title gives much better quality protection to legal estates and interests than it does to equitable interests. A legal lease granted for a term of seven years or less is an interest that overrides a registered transaction with the freehold, which means that

---

124 *Megarry & Wade*, above, footnotes omitted.
125 *Coatsworth v Johnson* (1886) 55 L.J.Q.B. 220.
126 (1882) L.R. 21 Ch.D.9.
127 Land Charges Act 1972 s.4(6).

the lease will bind a purchaser of the land even though it is not registered.[128] If a lease is granted for a term longer than seven years it must be registered with its own title otherwise it cannot take effect as a legal estate.[129] Thereafter all dealings with the landlord's freehold reversion will take effect subject to the lease.[130]

In registered land, in order to protect an equitable lease against a subsequent registered transaction with the estate, the contract may be registered against the title as a "notice".[131] The length of the equitable lease is irrelevant.[132] If an equitable lease is not so registered it may qualify as an overriding interest and bind a third party purchaser of the landlord's freehold reversion. However, the tenant must be in actual and discoverable occupation.[133]

D. PROBLEM SOLVING ON CREATION OF LEASES

LECTURER: Now let's try putting all this into practice and answering a problem question.

> **Fragment from a typical problem question**
> Davinder made an oral agreement to take a weekly tenancy of a flat and moved in immediately. Alistair, who is a musician, entered into a written agreement to rent a studio for five years to commence five months after the date of the agreement. No deed was ever executed. Alistair has moved into the studio.

STUDENT: Davinder's tenancy is a legal periodic tenancy. Although created entirely orally, and legal tenancies usually require a deed (LPA 1925 s.52), this tenancy falls within the s.54(2) exception. It is for a period of not more than three years. The relevant period here is a week, the tenancy thereafter taking effect from week to week until either landlord or tenant serves notice. The tenancy took effect "in possession", as we are told that Davinder "moved in immediately". I am assuming that he is paying the market rent for the premises and was not charged a lump sum in order to have a reduced rent payment.

LECTURER: And now what about Alistair?

STUDENT: Alistair's lease cannot be legal because it has not been granted by deed, required by LPA 1925 s.1, and LPA 1925 s.52.

---

128 Land Registration Act 2002 Sch.3, para.1, unless the lease is one of a number that must be registered as a registrable disposition irrespective of its length: see s.27(2).

129 Land Registration Act 2002 s.27. The registrar will then register the lease on the title to the freehold as a notice: Sch.3 para.3.

130 See Chapter 8 for the circumstances in which a lease must be registered with its own title, either when it is granted out of unregistered land for a period greater than seven years (see "First Registrations") or where it is granted out of land already registered for a term greater than seven years ("registrable dispositions").

131 s.32(3).

132 Although a legal lease cannot be registered as a notice if it is "granted for a term of years of three years or less from the date of the grant" and is not otherwise a registrable disposition (s.33(b) (for such leases see s.27(2)(b)(ii)–(v)), use of the word "granted" means that this limitation applies to legal leases not equitable ones.

133 Sch.3(2).

LECTURER: Good—and you do well to keep citing your authority, statutory or otherwise. But could the s.54(2) exception apply to Alistair's lease? What would be the legal effect if it did apply?

STUDENT: If s.54(2) applied Alistair would have a legal lease. However, it doesn't apply here. There are three criteria for s.54(2) to apply and Alistair's lease fails to satisfy two of them. The term of the lease was longer than three years, it is five years and the lease did not take effect "in possession": we are told that Alistair's right to use and enjoy the studio was "to commence five months after the date of the agreement".

LECTURER: However, even though the lease cannot be legal it might be recognised as an equitable lease under the doctrine of *Walsh v Lonsdale*. What you need to do is apply the requirements for equitable leases.

> You may wish to re-visit these criteria above and follow them through with our STUDENT.

STUDENT: Applying the required elements for an equitable lease, I am assuming that Alistair's "written agreement" complies with s.2 of the Law of Property (Miscellaneous Provisions) Act 1989, i.e. the document(s) are signed by him and his landlord and all the terms are contained in the document(s). Assuming that he has not breached any of his obligations under the lease (*Coatsworth v Johnson*) then Alistair will have an equitable lease.

LECTURER: This is concise and accurate but you have not really told me much about how the doctrine works.

STUDENT: Equity will say that because the contract for the lease is specifically enforceable, i.e. equity will make the parties perform what they said they were going to do and grant the lease as they promised, it will recognise the lease as existing: "equity looks on that as done which ought to be done".

LECTURER: Well done!

> Can you see how our STUDENT is beautifully making the transition from a "search for the right answer" to answering questions solely on the basis of the law?

(1) Revision Aid: A map of the rules on types of lease, essential characteristics and creation

1. TYPES OF LEASE → Fixed term tenancy

Periodic tenancy

> Do we know what type of lease it is and why?

2. ESSENTIAL   CHARACTERISTICS OF A LEASE

> These must be present for a lease to exist. It is important to be able to tell the difference between a lease and a licence: WHY?

a) The term must be certain ⟶

> *Lace v Chantler; Prudential Assurance v London Residuary Body.*

b) There must be "exclusive possession"

> First principles: *Let's understand what we are looking for*. What are the qualities of ownership and possession of land? *Street v Mountford*. In a real sense the tenant is an owner of the land, albeit temporarily and subject to certain restrictions: per Lord Templeman.

> Exclusive possession determined by looking at the facts objectively and considering the reality of the situation by the way the agreement for occupancy is carried out.

> SINGLE OCCUPIERS: Cases ask *to what extent is an occupier able to control who comes and goes: Street v Mountford*. Genuine provision of services negates control (*Abbeyfield v Woods*); but the clauses in the agreement must not be "sham": *Aslan v Murphy*.

> JOINT OCCUPIERS: All of the above considerations apply plus additional factors if the parties are to be joint tenants: *AG Securities v Vaughan*. Must have joint liability for rent and joint ability to exclude all including the landlord. Beware of "sham" clauses or "pretences": *Antonaides v Villiers*.

> EXCEPTIONS: Do any of the *Street   v   Mountford* "exceptions" apply? e.g. service occupancies.

3. HAS THE LEASE BEEN CREATED PROPERLY?

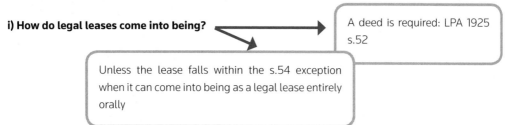

i) How do legal leases come into being?

A deed is required: LPA 1925 s.52

Unless the lease falls within the s.54 exception when it can come into being as a legal lease entirely orally

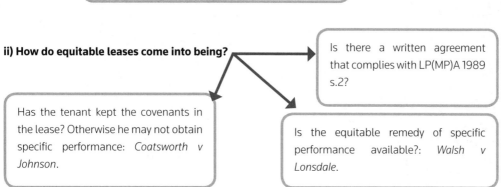

ii) How do equitable leases come into being?

Is there a written agreement that complies with LP(MP)A 1989 s.2?

Has the tenant kept the covenants in the lease? Otherwise he may not obtain specific performance: *Coatsworth v Johnson*.

Is the equitable remedy of specific performance available?: *Walsh v Lonsdale*.

Further reading

4

S. Bright, "Of Estates and Interests: A Tale of Ownership and Property Rights" in *Land Law Themes and Perspectives* (Oxford University Press, 1998).

S. Bridge, "Leases—contract, property and status" in L. Tee (ed.) *Land Law, Issues Debates Policy* (Willan Publishing, 2002).

M. Lower, "The Bruton Tenancy" [2010] Conv. 38.

Chapter 10

Leasehold Covenants

CHAPTER OVERVIEW

In this chapter you will find:

- Typical Landlord and tenant covenants
- The remedies for breach of covenant
- Instructions on how to solve a forfeiture problem like a land lawyer
- Constructed argument about reform proposals using Building Blocks
- The principles relating to transmission of leasehold covenants.

Covenants in Leases

1

Covenants are the "ground rules" of a tenancy.[1] Like any other contract a lease contains promises by the parties which lay down their rights and obligations. When a lease is entered into by a landlord and a tenant, there are usually sections in the tenancy agreement entitled Landlord's Covenants and Tenant's Covenants. The purpose of these covenants is to protect the interests of the landlord and tenant.

Tenant's Covenants

To pay rent.

Not to assign or sublet the premises without the prior permission of the landlord.

To allow the landlord to enter and view the state of repair of the premises.

Not to commit waste.

Landlord's Covenants

That the tenant shall have quiet enjoyment of the premises during the term.

To keep the structure and exterior in repair.

To keep in repair and proper working order all mechanical and electrical items.

To insure the premises with a reputable insurance company.

---

1   Gray & Gray, *Land Law Core Text,* 4th edn (Oxford University Press, 2006) p.537.

The tenant's covenants are very important to the landlord, particularly in respect of preserving the economic value of the house and to ensure that it is properly taken care of. The landlord's covenants are important to the tenant because they make sure he can live in the house in a reasonably comfortable environment.[2]

Covenants can be either expressly contained in the tenancy agreement (express covenants) or implied by law into the agreement (implied covenants). We will consider the most common covenants.

A. LANDLORD'S COVENANTS

(1) The covenant for quiet enjoyment[3]

The law implies into every tenancy agreement that the landlord will give the tenant quiet enjoyment of the land. This means that the landlord must not disturb the tenant's possession and occupation of the premises.[4] The word "quiet"

> "does not mean undisturbed by noise. When a man is quietly in possession it has nothing whatever to do with noise. 'Peaceably and quietly' means without interference – without interruption of the possession."[5]

The covenant for quiet enjoyment is a covenant that the landlord, or anyone lawfully claiming under him (such as other tenants of the same landlord) will not interfere with the tenant's "ability to use [the premises] in an ordinary lawful way."[6] It does not imply that the land is fit for the purpose for which it was let.[7] The landlord is liable for his actions, for those of his agents, and those of anyone claiming title under him.[8] Thus, the actions of tenants of the same landlord in adjoining flats can, in principle, amount to a breach by the landlord.[9]

In *Sanderson v Berwick-upon-Tweed Corporation*[10] a neighbouring tenant of the same landlord caused a flood on the complainant's agricultural land. It was held to be a breach of the covenant. A landlord who removed the doors and windows of the premises was also found in breach.[11]

---

2   Gray & Gray, above, p.537.
3   For further detail see M.Davey, *Landlord and Tenant Law* (London: Sweet & Maxwell, 1998); D. Williams, *Landlord and Tenant Casebook,* 3rd edn (Estates Gazette, 2002).
4   *Southwark Borough Council v Mills* [2001] 1 A.C. 1.
5   Per Kekewich J. *Jenkins v Jackson* (1888) 40 Ch.D. 71, p. 74 quoted *Southwark Borough Council v Mills* [2001] 1 A.C. 1. In *Kenny v Preen* [1963] 1 Q.B. 499, p.511 Pearson L.J. stated that "the word 'enjoy' used in this connection is a translation of the Latin word 'fruor' and refers to the exercise and use of the right and having the full benefit of it, rather than to derive pleasure from it": quoted by Lord Hoffman in *Southwark*, p.10; also Lord Millett p.22.
6   *Southwark Borough Council v Mills* [2001] 1 A.C. 1, p.10 per Lord Hoffmann.
7   *Southwark Borough Council*, above, p.10, per Lord Hoffmann; *Dennett v Atherton* (1872) LR 7 Q.B. 316.
8   *Southwark*, per Lord Hoffmann, p.22.
9   *Southwark*, per Lord Hoffmann, p.22.
10   (1884) 13 Q.B.D. 547.
11   *Lavender v Betts* [1942] 2 All E.R. 72.

There does not have to be direct physical interference in order to result in a breach of the covenant for quiet enjoyment.[12] For example, in *Kenny v Preen* the landlord sought to cause the tenant to leave by behaving in an intimidating way, e.g. by shouting at the door, threatening to evict her etc.[13]

In *Southwark Borough Council v Mills* the tenant complained that due to inadequate soundproofing she could hear the everyday activities from the other tenants of the council in the flats next door.[14] It was held that the landlord council was not in breach of the covenant. Although "regular excessive noise" could, in principal, amount to a breach of the covenant, it would have to amount to a nuisance.[15] Here, the ordinary activities of the neighbours, although distressing to the claimant, were not sufficient.

The covenant for quiet enjoyment is "prospective".[16] It "does not apply to things done before the grant of the tenancy, even though they may have continuing consequences for the tenant".[17] There will be no recourse against the landlord under this covenant if the defect that gave rise to the interference existed before the tenancy began.[18] There must be an "act or omission by the landlord or anyone lawfully claiming through him after the lease" is granted.[19] Thus, the tenant in *Southwark Borough Council v Mills* failed in her claim because the defect that caused the alleged interference existed prior to the grant of her tenancy. It was an old building with inadequate soundproofing. On this principle, *Southwark Borough Council* affirmed *Anderson v Oppenheimer*[20] in which a water pipe in the landlord's premises burst and flooded the tenant's premises below: "The water system was there when the tenant took his lease and he had to take the building as he found it".[21] In *Spoor v Green*[22] mining that caused subsidence was an existing defect so that the subsidence was not actionable under the covenant for quiet enjoyment.

The court will look at the common intention of landlord and tenant as to "the purposes . . . to which both intended the land to be put".[23] And if the landlord has not done anything that was outside this common intention, there will be no breach.[24] "[T]he landlord gives no implied

---

12   [2001] 1 A.C. 1; compare *Browne v Flower* [1911] 1 Ch. 219 (invasion of privacy insufficient).

13   [1963] 1 K.B. 499. Under s.1(3) of the Protection from Eviction Act 1977 a landlord will commit a criminal offence if in attempting to cause a residential tenant to leave rented premises, he interferes with the tenant's peace or comfort, or "withholds services reasonably required": Pearce and Stevens, *Land Law* 3rd edn (London: Sweet & Maxwell, 2004), pp.210–11.

14   The neighbours were tenants of the same landlord, Southwark Borough Council. Thus, they claimed their title under the landlord. Thus in principle their activities could be an interference on the part of the landlord with the complainant's enjoyment of her flat.

15   *Southwark Borough Council v Mills* [2001] 1 A.C. 1, per Lord Millett, p.23.

16   *Southwark Borough Council v Mills*, above, p.11 per Lord Hoffmann.

17   Above p.11 per Lord Hoffmann.

18   *Southwark*, above, p.11 per Lord Hoffmann.

19   Per Lord Hoffmann in *Southwark Borough Council v Mills* above, p.11.

20   (1880) 5 Q.B.D. 602.

21   *Southwark Borough Council v Mills* [2001] 1 A.C. 1, p.11 per Lord Hoffmann.

22   (1874) L.R. Exch. 99.

23   *Lyttelton Times Co Ltd v Warners Ltd* [1907] A.C. 476 PC (NZ), per Lord Loreburn L.C., quoted in *Southwark Borough Council v Mills* [2001] 1 A.C. 1, p.12 per Lord Hoffmann.

24   *Lyttelton Times Co Ltd v Warners Ltd* above per Lord Loreburn L.C.; *Southwark B.C. v Mills*, per Lord Millett, p.25.

warranty as to the condition or fitness of the premises [for its intended purpose]. *Caveat* lessee."[25] For example, in *Lyttelton Times Co Ltd v Warners Ltd*,[26] a landlord granted a tenancy of bedrooms to the neighbouring hotel. The bedrooms were above the landlord's printing works. The noise from the printing presses disturbed the occupiers of the rooms and the hotel complained that the operation of the presses was a breach of the covenant of quiet enjoyment. The Privy Council held that there was no breach. It was known by both parties that the landlord would continue operating their printing business: "[N]either has done or asks to do anything which was not contemplated by both, neither can have any right against the other".[27]

What we are looking at with the covenant of quiet enjoyment is essentially the obligations that landlord may be taken to have impliedly undertaken by the contract. Thus, the parties' common understanding of the purposes for which both landlord and tenant will be using their land, will be relevant in deciding whether the landlord has "interfered" with the tenant's use and possession. Therefore, the tenant in *Southwark Borough Council* was taken to have understood prior to entering into the tenancy that there would be other tenants in the same block. The council had committed no further act of interference apart from that resulting from a pre-existing defect. The policy behind the House of Lords' refusal to extend the covenant of quiet enjoyment to such cases as this was evident in the judgment of Lord Hoffmann. Had the tenant won her action the council would have been obliged to soundproof its property:

"I think that in a field such as housing law, which is very much a matter for the allocation of resources in accordance with democratically determined priorities, the development of the common law should not get out of step with legislative policy."[28]

(2) The covenant of non-derogation from grant

The law implies into every lease the covenant that the landlord will not derogate (take away) from his grant of the lease. The basis of this covenant is that the landlord is not permitted to "give with one hand and take away with the other".[29] This is where the landlord, after the grant of a tenancy, renders the land unfit for the purpose for which the tenant intended to use it. In this sense we can see that the covenant is akin to the covenant for quiet enjoyment. In *Aldin v Latimer, Clark, Muirhead & Co*,[30] a landlord was held in breach of this covenant where he leased land to a tenant who wished to use it for his timber business. After the grant the landlord built on his land blocking the flow of air to the tenant's timber-drying sheds. Effectively the landlord's actions rendered the land unfit for the purpose for which the tenant was intending to use it. However, before a landlord can be held liable he must know the purpose for which the tenant is intending to use the land. Finally, as with quiet enjoyment the covenant applies not only to the

---

25 *Southwark Borough Council v Mills* [2001] 1 A.C. 1, per Lord Hoffmann.
26 [1907] A.C. 476 PC (NZ).
27 [1907] A.C. 476 PC (NZ), per Lord Loreburn L.C.
28 Lord Millett, at p.26 stated that "Southwark London Borough Council has estimated that it would cost £1.271 billion to bring its existing housing stock up to acceptable modern standards".
29 *Southwark Borough Council v Mills* [2001] 1 A.C. 1, per Lord Millett.
30 [1894] 2 Ch. 437.

actions of the landlord but to the actions of those claiming title under him, e.g. another tenant of the same landlord.[31]

(3) Covenants as to the condition and repair of the premises

As to the landlord's responsibility for the state and condition of the premises the general position is that there is no contractual liability.[32] However, there are a number of repairing obligations that are implied into some leases.

(a) Furnished dwelling houses

If the property is a furnished dwelling house there is an obligation on the landlord to ensure at the start of the tenancy that the premises is fit for human habitation. Simply letting the premises in a state of disrepair, even if unsafe, will not be a breach of this covenant.[33] In *Smith v Marrable*[34] the landlord was found in breach of this covenant where there was an infestation of bugs on the premises. The covenant only means that the premises must be fit at the beginning of the tenancy. There is no obligation to ensure that the premises continue to be fit for human habitation during the tenancy.[35]

(b) Obligation to maintain common areas and means of access

Where the landlord retains ownership of common parts, such as a means of access to leased property, he has an obligation to keep these parts in repair. For example, the landlord of a block of flats must ensure that the stair way in the building is properly maintained as this provides essential access for tenants of the flats.[36] Whether or not such an obligation will be implied into a tenancy is a question of whether it is necessary: "All these are not just facilities, or conveniences provided at discretion: they are essentials of the tenancy without which life in the dwellings, as a tenant, is not possible".[37]

(c) Covenants implied to give "business efficacy" to the agreement

It may be necessary for the court to imply a covenant in order to make sense of the agreement entered into by the parties. In *Barrett v Lounova*[38] an obligation to repair the outside of the building was imposed on a landlord. This was to make the agreement workable. The tenant had agreed to keep the inside of the building in repair. Unless the landlord kept the exterior of the building in repair it would reach a stage when the tenant would be unable to comply with his covenant. The courts will not lightly imply a covenant to repair on these grounds.[39]

---

31   *Aldin v Latimer, Clark, Muirhead & Co* [1894] 2 Ch. 437; for further detail see Harpum, Bridge, Dixon, *Megarry & Wade Law of Real Property*, 7th edn (London: Sweet & Maxwell, 2008), para.19–015.
32   *Quick v Taff-Ely Borough Council* [1986] Q.B. 809.
33   *Maclean v Currie* (1884) Cab. & E. 361.
34   (1843) 11 M. & W. 5.
35   *Sarson v Roberts* [1895] 2 Q.B. 395: Harpum, Bridge. Dixon, *Megarry & Wade Law of Real Property*, para.19–019.
36   *Liverpool City Council v Irwin* [1977] A.C. 239.
37   Above; Pearce and Stevens, *Land Law*, p.213; also, Thompson, *Modern Land Law*, 4th edn (Oxford University Press, 2009), p.403.
38   [1990] 1 Q.B. 348.
39   For further detail see Harpum, Bridge, Dixon, *Megarry & Wade Law of Real Property*, para.19–021.

(d) Section 8 Landlord and Tenant Act 1985

Under this section there is implied a condition that the lease premises is fit for human habitation both at the start and during the tenancy. However, the section has exceptionally limited scope as it applies only to tenancies where the rent does not exceed £80 per annum in London and £57 per annum elsewhere.

(e) Obligation to repair dwelling-houses let for a period of less than seven years

By far the most significant implied repairing covenant is contained in s.11 of the Landlord and Tenant Act 1985. This is implied into all leases of dwelling-houses of terms of less than seven years. The landlord is not permitted to "contract out" of this obligation by imposing a covenant on the tenant that they should be responsible for the repairs covered by s.11.[40]

> **Landlord and Tenant Act 1985 s.11 Repairing obligations in short leases**
> "(1). . . there is implied a covenant by the lessor-
> - (a) to keep in repair the structure and exterior of the dwelling-house (including drains, gutters and external pipes),
> - (b) to keep in repair and proper working order the installations in the dwelling-house for the supply of water, gas and electricity and for sanitation (including basins, sinks, baths and sanitary conveniences, but not other fixtures, fittings and appliances for making use of the supply of water, gas or electricity), and
> - (c) to keep in repair and proper working order the installations in the dwelling-house for space heating and heating water."

In determining the standard of repair, the court will have regard to "the age, character . . . of the dwelling-house and the locality in which it is situated".[41] Where the s.11 repairing covenant applies the tenant is under a correlative obligation to allow the landlord, at a reasonable time of day, to "enter the premises comprised in the lease for the purpose of viewing their condition and state of repair".[42] The landlord must first give 24 hours' notice in writing to the occupier.[43] The landlord must have notice of the disrepair before he comes under the statutory obligation. Thus it is important that the tenant keep the landlord informed of any defects.[44]

As to the scope of the covenant, s.11(1)(a) provides that the landlord must "keep in repair the structure and exterior of the dwelling-house". Thus, for liability to arise there must be *disrepair*[45]

---

40   s.11(4).
41   Landlord and Tenant Act 1985 s.11(3).
42   Landlord and Tenant Act 1985 s.11(6).
43   s.11(6).
44   *McGreal v Wake* [1984] 1 E.G.L.R. 42, CA; further see D.Williams, *Landlord and Tenant Casebook*, p.168, who makes the comment that "[w]here the repairing liability is placed upon the landlord the golden rule is 'tell your landlord about the defects' ".
45   A deterioration: *Post Office v Aquarius Properties Ltd* [1987] 1 E.G.L.R.40, CA.

to the structure or exterior. In *Quick v Taff-Ely Borough Council*[46] the windows were inadequately constructed (being single glazed and metal frames) and the house had severe condensation. The tenant's living conditions were very bad, e.g. clothes and bedding were rotted. The landlord was not liable under a covenant to repair the structure and exterior of the house[47] because there was no damage to the windows themselves or to the structure and exterior.[48] "Structure and exterior" has been defined as anything that forms "a material or significant element in the overall construction".[49] For example in *Grand v Gill* it was held that plaster was not decorative finish but part of the structure.[50]

Under this covenant the landlord will not be required to carry out repairs that have become necessary due to the tenant's failure to use the property in a tenant-like manner.[51]

(4) Remedies for breach of the covenant and the "contractualisation" of leases

The tenant is usually entitled to damages and may obtain an injunction restraining a breach of the covenants of quiet enjoyment[52] and non-derogation. The tenant may obtain an order for specific performance of the landlord's repairing obligations, meaning that the landlord will be ordered to carry out the necessary repairs to the standard imposed by the statute.[53] If the tenant decides to carry out the repairs himself he may be able to deduct the cost from his future rent.[54]

If the breach is of a fundamental term of the lease then the tenant may be entitled to treat the tenancy as terminated. This is the contractual remedy of *repudiation*. In *Hussein v Mehlman*[55] the landlord had breached a repairing obligation and the premises were in such a state of disrepair that the tenant could no longer live there. It was held that the contractual doctrine of repudiation could apply to leases and that the tenant was entitled to repudiate the lease. This would mean that a tenant could legitimately hand the keys back to the landlord and regard his liability for the rent and other covenants as extinguished.[56] This may be criticised on the basis that leases are property rights and consequently, the law should not permit them to be brought

---

46 [1986] Q.B. 809.
47 At the time under the Housing Act 1961 s.32(1).
48 Also *Post Office v Aquarius Properties Ltd* [1987] E.G.L.R. 40, CA (on the meaning of disrepair) where there is a pre-existing defect that gives rise to the conditions complained of and there had been no deterioration to the building, then this is not "disrepair" and the landlord will not be obliged to take action. (Although it was a tenant's covenant in this case).
49 *Irvine's Estate v Moran* (1992) 24 H.L.R. 1, quoted in Harpum, Bridge, Dixon, *Megarry & Wade Law of Real Property*, para.19–030, n.173.
50 [2011] 3 All E.R. 1043 applying *Irvine's Estate v Moran* (1992) 24 H.L.R. 1
51 Landlord and Tenant Act 1985 s.11(2)(a). We will consider the extent of the tenant's implied covenant to use the property in a tenant-like way below.
52 *Lyttelton Times Co Ltd v Warners Ltd* [1907] A.C. 476 PC.
53 Landlord and Tenant Act 1985 s.17 (in relation to s.11).
54 *Lee-Parker v Izzet* [1971] 1 W.L.R. 1688.
55 [1992] 2 E.G.L.R. 87.
56 [1992] 2 E.G.L.R. 87: also S.Bridge, "Leases—contract, property and status" in L. Tee (ed.) *Land Law: Issues, Debates, Policy* (Willan Publishing, 2002), p.116.

to an end so readily and in accordance with contract principles.[57] As Bridge points out,[58] *Hussein v Mehlman*[59] has been applied by the Court of Appeal and to commercial leases.[60]

In *National Carriers Ltd v Panalpina (Northern) Ltd*[61] the House of Lords applied the contractual doctrine of frustration to leases, showing that the "process of contractualisation of leases was now growing apace".[62] Indeed, in *Southwark Borough Council v Mills*,[63] (the soundproofing case that we considered in the context of the landlord's covenant for quiet enjoyment) Lord Hoffmann in part standing back "from the technicalities of the law of landlord and tenant" adopted a contractual construction of the tenancy agreement. The landlord would not be liable under the covenant for quiet enjoyment where the interference was caused by activities within the common intention of both parties to the contract.

B. TENANT'S COVENANTS

(1) Rent

Rent is not an essential element of a tenancy.[64] Therefore, there is no such covenant to pay rent implied by law. However, in most leases there will be an express covenant in which the amount of rent is stipulated. There will usually be a provision that states whether rent is to be paid in advance or in arrears. If the lease is for a longer term it is usual to include a clause that provides for the amount of rent paid to be reviewed and increases made at certain dates throughout the tenancy.[65] This is known as "rent review".

"[T]he general purpose of a provision for rent review is to enable the landlord to obtain from time to time the market rent which the premises would command if let on the same terms on the open market at review dates."[66]

(2) Not to assign or sublet

An "assignment" is where the tenant transfers his interest under the lease to someone else, i.e. sells it and puts another tenant in his place. "Subletting" means that the tenant carves out of his own interest a tenancy of a shorter term than his own. We should remember that a lease is a property right. It is a natural incident of a property right to be able to alienate it (sell it) or to

---

57 S.Bridge, above p.116; M.Davey, *Landlord and Tenant Law*.
58 Above, p.116.
59 [1992] 2 E.G.L.R. 87.
60 e.g. *Re Olympic & York Canary Wharf Ltd (No. 2)* [1993] B.C.C. 159.
61 [1981] A.C. 675.
62 S.Bridge (above). See section 3, Ending of leases (below).
63 [1999] 4 All E.R. 449.
64 Law of Property Act 1925 s.205(1)(xxvii).
65 *British Gas Corporation v Universities Superannuation Scheme Ltd* [1986] 1 W.L.R. 398; *C.H.Bailey Ltd v Memorial Enterprises Ltd* [1974] 1 W.L.R. 728.
66 *British Gas Corporation v Universities Superannuation Scheme Ltd* above, p.401 per Sir Nicholas Browne-Wilkinson V.C. For further detail on rent review see D.Williams, *Landlord and Tenant Casebook*, Ch.3.

grant other interests out of it. Thus, if a landlord wishes to prevent the tenant from assigning or subletting he must include an express covenant to this effect. Such a covenant operates as a break on the tenant's normal property rights. It is common to find in a lease a covenant against assignment and subletting. Because sale and subletting are incidents of the leasehold estate, a breach of this covenant will not invalidate either the actual assignment or subletting.[67] But the landlord is entitled to a remedy.

(3) Not to commit waste

A lease may often include express covenants that require a tenant to keep the premises in repair with a common exclusion for "fair wear and tear". However, "[a]part from express contract, a tenant owes no duty to the landlord to keep the premises in repair".[68] There is a covenant implied into every tenancy that a tenant will not commit waste. "Waste" is defined as "any act which alters the nature of the land", e.g. spoiling it.[69]

> **Permissive waste**: defined as failing to do something which leads to damage to the property. For example, a tenant commits permissive waste if he fails to clean out the guttering and thereby causes water ingress.

> **Voluntary waste**: This is a positive act by the tenant which leads to damage.

(4) To use the property in a tenant-like manner

A tenant is subject to an implied obligation to use the premises in a "tenant-like" manner. In *Warren v Keen*[70] Denning L.J. said that this meant doing "the little jobs about the place which a reasonable tenant would do", e.g. unblocking sinks, mending lights, cleaning chimneys (when necessary), and, "if he is going away for the winter, turn off the water and empty the boiler":

> "In addition, he must not, of course, damage the house wilfully or negligently; and he must see that his family and guests do not damage it – if they do, he must repair it. But apart from such things, if the house falls into disrepair through fair wear and tear or lapse of time or for any reason not caused by him, the tenant is not liable to repair it."

In *Wycombe Health Authority v Barnett*[71] a tenant who stayed away from the leased premises for two nights in freezing weather was not held in breach of this covenant by failing to lag a water pipe or failing to keep the premises heated in order to prevent the pipe from bursting. It might be otherwise for lengthier periods of absence in very cold weather.[72]

---

67   *Scala House and District Property Co Ltd v Forbes* [1974] Q.B. 575; *Borthwick-Norton v Romney Warwick Estates Ltd* [1950] 1 All E.R. 798.
68   *Warren v Keen* [1954] 1 Q.B. 15, p.20 per Denning L.J.
69   Harpum, Bridge, Dixon, *Megarry & Wade Law of Real Property*, para.3–091.
70   [1953] 2 All E.R. 1118, p.1121.
71   [1982] 2 E.G.L.R. 35, CA.
72   [1982] 2 E.G.L.R. 35, CA.

C. REMEDIES FOR BREACH OF COVENANT

If the tenant breaches any of his covenants the landlord can obtain damages, specific performance, e.g. of a repairing covenant, or an injunction.[73]

(1) Distress

This remedy allowed the landlord to enter the premises and seize the tenant's goods to the value of unpaid rent. The Tribunals, Courts and Enforcement Act 2007 abolishes the remedy of distress,[74] although puts a different system in place for commercial property.[75]

(2) Forfeiture

Broadly speaking this is the leasehold equivalent of an action for repossession of the premises. If the tenant breaches a covenant, e.g. fails to pay rent, the landlord may be able to forfeit the lease. This means that he is entitled to terminate the lease prematurely and reclaim the premises. However certain conditions must be satisfied. Further, there are a number of ways in which statute and common law offer protection to tenants against forfeiture.

(a) Lease must contain a right of re-entry

The tenancy contract must have given the landlord a right of re-entry in the event of breach of the covenant. This is a right to forfeit the lease and re-enter the premises. It is common practice to include rights of re-entry in leases. If a particular obligation is construed as a "condition", i.e. it is fundamental to the tenancy, then a right of re-entry arises on the tenant's breach of that condition even if the landlord has not expressly reserved one in the lease.[76]

(b) Waiver

When the right of re-entry arises on breach of covenant the tenancy is not terminated automatically. The landlord has a choice whether to forfeit the lease or continue with it.[77] This "election" is the basis of the doctrine of waiver.[78] The landlord's right to forfeit the tenancy will cease if he waives the tenant's breach. He has thereby taken to have elected to continue with the tenancy. A waiver is an act done by the landlord that recognises the continued existence of the tenancy.[79] For example where the landlord makes an unequivocal demand for, and/or accepts, rent after the right of re-entry has arisen,[80] this will be taken as his affirmation of the tenancy:

---

73   Such a remedy would be appropriate, for example, in a case where the tenant has breached a covenant not to use the premises for illegal or immoral purposes and there is a continuing breach of covenant.

74   Tribunals, Courts and Enforcement Act 2007 s.71.

75   This system is called the "Commercial Rent Arrears Recovery": see Tribunals, Courts and Enforcement Act 2007 s.72; For further detail see Harpum, Bridge, Dixon, *Megarry & Wade Law of Real Property*, para.19–062.

76   E.g. non-payment of rent: *Rouf v Tragus Holdings Ltd* [2009] EWHC 96 (Ch) (periodic tenancy).

77   *Billson v Residential Apartments Ltd* [1992] 1 A.C. 494.

78   *David Blackstone Ltd v Burnetts (West End) Ltd* [1973] 1 W.L.R. 1487, p.1496 per Swanwick J.

79   *Matthews v Smallwood* [1910] 1 Ch. 777, per Parker J, p.786.

80   *David Blackstone Ltd v Burnetts (West End) Ltd* [1973] 1 W.L.R. 1487.

"[T]here is a fundamental inconsistency between contending that a lease has been [terminated] and demanding rent on the basis of its future continuance."[81]

This will be the case even if the demand is made by the landlord's agent and even without his knowledge of the demand.[82] A landlord who pursues the remedy of distress will have been taken to elect to continue the tenancy,[83] as will a landlord who takes proceedings to enforce another provision in the lease.[84] The test is objective and it does not matter that the landlord has no intention of waiving the breach.[85]

"Thus the landlord's acceptance of rent as the result of an error, or on a 'without prejudice' basis may indicate that the landlord had no intention to waive, but such circumstances do not, as a matter of law, prevent waiver."[86]

If the landlord is deemed to waive the breach he will no longer be able to take proceedings to end the lease. Thus, once a landlord is aware of his tenant's breach of covenant he will have to proceed very carefully in his dealings with the tenant if he is not to waive the breach inadvertently. It may well be unclear to the landlord what actions will amount to a waiver, so he will be unable to order his affairs accordingly: "Waiver is a trap for the unwary—whether they be landlords, or their lawyers".[87]

A waiver operates in relation to one specific breach and does not extend to future instances of breach.[88] Also, where the tenant's breach of covenant is continuous an act of waiver only operates up to the time of the act. If the breach continues after that point this is deemed to be a new breach that is not waived. For example, in *City and Westminster Properties (1934) Ltd v Mudd* a tenant breached a covenant to use the premises for commercial purposes only. The landlord waived the breach but the breach continued after the waiver. It was held that the act of waiver was not continuous unless the landlord "has. . . affirmatively consented" to the tenant continuing to use the premises as he has done.[89]

As we have seen above, the basis of the doctrine of waiver is election: once the landlord's right of re-entry has arisen he has a choice whether to continue with the tenancy or to end it. Thus, a

---

81   *David Blackstone Ltd v Burnetts (West End) Ltd* [1973] 1 W.L.R. 1487, p.1498 per Swanwick J; A landlord cannot accept rent and at the same time say that it is "without prejudice" to his right to forfeit: *Matthews v Smallwood* [1910] 1 Ch. 777; *Central Estates (Belgravia) Ltd v Woolgar (No. 2)* [1972] 1 W.L.R. 1048. For a recent case showing that acceptance of rent constitutes waiver of a breach see *Thomas v Ken Thomas Ltd* [2006] EWCA Civ 1504.

82   *David Blackstone Ltd v Burnetts (West End) Ltd* [1973] 1 W.L.R. 1487.

83   *Matthews v Smallwood* [1910] 1 Ch. 777.

84   *Cornille v Saha* (1996) 72 P. & C.R. 147: Harpum, Bridge, Dixon, *Megarry & Wade Law of Real Property*, para. 18–014.

85   *Cornille v Saha*, above.

86   *Osibanjo v Seahive Investments Ltd.* [2008] EWCA Civ 1282, para.4, per Mummery L.J. S.Bridge observes "Does [waiver's] unforgiving 'objective' application, without any reference to the parties' actual beliefs, really serve any useful purpose?", " 'Necessary and Proportionate': The Law Commission's Recommendations for the Reform of Forfeiture": S.Bridge, Law Commissioner, Lecture Given to the Property Bar Association, November 9, 2006, para. 1.17. See the Law Commission's website.

87   S. Bridge, above.

88   Law of Property Act 1925 s.148.

89   [1959] Ch. 129, p.145 per Harman J.

landlord can only be deemed to waive a breach, and thereby be taken to elect to continue with the tenancy, if he was aware of that breach. In *David Blackstone Ltd v Burnetts (West End) Ltd*[90] Swanwick J. observed

> "My view . . . is that an unambiguous demand for future rent in advance such as was made here does in law amount to an election and does constitute a waiver if, at the time when it is made, the landlord has sufficient knowledge of the facts to put him to his election."[91]

(c) Exercising the right of re-entry

A landlord may take possession peaceably or take court proceedings for possession of the premises. It is unlawful for a landlord to take peaceable possession of a dwelling-house where someone is lawfully residing on the premises. He must enforce his right of re-entry through the courts.[92]

(d) Procedures the landlord must follow if forfeiture is to be valid

There are rules that exist to protect tenants from losing the lease by forfeiture. The rules are different depending on the nature of the covenant breached.

(i) Forfeiture for non-payment of rent

In order the forfeit a lease for non-payment of rent the landlord must make a formal demand for the rent, although this requirement can be, and usually is, excluded by the terms of the lease. The tenant may be entitled to stop the forfeiture proceedings if he pays into court or to the landlord all the rent in arrears and costs of the action not less than five clear days before the trial.[93] Even if the county court grants the landlord a possession order if the tenant pays the arrears and costs before the date for execution of the order, the lease can be revived.[94] Equity may grant the tenant relief from forfeiture, which means that the lease will not be regarded as terminated, where the tenant pays the rent due and costs.[95]

(ii) Forfeiture for breaches of other covenants

If the tenant breaches a covenant other than the covenant to pay rent, the landlord will be unable to enforce a right of re-entry, either peaceably or by court action, unless he serves on the tenant a notice under s.146 of the Law of Property Act 1925.

---

90   [1973] 1 W.L.R. 1487, p. 1498.
91   Also *Matthews v Smallwood* [1910] 1 Ch. 777.
92   Protection from Eviction Act 1977 s.2.
93   County Courts Act 1984 s.138(2). If proceedings are in the High Court the tenant only has this right where rent is half a year in arrear: Common Law Procedure Act 1852 s.210: Harpum, Bridge, Dixon, *Megarry & Wade Law of Real Property*, para.18–022, observes that this has the unfortunate effect of putting a tenant who owes less rent in a worse position than a tenant who owes more.
94   Above para.18–022.
95   For a recent example see *Eastaugh v Crisp* [2007] EWCA Civ 638.

> **146 Restrictions on and relief against forfeiture of leases**
> "(1) A right of re-entry or forfeiture. . . . shall not be enforceable, by action or otherwise, unless and until the [landlord] serves on the [tenant] a notice-
> (a) specifying the particular breach complained of; and
> (b) if the breach is capable of remedy, requiring the [tenant] to remedy the breach;
> (c) in any case, requiring the [tenant] to make compensation in money for the breach."

The aim of s.146 is to give tenants "one last chance" to put things right and remedy their breach of covenant before the landlord is able to prematurely end the lease.[96] As Lindley L.J. stated in *Lock v Pearce*[97] "[t]he lessee is entitled to know what his landlord complains of". The tenant must be given reasonable time to comply with the terms of the notice.[98] What is "reasonable time" is a question of fact. It will depend on all the circumstances of the case including the extent of what is required by the tenant in order to remedy the breach, if anything.[99] For example, in *Expert Clothing Service & Sales Ltd v Highgate House Ltd*,[100] a tenant was in breach of a covenant to carry out reconstruction work on the leased premises. Slade L.J. thought that it would be reasonable for the landlord in that case to impose a short timescale for the tenant to carry out the work given that they had already had the premises for 15 months.

If, after the time has elapsed, the tenant still has not complied with the s.146 notice, the landlord can enforce his right of re-entry. At this point the tenant is no longer regarded as holding under the lease. He is a trespasser.[101] If the tenant complies with the notice, e.g. remedying the breach in a reasonable time, the landlord "is unable to prove that a condition precedent to his ability to seek to forfeit. . . has been fulfilled".[102] He or she will thus be unable to forfeit the lease.

A s.146 notice is void if it does not meet the requirements specified in that section. As we can see from the wording of s.146 it is only where a breach is capable of being remedied that the notice must require the tenant to remedy it. Thus, much case law has turned on the issue of whether a notice is defective because it failed to require the tenant to remedy the breach. The relevant test for whether a breach is capable of being remedied was stated in *Expert Clothing Service & Sales Ltd v Hillgate House Ltd*[103]:

---

96   *Expert Clothing Service & Sales Ltd v Highgate House Ltd* [1986] Ch. 340.
97   [1893] 2 Ch. 271, p. 279, per Lindley L.J.
98   s.146(1).
99   *Expert Clothing Service & Sales Ltd v Hillgate House Ltd* [1986] Ch. 340; *Scala House and District Property Co Ltd v Forbes* [1974] Q.B. 575.
100 [1986] Ch. 340.
101 *Jones v Carter* (1846) 15 M. & W. 718, per Parke B; affirmed *Billson v Residential Apartments Ltd* [1992] 1 A.C. 494, p.534 per Lord Templeman.
102 *Scala House and District Property Co Ltd v Forbes* [1974] Q.B. 575, per Russell L.J.
103 [1986] Ch. 340, per Slade L.J.

"if the section 146 notice had required the [tenant] to remedy the breach and the [landlords] had then allowed a reasonable time to elapse to enable the [tenant] fully to comply with the relevant covenant, would such compliance, coupled with the payment of any appropriate monetary compensation, have effectively remedied the harm which the [landlords] had suffered or were likely to suffer from the breach?"

The test is applicable to both positive and negative covenants alike.[104] Breach of a positive covenant is the failure to do something that has been promised to be done, e.g. to carry out reconstruction works.[105] Negative covenants are a promise that the tenant will *not do something* with the leased property, e.g. use it for commercial purposes. *Expert Clothing* involved breach of a positive covenant to carry out reconstruction work by a certain date, and that date had passed. The landlord could not show that he had suffered irremediable damage had they required the tenant to remedy the breach and allowed a reasonable time for them to do so.

In *Rugby School (Governors) v Tannahill*[106] one issue was whether the s.146 notice served by the School on the tenant for breach of a negative covenant was defective. In this case the tenant covenanted that they would not use the premises for illegal or immoral purposes. In breach of the covenant the tenant used the premises for prostitution. The School, who wished to forfeit the lease, had omitted to require the tenant to remedy the breach. However, if the breach was not capable of remedy this did not invalidate the notice. Although Greer L.J. did not accept the view that all negative covenants are automatically to be regarded as incapable of remedy, this particular breach was held to be irremediable because of the "stigma" created by the tenant's use of the premises: "The result of committing the breach would be known all over the neighbourhood and seriously affect the value of the premises".[107] Even if the tenant were to stop the immoral use, this would make no difference to the stigma. The breach was irremediable and consequently, the s.146 notice was not defective for omitting to require the tenant to remedy the breach. Consequently, the landlord was entitled to enforce their right of re-entry.

A breach of a covenant not to assign or sublet the premises is thought to be a "once and for all" breach that is not capable of remedy.[108] Such a breach "is not in any sense a continuing breach".

---

104   *Savva v Houssein* [1996] 2 E.G.L.R. 65, per Auld L.J.
105   *Expert Clothing Service & Sales Ltd v Hillgate House Ltd* [1986] Ch. 340.
106   [1935] 1 K.B. 87. If the answer to the question is "no" then the breach is not capable of being remedied. Remedy means to remove the mischief caused by the breach and not "to restore the matter wholly to the situation which it was in before the breach": *Savva v Houssein* [1996] 2 E.G.L.R. 65, per Staughton L.J.
107   [1935] 1 K.B. 87, p.90 per Greer L.J. See also *Hoffman v Fineberg* [1949] Ch. 245 (stigma caused by illegal gambling); *Egerton v Esplanade Hotels London Ltd* [1947] 2 All E.R. 88.
108   "An unlawful subletting is a breach once and for all. The subterm has been created": per Russell L.J., *Scala House and District Property Co Ltd v Forbes* [1974] Q.B. 575.

The sublease exists and cannot be undone.[109] Regarding positive covenants, just because a breach is a "once and for all" breach does not mean that it is incapable of remedy.[110] An example of a "once and for all breach" of a positive covenant would be to fail to carry out reconstruction work by a certain date.[111] It was thought that the matter here could have been remedied by doing the work, even if out of time. In *Expert Clothing*, Slade L.J. considered that the distinction with the "stigma" cases was that "[t]he harm had been irretrievably done".[112] It may be possible to comply with a positive covenant, even though out of time, and thereby remove the harm.[113]

On the interpretation of s.146(1)(c), the landlord only has to make a demand for compensation if he requires it. There is no obligation to do so if the landlord does not want compensation.[114]

(iii) Forfeiture for breach of a repairing covenant

For the protection of the tenant Parliament has introduced a specific provision that relates to enforcement of a tenant's covenant to repair. It applies where there is a lease of a house that has seven years or more to run and where three years or more of the lease remain unexpired. In such cases the landlord's s.146 notice must state clearly that the tenant may serve a counter notice within 28 days. If the tenant serves such a notice the landlord cannot enforce a right of re-entry or obtain damages for breach of covenant other than by court order.[115] The court will consider matters such as: whether the landlord is likely to suffer loss if the repairs are not carried out immediately, whether the expense of the repair is small in comparison to the cost of postponing the work, and any circumstances which render it just and equitable to enforce the right of re-entry.[116]

(e) Relief from forfeiture

Section 146 is intended to give the tenant the opportunity to remedy a breach of covenant before the landlord enforces his right of re-entry. It is also intended to give the tenant the opportunity to apply for relief from forfeiture.[117] Indeed, if the tenant applies for relief after service of a s.146 notice it can be a useful way of "setting in train the machinery by which the dispute between the landlord and the tenant can be determined by negotiation or by the court".[118] Once

---

109 Except on grounds of forfeiture by the sub-landlord, although this will require a breach of some covenant by the sub-tenant: *Borthwick-Norton v Romney Warwick Estates Ltd* [1950] 1 All E.R. 798.

110 *Expert Clothing Service & Sales Ltd v Hillgate House Ltd* [1986] Ch. 340, p.354 per Slade L.J.

111 *Expert Clothing* above.

112 [1986] Ch. 340, p.357.

113 [1986] Ch. 340, pp.355 and 357 citing *Hoffman v Fineberg* [1949] Ch. 245.

114 *Lock v Pearce* [1893] 2 Ch. 271; *Civil Service Co-operative Society Ltd v McGrigor's Trustee* [1923] 2 Ch. 347, both cases applied in *Rugby School (Governors) v Tannahill* [1935] 1 K.B. 87.

115 Leasehold Property (Repairs) Act 1938 s.1.

116 Leasehold Property (Repairs) Act 1938 s.1(5).

117 *Expert Clothing Service & Sales Ltd v Hillgate House Ltd* [1986] Ch. 340.

118 *Billson v Residential Apartments Ltd.* [1992] 1 A.C. 494, p.539 per Lord Templeman.

the landlord can enforce his right of re-entry the tenant is a trespasser.[119] "[T]he lease no longer exists".[120] If the court grants relief the tenant is then deemed to hold the premises under the lease again. Once a possession order is *executed* the tenant can no longer apply for relief from forfeiture.

Under s.146(2) of the Law of Property Act 1925 where the landlord is proceeding by court action for possession or by peaceable re-entry, the tenant may apply to the court for relief from forfeiture. The court has discretion to grant or refuse relief. The purpose behind s.146(2), and its predecessor Conveyancing Act 1881 ss.14(1) and (2), was that

"a tenant who had paid a large premium for a 999-year lease at a low rent could lose his asset by a breach of covenant which was remediable or which caused the landlord no damage. The forfeiture of any lease, however short, may unjustly enrich the landlord at the expense of the tenant".[121]

In exercising its discretion to grant relief the court will have regard "to the proceedings and conduct of the parties" in relation to the s.146 notice, "and to all the other circumstances" of the case. The grant of relief does not depend on the breach being remediable. A recent example of this jurisdiction is *Forcelux Ltd v Binnie*[122] in which a landlord claimed possession of a long lease on a flat after the tenant failed to pay ground rent and maintenance costs. The tenant was granted relief from forfeiture on the basis of the small amounts concerned and the disproportionate consequences of forfeiture. The tenant was able to pay the outstanding amounts.

The court has discretion to grant relief "on such terms, if any, as to costs, expenses, damages, compensation, penalty, or otherwise, including the granting of an injunction to restrain any like breach in the future, as the court, in the circumstances of each case, thinks fit".[123] Such conditions may include the payment of compensation to the landlord. Where the landlord is enforcing his right of re-entry by court proceedings, the tenant will no longer be able to apply for relief once the landlord has obtained a possession order.[124] If the landlord has taken possession peaceably, the tenant may apply for relief even after the landlord has taken possession.[125]

---

119   *Jones v Carter* (1846) 15 M. & W. 718, per Parke B; affirmed *Billson v Residential Apartments Ltd* [1992] 1 A.C. 494, per Lord Templeman.
120   *Billson v Residential Apartments Ltd* [1992] 1 A.C. 494, p.534 per Lord Templeman.
121   *Billson v Residential Apartments Ltd* [1992] 1 A.C. 494, p.535 per Lord Templeman.
122   [2009] EWCA Civ 854.
123   Law of Property Act 1925 s.146(2).
124   *Rogers v Rice* [1892] 2 Ch.170; *Billson v Residential Apartments*, above.
125   *Billson v Residential Apartments*, above.

(f) Application of the law of forfeiture

> **SPECIMEN PROBLEM: Mr Heath is a landlord who has leased a first floor flat to Peter and Alison for five years. The tenants covenant as follows**
>
> - To pay rent of £500 per month in advance;
> - Not to use the premises for illegal or immoral purposes;
> - To ensure that the premises is adequately ventilated (to protect the premises against damage from condensation).
>
> The lease contains a clause to the effect that "notwithstanding any provision as to the length of term the landlord shall have the right to terminate the lease and re-enter the leased premises should the tenants fail to comply with any of the above covenants".
>
> Peter and Alison moved into the flat and are using it as a base from which to sell pirate DVDs. They are three months in arrears in their rent payments and have failed to open a single window, so that there is now damage to the fabric of the walls caused by condensation.
>
> Advise Mr Heath who wishes to recover possession of the flat.

LECTURER: After reading this question and studying the preceding rules on forfeiture I think that you may well not know where to start! Like with any other legal problem we need to approach it systematically.

> **Here, we will only briefly sketch the rules, rather than go into the further detail you would need for a comprehensive solution to the problem. We will create a map to help you understand the workings of the rules.**

We must firstly remember what forfeiture *is*: it is a remedy by which Mr Heath can seek to end the tenancy *prematurely* for Peter and Alison's breach of the tenant's covenants under the lease: *Expert Clothing Service & Sales Ltd v Hillgate House Ltd*. Notice what I am doing here. I am not just giving a general description of the law—I am stating the consequences of the law for the parties.

STUDENT: I would have been tempted to begin by writing *about* forfeiture saying that it is a remedy and that it is like repossession of leased property.

LECTURER: I know. Many students feel the same. When you are answering a problem question you must never forget *what it is that you are actually doing*. You are providing a *solution*. So the first thing you need to ask is what the parties actually want to achieve. And then we need to pick our way through the law in order to look at its impact on the situation of Mr Heath and Peter and Alison. So at least we understand the first question we need to answer:

FIRST QUESTION: Has there been a breach of a tenant's covenant?

STUDENT: Actually Peter and Alison have breached all of the tenant's covenants listed here. There is breach of a covenant to pay rent in advance per month (they are three months in arrears).

LECTURER: And there is breach of a user covenant, i.e. not to use the premises in an illegal or immoral way. How?

STUDENT: They are using the flat as a base from which to sell pirate DVDs. This is illegal. And the other one is breach of a covenant to keep the premises in repair.

LECTURER: So now we move to the next stage. Forfeiture is not automatic. In order to terminate the lease of the flat prematurely Mr Heath must have what is known as a "right of re-entry". (Note again that I am stating the legal consequences of the rule for the parties.)

SECOND QUESTION: Does the landlord have a right of re-entry?

STUDENT: There is a right of re-entry contained in Peter and Alison's lease.

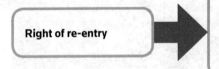

Right of re-entry → "Notwithstanding any provision as to the length of term or otherwise the landlord shall have the right to terminate the lease and re-enter the leased premises should the tenants fail to comply with any of the above covenants."

LECTURER: Once the breach has occurred what is the position that Mr Heath finds himself in? Does this mean that Peter and Alison's lease has terminated?

STUDENT: No, he may elect to re-enter and end the lease but he may also elect to continue with the tenancy. At this point he has a choice: *David Blackstone Ltd v Burnetts (West End) Ltd*.

LECTURER: As we are told that Mr Heath wishes to terminate Peter and Alison's lease why must he "tread carefully"?

STUDENT: He has to be careful that he does not commit some act that "waives" the breach, which means that Mr Heath will lose his right to terminate the lease for those breaches – unless they arise again after the waiver: *Matthews v Smallwood*.

> **LECTURER:** Our STUDENT has identified the way in which waiver works and remembered to state the legal consequences for the parties.

LECTURER: Good. And you are right to make sure that you cite the cases containing the relevant principles. Although there is more to the law of waiver than this, for the purposes of our map of the law let's move on and assume that Mr Heath has not committed any act to waive Peter and Alison's breaches of covenant.

> **THIRD QUESTION:** Has the landlord waived the breach?

LECTURER: A landlord can take possession of leased premises (we say "enforce his right of re-entry") peaceably by a court order for possession. Will Mr Heath be able to take peaceable possession here?

> **FOURTH QUESTION:** How can the landlord proceed to forfeit the lease?

STUDENT: Going into the premises himself and changing the locks! No. Section 2 of the Protection from Eviction Act 1977 would prevent Mr Heath from doing this because the flat is a dwelling house and Peter and Alison are lawfully residing there.

LECTURER: OK then. Mr Heath must obtain a court order for possession. In either case, before he can enforce his right of re-entry he must comply with certain procedures.

> **FIFTH QUESTION:** Has the landlord followed proper procedure?

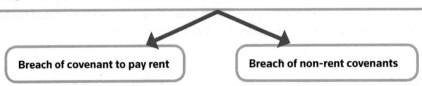

The procedure the landlord must comply with in order to be allowed to enforce his right of re-entry (through court of otherwise) DEPENDS ON THE COVENANT BREACHED

Breach of covenant to pay rent

Breach of non-rent covenants

LECTURER: Take Peter and Alison's failure to pay rent: this is a breach of a rent covenant.

STUDENT: Mr Heath must make a formal demand (unless the lease has excluded this requirement—we do not have enough detail in the problem). I would advise that Peter and Alison can stop proceedings by paying all the arrears and costs into court.

LECTURER: Now we have to consider the procedure that Mr Heath must follow in relation to Peter and Alison's breaches of the non-rent covenants: *the user covenant and the repair covenant.*

STUDENT: Mr Heath cannot prematurely end Peter and Alison's tenancy unless he has served them with a "section 146 notice". This must specify the breach of which Mr Heath complains. It must require this breach to be remedied (if the breach is capable of remedy) and if Mr Heath requires compensation, he must ask here for it to be paid. The notice must give Peter and Alison "reasonable time" to comply with its terms. This is a question of fact: *Expert Clothing Service & Sales Ltd v Hillgate House Ltd.* If the breaches are remediable, such as Peter and Alison's repair covenant, then it may be that a longer period will be reasonable: *Expert Clothing.* This means that they will have "one last chance" to comply with the covenants: *Expert Clothing.* Once the reasonable time has expired, if Peter and Alison are still in breach, Mr Heath will be able lawfully to enforce his right of re-entry and Peter and Alison will be trespassers: *Jones v Carter; Billson v Residential Apartments Ltd.*

LECTURER: Note that our STUDENT is stating the consequences of the rules to the parties.

LECTURER: Very good. Each time you introduce a new applicable rule you explain how it works in relation to the fictional parties, e.g. the way you treat the "reasonable time" rule. After arguing about how the rule might apply to the parties, e.g. here, breach of a repairing covenant is not irremediable but it may need a longer time for the defaulting tenants to comply with a legal problem solution should spell out the consequences of the legal rules to the fictional parties: which is what you do in your final sentence.

One issue here is that if Mr Heath has not asked Peter and Alison to remedy the breach the notice will be invalid if, in fact, the breach is remediable. However, if you are advising him at an early stage of proceedings, how might you draft the s.146 notice in such a way that

Mr Heath will not have to second guess whether Alison and Peter's various breaches of covenants would be deemed "remediable" by the courts.

> STUDENT writes: Your conduct amounts to a clear breach of the third covenant under the tenancy agreement, which stipulates that the tenant shall ensure that the flat is adequately ventilated. I require that this breach should be remedied, *if this is possible*, by your taking steps to repair the damage to the walls. I have notice that you are using the premises in a way that contravenes the second covenant in the tenancy agreement, i.e. not to use the flat for illegal purposes. I hereby require to take such steps, *if any are possible*, to remedy this breach.

LECTURER: Good. Now moving on to the next stage: Assuming Mr Heath has served a valid s.146 notice Peter and Alison can apply to the court for "relief from forfeiture" at any time prior to the granting to Mr Heath of a possession order.

> **SIXTH QUESTION:** Is the tenant entitled to relief from forfeiture?

LECTURER: Can you explain what "relief from forfeiture" means?

STUDENT: Once the landlord has properly served a s.146 notice he can proceed to enforce his right of re-entry. The lease is then regarded as terminated and the tenant a trespasser. If the court grants Peter and Alison "relief" then it means that the tenancy will not be regarded as ended and they will still have their lease.

LECTURER: Now tell me the circumstances in which the courts may grant relief from forfeiture (it is discretionary). Remember to use the rules to create an argument for or against the grant of relief in Peter and Alison's case.

STUDENT: Under s.146(2) the court may find it difficult to grant Peter and Alison relief from forfeiture. Although we are not told whether they attempt to remedy the breaches, in relation to the s.146 notice served by Mr Heath, they are in breach of several covenants. One of these is an illegal user covenant, which may have an impact on the value of the property (by analogy with the "stigma" cases). So arguably having regard to "all the circumstances" the court may hold it fairer to allow Mr Heath possession of the flat. This will particularly be the case if Peter and Alison do not attempt to redress the condensation problem or stop using the premises illegally, although the court could impose this as a condition for granting relief under s.146(2).

> **LECTURER:** Our STUDENT is not just listing the legal rules, but using them to see how they may work in Peter and Alison's case.

LECTURER: Good! Quite an imaginative argument!

What we are going to do now is critically evaluate the law of forfeiture. We will consider whether it is good and fair law as well as looking at the Law Commission's proposals for reform of the forfeiture rules.

(g) Reform of the law of forfeiture

LECTURER: Having now studied the law of forfeiture I have a question for you:

> **"I hazard the observation. If you were asked to devise a system whereby landlords could terminate tenancies where the tenant was in breach of obligation, you wouldn't come up with anything like this, not even in your wildest dreams."**
>
> **" 'Necessary and Proportionate': The Law Commission's Recommendations for the Reform of Forfeiture": Stuart Bridge, Law Commissioner, Lecture Given to the Property Bar Association, November 9, 2006. (See the Law Commission's website)**

I am sure that you have already appreciated that the law of forfeiture is difficult. Two major criticisms of the existing law of forfeiture are firstly that it is overly complex, and secondly that it can sometimes leave the landlord unjustly enriched at the expense of the tenant. The Law Commission said that it "is complex, it lacks coherence, and it can lead to injustice".[126] In its report, *Termination of Tenancies for Tenant Default*[127] the Law Commission concluded that "the time has come for the current law of forfeiture to be abolished and replaced by a simpler, more coherent statutory scheme".[128] The current law is opaque and "it is difficult for those who are unfamiliar with the system to understand what is involved in the forfeiture of a tenancy and to appreciate the consequences of the parties' actions".[129] The doctrine of waiver seems particularly difficult in this respect and may often operate as a trap for the unwary.[130]

Secondly where there is a long lease this represents a valuable asset for which the tenant has paid a considerable sum in advance. Thus, if the landlord can end the lease through forfeiture, for a relatively trivial breach of covenant, the tenant has lost a valuable asset.

(i) Critical thinking on the law of forfeiture and the Law Commission's observations

LECTURER: Before we look at the Law Commission's proposed scheme for reform can you hold these two criticisms against any of our Building Blocks and say whether you agree or

---

126   Law Commission, Consultation Paper *Termination of Tenancies for Tenant Default* (2004) Law Com No.174.
127   (2006) Law Com No.303.
128   Executive Summary para.1.3. The report includes a draft Landlord and Tenant (Termination of Tenancies) Bill.
129   Above para.1.5.
130   "'Necessary and Proportionate': The Law Commission's Recommendations for the Reform of Forfeiture": S.Bridge, Law Commissioner, Lecture Given to the Property Bar Association, November 9, 2006, para.1.17, hereafter cited as S.Bridge, "Necessary and Proportionate"; see the Law Commission's website.

disagree with the Law Commission's observations? Remember that if rules support or undermine any of our Building Blocks[131] we can say that they are good or bad fair or unfair accordingly.

STUDENT: Firstly I would choose BUILDING BLOCK NO 6:

BUILDING BLOCK NO 6: The Need for Certainty and Predictability in Land Law Rules
Land Law rules should be clear in how they apply to any given situation. This level of certainty will allow people to know the legal outcome of their actions. They will know where they stand. The law should not give them any "nasty surprises". The tenant's residential security is at stake as the law of forfeiture allows the landlord to evict the tenant before the lease is due to end. Landlords must be able to protect their ownership of the property and know when they can reclaim it. We can say that the law of forfeiture is good or bad fair or unfair depending on whether it supports or undermines this essential principle of certainty and predictability.

STUDENT: The Law Commission says that the law is complex and makes it difficult for ordinary landlords and tenants to appreciate the consequences of their actions. If this is true we can legitimately say that it is bad law as it undermines BUILDING BLOCK NO 6.

LECTURER: Can you verify the Law Commission's observation? Look back over the forfeiture law that we have studied.

STUDENT: The doctrine of "waiver" is very uncertain and unpredictable. A simple action like accepting rent or making a formal demand for rent can deprive the landlord of his right to end the lease prematurely.[132] Landlords will not necessarily appreciate that this will be the legal consequence of their actions. The law does not have sufficient *predictability*. This is not helped by the objective test for waiver. In determining whether the landlord has waived the breach the court looks to his conduct and not his intentions. Thus, a waiver can be entirely inadvertent.[133] Therefore the law of waiver does not allow parties to be able to predict the consequences of their actions.

LECTURER: You would need to introduce some cases to illustrate your point. But for now could you make similar arguments in relation to forfeiture procedure and s.146 notices?

STUDENT: It seems unjustifiable to have two sets of rules for forfeiture depending on the type of breach, i.e. whether a rent covenant or another type. Furthermore, there has been considerable uncertainty as to the content of the s.146 notice that the landlord must serve before he can repossess the property. Cases have shown that the idea of what is a "remediable breach" is uncertain.

---

131   For the full text of our Building Blocks and instruction on how to use them to create an argument see Chapter 1.
132   Bridge says that "[t]he landlord who knows (or ought to know) that the tenant is in breach of covenant has to tread very carefully indeed": "Necessary and Proportionate", para.1.17.
133   Bridge argues that "Does [the law's] unforgiving 'objective' application, without any reference to the parties' actual beliefs, really serve any useful purpose?" "Necessary and Proportionate", para.1.17.

If the breach is of a type deemed to be remediable then the landlord must ask the tenant to remedy it. If he has not done this then the notice is invalid and the landlord will be unable to repossess the premises: e.g. *Rugby School (Governors) v Tannahill*.[134] This seems like it is depriving the landlord of the right to protect his financial interests on a mere technicality! The application of the "test" for remediable breaches in *Expert Clothing Service & Sales Ltd v Hillgate House Ltd*[135] is far from clear, for instance a once and for all breach of a negative covenant is irremediable: *Scala House and District Property Co Ltd v Forbes*,[136] whereas the position is different with once and for all breaches of positive covenants. Taking all of this into account I think that the law in relation to s.146 of the Law of Property Act 1925 is far from being certain and predictable. It means that landlords can easily fall into the trap of serving defective notices.

"The law should be more transparent, so that those affected, landlords and tenants in particular, know what is happening, and what is expected of them. The law should be more accessible, so that the parties can readily discover what their rights and obligations are."

S.Bridge, "Necessary and Proportionate"

LECTURER: I think you have established your point fairly well, although in the problem solving exercise you managed to show me a way to overcome this. What about the Law Commission's unjust enrichment argument?

STUDENT: If there is a long lease (such as 999 years) and the tenant has paid a large sum up front, the landlord stands to gain a windfall by forfeiture. If the owner of the lease breaches a covenant then the owner of the freehold reversion could forfeit the lease and gain a valuable asset![137]

LECTURER: What you really need to be asking is whether reform is needed. Is the current law defective in protecting tenants under long leases in this respect?

STUDENT: Looking back over my notes I see that the purpose of introducing a statutory jurisdiction to provide relief from forfeiture under s.146(2) of the Law of Property Act 1925 was to avoid the situation whereby the landlord obtained a windfall in the case of forfeiture of a long lease: *Billson v Residential Apartments Ltd*, per Lord Templeman. And there is similar protection for termination for breach of repairing covenants. With long leases the tenant can require the landlord to obtain a court order in order that he may forfeit the lease. This means that the court will have an opportunity to scrutinise the case. In such a

134 [1935] 1 K.B. 87.
135 [1986] Ch. 340.
136 [1974] Q.B. 575.
137 (2006) Law Com. No.303.

case the court may consider whether the landlord will obtain a significant windfall and whether the forfeiture of the lease is really necessary in order to remedy the breach: Leasehold Property (Repairs) Act 1938.

LECTURER: Are these provisions defective?

STUDENT: Not really. They allow the courts to consider all the circumstances of the case.

LECTURER: But may the court expressly decline to award forfeiture if the remedy is not necessary in order to protect the value of the landlord's freehold reversion?

STUDENT: The jurisdiction is not as clear as it could be on such an important point. It may be that legislation should direct the courts to consider this matter expressly.

LECTURER: So your argument on this is based again on BUILDING BLOCK NO 6. For now let's look at the Law Commission's proposed new forfeiture scheme.

(ii) Proposed new statutory scheme for premature termination of a tenancy[138]

- The proposed scheme will abolish the law of forfeiture. In its place there will be "a statutory scheme enabling the landlord to 'terminate the tenancy for tenant default' ".[139] The scheme is intended to be confined to commercial tenancies and long residential tenancies.

> **Default = breach of a tenant's covenant.**

- A tenant default will allow the landlord to seek to end the tenancy prematurely.[140] There will be no need for the lease to include a right of re-entry.[141] The scheme confers a statutory right to take "termination action" to end the tenancy, and not a contractual right.[142] The two sets of rules that currently operate, forfeiture for failure to pay rent and forfeiture for breaches of other covenant, will be replaced by a single concept of "tenant default", i.e. a breach of a covenant or condition in the tenancy.[143]
- "[T]he tenant should be given an 'explanatory statement' explaining what can happen in the event of tenant default".[144] This ensures that the tenant is aware of the consequences of breach of covenant.

---

138 The Law Commission's proposals are contained in its report *Termination of Tenancies for Tenant Default* (2006) Law Com. No.303. The proposals have yet to be enacted into law.

139 S.Bridge, "Necessary and Proportionate", para.1.21. There are certain excluded tenancies, e.g. assured and assured shorthold tenancies.

140 S.Bridge, "Necessary and Proportionate", para.1.21.

141 S.Bridge, "Necessary and Proportionate", paras 1.26 and 1.28.

142 S.Bridge, "Necessary and Proportionate", paras 1.26 and 1.28.

143 Law Commission, *Termination of Tenancies for Tenant Default* (2006) Law Com. No.303, Executive Summary, para.1.9.

144 Above, para.1.9.

> **BUILDING BLOCK NO 6: The Need for Certainty and Predictability in Land Law Rules**
> From your knowledge of it so far, will this scheme produce sufficient certainty and predictability to allow ordinary landlords and tenants to know where they stand? Is it better than the old law in this respect?

- The landlord must serve on the tenant a tenant default notice informing the tenant of the impending action, detailing the nature of the breach, "any remedial action required and the date by which it should be completed".[145] The scheme will abolish the doctrine of waiver so that it will no longer be possible for a landlord to waive a breach of covenant,[146] but it "limits the period after a tenant default during which a tenant can be served with a tenant default notice".[147] The landlord must serve the notice within six months of the relevant tenant default.[148]

> The processes are clear then as to the rights of the landlord, but the tenant will not have "termination" hanging over his head forever!

> **BUILDING BLOCK NO 6: The need for certainty and predictability:**
> will this make good law?

> **The Law Commission:** "The primary purpose of the tenant default notice is to ensure that the tenant complies with the obligations under the tenancy". Also it will get the parties into discussion and negotiation: para. 1.13. This clearly shows the Law Commission's thinking is that premature termination of a long-term residential tenancy or a commercial tenancy should be a last resort.

> **Will this make good or bad law?**

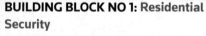

> **BUILDING BLOCK NO 1: Residential Security**
> The law is good if it gives protection to people's residential security. For the full text of this Building Block see Chapter 1.

---

145 Above, para.1.11.
146 The landlord and tenant can agree that breaches of certain covenants will not amount to a "tenant default": para.1.10.
147 Above, para.1.11.
148 S.Bridge, "Necessary and Proportionate", para.1.40.

- If the tenant fails to comply with their obligations "the landlord may make a termination claim" through the courts.[149] The court may make any order it thinks fit. It may make an order ending the tenancy, a "termination order"; Or it may make a "remedial order" which does not end the tenancy but requires the tenant to remedy the default within a stipulated time. The court may order sale of the tenancy and a distribution of the proceeds of sale. This is particularly valuable where there is a long lease and the tenant has paid a considerable capital sum for the lease.[150] Under the proposed scheme it is possible to end the tenancy without a court order (like peaceable re-entry), but only in limited circumstances.[151] The court should consider factors such as whether the tenant will "lose a significant capital asset as a result of a relatively trivial breach of covenant", i.e. whether the landlord will gain a disproportionate windfall.[152]

Transmission of leasehold covenants[153]

2

A. INTRODUCTION

What if the original tenant transfers ("assigns") his lease to another, e.g. he sells the lease, and the original landlord sells or otherwise disposes of the freehold reversion (we will also call this an assignment)? There will be a new tenant and a new landlord of the same premises.

Is the new tenant liable under the same covenants as the original tenant? Is the new landlord subject to the same obligations, e.g. repair, as the original landlord? Can the new landlord and tenant sue and be sued on the covenants in the lease?

| Original landlord | ⟶ | Assignee of the freehold reversion (new landlord) |

| Original tenant | ⟶ | Assignee of the lease (new tenant) |

---

149 Law Commission, *Termination of Tenancies for Tenant Default* (2006) Law Com. No.303, Executive Summary para.1.14. The Law Commission observes that the landlord is only able to make a termination claim "[i]f the service of a tenant default notice fails in its primary purpose": para.1.14. This underlines the fact that premature termination is a last resort under the proposed statutory scheme.

150 Above, paras 1.17–1.18. This order would avoid the landlord obtaining a "disproportionate windfall": para.1.18. If such a tenancy were ended by forfeiture the tenant would lose what he paid, subject of course to obtaining "relief" from forfeiture. As the Law Commission observe, this proposed scheme is more transparent in what it is seeking to achieve and why: above paras 1.5–1.6.

151 Above, paras 1.21–1.24: The "summary termination procedure".

152 S.Bridge, "Necessary and Proportionate", paras 1.47–1.48.

153 The law of transmission of leasehold covenants is a substantial topic and I can therefore only deal with it briefly. For more in-depth treatment see Kenny and Hewitson, *Blackstone's Guide to Landlord & Tenant Covenants: The New Law in Practice* (Blackstone Press, 1996); S.Bridge [1996] C.L.J. 313; M.Davey (1996) 59 M.L.R. 78.

The landlord must be able to enforce important covenants such as repair in order to protect the value of his freehold reversion. Likewise, the new tenant must be able to hold the landlord to his covenants in order that his interest is protected. Land is sold, and tenancies assigned, very frequently. It is difficult to imagine landlord and tenant law being workable if it did not make adequate provision for the *transmission* of the covenants under the lease to the new landlord and tenant. The Landlord and Tenant (Covenants) Act 1995 simplified the law and applies to the transmission of covenants in leases created on or after January 1, 1996. As there are many tenancies in existence that were granted before this Act (I call these pre-1996 tenancies) we need to consider the law prior to 1996.

B. THE LIABILITY OF THE ORIGINAL LANDLORD AND THE ORIGINAL TENANT UNDER A PRE-1996 TENANCY: PRIVITY OF CONTRACT

We must remember that a lease is also a contract and because of this it is subject to the doctrine of "privity of contract". This means that the contract is enforceable by and against the parties who entered into that contract, here the original landlord and tenant. The doctrine of privity of contract applies to leases created prior to the coming into force of the Landlord and Tenant (Covenants) Act 1995 (January 1, 1996).

The full logical implication of privity of contract is that the original landlord and tenant remain bound by the covenants under the lease for the full term, regardless of whether the landlord has sold the freehold reversion or the tenant has assigned the leasehold term.

> **Example**
> - There is a lease for a term of 99 years containing a covenant for the tenant to pay rent.
> - The tenant assigns the lease to T2 after 10 years has expired. T2 stops paying rent. However, T2 is insolvent so there is not much point in the landlord suing T2. He doesn't have any money!
> - The landlord can sue the original tenant for T2's non-payment of rent.[154]

This is a considerable liability for the original tenant. Likewise, if the landlord has assigned the freehold reversion and new landlord breaches a covenant then the original tenant can sue the original landlord. This was one of the major defects in the law that the 1995 Act was designed to remedy.

---

154   *Allied London Investments Ltd v Hambro Life Assurance Plc* (1985) 50 P. & C.R. 207.

C. TRANSMISSION OF LEASEHOLD COVENANTS PRE-1996: STATUTORY POSITION OF LANDLORD'S COVENANTS ON ASSIGNMENT OF THE FREEHOLD REVERSION

As far as concerns whether the *new* landlord or tenant can sue or be sued on the lease's covenants in leases created before 1996, obviously there is no privity of contract between assignees. If this were the end of the story the covenants could not be enforced by the new landlord and tenant once the original parties has assigned their interests.

Sections 141(1) and 142(1) of the Law of Property Act 1925 attach ("annex") the benefit and burden of the tenant's covenants to the freehold reversion so that an assignee of the landlord can sue the tenant on the tenant's covenants and be sued on the landlord's covenants.[155] For example a new landlord can pursue a claim against the tenant for, e.g. non-payment of rent.[156] If the new landlord commits a breach of a repairing covenant the tenant can sue the new landlord.[157] Both sections operate only if the covenant "touches and concerns" the land. We will consider the meaning of this phrase below.

D. TRANSMISSION OF LEASEHOLD COVENANTS: PRE-1996: ASSIGNEES OF THE ORIGINAL LANDLORD AND TENANT

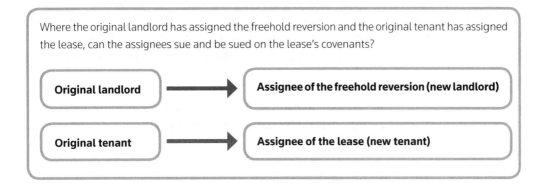

Where the original landlord has assigned the freehold reversion and the original tenant has assigned the lease, can the assignees sue and be sued on the lease's covenants?

| Original landlord | → | Assignee of the freehold reversion (new landlord) |
| Original tenant | → | Assignee of the lease (new tenant) |

Although there is no privity of contract where a tenancy or reversion has been assigned, land law has long held that where there is "privity of estate" then the covenants in the lease will be

---

155   s.141 and 142 are re-enacted versions of statutory provisions that date from The Grantees of Reversions Act 1540. This was before the common law (*Spencer's Case* (1583) 5 Co. Rep. 16a) held that covenants in leases would pass to those in privity of estate provided that they "touched and concerned" the land. For further detail see Harpum, Bridge, Dixon, *Megarry & Wade Law of Real Property*, paras 20–011, 20–046.

156   s.141(1): *Re King* [1963] Ch. 459.

157   s.142.

enforceable between assignees of the tenancy and the freehold reversion provided that the covenant "touches and concerns" the land.[158]

(1) Privity of estate

Privity of estate is present where both are party to the same leasehold estate: one landlord; the other tenant. Thus, where the tenant has assigned the lease the new tenant is in "privity of estate" with the landlord (although not privity of contract). Equally where both landlord and tenant have assigned their interests the new landlord and tenant are both in privity of estate. The covenants are only enforceable in privity of *estate*, which indicates that the lease must be legal.

(2) The covenant must "touch and concern" the land

Where there is privity of estate the covenants in the lease can be enforced by and against assignees provided that the covenant "touches and concerns" the land. In *P & A Swift Investments v Combined English Stores Group Plc*[159] Lord Oliver considered that a "satisfactory working test" for whether a covenant touches and concerns the land is as follows:

"(1) the covenant benefits only the [landlord] for the time being, and if separated from the reversion ceases to be of benefit to the [landlord];

(2) the covenant affects the nature, quality, mode of user or value of the land of the [landlord];

(3) the covenant is not expressed to be personal (that is to say neither being given only to a specific [landlord] nor in respect of the obligations only of a specific tenant);

(4) the fact that a covenant is to pay a sum of money will not prevent it from touching and concerning the land so long as the three forgoing conditions are satisfied and the covenant is connected with something to be done on, to or in relation to the land."

A useful test was established in *Hua Chiao Commercial Bank Ltd v Chiaphua Industries Ltd*[160] in which it was held that the requirement to pay a security deposit at the start of the tenancy (to be repaid at the end) was purely a personal obligation to make a payment. The covenant was not "reasonably incidental to the relation of landlord and tenant".

A covenant to pay rent clearly touches and concerns the land.[161] It relates to the payment in return for which the other is able to take possession of the land. It is fundamental to the owner of the freehold reversion. It is usually the whole point of granting the tenancy. Thus it is "reasonably incidental to the relation of landlord and tenant". A covenant that regulates the tenant's use of the premises, e.g. for residential purposes only also touches and concerns

---

158   *Spencer's Case* (1583) 5 Co. Rep. 16a.
159   [1988] 2 All E.R. 885, p. 890.
160   [1987] A.C. 99.
161   *Parker v Webb* (1693) 3 Salk. 5.

the land.[162] The covenant regulates how the tenant is able to make use of the land that is subject to the lease. It is thus incidental to the relation of landlord and tenant. In *Woodall v Clifton*[163] a covenant that gave the tenant an option to purchase the land he leased was held not to regulate the relationship between landlord and tenant. It related only to the *purchase* of the land by the tenant and not to the landlord and tenant relationship.

E. LEASES CREATED AFTER JANUARY 1, 1996[164]

(1) Enforceability of covenants by and against assignees of the freehold reversion and the lease: post-1996 tenancies

Under s.3(1) of the Landlord and Tenant (Covenants) Act 1995 the benefit (the ability to enforce the covenants) and the burden (liability to be sued for breach of a covenant) of the landlord and tenant covenants will pass to every assignee of the freehold reversion and every assignee of the lease.

In cases where the landlord has assigned the freehold reversion, the new landlord will be able to sue the tenant for breach of the tenant's covenants under the lease and is liable under the landlord's covenants.[165] If there is a right of re-entry contained in the lease enabling the landlord to forfeit the lease for the tenant's breach of covenant, this will attach to the reversion and pass to any new assignee.[166]

LANDLORD s.3(3)

Likewise where the tenant has assigned the lease the new tenant will be able to sue the landlord for breach of the landlord's covenants under the lease and is liable under the tenant's covenants.[167]

TENANT s.3(2)

There is no need to apply the old rules on privity of estate and no need to consider whether the covenant "touches and concerns" the land. Covenants which are "expressed to be personal" will not pass to assignees.[168]

---

162 *Wilkinson v Rogers* (1864) 2 De G.J. and S. 62.
163 [1905] 2 Ch. 257.
164 The date on which the Landlord and Tenant (Covenants) Act 1995 came into force.
165 Landlord and Tenant (Covenants) Act 1995 s.3(3).
166 s.4.
167 s.3(2).
168 s.3(6)(a).

> **Example**
> "For the benefit of the landlord *whilst he retains the freehold reversion*, X, as tenant, covenants to pay rent in advance rather than in arrears."
>
> The words in italics indicate that this covenant is only intended to be enforceable by the current landlord.

(2) The contractual liability of the original landlord and tenant

You will remember that one of the major defects of the pre-1996 law was that the original landlord and tenant remain liable to be sued on the covenants even after they have parted with their interests in the land. Thus, a tenant who assigned his lease could be sued by the landlord for the new tenant's breach of a covenant to pay rent years after the original tenant had ceased to hold the lease. This is a considerable injustice. The Landlord and Tenant (Covenants) Act 1995 changes this position both in regard to the original tenant and the original landlord. However, the situation is slightly different in relation to the landlord.

(a) The contractual liability of the original tenant after they have assigned the lease

When the original tenant assigns the lease they are released from the tenant's covenants as from the time of the assignment.[169] Consequently, they are not liable to be sued if the new tenant or his assignees breach a covenant.[170] Neither can the original tenant sue the original landlord for breach of a landlord's covenant.[171]

However, if a lease contains a covenant that a tenant can only assign with the consent of the landlord, the landlord can require the tenant to enter into an "authorised guarantee agreement" as a condition of giving their consent. An authorised guarantee agreement is an agreement by which the tenant guarantees that the new tenant will perform the covenants.[172]

> **Authorised Guarantee Agreement (AGA)**
> The tenant guarantees that the replacement tenant will pay the rent. If the replacement tenant breaches the covenant the original tenant will pay compensation to the landlord.

---

169   Landlord and Tenant (Covenants) Act 1995 s.5(2).
170   s.5(2)(a).
171   s.5(2)(b).
172   s.16(2); The 1995 Act imposes two further conditions to the validity of an authorised guarantee agreement. The landlord must make his consent subject to the tenant's entering into such an agreement and the agreement must be entered into pursuant to that condition: s.16(3); Kenny and Hewitson, *Blackstone's Guide to Landlord & Tenant Covenants: The New Law in Practice*, pp.31–32. For the terms that may be imposed by the landlord in the authorised guarantee agreement see s.16(5).

An authorised guarantee agreement can only operate to ensure that the original tenant guarantees the performance of the relevant covenant(s) by the immediate assignee and not any subsequent assignee.[173]

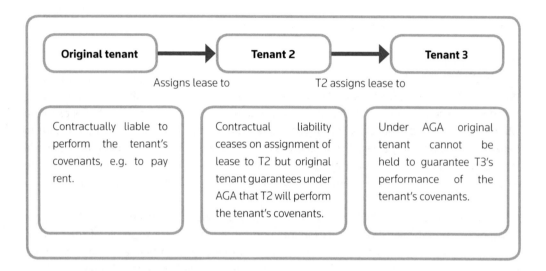

Original tenant	Tenant 2	Tenant 3
Assigns lease to	T2 assigns lease to	
Contractually liable to perform the tenant's covenants, e.g. to pay rent.	Contractual liability ceases on assignment of lease to T2 but original tenant guarantees under AGA that T2 will perform the tenant's covenants.	Under AGA original tenant cannot be held to guarantee T3's performance of the tenant's covenants.

(i) Overriding leases

If a tenant has paid compensation for his assignee's breach of a tenant's covenant he can obtain what is called an "overriding lease", i.e. he is entitled to get the landlord to grant him a lease of the reversion. The point of this is that the original tenant therefore becomes the landlord of the assignee (with all the same covenants) and can pursue remedies against the assignee for breach.[174]

(b) The contractual liability of the original landlord after they have assigned the freehold reversion

The position is not quite the same as that of the original tenant. Unlike the position of the tenant on an assignment of the lease, the landlord is not automatically released from his contractual liability under the landlord's covenants when he transfers the freehold reversion to another. However, the landlord may apply to be released.[175]

Once the landlord is released from the landlord's covenants he is no longer liable to be sued if the new landlord breaches the covenants, and he can no longer sue the tenant for breach of the

---

173   s.16(4).
174   Landlord and Tenant (Covenants) Act 1995 s.19. For further detail see Kenny and Hewitson, *Blackstone's Guide to Landlord & Tenant Covenants: The New Law in Practice*.
175   s.6(2).

tenant's covenants.[176] In order for the landlord to be released from the covenants he must serve on the tenant a notice informing him that he intends to assign the freehold reversion. In the notice the landlord must request to be released from the covenants.[177] The tenant then has four weeks to object to the release. If the tenant does not object then the landlord is released. If the tenant does object the landlord may apply to the county court, who may declare that it is reasonable for the landlord to be released from the covenants.[178]

(c) Excluded assignments

Under s.11 of the Landlord and Tenant (Covenants) Act 1995 there are certain situations in which the original landlord and tenant will not be released from their liability under the lease's covenants.[179] There will be no release where the assignment is by *operation of law*.[180] For example where a tenant is declared bankrupt, his interest under the lease vests in the trustee in bankruptcy by operation of law.[181] Also, there is no release where the assignment itself is made in breach of covenant.[182] For example, the tenant has assigned the lease unreasonably despite a covenant which prohibits assignment or subletting unless it is reasonable to do so.

Nevertheless, as soon as there is a further assignment after the excluded one the original assignor will be released from the covenants under the lease.[183] For example, if the original tenant assigns the lease in breach of a covenant not to assign or sublet, and the new tenant then assigns the lease then at this point the original tenant will be released from the tenant's covenants.

3

Ending of Leases

A. EXPIRY OF THE TERM

We must remember that a lease is an estate in land *for a time*. So the estate ends when the time has expired. A clause can be included in the agreement which allows landlord or tenant the right to end the tenancy after a certain point prior to the expiry of the contractual term, e.g. six months into a 12 month tenancy. This is known as a "break clause".

---

176 s.6(2).
177 s.8(1). The notice must be served no later than four weeks after the date of the assignment: s.8(1).
178 s.8(2).
179 s.11(2)(a).
180 s.11(1).
181 Kenny and Hewitson, *Blackstone's Guide to Landlord & Tenant Covenants: The New Law in Practice*, pp.22–25.
182 s.11(1).
183 s.11(2)(b); Kenny and Hewitson, above pp.22–25.

B. NOTICE

As we have seen a lease can be terminated by either party on giving notice to the other under the contract. In the case of any tenancy of a dwelling house four weeks' notice must be given, unless both parties agree a shorter period.[184]

The length of notice required by law to end a periodic tenancy is determined by the core period. Thus, to end a monthly periodic tenancy one month's notice must be given to expire at the end of the period.[185] A yearly tenancy requires six months notice.[186] Landlord and tenant can agree a different period of notice if they wish.[187] Periodic tenancies have no fixed duration at the outset. This is a tenancy initially for one period, e.g. a week or a month, and which automatically continues for another period until either landlord or tenant serves notice that they no longer wish the tenancy to continue. Thus, if there is more than one tenant and one serves notice to end the tenancy then this will be sufficient to terminate a periodic tenancy. Such tenancies only continue into a new period where all parties consent. Where one serves notice therefore, the requisite consent to the continuation of the periodic tenancy is absent.[188]

Notices to quit have been seen as problematic in some recent cases. For example, in *Alexander-David v Hammersmith and Fulham LBC*,[189] a local authority granted a tenancy to a minor, but because a minor cannot hold a legal estate in land[190] this meant that the local authority were holding the lease on trust for the minor. Accordingly it was held that the local authority could not serve a notice to quit under the terms of the agreement[191] because this would amount to a destruction of the subject matter of the trust. It would be a breach of trust. This clarifies the position for local authorities who grant tenancies to 16 and 17 year-olds. However, it is noted that should they grant genuine licences they will be able to terminate the agreement more readily.

C. FORFEITURE AND REPUDIATION

As we have seen above a tenancy can be brought to an end by forfeiture. It can also be brought to an end by the tenant under the contractual remedy of repudiation.[192]

Protection from Eviction Act 1977 s.5; Harpum, Bridge, Dixon, above, para.17–073.
185 *Javad v Aqil* [1991] 1 W.L.R. 1007.
186 *Prudential Assurance Co Ltd v London Residuary Body* [1992] 2 A.C. 386, per Lord Templeman.
187 Harpum, Bridge, Dixon, *Megarry & Wade Law of Real Property*, para.17–074.
188 *Hammersmith and Fulham LBC v Monk* [1992] 1 A.C. 478; *Harrow LBC v Qazi* [2003] UKHL 43.
189 [2009] EWCA Civ 259; [2010] Ch. 272.
190 Law of Property Act 1925 s.1(6).
191 It was a weekly periodic tenancy with a notice period of four weeks. The tenant had committed nuisance in breach of the tenancy agreement.
192 See section 1A in this Chapter.

D. FRUSTRATION

It has been held that the contractual doctrine of frustration applies to leases. "A contract will be described as 'frustrated' where, after the contract has been formed, an event occurs that is beyond the control of both parties and that has the effect of making the obligations under the contract impossible to perform."[193] For example, in *Taylor v Caldwell*[194] the claimants entered into a contractual licence to hire a music hall. The music hall burned down in a fire. It was held that the contract had been frustrated, which ended the obligations of both parties.[195] The effect of establishing a frustrating event is that the lease will end. The doctrine of frustration was held to apply to leases in *National Carriers Ltd v Panalpina (Northern) Ltd*.[196] On the facts of the case however the lease had not been frustrated. A tenant had been granted a 10-year lease of a warehouse. The local authority closed the access road which prevented the tenants from using the warehouse for two years. It was held that because there was still a number of years for which the tenant could use the warehouse, the lease had not been frustrated. The lease contract was not impossible to perform.

E. SURRENDER

A lease can be ended by "surrender", which means the giving up of the tenancy by mutual consent of landlord and tenant. This can be done either expressly or impliedly.

Further reading

Law Commission, *Termination of Tenancies for Tenant Default* (2006) Law Com. No.303.
S.Bridge, " 'Necessary and Proportionate': The Law Commission's Recommendations for the Reform of Forfeiture": S.Bridge, Law Commissioner, Lecture Given to the Property Bar Association, November 9, 2006 (The Law Commission's website).
S.Bridge, "Leases—contract, property and status" in L. Tee (ed.) *Land Law: Issue, Debates, Policy* (Willan Publishing, 2002).

---

193   R.Murray, *Contract Law: The Fundamentals* (London: Sweet & Maxwell, 2008), p.207.
194   (1863) 3 B. & S. 826.
195   (1863) 3 B. & S. 826; R. Murray, above p.208.
196   [1981] A.C. 675.

Chapter 11

Easements

CHAPTER OVERVIEW

In this chapter you will find:

- Instructions on how to think critically about the law of easements
- The four legal characteristics of an easement and case extracts
- How to think like a land lawyer about the four characteristics
- The legal methods by which an easement can be acquired
- Constructed argument using Building Blocks
- Constructed argument about the 2011 Law Commission reform proposals using Building Blocks.

Introduction

1

An easement is a limited right belonging to one landowner (usually a neighbour) over land belonging to another. They are not claims for possession or ownership of the land but the right to undertake some activity on the land.[1] An example would be a "right of way". Let's say that Alison owns a terraced house. She needs to be able to take her rubbish bin out on collection day. At the back of all the houses, between the houses and the gardens, there is a strip of land running the entire length of the houses. This land belongs to one of Alison's neighbours but Alison has a right of way over it. The plan of the path on the deeds/land register would look something like this:

---

1   *Copeland v Greenhalf* [1952] Ch. 488, p.498, per Upjohn J.

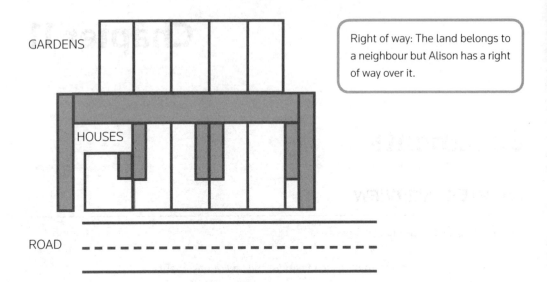

GARDENS

Right of way: The land belongs to a neighbour but Alison has a right of way over it.

HOUSES

ROAD

The land which has the right, e.g. to walk across the neighbour's land has the "benefit" of the easement. That land is called the "dominant tenement". The land over which the right is exercised has the "burden" of the easement. That land is referred to as the "servient tenement".

Examples of types of easement include a right of way,[2] use of a drive on the servient land for access to premises,[3] use of a coal shed on a neighbour's land for storage,[4] a right to park a car on land belonging to a neighbour,[5] a right to receive an amount of light through a defined channel, such as a window.[6] Neighbouring properties will not then be able to build on their land so as to obstruct the light to which the land is entitled.[7] Two slightly more unusual rights that have been established as easements are the right to use a lavatory[8] and the right to use a neighbour's kitchen for washing.[9]

A *positive* easement is where the dominant landowner has the right to do something on the servient land, e.g. a right of way, storage, or parking. A *negative* easement prevents the servient landowner from doing something, e.g. they cannot build an extension if their neighbour has an easement of light and the extension will take away their neighbour's light.

---

2   *Mills v Silver* [1991] 2 W.L.R. 324.
3   *Healey v Hawkins* [1968] 1 W.L.R. 1967.
4   *Wright v Macadam* [1949] 2 K.B. 744.
5   *London & Blenheim Estates Ltd v Ladbroke Retail Parks Ltd* [1994] 1 W.L.R. 31.
6   An easement of light: *Colls v Home and Colonial Stores Ltd* [1904] A.C. 179; *G & S Brough Ltd v Salvage Wharf Ltd* [2010] Ch. 11.
7   *Allen v Greenwood* [1979] 1 All E.R. 819.
8   *Miller v Emcer Products Ltd* [1956] Ch 304.
9   *Heywood v Mallalieu* (1883) 25 Ch. D. 357.

> **BUILDING BLOCK NO 4: Ideas of Ownership**
> As you can imagine, Land Law does not like restricting a landowner's freedom to do what he likes on his land—so negative easements are much less frequently recognised by law.

A. CRITICAL THINKING: BUILDING BLOCKS AND THE LAW OF EASEMENTS

At this point the nature of an easement becomes clear. It is a limited right to do some restricted activity on land belonging to another. Easements enable people (such as Alison in the above example) to make better use of their own land. They can allow people to walk over neighbouring land for purposes of access, store things in a limited area of it, park their cars on it or drive over it etc. No plot of land is the same and land can be used in many different ways. For example, the owner of a large park may wish to sell off part of the land for building houses and grant to the new owners of the houses the right to use the rest of the park as a pleasure park.[10] Although such rights can come into being contractually or by deed, as well as by implication of law, unless Land Law recognises the right as an *easement* they are likely to be extinguished pretty quickly. They will not endure from one transfer of the servient land to the next. Only property rights such as easements are capable of doing this. Consequently, a landowner (A) may be given a right to store coal in his neighbour's cellar, but unless it is recognised as an easement, A will not be able to store the coal once his neighbour sells his land.

> **BUILDING BLOCK NO 7: Land Law is "facilitative" (P.Birks) and should give effect to what people want and need to do with their land**
> Our Building Blocks are essential policies and principles of Land Law. We hold the rules of Land Law up against the Building Blocks and think about whether the rules support or undermine them. We can legitimately say that the rules are good or bad fair or unfair accordingly. See Chapter 1 for further details on how to create argument with Building Blocks. One essential aim of Land Law is to give effect to people's intentions, i.e. to facilitate what they want to do with their land. We expect to see that the rules are sufficiently adaptable to recognise different types of easement for different types of land use. So we can hold the rules that we are about to learn against this aim and consider whether they give effect to it or are too restrictive so as to undermine it.

Indeed, when easements of storage were recognised as capable in principle of existing as easements, these observations were made:

---

10   *In Re Ellenborough Park* [1956] Ch. 131.

"There is no reason why there should not be a valid easement for the purpose of storing on the land . . . trade goods and produce . . . 'The law must adapt itself to the conditions of modern society and trade, and there is nothing in the purposes for which the easement is claimed inconsistent in principle with a right of easement as such.' "[11]

In *Dyce v Hay*, Lord St. Leonards L.C. stated that "The categories of . . . easements must alter and expand with the changes that take place in the circumstances of mankind".[12] Indeed, it has been observed that "[t]he industrial revolution, which caused the growth of large towns and manufacturing industries, naturally brought into prominence such easements as ways, watercourses, light, and support".[13]

(1) Easements are property rights not personal rights

An easement is a property right. This means that it is capable of being transferred with the land and of binding all future owners of the land. If I have an easement to walk over my neighbour's land and my neighbour sells her house, my neighbour's purchaser may have to give effect to my right. My right is not a purely personal one that binds only me and my neighbour. It is a property right capable of attaching to the land itself and surviving subsequent transfers. Consequently strict criteria must be observed before an easement can come into existence. In order to be an easement the right claimed must possess certain "characteristics"[14] and must have been granted or otherwise come into being in one of the ways recognised by law.[15] Unless these criteria are satisfied the right cannot be an easement. It is possible that there may be a contractual right to use the land in a particular way, but the right is not an easement, a property right, and will bind only the contracting parties.[16]

> **BUILDING BLOCK NO 5: Property Rights and the Protection of Purchasers**
> We have seen that the acquisition of land is an important part of our society and economy: see Chapter 1. If a purchaser of the land is bound potentially by many property rights it makes the sale and transfer of land difficult. As a matter of policy this should be avoided. Thus if the law allows too many different types of easement to come into being too easily, this may potentially mean that there are many more property rights capable of binding purchasers of the land. This may overly restrict what landowners can do with their land and may make it more difficult for the land to be sold. Thus we say that law is good if it prevents this from happening. Because an easement is a property right the rules that recognise their existence must be fairly restrictive.

---

11   *Copeland v Greenhalf* [1952] Ch. 488, p.495, per Lord Upjohn quoting Osborne C.J. in the Privy Council case of *Attorney-General of Southern Nigeria v John Holt & Co (Liverpool) Ltd* [1915] A.C. 599.
12   1 Macq. 305, p.312.
13   Evershed M.R. *Re Ellenborough Park* [1956] 1 Ch. 131, p.162.
14   *In Re Ellenborough Park* [1956] Ch. 131; *London & Blenheim Estates Ltd v Ladbroke Retail Parks Ltd* [1994] 1 W.L.R. 31, p.36, per Peter Gibson L.J.
15   For example *Wheeldon v Burrows* (1879) L.R. 12 Ch.D 31.
16   *Re Ellenborough Park* [1956] 1 Ch. 131, p.141, per Danckwerts J., quoting Cheshire, *Modern Real Property* (7th edn.) *Ashburn Anstalt v Arnold* [1989] Ch. 1.

So immediately we see that there must be a "trade off", or balance struck, in the rules relating to easements. They must be sufficiently adaptable to give effect to the numerous purposes for which people own land, yet they cannot allow the recognition of too many different types of easement that may bind the title to the servient land and, perhaps, be overly restrictive of what the servient owner can do with his land.

B. EASEMENTS CAN BE "EXPRESSLY" OR "IMPLIEDLY" CREATED

An easement can come into being because the servient landowner has expressly created it, e.g. a landowner sells off part of his land and grants a right of access to the sold land over land that he has retained. This is an example of what we call a "grant" of an easement. However as part of the sale he may also "reserve" an easement for himself, e.g. he may in the conveyance expressly provide that he has a right of way for purposes of access to his land over the land that he sells. This is known as a "reservation" of an easement.

The law recognises that easements can come into being by implication into a conveyance of land (implied grants or reservations),[17] i.e. without having been expressly mentioned, or entirely informally, i.e. by continued use of the right for a certain number of years: which is known as "prescription".

EXAMPLE: Reservation of an easement
A landowner sells a house and part of his garden to a purchaser. He has retained part of the garden and needs access to the road

ROAD

SELLER SELLS HOUSE AND GARDEN TO PURCHASER

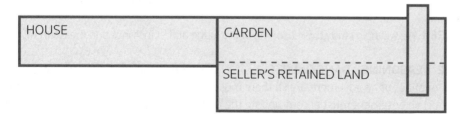

In the conveyance to the purchaser of the house and garden the seller reserves a right of access over the garden that he has sold in order that he may get to the road.

---

17   For example under the Law of Property Act 1925 s.62.

An easement must possess the four characteristics from the case of Re Ellenborough Park

Before a right or limited use of someone's land can be recognised by law as an easement it must bear what we call the "four characteristics of an easement".

(1) there must be a dominant and a servient tenement:

(2) an easement must "accommodate" the dominant tenement:

(3) the dominant and servient owners must be different persons, and

(4) a right over land cannot amount to an easement, unless it is capable of forming the subject-matter of a grant.[18]

However, before we consider these criteria in detail we will look at the case of *Re Ellenborough Park* itself in order to see the reason for their existence. All the characteristics of an easement, which must be established before a claimant can successfully claim that he has an easement over his neighbour's land, stem from the idea that easements are rights capable of permanently affecting the title to the land, and with it, every subsequent purchaser. The reasoning behind requiring four "characteristics" to be established is that a use of another's land in order to be capable of existing as a right that binds his title must be defined, limited and restricted in scope.

A. CASE STUDY 1: RE ELLENBOROUGH PARK

> **THE FACTS**: The owner of the White Cross Estate sold a considerable part of the estate in plots and houses were built on the plots. The part the owner retained was open ground and fronted onto the houses. This open ground became known as Ellenborough Park: it was a pleasure garden well-stocked with shrubs and plants. The conveyances of the plots purported to grant easements to the owners of the houses to use Ellenborough Park as a pleasure ground, e.g. to walk in it, rest in it, and use any facilities provided.[19] The material issue in the case was whether use of another's land for such a purpose was capable of amounting to an easement.

> LECTURER: We will now study the reasoning of the judge at first instance and the Court of Appeal

> **THE REASONING: DANCKWERTS J.** at first instance (pp.140–151): "The essential qualities of an easement are (1) there must be a dominant and a servient tenement; (2) an easement must accommodate the dominant tenement, that is, be connected with its enjoyment and for its benefit; (3) the dominant and servient owners must be

---

18   *Re Ellenborough Park* [1956] 1 Ch. 131, per Evershed M.R.

19   [1956] 1 Ch. 131, p.168.

different persons; and (4) the right claimed must be capable of forming the subject-matter of a grant . . . 'if [a right] lacks one or more of those characteristics, it may, indeed, be enforceable between the contracting parties, but it cannot, like an easement, be enforceable by or against third parties.' [quoting Cheshire]

In the present case. . . . [t]here is an express grant of 'the full enjoyment of the pleasure ground [Ellenborough Park]' . . . Presumably this means the right to enjoy the ground as a pleasure ground in all the ways in which a pleasure ground would normally be enjoyed, which would no doubt include the right to walk about on any parts not covered by flower beds and the like, and to sit down on appropriate parts of the ground and possibly to picnic there."

LECTURER: What is the main argument being outlined here?

STUDENT: Whether the right claimed in this case, i.e. the right to use Ellenborough Park as a pleasure ground, satisfies the four characteristics of an easement so that it can be a right that binds the title to the servient land.

DANCKWERTS J. CONTINUES: "Dr. G. R. Y. Radcliffe, in his book on Real Property Law . . . after observing that 'The English law of easements is very largely derived from the Roman law of servitudes, and is governed by the general consideration that it is not desirable on grounds of public policy that landowners should be able to subject their land to new and strange burdens', postulates as one of the qualities of an easement that 'The easement must be calculated to benefit the dominant tenement as a tenement [land], and not merely to confer a personal advantage on the owner of it.' This I find somewhat difficult to apply, for it seems to me that the benefit received from a right of way is necessarily a benefit to the owner or occupier of the tenement rather than to the tenement itself . . . But Dr Radcliffe continues: 'This principle is directly derived from the Roman law of servitudes and is well illustrated by the Roman Jurist Paul when he says that you cannot have a servitude giving you the right to wander about and picnic in another man's land' . . . If this is true of the English law of easements, it is apt to the situation with which I have to deal . . .'"

LECTURER: So what is the issue here?

STUDENT: An easement must be of benefit to the land and not confer a purely personal benefit on the owner. This is one of the "four characteristics" that must be present before an easement will be recognised to exist.

LECTURER: This is the second of the four characteristics: The right must "accommodate" the dominant tenement, i.e. be of benefit to it. Danckwerts J. found the test that the right must benefit the land and not be purely personal a difficult test to apply. Why?

STUDENT: Because it is always the people who own the land that will benefit in some way.

LECTURER: Let's see then how the judge interprets and applies this test.

DANCKWERTS J. CONTINUES: "In Theobald, The Law of Land . . . it is stated that an easement 'must be a right of utility and benefit and not one of mere recreation and amusement.' Two authorities are quoted for this statement. *Solomon v Vintners' Company* (1859) is one of them.

[After reviewing the cases that stated it was not possible to have an easement to wander aimlessly over another's land, and cases (much nearer the present one) which held that the use ornamental gardens was capable of amounting to an easement, Danckwerts J continued] I find it difficult to see what are the objections to a right to use neighbouring land for the purpose of enjoying air and exercise and similar amenities. Further, it is evident that the attachment of such amenities to the ownership of a particular house may add considerably to the value and the enjoyment of the house. As regards fettering the land which is the subject of the rights, the covenants entered into by the vendors in the present case prevent them or their successors in title building upon the site of the pleasure ground, and its existence as a pleasure ground in accordance with the intentions of the grantors is patent to anyone who visits the locality. I must confess that I have a leaning towards the intentions of the parties to transactions being carried out, if this is legally possible, and a dislike of seeing them defeated by the technicalities of suggested rules of law . . . I am not anxious to deprive the owners of the plots on the former White Cross Estate of the rights which the vendors' conveyances from 1855 to 1864, or thereabouts, attempted to give them . . . [. . .]

Accordingly, the conveyances of parts of the White Cross Estate conferred on the purchasers and their successors in title legal and effective easements to use the pleasure ground known as Ellenborough Park."

LECTURER: So what was the conclusion? Could the right claimed exist as an easement and why?

STUDENT: Yes. The legal reason was that the right to use the pleasure ground, when defined and attached to the houses as it was, satisfied the four characteristics of an easement. Particularly it satisfied the characteristic that the right benefited the houses themselves and was not just a personal benefit to the owners. It added to the value and enjoyment of the houses.

LECTURER: In technical terms we say that the right "accommodates the dominant tenement". Can you identify how Danckwerts J. balanced the two policy factors that we considered above, i.e. that easements should not be recognised too easily because they bind title to the servient land and affect every subsequent purchaser (BUILDING BLOCK NO 5) and Land Law rules should give effect to people's intentions, i.e. to what they want to do with the land (BUILDING BLOCK NO 7).

STUDENT: Danckwerts J. acknowledged that to allow the easement would mean that the servient owners could not build on the park. This would restrict its development. But he indicates that this would be obvious to anyone, including future purchasers of the servient land, that it is a pleasure park. He implies that the easement would not be too difficult to find out about. Because of this I think that the recognition of the right does not severely undermine BUILDING BLOCK NO 5.

BUILDING BLOCK NO 5: Property Rights and the Protection of Purchasers

If the law allows the parties to create many new types of right that may bind future purchasers of land, it may make the land more difficult to sell. This lies behind the basic thrust of the law of easements, that only definite and restricted rights can be recognised as easements.

LECTURER: And how did Danckwerts J. justify his decision to uphold the right as an easement?

STUDENT: Because it meant that the law would respect the intentions of the parties and allow them to create the easement that they wanted to in favour of the owners of the houses. It allowed them to use the land as they wished.

BUILDING BLOCK NO 7: Land Law is "facilitative" and should give effect to people's intentions regarding their land

It is a major function of Land Law to support what people want to do with their land. We can therefore legitimately say that Danckwerts J.'s final reasoning, because it supported this Building Block, is good and fair law.

Danckwerts J.'s decision in *Re Ellenborough Park* was affirmed on appeal, in which Evershed M.R. elaborated on what is meant by the requirement that the "right must accommodate the dominant tenement".

> **DANCKWERTS J. CONTINUES:** "We pass . . . to a consideration of . . . the accommodation of the alleged dominant tenements by the rights . . . [Quoting from Cheshire's *Modern Real Property*] After pointing out that 'one of the fundamental principles concerning easements is that they must be not only appurtenant to a dominant tenement, but also connected with the normal enjoyment of the dominant tenement' . . . the author proceeded: 'We may expand the statement of the principle thus: a right enjoyed by one over the land of another does not possess the status of an easement unless it accommodates and serves the dominant tenement, and is reasonably necessary for the better enjoyment of that tenement, for it has no necessary connexion therewith, although it confers an advantage upon the owner and renders his ownership of the land more valuable, it is not an easement at all, but a mere contractual right personal to and only enforceable between the two contracting parties.' [. . .]
>
> On these facts [counsel] submitted that the requisite connexion between the right to use the park and the normal enjoyment of the houses which were built around it or near it had not been established. He likened the position to a right granted to the purchaser of a house to use the Zoological Gardens free of charge or to attend Lord's Cricket Ground without payment. Such a right would undoubtedly, he said, increase the value of the property conveyed but could not run with it at law as an easement,

because there was no sufficient nexus between the enjoyment of the right and the use of the house. It is probably true, we think, that in neither of [counsel's] illustrations would the supposed right constitute an easement, for it would be wholly extraneous to, and independent of, the use of a house as a house, namely, as a place in which the householder and his family live and make their home; and it is for this reason that the analogy which [counsel] sought to establish between his illustrations and the present case cannot, in our opinion, be supported. A much closer analogy . . . is the case of a man selling the freehold of part of his house and granting to the purchaser, his heirs and assigns, the right appurtenant to such part, to use the garden in common with the vendor and his assigns. In such a case, the test of connexion, or accommodation, would be amply satisfied; for just as the use of a garden undoubtedly enhances, and is connected with, the normal enjoyment of the house to which it belongs, so also would the right granted, in the case supposed, be closely connected with the use and enjoyment of the part of the premises sold. Such, we think, is in substance the position in the present case. The park became a communal garden for the benefit and enjoyment of those whose houses adjoined it or were in its close proximity. Its flower beds, lawns and walks were calculated to afford all the amenities which it is the purpose of the garden of a house to provide; and apart from the fact that these amenities extended to a number of householders, instead of being confined to one (which on this aspect of the case is immaterial), we can see no difference in principle between Ellenborough Park and a garden in the ordinary signification of that word. It is the collective garden of the neighbouring houses, to whose use it was dedicated by the owners of the estate and as such amply satisfied, in our judgment, the requirement of connexion with the dominant tenements to which it is appurtenant". . .

LECTURER: So, the right to use Ellenborough Park as a pleasure park could only be an easement belonging to the neighbouring houses if it sufficiently "accommodated" them. This is one of the four characteristics that must be present before an easement can be said to exist. What was the relevant test for this?

STUDENT: The right claimed must have a "connection" with the land itself. It must facilitate the normal enjoyment of that land.

LECTURER: And how did Evershed M.R. apply this test to the facts?

STUDENT: The right to use a pleasure park enhanced the ownership of the houses. It was similar to having a garden attached to a house: "the use of a garden undoubtedly enhances, and is connected with, the normal enjoyment of the house to which it belongs".

LECTURER: According to Evershed M.R. is it sufficient that the right enhanced the value of the land?

STUDENT: It is not sufficient to show that "the right increased the value of the property conveyed, unless it is also shown that it was connected with the normal enjoyment of that property". This is why Evershed M.R. thought it important to establish that the use of a garden or pleasure park enhanced the use of the houses by the householders.

LECTURER: The opposing barrister put forward two "analogies" that purported to show that the right claimed by the owners of the houses could not be an easement.

STUDENT: He said that the right to use Ellenborough Park was the same as being granted a right to go to Lord's Cricket Ground or attend the Zoological Gardens free of charge.

LECTURER: And what was his point? Why did this comparison advance his argument?

STUDENT: Because the rule is that there must be a connection between the right claimed and the land. With counsel's analogies a purchaser of a house who was granted these rights could show no connection between the ordinary use of the house and the purpose of going to Lord's Cricket Ground etc. It may be a personal benefit but it is not connected with their use of the house *as a house*.

LECTURER: But Evershed M.R. ultimately rejected these analogies. He thought the right to use a park was sufficiently different, i.e. it *was* connected with the use of the houses (see above).

> The use of analogies can be a powerful way of supporting your argument. But as we see, it did not work here.

The Court of Appeal then considered how the present case differed from another case that the opposing barrister had cited in support of the conclusion that there was no connection between the right and the dominant tenement: *Hill v Tupper*.[20] Evershed M.R. "distinguished" *Hill v Tupper*.

> **"Distinguished"** in legal problem-solving is where a court in a later case considers that although the same rule applies as that applied in a previous case, e.g. the right must be seen to have sufficient connection with the dominant land in order to be recognised as an easement, the previous case was so materially different that the court is justified in coming to a different conclusion in the present case.

EVERSHED M.R. CONTINUES: "[Counsel] referred us to, and to some extent relied upon, *Hill v Tupper*, but in our opinion there is nothing in that case contrary to the view which we have expressed. In that case, the owner of land adjoining a canal was granted the exclusive right to let boats out for hire on the canal. He did so and then sought to restrain a similar activity by a neighbouring landowner. He sought to establish that his grant constituted an easement but failed. Pollock CB said in his judgment: 'It is not competent to create rights unconnected with the use and enjoyment of land, and annex them to it so as to constitute a [property right] in the grantee.' It is clear that what the [claimant] was trying to do was to set up, under the guise of an easement, a monopoly which had no normal connexion with the ordinary use of his land, but which was merely an independent business enterprise. So far from the right claimed subserving or accommodating the land, the land was but a convenient incident to the exercise of the right . . ."

---

20   (1863) 2 H. & C. 121.

LECTURER: On what basis did Evershed M.R. think that the present case was different from *Hill v Tupper*? Here I am asking you how he managed to "distinguish" *Hill v Tupper*.

STUDENT: The point of difference was that in *Hill v Tupper* there was no real connection between the *exclusive* right to use his neighbour's canal to put boats on it for his business, and the use of his land. It did not enhance the use and enjoyment of his *land*—the exclusivity enhanced his *business*.

LECTURER: And the right to use Ellenborough Park was materially different because there was such a connection between the right to use the park (as a garden) and the ordinary use of a house.

B. THE FOUR CHARACTERISTICS

So as we have seen, in order for a right over land to qualify as an easement the right must possess the four characteristics of an easement, as laid down in *Re Ellenborough Park*.[21]

(1) There must be a dominant and a servient tenement

The first of these characteristics is that there must be a dominant and a servient tenement.[22] As we have seen above, the dominant land is the land to be benefited by the right (e.g. the houses in *Re Ellenborough Park*) and the servient land is the land which is burdened and which must give effect to the right (e.g. Ellenborough Park in that case). Another way in which you will find that land lawyers express this principle is to say that an easement cannot exist *in gross*, i.e. without the benefit being attached to any plot of land. In *London & Blenheim Estates Ltd v Ladbroke Retail Parks Ltd* a right to park cars was granted before the company became owners of the dominant tenement. Because of this the claim for an easement failed.[23]

> **The reason for the existence of the requirement of a dominant tenement has to do with our BUILDING BLOCKS NO 5 and 6.**

In *London & Blenheim Estates Ltd v Ladbroke Retail Parks Ltd*[24] Peter Gibson L.J. made the point that without the requirement for a dominant tenement the law would be rendered uncertain. Quoting Fox L.J. in *Ashburn Anstalt v Arnold*[25] to the effect that "[i]n matters relating to the title to land certainty is of prime importance", he reasoned that without the requirement of a dominant tenement any number of people may be able to claim rights over the servient land that could bind purchasers of that land. The precise number may be difficult for the owner to

---

21 [1956] Ch. 131.
22 *London & Blenheim Estates Ltd v Ladbroke Retail Parks Ltd* [1994] 1 W.L.R. 31, pp.36–37, per Peter Gibson L.J; *Rangeley v Midland Railway Co* (1868) L.R. 3 Ch. App. 306.
23 [1994] 1 W.L.R. 31, per Peter Gibson L.J., pp. 37–38.
24 [1994] 1 W.L.R. 31, p.37.
25 [1989] Ch. 1, p.26.

quantify. Thus, the requirement of a dominant tenement operates as a brake on the number of easements that can come into existence and bind the servient land. Easements can only be claimed by someone who owns land that is benefited by that right.

> **BUILDING BLOCK NO 6: The Need for Certainty and Predictability in Land Law Rules**
> A basic aim of any good legal system is that it's rules should allow people to predict the outcome of their actions. The rules of Land Law should tell people precisely what rights bind them and how many. Rules are good and fair if they allow for the achievement of this aim.

So we can say that this requirement for a dominant tenement is good law because it ensures that the number of easements that can bind the servient tenement is not unpredictable. Referring to this issue Cresswell J. in *Ackroyd v Smith*[26] made the point that without the necessity for a dominant tenement "the owner of the land [may] render it subject to a new species of burden, so as to bind it in the hands of [a purchaser]". The point being made here is that without the restriction of having to prove that the right benefited particular land, a new species of property right could be created, which could add greatly to the number of property rights that would bind a purchaser of the land.

> **BUILDING BLOCK NO 5: Property Rights and the Protection of Purchasers**
> We can say the law is good if it prevents too many property rights from coming into being.

So all in all I think we can say that the requirement for a dominant tenement is a well-justified rule.

(2) An easement must "accommodate" the dominant tenement[27]

There must be sufficient connection between the activity claimed as an easement and the use of the dominant land. In short the right must "accommodate the dominant tenement". For example, rights of a purely recreational nature such as the right to play games, or a right to attend a cricket ground, will not possess sufficient connection with ownership of the house or land. They "would be wholly extraneous to, and independent of, the use of a house as a house, namely, as a place in which the householder and his family live and make their home".[28] As we saw in *Re Ellenborough Park* itself the right to use a pleasure ground was successfully claimed as a valid easement by the owners of the nearby houses. The right was held to be of sufficient connection with the houses themselves as it would always increase the enjoyment of a house if the owner was able to use a garden.

---

26   (1850) 10 C.B. 164, p.188.
27   *Re Ellenborough Park* [1956] 1 Ch. 131, per Danckwerts J., p.140; *Ackroyd v Smith* (1850) 10 C.B. 164.
28   Example of a purely personal right given in *Re Ellenborough Park* [1956] 1 Ch. 131, per Evershed M.R.

So if you are claiming a right across land belonging to another, that right must be connected with the use and enjoyment of your land.[29] The right has to do more than merely render your land more valuable.[30]

(a) What benefits the land is a question of fact

Whether a right can be said to "accommodate the dominant tenement" is clearly dependent on the facts of the case, i.e. what was the land being used for?[31] If the dominant land is residential housing it is easier to argue that the right to use a neighbour's park for recreation "accommodates the dominant tenement". The ordinary use of land as a garden is connected directly with residential houses. In *Moody v Steggles*[32] the owners of a public house claimed an easement to place a sign advertising the public house on a wall of a nearby property. It was held that this was sufficiently connected with the land as it was used entirely as a public house. In *PropertyPoint Ltd v Kirri*[33] the right to drive onto the servient land in order to turn vehicles around was held to be sufficiently connected with the enjoyment of adjacent dominant land.

(b) Purely recreational rights

In *Re Ellenborough Park*, the right in question, i.e. use of the servient land in a similar way to that of a garden, was capable of benefiting the dominant land itself, rather than being regarded as a purely personal benefit. It benefited the land because it allowed rest and limited leisure activities that would enhance the ownership of the house for the householders, such as picnicking on the land. It was considered material that the right was thus defined and limited. But ill-defined rights, such as rights to wander unrestrictively,[34] or other rights of a purely recreational nature do not possess sufficient connection with ownership of the house or land. They "would be wholly extraneous to, and independent of, the use of a house as a house, namely, as a place in which the householder and his family live and make their home".[35]

The land enjoying the right does not have to be directly adjacent to the plot of land over which the right is enjoyed, provided there is "the presence of the necessary 'nexus' between the subject-matter enjoyed and the premises to which the enjoyment is expressed to belong".[36]

(c) Case study 2: Hill v Tupper

In *Hill v Tupper*[37] the claimant was the owner of land which fronted onto the Basingstoke Canal. He was granted by the Canal Company an exclusive right to put pleasure boats on the canal for profit. The owner of an adjacent Inn, which also fronted the canal started also to put boats on the canal for profit. Effectively it was argued that the claimant had a right to the exclusive use of

---

29   *Ackroyd v Smith* (1850) 10 C.B. 164.
30   *Re Ellenborough Park* above, p.173, per Evershed M.R.
31   *Re Ellenborough Park* above, p.162, per Evershed M.R.
32   (1879) L.R. 12 Ch. D. 261.
33   [2009] EWHC 2958.
34   A privilege of wandering at will all over the land: "Jus spatiandi".
35   Above, p.174, per Evershed M.R.
36   *Re Ellenborough Park* above, p.175, per Evershed M.R. *Bailey v Stephens* (1862) 142 E.R. 1077.
37   (1863) 2 H. & C. 121.

land for a particular purpose, unconnected with the normal use and enjoyment of his own land, and that this attached to his land as an easement and stopped the adjacent landowner from likewise putting pleasure boats on the canal for profit. Because this right of exclusive use was unconnected with the use and enjoyment of the claimant's *land*, and only benefited his business, it was held to be a licence not an easement. It was purely a personal right between the claimant and the Canal Company. Pollock C.B. held that

> "it is not competent to create rights unconnected with the use and enjoyment of land, and annex them to it so as to constitute a property in the grantee. This grant merely operates as a licence . . . on the part of the grantors, and is binding on them as between themselves and the grantee".[38]

The claimant grantee had no property right to assert against others and prevent them from putting boats on the canal.

LECTURER: The significance of this decision was that it shows that, although the courts do recognise new types of easement, they take a restrictive approach—not allowing too many rights to exist as easements, because these will affect future purchasers of the servient land. Pollock C.B. had observed that "If the [claimant's] contention were correct, the number and variety of rights which might thus be created over land for a particular purpose would be infinite".[39]

Do you think this is good and fair law, or do you think the canal boat business owner should have won the case? Remember that we can say that a rule is good or bad depending on the extent to which it supports the policies, principles and aims of Land Law contained in our Building Blocks.[40]

STUDENT: I think that we can say that the case is good law on the basis of our BUILDING BLOCK NO 5.

An important policy reason lay behind this decision that had to do with our **BUILDING BLOCK NO 5: Property Rights and the Protection of Purchasers**. If it was no longer necessary to prove that there was a connection between the land itself and the right this would allow a great deal more easements to come into being. The more types of right that are recognised as easements the more potential property rights there are to affect future purchasers of the servient land. Title to the land may then become bogged down with rights *thus making land harder to sell because this would effectively restrict the owner's ability to use his land.*

---

38 Above, p.127.
39 Above p.126.
40 For further instructions on how to use our BUILDING BLOCKS to create an argument including the full text of the aims and policies in our BUILDING BLOCKS see Chapter 1.

LECTURER: I think that we can use other Building Blocks too.

STUDENT: I would argue that had the decision allowed the claimant's right to be an easement it would have created great uncertainty in the law. If it was no longer necessary to prove a connection between the right claimed and the use and enjoyment of the dominant tenement as observed in *Hill v Tupper* "the number and variety of rights which might thus be created over land for a particular purpose would be infinite". It would be difficult to assess the number of rights that may bind the servient tenement. Thus, *Hill v Tupper* is good law on the basis of BUILDING BLOCK NO 6.

BUILDING BLOCK NO 6: The Importance of Certainty and Predictability in Land Law Rules:

Rules must provide clear outcomes so that future owners of land can predict exactly what their legal position is in relation to other people.

LECTURER: And now on a matter of legal reasoning, how can *Hill v Tupper* be properly "distinguished" from *Moody v Steggles*?

> In *Moody v Steggles* (1879) LR 12 Ch. D. 261 the owners of a public house *successfully* claimed an easement to place an advertising sign on a wall of a nearby house. There was sufficient connection between the right and the land because it was used entirely as a public house. The sign was advertising the public house.

> **"Distinguished"** in legal problem-solving is where a court deciding a case considers that although the same rule applies as that applied in a previous case, e.g. the right must be seen to have sufficient connection with the dominant land in order to be recognised as an easement, that previous case has factors that are *so materially different* from the present case that the court feels justified in coming to a different conclusion in the present case.

STUDENT: Initially *Moody v Steggles* seems to be similar to *Hill v Tupper* because the easement was to advance the claimant's business in both cases.

LECTURER: But it was not this factor which *per se* precluded the right in *Hill v Tupper* from being held to be an easement.

STUDENT: It was that fact that the exclusive right to put boats on the canal had no connection with the claimant's land. This was the "material" factor that led the judge to decide what he did.

LECTURER: And so can we "distinguish" *Moody v Steggles*? Was this case materially different?

STUDENT: Yes I think it was. In that case the whole function of the land was a public house. Thus there was a sufficient connection between the use and enjoyment of the land as a public house and the easement to display the sign advertising the pub.

> "[T]he house can only be used by an occupant, and that the occupant only uses the house for the business which he pursues, and therefore in some manner (direct or indirect) an easement is more or less connected with the mode in which the occupant of the house uses it."[41]

(3) The dominant and servient owners must be different persons: the unity of seisin rule

The third of the *Re Ellenborough Park* characteristics is that the dominant and servient tenements must be owned by different people. The Law Commission observes that

> "the rule is that an easement or profit cannot exist where the dominant and servient tenements are in common ownership and possession."[42]

It is not required that dominant and servient owners must be freehold owners. One can be a tenant under a lease. The principle is that you cannot have an easement over your own land. The nature of an easement is that it is a limited right exercised over land belonging to *another*. So that if you walk across your own land to get to your house on the other side of another piece of land that you own, you are able to walk across the land *because you own it* and not because you have any other sort of right over it.[43] However, if there are two plots of land owned by the same person and that person uses one plot to get to the other this has sometimes been referred to as a "quasi-easement". This may have significance if the owner of the plots sells one to another person. The purchaser may then be able to have the right to walk over the other one, just as the original owner did, as a proper fully-fledged easement.[44]

The Law Commission recommends abolition of this requirement in order to permit a person to create an easement over his own land where both dominant and servient plots are registered with separate title numbers.[45] *Why?* One principal difficulty with the current law concerns the situation where a property developer builds a number of houses as a residential housing estate. Once the plots are sold off the owners of the houses may need easements, such as rights to drive over a common road, rights of way over a neighbour's driveway, rights of drainage, and so forth. The problem arises before the plots are sold by the developer, the common owner, to

---

41 *Moody v Steggles* (1879) LR 12 Ch.D 261, p. 266.

42 Law Commission, *Making Land Work: Easements, Covenants and Profits-à-Prendre* (2011) Law Com No.327, para.4.21. This is known as the "unity of seisin" rule.

43 Stevens and Pearce, *Land Law*, 3rd edn (London: Sweet & Maxwell, 2004), p. 407.

44 Dependent on the rule in *Wheeldon v Burrows* (1879) L.R. 12 Ch. D. 31. See below.

45 Law Commission Final Report *Making Land Work: Easements, Covenants and Profits-à-Prendre* Law Com No.327 (2011), para.1.14, paras 4.19–4.51 and the preceding Law Commission Consultation Paper *Easements, Covenants and Profits-à-Prendre*, Law Com No.186 (2008), para.3.66.

separate purchasers. He or she cannot grant easements over the plots before they are sold because the developer is the common owner of all the plots.

> **Example**
>
> A developer owns land and has built two houses on it. He wishes for each to have a right of access over the other's part of the shared driveway. He can sell one of the plots subject to and with the benefit of easements. But how would the other plot gain the easements unless he could grant them over the other plot when he was still the owner of it? And housing estates usually involve many more houses than this.
>
> Law Commission, *Making Land Work: Easements, Covenants and Profits-à-Prendre* (2011) Law Com No.327, paras 4.27–4.31.

LECTURER: Do you think that abolishing the *unity of seisin* rule in registered land would make good law reform? Hold it against our Building Blocks. We can say that it is good or bad depending on the extent to which it supports or undermines the basic aims of Land Law, i.e. what Land Law *should* achieve.

STUDENT: Where both dominant and servient plots are registered, the requirement for both plots to be separately owned serves no useful function of certainty or predictability. The easements would be registered on the titles for all to see. The people buying the land would then be fully aware of the benefits and burdens on the titles.

LECTURER: And to add to your argument the easements would still have to meet the requirement of a necessary connection between the land and the right, as well as the other *Re Ellenborough Park* criteria.

STUDENT: And so the abolition of this single characteristic is unlikely to lead to the creation of a great deal more rights that bind title, or make those rights any more uncertain or ill-defined. So the Law Commission's proposal would not violate Building Blocks 5 and 6.

BULDING BLOCK NO 5: Property Rights and the Protection of Purchasers	**BUILDING BLOCK NO 6:** The Need for Certainty and Predictability in Land Law Rules

LECTURER: Indeed, abolishing the rule that the dominant and servient owners must be different people could make it easier to give effect to people's intentions regarding the land, taking the example of property developers above.

STUDENT: I think that if the law were not changed in the way that the Law Commission recommends it may mean that many important and necessary easements would be invalidated by a technical rule.[46]

---

46 Although if title to the land were registered the validity of the easement would be guaranteed by the Land Registry because an easement is a "registrable disposition" (Land Registration Act 2002 s.58), "there is an expense for customers because costs to the indemnity fund will be passed on in terms of levels of fees" Law Com No.327 (2011), para.4.32.

LECTURER: What other unfortunate consequence may result from the unity of seisin rule. Here is a clue—it is a rule that will mean a potential right over someone else's land may be invalid.

STUDENT: With property development throughout the country—the rule may result in expensive litigation years after the original houses were sold.[47]

> **BUILDING BLOCK NO 7: Land Law is "facilitative" and should give effect to what people want to do with their land:**
>
> Land Law is facilitative (Birks). So we expect to see that the rules relating to easements give effect to what people want to do with their land. If they do—we can say that they are good law. As the Law Commission puts it, the law should "Make Land Work".

STUDENT: So our considered view is that this would be good law reform.

(4) A right over land cannot amount to an easement, unless it is capable of forming the subject matter of a grant

The fourth of the *Re Ellenborough Park* characteristics is that a right can only be recognised as an easement if it is capable of forming the subject matter of a grant. This has a particular meaning. The activity claimed as the easement, must be narrowly circumscribed, restricted in scope, and capable of being defined in certain and defined terms. In short it must be capable of being written down in a deed as a third party right over land belonging to another. For example, the right to use a pleasure garden was held in *Re Ellenborough Park* to be "a common and clearly understood conception". It was narrow in scope and therefore sufficiently definable: "the subject matter of the grant in question [is] the provision for a limited number of houses in a uniform crescent of one single large but private garden".[48] Another way in which land lawyers have described this requirement is by saying that *the right must be a right known to the law*. In *Re Ellenborough Park* Evershed M.R. said that in order to satisfy this fourth characteristic it is necessary to consider "whether the right conferred is too wide and vague [and] whether it is inconsistent with the proprietorship or possession of the alleged servient owners". So this fourth characteristic thereby describes the true nature of an easement—a limited third party right over land belonging to another. Hence Evershed M.R.'s comment that the right should not take up the entire use of the land, as a freehold owner would use his land. Rights such as easements and restrictive covenants are , by nature, not *ownership* of the servient land.

---

47   For example see the anecdotes cited by the Law Commission, *Making Land Work: Easements, Covenants and Profits-à-Prendre* (2011) Law Com No.327, para.4.32.
48   *Re Ellenborough Park* [1956] Ch. 131, per Evershed M.R. from p.176.

> **Capable of forming the subject matter of a grant**
> The right claimed must be sufficiently limited and definable: A right that "could readily be included in a lease or conveyance by the insertion of appropriate words". It is a right known to the law: *Wright v Macadam* [1949] 2 K.B. 744, CA, p.752, per Jenkins L.J.

We will now consider the different aspects of this requirement that the right, in order to be recognised as an easement must be *capable of forming the subject matter of a grant*.

(a) There must be a capable grantor and grantee

Because the right must be capable of forming the subject matter of a grant there must be a capable grantor of the right and a capable grantee to receive it. For example, no easement can arise where the owner of the servient tenement has no power to grant an easement, e.g. a statutory corporation may have no power to grant easements.[49] At the time at which the easement is said to have arisen there must also be a person capable of receiving the benefit of an easement. "A fluctuating body of persons, such as 'the inhabitants for the time being of the village of X', cannot claim an easement, for no grant can be made to them".[50]

(b) The right must be sufficiently definable and limited

In order to exist as an easement, the right must be sufficiently definable and limited. As is often said: *it must be of a nature that is recognised by law*. It is possible for an entirely novel type of right to be recognised as an easement, provided it possesses this characteristic. Indeed, the categories of easements are not closed. It must be possible for the law of easements to develop and accommodate new land uses. In *Dyce v Hay*[51] Lord St. Leonards L.C. stated that

> "The category of servitudes and easements must alter and expand with the changes that take place in the circumstances of mankind. The law of this country. . . frequently moulds its practical operation without doing any violence to its original principles."

There are many common types of use of another's land that have already been found to be sufficiently capable of definition and limited in scope to be easements. For example, a right of way across the servient land to access the dominant land is perhaps the most commonly recognisable easement, as seen in the case of *Harris v Flower*.[52] In this case it was held that the scope of the right must be definable and circumscribed. It was held that a right of way can only be used to access the dominant tenement and not other lands belonging to the dominant owner. Another type of use recognised as an easement is a right belonging to the dominant land owner to store items, such as trade goods, on the servient land.[53] The right to use a lavatory on

---

49   Harpum, Bridge and Dixon, *Megarry & Wade Law of Real Property*, 7th edn (London: Sweet & Maxwell, 2008), para.27-018, citing *Derry v Sanders* [1919] 1 K.B. 223 and *Mulliner v Midland Ry* (1879) 11 Ch.D 611 respectively.
50   Above, para.27-019.
51   House of Lords, (1852) 1 Macq. 305 p.312.
52   (1904) 74 L.J. Ch. 127.
53   *Wright v Macadam* [1949] 2 K.B. 744; *Grigsby v Melville* [1972] 1 W.L.R. 1355.

the servient land has been held capable of amounting to an easement.[54] With increasing density of building following the industrial revolution the law recognised that a right to support from a neighbouring house is capable of existing as an easement.

"It is settled law. . . that a man who has his house next to another for many years, so that it is dependent on it for support, is entitled to have that support maintained. His neighbour is not entitled to pull down his house without providing substitute support in the form of buttresses or something of the kind".[55]

An easement of car parking can now exist,[56] a right that is extremely beneficial if the dominant land does not otherwise have parking facilities.[57]

GOOD LAW?

BUILDING BLOCK NO 7: Land Law is "facilitative" and should give effect to what people want to do with their land

No plot of land is the same and land can be used in many different ways. Land Law is facilitative (Birks). As we see here the rules relating to easements are plainly capable of giving effect to what people want to do with their land. Thus, they are good law because they support this Building Block.

Nevertheless, it is important to remember that as with any right that you would expect to find expressed in a deed, it is usually only valid if the terms of the right are expressed with certainty and have clearly defined parameters. For instance, the right to a "view" was held insufficiently definable in *William Aldred's Case*.[58] The only way of giving effect to such a right is "to get your neighbour to make a covenant with you that he will not build so as to block your view".[59] Similarly a right to wind and air through an undefined channel is too ill-defined to amount to a right recognised by law as an easement. In *Webb v Bird*[60] a mill owner claimed unsuccessfully against a neighbour who built on his land and blocked the flow of air to his windmill. It is only possible to have an easement for a flow of air through a definite channel or aperture.[61] In *Phipps v Pears*,[62]

---

54   *Miller v Emcer Products Ltd* [1956] Ch. 304.
55   *Phipps v Pears* [1965] 1 Q.B. 76, p.82, per Lord Denning M.R. (although the case turned on another point); *Dalton v Angus* (1880–81) L.R. 6 App. Cas. 740, HL, p.763, per Lindley J; *Lloyds Bank Ltd v Dalton* [1942] Ch. 466.
56   *London and Blenheim Estates Ltd v Ladbroke Retail Parks Ltd* [1994] 1 W.L.R. 31.
57   In *PropertyPoint Ltd v Kirri* [2009] EWHC 2958 the right to drive onto the servient land in order to turn vehicles around was capable of amounting to an easement.
58   (1610) 9 Co. Rep. 57b; also *Bland v Moseley* (1587) cited in 9 Co. Rep. 58a.
59   *Phipps v Pears* [1965] 1 Q.B. 76, p.83, per Lord Denning M.R. For the binding effect of freehold covenants as property rights see that chapter.
60   (1862) 13 C.B. 841.
61   *Harris v De Pinna* (1886) L.R. 33 Ch.D 238, pp.250–1 per Chitty J.
62   [1965] 1 Q.B. 76.

a house owner demolished his house and left the wall of an adjacent house exposed to the weather. Lord Denning M.R. held that "[t]here is no such easement known to the law as an easement to be protected from the weather". "[I]f we were to stop a man pulling down his house, we would put a brake on desirable improvement."[63]

LECTURER: Is this good or bad law?

STUDENT: Clearly if easements such as the right to receive a general flow of air, the right to a "nice" view, and such a generalised right to "protection" from the weather, could exist it would inhibit the servient landowner from doing things on his land, from developing it and from using it in accordance with his intentions.

LECTURER: Thus, in requiring the claimed right to be definable in nature and limited in scope, we can say that the law supports BUILDING BLOCK NO 4: Ideas of Ownership—people's ownership should not be restricted unduly.

STUDENT: It also supports BUILDING BLOCK NO 6 because it ensures that only defined rights can be recognised as affecting the servient land. If the servient owner's land were affected by vague and ill-defined rights, the extent to which he/she would be in breach of those rights would be unpredictable. The above rules give sufficient certainty.

LECTURER: It also supports BUILDING BLOCK NO 5 because the law ensures that the title to the servient land is not bound by too many rights that are difficult to define, and which may affect a purchaser of that land.

The courts are particularly reluctant to recognise new "negative" easements, i.e. where the servient landowner is *prohibited* from doing something on his land, such as building. This is often regarded as a proper context for *covenants* between landowners and not easements.[64] Although the law recognises an easement of light to a building, so that the owner of adjacent land cannot build or otherwise obstruct that flow of light, the courts have narrowly circumscribed such a right. The dominant tenement is not entitled to unlimited light. "Light, like air, is the common property of all, or, to speak more accurately, it is the common right of all to enjoy it, but it is the exclusive property of none."[65] The right to light must be limited and defined otherwise the development of land and building would be unjustifiably restricted.[66] Consequently, there is only a right to light through a defined window.[67] The relevant test is not so much whether the neighbour has built so as to block the light to the dominant tenement, but whether there is sufficient light left after the building for the ordinary use of the dominant land.[68] The measure of light to which the dominant tenement is entitled is "what is required for the ordinary purposes of inhabitancy or business of the tenement according to the ordinary notions of mankind".[69]

---

63   [1965] 1 Q.B. 76, per Lord Denning M.R. The house in the case was below current standards and needed to be rebuilt.
64   *Phipps v Pears* [1965] 1 Q.B. 76, p.83, per Lord Denning M.R.
65   *Colls v Home and Colonial Stores Ltd* [1904] A.C. 179 pp. 182–3, per Earl of Halsbury L.C.
66   Above, p.183.
67   *Colls v Home and Colonial Stores Ltd* above, pp.185, per Earl of Halsbury L.C.
68   Also *Carr-Saunders v Dick McNeil Associates Ltd* [1986] 1 W.L.R. 922.
69   *Colls v Home and Colonial Stores Ltd* [1904] A.C. 179, p.204, per Lord Davey. The right to light is often referred to as "ancient lights" when the right comes into being through long user, i.e. "prescription". *Allen v Greenwood* [1979] 1 All E.R. 819, p.824, per Goff L.J. also *City of London Brewery Co v Tennant* [1973] L.R. 9 Ch. App. 212; *Kelk v Pearson* [1871] L.R. 6 Ch. App. 809.

Thus, what is held to be the "ordinary" level of light to a building will depend on the nature of the property and what it has been used for. In *Allen v Greenwood*[70] a greenhouse on the dominant tenement was held to be entitled to a high level of light as this was necessary for its ordinary use as a greenhouse.[71]

> Hold the law in this paragraph against our Building Blocks, think about the connection between the law and the Building Blocks, and see whether it supports or undermines the aims and principles contained therein. We can say that the law is good or bad accordingly.

BUILDING BLOCK NO 5: Property Rights and the Protection of Purchasers
Easements are property rights and thus bind the title of the servient land. Property rights should not be too readily recognised as this would "clog" the title to the land and, perhaps, make it difficult to sell, particularly if the rights are restrictive of what the owner can do with his land. Does the above law support this policy?

(c) A right must not amount to exclusive possession or excessive use of the servient land

In order to be recognised as an easement a right must not entitle the dominant owner to possession or too extensive use of the servient land. Neither must the right have the effect of excluding the servient owner. Easements, by definition, are supposed to be a limited right to use land belonging to *another* for a single purpose.

> **What should easements *look like*?**
> **The right is restricted in purpose and limited in scope. It is not exclusive of others. The owner of an easement cannot stop others from using the land: S.Bright, "Of Estates and Interests: A Tale of Ownership and Property Rights" in *Land Law Themes and Perspectives*, p.538. Easements concern one purpose only and not open-ended use, e.g. access: S.Bright, above, p.534.**

Just as we saw that the rights of a tenant under a lease had to look like BUILDING BLOCK NO 4: Ideas of Ownership, the rights of someone claiming an easement *must not look like ownership*:

---

70   *Allen v Greenwood* [1979] 1 All E.R. 819.
71   *Allen v Greenwood* [1979] 1 All E.R. 819, p.825, per Goff L.J.

> **BUILDING BLOCK NO 4: Ideas of Ownership**
>
> The idea of ownership or possession is *exclusive control* over land. It is open-ended: "Ownership itself is a set of open-ended use privileges and open-ended powers to control the use made by others of the property" (Bright). Thus, *ownership* gives the owner control over who can come and go on the property. This control, at least as far as the freehold estate is concerned means open-ended uses of that land.

This idea that an easement must not amount to possession and open-ended use of the servient tenement, was what Evershed M.R. meant when in *Re Ellenborough Park*[72] he stated that the right claimed as an easement must not be "inconsistent with the proprietorship or possession of the alleged servient owners".

STUDENT: This is a bit like Lord Templeman's saying in *Street v Mountford* when we did leases: You cannot call some use of land an easement if it exhibits the characteristics of something else. If I have made a five-pronged instrument for manual digging I cannot call it a "spade".

LECTURER: So when we consider the reasoning in the cases below we will hold it up against these ideas of the true nature of an easement and of ownership and see whether the judges got it right!

Finally, it is worth noting that the courts have had some difficulty in defining what amounts to a use of the land which is too extensive and thus "inconsistent with the proprietorship or possession of the servient owner". This has led to a real practical difficulty with easements of car-parking and even throws some doubt upon whether a right to park a car in a defined space can ever exist as an easement. But before considering this issue in greater detail we will examine the cases that apply this "exclusive use" principle.

(i) Cases which demonstrate this principle

In *Copeland v Greenhalf*[73] the claimant, Mrs Copeland, was the owner of an orchard and an adjoining strip of land 150ft by 15-35ft. The defendant was a wheelwright with a business across the road from the orchard and he used the strip of land to store his customer's vehicles awaiting repair and collection. Mrs Copeland brought an action against the defendant preventing him from using the land. He claimed that he had an easement by prescription (acquired by long use of the strip).[74] Although in principle it is possible to have an easement to store trade goods,[75] the defendant's claim failed on the basis that the right did not satisfy the requirement that it should be sufficiently definable and certain and limited in scope. It was therefore not in the nature of an easement. The right claimed was uncertain in scope as the defendant used the land for many different types of vehicle beyond the remit of his business. The extent to which he used the land was undefined: he left the vehicles all over the land in different places, leaving Mrs Copeland an

---

72   [1956] Ch 131.
73   [1952] Ch. 488.
74   We will consider prescription as a method of acquisition of easements below.
75   *Pye v Mumford* (1848) 11 Q.B. 666.

"ill defined" access.[76] Effectively his use amounted to possession of the strip, excluding the servient owner. Upjohn J. thus concluded:

"I think that the right claimed goes wholly outside any normal idea of an easement, that is, the right of the owner or the occupier of a dominant tenement over a servient tenement. This claim. . . really amounts to a claim to a joint user of the land by the defendant. Practically, the defendant is claiming the whole beneficial user of the strip of land on the south-east side of the track there; he can leave as many or as few lorries there as he likes for as long as he likes; he may enter on it by himself, his servants and agents to do repair work thereon. In my judgment, that is not a claim which can be established as an easement. It is virtually a claim to possession of the servient tenement, if necessary to the exclusion of the owner; or, at any rate, to a joint user, and no authority has been cited to me which would justify the conclusion that a right of this wide and undefined nature can be the proper subject matter of an easement. It seems to me that to succeed, this claim must amount to a successful claim of possession by reason of long adverse possession."[77]

LECTURER: And so we see that before a right can be recognised as an easement it must be of a nature "known to the law". In short, it must be defined, limited and, if such was necessary, capable of being written down in a deed. How does Upjohn J. confirm this?

STUDENT: In his first sentence he defines the nature of an easement as being a right *over* land belonging to another.

LECTURER: And not a claim to possession of the land itself. This clearly agrees with the idea of what an easement *is*.

Like this

First principle of an easement: An easement is a limited right over land belonging to another. It is not a right to possession and control of the servient land: Bright, "Of Estates and Interests: A Tale of Ownership and Property Rights" in *Land Law Themes and Perspectives*, p.538. Easements concern one purpose only and not open-ended use: S.Bright, above p.534.

Not like this

BUILDING BLOCK NO 4: Ideas of Ownership

The idea of ownership is *control* over land. It is open-ended: "ownership itself is a set of open-ended use privileges and open-ended powers to control the use made by others of the property". Thus, *ownership* gives the owner control over who can come and go on the property. It also permits open-ended uses of that land, exploitation of value, sale etc.

---

76   [1952] Ch. 488, p.497, per Upjohn J., discussing the arguments of counsel.
77   [1952] Ch. 488, p.498, per Upjohn J. Although it might be suggested that Upjohn J. appeared to limit his reasoning on the exclusive use of the strip of servient land to claims made by prescription, *Moncrieff v Jamieson* [2007] 1 W.L.R. 2620, House of Lords, held that an easement must exhibit the same characteristics whether acquired by grant, express or implied, or prescription: per Lord Scott, p.2643; also Brightman J. in *Grigsby v Melville* [1972] 1 W.L.R. 1355, p.1364.

LECTURER: And so we see *why* the defendant's use of the land in *Copeland v Greenhalf* could not amount to an easement. Hold Upjohn J.'s reasoning against these ideas of what an easement is and show why.

STUDENT: His use was open-ended. He put vehicles in different places all over the land and left Mrs Copeland, the owner of the servient tenement with an undefined and ever changing access to it because of this. He was in control of the land not her. He was in exclusive possession. The purpose of leaving the vehicles on the land was also uncertain as it went way beyond the purposes of his business as a wheelwright. Therefore as the very nature of an easement is a right over someone else's land *for a limited purpose*—there was no certain and definable purpose for the storage in this case.

LECTURER: And thus the Wheelwright's claim could not be brought within the definition of easements "known to the law". And turning to our Building Blocks is this good law?

STUDENT: The obvious one here is BUILDING BLOCK NO 6: The Importance of Certainty and Predictability in Land Law Rules.

> **BUILDING BLOCK NO 6: The Need for Certainty and Predictability in Land Law Rules**
> People need to know the clear effects of rules of law. Otherwise they will be uncertain as to the consequences of their actions.

Had such a right for such an ill-defined purpose as the one in *Copeland v Greenhalf* been held to exist as an easement, no landowner could be sure of when and how he could use his land. He might be violating the easement all the time! On the basis of BUILDING BLOCK NO 6 therefore, *Copeland v Greenhalf* is good law.

LECTURER: What about BUILDING BLOCK NO 5?

> **BUILDING BLOCK NO 5: Property Rights and the Protection of Purchasers:**
> Easements are property rights and thus bind the title of the servient land. Property Rights should not be too readily recognised as this would "clog" the title to the land and, perhaps, make it difficult to sell, particularly if the rights are restrictive of what the owner can do with his land.

STUDENT: Well, if *Copeland v Greenhalf* had been decided the other way rights could exist which were profoundly restrictive of what the servient owner could do on her land. Imagine the situation if Mrs Copeland had tried to sell that plot of land with such a right over it. An easement is a property right which would bind the title to the servient land. It would probably make it difficult to sell. On the basis of BUILDING BLOCK NO 5 I would again conclude that *Copeland v Greenhalf* is good law.

In *Grigsby v Melville*[78] the defendants had been using the claimant's cellar for storing bottles and other things. They claimed an easement of storage. The claim failed, inter alia, because their use of the cellar was so extensive that it would amount to exclusive use. Brightman J. applied *Copeland v Greenhalf*[79] and held that because the defendants were claiming an unlimited right to store items in the cellar, to the exclusion of the servient owner, it could not be an easement.

LECTURER: Which one of our Building Blocks does this reflect?
STUDENT: BUILDING BLOCK NO 6

BUILDING BLOCK NO 6: The Need for Certainty and Predictability in Land Law Rules
People need to know the clear effects of rules of law. Otherwise they will be uncertain as to the consequences of their actions.

Because the right claimed to store any items in the cellar, to whatever extent the claimant pleased, it would be unpredictable as to when the servient owner was interfering with the right. Also, it would be unclear as to what type of right it was. A claim to exclusive use like this, i.e. possibly to the exclusion of the servient owner, has some of the characteristics of ownership. Easements are not exclusive rights. They are limited third party rights to do something on land belonging to another. If this case had been decided the other way, it would have blurred the distinction between easements and ownership of the fee simple.

LECTURER: So the point of the requirement that the right must be "one known to the law" before it can be an easement, i.e. it must be definable in extent, is to keep a definite distinction between the fee simple estate and a limited third party right.

STUDENT: It feels a little like the requirement for certainty of term in leases: *Prudential Assurance Co Ltd v London Residuary Body*.[80] Otherwise there would be nothing to separate a lease conceptually from a fee simple.

---

78   [1972] 1 W.L.R. 1355.
79   [1952] Ch. 488.
80   [1992] 2 A.C. 386.

An easement should look like this

First principle of an easement: An easement is a limited right over land belonging to another. It is not a right to possession and control of the servient land: Bright, "Of Estates and Interests: A Tale of Ownership and Property Rights" in *Land Law Themes and Perspectives*, **p.538. Easements concern one purpose only and not open-ended use: S.Bright, above p.534.**

Not like this

BUILDING BLOCK NO 4: Ideas of Ownership
The idea of ownership is *control* over land. It is open-ended:
"Ownership itself is a set of open-ended use privileges and open-ended powers to control the use made by others of the property."
Thus, *ownership* gives the owner control over who can come and go on the property. It also permits open-ended uses of that land, exploitation of value, sale etc.

LECTURER: Indeed, in *Dyce v Hay*,[81] the sidenote to the report states that "There can be no prescriptive right in the nature of a servitude or easement so large as to preclude the ordinary uses of property by the owner of the lands affected".

By apparent contrast in *Wright v Macadam*[82] the Court of Appeal held that a right claimed by a tenant to store coal in a shed on the landlord's servient land could be recognised as an easement. Potentially this could have been so extensive as to amount to exclusive use. *Wright* was not considered in *Copeland v Greenhalf*. However, Brightman J. in *Grigsby v Melville*[83] explained that *Copeland v Greenhalf*[84] was not inconsistent with *Wright v Macadam*. He stated that "it is a little difficult to know whether the tenant had exclusive use of the coal shed or of any defined portion of it"[85] as the "exclusive use" point had not been cited to the Court of Appeal or discussed. In *London & Blenheim Estates Ltd v Ladbroke Retail Parks Ltd*[86] Judge Paul Baker Q.C. stated that: "A small coal shed in a large property is one thing. The exclusive use of a large part of the alleged servient tenement is another".[87] The relevant test is whether the servient owner is left without any reasonable use of his land. Judge Paul Baker Q.C. observed:

---

81   (1852) 1 Macq 305.
82   [1949] 2 K.B. 744.
83   [1972] 1 W.L.R. 1355.
84   [1952] Ch. 488.
85   [1972] 1 W.L.R. 1355, p. 1364. In *Wright v Macadam* [1949] 2 K.B. 744 the Court of Appeal were entirely occupied with the question of whether the right had been acquired under Law of Property Act 1925 s.62 (see below).
86   [1992] 1 W.L.R. 1278, p.1288.
87   On the point of the nature of the servient tenement this has been thought to be wrong. Lord Scott pointed out in *Moncrieff v Jamieson* [2007] 1 W.L.R. 2620, House of Lords, the "servient tenement" is properly regarded as the area of land over which the easement is exercised and "not the totality of the surrounding land over which the servient owner happens to be the owner": above, p.2642. However, this is a Scottish case so only persuasive authority.

"The essential question is one of degree. If the right granted in relation to the area over which it is to be exercisable is such that it would leave the servient owner without any reasonable use of his land, whether for parking or anything else, it could not be an easement though it might be some larger or different grant."[88]

This test, which has become known as the "ouster principle",[89] was applied in *Batchelor v Marlow*,[90] in which the defendants claimed an easement by prescription to park up to six cars on a strip of land between the hours of 8:30am to 6:00pm Mondays to Fridays. The land would only accommodate six cars. Tuckey L.J.[91] held that although an easement to park a car in a defined area is recognised in principle[92] the right claimed would leave the servient owner without any reasonable use of his land. The servient owner would no doubt be able to exercise certain powers over the land, the examples given in the case being to concrete over the land in a way that would not interfere with the defendants' car parking, to charge others for parking outside these hours, to sell it to the defendants etc. However, Tuckey L.J. concluded that the servient owner's ownership of the land was effectively "illusory".[93]

In one sense, the parking rights of the defendants concerned a limited and definable purpose: car-parking. They could not use the land for other purposes. However, because they were claiming parking rights over the whole area during the specified times, the right would have effectively excluded others from exercising the same right.

"[The servient owner] has no use at all during the whole of the time that parking space is likely to be needed. But if one asks the question whether the [servient owner] has any reasonable use of the land for any other purpose, the answer is even clearer. His right to use his land is curtailed altogether for intermittent periods throughout the week. Such a restriction would, I think, make his ownership of the land illusory."[94]

However, it was not so much the fact that the dominant owners were taking all the available car parking space that was considered significant *per se* it was the impact of the use of all the space upon the value and usability of the land. The servient owner's intentions for the land use as a whole and it's value would be significantly curtailed. If the parking rights had been recognised

---

88   [1992] 1 W.L.R. 1278, p. 1288. The most likely modern meaning of the latter part of the quotation is that the right could not be an easement if it involves exclusivity, but it might be expressly granted as a different type of right, such as joint use of land: *London & Blenheim Estates Ltd v Ladbroke Retail Parks Ltd* [1992] 1 W.L.R. 1278, p.1288, per Judge Paul Baker Q.C.

89   See the Law Commission Final Report, *Making Land Work: Easements, Covenants and Profits-à-Prendre* (2011) Law Com No.327, paras 3.188–3.211. The Law Commission draws a distinction between the principle that an easement must not confer exclusive possession and this ouster principle, i.e. that the right claimed must not leave the servient owner without reasonable use of his or her land. I suggest that this distinction is highly problematic.

90   *Batchelor v Marlow* [2003] 1 W.L.R. 764.

91   Who gave the leading judgment with whom Kay and Henry L.JJ. simply agreed.

92   *London & Blenheim Estates Ltd v Ladbroke Retail Parks Ltd* [1992] 1 W.L.R. 1278.

93   [2003] 1 W.L.R. 764, p.768.

94   [2003] 1 W.L.R. 764, p.768 per Tuckey L.J.

no other use could be made of the land in terms of development,[95] and it's value would be diminished considerably.[96]

> "The [servient owner] could of course park himself at night or the weekends but the commercial scope for getting others to pay for doing so must be very limited indeed. I cannot see how the plaintiff would benefit from concreting over the land".[97]

It is not difficult to make the step from this to saying that the defendants in *Batchelor v Marlow* were in de facto control, or possession, of the land. This did not look like a "limited third party right". It looked like ownership.[98]

An easement should look like this

First principle of an easement: An easement is a limited right over land belonging to another. It is not a right to possession and control of the servient tenement to the exclusion of the servient owner: Bright, "Of Estates and Interests: A Tale of Ownership and Property Rights" in *Land Law Themes and Perspectives*, p.538. Easements concern one purpose only and not open-ended use: S.Bright, above p.534.

Not like this

BUILDING BLOCK NO 4: Ideas of Ownership

The idea of ownership is *control* over the land. It is open-ended: "Ownership itself is a set of open-ended use privileges and open-ended powers to control the use made by others of the property." (Bright) Thus, *ownership* gives a person control over the land, i.e. limit the use made of it by others, and claim rights to exploit that land, e.g. sale.

In *Moncrieff v Jamieson*[99] Lord Scott doubted whether *Batchelor v Marlow* had been correctly decided.[100] In this case the alleged dominant tenement was a property on the sea front "sandwiched" between a cliff and the sea. The servient tenement was at the top of the cliff and

---

95   "If the defendants' right to park in this way is upheld the adjoining land. . . will probably not be able to be developed since the present planning permission for its development requires the [disputed land] to be used as a small roundabout or turning circle in connection with the development": per Tuckey L.J. above p.766.

96   "Sale to the defendants would amount to a recognition that the rights they asserted had given them in practice a beneficial interest and no doubt the price would reflect this fact": per Tuckey L.J. above p.768.

97   Above, p.768.

98   Luther, "Easements and Exclusive Possession" (1996) 16 L.S. 51 makes the point that the question of what the dominant landowner is able to do on the land may sometimes be the same as asking what the servient landowner *cannot* do.

99   [2007] 1 W.L.R. 2620, p.2643.

100   *Moncrieff v Jamieson* concerned Scots Law and as such is not binding authority. The *Batchelor v Marlow* test still applies: *Virdi v Chana* [2008] EWHC 2901; *Polo Woods Foundation v Shelton-Agar* [2009] EWHC 1361 (Ch), per Warren J. on appeal from the Deputy Adjudicator of H.M. Land Registry, paras 262–265 (in the context of a profit à prendre for the grazing of horses on the servient land).

there was no vehicular access to the dominant property except across the servient tenement. The main public road was 150 yards away. The previous owners of the servient tenement had granted the claimants, the owners of the dominant property, a right of vehicular access to the public road. The claimants began to park their cars at the top of the cliff, on the servient land, at the point nearest to their property so that they would only have a short walk down the incline to get to their house. They would otherwise have to park on the public road, walk 150 yards all the way back over the vehicular access route to their property "in all weathers and in times of darkness as well as in daylight, over . . . a significantly steep descent or climb in open and exposed country".[101] The defendants disputed that the claimants were allowed to use the access in order to park their cars as they now wanted to enclose the parking area in their garden.

One of the defendants' arguments was that the claimants' right to park in the space at the end of the access route would deprive them "of any reasonable use of that land", arguing on the basis of the tests laid down in *London & Blenheim* and *Batchelor v Marlow*. Lord Scott criticised the test. It should be possible to grant the sole use of the area concerned, for car parking or another defined purpose, provided that the servient owner is still in "control" of the land. In this case the owners of the land in question still retained control of it, so it was not fatal to the claim of an easement that the area could at times be taken up entirely with the dominant owners' cars. Commenting on the *Batchelor v Marlow* test, Lord Scott observed:

> "I can think of no reason why, if an area of land can accommodate nine cars, the owner of the land should not grant an easement to park nine cars on the land. The servient owner would remain the owner of the land and in possession and control of it. The dominant owner would have the right to station up to nine cars there and, of course, to have access to his nine cars. How could it be said that the law would recognise an easement allowing the dominant owner to park five cars or six or seven or eight but not nine? I would, for my part, reject the test that asks whether the servient owner is left with any reasonable use of his land, and substitute for it a test which asks whether the servient owner retains possession and, subject to the reasonable exercise of the right in question, control of the servient land."[102]

Lord Scott's analysis of the *Batchelor v Marlow* case appears cursory and it is doubtful whether his alternative "retention of control" test really says anything different, or that *Batchelor v Marlow* would have been decided any differently under his "control" test. It is submitted that the *Batchelor v Marlow* test does not prevent an easement to park a car in a single space or five cars on land that only accommodates five cars.[103]

---

101 *Moncrieff v Jamieson* [2007] 1 W.L.R. 2620, p.2631, per Lord Hope.
102 [2007] 1 W.L.R. 2620, p. 2642. Lord Scott relied on Alexander Hill-Smith's article "Rights of Parking and the Ouster Principle after Batchelor v Marlow" [2007] Conv. 223.
103 See *Virdi v Chana* [2008] EWHC 2901.

The way in which the Court of Appeal in *Batchelor* articulated the test and applied it to the facts showed that the Court was reasoning from first principles. Thus, even if one substituted the test of "reasonable use" for the question *does the servient owner retain possession and control* the effect is the same. The use of the land made by the claimants, because it substantially affected the value of the servient land and the developmental use that could be made of it meant that the servient owner's "control" or possession over the land was materially diminished. This would have been the same if the easement was for five cars in a space that would accommodate six. Although because the right was so extensive that it meant the servient owners were excluded from the land during a considerable amount of time, there appeared to be more at stake than this. There were some peripheral uses to which they could put the land, but nothing that they wanted to do, could do, or had planned to do by way of developing the land. One of the "control" powers of land ownership is sale, and, according to *Batchelor v Marlow* this right was fettered by the extensive parking claim. Its developmental value would be affected by the parking rights, and if the servient land was sold to the dominant owner this "would amount to a recognition that the rights they asserted had given them in practice a beneficial interest and no doubt the price would reflect this fact".[104]

In *Moncrieff v Jamieson* although the right to park could have used up the entire space from time to time, the right did appear less extensive,[105] and in any case, did not affect the control powers of the owner in the same way. From the report, it is fair to assume that the use to which the servient owner could put the land was limited anyway. It is unlikely they could have sold it separately, or that the claimants' right would have diminished the overall value of the servient tenement. It was not part of development land. Thus, in balance with what could not be done with the land, the servient owner's ability to concrete over the area or undertake other such improvements did not amount to a material diminution in their control powers. The inability to enclose the servient land as part of their garden was not material in this respect. Although the test applied by the House of Lords in this case was whether the servient owners retained possession and control of their land, it is submitted that the same result ought to have been reached on the *Batchelor v Marlow* test.[106] The uses to which the land could have been put were limited anyway and the right claimed left sufficient "reasonable use" of the servient tenement.

In the face of either test the right claimed *looked like* a limited third party right over land of another.[107]

---

104 In relation to earlier cases see Luther, "Easements and Exclusive Possession" (1996) 16 L.S. 51.

105 In relation to a similar principle of Scots law Lord Hope had shown that the claimant's use of the servient land would not be an "unacceptable burden". The right was limited in that the only vehicles that could be parked there were ones used to access the road and the dominant property, i.e. the right to park was incidental to the right of vehicular access: [2007] 1 W.L.R. 2620, pp. 2633, per Lord Hope.

106 *Virdi v Chana* [2008] EWHC 2901 (considered immediately below) the same result would have been reached on either test: paras 23–24. Also Luther (1996) 16 L.S. 51.

107 In its earlier report on easements, the Law Commission considered it desirable to return to the first principle of what an easement looks like: Law Com No. 186 (2008).

Like this

> **First principle of an easement: An easement is a limited right over land belonging to another. It is not a right to possession and control: Bright, "Of Estates and Interests: A Tale of Ownership and Property Rights" in *Land Law Themes and Perspectives*, p.538. Easements concern one purpose only and not open-ended use: S.Bright, above, p.534.**

Not like this

> **BUILDING BLOCK NO 4: Ideas of Ownership:** The idea of ownership is *control* over land. It is open-ended: "Ownership itself is a set of open-ended use privileges and open-ended powers to control the use made by others of the property". (Bright) Thus, *ownership* gives the owner control: he can prevent others from doing similar things with the land and can use it himself, e.g. for exploitation of value, sale etc.

In *Virdi v Chana*[108] and *Polo Woods Foundation v Shelton-Agar*[109] it was held that the Court of Appeal's test in *Batchelor v Marlow* is still the correct test to apply in order to determine whether the right claimed amounts to exclusive use or possession of the servient tenement. *Moncrieff v Jamieson* is a Scottish case and therefore not binding authority. In *Virdi v Chana*[110] the whole question of the appeal was whether it was possible to have an exclusive right to park in a defined space. There was only room for one car in the space and the land could not have been used for much else. Was this in the nature of an easement or too extensive? His Honour Judge Purle Q.C distinguished *Batchelor v Marlow*.[111] He defined the "ouster principle" as recognising that "an easement cannot be claimed if its effect is to deprive the servient owner of the benefits of ownership". As the servient owners could not have used the space for anything else anyway, the car parking easement did not affect their ownership powers. The servient owner could go onto the land and tend to trees and shrubs, provided that this did not interfere with the easement. Thus, the exercise of the easement was an acceptable limitation.[112] Again one gets the impression that in deciding whether the exercise of the right in question has the effect of rendering the servient owner's ownership "illusory" the courts conduct a weighing exercise. Firstly one considers the nature and uses of the relevant land and then whether the easement constitutes a proportional limitation on these uses. On this basis it appears, *Batchelor v Marlow* was distinguishable.[113]

---

108   [2008] EWHC 2901.
109   [2009] EWHC 1361 (Ch).
110   [2008] EWHC 2901.
111   [2008] EWHC 2901, paras 18–19.
112   paras 20–21.
113   For some similar arguments see Luther, "Easements and Exclusive Possession" (1996) 16 L.S. 51, relating to an evaluation of what the courts should be looking for.

Finally, despite what Lord Scott says about the servient tenement only being the land over which the right is exercised and not the entire land, it is difficult to assess questions of the servient landowner's control without considering the use he makes of his entire surrounding land.[114] In *Grigsby v Melville* the claimants of the easement were attempting to occupy the whole of a cellar that ran all the way underneath the servient owner's living room. This was an attempt to control the entire basement of a house. In *Wright v Macadam* the tenant's right to use a small coal shed affected the servient owners' use of their land in a much less significant way. Whether the servient landowner is left with "reasonable use" of land must therefore vary significantly from case to case. There will be a variety of factors relevant. *Gale on Easements*[115] states that "[t]he line is difficult to draw, and each new case would probably be decided on its own facts in the light of common sense". Indeed in *Moncrieff v Jamieson* the House of Lords was impressed by the "unusual circumstances" of the case and the "great inconvenience" to the dominant owners if the easement had not been allowed.

(d) Law Reform
The Law Commission has concluded that there is at present so much uncertainty about the test to determine whether a right would amount to "excessive use" of the servient land that it is open to doubt whether it is possible to have an easement to park a car in a defined space.[116] The Law Commission consider both the *London & Blenheim* test and the *Moncrieff v Jamieson* test to be problematic[117] and suggest that the rule that the easement must not leave the servient owner without reasonable use of their land should be abolished.[118] The recommendations in the earlier Law Commission report seem less counter-intuitive.[119] In this earlier report the Law Commission suggests a return to first principles, i.e. the right must "look like" a limited right in the land and "not look" like ownership. But for reasons given above this does seem pretty much what the courts are doing anyway.

(e) A right must not impose expenditure on the servient owner
An easement cannot impose positive action on the servient owner in order for the right to be enjoyed by the dominant owner.[120] Thus, a dominant owner entitled to a right of support does not oblige the servient owner to keep his/her house in repair – he is only obliged not to demolish it.[121] However, it is possible to have an easement requiring the owner of the servient tenement to repair a fence, but only where the purpose is to keep in livestock.[122] Thus, in *Jones v Pritchard*[123] it was held that the owner of the servient tenement over which a right of way is exercised is not

---

114   See Luther, (1996) 16 L.R. 51; although there might be extreme cases where the total land owned by the servient landowner is so extensive that the land over which the easement is exercised bears little relation to the rest.

115   17th edn (London: Sweet & Maxwell, 2002), p. 30, quoted *Batchelor v Marlow*, p.767.

116   Law Commission, *Making Land Work: Easements, Covenants and Profits-à-Prendre* (2011) Law Com No.327; Law Com No.186 (2008), paras 3.42–3.44. For reasons given above I would disagree with this conclusion. We will study these reforms below.

117   Law Com No.186 (2008), para.3.47; also Jackson, Stevens and Pearce, *Land Law*, 4th edn (London: Sweet & Maxwell, 2008).

118   See below. The rule that the easement must not amount to *exclusive possession* of the servient land is to be retained.

119   Law Commission Consultation Paper *Easements, Covenants and Profits-à-Prendre* Law Com No. 186 (2008).

120   *Moncrieff v Jamieson* [2007] 1 W.L.R. 2620, p.2636, per Lord Scott.

121   Clarke and Greer, *Land Law Directions,* 2nd edn (Oxford University Press, 2010) p.307.

122   *Crow v Wood* [1971] 1 Q.B. 77; M.Thompson, *Modern Land Law*, 4th edn (Oxford University Press, 2009), pp.502–3.

123   [1908] 1 Ch. 630.

obliged to keep the driveway in repair. However, the dominant owner is entitled if they wish to undertake repairs on the servient land in order that they may exercise their right.[124]

C. EASEMENTS COMPARED WITH OTHER RIGHTS

(1) Public rights

Whereas easements are specific and attached to a dominant plot of land, public rights over certain land may be exercised by any member of the public. They do not need to own adjacent land that benefits from the right. For instance there are public rights to fish on the foreshore (the land between high tide and low), and public rights of way: "highways" (roads) and rights to walk on the footpaths.[125]

Members of the public have certain rights of way over countryside and common land for recreation.[126]

(2) Rights incident to ownership of land: natural rights

A landowner has a natural right to support for his land, i.e. "upper from lower strata, and soil from adjacent soil". This is separate from any question of an easement.[127] However, this right of support does not extend to support for buildings on the land,[128] unless there is damage to a building caused by loss of support to the land. For example, in *Holbeck Hall Hotel Ltd v Scarborough Borough Council*,[129] a local authority who owned land between the sea front and the plaintiff's hotel was held to have a duty of care when the hotel was seriously damaged due to coastal erosion. They were under a duty to prevent foreseeable damage. However, the local authority was unaware of the extent of the geological problem and it was held that the duty may be restricted to "warning claimants of such risk as they were aware of or ought to have foreseen and sharing such information as they had acquired". A landowner also has a natural right to receive water where it flows through a defined channel.[130]

(3) Restrictive covenants

A restrictive covenant is a promise by one landowner for the benefit of a neighbouring landowner that they will not do something on their land, e.g. build on it. Like an easement a covenant can restrict the burdened landowner's ability to use his land, and they are property rights that run with the burdened land. There is a significant difference: covenants must be brought into being expressly whereas easements, as we shall see, can come into being entirely informally.

---

124 *Moncrieff v Jamieson* [2007] 1 W.L.R. 2620, p. 2636, per Lord Scott.
125 C.Harpum, S.Bridge and M.Dixon, *Megarry & Wade Law of Real Property*, para. 27–024.
126 Countryside and Rights of Way Act 2000; *Oxfordshire CC v Oxford City Council* [2006] UKHL 25; R.Meager [2006] Conv. 265; the Commons Act 2006.
127 *Dalton v Angus* (1880–81) L.R. 6 App. Cas. 740, p. 791, per Lord Selborne L.C.
128 *Dalton v Angus*, above; *Bonomi v Backhouse* (1861) 11 E.R. 825; *Caledonian Railway Co v Sprot* (1856) 2 Macq 449.
129 [2000] 2 All E.R. 705.
130 *Palmer v Bowman* [2000] 1 All E.R. 22.

Easements are more circumscribed, i.e. a right to light entitles the dominant landowner to a certain amount of light that is necessary for the reasonable enjoyment of his land. His neighbour can build as long as he does not block that amount of light. On the other hand a covenant is a promise restricting use of land automatically, e.g. not to build. Easements are expressed in terms of what the dominant land is entitled to, e.g. light. With covenants the benefited land is entitled to the promise, to restrict all building. This may be a way of preserving a highly intangible benefit (such as a view) that is not known to the law of easements.

(4) Licences

A licence is permission to enter upon another's land. It is "precarious" in the sense that permission to do so can be withdrawn at any time. There is no need for a dominant tenement and licences do not bind third party purchasers of land.[131]

(5) Profits-à-prendre

Initially easements and profits look the same in nature. However they are not. Easements are the right to undertake a limited activity on another's land, such as walking over it to get access to a house or parking a car on it or storing goods on the land. Profits are the right to take something from land belonging to another.[132]

3   The easement must be created, or come into being, in one of the ways recognised by law

Once you have established that your client's use of his neighbour's land has the characteristics of an easement it is necessary then to go on to establish that it has been acquired in one of the following ways.

A. EXPRESS GRANT/RESERVATION

An easement could be expressly granted where there are two separate owners of two plots of land one may grant an easement over his land, such as a right of way, to the other. However, a very common type of express grant or reservation is where the dominant and servient land were originally in common ownership of one person who then sells part of the land to a purchaser and grants easements for the benefit of the purchaser over his retained land. For example, a larger building is turned into three terraced houses. The owner then sells two of the houses to purchasers. It is usual for the seller to grant necessary easements, such as the right for drainage pipes to run under his retained land, or a right of access round the back of his property.

---

131   *Ashburn Anstalt v Arnold* [1989] Ch. 1.
132   *Polo Woods Foundation v Shelton-Agar* [2009] EWHC 1361. We will consider profits below.

It may likewise be the case that the owner of land who is selling part of it in this way may need easements himself over the part of the land or houses that he sells. Thus it is usual in the deed of conveyance of those houses for the seller to "reserve" easements for the benefit of *his retained land* over the part of the land sold to the purchaser. This is known as a "reservation".

Example: A landowner sells part of his land comprising a house and garden to a purchaser. He reserves a right of access to the road across the land sold for the benefit of his retained land

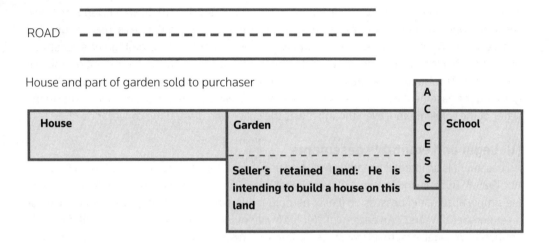

ROAD

House and part of garden sold to purchaser

| House | Garden | ACCESS | School |

Seller's retained land: He is intending to build a house on this land

Indeed, the seller of land, if he wishes to reserve easements for the benefit of his retained land over the land that he sells, is under a duty to do so expressly in the conveyance of that land.[133] The law will not do it for him. In *Re Webb's Lease* it was stated that there is a general rule that "a grantor, whether by way of conveyance or lease, of part of [land] in his ownership, cannot claim any easement over the part granted for the benefit of the part retained, unless it is expressly reserved out of the grant".[134] This "is founded upon a maxim which is as well established by authority. . . that a grantor shall not derogate from his grant".[135] He cannot give the ownership of the land with one hand and detract from it with the other by claiming an easement over it. If he wanted such an easement he should have reserved it in the conveyance.[136] This general rule has two very limited exceptions: the doctrines of necessity and common intention, which we shall consider below.

Prior to 1925 it was a complicated matter to reserve an easement. Because the owner of the *servient* land is the one who must grant the easement over that land: i.e. the purchaser in the

---

133   *Wheeldon v Burrows* (1879) L.R. 12 Ch.D. 31, p.49, per Thesiger L.J.
134   *Re Webb's Lease* [1951] Ch. 808, per Jenkins L.J. *Wheeldon v Burrows* (1879) L.R. 12 Ch. D 31.
135   *Wheeldon v Burrows* (1878) L.R. 12 Ch.D. 31, p.49, per Thesiger L.J.
136   *Suffield v Brown* 4 D. J. & S. 185, per Lord Westbury; *White v Bass* (1862) 7 H. & N. 722, p.730, per Baron Martin; *Sovmots Investments Ltd v Secretary of State for the Environment* [1977] 2 W.L.R. 951.

above example, "a person [the seller] could not grant to himself",[137] the new purchaser, upon conveyance of the land to him, would then have to execute a deed in order to grant the easement to the seller. However, s.65(1) of the Law of Property Act 1925 provides that this is not necessary. It is possible, by this provision, to reserve an easement in the seller's conveyance of the land.

> "A reservation of a legal estate shall operate at law without any execution of the conveyance by the grantee of the legal estate out of which the reservation is made, or any regrant by him, so as to create the legal estate reserved".

Thus where a seller reserves an easement in the conveyance of the servient land, the new servient owner is treated by law as making the grant to the seller. This has an unusual consequence. Whenever there is an ambiguity in a contract or grant the ambiguity is construed against the person making the grant, i.e. the interpretation least favourable to that person will be adopted. This is the *contra proferentum* rule. Thus, as the servient owner is treated as the one granting the easement then the terms of the easement will be construed most favourably to the seller of the servient land, even though it was the seller who drafted the conveyance.[138]

(1) Legal and equitable easements

An easement is an interest capable of existing as a legal interest under s.1 of the Law of Property Act 1925.[139] But it is only capable of being legal if it is "for an interest equivalent to an estate in fee simple absolute in possession [i.e. of perpetual duration] or a term of years absolute [i.e. for a set number of years]". An easement "for life" will not qualify as a legal interest, but it may be equitable. A legal easement must be granted or reserved by deed.[140] Expressly grants or reservations of easements are often made in the deed of conveyance of the land itself. This satisfies the requirement. As far as registered land is concerned the express grant or reservation of an easement is a disposition that must be completed by registration.[141] If it is not registered with the burden on the servient title and the benefit against the dominant title then the easement will take effect only as an equitable easement.[142]

B. IMPLIED GRANT/RESERVATION

In certain situations the law will imply an easement into a deed of conveyance. For example, where the dominant and servient land were originally in common ownership of one person, who sold parts of it off to separate purchasers, and the conveyance makes no mention of any

---

137 Harpum, Bridge and Dixon, *Megarry & Wade Law of Real Property*, para.28–006, citing *Durham & Sunderland Ry v Walker* (1842) 2 Q.B. 940.
138 *St Edmundsbury and Ipswich Diocesan Board of Finance v Clark* [1975] 1 W.L.R. 468; M.Thompson, *Modern Land Law*, p.511.
139 s.1(2)(a). See Chapter 2.
140 Law of Property Act 1925 s.52.
141 Land Registration Act 2002 s.27(2)(d); Sch.2(7).
142 Land Registration Act 2002 s.27(1); Sch.2 para.7.

easements, the law may nonetheless recognise certain easements in favour of the land sold over the land retained by the seller. The circumstances in which the law implies a *reservation* of an easement in favour of the seller's retained land are much more restrictive. Implied grants and reservations, because they are implied into the deed itself, are legal easements, provided of course the easement is capable of being legal under s.1(2)(a) of the Law of Property Act 1925.

Example: Methods of implied grant and reservation

Implied grant
- **The doctrine of necessity**
- **Common intention**
- **The rule in** *Wheeldon v Burrows*
- **s.62 of Law of Property Act 1925**

Implied reservation
- **Necessity**
- **Common intention**

---

(1) Implied grant and reservation of easements

It is simpler to deal first with the methods by which it is possible to imply a reservation as well as a grant of an easement: *necessity* and *common intention*.

(a) The doctrine of "necessity"

Where a person owns land and then sells part of that land to a purchaser, it is important that he grants easements over his land for the benefit of the land sold, for example, rights of access and drainage over his land where this is necessary for the enjoyment of the purchaser's land. Similarly it is important when he sells part of his own land to contemplate what rights he may need over the land sold. He may need to get to his own land via the land sold, he will need rights of drainage, and may need rights of support to structures on his land—if supported currently by structures on the part of the land that he sells.[143] However, sometimes the conveyance of the land makes no mention of any easements. In certain circumstances the law will recognise that an easement has come into existence even though it was not expressly granted or reserved in the conveyance if it can be shown to be *necessary* to the use of the land sold or retained. This has been said to be a matter of common sense.[144] For example, where land is transferred it may be possible to imply an easement of necessity where, following the transfer, one of the plots would be landlocked, i.e. without any means of access.[145]

In *Manjang v Drammeh*,[146] Lord Oliver in the Privy Council stated the elements required before the law will imply an easement of necessity:

---

143   For example, *Union Lighterage Company v London Graving Dock Company* [1902] 2 Ch. 557.
144   *Barry v Hasseldine* [1952] Ch. 835, p.839 per Danckwerts J.
145   *Nickerson v Barraclough* [1981] Ch. 426.
146   (1991) 61 P. & C.R. 194, pp.196–7.

"There has to be found, first, a common owner of a legal estate in two plots of land. It has, secondly, to be established that access between one of those plots and the public highway can be obtained only over the other plot. Thirdly, there has to be found a disposition of one of the plots without any specific grant or reservation of a right of access."[147]

The question is then a matter of construction of the conveyance in the light of the surrounding circumstances of the case in order to determine whether it is possible to imply such an easement. For instance, if the terms of the conveyance clearly and unambiguously preclude the grant or reservation of access then the law will not intervene.[148] Before such an easement will come into being it must be *impossible* to use the land as intended unless an easement is implied.[149] Thus, where it is a right of way in dispute concerning either the land sold or the land retained, the alleged dominant land must be literally landlocked with no legal rights of access elsewhere. In *Union Lighterage Company v London Graving Dock Company*,[150] Stirling L.J. stated that

"In my opinion an easement of necessity. . . means an easement without which the property retained cannot be used at all, and not one merely necessary to the reasonable enjoyment of that property."

So where there is an alternative way available, even if inconvenient, there will be no right of way implied under the doctrine of necessity.[151] Thus in *Union Lighterage Company v London Graving Dock Company*[152] no easement of support was reserved to a dock when its owner sold the adjacent wharf. The dock was physically supported by tie-rods fastened underneath the wharf.

"So here it may be that the tie-rods which pass through the plaintiffs' property are reasonably necessary to the enjoyment of the defendants' dock in its present condition; but the dock is capable of use without them, and I think that there cannot be implied any reservation in respect of them."[153]

(b) Common intention

An easement may be implied where it is necessary in order for the land to be used *for the purpose for which the land was granted or retained*.[154] There is no need to prove strict "necessity" as above.

---

147   It is possible for other rights than rights of way to be implied under this doctrine.

148   *Nickerson v Barraclough* [1981] Ch. 426.

149   *Adealon International Corp Proprietary Ltd v Merton LBC* [2007] 1 W.L.R. 1898. But compare *Sweet v Sommer* [2004] EWHC 1504 in which Hart J. recognised an easement of necessity for access by vehicles, even though the land was capable of use without such access. The case went to appeal [2005] EWCA Civ 227 but was decided on different grounds.

150   [1902] 2 Ch. 557, p.573.

151   *Nickerson v Barraclough* [1980] Ch. 325, p.334, per Sir Robert Megarry V.C. *Manjang v Drammeh* (1991) 61 P. & C.R. 194. In *MGA Engineering Ltd v Trimster Co Ltd* (1987) 56 P. & C.R. 1, there was no easement of necessity implied. There was an alternative access on foot, albeit "inconvenient"; also *Barry v Hasseldine* [1952] Ch. 835.

152   [1902] 2 Ch. 557, p.573.

153   Above per Stirling L.J.

154   *Jones v Pritchard* [1908] 1 Ch. 630; *Lyttleton Times Co Ltd v Warners Ltd* [1907] A.C. 476.

In *Wong v Beaumont Property Trust Ltd*[155] the claimant and defendant entered into a lease of some basement rooms. It was known to both parties that the purpose of the lease was so that the claimant could use the premises to run a Chinese restaurant. However, the then current health regulations showed that the premises were inadequately ventilated and that the proposed ventilation system would require a ventilation duct to be fastened to the rear of the landlord's property. The lease contained no such easement for the benefit of the claimant's premises and the landlord refused to allow it. Lord Denning M.R. relied on the law as stated by Lord Parker in *Pwllbach Colliery Co Ltd v Woodman*[156]:

> "The law will readily imply the grant or reservation of such easements as may be necessary to give effect to the common intention of the parties to a grant of real property, with reference to the manner or purposes in and for which the land granted . . . is to be used. But it is essential for this purpose that the parties should intend that the subject of the grant . . . should be used in some definite and particular manner. It is not enough that the subject of the grant . . . should be intended to be used in a manner which may or may not involve this definite and particular use."[157]

Lord Denning M.R. held that the plaintiff had an easement to attach a ventilation duct to the landlord's property. The running of a restaurant was the "definite and particular manner" in which the parties had intended the premises to be used. The premises could not be used in this manner unless a ventilation duct was installed, and in the lease the plaintiff had covenanted not to cause any nuisance and smells. In *Davis v Bramwell*[158] the Court of Appeal implied a wider access way because at the time of the transfer it was the parties' common intention that the land should be used as garage premises. This required a wider access route for safety reasons so that large vehicles could access the garage.

Where it is argued that an easement is *reserved* under this ground it is for the seller of the alleged dominant plot to prove ("and prove clearly"!)[159] that at the time that he sold that part of his land there was a common intention that his retained land was to be used for a definite and particular purpose and that an easement is necessary in order to give effect to this intention.[160] It is more difficult to imply a reservation under this ground.[161] It must be the case that "the facts are not reasonably consistent with any other explanation".[162] It will be remembered that the reservation of an easement by common intention is an exception to the general rule that "[i]f the [grantor of land] intended to reserve any such rights over the [land] it was his duty to reserve

---

155   [1965] 1 Q.B. 173.
156   [1915] A.C. 634.
157   Relied on by Lord Denning M.R. in *Wong v Beaumont Property Trust Ltd* [1965] 1 Q.B. 173, p.180 (editing supplied).
158   [2007] EWCA Civ 821.
159   *Re Webb's Lease* [1951] Ch. 808, per Jenkins L.J.
160   *Aldridge v Wright* [1929] 2 K.B. 117.
161   *Peckham v Ellison* [2000] 79 P. & C.R. 276.
162   *Peckham v Ellison* above.

them expressly in the [conveyance]".[163] The law will not imply them. In *Re Webb's Lease*,[164] the defendant was the owner of a three storey building and leased the upper floors to the claimant. During the lease the defendant had continued to display advertising posters on the external walls of the claimant's premises. The defendant had not reserved an easement to do this in the lease and the claimant objected. Jenkins L.J. held that an easement to display the posters was not necessary to the defendant's intended use of the ground floor for his business. Even the poster that advertised his business was not necessary to the running of that business.

Easements that have been reserved under this ground include easements of support,[165] and similar easements. In *Jones v Pritchard* when the owner of two semi-detached houses sold one to a purchaser, an easement was implied that the seller could continue to use the shared chimney.[166]

The doctrine of common intention will also apply to give effect to another right granted.[167] Thus, if the owner of land has granted someone the right to draw water from land the law may imply an easement for the grantee to walk onto the land for that purpose. This would give effect to the parties' common intention at the time of the grant.

(c) *The rule in Wheeldon v Burrows*[168]

There are two further rules by which easements can be impliedly granted: the rule in *Wheeldon v Burrows* and the rule under s.62 of the Law of Property Act 1925. These rules can only be used to imply a grant of an easement and not a reservation.

Where a person owns land and divides it up, selling part of it to a purchaser, the law will in certain circumstances imply easements in favour of the purchaser's land over the seller's retained land. In *Wheeldon v Burrows*[169] Thesiger L.J. laid down the general principle that

> "on the grant by the owner of a tenement or part of that tenement as it is then used and enjoyed, there will pass to the grantee all those continuous and apparent easements (by which, of course, I mean quasi easements), or, in other words, all those easements which are necessary to the reasonable enjoyment of the property granted, and which have been and are at the time of the grant used by the owners of the entirety for the benefit of the part granted."

In short, where land is in common ownership and the owner sells or leases part of it, the grantee will obtain all those easements previously enjoyed by the common owner over his own land. For

---

163   *Re Webb's Lease* [1951] Ch. 808, per Jenkins L.J.
164   [1951] Ch. 808.
165   *Jones v Pritchard* [1908] 1 Ch. 630.
166   *Jones v Pritchard* [1908] 1 Ch. 630.
167   *Pwllbach Colliery Co Ltd v Woodman* [1915] A.C. 634, per Lord Parker.
168   (1879) L.R. 12 Ch.D. 31.
169   (1879) LR 12 Ch.D. 31, p.49.

example an owner of two plots of land frequently walks across Plot A to get to Plot B. If he sells Plot B the purchaser will acquire an easement over Plot A. Whilst the two plots of land are in common ownership we do not refer to the owner's activities on his own land as "easements", because as you know, for an easement to exist the dominant and servient land must have different owners. We call them "quasi easements". Let's consider another example. Jason owns a large plot of land divided into a park area and a house and garden. He regularly walks across the park to get from his house to the public road and back again. Drainage and water pipes that service the house run across part of the park. In 2010 Jason sells the house and garden to Amerjit. The rule in *Wheeldon v Burrows* provides that easements of access and drainage over the park pass to Amerjit provided that they had been used by Jason at the time of the grant of the house and garden to her. The rule in *Wheeldon v Burrows* only applies only where both plots of land were in common ownership prior to the transfer of the quasi-dominant plot. The other conditions are that the easements must be continuous and apparent and necessary to the reasonable enjoyment of the property.

The rule in *Wheeldon v Burrows* is founded on the principle of non-derogation from grant.[170] The principle is that an owner of land should not be allowed to sell or lease that land and at the same time detract from the utility of the land. It is implied that he intended to grant the land *as it was used at the time of the grant*, i.e. with all the rights of access, drainage, storage etc.[171] The principle is that the grantee should acquire the land in no lesser form and utility than it had when held by the common owner prior to the grant. The easements necessary for this purpose will be implied into the grant.

(i) Continuous and apparent

In order for an easement to be implied into a conveyance of the dominant land the common owner's use of the retained land must have been "continuous and apparent". This means that there should be permanent evidence of the right on the servient tenement "which would be seen on inspection and which is neither transitory nor intermittent".[172] An example of this would be a pathway, road or a drain.[173] In *Sovmots Investments Ltd v Secretary of State for the Environment*[174] a shopping and showroom complex had a number of residential maisonettes. When the maisonettes were compulsorily acquired by the council it was held that easements of access, support and drainage did not pass to the council under the rule in *Wheeldon v Burrows*. The reason, amongst others, was that the maisonettes were unoccupied and unused at all by the owners. Lord Wilberforce stated that "for the rule to apply there must be actual, and apparent, use and enjoyment at the time of the grant".[175]

---

170   *Wheeldon v Burrows* (1879) LR 12 Ch.D. 31, p.49, per Thesiger L.J. *Borman v Griffith* [1930] 1 Ch. 493, p.499, per Maugham J.
171   *Sovmots Investments Ltd v Secretary of State for the Environment* [1977] 2 W.L.R. 951, p.168, per Lord Wilberforce.
172   *Ward v Kirkland* [1967] Ch. 194, pp.224–5, per Ungoed-Thomas J.
173   *Ward v Kirkland*, above also *Wheeler v J.J. Saunders Ltd* [1996] Ch. 19.
174   [1977] 2 W.L.R. 951.
175   [1977] 2 W.L.R. 951, p.169, per Lord Wilberforce.

(ii) Necessary for the reasonable enjoyment of the land

In *Wheeldon v Burrows* it was stated that for an easement to pass to the grantee of land it must be "necessary to the reasonable enjoyment of the property granted". Clearly this does not imply necessity in the strict sense above. What is necessary for the reasonable enjoyment of the land will depend on the purpose for which the property is intended to be used. Thus, it is a question of construing the relevant grant and its surrounding circumstances in order to determine the intended use of the property and what is required for its reasonable enjoyment. In *Borman v Griffith*[176] a right to use a private road was implied in favour of the claimant, as there was no other way that would accommodate the large vehicles used by the claimant's business as a poultry farmer. The purpose to which the claimant was intending to put the land was known to both parties at the time. Conversely, in *Wheeler v J.J. Saunders Ltd*[177] it was held that the claimants had acquired no access route because there was another means of access that did just as well. Thus, it was not necessary for the reasonable enjoyment of the property.

There has been some doubt as to whether it is necessary to prove that the rights are continuous and apparent *and* necessary for the reasonable enjoyment of the land, or whether one of these requirements will suffice. Lord Wilberforce in *Sovmots Investments Ltd v Secretary of State for the Environment*[178] treated the meaning of these requirements as interchangeable. They are both aimed at proving that the grantee of the quasi-dominant plot should acquire the land in the state in which it was used and enjoyed when it was in common ownership. The grantor cannot be allowed to take away from what was granted by claiming that those rights were not implied into the conveyance. This is consistent with the way in which the rule was expressed in *Wheeldon v Burrows* itself in which Thesiger L.J. had stated that a grant will included continuous and apparent easements "or, in other words, all those easements which are necessary to the reasonable enjoyment of the property granted".[179]

(iii) The scope of the rule in Wheeldon v Burrows

The rule in *Wheeldon v Burrows* applies to conveyances of land, i.e. transfers of the fee simple and leases, and to contracts for the sale of land or contracts for leases. Thus, unlike s. 62 of the Law of Property Act 1925, considered below, there is no requirement for there to be a conveyance. However, it only applies to *voluntary* conveyances/contracts. It does not create easements where the dominant land is subject to a compulsory purchase order.[180] The rule applies to create legal and equitable easements. For example, if the interest in the land transferred is only equitable, the easement created thereunder will only be equitable, e.g. a contract for a lease that becomes an equitable lease under the doctrine of *Walsh v Lonsdale*.[181]

---

176   [1930] 1 Ch. 493.
177   [1996] Ch. 19, p.25 per Staughton L.J.
178   [1977] 2 W.L.R. 951, p.168–9.
179   In *Ward v Kirkland* [1967] Ch. 194, p.224 Ungoed-Thomas J. thought it possible that the requirements referred to different types of easement, the requirement of necessity for the reasonable enjoyment of land applying to negative easements.
180   *Sovmots Investments Ltd v Secretary of State for the Environment* [1977] 2 W.L.R. 951.
181   See also Clarke and Greer, *Land Law Directions*, p.323 which also takes this point.

(d) Section 62 of the Law of Property Act 1925

Section 62(1) of the Law of Property Act 1925 provides that

"A conveyance of land shall be deemed to include and shall by virtue of this Act operate to convey, with the land, all buildings, erections, fixtures, commons hedges, ditches, fences, ways, waters, water-courses, liberties, privileges, easements, rights, and advantages whatsoever, appertaining or reputed to appertain to the land, or any part thereof, or, at the time of conveyance, demised, occupied, or enjoyed with, or reputed or known as part or parcel of or appurtenant to the land or any part thereof."[182]

Section 62 operates where two plots of land are in the common ownership of one person and another person is occupying one of these plots, whether by virtue of a lease or otherwise. That person may be exercising rights, liberties or privileges over the other plot, for example walking across the yard or storing items on the other plot. Section 62 works as follows: if the owner then conveys the plot of land occupied, e.g. by renewing the lease if the occupier is a tenant, by creating a lease in favour of the occupier (if the occupier is a licensee), or by selling the land to a tenant of the plot, then upon that conveyance, all rights, liberties and privileges exercised by the occupier become full easements, i.e. property rights that bind the sellor's/lessor's retained land. The rights exercised prior to the conveyance may or may not be actual easements. They may be purely licences. The owner may simply have given permission for the occupier to use his land temporarily, which he could have revoked at any time. Nevertheless, when the land is sold or leased to the occupier, these rights are "upgraded" to full easements.

> **Example**
> In *Wright v Macadam* [1949] 2 K.B. 744 a landlord owned two adjoining properties and leased one to a tenant. The tenant had been given permission by her landlord to store coal in a shed on his retained land. When the landlord renewed the lease in favour of the tenant s.62 gave the tenant a full easement of storage.

There is some overlap with the rule in *Wheeldon v Burrows* but there are also significant differences, which we examine below. Both rules are based on the principle of non-derogation from grant.[183] Thus, in *Wright v Macadam*, when the landlord renewed the lease to the tenant he was deemed to intend that upon creation of the lease the land should be capable of being enjoyed and used in the way that it was before. We will now look at the scope of s.62 in more detail.

---

182   The Law Commission observes that because it implies terms into an express grant s.62 is "better regarded as an aspect of the express creation of easements rather than as a form of implication". Law Commission, *Making Land Work: Easements Covenants and Profits-à-Prendre*, Law Com No.327 (2011), para.3.11.
183   *Wright v Macadam* [1949] 2 K.B. 744, CA, pp.751–2, per Jenkins L.J.

(i) There must be a conveyance

We see that it is only a "conveyance" of the dominant land that will be deemed under s.62 to include the rights previously enjoyed with the land.[184] This means the creation of a legal estate in the land and requires a deed under s.52 of the Law of Property Act 1925. It includes a lease. Thus, if David was the owner of two plots of land and Gill had been his tenant of one plot, if he renews the lease by deed this will operate to convey all those rights, liberties and privileges that had operated for the benefit of Gill's land prior to the renewal, for example rights of support and access. A contract for a lease, which creates an equitable lease under the doctrine of *Walsh v Lonsdale*[185] is not sufficient.[186]

In *Sovmots Investments Ltd v Secretary of State for the Environment*[187] Lord Keith and Lord Fraser considered that s.62 did not apply where the conveyance of the dominant land was forced under a compulsory purchase order. Thus, the conveyance must be voluntary. The basis for this appears to be that the intention imputed to a voluntary grantor that the land should be capable of being used and enjoyed in the same way after his grant, cannot be imputed in cases of a forced transfer. In *Kent v Kavanagh*[188] it was held that s.62 *did* apply where a tenant under a long lease at a low rent has power under the leasehold enfranchisement legislation to acquire the landlord's freehold title.[189] There was enough in the Leasehold Enfranchisement Act 1967 to suggest that freeholders should not be taken to intend to derogate from their grant.

(ii) The relevant time to assess whether rights existed so as to pass under the conveyance

Section 62 states a conveyance of land will be deemed to include rights appertaining to the dominant land "at the time of the conveyance". The courts will look at whether the rights existed at this time.[190] In *Green v Ashco Horticulturalist Ltd*[191] it was held that in order to determine whether the right was in existence the courts should look also at a reasonable period prior to the conveyance. Just because the right was unused for a short period does not mean that it ceases to exist so that it will be unable to pass under s.62.[192]

(iii) Section 62 passes rights previously enjoyed even if they were not full easements

Section 62 passes *all rights* that had previously been enjoyed, even if they were not full easements and were enjoyed only with the permission of the owner of the servient land.[193]

---

184 The meaning of "conveyance" is contained in Law of Property Act 1925 s.205.
185 (1882) L.R. 21 Ch. D. 9, see Chapter 9.
186 *Borman v Griffith* [1930] 1 Ch. 493.
187 [1977] 2 W.L.R. 951.
188 [2007] Ch. 1.
189 Chadwick L.J. distinguished the *Sovmots* case: [2007] Ch. 1, pp.19–20.
190 Provided, of course they were not excluded by the terms of the conveyance: *Goldberg v Edwards* [1950] Ch. 247, pp.256–7 per Evershed M.R., p. 259 per Cohen L.J. Law of Property Act 1925 s.62(4).
191 [1966] 2 All E.R. 232.
192 *Pretoria Warehousing Co Ltd v Shelton* [1993] E.G. 120; A.Dowling [1994] Conv. 238, p.239.
193 For recent discussion of this principle see *Campbell v Banks* [2011] EWCA Civ 61.

"the right, in order to pass, need not be one to which the owner or occupier for the time being of the land has had what may be described as a permanent title. A right enjoyed merely by permission is enough."[194]

In *International Tea Stores Co v Hobbs*[195] a person owned two adjacent houses and let one to a business. The tenants had permission to walk across the yard of the landlord's house. The owner sold the leased house to the tenants and the conveyance did not refer to a right of way over the owner's retained house. It was held that the former tenants had acquired an easement over the yard. Farwell J. stated that the material question is one of fact as to whether the right is enjoyed at the time of the conveyance. It matters not whether it is exercised as of right or by permission.[196] Thus, in *White v Williams*[197] Younger L.J. held that "[i]t matters not ... whether the user is continuous and permanent or permissive and precarious". So there is no requirement for the right to be "continuous and apparent"[198] provided the right is of the nature of rights known to the law, i.e. it satisfies the four *Re Ellenborough Park* characteristics,[199] and the person executing the conveyance has power to make such a grant of an easement.[200]

In *Wright v Macadam*[201] the claimant was a tenant of Macadam and was permitted to store coal in his shed on his adjacent land. When he renewed the lease there was no mention made of the use of the shed. The Court of Appeal held that the claimant had acquired an easement of storage in relation to the shed. In *Goldberg v Edwards*[202] a tenant was allowed into possession prior to the granting of a lease. He was allowed to use a passage way as access to the leased premises. When the lease was executed six months later the conveyance was deemed to include a right of way to use the passage way. Evershed M.R. stated that

"it has to be assumed that the terms of the bargain are intended to be in accordance with the rights or privileges which the tenant is allowed to enjoy in fact."[203]

LECTURER: Is this good or bad law so far?
STUDENT: From a point of view of ensuring that following a conveyance of the land it can still be used as the parties intended it to be, s.62 is good law. Even where the conveyance makes no mention of any easements that are to pass with a conveyance of the land, s.62 ensures that all privileges and rights that were used before the conveyance can be claimed as rights

---

194 *Wright v Macadam* [1949] 2 K.B. 744, CA, p.748, per Jenkins L.J.
195 [1903] 2 Ch. 165, per Sir George Farwell; The right in this case was claimed under the Conveyancing and Law of Property Act 1881 s. 6, which was replaced by Law of Property Act 1925 s. 62. The effect is the same: *Wright v Macadam* [1949] 2 K.B. 744, CA, p.748, per Jenkins L.J.
196 [1903] 2 Ch. 165. Also *Kay v Oxley* L.R. 10 Q.B. 360, p.368, per Blackburn J. *Wall v Collins* [2008] 1 All E.R. 122.
197 [1922] 1 K.B. 727, p. 740, citing *International Tea Stores Co v Hobbs* [1903] 2 Ch. 165.
198 *Ward v Kirkland* [1967] Ch. 194, p.229 per Ungoed-Thomas J.
199 *Wright v Macadam* [1949] 2 K.B. 744, CA, p.752, per Jenkins L.J. *International Tea Stores Co v Hobbs* [1903] 2 Ch. 165, per Farwell J. *Burrows v Lang* [1901] 2 Ch. 502.
200 Law of Property Act 1925 s.62(5).
201 [1949] 2 K.B. 744.
202 [1950] Ch. 247.
203 [1950] Ch. 247, p.257.

afterwards. This gives effect to the parties' expectations as to the use of land. It is therefore good law in accordance with BUILDING BLOCK NO 7.

> **BUILDING BLOCK NO 7: Land Law is "facilitative" and should give effect to what people want to do with their land**
> We can legitimately say that Land Law rules are good if they give effect to people's intentions behind the sale and purchase of land. Land Law is facilitative (Birks).

LECTURER: Good, but this is very far from being the only argument possible about s.62. Remember that easements are property rights that bind third party purchasers of the servient land. BUILDING BLOCK NO 5 tells us the policy that it is important that purchasers are aware of rights that will bind them following a transfer. Also as we have seen judges are usually reluctant to allow too ready a creation of property rights.

So looking at the law in relation to s.62 so far, is it good or bad? Hold the cases against BUILDING BLOCK NO 5 and think about the connection between them. Do they support or undermine it?

> **BUILDING BLOCK NO 5: Property Rights and the Protection of Purchasers**
> Easements are property rights and thus bind the title of the servient land. Property rights should not be too readily recognised as this would "clog" the title to the land and, perhaps, make it difficult to sell, particularly if the rights are restrictive of what the owner can do with his land.

STUDENT: Well, cases such as *Wright v Macadam* and *International Tea Stores Co v Hobbs* show that really small rights that were not really rights at all and only enjoyed with the permission of the owner, can on the conveyance of the dominant land become full property rights (easements) which will bind the servient land whether the owner likes it or not. It will also bind subsequent purchasers from him which might, depending on the precise content of the rights concerned, make his land more difficult to sell. This is bad law as it undermines BUILDING BLOCK NO 5: Property Rights and the Protection of Purchasers.

LECTURER: Good, in fact in *Wright v Macadam*, Tucker L.J. stated that

> "The result is that the defendant, through his act of kindness in allowing this lady to use the coal shed, is probably now a wiser man, and I may perhaps regret that the decision in this case may tend to discourage landlords from acts of kindness to their tenants. But there it is: that is the law."

LECTURER: As far as concerns subsequent purchasers of the servient land does registered land law offer any protection to purchasers from the possibility of being bound by easements that come into being so easily as a result of s.62?

STUDENT: In registered land law, impliedly granted easements are overriding interests, i.e. they do not have to be registered in order to bind a purchaser of the servient land. Thus, because s.62 allows many rights to be transformed into easements there are many more possibilities that a purchaser will be bound by property rights. However, in registered land, in order for an easement to be overriding (unless it has been exercised within the last year) it must be "obvious on a reasonably careful inspection" of the land.[204] This offers some protection to purchasers and means that even though s.62 may have the effect of creating more property rights, a purchaser will not be bound unless he could have found evidence of the right and thus known of its existence. Therefore, s.62 does not undermine BUILDING BLOCK NO 5 as much as it could have done.

So the main problem with s.62 is that it allows property rights to come into being without people being aware of it, as in *Wright v Macadam*.

LECTURER: And so s.62 could also be dangerous if the servient plot were sold simultaneously with the conveyance of the dominant plot.[205] Accordingly the Law Commission says that s.62 "suffers from a number of serious defects"[206]: "The principal problem is that it transforms precarious interests, such as licences, into property rights".[207] The Law Commission says that this makes s.62 a "trap for the unwary".

Although it has been stated that s.62 works no injustice because the owner, when conveying the quasi-dominant land to the occupant/tenant, can always protect himself by excluding the possibility of an easement in the terms of the conveyance,[208] he may not always appreciate the need to do this, as was clearly the case in *Wright v Macadam*.[209]

(iv) There must be prior diversity of occupation

It is clear from the words of s.62 that even though the two plots of land are in common ownership, there must be a person other than the owner occupying the alleged dominant plot prior to the conveyance. This is known as the rule in *Long v Gowlett*.[210] Section 62 states that easements, rights, liberties and privileges appertaining to the land pass on a conveyance of the land. Without separation of possession there can be no "right" or even "liberty" or "permission". There must be someone to give and to receive it. There can be no jural right without a corresponding burden being suffered by another party. Legally you cannot burden yourself with your own actions (Hohfeld).

In *International Tea Stores Co v Hobbs*[211] Farwell J. appears to take the point that without separation of possession no right could be exercised for the convenience of the dominant

---

204 Land Registration Act 2002 Sch.3 para.3.
205 See e.g. Sargant J. in *Long v Gowlett* [1923] 2 Ch. 177, p.203.
206 (2008) Law Com No.186, para.4.73.
207 para.4.73.
208 *Goldberg v Edwards* [1950] Ch. 247, p.257 per Evershed M.R.
209 [1949] 2 K.B. 744, p.754, Tucker L.J.
210 [1923] 2 Ch. 177.
211 [1903] 2 Ch. 165, p.171.

tenement at the time of the conveyance. In *Sovmots Investments Ltd v Secretary of State for the Environment*[212] Lord Wilberforce stated that

> "The reason is that when land is under one ownership one cannot speak in any intelligible sense of rights, or privileges, or easements being exercised over one part for the benefit of another. Whatever the owner does, he does as owner and, until a separation occurs, of ownership or at least of occupation, the condition for the existence of rights, etc., does not exist".

In *Long v Gowlett*[213] Sargant J. stated the rationale behind the rule in the following way:

> "As it seems to me, in order that there may be a 'privilege, easement or advantage' enjoyed with Whiteacre over Blackacre so as to pass under the statute, there must be something done on Blackacre not due to or comprehended within the general rights of an occupying owner of Blackacre, but of such a nature that it is attributable to a privilege, easement, right or advantage, however precarious, which arises out of the ownership or occupation of Whiteacre, altogether apart from the ownership or occupation of Blackacre."

For example, in *Wright v Macadam* the landlord was the freehold owner of both plots, but he had leased Plot B to a tenant who was, by virtue of the lease, in occupation.

It has been argued that s.62 should operate to convey continuous and apparent easements, even where the dominant plot is not in separate occupation of a tenant or a licensee.[214] However, as this situation is covered by the rule in *Wheeldon v Burrows*, so that no injustice is likely to be done, and as it is inconsistent with the plain wording of s. 62, it is submitted that the rule in *Long v Gowlett* is the preferable approach.

(v) Contrary intention

Because s.62 is based on the implied intentions of the parties, that the conveyance of land should include all those rights exercised for the benefit of the land granted over the land of the grantor, a right will not pass under s.62 where there is a contrary intention.[215] Section 62 will not operate where the parties to the conveyance clearly intend that the right should not pass. This may be expressed in the conveyance itself or derived from the surrounding circumstances of its execution. In *Birmingham & Dudley District Banking Co v Ross*[216] a builder bought land and built

---

212   [1977] 2 W.L.R. 951, p.169.
213   [1923] 2 Ch. 177, p.201.
214   *Broomfield v Williams* [1897] 1 Ch. 602; *Platt v Crouch* [2003] EWCA 1110; The argument is put forward by M.Thompson, *Modern Land Law*, pp. 516–7, citing Roch L.J. in *Payne v Inwood* (1996) 74 P. & C.R. 42, p.47, where the point was that s.62 requires there to have been some use of the putative dominant tenement for the purposes claimed "call it a liberty, privilege, advantage, easement or quasi-easement". The *Long v Gowlett* point was not discussed directly here. In the recent case of *Campbell v Banks* [2011] EWCA Civ 61, Mummery L.J. clearly regarded the point of whether diversity of occupation was necessary to be "in question", but it was not necessary to decide the point in that appeal.
215   Law of Property Act 1925 s.62(4); *Wright v Macadam* [1949] 2 K.B. 744, CA, pp.751-2, per Jenkins L.J.
216   (1888) 38 Ch.D 295.

houses on it. It was known by all that he was going to build further houses in a certain place that might diminish the light into the original houses. When he built the remaining houses this obscured the light into the living rooms of the original three houses. The right to light that they previously enjoyed was clearly shown to have been intended by all to be temporary.[217] Thus, it did not pass on the conveyance of the first houses. It has been said that the burden of proving contrary intention is heavy.[218]

Acquisition of easements by prescription

4

An easement may be acquired where the right has been exercised for a long period of time. We refer to this as *long user*.[219] This is known as acquisition by *prescription* and easements that are acquired in this way come into being entirely informally. As the Law Commission points out in its recent report on easements,[220] there are two common features associated with all methods of acquiring an easement by prescription. Firstly "is the legal fiction that prescriptive use is evidence that an easement was, at some point, expressly granted". Thus when the owner of the alleged dominant tenement has exercised the right claimed for a long period, usually 20 years, the law presumes that he or she is doing so because the right has been expressly granted at some point. The other feature common to all methods of prescription, which flows from the first one, "is the requirement that the claimed right must have been exercised in a particular way",[221] i.e. the person claiming the easement by prescription must have exercised the claimed right *as if he or she had an entitlement to do so*.

In order to claim an easement by prescription it is necessary for the claimant to establish firstly that he has exercised the alleged right *as of right*, and secondly that the easement has been acquired by one of the three methods of prescription considered in section C) below. Easements acquired by way of prescription are legal easements. As with all easements, a right claimed through prescription must first satisfy the *Re Ellenborough Park*[222] criteria.

A. THE EXERCISE OF THE CLAIMED RIGHT MUST BE "AS IF OF RIGHT": NEC VI NEC CLAM NEC PRECARIO

Before a claim to an easement will succeed on the basis of long term use of the servient land, the claimant must have used the alleged right over the servient land *nec vi nec clam nec precario*,

---

217 (1888) 38 Ch.D 295, p.307, per Cotton L.J.
218 *Pretoria Warehousing Co Ltd v Shelton* [1993] E.G. 120; A.Dowling [1994] Conv. 238, p.239.
219 User means "use".
220 Law Commission, *Making Land Work: Easements, Covenants and Profits-à-Prendre* (2011) Law Com No. 327, para. 3.86.
221 Law Commission, *Making Land Work*, above.
222 [1956] Ch. 131.

i.e. without force, without secrecy, without permission.[223] In short he must have used the land as of right, i.e. as *if* he had a *right* or *entitlement* to do so. In *R (Lewis) v Redcar and Cleveland Borough Council (No. 2)*[224] the Supreme Court stated that the person claiming an easement must use the alleged servient land "openly and in the manner that a person rightfully entitled would have used it".[225] The principle at the heart of all prescriptive claims is that the servient owner has *acquiesced* in the claimant's right to use his land. He cannot have done this if he did not know about the use or if the use was with his consent or permission.[226] If you have a right you do not need permission.[227] In *R v Oxfordshire County Council, ex p. Sunningwell Parish Council* Lord Hoffmann observed:

> "The unifying element in these three vitiating circumstances was that each constituted a reason why it would not have been reasonable to expect the owner to resist the exercise of the right – in the first case, because rights should not be acquired by the use of force, in the second, because the owner would not have known of the user and in the third, because he had consented to the user, but for a limited period."[228]

The test is objective. Thus, in *London Tara Hotel Ltd v Kensington Close Hotel Ltd*[229] a right by prescription was established after 20 years continuous use without force, stealth/secrecy, or permission, even though the servient landowner subjectively believed that he had given a personal licence. In fact the licence did not cover the present dominant owner—only his predecessor in title.

Clearly therefore, the claimant's exercise of the right must be uninterrupted for the full prescription period. This simply means that if the servient owner interrupts the use of the right, e.g. by erecting a barrier, then although the claimant can start the use again where the interruption ceases, the time which the right was exercised before the interruption cannot be added to time which the right was exercised after the interruption.

(1) Nec vi—without force

We will now examine these three requirements. Firstly, the right claimed must not have been exercised by force. Thus, if a claimant demolishes a fence in order to exercise a right of way his claim will fail.[230] Force does not mean merely physical force.[231] If the claimant continues to use

---

223   This "tripartite test" is said to be established by high authority, e.g. *Gardner v Hodgson's Kingston Brewery Co Ltd* [1903] A.C. 229: per Lord Walker in the Supreme Court in *R (Lewis) v Redcar and Cleveland Borough Council (No. 2)* [2010] UKSC 11, para.20.
224   [2010] UKSC 11 (Supreme Court, formerly House of Lords).
225   Per Lord Walker para.19, quoting Parke B. in *Bright v Walker* 1 Cr. M. & R. 211, p.219.
226   *Sturges v Bridgman* (1879) LR 11 Ch.D 852, p.863, per Thesiger L.J. Also *Davis v Du Paver* [1953] 1 Q.B. 184, p.210, per Morris L.J. *Mills v Silver* [1991] Ch. 271, CA, p.280 per Dillon L.J.
227   Law Commission, *Making Land Work: Easements, Covenants and Profits-à-Prendre* Law Com No.327 (2011), para.3.92.
228   [2000] 1 A.C. 335, pp.350–351, quoted by Lord Walker in the Supreme Court in *R (Lewis) v Redcar and Cleveland Borough Council (No. 2)* [2010] UKSC 11, para.18; also Thesiger L.J. in *Sturges v Bridgman* (1879) LR 11 Ch.D. 852, p.863.
229   [2011] 1 P. & C.R. DG16, per Roth J.
230   *Newnham v Willison* (1987) 56 P. & C.R. 8. Or breaks down a gate: *Bright v Walker* (1834) 1 Cr. M. & R 211.
231   *R (Lewis) v Redcar and Cleveland Borough Council (No. 2)* [2010] UKSC 11, para.91, per Lord Rodger.

the land after protests by the alleged servient owner then this amounts to using the land with force. As Lord Rodger observed obiter in the Supreme Court "user is only peaceable (nec vi) if it is neither violent nor contentious".[232] The principle is that if use is with force it cannot be reasonable for a right to be acquired against the servient owner.[233]

(2) Nec clam—without stealth/secrecy

Secondly the alleged dominant owner's use of the land must be open and of a nature that would give the servient owner knowledge that a continuous right was being asserted and which might ripen into a legal right against him: *nec clam* (without stealth). The servient owner must have the opportunity to object to the use and to interrupt it. Otherwise he cannot be said to have *acquiesced* in the claimant's entitlement to the use of his land, and because of this, the law could not attribute use to a presumed grant.[234] *But what knowledge must be proved against the servient owner?* In *Union Lighterage Co v London Graving Dock Co*[235] Romer L.J. stated that

> "On principle, it appears to me that a prescriptive right to an easement over a man's land should only be acquired when the enjoyment has been open – that is to say, of such a character that an ordinary owner of the land, diligent in the protection of his interests, would have, or must be taken to have, a reasonable opportunity of becoming aware of that enjoyment."[236]

Therefore, the person claiming the easement must use the servient land openly and in a manner that signifies to the reasonable servient owner that a right to use his land is being asserted against him. This is a question of fact.

Let's consider some examples: in *Mills v Silver*[237] an open but intermittent use of a track for a period in excess of 20 years was held to be sufficient. In *Hollins v Verney*,[238] a claim failed because the land was used rotationally with 13 year gaps in between. Use was insufficiently "open". In *Llewellyn v Lorey*[239] it was argued that the owners of a farm had acquired a right to use heavy business vehicles on a road on the servient land. However, there was insufficient evidence of use of the road by that type of vehicle. If the use of land concerns support for a structure the alleged servient owner must be aware that "his building is in fact supporting the dominant tenement".[240] In *Dalton v Angus*[241] Lord Selborne L.C. stated that it can be presumed that a person knows that "according to the laws of nature, a building cannot stand without vertical or (ordinarily) without

---

232 *R (Lewis) v Redcar and Cleveland Borough Council (No.2)* [2010] UKSC 11, para.90, relying on *Gale on Easements*, 18th edn (London: Sweet & Maxwell, 2008).
233 *Dalton v Henry Angus & Co* (1880–81) LR 6 App. Cas. 740; *Smith v Brudenell-Bruce* [2002] 2 P. & C.R. 4.
234 *Llewellyn v Lorey* [2011] EWCA Civ 37.
235 [1902] 2 Ch. 557, p.570.
236 Also *Hollins v Verney* (1883–84) 13 QBD. 304, p.315, per Lindley L.J. relied on in *Mills v Silver* per Parker L.J. *R v Oxfordshire C.C., ex p. Sunningwell Parish Council* [2000] 1 A.C. 335; *Davis v Du Paver* [1953] 1 Q.B. 184, p.210 per Morris L.J.
237 [1991] Ch. 271, CA.
238 (1884) 13 Q.B.D. 304.
239 [2011] EWCA Civ 37.
240 *Lloyds Bank Ltd v Dalton* [1942] Ch. 466, per Bennett J.
241 (1880–81) LR 6 App. Cas. 740, p.801.

lateral support". Thus, in *Union Lighterage Co v London Graving Dock Co*[242] the supports were invisible so the claim failed.

As the law of prescription is based on an assumed grant, and on the acquiescence of the servient owner, the state of mind of the user of the right is irrelevant.[243] Thus it is of no importance that the claimant mistakenly believed that he had such a right,[244] or that the claimants of the right "deferred" to other users of the land. In *R (on the application of Lewis) v Redcar and Cleveland BC*[245] the Supreme Court held that just because the people claiming the right showed deference to others using the same land, this did not prevent the use from being "as of right" in this case. The question is *how* the land is used and whether the use conveys to the mind of the servient owner that the land is being used as if the claimants had a right to use it. The claimants were regularly walking across the land and using it for various recreational purposes. A reasonably diligent landowner would have noticed that a continuous right of enjoyment was being asserted and unless they wanted to become established by law they must object to it.[246]

(3) Nec precario—without permission

Thirdly, the right claimed should not be enjoyed *prècario*, i.e. with the permission of the servient owner.[247] In *Gardner v Hodgson's Kingston Brewery*[248] Earl of Halsbury L.C. stated that the necessary quality of use required for an easement by prescription is the use of the land *as if* the claimant had a right to do so. Thus, use is

> "against the will of the person over whose property it is sought to be exercised. It does not and cannot mean an user enjoyed from time to time at the will and pleasure of the owner of the property over which the user is sought."

So there can be no easement by prescription if use of the land is attributable to a temporary licence to use the land in a particular way.[249] In *Patel v W.H.Smith (Eziot) Ltd*[250] the claimants argued that they had a prescriptive right to park cars on the servient land. The claim was rejected because the claimants' solicitors had during the 20 year period attempted repeatedly to negotiate for a licence (permission) to park their cars, acknowledging explicitly that their clients had no "right" to park. As the Law Commission observes, "if you have a right you do not need permission".[251] Permission can be implied from the circumstances of the case but it requires an

---

242   [1902] 2 Ch. 557, p.570.
243   *London Tara Hotel Ltd v Kensington Close Hotel Ltd* [2011] 1 P. & C.R. DG16, per Roth J.
244   *Bridle v Ruby* [1989] Q.B. 169, confirmed by the House of Lords in *R v Oxfordshire C.C., Ex p. Sunningwell Parish Council* [2000] 1 A.C. 335.
245   [2010] UKSC 11; [2010] 2 A.C. 70.
246   Although the case concerned the registration of rights to common land under the Commons Act 2006 the principle that the user must be "as of right" is the same.
247   *Ward v Kirkland* [1967] Ch. 194; *Healey v Hawkins* [1968] 1 W.L.R. 1967, p.1973 per Goff J.
248   [1903] A.C. 229, p.231 HL, considered in *Mills v Silver* [1991] Ch. 271, CA.
249   *Gardner v Hodgson's Kingston Brewery Co Ltd* [1903] A.C. 229, p.239 per Lord Lindley. This is provided that user was exercised in accordance with the licence and not outside its scope: *Thomas W. Ward Ltd v Alexander Bruce (Grays) Ltd* [1959] 2 Lloyd's Rep 472; *Mills v Silver* [1991] Ch. 271, CA, p.282 per Dillon L.J.
250   [1987] 1 W.L.R. 853.
251   *Making Land Work, Easements, Covenants and Profits-à-Prendre* (2011) Law Com No.327.

overt or positive act by the servient landowner. In *London Tara Hotel Ltd v Kensington Close Hotel Ltd*[252] a personal licence given to the user's predecessor in title was not taken to be implied permission as far as concerned the successor's use of the same right.

Once permission has been given, the use of the land is not capable of itself "of ripening into a right". It must be established that permission has been revoked and user then continued for 20 years after the revocation.[253]

(4) Interruption and objection

Finally, the right must be exercised without objection and without interruption by the servient owner. Only in this way can the servient owner be said to have *acquiesced* in the use of his land.[254] It is not sufficient for the servient owner within the 20 year period to have the *ability* to object, to say effectively "I tolerated the use".[255] If he is to defeat the prescriptive claim he must object to the use and interrupt it. For example, he must erect a physical obstruction to an access path, or lock a door to a shed that is being used for storage.[256]

> Provided that the user is enjoyed "as of right" and the nature of the easement claimed satisfies the four characteristics laid down in *Re Ellenborough Park*, i.e. it is of the nature of rights known to the law, then it is possible for the claimant to acquire an easement by prescription. This must be done in one of the three methods considered below.

B. THE CLAIM MUST BE ESTABLISHED BY AND AGAINST A FEE SIMPLE OWNER

A right to an easement by prescription must be acquired by the freehold owner of the dominant tenement against the freehold owner of the servient tenement.[257] Tenants, even under very long leases, cannot acquire easements by prescription against each other,[258] and a tenant cannot acquire an easement by prescription over his landlord's adjacent land.[259] However, where the servient tenement is in the possession of a tenant, an easement by prescription may still be acquired against the freehold owner if he knew about the use and could have prevented it.[260] This rule, that the claim to an easement by prescription must be pursued by and against a

---

252 [2011] 1 P. & C.R. DG16, per Roth J.
253 *Healey v Hawkins* [1968] 1 W.L.R. 1967, p.1973 per Goff J.
254 *Mills v Silver* [1991] Ch. 271, CA, p.290 per Parker L.J.
255 *Mills v Silver* above p.281 per Dillon L.J., overturning the judge at first instance on this point.
256 See below for ways of obstructing rights to light.
257 *Ward v Kirkland* [1961] 1 Ch. 194.
258 *Simmons v Dobson* [1991] 1 W.L.R. 720; *Kilgour v Gaddes* [1904] 1 K.B. 457.
259 Thus in *Wright v Macadam* [1949] 2 K.B. 744, where a tenant successfully claimed an easement to store coal in a shed on her landlord's adjacent land under Law of Property Act 1925 s.62, that tenant would have been unable to establish an easement by prescription (had she used the shed for the requisite period).
260 *Williams v Sandy Lane (Chester) Ltd* [2006] EWCA Civ 1738.

freehold owner, has been described recently by Lord Millett as "counter-intuitive and contrary to the policy of the law".[261]

C. ACQUISITION OF THE RIGHT

Once it is established that a right as been exercised uninterrupted, there are three ways of claiming a right through prescription. Firstly, at common law in order to establish an easement by prescription it was necessary to show that the relevant use of the servient land, e.g. as a right of way, had continued since *time immemorial*, i.e. as far back as legal memory goes. The date established for the commencement of legal memory was the beginning of the reign of King Richard I (1189).[262] Thus the right must have been exercised since 1189. This is probably impossible to establish. Thus the law presumes that the right had been enjoyed since 1189 if it has been enjoyed for 20 years. However this presumption is easily rebutted by proof that the right *could not* have been enjoyed since time immemorial, e.g. a right of access to a building where that building had been built since 1189.[263] Consequently this common law method of acquiring an easement by prescription is extremely limited. The Law Commission considered this to be "probably the least satisfactory" of the three methods of prescription.[264]

(1) The fiction of a lost modern grant

"As time marched on and the limit of legal memory slipped further into the past, the vulnerability of a claim based on prescription at common law increased."[265] It became easier to prove that the right could not have been enjoyed since legal memory began in 1189. It accordingly became more difficult as time went on to establish an easement by prescription.[266] For example in *Hulbert v Dale*[267] the use of a road could only have existed for about 100 years so a claim on this common law ground of prescription failed.[268] Thus, the courts invented the doctrine, or rather "fiction", of the *lost modern grant*.[269] If user as of right continues for 20 years the court may presume that there was a grant of the right before such use commenced but that the grant has been lost or destroyed.[270] In this way the claimant can acquire an easement. In *Hulbert v Dale*[271] a lost grant of a right of way was established, giving the claimant an easement by prescription. The use of the road by successive owners of the dominant property had continued as of right for a century.

261　*China Field Ltd v Appeal Tribunal (Buildings)* [2009] HKCU 1650, Hong Kong's highest Court of Appeal: cited and quoted by the Law Commission (2011) Law Com No.327, para.3.145. The Law Commission does not make proposals for reform of this rule.

262　Discussed briefly in *Hulbert v Dale* [1909] 2 Ch. 570, CA; *Bryant v Foot* (1867) L.R. 2 Q.B. 161.

263　*Duke of Norfolk v Arbuthnot* (1880) 5 C.P.D. 390.

264　Law Commission, *Making Land Work: Easements, Covenants and Profits-à-Prendre* Law Com No.327 (2011), para.3.98.

265　Law Commission, *Making Land Work: Easements, Covenants and Profits-à-Prendre* Law Com No.327 (2011), para.3.99.

266　*Bryant v Foot* (1867) L.R. 2 Q.B. 161.

267　[1909] 2 Ch. 570.

268　Although the claim succeeded on other grounds.

269　*Bryant v Foot* (1867) L.R. 2 Q.B. 161; *Healey v Hawkins* [1968] 1 W.L.R. 1967.

270　*Tehidy Minerals v Norman* [1971] 2 Q.B. 528; *Polo Woods Foundation v Shelton-Agar* [2009] EWHC 1361; [2010] 1 P. & C.R. 12.

271　[1909] 2 Ch. 570.

So how could the owner of the alleged servient tenement prevent the claimant from establishing an easement by prescription on this ground? The presumption of a lost grant cannot be rebutted by evidence that no grant was in fact made.[272] The only way of rebutting the presumption that there was a grant, but it has been lost, is to establish that it was *impossible* for such a grant to have been made.[273] For example, as the doctrine of lost modern grant operates by way of a presumption that an express grant of the easement was once made, the claim can be defeated by proving that the person who could have made the grant prior to the 20-year period did not have the capacity to do so,[274] e.g. an authority with no power to grant easements. Unlike under the Prescription Act 1832, as we shall see below, it is not necessary to establish that the user carried on for the 20 years immediately before the bringing of the court action to establish the right. Any period of 20 year user as of right will be sufficient to establish an easement by prescription.[275]

The judicial fiction of the lost modern grant probably does not reflect a great deal of credit on our legal system. In *A-G v Simpson*[276] Farwell J. stated that "it cannot be the duty of a judge to presume a grant of the non-existence of which he is convinced".

(2) Prescription Act 1832

As well as these two common law methods of prescription, there is a statutory method under the Prescription Act 1832.

(a) Easements other than rights to light

Where a right of way or other matter has been continuously enjoyed *as of right* for a period of 20 years *next before action*, an easement can be acquired under the Prescription Act 1832.[277] We will look at each element of this statutory prescriptive claim in turn. Firstly, the claimant of the easement must establish that he has used the alleged servient land as if he had an entitlement to do so, i.e. without force, without secrecy, and without permission. We looked at this in detail above. Secondly, the claimant's use of the land, for example as a right of way, must have been continuous.[278] During the 20 year period the claimant's exercise of the right must have been uninterrupted by the owner of the alleged servient tenement.[279] If the enjoyment of the right is interrupted then this will prevent the claimant from acquiring an easement by prescription. For example, to interrupt the exercise of a right of way the servient owner may erect a barrier.

---

272 *Bridle v Ruby* [1989] Q.B. 169, in which the reservation of an easement had been physically deleted from the relevant conveyance of the land. The claimant had continued to use the right in the mistaken belief as to the validity of the easement: See Law Commission, *Making Land Work, Easements, Covenants and Profits-à-Prendre* (2011) Law Com No.327, para.3.101.

273 *Tehidy Minerals v Norman* [1971] 2 Q.B. 528.

274 *Housden v Conservators of Wimbledon and Putney Commons* [2008] EWCA Civ 200; *Tehidy Minerals v Norman* [1971] 2 Q.B. 528.

275 *Tehidy Minerals v Norman* [1971] 2 Q.B. 528; *Healey v Hawkins* [1968] 1 W.L.R. 1967, p.1976, per Goff J. *Hulbert v Dale* [1909] 2 Ch. 570.

276 [1901] 2 Ch. 671, quoted E.H.Burn, *Maudsley & Burn's Land Law Cases and Materials*, 8th edn (Oxford University Press, 2004); also *Bryant v Foot* (1867) L.R. 2 Q.B. 161.

277 Prescription Act 1832 s.2.

278 *Llewellyn (Deceased) v Lorey* [2011] EWCA Civ 37; (2011) Law Com No.327, para.3.103.

279 Prescription Act 1832 s.2.

Section 4 of the Prescription Act 1832 provides that the dominant owner must have acquiesced in, or submitted to, the interruption for a year. Otherwise he or she may still claim a prescriptive easement.[280] In common with the other methods of acquiring an easement by prescription it does not matter if either the dominant or the servient tenement has changed ownership over the 20 year period, provided the use has continued as of right.

Thirdly, in order to establish a right under the Prescription Act 1832 it must be shown that the right has been enjoyed for 20 years *next before action*.[281] This means that the claimant must show user as of right up to the date on which court proceedings concerning the right were issued.[282] In *Hulbert v Dale*[283] the user had continued as of right for a century apart from a break of 16 years which occurred in the 20 years immediately before the bringing of the legal action to establish the right. Thus, there could be no claim under the Prescription Act 1832. However, a claim of lost modern grant succeeded (see above).

The effect of establishing 20 years uninterrupted and continuous use under the Prescription Act 1832 is that a claim to an easement cannot be defeated by showing that it cannot have existed since 1189. However, the right can be defeated in other ways permitted at common law. For example, prescription is based on the fiction that a grant was made, evidenced by the continuous use as of right. Thus, the claim to an easement can be defeated by evidence that at the relevant time the servient tenement was owned by someone incapable of making such a grant.[284]

After a period of 40 years, s.2 of the Prescription Act 1932 deems the right to be "absolute and indefeasible". The only way of defeating a right enjoyed uninterrupted for 40 years is to show that it was enjoyed by the express consent or agreement of the servient owner *in writing*.[285] What constitutes "agreement or consent"? Any agreement purporting to defeat a prescriptive claim should be construed with reference to the consequences to the parties, the idea being that the agreement should show the use of the right of way, light, or storage etc. to be permissive only. Thus, an express provision in a grant of the land or other agreement that the grantor is at liberty to build so as to obstruct the right should be sufficient.[286]

(b) Rights to light

The position with regard to rights to light is different. The Prescription Act 1832 provides that where a right to light is enjoyed without interruption for a 20 year period next before action, then

---

280 Prescription Act 1832 s.4; *Ward v Kirkland* [1967] Ch. 194, p.231 per Ungoed-Thomas J.
281 Prescription Act 1832 s.4.
282 *Mills v Silver* [1991] Ch. 271, CA, p.278, per Dillon L.J.
283 [1909] 2 Ch. 570.
284 *Housden v Conservators of Wimbledon and Putney Commons* [2008] EWCA Civ 200; Law Commission, *Making Land Work: Easements, Covenants and Profits-à-Prendre* (2011), para.3.87.
285 For this particular time period this modifies the requirement that the claim to the right can be defeated by permission: *nec precario* (see above). After 40 years continuous user the giving of oral permission by the servient owner will no longer defeat the claim to a prescriptive easement.
286 *Mitchell v Cantrill* (1887) 37 Ch. D. 56, pp.59–60 per Cotton L.J. *Willoughby v Eckstein* [1937] Ch. 167, both cases considered in *G & S Brough Ltd v Salvage Wharf Ltd* [2010] Ch. 11.

the dominant owner will have acquired an easement of light by prescription. Unlike all other easements a right to light will be deemed "absolute and indefeasible" after 20 years[287] unless it is shown that it was enjoyed with the *written* consent of the servient owner.[288] There is no need to prove that the right is exercised *as of right*, i.e. without secrecy or force.[289]

A right of light will be so acquired by prescription unless during the 20 period it has been interrupted. As with easements other than light, the interruption must have been submitted to or acquiesced in by the dominant owner for a period of one year after he had notice of the interruption.[290] Because it is difficult to obstruct or interrupt the use of light to a property, s. 2 of the Rights of Light Act 1959 provides that a person who is the owner of land "over which light passes to a dwelling house, workshop or other building" can apply to the local authority to register a light obstruction notice.[291] The effect of this is the same as if a physical obstruction had been erected in the dimensions required to obstruct the light.[292]

(3) Prescription and illegal use

An easement cannot be acquired by prescription where the use of land claimed is illegal. In *Bakewell Management Ltd v Brandwood*[293] the claimant had been driving across common land to his home. The House of Lords held that even though the driving of vehicles across common land without lawful authority constituted a criminal offence,[294] the grant of an easement would constitute "lawful authority". Thus, an easement by prescription was allowed.[295]

Easements and land transfer

5

An easement is capable of being a legal interest in land under s.1(2)(a) of the Law of Property Act 1925. It is necessary for the easement to be created by deed under s.52 of the Law of Property Act 1925. Express grants or reservations of an easement by deed will give rise to legal easements, provided that the easement is of perpetual duration or for a term of years.[296] It is more usual for the easement to be granted or reserved as part of the deed of conveyance of the land itself, which will automatically comply with s.52. An easement will not be legal but may be

---

287   Prescription Act 1832 s.3.
288   Prescription Act 1832 s.3; *Colls v Home and Colonial Stores Ltd* [1904] A.C. 179, per Lord Macnaghten, pp.190–1.
289   *Colls v Home and Colonial Stores Ltd* [1904] A.C. 179: Law Commission, *Making Land Work: Easements, Covenants and Profits-à-Prendre* (2011) Law Com No.327, para.3.107; Under the Prescription Act 1832 s.3, a tenant can acquire a right to light over their landlord's adjacent property: Law Commission, ibid., para.3.108
290   Prescription Act 1832 s.4.
291   The notice once registered will be a local land charge: Rights of Light Act 1959 s.2(4)(a).
292   Rights of Light Act 1959 s.3. See *G & S Brough Ltd v Salvage Wharf* [2010] Ch. 11, CA.
293   [2004] 2 A.C. 529.
294   Law of Property Act 1925 s.193(4).
295   See also *Making Land Work: Easements, Covenants and Profits-à-Prendre*, Law Com No.327 (2011), para.3.96.
296   Law of Property Act 1925 s.1(2)(a).

equitable if it is not of perpetual duration or for a term of years, e.g. an easement "for the life of Harry". Also if the easement is not granted by deed an equitable easement may be recognised where there is an agreement to grant an easement that satisfies s. 2 of the Law of Property (Miscellaneous Provisions) Act 1989.[297]

Implied grants and reservations, for instance, under the doctrines of necessity, common intention and *Wheeldon v Burrows*,[298] will give rise to legal easements as they are implied into the deed of conveyance.[299] Easements acquired under s. 62 of the Law of Property Act 1925 will be legal easements as they are deemed to be included in the deed of conveyance.[300] It is possible to acquire an equitable easement under the rule in *Wheeldon v Burrows*, e.g. where the quasi-dominant plot is for example let under an agreement for a lease, thereby creating an equitable lease under the doctrine in *Walsh v Lonsdale*.[301] Any easement that comes into being will also be equitable. Easements acquired by prescription will give rise to legal easements as they are acquired only by and against a freehold owner and will be, by definition of the rationale of prescription, of perpetual duration. A grant is presumed and thus the deed requirement is met.

A. WHERE TITLE TO LAND IS UNREGISTERED

If the easement is legal it will "bind the whole world", i.e. anyone who comes to own the servient tenement will have to give effect to it. If the easement is equitable in order to bind subsequent purchasers for money or money's worth of a legal estate it must be registered as a Class D(iii) land charge.[302] Otherwise a purchaser of the legal estate will take free from it, whether he has notice thereof or not.[303]

B. WHERE TITLE TO LAND IS REGISTERED

(1) Where the servient land is registered for the first time: first registrations

A legal easement, whether expressly or impliedly granted will be bind the title to the servient land when that title is registered for the first time. It does not matter whether the easement is registered or not, it is an overriding interest.[304] Equitable easements do not override first registration of the title. However, if, whilst the servient land was unregistered, the right had

---

297   Under the doctrine of *Walsh v Lonsdale* (1882) L.R. 21 Ch. D. 9. See Chapter 3.
298   (1879) 12 Ch. D 31.
299   They can only be legal if they are of perpetual duration of for a term or years: Law of Property Act 1925 s.1(2)(a).
300   The Law Commission considered that easements acquired under s.62 are properly regarded as a species of express rather than implied grant: *Making Land Work: Easements, Covenants and Profits-à-Prendre* (2011) Law Com No.327.
301   (1882) L.R. 21 Ch. D. 9. Also Clarke and Greer, *Land Law Directions*.
302   Land Charges Act 1972 ss.2(5), 4(6). See Chapter 7.
303   Law of Property Act 1925 s.199(1)(i).
304   Land Registration Act 2002 Sch.1 para.3.

been registered as a Class D(iii) land charge then the purchaser will take subject to the easement and the land registrar will enter it as a notice on the charges register of the servient title. It will then bind all future dealings with the land: "registrable dispositions".[305]

(2) Expressly granted/reserved legal easements: where the servient title is already registered

An expressly granted or reserved legal easement is a registrable disposition. The burden of the easement must be entered as a notice on the title of the servient tenement, and the benefit registered on the title to the dominant tenement, if that title is also registered.[306] Otherwise the easement does not take effect as a legal easement. It remains equitable until the registration requirements are met.[307] The effect of registration of a legal easement as a registrable disposition is that its validity is guaranteed by the Land Registry.[308] Once registered, all future transactions with the servient land will take effect subject to the easement.[309]

(3) Impliedly granted/prescriptive easements: where the servient title is already registered

An impliedly granted or reserved legal easement, including one which arises by virtue of s.62 of the Law of Property Act 1925, or an easement arising by prescription, is an overriding interest that binds all subsequent purchasers of the servient land for valuable consideration.[310] As we saw in Chapter 8 this means that the easement will bind a purchaser of the servient land even though that right is not registered against the title. Overriding interests are the "crack in the mirror" of the aim of the Land Registration Act 2002, i.e. that the land register should be an accurate reflection of all the interests that are going to bind future purchasers of that land. Such an easement however, will not be overriding if at the time of the transaction with the land, it is not within the actual knowledge of the purchaser and "would not have been obvious on a reasonably careful inspection of the land over which the easement . . . is exercisable".[311]

Even where the easement *is not* within the actual knowledge of the purchaser and *not* obvious on inspection, the easement will still be overriding if it has been exercised within a year prior to the disposition of the servient land.[312] Thus, easements which are vital to the use of the property,

---

305   Land Registration Act 2002 ss.29(2)(a)(i) and 30(2)(a)(i).

306   s.27(2)(d), Sch.2 para.7.

307   s.27(1).

308   Land Registration Act 2002 s.58; The "Insurance Principle" applicable to all dispositions of land required to be registered (Land Registration Act 2002 ss.4 and 27); see also Law Commission, *Making Land Work: Easements Covenants and Profits-à-Prendre*, Law Com No.327 (2011), para.2.12. It appears to be assumed that in order to be so guaranteed the easement in question must still comply with the characteristics of an easement: otherwise it cannot exist at all. However, the Law Commission propose that the law be amended to make this point explicit, i.e. that s.58(1) of the Land Registration Act 2002 (the section that confers the right on the registered grantee/transferee of a registered estate or interest whether he was entitled to it under the ordinary law or not) does not operate "to create an easement that does not accommodate and serve the dominant land": above para.4.17; see the Law Commission's proposed legislation the Law of Property Bill 2011, Sch.3, para.16(3)(b).

309   Land Registration Act 2002 ss.29(2), 30(2).

310   Land Registration Act 2002 s.27, Sch.3 para.3.

311   Sch.3, para.3(1).

312   Land Registration Act 2002 Sch.3, para.3(2). The same provisions of Sch.3, para.3 apply to legal profits-à-prendre.

such as the right for a drain to run under the land, remain overriding interests. Such rights are clearly not visible and will probably not be within the actual knowledge of a purchaser. Thus it was necessary to preserve them. Provided they have been exercised within a year prior to the transaction with the servient land, they will continue to bind purchasers.

(4) Equitable easements: where the servient title is already registered

An equitable easement, expressly granted or impliedly granted, is a right that must be protected by entry of a notice on the servient title. Otherwise it will not bind subsequent purchasers of the servient plot.[313]

6 Extinguishment of easements

An easement can come to an end in several ways. Firstly by express release by deed. Effectively the owner of the dominant tenement releases the servient tenement from the obligation. The Law Commission have pointed out that an express release is not a dealing with land that is required to be registered. So the easement may continue to appear on the title to the servient land, with its validity guaranteed by the state, when in fact the easement has long since ceased to exist.[314]

An easement can be extinguished by "abandonment" e.g. "where there is some act or omission on the part of the owner of land benefited by it, accompanied by an intention to abandon the right".[315] However, an easement will not be treated as impliedly extinguished on this ground if it is possible in changed circumstances in the future for the easement to again be usable. In *Jones v Cleanthi*[316] the servient owner was obliged by statutory fire regulations to build a wall that had the effect of blocking the claimant's right. The easement was held not to have been extinguished because the fire regulations might change in the future and it may again be possible for the easement to be used. It is said that it is difficult to prove that an easement has been abandoned.[317] Simply proving that the easement has not been used will not suffice.[318] The Law Commission recommends that there should be a rebuttable presumption that an easement has been abandoned where it "has not been used for a continuous period of 20 years".[319]

An easement will be treated as extinguished where the dominant and servient lands come into the common ownership and possession of the same person.[320] As we have seen, before an

313   For a description of what a "notice" is and how notices work see Chapter 8.
314   Law Commission, *Making Land Work: Easements Covenants and Profits-à-Prendre*, Law Com No.327 (2011), para.2.66.
315   Law Com No.327, para.3.213.
316   [2006] EWCA 1712.
317   Law Com No.327 (2011), para.2.67.
318   See *Benn v Hardinge* (1993) 66 P. & C.R. 246.
319   Law Com No.327 (2011), para. 3.230; See the proposed legislation: the Law of Property Bill 2011, cl.27.
320   See the Law Commission (2011) Law Com No.327, para.4.22.

easement can be said to exist the dominant and servient tenements must be in the ownership and possession of different persons: the *unity of seisin* rule.[321]

Profits-à-prendre

7

Initially easements and profits look the same in nature. However they are not. Profits are the right to *take something* from land belonging to another.[322] For example, a profit of pasturage is a right to graze horses or other animals on the servient land.[323] A profit of piscary is the right to take fish from land belonging to another. A profit of turbary is the right to take peat or turf.

> "A *profit-à-prendre* is a right to take something off another person's land. It may be more fully defined as a right to enter another's land to take some profit of the soil, or a portion of the soil itself, for the use of the owner of the right."[324]

A "several" profit is where the owner of the profit can exclude the servient owner, so that the servient owner cannot similarly graze his horses on his land, or fish in a stream on his land etc. A profit "in common" is where the servient owner is not excluded.[325]

A profit must satisfy the criteria laid down in *Re Ellenborough Park*.[326] For instance, profits must be limited in scope, e.g. there cannot be a right to graze an unlimited number of animals.[327] There is one exception. We have seen that an easement cannot exist unless there is a dominant and a servient tenement, the first of the *Re Ellenborough Park* criteria. The situation is different with profits-à-prendre. It is possible for a profit to exist *in gross*, i.e. without the owner having to prove that he owns land that is benefited by the right.

A profit a prendre is a legal interest in land under s.1(2)(a) of the Law of Property Act 1925. Where the servient land is registered the express grant or reservation of a profit is a disposition that is required to be completed by registration before it can be legal.[328] However, once it is so

---

321 *Re Ellenborough Park* [1956] Ch. 131.
322 *Polo Woods Foundation v Shelton-Agar* [2009] EWHC 1361; [2010] 1 P. & C.R. 12
323 Above.
324 Halsbury's Law of England (Vol. 16(2), para. 254) relied on in *Polo Woods Foundation v Shelton-Agar*, above; *Duke of Sutherland v Heathcote* [1892] 1 Ch. 475.
325 Law Commission, *Making Land Work: Easements Covenants and Profits-à-Prendre*, Law Com No.327 (2011), para.2.32.
326 [1956] Ch. 131.
327 *Anderson v Bostock* [1976] 1 Ch. 312; *Harris v Earl of Chesterfield* [1911] A.C. 623; *Polo Woods Foundation v Shelton-Agar*, above.
328 Land Registration Act 2002 s.27(1); s.27(2)(d); if the profit is in gross the interest must be registered with title in its own right (unless it has been granted for a period not exceeding seven years) and a notice entered against the title to the servient land: Sch.2 para.6; if the profit is attached to a dominant tenement, as with easements, a notice must be registered in the charges register of the title to the servient tenement and the owner of estate with the benefit of the profit must be registered as its proprietor: Sch.2 para.7. The benefit is registered on title to the dominant land.

registered its validity is guaranteed by the Land Registry. If a profit comes into being by implication or prescription it can be an interest which overrides all subsequent dealings with the servient land under Sch.3 para.3 of the Land Registration Act 2002. It will be overriding unless the purchaser of the servient land does not actually know about the profit and where the profit would not have been obvious on a reasonably careful inspection of the land. However, even if the purchaser did not know about the right and it was not obvious, the profit will still be overriding if it has been exercised in the period of one year prior to the disposition.[329]

<h1>8   Reform of the law of easements</h1>

On June 8, 2011 the Law Commission published its final report *Making Land Work: Easements, Covenants and Profits-à-Prendre*,[330] which makes recommendations for reform of the law in this area. Its aim is to "modernise and simplify some very long-established law which is causing difficulty—and unnecessary cost—by its complexity and antiquity".[331] The Law Commission attach to its Final Report a draft bill: the Law of Property Bill 2011.

A. CRITICAL THINKING: THE LAW REFORM[332]

LECTURER: Let's consider the Law Commission's arguments and proposals for reform against our Building Blocks. We will create argument about whether the law of easements is good or bad depending on the extent to which it supports or undermines any of our Building Blocks.[333]

(1) Problems with the law relating to implied grants

The Law Commission considers that the rules for implying an easement into a grant of land serve a useful function, but are over-complicated:

"[I]t is generally agreed that implication is a useful safeguard, enabling the creation of rights that would have been created expressly but for inadvertence or ignorance and thereby preventing land from falling into disuse or becoming unmarketable."[334]

---

329   Sch.3 para.3(2).
330   Law Com No.327 (2011), following its Consultation Paper *Easements, Covenants and Profits-à-Prendre*, Law Com No.186 (2008). This project followed the earlier Working Paper *Transfer of Land: Appurtenant Rights* (1971) Law Com Working Paper No. 36 and *Transfer of Land: The Law of Positive and Restrictive Covenants* (1984) Law Com No.127 (covenants only).
331   Law Com No.327 (2011), para.1.14.
332   Many of the arguments in this dialogue take points from the Law Commission's Report *Making Land Work: Easements, Covenants and Profits-à-Prendre* (2011) Law Com No.327.
333   For the full text of our Building Blocks plus instructions on how to use them to build argument see Chapter 1.
334   Law Com No.327, para.3.25.

LECTURER: Let's review this law. Can you give me a brief sketch of the law relating to the implied grant/reservation of easements?

STUDENT: I agree that the law of implied grants/reservation provides a useful function in land ownership. It is not always reasonable to expect people to grant or reserve every right that they may need. However, the current law on implied grants/reservations does not appear to have any unifying principles and they seem to undermine rather than support our Building Blocks. Necessity and common intention are both very restricted grounds on which to claim an easement. Land must be absolutely useless without the easement and, for common intention both parties must have in mind the purpose for which the land is to be used.

LECTURER: What situations does this not cover?

STUDENT: The grant or reservation of an easement may not be strictly necessary (in the above sense) but it may still be important for the reasonable use and enjoyment of the land. As far as common intention is concerned, if the conveyance was made a long time ago it might not be easy to prove what the parties intended, or it might not be easy to derive any coherent intentions from the transaction. Thus, there would be no easement on the "common intention" ground.

LECTURER: So we can see here that the law is not giving effect to the type of right that people would reasonably expect to be present when they buy land. The law therefore violates BUILDING BLOCK NO 7.

> **BUILDING BLOCK NO 7: Land Law is "facilitative" and should give effect to people's intentions and expectations regarding their land**
> It is a major function of Land Law to support what people want to do or expect to be able to do with their land—as the Law Commission puts it to *make land work*.

Don't forget that you would need to cite cases and some of the reasoning in the cases in order to support this argument.

Now let's look at the rule in *Wheeldon v Burrows*.

STUDENT: In order to acquire an easement under the rule in *Wheeldon v Burrows* there must have been common ownership and possession of the alleged dominant and servient land. Before sale or lease of the quasi-dominant plot, the common owner must have exercised a quasi-easement over the other plot. When the quasi-dominant plot is sold the purchaser, lessee or donee, will be able to exercise that quasi-easement as a full easement provided that it is "continuous and apparent" and "necessary for the reasonable use and enjoyment of the land".

LECTURER: Is this good law? Does this law support or undermine BUILDING BLOCK NO. 7 (above)?

STUDENT: I'm not sure how to go about creating an argument on *Wheeldon v Burrows* in relation to this BUILDING BLOCK.

LECTURER: Go through the rules you have just stated very carefully—hold them against the Building Block—thinking all the time about the connection between the rule and the Building Block. This is the *imaginative* part of creating an argument.

> **Using imagination in argument**
> Think about what it is we are arguing about. We are basically trying to assess how useful the rule in *Wheeldon v Burrows* is. Does it *make land work* for people? How many situations does it cover? In how many possible situations are parties left without easements when they need them in order to use the land in accordance with their expectations?

STUDENT: *Wheeldon v Burrows* only works to give easements to a purchaser of land where the seller owns and occupies both the sold plot and the adjacent plot over which the easement is claimed *and* where he exercised quasi-easements over his own land. This is quite a narrow situation. Thus, it may not help, for example, a property developer who has built a new housing estate and is selling off the houses one-by-one. Those houses would need easements, of access, drainage and so forth and the developer would not have used such rights as he has just created the housing estate. It is like the *Sovmots* case.

LECTURER: And I'm sure you can find other situations that *Wheeldon v Burrows* does not cover from reading journals such as *The Conveyancer and Property Lawyer* and the recent Law Commission report.

Now think about the type of easement that people will need when they buy land—how might the requirements of the rule in *Wheeldon v Burrows* preclude important types of easement that people will expect to be able to have when they buy land?

STUDENT: Invisible rights such as rights of drainage and some easements of support may not be "apparent" on inspection of the land. If it is necessary to prove *both* that the quasi-easement is continuous and apparent *and* that it is necessary for the use of the land (the current law is uncertain in this respect), then *Wheeldon v Burrows* will not work to give to the purchaser of the dominant land these very important easements.[335]

LECTURER: Good—Now let's look at s.62 of the Law of Property Act 1925. First of all give me a summary of the way the section works to imply easements into a conveyance of land.

STUDENT: Under s.62 of the Law of Property Act 1925 a conveyance of land will be deemed to include all easements that benefit the land. This section has been interpreted to mean that lesser rights, such as licences or mere kindly permission by the servient owner, will be transformed into full easements when the dominant plot is conveyed. The rule is that prior to the conveyance the dominant and servient lands must be owned by the same person but the dominant plot should be occupied by another, such as a tenant or licensee of the owner (the rule in *Long v Gowlett*). And when that tenant's lease is renewed or the dominant land is sold to the occupier/tenant, he will gain as easements all rights and privileges that were exercised prior to the conveyance.

LECTURER: Therefore s.62 of the Law of Property Act 1925 looks broader in application as to the easements that will be implied into conveyances of land. But it only applies where there is a prior diversity of ownership and occupation.

STUDENT: So s.62 will only imply easements in the context of a very limited factual situation. Does this support or undermine BUILDING BLOCK NO 7?

---

335   I am indebted to Jackson, Pearce and Stevens, *Land Law* for this argument.

> **BUILDING BLOCK NO 7:** Land Law is "facilitative" and should give effect to people's intentions and expectations regarding their land
>
> It is a major function of Land Law to support what people want to do or expect to be able to do with their land—as the Law Commission puts it to *make land work*.

Section 62 could potentially have such a useful function. As we have said above it is not reasonable to expect people to always think of everything when land is transferred. The conveyance may omit rights that are necessary to the use and enjoyment of that land, for example rights of drainage and support. However, because of the requirement that the dominant and servient lands should be owned and occupied by different persons (the rule in *Long v Gowlett*) the usefulness of s.62 may be limited.

LECTURER: Possibly—but to strengthen your argument you need to think of situations in which easements need to be implied into conveyances but that will fail to comply with the rule in *Long v Gowlett*.

STUDENT: Where there is a common seller of land, and the dominant plot is not occupied by a separate person at the time of the conveyance, then s.62 will not be of much help. For example it is unlikely that a property developer will allow purchasers of the houses into occupation prior to the conveyance. Thus, s.62 will not imply easements that are necessary to the use and enjoyment of the land, such as rights of drainage and support. Neither may *Wheeldon v Burrows* (see above).

LECTURER: So the question of whether the purchaser acquires important easements, that he or she would reasonably expect to enjoy on the purchase of the land, such as drainage and support, is left in the perilous territory of "necessity" and "common intention".

STUDENT: So I think we could legitimately conclude that in this respect Land Law undermines BUILDING BLOCK NO 7 and is therefore bad law.

LECTURER: In terms of ensuring that Land Law meets the reasonable expectations of sellers and purchasers of land, in terms of the rights that they would expect to enjoy, there is another significant defect in the current law. Think about the *seller's* reasonable expectations when he sells off part of his or her land.

STUDENT: Because of the principle of non-derogation from grant it is much harder to imply a reservation of an easement than a grant. This seems unfair on sellers of land who legitimately omit to reserve easements for the benefit of their own land over the land sold. Yet they will expect to use and enjoy the land and easements (such as access) may be necessary for this purpose, and there may be situations in which it is difficult to prove either strict necessity or that the easement was within the common intention of the parties.

Because Land Law makes it harder to imply a reservation of an easement it undermines BUILDING BLOCK NO 7: The law should give effect to landowners' reasonable expectations. It is not always reasonable to expect people to reserve in a formal way every right they need or expect to have.

LECTURER: Good, you have argued well. Now we must think about whether the law relating to the implied grant and reservation of easements supports or undermines any of our other

BUILDING BLOCKS. Hold up the rules you have just discussed against BUILDING BLOCK NO 6 and think about the possible connections between them.

BUILDING BLOCK NO 6: The Importance of Certainty and Predictability in Land Law Rules

People need to know the clear effects of rules of law. Otherwise they will be uncertain as to the consequences of their actions. People should not have to litigate in order to know where they stand and what the law is.

STUDENT: Well, there is a lack of clarity over the elements that need to be proved in *Wheeldon v Burrows*. And the transforming of precarious rights into full easements under s.62 of the Law of Property Act 1925 is a "trap for the unwary".[336]

LECTURER: But to make your argument properly you need to give an example of what you mean by this and demonstrate how it undermines BUILDING BLOCK NO 6.

STUDENT: In *Wright v Macadam*[337] the landlord's act of kindness to his tenant in allowing her to store coal in his shed became a full easement when the lease was renewed, doubtless to the surprise of both parties. Many people may give their tenants next door permission to do things on their land—simply out of kindness. And then they find that when they renew the lease those "permissions" have become full rights belonging to the tenant—ones that the tenant can exercise against the will of the landlord! This is not what most people would expect. They will be fully unaware of the consequences of their actions, although it may be said that the rule is clear.

LECTURER: And we have seen above how this rule, the transforming of precarious benefits into full easements, may operate to create many new easements. Can you see that s.62 therefore undermines another of our Building Blocks?

STUDENT: Yes, many rights will be transformed into easements—full property rights that bind the servient tenement.

BUILDING BLOCK NO 5: Property Rights and the Protection of Purchasers

If a purchaser of the land is bound potentially by many property rights it makes the sale and transfer of land difficult. As a matter of policy this should be avoided. Thus if the law allows too many different types of easement to come into being too easily, this may potentially mean that there are many more property rights capable of binding purchasers of the land. This may overly restrict what landowners can do with their land and may make it more difficult for the land to be sold. Thus we say that law is good if it prevents this from happening. Because an easement is a property right the rules that recognise their existence must be fairly restrictive.

---

336   Law Commission, *Making Land Work: Easements, Covenants and Profits-à-Prendre* (2011) Law Com No.327.
337   [1949] 2 K.B. 744.

Although our STUDENT is doing very well in creating argument there is more detail, imaginative argument, and case law that could be discussed. Treat our Building Blocks as your starting point.

(a) New rules for implication of easements into a grant of land

The Law Commission proposes that a single test replaces the current complicated grounds of necessity, common intention and the rule in *Wheeldon v Burrows*.[338] This is found in clause 20 of the draft Law of Property Bill 2011.

The grant of an estate in land will be deemed to include an easement that is necessary for the reasonable use of either the land granted or the land retained. The new test will operate to imply both grants and reservations of easements. Thus, reservations of easements under the new law will be implied much more readily. When deciding whether an easement is reasonably necessary the factors the courts should bear in mind are

"(1) the use of the land at the time of the grant;
(2) the presence on the servient land of any relevant physical features;
(3) any intention for the future use of the land, known to both parties at the time of the grant;
(4) so far as relevant, the available routes for the easement sought; and
(5) the potential interference with the servient land or inconvenience to the servient owner."[339]

These factors replicate "the most useful and practical features of the current law" so that the courts should consider issues such as the commonly intended use of the land and the possibility of alternative routes, e.g. for a right of way. Thus if there is a practicable alternative route then the court may come to the conclusion that the litigated right is not necessary for the use of the land.[340] Any physical sign on the servient tenement that the right is used may well be relevant in proving that it is necessary for the use of the dominant land.[341]

The new test will replace the old law.[342] An easement will not be impliedly granted or reserved if the conveyance excludes it.[343]

---

338   (1879) L.R. 12 Ch.D. 31.
339   Law Com No.327, para.3.45.
340   See for example the approach taken in *Wheeler v J.J. Saunders Ltd* [1996] Ch. 19.
341   The likely function of this requirement in the rule in *Wheeldon v Burrows* (1879) L.R. 12 Ch.D 31: See for example Lord Wilberforce in *Sovmots Investments Ltd v Secretary of State for the Environment* [1977] 2 W.L.R. 951, p.168–9.
342   Law of Property Bill 2011, c.20(4).
343   C.20(3).

CRITICAL THINKING: Re-read the dialogue above—Use the same Building Blocks to create an argument about whether the Law Commission's proposal makes the law better or worse

> **BUILDING BLOCK NO 7:** Land Law is "facilitative" and should give effect to people's intentions and expectations regarding their land

> **BUILDING BLOCK NO 6:** The Importance of Certainty and Predictability in Land Law Rules

> **BUILDING BLOCK NO 5:** Property Rights and the Protection of Purchasers

(2) Reform of section 62

As we saw above, s.62 of the Law of Property Act 1925 will transform lesser rights, such as licences, into full easements upon a conveyance of the dominant land. The Law Commission concluded that s.62, in this respect, operated as a "trap for the unwary".[344] Thus, the Law Commission proposes that s.62 will no longer "operate to transform precarious benefits into legal easements" on conveyance of the land.[345] If such an easement is necessary for the reasonable use of the land conveyed or retained, it can be implied under clause 20 of the Law of Property Bill 2011 (above). Thus, the removal of the transformational effect of s.62 is not likely to work serious hardship.[346]

Is this good law?

> Hold this reform against our Building Blocks and think about the connection between them. Which does it support or undermine and why?

BUILDING BLOCKS

(3) Critical Thinking: reform of prescription

The law of prescription is unnecessarily complicated and confused, with overlapping common law and statutory grounds, and reliance on the unbelievable fiction of "lost modern grant".

---

344 Law Com No.327 (2011), para.3.59.
345 Law of Property Bill 2011, cl.21(1)(a).
346 Law Com No.327 (2011), para.3.62.

"The rapid expansion of home ownership, the increasing pressures on land available for development and the almost universal reliance on cars for travel outside the city all mean that the need for a simpler law of prescription has become of more rather than less concern."[347]

However, the Law Commission does not recommend that prescription be abolished.[348] "Prescription regularises the use of land and ensures that use that has continued uncontroversially over long periods does eventually become legitimate and secure".[349] Transfers of land may omit to create important easements, such as easements of light and rights of drainage. In this respect allowing an easement to be acquired by prescription fills an important gap, particularly "in the context of urban development".[350]

LECTURER: Let's consider whether we agree with these criticisms of the law of prescription. Once again can you give me a brief summary of the rules so that we can hold them against our Building Blocks and create an argument.[351]

> Here is a brief summary of the rules of prescription that we will hold against our Building Blocks.

STUDENT: An easement can be acquired where the right has been exercised continuously over a long period. In order to acquire a prescriptive easement the dominant owner's exercise of the right claimed must be "as of right" or "nec vi, nec clam, nec precario" (without force, without secrecy (stealth) and without permission). The basis of prescription is that the right was once properly granted. Thus, it is necessary to show that the servient owner(s) acquiesced in the continued use of their land. Once this is established it is necessary for the claimant of the easement to show that it has been acquired in one of three ways: 1. Because it has been exercised since time immemorial; 2. Under the doctrine of lost modern grant, and 3. Under the Prescription Act 1832.

LECTURER: Now we need to create an argument about the law. Which of our Building Blocks does the current law of prescription support or undermine?

STUDENT: The problem appears to be a lack of clarity and transparency in the law. The doctrine of "lost modern grant" is still relied on in modern cases, for example, where an easement cannot be acquired under the Prescription Act 1832 because the 20 year period relied upon

---

347 *Housden v Conservators of Wimbledon and Putney Commons* [2008] EWCA Civ 200, per Mummery L.J. quoted by the Law Commission in its Final Report *Making Land Work: Easements, Covenants and Profits-à-Prendre* Law Com No.327 (2011), para.3.72.

348 Law Com No.327 (2011), para.3.80.

349 Law Com No.327 (2011), para.3.6.

350 Law Com No.327 (2011), paras 3.77–3.81.

351 Again many of the arguments developed here are taken from points raised by the Law Commission: *Making Land Work: Easements, Covenants and Profits-à-Prendre* (2011) Law Com No.327.

by the claimant does not take place immediately before the legal action (a requirement under the Prescription Act). This doctrine relies entirely on a rather implausible fiction that a grant of the easement was once made but that it has been lost or destroyed. Even where it is proven positively that a grant was *not made* the courts still presumes that one existed.

LECTURER: Good point but make sure that you substantiate your argument with real illustrations from the cases. And in the cases we see that a claimant will often plead all three grounds of acquisition in the alternative—in short hoping that if they throw enough mud at the wall some of it will stick.

STUDENT: So I think that the law of prescription is bad law because it undermines BUILDING BLOCK NO 6.

BUILDING BLOCK NO 6: The Importance of Certainty and Predictability in Land Law Rules

People need to know the clear effects of rules of law. Otherwise they will be uncertain as to the consequences of their actions. People should not have to litigate in order to know where they stand and what the law is.

LECTURER: Yes, I agree with you in principle. But I think we have reached the stage now where you need to be a little more sophisticated in your argument. Apart from the need to illustrate these complexities by using some choice case law examples, I think we need to develop our argument further. By using *imaginative argument* we can really start to use the Building Blocks as strong evidence for an argument that the law is good or bad. This is all about knowing what questions to ask.

Imaginative argument as asking questions: Here, we need to consider the people and organisations that are affected by a lack of certainty and clarity in the law and show just how the law adversely affects *them*.

This is similar to what the Law Commission call an "impact assessment"

STUDENT: Firstly then I will consider the litigants themselves: In a prescription case the arguments raised in court are likely to be more complex than they need to be, because of the three separate and overlapping doctrines pleaded. This results in less certainty and more legal costs. It may be difficult for solicitors to advise their clients accurately (or at least inexpensively) as to whether they have an easement or not.

LECTURER: Now I want you to think about what effect the complexity of prescription law might have on the Land Registry, which, of course, plays an important role in the transfer of land.

What is the role of the Land Registry—it is not just an organisation that records details about the land?

STUDENT: No, when a registrable disposition (such as an easement) is registered the Land Registry guarantees that it is valid. So the easement will come into being *because it is registered*.

LECTURER: What is the effect of this for the owner of the servient land?

STUDENT: They will be bound by the easement and will have to allow it. And by virtue of s.29 of the Land Registration Act 2002 the easement will bind all future owners of the servient land.

LECTURER: So how will the complexities in the law of prescription make life difficult for the Land Registry?

STUDENT: Oh I see! When a person applies to register an easement, or wishes to register an easement on the transfer of the dominant title, the Land Registry will have to apply complex law in order to determine whether the easement is valid. This increases the risk that they will make a mistake. They might register an easement which is not in reality valid.

LECTURER: And why is it so critical that they do not make a mistake?[352]

STUDENT: Because of the principle of "title by registration", i.e. the effect of substantive registration. Once it is registered this gives the claimant an easement, whether it was valid under ordinary principles or not: Land Registration Act 2002, s.58.[353]

LECTURER: This only applies to registrable dispositions. Is an easement one of these?

STUDENT: Yes an easement is a registrable disposition.[354]

LECTURER: The "Insurance Principle" of land registration means that the Land Registry guarantees the validity of a registered disposition. What is the effect of this?

STUDENT: If an easement is mistakenly registered they may have to pay an indemnity to anyone who has suffered loss as a result.

LECTURER: And where the complexity of the law means that the Land Registry has an increased burden to pay compensation who are the people most likely to be affected by this?

STUDENT: They may pass on any increase in costs by way of fees to clients.[355] And this affects anyone who deals with the Land Registry, e.g. ordinary residential purchasers.

LECTURER: So let's summarise the results of our "impact assessment" concerning the way in which the current law of prescription undermines BUILDING BLOCK NO 6.

---

352 For the following argument in a similar context see Law Com No.327 (2011).

353 See Chapter 8. It is thought that this principle would not apply to confer a valid easement where the right is not one that *could be* created under ordinary principles, e.g. the right does not "accommodate the dominant tenement" under *Re Ellenborough Park* principles: See Law Com No.327. The point has never been formally settled so the Law Commission propose legislation to put the matter beyond doubt.

354 Land Registration Act 2002 s.27(2)(d); The principle of "title by registration" applies only to registrable dispositions and not to other interests such as restrictive covenants and estate contracts: Land Registration Act 2002 s.32(3).

355 Law Com No.327.

> **STUDENT:** Ordinary litigants will not fully know where they stand and will often have to argue the three methods of prescription in the alternative. The result of this is that litigation may cost more than it needs to in order to determine the validity of an easement. The complexity or lack of clarity and simplicity in the law could lead to mistakes by the Land Registry, which impact not only servient landowners but everyone.

LECTURER: I think you have argued very well that the law of prescription undermines BUILDING BLOCK NO 6. We can legitimatly conclude therefore that it is bad law. You have demonstrated an ability to use the Building Blocks as a starting point and not a finishing point.

> **BUILDING BLOCK NO 6: The Importance of Certainty and Predictability in Land Law Rules**
> People need to know the clear effects of rules of law. Otherwise they will be uncertain as to the consequences of their actions. People should not have to litigate in order to know where they stand and what the law is.

LECTURER: Are there any difficulties with the "next before action" rule?

STUDENT: It may preclude people from acquiring an easement because they can only show 20 years continuous use at some earlier period. Thus they will not acquire an easement that they have effectively been using and which is probably necessary for the enjoyment of their land—or at the very least the claimant will have to rely on one of the archaic common law methods of establishing prescription. So we might say that the law is not good because it does not efficiently give people the rights that they would expect to have in order to enjoy their land properly. The law of prescription therefore also undermines BUILDING BLOCK NO 7.

> **BUILDING BLOCK NO 7: Land Law is "facilitative" and should give effect to people's intentions and expectations regarding their land**
> It is a major function of Land Law to support what people want to do or expect to be able to do with their land—as the Law Commission puts it to *make land work*.

LECTURER: These are good arguments. But remember that in order to develop your points fully and effectively you will need to cite cases that show these difficulties. You will also find them talked about in the Law Commission Report and in the law journals.

The Law Commission concluded that some reform of the law of prescription is necessary. The law is currently so complicated that "[a] single set of rules would have an immediate beneficial impact on the workload of all aspects of the legal system involved in the law of prescription".[356] The Law Commission recommends that the current law of prescription is abolished and replaced with a single statutory scheme of prescription. This scheme is aimed at simplifying the law of prescription, avoiding litigation because of its clarity, and "ensuring that the scope for prescription is not extended".[357] The proposed scheme is contained in the Law of Property Bill 2011, clauses 16, 17 and 18.

There is a requirement of "qualifying use" of the servient tenement, i.e. that the right claimed should be exercised for 20 years continuously, without interruption,[358] and be exercised without force, stealth (secrecy) and permission.[359] Prescription will no longer be based on the acquiescence of the servient owner in the exercise of the right.[360] There is no requirement that the use should take place immediately before the legal action to establish the right.[361] Rights to light will have to establish the same elements. They will not be treated differently. As under the current law, the easement must be established by a freehold owner against a freehold owner, and an easement cannot be acquired where at the relevant time the servient owner had no capacity to grant the easement.

Building Blocks: Will this proposed reform make good law?

Hold this reform against our Building Blocks and think about the connection between them. Which does it support or undermine and why?

BUILDING BLOCKS

(4) Profits-à-prendre

Because profits-à-prendre are not "essential to make land usable" and they are often onerous to the servient landowner, i.e. they must allow something to be taken from their land, the Law Commission recommends that profits should only be capable of being created expressly or by statute. They should no longer be capable of coming into being by implied grant or by prescription.[362]

---

356 Law Com No.327 (2011), para.3.110.
357 Law Com No.327 (2011), para.3.116.
358 This simply means that if the servient owner interrupts the use of the right, e.g. by erecting a barrier, then although the claimant can start the use again where the interruption ceases, the time which the right was exercised before the interruption cannot be added to time which the right was exercised after the interruption.
359 The meaning of these requirements being established by the current law (above).
360 Although as the Law Commission acknowledges this requirement is largely only a reflection of use without force, stealth or permission and not a separate criterion: para.3.121.
361 Law Com No.327 (2011), para.3.131.
362 Law Com No.327 (2011), para.3.7.

(5) Car-parking easements and the abolition of the ouster principle

The Law Commission noted that the way in which the courts had applied the "ouster" or "excessive use" principle may have the effect of precluding a right to park a car from existing as a valid easement.[363] This would cause considerable difficulty in practice because not only has it been noted that an easement to park a car can add 6.5 per cent to a property's value,[364] but that "Land Registry data . . . suggests that over 7,500 exclusive rights to park were created in 2009/10".[365] Thus, there should be no legal doubt cast over the validity of these rights as easements.

The problem has been caused by a principle connected with the fourth criterion in *Re Ellenborough Park*, i.e. that a right, in order to be recognised as an easement, must be capable of forming the subject matter of a grant. It must be definable and limited in scope. Thus, the right claimed must not involve excessive use of the servient tenement. This was recognised in cases such as *Copeland v Greenhalf*,[366] *Grigsby v Melville*[367] and *Batchelor v Marlow*.[368] In respect of the requirement that the right claimed must not be an excessive use of the servient tenement, the Law Commission saw this as two separate rules: firstly, the right claimed must not amount to exclusive possession of the servient tenement, exclusive possession being "the right to exclude others, involving both factual control and the legal ability to exclude others".[369] This is freehold or leasehold ownership. It is not an easement, which, by nature is a more limited right. Secondly, the dominant owner's use of the land, whether to park a car or store items etc, "must not leave the servient owner without any reasonable use of his or her land".[370] This second principle is often referred to as the "ouster principle".

The Law Commission considers that the ouster principle gives rise to problems, particularly where a purported easement grants rights to make extensive use of the servient land, e.g. a right to park in a defined space. The dominant owner is effectively making almost exclusive use of that particular space.[371] In *Batchelor v Marlow* it was held that a right to park six cars on land that could only accommodate six cars for 9.5 hours a day Monday-Friday, was not capable of being an easement. The right did not leave the servient owner with reasonable use of his land. Thus the Law Commission considers it arguable that a right to park a car, under the existing law, may not always be held to be a valid easement, the servient owner being left with very little use of the land.[372] At any rate the position is unclear and this "lack of clarity puts many valuable parking rights at risk".[373]

---

363 See above, p.605.
364 Law Com No.327 (2011), para.1.4.
365 Law Com No.327 (2011), para.3.204.
366 [1952] Ch. 488.
367 [1972] 1 W.L.R. 1278.
368 [2001] EWCA Civ 1051; see above, p.606.
369 Law Com No.327 (2011), para.3.193.
370 Law Com No.327 (2011), para.3.196.
371 Law Com No.327 (2011), para.3.199.
372 Although the right to park a car anywhere in a much larger space in the servient tenement would not amount to excessive use and would therefore be valid.
373 Law Com No.327 (2011), para.3.204.

Accordingly the Law Commission proposes the abolition of the ouster principle but the retention of the principle that the right must not confer exclusive possession.[374] Thus, provided that the right claimed does not permit the dominant owner to exclude the servient owner from his land, then the right can exist as an easement—however extensive it may be. This would have the effect of overruling *Batchelor v Marlow*.

The difficulty with this reform is that it misidentifies the nature of the problem. As seen above the courts take a much broader and common-sense approach to the question of whether the right claimed amounts to a use that is too extensive. We have compared each case dealing with this issue against fundamental ideas of ownership and easements and seen that cases such as *Batchelor v Marlow* and *Copeland v Greenhalf*, and even *Grigsby v Melville* showed that it was the dominant owners who were in effective control of the land. Although the servient owners were not excluded in the sense that they could have walked upon their land whenever they wished, the dominant owners could not have kept them out, the dominant owners were able to assume an effective control over the land which negated any rational idea of the rights conferred by ownership.[375] If control of the land is at the heart of possession/ownership of the freehold estate then the Law Commission's proposal makes no sense. *Batchelor v Marlow* was perfectly clear that leaving the servient owner "without reasonable use" of his land (the ouster principle) meant in this case that the servient owner's ownership was "illusory". He had virtually no meaningful control powers left.[376] Under the new reform the dominant owner can now exercise rights that leave the servient owner without reasonable use of his land, provided what he is doing does not amount to excluding the servient owner himself. One ventures to ask the Law Commission *what is left?*

---

374   Law of Property Bill 2011, cl. 24.
375   Above, p.606.
376   Indeed, in *Virdi v Chana* [2008] EWHC 2901, para.14, His Honour Judge Purle Q.C. defined the "ouster principle" as recognising that "an easement cannot be claimed if its effect is to deprive the servient owner of the benefits of ownership".

Chapter 12

Freehold Covenants

CHAPTER OVERVIEW

In this chapter you will find:

- Illustrated discussion on the rules for running the benefit and burden of restrictive covenants
- Critical thinking with Building Blocks
- Critical thinking about the legal problems with positive covenants
- Consideration of the Law Commission's recent reform proposals.

Introduction

1

A covenant is a promise made by a landowner usually contained in a deed.[1] It is a promise either to do something on the land, such as maintain a driveway, or *not to do* something on the land, for example, use the land for business purposes or build on it. A covenant is made for the benefit of a neighbouring piece of land, and in this way it is similar to an easement, which must "accommodate the dominant land".[2] In Chapter 10 we considered covenants between a landlord and a tenant. This Chapter concerns covenants between neighbouring freehold owners of land. Positive covenants require the burdened landowner to do something. Restrictive covenants are covenants that restrict the owner's use of the land. They prevent her from doing something. We are largely concerned with restrictive covenants, as these may be enforced against successors in title to the burdened land. This makes them property rights.[3] If you remember from Chapter 2, a restrictive covenant is always an equitable interest in land. It is not in the list of interests that are capable of existing as legal interests provided for by s.1(2) of the Law of Property Act 1925.[4]

---

1   Law Commission, *Making Land Work: Easements, Covenants and Profits à Prendre* (2011, Law Com No.327), para.2.37.
2   See *Re Ellenborough Park* [1956] Ch. 131.
3   Law Commission, above, para.2.37.
4   Law of Property Act 1925 ss.1(2) and (3).

Covenants help to regulate the use of land and to preserve the character of a neighbourhood.[5] Covenants are often created when a landowner sells part of his land to another, or when a property developer builds a housing estate. The latter will want to preserve the character of the estate, for example by preventing the purchasers of the houses from building any further on the land.

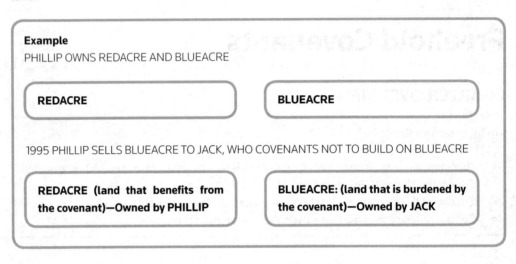

Example

PHILLIP OWNS REDACRE AND BLUEACRE

> **REDACRE**

> **BLUEACRE**

1995 PHILLIP SELLS BLUEACRE TO JACK, WHO COVENANTS NOT TO BUILD ON BLUEACRE

> **REDACRE (land that benefits from the covenant)—Owned by PHILLIP**

> **BLUEACRE: (land that is burdened by the covenant)—Owned by JACK**

"Covenants have their origin in the law of contract".[6] In our example above the covenantor (Jack) and covenantee (Phillip) have entered into a contract. The promises were made under the deed of conveyance of Blueacre to Jack and are enforceable by the parties themselves, as a contract. So if Jack breaches the covenant and builds three houses on Blueacre, then Phillip may sue Jack for breach of contract. However, under the doctrine of privity of contract only Jack and Phillip may sue or be sued on the contract.[7] Thus, if Jack sells Blueacre to Alison and Phillip sells Redacre to Mr Smith, under the doctrine of privity of contract Mr Smith cannot sue Alison for breach of contract if she builds on Blueacre.

However, there are limited circumstances in which someone other than the covenantee can enforce the benefit of the covenant. Under s.56 of the Law of Property Act 1925,

> "A person may take an immediate or other interest in land, or other property, or the benefit of any condition, right of entry, agreement over or respecting land, although he may not be named as a party to the conveyance or other instrument."

Although this may look like s.56 allows a covenant to be enforced by successors in title to the benefited land,[8] and thus it would have meant that Mr Smith (in our example) could take the

---

5   Gray and Gray, *Elements of Land Law,* 4th edn (Oxford University Press, 2004).
6   Law Com No.327 (2011), para.2.37.
7   Law Com No.327 (2011), para.2.37.
8   M.P.Thompson, *Modern Land Law,* 4th edn (Oxford University Press, 2009), p. 527—and was at one time interpreted in this way: *Drive Yourself Car Hire Co (London) Ltd v Strutt* [1954] 1 Q.B. 250 also *Stromdale & Ball Ltd v Burden* [1952] Ch. 223.

benefit of the covenant and enforce it against Jack (but not Alison), it does not have this effect. The section was only designed to change an old common law rule that "no one can sue on a covenant in a [deed] who is not mentioned as a party to it".[9] Section 56 does not have the broad effect contended at the start.[10] All it means is that a person does not need be named as a party to the deed if the covenant purports to have been made with him. Thus, if Jack had covenanted with Phillip for the benefit of Phillip's land and with X for the benefit of his adjoining land, then X, even though not a party to the deed, may take the benefit of the covenant. The covenant must purport to be made with X.[11] Because of this the party claiming the advantage of s.56 must have been identifiable at the time of the original conveyance.[12]

However, under the Contracts (Rights of Third Parties) Act 1999[13] a "person who is not a party to a contract" may enforce it, if "the contract expressly provides that he may, or . . . [a] term purports to confer a benefit on him".[14] Thus, for a covenant created after May 11, 2000 the benefit may be enforced by a person even though the covenant is not made *with* him or her, provided it confers a benefit on him or her. The third party need not even be in existence at the time.[15]

A. COVENANTS CAN BE PROPERTY RIGHTS

Under certain circumstances it is possible for freehold covenants to be enforceable by and against successors in title to the original covenantee and covenantor. The benefit is capable of being "annexed" to the land and the burden can pass to successors in title under the rule in *Tulk v Moxhay*,[16] provided the covenant "touches and concerns" the land. Thus, if (taking our example above) Jack sells Blueacre to Alison and Phillip sells Redacre to Mr Smith, it may be possible for Mr Smith to sue Alison for breach of covenant if she builds on Blueacre. And thus, once it is possible for the burden of the covenant to run with the land and be enforceable against purchasers of the land, it is a property right.[17]

---

9   *Forster v Elvet Colliery Co Ltd* [1908] 1 K.B. 629, p.639 per Farwell L.J.
10   *Beswick v Beswick* [1968] A.C. 58.
11   *White v Bijou Mansions Ltd* [1938] Ch. 351, per Simonds J. Also E.H.Burn, *Maudsley & Burn Land Law Cases and Materials*, 8th edn (Oxford University Press, 2004), pp.992–3.
12   *Amsprop Trading Ltd v Harris Distribution Ltd* [1997] 1 W.L.R. 1025.
13   The Act applies to contracts that come into being after May 11, 2000.
14   s.1.
15   Contracts (Rights of Third Parties) Act 1999 s.1(3).
16   (1848) 2 Ph. 774.
17   Law Com No.327 (2011), para.2.41.

Example

In 1998 Phillip sells Redacre to Mr Smith and Jack sells Blueacre to Alison who proceeds to build three houses on Blueacre in breach of the covenant. The burden of the covenant must pass to Alison before she can be sued for breach.

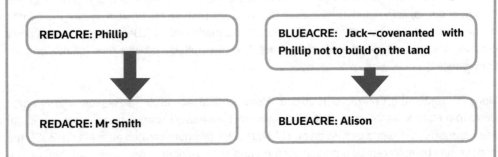

A covenant is capable of being a property right which attaches to the burdened land and can be enforced against successors in title. If this is the case and the burden of the covenant has run with Blueacre, Alison can be sued for breach. But if Redacre, the benefited land, has also changed hands it must also be proven that the benefit of the covenant has run with Redacre.

It is essential to be able to identify someone who can enforce the benefit of the covenant against someone who is subject to the burden of the covenant. Without both the covenant is unenforceable. There are different rules for running the benefit and running the burden, so we must consider the benefit and burden separately. There are different rules at common law and in equity. Therefore we will need to consider four sets of rules.

 Rules for running the benefit and burden of covenants

A. THE BURDEN

(1) Running the burden at common law

The burden of a covenant can never pass to a new owner of the land at common law. The common law sees the covenant as a contract and will not enforce the burden against anyone who is not a party to the contract.[18] This rule was confirmed by the House of Lords in *Rhone v*

---

18   *Austerberry v Corporation of Oldham* (1885) L.R. 29 Ch. D 750.

Stephens.[19] In this case there were two adjoining houses. There was a covenant that one of the owners would keep the shared roof in repair. This was unenforceable against successors in title to the burdened land. The common law will not impose such legal obligations on people who have not agreed to undertake them.

> **Thus, to take our example above, under the common law the burden of Jack's covenant with Phillip restricting the use of Blueacre will not be enforceable against Alison.**

(2) Running the burden in equity

The rule in *Tulk v Moxhay*[20] provides that under certain circumstances the burden of a covenant can run with the land and pass to successors in title of the burdened land. In this case Tulk sold an open plot of land in Leicester Square to a purchaser, who covenanted to "keep and maintain the said piece of ground . . . in an open state, uncovered with any buildings". The burdened land then passed through several successors in title to the defendant. The defendant knew of the covenant but claimed that it did not bind him as a successor in title to the burdened land. Lord Cottenham L.C. held that the defendant was bound by the covenant:

> "the question is . . . whether a party shall be permitted to use the land in a manner inconsistent with the contract entered into by his vendor, and with notice of which he purchased. Of course, the price would be affected by the covenant, and nothing could be more inequitable than that the original purchaser should be able to sell the property the next day for a greater price, in consideration of the assignee being allowed to escape from the liability which he has himself undertaken."[21]

Lord Cottenham L.C. considered that it was important for covenants to be enforceable between successors in title. Otherwise "it would be impossible for an owner of land to sell part of it without incurring the risk of rendering what he retains worthless".

Before considering the conditions that now must be satisfied before the burden of a freehold covenant can run with the burdened land to successors in title, it is necessary to note one point. You will see that the defendant was bound by the covenant in *Tulk* because he had notice of it. This does not apply in modern land law. It is now irrelevant that a purchaser had notice of a covenant. In order to bind a purchaser, the burden of the covenant must be registered, as a "notice" in registered land law,[22] and as a class d(ii) land charge in unregistered land law.[23]

---

19 [1994] 2 A.C. 310.
20 (1848) 2 Ph. 774.
21 Quoted in E.H.Burn, *Maudsley & Burn Land Law Cases and Materials*, pp.942–3; also *Formby v Barker* [1903] 2 Ch. 539; *Re Nisbet and Potts' Contract* [1905] 1 Ch. 391.
22 Land Registration Act 2002 ss.29 and 30.
23 Land Charges Act 1972 s.2(5).

There are a number of conditions that must be satisfied before the burden of a covenant will run with the land under the rule in *Tulk v Moxhay*.

(a) The covenant must be restrictive

The burden of positive covenants can never run with the land.[24] The House of Lords reaffirmed this rule in *Rhone v Stephens*[25] in which it was held that a covenant to keep a roof in repair was unenforceable because it was positive rather than restrictive. A positive covenant requires the burdened landowner to undertake some activity or expenditure, for example, maintain a fence or roof, or build a wall.[26] A restrictive covenant *prevents* the burdened landowner from doing something on his land. What is "positive" or "restrictive" does not depend on the words used. It is a question of the *substance* of what is agreed.[27]

> **BLUEACRE:** Had Jack covenanted to "maintain Blueacre free from buildings" this would be in substance restrictive, despite the apparent positive words of the covenant.

The principle that holds that the burden of a positive covenant will not run with the burdened land is so entrenched that the House of Lords considered it was a matter for parliament to reform the law.[28]

There are a number of indirect methods of enforcing positive covenants that we will consider in section 3 below.

(i) Critical Thinking

The rule that only restrictive covenants run with the land serves to maintain a system of property rights that is certain and predictable. If positive burdens could bind successors in title, this would create an undesirable number of property rights that impose onerous obligations on landowners. So this is potentially good law on the basis of two of our Building Blocks. We might argue that this rule preventing the burden of positive covenants from running with the land is good and fair law because it contains the number of rights that can come into existence as property rights. It is clear and predictable.

> **BUILDING BLOCK NO 6: The Need for Certainty and Predictability in Land Law Rules**
> If the rules are clear as to how they will apply in future cases, i.e. if they allow people (e.g. purchasers or occupiers) to predict the outcome of their actions then they are good law.

---

24 *Austerberry v Corporation of Oldham* (1885) L.R. 29 Ch.D 750.
25 [1994] 2 A.C. 310.
26 *Haywood v Brunswick Permanent Building Society* (1881–82) L.R. 8 QBD 403.
27 *Haywood v Brunswick Permanent Building Society*, above.
28 [1994] 2 A.C. 310, p.321 per Lord Templeman. We will consider recent proposals for reform below.

We might also say that this is good for purchasers of land in general as it means that fewer rights can be made to bind the land and the rights that do bind the land, will not impose positive obligations on the new owner.

> **BUILDING BLOCK NO 5: Property Rights and the Protection of Purchasers and Mortgage Lenders**
> We can argue that a development of a rule in a case or statute is good or bad fair or unfair, depending on the extent to which it supports or undermines the idea that rules of Land Law should protect a purchaser or mortgage lender from being bound by prior interests in the land. This is the policy behind the 1925 property legislation.

On the other hand, as we saw above, a covenant must be registered in order for the burden of the covenant to bind successors in title. Thus, a purchaser will have a ready means of ascertaining whether there are any rights that will bind him after the purchase. Furthermore, the rule that prevents the burden of positive covenants from running with the land has been said by the Law Commission to be a "major weakness in English law".[29] The rule means that repairing obligations cannot be enforced once the burdened land is sold. The rule is

"the principal reason why freehold flats are inadvisable (since the physical interdependence of the property means that the owners of the flats must be required to take positive steps to maintain their property and any common parts such as the roof)".[30]

(b) It is necessary for there to be land that is benefited by the covenant

In order for the burden of a restrictive covenant to be enforceable, the covenant must have been entered into for the benefit of identifiable land. In *London County Council v Allen*[31] the defendant had covenanted not to build on part of his land, in order to allow the LCC to widen a road.[32] His wife then became owner of the land and built upon it in breach of the covenant. It was held that the plaintiff local authority could not sue on the covenant because they had not retained any land that benefited from the covenant. Scrutton J. considered the decision "regrettable" as the covenantee's wife had taken the land knowing of the covenant and the covenant served a useful public purpose. However, the material point was that a restrictive covenant is an "equitable interest analogous to a negative easement", which cannot exist unless the easement is of benefit to dominant land.[33]

Consequently, the covenant must "touch and concern" the benefited land.[34] This is similar to the requirement in the law of easements that the right claimed as an easement must benefit

---

29   Law Commission, *Making Land Work: Easements, Covenants and Profits à Prendre* (2011, Law Com No.327), para.2.41.
30   Law Com No.327, para.2.41.
31   [1914] 3 K.B. 642.
32   *Maudsley & Burn*, above, p.943.
33   [1914] 3 K.B. 642; also, *Formby v Barker* [1903] 2 Ch. 539.
34   *Smith and Snipes Hall Farm Ltd v River Douglas Catchment Board* [1949] 2 K.B. 500; *P & A Swift Investments v Combined English Store Groups* [1989] A.C. 632; *Rogers v Hosegood* [1900] 2 Ch. 388.

the dominant tenement.[35] This means that the land itself must benefit from the covenant. It must not confer a purely personal advantage on the owner, e.g. a covenant to pay for the owner to go to Lords Cricket ground. The covenant will not touch and concern the alleged benefited land if there is insufficient proximity with the burdened land.[36]

> In our example, with Phillip and Jack, the covenant by Jack to restrict the amount of building on Blueacre is clearly of benefit to Redacre and not just to Phillip. A covenant restricting the amount of buildings on land is likely to preserve the amenity and value of the benefited land.

> We will consider more on this requirement that the covenant must "touch and concern" the land below.

(c) It must be intended for the covenant to run with the land

The covenant must be intended by the parties to be enforceable against successors in title of the burdened land, thus creating a property right.[37] In the case of covenants made after 1925, the intention to bind successors is implied unless there is something in the documentation that displays a contrary intention. Section 79 of the Law of Property Act 1925 provides that

> "A covenant relating to any land of a covenantor or capable of being bound by him, shall unless a contrary intention is expressed, be deemed to be made on behalf of the covenantor on behalf of himself his successors in title and the persons deriving title under him or them and, subject as aforesaid, shall take effect as if such successors and other persons were expressed."[38]

Section 79 will not imply an intention that the burden should run with the land where the covenant in the deed shows a contrary intention. It need not be stated expressly that "the covenant is made with the intention that it should be personal only and should not bind successors in title to the burdened land", although this of course, would suffice. It can be implied from the wording and the context of the deed. What we are looking for is an intention that the covenant "on its natural construction, is manifestly intended to be personal only".[39]

---

35   *Re Ellenborough Park* [1956] Ch. 131, i.e. the right must "accommodate the dominant tenement". See Chapter 11.
36   *Kelly v Barrett* [1924] 2 Ch 379.
37   M.P.Thompson, *Modern Land Law*, p.534.
38   In *Rhone v Stephens* [1994] 2 A.C. 310 the House of Lords confirmed that s.79 does not have the "effect of making the burden of positive covenants run with the land": per Lord Templeman; also *Jones v Price* [1965] 2 Q.B. 618.
39   *Re Royal Victoria Pavilion, Ramsgate* [1961] Ch. 581, p.589 per Pennycuick J.

> If Jack had covenanted with Phillip to the effect that "Jack covenants with Phillip for the benefit of Redacre, that Jack will not build on Blueacre", the implication is that it is intended to bind Jack and Jack only—not his successors in title.
>
> *Re Royal Victoria Pavilion, Ramsgate* [1961] Ch. 581

(d) The covenant must be registered

As we saw above under the case of *Tulk v Moxhay* it used to be the case that the burden of the covenant would only bind a successor in title if they had notice of the covenant.

(i) Restrictive covenants entered into post-1925

Since the 1925 property legislation curtailed the operation of the doctrine of notice,[40] the following rules apply: in unregistered land a restrictive covenant should be registered as a Class D(ii) land charge. If it is not so registered it will not bind a purchaser of the burdened land for money or money's worth.[41] If it is registered, the registration is deemed to constitute actual notice and any purchaser of the burdened land will be bound by it.[42] In registered land a restrictive covenant should be protected by entry of a notice against the title to the burdened land on the land register. It will then bind all further dealings with that title.[43] A covenant is not an overriding interest. Thus, if it is not registered it will not bind a purchaser of the burdened land.

(ii) Restrictive covenants entered into before 1925

For covenants created before the 1925 legislation came into force the doctrine of notice determines the issue of whether a purchaser of the burdened land is bound by it.

B. THE BENEFIT

It is insufficient merely to prove that the burden of the covenant has passed to a successor in title. It must also be shown that there is someone to enforce the benefit of the covenant. Thus it is necessary to show that the benefit runs with the land.

(1) Running the benefit at law

Since 1368 it has been possible for the benefit of a freehold covenant to pass with the land to successors in title of the covenantee.[44] However, certain conditions must be satisfied. The leading case is *Smith and Snipes Hall Farm Ltd v River Douglas Catchment Board*.[45] The

---

40   See Chapters 7 and 8.
41   Land Charges Act 1972 s.4(6).
42   Law of Property Act 1925 s.198.
43   Land Registration Act 2002 ss.29 and 30.
44   *The Prior's Case* (1368) Y.B. 42.
45   [1949] 2 K.B. 500.

defendants covenanted with adjoining landowners that they would widen and maintain the river banks of the Eller Brook. The first plaintiff was a purchaser from one of the original covenantee landowners. He granted a lease of the land to Snipes Hall Farm. The plaintiffs' land was flooded as the defendant Board had not maintained the banks as required by the covenant.[46] It was held that the covenant could be enforced by both plaintiffs. The case laid down four criteria that must be met before the benefit can be enforced by a successor in title to the original covenantee.

(a) The covenant must be one that "touches and concerns" the land

In *Smith and Snipes Hall Farm Ltd v River Douglas Catchment Board*[47] Tucker L.J. described the requirement that the covenant must touch and concern the land in the following way:

> "It is first necessary to ascertain from the deed that the covenant is one which 'touches or concerns' the land, that is, it must either affect the land as regards mode of occupation, or it must be such as per se, and not merely from collateral circumstances, affects the value of the land".[48]

In *Smith and Snipes Hall Farm* the covenant to maintain the riverbank clearly touched and concerned the land. Tucker L.J. observed that "[i]t affects the value of the land per se and converts it from flooded meadows to land suitable for agriculture".

In *P & A Swift Investments v Combined English Stores Group Plc*[49] Lord Oliver considered that a "satisfactory working test" for whether a covenant touches and concerns the land is as follows:

> "(1) the covenant benefits only the [covenantee] for the time being, and if separated from the [land] ceases to be of benefit to the covenantee;
> (2) the covenant affects the nature, quality, mode of user or value of the land of the [covenantee];
> (3) the covenant is not expressed to be personal (that is to say neither being given only to a specific [covenantee] nor in respect of the obligations only of a specific [covenantor]);
> (4) the fact that a covenant is to pay a sum of money will not prevent it from touching and concerning the land so long as the three forgoing conditions are satisfied and the covenant is connected with something to be done on, to or in relation to the land."

---

46   E.H.Burn, *Maudsley & Burn Land Law Cases and Materials*, p.951.
47   [1949] 2 K.B. 500.
48   [1949] 2 K.B. 500, p.506, citing *Congleton Corpn v Pattison* (1898) 10 East 135; *Rogers v Hosegood* [1900] 2 Ch. 395.
49   [1989] A.C. 632, p.642.

In our example above we saw how the restrictive building covenant between Jack and Phillip "touched and concerned" the land. A covenant that restricted the covenantor from building on the land would affect the mode of occupation of the benefited land. It would prevent the land from becoming densely built up and crowded. It is also possible that it would prevent the benefited land from losing value, which might happen if the adjoining land was built upon.

In relation to the *P & A Swift Investments* test it is clear that a covenant restricting building on Blueacre will only benefit Phillip *whilst he is the owner of Redacre*. The covenant is not expressed to be personal, i.e. there is nothing implied in the deed that suggests that the covenant is only intended to be enforceable between Phillip and Jack. Thus, it appears that the covenant touches and concerns the benefited land.

There are just two final observations to be made. You may remember that the burden of a positive covenant can never run with the land. But where the original covenantor has not sold the land, he can bind himself to a positive covenant and this may be enforced against him under the *Smith and Snipes Hall Farm* rules by successors in title to the benefited land. Indeed in that case the covenant in question was a positive covenant. Thus, a covenant to pay money would touch and concern the land provided that it affected the land in some way, e.g. a payment towards maintenance.

Secondly, *Smith and Snipes Hall Farm* established that it is not necessary for the covenantor to retain any land. This is unlike the rule that stipulates that in order to run the burden in equity the covenantee must retain land to be benefited. This is because when you are looking at running the burden this effectively means that a covenant is turned into a property right, i.e. the burden of an obligation capable of binding successors in title. The rule has the effect of limiting the ambit of the burdened landowner's obligations. The same restriction is not needed when looking at allowing the enforcement of the benefit by successors in title *against the original covenantor*.

(b) The land must be identifiable

The land to be benefited must be identified in the deed, for example in extent and situation.[50] This can be clarified through use of extrinsic evidence.[51]

(c) The successor must have a legal estate in the land derived from the legal estate of the original covenantee

In the *Smith and Snipes Hall Farm* case both plaintiffs had a legal estate. Smith had acquired the freehold from one of the covenantee landowners and Snipes Hall Farm was Smith's tenant

---

50   *Smith and Snipes Hall Farm Ltd v River Douglas Catchment Board* [1949] 2 K.B. 500.
51   [1949] 2 K.B. 500, per Tucker L.J.

under a legal lease. Denning L.J. held that the tenant could sue on the covenant. It used to be thought that the successor in title must have the same legal estate as the predecessor, i.e. the freehold, but now it is only necessary that the successor derived his legal estate from either the original covenantee or his successor, i.e. a tenant of such persons. Denning L.J. held this to be the effect of s.78(1) of the Law of Property Act 1925:

"A covenant relating to any land of the covenantee shall be deemed to be made with the covenantee and his successors in title and the *persons deriving title under him* or them, and shall have effect as if such successors and other persons where expressed."[52]

(d) Intention that the benefit of the covenant shall run with the land

It is necessary that the covenant in the deed "shows an intention that the benefit of the obligation. . . shall attach [to the land] into whosesoever hands the lands shall come".[53] In *Smith and Snipes Hall Farm* the deed stipulated that in return for monetary payment from adjoining landowners the defendants covenanted with those landowners to carry out work on the riverbanks on the Eller Brook and to maintain the work for all time. It was held that this showed sufficient intention that the obligation should be enforceable by all future owners of the benefited land.[54]

> A statement in the deed that the covenantor *covenants with the covenantee and his successors in title and heirs and assigns* will also show that the benefit is intended by the original parties to run with the land.

However, even if there is no express intention that the benefit should run with the land this is implied into the covenant by s.78 of the Law of Property Act 1925.[55] Section 78(1) provides that

"A covenant relating to any land of the covenantee shall be deemed to be made with the covenantee and his successors in title and the persons deriving title under him or them, and shall have effect as if such successors and other persons were expressed."

This will only have the effect of implying an intention into the covenant that the benefit should be enforceable by successors in title to the benefited land insofar as there is no intention to the contrary in the deed itself. For example, if a covenant between Phillip and Jack that "Jack agrees not to build on Blueacre for the benefit of Redacre only and insofar as Phillip retains the ownership of Redacre", this would show that the parties did not intend the benefit to run with Redacre and benefit all future owners of the land. In effect the covenant is expressed to be personal.[56]

---

52   Emphasis added.
53   *Smith and Snipes Hall Farm Ltd v River Douglas Catchment Board* [1949] 2 K.B. 500, p.506 per Tucker L.J.
54   Above, p.506, per Tucker L.J.
55   *Federated Homes v Mill Lodge Properties* [1980] 1 W.L.R. 594.
56   *Crest Nicholson v McAllister* [2004] EWCA Civ 410.

However, for s.78 to operate to imply an intention that the benefit should run, it is still necessary for the benefited land to be identified in the deed that creates the covenant, with the help of extrinsic evidence if necessary,[57] and that the covenant should "touch and concern" the land.[58] We considered these requirements above.

(e) Summary

If these four conditions in *Smith and Snipes* are satisfied a successor in title of the original covenantee can enforce the covenant against the original covenantor.

Example

As you may remember from our example Phillip was originally the owner of both Redacre and Blueacre. Phillip sells Blueacre to Jack, who, for the benefit of Redacre, covenants not to build on Blueacre. Then Phillip sells Redacre to Mr Smith and let's say that Jack has not sold Blueacre and remains the owner.

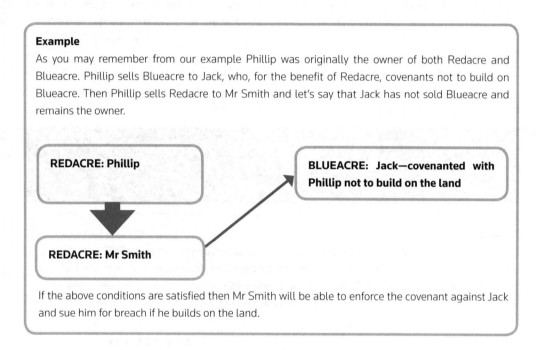

If the above conditions are satisfied then Mr Smith will be able to enforce the covenant against Jack and sue him for breach if he builds on the land.

If you are seeking to enforce a covenant not only by a successor in title to the benefited land but against a successor in title to the burdened land, it must be proven that the benefit runs in equity. This is because it is necessary to prove that both benefit and burden have run with the land, and that both benefit and burden have run through the same set of rules, i.e. either at common law or in equity. Thus, because the burden of a covenant is unenforceable at law against successors in title, if the burdened land has been sold then it is necessary to run the benefit in equity.[59]

---

57   Implied in *Smith and Snipes*, above p.509, per Tucker L.J. and confirmed in *Crest Nicholson v McAllister* [2004] EWCA Civ 410.
58   *Smith and Snipes Hall Farm Ltd v River Douglas Catchment Board* [1949] 2 K.B. 500, p.506, per Tucker L.J. *Federated Homes v Mill Lodge Properties* [1980] 1 W.L.R. 594.
59   *Renals v Cowlishaw* (1878) L.R. 9 Ch. D 125; *Re Union of London and Smith's Bank Ltd's Conveyance, Miles v Easter* [1933] Ch. 611.

Thus, if in our example, Jack had sold Blueacre to Alison, who then built on the land, Mr Smith could sue Alison for breach of covenant only if he could prove that the benefit transmitted to him under the equity rules and the burden had passed to Alison under the *Tulk v Moxhay* rules (above).

(2) Running the benefit in equity

Firstly it must be proven that the covenant "touches and concerns" the benefited land, in accordance with the tests above. Then it must be shown that the covenant has been *annexed* (attached) to the land, or has been *assigned* to the claimant by her predecessor in title to the benefited land, or the covenant was intended to be enforced as part of a *building scheme*.[60]

(a) Annexation

If the benefit of the covenant has been "annexed" to the land this means that it has become attached to the land and will therefore be enforceable by every successor in title to the original covenantee, provided that the burden also runs with the land.

The covenant runs "because the purchaser has bought something which inhered in or was annexed to the land bought".

Rogers v Hosegood [1900] 2 Ch.388, per Collins L.J.

Example

As you may remember from our example Phillip was originally the owner of both Redacre and Blueacre. Phillip sells Blueacre to Jack, who, for the benefit of Redacre, covenants not to build on Blueacre. Then Phillip sells Redacre to Mr Smith and let's say that Jack has now sold Blueacre to Alison, who shows signs that she is going to build on the land in breach of the covenant.

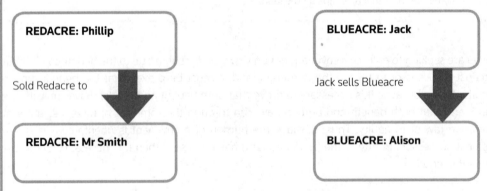

REDACRE: Phillip

Sold Redacre to

REDACRE: Mr Smith

BLUEACRE: Jack

Jack sells Blueacre

BLUEACRE: Alison

If you can show that the burden of the restrictive building covenant has run with Blueacre under rules in *Tulk v Moxhay* (1848) 2 Ph. 774 (above), then Mr Smith will be able to enforce the covenant if it "touches and concerns" the land and it has been "annexed" to Redacre.

---

60   *Renals v Cowlishaw* (1878) L.R. 9 Ch. D 125.

There are two ways in which the benefit of a covenant can be annexed to the covenantee's land:

- Express annexation
- Statutory annexation by s.78 of the Law of Property Act 1925.

(i) Express annexation

For an express annexation there must be an intention expressed in the covenant that the benefit should be annexed to the land. This requires statements to the effect that the covenant is intended to run with the land and to be enforceable by every future successor in title.[61] Thus, in *Rogers v Hosegood*,[62] there was held to be sufficient intention to annex the benefit of the covenant when it stated that it was the intention that the covenants "might enure to the benefit of [the covenantees] their heirs and assigns and others claiming under them to all or any of their lands adjoining or near to the [burdened land]". It is also necessary that the benefited land is identified in the deed that creates the covenant.[63] An intention to annex can be construed from the conveyance that contained the covenant "in the light of the surrounding circumstances".[64] Essentially therefore the circumstances surrounding the execution of the covenant can be used to determine the meaning of the words in the conveyance.

The express annexation rules caused problems where part of the benefited land was sold. The benefit did not transmit with part of the land.[65] The problem was often solved by stating that the covenant was annexed to each and every part of the land.

(ii) Statutory annexation of benefit

The problem of finding an express annexation has been removed by s.78 of the Law of Property Act 1925 and the interpretation of its effect by the Court of Appeal in *Federated Homes v Mill Lodge Properties*.[66] If you remember s.78(1) provides that "[a] covenant relating to any land of the covenantee shall be deemed to be made with the covenantee and his successors in title and the persons deriving title under him or them, and shall have effect as if such successors and other persons were expressed".

In *Federated Homes* the land in question was a large building plot subject to a limit on the total number of houses that could be built. It was sold in three parts: Blue, Green and Red. The purchasers of the Blue land, Mill Lodge Properties, covenanted not to build any more than 300 houses on the land. If they exceeded this number it would reduce the number that the owners of the Red and Green land were allowed to build. There was no express annexation.[67] The question was whether the covenant had been annexed to the benefited land by s.78.

---

61 *Federated Homes v Mill Lodge Properties* [1980] 1 W.L.R. 594.
62 [1900] 2 Ch. 388.
63 *Renals v Cowlishaw* (1879) 11 Ch.D. 866—the land was not identified in the conveyance which contained the covenant so that the benefit was not annexed.
64 *J.Sainsbury Plc v Enfield London Borough Council* [1989] 1 W.L.R. 590, per Morritt J.
65 *Re Ballard's Conveyance* [1932] Ch. 473.
66 [1980] 1 W.L.R. 594; G. Newsom "Universal Annexation" (1981) 97 L.Q.R. 32; E.H.Burn, *Maudsley & Burn's Land Law Cases and Materials*, p.959.
67 Although the Green land had an unbroken chain of assignments: [1980] 1 W.L.R. 594, p.603.

It was held that provided the covenant touched and concerned the land, i.e. in the terms of s. 78 "related to the land of the covenantee", which it did, s.78 had the effect of annexing the benefit of the covenant to the land.[68] There is no need for express words that state that the covenant should be for the benefit of the land and thus enforceable by successors in title. Once it is proved that the covenant touches and concerns the land (which this one did), then the benefit of any restrictive covenant is annexed to the land of the covenantee: it runs with the land for the benefit of successors in title. Brightman L.J. reasoned that s.78 says that the covenants shall be enforceable by all successors in title and persons deriving title under the original covenantee. This includes everyone who could possibly come to own or occupy the benefited land.[69] Thus, as Brightman L.J. states, this must have the effect of meaning that the covenant runs with the land.[70]

Brightman L.J. also observed that s.78 annexed the benefit of a covenant to each and every part of the land, and not just to the whole of the land. Consequently, if part of the benefited land is sold off, the benefit will run with that part.

(iii) Identification of benefited land

In *Federated Homes* Brightman L.J. did not find it necessary to consider whether, under s.78, it remained necessary that the conveyance containing the covenant identified the benefited land, with the aid of extrinsic evidence if necessary.[71] In *Crest Nicholson v McAllister*[72] it was confirmed that such identification is necessary.

(iv) Section 78 subject to a contrary intention

Although it is not stated explicitly in s.78, the section will not operate to annex the benefit of a covenant if there is a contrary intention expressed in the conveyance containing the covenant. This appears self evident from the wording of the section itself. Where a covenant is expressed to be personal it cannot be said to "relate to the land of the covenantee" or to operate for the benefit of successors in title. It was held in *Roake v Chadha*[73] that if the covenant shows the intention that it is not to be annexed to the land, then s.78 will not operate to annex it. In this case, the covenant was expressed in the following terms:

> "this covenant shall not enure for the benefit of any owner or subsequent purchaser of any part of the estate unless the benefit of this covenant shall be expressly assigned".

Judge Paul Baker Q.C. stated that it was clear from the reasoning in *Federated Homes* that it is still necessary "to consider the covenant as a whole to determine its true effect". Section 78 deems a covenant to have been made with the covenantee's successors in title etc. The covenant

---

68   [1980] 1 W.L.R. 594, p.604, per Brightman L.J.
69   Law of Property Act 1925 s.78(2).
70   [1980] 1 W.L.R. 594, p.605, per Brightman L.J.
71   The covenant in that case clearly *did* identify the land.
72   [2004] 1 W.L.R. 2409; see J.Howell [2004] Conv. 507.
73   [1984] 1 W.L.R. 40.

in *Roake* clearly showed that it *was not intended* to benefit those persons without an assignment. It was held that the benefit of the covenant did not run with the land under s.78.

The Court of Appeal in *Crest Nicholson v McAllister*[74] confirmed that where a covenant shows the intention that it should not run with the land, s.78 will not apply. Covenants expressed to be personal will exclude the operation of s.78. In *Sugarman v Porter*,[75] the wording of the relevant covenant was that the covenant would benefit the seller's retained land whilst it remained *unsold*. It was held to be personal to the vendor and expressly intended not to benefit successors in title. This was sufficient contrary intention to exclude s.78.

(b) Assignment of the benefit

In the unlikely event that it is impossible to establish statutory annexation of the benefit of the covenant, it will not be enforceable by a successor in title to the benefited land unless he can show that it has been expressly assigned to him by the original covenantee or by an unbroken chain of assignments each time the benefited land changed hands.[76]

An assignment is where the current owner of the benefited land transfers the benefit of the covenant to his purchaser or other successor in title. It is a transfer of the benefit of a contract.[77] As such therefore, the benefit is not attached to the land so as to transfer to all future successors in title. The benefit must be assigned every time the land changes hands in order that the covenant is enforceable by the current owner of the benefited land. The assignment of the covenant must happen at the same time as the transfer of land[78] and it must identify the benefited land.[79]

(c) Building schemes

Where there is a "building scheme", restrictive covenants are mutually enforceable between the participants. This allows for the situation where a developer owns land and has created a housing estate. He then sells each plot to individual purchasers. It is vital that the covenants attach to the various plots of land. It may be necessary to restrict building on the estate and to maintain the character of the neighbourhood. For example, there may be covenants against building a wall in the front garden. In this situation the normal rules of the running of covenants function inadequately. As the conveyances to the purchasers are made at different times it is difficult to get the benefit and burden of covenants to run with the land. In *Baxter v Four Oaks Properties Ltd*,[80] Cross J. stated that

---

74   [2004] 1 W.L.R. 2409.
75   [2006] EWHC 331.
76   E.H.Burn, *Maudsley and Burn's Land Law Cases and Materials*, p.956.
77   See Harpum, Bridge and Dixon, *Megarry and Wade Law of Real Property*, 7th edn (London: Sweet & Maxwell, 2008) para.32–010.
78   *Re Union of London and Smith's Conveyance, Miles v Easter* [1933] Ch 611.
79   *Miles v Easter*, above; *Newton Abbot Co-operative Society Ltd v Williamson and Treadgold Ltd* [1952] Ch. 286.
80   [1965] Ch. 816, p.825.

". . . for well over 100 years past where the owner of land deals with it on the footing of imposing restrictive obligations on the use of various parts of it as and when he sells them off for the common benefit of himself (in so far as he retains any land) and of the various purchasers inter se a court of equity has been prepared to give effect to this common intention notwithstanding any technical difficulties involved."

> If a building scheme is established restrictive covenants are mutually enforceable between the participants to the scheme. Thus, a covenant not to build a wall in your front garden would be enforceable against you. But you would also be able to prevent your neighbour from building a wall. The same would apply to successors in title to the various plots of land.

Equity originally took a strict view as to when covenants could be said to have been annexed as part of a building scheme. In *Elliston v Reacher*[81] four criteria were established: firstly, there must be a common vendor from whom all the claimants and defendants derive their titles. Secondly, the common vendor, prior to selling the land, must have laid the estate out in lots for sale and subjected the lots "to restrictions intended to be imposed on all the lots". Thirdly, the common vendor must have intended the restrictions to benefit all the lots, for example by enhancing their value. Fourthly, the lots must have been purchased on the understanding that the restrictions were to be for the benefit of all the lots.

(i) A broader approach

In *In re Dolphin's Conveyance*[82] Stamp J. held that the essence of a "building scheme" was an intention

> "to lay down what has been referred to as a local law for the estate for the common benefit of all the several purchasers of it. The purpose of the covenant by the vendors was to enable each purchaser to have, as against the other purchasers, in one way or another, the benefit of the restrictions to which he had made himself subject."

This case took a broader approach to the finding of a building scheme. The essential requirement is *mutuality*. It is clear that there must be an intention to impose the benefit of the covenants on all the purchasers. It was held that it is not necessary for the land to have been laid out in lots or for there to be a common vendor. The essential principle, as stated in *Baxter v Four Oaks Properties Ltd*,[83] is that there is a common intention that the covenants should be mutually enforceable between all the purchasers.[84] Thus it is vital that, in accordance with the last of the *Elliston v Reacher* criteria, the purchasers buy their lots on the understanding that the restrictions

---

81   [1908] 2 Ch. 374, per Parker J.
82   [1970] Ch. 654, p.662.
83   [1965] Ch. 816.
84   *Reid v Bickerstaff* [1909] 2 Ch. 305: "Reciprocity is the foundation of the idea of a scheme".

were to benefit all the other lots. In *Reid v Bickerstaff*,[85] it was held that "there must be a defined area within which the scheme is operative".[86] The purchaser must "know both the extent of his burden and the extent of his benefit".

In *Emile Elias & Co Ltd v Pine Groves Ltd*,[87] the covenants were not uniform. Some imposed an obligation not to build and others restricted the use of the land in a different way. This made it difficult to find the necessary element of common intention that the covenants were to create a local law by which all the owners of the houses had reciprocal rights and obligations.[88] However, this does not necessarily mean that the covenants must be *identical*.[89]

Positive covenants

3

A. PROBLEMS WITH ENFORCEABILITY OF POSITIVE COVENANTS

As we have seen the burden of a positive covenant cannot run either at common law or in equity. As Lord Templeman observed in *Rhone v Stephens*[90]

> "For over 100 years it has been clear and accepted law that equity will enforce negative covenants against freehold land but has no power to enforce positive covenants against successors in title of the land. To enforce a positive covenant would be to enforce a personal obligation against a person who has not covenanted. To enforce negative covenants is only to treat the land as subject to a restriction."

Thus, to take our example above, if Jack had covenanted to maintain a shared driveway between Blueacre and Redacre the burden would not run with Blueacre. Therefore, future purchasers from Jack would not be liable on the covenant if they refused to maintain the driveway. The Law Commission has perceived this rule to be problematic and in need of reform.[91]

---

85   [1909] 2 Ch. 305.
86   Per Cozens-Hardy M.R., p. 319. See E.H. Burn, *Maudsley and Burn's Land Law Cases and Materials*, pp.983–4.
87   [1993] 1 W.L.R. 305 P C.
88   Above p.311, per Lord Browne-Wilkinson.
89   *Emile Elias & Co Ltd v Pine Groves Ltd*, above, p.311, per Lord Browne-Wilkinson.
90   [1994] 2 A.C. 310, p.321.
91   Law Com No.327, para.2.41.

> The rule means that repairing obligations cannot be enforced once the burdened land is sold. Thus, where properties are interdependent, such as flats, the owner of a lower flat cannot enforce a repairing covenant against the owner of the higher flats. Thus, if the roof and other common parts get into a state of disrepair and devalue the lower floor flats, there is nothing that the owners of the lower flats can do about it.

There are legal methods of ensuring that positive covenants are enforceable against successors in title to the burdened land, but these methods are artificial and impractical. The lack of any direct method of enforcing positive covenants was one of the principal reasons for the introduction of the "Commonhold" system of land ownership.[92]

B. INDIRECT METHODS OF ENFORCEMENT

(1) A chain of indemnities

To take our example from above, as the original covenantor, Jack will remain liable on any positive covenant he entered into with Phillip. So that if Jack sold Blueacre to Alison and she breaches the covenant, Phillip can still sue Jack for breach of covenant. So when Jack sold Blueacre to Alison he might include in the conveyance a clause by which Alison promises to repay Jack if he is sued by Phillip for her breaches of covenant. If Alison then sells Blueacre she may include a similar "indemnity" clause in her conveyance to that purchaser. Thus, if Jack is sued for that purchaser's breach of covenant, he will sue Alison and Alison will sue her purchaser. The disadvantage of this method is that eventually there will be a break in the chain—someone will forget to include the indemnity clause or one of the parties may not be traceable or may have gone bankrupt.

(2) The doctrine of mutual benefit and burden

The case of *Halsall v Brizell*[93] stated the principle that a landowner who takes the benefit of a deed must also bear the corresponding burden.

> Thus, if under a conveyance of Blueacre, Jack had been granted the right to use a shared driveway, and he covenants to repair that driveway, the repair covenant may be enforced against him. He is taking the benefit of the right to use the driveway so he must bear the corresponding burden of repairing it. This would also apply to purchases from Jack.

---

92   See Chapter 2.
93   [1957] Ch 169.

In *Halsall v Brizell* the purchasers of plots of land were granted the right to use private roads, sewers, and a promenade. They covenanted to contribute to the maintenance of roads, sewers, promenade and sea wall. It was held that if the purchasers wanted to use the roads etc., they were bound by the condition in the deed. Hence, "the defendant could not exercise the rights without paying his costs of ensuring that they could be exercised".[94]

The doctrine of mutual benefit and burden has received a narrow interpretation by the courts. The House of Lords has held that the benefit claimed must bear some relation to the obligation of maintenance. The person sought to be held to the repairing obligation must also have some real choice about whether to take the benefit or not, and pay any corresponding maintenance. In *Rhone v Stephens*,[95] a house had been divided into two separate dwellings: A larger dwelling and a cottage. The owner sold the cottage to a purchaser and covenanted to repair the shared roof. Eventually the roof fell into disrepair and the cottage ceiling leaked. It was held that the repairing covenant was not enforceable through the principle in *Halsall v Brizell*. Lord Templeman observed that[96]:

"It does not follow that any condition can be rendered enforceable . . . The condition must be relevant to the exercise of the right. In *Halsall v Brizell* there were reciprocal benefits and burdens enjoyed by the users of the roads and sewers. . . the defendant could, at least in theory, choose between enjoying the right and paying his proportion of the cost or alternatively giving up the right and saving his money."

The defendant in this case could not be deprived of any benefit if he failed to repair the cottage roof. The only benefit he gained under the deed of conveyance was a right to support for the house. He could not refuse this. Furthermore, there was no correlation between having the benefit of support from the cottage and the obligation to repair the *roof* of that cottage. The same reasoning was applied in the case of *Thamesmead Town v Allotey*.[97]

(3) The grant of a long lease

If instead of selling the freehold of the cottage in *Rhone v Stephens*, the owner had granted a long lease, and then entered into repairing covenants for the roof etc, the purchaser of the lease would have been able to enforce the covenant to repair the roof. Leasehold covenants are enforceable between the original landlord and tenant and assignees of the lease and the freehold reversion.

(4) A right of re-entry

It is possible to create a right of re-entry when the freehold estate is transferred. This means that the estate can be terminated for failure to comply with positive covenants specified. The deed could then impose the condition that certain repairs to the land be undertaken. A right of

---

94 *Rhone v Stephens* [1994] 2 A.C. 310, p.322, per Lord Templeman.
95 Above.
96 [1994] 2 A.C. 310, pp.322–3.
97 [1998] 3 E.G.L.R. 97.

re-entry is an interest in land capable of binding successors in title. In this way it is an indirect method of enforcing positive obligations on freehold landowners. A rentcharge is where the freehold estate is made subject to the payment of money, e.g. for repairs. They are enforced by rights of re-entry.

4   Remedies for breach of covenant

The usual remedy for breach of covenant is an injunction. An injunction can be prohibitory, which orders the defendant to discontinue a breach of covenant or refrain from breaching it, for example, if the defendant is threatening to build on his land in breach of a restrictive covenant then the court may order her to refrain from doing so. If the defendant is already building in breach of covenant than the court may order that she stops building. An injunction can also take mandatory form, which requires the defendant to do some positive act, for example demolish a building that has been erected in breach of covenant.[98] The court is not obliged to award an injunction, as it is an equitable discretionary remedy. The court may refuse an injunction where the claimant has delayed in bringing the action,[99] or where there is hardship to the defendant.[100] However, it is only in exceptional circumstances that an injunction will not be awarded.[101]

The court has jurisdiction to award common law damages instead of an injunction. However, as a restrictive covenant is exclusively *equitable* in nature, this jurisdiction is unavailable.[102] Nevertheless, under s. 50 of the Supreme Court Act 1981[103] the court has jurisdiction to award damages in lieu of an injunction, where damages are unavailable at common law. In *Shelfer v City of London Lighting Co*[104] the court established the principles on which the court may award damages instead of an injunction: damages may be awarded instead of an injunction where the injury to the claimant's right is a small one and is capable of being quantified and compensated by a small monetary payment. If this is the case, and it would be oppressive to the defendant to award an injunction, the court may award damages instead.

An example of this jurisdiction is *Wrotham Park Estate Ltd v Parkside Homes*.[105] There was a restrictive covenant that restricted building save in accordance with a specific plan. The

---

98   See Hanbury and Martin, *Modern Equity*, 18th edn (London: Sweet & Maxwell, 2009), pp.794–796.
99   *Bates v Lord Hailsham of St Marylebone* [1972] 1 W.L.R. 1373. There must be "inordinate" delay: *H.P. Bulmer Ltd & Showerings Ltd v Bollinger SA* [1977] 2 C.M.L.R. 625, per Goff L.J. Hanbury and Martin, *Modern Equity*, p.833.
100   *Shell UK Ltd v Lostock Garages Ltd* [1976] 1 W.L.R. 1187: Hanbury and Martin, above, p.836.
101   *Watson v Croft Promo-Sport Ltd* [2009] EWCA Civ 15.
102   See Hanbury and Martin, *Modern Equity*, pp.838–9.
103   Its predecessor was Lord Cairn's Act, the Chancery Amendment Act 1858.
104   [1895] 1 Ch. 287.
105   [1974] 1 W.L.R. 798.

defendant, a property developer, built several houses in breach of this requirement. The court refused a mandatory injunction on the basis that it was reluctant to order the demolition of much-needed housing[106]: Brightman J. observed:

> "I cannot close my eyes to the fact that the houses now exist. It would, in my opinion, be an unpardonable waste of much needed houses to direct that they now be pulled down and I have never had a moment's doubt during the hearing of this case that such an order ought to be refused. No damage of a financial nature has been done to the plaintiffs by the breach of the lay-out stipulation. The plaintiffs' use of the Wrotham Park Estate has not been and will not be impeded. It is totally unnecessary to demolish the houses in order to preserve the integrity of the restrictive covenants imposed on the rest of area 14. Without hesitation I decline to grant a mandatory injunction."[107]

As to the quantum of damages, the claimant can obtain the amount that could reasonably have been charged to release the defendant from the covenant.[108]

Discharge or modification of a restrictive covenant

5

Covenants can last forever. However, "changes in the environment may render them obsolete or may make their enforcement anti-social".[109] Under s.84 of the Law of Property Act 1925, the Lands Chamber[110] has the power to discharge or modify a restrictive covenant on the following grounds:

- Where the covenant is obsolete "by reason of changes in the character of the property or the neighbourhood or other circumstances of the case".[111]
- Where the covenant "would impede some reasonable user of the land".[112] A covenant can be discharged or modified on this ground if it confers no practical benefits on the person entitled to the benefit, is contrary to the public interest, and can be adequately compensated with a monetary payment.[113]

---

106 See also *Jaggard v Sawyer* [1995] 1 W.L.R. 269. The situation may be different where the defendants have erected the building in bad faith, blatantly aware that they were in breach of covenant: *Daniells v Mendonca* (1999) 78 P & CR 401: Hanbury and Martin, *Modern Equity*, p.840.

107 [1974] 1 W.L.R. 798, p. 811.

108 Hanbury and Martin, above, pp.842–845; *Wrotham Park Estate Ltd v Parkside Homes* [1974] 1 W.L.R. 798.

109 C.Harpum, S.Bridge, M.Dixon, *Megarry and Wade Law of Real Property*, para.32–085.

110 Formerly the Lands Tribunal: Tribunal Procedure (Upper Tribunal) (Lands Chamber) Rules 2010.

111 Law of Property Act 1925 s.84(1)(a).

112 s.84(1)(aa).

113 Law of Property Act 1925 s.84(1A). An application to discharge a covenant restricting parking was refused in *Re Marshall's Application* [2011] UKUT 69 (LC) because it still secured a practical benefit to the dominant land. If vehicles were allowed to park in the space concerned the owners of the benefited land would be unable to turn their vehicles in the space.

- Where the person entitled to the benefit agrees, "either expressly or by implication, by their acts or omissions". The person entitled to the benefit must be of full age and capacity.[114]
- Where "the proposed discharge or modification will not injure the persons entitled to the benefit of the restriction".[115]

6 Reform of covenants

The Law Commission has recently published a report recommending large scale reform of the law of freehold covenants: *Making Land Work: Easements, Covenants and Profits à Prendre* (2011).[116] The Law Commission criticised the "differing and complicated rules for the running of the benefit and burden of restrictive covenants",[117] the fact that the "contractual liability between the original parties to a covenant persists despite changes in the ownership of the land",[118] and the fact that the burden of a positive covenant cannot be made to bind successors in title.[119] For example, there is no way of enforcing directly a covenant to repair a fence.

For the future, the Law Commission recommends the introduction of a power to create a new interest in land: a positive or negative "land obligation".[120] For example, a negative land obligation would be an obligation not to do something on the burdened land. This will take effect as a legal interest in land under s.1(2)(a) of the Law of Property Act 1925.[121] It will thus bind successors in title without recourse to the current complicated rules on the running of covenants. Further, it will not have its origins in contract.[122] Like an easement, its origins will "lie in grant".[123] Thus, there is no privity of contract, or continuing contractual liability on the part of the burdened landowner. Whether title to the land is registered or not, enforceability of land obligations will depend on their registration.[124] If title to the benefited land is registered, the benefit must be

---

114   s.84(1)(b).
115   s.84(1)(c).
116   Law Com. No.327 (June 7, 2011).
117   para.5.4; 5.7.
118   para.5.4.
119   para.5.4.
120   para.6.14.
121   Thus, the land obligation, in order to be a legal interest must be created for either a perpetual duration or for a defined time period, as required by s.1(2)(a). To be properly created as a legal interest, it must be granted by deed (Law of Property Act 1925 s.52) and completed by registration under Land Registration Act 2002 s.27: Law Com. No.327, para.6.46.
122   para.5.74.
123   Law Com. No.327, para.6.7; Accordingly, it must be sufficiently clearly defined, as in the *Re Ellenborough Park* [1956] Ch. 131 fourth characteristic of an easement. Thus, maintenance obligations must specify exactly "when it is to be done and what is to be done": Law Com No.327, para.6.42.
124   They will not be overriding interests: Law Com. No.327, para.6.67. However, it is important to note that the new land obligation can be created regardless of whether land is registered or unregistered. In unregistered land, even though a legal interest, a land obligation would thus be required to be registered under the Land Charges Act 1972. Otherwise it would be void as against purchasers of the burdened land: Law Com. No.327, para.6.54–6.56.

registered as a registrable interest under the Land Registration Act 2002.[125] The dominant and servient land must be in separate ownership or possession.[126] However, there will be no need for this requirement where the benefited and burdened titles are registered.[127]

Because of the need to protect purchasers and to prevent the burdened land from becoming unmarketable, a land obligation must satisfy certain characteristics. It must benefit an estate in land, whether freehold or leasehold.[128] The right must "touch and concern" the land.[129] The existing test under the current law will be applicable here.[130] There are also further requirements before a right can be created as a land obligation. A positive land obligation must involve "an obligation to do something on the land burdened by the obligation, or in relation to any structure or feature that marks, or lies on, or is treated as marking, or lying on, the boundary of the land burdened by the obligation and the land in which the benefited estate subsists". It includes "an obligation to make a reciprocal payment".[131]

A. CRITICAL THINKING AND BUILDING BLOCK NO 4

> What is the purpose of the "touch and concern" requirement and this "functional" definition of a land obligation?

It's purpose is to meet the usual concern that Land Law should not permit too many property rights, i.e. so that purchasers of the land will not be taken unawares by rights that bind them.[132] They are limiting criteria. The Law Commission also observes that:

> "[A] pervasive technique for controlling the impact of binding positive obligations is registration . . . only a really careless purchaser could be caught out by an unexpected burden".[133]

---

125   It will therefore fall within Land Registration Act 2002 s.2(a)(v): See Law Com. No.327, para.6.12. If the land obligation does not touch and concern the land it will not be assumed to be valid under Land Registration Act 2002 s.58: para.6.78.
126   Law of Property Bill 2011, cl.22.
127   Law Com. No.327 para.6.83.
128   Law of Property Bill 2011, cl.1(2); Law Com. No.327, para.6.17. Thus, like with the law of easements, there must be a dominant and a servient tenement.
129   Law of Property Bill 2011, cl.1(2); Again similar to the law of easements that requires the right to "accommodate the dominant tenement": Re Ellenborough Park [1956] Ch. 131.
130   Law Com. No.327, para.6.19.
131   Law of Property Bill 2011, cl.1(3). A reciprocal payment might be to pay half the cost of maintaining a fence or shared boundary: Law Com No.327, para.6.30.
132   para.5.54.
133   para.5.58. The object of the limiting criteria is to ensure that land does not become "unmarketable" by the presence of too many land obligations: para.5.60.

B. WHY DOES A LAND OBLIGATION NEED TO BE A LEGAL INTEREST IN LAND?

Currently a covenant is only an equitable interest and this means that the benefit cannot be registered against the title to the benefited land.[134] Of course the burden of the covenant can be registered using the mechanism of a "notice".[135] But a notice is registered against the title to the *burdened* land. Thus, there is no public record of the benefited land.[136] Consequently, it would be difficult for the burdened landowner to know with whom to "negotiate a release" of the covenant if necessary. So it is important that the benefited land can be identified more clearly than it can be under the current law, which allows identification by evidence extrinsic to the original deed of conveyance.[137]

C. RELATIONSHIP WITH THE CURRENT RULES

The Law Commission's proposals are intended to have prospective effect only. Once the new regime is enacted it will not be possible for a covenant to be created in accordance with the *Tulk v Moxhay* rules.[138] However, there will be very many old-style covenants, created before the new regime, the enforceability of which must be determined by the *Tulk v Moxhay* rules.[139]

D. EXTENSION TO SECTION 84 OF THE LAW OF PROPERTY ACT 1925

Covenants are effectively permanent. However, because of changes in circumstances, as well as in the nature and use of land, covenants can become highly burdensome and may restrict legitimate development. We have seen that the court has power to modify and discharge restrictive covenants under s.84 of the Law of Property Act 1925. The Law Commission recommends an extension to this jurisdiction. Positive land obligations in particular might need to be discharged and modified.

---

134   Land Registration Act 2002 s.2.
135   See Chapter 8.
136   Law Com No.327, para.5.5.
137   para.5.61–5.62.
138   An attempt to create a covenant after the regime comes into force will take effect as a land obligation, provided the above criteria are met and the covenant is not expressed to be personal: Law of Property Bill 2011, cl.2; Law Com. No.327, para.6.37.
139   para.5.82.

Chapter 13

Mortgages

CHAPTER OVERVIEW

In this chapter you will find:

- The aims of mortgage law and now they will help you create argument
- The nature of a mortgage and the rights of the borrower
- Consideration of how mortgages are created and the rights and powers of the legal mortgage
- The doctrine of undue influence
- Critical thinking and constructed argument with Building Blocks.

Introduction

1

A. A MORTGAGE IS A "SECURITY" INTEREST IN LAND

A mortgage is a package of rights over land. It is usually granted by a borrower to a lender in return for a loan. This package of rights includes the right to take possession of the borrower's land and to sell it in order to repay the debt owed. When I borrow money from a bank I enter into a contract by which I am obliged to repay that money, usually in monthly instalments and at a rate of interest. The bank has the right to sue me under the contract if I fail to make the repayments. So far, what we are talking about is an "unsecured loan". The bank can sue me in order to get its money back, but it has no other way of recouping its investment should I default on the loan agreement.

A mortgage is an interest in land that is usually granted as "security" for a loan, i.e. it is an additional way that the bank can recoup its money. This time it is not dependent on suing the borrower, who, after all, may be insolvent by this time. A mortgage is "real" security, which means that the lender has rights over the borrower's *land*. It is also possibly to give "personal" security for a loan, which is where a third party agrees to guarantee the loan. If the principal borrower defaults the lender can sue the third party.[1] A mortgage can be used for a variety of purposes, e.g. to finance the purchase of a home or later improvements to that home, or as a vehicle to obtain finance to start a small business.[2]

> **Terminology**
> Mortgagor: The person who grants the mortgage (the borrower).
> Mortgagee: The person or institution who is granted the mortgage (the lender).

B. MORTGAGES AND OWNER OCCUPATION

A mortgage is often used to purchase a home. It is a feature of society in this country that most people own rather than rent their own homes. One judge remarked that "[t]he mass diffusion of home ownership has been one of the most striking social changes of our own time".[3] However, the majority of people who buy a house, particularly those starting out on the property ladder, cannot afford to purchase a house without the aid of a loan from a bank or a building society.

"A feature of home ownership in the United Kingdom is the relatively large number of homes purchased with a mortgage. Approximately three quarters of house purchases are financed with a mortgage loan facility. In 2002, 76 per cent of loans for home purchase were obtained through banks and 17 per cent through building societies."[4]

Banks and building societies may lend a person a sum of money approximately equivalent to three times their income.

C. CRITICAL THINKING: LAW OF MORTGAGES

The law of mortgages is partly concerned with when the lender can exercise his rights to take possession and sell mortgaged property. A lender has the right to sell the mortgaged property if the borrower fails to pay the loan secured by the mortgage. Repossession will have drastic consequences for the borrower as it means that they will lose their home.

---

1   For a detailed description on these different forms of security see N. Jackson, J. Stevens, and R. Pearce, *Land Law*, 4th edn (London: Sweet & Maxwell, 2009), Ch.17 Mortgages.
2   M.P.Thompson, *Modern Land Law*, 4th edn (Oxford University Press, 2009), p.424.
3   *Midland Bank Plc v Cooke* [1995] 4 All E.R. 562, p.575A per Waite L.J.
4   Central Statistical Office Social Trends 27 (2004), quoted in E.H.Burn, *Maudsley and Burn's Land Law Cases and Materials*, 8th edn (Oxford University Press, 2004) p.790.

> "The warning given with every mortgage is that 'your home is at risk if you do not keep up repayments on a mortgage or other loan secured on it'".
>
> Central Statistical Office Social Trends 27 (2004), quoted in E.H. Burn, *Maudsley and Burn's Land Law Cases and Materials*, p.791

We need to consider the safeguards the law puts in place to ensure that the lender cannot take possession of the house too readily; that the borrower is given sufficient opportunity to remedy the default and catch up on his or her loan repayments. Does the law give sufficient protection to the borrower and his/her family? After all, the mortgage was originally granted to enable them to buy a home in which to live with their family. They bought the house in order to have residential security.[5] This is now a main purpose why people own land in this country. Thus we can say legitimately that the rules of the Law of Mortgages are good and fair if they provide adequate safeguards for the borrower before allowing the mortgagee to take possession and sell the house.

> **BUILDING BLOCK NO 1: Residential Security**
> We can legitimately say that where the rules operate in the context of owner occupation of property, they are good and fair if they give effective protection to people's residential security. Land Law now operates in the context of owner occupation. When people are using land ownership to build a home this is a significant part of their lives.

However, looking at the law from the lender's point of view, there are important reasons why the law of mortgages needs to give protection to institutions that lend money on the security of land.

> In the context of the doctrine of undue influence (which we consider below), Lord Nicholls explained that unless banks can have confidence that mortgages are enforceable they "will not be willing to lend money on the security of a . . . house or flat".
>
> *Royal Bank of Scotland Plc v Etridge (No.2)* [2002] 2 A.C. 773, para.35

Either a loan is needed in order to purchase the house in the first place, or, as is becoming increasingly common, a second mortgage is used to secure a loan to set up a small business, or to expand an existing business.[6] Unless the rules of Land Law make sure that lenders can readily get their money back by selling the house, banks and building societies may become reluctant to give loans to owner occupiers and small businesses in the future. This would have significant impact on the country's economy.[7]

---

5   Expression and idea of "residential security": K.Gray and P.Symes, *Real Property and Real People* (London: Butterworths, 1981).
6   As was the case in *Williams & Glyn's Bank Ltd v Boland* [1981] A.C. 487.
7   Also K.Gray and S.F.Gray, *Elements of Land Law*, 4th edn (Oxford University Press, 2004), pp. 1625–6, quoting *Barclays Bank Plc v O'Brien* [1994] 1 A.C. 180, per Lord Browne-Wilkinson.

> **A balance between Building Blocks**
> A balance must be struck therefore between BUILDING BLOCK NO 1 and BUILDING BLOCK NO 4. The Law of Mortgages should make sure that it is not too restrictive and does in fact allow lenders to take possession of security and sell mortgaged houses, as observed by Lord Nicholls in the House of Lords in *Royal Bank of Scotland Plc v Etridge (No.2)* [2002] 2 A.C. 773, para.37.

D. TYPES OF MORTGAGE CONTRACT

The loan secured by the mortgage, for example £100,000 for the purchase of a house, is usually paid back over a period of time on monthly instalments. Often this is over a term of 20 or 25 years (referred to as the "mortgage term"). The loan can be repaid in a variety of ways. For example, the borrower's monthly payment may include interest payments and payment of part of the capital debt owed to the lender. This is known as a "repayment mortgage". A borrower may make monthly payments consisting of the interest due on the loan ("interest only" mortgages), in which case they would need to make some arrangement for repaying the capital at the end of the mortgage term.

2 The creation and registration of a legal mortgage

A. THE METHODS OF CREATING A MORTGAGE

Prior to 1925 mortgages could be created by the borrower transferring his fee simple to the lender in return for a loan. Upon repayment of the loan the lender would transfer the land back to the borrower. It is now no longer possible to create a mortgage in this way. Under s. 85 of the Law of Property Act 1925, a mortgage can only be created by the borrower executing "a charge by deed expressed to be by way of legal mortgage", or by the grant of a lease in favour of the mortgagee for 3000 years, subject to a provision that the lease shall end when the borrower has paid off the loan. It is no longer possible to create a mortgage by conveyance of the fee simple estate.[8] Where title to the borrower's estate is registered, he does not have the power to create a mortgage by long lease.[9] The only way in which a mortgage of registered land can be created is by way of a charge expressed to be by way of legal mortgage.

---

8   Law of Property Act 1925 s.85(2).
9   Land Registration Act 2002 s.23(1).

B. THE FORMALITIES FOR THE CREATION OF A LEGAL MORTGAGE

(1) Legal interests in land must be created by deed

A charge by way of legal mortgage is a legal interest in land and thus it must be created by deed.[10] It must state in the deed that it is intended to take effect as a legal mortgage.[11] When a charge is created properly in this way the lender has all the rights and remedies of a legal mortgagee. Section 87(1) of the Law of Property Act 1925 provides that "where a legal mortgage of land is created by a charge by deed expressed to be by way of legal mortgage, the mortgagee shall have the same protection, powers and remedies (including the right to take proceedings to obtain possession from the occupiers)" as a mortgage created under the general law.

(2) Registration requirements

Where a legal charge is granted in respect of a registered estate it is a "registrable disposition".[12] Thus, it cannot operate as a *legal* charge unless the registration requirements are met.[13] The mortgagee must be entered in the register as proprietor of the charge and will then have all the powers that a legal mortgagee has under the general law, including the right to take possession and sell mortgaged property.[14] Where a legal charge is granted in respect of an estate in land, and title to that estate is unregistered, the grant triggers compulsory first registration of the mortgaged estate.[15] However, this is only the case if the mortgage is a *protected first legal mortgage*.[16]

C. EQUITABLE MORTGAGES

An equitable mortgage can come into being in one of the following situations. Firstly, where a mortgage of registered land is not completed by registration it will not operate at law. It will take effect as an equitable mortgage.[17] Secondly, if a mortgage is created of an equitable interest it will only take effect as an equitable mortgage. For example, a couple are joint registered proprietors of their house. As we saw in Chapter 5, the Law of Property Act 1925 imposes a trust in all cases of co-ownership. So the joint registered proprietors will hold on trust for each other. If one forges the other's signature on a mortgage deed that mortgage cannot take effect as a mortgage of the legal estate. Both parties have to act jointly. However, the effect of the transaction is that the mortgage takes effect against the forger's equitable interest.[18]

---

10   Law of Property Act 1925 ss.1(2)(c) and 52.
11   Law of Property Act 1925 s.85(1) states that the deed must be "expressed to be by way of legal mortgage".
12   Land Registration Act 2002 s.27(f).
13   s.27(1), 51.
14   Land Registration Act 2002 s.52, subject to any entry on the register restricting those powers.
15   s.4(1)(g), provided that estate is an unregistered legal freehold or leasehold estate. If the latter, the lease must have more than seven years left to run: Land Registration Act 2002 s.4(2).
16   See section 6 of this chapter, p.731.
17   Land Registration Act 2002 s.27(1).
18   *Mortgage Corporation v Shaire* [2001] Ch. 743; The forger is, by the grant of the charge, taken to grant everything that is in *his or her* power to grant: Law of Property Act 1925 s.63.

Thirdly, if the borrower enters into an enforceable contract to grant a mortgage[19] but fails to execute a deed of grant then this may take effect as an equitable mortgage.[20]

(1) Rights of an equitable mortgagee

Unlike a legal mortgage, as we shall see below, an equitable mortgagee does not have an automatic right to take possession and sell mortgaged property. The equitable mortgagee will need to apply to the court for an order of sale of the property under s.14 of the Trusts of Land and Appointment of Trustees Act 1996.

3 Only a mortgage, not ownership of the land: the borrower's equity of redemption

The borrower must always have the right to pay off the debt to the lender and get back the mortgaged property unencumbered by the mortgage. This is known as the borrower's "equity of redemption". The borrower has this right even after the contractual date for repaying the mortgage has passed. The equity of redemption is an interest in land.[21] The equity of redemption stems from the time where mortgages were created by a conveyance to the lender of the borrower's estate in the land. Equity had to safeguard the borrower's right to pay off the loan and get back his land. A mortgage was only security for the loan. A mortgagee was not the *owner* of the land.

> **Because of this, the courts have protected the borrower's right to pay off the mortgage and to get back the estate free from the lender's rights.**

The courts have taken the view that the rights of the lender under the mortgage should extend no further than necessary to allow the lender security for a loan. All the terms included in the mortgage contract must be consistent "with the nature of a mortgage", i.e. they must not restrict the borrower's right to redeem the mortgaged property. Otherwise they will be held void.[22] In the courts' terminology, there must be no "clog or fetter" on the equity of redemption.[23] The courts have struggled with this doctrine. They are understandably reluctant to render void terms

---

19   The contract must comply with Law of Property (Miscellaneous Provisions) Act 1989 s.2, which requires contracts for the creation or disposition of an interest in land to be in writing, to contain all the terms of the agreement, and to be signed by both parties. See Chapter 3.

20   Under the doctrine in *Walsh v Lonsdale* (1882) L.R. 21 Ch. D. 9. It is no longer possible to create an equitable mortgage by deposit of the title deeds with the lender: *Bank of Kuwait v Sahib* [1996] 3 All E.R. 215.

21   *Casborne v Scarfe* (1738) 1 Atk 603, per Lord Hardwicke.

22   E.H.Burn, *Maudsley and Burn's Land Law Cases and Materials*, p.802.

23   For example, *Santley v Wilde* [1899] 2 Ch. 474.

that have been freely negotiated and which would otherwise comprise a "perfectly fair bargain" that was entered into by parties who knew what they were doing.[24]

A. THE RIGHT TO REDEEM MUST NOT BE RENDERED ILLUSORY

Where there is a term which renders the right to redeem illusory, i.e. non-existent, the term will be struck out unless it forms part of a bargain that is separate from the mortgage transaction itself. A postponement of the right to redeem may be held valid, unless it is part of a bargain that is "oppressive or unconscionable".

A term of the mortgage must not negate entirely the borrower's right to redeem the mortgaged property. A mortgage cannot be made irredeemable.[25] In *Fairclough v Swan Brewery Co Ltd*,[26] the appellant had a 17-and-a-half year lease of property. He mortgaged this to the respondent. There was a term in the mortgage to the effect that the borrower was not allowed to redeem the mortgage until six weeks before the lease was to end. The Privy Council held the term to be void.

The position was different in *Knightsbridge Estates Trust Ltd v Byrne*.[27] In this case the borrowers agreed to pay back the loan over 40 years and the lender agreed to accept instalments every six months. A term of the agreement prevented the borrowers from paying off the loan before this time. It was held that this was a valid arrangement and the plaintiffs were bound by it.[28] *So what was the difference?* Sir Wilfred Greene M.R. stated that "in the absence of compelling authority we are not prepared to say that such an agreement cannot lawfully be made". The court should have regard to the "business realities" of the case. This was the only way in which the borrowing company could raise money and they successfully stipulated for terms that reflected their own interests. The lending company wanted a long term investment and thus "the resulting agreement . . . has none of the features of an oppressive bargain where the borrower is at the mercy of an unscrupulous lender".

> "Any other answer would place an unfortunate restriction on the liberty of contract of competent parties who are at arm's length."[29]

Both parties entered into the agreement knowing what they were getting into. And both had the bargaining strength to impose their own terms.

---

24   *Samuel v Jarrah Timber and Wood Paving Corporation Ltd* [1904] A.C. 323, per Earl of Halsbury. See also a recent criticism in *Jones v Morgan* [2002] E.G.L.R. 125, para.86 per Lord Phillips M.R.

25   *Kreglinger v New Patagonia Meat and Cold Storage co Ltd* [1914] A.C. 25, per Viscount Haldane; *Salt v Marquess of Northampton* [1892] A.C. 1.

26   [1912] A.C. 565.

27   [1939] Ch. 441, Court of Appeal.

28   E.H.Burn, *Maudsley and Burn's Land Law Cases and Materials*, p. 808.

29   *Knightsbridge Estates Trust Ltd v Byrne* [1939] Ch. 441, p.457 per Sir Wilfrid Greene M.R.

So restrictions on the borrower's right to redeem are permissible, provided they are not oppressive. Sir Wilfrid Greene reconciled this case with *Fairclough v Swan Brewery Co Ltd* on the basis that the clause in that case rendered the right to redeem "illusory", i.e. at the point at which redemption was allowed, six weeks prior to the termination of the borrower's lease there was virtually nothing left of the borrower's interest in the land.

> **Freedom of Contract**
> The courts are influenced by the ideology of "freedom of contract", i.e. that parties should have the freedom to fix whatever terms they please. The reluctance of the courts to strike out terms of a mortgage transaction stems from the perception that rules of equity should not interfere with this freedom without due cause.

Options granted to the lender to purchase mortgaged property will be held void as they effectively render the property irredeemable, by allowing the lender to purchase (or otherwise gain) the land. However, this will only be the case if the term forms part of the mortgage transaction itself. *Samuel v Jarrah Timber and Wood Paving Corporation Ltd*[30] concerned a mortgage of debenture stock. As part of the contract the borrower had granted the lender an option to purchase the stock. Effectively therefore, if the lender exercised this option the borrower would be unable to get its property back once the loan was paid off. The House of Lords reluctantly held the option to be void. The Earl of Halsbury L.C. held that the position would have been different if the option had been granted as a separate agreement.[31]

In *Jones v Morgan*,[32] the Court of Appeal held void a term that gave the lender the right to purchase part of mortgaged land. The term was contained in an agreement that was entered into in 1997, three years after the original mortgage transaction. However, the 1997 agreement was entered into in order to obtain further finance from the lender and to vary the terms of the loan. It was in substance part of the original mortgage arrangement. Consequently, the Court of Appeal held that the term was void as it restricted the borrower's right to redeem the land.[33] In *Reeve v Lisle*[34] an option to purchase mortgaged property was upheld because it was granted as a separate agreement after the mortgage.

B. OPPRESSIVE OR UNCONSCIONABLE BARGAINS

Even where the agreement between borrower and lender does not render the right to redeem illusory, a term may be void if it imposes oppressive or unconscionable terms. What is oppressive depends on the relative bargaining strengths of the parties.

---

30   [1904] A.C. 323.
31   See also C below.
32   [2001] 1 E.G.L.R. 125.
33   Per Lord Phillips M.R., para.86, Pill L.J. dissenting.
34   [1902] A.C. 461.

Equity will not allow the enforcement of a term in the mortgage transaction if it is oppressive or unconscionable. The test is not one of *reasonableness*.[35] It is whether the terms of the mortgage transaction are "oppressive or unconscionable".[36] Effectively the courts are looking for one party taking advantage of another.

> "The classic example of an unconscionable bargain is where advantage has been taken of a young, inexperienced or ignorant person to introduce a term which no sensible well-advised person or party would have accepted."
>
> *Multiservice Bookbinding Ltd v Marden* [1979] Ch. 84, p.110 Per Browne-Wilkinson J.

In *Cityland and Property (Holdings) Ltd v Dabrah*[37] the defendant had purchased a house from the plaintiffs, part of the balance for which was secured on the house by way of mortgage. As part of the mortgage contract the defendant agreed to pay a premium of what amounted to 57 per cent of the loan amount. It was held to be an unconscionable bargain.

In *Multiservice Bookbinding Ltd v Marden*,[38] Browne-Wilkinson J. upheld a mortgage arrangement between two business people, independently advised by their solicitors. The agreement included a clause that linked the interest payable to the Swiss Franc, which increased considerably the amount of interest payable on the capital debt. It also provided that the mortgaged property could not be redeemed for 10 years, and that arrears of interest were added to the capital so that they also accrued interest. Browne-Wilkinson J. held that these terms were not oppressive or unconscionable. They did not have the necessary feature of a mortgagee taking advantage of an inexperienced mortgagor. It was certainly a hard bargain but the borrower and lender were in equal bargaining positions and the borrower had independent advice.

C. CASES WHERE THE MORTGAGEE OBTAINS A COLLATERAL ADVANTAGE

A collateral advantage exists where the mortgagee obtains some benefit from the transaction additional to its security, such as a sharing of profits or an option to purchase certain products, or a requirement that certain products should be purchased from the mortgagee. These terms will be held void if they are oppressive or unconscionable. They will not be void if they form part of a bargain that is separate from the mortgage transaction.

---

35   *Knightsbridge Estates Trust Ltd v Byrne* [1939] Ch. 441, per Sir Wilfrid Greene M.R.
36   *Knightsbridge,* above.
37   [1968] Ch. 166.
38   [1979] Ch. 84.

In *Noakes & Co Ltd v Rice*[39] the mortgagor of a public house undertook to purchase liquor solely from the mortgagee brewery.[40] The House of Lords held that if the collateral advantage continues after the loan has been paid off the mortgagor is not getting his property back in the condition that he mortgaged it. The lender has obtained something more than a mortgage. Such a collateral advantage is in the nature of "interest" paid on the loan, "and no more payable after the principal is paid off than interest would be".[41]

> "Once a mortgage always a mortgage and nothing but a mortgage"
>
> Lord Davey *Noakes & Co Ltd v Rice* [1902] A.C. 24

The principle is also seen in *Biggs v Hoddinott*,[42] in which a stipulation that the borrower would buy the mortgagee's liquor during the currency of the mortgage was upheld.

In *Kreglinger v New Patagonia Meat and Cold Storage Co Ltd*[43] the respondents ran a meat packing business. They had borrowed money from the appellants, who sold wool. As part of a mortgage transaction the meat company agreed to sell sheepskins to the woolbrokers. The woolbrokers agreed not to call in the loan for a specified period, although the meat company could pay off the loan at any time. When the meat company paid off the loan they claimed that the woolbrokers' option to purchase the sheepskins ended with their security. Viscount Haldane L.C. upheld the option for the agreed period. The bargain was not oppressive or unconscionable. The option to purchase the sheepskins was independent of the mortgage. The option was entered into as a commercial agreement by two parties dealing at arm's length. It was not a term that was imposed as part of the mortgage. This is a question of substance rather than the form of the agreement:

> "The question is in my opinion not whether the two contracts were made at the same moment and evidenced by the same instrument, but whether they were in substance a single and undivided contract or two distinct contracts."

Here it was the intention of the woolbrokers to obtain this option as a condition for giving the loan. It was held that the law should give effect to this intention. So the mortgage was seen as a separate part of the transaction "not to interfere" with the option.

---

39   [1902] A.C. 24.
40   Such an agreement is called a *solus* tie.
41   Per Lord Davey.
42   [1898] 2 Ch. 307.
43   [1914] A.C. 25.

> **A change in public policy**
> Viscount Haldane L.C. intimated obiter that it would be permissible for a collateral advantage to continue after the loan had been paid off as long as it was not "oppressive or unconscionable", and that this would be the case even if the advantage was part of the mortgage transaction itself. A change in public policy and the fact that the mortgage is often used as part of ordinary commercial transactions means that the courts should not view additional advantages as necessarily wrong and usurious, exacting benefits from a borrower who has fallen on hard times—as may have been the case in the earlier equity cases of the seventeenth, eighteenth and nineteenth centuries. The court should strike out a term if it was proven as a fact to be "oppressive or unconscionable". But not otherwise. The courts should give effect to the intentions behind commercial transactions.

D. AN "UNFAIR RELATIONSHIP BETWEEN DEBTOR AND CREDITOR"

Under the Consumer Credit Act 1974 the court had jurisdiction to reopen an "extortionate credit bargain", i.e. if it was "grossly exorbitant, or otherwise grossly contravene[d] ordinary principles of fair dealing".[44] Section 138(1), provided that in deciding whether to reopen a credit bargain the court should consider the degree of risk taken by the lender, and the age and experience, health and financial circumstances of the borrower. The Consumer Credit Act 2006 repeals s.138 with effect from April 2008. It introduces a jurisdiction for the courts to intervene where there is an "unfair relationship between creditor and debtor".[45]

Rights of the legal mortgagee: enforcing the security

4

A mortgage is a bundle of rights and powers given to a lender for the purpose of realising his security, i.e. using the borrower's land in order to recoup its loan investment should the borrower default on the loan repayments. Many mortgages exist in the context of residential home owner-occupied property. They have often been used in order to purchase the home in the first

---

44   s.138. This did not apply to building societies or local authorities.
45   The Consumer Credit Act 2006 repeals s.138 and replaces it with s.140A(1). It came into force on April 6, 2008. Not all mortgages fall within this Act, for instance, first mortgages of residential property that are regulated under the Financial Services and Markets Act 2000: Harpum, Bridge, Dixon, *Megarry & Wade Law of Real Property*, 8th edn (London: Sweet & Maxwell, 2008), para.25–118.

place. Our issue is really where the law draws the line in relation to protecting a borrower and their family from being evicted from their home.

A. THE RIGHT TO SUE ON THE PERSONAL COVENANT TO REPAY

As part of the mortgage transaction a borrower will covenant to repay the loan, in the manner stipulated (e.g. in monthly instalments) plus an amount of interest. Thus, if the borrower fails to repay the loan in accordance with the covenant then he or she is in breach of the agreement. Consequently, this will give the lender the right to sue the borrower for outstanding sums. This is useful in cases of "negative equity", e.g. where the house is worth less than the debt owed by the borrower to the bank. In such cases the lender can bring an action against the borrower to recover the amount outstanding.[46] This was the situation in *Palk v Mortgage Services Funding Plc*[47] in which there was approximately £75,000 negative equity.

B. THE MORTGAGEE'S RIGHT TO POSSESSION

A mortgagee has an automatic right to possession of mortgaged property. This arises because the mortgagee has rights that the Law of Property Act 1925 equates to an estate in the land.[48] There does not have to be any default by the borrower on the terms of the agreement before the mortgagee can exercise this right. As has been famously said in *Four-Maids Ltd v Dudley Marshall (Properties) Ltd*,[49] "The mortgagee may go into possession before the ink is dry on the mortgage".[50] It is possible for the mortgagee to "contract out" of this right to the effect that the mortgagee will only take possession if the borrower fails to meet the loan repayments.

> **Remember what "possession" actually *means***
> Possession is, in effect, *ownership*: the right to control the land. It is the right to choose what is done on the land, who can enter or not, and the right to take profit from the land.

It may be useful for a mortgagee to go into possession of mortgaged business premises and manage the business in order to pay off the loan.[51] However, in mortgages of residential property

---

46   Where the claim relates to the capital amount owed the claim must be brought within 12 years: *West Bromwich Building Society v Wilkinson* [2005] 1 W.L.R. 2303. Arrears of interest must be claimed within six years.
47   [1993] Ch.330.
48   Law of Property Act 1925 s. 87. See *Four-Maids Ltd v Dudley Marshall (Properties) Ltd* [1957] Ch. 317.
49   [1957] Ch. 317.
50   Per Harman J.
51   Ministry of Justice Consultation Paper, *Mortgages Power of Sale and Residential Property*, p.41: "Until late in the 19th century it was common practice for the lender to take actual possession of the property during the period of the loan, to rent it out or derive some other income from it".

it is usual for the mortgagee to allow the borrower to have possession, unless and until he fails to pay the instalments. Otherwise, if the lender could take possession immediately it would defeat the purpose of the loan.[52]

The usual reason a mortgagee will enter into possession of mortgaged property is in order to exercise the power of sale. In this way the lender will be able to get back its money. Although it is not necessary for a mortgagee to enter into possession in order to exercise the power of sale, many will do so in order to sell the property with vacant possession.[53] In strict legal theory if a mortgagee can sell to a buyer who does not demand vacant possession, he can simply exercise his statutory power of sale (see below) without obtaining possession.[54]

(1) Duties of the mortgagee in possession

A mortgagee in possession comes under strict duties. The right must be exercised in good faith. For example, it must be exercised for the purpose of enforcing the lender's security, e.g. obtaining repayment of the loan monies or to ensure that the borrower's business is being run appropriately. It should not be used as a means of defeating the right of another, which has little to do with the mortgagee's security.[55] Furthermore, if a mortgagee goes into possession of mortgaged property he will be held to account for the profits he ought to have received had he managed the property diligently. In *White v City of London Brewery Co*,[56] a mortgagee took possession of a public house. They leased it subject to a requirement that the tenants had to purchase beer from the mortgagee brewery. They were able to and should have leased it free from the condition. Had they done so they would have obtained higher rent. The mortgagees were held accountable for the difference. Because of the onerous nature of this duty, mortgagees will generally only take possession with a view to immediate sale of mortgaged property. If a mortgagee wishes to ensure that the borrower's business is being run properly it is more usual to appoint a receiver.[57]

(2) How can a mortgagee take possession?

A mortgagee can obtain a court order for possession or can take possession under its common law right. Thus, a mortgagee does not need to obtain a court order to take possession of mortgaged property,[58] although it is more usual to obtain one.

(3) Possession through a court order

A mortgagee can apply to the court for an order for possession of mortgaged property. Where this concerns residential property there are two possible outcomes to the hearing.[59] Firstly, the

---

52   Ministry of Justice Consultation Paper, *Mortgages Power of Sale and Residential Property*, para.42.
53   Above.
54   *Horsham Properties Group Ltd v Clark and Beech* [2008] EWHC 2327 (Ch). *Horsham* involved a "buy-to-let" mortgaged property under which the borrowers did not occupy the property. Mortgage lenders' internal regulation strongly prohibits this practice as far as residential mortgages are concerned (see below).
55   *Quennell v Maltby* [1979] 1 W.L.R. 318; *Downsview Nominees Ltd v First City Corp Ltd* [1993] A.C. 295.
56   (1889) 42 Ch.D 237.
57   The mortgagee's right to appoint a receiver is considered below.
58   *Ropaigealach v Barclays Bank Plc* [2000] Q.B. 263, p.271, per Chadwick L.J.
59   These outcomes are usefully detailed in Ministry of Justice, *Mortgages Power of Sale and Residential Property – Consultation Paper*, paras 58–9.

court can award an outright possession order and require the occupier to vacate the property, normally within 28 days. This will usually be the case where the borrower has failed to attend the hearing and/or there is little prospect of the arrears being repaid. Secondly, the court may grant a postponed or suspended possession order, or adjourn proceedings, under s.36 of the Administration of Justice Act 1970 (see below). Apart from s.36, the court has a limited inherent jurisdiction to stay a possession order.[60]

(a) Mortgage Pre-Action Protocol for institutional mortgagees

The Mortgage Pre-Action Protocol for institutional mortgagees was issued by the courts to residential mortgage lenders in respect of taking court action for possession following mortgage arrears. The Protocol highlights "concerns that possession orders were being obtained in cases where other remedies had not been exhausted".[61] The message that the courts are thereby giving to mortgage lenders is that *repossession should be a last resort*. The Protocol applies to first mortgages that are granted to finance the purchase of owner-occupied housing. It sets out the action a lender should take "prior to the start of a possession claim", for example the lender should attempt to discuss the problem and possible solutions with the defaulting borrower.[62]

> **BUILDING BLOCK NO 1: Residential Security**
> We can say that the law is good depending on the extent to which it supports the policy aim that the law should protect residential security. If the Pre-action Protocol is effective, we can therefore say that the law on mortgage repossessions is good law.

> The Ministry of Justice observed that the Protocol "appears to have been successful in reducing the number of possession order cases going to court": Ministry of Justice Consultation Paper, *Mortgages Power of Sale and Residential Property*, para.11.

(b) The court's jurisdiction under section 36 of the Administration of Justice Act 1970

As we have seen, under a mortgage of residential property, the mortgagee will not often take possession of the mortgaged property unless the borrower defaults on the loan repayments that are secured by the mortgage. Even then, under s.36 of the Administration of Justice Act 1970 the court has power to suspend a possession order where the mortgagee applies for a court order. Where there is a mortgage of a dwelling-house and the mortgagee brings an action for possession, the court may adjourn the proceedings, or "on giving judgment, or making an order, for delivery of possession of the mortgaged property. . . may stay or suspend execution of the judgment or order, or postpone the date for delivery of possession. . . for such period or

---

60   *Birmingham Citizens Permanent Building Society v Caunt* [1962] Ch. 883.
61   Ministry of Justice, *Mortgages Power of Sale and Residential Property – Consultation Paper*, para.11.
62   *Pre-action protocol for possession claims based on mortgage or home purchase plan arrears in respect of residential property*, paras 1.1, 3, 5 and 7.

periods as the court thinks reasonable". The court has no such jurisdiction where the mortgagee has exercised his common law right of possession. The powers of the court are "only capable of being exercised in the context of existing proceedings in which a claim for possession is made".[63] However, the court can only suspend or postpone a possession order where the borrower can show that he or she is "likely to be able within a reasonable period to pay any sums due under the mortgage or to remedy a default consisting of a breach of any other obligation arising under or by virtue of the mortgage".

(i) "Any sums due"

In *Halifax Building Society v Clarke*[64] it had been held that "any sums due" meant not only the amount that the borrower is in arrears, but the whole amount of the capital debt. In this case the loan was repayable in instalments, as is typically the case, and the mortgage in question had a clause that provided that the whole amount became "due" in the event that the borrower defaulted on the instalments. The effect of this is that it would have been much harder for the typical domestic mortgagor to show that they could pay "any sums due" within a reasonable period. Thus, parliament enacted the Administration of Justice Act 1973, s. 8 which provides that "any sums due" refers only to missed payments, which reversed *Clarke*.

(ii) "Within a reasonable period"

In order for the court to be able to exercise its discretion to suspend or postpone a possession order, the borrower must show that he is able to pay off the arrears *within a reasonable period*. Naturally they must also be able to pay the regular monthly instalments so that they do not fall behind again.[65] Originally the courts applied a period of 2–4 years. The borrower had to show that he could pay the arrears in this time as well as making his normal mortgage instalments. However, the leading case of *Cheltenham & Gloucester Building Society v Norgan*[66] took a more lenient approach. Waite L.J. held that the starting point for the court in considering whether to exercise its jurisdiction to postpone or suspend a possession order for mortgaged residential property would be the whole remaining term of the mortgage.

> "It does seem to me that the logic and spirit of the legislation require that the court should take as its starting point the full term of the mortgage and pose at the outset the question: 'Would it be possible for the mortgagor to maintain payment-off of the arrears by instalments over that period?' "

Waite L.J. concluded that as a result of this approach the court should

> "demand a more detailed analysis of present figures and future projections than it may have been customary for the courts to undertake until now. There is likely to be a greater need to require of mortgagors that they should furnish the court with a detailed 'budget' ".

---

63   *Ropaigealach v Barclays Bank Plc* [2000] Q.B. 263, p.271, per Chadwick L.J.
64   [1973] Ch. 307.
65   *Zinda v Bank of Scotland Plc* [2011] EWCA Civ 706.
66   [1996] 1 All E.R. 449.

Thus the court will not act speculatively. The borrower must present detailed facts and figures that show that he or she can pay off the arrears at the same time as maintaining their originally agreed mortgage instalments. The court must also consider the adequacy of the mortgagee's security and whether it is vulnerable because at some point in the near future there is a realistic chance that the house may be worth less than the amount secured on it. This is a factor in considering what may amount to a "reasonable period" to allow the borrower to pay off any arrears.

However, although the case took a lenient approach to what could be held to be a "reasonable period" the *quid pro quo* for the borrower is that once there has been one suspension of a possession order, and the borrower then defaults again on his agreed payment plan, then the courts are highly unlikely to suspend possession again. Waite L.J. stated that

> "the section 36 powers (although of course capable in theory of being exercised again and again) should not be employed repeatedly to compel a lending institution which has already suffered interruption of the regular flow of interest to which it was entitled under the express terms of the mortgage to accept assurances of future payment from a borrower in whom it has lost confidence."

Thus, in *Halifax Plc v Okin*[67] the court declined to exercise the powers under s.36 as the borrower's history of payment was very poor and the borrower had had a previous postponement of possession and had defaulted on an agreed payment plan.[68]

It is important to remember that the courts will not invariably allow the borrower the whole remaining term of the mortgage to pay off the arrears. This will depend on many factors, such as the adequacy of the mortgagee's security. The remaining term of the mortgage is a starting point only. Indeed the Ministry of Justice Consultation Paper, *Mortgages Power of Sale and Residential Property*[69] observes that "normal practice appears to be that arrears are likely to be spread over two to four years".

(iii) Allowing a short postponement in order to permit the borrower to sell the mortgaged property

If the borrower has no prospect of being able to pay the arrears of capital and interest that have accrued on the loan, or cannot continue to service the loan by making the repayments as they fall due in the future, then it is possible that the borrower may wish to sell the mortgaged property himself or herself, in order to avoid a forced sale. In limited circumstances the court will, under s.36, suspend or postpone a possession order for a short period in order to allow the borrower to sell the house. Some cases have been prepared to postpone possession for 3–5 years.[70] Generally,

---

67   [2007] EWCA Civ 567.
68   Also *Zinda v Bank of Scotland Plc* [2011] EWCA Civ 706.
69   para.55.
70   *Bristol and West Building Society v Ellis* (1996) 73 P. & C.R. 158, although on the facts of the case possession was not postponed. Compare the contemplated period of postponement of six months to a year in *National and Provincial Building Society v Lloyd* [1996] 1 All E.R. 630.

there are two considerations here: firstly, the adequacy of the mortgagee's security and secondly, whether or not there is a realistic prospect of a sale occurring.

If a sale of the mortgaged property is unlikely at the time of the court action to realise enough to discharge the debt to the lender, plus arrears and costs, then the court is likely to award the mortgagee possession in order to conduct the sale themselves.[71]

> **"Negative equity"**
> In such cases it may be said that the mortgagee's security is *vulnerable*, i.e. sale of the mortgaged property will not discharge the loan. This means that the borrower has what is called "negative equity" in the property, i.e. the house is worth less than the amount owed to the lender.

Indeed in *Bristol & West Building Society v Ellis*[72] Auld L.J. observed

"all depends on the individual circumstances of each case, though the important factors in most are likely to be the extent to which the mortgage debt and arrears are secured by the value of the property and the effect of time on that security. . . Where there is likely to be considerable delay in selling the property and/or its value is close to the total of the mortgage debt and arrears so that the mortgagee is at risk as to the adequacy of the security, immediate possession or only a short period of suspension may be reasonable. Where there has already been considerable delay in realising a sale of the property and/or the likely sale proceeds are unlikely to cover the mortgage debt and arrears or there is simply no sufficient evidence as to sale value, the normal order would be for immediate possession".

Thus, in addition to the security issue, before the courts will consider postponing a possession order to allow the borrower conduct of the sale, a sale must be a likely prospect. In *Target Homes Ltd v Clothier*[73] possession was postponed. An offer for the property had already been received and there was evidence from an estate agent that the price obtained by a sale would discharge the loan and pay off the arrears.

(c) Critical Thinking

LECTURER: Now hold your understanding of the law established by s.36 of the Administration of Justice Act 1970 against the Building Blocks. We can say that it is good law if it supports the Building Blocks below bad law if it undermines them.

---

71 *Cheltenham and Gloucester Plc v Krausz* [1997] 1 All E.R. 21.
72 (1996) 73 P. & C.R. 158.
73 [1994] 1 All E.R. 439.

STUDENT: The reasoning in the cases we have just examined clearly supports BUILDING BLOCK NO 1. I think that although any possession order and forced sale severely undermines the borrower's residential security, as it effectively means that the borrower and his or her family will lose their home, the law puts safeguards in place before allowing the grant of a possession order.

LECTURER: And what are these safeguards?

STUDENT: Well, a court will postpone possession if the borrower can show a reasonable prospect of being able to catch up on their mortgage payments, and pay off any arrears within a reasonable period. And the court in *Cheltenham & Gloucester v Norgan*[74] gave "reasonable period" a very broad interpretation.

LECTURER: And the courts, through the Pre-Action Protocol, have given the strong message that repossession of mortgaged property should be an action of last resort, to be used only after the lender has attempted through negotiation with the borrower, to resolve any difficulties of payment that the borrower may have. The lender might offer to restructure the mortgage and the loan repayments in order to assist the borrower, for example, the loan might be taken over a longer period.

So does the law so far support or undermine BUILDING BLOCK NO 1?

STUDENT: The law and the Pre-Action Protocol shows a deep respect for the borrower's residential security, by trying to allow the borrower every chance of catching up on their arrears before allowing a repossession.

LECTURER: But as you know from our Building Blocks and the way in which we use them to construct an argument, this is very far from being the end of the story. The law, in order to be argued to be good and fair, must consider all the relevant "stakeholders", i.e. all the competing policy interests.

So the law must also adequately serve the policy contained in BUILDING BLOCK NO 5.

BUILDING BLOCK NO 5: The Protection of Mortgage Lenders

Either a loan is needed in order to purchase the house in the first place, or, as is becoming increasingly common, a second mortgage is used to secure a loan is used to set up a small business, or to expand an existing business. Unless the rules of Land Law make sure that lenders can readily get their money back by selling the house, banks and building societies may become reluctant to give loans to owner occupiers and small businesses in the future. This would have significant impact on the country's economy: see also K.Gray and S.F.Gray, *Elements of Land Law*, pp.1625–6, quoting *Barclays Bank Plc v O'Brien* [1994] 1 A.C. 180, per Lord Browne-Wilkinson. See also Lord Nicholls' comments in *Royal Bank of Scotland Plc v Etridge (No.2)* [2002] 2 A.C. 773, para.35.

STUDENT: I think that the law supports the policy in BUILDING BLOCK NO 5. The courts try to ensure that repossession is a last resort. Even though possession may be postponed, this will not be the case unless the lender is getting payment on the loan, hence the need for the

---

74   [1996] 1 All ER 449.

borrower to show that they can pay back the arrears over a reasonable period. And even though the arrears can be stretched over the entire remaining period of the mortgage loan, this will not always be the case (as shown by the Ministry of Justice Consultation Paper, *Mortgages Power of Sale and Residential Property*, para.55, described above). And the borrower must still be making payment of interest, capital and arrears. Thus, the lender will not be "kept out of their money", as was said in the cases that decided whether co-owned property should be sold under s.15 of the Trusts of Land and Appointment of Trustees Act 1996. Furthermore, the courts have shown that a dominating consideration in deciding what is a "reasonable period" is whether the house is adequate security for the loan. A much shorter period may be set where the borrower is in negative equity: *Cheltenham & Gloucester v Norgan*.

All of this shows that the law supports the needs of banks and building societies. The law tries to ensure that they are being paid a return on their loan and that their investment is safe. I think that the law strikes a good balance between BUILDING BLOCK NO 1 and BUILDING BLOCK NO 5.

LECTURER: So the law supports the interests of both its "stakeholders".

(d) Where the borrower wants to sell against the wishes of the mortgagee

It might be the case that the borrower wishes the mortgaged property sold and the lender wishes to wait and see if the property market improves. Here the borrower is seeking to sell the property himself *against the wishes of the mortgagee*.

> Section 91(2) of the Law of Property Act 1925 provides that in an action relating to the mortgaged property, at the request of any person interested in the right of redemption or the mortgage money, the court may direct a sale, "notwithstanding that any other person dissents". The court "may direct a sale of the mortgaged property, on such terms as it thinks fit".

Thus, at the request of the borrower the court can order a sale of the mortgaged property even though the lender objects to the sale. In *Palk v Mortgage Services Funding Plc*,[75] the Palks had originally borrowed £300,000, secured on the family home. They did not make many repayments before defaulting. The debt to the mortgagees mounted to nearly £360,000 and the Palks themselves had arranged to sell the property for £283,000. The mortgagee obtained possession but wished to wait until the property market improved before selling the house. Until then the mortgagees wished to rent out the property. However, the rental income did not come close to covering the mounting debt that the Palks owed. Thus, each year they would get further and further into debt. The Court of Appeal held that the property should be sold. It was said that the lender could back its own judgment on the property market and purchase the property. The decision in *Palk* was clearly fair in the circumstances, but usually, where the borrower is in negative equity, the court will refuse to allow the borrower conduct of the sale.[76]

---

75   [1993] Ch. 330.
76   *Cheltenham and Gloucester Plc v Krausz* [1997] 1 All E.R. 21.

Indeed, in *Toor v State Bank of India*,[77] the court refused to compel a mortgagee to sell the mortgaged property to a family friend of the borrower. It was stated that under s.91 the court would only compel a mortgagee to sell against its wishes if the circumstances were exceptional or it would be unfair to the mortgagor to decline to compel a sale, as in the *Palk* case. It was also stated that the court should be cautious when the borrower is advocating a sale to persons connected with them, e.g. family friends. It may simply be a way to avoid eviction.

(4) The "Horsham loophole"[78]

As we have seen above, the court only has jurisdiction to come to the assistance of the borrower and suspend or postpone a possession order where the mortgagee applies for a court order of possession.[79] A mortgagee has a common law right of possession that arises automatically "as soon as the ink is dry on the mortgage".[80] Thus it is not necessary to obtain a court order for possession.

In *Horsham Properties Group Ltd v Clark and Beech*[81] property was purchased with the aid of a mortgage in order that the property could be rented out. This is a commercial venture. The property was not purchased as a residence. A mortgage used to secure funding to purchase property in these circumstances is often referred to as a "buy-to-let" mortgage. When the borrowers defaulted on the loan the lender simply sold the property under its statutory power of sale[82] without obtaining possession. At the time the buyer did not demand possession, but they later obtained a possession order against the borrowers, who had by this time moved into the mortgaged property.[83]

> Thus, possession was obtained as against the borrowers without the latter having the opportunity to go to court and argue that the possession order should be postponed or suspended under s.36 of the Administration of Justice Act 1970.

One argument raised by one of the borrowers was that English property law thereby deprived her of her possessions under the Human Rights Act 1998. The court rejected this argument and held that the borrower's rights to the mortgaged property had always been subject to the mortgage agreement. Allowing an automatic right of possession was part of the nature of a mortgage.

We should note that the mortgage in *Horsham* was granted to secure what was essentially a commercial venture. There were fears that mortgagees would begin to take similar action with

---

77   [2010] EWHC 1097 (Ch).
78   The expression was used in the Ministry of Justice Consultation Paper, *Mortgages Power of Sale and Residential Property*.
79   *Ropaigealach v Barclays Bank Plc* [1999] 4 All E.R. 235.
80   *Four-Maids Ltd v Dudley Marshall Ltd* [1957] Ch. 317.
81   [2008] EWHC 2327 (Ch); [2009] 1 P & C.R. 8; *Times*, October 29, 2008.
82   Which we will consider below.
83   This was prohibited under the mortgage agreement, see Ministry of Justice Consultation Paper, *Mortgages Power of Sale and Residential Property*, para.37.

regard to residential property, and thus, exercise their power of sale without taking possession and without giving borrowers the opportunity to apply for the court's assistance under s.36 of the Administration of Justice Act 1970. There was an attempt at law reform, requiring mortgagees of a dwelling-house to first obtain a court order before exercising their statutory power of sale. The court would then be able to suspend or postpone the exercise of the power on the same grounds covered by s.36.[84] But it appears that the mortgage industry may itself provide effective regulation against this, and the attempt at legislative reform has been abandoned.[85] The Council of Mortgage Lenders, the regulatory body for institutional mortgagees, has stated that its members would not seek to obtain possession of a dwelling without a court order in cases where the mortgaged property is the borrower's residence.[86]

> "In November 2008 the Financial Services Authority wrote to the heads of all lending institutions in the UK, stating that if lenders were to employ the power of sale in situations where a court order for possession would have been denied, the Authority would be inclined to view such actions as unfair practices".
>
> Ministry of Justice Consultation Paper, *Mortgages Power of Sale and Residential Property*, para.67

(5) Repossessions and unauthorised tenancies of mortgaged property

Where a borrower has granted an unauthorised lease of a mortgaged dwelling house, the tenant has a statutory right to apply to the court to suspend a possession order. The court may postpone possession for a period not exceeding two months.[87]

C. THE RIGHT TO APPOINT A RECEIVER

Where the borrower is in default so that it gives rise to the mortgagee's power of sale, the mortgagee may appoint a receiver.[88] A receiver is a person who goes into possession of mortgaged property and has powers to manage the property. Under s.109(2) of the Law of Property Act 1925 the receiver is deemed to be the agent of the borrower, who is "solely responsible for the receiver's acts or defaults".[89] Thus, if the receiver manages the property negligently, the mortgagee will not be responsible to the borrower. This is why many mortgagees would choose to appoint a receiver instead of going into possession and managing mortgaged property themselves. When a mortgagee is in possession they come under a strict duty to the borrower to manage the property diligently.[90]

---

84 The Home Repossession (Protection) Bill 2009.
85 The bill was withdrawn before its second reading in the commons.
86 Ministry of Justice Consultation Paper, *Mortgages Power of Sale and Residential Property*, para.65.
87 Mortgage Repossessions (Protection of Tenants etc) Act 2010.
88 Law of Property Act 1925 s.109(1). The appointment must also be made in writing. The mortgagee has the power to appoint a receiver under Law of Property Act 1925 s.101(1)(iii).
89 Unless it is stated otherwise in the mortgage deed.
90 *White v City of London Brewery Co* (1889) 42 Ch.D 237, see above in this chapter section 4B.

The receiver owes his primary duty to the mortgagee: "In exercising his powers of management the primary duty of the receiver is to try and bring about a situation in which interest on the secured debt can be paid and the debt itself repaid".[91] However, the receiver owes secondary duties to the borrower. He must manage the property in good faith, e.g. for the purposes of fulfilling his primary duty.[92] "Bad faith" has been defined as "some dishonesty or improper motive".[93] He is also under a duty to manage the property with due diligence.[94] Although the receiver is not obliged to carry on the business of the borrower, if he chooses to continue the business, "due diligence requires reasonable steps to be taken in order to try to do so profitably".[95] In *Medforth v Blake*[96] a mortgagee had appointed a receiver who had gone into possession and carried on the business of the mortgagor: a pig-farming business. The receivers had failed to obtain available discounts on pig feed. The Court of Appeal held that the receivers had breached their duty to the borrowers.

D. POWER OF SALE

In many cases a mortgagee will take possession of mortgaged property in order to sell it and recoup the debt owed by the borrower. However, the mortgagee does not own the estate in the land; the borrower does. Thus, the lender will need a power of sale. A mortgagee has a statutory power of sale under s.101 of the Law of Property Act 1925. However, before the power can be properly exercised by the lender, it must have "arisen" and become "exercisable".[97]

(1) When the mortgagee's power of sale arises

Section 101 of the Law of Property Act 1925 imposes two conditions:

- The legal mortgagee has a power to sell mortgaged property only when the mortgage money *has become due*. In a mortgage deed there will usually be a term stating that the money falls due to be repaid after six months. This of course does not mean that the borrower has to repay the money at this time. The objective of such a clause is to ensure that the mortgagee's power of sale arises.
- The statutory power of sale only arises where the mortgage is created by deed.[98]

---

91   *Medforth v Blake and Others* [2000] Ch. 86, per Sir Richard Scott V.C. p.102.
92   *Kennedy v De Trafford* [1897] A.C. 180, per Lord Herschell.
93   *Medforth v Blake*, above, per Sir Richard Scott V.C. p.103.
94   *Medforth v Blake* above, per Sir Richard Scott V.C. p.102. Duty of the receiver to the borrower goes beyond the need to act in good faith: *Knight v Lawrence* [1993] B.C.L.C. 215.
95   Above.
96   [2000] Ch. 86.
97   The mortgagee's powers conferred by the Law of Property Act 1925, including the power of sale and the power to appoint a receiver, can be varied and extended by the mortgage deed: Law of Property Act 1925 s.101(3).
98   Law of Property Act 1925 s.101(1). Although the mortgage must be created by deed for the power of sale to arise, if the mortgage itself is equitable through want of registration, but is still created by deed, then the power of sale still arises: *Swift 1st Ltd v Colin* [2011] EWHC 2410.

If the mortgagee attempts to sell the mortgaged property *before* he has acquired a power of sale, it is clear that the borrower's estate in the land does not pass to the purchaser. The lender has no power to make this happen. All a purchaser will acquire is the mortgagee's interest in the land. Thus, a purchaser from a mortgagee conducting a forced sale must check that the contractual date for redemption of the mortgage is passed.[99]

(2) When the power of sale becomes exercisable

Before selling the mortgaged property, the lender must make sure that its power of sale has become *exercisable*. This will be the case if one of the conditions laid out in s.103 of the Law of Property Act 1925 is satisfied. Section 103 provides that a mortgagee shall not exercise the power of sale unless and until:

(i) The lender has served notice on the mortgagor requiring payment and there has been a default in the payment of the mortgage money for three months after the notice was served; or

(ii) There is interest under the mortgage in arrear and "unpaid for two months after becoming due"; or

(iii) There has been a breach of some term of the mortgage, other than the requirement to pay the mortgage money or interest.

(3) The position of the purchaser from the mortgagee

Where the mortgagee has exercised his power of sale, s.104(1) of the Law of Property Act 1925 determines that the purchaser will acquire the mortgaged estate "freed from all estates, interests, and rights to which the mortgage has priority, but subject to all estates, interests, and rights which have priority to the mortgage". The effect of the mortgagee exercising the power of sale is to extinguish the borrower's equity of redemption.[100] The purchaser will acquire a good title to the estate free from any interest in the land which did not bind the mortgagee. However, if the lender took his mortgage subject to a prior right in the borrower's land, then he cannot sell the estate free from that right.

> **Example**
> It might be the case that prior to the mortgage, another person had acquired a beneficial interest in the land by contribution to the purchase. This may be an overriding interest that bound the mortgagee under the provisions of Sch.3 of the Land Registration Act 2002, when the mortgage was granted. If such is the case then the lender is bound by that right and could not convey the land to a purchaser free from it. In fact, they would not have the prior right to possession of the land in this example. For the rules relating to which interests in the land have priority over a later mortgage lender see Chapters 7 and 8.

---

99   See C.Harpum, M.Dixon, S.Bridge, *Megarry and Wade Law of Real Property*, para.25–016: "Proof of title is thereby simplified, for the existence of the power of sale is proved by the form of the mortgage and the redemption date specified in it".

100   *National and Provincial Building Society v Ahmed* [1995] 2 E.G.L.R. 127.

A purchaser from the mortgagee does not have to enquire into whether the power of sale has become exercisable. The purchaser will obtain a good title notwithstanding that the power was not exercisable.[101] The borrower will have a right of action against the lender for damage suffered as a result of an unauthorised, improper or irregular exercise of the power of sale.[102]

(4) Mortgagees' duties in conducting a sale of mortgaged property

A Forced sale will have terrible consequences for the borrower because they will lose their home. However, if the house is worth more than the debt secured on it then the borrower will be concerned that he comes out of the sale with as much money as possible. It may enable them to start afresh. If the price that is realised by the mortgagee's sale is less that the amount required to discharge the debt, interest and costs, then the lender is able to sue the borrower on his covenant to repay. Taking all of this into consideration therefore, the price obtained by a forced sale is of major significance to the borrower. As Dixon observes,[103]

> "Quite naturally, the borrower facing a forced sale of its paramount legal title, in circumstances where it has no control over the conduct of the sale, often suspects both the motives of the lender and its diligence in finding a buyer. After all, the interests of the parties often will not coincide: the lender may prefer a quick escape with its debt paid, while the borrower wants to avoid a shortfall and even gain a decent surplus."

A mortgagee is not by law permitted to sell the mortgaged property at a "knock-down" price, simply to repay the debt.[104] As to the nature of the mortgagee's duties, it was confirmed in *Silven Properties v Royal Bank of Scotland*,[105] that the mortgagee's duties in the conduct of a sale are not tortious duties, as for instance the duty of care in the tort of negligence – attributable to the "neighbour principle".[106] They are equitable. The other preliminary observation is that it is often said that a mortgagee is not "trustee" of the power of sale.[107] You may remember that a trustee is under strict equitable duties which, broadly conceived, mean that he must put the interests of the beneficiaries above his own interests. He is not entitled to prefer his own interests. A mortgagee is in a different position. When exercising the power of sale, he is under no such obligation to put the borrower's interests first.[108] The power of sale "is given to the mortgagee for his own benefit to enable him to realise his security".[109] Subject to the two duties discussed below, he *is* entitled to prefer his own interests.

---

101   Law of Property Act 1925 s.104(2), unless the purchaser is actually aware that the power of sale has not become exercisable, e.g. none of the three conditions in s.103 has been satisfied. In such a case the purchaser will not acquire a good title: *Lord Waring v London and Manchester Assurance Co Ltd* [1935] Ch. 310.

102   Law of Property Act 1925 s.104(2).

103   M.Dixon, "Mortgage Duties and Commercial Property Transactions" [2006] Conv. 278.

104   *Palk v Mortgage Services Funding Plc* [1993] Ch. 330, pp.337–8, per Sir Donald Nicholls V.C. *Predeth v Castle Phillips Finance Co Ltd* [1986] 2 E.G.L.R. 144.

105   [2004] 1 W.L.R. 997, also *Medforth v Blake* [2000] Ch. 86, per Sir Richard Scott V.C. p.97; *Downsview Nominees Ltd v First City Corporation* [1993] A.C. 295, Privy Council, per Lord Templeman.

106   *Medforth v Blake* [2000] Ch.86, per Sir Richard Scott V.C. p. 97.

107   *Nash v Eads* (1889) 25 S.J. 95, per Sir George Jessel M.R.

108   *Raja v Austin Gray* [2003] 1 E.G.L.R. 96, para.59, per Peter Gibson L.J.

109   C.Harpum, M.Dixon, S.Bridge, *Megarry and Wade Law of Real Property*, para.25–018.

The mortgagee's duties
Cuckmere Brick Co Ltd v Mutual Finance [1971] Ch. 949 confirmed that in selling the mortgaged property the mortgagee must act in good faith and take reasonable care to obtain a proper price for the property.

Firstly therefore, the mortgagee must exercise the power of sale in good faith.[110] Thus, it must be exercised for a proper purpose and not for a purpose unconnected with the realisation of the mortgagee's security.[111] An example of "bad faith" would exist where the mortgagee exercises his power of sale not because he wishes to obtain his money but because he wishes to defeat another person's option to purchase the property.[112]

Secondly, the mortgagee must take reasonable care to obtain a proper price or "market value" for the property.[113] If it breaches this duty of reasonable care and the sale realises less than a "proper price", the mortgagee will be liable to account to the mortgagor, and anyone else with an interest in the equity of redemption, for the difference.[114] In *Cuckmere Brick Co Ltd v Mutual Finance*,[115] Salmon L.J. observed that

"The mortgagor is vitally affected by the result of the sale but its preparation and conduct is left entirely in the hands of the mortgagee. . . it would be strange indeed if he were under no legal obligation to take reasonable care to obtain what I call the true market value at the date of the sale."

The mortgagee must be shown to have failed to take proper care in the conduct of the sale, e.g. in marketing the property. So the question that the court will ask is whether the mortgagee's conduct of the sale was likely to achieve the best price reasonable obtainable.[116] As to what amounts to "reasonable care" the mortgagee is free to sell the property whenever he wishes, even if the timing is poor. He is not obliged to wait until he could obtain a better price.[117] Neither is the mortgagee under any duty to improve the mortgaged property before selling it, in order to obtain a better price.[118] For example, he is under no duty to spend money applying for planning permission in order to improve the price or marketability of the property.

---

110   *Kennedy v De Trafford* [1897] A.C. 180, HL.
111   M.Dixon [2006] Conv. 278.
112   *Meretz Investments NV v APC Ltd* [2006] EWHC 74.
113   *Silven Properties v Royal Bank of Scotland* [2004] 1 W.L.R. 997—for a useful review of the current authorities; *Cuckmere Brick Co Ltd v Mutual Finance* [1971] Ch. 949; *Medforth v Blake* [2000] Ch 86.
114   *Silven Properties v Royal Bank of Scotland* [2004] 1 W.L.R. 997, para.19.
115   [1971] Ch. 949.
116   *Bishop v Blake* [2006] EWHC 931; M.Dixon [2006] Conv. 278.
117   *Tse Kwong Lam v Wong Chit Sen* [1983] 1 W.L.R. 1349, p.1355; *Silven Properties*, above, para.15, also *South Sea Bank Ltd v Tan Soon Gin* [1991] 1 A.C. 531, both disapproving Lord Denning MR's comments that although a mortgagee can choose the timing of the sale, he cannot choose the *worst* time: *Standard Chartered Bank v Walker* [1982] 1 W.L.R. 1410, pp.1415–1416.
118   *Silven Properties v Royal Bank of Scotland* [2004] 1 W.L.R. 997, para.16.

The mortgagee must expose the property to the market for a reasonable length of time and advertise the property sufficiently.[119] In *Bishop v Blake*[120] a mortgagee was in breach of the duty to take reasonable care when she sold a mortgaged inn to the existing tenants at substantially less than market value. The property was advertised in a relevant periodical but only very briefly, and without sufficient contact detail. Thus, only the most alert reader would have spotted the advert. In *Cuckmere Brick Co Ltd v Mutual Finance*[121] the plaintiffs owned development land, which they had mortgaged to the defendants for a £50,000 loan. The plaintiffs had planning permission to build 100 flats but obtained further planning permission to build houses on the site. The mortgagees exercised their power of sale and sold the land through auction. They had advertised the property and mentioned the planning permission for the houses, but failed to mention the planning permission for the flats. It was held that the mortgagees were in breach of their duty to obtain the true market value of the land. They were held liable to account to the plaintiffs for the difference between the price actually realised at auction (£44,000) and the assessment of its true market value (£65,000).

(5) Mortgagee cannot purchase mortgaged property itself

A mortgagee or its agent cannot itself purchase mortgaged property. Such a sale may be set aside.[122] The mortgagee may sell to an associate, provided it had taken steps to realise the true market value.[123]

(6) Application of the proceeds of sale

Once the mortgaged property has been sold, the mortgagee holds the proceeds of sale on trust and must apply them as provided in s.105 of the Law of Property Act 1925.

The mortgagee must firstly discharge any prior incumbrances that were not made part of the sale, i.e. prior incumbrances are rights in the land that have priority to their mortgage.

> For example, it may be the case that a house is subject to three registered charges and it is the second lender who is selling the house. The second lender must pay off the first mortgage out of the sale proceeds before he can use those proceeds to pay off the debt owed to him.

The selling mortgagee must then pay the costs, charges and expenses properly incurred by the sale. Then he is to discharge the loan, interest and costs, including any unpaid arrears. Then he must discharge any mortgage that takes priority after his own.

---

119   *Skipton Building Society v Stott* [2000] All E.R. 779, CA—property sold to a neighbour and not advertised. Mortgagee held to be in breach of duty.
120   [2006] EWHC 931. M.Dixon [2006] Conv. 278.
121   [1971] Ch. 949.
122   *Farrar v Farrars Ltd* (1888) 40 Ch.D 395.
123   *Tse Kwong Lam v Wong Chit Sen* [1983] 1 W.L.R. 1349.

> Thus, in our example, the selling mortgagee is the second lender. He firstly discharged the first mortgage that had priority to his own, and then paid off his loan. Now he is to pay off the debt owed by the borrower to the third lender.

Any money remaining from the sale shall then be paid to the borrower.

E. FORECLOSURE

When the legal date for redemption has passed the mortgagee can apply to the court for a foreclosure order. However foreclosure actions are very rare.[124] A mortgagee must obtain a court order for foreclosure. Where an order for foreclosure is made absolute it extinguishes the borrower's equity of redemption. By the court order the mortgagee gains the whole interest in the mortgaged property.[125] Section 88(2) of the Law of Property Act 1925 provides that "[w]here any such mortgagee obtains an order for foreclosure absolute, the order shall operate to vest to fee simple in him". The mortgage term is merged into the fee simple. The effect of this provision is that the borrower loses the right to have any increase in value of the property over and above the debt. The effect is also to extinguish the borrower's personal covenant to repay the loan.

When the lender applies for a court order for foreclosure, if the court is satisfied that the contractual date for redemption has arisen, it may make an order of foreclosure *nisi*, in which it will stipulate a date by which, if he is to avoid foreclosure, the borrower must pay the sum outstanding to the lender. If the borrower fails to make payment by this date, the order is made *absolute*.

> The court can order sale instead of foreclosure under s.91(2) of the Law of Property Act 1925: *Twentieth Century Banking Corp Ltd v Wilkinson* [1977] Ch. 99.

Enforcement of mortgages and the doctrine of undue influence

5

In section 4 above we considered the remedies available to a mortgagee to enforce its security. The borrower can be sued on the personal covenant to repay the loan, on the basis of breach of contract. The lender also has various mean by which it may choose to enforce the security for the

---

124   *Palk v Mortgage Services Funding Plc* [1993] Ch. 330.
125   For a history of foreclosure see Harpum, Bridge and Dixon, *Megarry and Wade Law of Real Property*, para.25–006.

loan. It may take possession of mortgaged property and sell it with vacant possession to a purchaser.

However, where a mortgage has been entered into as a result of fraud, misrepresentation or undue influence, the borrower may be able to set aside the mortgage, meaning that it is unenforceable against them.[126] Undue influence is where a person's intention to enter into a transaction has been procured by unacceptable means.[127] In *Royal Bank of Scotland Plc v Etridge (No.2)*,[128] Lord Nicholls states that "[t]he means used is regarded as an exercise of improper or 'undue' influence, and hence unacceptable. . . the consent thus procured ought not fairly to be treated as the expression of a person's free will". Thus, where there is undue influence, it means that the borrower did not enter into the transaction with their own free will and consent.

In this context, undue influence "arises out of a relationship between two persons where one has acquired over another a measure of influence, or ascendancy, of which the ascendant person then takes unfair advantage".[129] This would be the case where one person reposes trust and confidence in the other to look after their affairs and the other takes advantage of this.[130] In *Royal Bank of Scotland Plc v Etridge (No.2)*,[131] Lord Nicholls stated that:

"Several expressions have been used in an endeavour to encapsulate the essence: trust and confidence, reliance, dependence or vulnerability on the one hand and ascendancy, domination or control on the other. None of these descriptions is perfect. None is all embracing. Each has its proper place."

Example

A husband and wife owned their own home as joint registered proprietors. The husband wanted to borrow heavily from the bank in order to expand his business. In return the bank wanted a mortgage on the house. The husband said that this was really the only way of saving the business, and that if she did not agree to the mortgage, he would go bankrupt anyway. This was not true. However, because the wife left all financial matters to her husband, she believed him and signed the mortgage deed. The husband's business failed and the bank now want possession of the house.

In this example the wife's signature on the mortgage deed was procured by undue influence. The husband had a measure of ascendancy over his wife in matters of finance and he took unfair advantage of it.

---

126   *First National Bank Plc v Achampong* [2003] EWCA Civ. 487; *Barclays Bank Plc v O'Brien* [1994] 1 A.C. 180.
127   *Huguenin v Baseley* (1807) 14 Ves. 273, p.300.
128   [2002] 2 A.C. 773, para.7.
129   *Royal Bank of Scotland Plc v Etridge (No. 2)* [2002] 2 A.C. 773, para.8, per Lord Nicholls.
130   Above, para.9; *Allcard v Skinner* (1887) 36 Ch.D. 145.
131   [2002] 2 A.C. 773, para.11.

Although it is important for the purposes of this doctrine to establish the existence of undue influence, the question with which we are concerned is whether the presence of undue influence affects the enforceability of the mortgage. *Will the bank in our example above be able to take possession and sell the house?*

The effect of establishing that the undue influence infects the mortgagee is that the mortgage cannot be enforced by the lender against the victim (the wife in our example). This means that the lender will not acquire the rights and remedies of a legal mortgagee. It requires both or all the owners of the legal estate to jointly create a legal mortgage, and one of the owners of the legal estate has effectively not joined the transaction. However, the bank will have acquired rights. The mortgage will take effect against the husband's equitable interest, and the bank will be able to apply for an order of sale under s.14 of the Trusts of Land and Appointment of Trustees Act 1996.[132] However, as we saw in Chapter 5, sale is not an automatic result of such an application.

(1) Surety transactions and joint loans

The type of transaction in our example was what we call a surety transaction. These are tripartite transactions[133] involving a principal borrower (the husband in our example), whose debts are being guaranteed or to whom a loan is being made for their business; the creditor, i.e. the person making the loan, and the surety or "guarantor" (the wife). A surety stands to take no advantage from the transaction. He or she is simply guaranteeing that the principal borrower will repay the loan, i.e. the mortgage will give the bank rights over the surety's house should the principal borrower default on the loan agreement. As Lord Nicholls observes in *Royal Bank of Scotland Plc v Etridge (No.2)*,[134] surety transactions

> "involve the debtor as well as the creditor and the guarantor. The guarantor enters into the transaction at the request of the debtor. The guarantor assumes obligations. On the face of the transaction the guarantor usually receives no benefit in return unless the guarantee is being given on a commercial basis. Leaving aside cases where the relationship between the surety and the debtor is commercial, a guarantee transaction is one-sided so far as the guarantor is concerned."

A surety transaction is different from the situation where a loan is made to the couple jointly, ostensibly for their joint purposes.[135]

(2) The structure of the law of undue influence

In most of these cases it is not the lender who is exerting undue influence but the principal borrower. Thus, we need to study the principles that tell us: firstly, how we can ascertain whether

---

132   *First National Bank Plc v Achampong* [2003] EWCA Civ 487.
133   *Royal Bank of Scotland Plc v Etridge (No.2)* [2002] 2 A.C. 773.
134   [2002] 2 A.C. 773, para.43.
135   *CIBC Mortgages Plc v Pitt* [1994] 1 A.C. 200, e.g. a joint loan to purchase a holiday home.

the transaction has been procured by undue influence, and secondly, whether the mortgagee is affected by the undue influence, so that the mortgage is unenforceable against the victim of undue influence.

> The difference between surety transactions and joint loans is important when we consider whether the lender has become affected by the undue influence.

(3) Critical Thinking

LECTURER: This is yet another situation in which the law must strike a balance between the need for an innocent lender to get its money back and the need to protect the surety/victim. Can you see how the doctrine of undue influence engages BUILDING BLOCK NO 2?

BUILDING BLOCK NO 2: Ideas of Justice

Rules are good and fair if they take account of moral justice: Every person should be accorded the freedom of their will and autonomous choice. Thus, if people deal with each other and with their property in a way that violates the will of another then the law should offer that other some remedy.

STUDENT: It is a clear case where one person's will and free choice has been violated by another. Undue influence is where one person has domination and control over the actions of another, and then takes advantage of that by preferring their own interests and manipulating the other into the transaction. Land Law would be very bad if it didn't protect the victim of the undue influence.

LECTURER: And what form do you think this protection should take?

STUDENT: The victim should not be bound by the mortgage. In our example of the husband and wife the bank should not be able to evict the wife from her home, threatening her residential security, where she did not freely enter into the transaction. So I think that the law is bad unless it prevents the lender from enforcing the mortgage. It would also be bad on the basis of BUILDING BLOCK NO 1.

BUILDING BLOCK NO 1: Residential Security

We can legitimately say that where the rules operate in the context of owner occupation of property, they are good and fair if they give effective protection to people's residential security. Land Law now operates in the context of owner occupation. **For the full text of our Building Blocks and instructions on how to use them to construct an argument see Chapter 1.**

LECTURER: But I think you know enough about Land Law now, and about creating arguments about it, to know that it can't be packaged quite so neatly. It doesn't quite work like this. The law cannot give protection to the interests of one of its "stakeholders" at the almost total expense of others. What other class of litigant might need some consideration under the doctrine of undue influence? I'm thinking of another innocent party in these disputes.

STUDENT: Well banks and building societies are affected as the doctrine of undue influence may stop them from enforcing their mortgages and realising their security.

LECTURER: And which of our Building Blocks does this engage?

STUDENT: BUILDING BLOCK NO 5.

BUILDING BLOCK NO 5: The Protection of Mortgage Lenders

Unless the rules of Land Law make sure that lenders can readily get their money back by selling the house, banks and building societies may become reluctant to give loans to owner occupiers and small businesses in the future. This will affect our economy: *Royal Bank of Scotland Plc v Etridge (No.2)* [2002] 2 A.C. 773.

LECTURER: So if the law always sides with the victim of the undue influence, preventing the lender from enforcing its mortgage, what might be the result?

STUDENT: Lenders would be very wary about lending money to a couple, or they may not be willing to accept a surety arrangement. This may stop many people from obtaining loans in order to start up or expand businesses. And this will have a knock-on effect for the economy.

LECTURER: So we see here that the law clearly must offer the victim of the undue influence some degree of protection. But there must be limits to that protection. There should be a point at which lenders are allowed to enforce mortgages against co-owners and sureties.

As Lord Nicholls states in *Royal Bank of Scotland Plc. v Etridge (No.2)* [2002] 2 A.C. 773, paras 34–37, we must consider whether the law strikes the right balance.

If you were designing the system when might you cease to offer protection to the lender?

STUDENT: I think when the lender knew that the surety wife did not consent to the transaction. The lender should be expected to make some enquiries prior to the mortgage. It's like *Williams & Glyn's Bank Ltd v Boland* all over again.

LECTURER: How so?

STUDENT: The question was whether the bank was bound by Mrs Boland's prior right in the land. The House of Lords had to consider the same policy interests. It said that banks should be expected to make some enquiries prior to taking a mortgage on the house. They must to an extent protect their own interests.

LECTURER: Yes, *to an extent*. But there are important rules within the Land Registration Act 2002 that protect purchasers and mortgage lenders from being bound by prior rights.

The position under that Act too is that the law must strike a balance between the need to protect residential security, or ideas of justice, and the need to ensure that banks keep lending money to home owners.[136]

So you accept that there must be some protection for the lender so as not to violate the policy in BUILDING BLOCK NO 5. It's good to see you asking questions and arguing imaginatively in order to consider how far the law should go in protecting lending institutions.

STUDENT: Yes, as it says in chapter one, the law should not protect a class of litigant to the extent to which they could themselves have guarded against the situation.

LECTURER: The question then remains: *what can lending institutions be expected to do in order to guard against the possibility of undue influence?* We will now see what the law does.

A. THE STARTING POINT—BARCLAY'S BANK PLC V O'BRIEN[137]

In *Barclay's Bank Plc v O'Brien* the House of Lords clarified the principles that applied within the doctrine of fraud, misrepresentation and undue influence. The structure of the rules that we are about to consider derive from this case as subsequently re-evaluated by the House of Lords in *Royal Bank of Scotland Plc v Etridge (No.2)*.[138]

Firstly, it must be proven that there is misrepresentation or undue influence that has caused the victim to enter into the mortgage transaction. Undue influence is where pressure is exercised by one legal owner over another to get them to enter into a joint loan, or by the principal borrower against a surety in order to get them to offer their house as security for a loan to the principal borrower. The doctrine of undue influence extends to all fact situations and not merely to husband and wife. Thus, a son could exercise undue influence over his mother in order to get her to mortgage her house,[139] or a father his inexperienced children,[140] or a nephew his uncle,[141] or an employer their employee.[142]

Secondly, once undue influence has been proven, the perpetrator (e.g. the husband in our above example) will not be able to enforce the transaction against the victim, e.g. the wife. However, this is not usually the victim's concern in such cases. He or she wants to set the mortgage aside *as against the lending bank*.[143]

So we need to examine (1) How undue influence is established; and (2) When the transaction can be set aside as against the lender, i.e. when is the lender affected by the undue influence?

---

136   See Chapter 8.
137   [1994] 1 A.C. 180
138   [2002] 2 A.C. 773.
139   *Abbey National Bank Plc v Stringer* [2006] EWCA Civ 338.
140   *Bainbrigge v Browne* (1881) 18 Ch. D 188.
141   *Goodchild v Bradbury* [2006] EWCA Civ 1868.
142   *Credit Lyonnais Bank Nederland N.V. v Burch* [1997] 1 All E.R. 144.
143   *Barclays Bank Plc v O'Brien* [1994] 1 A.C. 180, per Lord Browne-Wilkinson, p.191.

Example

Mr and Mrs O'Brien co-owned their home. Mr O'Brien wanted to mortgage the house in order to guarantee his company's debts. He told his wife that the amount of the debt was £60,000 and that the mortgage was a short-term arrangement. In fact it was £135,000 and it was not short term. The House of Lords held that Mrs O'Brien had entered into the transaction as a result of the misrepresentation and that the bank, having notice of her rights, could not enforce the mortgage against her.

(1) How undue influence is established

In cases of this nature it is firstly necessary to establish that the mortgage was entered into as a result of undue influence. In the House of Lords in *Royal Bank of Scotland Plc v Etridge (No.2)*,[144] Lord Nicholls defined undue influence as arising

> "out of a relationship between two persons where one has acquired over another a measure of influence, or ascendancy, of which the ascendant person then takes unfair advantage."

Thus, the husband in our example attained ascendancy over his wife by looking after their finances and by lying to her about the importance of the transaction. There are two methods by which a claimant can prove undue influence. Firstly, by proving as a question of fact that ascendancy existed within her relationship and that the dominant person took advantage of this in order to obtain her consent to the transaction. The expression is "actual undue influence". This refers to the situation where the victim *actually proves* that her free will has been overcome and that the mortgage transaction was not an expression of her true will and consent. Indeed, in *Royal Bank of Scotland Plc v Etridge (No.2)*[145] Lord Nicholls stated that as a general rule "the burden of proving an allegation of undue influence rests upon the person who claims to have been wronged".

That said, there is a second class of case in which the law will make a presumption in the complainant's favour.

(a) Actual undue influence

In *Drew v Daniel*,[146] Ward L.J. defined undue influence: "something has to be done to twist the mind of a donor". "The vulnerability of one party must feature in [the] analysis. So does the forcefulness of the personality of the other".[147] Thus, proving the existence of undue influence depends on many factors such as the parties' personalities and the nature of their relationship.[148]

---

144   [2002] 2 A.C. 773, para.8.
145   [2002] 2 A.C. 773, para.13.
146   [2005] 2 P. & C.R. DG14.
147   [2005] 2 P. & C.R. DG14.
148   *Royal Bank of Scotland v Etridge* [2002] 2 A.C. 773, para.13, per Lord Nicholls.

> Thus, undue influence may be established where it is shown that an elderly mother who did not understand finances but who was devoted to her son, had mortgaged her house because her son kept on telling her that he would go bankrupt and would be destitute unless she did so.

It is not necessary to find that the claimant's will was completely overborne. There may simply be facts withheld, or misrepresentations made that meant that the complainant's signature was not a conscious exercise of her will and consent.[149] In *Etridge* Lord Nicholls observed that where a husband and wife are discussing the possibility of a legal charge over their home to secure finance for the husband's business, a degree of latitude is expected. The husband may well be overly optimistic about the prospects of this business. He may well exaggerate. This is only normal and is not to be labelled undue influence.[150]

"Statements or conduct by a husband which do not pass beyond the bounds of what may be expected of a reasonable husband in the circumstances should not, without more, be castigated as undue influence. Similarly, when a husband is forecasting the future of his business, and expressing his hopes or fears, a degree of hyperbole may be only natural. Courts should not too readily treat such exaggerations as misstatements".

However, there may well be a finding of undue influence where a husband has given inaccurate details about the transaction in order to procure his wife's consent. And where the husband clearly puts his interests first and "makes a choice for both of them on that footing" even though the wife reposes trust in him "for the management of their financial affairs".[151]

"Such a husband abuses the influence he has. He fails to discharge the obligation of candour and fairness he owes a wife who is looking to him to make the major financial decisions."[152]

In *Hewett v First Plus Financial Group Plc*[153] the Court of Appeal held that a husband had breached his duty of candour towards his wife. He had told her that a mortgage on the house was the only way in which his mounting credit card debts could be managed, which was false, and he failed to disclose that he was having an affair at the time. She trusted him about financial matters and made the decision to enter into the mortgage because she thought they were both committed to their family life.

---

149   *Drew v Daniel* [2005] EWCA Civ 507; *Hewett v First Plus Financial Group Plc* [2010] EWCA Civ 312.
150   *Royal Bank of Scotland v Etridge* [2002] 2 A.C. 773, para.32 per Lord Nicholls.
151   *Royal Bank of Scotland v Etridge* [2002] 2 A.C. 773, para.33.
152   *Royal Bank of Scotland v Etridge*, above, para.33.
153   [2010] EWCA Civ 312, facts on *Westlaw* case summary.

In order to establish undue influence the victim does not need to prove that the transaction is disadvantageous to them.[154]

(b) Presumed undue influence

There are two sets of circumstances in which the law presumes certain facts favourable to the claimant, but the nature of the presumption is different in each case.[155]

(i) An irrebuttable presumption of trust and confidence within the relationship

Where there is a surety arrangement or other transaction within certain specific relationships the law will irrebuttably presume that the claimant reposed trust and confidence in the other party.[156] The complainant does not have to prove this. The law will then presume that an unusual transaction or gift within the context of that relationship could only have been procured by the undue influence of the ascendant party. Examples of relationships that fall into this category are doctor and patient, parent and child, guardian and ward, solicitor and client, trustee and beneficiary. The relationship of husband and wife does not fall into this category.[157] As Lord Nicholls reasoned in *Royal Bank of Scotland Plc v Etridge (No.2)* the law is "sternly protective" of certain relationships within which large gifts are not normally given by the dependent person.[158]

The complainant must show that the transaction in question "calls for explanation" before the presumption of undue influence arises, as is the case with the second category.[159] So we will examine this below. Moderate gifts, even by a client to a solicitor, will not give rise to a presumption of undue influence, e.g. a small legacy where the solicitor agrees to act as executor.[160] Thus, where the presumption arises, the other party must show that the transaction was entered into as a result of an independent exercise of the complainant's will. In *Pathania v Adedeji*[161] the presumption of undue influence was not rebutted where a solicitor charged an unusually high interest rate when he took a charge on the client's house in return for a loan. The solicitor rebutted the presumption of undue influence in relation to the transaction itself as the client had been an experienced doctor, who had gained benefit from the transaction and had read and reflected on the documents for a considerable period of time.

(ii) An evidential presumption

If the complainant does not fall within one of the categories of relationship above, undue influence may be presumed where she proves

---

154 *CIBC Mortgages Plc v Pitt* [1994] 1 A.C. 200; *Royal Bank of Scotland Plc v Etridge (No.2)* [2002] 2 A.C. 773, para.12, per Lord Nicholls, para.156, per Lord Scott, hereafter *Etridge*.

155 *Etridge*, para.18, per Lord Nicholls. In *Barclays Bank v O'Brien* Lord Browne-Wilkinson held that these were Class 2(A) and 2(B) respectively.

156 *Etridge*, para.18, per Lord Nicholls.

157 *Yerkey v Jones* (1939) 63 C.L.R. 649, cited in *Etridge*, para.19.

158 [2002] 2 A.C. 773, para.18, per Lord Nicholls.

159 It is not out of the question for a gift to arise within unusual circumstances in one of the "irrebuttable" types of relationship, although it would probably be a lot easier for the complainant to prove that the transaction goes above and beyond what would normally be expected in that type of relationship. See also C.Harpum, S.Bridge, M.Dixon, *Megarry & Wade Law of Real Property* para.25–123.

160 *Etridge* [2002] 2 A.C. 773, para.156, per Lord Scott.

161 [2010] EWHC 3085.

- that she placed trust and confidence in the perpetrator in relation to her financial affairs and
- that there is a transaction which "calls for explanation".

Once these two factors are established the burden of proving undue influence is reversed and placed upon the alleged perpetrator. As Lord Nicholls stated in *Royal Bank of Scotland Plc v Etridge (No.2)* the court will "infer that, in the absence of a satisfactory explanation, the transaction can only have been procured by undue influence".[162] It is then up to the person alleged to have committed the undue influence to prove that the complainant entered into the transaction of his or her own free will.[163] How this is to be done remains a question of fact in each case. They must show that the transaction was made independently of any influence that they were able to exercise.[164] The alleged perpetrator of the undue influence may show that the complainant was independently advised prior to entering into the transaction. However, independent advice does not have the automatic effect of establishing that the complainant entered into the transaction of his or her own free will. The importance of independent advice depends on all the circumstances of the case. In *Etridge* Lord Nicholls observed that

"In the normal course advice from a solicitor or other outside adviser can be expected to bring home to a complainant a proper understanding of what he or she is about to do. But a person may understand fully the implications of a proposed transaction, for instance, a substantial gift, and yet still be acting under the undue influence of another."[165]

(iii) Trust and confidence in the other party in relation to management of financial affairs
Even where the relationship between the parties is not of the type giving rise to an automatic presumption of trust and confidence, the burden of proving undue influence will be reversed where the complainant establishes that he or she reposed trust and confidence in the other party in relation to the management of their financial affairs and that there is a transaction which calls for explanation.[166] In respect of establishing trust and confidence for example, a wife might establish that her husband was usually the one to look after the financial side of their lives, and that she habitually left these matters to him. An elderly mother might prove that she put trust and confidence in her son because she spoke little English, and did not understand the nature of complex financial transactions.[167]

In *Thompson v Foy*,[168] the presumption of undue influence was not established. A mother transferred her house to her daughter on the basis of a repeated promise from her daughter that she would be paid the value of her share in the house. The daughter failed to do this and

---

162 [2002] 2 A.C. 773, para.14, per Lord Nicholls.
163 *Goodchild v Bradbury* [2006] EWCA Civ 1868.
164 *Smith v Cooper* [2010] EWCA Civ 722.
165 *Etridge*, para.20 per Lord Nicholls.
166 *Etridge*, para.14, per Lord Nicholls.
167 *Abbey National Bank Plc v Stringer* [2006] EWCA Civ 338.
168 [2009] EWHC 1076.

the mother sought to have the transaction set aside for undue influence. It was held that the mother understood that she had been taking a risk in transferring her house to her daughter. The trust and confidence that she placed in her daughter to pay her the value of her share was no more than existed in the ordinary mother/daughter relationship.

(iv) The transaction calls for explanation

Under the law as stated in *Barclays Bank Plc v O'Brien*,[169] a person seeking to raise the presumption of undue influence also had to prove that the transaction in question operated to their "manifest disadvantage". This could in theory make it difficult for a wife to raise the presumption where she mortgages her house to guarantee her husband's business debts. The wife in such cases would not be *disadvantaged*. His business might prosper and she will benefit. As Lord Nicholls observed in *Etridge* "[o]rdinarily, the fortunes of husband and wife are bound up together. . . the wife has a lively interest in doing what she can to support the business".[170] Thus, it was held in *Etridge* that what the complainant must prove is that there is a transaction that "calls for explanation", i.e. one that is "not readily explicable by the relationship of the parties".[171]

> A transaction that is "immoderate and irrational": *Bank of Montreal v Stuart* [1911] A.C. 120 per Lord Macnaghten.
>
> In *Allcard v Skinner* (1882) 36 Ch. D 145 Lindley L.J. defined the concept of a transaction which calls for explanation:
>
> > "But if the gift is so large as not to be reasonably accounted for on the ground of friendship, relationship, charity, or other ordinary motives on which ordinary men act, the burden is upon the donee to support the gift."

For example, an uncle gave to his nephew a valuable piece of development land adjacent to his own property, and which had the potential, if built upon, to devalue his property.[172] This was held to be beyond what even a close uncle would give to a nephew as a wedding present. In *Abbey National Bank Plc v Stringer*[173] an elderly mother mortgaged her house, putting her home at risk, at the request of her son in order to finance "a new business of which she knew nothing". The Court of Appeal held that this was a transaction that went beyond a mother's generosity. By contrast in *Turkey v Awadh*[174] an agreement that a couple would transfer ownership of a house

---

169   [1994] 1 A.C. 180.
170   *Etridge*, para.28. The "manifest disadvantage" description had been used in *National Westminster Bank Plc v Morgan* [1985] A.C. 686. Lord Nicholls in *Etridge* commented that *Morgan* in reality sought to apply the test for a transaction that calls for explanation, but had simply attached an inappropriate label to it, referring to "disadvantage". The courts prior to this would allow the presumption where there was some transaction that could not be explained on the basis of the parties' relationship: *Etridge*, para.29, per Lord Nicholls referring to *Allcard v Skinner* (1882) 36 Ch. D 145.
171   *Etridge*, para.21, per Lord Nicholls.
172   *Goodchild v Bradbury* [2006] EWCA Civ 1868.
173   [2006] EWCA Civ 338, per Lloyd L.J.
174   [2005] EWCA Civ 382.

to their father if he would pay the mortgage was held to be an ordinary transaction. The couple were in considerable financial difficulty and nature of the family's relationship meant that the couple would probably remain in occupation.

Transactions involving husband and wife need to be scrutinised carefully as wives may execute a mortgage to support their husbands' business debts for many reasons even though they "may be less optimistic than their husbands about the prospects of the husbands' businesses". They may wish to support their husbands. Thus, despite risks to themselves and their families, the mortgage may not necessarily be unaccountable on grounds of the relationship.[175]

(2) When can the transaction be set aside as against the lender?

Once a complainant has successfully proved undue influence, whether as a question of fact or by the use of one of the presumptions above, the perpetrator of the undue influence cannot enforce the transaction against them. However, in most such cases it is not the person who has inflicted the undue influence that is attempting to enforce the mortgage. It is the lender.

> So the question with which we are concerned in this section is the *circumstances in which the undue influence will affect the mortgagee so that they cannot enforce their mortgage against the wife.*

(a) Critical Thinking

LECTURER: As we saw earlier, if you want to create an argument about the law of undue influence you must consider whether it supports or undermines two of our Building Blocks. You are now well used to the idea that these two Building Blocks pull in opposite directions. So the law must strike a balance between them. Firstly, in *Etridge* Lord Nicholls observes (para.36)

"One party may take advantage of the other's vulnerability. . . It is all too easy for a husband, anxious or even desperate for bank finance, to misstate the position in some particular or to mislead the wife, wittingly or unwittingly, in some other way. The law would be seriously defective if it did not recognise these realities."

STUDENT: I think that unless the law protects a claimant from having his or her home taken away as a result of undue influence then the law is effectively allowing blatant violations of people's free will and autonomy.

---

175   *Etridge*, para.30, per Lord Nicholls.

> **BUILDING BLOCK NO 2: Ideas of Justice**
>
> Every person should be accorded the freedom of their will and autonomous choice. Thus, if people deal with each other and with their property in a way that violates the will of another then the law should offer that other some remedy.
>
> Josef Pieper, the moral philosopher, affirms the view that God created us as separate beings with a creative will of our own: "[i]t is through creation that the created being first comes to have his rights": Pieper, *The Four Cardinal Virtues* (first paperback edition 1966, reprinted 2006), pp.44–46. And it is for this reason that each person should be respected as "master of his own actions" and choices.
>
> This is a person's "due" respect. A person's freedom of will should be respected because he or she "is a *person* – a spiritual being, a whole unto himself, a being that exists for itself and of itself, that wills its own proper perfection. Therefore, and for *that very reason* something *is* due to man in the fullest sense, *for that reason* he does inalienably have a *suum*, a 'right' which he can plead against everyone else, a right which imposes upon everyone of his partners the obligation at least not to violate it."
>
> Josef Pieper, *The Four Cardinal Virtues*, p.50
>
> When the will is properly active, the personality can move forward, direct, press through difficulty, initiate change. Thus, a person must be accorded freedom of the will.

LECTURER: If a person is prevailed upon to enter into a mortgage in such a way that their signature on that mortgage cannot be said to be a proper expression of their will, then the mortgage cannot be seen as a decision of their own personality. Can you see how the exercise of undue influence over a person is morally unjust?

STUDENT: It is a violation of their personhood. They have made a significant life choice in which their own independent will had no part.

LECTURER: And so if we are to take seriously the idea that a person must have freedom to create and develop his or her own being, then a person should be held accountable only for those actions that spring from their own will.

STUDENT: Hence why it makes good law to prevent the mortgage from being enforced by the lender against them.

LECTURER: But on the other hand, banks rely upon enforcing mortgages by repossession and selling houses in order that they may recoup their initial loan money. If the courts place too many restrictions on their ability to enforce a mortgage, they may become reluctant to lend money in the future. In *Etridge*, Lord Nicholls made this observation (paras 34–35):

"Bank finance is in fact by far the most important source of external capital for small businesses with fewer than ten employees. These businesses comprise about 95% of all businesses in the country, responsible for nearly one-third of all employment. Finance raised by second mortgages on the principal's home is a significant source of capital for the start-up of small businesses.

If the freedom of home-owners to make economic use of their homes is not to be frustrated, a bank must be able to have confidence that a wife's signature on the necessary guarantee and charge will be as binding upon her as is the signature of anyone else on documents which he or she may sign. Otherwise banks will not be willing to lend money on the security of a jointly owned house or flat."

STUDENT: Lord Nicholls is basically talking about the idea in our BUILDING BLOCK NO 5.

LECTURER: And so we see that in determining when a mortgage can or cannot be enforced by a lender against the victim of undue influence, the law must strike a balance between these two Building Blocks.

(b) The law

(i) Circumstances in which a mortgagee is affected by the undue influence

In *Barclays Bank v O'Brien*[176] Lord Browne-Wilkinson identified that a mortgage transaction is unenforceable by the lender against the victim of undue influence, e.g. a wife, if the husband was acting as the lender's agent "in procuring the wife to stand as surety",[177] or if the lender had actual or constructive notice of the undue influence exercised by the husband. This use of the concept of constructive notice is unconventional,[178] given that it is usually applied to determine whether a later purchaser will take land free from an earlier property right. Lord Browne-Wilkinson concluded that a lender would have constructive notice of undue influence, or would be "put on inquiry" that the wife's consent to a surety agreement was not genuine, where:

"(a) the transaction is on its face not to the financial advantage of the wife: and (b) there is a substantial risk in transactions of that kind that, in procuring the wife to act as surety, the husband has committed a legal or equitable wrong that entitles the wife to set aside the transaction."

In this situation the mortgagee will have constructive notice of the undue influence and must therefore take "reasonable steps to satisfy himself that the wife's agreement to stand surety has been properly obtained".[179] Unless the mortgagee takes such steps it will be unable to enforce the mortgage against the potential victim of the undue influence.

In the later House of Lords decision in *Royal Bank of Scotland Plc v Etridge (No.2)*[180] it was held that a mortgagee will always be put on inquiry whenever a wife offers to stand surety for her husband's debts.[181] This is because the transaction is one-sided and the lender knows

---

176   [1994] 1 A.C. 180, per Lord Browne-Wilkinson.

177   Lord Browne-Wilkinson thought that such cases would be "of very rare occurrence".

178   See Lord Nicholls' comments to this effect in *Etridge* [2002] 2 A.C. 773, para.39.

179   *Barclays Bank v O'Brien* [1994] 1 A.C. 180, p.196, per Lord Browne-Wilkinson, quoted in *Etridge*, para.38, per Lord Nicholls.

180   [2002] 2 A.C. 773: *Etridge*.

181   Although Lord Nicholls concluded that the expression "put on inquiry" is strictly "a misnomer": para.44. His lordship thought that the use of the concept of constructive notice was inappropriate, but that *O'Brien* had not taken the law in the wrong direction.

this.[182] This applies to any situation, whether it is a wife or husband standing surety. It applies where a couple is unmarried and regardless of whether they are heterosexual or homosexual. It is not even necessary that the parties live together.[183]

> **The bank is put on inquiry that undue influence exists whenever it knows that one party to a relationship is standing surety for the other and the relationship between the debtor and surety is non-commercial: para. 109, per Lord Hobhouse; para.87, per Lord Nicholls.**

Lord Hobhouse in *Etridge* thought that this "low threshold" for when the bank is put on inquiry is justified as "it assists banks to put in place procedures which do not require an exercise of judgement by their officials".[184] Otherwise, such judgement would involve banks in inappropriate personal inquiries into the nature of the parties' relationship.

Lord Nicholls drew a sharp distinction between these surety cases and cases where a loan is made to a couple jointly, i.e. and secured on their family home.[185] Here the underlying rationale is that there is nothing to alert the lender to the possibility of undue influence. The loan is ostensibly for the couple's joint benefit. It is not a one-sided transaction. In joint loan cases "the bank is not put on inquiry, unless the bank is aware the loan is being made for the husband's purposes, as distinct from their joint purposes".[186]

(ii) Steps the bank must take once put on inquiry[187]
So what is the effect of the bank's being put on inquiry that the wife's signature on the document might not represent her consent? In order to then be able to enforce the mortgage against the potential victim of the undue influence, the lender must take certain steps.

With regard to transactions that occurred prior to *Etridge* the bank will be able to enforce the mortgage if it obtains confirmation from a solicitor advising the wife that she has been advised as to the consequences of the mortgage.[188] As far as concerns transactions that took place

---

182   *Etridge* para.43, per Lord Nicholls. Lord Nicholls considered that this was essentially what was held in *Barclays Bank v O'Brien* and that Lord Browne-Wilkinson in the quotation above was simply articulating the underlying rationale in such surety cases.

183   *Etridge*, para.47, also para.87.

184   [2002] 2 A.C. 773, para.108.

185   For the difference between joint loans and surety cases see above in this Chapter section 5.

186   *Etridge*, para.48, citing *CIBC Mortgages Plc v Pitt* [1994] 1 A.C. 200.

187   Although throughout I use the language of "husband and wife" this law is not limited to sexual relationships: *Etridge*, para.82 per Lord Nicholls. It has been applied in the context of the relationship of employer/employee: *Credit Lyonnais Bank Nederland NV v Burch* [1997] 1 All E.R. 144.

188   *Etridge*, para.79(2) per Lord Nicholls.

post-*Etridge* Lord Nicholls considered it impractical for banks to ascertain whether the wife entered into a transaction as a result of undue influence. Such an inquiry would be "intrusive" and impractical.[189] What is required is that the bank takes steps to ensure that the wife has been advised in a meaningful way about the risks she is running by executing a charge over her home.[190] The bank is not expected to give the advice itself, but may rely on the written confirmation from a solicitor advising the wife that the implications of the mortgage have been explained to her. The bank must tell the wife that it will need this written confirmation from a solicitor and that the purpose of the bank obtaining this letter is so that the mortgage will be enforceable against her and that she will be unable to argue to the contrary on the basis of undue influence. So the bank should then ask the wife to nominate a solicitor.[191] The bank should not proceed with the transaction unless the wife responds.[192] It is not necessary for the wife to be advised by a different solicitor from the one advising the husband, provided the solicitor considers that there is no conflict of interest.[193]

> In sharp contrast with *O'Brien*, in *Etridge* Lord Nicholls stated that it was important for the wife to understand *why* she was being asked to obtain separate legal advice. The idea is that the wife understands that once the bank has the letter from the solicitor that she has been advised about the effect of the mortgage on her house, the wife will not be able to challenge the mortgage on grounds of undue influence.

The bank must ensure that the solicitor is in possession of all the necessary information, which may include details concerning the husband's present indebtedness to the bank and the terms of the proposed new loan or overdraft facility.[194] If the husband refuses to give consent to this disclosure, then the bank should not proceed with the mortgage.

(iii) The role of the solicitor

The solicitor must have a face-to-face meeting with the wife, without her husband present. Before acting for the wife the solicitor must obtain any necessary information from the bank, and if the bank declines then the solicitor should refuse to confirm that the wife has been properly advised. The solicitor must be in possession of the facts.[195]

---

189   *Etridge*, para.53, per Lord Nicholls.
190   Above, para.54.
191   *Etridge*, para.79(1).
192   *Etridge*, para.79(1).
193   *Etridge*, para.73.
194   *Etridge*, para.79(2). It is the bank that will be in possession of valuable background to the transaction and the history of the husband's business. It is this information that is needed to ensure that the wife is properly advised about the execution of the charge. The extent of the pressure that she may be under and the extent of the financial needs of the husband are disclosed by this background information. The solicitor is only likely to have possession of the documents that are to be signed. See Lord Hobhouse, *Etridge* [2002] 2 A.C. 773, para.114.
195   *Etridge*, paras 67–8.

In general terms, the role of the solicitor is to bring home to the wife the risks she is running by the transaction and that the purpose of his role is to ensure that the bank can enforce the charge against her, should it become necessary to do so.[196] The solicitor should not refuse to confirm to the bank that he has given advice to the wife, just because he decides that the transaction is very unwise. It is the wife's decision as to whether she wishes to proceed—unwise or not.[197] He may give clear reasons why he considers the transaction to be damaging to the wife's financial interests. Exceptionally, if it is "glaringly obvious that the wife is being grievously wronged. . . the solicitor should decline to act further."[198]

As to the content of the advice, the solicitor must explain to the wife, in non-technical language, the nature and implications of the transaction. In *Etridge* Lord Nicholls laid out the typical "core minimum" advice that the solicitor should give[199]:

- The solicitor must explain the documents and their consequences, i.e. that the bank will be able to repossess her home if her husband's business fails.
- The wife should be told the terms of the loan to the husband and the extent of her liability. She must be advised that the bank might increase the amount covered by the charge without reference to her.[200] The solicitor should discuss with the wife the value of the house, compared with the amount of the loan or overdraft. He should also discuss the couple's assets and whether, should it become necessary, they have other assets that could be sold in the event that the business fails.
- The solicitor should make sure that the wife understands that she has a choice as to whether to sign the mortgage, i.e. that it is *her* decision.
- At the end, the solicitor should ask the wife if she wishes to go ahead with the mortgage. He must obtain her authority to write to the bank confirming that he has explained the nature and implications of the transaction. She should be asked whether she wishes the solicitor to negotiate more favourable terms with the bank, such as "the sequence in which the various securities will be called upon".[201]

---

196 para.64.
197 *Etridge*, para.61.
198 para.62.
199 para.65.
200 Some of the wives involved in the *Etridge* case (there were several cases tested) had signed "all monies" guarantees. This means that the charge extended to further advances by the bank to the husband and that there was no upper limit on the amount guaranteed. Lord Hobhouse remarked ([2002] 2 A.C. 773, para.112) that "banks have acknowledged that such guarantees are likely to be unnecessary and unjustifiable where private sureties are sought. They should be subject to a stated monetary limit on the surety's liability and any legal adviser should so advise a private client".
201 *Etridge*, para.165.

6 Priority of mortgages

It is important to a mortgage lender that they take their charge free from prior rights in the land, such as a beneficial interest under a trust or a prior lease. The whole idea of security conferred by a mortgage is that the lender will be able to sell the land and recoup the debt owed by the borrower in the event that the latter defaults. Therefore the lender will be keen to establish that there is no-one with a prior right in the land that can potentially stop them from enforcing their security.[202] It is also possible that there are other mortgages on the land. So it is important to know the order in which they rank in priority, i.e. if the house must be sold what is the order in which various lenders can claim their debt out of the proceeds of sale. If there is insufficient money to go round, then this order becomes crucial.

A. REGISTERED LAND

Where a legal mortgage/charge is granted in respect of a registered estate in land it is a "registrable disposition".[203] Thus, it cannot operate as a *legal* charge unless the registration requirements are met.[204] The mortgagee must be entered in the register as proprietor of the charge and will then have all the powers that a legal mortgagee has under the general law, including the right to take possession and sell mortgaged property.[205]

Registered charges—the priority rule
Once the charge is registered the lender then has the protection of the special priority rule contained in s. 30 of the Land Registration Act 2002. The lender will take its charge free from all third party interests and other charges, with the following exceptions:

- The owner of the registered charge will be subject to third party rights that are registered as a "notice" in the charges register;
- He will also take subject to registered charges that have been registered prior to the registration of his charge. Mortgages rank in priority in the order in which they are registered: Land Registration Act 2002 s.48;
- The owner of the registered charge will also take subject to an overriding interest that falls within any of the paragraphs of Sch.3.

This is how Mrs Boland managed to establish that her beneficial interest bound the bank in *Williams & Glyn's Bank Ltd v Boland* [1981] A.C. 487.

---

202 As seen in *Williams & Glyn's Bank Ltd v Boland* [1981] A.C. 487.
203 Land Registration Act 2002 s.27(f).
204 s.27(1), 51.
205 Land Registration Act 2002 s.52, subject to any entry on the register restricting those powers.

This gives the lender extensive protection from being bound by prior rights in the land that may prevent it from taking possession of the land and selling it in order to realise its security. It also allows the lender's charge to take priority over any earlier registered charges or later charges, whether registered or not.

(1) Equitable mortgages

As we have seen in section 2C above in this chapter, it is possible to have an equitable mortgage. Although an equitable mortgagee does not have the automatic right to possession of the mortgaged estate, it is still a security interest in the borrower's estate which entitles the lender to payment out of the proceeds of sale.

- An equitable mortgage is not a registrable disposition. Thus, in order to take priority over a later registered estate or charge, the equitable mortgage must be registered as a "notice" on the charges register. It will then bind all future registered dealings with the land.[206]
- If the equitable mortgage is not so registered then later registered dispositions, such as a further registered charge, will take priority over that mortgage.

B. UNREGISTERED LAND

- Where a first legal mortgage is granted the lender is entitled to take possession of the title deeds. The mortgage is a legal interest that will bind the world. This means that all later dealings with the mortgaged estate, including later mortgages, will take effect subject to the mortgage. However, it will only bind the whole world if the lender has the title deeds.
- A mortgagee with the title deeds will lose priority to a later mortgagee if he was fraudulent or grossly negligent in parting with the title deeds.
- However, a first mortgagee may not take possession of the title deeds. And a second or later mortgagee will usually be unable to take possession (because the first mortgagee will have the deeds). Where a legal mortgage is created but the lender does not take possession of the title deeds, this is known as a "puisne" mortgage, which must be registered as a class C(i) land charge.[207] It will not bind a purchaser for value, including a later mortgagee, unless it is registered.[208]

C. COMPULSORY FIRST REGISTRATION

Where a legal charge is granted in respect of an estate in land, and title to that estate is unregistered, the grant triggers compulsory first registration of the mortgaged

---

206   Land Registration Act 2002 ss.29, 30 and 32(1).
207   This is an exception to the usual rule that legal interests bind the whole world.
208   Land Charges Act 1972 s.4.

estate.[209] However, this is only the case if the mortgage is a *protected first legal mortgage*. "First protected" means that the mortgage is to take effect as a mortgage protected by deposit of the title documents of the mortgaged estate with the lender and the mortgage ranks first in priority above any other mortgages on the estate that exist at the time of creation.[210] The mortgagor is obliged to register title to the estate that is the subject of the mortgage and when the estate becomes registered the mortgagor must register the charge against the title and the mortgagee as proprietor of the charge.[211]

D. TACKING

Tacking is where a further loan by the same lender is secured by their original charge on the land.

Let's say that in 2001 Floyds Bank lends Martin £100,000 and takes a charge over his home. In 2010 Martin wants another loan. He approaches Floyds Bank who gives him a further advance of £50,000. This amount can be "tacked" onto Floyds' first charge, which means that the original charge now secures Martin's indebtedness to them of £150,000. The issue of tacking becomes important where there are other lenders involved to whom Martin has granted charges in the intervening period. If in 2006, Martin had borrowed £50,000 from the Edgestow Bank, who then had a charge that ranked second in priority to Floyds', the Edgestow Bank is likely to be affected by any subsequent tacking by Floyds Bank in 2010. Once the second loan is "tacked" onto the first charge the value of the security of the intervening lender (Edgestow) is reduced.

> Thus, if Martin's house is sold in order to pay off these debts and the sale realises £170,000, Floyds will be able to claim the full amount of their loans (£150,000) and Edgestow will only be entitled to £20,000.

(1) Registered land

In registered land the question of whether a lender is entitled to "tack" further advances to an existing charge is regulated by s.49 of the Land Registration Act 2002. Generally it is only possible to tack a further advance onto an existing charge where the subsequent chargee agrees.[212] However, the section adds a number of ways in which tacking may occur.

---

209   Land Registration Act 2002 s.4(1)(g), provided that estate is an unregistered legal freehold or leasehold estate. If the latter, the lease must have more than seven years left to run: Land Registration Act 2002 s.4(2).
210   Land Registration Act 2002 s.4(8)(a) and (b); C.Harpum and J.Bignell, *Registered Land: Law and Practice under the Land Registration Act 2002* (Jordan Publishing, 2004), para.2.19.
211   Land Registration Act 2002 s.6(2); Sch.2, para.8.
212   Land Registration Act 2002 s.49(6).

- A mortgagee may make a further advance on the security of a "charge ranking in priority to a subsequent charge" if he does not have notice from that lender that the subsequent charge has been created.[213]
- Tacking may occur if a loan is made in pursuance of an obligation to make further advances and that obligation was entered in the register at the time of creation of the later charge.[214]
- Tacking may also occur where the parties agreed a maximum limit "for which the charge is security" and that agreement was entered on the register at the time the subsequent charge was created.[215]

---

213 Land Registration Act 2002 s.49(1).
214 s.49(3).
215 s.49(4).

INDEX